Economics and the Interpretation and Application of U.S. and E.U. Antitrust Law

Richard S. Markovits

Economics and the Interpretation and Application of U.S. and E.U. Antitrust Law

Volume I Basic Concepts and Economics-Based Legal Analyses of Oligopolistic and Predatory Conduct

Springer

Richard S. Markovits
School of Law
The University of Texas
Austin
USA

Foreword to the Two-Study Project

The two-volume law study now being published—ECONOMICS AND THE INTERPRETATION AND APPLICATION OF U.S. AND E.U. ANTITRUST LAW[1]—is the first component of a two-study project whose second (policy) component is entitled THE WELFARE ECONOMICS OF ANTITRUST POLICY AND U.S. AND E.U. ANTITRUST LAW: A SECOND-BEST-THEORY-BASED ECONOMIC-EFFICIENCY ANALYSIS. Although each of the two studies in the project is freestanding in the sense that each can be read independently, each builds on the other. Thus, the law study's analyses of the organizational-economic-efficiency defense that I argue should as a matter of law be read into the U.S. Clayton Act,[2] the efficiency defense that U.S. courts interpret the Sherman Act[3] to recognize, the efficiency defenses that the United States Department of Justice (DOJ)/Federal Trade Commission (FTC) Horizontal Merger Guidelines[4] indicate these institutions will accept, the "improving the production

[1] Throughout the text that follows, "U.S." will stand for the United States of America, "E.U." will stand for the European Union, and "E.C." (with periods) will stand for the European Communities. The letters "EC" without periods will stand for the European Commission. After the ratification of the Treaty of Lisbon on December 1, 2009, European Communities (E.C.) arrangements were redesignated European Union (E.U.) arrangements. The text and footnotes that follow usually avoid distinguishing between E.C. and E.U. law or decisions by using the symbol E.C./E.U. to refer to them. The subtitle of the first volume of the law study to whose main title this footnote is attached is ON THE LEGITIMATE FUNCTIONS, POSSIBLE MONOPOLIZING OR ABUSIVE CHARACTER, AND COMPETITIVE IMPACT OF BUSINESS CONDUCT. The subtitle of the second volume of the law study is ECONOMICS-BASED LEGAL ANALYSIS OF MERGERS, VERTICAL PRACTICES, AND JOINT VENTURES.

[2] Clayton Act, 38 Stat. 730 (1914) (codified as amended at 15 U.S.C. Sections 12-27) (hereinafter Clayton Act).

[3] Sherman Act, 26 Stat. 209 (1890) (codified as amended at 15 U.S.C. Sections 1-11) (hereinafter Sherman Act).

[4] Department of Justice and Federal Trade Commission 1992 Horizontal Merger Guidelines (hereinafter 1992 Horizontal Merger Guidelines), 4 Trade Reg. Rep. (CCH) Section 13,104 (1992), 57 Fed. Reg. 41,532; 1997 Revision of the 1992 Horizontal Merger Guidelines, available at http://www.justice.gov/atr/public/guidelines/hmg.pdf; and Department of Justice and Federal Trade Commission 2010 Horizontal Merger Guidelines (hereinafter 2010 Horizontal Merger

or distribution of goods" and "promoting technical or economic progress" defences (exemptions) promulgated by Article 101(3) of the 2009 Treaty of Lisbon[5] (formerly Article 81(3) of the 1957 Treaty of Rome[6]), the efficiency defence included in the European Commission's (EC's) Guidelines on the Assessment of Horizontal Mergers,[7] and the efficiency defence promulgated by the European Community's Merger Control Regulation (EMCR)[8] rely on the summary that its Chap. 1 provides of the policy study's more detailed discussion of the "correct" definition of "the impact of a natural event, non-government act, or government policy (hereinafter policy) on economic efficiency" and on the summary that Chap. 5 of the law study provides of the policy study's more detailed account of the various categories of economic inefficiency that are *ex ante* economically efficient to distinguish. Similarly, the policy study's analyses of the economic efficiency of preventing all or specified subsets of the various sorts of business conduct antitrust law covers make use of the conclusions that the law study reaches about the definitions of various legal concepts that are correct as a matter of law and about the determinants of various economic impacts of the relevant categories of conduct. More specifically, the policy study makes use of the law study's definitions of such (cognate) legal concepts as (1) monopolizing conduct,[9] attempts to monopolize,[10] contracts, combinations, or conspiracies in restraint of trade,[11] conduct whose object is the prevention or restriction of competition,[12] and exclusionary abuses (of a dominant position),[13] (2) conduct that lessens competition,[14] conduct whose effect is the prevention or restriction of competition,[15] and conduct that impedes effective competition,[16] and (3) unfair methods of competition[17] and conduct

Guidelines) available at http://www.justice.gov/atr/public/guidelines/hmg-2010.pdf (August 19, 2010).

[5] Treaty of Lisbon Amending the Treaty on European Union and the Treaty Establishing the European Community (hereinafter 2009 Treaty of Lisbon), 2007 OJ C306 p. 1 (December 13, 2007).

[6] Treaty Establishing the European Economic Community (hereinafter Treaty of Rome), 298 U.N. T.S. 11 (March 25, 1957).

[7] EC Guidelines on the Assessment of Horizontal Mergers, C31/5 OJ (2004).

[8] Council Regulation 139/2004 on the Control of Concentrations Between Undertakings, OJ L24/1 (May 1, 2004) (hereinafter EMCR).

[9] Sherman Act at Section 2.

[10] *Id.*

[11] *Id.* at Section 1.

[12] 2009 Treaty of Lisbon at Article 101(1).

[13] 2009 Treaty of Lisbon at Article 102.

[14] Clayton Act at Sections 2-7.

[15] 2009 Treaty of Lisbon at Article 101(1).

[16] EMCR at Article 2.

[17] Federal Trade Commission Act, 38 Stat. 717 (1914) (codified as amended at 15 U.S.C. Sections 41-45) (hereinafter FTC Act).

whose object or effect is to distort competition.[18] The policy study also makes use of the law study's many analyses of (1) the legitimate private functions of each category of conduct covered by U.S. antitrust law and/or E.C./E.U. competition law, (2) the conditions under which each such category of conduct can correctly be said to be monopolizing, to have as its object the prevention or restriction of competition, or to constitute an exclusionary abuse, (3) the determinants of the impact of each such category of conduct on the intensity of price competition, (4) the determinants of the impact of each such category of conduct on the intensity of the kind of competition that firms wage by increasing the quality or variety of their product variants or distributive outlets or by increasing the average speed with which they can supply their products and services throughout a fluctuating-demand cycle by adding to their capacity and inventory (which I call quality-or-variety-increasing-investment [QV-investment] competition), and (5) the ways in which those categories of relevant conduct that can distort competition can do so and the circumstances in which each will do so.

This Foreword to the Two-Study Project is designed to summarize the coverage of both the law-study and the policy-study components of this project and to explain why I think that all the analyses the project contains will be useful as well as intellectually interesting to the various categories of readers I hope the two studies will attract. The Foreword's summary of the two studies will take the form of lists of the sets of related questions they respectively address.

Before proceeding to delineate those lists, some encouragement and advice. I start with the encouragement. Although I include in the Foreword definitions of all the concepts that play a critical role in the articulation of the questions its lists delineate—definitions that I hope are sufficiently clear to make the questions comprehensible—all these concepts will be defined in a more elaborated way that often includes illustrations the first time they are used in the studies that employ them. The studies will therefore be much more easily and fully comprehensible than the question-lists that summarize their coverage. Now the advice. Readers who do not want to incur the cost of obtaining in advance information about the issues that this project addresses and the distinctions, concepts, conceptual systems, and theories the studies will articulate, define, explain, and employ can proceed directly to the Foreword to this Law Study.

Inter alia, this book on Economics and the Interpretation and Application of U.S. and E.U. Antitrust Law addresses the following 18 sets of issues:

(1) Why is it correct as a matter of U.S. law to interpret the Sherman Act's prohibition of "contracts, agreements, or conspiracies in restraint of trade," acts of monopolization, and "attempts to monopolize" to promulgate a test of illegality according to which covered conduct is illegal if and only if its perpetrator's or perpetrators' *ex ante* perception that it was *ex ante* profitable was critically affected by its/their belief that it would or might increase its/

[18] 2009 Treaty of Lisbon at Article 101(1).

their profits by reducing the absolute attractiveness of the best offers against which it/they would have to compete in some way that would render the conduct profitable though economically inefficient if its profitability would not otherwise have deviated from its economic efficiency? Why does the above operationalization of the Sherman Act's specific-anticompetitive-intent test of illegality include the requirement articulated by the text that begins with "in some way" in the preceding formulation? Is the U.S. Supreme Court's practice of dismissing any monopolization or "attempt to monopolize" case before evidence of wrongdoing is submitted if the private plaintiff or government has not demonstrated that the defendant(s) had market power prior to (after?) engaging in the allegedly-illegal conduct sound as a matter of economics or correct as a matter of U.S. law? What is the relationship between this Sherman Act specific-anticompetitive-intent test of illegality and the test of *prima facie* illegality promulgated by Article 101(1) of the 2009 Lisbon Treaty's prohibition of exemplars of covered conduct that "have as their object" the "prevention" or "restriction" of competition and Article 102 of the 2009 Lisbon Treaty's prohibition of any exclusionary abuse by a dominant firm (or, by interpretation, by any set of collectively-dominant rivals)?

(2) Why is it correct as a matter of U.S. law to interpret the Clayton Act's prohibition of covered conduct whose "effect may be to lessen competition or tend to create a monopoly" to declare such conduct *prima facie* illegal if but only if it imposes a net equivalent-dollar loss on the customers of the perpetrator or perpetrators and the customers of its/their product-rivals (all taken together) by reducing the absolute attractiveness of the best offer they respectively receive from any inferior supplier? Why in particular is this operationalization of the Clayton Act's test of *prima facie* illegality superior to the "decrease in unit-output," "increase in price," "increase in price *minus* marginal cost (P–MC)," "increase in (P–MC)/P," "increase in buyer welfare," and "increase in seller profits" operationalizations of the Clayton Act's test of illegality that some scholars and some U.S. courts have proposed or used? Why is it correct as a matter of U.S. law to assess the competitive impact of a merger or acquisition or any other relevant unit of conduct by comparing the state of the world such conduct generated or would generate with the state of the world that would have resulted had the defendant(s) done nothing as opposed to by comparing it with the state of the world that would have resulted had the defendant(s) made the most-competition-enhancing choice they could have made that would have been more profitable than doing nothing? Do any features of the 2009 Treaty of Lisbon or its or its predecessors' interpretation by the European Commission (EC) or E.C./E.U. courts favor the conclusion that, under E.C./E.U. competition law, the baseline for competitive-impact assessment is the state of the world that would have resulted from the defendant's or defendants' making the most-pro-competitive choice that would have been more profitable for it/them to make than choosing to do nothing? Why is it correct as a matter of U.S. law to read the part of the Clayton Act's text that states that covered conduct is illegal only if its effect

may be "substantially to lessen competition or to tend to create a monopoly" "*in any line of commerce or in any section of the country*" (emphasis added) to imply that covered conduct that has or may have such an effect in one product or geographic market violates the Act even if on balance it does not lessen competition or tend to create a monopoly? What is the relationship between the correct interpretation of this portion of the Clayton Act's text and the "more than *de minimis* effect" doctrine of E.C./E.U. competition law? Why is it correct as a matter of U.S. law to conclude that the Clayton Act legality of various vertical practices depends on the competitive impact of a rule permitting all members of a set of product-rivals to engage in the practice as opposed to the competitive impact of an individual firm's engaging in the practice? Relatedly, why is it incorrect as a matter of U.S. law to interpret the Clayton Act to authorize U.S. courts to engage in pari-mutuel handicapping—to prohibit well-established firms from making use of various contractual arrangements and sales/consignment policies to increase their business' proficiency in order to protect marginal and potential competitors while allowing marginal competitors and new entrants to use such contractual arrangements and sales/consignment policies to help them survive?

(3) Why may the specific-anticompetitive-intent test of illegality and the lessening-competition test of illegality just operationalized yield different conclusions about the legality of given conduct? What is the relationship between each of these tests of illegality and the economic-inefficiency test of illegality that some U.S. antitrust economists and legal scholars claim or implicitly assume U.S. antitrust law promulgates or U.S courts should read the U.S. antitrust statutes to promulgate?

(4) What is the legally-correct operationalization of Article 101's prohibition of exemplars of covered conduct that "have as their object or effect" "the distortion of competition"? What is the relationship between this test of illegality and the test of illegality promulgated by the U.S. Federal Trade Commission Act's prohibition of "unfair methods of competition"?

(5) Can a justiciable operationalization be given to Article 102's prohibition of "exploitative abuses"? If so, what is that operationalization? Does U.S. antitrust law promulgate any such test of illegality?

(6) What is the relationship between the efficiency defense that U.S. courts have recognized in Sherman Act cases, the organizational-economic-efficiency defense that I find correct as a matter of law to read into the Clayton Act, the efficiency defenses recognized by the various U.S. Horizontal Merger Guidelines, the efficiency defence promulgated by Article 101(3) of the 2009 Treaty of Lisbon, the "competition on the merits" defence the EC and E.C./E.U. courts at least sometimes recognize in Article 102 exclusionary-abuse cases, and the efficiency defence promulgated by the EMCR?

(7) Does the U.S. Sherman Act cover all business conduct or does it not cover unsuccessful attempts to enter into price-fixing or other-term-fixing agreements and natural oligopolistic behavior—*i.e.*, conduct initiated by an actor that would not have found the conduct *ex ante* profitable but for its belief

job for a substantial period of time if all initial bids are rejected, a medical professional association's refusing to supply insurers with information the insurers claim they need to assess whether particular medical services are in specific cases covered by insurance, or a professional association's forbidding any member from making a price-offer for his or her services until the prospective employer has, after interviewing the members, expressed an intention to hire him? What Sherman-Act-licit and Sherman-Act-illicit functions can be performed by inter-seller exchanges of information on past prices, future prices, costs, inventories, and production-plans? Why is the ability of exchanges of information on these parameters to perform both licit and illicit functions enhanced by the identification of the sellers and/or buyers to which the information relates? Are information exchanges in which such party-identities are revealed more likely or less likely to be monopolizing than those in which party-identities are not revealed? Why may it be profitable for one or more rivals to contrive changes in the non-price terms buyers are offered, non-QV-investment-generated changes in the attributes of the products that are on offer or in buyer perceptions of the relevant products' attributes, reductions in the quantity or changes in the product-space location of the QV investments that are made, or reductions in the quantity or changes in the character of the production-process-research (PPR) projects that are executed? When may the above effects be generated by natural oligopolistic interactions? What kinds of price-related evidence on bidding patterns have U.S. and E.C./E.U. courts concluded favor the conclusion that the relevant sellers were engaging in illegal oligopolistic pricing? Is this type of evidence as probative as the courts that based their decisions on it claimed? Do the various so-called plus factors that U.S. courts claim favor the conclusion that one or more defendants have practiced contrived oligopolistic pricing actually favor that conclusion? Is the U.S. case-law on inter-rival information exchanges correct as a matter of economics or law? Is the U.S. and E.C./E.U. case-law on rival efforts to standardize quality or establish what purport to be minimum quality standards correct as a matter of law? Have the U.S. or E.C./E.U. courts or antitrust-enforcement agencies taken positions on oligopolistic interactions that reduce the quantity or change the product-space location of the QV investments that are made or of the PPR projects that are executed? Are any such positions that have been taken correct as a matter of law?

(13) What definition of predatory conduct operationalizes this concept to cover behaviors that violate the Sherman Act's specific-anticompetitive-intent test of illegality, Article 101's "have as their object the prevention or restriction of competition" test of *prima facie* illegality, and Article 102's exclusionary-abuse test of illegality? What kinds of behaviors can be predatory? What are the determinants of the profitability of predatory pricing? What arguments have economists and antitrust-law scholars made to support their conclusion that predatory pricing is virtually never profitable or practiced, and what are the deficiencies of these arguments? Why is "limit pricing"—the alleged practice in which established firms charge lower prices than they would

otherwise have found profitable to deter entry—predatory? Why is limit pricing unlikely to be effective, unlikely to be more profitable than allowing entry to occur even when it would be effective, and unlikely to be more profitable than various other moves that incumbents can make to deter entry (*e.g.*, making [limit] QV investments) even if it would be more profitable than allowing entry to occur? What kinds of evidence favor the conclusion that one or more defendants have engaged in predatory pricing? What tests have scholars recommended courts use and have U.S. and E.C./E.U. courts actually used to determine whether predatory pricing has been practiced, and what are the flaws in these tests? Under what circumstances will advertising expenditures be predatory? Is the U.S. and E.C./E.U. antitrust case-law on advertising correct as a matter of law? How should the concepts of "predatory QV investments" and "predatory cost-reducing investments" be defined for all such investments as defined to violate the specific-anticompetitive-intent test of illegality? How do these definitions differ from the limit-investment definition of a predatory QV investment advocated by some leading economists (according to which a QV investment would be deemed predatory if and only if the investor's *ex ante* perception that it was *ex ante* profitable depended on the investor's belief that it would or might deter a rival QV investment)? Under what circumstances will QV investments (including investments in product R&D), production-process research, and investments in plant modernization (all of which obviously create some Sherman-Act-licit profits) violate the Sherman Act's test of illegality (be predatory)? What are the Sherman-Act-licit functions of refusals to deal? Under what conditions will refusals to deal violate the Sherman Act (be predatory)? Is the "essential-facilities" doctrine (which imposes an obligation on owners of certain [ill-specified] types of facilities in certain types of [ill-specified] situations to make them available to competitors [on "reasonable" terms]) correct as a matter of law? What are the non-monopolizing (legitimate) private functions of so-called systems rivalry—the practice in which the producer of one product makes changes in that product that render incompatible complements produced by independents and perhaps keeps those changes secret, prohibits buyers of its product from purchasing complementary goods or (aftermarket) services from independents, or refuses to supply repair or maintenance materials or know-how to independent aftermarket-service providers—and under what conditions will "systems rivalry" be predatory? Is the U.S. case-law on systems rivalry sound as a matter of economics and correct as a matter of law? Is the "quantitative substantiality" test that U.S. courts formerly used to determine the legality of long-term full-requirements contracts economically and therefore legally sound? Is the "qualitative substantiality" test that U.S. courts currently use to determine the legality of long-term full-requirements contracts economically and therefore legally sound—in particular, does this test take account of the fact that not all suppliers in any market are equally-well-placed to obtain the patronage of given buyers? Why does Article 101 of the 2009 Treaty of Lisbon not cover many types of predation?

What is the relationship between the U.S.' "essential-facilities" doctrine and the EC's claim that Article 102 imposes a legal duty on dominant firms to preserve competition in the areas of product-space in which they are dominant? What is the relationship between this EC claim and the EC's acknowledgement that Article 102 does not prohibit competition on the merits?

(14) What Sherman-Act-licit private functions can horizontal mergers or acquisitions perform? What determines the extent to which a horizontal merger or acquisition will increase its perpetrators' profits by performing each of these functions? What in particular determines the extent to which the economic efficiencies a horizontal merger or acquisition generates will increase the profits of the merger partners? What determines the impact of a horizontal merger or acquisition that generates no economic efficiencies on (A) the highest non-oligopolistic prices of the merged firm (relative to the highest non-oligopolistic prices of the merger partners), (B) the amount of oligopolistic margins the merged firm can obtain naturally (relative to the amount that the merger partners could have obtained), (C) the amount of oligopolistic margins the merged firm would find profitable to contrive and would contrive (relative to the amount that the merger partners would have found profitable to contrive and would have contrived), (D) the highest non-oligopolistic prices of the merged firm's rivals, (E) the natural oligopolistic margins of the merged firm's rivals, (F) the contrived oligopolistic margins of the merged firm's rivals, and (G) the intensity of the QV-investment competition that the merged firm and its rivals will face (relative to the intensity of such competition that the merger partners and the merged firm's rivals faced or would face absent the merger)—*inter alia*, the merger's impact on the retaliation barriers that the merged firm would face (relative to those that would have been faced by the merger partners), its impact on the retaliation barriers to new entry that would face the relevant potential competitors of the merged firm, its impact on the retaliation barriers to expansion that would face the merged firm's established rivals, its impact on the monopolistic QV-investment disincentives the merged firm would face because its contemplated QV investment would reduce the profit-yields of its other QV investments in the relevant area of product-space by more than they would otherwise be reduced by any rival QV investment the contemplated investment would deter (relative to the monopolistic QV-investment disincentives a relevant merger partner would otherwise have faced), or its impact on the monopolistic QV-investment incentives the merged firm would face because its contemplated QV investment would (in effect) increase its other QV investments' profit-yields because its QV investment would reduce those yields less than they would otherwise be reduced by the rival QV investment(s) the QV investment in question would deter (relative to the monopolistic QV-investment incentives a relevant merger partner would otherwise have faced)? What determines the impact of the economic efficiencies a horizontal merger or acquisition generates on the prices charged by the merged firm relative to those that would have been charged by the merger partners, on the prices

charged by the merged firm's rivals, and, derivatively, on the merged firm's profits and the merger's net equivalent-dollar impact on the customers of the merged firm and the customers of the merged firm's product-rivals? What determines the impact of the economic efficiencies a horizontal merger generates on equilibrium QV investment in the relevant area of product-space (on the quality and variety of the products on offer to the customers of the merged firm and the customers of its product-rivals) and, derivatively, on the merged firm's profits and the merger's net equivalent-dollar impact on the customers of the merged firm and the customers of the merged firm's product-rivals? What market-oriented protocol did U.S. courts traditionally use to predict or post-dict the competitive impact of a horizontal merger or acquisition, and what were the deficiencies of this market-oriented approach? What are the most important features of the pre-merger notification systems of the U.S. and the E.C./E.U., and how do they differ from each other? What market-oriented approach did the U.S. 1992 Horizontal Merger Guidelines state that the Department of Justice (DOJ) and Federal Trade Commission (FTC) would use to predict the competitive impact of any horizontal merger or acquisition, and what were the deficiencies of this approach? What approaches did the DOJ and FTC actually take to predicting the competitive impact of horizontal mergers and acquisitions post-1992, and what were the strengths and weaknesses of these approaches? To what extent were the approaches just described not market-oriented? Why is it correct to say that—although the 2010 U.S. Horizontal Merger Guidelines continue to devote considerable attention to market definition—they essentially abandon the elements of the 1992 Guidelines' approach to the analysis of the competitive impact of horizontal mergers and acquisitions that were market-oriented? How do the test of *prima facie* illegality and the economic-efficiency defence promulgated by the EMCR differ from their 2009 Treaty of Lisbon Article 101 counterparts? How do the European Commission's Horizontal Merger Guidelines' market-aggregated-data-focused decision-rules differ from their 1992 U.S. Horizontal Merger Guidelines' counterparts? Why is it correct to say that the EC Guidelines give the impact of a horizontal merger on quality and variety more weight than any U.S. Guidelines do? What features of the EC's approach to defining markets seem likely to lead the Commission to abandon its market-oriented approach to predicting the competitive impact of horizontal mergers? Why will the EC's consideration of the problems it acknowledges will arise when the relevant products constitute an (unbroken) "chain of substitutes" tend to lead it to conclude that it should reject all market-oriented approaches to predicting the competitive impact of horizontal mergers? Why is it correct to say that the current EC approach to analyzing the competitive impact of horizontal mergers is less market-oriented than is the approach of the 1992 U.S. Guidelines but more market-oriented than is the approach of the 2010 U.S. Guidelines?

(15) Why can conglomerate mergers and acquisitions of all types yield their participants all the categories of Sherman-Act-licit profits that horizontal

mergers and acquisitions can yield their participants? Why can product-diversification and geographic-diversification conglomerate mergers that do not eliminate an effective potential competitor create a merged firm that is more able to profit from practicing contrived oligopolistic pricing, raising retaliation barriers to rival QV investments, and practicing predation than the merger partners were? What are the determinants of the extent to which any such conglomerate merger will make strategic behavior of each of the above kinds more profitable for the merged firm than it would have been for the merger partners? How can conglomerate mergers affect the ability of the merged firm's rivals to practice contrived oligopolistic pricing, raise retaliation barriers to expansion, and engage in predation? What are the determinants of the sign and magnitudes of these effects? What determines the effectiveness of the best-placed potential entrant into any area of product-space? When will limit pricing deter entry, be more profitable than allowing entry to occur, and be more profitable than limit investing? When will it be profitable for an established firm faced with a threat of entry to make one or more limit QV investments? Why may a conglomerate merger that eliminates an effective potential competitor still increase QV-investment competition? What are the determinants of the overall impact of such a conglomerate merger on QV-investment competition? Is it accurate as a matter of economics to assume (as the DOJ once indicated it would assume) that the best-placed, second-placed, and third-placed potential entrant into any area of product-space will always be an effective potential competitor and that no lower-placed potential entrant will ever be an effective potential competitor? Are the U.S. courts correct in assuming that in a wide variety of circumstances established firms will respond to the threat of entry by engaging in limit pricing and will (at least sometimes) perceive potential competition to be effective when entry would not occur even if they did nothing to prevent it? Are the U.S. courts correct in assuming that limit pricing is pro-competitive as opposed to being predatory? As a matter of economics, is the U.S. Supreme Court's claim that any tendency of a conglomerate merger to make reciprocal trading more feasible for the merged firm than it would be for the merger partners favors the conclusion that the merger violates the Sherman Act's test of illegality or the Clayton Act's test of *prima facie* illegality correct as a matter of economics? Is the so-called toe-hold merger doctrine promulgated by several lower U.S. courts (under which a firm that wants to execute a geographic-diversification merger or acquisition with a medium-sized or large "partner" will be allowed to do so only if it can prove that it made a reasonable effort to identify a smaller firm that it could buy or merge with profitability and failed to do so) correct as a matter of economics (in the sense of being likely to increase competition) and correct as a matter of U.S. law (even if it would be likely to increase competition)? Is there any difference between the U.S. Supreme Court's claim (in one case) that any tendency of a conglomerate merger to create a merged firm that is more likely than its antecedents to engage in reciprocity counts against its legality under U.S. antitrust law and the repeated claim of both the EC and E.C./E.U. courts that any tendency of a conglomerate merger to create a merged firm that will practice more reciprocity and enter into more tying agreements counts against the merger's legality under E.C./E.U. competition law? Why is it correct to say that, although—unlike their U.S. counterparts and academic economists—the EC and the E.C./E.U. courts have recognized that conglomerate mergers can increase the extent of contrived oligopolistic pricing and other sorts of strategic conduct, the E.C./E.U. authorities have misunderstood how conglomerate mergers can produce these effects and therefore have reached incorrect conclusions about the circumstances in which they are likely to do so?

(16) What Sherman-Act-licit functions can be performed by vertical integration (achieved by merger/acquisition or internal growth)? Which of these licit functions can be performed by various pricing-techniques, contract-of-sale provisions, and consignment or sales policies—in particular, by conventional price discrimination, perfect price discrimination, charging a combination of a lump-sum fee and supra-marginal-cost per-unit price, tie-ins, reciprocity, systems rivalry, minimum-price-setting resale price maintenance, maximum-price-setting resale price maintenance, vertical territorial restraints and customer-allocation clauses, manufacturer subsidies of reseller advertising-and-promotion expenditures, slotting arrangements, single-brand and non-single-brand exclusive dealerships, long-term full-requirements contracts, and sales/consignment policies of cutting off distributors/consignees that do not act in particular (recommended?) ways? What are the various ways in which vertical mergers/acquisitions or vertical integration through internal growth can *ceteris paribus* critically inflate the integrator's profits by reducing the absolute attractiveness of the best offers against which the integrator will have to compete? Under what conditions will vertical integration by merger/acquisition or internal growth manifest its perpetrator's specific anticompetitive intent? Why may vertical integration "distort competition" even if it does not lessen competition in the Clayton Act sense? Under what conditions will the various pricing-techniques, contract-of-sale provisions, and sales/consignment policies just listed manifest their perpetrator's specific anticompetitive intent? How can a firm's vertical merger(s)/acquisition(s) or vertical integration through internal growth lessen competition in the Clayton Act sense, and under what conditions will it do so? Under what conditions will a rule allowing all members of a set of product-rivals to use the just-listed contract-of-sales provisions and sales/consignment policies lessen competition in the Clayton Act sense? Why are all of the business behaviors listed above covered by the Sherman Act? Which of the various surrogates for vertical integration listed above are never covered by the Clayton Act, and which are covered by the Clayton Act only when they involve a full-requirements contract? Why is it correct as a matter of U.S. antitrust law to conclude that the question in many Clayton Act cases is the impact on competition of a general rule allowing all members of a set of product-rivals to use a particular surrogate for vertical integration as opposed to the impact on competition of

an individual firm's use of that vertical-integration surrogate? Have the U.S. courts and the DOJ and FTC reached correct conclusions about the conditions under which vertical integration or long-term full-requirements contracts will foreclose competitors and lessen competition (and perhaps manifest specific anticompetitive intent)? Why are the distinctions between (A) a contractual provision and a sales policy and (B) a sales policy that includes a verbally-articulated threat and one that does not—distinctions that U.S. courts once found legally critical—legally irrelevant? Why is the distinction (which U.S. courts once thought legally critical) between a producer's controlling the conduct of an independent distributor to which it sold its product and controlling the conduct of an independent distributor to which it consigned its product legally irrelevant? Why is the leverage theory of tie-ins and reciprocity (which the U.S. courts propounded and continue to endorse) incorrect as a matter of economics (despite some modern economists' attempt to justify it) and therefore incorrect as a matter of law? Why is the contention, formerly made by the U.S. Supreme Court, that the antitrust illegality of resale price maintenance is a corollary of the conclusion that U.S. antitrust law prohibits horizontal price fixing incorrect as a matter of law? Why is the U.S. Supreme Court's holding that the legality of minimum-price-fixing resale price maintenance depends in individual cases on whether the practice increases inter-brand competition by more than it decreases intra-brand competition incorrect as a matter of law? Does the fact that the E.C. and E.U. were created in part to promote social and political integration bear on the legality under E.C./E.U. competition law of a manufacturer's prohibiting distributors in one member country from reselling its products to distributors or final consumers in another member country (from prohibiting "parallel trade")—*i.e.*, if decisions declaring manufacturers' efforts to prevent parallel trade illegal would increase parallel trade, would that fact imply that such decisions are correct as a matter of E.C./E.U. competition law? Even if the answer to the immediately-preceding question were affirmative, would the legal significance of that conclusion be vitiated if manufacturers would respond to such a legal ruling by making other arrangements that prevented the ruling from increasing the extent to which their goods were sold in multiple member-countries? What business decisions might manufacturers make if they could not contractually prohibit their independent distributors from making sales in other E.U.-member-countries to prevent such cross-country sales from being made? Is the legality of various surrogates for vertical integration under E.C./E.U. competition law affected by the fact that clause (e) of now-Article 101 and clause (d) of now-Article 102 imply that many of these practices impose (supplemental) obligations that "by their nature or according to commercial usage. . .have no connection with the subject of. . .[the] contracts" that impose them—even though both of these claims are incorrect as a matter of both economics and business practice? Is the legality of the various pricing-technique, contractual-term, and sales/consignment-policy surrogates for vertical integration under Article 102 of the 2009 Treaty of Lisbon affected by the fact that that Article promulgates an "exploitative-abuse" (as well as an "exclusionary-abuse") test of illegality? Has the economic analysis of the Sherman-Act-licit functions of vertical integration and its pricing-technique, contractual-provision, and sales/consignment-policy surrogates and of the conditions under which various types of such conduct will lessen competition or manifest specific anticompetitive intent had less of an impact on the EC's and E.C./E.U. courts' pronouncements about the legality of such conduct under E.C./E.U. competition law than it has had on the DOJ/FTC's pronouncements and enforcement decisions and the U.S. courts' holdings and antitrust-law decisions on such conduct (for reasons that cannot be explained by any differences between U.S. and E.C./E.U. antitrust law as written and correctly interpreted and applied)?

(17) What specific kinds of joint ventures are respectively horizontal, conglomerate, and vertical? What specific kinds of joint ventures are respectively full-function and partial-function joint ventures? What Sherman-Act-licit functions can be performed by joint ventures and the restraints that joint-venture agreements impose on the joint venture and its parents? What are the determinants of whether and the extent to which a joint venture and the restraints a joint-venture agreement imposes will perform each of the Sherman-Act-licit functions in question? How can joint-venture agreements that impose no restraints on the joint venture and its parents increase competition or decrease competition? What are the determinants of whether and the extent to which such a joint-venture agreement increases or decreases competition in each of these ways? How can the restraints that a joint-venture agreement imposes on the joint venture and/or its parents increase or decrease competition? What are the determinants of whether and the extent to which such restraints increase or decrease competition in each of the ways in question? If the conclusion that a restraint imposed by a joint-venture agreement is "ancillary" implies that the restraint is lawful, how should the concept of an ancillary restraint be defined for use in antitrust cases in which the applicable test of illegality is respectively the "lessening-competition" test and "the specific-anticompetitive-intent" test? Why is it not possible to predict the competitive impact of a joint-venture agreement and any restraints it imposes without taking account of the details of the business conditions facing the joint venture, its parents, and its and its parents' rivals—*i.e.*, why is it not possible to filter out joint-venture cases acceptably accurately before taking evidence on the details of the joint-venture situation? Why does the Sherman Act but not the Clayton Act cover joint ventures? Have the U.S. courts clearly or legally-correctly defined the concept of "ancillary restraints" in the Sherman Act opinions that use this concept? Why is it correct to say that in some joint-venture cases U.S. courts reached incorrect legal conclusions (A) because they failed to recognize the legal salience of the distinction between business choices that are designed to or do reduce intra-brand competition and business choices that are designed to or do reduce inter-brand competition, (B) because they accepted limit-price theory and assumed that limit pricing was lawful, and (C) because they accepted the "essential-facilities" doctrine? Why is it

correct to say that, in one joint-venture-like collaborative-arrangement case, the U.S. Supreme Court reached the legally-correct decision that the conduct at issue was lawful because it refused to acknowledge that the conduct entailed the use of tie-ins in circumstances in which its own doctrine deemed the tie-ins *per se* illegal? Why is it correct to say that—although the DOJ has recognized many of the Sherman-Act-licit functions that joint ventures can perform as well as the possibility that joint ventures can increase contrived oligopolistic pricing and predatory conduct—its pronouncements on joint ventures are undermined by the Division's assumption that the legality of joint ventures depends on their competitive impact, its market-oriented approach to predicting the impact of joint ventures on price competition, and its failure to address the impact of joint ventures on QV-investment competition? Why is it correct to say that, in the one joint-venture case the FTC handled,[19] the Commission overstepped its legal authority by conditioning its grant of a consent decree to a joint venture on the joint venture's and its parents' accepting various restrictions on their conduct? Why is it correct to conclude that Article 101 of the 2009 Treaty of Lisbon does cover joint ventures? Why is it correct to conclude that in some circumstances joint ventures will violate Article 102 of the 2009 Treaty of Lisbon? Why does the passage of the EMCR not render the preceding two conclusions unimportant? Why may the EC be correct in resolving some Article 101 production and R&D joint-venture cases by declaring the joint venture lawful but limiting the length of time during which the parents may (in essence) agree not to compete against each other as distributors of the jointly-produced or jointly-discovered product when no similar resolution of Sherman Act cases would be correct as a matter of U.S. law? Why have the EC and the E.C./E.U. courts been too likely to conclude that a joint venture would reduce the intensity of QV-investment competition in the joint venture's market (though they deserve credit for addressing this possibility, which their U.S. counterparts ignore)? How have the EC and the E.C./E.U. courts misanalysed the likelihood that joint ventures will increase the incidence of contrived oligopolistic pricing? What economic and legal mistakes undermine the EC's and E.C./E.U. courts' analyses of the legality of joint-buying arrangements (just as they undermine their U.S. counterparts' analyses of the legality of horizontal mergers and joint-buying arrangements)? What economic and legal errors do the EC and the E.C./E.U. courts make when discussing the possibility that a joint venture may prevent, restrict, or distort competition by "foreclosing" the parents' rivals from making sales to the joint venture and possibly to its parents or by making purchases from the joint venture or possibly from its parents? Why is the EC too optimistic about the likelihood that an R&D joint venture that will reduce the extent to which economically-inefficiently-duplicative R&D is executed will qualify for an Article 101(3) exemption? In what respects are the EC's and

[19] General Motors Corp., 103 F.T.C. 374 (1984).

E.C./E.U. courts' analyses of the legality of joint ventures market-oriented? What evidence supports the conclusion that the EC and the E.C./E.U. courts have adopted a pari-mutuel approach to R&D joint-venture cases—*i.e.*, that they allow small companies to create such joint ventures to enable them to improve their competitive positions while prohibiting large companies from doing so? Has the EC's and the E.C./E.U. courts' treatment of the "ancillarity" issue been more precise or appropriate than that of their U.S. counterparts?

(18) What are the most important differences between E.C./E.U. competition law correctly interpreted and applied and U.S. antitrust law correctly interpreted and applied both pre-EMCR and post-EMCR? Historically, what errors were made in common (A) by U.S. courts and the DOJ and FTC and (B) by E.C./E.U. courts and the EC when interpreting and applying respectively U.S. antitrust law and E.C./E.U. competition law? What error have the U.S. courts made when interpreting and applying the Sherman Act that brings U.S. antitrust law as interpreted and applied closer to E.C./E.U. competition law as written than U.S. antitrust law as written is to E.C./E.U. competition law as written? Over the past 20 years or so, what errors of interpretation and application have the U.S. authorities corrected that their E.C./E.U. counterparts continue to make? Why is there reason to believe that the divergence between U.S. and E.C./E.U. competition law as actually interpreted and applied that has been generated by the U.S. authorities' correction of errors of interpretation and application that their E.C./E.U. counterparts continue to make may be relatively short-lived?

The policy-component of this two-study project addresses the following sets of questions:

(1) What definition of "the impact of a natural event, non-government act, or government policy (hereinafter policy) on economic efficiency" creates the conception of this concept that is most useful for policy evaluation and is most consonant with economists' and the general policy audience's intuitive understanding of the concept? How should this definition's equivalent-variation operationalizations of a policy's winners' equivalent-dollar gains and losers' equivalent-dollar losses be elaborated? Should the external preferences of individuals—their positive and negative evaluations of a policy's impact on others—be counted in any economic-efficiency calculation? Why are the Pareto-superior/Pareto-inferior definition of the impact of a policy on economic efficiency and the Kaldor-Hicks, Scitovsky, and potentially-Pareto-superior tests for the economic efficiency of a policy "incorrect"—*i.e.*, why is the conception of the concept they define neither useful nor compatible with intuitive understanding? Why is the claim that "the impact of a policy on economic efficiency" cannot be defined non-arbitrarily because there is no non-arbitrary way to resolve the offer-asking problem incorrect?

(2) Why is it useful to analyze the overall impact of a policy on economic efficiency by analyzing its impact on various subcategories of economic inefficiency—*e.g.*, on the economic inefficiency caused by (A) the allocation of resources among alternative unit-output-increasing uses (UO-to-UO allocations), (B) the allocation of resources among alternative QV-investment-creating uses (QV-to-QV allocations), (C) the allocation of resources among alternative production-process-research-executing (PPR-executing) uses (PPR-to-PPR allocations), (D) the allocation of resources among unit-output-increasing, QV-investment-creating, and PPR-executing uses, (E) producers' choices to use one known production process rather than another, and (F) the allocation of final goods and services among final consumers?

(3) What are the types of imperfections that can generate economic inefficiency by causing the profitability (private attractiveness) of a resource-allocating choice to diverge from its economic efficiency and/or by inducing a relevant resource allocator to make a resource-allocating choice that was not the most profitable (most attractive) choice available to him, her, or it (what are the various types of Pareto imperfections)? How would an individual exemplar of each type of Pareto imperfection[20] cause each category of economic inefficiency just identified in an otherwise-Pareto-perfect economy? How do the multiple exemplars of all types of Pareto imperfections that are present in any actual economy interact to cause each category of economic inefficiency just identified?

(4) What is the relationship between the preceding analysis and the central claim of The General Theory of Second Best[21] that, given a series of optimal conditions, if one or more of those conditions cannot be or will not be fulfilled, there is no general reason to believe that increasing the extent to which the remaining conditions are fulfilled will even tend to bring one closer to the optimum? What does The General Theory of Second Best imply about the soundness of the following contention: the fact that "perfect seller competition" is a Pareto-optimal condition implies that any policy that will increase seller competition will increase economic efficiency on that account (though those who make this claim acknowledge that the related increase in economic efficiency might be smaller than the sum of the allocative transaction costs the policy generated and any losses in economic efficiency it yielded by precluding firms from taking

---

[20] Seven types of Pareto imperfections are conventionally distinguished: imperfections in seller competition, imperfections in buyer competition, (real) externalities, taxes on the margin of income, imperfections in the information available to economic choosers that is relevant to their identifying the choice that most satisfies their "preferences" (non-sovereignty), non-maximization, and buyer surplus that would cause economic inefficiency in an otherwise-Pareto-perfect economy (sometimes mislabeled, public goods). Some would say that one should also list the allocative transaction costs that would have to be generated to eliminate the other types of Pareto imperfections as an eighth type of Pareto imperfection.

[21] See R.G. Lipsey and Kelvin Lancaster, *The General Theory of Second Best*, 24 Rev. Econ. Stud. 11 (1956), for the first formal statement of the theory.

advantage of economies of scale and combining assets that are complementary for non-scale reasons)? Granting that it would not be *ex ante* economically efficient (even if it were possible) to assess the economic efficiency of any antitrust (or other) policy by analyzing its impact on each category of economic inefficiency whose magnitude it might affect perfectly accurately by executing perfect analyses of all relevant theoretical issues and generating perfectly-accurate estimates of the magnitudes of each parameter whose relevance the theory establishes (by executing what I call second-best-economic [allocative]-efficiency analyses), why does this reality not imply the *ex ante* economic efficiency of analyzing the economic efficiency of reducing the incidence or magnitude of any type of Pareto imperfection on the assumption that the target imperfection in question is the only Pareto imperfection in the economy (that the economy is otherwise-Pareto-perfect)—*i.e.*, does not imply the *ex ante* economic efficiency of what I call first-best-economic-efficiency analyses? Why, to the contrary, do the theory and facts that justify the corollary of The General Theory of Second Best that relates to the prediction or post-diction of the impact of any policy on economic efficiency imply the *ex ante* economic efficiency of a protocol that takes account not just of all categories of economic inefficiency, the ways in which individual exemplars of each type of Pareto imperfection can cause each category of economic inefficiency in an otherwise-Pareto-perfect economy, and the ways in which the extant imperfections interact to cause each category of economic inefficiency but also of the allocative (economic-efficiency) benefits and costs of doing additional theoretical work and collecting additional data on the parameters whose relevance theory establishes—*i.e.*, of what I call third-best-allocative-efficiency analysis?

(5) Why might it be *ex ante* third-best economically efficient to analyze the impact of a policy on the magnitudes of UO-to-UO, QV-to-QV, PPR-to-PPR, QV-to-UO and UO-to-QV, QV-to-PPR and PPR-to-QV, and UO-to-PPR and PPR-to-UO misallocation by predicting or post-dicting the policy's impact on the "percentage-distortions in the profits yielding by" the "marginal exemplars" of the resource-uses involved in each category of resource allocation just listed where "the percentage-distortion in the profits yielded by" any resource-use equals the ratio of *the difference between the profits that resource use yielded and the economic efficiency of that resource use* to *the allocative cost of the resource use in question (the allocative value the resources "consumed" by that use would have generated in their actual alternative uses)* and "the marginal exemplars of any resource use" is defined to be the exemplars of that resource-use that are least profitable but not unprofitable (*i.e.*, does not refer to the relevant resource use's magnitude [allocative cost])? Why, more specifically, might it be *ex ante* third-best economically efficient to analyze the economic efficiency of the impact of any policy on the above categories of resource allocation by focusing on its impact on the weighted mean, weighted mean deviation, and weighted-average squared deviation of either the positive or the negative segment of the distribution of percentage-distortions in the profits yielded by the marginal exemplars of some of the categories of resource

allocation just listed and of both the positive and the negative segment of the distribution of percentage-distortions in the profits yielded by the marginal exemplars of other of the categories just listed where the weight to be assigned to any percentage-distortion figure, deviation from the weighted mean of the positive segment of a distribution of percentage-distortions in the profits yielded by a specified type of resource allocation, and squared deviation from the weighted mean of such a distribution-segment equals the allocative cost of the relevant resource uses? Why does this approach seem less promising when the economic efficiency of a policy's impact on the amount of misallocation generated by producer choices among known production-techniques or the allocation of goods among final consumers is at issue? What is the *ex ante* economically-efficient way to assess the impact of a policy on the magnitudes of these other categories of economic inefficiency? What is the overall distortion-analysis protocol for predicting the (total) economic efficiency of any policy?

(6) What facts does the distortion-analysis protocol for economic-efficiency assessment imply are relevant to the prediction or post-diction of the economic efficiency of prohibiting and preventing all exemplars of all variants of monopolizing conduct, all exemplars of all variants of conduct that reduce competition overall, and all exemplars of all variants of conduct that distort competition? Given the information currently available and taking into consideration the likely success and allocative-transaction-cost consequences of efforts to bar or prosecute all such exemplars of conduct, would such efforts be likely to be economically efficient? What facts would be relevant to assessing the economic efficiency of various more selective efforts to deter monopolizing conduct, conduct that lessens competition, and conduct that distorts competition? Which more selective policies seem likely to be not just more economically efficient than non-selective policies of these sorts but economically efficient?

(7) What facts does the distortion-analysis protocol for economic-efficiency assessment imply are relevant to the prediction or post-diction of the economic efficiency of the various provisions of U.S. and E.C./E.U. antitrust law as correctly interpreted and applied and as actually interpreted and applied? Given the information currently available, which of these legal provisions (as correctly and as actually interpreted and applied) seem likely to increase economic efficiency and which seem likely to decrease economic efficiency?

(8) What non-antitrust policies (*e.g.*, anti-pollution, other sorts of tax, and intellectual-property policies) might reduce the magnitudes of one or more of the categories of economic inefficiency whose magnitudes antitrust policies can affect?

(9) What objectives other than increasing economic efficiency might antitrust policies be designed to secure? How might these distributive-value and political-process-value objectives affect the overall evaluation of the various antitrust policies that could be adopted and the antitrust laws of the U.S. and E.C./E.U. as correctly interpreted and applied and as actually interpreted and applied?

At the risk of being not only obvious but annoyingly repetitive, I will now explain why this project's analyses of the preceding questions have practical value for its various potential readers. I start with Antitrust Economics (Industrial Organization) economists and experts in Welfare Economics. Scholars and students of Antitrust Economics should profit from the law study's operationalizations of the U.S. and E.C./E.U. laws' tests of illegality and the policy study's analyses of the economic efficiency of increasing competition. Many antitrust economists (often under the influence of misguided legal scholars) assume that U.S. and E.C./E.U. antitrust law promulgate an economic-inefficiency test of illegality. And many experts in antitrust (and welfare) economics assume that increases in competition always tend to increase economic efficiency—*i.e.*, ignore The General Theory of Second Best. Antitrust Economics scholars and students should also profit from the law study's operational definitions of "contrived and natural oligopolistic conduct," "predatory conduct" in general and "predatory QV investments" and "predatory cost-reducing investments" in particular. *Inter alia*, such potential readers should also find valuable the following elements of the law study's analyses: (1) the distinction between individualized-pricing situations and across-the-board-pricing situations, (2) the concept of a best-placed seller's basic competitive advantage in its relations with a particular buyer—the sum of its buyer preference advantage and marginal cost advantage over its closest rival for that buyer's patronage, (3) the individualized-pricing-situation concept of the contextual marginal costs that the second-placed supplier of a particular buyer would have to incur to charge that buyer to match the highest non-oligopolistic-price-containing offer of the buyer's best-placed supplier because the second-placed supplier's relevant price was discriminatory or violated a maximum or minimum price regulation, (4) the concept of an individualized pricer's highest non-oligopolistic price to a buyer it was best-placed to supply—the price the best-placed seller would find most profitable to charge that buyer if its rivals believed that it could not react to their responses to that price, (5) the concept of the highest non-oligopolistic price for an across-the-board pricer to charge, (6) the definition and analysis of the determinants of the magnitude of the across-the-board-pricing counterpart to the individualized-pricing concept of the contextual marginal costs that a second-placed supplier will have to incur to match the highest-non-oligopolistic-price-containing offer of the best-placed supplier of a particular buyer, (7) the definition of QV-investment competition, (8) the definitions of the various intermediate determinants of the intensity of QV-investment competition, (9) the analysis of the ways in which (in different situations) these determinants will interact to determine the intensity of QV-investment competition, (10) the analyses of the evidence that does and does not favor or establish the conclusion that a particular seller has engaged in contrived or natural oligopolistic pricing, charged a predatory price, or made a predatory QV or cost-reducing investment, (11) the analyses of the legitimate functions of horizontal and conglomerate mergers and acquisitions (some of which are standard and some of which are not), (12) the demonstration that, regardless of whether one uses an ideal-type or functional criterion to evaluate market definitions and market-definition protocols, market definitions are inherently arbitrarily not just at their periphery but comprehensively, (13) the analyses of the determinants of the impact of a horizontal or conglomerate merger on price competition (on the highest non-oligopolistic prices, natural oligopolistic margins, and contrived oligopolistic margins of the merged firm relative to those of its merger-partner antecedents and on the highest non-oligopolistic prices, natural oligopolistic margins, and contrived oligopolistic margins of the merged firm's rivals), (14) the analyses of the determinants of the impact of a horizontal or conglomerate merger on QV-investment competition, (15) the explanation of why limit pricing will rarely deter entry, will be extraordinarily unlikely to be more profitable than allowing entry to occur even when it would deter entry, and will be even less likely to be more profitable than limit investing even if it was equally-effective as limit investing at deterring entry, (16) the standard and non-standard analyses of the legitimate functions of vertical integration and the pricing-techniques, contractual clauses, and non-contractual sales/consignment policies that are surrogates for vertical integration, (17) the analyses of the conditions under which vertical integration and its various surrogates will reduce or distort competition, (18) the demonstration that even joint ventures that impose no restraints on the conduct of the joint venture and/or its parents can either increase or decrease competition, that the restraints imposed by joint-venture agreements can either increase or decrease competition, and that, in order to determine the competitive impact of a joint venture without its restraints or the restraints any joint-venture agreement imposes, one must execute an analysis that focuses on the specific facts of the case at hand, (19) the demonstration that market-oriented protocols for determining the antitrust legality of business conduct (including all those used by U.S. and E.C./E.U. courts, the DOJ and FTC, and the EC as well as all those proposed by economists and economics-conversant legal scholars) cannot be cost-effective both because the market definitions they use are arbitrary and because data on the market-aggregated parameters on which they focus have less predictive power than do data on the non-market-aggregated parameters that should be used to define the relevant market(s), and (20) the critiques of various doctrines promulgated by U.S. and E.C./E.U. courts and U.S. and E.C./E.U. antitrust-enforcement "agencies," including not only the limit-pricing doctrine but the leverage theory of tie-ins and reciprocity, the various foreclosure "theories" applied to long-term requirements-contracts and vertical integration, the U.S. courts' essential-facilities doctrine and the EC's claim that dominant firms have a special obligation to promote competition, the U.S. courts' toe-hold-merger doctrine, the claim that U.S. antitrust law and E.C./E.U. competition law are as concerned with decreases in intra-brand competition as they are with decreases in inter-brand competition, and the EC's claim that the Treaty is intended *inter alia* to promote parallel trading and R&D.

Welfare economists and welfare-economics students should profit from the policy study's (1) correct definition of a policy's impact on economic efficiency and its critiques of the Pareto-superior/Pareto-inferior, Kaldor-Hicks, Scitovsky, and potentially-Pareto-superior operationalizations of this concept, (2) identification of the categories of economic inefficiency that are economically efficient to distinguish and analyze, (3) analyses of the different ways in which an economy's various Pareto imperfections interact to cause each of these categories of economic inefficiency, (4) account and justification of the distortion-analysis protocol for assessing the economic efficiency of any policy, (5) analyses of the economic efficiency of various possible and extant antitrust policies, (6) critiques of various canonical analyses of the economic efficiency of particular antitrust policies and of pro-competition policies more generally, (7) discussion of the various non-antitrust (*e.g.*, anti-pollution, other sorts of tax, and intellectual-property) policies that can be designed to reduce various categories of economic inefficiency that imperfections in competition can cause, and (8) accounts of the non-economic-efficiency goals that antitrust policies can achieve and the significance of the fact that antitrust policies can achieve such goals for such policies' overall desirability.

Even businessmen who do not want to take advantage of the law study's analyses of the determinants of the profitability of various illegal practices will be able to profit from the law book—in particular, from its (1) account of the legitimate ways that the categories of conduct that antitrust laws cover can increase the profits of their perpetrator(s), (2) analyses of the determinants of the extent to which each such category of conduct will yield its perpetrator or perpetrators legitimate profits in each of the ways it can, (3) articulation of the U.S. antitrust law's and E.C./E.U. competition law's conduct-coverage, tests of illegality, and recognized defenses, (4) delineation of the appropriate ways to analyze the legality of all categories of business conduct under U.S. and E.C./E.U. antitrust law as correctly interpreted and applied and as actually interpreted and applied, and (5) critiques of U.S. and E.C./E.U. antitrust case-law and DOJ/FTC and EC legal guidelines and other sorts of position-pronouncements. I should add that businessmen should be interested in the errors that antitrust courts and antitrust-enforcement "agencies" make not only for straightforward reasons but also because some of those errors make it likely that certain categories of conduct will be held illegal even though other categories of conduct that are functionally identical will be held lawful—*i.e.*, put businesses in a position in which they can reduce their prospect antitrust liabilities by substituting one category of conduct that performs a given function for another category of conduct that performs the same function. For three reasons, businessmen should also be interested in the policy book's analyses of the economic efficiency of various categories of business conduct and of various categories of antitrust policies: such analyses (1) may reveal whether contemplated conduct would qualify for an antitrust defense or should not be deemed to be monopolizing or exclusionarily abusive in the first place, (2) may help the businessmen argue more effectively for antitrust-reform legislation that would be in their interest, and (3) may help them secure more favorable decisions from enforcement agencies (more favorable merger rulings, prosecution decisions, and settlement offers).

Antitrust lawyers and law students should be interested in the analyses of the law study and the analyses of the policy study for virtually the same reasons that these analyses should be valuable to businessmen. The only differences are that lawyers may be less likely to advise businessmen about the profitability of various kinds of illegal conduct than businessmen are to engage in such conduct and that lawyers may have more to learn than businessmen about the legitimate ways in which various categories of conduct can increase business profits and the determinants of the extent to which given conduct will increase business profits in each legitimate way.

Antitrust-law judges and antitrust-enforcement-agency personnel should be interested in the law study's analyses because they are obligated to interpret and apply their legal system's antitrust law correctly. To the extent that antitrust-enforcement-agency personnel are authorized to exercise discretion when enforcing their legal system's antitrust law, operate under a budget-constraint that requires them to be selective when enforcing the law, or are expected to make recommendations for antitrust-law reform, such agency personnel should also be interested in the policy study's economic-efficiency analyses and discussion of the possible non-economic-efficiency goals of antitrust. Legislators and members of the policy audience should find both studies valuable because these individuals will want both (1) to correct the errors that the courts and antitrust-enforcement agencies make when interpreting and applying the law and (2) to reform the written law to make it more economically efficient or desirable overall.

Finally, antitrust-law professors should be interested in the analyses of both the law study and the policy study because their analyses will improve their teaching of antitrust law and antitrust policy, their scholarship, and the private and public consulting-work they do.

Foreword to This Law Study

This Law Study's Business-Conduct-Coverage and Distinctive Features

This study analyzes the non-monopolizing (Sherman-Act-licit) private functions, possible monopolizing or abusive character, competitive impact, and possible competition-distorting effects of the various categories of business conduct that U.S. and/or E.C./E.U. antitrust law covers. More specifically, it addresses these issues as they apply to

(1) the exploitative abuse of a dominant position or of monopoly power,
(2) the various types of oligopolistic conduct in which firms can engage,
(3) the various types of predatory conduct in which firms can engage and some types of business conduct that have been incorrectly characterized as predatory,
(4) horizontal mergers and acquisitions,
(5) conglomerate mergers and acquisitions,
(6) various pricing-technique, contract-term, and sales/consignment-policy surrogates for vertical integration—price discrimination of different sorts, tie-ins, reciprocity, systems rivalry, resale price maintenance, vertical territorial restraints and customer-allocation clauses, long-term full-requirements contracts, single-brand and non-single-brand exclusive dealing, subsidies to independent-distributor advertising and in-store-promotion expenditures, slotting arrangements, and sales and consignment policies of supplying only those independent distributors or using only those independent consignees whose pricing, promotion, and other choices the supplier deems appropriate,
(7) vertical mergers and acquisitions and vertical integration through internal growth,
(8) horizontal, conglomerate, and vertical joint ventures (including R&D joint ventures and patent pools) and related types of inter-firm collaborative arrangements, and
(9) inter-rival exchanges of information, efforts by rivals to establish quality standards, and attempts by rivals to increase the profitability of their product

and production-process research-portfolio without making it smaller by making it less duplicative.

In addition to developing its own economic analyses of the non-monopolizing private functions, possible monopolizing character, competitive impact, and possible competition-distorting effects of these categories of business conduct and explaining how their legality under U.S. and E.C./E.U. antitrust law should be analyzed, it criticizes the standard economic analysis of many of these types of conduct, the conclusions that economists and legal scholars have reached about the way in which courts should analyze their legality, and the ways in which U.S. and E.C./E.U. antitrust agencies and courts have actually handled such conduct.

There is nothing unusual about the set of business practices this law study investigates or the broad issues it addresses. However, the study's approach to these issues is in several respects unique. This Foreword provides preliminary accounts of the study's five major distinguishing features. The separate Introductions to this study's two parts and its Contents contain respectively chapter-by-chapter and section-by-section summaries and outlines of the study's coverage.

This law study's first major distinguishing feature is its explicit definition of various key antitrust-economics concepts. The study provides a basis for its definitions by delineating the criteria one should use to evaluate definitions of the kinds of concepts in question—*viz.*, (1) the extent to which the definition conforms with professional and, when relevant, popular usage and intuitive understanding and (2) the extent to which the definition creates a concept that can play a useful role in a valuable analysis. It then articulates operational definitions of such concepts as "the impact of a choice or policy on economic efficiency," "the impact of a choice or policy on the intensity of competition," "monopolization," "the distorting effect of conduct on competition," "oligopolistic conduct," and "predatory conduct" and applies the criteria it has delineated to justify the definitions it proposes.

This feature of this law study rectifies a deficiency in the literature: economists and lawyers that use economics to execute antitrust-law analyses (1) have never articulated explicit definitions of "oligopolistic conduct" or "predatory conduct," have delineated operational definitions of some categories of predatory conduct that are "incorrect" in the sense in which I use this modifier, and have articulated various underspecified, inconsistent, and I believe "incorrect" operationalizations of "the impact of a choice on the intensity of competition" and "the impact of a choice on economic efficiency" and (2) have never discussed the criteria one should use to evaluate definitions of these sorts of concepts and, relatedly, have never tried to justify the definitions of these concepts they have implicitly or explicitly adopted.

Even at this juncture, an example may be useful. This law study defines a choice to be a "primary oligopolistic choice" if and only if the chooser's *ex ante* perception that it would be profitable was critically affected by its perception that its rivals would or might realize that it could react to their responses to the choice in question. The study further refines this concept to distinguish between primary oligopolistic choices to initiate a "contrived" oligopolistic interaction and primary oligopolistic choices to initiate a "natural" oligopolistic interaction. On this study's definition, an oligopolistic interaction is "contrived" if its initiator induced the responder to believe that the initiator would or might react to its response in a way that would render unprofitable for the responder a non-cooperative response the responder would otherwise have found profitable by promising to reciprocate to the responder's otherwise-unprofitable[22] cooperation (*i.e.*, to react to a cooperative response in an inherently-unprofitable way that would benefit the cooperative responder) and/or by threatening to retaliate[23] against a responder that made a non-cooperative response (*i.e.*, to react to a non-cooperative response in an inherently-unprofitable way that would impose losses on the non-cooperative responder). By way of contrast, on this study's definition, an oligopolistic interaction is "natural" if its initiator did not have to rely on any such anticompetitive promise and/or threat to induce the responder to conclude that the initiator would react to the responder's cooperative and non-cooperative responses in ways that would render unprofitable for the responder non-cooperative responses the responder would otherwise find profitable—more positively, if the initiator could rely on the responder's realization that it would be both possible and inherently profitable for the initiator to react to a non-cooperative response in a way that would render unprofitable for the responder a non-cooperative response the responder would otherwise find profitable (*e.g.*, on the responder's realization that the relevant buyer would give the initiator the opportunity to rebid and that the initiator would find it inherently profitable to beat any non-cooperative response-offer the responder would otherwise find profitable to make to the buyer in question).

As we shall see, although some oligopolistic pricing models focus on conduct that is oligopolistic in my sense, other so-called oligopolistic pricing models focus on conduct that is not oligopolistic in my sense—specifically, focus on conduct that is

---

[22] In my vocabulary, a business believes that a choice it is contemplating making is "inherently profitable" if its perception that the choice will be profitable does not depend on any tendency it believes the choice may have to reduce the absolute attractiveness of the offers against which the business will have to compete in the future in some way that would tend to make the choice more profitable than economically efficient in an otherwise-Pareto-perfect economy—most commonly, by driving a rival out or inducing a rival to compete less hard against it. By way of contrast, in my vocabulary, a business choice is said to be "strategic" if the business' *ex ante* perception that the choice would be profitable is critically affected by the business' belief that the choice will or may reduce the absolute attractiveness of the offers against which it will have to compete in the future in some way that would tend to make the choice more profitable than allocatively efficient in an otherwise-Pareto-perfect economy. For an explanation of the point of the qualification articulated at the end of the preceding sentence, see Chaps. 3 and 4 *infra*.

[23] In my usage, a business' response to a rival's choice is said to be retaliatory if it is a strategic response that is designed to increase the retaliator's future profits by deterring rivals that it does not drive out from competing as hard against the retaliator in the future as they would otherwise have done. This usage distinguishes "retaliatory responses" not only from non-strategic responses but also from "predatory" strategic responses—*i.e.*, responses made by actors that would not have found them profitable *ex ante* but for their belief that they would or might increase their profits in the long run by driving a rival out or deterring a rival from entering when this effect would make the choice in question profitable though economically inefficient in an otherwise-Pareto-perfect economy.

influenced by the actor's realization that the payoff to its choice will be affected by the response it elicits from one or more particular, identifiable rivals. As we shall also see, economists and lawyers have also not distinguished contrived and natural oligopolistic interactions. This study explains why (1) the distinction between the three-stage interaction I denominate "oligopolistic" and the two-stage interaction that some economists call oligopolistic is legally salient under both U.S. and E.C./E.U. antitrust law and (2) the distinction between oligopolistic interactions that are contrived and natural in my sense are legally critical under U.S. but not E.C./E.U. antitrust law, correctly interpreted and applied.

This law study's second major distinguishing feature is its recognition that the economy generates a wide variety of categories of economic inefficiency whose magnitudes business conduct and antitrust policies can affect and that the impact of business conduct on the magnitudes of only some of these categories of economic inefficiency is relevant to the conduct's legality under either U.S. antitrust law or E.C./E.U. competition law. Thus, the study explains why the impact that business conduct has on the amount of misallocation the relevant economy generates (1) by producing the goods it does produce in economically-inefficient proportions, (2) by allocating too many resources from the perspective of economic efficiency to the creation of quality and variety in some areas of product-space relative to the amount of resources it allocates to creating quality and variety in other areas of product-space, (3) by allocating too many resources from the perspective of economic efficiency to research designed to discover more-economically-efficient production processes to use to produce goods in some areas of product-space relative to the amount of resources it allocates to research designed to discover more-economically-efficient production processes to produce goods in other areas of product-space, and (4) by allocating resources among unit-output-increasing, quality-or-variety-creating, and production-process-research-executing uses in economically-inefficient proportions is irrelevant to its legality under both U.S. antitrust law and E.C./E.U. competition law, while any tendency business conduct has to increase economic efficiency (A) by increasing the proficiency with which its perpetrator or perpetrators produce their products using known technologies, distribute their products, and finance their operations, (B) by increasing the intrinsic economic efficiency of the product and production-process-research projects they undertake, (C) by increasing the proficiency with which they execute the research projects they undertake, and (D) by increasing the economic efficiency of the portfolio of research projects a group of businesses execute by enabling them to avoid executing a set of projects that is less economically efficient than an alternative set of the same magnitude could be because the projects they executed were economically-inefficiently duplicative is relevant to its legality under U.S. antitrust law and E.C./E.U. competition law.

The law study's third major distinguishing feature is the conceptual system it uses to analyze the impact of conduct on the intensity of price competition. Conventional analyses (1) focus on the total difference between price and marginal cost and (2) do not analyze separately the determinants of the intensity of price competition in individualized-pricing contexts (in which sellers set separate terms of sale [including prices] to each of their potential customers) and in across-the-board-pricing contexts (in which sellers set terms of sale [including price-terms] that apply to all buyers). This study distinguishes a number of components of the gap between price (P) and marginal cost (MC) and focuses separately on individualized-pricing and across-the-board-pricing contexts. Chapter 2 delineates in detail all the components of the difference between a seller's actual price and marginal cost that are useful to distinguish, including various components of the gap between a seller's actual price and the price it would find most profitable to charge if no-one made any relevant error and its rivals assumed that it could not react to their responses to its price (the firm's NEHNOP or no-error highest-non-oligopolistic price) and various components of the gap between a firm's NEHNOP and its conventional marginal cost. I argue that one should distinguish the components in question because only by doing so can one understand the relationships between or among the components in question, accurately predict the impact of various types of conduct such as horizontal mergers on the prices the merger partners and their independent rivals charge, or accurately assess whether the price a given seller is charging is "oligopolistic" or "predatory." The study focuses separately on individualized-pricing and across-the-board-pricing contexts because some of the components of the P–MC gap of a seller that is setting individualized prices that are useful to distinguish have no exact across-the-board-pricing counterpart, because the determinants of the magnitudes of some of the components of the gap between an individualized-pricing seller's P–MC gap are different from the determinants of the magnitudes of the counterpart components of an across-the-board-pricing seller's P–MC gap, and because one therefore cannot accurately predict the impact of given conduct on the P–MC gap of its perpetrator(s) and its (their) rivals or accurately assess whether a given seller's price is oligopolistic or predatory without paying attention to this distinction between individualized and across-the-board pricing.

The law study's fourth major distinguishing feature is (1) the fact that it analyzes the impact of business choices and government policies not only on price competition but also on what I call quality-or-variety-increasing-investment (QV-investment) competition—the process through which firms compete away their potential supernormal profits by increasing the quality or variety of the products they offer for sale or the distributive outlets they operate—and (2) the conceptual system it uses to analyze the impact of business choices or government decisions on QV-investment competition. This system defines eleven determinants of the intensity of QV-investment competition in any arbitrarily-designated area of product-space (ARDEPPS)[24]: four barriers to entry, four barriers to expansion, the monopolistic QV-investment incentive a potential QV investor that is already operating in the

[24] The text refers to an arbitrarily-designated portion of product-space rather than a market because, for reasons that the text of this Introduction outlines below and Chap. 6 explains in detail, regardless of the plausible criterion one uses to evaluate any set of market definitions, market definitions are inherently arbitrary not just at their periphery but comprehensively.

relevant area of product-space may face, the monopolistic QV-investment disincentive such a potential QV investor may face, and the natural oligopolistic QV-investment disincentives that two or more such potential QV investors may face.[25]

Obviously, economists recognize that firms engage in QV-investment competition as well as price competition. However, because they think that (1) the intensities of price and QV-investment competition are determined by the same factors in the same ways, (2) increases of the same magnitude in price and QV-investment competition (*i.e.*, of equal net equivalent-dollar value to relevant buyers) have the same positive impact on economic efficiency, and (3) increases of the same magnitude in price and QV-investment competition have the same impact on the distribution of income and/or its desirability, they see no need to analyze the impact of any business choice or government decision on the intensity of QV-investment competition—*i.e.*, they believe that one can learn everything one needs to know about the competitive impact, economic efficiency, distributive desirability, and overall desirability of any business choice or government decision by analyzing its impact on price competition. I disagree with this conclusion because I reject all of its predicates. In particular, I believe that

(1) as Chap. 2 makes clear, the determinants of the impact of a business choice or government decision on the intensity of price competition are different from the determinants of such a choice's impact on the intensity of QV-investment competition and a given choice can increase price competition while decreasing QV-investment competition and *vice versa*;
(2) for reasons that THE WELFARE ECONOMICS OF ANTITRUST POLICY AND U.S. AND E.U. ANTITRUST LAW explains in great detail, although increases in price competition almost always increase economic efficiency in any actual, highly-Pareto-imperfect economy, increases in QV-investment competition usually decrease economic efficiency on balance in any actual economy; and
(3) because increases in price competition usually benefit the poor more than do increases in QV-investment competition that confer the same net equivalent-dollar gains on relevant consumers, both the distributive impact of and the distributive desirability from a wide variety of normative perspectives of increases in the two types of competition are almost certainly quite different.

This law study, therefore, analyzes the impact of the business choices and government decisions it examines on QV-investment competition as well as on price competition, and its policy companion analyzes separately the economic

[25] Chapter 2 carefully defines all of these concepts. I should point out that this conceptual system is unique. Admittedly, economists do talk about "barriers to entry." However, they do not define such barriers in the way I have done—indeed, do not define them clearly or consistently and do not use them to analyze QV-investment competition (use them instead to predict whether established firms will engage in "limit pricing"—*i.e.*, will charge lower prices than they would otherwise charge to deter new entry). Moreover, to my knowledge, economists have never discussed either the barriers to expansion established firms face or any of the QV-investment incentives and disincentives I identify.

efficiency/overall desirability of any tendency that relevant business choices and government decisions have on QV-investment competition and price competition. For this purpose, I have developed another unique conceptual scheme.

The law study's fifth major distinguishing feature is its rejection of market-oriented approaches to (1) the measurement of a firm's monopoly, oligopoly power, and total economic power, (2) the analysis of the monopolizing character of any type of business conduct, and (3) the prediction of the competitive impact of any type of business conduct. None of the analyses this study executes uses such an approach—*i.e.*, bases predictions or post-dictions on any kind of market-aggregated data (*e.g.*, on market-share figures, four-firm or eight-firm seller-concentration ratios, post-merger Hirschman-Herfindahl Indices [HHIs—the sum of the squares of the market shares of all firms placed inside an allegedly-relevant market], or merger-induced increases in HHIs). Admittedly, the study's definitions of barriers to entry and expansion and its analyses of the impact of business choices and government decisions on the intensity of QV-investment competition do make reference to arbitrarily-designated areas of product-space (ARDEPPSes). However, my use of these concepts is not inconsistent with my claim that the study consistently rejects market-oriented approaches. At no point do I propose doing anything that requires the oxymoronic non-arbitrary definition of an ARDEPPS—*i.e.*, my use of the concept of an ARDEPPS is always purely heuristic.

As Chap. 6 explains, I reject market-oriented approaches to any of the issues with which this study and/or its policy sequel is concerned for two partially-overlapping reasons. First, I reject market-oriented approaches to any type of antitrust-economics analysis because, regardless of whether one evaluates sets of market definitions (protocols for market definition) by the extent to which the market definitions (the protocols that yield them) (1) satisfy professional (and perhaps popular) assumptions about the competitiveness of products placed within the same market and the difference between the competitiveness of products placed in the same market and the competitiveness of products placed in different markets or (2) play a useful role in a valuable analytic protocol,[26] market definitions (the choice among alternative approaches to market definition) are arbitrary not just at their periphery but comprehensively. Second, I reject market-oriented approaches to antitrust-economics analyses because, even if (contrary to my conclusion) some set of market definitions could be shown to be superior to all its alternatives, market-oriented approaches would not be cost-effective. In my judgment, regardless of the question at issue, market-oriented approaches always achieve the remarkable double of increasing cost while decreasing accuracy because (1) market definitions are costly and (2) the non-market-aggregated data one uses to define relevant markets have more predictive power than the market-aggregated figures

[26] Note that the criteria in question are exemplars of the two criteria by which I think one should evaluate any conceptual definition of the type to which the concept of a market belongs: respectively, (1) is the definition consistent with professional and, when relevant, popular usage and intuitive understanding and (2) will the definition create a concept that can perform a valuable role in a useful analysis.

(on market shares, market-concentration ratios, and HHIs) that market-oriented approaches use market definitions to generate.

Six final introductory points. First, I want to admit at the outset that the question to ask about conceptual systems and analytic approaches is not whether they are "right" or "wrong" but whether they are useful—whether (1) the conceptual systems call attention to important issues that could not be articulated without them (or, at least, without paying attention to the distinctions they draw) and (2) whether the conceptual systems and theoretical approaches enable the analyst to resolve more accurately or cost-effectively both the novel issues the conceptual systems enable the analyst to identify and important issues that have been or can be articulated without making reference to any of the conceptual innovations under scrutiny. Second, I want to assure readers that all the innovative concepts and approaches just outlined will be described and discussed in far more detail in the chapters that follow. Third, and relatedly, I want to point out that readers will not be able to assess the value of the distinguishing conceptual and analytic features of this study until they have seen them in use (until they have read the study). The proof of this pudding is in the eating. Fourth, another vocabulary point: in both this law study and its policy companion, the text will refer to the Antitrust Division of the United States Department of Justice (DOJ), the United States Federal Trade Commission (FTC), and the European Commission (the EC) as "antitrust-enforcement agencies." I admit that, in at least two respects, this designation is somewhat misleading: (1) technically, the United States Department of Justice in general and its Antitrust Division in particular are prosecutorial offices, not (administrative) "agencies," and (2) the EC may well have legislative power, not just the power to find the internal-to-law correct interpretations and applications of the Treaty and EMCR, to investigate possible violations, and to prosecute violators. Fifth, the most relevant sections of the U.S. Sherman Antitrust Act, the U.S. Clayton Antitrust Act, the U.S. Federal Trade Commission Act, the 1992 Horizontal Merger Guidelines promulgated jointly by the DOJ and FTC, the 1997 Revision of those Guidelines, the 2010 Horizontal Merger Guidelines promulgated jointly by the DOJ and FTC, Article 101 of the 2009 Treaty of Lisbon, Article 102 of the 2009 Lisbon Treaty, the EC Concentration Guidelines, and the E.C. Merger Control Regulations (EMCR) are quoted in the study's text (most prominently in Chaps. 3, 4, and 13) as opposed to being reproduced in an appendix. Sixth, because the two volumes in which this study is being printed have been given different ISBN numbers, the first page of Vol. 2 must begin with page-number 1. In the Index (which appears in both volumes), upright page-numbers refer to pages in Vol. 1, and italicized page-numbers refer to pages in Vol. 2.

Contents

Part I
Introduction to Part I: Basic Concepts and Approaches

Part I defines the basic concepts this study uses and outlines the protocols it follows when analyzing the issues it addresses. Chapter 1 has two sections. Section 1 delineates the monetized definition of "the impact of a choice on economic efficiency" that is correct in the sense of best fitting professional and public intuitive understanding and creating a concept that is most useful. Section 2 argues that this definition conforms to professional and popular understanding and is more useful than any alternative definition that could be devised.

I should admit that, for two reasons, I find the fact that this two-volume study begins with a discussion of economic efficiency somewhat disconcerting:

1. one of the defining characteristics both of this study and of the two-study series to which it belongs is the strong distinction I draw between the analysis of antitrust law and the analysis of antitrust policy, and
2. although the desirability of antitrust policies that prohibit particular types of business conduct either always or in specifiable circumstances depends to a very considerable extent on their economic efficiency, the legality of business conduct under either U.S. antitrust law or E.C./E.U. competition law depends to a far lesser extent on its economic efficiency or the economic efficiency of prohibiting it.

Nevertheless, for four reasons, it makes sense for me to begin by defining the concept of the impact of a choice on economic efficiency:

1. the correct definitions of an "agreement in restraint of trade,"[27] an "attempt to monopolize,"[28] an "agreement. . .that has as its object. . .the prevention, restriction or distortion of competition,"[29] and an exclusionary "abuse" of a dominant position[30] all make reference to the economic efficiency of the conduct in

[27] See Sherman Act Section 1.

[28] See Sherman Act Section 2.

[29] See Article 101 of the 2009 Lisbon Treaty.

[30] See Article 102 of the 2009 Lisbon Treaty.

question (or, to be more precise, to whether it would be economically efficient in an otherwise-Pareto-perfect economy);

2. I believe that, correctly interpreted as a matter of law, the U.S. Clayton Act would be read to include what I term an "organizational-economic-efficiency" defense;
3. Section 3 of Article 101 of the 2009 Lisbon Treaty creates a more limited economic-efficiency-related defense for covered practices that "contribute[] to improving the production or distribution of goods" or that "promot[e] technical or economic progress. . ."; and
4. the E.C. Merger Control Regulations (EMCR)[31] and the U.S. 1992 Horizontal Merger Guidelines[32] both establish economic-efficiency defenses for the mergers they cover.

Chapter 2 delineates the vocabulary of competitive-impact analysis. Section 1 operationalizes the concepts "the impact of a choice on price competition" and "the impact of a choice on QV-investment competition" as they should be defined in the antitrust-law context. Section 2 delineates the conceptual schemes I use to break down the difference between price and marginal cost respectively in individualized-pricing and across-the-board-pricing contexts. Section 3 defines the various possible causes of QV-investment competition's being imperfect, illustrates the way in which they interact to cause actual QV investment to fall below the level of QV investment that would result in the most-supernormally-profitable projects in the relevant area of product-space just breaking even over their lifetimes, and distinguishes three different types of QV-investment equilibria that can obtain in a given area of product-space.

Chapter 3 focuses on the concepts "monopolizing conduct" and "attempt to monopolize." After explaining that the U.S. Sherman Antitrust Act promulgates an anticompetitive-intent test of illegality that (with one possible exception) prohibits all monopolizing conduct and attempts to monopolize, Chap. 3 provides an operational definition of the concepts in question.

Chapter 4 delineates and discusses the conduct-coverage of, tests of illegality promulgated by, and defenses recognized by U.S. antitrust law and E.C./E.U. competition law. Section 1 focuses on U.S. antitrust law—in particular, on the Sherman Antitrust Act and the Clayton Antitrust Act. In addition to explaining the conclusions about these statutes' conduct-coverage, tests of illegality, and defenses that are correct as a matter of law, Section 1 discusses various errors that U.S. judges and scholars have made when discussing these issues. Section 2 focuses on E.C./E.U. competition law—in particular, on Article 101 of the 2009 Lisbon Treaty, on Article 102 of the Treaty, and on the E.C. Merger Control Regulations (EMCR) promulgated by the Council of Ministers. In addition to explaining the conduct that these three law-sources respectively cover, the tests of illegality they

[31] See EMCR.

[32] See Section 4 of the 1992 Horizontal Merger Guidelines as revised in 1997.

respectively promulgate, and the defences (British spelling) they respectively recognize, this section discusses various errors that the EC and E.C./E.U. courts have made when addressing these issues. Section 3 discusses the differences between the conduct-coverage of, tests of illegality promulgated by, and defenses (defences) recognized by U.S. antitrust law and E.C./E.U. competition law.

Chapter 5 analyzes the relationship between (1) the impact of business conduct that is covered by antitrust law on the magnitudes of various categories of economic inefficiency and (2) the legality of that conduct under the U.S. Sherman Act, U.S. Clayton Act, Articles 101 and 102 of the 2009 Lisbon Treaty, and the EMCR. Section 1 delineates four general categories of economic inefficiency that economies can generate whose magnitudes business conduct can affect. Section 2 lists the categories of economic-efficiency gains and losses that business conduct can yield whose generation is irrelevant to the conduct's legality under either U.S. antitrust law or E.C./E.U. competition law. And Section 3 lists the various categories of economic-efficiency gains that business conduct can yield whose generation may critically affect the conduct's legality under various provisions of U.S. and E.C./E.U. antitrust law.

Chapter 6 explains why I believe that, regardless of the defensible criterion one uses to assess one or more market definitions or an approach to market definition, market definitions are inherently arbitrary, not just at their periphery but comprehensively. Section 1 establishes this conclusion on the assumption that the applicable criterion is an ideal-type criterion that focuses on professional and popular assumptions about the competitiveness of the various products placed inside a given market and the difference between the competitiveness of such products and the competitiveness of products placed in different markets. Section 2 establishes this conclusion on the assumption that the relevant criterion is functional—*i.e.*, evaluates a market definition or market-definition approach by its ability to play a useful role in a valuable analytic protocol.

Chapter 7 focuses on the various ways in which economists, the U.S. antitrust-enforcement agencies, and U.S. and E.C./E.U. courts have defined or operationalized the concept of a "market." Section 1 reviews the way in which Chap. 6 argued the concept of an economic market should be defined (if the concept is to be used in any analytic protocol), states and criticizes the classical definition of an economic market (an area of product-space that contains products—defined in terms of their attributes and the geographic locations of their sellers and buyers—whose product-prices tend to uniformity), discusses briefly the fact that economists have disagreed about whether any classically-defined economic market exists, considers an alternative definition of an economic market that is less comprehensive in that it focuses on the market into which it would be analytically useful to place an individual product or product/seller combination, and finally discusses the concept of an "antitrust market" (a set of sellers and buyers that is defined to yield market-aggregated data that allegedly can play a useful role in a defensible protocol for analyzing the antitrust legality of one or more types of business conduct)—a variant of which appears to have been incorporated into the 1992 and 2010 U.S. Horizontal Merger Guidelines. Section 2 criticizes both the abstract definition of the concept of an "antitrust market" that the 1992 and 2010 U.S. Horizontal Merger Guidelines promulgate and the protocol that the 1992 Guidelines explicitly and incorrectly claim and the 2010 Guidelines appear to assume will enable its user to delimit the market that conforms best with this abstract definition. Section 3 discusses the various techniques that economists have proposed using or have actually used to define markets. Section 4 examines the various approaches to market definition that U.S. federal courts have taken. Finally, Section 5 addresses the approach that the European Commission and E.C./E.U. courts (as contrasted with the national courts of the members of the European Communities) have taken to market definition.

Consistent with Chap. 6's account of economists' implicit assumptions about the characteristics of ideal economic markets and explanation of why, regardless of whether they are evaluated by ideal-type or functional criteria, market definitions are inherently arbitrary not just at their periphery but comprehensively, Chap. 7 argues that (1) the classical definition of an economic market mis-states the defining characteristics of a market that conforms to the classical ideal-type market, (2) those economists that claim that, in the real world, classical economic markets—*i.e.*, markets that satisfy the ideal-type notions that underlie the classical definition—can be delimited non-arbitrarily are mistaken, (3) the concept of an "antitrust market" is misguided because, regardless of how markets are defined, they cannot play a useful role in a valuable analytic protocol, (4) the 1992 and 2010 U.S. Horizontal Merger Guidelines' abstract definition of an "antitrust market" is unnecessarily deficient and the 1992 Guidelines' protocol for identifying markets that satisfy its abstract definition often will not do so, (5) the various techniques that economists have used to define markets cannot bear scrutiny, and (6) the various approaches that U.S. courts, U.S. antitrust-enforcement agencies, E.C./E.U. courts, and the European Commission have taken to market definition are also indefensible.

Chapter 8 focuses on the concept of a firm's market power. Section 1 provides operational definitions of the concepts of a firm's monopoly power, oligopoly power, and total (market) power over price, over QV investment, and over price and QV investment combined in a given ARDEPPS. Section 2 delineates and criticizes the abstract definition and market-share-oriented operational definitions that U.S. courts have given to a firm's market power and the primarily-market-share-oriented operational definition that E.C./E.U. courts and the EC have given to the related concept of a firm's market dominance. Section 3 explains in great detail why—even if markets are defined as well as they can be for this purpose—one will not be able to accurately infer a firm's monopoly, oligopoly, or market power over price, QV investment, or price and QV investment combined from its market share. The Conclusion of Chap. 8 points out that market-share-oriented approaches to market-power or market-dominance estimation are not only inaccurate but unnecessarily expensive. A firm's market power or market dominance can be estimated not only more accurately but also more cheaply by estimating directly such things as the firm's P–MC gaps (OCAs, NOMs, and COMs) and supernormal rates-of-return. The market-share-oriented approach to market-power or market-dominance estimation already collects data on many of these parameters in the course of defining the relevant market. Rather than using this data directly and supplementing it with data on other parameters, it uses the non-aggregated data indirectly to define a relevant market and calculate market-share figures from which it derives market-power/market-dominance conclusions. This circuitous approach consumes a lot of resources to convert non-aggregated data that reveals more about a firm's market power into market-aggregated data that reveals less about the firm's market power. Like the market-oriented approach to horizontal-merger competitive-impact analysis that Chap. 12 analyzes, the market-share-oriented approach to market-power/market-dominance estimation achieves the remarkable double of increasing cost while decreasing accuracy.

Chapter 9 explains why the definitions its predecessors give to "monopolizing conduct," "abusive conduct," "competitive impact," and "economic efficiency" and the protocols they delineate for analyzing the monopolizing character, abusiveness, competitive impact, and economic efficiency of any business choice imply the need to analyze these issues separately.

Chapter 1
The "Correct" Definition of "the Impact of a Choice on Economic Efficiency"

1. The Correct Definition of Economic Efficiency

Defined in the way that conforms with professional and popular understanding and creates a concept that is most useful, the impact of a choice on economic efficiency equals the difference between the equivalent-dollar gains the choice confers on its beneficiaries (the winners) and the equivalent-dollar losses it imposes on its victims (the losers).[33] More controversially, in this formulation, a winner's equivalent-dollar gain equals the number of dollars that would have to be transferred to him to leave him as well-off as the choice would leave him if

(1) he did not agree to the transfer;
(2) he either was intrinsically indifferent to the substitution of the transfer for the private choice or government decision (hereinafter choice) in question or was unaware of the linkage between the transfer and the relevant choice's rejection;
(3) his distributive attitude toward such transfers, non-parochial distributive preferences, or normative distributive commitments gave him no reason to prefer the transfer to the choice or vice versa; and
(4) the transfer would not benefit or harm him indirectly by changing the conduct of others by altering their income and/or wealth.

Similarly, in this formulation, a loser's equivalent-dollar loss equals the number of dollars that would have to be withdrawn from him to leave him as poorly-off as the choice would leave him under the four assumptions just delineated.

---

[33] I use the expressions *equivalent*-dollar gains and losses because many of the relevant effects of the choices whose economic efficiency is analyzed are not direct monetary effects. Indeed, in some instances, a winner may not even be able to capitalize his equivalent-dollar gain. Take, for example, the equivalent-dollar gain that the owner of swampland who values it positively (for sentimental reasons) despite the fact that its market value is zero obtains from an environmental policy that cleans up the water in the swamp and/or the air over the swamp. If the policy does not improve the property sufficiently for it to have a positive market value post-policy, this winner will not be able to capitalize his equivalent-dollar gain.

R.S. Markovits, *Economics and the Interpretation and Application of U.S. and E.U. Antitrust Law*, DOI 10.1007/978-3-642-24307-3_1,

The preceding operationalizations measure the relevant equivalent-dollar gains and losses by what economists call the equivalent variations in the relevant winners' and losers' wealths and then elaborate on the definition of the equivalent variations in question. I will now justify the four assumptions that this equivalent-variation operationalization of a choice's winner's equivalent-dollar gain and a choice's loser's equivalent-dollar loss incorporates. For two reasons, the equivalent-dollar gain obtained by each beneficiary of a choice should be measured on the assumption that he did not voluntarily agree to accept money in exchange for his essential consent to the choice's rejection, and the equivalent-dollar loss sustained by each victim of a choice should be measured on the assumption that he did not voluntarily agree to sell for money his essential consent to the choice's being made and implemented: (1) in practice, the choice's winners and losers will not have engaged in such voluntary market transactions, and (2) in some relevant instances, some winners and losers would find engaging in such voluntary market transactions intrinsically costly or valuable. Take, for example, a choice that would benefit a parent by preventing his or her child from being injured or becoming ill. To the extent that, for self-definitional reasons, the parent would place a negative value on voluntarily exchanging the choice for a money payment, any operationalization of the parent's equivalent-dollar gain that equated that gain with the number of dollars for which the parent would be indifferent to voluntarily surrendering the policy, when in fact no such consensual exchange would occur, would overestimate the equivalent-dollar gain the choice would confer on the parent even if he or she were a sovereign maximizer (since the figure the operationalization yielded would be increased by the number of dollars the parent would have to be paid to offset the "cost" to him of voluntarily engaging in the [counterfactual] voluntary transaction in question). Such an operationalization would also yield overestimates of the equivalent-dollar gains that would be generated by choices that would protect a winner's own health or a family heirloom when the winner did not actually trade the choice for money to the extent that, for self-definitional reasons, the winner respectively (1) would disvalue voluntarily selling his or her health (endangering his health for a money payment) and (2) identified with his family and found it costly to sell his heritage. I hasten to add, however, that the counterfactual, voluntary-market-transaction operationalization of a winner's equivalent-dollar gain could also underestimate the dollar gain the choice actually conferred on its beneficiaries—in particular, would underestimate that gain when the beneficiary would positively value voluntarily trading the choice for money since in these circumstances the sum he would have to be paid to induce him to forego engaging in such a transaction would be reduced by the positive equivalent-dollar value he would place on the act of engaging in the relevant counterfactual voluntary transaction. This outcome would occur, for example, in a case in which the choice would protect a beneficiary's health if the beneficiary (1) valued being a good family-provider or valued the welfare of his wife and children and (2) believed that the money he could obtain by trading a choice (a government policy or a private accident-or-pollution-loss-avoidance move) that would protect his health would benefit his family more than family members would be harmed by the pain, worsened health, and reduction in future earning power he would experience if the choice were rejected.

Obviously, a counterfactual, voluntary-market-transaction operationalization of the equivalent-dollar loss a private choice or government decision would impose on its victims will also mismeasure that loss when the victim would find agreeing to make a payment to prevent the private choice's execution or public policy's adoption either costly or beneficial in itself (independent of its material impact on him). Thus, such an operationalization would underestimate the equivalent-dollar loss a choice would impose on its victims to the extent that the amount that they should be indifferent to paying to block the choice would be reduced by their placement of a negative value on making such voluntary payments—as they might if they thought that the government (private actor) ought to and/or was morally obligated to reject the policy (private choice) without such a transfer's being made. Particularly when the transfer would go to a perceived wrongdoer (the person that or private organization that would otherwise make the harmful choice in question), its potential victim may disvalue making any payment to prevent it because the victim disvalues rewarding wrongdoers or believes that making such a payment would amount to giving in to extortion and disvalues doing so.

Second, the relevant money transfers should be calculated on the assumption that the private choice's or government decision's winners and losers would perceive no linkage between its rejection and any related transfers that one would imagine being made respectively to them and from them. Even if the relevant operationalizations did not assume that the winners (losers) voluntarily agreed to accept (make) the payments in question to forego (prevent) the relevant private choice or government decision, operationalizations would mismeasure the equivalent-dollar gains and losses the choice would generate to the extent that some winners or losers would find the relevant nonconsensual transfers intrinsically valuable or distasteful. Thus, an operationalization of the equivalent-dollar gains that would be generated by a private choice or government decision that would prevent a child's being injured (or would reduce the probability that a child would be injured) that assumed that the child's parents would be aware of the linkage between any transfer to them and the choice's rejection would overestimate the equivalent-dollar gain it would confer on the parents to the extent that the parents would find it intrinsically costly to accept "blood money" *ex post* as compensation for exposing their child to injury or a greater risk of injury (for the choice's rejection) even if they did not agree *ex ante* to trade the choice for the money payment.

Third, the relevant money transfers should be measured on the assumption that the winners and losers in question would not find them valuable or costly because they approved or disapproved of the relevant private party's or their government's executing such transfers for reasons that do not relate to their direct parochial interests. Since the money transfer that is being said to be equivalent to the relevant party's equivalent-dollar gain or loss is purely hypothetical, its calculation should not be affected by any such attitudes, distributive preferences, or distributive moral commitments.

Fourth, since (1) the relevant money transfers are purely hypothetical and could be financed in different ways that would have different distributive impacts and hence have different effects on the choices that people make by altering their income/wealth positions and (2) the indirect behavioral consequences of the transfer's distributive impact not only (A) could benefit or harm the individual winners and losers of the policy or choice but (B) could also produce a net equivalent-dollar impact on all such individuals combined, the equivalent-dollar gains and losses any private choice or government decisions would generate should be measured on the assumption that it would not produce any net equivalent-dollar effects on its winners and losers in this indirect way.

Points (2)(A) and (2)(B) in the preceding sentence require some explanation. I will use two illustrations to explain point (2)(A).

Assume first that

(1) the beneficiary of a particular government policy owns a business;
(2) the business in question faces imperfect price competition;
(3) the hypothetical money transfer to him would be financed in a way that reduces the wealth of one of his customers; and
(4) this reduction in his customer's wealth would reduce the latter's demand for the beneficiary's product or services.

In this case, the transfer would hurt its direct beneficiary indirectly by reducing the profits his business earned.

Assume, alternatively, that

(1) the victim of a particular government policy was different from the victim of the hypothetical dollar transfer that the policy's beneficiary would find equivalent to the policy;
(2) unlike the victim of the actual policy, the victim of the hypothetical transfer would in any event drive his car by the residence of the policy's beneficiary;
(3) the equivalent-dollar loss the hypothetical transfer would impose on its victim would induce him to (make it profitable for him to) purchase and operate a more polluting and breakdown-prone car (make it personally attractive for him to buy a cheaper car, whose use was more externality prone); and
(4) the actual policy would not affect its beneficiary by generating such secondary-feedback effects.

In this case, unlike the actual policy, the hypothetical money transfer would hurt its direct beneficiary indirectly by increasing the equivalent-dollar loss its direct victim imposed on him by driving in his neighborhood.

Point (2)(B) in the relevant sentence—*viz.*, that the indirect effect of the hypothetical money transfers on the policy's winners and losers may not offset each other perfectly (may not produce the same net total dollar effect on the policy's winners as on the policy's losers)—requires a more abstract explanation. Admittedly, in an otherwise-Pareto-perfect world, allocative-transaction-costless money transfers will not produce any net equivalent-dollar effects—*i.e.*, the economy will be maximally-economically efficient (will contain no resource misallocation) regardless of the initial endowments of its participants. However, for two reasons, this proposition does not imply that the relevant money transfers will have no net equivalent-dollar impact on the policy's winners and losers. First, since, in our actual Pareto-imperfect world, the amount of economic inefficiency will often be affected by the distribution of initial endowments, allocative-transaction-costless money transfers can either increase or decrease economic efficiency[34] and hence can affect the difference between the policy's winners' equivalent-dollar gains and losers' equivalent-dollar losses even if they do not have any net equivalent-dollar impact on other individuals. Second, even when the money transfers in question do not affect allocative efficiency, the net equivalent-dollar impact of the combination of the policy and transfers on the policy's winners and losers will be different from that of the policy when the transfers have a net equivalent-dollar impact on people who would neither gain nor lose from the policy.

2. Why My Definition Is Correct

This chapter began by asserting that the definition of economic efficiency just delineated is appropriate or "correct" because it conforms with professional and popular understanding and defines the concept in the way that is most useful. Both of these claims require some justification.

In my judgment, both professional economists and members of the general public assume that the "dollar gain" a choice confers on each of its beneficiaries equals the number of dollars whose transfer to the beneficiary would be equivalent to the choice and that the dollar loss a choice imposes on each of its victims equals the number of dollars whose withdrawal from the victim would be equivalent to the choice—*i.e.*, equate what I denominate the equivalent-dollar gains and losses a choice generates with the equivalent variations in the relevant parties' wealths. The definition I have proposed conforms with this understanding.

The fact that my definition conforms with professional and popular understanding also contributes towards its usefulness. Three types of enquiries make use of economic-efficiency conclusions and, in each, economic efficiency must be defined in the way I have proposed for such conclusions to play a useful role.

First, economic-efficiency conclusions can play a role in the analysis of the moral desirability of a choice from a utilitarian perspective. At least, one way to determine the impact of a choice on the total utility or average utility of all creatures whose utility is deemed to be morally relevant is (1) to determine the equivalent-dollar gains and losses the choice generates—figures that economic-efficiency analyses of certain types can provide, (2) to determine the average number of units of utility (the

[34] For example, in a Pareto-imperfect world, allocative-transaction-costless money transfers can affect economic efficiency by altering the amount of misallocation their winners and losers cause by making externality-generating consumption decisions by changing their wealth and thereby the consumption choices that are in their individual interests. For an example that illustrates this possibility, see the paragraph of the text that precedes the paragraph to which this note is attached.

average number of "utils") the choice's beneficiaries obtained from the equivalent dollars the choice conferred on them and the average util-value of the equivalent-dollar losses the choice imposed on its victims, and (3) compare the product of the total equivalent-dollar gains generated and the average util-value of those equivalent-dollar gains with the product of the total equivalent-dollar losses generated with the average util-value of the equivalent-dollar losses. Whenever this circuitous method of utilitarian evaluation promotes utility more than a protocol of measuring util gains and losses directly,[35] variants of economic-efficiency analysis that yield conclusions about the total equivalent-dollar gains and losses generated or the ratio of those equivalent-dollar gains to those equivalent-dollar losses will make a positive contribution to utilitarian evaluation. Obviously, however, to do so, the relevant economic-efficiency analyses must define the equivalent-dollar gains and losses in the way that conforms with the understanding of utilitarians, who will proceed by placing weights on the equivalent dollars gained and lost equal to their average util-value.

Second, a variant of economic-efficiency conclusions may be relevant to the liberal analysis of the justness of certain choices in moral-rights-based societies[36] that are committed to liberalism[37] and to the moral desirability of a choice from a

---

[35] I believe this condition will often be fulfilled. In my judgment, an evaluative protocol that combines the distortion-analysis approach to economic-efficiency analysis that is third-best allocatively efficient (which THE WELFARE ECONOMICS OF ANTITRUST POLICY AND U.S. AND E.U. ANTITRUST LAW will delineate in detail) with an analysis of the characteristics of a choice's winners and losers that bear on the relative magnitudes of the average util-value of their respective equivalent-dollar gains and losses will promote the utilitarian goal of maximizing total or average utility more than would an evaluative protocol that seeks to determine the effect of choices on total or average utility directly.

[36] Rights-based societies are societies whose members and governments (1) draw a strong distinction between prescriptive-moral discourse about moral rights (about the just) and prescriptive-moral discourse about what morally ought to be done when justice considerations are not determinative (about the good) and (2) are committed to instantiating their justice-commitments even when the good as legitimately conceived must be sacrificed to do so.

[37] In my usage, liberalism is a moral norm that gives lexical priority to individuals' having and seizing the opportunity to lead a life of moral integrity—*i.e.*, to individuals' taking their moral obligations seriously and taking seriously as well the dialectical task of choosing a conception of the good and leading a life that conforms to this conception. On this account, liberalism commits its adherents and the members of, participants in, and governments of liberal, rights-based societies to treating all moral-rights bearers with appropriate, equal respect and for showing appropriate (in the case of individuals) or appropriate, equal (in the case of government) concern for them as well, in part for their utility as economists understand this concept but pre-eminently for their having and seizing the opportunity to lead a life of moral integrity. For a more detailed discussion of liberalism and its concrete corollaries, see RICHARD S. MARKOVITS, MATTERS OF PRINCIPLE: LEGITIMATE LEGAL ARGUMENT AND CONSTITUTIONAL INTERPRETATION 34–53, 196–209, 274–96 (hereinafter MATTERS OF PRINCIPLE) (NYU Press, 1998) and Richard S. Markovits, *Liberalism and Tort Law: On the Content of the Corrective-Justice-Securing Tort Law of a Liberal, Rights-Based State*, 2006 ILL. L. REV. 243 (2006).

liberal perspective in societies of other types.[38] More specifically, liberalism may imply that individuals should make and that the members of and participants in a liberal, rights-based society are morally obligated to make an accident-or-pollution-loss-avoidance move that would increase its beneficiaries' "mere utility"—*i.e.*, that would not increase their capacity to lead lives of moral integrity—if and only if (roughly speaking) the actor in question should perceive the move to be (in essence) economically efficient. For current purposes, the salient point is that since the argument for this conclusion uses the expression "increase in economic efficiency" in the way in which that concept is commonly understood, economic efficiency must be defined in the way in which this chapter defines it for the concept to play a useful role in this type of liberal analysis.

Third, the concept of economic efficiency plays a significant role in the interpretation and application of legislation, administrative regulations, or judicial decisions that either explicitly articulate an economic-efficiency test of illegality or benefit-eligibility or are properly interpreted[39] to have implicitly promulgated an economic-efficiency decision-criterion. In either eventuality, if I am right in contending that the relevant laws' creators understood "economic efficiency" in the way in which this chapter defines this concept, the legal interpretations and applications in question should be based on this definition as well.

* * *

THE WELFARE ECONOMICS OF ANTITRUST POLICY AND U.S. AND E.U. ANTITRUST LAW will elaborate substantially on this chapter's brief treatment of the definition of economic efficiency. *Inter alia*, it will discuss whether equivalent-dollar gains and losses that derive from individuals' placing positive or negative values on the gains

---

[38] Not all societies are moral-rights-based, and not all moral-rights-based societies are committed to a liberal conception of justice. As to the first point: (1) some societies of moral integrity (*i.e.*, societies that have moral commitments and fulfill them to a sufficient extent to deserve this characterization) are moral-goal-based (*i.e.*, are committed to achieving a goal that qualifies as "moral" but do not draw a strong distinction between the just and the good) and (2) other societies (which are not societies of moral integrity) are (A) immoral—*i.e.*, are committed to securing an immoral goal—or (B) amoral—*i.e.*, are committed to securing a goal that is neither moral nor immoral or vary the alleged moral justification of their choices in an *ad hoc* way. As to the second point: (1) although I am aware of attempts to derive an "objectively-true" and hence universally-applicable concept of justice from the concept of the moral, from the concept of human flourishing, from the concept of freedom, and from the concept of human nature, I have never been convinced by any such Foundationalist, Aristotelian, Kantian, or Natural-Rights argument, and (2) in light of that fact, I feel compelled to admit that my own predilection for a liberal conception of justice cannot ultimately be justified—that rights-based societies can legitimately base their justice-commitments on other defensible moral norms (for example, on various nonliberal conceptions of egalitarianism). The point of the last part of the sentence of the text to which this footnote is attached is that, in immoral societies, amoral societies, and rights-based societies whose justice-commitments are not liberal, it will still be possible to evaluate the moral desirability of a choice from a liberal perspective (though, in nonliberal rights-based societies, it will not be morally permissible—*i.e.*, it will be moral-rights-violative—to make choices that liberalism commends if they violate the justice-commitments of the societies in question).

[39] For an account of proper legal interpretation and application, see MATTERS OF PRINCIPLE 57–76.

or losses a choice confers on others are properly considered in any economic-efficiency calculation, how the definition of "the impact of a choice on economic efficiency" that I believe is correct differs from, and is superior to, four alternative definitions or operationalizations of that concept that economists have proposed, and why I reject the claim that definitions of the concept of "the impact of a choice on economic efficiency" are inherently arbitrary because there is no non-arbitrary way of resolving the so-called offer/asking problems (roughly speaking, whether one should define parties' gains and losses by the equivalent variations or compensating variations in their wealths).

Chapter 2
The Components of the Difference Between a Firm's Price and Conventional Marginal Costs and the Intermediate Determinants of the Intensity of Quality-and-Variety-Increasing-Investment Competition

Industrial Organization economists devote considerable attention to analyzing the competitive impact of various types of business conduct, and the antitrust laws of the United States and the E.U. make the legality of various types of business conduct depend (sometimes *inter alia*) on their competitive impact.[40] Surprisingly, neither Industrial Organization economists, nor the antitrust laws in question, nor the lawyers and judges that interpret and apply these laws have satisfactorily defined the concepts of the intensity of competition they use. The definitions that have been proposed for (1) the impact of conduct on price competition have been incomplete, inconsistent, and/or inappropriate[41] and (2) the concepts of the impact of conduct on QV-investment competition and the impact of conduct on price and QV-investment competition combined have been totally ignored. Chapter 4 will

[40] See, *e.g.*, (1) the Clayton Act, whose specific provisions make the legality of the conduct they cover depend on whether their "effect. . .may be to substantially lessen competition or tend to create a monopoly," (2) Article 101 of the 2009 Lisbon Treaty, which makes the legality of "agreements between undertakings, decisions by associations of undertakings and concerted practices" depend on whether they "have as their object or effect the prevention, restriction or distortion of competition," (3) one branch of Article 102 of the 2009 Lisbon Treaty, which (as interpreted and applied) makes the legality of the conduct of a dominant firm or a collectively-dominant set of firms depend on whether the conduct "has the effect of hindering the maintenance of the degree of competition still existing in the market or the growth of that competition," and (4) the European Merger Control Regulation (EMCR), which makes the legality of the mergers, acquisitions, and full-function joint ventures it covers depend on whether they "significantly imped[e] effective competition." See Manufacture Française des Pneumatiques Michelin v. Commission (Michelin II), Case T-203/01, ECR-II 4071 § 54 (2003). For a more detailed discussion of the conduct-coverage, the tests of illegality promulgated by, and the defenses recognized by the Clayton Act, the Sherman Act, Articles 101 and 102 of the 2009 Lisbon Treaty, and the E.C./E.U. Merger Control Regulation (EMCR) as written, interpreted, and applied, see Chap. 4.

[41] For a detailed analysis of the various ways in which economists and lawyers who are conversant with economics have assumed that the Clayton Act concept of "lessening competition" should be operationalized, see Richard S. Markovits, *Some Preliminary Notes on the U.S. Antitrust Laws' Tests of Illegality*, 27 STAN. L. REV. 841-844-50 (1975) and the summary of this discussion in Subsection 1B(2) of Chap. 4.

R.S. Markovits, *Economics and the Interpretation and Application of U.S. and E.U. Antitrust Law*, DOI 10.1007/978-3-642-24307-3_2,

offer a definition of "the impact of a choice on competition" that I think correctly operationalizes this concept in both the U.S. antitrust-law context and the E.C./E.U. competition-law context.

This chapter tries to remedy another set of related deficiencies in the current treatment of the concept "the intensity of completion": the failure of economists or lawyers (1) to distinguish various components of the gap between a seller's price and marginal cost that need to be separately analyzed, regardless of whether the goal is to predict the competitive impact of some conduct or natural event, to study its economic efficiency, to assess (in the case of conduct) its legality, or to predict its distributive impact or distributive desirability and (2)(A) to define the intermediate determinants of the intensity of QV-investment competition in any arbitrarily-defined (see Chap. 6) area of product-space and (B) to analyze the way in which the various determinants of the intensity of QV-investment competition in any area of product-space interact to determine the intensity of QV-investment competition in that area, regardless of how that intensity is operationalized.

Section 2.1 develops a conceptual scheme for analyzing the intensity of price competition or the impact of any conduct on that intensity, regardless of how the intensity of price completion is defined, and analyzes the connection between the various components of this scheme. Section 2.2 delineates the intermediate determinants of the intensity of QV-investment competition in any (arbitrarily-designated) area of product-space and explains how these determinants interact to determine that intensity, regardless of how it is defined.

1. The Price-Competition Conceptual Scheme

Economists and antitrust lawyers who have analyzed the impact of particular business conduct on the intensity of price competition have almost always focused exclusively on the overall gap between the price or prices that particular sellers charged and their respective marginal costs. Because (1) different factors determine the magnitudes of the various components of this P–MC gap that should be distinguished, (2) the law of various countries places a different significance on various such components' having non-zero values, and (3) changes in the magnitude of different components of a seller's P–MC gap have different economic-efficiency implications, I have developed two price-competition conceptual systems that subdivide the standard P–MC gap to facilitate the relevant micro-economic, legal, and economic-efficiency analyses.

However, before proceeding to give an account of these conceptual systems, I need to define or comment on three concepts or pairs of concepts that this account implicates. The first is the pair of concepts "individualized pricing" and "across-the-board pricing." In my vocabulary, a seller is said to be engaging in "individualized pricing" if it sets the price it charges each of its potential customers separately. By way of contrast, a seller is said to be engaging in across-the-board pricing if it establishes a single set of terms that applies to all its potential customers. As we shall see, this distinction is important because the conceptual scheme that is best adapted to individualized-pricing situations is different from its across-the-board-pricing counterpart.

The second is the pair of related concepts "strategic" decisions and "inherently-profitable" decisions. In my usage, the expression "strategic decision" refers to decisions whose subjective *ex ante* profitability is critically affected by the "strategic advantages" it is expected to generate for the business decisionmaker in question. The "strategic advantages" a decision generates for a business decisionmaker are the advantages it yields that actor (1) by deterring one or more of its rivals from undercutting it by inducing the rival or rivals in question to increase their estimate of the costs they will have to incur to undercut the actor in question because such undercutting will induce it to retaliate and/or deter it from cooperating with them—*i.e.*, by inducing the rival or rivals in question to forego "inherently-profitable" (see below) opportunities to undercut it—or (2) by inflating its profits by driving one or more rivals out of business or deterring a potential or established competitor from making a QV investment in its area of product-space in circumstances in which the exited rival or deterred investment either will not be replaced or will be replaced by a rival that or investment that will reduce the relevant business decisionmaker's profits to a lesser extent. Relatedly, the expression "inherently profitable" decisions will be used to refer to business decisions made by actors whose *ex ante* perception that the decisions would be profitable did not depend on their belief that the decisions might yield strategic gains.

The third concept that requires elucidation is "oligopolistic conduct." As I indicated in the Introduction to Part I of this study, on my definition, a seller is said to have initiated an oligopolistic-conduct sequence if and only if *ex ante* it perceived the profitability of its move to be critically affected by the fact that its rivals' responses to its conduct will or may be influenced by their realization that it can react to their responses.[42] I want to emphasize at the outset that this definition of

[42] Economists have never explicitly defined the concept "oligopolistic conduct"—*i.e.*, have defined it only implicitly through usage (by developing pricing models they denominate "oligopolistic"). My definition is narrower than its standard counterpart, which defines a choice to be oligopolistic when the actor realizes that its pay-off will be affected either by the choices that identifiable rivals have already made or (somewhat more narrowly) by the responses the choice elicits from one or more identifiable rivals—*i.e.*, to be oligopolistic when it manifests simple, two-stage recognized interdependence rather than the more-complex, three-stage type of recognized interdependence that is the identifying characteristic of the conduct I call "oligopolistic." Thus, the interdependence that is the basis of the leading conjectural-variations models of oligopolistic pricing is backward-looking: in the Cournot model, each firm assumes that its output-decision will not affect its rivals' output choices; in the Bertrand model, each firm assumes that its price decision will not affect its rivals' price decisions; and in the Stackelberg model, a leader-firm profits from the fact that its followers behave in the way that the Cournot model assumes. The interdependence that many of the more modern, game-theoretic, "oligopolistic-pricing" models posit, though forward-looking, is also two-stage (simple) recognized interdependence. For a discussion of several of these game-theoretic models that substantiates this conclusion, see DAVID CARLTON AND JEFFREY PERLOFF, MODERN INDUSTRIAL ORGANIZATION 380–903 (Harper Collins Pub., 1990). I hasten to add that some oligopolistic-pricing models do focus on the kind of three-stage interdependence

"oligopolistic conduct" in general and of "oligopolistic pricing" in particular is more restrictive than the definitions economists generally employ.

A. The Price-Competition Conceptual Scheme for Individualized-Pricing Situations

I will begin by describing the conceptual scheme I use to analyze the competitiveness of *individualized* prices and the impact of given transactions or practices on the competitiveness of *individualized* prices. I will then describe the conceptual scheme I use when pricing is done on an across-the-board basis.

My individualized-pricing conceptual system focuses on the gap between the price that a seller that is (privately) best-placed to supply a given buyer[43] charges that buyer and the conventional marginal costs that seller must incur to supply the buyer in question. My system subdivides the relevant P–MC gap into three major and a larger number of smaller components. The three major components are formed by inserting a seller's "highest non-oligopolistic price" (HNOP) and "no-error highest non-oligopolistic price" (NEHNOP) between its actual price and its conventional marginal costs. In an individualized-pricing context, the HNOP is defined to be the highest price that would be profitable for a seller that was best-placed to supply a particular buyer to charge that buyer if its rivals would always respond to its moves on the assumption that it could not react to their responses. The NEHNOP is defined to be the highest price that would be profitable for a seller that was best-placed to supply a particular buyer to charge that buyer if neither it, nor any of its rivals, nor any relevant buyer made any *ex ante* error and its rivals would always respond to its moves on the assumption that it could not react to their responses.

I will now delineate the various subcomponents respectively of NEHNOP–MC, HNOP–NEHNOP, and P–HNOP. In individualized-pricing situations, the

---

that makes conduct oligopolistic in my sense. See, *e.g.*, George Stigler, *A Theory of Oligopoly*, 72 J. POL. ECON. 44 (1964). In my judgment, my definition of "oligopolistic" is superior to (more useful than) its broader standard counterpart for two reasons. First, because (1) the standard definition labels as "oligopolistic" all pricing and advertising choices made by sellers that do not face perfect price competition and all QV-investment decisions made by sellers that do not face perfect QV-investment competition and (2) virtually no sellers face perfect price or QV-investment competition, the standard definition is too inclusive to be useful. Second, because the standard definition covers behaviors that manifest simple recognized interdependence as well as other, more-complicated kinds of interdependence, it is deficient in that it fails to capture the characteristics of particular pricing sequences that make them illegal under U.S. antitrust law or appropriate targets for prohibitory legislation.

[43] The seller that is privately-best-placed to supply a buyer in an individualized-pricing context is the seller that would find it inherently profitable to supply that buyer on terms contained in an offer that no rival would find inherently profitable to beat. For the definition of "inherently profitable," see the paragraph of the text that immediately precedes the paragraph that contains footnote-number 3.

NEHNOP–MC gap is first subdivided into (a) the best-placed seller's basic competitive advantage (BCA) when dealing for the patronage of the relevant buyer and (b) the contextual marginal costs (CMC) that the second-placed seller would have to incur to match (or infinitesimally beat) the best-placed seller's NEHNOP. Obviously, several terms in the preceding sentence require elucidation. I will analyze the concept "basic competitive advantage" on the assumption that neither the best-placed supplier of a given buyer nor its closest rival for that buyer's patronage (the second-placed supplier of that buyer) will have to incur any contextual marginal costs (see below) to supply the buyer in question on relevant terms. In this case, the best-placed supplier's BCA would equal the amount by which it was (privately) better-placed than anyone else to supply the buyer in question—the amount by which it could raise its price above its marginal costs of production and distribution without making it inherently profitable for any rival to "steal" the customer in question by beating its offer. This amount is equal to the sum of the buyer preference advantage (disadvantage) the best-placed supplier has over its closest rival for the relevant buyer's patronage at the relevant set of prices (the $BPA_{\#1}$—the additional amount of money that it would be inherently profitable for the buyer to pay to obtain its best-placed supplier's product variant or service variant rather than its second-placed supplier's product variant or service variant if the buyer's preference-perception were accurate) and the best-placed supplier's (conventional) marginal cost advantage (disadvantage) over its closest rival for the relevant buyer's patronage ($MCA_{\#1}$—the amount by which the marginal or incremental costs the best-placed supplier of the buyer in question would have to incur to supply the buyer in question were lower than the marginal or incremental costs its closest rival for that buyer's patronage would have to incur to supply him). As the preceding statement implies, a seller may enjoy a BCA in its relations with a particular buyer because it has both a BPA and an MCA, because its buyer preference disadvantage (BPD) is smaller than its MCA, or because its BPA exceeds its marginal cost disadvantage (MCD).

The second component of the NEHNOP–MC gap I find worth distinguishing in individualized-pricing contexts is the contextual marginal costs of the second-placed supplier of the buyer in question ($CMC_{\#2}$). Contextual marginal costs are the extra costs a seller has to bear because the price it is charging the buyer in question might expose the seller to some risk of cross-selling (*i.e.*, arbitrage) (to the extent that the price it is charging is discriminatory or multi-part [contains a lump-sum fee as well as a per-unit price]), might induce its other customers to intensify their bargaining (by putting the lie to its statements about its costs, by leading them to conclude that it has been treating them unfairly, or by suggesting that it can in fact be bargained down), and/or might expose it to *ex ante* legal-liability costs (to the extent that the price may appear to some to involve illegal price discrimination or some other price-regulation violation). Such costs are said to be "contextual" because they depend on various features of the context in which they are charged—*inter alia*, the prices the relevant seller is charging other buyers, various features of the legal milieu (*e.g.*, the existence of price-discrimination prohibitions or maximum or minimum price regulations), what the seller has told its other customers about its own costs, *etc*. In individualized-pricing situations, a #2 seller (a seller that is second-placed to obtain the relevant buyer Y's patronage) is likely to have to incur CMC to quote Y a price that makes #2's offer as attractive to Y overall as the offer Y received from its best-placed supplier (#1) because the price-component of #2's "matching" offer to Y is likely to be discriminatory—*i.e.*, is likely to be lower than the price #2 charges those buyers it is best-placed to supply.

Unfortunately, once one recognizes the existence of contextual marginal costs, a series of additional, related terms have to be introduced: (1) the contextual marginal cost advantage or disadvantage (CCA or CCD) of a best-placed supplier in an individualized-pricing context ($CCA_{\#1} = CMC_{\#2}–CMC_{\#1}$), (2) the overall marginal cost a firm would have to incur to supply a particular buyer on specified terms ($OMC = MC + CMC$), and (3) the overall competitive advantage a best-placed seller enjoys in its relations with a particular buyer ($OCA_{\#1} = BCA_{\#1} + CCA_{\#1}$). The text that follows will sometimes make reference to relationships that involve these concepts—in particular, will sometimes make use of the facts that (1) $CMC_{\#2} = CMC_{\#1} + CCA_{\#1}$, (2) $OCA_{\#1} = BCA_{\#1} + CCA_{\#1}$, and (3) $(NEHNOP–MC)_{\#1} = OCA_{\#1} + CMC_{\#1}$. In the end, then, my conceptual system subdivides each of the two subcomponents of the NEHNOP–MC gap ($BCA_{\#1}$ and $CMC_{\#2}$) into two parts: $BCA_{\#1} = BPA_{\#1} + MCA_{\#1}$ and $CMC_{\#2} = CMC_{\#1} + CCA_{\#1}$.

In my scheme, the second major component of the P–MC gap is the HNOP–NEHNOP gap. This gap reflects various errors that can cause a best-placed seller's actual price to exceed or differ from its NEHNOP for non-oligopolistic reasons. My conceptual system distinguishes three subcomponents of the HNOP–NEHNOP gap—*i.e.*, three categories of errors that can cause a seller's HNOP to exceed or differ from its NEHNOP: (1) buyer-error-generated HNOP–NEHNOP gaps or margins ($BEM_{\#1}$); (2) rival-error-related HNOP–NEHNOP gaps or margins ($REM_{\#1}$); and (3) best-placed-supplier-error-related HNOP–NEHNOP gaps or margins (#1EM). In my system, the total extra margin a best-placed seller obtains because of all relevant actors' errors—Its HNOP–NEHNOP gap—is symbolized by $\Sigma EM_{\#1}$. I will now comment on each of the three subcomponents of $\Sigma EM_{\#1}$ in turn.

I will restrict my comments about the relevant buyer-error margin to a few remarks about the contestability of the usefulness of the concept. Admittedly, if the buyer preferences that played a role in the analysis of the determinants of a best-placed individualized pricer's NEHNOP–MC gap are defined to refer to the buyer's perceived preferences as opposed to the preferences it would have if it were a sovereign maximizer, then the NEHNOP would already reflect any buyer errors that affected the price that a best-placed individualized pricer charged the buyer in question. However, for linguistic reasons and because the reality of buyer errors is sometimes relevant to both policy analyses and the determination of existing legal rights, it is useful to assume that the buyer preferences that lie behind the BPAs that are a component of a best-placed individualized pricer's NEHNOP are the monetized preferences of a sovereign maximizer and to handle separately the buyer errors that may enable such a best-placed seller to obtain higher prices from the erring customer than it otherwise could (or, for that matter, that may preclude it from obtaining as high a price from a buyer it was "objectively" privately-best-placed to supply as it otherwise could).

I will confine my comments about the relevant rival-error margin to a brief account of the various types of rival errors that can cause a best-placed seller's HNOP to exceed or differ from its NEHNOP. In an individualized-pricing context, a best-placed seller's closest competitor for a particular buyer's patronage (#2) may make at least four different types of errors that will enable the best-placed seller to obtain a price above its NEHNOP. First, #2—the rival that is second-placed to obtain the relevant buyer's patronage—may overestimate the overall marginal costs #2 would have to incur to supply the buyer in question at the price it would have to charge to beat the relevant best-placed-supplier's (#1's) offer (in which case #2 would fail to beat #1's offer despite the fact that it would beat it if it realized the inherent profitability of doing so); second, #2 may underestimate the relevant buyer's preference for #1's product or service in circumstances in which #2 will not have the opportunity to make a second bid for the relevant buyer's patronage (in which case #2 will make an offer to the buyer in question that will fail to obtain its patronage despite the fact that #2 believed that its offer would be successful and could in fact have profited by making a more attractive offer that would have been successful); third, #2 may critically overestimate the probability that #1 will beat any undercutting offer whose acceptance #2 would find profitable because #2 overestimates the probability that #1 will have the opportunity to change its initial offer to that buyer and/or the probability that #1 will find it inherently profitable to beat any relevant underbid #2 would otherwise find it profitable to make (in which case #2 will be deterred from making what would have been a successful, profitable underbid by the fact that the pricing and bidding costs it would have to incur to do so exceed its estimate of the weighted-average profits such a bid would yield it if pricing and bidding costs were zero [given its estimate of the probability that its undercutting offer will be accepted], though such bidding costs are in fact less than the weighted-average profits it should expect to make by undercutting #1's initial offer [bidding costs aside], given the actual [higher] probability that its undercutting offer will be accepted); and fourth, #2 may critically overestimate the sum of (1) the benefits #1 will allow it to obtain by engaging in reciprocal collaboration if #2 does not undercut #1's bid and (2) the costs #1 will impose on it by retaliating if #2 does undercut #1's bid (in which case #2 will be deterred from making a successful underbid that would have been profitable [strategic costs considered] by its misperception of the likelihood and/or likely extent of #1's relevant contrived oligopolistic reactions to #2's various possible responses to #1's initial price).

The third type of error that can cause a best-placed individualized pricer's HNOP to exceed its NEHNOP are errors that #1 makes itself. Thus, #1 may charge an individualized *supra*-NEHNOP price because it has overestimated its NEHNOP (its closest rival's MC, CMC, or BPD) and/or has incorrectly concluded that its closest rival will make errors that will enable it to get away with a price that that rival could have profited *ex ante* by undercutting (on the current assumption that the #1 seller did not intend to engage in oligopolistic conduct). As we shall see, such errors by #1 may not cause it to lose the sale in question if its rivals conclude that its price was intended to communicate its intention to retaliate against their undercutting and/or reciprocate to their not undercutting—that its price was contrived oligopolistic rather than mistaken.

Before proceeding to the P–HNOP component of an individualized pricer's P–MC gap, two additional points should be made about the HNOP–NEHNOP gap. First, although the preceding discussion presupposed that any errors that the best-placed individualized pricer and its rivals might make would always cause it to charge prices above the NEHNOP, that supposition is unjustified. Thus, if the best-placed supplier realized that its closest rival for the relevant buyer's patronage underestimated the marginal cost that that rival would have to incur to supply the buyer in question or if the best-placed supplier itself underestimated its closest rival's relevant marginal cost or its own BPA over that rival in relation to the relevant buyer, the best-placed supplier would tend on those accounts to charge the buyer a price below its NEHNOP.

Second, it is important to note that although the set of errors that affect a best-placed individualized pricer's HNOP–NEHNOP gap include errors its rivals make about its oligopolistic intentions, it does not include the errors it may make that affect whether it seeks to obtain an oligopolistic margin (OM) or the size of the OM it seeks to obtain.

In my scheme, the third major component of the gap between the price an individualized pricer actually charges a buyer it is best-placed to supply and the conventional marginal costs it would have to incur to supply that buyer are the oligopolistic margins it seeks to obtain from the buyer in question—*i.e.*, the extra sum it tries to obtain from this buyer because it believes that its closest rival or rivals for the relevant buyer's patronage will be deterred from making what would otherwise be a profitable undercutting response to any price it charges above its HNOP by a correct realization that it will react to such a response in a way that makes undercutting unprofitable for them. When the best-placed seller believes that its rivals will be deterred from undercutting it by their correct perception that it will react to such undercutting by making a move that is inherently profitable for it, the margin that it believes its ability to react will enable it to obtain is called a natural oligopolistic margin (NOM) and the best-placed seller's act of setting a price that relies on its rivals' being deterred from undercutting by their realization that it would react to their undercutting by making an inherently-profitable move that would make their undercutting unprofitable for them is called natural oligopolistic pricing (NOP). When the best-placed seller believes that its rivals will be deterred from undercutting it by their correct perception that it would react to such undercutting by making an inherently-unprofitable (strategic) move that would render undercutting unprofitable for them, the margin the anticipated strategic reaction enables the best-placed firm to obtain is called a contrived oligopolistic margin (COM), and the best-placed seller's act of setting a price that relies on its rival's or rivals' justified belief that it would react strategically to undercutting (as well as any collaborative response its rivals make and any strategic move it makes in reaction to their collaboration or undercutting) is called contrived oligopolistic pricing (COP). In my system, the total oligopolistic margin a best-placed seller obtains from a buyer it is best-placed to supply is symbolized as $\Sigma OM_{\#1} = NOM_{\#1} + COM_{\#1}$.

One additional point needs to be made about the situation that will prevail when $P_{\#1}$ exceeds $HNOP_{\#1}$. As you will recall, my original discussion of $CMC_{\#1}$ assumed that the best-placed seller was charging its HNOP, and my discussion of $CMC_{\#2}$ assumed that the second-placed seller was matching or infinitesimally beating an offer by #1 to supply the relevant buyer at #1's HNOP. If $P_{\#1}$ exceeds $HNOP_{\#1}$, that fact will affect both its CMC and the CMC its closest rival for the relevant buyer's patronage will have to incur to match #1's offer. In particular, #1's higher (supra-HNOP) price will reduce $CMC_{\#1}$ if it is less discriminatory than its HNOP or is less far below, equal to, or above a legally-required minimum price, while a $P_{\#1}$ that exceeds $HNOP_{\#1}$ will increase $CMC_{\#1}$ if it is more discriminatory or exceeds a maximum-price regulation. In general, #1's supra-HNOP price will tend to reduce $CMC_{\#2}$ by reducing the extent to which #2's matching-offer price discriminates in the relevant buyer's favor and may tend to reduce $CMC_{\#2}$ as well by reducing or eliminating any positive difference between the price #2 will have to charge to match #1's offer and some required minimum price though it may increase $CMC_{\#2}$ by increasing the positive difference between #2's matching-offer price and a maximum allowed price.

Chart I presents the conceptual scheme just delineated. It is accompanied by a glossary of all the symbols my individualized-pricing price-competition scheme involves. Before proceeding, I should point out that the preceding account of the determinants of an individualized pricer's P–MC gap has ignored the reality that such a pricer's actual price may also be influenced by conventional individual-product "promotional," product-line promotional, institutional promotional, network-building, "learning-by-doing," and "keeping-in-touch" considerations.[44]

---

[44] A seller is properly said to be engaging in (conventional single-product) "promotional pricing" at time t(0) when it lowers the price of its product X at t(0) to a level that would not otherwise be profitable because it expects the additional sales of product X that the price-reduction enables it to make at t(0) to increase the profits it makes at t(1. . .n) by increasing the demand it will face in relation to product X at t(1. . .n) for any or all of the following three reasons: (1) because it increases the demand that the additional buyer(s) the price-reduction enables it to sell X to at t(0) will have for product X at t(1. . .n)—"try it, you'll like it"; (2) because it increases the demand that other buyers will have for product X at t(1. . .n) by increasing the positive information they receive about X from the additional buyer(s) to which its price-reduction enabled it to sell X to at t(0) or from someone with whom these buyers talked or who observed these buyers using X or by observing themselves the way in which X performed for these additional buyers; and/or (3) because it increases the demand that other buyers will have for X at t(1. . .n) because they want to be identified with the additional buyers its price-reduction induced to buy X at t(0) or with particular attributes of these buyers. A seller is properly said to be engaging in product-line promotional pricing of product X1 at time t(0) when it charges a lower price for X1 because it expects that the additional sales of X1 that the reduction in X1's price will enable it to make of X1 at time t(0) will increase the demand curve it faces for products X2. . .n at time t(0) and subsequently because buyers have a preference for multiple members of the same product-line (1) because they find a matching set more aesthetically attractive than an unmatched collection, (2) because the proper way to use each member of a given product-line is the same while the proper method of using different product-lines varies from product-line to product-line and it is costly to learn how to use

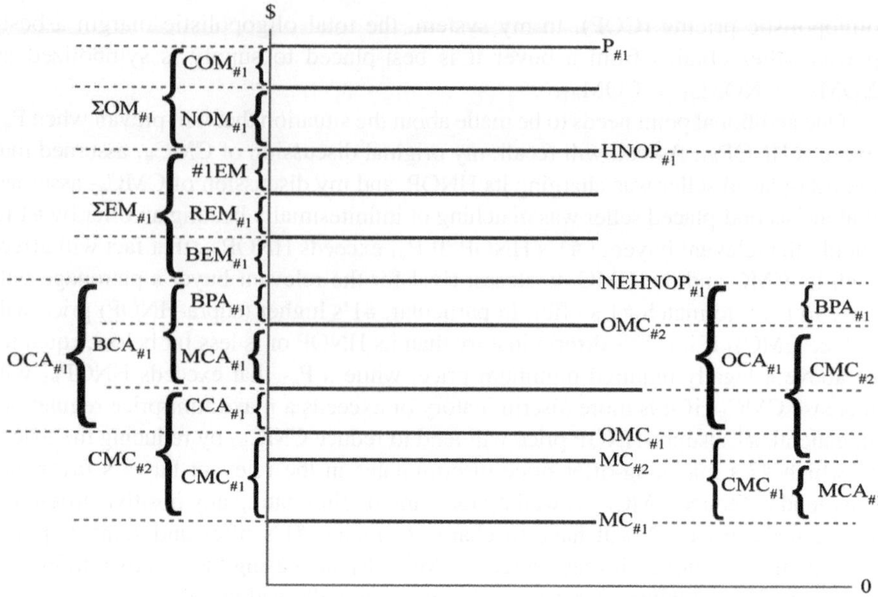

Chart I The components of the gap between a best-placed seller's actual individualized price and its (conventional) marginal cost

---

the products in a product-line whose products one has not yet used, and/or (3) because the members of any given product-line have the same strengths and weaknesses and such strengths and weaknesses differ among rival product-lines and it is costly to learn the strengths and weaknesses of a product-line whose products one has not yet used. I should add that the benefits of product-line promotional pricing will tend to be higher to the extent that the additional purchases of X2...n made by a buyer of X1 that has been induced to purchase X1 by a reduction in its price induces other buyers to purchase a member of the product-line X1...n. A seller is properly said to be engaging in institutional promotional pricing if it charges a lower price for product X at time t(0) than it otherwise would have found profitable because it expects that the extra sales the price-reduction will enable it to make of X will increase the demand it faces for all its products (regardless of whether they are in the same product-line as X) because product X is a good product and any buyer that consumes it will revise upward its estimate of the quality of all of the seller's products as will anyone that is told of its performance by its actual consumer or that observes its performance by its actual consumer in circumstances that enable the observer to evaluate its performance. A seller is properly said to be engaging in network-building pricing of product X when it charges a lower price for product X than it would otherwise find profitable because the objective value of product X to an individual buyer increases with the number of other buyers (*i.e.*, users) of the product. A seller is properly said to be engaging in "learning-by-doing" pricing when it lowers its price at t(0) because it expects the additional sales that the price-reduction enables it to make at t(0) will increase the profits it makes at t(1...n) by reducing the costs it will have to incur to produce various relevant outputs of its product at t(1...n) or by enabling it to discover a somewhat-different product variant that it could produce at t(1...n) on which it would face a more attractive DD/MC combination. A competitive inferior is properly said to be engaging in "keeping-in-touch" pricing if it incurs the cost of making a bid that it knows will not be accepted to secure the advertising-like benefits such a bid will generate by making it more likely that the buyer will solicit bids from it in the future and/or to pay more attention to its bids in the future by inducing the buyer to have a better opinion of it than it otherwise would have.

Glossary of Symbols

(1) $P_{\#1}$—the best-placed seller's actual price

(2) $COM_{\#1}$—the best-placed seller's attempted contrived oligopolistic margin

(3) $NOM_{\#1}$—the best-placed seller's attempted natural oligopolistic margin

(4) $\Sigma OM_{\#1}$—the best-placed-seller's attempted oligopolistic margin = $NOM_{\#1} + COM_{\#1}$

(5) $HNOP_{\#1}$—the best-placed seller's highest non-oligopolistic price = $(P_{\#1} - \Sigma OM_{\#1})$

(6) #1EM—the additional margin that the best-placed seller's errors about its NEHNOP, BEM, or $REM_{\#1}$ (see item [7] in this list) lead it to believe it can obtain non-oligopolistically

(7) $REM_{\#1}$—the additional margin the best-placed seller can obtain because of errors its rivals make

(8) $BEM_{\#1}$—the additional margin the best-placed seller can obtain because of errors the relevant buyer makes

(9) $\Sigma EM_{\#1}$—the total additional margin the seller's actual price contains because of errors its customers make, its rivals make, or it makes on issues that do not cause it him to try for additional or higher OMs = HNOP–NEHNOP (see item [10] in this list)

(10) $NEHNOP_{\#1}$—the price that would be the best-placed seller's HNOP if no-one made any relevant errors = $(HNOP_{\#1} - \Sigma EM_{\#1})$

(11) $BPA_{\#1}$—the best-placed seller's buyer preference advantage over its closest rival for the relevant buyer's patronage

(12) $MCA_{\#1}$—the best-placed seller's (conventional) marginal cost advantage over this closest rival for the relevant buyer's patronage

(13) $BCA_{\#1} = BPA_{\#1} + MCA_{\#1}$—the best-placed seller's basic competitive advantage over its closest rival for the relevant buyer's patronage

(14) $CCA_{\#1}$—the best-placed seller's contextual (marginal) cost advantage over its closest rival for the relevant buyer's patronage when the best-placed seller is charging its NEHNOP and this closest rival is matching that offer

(15) $OCA_{\#1} = BCA_{\#1} + CCA_{\#1}$—the best-placed seller's overall competitive advantage over this closest rival for the relevant buyer's patronage when the best-placed seller is charging its NEHNOP

(16) $CMC_{\#1}$—the contextual marginal costs the best-placed seller would have to incur to supply the relevant buyer at its NEHNOP

(17) $MC_{\#1}$—the conventional marginal cost the best-placed seller (#1) would have to incur to supply the buyer in question

(18) $OMC_{\#1} = MC_{\#1} + CMC_{\#1}$—the best-placed seller's overall marginal cost if it charges the relevant buyer its NEHNOP

(19) $MC_{\#2} = MC_{\#1} + MCA_{\#1}$—the conventional marginal cost the second-placed seller (#2) would have to incur to supply the relevant buyer

(20) $CMC_{\#2}$—the contextual marginal costs the second-placed seller would have to incur to match or infinitesimally beat the best-placed seller's NEHNOP-containing offer to the relevant buyer

(21) $OMC_{\#2} = MC_{\#2} + CMC_{\#2} = MC_{\#1} + MCA_{\#1} + CMC_{\#2}$—the overall marginal costs the second-placed seller would have to incur to match or infinitesimally beat the best-placed seller's NEHNOP-offer to the relevant buyer

Not Represented: the contextual marginal costs and hence overall marginal costs that the best-placed seller would have to incur to make a sale or even an offer to the relevant buyer at a price that exceeded its NEHNOP or the contextual marginal and hence overall marginal costs that a second-placed seller would have to incur to match or infinitesimally beat any offer by a best-placed seller to the relevant buyer that contained a price that exceeded the latter's NEHNOP

N.B. $P_{\#1} - MC_{\#1} = CMC_{\#2} + BCA_{\#1} + \#1EM + REM_{\#1} + BEM_{\#1} + NOM_{\#1} + COM_{\#1} = CMC_{\#1} + OCA_{\#1} + \Sigma EM_{\#1} + \Sigma OM_{\#1}$

B. The Price-Competition Conceptual Scheme for Across-the-Board-Pricing Situations

My breakdown of the gap between an across-the-board pricer's P–MC gap is very similar to its individualized-pricing counterpart. Once more, the P–MC gap is subdivided into P–HNOP, HNOP–NEHNOP, and NEHNOP–MC components. Once more, P–HNOP = NOM + COM, and HNOP–NEHNOP = ΣEM. However, at least five differences between the across-the-board-pricing and individualized-pricing (P–MC)-gap breakdown are worth pointing out. First, because any across-the-board price that a seller charges will apply to some buyers that it is not "best-placed to serve" in any sense in which that expression might be usefully defined, I use the symbol S (for seller) rather than the symbols #1, #2, . . . #N to refer to any across-the-board pricer whose HNOP or NEHNOP I am considering. Second, and relatedly, the #1EM subcomponent of the individualized HNOP–NEHNOP gap is replaced by a seller-error-margin (SEM) subcomponent in the across-the-board pricing conceptual scheme. Third, and also relatedly, although I recognize that the following usage may be confusing and therefore not advisable, in across-the-board-pricing contexts, the analysis of the breakdown of an across-the-board-pricing seller's NEHNOP–MC gap will refer to it and its rivals' across-the-board-pricing BCA/BCD distributions where each across-the-board-pricing BCA or BCD (basic competitive disadvantage) that any S has in its relations with any particular buyer is equated with the sum of its BPA or BPD in relation to that buyer and the MCA or MCD it would have in relation to that buyer *if the marginal costs that the seller in question and each of its rivals would have to incur to supply a unit of their respective products to that buyer (assuming the buyer paid the delivery costs) were equated with the marginal costs each such S would have to incur to supply the last unit of its product it would supply if all of them charged the prices that would equal their NEHNOPs if they announced their prices in the order in which they actually announced their prices.* This definition would not be problematic if, as there is some reason to believe is often the case, the MC curves of all the relevant sellers were horizontal over the relevant ranges of output. However, when the relevant MC curves are not horizontal over the relevant ranges of output, this component (though still useful as a descriptive concept) cannot be used in any protocol for identifying a particular across-the-board pricer's HNOP: if the goal is to calculate a particular seller S*'s HNOP, one cannot do so through a protocol of measuring the components of its HNOP–MC gap if the definition of one of these components assumes that one already knows the HNOP not only of S* but also of each of its rivals. Fourth and again relatedly, the across-the-board-pricing counterpart to the BCA component of the gap between a best-placed seller's NEHNOP and MC in an individualized-pricing situation is the difference between the across-the-board price each across-the-board-pricing S* would charge if it and its rivals knew that it could not react to its rivals' responses and they charged its customers' prices equal to their conventional marginal costs. This component will depend not just on the relevant S*'s across-the-board-pricing BCA/BCD distribution as defined above but also on the way in which that S*'s and its rivals' marginal costs vary above and below the unit outputs they would respectively produce if none behaved oligopolistically and they announced their prices in the order in which they actually did announce them. And fifth, the across-the-board-pricing counterpart to the $CMC_{\#2}$ subcomponent of the individualized-pricing NEHNOP–MC gap is replaced by an analogous subcomponent that also equals the extra margin that the seller in question finds profitable to charge because its rivals are charging its customers prices that exceed their respective conventional marginal costs. However, whereas (1) in the normal individualized-pricing situation, a best-placed supplier's closest rival will usually charge the #1's customers prices above the #2's conventional marginal costs if the #1 charges its NEHNOP to the relevant buyer because (A) the individualized price the #2 will have to charge the relevant buyer to match the #1's NEHNOP-containing offer to that buyer will discriminate in the relevant buyer's favor and (B) sellers (including #2) will normally have to incur arbitrage-related, goodwill-related, bargaining-related, and/or law-related CMC to discriminate in favor of a buyer (to charge that buyer a lower price than the seller is charging other buyers—in particular, is charging other buyers that the seller is best-placed to supply), (2) in across-the-board-pricing situations, the rivals of each seller S* will be charging that seller's potential customers prices above their respective conventional marginal costs because (A) by definition, in such situations, these rivals will be charging their own customers the same price they are charging the relevant S*'s customers and (B) charging buyers that would be willing to pay them prices in excess of their respective conventional marginal costs prices equal to their respective marginal costs will be "costly" to them in that (1) each rival of each S* would on this account charge supra-marginal-cost prices to that S*'s potential customers even if each such rival believed that the other rivals of the S* in question would equate their prices with their respective marginal costs and (2) each rival of each S* would also be charging prices that exceed the rival's marginal costs because each of them would realize that in reality its rivals (often the S*'s other rivals) would also be charging the relevant rival's customers (across-the-board) prices that exceed their respective marginal costs.

I will now proceed to describe the protocol for determining the NEHNOP array for a relevant set of across-the-board-pricing sellers. (For simplicity, I will henceforth assume that no relevant errors are being made and therefore focus on the HNOP array for such sellers.) I will then delineate and explore two simple examples that illustrate the protocol, reveal the relevance of various determinants of the gap between the prices in an across-the-board-pricing HNOP array and the respective seller's marginal costs, and reveal as well the fact that the HNOP–MC gap for across-the-board pricers will almost always substantially exceed their average and even their highest across-the-board-pricing BCA in their relations with those buyers in relation to which (on my admittedly-awkward definition) they have a (positive) across-the-board-pricing BCA.

I will start by providing an account of how one would calculate the array of across-the-board-pricing HNOPs for a set of across-the-board pricers. To generate conclusions about such an HNOP array, one would have to know (1) the order in which the relevant sellers announced their prices, (2) each relevant seller's across-the-board BPA/BPD array, and (3) each relevant seller's MC curves over the relevant range of unit outputs.

I will start by describing the protocol for calculating the across-the-board-pricing HNOP array for duopolists—X1, which produces product A1, and X2, which produces product A2. I will assume that (1) X1 announces its price for A1 before X2 announces its price for A2, (2) X1 knows that X2 realizes that X1 will not react to X2's response to X1's price, and (3) X1 and X2 have perfect information about their respective BPA/BPD arrays and the shapes of their respective MC curves over the relevant range of outputs. On these assumptions, X1 will identify its profit-maximizing (HNOP) price $P1^*$ by (1) determining for each price P1 it could charge the price P2 that X2 would find most profitable to charge in response, (2) calculating the unit sales it would make if it charged the P1 in question and X2 made its profit-maximizing price-response, (3) calculating the profits that it would make by charging the particular price P1 in question, given the unit sales X1 would make at that price and its marginal costs over the relevant output-range, and (4) identifying the price $P1^*$ that would yield it the highest profits in the circumstances in question. X2 would, of course, determine the price P2 that would be most profitable for it to charge in response to any price that X1 charged if X1 would not react to X2's price-response by (1) determining for each such price P2 that it could charge in response to the particular price P1 that X1 set for A1 the unit sales that it would make if it charged that P2, (2) calculating the profits it would make if it charged that price P2 in response to X1's price P1, given the marginal costs it would have to incur to supply the units it would sell if X1 charged that P1 and it responded with that P2, and (3) identifying the price that would yield it the highest profits if X1 charged the P1 in question. The relevant HNOP array would than consist of the price $P1^*$ that X1 would find most profitable if it could not engage in oligopolistic pricing and the price $P2^*$ that X2 would find most profitable to charge in response to X1's price $P1^*$ if X1 could not engage in oligopolistic pricing.

The relevant protocol is more complicated but essentially no different in across-the-board-pricing situations in which three or more relevant sellers are operating. The complication is that, in the three-seller case in which X1, X2, and X3 announce their binding prices in that order, X2's calculation of the price P2* that would constitute its profit-maximizing price-response to any price P1 that X1 might charge would take into account the response that X3 would find most profitable to make if X1 charged the P1 in question and X2 responded to X1's price P1 with a particular price P2 and neither X1 nor X2 would react to X3's response to their prices. Concomitantly, X1's calculation of its HNOP would have to take account of X2's prospective analysis of X3's profit-maximizing response to any price P2 that X2 could charge in response to any price P1 X1 charged on the assumption that X1 would not react to X2's and X3's responses to its price P1 and that X2 would not react to X3's response to X2's price (itself made in response to X1's price).

Although the relevant calculations will become highly complex as the number of rival sellers increases, if one had the relevant data, computer programs could be designed to generate HNOP-array conclusions quickly and without much expense. I should point out that there is little reason to believe that HNOP calculations will be less practicable in across-the-board-pricing contexts than in individualized-pricing contexts: the protocol I delineated for calculating individualized HNOPs was a protocol for calculating the HNOP for a best-placed single individualized-pricing seller to charge an individual buyer it was best-placed to supply whereas the protocol just delineated for calculating the HNOP array in an area of product-space in which across-the-board prices are being charged is a protocol for determining the prices that all relevant sellers in that area of product-space would be charging all relevant buyers. I do not want the wrong conclusions to be inferred from the preceding point. The fact that I do not think that it would be less practicable to determine the HNOPs of all the sellers that operate in a given area of product-space if they are setting across-the-board prices than if they are setting individualized prices has no bearing on whether I think it practicable to calculate such HNOP arrays in either type of pricing context. In fact, as I will argue in Sects. 2 and 3 of Chap. 10, I do not think it practicable to calculate HNOPs in either pricing context—*i.e.*, I do not think that in either individualized-pricing or across-the-board-pricing contexts, it will be cost-effective to determine whether a seller is charging an oligopolistic price by comparing its actual price with an estimate of its HNOP.

I will now develop and explore two highly-simplified examples (1) to illustrate the HNOP-calculation protocol respectively in duopoly and three-seller cases and (2) to reveal that, as the preceding discussion of the across-the-board-pricing counterpart to the $CMC_{\#2}$ component of a best-placed individualized pricer's HNOP–MC gap implied, the across-the-board-pricing HNOP–MC gaps for across-the-board pricers will almost always be higher not only than the average across-the-board-pricing BCA any such pricer enjoys in its relations with those buyers for which it has such a BCA but also than the highest such BCA an across-the-board pricer enjoys.

I will then explain (1) the various across-the-board-pricing-BCA/BCD-related determinants of the HNOP–MC gap of an across-the-board-pricing seller other than its highest and average across-the-board-pricing BCA in its relations with buyers for which it has a positive across-the-board-pricing BCA and (2) why the average across-the-board-pricing HNOP–MC gap for a set of across-the-board-pricing rivals will depend not only on their BCA/BCD distributions but also on the order in which they announce their prices. Considerations of space and reader patience have led me to conclude that I should not create and explore numerical examples to illustrate these points.

To ease the exposition, the examples I will use to illustrate the HNOP-calculation protocol respectively in duopoly and three-seller situations incorporate the usually-unrealistic assumption that only one of the set of across-the-board-pricing sellers in each case has any across-the-board-pricing BCAs (in fact, BPAs) in its relations with all the buyers concerned. This assumption does not critically affect any significant conclusion I use these examples to generate.

The first example is a simple duopoly case in which (1) there are two sellers X1 and X2 that respectively produce product variants A1 and A2, (2) X1 announces its price before X2 announces its price, (3) X1's and X2's marginal costs are constant over the relevant output ranges and both equal 1 cent, (4) there are 40 buyers Y1-40 each of which will purchase one unit of either A1 or A2, regardless of the prices that are being charged for these products within the relevant range, (5) buyers Y1-20 are indifferent between X1's product A1 and X2's product A2, (6) X1 has a BPA over X2 in its relations with buyers Y21-40—in particular, a BPA that is 1 cent for buyers Y21-22 and increases by 1 cent for each successive pair of buyers from buyers Y23-24 through buyers Y39-40. (Thus, X1's BPA is 2 cents for buyers Y23-24 and 10 cents for buyers Y39-40.) In addition to assuming that (7) X1 knows that X2 knows that X1 will not react to any across-the-board price P2 X2 charges in response to any across-the-board price P1 X1 sets and (8) X1 and X2 are perfectly informed about (A) both of their BPA/BPD distributions and (B) their actual MC curves over the relevant ranges of output, the analysis that follows also assumes that (9) prices cannot contain any fractional part of a cent, (10) if X1 and X2 make equally-attractive offers to any buyer, each will have a 50 % chance to obtain that buyer's patronage, (11) X1 and X2 are both risk-neutral, and (12) X1 and X2 will both prefer to earn the same profits on higher unit-sales than on lower unit-sales (because [1] they will have to provide more working capital to produce and sell more units in that they will have to pay the cost of producing and selling those units before they obtain the revenue from selling them and [2] they are just satisfied by as opposed to being indifferent toward the normal rate-of-return they will earn on that working capital when their sales cover their marginal costs, which include the cost of the associated working capital to them). Thus, if X2 matches X1's price, X2 will expect to sell 10 units to Y1-20; if X2 beats X1's price by 1 cent, X2 will expect to sell a total of 20 units to Y1-20 and a total of one unit to Y21-22; if X2 beats X1's price by 2 cents, X2 will expect to sell a total of 20 units to Y1-20, a total of two units to Y21-22, and a total of one unit to Y23-24; and so on and so forth.

We should now be able to calculate X1's and X2's across-the-board-pricing HNOPs in this case—*i.e.*, to determine (1) the price $P1^*$ that X1 will find most profitable to charge for A1 when no-one makes any mistakes, X1 sets its price for A1 before X2 sets its price for A2, and X1 cannot react to X2's response to X1's price and (2) the price $P2^*$ that on those assumptions X2 will find most profitable to charge for A2 in response to X1's price of $P1^*$ for A1. To do so, I will simply follow the protocol previously delineated—*i.e.*, I will calculate for each across-the-board price P1 that X1 could charge the price P2 that X2 would find most profitable to charge in response, the number of units of A1 that X1 would sell if it charged that P1 and X2 responded with that P2, and the profits that X1 would make by selling that number of units at that price P1.

I will assume that X1 will begin by considering the profits it would make in the case described if it charged a price of 1 cent for A1 and proceed by calculating the profits it would make in this case if it charged prices of 2 cents, 3 cents, 4 cents. . .for A1. I will not consider the possibilities that X1 or X2 might charge a price below their marginal cost of 1 cent (*i.e.*, on our assumption that prices cannot contain any fraction of a cent, a price of zero cents) because any such price would clearly be unprofitable for any seller (on my implicit assumption that it would not be promotional and explicit assumption that it would not be retaliatory).

In the case I have described, X1 will begin its calculation of the most profitable price it could charge for A1 if it could not practice oligopolistic pricing by determining that, if it sets its price for A1 at its marginal cost of 1 cent, (1) X2 will respond by charging a price of 1 cent for its product A2 and (2) X1 will sell 30 units of A1 (a total of 10 units to Y1-20 and a total of 20 units to Y21-40) but will make no profits on those sales (since the price of 1 cent just equals the marginal costs X1 must incur to produce and sell each of the 30 units in question). X1's conclusion that X2 will respond to its price of 1 cent for A2 by charging a price of 1 cent for A2 reflects the following calculations: (1) if X2 responds by charging 1 cent for A2, it will sell a total of 10 units to Y1-20 and will just break even on those sales (an outcome that I am assuming X2 will find better than making no sales) and (2) if X2 responds by charging 2 cents or more for A2, X2 will sell no units of A2 (given A1's price of 1 cent) and incur no loss and obtain no profits.

X1 would then determine the profits it would realize if it charged a price of 2 cents for A1. In particular, X1 would determine that, if it charged 2 cents for A2, X2 would respond by charging a price of 2 cents for X2's product A2, X1 would sell 30 units of A1 (a total of 10 units to Y1-20 and a total of 20 units to Y21-40) and would realize 30 cents in operating profits = (30 units)(2 cents–1 cent). X1's conclusion that X2 would respond to a price of 2 cents for A1 by charging 2 cents for A2 reflects the following calculations: (1) if X2 responded with a price of 1 cent, X2 would sell 21 units of A2 (20 units to Y1-20 and one unit to Y21-22) but would realize no operating profits on any of these sales (since X2's marginal costs are 1 cent on each of those units); (2) if X2 responded with a price of 2 cents, X2 would sell 10 units of A2 to Y1-20 and no units to anyone else and would realize 10 cents = (10 units)(2 cents–1 cent) profits on those sales; and (3) if

X2 responded with a price of 3 cents or more, it would sell no units of A2 and therefore earn no profits.

X1 would then determine the profits it would realize if it charged a price of 3 cents for A1. In particular, X1 would determine that, if it charged 3 cents for A1, X2 would respond by charging a price of 2 cents for A2, X1 would sell 19 units of A1 (a total of one unit to Y21-22 and a total of 18 units to Y23-40) and would realize 38 cents = (19 units)(3 cents–1 cent) in profits. X1's conclusion that X2 would respond to X1's price of 3 cents for A2 by charging 2 cents for A2 reflects the following calculations: (1) if X2 responded by charging 1 cent for A2, X2 would sell 23 units of A2 (a total of 20 units to Y1-20, a total of two units to Y21-22, and a total of one unit to Y23-24) but would earn no profits on those sales; (2) if X2 responded by charging 2 cents for A2, X2 would sell 21 units of A2 (a total of 20 units to Y1-20 and a total of one unit to Y21-22) and would realize 21 cents = (21 units)(2 cents–1 cent) in profits on those sales; (3) if X2 responded by charging a price of 3 cents for A2, X2 would sell 10 units of A2 (a total of 10 units to Y1-20 and no units to anyone else) and would realize 20 cents = (10 units) (3 cents–1 cent) in profits on those sales; and (4) if X2 responded by charging a price of 4 or more cents for A2, X2 would make no sales of A2 and would realize no profits on A2. X1 will therefore conclude that on our assumptions it will be more profitable for it to charge a price of 3 cents for A1 than to charge a price of 2 cents for A1.

X1 would then proceed to calculate in the above way for each price above 3 cents it might charge for A1 (1) the price that X2 would find most profitable to charge in response on our assumptions, (2) the unit sales that X1 would make at the price of A1 in question, given X2's response, and (3) the profits X1 would realize by charging the price in question—(the difference between the price in question and X1's constant marginal costs of 1 cent) *times* (the number of units of A1 that X1 would sell if it set the relevant price for A1). There are limits to how tedious even I am willing to be. If one made all the relevant calculations, one would discover that the most profitable price for X1 to charge on our assumptions—*i.e.*, X1's HNOP in the case in question—is 17 cents: if X1 charges 17 cents for A1, X2's most profitable response will be to set A2's price at 14 cents, X1 will sell 15 units of A1 (a total of one unit to Y25-26 and a total of 14 units to Y27-40) and will realize $2.40 on its sales of A1—(17 cents–1 cent) (15 units). In this case, therefore, the HNOP array is 17 cents for X1's product A1 and 14 cents for X2's product A2.

It may be worthwhile to point out that in this case (1) the gap between X1's HNOP and MC (16 cents = 17 cents–1 cent) is higher not only than X1's average across-the-board-pricing BCA in its relations with those buyers for which X1 has a positive across-the-board BCA (buyers Y21-40, in relation to which X1's average BCA is 5 [1/2] cents) but also than X1's highest across-the-board-pricing BCA in its relations with any buyer (the 10 cent BCA X1 enjoys in its relations with Y39-40) and (2) the gap between X2's HNOP and MC (13 cents = 14 cents–1 cent) is higher than its average and highest across-the-board-pricing BCA in its relations with buyers for which it has a positive BCA of this kind (zero and zero, since *X*2 enjoys no such BCA in relation to any buyer). In the duopoly case just analyzed, these outcomes reflect the facts that (1) X1 can take a "piggyback ride" on X2's decision to charge a price for A2 (14 cents) that exceeds X2's marginal costs of 1 cent and (2) *X2* can take a "piggyback ride" on X1's decision to charge X2's potential customers a price for X1 (17 cents) that exceeds X1's marginal costs (1 cent).

The second example is a three-seller example that is designed *inter alia* to concretize the protocol for calculating the HNOP array of a set of three or more across-the-board-pricing rivals. This case assumes that (1) there are three rival sellers X1, X2, and X3 that respectively produce product variants A1, A2, and A3; (2) X1 announces its price first, X2 announces its price second, and X3 announces its price third; (3) X1, X2, and X3 all face the same marginal-cost curve—an MC that is horizontal over the relevant range at the height of 1 cent, (4) only three buyers—Y1, Y2, and Y3—are interested in purchasing A1, A2, or A3, and each of these buyers will purchase one and only one unit of one of the products in question, regardless of the prices that are charged for them over the relevant range, (5) buyer Y1 has a 4 cent buyer preference for A1 over both A2 and A3—*i.e.*, X1 has a 4 cent BPA (and across-the-board-pricing BCA) over X2 and X3 in their relations with buyer Y1, buyer Y2 has a 1 cent buyer preference for A1 over both A2 and A3—*i.e.*, X1 has a 1 cent BPA (and across-the-board-pricing BCA) over both X2 and X3 in their relations with buyer Y2, and buyer Y3 also has a 1 cent buyer preference for A1 over both A2 and A3—*i.e.*, X1 has a 1 cent BPA (and across-the-board-pricing BCA) over both X2 and X3 in their relations with buyer Y3, (6) X1, X2, and X3 are perfectly informed about their own BPA/BPD positions and marginal costs and about each other's BPA/BPD positions and marginal costs, (7) X1 cannot react to X2's response to X1's price or to X3's response to the prices it and X2 charge, X2 cannot react to X3's response to X2's price, and X1, X2, and X3 are all aware of the above realities, (8) prices must be in whole-cent denominations, (9) if two sellers make equally-attractive offers to any buyer, each will have a 50 % chance of obtaining that buyer's patronage, and if three sellers make equally-attractive offers to any buyer, each will have a 1/3 chance of obtaining that buyer's patronage, (10) X1, X2, and X3 are all indifferent to risk, and (11) X1, X2, and X3 would rather cover their marginal (variable) costs on positive sales than make no sales at all, and X1, X2, and X3 would rather earn given profits on higher unit-sales than on lower unit-sales because they are just satisfied by rather than indifferent to any normal returns they realize on the working capital required to finance production and sales. As always, the prices that X1, X2, and X3 will find most profitable to charge in these circumstances will constitute their across-the-board-pricing HNOP array on the assumptions in question—*inter alia*, when they are announcing their prices in the stipulated order.

Once more, I will assume that X1 (1) will proceed by considering in the stated order the unit-sales it will make and profits it will earn if it charges a price of 1 cent, 2 cents, 3 cents. . .for A1 when these outcomes will depend *inter alia* on the ways in which X2 and X3 will respond sequentially to that price under the circumstances in question where X2's response will partly depend on X2's conclusions about the way in which X3 will respond to X2's responding to each price P2 that X2 could charge for A2 in response to X1's charging a particular price for A1 and then

(2) charge the price $P1^*$ that will yield it the most profits, given the responses from X2 and X3 that the various prices P2 and P3 that each P1 would elicit. $P1^*$ will be X1's HNOP, and the prices $P2^*$ and $P3^*$ that X2 and X3 will sequentially find are their most profitable price responses respectively to $P1^*$ and to $P1^*$ and $P2^*$ will be their HNOPs.

On this example's assumptions, if X1 charges 1 cent for A1, X2 and X3 will not be able to make any sales of their respective products A2 and A3 unless they charge a price at least 1 cent below 1 cent, which they obviously will not find profitable to do. Hence, X1 will conclude that if it sets A1's price at 1 cent, it will sell three units of A1 (one unit each to Y1, Y2, and Y3) but will make no profits on those sales since one cent also equals X1's marginal costs for each of the units in question.

X1 would then determine that, if it charged a price of 2 cents for A1, (1) X2 would respond by charging a price of 1 cent for A2 and X3 would respond to X1's price of 2 cents for A1 and X2's price of 1 cent for A2 by charging a price of 1 cent for A3, (2) X1 would sell (expect on the weighted average to sell) 1(2/3) units of A1—one unit to Y1 and 1/3 of a unit to each of Y2 and Y3, and (3) X1 would make 1(2/3) cents profits on the sales in question. X1's conclusion that X2 and X3 would respond to a price of 2 cents for A1 by charging respectively and sequentially 1 cent for A2 and 1 cent for A3 would be based on the following calculations: (1) if X2 responded to X1's price of 2 cents for A1 by charging a price of 2 cents or more for A2, X2 would make no sales of A2 and no profits on A2, regardless of how X3 responded; (2) if X2 responded to X1's price of 2 cents for A2 by charging 1 cent for A2, X3 would respond by charging a price of 1 cent for A3 and that would result in X2's making weighted-average-expected sales of 2/3 of one unit—1/3 of a unit to Y2 and 1/3 of a unit to Y3—on which it would just break even (since the price of 1 cent just covers X2's marginal costs of 1 cent for any relevant unit of A2). The conclusion that X3 would respond to X1's charging 2 cents for A1 and X2's charging 1 cent for A2 is based on the following calculations: (1) if X3 responded to X1's charging 2 cents for A1 and X2's charging 1 cent for A2 by charging 2 cents or more for A3, it would make no sales of A3, and (2) if X3 responded by charging 1 cent for A3, X3 would expect on the weighted average to sell 2/3 of a unit of A3 (none to Y1, 1/3 to Y2, and 1/3 to Y3), X3 would break even on those sales, and on assumption (11) X2 would prefer to break even on positive sales than to make no sales. Assumption (11) implies not only that (1) X3 will prefer to respond to a price of 2 cents for A1 and a price of 1 cent for A2 by charging a price of 1 cent for A3 rather than by not bidding for the relevant buyers' patronage at all or charging a price of two or more cents for A3 but also that (2) X2 will prefer to respond to a price of 2 cents for A1 with a price of 1 cent for A2 that would induce X3 to set a price of 1 cent for A3 rather than by not bidding for Y1-3's patronage at all or charging a price for A2 of 2 cents or higher, which would result in X2's making no sales to Y1-3.

X1 would then determine that, if it charged a price of 3 cents for A2, (1) X2 would respond by charging a price of 2 cents for A2 and X3 would respond to X1's and X2's decisions by charging a price of 2 cents for A3, (2) if X1 charged a price of 3 cents for A2, it would therefore make 1(2/3) units of sales—would sell one unit to Y1 and 1/3 or a unit to each of Y2 and Y3, and (3) X1 would earn (weighted-average-expected) profits of 3(1/3) cents = (2 units) (1[2/3] cents). X1's conclusions about how X2 and X3 would respond to its setting A1's price at 3 cents would reflect the facts that (1) if either of them charged 1 cent for A2 and A3 respectively, that firm would make no profits on the resulting sales, (2) if either charged 3 cents or more for A2 and A3 respectively, that firm would make no sales, but (3) if they respectively charged a price of 2 cents for A2 and A3, each would expect to sell on the weighted average 2/3 of a unit of its product—1/3 of a unit to Y2 and 1/3 of a unit to Y3—and would realize weighted-average-expected profits of 2/3 cents.

On my account, X1 would then proceed to determine that, if it charged a price of 4 cents for A1, (1) X2 and X3 would successively charge 2 cents for A2 and 2 cents for A3, (2) X1 would sell one unit of A1 (to Y1), and (3) X1 would realize 3 cents profits on that sale (less profits than X1 could earn by charging 3 cents for A1). X1's conclusion that X2 and X3 would respond sequentially to its charging 4 cents for A1 by charging respectively 2 cents for A2 and 2 cents for A3 is based on the following calculations: (1) X2 will not charge 1 cent for A2 in response to X1's pricing A1 at 4 cents because, regardless of how X3 would respond, X2 would not make any profits by selling A2 for 1 cent (since its marginal cost for each relevant unit of A2 is 1 cent); (2) X2 will not charge 4 cents or more for A2 if A1 is priced at 4 cents because, if it did, it would make no sales of A2 and therefore no profits; (3) X2 will find it more profitable to charge 2 cents than 3 cents for A2 because (A) if X2 charges 3 cents for A2, X3 will find it more profitable to charge 2 cents for A3 since doing so would result in its selling two units of A3 (one unit to Y2 and one unit to Y3) and earning 2 cents in profits than to charge 3 cents for A3 since doing so would result in its selling 2/3 of a unit of A3 (1/3 of a unit to Y2 and 1/3 of a unit to Y3) and earning 1(1/3) cents in profits and (B) if X2 charges 2 cents for A2, X2 will also find it most profitable to charge 2 cents for A3 since doing so will enable it to sell one unit of A3 (1/2 of a unit to Y2 and ½ of a unit to Y3) and to earn 1 cent profits while charging 3 cents or more for A3 would result in its making no sales of A3 and charging 1 cent for A3 would result in its making no profits on the two units of A3 it would sell at that price (inasmuch as X3 must also incur 1 cent in marginal costs to produce each unit of A3 in question), and (4) for the reasons just articulated, if X1 charges 4 cents for A1 and X2 charges 2 cents for A2, X3 will charge 2 cents for A3.

However, although X1 would conclude that in the situation in question it would be more profitable for it to charge 3 cents than 4 cents for A1, X1 would conclude that a price of 5 cents for A1 would be even more profitable. This conclusion reflects the fact that, if X1 charges 5 cents for A1, (1) X2 will charge 2 cents for A2, and X3 will charge 2 cents for A3, (2) X1 will therefore still sell one unit of A1 (to Y1) but now (3) will realize 4 cents profits on that sale. X1's conclusions about X2's and X3's responses to its pricing A1 at 5 cents will reflect the following calculations: (1) X2 will not respond to a price of 5 cents for A1 by charging a price of 1 cent for A2 because that price will yield X2 no profits and (as we shall see) X2's decision to charge a price of 2 cents for A2 will yield it some profits; (2) X2 will not respond to a price of 5 cents for A1 by charging 5 cents or more for A2 because, if it does, it will make no sales of A2 and hence no profits on A2; and (3) X2 will not respond to a price of 5 cents for A1 by charging prices of 4 or 3 cents for A2 because, if it does, X3 will find it most profitable to respond to such prices by charging a price for A3 that precludes X2 from making any sales of or any profits on A2: thus, (A) if X2 charges 4 cents for A2, X3 will know that (i) if it charges 4 cents for A3, it will sell 2/3 of a unit of A3 (1/3 to Y2 and 1/3 to Y3) and realize 2 cents = ([2/3] of a unit)(4 cents–1 cent) profits whereas [ii] if it charges 3 cents for A3, it will sell two units of A3 (one unit each to Y2 and Y3), leaving X2 with no sales of A2, and realize 4 cents = (2 units)(3 cents–1 cent) profits and (B) if X2 charges 3 cents for A2, X3 will know that (i) if it charges 3 cents for A3 it will sell (expect to sell on the weighted average) one unit of A3 (1/2 of a unit to Y1 and 1/2 of a unit to Y2) and realize 2 cents = (one unit)(3 cents–1 cent) profits whereas (ii) if X3 charges a price of 2 cents for A3, it will sell two units of A3 (one each to Y1 and Y2), thereby leaving X2 with no sales of A2, and also realize 2 cents = (one unit)(2 cents–1 cent)—an outcome I am assuming X3 would prefer in that X3 would prefer to realize the same profits on higher unit-sales. Thus, X2 will charge a price of 2 cents for A2 if X1 has priced A1 at 5 cents because, if X2 charges a price of 2 cents for A2, X3 will charge a price of 2 cents for A3 and X2 will sell one unit of A2 (1/2 a unit to Y2 and 1/2 a unit to Y3) and make 1 cent in profits = (one unit) (2 cents–1 cent) whereas, if X2 charges a price of three or more cents for A2, X3 will charge 2 cents for A3 and X2 will make no sales of A2 and earn no profits. Hence, if X1 charges a price of 5 cents for A1, X2 and X3 will charge 2 cents for their products, X1 will sell one unit of A1 and realize 4 cents in profits on that sale—more profits than it would realize by charging any lower price for A1.

In fact, on the assumptions of this second case, 5 cents will be X1's most profitable price and concomitantly its HNOP. To give you some sense of why this is so, I will explore the consequences of X1's charging a price of 6 cents for A1. If X1 charges a price of 6 cents for A1, X2's analysis of the most profitable response for X3 to make to the various prices that *X*2 could charge for A2 will lead X2 to conclude that its most profitable response to X1's price of 6 cents for A1 is 2 cents. X2 will reach this conclusion by making the following calculations: (1) if X2 charges 2 cents for A2 after X1 has priced A1 at 6 cents, (A) X3 will charge 2 cents for A3 because at that price it will sell 1(1/3) units of A3 (1/3 of a unit to Y1 and 1/2 of a unit to each of Y2 and Y3) and earn 1(1/3) cents by doing so whereas (B) if X3 charges a price above 2 cents for A3 it will make no sales of and hence no profits on A3 so that if X2 responds to X1's pricing A1 at 6 cents by charging 2 cents for A2, X2 will sell 1(1/3) units of A2 (1/3 of a unit to Y1 and 1/2 of a unit to Y2 and Y3) and earn 1(1/3) cents by doing so, (2) if X2 responds to X1's decision to charge 6 cents for A1 by charging 3 cents for A2, X3 will respond to those prices by charging 2 cents for A3 because X3 will realize that (A) if it charges 4 cents or more for A3, it will make no sales of that product, (B) if it charges 3 cents for A3, it will sell one unit of A3 (1/2 a unit to each of Y2 and Y3) and realize a total of 2 cents profits on A3, and (C) if it charges 2 cents for A3, it will sell 2(1/3) units of A3 (1/3 of a unit to Y1 and one unit each to Y2 and Y3) and realize a total of 2(1/3) cents profits on those sales so that, if X2 responds to X1's price of 6 cents for A1 by charging 3 cents for A2, it will make no sales of and no profits on A2. Note, too, that if X2 responds to X1's setting a price of 6 cents for A1 by charging a price of 4 cents for A2 it will also make no sales of or profits on A2 because X3 will respond by charging a price of 3 cents for A2. This last conclusion reflects the following calculations: on our assumptions, (1) if X3 charges a price of 4 cents for A3 after X1 has announced a price of 6 cents for A1 and X2 has announced a price of 4 cents for A2, X3 will sell one unit of A3 (1/2 unit to Y2 and 1/2 unit to Y2) and will make 3 cents profits; (2) if X3 charges a price of 3 cents for A3 after A1 is priced at 6 cents and A2 at 4 cents, X3 will sell two units of A3 (one unit to each of Y1 and Y2) and realize 6 cents = (2 units)(4 cents–1 cent) profits on those sales; and (3) if X3 charges a price of 2 cents for A3 after A1 is priced at 6 cents and A2 is priced at 4 cents, X3 will sell 2(1/2) units of A3 (1/2 unit to Y1 and one unit each to Y2 and Y3) and earn 2(1/2) cents = (2[1/2] units)(2 cents–one sent) profits. Note, finally, that, if X2 responds to X1's charging 6 cents for A1 by charging 5 cents for A2, X2 will also make no sales of or profits on A2 because, on our assumptions, X3 will find it most profitable to respond by charging 4 cents for A3. Thus, on our assumptions, (1) if X3 responds by charging 5 cents for A3, it will sell 2/3 of a unit of A3 (1/3 of a unit to each of Y2 and Y3) and realize 3(1/3) cents = (2/3 of a unit)(5 cents–1 cent) profits; (2) if X3 responds by charging 4 cents for A3, it will sell two units of A3 (one unit to each of Y2 and Y3) and earn 6 cents = (two units)(4 cents–1 cent) profits; (3) if X3 responds by charging 3 cents for A3, it will still sell only two units of A3 (to the same buyers) and earn 4 cents = (2 units)(3 cents–1 cent) profits; and (4) if X3 responds by charging 2 cents for A3, it will sell 2(1/2) units of A3 (1/2 a unit to Y1 and one unit each to Y2 and Y3) and earn 2(1/2) cents = (2[1/2] units)(2 cents–1 cent). Hence, on the assumptions of our second example, if X1 charges 6 cents for A2, X2 will respond with a price of 2 cents for A2, and X3 will then charge 2 cents for A3. The result will be that X1 will sell only 1/3 of a unit of A1 (to Y1) and will realize 5/3 cents = ([1/3] unit)(6 cents–1 cent) profits if it charges 6 cents for A1—less profits than X1 would earn on A1 if it charged 5 cents for that product.

Any price above 6 cents that X1 might charge for A1 would result in its making no sales of or profits on A1. This conclusion follows from the fact that on our assumptions X3 would always find it profitable to undercut any price above 2 cents X2 might charge for A2 (thereby causing X2 to make no sales of or profits on A2)—*i.e.*, from the fact that on our assumptions X2 and X3 would respond to any price X1 might charge above 6 cents with two-cent prices that would deprive X1 of any sales of or profits on A1 and yield X2 and X3 each sales of 1(1/2) units (since their 2-cent prices would beat X1's price by more than X1's 4-cent BPA in its relations with Y1) and profits of 1(1/2) cents. Hence, in this second example, the across-the-board-pricing HNOP array is 5 cents for X1, 2 cents for X2, and 2 cents for X3. In this case, X1's HNOP–MC gap of 4 cents equals its highest across-the-board-pricing BCA (its BPA of 4 cents in its relations with Y1) but is higher than its average such BCA in its relations with those buyers for which it has such a BCA (2 cents). X2's and X3's HNOP–MC gap (1 cent) obviously exceeds their highest and average across-the-board-pricing BCAs (which, for each, are zero and zero).

(Before proceeding, I should point out that the no-oligopolistic-pricing outcomes in the duopoly and three-seller cases just analyzed would be economically inefficient if the economy did not contain Pareto imperfections that caused the sellers [X2 and X3] that had across-the-board-pricing BCDs in their relations with particular buyers to be allocatively at-least-as-well-placed to supply those buyers as was the seller [X1] that had an across-the-board-pricing BCA in its relations with the buyers in question. Thus, in the duopoly case, the fact that in the relevant non-oligopoly equilibrium, X2 [1] will sell one unit to each to Y21 and Y22 despite the fact that it has a 1 cent across-the-board-pricing BCD in its relations with them, [2] will sell one unit each to Y23 and Y24 despite the fact that it has a 2-cent across-the-board-pricing BCD in its relations with them, and [3] will sell a total of one unit to Y25 and Y26 despite the fact that it has a 3-cent across-the-board-pricing BCD in its relations with them that would [in an otherwise-Pareto-perfect economy] be associated respectively with 2 cents = [two units][1 cent] *plus* 4 cents = [two units][2 cents] *plus* 3 cents = [one unit][3 cents] = 9 cents in economic inefficiency. And in the three-seller example, the fact that, in the relevant non-oligopoly equilibrium, [1] X2 and X3 will each sell 1/2 of a unit to Y2 and 1/2 of a unit to Y3 despite the fact that both sellers have a 1-cent across-the-board-pricing BCD in their relations with Y2 and Y3 implies that a total of 2 cents in economic inefficiency would be generated by their supplying these buyers if these sellers' private BCDs equaled their allocative counterparts. [Admittedly, since the assumption of our duopoly and three-seller examples that the relevant buyers' total unit purchases of the product variants will not be affected by those product variants' prices over the relevant range does not rule out the possibility that the unit-sales of A1 would be below three units if X1 would find it profitable to charge a price that exceeds the price that is its HNOP when X2 in the duopoly case and X2 and X3 in the three-firm case are present and they announce their prices in the sequence stipulated if it were freed from X2's competition in the duopoly case or X2's and X3's competition in the three-firm case, X2's or X2's and X3's operation might in the respective cases reduce misallocation by preventing X1 from reducing its output of A1 below the three total units of A1, A2, and A3 that will be produced if X1 and X2 or X1, X2, and X3 are operating respectively in the duopoly and three-seller cases. But even if that is the case, *inter alia*, because other imperfections do not reduce the economically-efficient output of A1 below 3 units, the duopoly and three-seller no-oligopolistic-pricing equilibria in question would be economically inefficient: even if X2's operation in the duopoly case and X2's and X3's operation in the three-seller case do prevent X1 from underproducing A1 from the perspective of economic efficiency, their operation will achieve this result only by causing another type of misallocation.])

I now want to delineate and explain three points about the determinants of a set of across-the-board-pricing rivals' HNOP–MC gaps. First, these gaps depend on the order in which the sellers in question announce their prices. In particular, such a set of rivals' HNOP–MC gaps will tend to be higher the greater the extent to which the firms for which the following ratio is low announce early in the relevant sequence: the ratio of (the frequency with which the relevant firm has an across-the-board-pricing BCA) to (the frequency with which it has the lowest or close-to-lowest across-the-board-pricing BCD). This conclusion reflects the fact that any seller for which this ratio is lower has more of an incentive than do its rivals to undermine their prices since the amount of potential profits it will lose by charging a lower across-the-board price to buyers that would have been willing to pay it a higher price will be small relative to the amount of additional sales and related profits it will be able to make by charging (roughly speaking) a lower price than its earlier-announcing rivals charged.

Second, in what I take to be the not-uncommon special case in which the relevant across-the-board pricers face constant marginal costs over their respective relevant output ranges, each seller's HNOP–MC gap will depend on its and the other relevant sellers' respective across-the-board-pricing BCA or BCD in relation to each relevant buyer. Thus, in such a situation, a given such seller's HNOP–MC gap depends not only on (1) its positive across-the-board-pricing BCA array but on (2) the across-the-board-pricing BCD positions of rivals whose across-the-board-pricing BCDs in relation to buyers for which it has an across-the-board-pricing BCA are not lowest as well as on (3) the across-the-board-pricing BCA positions that firms that have across-the-board-pricing BCDs in relation to buyers in relation to which it has an across-the-board-pricing BCA enjoy in relation to buyers for which they have across-the-board-pricing BCAs and (4) the across-the-board-pricing BCD positions that rivals occupy in their relations with buyers in relation to which other rivals have across-the-board-pricing BCAs. The immediately-preceding, unfortunate sentence is a corollary of the earlier discussion of the across-the-board-pricing counterpart to the $CMC_{\#2}$ component of an individualized-pricing seller's HNOP–MC gap in its relations with a buyer it is best-placed to supply. (The second point in the sentence before last is reflected in the fact that, if I adjusted the three-seller example so that X2 and X3 had respectively 1-cent and 3-cent BCDs in relation to Y2 and Y3 rather than both having 1-cent BCDs in relation to those buyers, X1's HNOP would be considerably higher because X3 would put *X*2 under less pressure to charge a low price for A2 in response to any price P1 X1 charged for A1.)

Third, in the general case in which the relevant sellers' marginal costs can vary from output-unit to output-unit, the HNOP–MC determinants on which it is cost-effective to focus are (1) the BPA or BPD of each seller in relation to each relevant buyer and (2) the MC curves of the relevant sellers over the relevant output ranges.

* * *

The price-competition conceptual schemes this section has delineated will be used for many purposes in this study—*inter alia*,

(1) to explain why market definitions are inherently arbitrary, not just at their periphery but comprehensively, and, relatedly, to explain why the two approaches to market definition that both the 1992 and the 2010 US DOJ/FTC Horizontal Merger Guidelines prescribe cannot be defended;
(2) to generate operational definitions of a firm's monopoly and/or oligopoly control over price;

(3) to generate an operational definition of a firm's highest non-oligopolistic (lowest non-predatory) price;
(4) to structure my analysis of the determinants of the feasibility of natural oligopolistic pricing and the profitability of contrived oligopolistic and predatory pricing;
(5) to structure my analysis of the kinds of evidence that can properly be used in court to prove that firms have engaged in contrived oligopolistic or predatory pricing;
(6) to structure my critiques of various protocols that others have argued courts should use to determine whether firms have engaged in contrived oligopolistic or predatory pricing;
(7) to structure my analysis of the factors that determine the impact of horizontal mergers, acquisitions, or joint ventures on the intensity of price competition;
(8) to structure my critiques of the traditional approach to predicting the impact of horizontal mergers on price competition and the approach to this issue taken both by the U.S. 1992 and 2010 Horizontal Merger Guidelines and by the European Commission;
(9) to structure my analysis of the impact of conglomerate mergers, acquisitions, and joint ventures that do and do not involve potential competitors (including geographical-diversification conglomerate mergers) on price competition;
(10) to structure my critique of the traditional analysis of the impact of conglomerate mergers on price competition (including limit-price theory); and
(11) to structure my analysis of the determinants of the most-inherently-profitable (non-monopolizing) pricing strategy for firms to employ in different situations.

2. The QV-Investment-Competition Conceptual Scheme

As we have seen, (1) "QV investments" are investments that create additional or superior product variants, additional or superior distributive outlets, or additional capacity and/or inventory (which enable their owner to provide faster average speed of supply during a fluctuating-demand cycle), and (2) "QV-investment competition" is the process through which the supernormal profits that a QV investment could generate are eliminated by the introduction of additional QV investments into the relevant area of product-space—*i.e.*, by new entries by the relevant QV investor's potential competitors and by (QV-investment) expansions by the QV investor itself or by its established rivals. This section of Chap. 2 delineates the conceptual scheme I use to analyze QV-investment competition. More specifically, this section (1) defines the various intermediate determinants of QV-investment competition in any area of product-space and (2) distinguishes three different types of QV-investment equilibria that may be established and analyzes the different ways in which the intermediate determinants just listed interact to generate them.

This definitional and analytic work is long overdue. Although economists do sometimes refer to one set of the relevant determinants—"barriers to entry"—different economists define "the barriers to entry" to which they refer differently, and all economists that use this concept do so to analyze the supposed effect of such barriers on the competitiveness of prices (usually, on whether so-called limit pricing is practiced) rather than on the competitiveness of QV investment. Moreover, to my knowledge, no economist has ever focused on the other two major categories of intermediate determinants of the intensity of QV-investment competition—*viz.*, (1) barriers to expansion and (2) monopolistic or natural oligopolistic QV-investment disincentives and monopolistic QV-investment incentives. Indeed, to my knowledge, no economist has ever attempted to execute an analysis of competition that focuses separately on QV-investment competition. These omissions are important not just because QV-investment competition is a significant social phenomenon but also because (1) the determinants of the intensity of QV-investment competition are different from the determinants of the intensity of price competition and given practices or transactions can increase price competition while decreasing QV-investment competition or *vice versa*, (2) increases in QV-investment competition will often reduce economic inefficiency in our Pareto-imperfect economy while increases in price competition will always or virtually always increase economic efficiency in our Pareto-imperfect economy, and (3) increases in QV-investment competition have a different distributive impact from that of increases in price competition and, from various value-perspectives, this difference will sometimes critically affect the desirability of increasing one or the other of these types of competition.

Before proceeding, two additional pieces of terminology need to be explained. The first is the concept of an "ARDEPPS." By its very nature, QV-investment competition is not individual-buyer or individual-product specific—*i.e.*, QV-investment competition is a process that takes place in an area of product-space. The determinants of the intensity of QV-investment competition (however that intensity is defined) will, therefore, be aggregated concepts. Unfortunately, Chap. 6's demonstration that it is not possible to define markets non-arbitrarily implies that it is also not possible to define non-arbitrarily the area of product-space within which QV-investment competition takes place. To remind readers both (1) that the domain of QV-investment competition is an area of product-space and (2) that the "relevant" area of product-space cannot be defined non-arbitrarily, I will use the acronym "ARDEPPS" to refer to the arbitrarily-designated portion of product-space within which QV-investment competition takes place. I should emphasize at the outset that my use of the concept of an ARDEPPS and correlatively of various ARDEPPS-aggregated concepts does not make me vulnerable to the same criticisms this study makes of market-oriented approaches to firm-economic-power assessment or competitive-impact prediction. At no point will any of the protocols I delineate for executing any type of analysis presuppose the non-arbitrary definition of any area of product-space: all uses I make of the concept of an ARDEPPS and various correlative ARDEPPS-aggregated concepts are purely heuristic.

The second set of vocabulary that must be discussed relates to the time-period to which the curves and concepts I am about to define refer. Unfortunately, this time-period question is quite complicated. Even if one assumes (contrary to fact—see below) that a static equilibrium will eventually be established, the lifetime of at least some of the QV-investment projects in an ARDEPPS can be divided into three different periods: (1) the period before the period on which the analysis is focusing—the "pre-analysis period"—at the end of which the ARDEPPS contains some QV investments and its established firms are considering whether to expand their QV-investment holdings in the ARDEPPS themselves or perhaps to allow entry to take place; (2) the "analysis period," which extends from the end of the pre-analysis period to the establishment of the hypothesized static equilibrium; and (3) the post-equilibrium period. The time-period problem reflects the fact that, since the rate-of-return that various individual QV investments generate will often vary from period to period, it is essential to specify the time-period to which any curve or concept refers.

The period on which an analysis should focus depends on the question the analysis is trying to answer. If the question is "do pioneers (early entrants) have systematic advantages over copycats (latecomers)," the appropriate focus is on lifetime rates-of-return (though one must take account of the possibility that any correlation between an investor's lifetime rate-of-return and its date of entry may be false—*i.e.*, that pioneers may have attributes that give them an advantage over copycats that do not depend on the pioneers' entering earlier). If the question is "why does no-one enter or expand despite the fact that the established firms are realizing lifetime supernormal rates-of-return on some projects," the appropriate focus is also on lifetime rates-of-return. If, however, perhaps because of the difficulty of establishing the rates-of-return that existing projects generated in the past, the question is "why does no-one enter or expand despite the fact that the established firms would be said to be realizing supernormal rates-of-return on some projects post-equilibrium if one ignored the subnormal profits the projects in question generated in the pre-equilibrium period," the appropriate focus is on the post-equilibrium rate-of-return. Although, in practice, lawyers and applied economists who are concerned with the concept of barriers to entry seem to have this third question in mind, I have chosen to define the curves in all the QV-investment diagrams I use to refer to lifetime profit-rates. Primarily, my choice reflects the fact that the use of the most-likely alternative time-period would complicate the definition of a number of other concepts that I have developed—*e.g.*, would create the possibility that a QV investment whose post-equilibrium supernormal profit-rate is highest does not belong to the set of projects that are most profitable over their lifetimes. I should emphasize that no conclusion I reach will turn on the time-period in terms of which the relevant curves and concepts are defined.

A. The Intermediate Determinants of the Intensity of QV-Investment Competition

I have found it useful to distinguish 11 intermediate determinants of the intensity of QV-investment competition—four barriers to entry, four counterpart barriers to expansion, the monopolistic QV-investment incentives or disincentives that a potential QV-investment expander may face, and the natural oligopolistic QV-investment disincentives that two or more potential QV-investment expanders may face. All barriers to entry and expansion cause the "nominal" or "conventional book" supernormal profit-rate a potential entrant or expander would expect to realize on its new QV investment to be lower than the lifetime supernormal rate-of-return that would be generated by the most-profitable QV investments in the relevant area of product-space at the original QV-investment level. In this last sentence, the word "nominal" and the expression "conventional book" indicate the fact that the relevant calculations ignore any monopolistic QV-investment incentives or disincentives and any oligopolistic QV-investment disincentives a potential expander may have to make a particular QV investment. Somewhat optimistically, I am assuming that "conventional book" supernormal-profit calculations will take into account any positive contribution a relevant QV investment makes to the profit-yields of one or more of the investor's other QV investments by generating traditional joint cost-reduction economies or increasing the demand for its other products by filling out its product-line or increasing its reputation for quality. The monopolistic QV-investment incentives, monopolistic QV-investment disincentives, and (natural) oligopolistic QV-investment incentives a QV investor faces on a particular QV investment all reflect the fact that for reasons that will be delineated below (reasons that are unrelated to its generating traditional joint-cost economies or increasing the demand for the investor's other products by filling out its product-line or increasing its reputation for quality), the QV investment in question will affect the profit-yields of the investor's other projects and, in the case of natural oligopolistic QV-investment disincentives, will yield lower nominal profits itself because it will induce the execution of a rival QV investment that would not otherwise have been made. After defining the four different types of barriers to entry or expansion that a QV investor may face, this section defines the monopolistic QV-investment incentives and disincentives and the natural oligopolistic QV-investment disincentives a QV-investment expander may face.

(1) The Profit-Rate-Differential Barrier to Entry or Expansion—Π_D

The Π_D barrier faced by a particular potential entrant or expander on the most-privately-attractive QV-investment project available to it at the relevant point in time indicates the amount by which the weighted-average lifetime rate-of-return[45]

[45] Throughout this text, the expressions "rate-of-return" or "profit-rate" are being defined in the way that lawyers use them—*viz.*, to refer to rates that are gross of capital costs. The expressions

gross of capital costs that that project would be expected to generate in the absence of retaliation at any relevant ARDEPPS QV-investment level would be lower than its counterpart at that ARDEPPS QV-investment level for the most-profitable QV-investment project or projects already in the relevant area of product-space.[46] I will first discuss Π_D barriers to entry and then discuss Π_D barriers to expansion.

Π_D barriers may confront potential entrants—even-best-placed potential entrants—for a wide variety of reasons: (l) because the established firms were able to occupy some locations in product-space that were inherently more profitable than any the best-placed potential entrant could occupy; (2) because the established firms were able to obtain patents at a lower cost than the cost the best-placed potential entrant would have to incur to invent around them, buy them, or buy the right to use them; (3) because the established firms were able to obtain natural resources more profitably than the best-placed potential entrant can now obtain them; (4) because the established firms had more profitable reputation-building options available to them than were available to the potential entrant that was best-placed to enter the ARDEPPS in question at a particular point in time (because, *e.g.*, it was cheaper and more feasible for a pioneer to establish a reputation for quality and reliability than for the potential competitor that was best-placed to enter at some point in time to match it—that the advantages of being an old reliable are greater than the disadvantages of being lumbered with a reputation for low or inconsistent quality long after the pioneer's product-quality and quality-control improved); and/or (5) because the managers of the ARDEPPS' pioneers have managed and will manage its most-profitable projects better over their lifetimes than their managerial counterparts for the ARDEPPS' best-placed potential competitor will manage its most-privately-attractive project and only part of the managerial-productivity difference in question is offset by compensation-differences (a possibility that reflects two facts: the fact that the pioneers' managers learned the business in competition with other neophytes [a factor that is admittedly offset by the copy-cat's ability to learn from the pioneers' early experience] as well as the fact that, since part of any company's managers' knowledge is company-specific, managers cannot obtain compensation equal to their contribution to their company's profits [their compensation aside]). In practice, the size of the Π_D barrier facing an ARDEPPS' best-placed potential entrant will tend to be lower when that firm is not an entirely-new business concern but a well-established firm operating in a related field or geographic area that is considering product or geographic diversification.

"supernormal" rate-of-return or "supernormal" profit-rate refer to rates whose calculation takes capital costs into consideration (to rates that economists would use the expression "rate-of-return" or "profit-rate" to signify).

[46] In my terminology, the most-profitable QV-investment projects in any area of product-space are those with the highest, identical supernormal rate-of-return. For expositional reasons, I will assume (often counterfactually) that all these projects have the same weighted-average-expected rates-of-return (gross of capital costs) and the same normal rate-of-return.

Π_D barriers may also confront firms established in the relevant ARDEPPS that are considering QV-investment expansions. The Π_D barrier to expansion facing a firm that is established in the relevant ARDEPPS on the privately-most-attractive QV-investment project it could introduce into that ARDEPPS is defined precisely the same way as the Π_D barrier to entry facing a potential competitor.

The Π_D barrier facing an ARDEPPS' best-placed potential expander at any point in time will tend to be smaller than the Π_D barrier facing its best-placed potential entrant at that time because the experience of operating in an ARDEPPS contributes to the insiders' ability to conceive and execute new projects in it. However, this difference will tend to be smaller when the best-placed potential entrant is an established firm operating in a related area. It will also tend to be smaller when the QV investment in question would not be the first that the best-placed potential expander would be making in a relatively short time-period. A firm that is expanding rapidly will face a higher Π_D barrier on an additional expansion both because the nth-best project a management devises will usually be worse than its (n-1)th-best project and because firms execute projects less efficiently when they are expanding rapidly.

Although the Π_D barrier facing an ARDEPPS' best-placed potential expander at any point in time—$(\Pi_D)_E$ where the subscript E stands for "established firm"—will *tend to be* lower than the Π_D barrier facing its best-placed potential entrant at that point in time—$(\Pi_D)_N$ where the subscript N stands for new entrant, there clearly will be situations in which $(\Pi_D)_N$ is lower than $(\Pi_D)_E$. In particular, this relationship may prevail in two types of situations: (1) when a potential competitor has made a technological, promotional, or distributive breakthrough and (2) when equilibrium QV investment is rising rapidly in the ARDEPPS in question (because "ARDEPPS demand" is rising rapidly and/or costs are falling rapidly). In this latter case, the Π_D barriers facing the established firm that is best-placed at the relevant point in time to execute an expansion that would deter an entry may be high because all the established firms may have had to expand quite rapidly to raise QV investment in the ARDEPPS to the prevailing non-equilibrium level so that the Π_D barrier to each's making yet another QV investment was considerably higher than the Π_D barrier each faced on its first or even last fairly-recent expansion.

(2) The Risk Barrier to Entry or Expansion—R

R indicates the amount by which in the absence of retaliation the normal rate-of-return for the project in question would be higher than its counterpart for the relevant most-profitable projects. A best-placed potential competitor will confront a risk barrier to entry to the extent that the profitability of its project is more uncertain than was the lifetime profitability of the most-profitable projects in the ARDEPPS in question, to the extent that the best-placed potential competitor is more risk-averse than the established owners of an ARDEPPS' most-profitable projects, and to the extent that the best-placed potential entrant is less able than the owners of the ARDEPPS' most-profitable projects to make investment-portfolio moves that reduce the contribution of the project in question to the overall risk they respectively faced. In practice, once more, the size of the relevant R is likely to be lower when the best-placed potential entrant into the ARDEPPS in question is a large established firm that sells similar goods or services in the same territory or the same goods or services in other territories: such potential entrants will tend to be less uncertain about the outcomes of their contemplated entry, less risk-averse, and more able to reduce risk by compiling appropriate investment portfolios than are entirely-new potential entrants.

Not only potential entrants but also potential QV-investment expanders can face R barriers. For the same reason that the Π_D faced by a potential expander will tend to be lower than the Π_D barrier faced by an already-established firm that is not operating in the ARDEPPS in question and for the same reason that these latter barriers in turn tend to be lower than the Π_D barrier faced by an entirely-new company, the R barrier faced by established firms will tend to be lower than those facing potential entrants that are established elsewhere and *a fortiori* than those facing entirely-new-firm potential entrants. Once again as well, the R barrier that an established firm will face on an nth expansion in any time-period will tend to increase with n both because the nth expansion will tend to be inherently more risky than the (n-1)th new project and because the nth new project will tend to be executed with less-experienced personnel whose performance is riskier than the performance of the personnel that would execute the (n-1)th new project.

(3) The Scale Barrier to Entry or Expansion—S

S indicates the amount by which the relevant new entry or expansion would reduce the supernormal profit-rate generated by all projects in the relevant area of product-space (assuming, for simplicity, that the new project has an equal effect on all such projects)[47] by increasing the amount of QV investment and (in the case of new entry) the number of independent sellers that the ARDEPPS contains. Any QV investments that are added to an ARDEPPS will decrease their predecessors' rates-of-return by reducing the average BPA of best-placed products in the ARDEPPS in question, by lowering the average natural and contrived oligopolistic margins in the ARDEPPS, and (usually) by increasing the average total cost of each product in the ARDEPPS by reducing the quantity of each that is sold. Although a potential competitor or expander could reduce S by reducing the scale of its entry or expansion below the minimum scale that would minimize the $(\Pi_D + R)$ barriers it faced, I will assume that no entrant or expander will do so—that each entry and expansion takes place at or above the scale that minimizes the sum of the investor's Π_D and R barriers. Admittedly, this assumption is not consistent with my current

[47] This assumption is admittedly unrealistic. Indeed, the fact that projects in a given area of product-space will have different effects on the rates-of-return generated by the various other projects in that area of product-space plays a significant role in my argument for the inevitable arbitrariness of market definitions and underlies my claim that, in some circumstances, potential expanders have monopolistic QV-investment incentives to make a particular QV investment.

static assumptions. However, it is quite realistic in the normal "dynamic" case in which "demand" for each relevant set of products increases through time since the prospect of such increases and the concomitant tendency of equilibrium QV investment to rise through time in the relevant area of product-space reduces the benefits of investing at less than minimum efficient scale by implying that in the medium or long run the larger magnitude of a QV investment of minimum efficient scale will not reduce the rate-of-return it generates by increasing total QV investment in the ARDEPPS in which it is located. The S barrier faced by potential entrants that are well-established in related fields and *a fortiori* the S barrier faced by potential established expanders will tend to be lower than those facing entirely new companies because the Π_D-cost to the former two types of firms of investing at lower scales will tend to be lower than those facing entirely new companies—*i.e.*, because such established firms may be able to take advantage of joint economies in production, promotion, and distribution.

(4) The Retaliation Barrier to Entry or Expansion—L

The retaliation or L barrier facing a potential entrant or potential expander indicates the amount by which the expected supernormal rate-of-return for the new QV investment in question is reduced by the possibility of retaliation. I will assume for simplicity that the supernormal rate-of-return that will be generated by the set of most-profitable projects in the ARDEPPS will not be reduced by retaliation. On this assumption, L_N and L_E at any ARDEPPS QV-investment level will respectively equal the amount by which the prospect of retaliation will reduce the supernormal rate-of-return the best-placed potential competitor or the best-placed potential expander at that QV-investment level should expect to realize on the most-privately-attractive QV investment it can make in the ARDEPPS in question. For simplicity, I will also assume that the prospect of retaliation will affect the attractiveness of making a QV investment exclusively by reducing the potential competitor's or expander's gross-of-capital-cost expected rate-of-return on that investment—*i.e.*, I will ignore the extent to which the prospect of retaliation increases the risk costs of making the QV investment in question. It is difficult to tell whether the retaliation barriers facing a potential entrant that is well-established in other areas or by a potential expander will be lower than those facing an entirely-new potential entrant. On the one hand, already-established firms may have "Don't Tread on Me or Don't Try to Deter Me" reputations, the ability to survive retaliation, or the ability to retaliate against retaliators that deter retaliation. On the other hand, well-established potential entrants and *a fortiori* potential expanders provide retaliators with more targets.

(5) The Monopolistic QV-Investment Disincentives—$M > 0$—and Incentives—$M < 0$—That a Potential Expander May Face

The monopolistic QV-investment incentives and disincentives (*M*) a potential expander may face reflect the effect the relevant QV investment has on the profit-yields of the expander's pre-existing (or, more generally, pre-existing and other future) projects in the relevant ARDEPPS not by generating joint-cost economies or increasing the demand for the investor's other products by filling out its product-line or enhancing its reputation for quality but

(1) by taking sales away from those projects directly,
(2) by inducing established rivals to make non-retaliatory responses that do not involve their increasing their QV investments in the relevant area of product-space but that do reduce the expander's pre-existing projects' profit-yields, and
(3) by deterring established or potential competitors from making additional QV investments in the relevant area of product-space.

When a potential expander's QV investment would do more damage to its pre-existing projects' profit-yields in the above ways (in comparison with the *status quo ante*) than would have been done by any QV investments it deters others from making, the potential expander will face a QV-investment disincentive equal to the amount by which these effects reduce the actual supernormal rate-of-return its project should be expected to generate *ex ante* below the supernormal rate-of-return it should have been expected to generate absent these effects. When the project in question will do less damage in the above ways to the profit-yields of the relevant expander's pre-existing projects than would otherwise have been done by the QV investments of others that its expansion would deter, the potential expander will have a QV-investment incentive.

(6) The (Natural) Oligopolistic QV-Investment Disincentives—*O* > 0—That a Potential Expander May Face

A potential expander will be said to face (natural) oligopolistic QV-investment disincentives when, rather than deterring others from making QV investments, its expansion will induce an established rival to make a QV investment that that firm would otherwise not have made. On my definition, the *O*s a potential expander faces equal (1) the amount by which its QV investment will reduce its pre-existing projects' profit-yields (A) by taking sales away from those projects directly and inducing others to make QV investments that take sales away from those projects directly and (B) by inducing established rivals to make non-retaliatory, non-QV-investment responses to the investment expansion in question and the expansions it induces others to make *plus* (2) the amount by which the QV investment its relevant QV investment induces others to make reduces the nominal profits its relevant QV investment generates both (A) directly and (B) by inducing still others to react to the induced QV investment by making non-retaliatory changes in their prices and other non-QV-investment choices. This definition implies that the "nominal profits" yielded by an expansion that will induce someone to make a QV investment it would not otherwise have made are defined to equal the profits the expansion in question would yield if, counterfactually, it would not cause any additional QV investments to be made in the relevant area of product-space and the *O*s that will be said to face a potential expander in this position will be defined to equal the amount by which the supernormal rate-of-return the expansion in question should be expected to generate *ex ante* will be reduced by the four effects just listed.

B. The Three Different Types of QV-Investment Equilibria and the Conditions for Their Generation

I will now use the preceding concepts to analyze three different types of QV-investment equilibria it is useful to distinguish. I begin by defining four different QV-investment-level concepts and explaining two diagrams that play important roles in the analyses that follow. The first relevant QV-investment level is the lowest equilibrium QV-investment level in a given ARDEPPS. The adjective "lowest" is included because, given the presence of economies of scale in making a QV investment, there will often be a range of ARDEPPS QV-investment levels at which all QV investments that have been made are profitable and no QV investment that has not been made would be profitable. In the text that follows, the expression "equilibrium QV-investment level" will always refer to the lowest equilibrium QV-investment level in the ARDEPPS in question.

Second, some of the analyses that follow will make reference to the (lowest) entry-preventing QV-investment level. This is the lowest level of QV investment that will render unprofitable the most-profitable QV investment any potential competitor could introduce into the ARDEPPS at the time of analysis.

Third, some of the analyses that follow will make reference to the relevant ARDEPPS' (lowest) entry-barred expansion-preventing QV-investment level. This level is calculated on the normally-counterfactual assumption that something (usually a legal prohibition or bar) prevents any new entry from being executed at or after the time of analysis even if one or more potential competitors would otherwise have found entry profitable. In many situations, the relevant ARDEPPS' entry-barred expansion-preventing QV-investment level is higher than the level of QV investment in the ARDEPPS at the time of analysis—*i.e.*, some expansions will have to be executed after the time of analysis to raise total QV investment in the ARDEPPS to the entry-barred expansion-preventing QV-investment level.

The fourth and final QV-investment level to which some of the analyses that follow will refer is the "actual, competitive" QV-investment level. This is the level of ARDEPPS QV investment at which the ARDEPPS' most-profitable projects will generate a normal rate-of-return over their lifetimes, given the relationship between price and marginal cost at different QV-investment levels in the ARDEPPS in question. The first adjective in the expression "actual, competitive QV-investment level" refers to the assumption that is being made about the competitiveness of pricing. The second, to the assumption that is being made about the competitiveness of QV investment.

I will now turn to the two diagrams to illustrate the analysis of the three types of QV-investment equilibria it is useful to distinguish. Diagrams I and II illustrate the individual determinants of the intensity of QV-investment competition in any

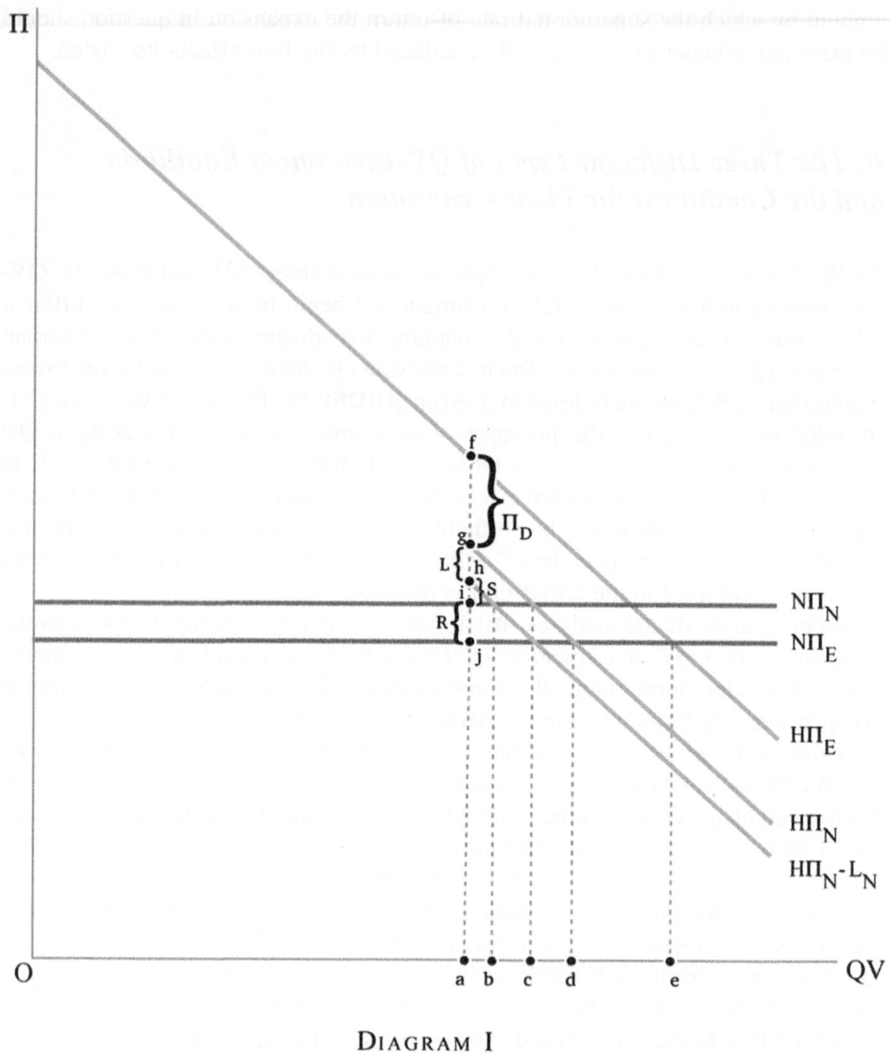

Diagram I The determinants of the entry-preventing QV-investment level

ARDEPPS, the different types of QV-investment equilibria that can be established in any ARDEPPS, and the complex relationship between the various individual determinants or sets of determinants in question on the one hand and the three types of equilibria I will distinguish on the other.

Diagram I contains two highest-profit-rate (HΠ) curves and two normal-profit-rate (NΠ) curves. I will begin by analyzing the HΠ curves and then proceed to the NΠ curves.

$H\Pi_E$ (recall: the subscript "E" stands for "established firms") indicates the relationship between the equilibrium QV-investment level in the ARDEPPS and the "gross" weighted-average-expected lifetime rate-of-return (gross of capital costs) the established owner(s) of the most-(supernormally)-profitable (hereinafter "most-profitable") QV-investment project(s) in the ARDEPPS would expect to realize on these project(s) if they faced no retaliation barriers and faced neither monopolistic nor natural oligopolistic QV-investment disincentives nor monopolistic QV-investment incentives on the investments in question.[48] It should be emphasized at the outset that the height of the $H\Pi_E$ curve at any given QV-investment level does not in general indicate the gross lifetime rate-of-return expected to be yielded by the QV investment that would bring ARDEPPS QV investment to that level. Indeed, the gross rate-of-return that its owner should expect this last QV investment to generate over its lifetime at the relevant ARDEPPS QV-investment level will equal the height of the $H\Pi_E$ curve at that QV-investment level only if the investment in question belongs to the set of most-profitable QV-investment projects in that ARDEPPS. In most situations, the analysis of the relationship between the equilibrium-QV-investment level and the actual, competitive QV-investment level (the QV-investment level at which the ARDEPPS' most-profitable QV investments yield just a normal rate-of-return—Oe in Diagram I, the QV-investment level at which the $H\Pi_E$ curve cuts the $N\Pi_E$ curve [see below] from above) will focus on the height of the $H\Pi_E$ curve at QV-investment levels that exceed the sum of the QV investments in the ARDEPPS that are most profitable. I have stressed this point because this feature of the $H\Pi_E$ curve distinguishes it from the demand curves with which economists are accustomed to dealing. The height of the demand curve at quantity "X" indicates the price for which the "X"th unit (the unit that raises the relevant output to X) can be sold. By way of contrast, the height of the $H\Pi_E$ curve at QV-investment level "X" does not in general tell you the gross (of capital costs) rate-of-return that is expected to be generated by the "X"th QV investment (more precisely, the QV investment that raises total QV investment in the ARDEPPS to "X"): what changes as one moves to the right along an $H\Pi_E$ curve is the total QV investment in the relevant ARDEPPS, not the identity of the QV investment(s) to which the information provided by the height of the curve applies.

$H\Pi_N$ (recall: the subscript "N" stands for "new entrant") indicates the relationship between (1) the "gross" weighted-average-expected lifetime rate-of-return (gross of capital costs) that the potential entrant that was best-placed to enter the relevant ARDEPPS at the time of analysis should anticipate realizing on the most-privately-attractive QV investment it could make within the ARDEPPS if it did not face any retaliation barriers to entry and (2) various hypothetical equilibrium QV-investment levels in that ARDEPPS. The expression "best-placed potential

[48] Although the identity of the projects that are most profitable may vary either with the equilibrium level of QV investment in the ARDEPPS or with changes in the ARDEPPS' structure that do not alter its equilibrium QV-investment level, I will ignore this possibility in the text that follows.

competitor" refers to the potential competitor that can make a QV investment in the relevant ARDEPPS whose *ex ante* supernormal profit-rate exceeds or equals its counterpart for any QV investment that any other potential competitor can introduce into the ARDEPPS in question at the time of analysis. The $H\Pi_N$ curve resembles the $H\Pi_E$ curve in that its height at any ARDEPPS-QV-investment level indicates the rate-of-return that a given project (the most-supernormally-profitable project that can be introduced by any potential competitor at the time of analysis) would yield if it raised ARDEPPS QV investment to the indicated level—*i.e.*, the identity of the QV-investment project to which the varying height of the $H\Pi_N$ curve applies does not vary as one moves to the right along the $H\Pi_N$ curve.[49]

Four further points should be made about the $H\Pi_E$ and $H\Pi_N$ curves. First, the height of the $H\Pi_E$ and $H\Pi_N$ curves at any given QV-investment level increases as the prices of the products in the ARDEPPS rise from competitive to monopolistic levels (from the products' respective marginal costs to the levels that maximize the total supernormal profits that the ARDEPPS' QV investors realize, given the amount of QV investment in the ARDEPPS). The $H\Pi_E$ and $H\Pi_N$ curves in Diagram I (and the $H\Pi_E$ curve in Diagram II—see below) are constructed on realistic assumptions about the prices that will be charged at different QV-investment levels in the relevant ARDEPPS—*i.e.*, are in this sense actual $H\Pi_E$ and $H\Pi_N$ curves.[50] Second, relatedly, and somewhat inconsistently, my construction of the $H\Pi_E$ and $H\Pi_N$ curves in Diagram I assumes that their heights at any given QV-investment level will not depend on the percentage of ARDEPPS QV investment that has been made by new entrants as opposed to expanding established firms. This clearly unrealistic assumption is made for expositional reasons and is relaxed when appropriate—for example, when analyzing QV-investment incentives and disincentives.[51]

---

[49] Unless otherwise indicated, the analyses that follow assume (admittedly sometimes counterfactually) that QV investments will be introduced into an ARDEPPS in the order of their profitability.

[50] Thus, one might also construct a "monopolistic" and a "competitive" $H\Pi_E$ curve for a particular ARDEPPS. The former would indicate the rate-of-return the ARDEPPS' most-profitable projects would yield as its QV-investment level varied if prices in the ARDEPPS were always perfectly monopolistic (maximized the profits that the ARDEPPS' constituent firms realized, given the ARDEPPS' QV-investment level). The latter would indicate the rate-of-return the ARDEPPS' most-profitable projects would yield as its QV-investment level varied if prices in the ARDEPPS were always perfectly competitive (equaled the respective products' marginal costs). The monopolistic $H\Pi_E$ curve will tend to be higher to the extent that the monopolist is able to increase its returns on a given amount of QV investment (1) by charging supra-marginal-cost prices for its products and services and/or (2) by making a less-overlapping set of QV investments (by offering a set of products and services whose members' appeal overlaps to a lesser extent than the appeal of its competitive counterparts). Obviously, all actual $H\Pi_E$ curves will start at the height of the monopolistic $H\Pi_E$ curve (since prices will be monopolistic when the ARDEPPS contains one QV investment) and progressively converge on the competitive $H\Pi_E$ curve as one moves to the right.

[51] In practice, the rate at which any given actual $H\Pi_E$ curve converges on the lower, competitive $H\Pi_E$ curve will increase *inter alia* with the percentage of any additional QV investments made by new entrants because a new entry will militate more against contrived oligopolistic pricing than an

Third, the downward slope of both the $H\Pi_E$ and $H\Pi_N$ curves reflects the fact that the introduction of additional product variants, outlets, or capacity will lower the rates-of-return generated by the ARDEPPS' pre-existing QV investments (including those that are "most profitable") both (1) by reducing the prevailing price level in the ARDEPPS (by reducing BCAs and perhaps NOMs and/or COMs as well) and (2) by increasing the "per-unit" average total cost of using the pre-existing QV investments because the unit sales the new QV investment takes from its predecessors exceed the additional units the new QV investment's introduction causes its predecessors to sell by inducing the owners to lower their prices. I should note that the expression "per unit" is enquoted in the preceding sentence to reflect the fact that when demand fluctuates through time the relevant "product" will change when the average rate of capacity-utilization drops since this drop will be associated with an increase in the average speed of supply through a fluctuating-demand cycle.[52]

Fourth, Diagram I's assumption that the $H\Pi_E$ and $H\Pi_N$ curves are linear and parallel is not intended to be realistic. This assumption has been adopted solely to ease construction and facilitate textual exposition. It does not critically affect any significant conclusion. The distance between $H\Pi_E$ and $H\Pi_N$ at any given QV-investment level equals the profit-rate-differential (Π_D) barrier to entry faced by the relevant ARDEPPS' best-placed potential competitor at the time of analysis. Diagram I's construction of $H\Pi_N$ parallel to $H\Pi_E$ assumes that this Π_D barrier to entry will not vary with the ARDEPPS' QV-investment level, assuming (as I will) that variations in the pre-existing relevant QV-investment level will not change the identity of the ARDEPPS' most-profitable projects or the most-privately-attractive project that could be introduced by any potential competitor. In Diagram I, $\Pi_D = fg$.

As I have already indicated, Diagram I also contains two $N\Pi$ curves. $N\Pi$ indicates the normal rate-of-return (the minimum weighted-average-expected rate-of-return needed to induce investment, which varies *inter alia* with the riskiness of the QV-investment project in question). $N\Pi_E$ indicates the rate-of-return that owners of the ARDEPPS' most-profitable projects will consider normal on these investments if those investments would generate no retaliation. $N\Pi_N$ indicates the rate-of-return that the ARDEPPS' best-placed potential entrant would find normal for the most-privately-attractive project it could execute to enter the ARDEPPS in question if that entry would generate no retaliation. Diagram I's construction of the two $N\Pi$ curves as horizontal implies that the riskiness of the relevant QV investments

---

equally-large QV-investment expansion by a new entrant would (and because an expander will tend to choose a location in product-space that reduces BCAs less than they would be reduced by the equally-large but differently-located QV investment a new entrant would make).

[52] Admittedly, since the presence of additional product variants or distributive outlets in the early stages of an ARDEPPS' formation may increase the sales of their predecessors by making more consumers aware of the ARDEPPS' product or by increasing consumer-confidence in the quality and reliability of all products produced by the ARDEPPS, the $H\Pi$ curves may slope upward over a low range of ARDEPPS QV investment. Diagram I ignores this possibility. The text that follows also ignores the fact that such new product variants may have different effects on the rates-of-return generated by what originally were the most-profitable QV investments in the ARDEPPS.

will not vary with the QV-investment level of the ARDEPPS. This assumption will not always be realistic—*e.g.*, would be unrealistic if an ARDEPPS' constituent firms would clearly be able to contrive OMs when QV investment is low (because only a few firms are in the relevant ARDEPPS at such times), would clearly be unable to contrive OMs when QV investment is high (because the additional QV investments are made by new entrants and most or all products in the ARDEPPS other than the product that is best-placed in relation to each relevant buyer are second-placed or close-to-second-placed to obtain the patronage of the buyer in question), and may or may not be able to contrive OMs when QV investment is middling (to the extent that in such situations the number of firms that are second-placed or close-to-second placed is middling). In such situations, the relevant NΠ curves would be horizontal at low and high QV-investment levels but have a bubble in the middle. The assumption that the NΠ curves are horizontal is adopted primarily for expositional reasons but also because, as we shall see, the three generalizations in the preceding sentence are extremely crude. In any event, Diagram I's assumption that the NΠ curves are horizontal does not critically affect any significant conclusion. The vertical distance between $N\Pi_N$ and $N\Pi_E$ in Diagram I indicates the risk barrier to entry (R). The assumption that $N\Pi_N$ and $N\Pi_E$ are horizontal implies that this risk barrier will not vary with the ARDEPPS' QV-investment level. In Diagram I, R = ij.

Diagram I also illustrates the remaining two barriers to entry I find useful to distinguish—the retaliation barrier to entry (L or L_N where the subscript "N" indicates that the relevant barrier relates to the position of a new entrant) and the scale barrier to entry (S or S_N). I will assume that the owners of the ARDEPPS' most-profitable projects face no retaliation barriers on those QV investments. On that assumption, L_N indicates the amount by which the best-placed potential entrant's *ex ante* supernormal rate-of-return is reduced by the possibility that the established firms may retaliate against its entry. Although in reality the prospect of retaliation will reduce the best-placed potential competitor's *ex ante* supernormal rate-of-return both by reducing its weighted-average-expected gross rate-of-return and by increasing its risk costs, for simplicity Diagram I assumes that the L_N barrier will affect only the weighted-average-expected gross rate-of-return of the best-placed potential competitor—that the possibility of retaliation will not raise the best-placed potential entrant's R barrier. For this reason, the L barrier in Diagram I is represented as a vertical distance (hi) between the $H\Pi_N$ and ($H\Pi_N$-L_N) curves. Also for simplicity, Diagram I assumes in addition that the L_N barrier does not vary with the ARDEPPS' QV-investment level. In Diagram I, L = gh.

The final barrier to entry is the scale barrier (S_N). It reflects the fact that, since entry is lumpy (since there are economies of scale in entry), any QV investment a potential competitor finds profitable to introduce will reduce not only the supernormal rate-of-return it realizes on its new entry (below the rate it would have realized post-entry on its entry if its entry would not raise total QV investment in the ARDEPPS) but the supernormal rate-of-return generated by all pre-existing QV investments in the ARDEPPS by raising the ARDEPPS' QV-investment level. In a static world, a potential competitor might well find it profitable to reduce the S_N

barrier it faced by entering with a smaller QV investment whose size causes it to face higher ($\Pi_D + R$) or ($\Pi_D + R + L$) barriers than it would face if it entered with a larger QV investment. However, since in our actual, dynamic world ARDEPPS $H\Pi_E$ and $H\Pi_N$ curves tend to rise through time because "ARDEPPS demand curves"[53] tend to rise through time and ARDEPPS cost curves tend to decrease through time, the S-barrier advantage such a choice would yield is unlikely to survive long enough to make such a trade-off worthwhile (since the extra QV the larger entry would introduce will reduce the amount of additional investment by others the relevant increase in demand will stimulate). I will therefore assume that potential competitors will always choose to enter on a scale that is at least large enough to minimize the sum of the ($\Pi_D + R$) barriers they face (hereinafter the "minimum efficient scale"). In Diagram I, the minimum efficient scale is assumed to be ab and the associated scale barrier—S—equals (ab *times* the slope of the $H\Pi_N$ curve [which Diagram I assumes does not vary with the ARDEPPS' QV-investment level]) = hi.

It should now be possible to use Diagram I to illustrate some of the QV-investment levels that play a significant role in the analysis that follows. First, in Diagram I, Oe—the level of QV investment at which $H\Pi_E$ and $N\Pi_E$ intersect—is the "actual," competitive level of QV investment (where the first adjective refers to the competitiveness of pricing at the relevant QV-investment level and the second, to the competitiveness of QV investment at that QV-investment level). QV investment is said to be "competitive" when it is at the level at which any firm that owned a most-profitable project would realize a normal rate-of-return on that project. Second, in Diagram I, Oa (actually, an investment-level infinitesimally above Oa) the quantity of QV investment that equals the quantity at which ($H\Pi_N$–L_N) falls just below $N\Pi_N$ (Ob) *minus* the minimum efficient scale of entry (ab)—is the "entry-preventing QV-investment level," the lowest level of QV investment whose attainment would result in the best-placed potential competitor's confronting an *ex ante* subnormal rate-of-return on its most-privately-attractive project.

Thus, Diagram I indicates that in the circumstances it portrays the relevant barriers to entry permit the established firms to restrict their QV investment

[53] A "demand curve" is a diagrammatic representation of a schedule indicating the quantity of an indicated product that will be sold at different prices. Demand curves are usually constructed in diagrams whose vertical axis measures some monetary unit (say dollars—$) and whose horizontal axis measures the quantity of the good in question (Q). Economists distinguish between the demand curve a given seller of a particular product faces when selling that product—the "firm" demand curve—and the demand curve faced by an industry whose members produce identical physical products with identical images that they distribute from an identical location—so-called industry demand curves. The text enquotes the expression "ARDEPPS demand curve" because in all or virtually all cases the sellers in a given ARDEPPS will be producing physically-different products, will be producing products with different "images," and/or will be distributing their products from different locations among which relevant buyers will not be indifferent. Since the "products" in the ARDEPPS are different, there will usually be no straightforward ARDEPPS counterpart for the traditional notion of an industry demand curve. My use of the concept of an "ARDEPPS demand curve" should therefore be regarded as purely heuristic.

(infinitesimally less than) ea below the actual, competitive level Oe without making it profitable for any potential competitor to enter. Of this amount ea, de reflects the profit-rate-differential barrier Π_D (the difference between the intersection of $H\Pi_E$ and $N\Pi_E$ on the one hand and $H\Pi_N$ and $N\Pi_E$ on the other); cd reflects the risk barrier R (the difference between the intersection of $H\Pi_N$ and $N\Pi_E$ on the one hand and $H\Pi_N$ and $N\Pi_N$ on the other); bc reflects the retaliation barrier L (the difference between the intersection of $H\Pi_N$ and $N\Pi_N$ on the one hand and $[H\Pi_N-L_N]$ and $N\Pi_N$ on the other); and ab reflects the scale barrier S (assuming that ab is the minimum efficient scale of entry in QV-investment terms and that entry will always take place at at least minimum efficient scale).

Diagram I also indicates that in the circumstances it portrays, the established firms can realize a supernormal rate-of-return infinitesimally below $(fj = [\Pi_D + R + S + L]_N)$ on their most-profitable projects without making it profitable for a potential competitor to enter their ARDEPPS. In brief, this conclusion reflects the fact that $(\Pi_D + R + L + S)_N$ equals the difference between the established firms' pre-entry lifetime supernormal profit-rate on their most-profitable projects and the best-placed potential competitor's expected post-entry supernormal profit-rate—the supernormal profit-rate the best-placed entry would generate if its execution would bring the ARDEPPS into equilibrium. A numerical example might make this point more comprehensible. Assume that the lifetime supernormal profit-rate that the established firms that owned most-profitable QV investments would realize on these projects if the pre-entry QV-investment level in the ARDEPPS were the ARDEPPS' equilibrium QV-investment level was 8.25 % and that $(\Pi_D + R + S + L)_N = (5\,\% + 2\,\% + 1\,\% + .26\,\%) = 8.26\,\%$. In such a case, the fact that the established firms would realize a lifetime supernormal profit-rate of 8.25 % on any most-profitable projects they owned if the pre-entry QV-investment level were the equilibrium QV-investment level would not imply that new entry would be profitable: in fact, the best-placed potential competitor would anticipate realizing a .01 % subnormal profit-rate if it entered. Thus, if $N\Pi_E = 10\,\%$ and the established firms' lifetime gross rate-of-return would therefore be 18.25 % on any most-profitable projects they owned if QV investment were in equilibrium at the pre-entry level, entry would not be profitable because the best-placed potential competitor's weighted-average-expected gross rate-of-return $(18.25\,\%-[\Pi_D]_N-S_N-L_N] = 18.25\,\%-5\,\%-1\,\%-.26\,\% = 11.99\,\%)$ would be lower than the normal rate-of-return for the privately-best project it could introduce into the ARDEPPS in question $(N\Pi_E + R_N = 10\,\% + 2\,\% = 12\,\%)$.

Diagram II illustrates the various barriers to expansion, monopolistic QV-investment incentives, and monopolistic and oligopolistic QV-investment disincentives that may confront the established firms that are successively-best-placed to add QV investments to their ARDEPPS after the time of analysis. In fact, Diagram II illustrates the *M*s and *O*s that the relevant successive, best-placed potential expanders will face both given the actual entry situation and on an artificial (*i.e.*, usually counterfactual) assumption that entry is barred (for example, because some law effectively prohibits entry, regardless of whether entry would be profitable absent the law in question). Diagram II also illustrates the determinants of the

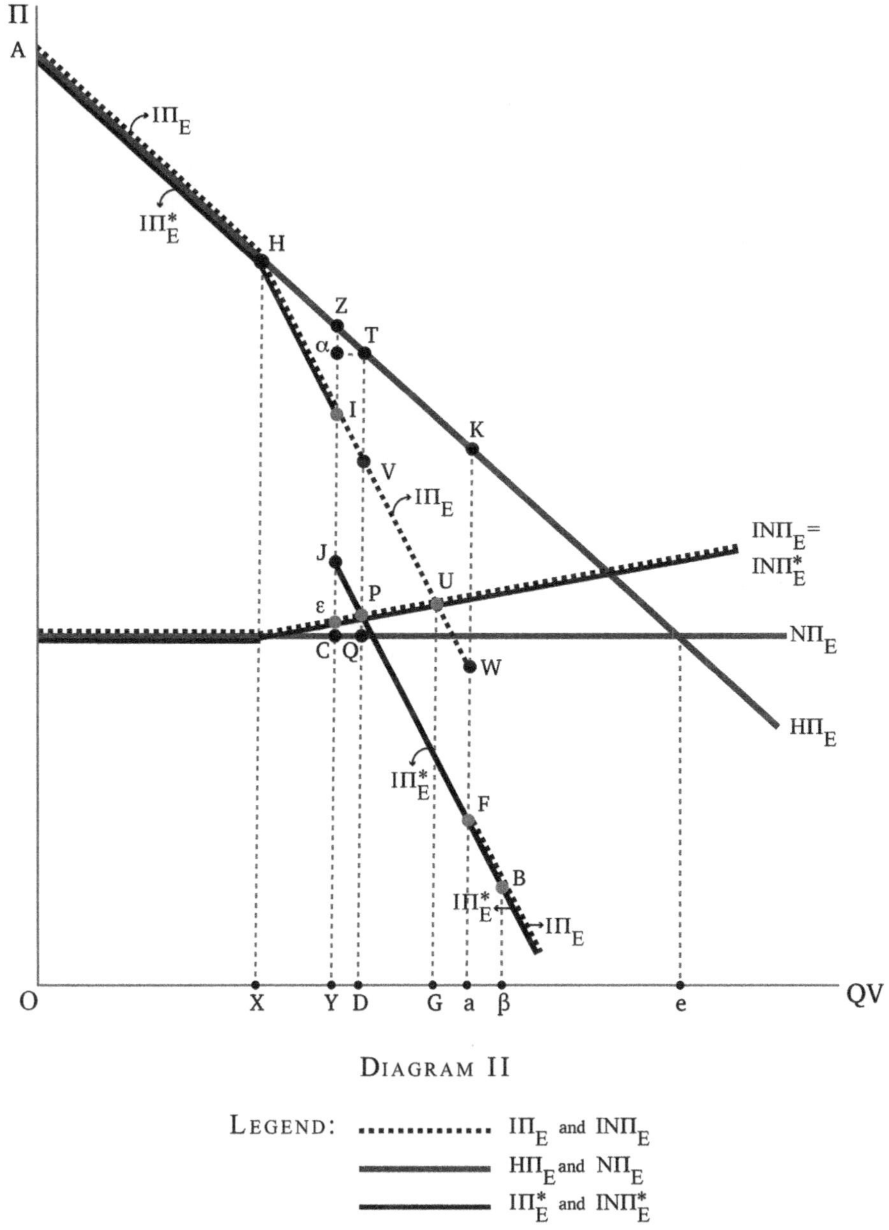

Diagram II The determinants of the entry-barred, expansion-preventing QV-investment level

entry-barred expansion-preventing QV-investment level (the level of QV investment at which expansion would cease if entry were barred at the time of analysis), given the $H\Pi_E$ and $N\Pi_E$ curves in question. In combination with Diagram I, Diagram II will also be used to illustrate the analysis of (1) the conditions under which potential competition is effective (*viz.*, the conditions under which the entry-preventing QV-investment level is higher than the entry-barred expansion-preventing QV-investment level), (2) whether and the extent to which an ARDEPPS' established firms will find it profitable to respond to potential competition by making QV investments whose profitability is critically affected by the fact that they would deter new entry, and relatedly (3) the relationship between (A) the entry-preventing QV-investment level and the entry-barred expansion-preventing QV-investment level on the one hand and (B) the equilibrium QV-investment level in the ARDEPPS in question on the other hand.

Diagram II incorporates the $H\Pi_E$ and $N\Pi_E$ curves that Diagram I contains. In addition, Diagram II contains three "incremental" curves—the $I\Pi_E^*$ curve, the $I\Pi_E$ curve, and the $IN\Pi_E = IN\Pi_E^*$ curve. $I\Pi_E^*$ indicates the actual incremental (hence "I") lifetime rate-of-return (gross of capital costs) that the established firm that would be best-placed to expand the ARDEPPS' QV investment to various levels if no entry could take place after the beginning of the analysis period—*i.e.*, if entry were barred (hence the asterisk)—should expect to realize on this expansion. $I\Pi_E$ indicates the same information, given the actual position of potential competitors. The $IN\Pi_E$ and $IN\Pi_E^*$ curves respectively indicate the normal rate-of-return for the successive best-placed QV-investment expansions that could be executed by the relevant ARDEPPS' established firms, respectively on actual-condition-of-entry and entry-barred assumptions. For simplicity, I have assumed that these two normal rates-of-return are equal—that the $IN\Pi_E = IN\Pi_E^*$ curves coincide. It is critical to emphasize that the different points on the $I\Pi_E$, $I\Pi_E^*$, and $IN\Pi_E = IN\Pi_E^*$ curves provide information about the different, successive, most-privately-attractive expansions the ARDEPPS' established firms would or could undertake. In this respect, the incremental curves resemble demand curves rather than $H\Pi_E$, $N\Pi_N$, $N\Pi_E$, and $N\Pi_N$ curves, whose points indicate the gross rate-of-return that *a given, unchanging* QV investment or group of investments—the most-profitable QV investment or investments in the relevant ARDEPPS—would generate or would have to be expected to generate to be privately attractive at different equilibrium QV-investment levels.

I will now consider the $I\Pi_E$ and $I\Pi_E^*$ curves in Diagram II. In Diagram II, $I\Pi_E$ is the disjointed line AHIVUWFB, while $I\Pi_E^*$ is the disjointed line AHIJPFB. As I have already indicated, by definition, $I\Pi_E^*$ differs from $I\Pi_E$ in that $I\Pi_E^*$ is the incremental profit-rate curve that would be applicable if (usually counterfactually) entry were barred while $I\Pi_E$ is the incremental profit-rate curve that actually is applicable—*i.e.*, that is constructed on realistic assumptions about the entry-preventing QV-investment level (in Diagram II, Oa). This difference causes the two curves to diverge whenever the monopolistic QV-investment incentives, monopolistic QV-investment disincentives, or natural oligopolistic QV-investment disincentives confronting the ARDEPPS' best-placed potential expander at a relevant QV-investment level are affected by the possibility of entry—*viz.*, in virtually all situations in which the established firm that would be best-placed to expand ARDEPPS QV investment from some level below the entry-preventing level would face *M* disincentives, *M* incentives, or *O* disincentives if entry were barred. This conclusion reflects the fact that in the vast majority of such cases the possibility of entry will affect the existence or magnitude of the incentives and disincentives in question. I will return to this issue when explaining the divergence between $I\Pi_E$ and $I\Pi_E^*$ between QV-investment levels OY and Oa.

I will discuss separately three pairs of segments of the $I\Pi_E$ and $I\Pi_E^*$ curves that Diagram II contains. The first pair of segments contains the portions of the curves between ARDEPPS QV-investment levels zero and OY. Between these two levels, $I\Pi_E$ and $I\Pi_E^*$ coincide. Their coincidence reflects an assumption that the established firms that would be successively best-placed to raise ARDEPPS QV investment from zero to OY would not have an *M* incentive, *M* disincentive, or *O* disincentive to make the investments in question, regardless of whether the entry-preventing QV-investment level was Oa or entry was assumed to be barred. Diagram II constructs $I\Pi_E$ and $I\Pi_E^*$ to coincide with $H\Pi_E$ between QV-investment levels zero and OX. This construction assumes not only that (*M* or *O*) and (M^* or O^*) are zero between those QV-investment levels but that Π_D and L are also zero over this QV-investment range—that the projects that create the first OX in QV investment in the ARDEPPS in question are all most-profitable projects (given the diagram's assumption [see below] that R is also assumed to be zero for the QV investments in question) and that the relevant established firms face no retaliation barriers on the QV investments in question. However, although Diagram II also constructs $I\Pi_E$ and $I\Pi_E^*$ to coincide with each other between QV-investment levels OX and OY, it constructs both to be progressively lower than $H\Pi_E$ as one moves from QV-investment level OX to QV-investment level OY. This divergence could reflect the fact that Π_D becomes increasingly positive for the ARDEPPS' successive best-placed potential expanders as one moves progressively above OX, the fact that L becomes increasingly positive for the ARDEPPS' successive best-placed potential expanders as one moves progressively above OX, or the fact that (Π_D + L) becomes increasingly positive for the ARDEPPS' successive best-placed potential expanders as one moves progressively above OX. However, for simplicity, I will assume that L_E is zero throughout and that all the divergences between $H\Pi_E$ and $I\Pi_E$ or $I\Pi_E^*$ at all QV-investment levels above OX that cannot be attributed to *M* disincentives (see below) reflect Π_D barriers.

The second segments of $I\Pi_E$ and $I\Pi_E^*$ in Diagram II contain the portions of the curves between QV-investment levels OY and Oa. In Diagram II, $I\Pi_E^*$ diverges from $I\Pi_E$ at QV-investment level OY. In particular, although $I\Pi_E$ drops continuously progressively below $H\Pi_E$ to the right of QV-investment level OY, $I\Pi_E^*$ first jumps discontinuously from point I to point J at QV-investment level OY before declining continuously to the right of point J in precisely the same way that $I\Pi_E$ does. ($I\Pi_E^*$ is parallel to $I\Pi_E$ between QV-investment levels OY and Oa.) This construction reflects three assumptions.

First, it assumes that although the established firms that would be best-placed to add the successive QV investments to the ARDEPPS in question that would raise its QV-investment level to OY would not face *M* incentives, *M* disincentives, or *O* disincentives on those investments even if entry were barred (because, I am assuming, their failure to make an additional QV investment would induce an established rival to make an equally-large QV investment that would be equally damaging to the actual investor's other QV investments' profit-yields as its own expansion would be [relative to the *status quo ante*]), at QV-investment level OY, each successive best-placed potential expander would face *M* disincentives if entry were barred because each would know that it was the only established firm that could earn normal returns on any additional project it introduced into the relevant area of product-space—*i.e.*, that its decision not to expand would not induce any established rival to expand instead. I hasten to point out that, given that the entry-preventing QV-investment level in Diagram II—Oa—is higher than OY, no similar *M* disincentives will cause $I\Pi_E$ to drop continuously at point I: at least if one assumes that the new entry that would actually take place because the established firm that was best-placed to raise ARDEPPS QV investment above OY failed to do so would be equally damaging to the profit-yields of this potential expander's other projects, the relevant potential expander would face no *M* disincentives (and no *M* incentives) at QV-investment level OY on the realistic entry assumptions on which $I\Pi_E$'s construction is based, though it would face them on the counterfactual entry-barred assumption on which $I\Pi_E^*$'s construction is based.

Second, $I\Pi_E^*$'s construction between QV-investment levels OY and Oa is based on the assumption that the successive best-placed expanders in question would face the same *M* disincentives on their QV-investment projects. This assumption is unrealistic (since on our assumptions the successive expansions in question will be made by the same firm, the *M* disincentives that firm faces will tend to increase as one moves to the right because the number of pre-existing projects it owns [whose profit-yields an expansion will reduce] will increase as one moves to the right), but the assumption's lack of realism does not affect any significant conclusion I generate.

Third, the construction of $I\Pi_E$ and $I\Pi_E^*$ between OY and Oa also reflects the continuance of our assumptions that Π_D increases progressively as one moves to the right of OX and that L equals zero.

The third segments of the $I\Pi_E$ and $I\Pi_E^*$ curves in Diagram II contain the portions of the curves that lie between QV-investment levels Oa and Oβ. The critical point is that between QV-investment levels Oa and Oβ, $I\Pi_E$ coincides with $I\Pi_E^*$ once more—*i.e.*, that at QV-investment level Oa, $I\Pi_E$ drops discontinuously from point W above $I\Pi_E^*$ to point F on $I\Pi_E^*$. This drop reflects the fact that, once the entry-preventing QV-investment level Oa is reached, the entry-barred assumption becomes irrelevant since the established firm's failure to expand the ARDEPPS' QV investment beyond Oa will not induce entry. The fact that the coincident segments of $I\Pi_E$ and $I\Pi_E^*$ to the right of QV-investment level Oa continue to drop further below $H\Pi_E$ between points F and B (between QV-investment levels Oa and Oβ) reflects my continuing assumptions that Π_D rises progressively as one moves to the right beyond QV-investment level OX and that L is zero throughout.

Finally, since as already stated $IN\Pi_E$ and $IN\Pi_E^*$ indicate the normal rates-of-return for the expansions that would successively be the most-privately-attractive expansions any established firm could execute if entry respectively were not and were barred, R_E and R_E^* at any QV-investment level will respectively equal $IN\Pi_E$–$N\Pi_E$ and $IN\Pi_E^*$–$N\Pi_E$ at that level. In what follows, I will assume that $IN\Pi_E = IN\Pi_E^*$ and that R_E therefore equals R_E^*. For simplicity, Diagram II is also constructed on the assumption that the risk barrier to expansion appears at precisely the same QV-investment level at which the Π_D barrier to expansion appears—that the first QV-investment expansion for which $I\Pi_E < H\Pi_E$ (because $\Pi_D > 0$) is the first QV-investment expansion for which $IN\Pi_E > N\Pi_E$ (because $R_E > 0$). In particular, in Diagram II, the QV-investment expansion for which these two barriers appear is the expansion that would raise the total amount of QV investment in the ARDEPPS to a level above OX.

In order to use Diagram II to illustrate the determinants of the lowest entry-barred expansion-preventing QV-investment level, one additional piece of information must be supplied—information on the scale of the expansion that would be best-placed to raise total QV investment in the ARDEPPS above the entry-barred expansion-preventing QV-investment level. Diagram II assumes that this scale will be YD, the minimum efficient scale of expansion. YD is constructed to be slightly lower than ab in Diagram I because the minimum efficient scale of expansion will tend to be lower than the minimum efficient scale of entry (ab) since established firms will be more able than potential competitors to take advantage of economies of scale in production, promotion, and distribution by producing, promoting, and distributing their new products together with their old. In any event, if the expansion that would be best-placed to raise QV investment in the ARDEPPS in question above the entry-barred expansion-preventing QV-investment level would take place at a scale of YD, the (lowest) entry-barred expansion-preventing QV-investment level would be infinitesimally above $OY = OD–YD$ where OD is the QV-investment level at which the $I\Pi_E^*$ curve cuts the $IN\Pi_E^*$ curve from above (at point P) and YD is the minimum scale at which any expansion of ARDEPPS QV above OD would take place if entry were barred. In what follows, I will assume that the entry-barred expansion-preventing QV-investment level in the ARDEPPS in question is (infinitesimally above) OY—*i.e.*, that the lumpiness of QV investments will not cause this level to diverge from OY. At a QV-investment level (infinitesimally above) OY, the established firms that owned most-profitable projects would be realizing a supernormal profit-rate infinitesimally less than ZC on these QV investments. Despite this fact, no established firm would find it profitable to expand because the sum of the barriers to expansion and monopolistic QV-investment disincentives that the best-placed potential expander at OY would face would equal ZC. Thus, in Diagram II, the value of the barriers and disincentives that would affect this next expansion are as follows: S_E for an expansion of scale YD equals $Z\alpha$ (the difference between the vertical coordinates of points Z and T on $H\Pi_E$),[54] $(\Pi_D + L^*)_E = TV$ (the vertical distance between the $H\Pi_E$ and $I\Pi_E$ curves

[54] I should note that one should not count as part of the scale barrier that would confront the established firm that was contemplating making a QV investment that would raise the total QV investment of the ARDEPPS in question from OY to OD the amount by which the R barrier to expansion at QV-investment level OD exceeds the R barrier to expansion at QV-investment level OY—PQ–εC—because on the assumptions of Diagram II the expansion in question will not raise the risk costs of any pre-existing QV investment. However PQ–εC is a component of the risk barrier R faced by the established firm that is best-placed to increase the ARDEPPS' QV-investment level from OY to OD: the other component of that risk barrier is εC (the risk barrier to the execution of the expansion that would be best-placed to raise the ARDEPPS'

at QV-investment level OD), $M^* = $ VP (the vertical distance between curves $\text{I}\Pi_{\text{E}}$ and $\text{I}\Pi^*_{\text{E}}$ at QV-investment level OD), and R = PQ = εC + (PQ–εC) (the vertical distance between curves $\text{IN}\Pi^*_{\text{E}}$ and $\text{N}\Pi_{\text{E}}$ at QV-investment level OD). An inspection of Diagram II reveals that ZC = Zα + TV + VP + PQ.

Now that Diagrams I and II and the various barriers, (dis)incentives, and QV-investment levels they illustrate have been explained, it should be possible to analyze the determinants of the equilibrium QV-investment level in an ARDEPPS with a given actual, competitive QV-investment level and correlatively the determinants of the lifetime supernormal profit-rate that will be generated in equilibrium by the most-supernormally-profitable QV investments in the ARDEPPS in question. In addition to the assumptions on which (as I have explained) the construction of Diagrams I and II are based, the analysis that follows is based on four further assumptions.

The first is that at the time of the analysis QV investment in the ARDEPPS in question has not yet attained its static equilibrium level. New QV investments that are introduced into this ARDEPPS may be introduced either by firms that are already established in the ARDEPPS (in which case they will be described as QV-investment expansions) or by potential entrants (in which case they will be described as new entries). QV-investment expansions that would not have been executed but for their tendency to deter someone else (either an established firm or a potential competitor) from making a QV investment will sometimes be described as "limit investments."

The second is that, although I will continue to assume generally that QV investments are introduced into any ARDEPPS in the order of their profitability, I will also assume (somewhat inconsistently) that whenever an established firm finds an expansion profitable and a potential competitor finds an entry profitable, any relevant QV investment that is executed will be made by the established firm (regardless of whether it is more profitable than the deterred QV investment of the potential competitor). This expositionally-useful assumption has some basis in reality. Although the following justification is somewhat undercut by the fact that an ARDEPPS' best-placed potential competitors are normally-existing companies operating in nearby geographic "markets" or related product "markets," I suspect that established firms usually learn of QV-investment opportunities (*i.e.*, that a QV investment that would create a particular type of product or distributive outlet would be profitable) sooner than do potential competitors and can commit themselves to making or completing the relevant type of QV investment before outsiders can do so.

The third additional assumption is that QV investments are sufficiently immobile that it will never be inherently profitable for someone to make a QV investment on the assumption that its execution will induce an established QV investment to be withdrawn. This third assumption will be more realistic the more use-specific the established QV investments. Thus, QV investments in product or outlet design are least likely to be withdrawn because they cannot be converted into alternative uses.

QV-investment level to OY). For convenience, however, I am classifying this component of the scale barrier to the relevant expansion to be a component of the risk barrier to that expansion.

QV investments in physical distributive outlets will be more likely to be withdrawn to the extent that they can be (profitably) used to distribute either products that would be rivalrous with the product their creator built them to distribute or completely-different, non-rivalrous products. QV investments in capacity-increasing machinery will be more likely to be withdrawn to the extent that the machinery can be used equally well to produce other products, to the extent that their alternative users are geographically proximate to the actor that invested in them, and to the extent that the cost of transporting them any distance is low. QV investments in capacity-increasing plants will be more likely to be withdrawn to the extent that the plants are physically and geographically equally suitable for producing other products.

The fourth and final additional assumption is that all the expansions that could be made in or entries that could be made into the ARDEPPS in question after the time of analysis will have the same QV-investment magnitude. This assumption is made purely for expositional reasons: it enables me to refer to the number of entries that could be made absent established-firm expansions and the number of expansions that would deter a given number of entries rather than the total monetary magnitudes of the investments in question.

On the above assumptions, I will now analyze the determinants of the lifetime supernormal rate-of-return that will be generated by an ARDEPPS' most-profitable projects in equilibrium. The fact that I am focusing on this variable does not imply my belief that, in the context of antitrust-law analysis, the intensity of QV-investment competition should be defined in terms of the highest supernormal lifetime rate-of-return any relevant project generates. I have adopted this focus because the analysis it requires me to execute is germane to the issues that the relevant antitrust laws make legally salient—in Clayton Act analysis, the effect a practice or transaction will have on the equivalent-dollar welfare of the customers of the actor(s) and the customers of the actors' product-rivals by reducing the absolute attractiveness of the best offer they respectively receive from any inferior supplier[55] and, in Sherman Act analysis, the tendency of a practice or transaction to inflate the actor or actors' profits critically by reducing the attractiveness of the offers against which it or they have to compete. Since, in one sense, the determinants of this highest supernormal profit-rate will depend on which of three "types" of equilibria is established in the ARDEPPS in question, the analysis that follows will analyze these three types of equilibria separately.

(1) Equilibria in Which QV Investment Exceeds the Entry-Preventing Level at the Time of Analysis

The first set of equilibria worth distinguishing in this context are equilibria at a level of QV investment that is higher than the level that would prevent all entry at the time of analysis. An equilibrium will be established above the time-of-analysis

[55] In my terminology, a buyer's "inferior suppliers" are the potential suppliers that are worse-than-best-placed to supply it.

entry-preventing QV-investment level in two sets of circumstances. First, such an equilibrium will be established when (unlike in Diagram II) the entry-barred expansion-preventing QV-investment level is higher than the entry-preventing QV-investment level.

Second, such an equilibrium will be established when (unlike in Diagram II) (1) the entry-barred expansion-preventing QV investment level is lower than the entry-preventing QV-investment level or (2) one or more established firms find it profitable to expand sufficiently to prevent all entry—a possibility that may reflect the fact that the threat of entry may critically reduce the monopolistic QV-investment disincentives the potential expander faces, indeed may cause it to have monopolistic QV-investment incentives to make the relevant investment—and the lumpiness of QV investments (the fact that there are economies of scale in making such investments) makes it profitable for the expander that executes the equilibrating QV investment in the relevant ARDEPPS to make an investment that will raise QV investment in the ARDEPPS in question above the entry-preventing level.

The lifetime supernormal profit-rate that will be yielded by an ARDEPPS' most-profitable projects in either of the two situations just described will equal the sum of (1) the supernormal profit-rate the investor whose expansion brought the ARDEPPS into equilibrium anticipated realizing on this QV investment *plus* (2) the sum of the (Π_D + R) barriers to expansion it faced on the expansion that brought the ARDEPPS into equilibrium *plus* (3) (A) the monopolistic QV-investment disincentives it faced on that investment or *minus* (3) (B) the monopolistic QV-investment incentives it had to make that investment. The (Π_D + R) expansion barriers must be added to the expander's supernormal rate-of-return to calculate the most-profitable projects' equilibrium supernormal rate-of-return because, by definition, the most-profitable projects' profits are not reduced by any such barriers. In the normal situation in which the number of QV investments in an ARDEPPS in equilibrium exceeds the number of most-profitable QV investments it contains, the equilibrium supernormal rate-of-return of the most-profitable projects will also be augmented by any positive difference between the monopolistic QV-investment incentive their makers had to make them and any monopolistic QV-investment incentive the last expander had to make its last QV investment or the sum of the monopolistic QV-investment incentive the owner of the relevant most-profitable project had to execute the project and any monopolistic QV-investment disincentive that faced the expander that established the ARDEPPS' QV-investment equilibrium on that equilibrating investment.

(2) Equilibria at the Time-of-Analysis Entry-Preventing QV-Investment Level

The second set of equilibria worth distinguishing in this context are equilibria at the time-of-analysis entry-preventing QV-investment level. Such equilibria can prevail in four situations. First, this type of equilibrium can result when (unlike in Diagram II) the entry-barred expansion-preventing QV-investment level at the time of analysis happens to equal the time-of-analysis entry-preventing QV-investment level.

Second, this type of equilibrium can result when the threat of entry makes it individually profitable for various established firms to make enough QV investments to bring total QV investment in the relevant ARDEPPS to the entry-preventing level despite the fact that (as in Diagram II) the entry-barred expansion-preventing QV-investment level is lower than the time-of-analysis entry-preventing QV-investment level. As already indicated, potential competition can make it profitable for established firms to make QV investments that would not otherwise have been profitable because the threat of entry will reduce or eliminate what may otherwise have been critical monopolistic QV-investment disincentives—indeed, may cause an established firm to have (critical or non-critical) monopolistic QV-investment incentives. This type of equilibrium is most likely to prevail when (1) the number of QV-investment expansions that the established firms must execute to deter all entry at the time of analysis is as large or almost as large as the number of new entries that would result if the established firms did not make any additional (limit) investments to deter entry and (2) the sum of the barriers to expansion that will face the established firm that will be best-placed to make the last QV investment necessary to deter all entry does not significantly exceed the sum of the barriers facing the best-placed potential competitor. The first of these conditions is most likely to be satisfied when QV investment at the time of analysis is close to the entry-preventing level or the number of potential entrants that are equal-best-placed to enter or close-to-best-placed to enter equals the number of limit investments the established firms must execute to deter all entry. If I relax the assumption that the equilibrium in question must be static, the second of the above two conditions is most likely to be satisfied if "demand" for the products of the ARDEPPS is not rapidly increasing or costs in the ARDEPPS are not rapidly falling: if demand increases and/or costs fall, the actual dynamic equilibrium may be rising sufficiently rapidly to increase the number of expansions that the established firms must execute quickly to deter entry to the point that the Π_D and R barriers they would confront on their last limit investments would become prohibitively higher than the barriers faced by the best-placed potential entrant (given that the efficiency with which any given company can execute an internal expansion will tend to be inversely related to the rate at which it will have to grow to execute the expansion in question).

Third, an equilibrium may be established at the time-of-analysis entry-preventing QV-investment level if (1) as in Diagram II, the time-of-analysis entry-barred expansion-preventing QV-investment level is lower than the time-of-analysis entry-preventing QV-investment level, (2) the established firms do make some (limit) QV investments to deter some entry but not enough to deter all entry, and (3) the number of new entries that are executed equals the difference between the number of limit investments the established firms would have to execute at the time of the analysis to deter all entry and the number of limit investments the established firms did execute post-analysis. This result is likely to obtain if (1) the barriers to expansion facing the successively-best-placed potential expanders rise so that at some QV-investment level below the entry-preventing level the barriers facing the best-placed potential expander exceed the barriers facing the best-placed potential entrant sufficiently to outweigh any monopolistic QV-investment incentive the potential expander may have to execute an additional expansion and (2) the number of equally-best-placed potential entrants equals or exceeds the difference between the number of QV-investment expansions the established firms must execute at the time of analysis to deter all entry and the number of such investments the established firms actually do execute.

Fourth, an equilibrium may also be established at the time-of-analysis entry-preventing QV-investment level if (1) as in Diagram II, the time-of-analysis entry-barred expansion-preventing QV-investment level is lower than the time-of-analysis entry-preventing QV-investment level, (2) the established firms make no limit QV investments (because the barriers to expansion they face are sufficiently higher than the barriers confronting the best-placed potential entrant to outweigh any monopolistic QV-investment incentives they may have to expand—*i.e.*, if the relevant barriers are prohibitive), and (3) actual entry brings QV to the entry-preventing level (because the number of equally-best-placed potential entrants equals or exceeds the difference between the number of QV investments the established firms own in the relevant ARDEPPS and the number that is entry-preventing).

In any event, if an equilibrium is established in an ARDEPPS at the entry-preventing QV-investment level and we assume that the owners of the ARDEPPS' most-profitable projects faced neither monopolistic QV-investment incentives nor monopolistic QV-investment disincentives in relation to them, the most-profitable projects in the ARDEPPS in question will all generate a supernormal rate-of-return equal to the sum of the $(\Pi_D + R + S + L)_N$ barriers confronting the potential competitor that was best-placed to enter the relevant ARDEPPS at the time of the analysis, regardless of which of the four scenarios just described brought the ARDEPPS to this equilibrium. If some entries have been executed, the new entrant will anticipate realizing a supernormal rate-of-return equal to the S barrier it faced so that the most-profitable projects' equilibrium supernormal rate-of-return will also equal the sum of the $(\Pi_D + R + L)_N$ barriers confronting the time-of-analysis best-placed potential competitors and the supernormal profit-rate the actual new entrants anticipated realizing on their entries. If some expansions have been executed, the least profitable expansion to have been executed will yield an anticipated supernormal rate-of-return equal to (1) the S barrier that the best-placed potential entrant faced *plus* (2) the difference between the sum of the $(\Pi_D + R + L)_N$ barriers confronting the potential competitors that were best-placed to enter the ARDEPPS in question at the time of analysis and the sum of the $(\Pi_D + R + L)_E$ barriers the firm that executed this expansion faced on the QV investment in question *plus* or *minus* any QV-investment incentives or disincentives the relevant investor had to execute the expansion in question (which I am assuming are zero). In such cases, the most-profitable projects' equilibrium supernormal rate-of-return will also equal (1) the supernormal rate-of-return the last expander anticipated realizing on this last expansion *plus* (2) the $(\Pi_D + R + L)$ barriers it faced on this expansion *plus* or *minus* (3) the QV-investment disincentives or incentives the last expander faced on the last expansion.

(3) Equilibria at QV-Investment Levels That Are Lower Than the Time-of-Analysis Entry-Preventing QV-Investment Level

The third set of QV-investment equilibria worth distinguishing in this context are equilibria at a QV-investment level that is lower than the level that would prevent all entry at the time at which the relevant investigation was being executed. This type of equilibrium will tend to be established when (1) as in Diagram II, the entry-barred expansion-preventing QV-investment level is lower than the entry-preventing QV-investment level and (2) the difference between the number of QV investments that would be entry-preventing in the ARDEPPS in question at the time of analysis and the number of QV investments that would be expansion-preventing if entry were barred is bigger than the sum of the limit investments the established firms will make (the QV investments that will be induced by the prospect of entry) and the number of new entries that potential competitors will find profitable to execute after the established firms have made the limit investments they will find profitable to make. Not surprisingly, the analysis of the factors that determine the equilibrium that will obtain in this type of situation is quite complicated. Put crudely, the outcome depends on four factors:

(1) the difference between the number of limit investments that the established firms must make to deter all entry at the time of analysis (say, total limit QV investments, ΣLQV) and the number of entries that will be executed if the established firms make no limit investments—which, given ΣLQV, will depend on the number of potential competitors that are equal-best-placed to enter at the time of analysis (up to ΣLQV) and the rate at which the relevant barriers rise for the successive worse-than-best-placed potential entrants
(2) the difference between the $(\Pi_D + R + S + L)_E$ barriers that would have confronted the established firm that would have executed the last expansion in the ARDEPPS in question had entry been barred and the $(\Pi_D + R + S + L)_N$ barriers facing the established firms' best-placed potential competitors at the time of analysis,
(3) the rate at which the relevant barriers rise as one moves down the list of successive best-placed potential expanders in the ARDEPPS in question, and
(4) in practice, though for the most part I have been ignoring this consideration, the extent of any monopolistic QV-investment incentives the successive best-placed potential expanders have to substitute their respective individual expansions for the rival expansion or entry their respective expansions would deter.

In any event, if an equilibrium is established at a QV-investment level that is lower than the time-of-analysis entry-preventing QV-investment level, the most-profitable projects' equilibrium supernormal rate-of-return will equal (1) the supernormal rate-of-return the last entering potential competitor anticipated on its investment *plus* (2) the sum of the $(\Pi_D + R + L)_N$ barriers to entry it faced on that investment. In such situations, the most-profitable projects' equilibrium supernormal rate-of-return will also equal (1) the supernormal rate-of-return the last expanding established firm anticipated realizing on this last investment *plus* (2) the $(\Pi_D + R + L)_E$ barriers to expansion it faced on this investment *plus* or *minus* (3) any QV-investment disincentives or incentives it had to make this investment (which I am assuming to be zero).

* * *

This section defined and diagrammatically illustrated the various intermediate determinants of the intensity of QV-investment competition as well as a number of QV-investment levels that play a role in QV-investment-competition analysis. It also explained and diagrammatically illustrated the relationship between the above determinants and the QV-investment levels in question.

The QV-investment-competition-related vocabulary and analyses this section respectively delineated and executed will be used for many purposes in this study—*inter alia* (1) to demonstrate that market definitions are inherently arbitrary, (2) to articulate the distinction between natural and contrived oligopolistic QV-investment restrictions, (3) to criticize various proposed tests for contrived (or natural or contrived) oligopolistic pricing, (4) to articulate correct definitions of predatory QV investments and predatory cost-reducing investments, (5) to criticize various proposed tests for predatory pricing, (6) to articulate the conditions under which "systems rivalry" will and will not be predatory, (7) to structure the analysis of the impact of horizontal mergers, acquisitions, and joint ventures on QV-investment competition, (8) to reveal the conditions under which and the way in which potential competition will be effective, to criticize the 1992 Horizontal Merger Guidelines' position on this issue, and to criticize various arguments that have been made for the profitability of limit pricing and various ways in which some scholars have claimed limit-price theory could be tested, and (9) to structure the analysis of the conditions under which conglomerate mergers, acquisitions, and joint ventures that do or do not involve potential competitors will decrease QV-investment competition.

* * *

Chapter 2 has defined a large number of concepts that the study will use to analyze a wide variety of micro-economic, antitrust-law, and antitrust-policy issues. As I indicated in this study's introduction, these types of conceptual innovations are neither right nor wrong. The relevant question is whether they are useful. I think that Part II of this study demonstrates the utility of these conceptual innovations by demonstrating that they enable me to formulate important new questions and to give more accurate answers than could otherwise be provided both to those questions and to questions that can be formulated without them.

Chapter 3
How "Monopolizing Conduct," "Attempts to Monopolize," and "Exclusionary or Foreclosing Conduct" Should Be Defined by Economists

Economists who specialize in Industrial Organization or Antitrust Economics often analyze whether particular conduct can properly be said to involve monopolization, to constitute an attempt to monopolize, to be exclusionary, or to foreclose competition. In my judgment, American economists address these issues because Section 2 of the U.S. Sherman Act makes it illegal for anyone to monopolize or attempt to monopolize and because any time that a U.S. court or antitrust-enforcement agency characterizes conduct as being exclusionary or states that conduct forecloses competition it does so to justify the conclusion that the conduct violates Section 2 of the Sherman Act. European economists focus on these issues not only because of U.S. legal usage but also because Article 102 of the 2009 Treaty of Lisbon prohibits dominant firms from committing exclusionary abuses of their dominant position, because (as Chap. 4 argues) the "hav[ing] as an object... the prevention or restriction... of competition" branch of Articles 101(1)'s test of *prima facie* illegality is identical to the Sherman Act's test of illegality, and because the EC frequently expresses concern that particular types of conduct will foreclose competition.

Although this chapter might be criticized for duplicating Chapter 4's discussions of the Sherman Act's test of illegality, the "object" branch of now-Article 101(1)'s *prima facie* test of illegality, and the exclusionary-abuse branch of now-Article 102's test of illegality, I concluded that it would be cost-effective to anticipate those discussions by indicating how economists should define these concepts not only to make their claims legally relevant but to highlight a distinction between conduct that "lessens competition" and conduct that manifests "specific anticompetitive intent," which is important for moral as well as legal analysis.

I start with the (Sherman Act) concept of monopolizing conduct. A seller is properly said to have committed a monopolizing act (or to have engaged in a more general, monopolizing practice) if and only if its *ex ante* perception of its choice's profitability was "*ceteris paribus* critically inflated" by its belief that the conduct might benefit the seller by increasing the demand curve it would face in the future by reducing the absolute attractiveness of the offers against which it would have to compete. In other words, monopolizing acts are acts committed with what lawyers call the "specific intent" to

R.S. Markovits, *Economics and the Interpretation and Application of U.S. and E.U. Antitrust Law*, DOI 10.1007/978-3-642-24307-3_3,

reduce the absolute attractiveness of the offers against which the actor will have to compete (*i.e.*, are acts committed that the actor would not have committed but for its belief that they would or might have this effect) in circumstances in which the effect in question would *ceteris paribus* critically inflate the profitability of the acts concerned. Each component of the expression "*ceteris paribus* critically inflated" needs to be explicated. In my terminology, the profits yielded by a choice are said to be "inflated" if they exceed its economic efficiency; the profits a choice yields are said to be "critically inflated" if the relevant profit-inflation caused the choice to be profitable despite the fact that it is economically inefficient; and the profits a choice yields are said to be "*ceteris paribus* critically inflated" by one of its effects or tendencies (or by one or more Pareto imperfections) if the effect or tendency (or imperfection[s]) in question would critically inflate the profits of the choice in question if nothing else "distorted" those profits—*i.e.*, if nothing else caused them to diverge from the choice's economic efficiency.

I believe that this specific-intent definition of monopolizing conduct captures professional legal understanding. I also believe that it is consistent with the relevant portion of the more general public's intuitive grasp of the concept, including their perception that such conduct is bad. Monopolizing conduct is understood to be bad both because it is presumptively economically inefficient and because, from any plausible conception of distributive justice, it is unjust. Thus, by definition, in an otherwise-Pareto-perfect economy and (I suspect) in most instances in our actual, highly-Pareto-imperfect economy as well, monopolizing conduct is economically inefficient (1) because it would be unprofitable but for its tendency to reduce the absolute attractiveness of the offers against which its perpetrator(s) must compete and (2) because its tendency to reduce the absolute attractiveness of the offers against which its perpetrator(s) must compete will generally reduce economic efficiency at the same time as it yields its perpetrator's or perpetrators' profits. Relatedly, monopolizing conduct is always distributively unjust in an otherwise-distributively-perfect economy and (I suspect) is virtually always distributively unjust in our actual, highly-distributively-imperfect economy (1) because it rewards its perpetrators for doing something that is economically inefficient and has no other redeeming consequence and (2) because it imposes losses on the customers of its perpetrator(s) and (when the monopolizing conduct in question is predatory) on the targets of its perpetrator(s) for no good reason at all.

The definition of monopolizing conduct just delineated has both negative and positive concrete implications. Negatively, it implies that business conduct should not be characterized as "monopolizing" if its perpetrator believed *ex ante* that it would be rendered at least normally profitable (1) by its enabling the perpetrator to make its product more attractive and/or to reduce its costs, (2) by its enabling the perpetrator to take better advantage of a given demand-curve/marginal-cost-curve (DD/MC) combination, (3) by its enabling the perpetrator to secure a tax benefit, and/or (4) by its enabling the perpetrator to liquidate financial or real assets on terms that were not critically affected by any tendency the sale had to reduce the absolute attractiveness of the offers against which the buyer would have to compete. Positively, it implies that at least the following types of conduct are properly said to be "monopolizing": (1) contrived oligopolistic conduct, whose *ex ante* perpetrator-perceived profitability is critically affected by its deterring rivals from making as attractive offers to its perpetrator’s customers as those rivals would otherwise have made, (2) predatory conduct, whose *ex ante* perpetrator-perceived profitability is critically affected by its driving a rival out (or causing a rival to locate or relocate further away in product-space from the perpetrator’s operations than the rival would otherwise have done), (3) horizontal mergers and acquisitions whose *ex ante* merger-partner-perceived profitability is critically affected by their freeing their participants from each other’s competition and/or increasing the profits their participants can realize by engaging in contrived oligopolistic or predatory conduct, (4) conglomerate mergers whose *ex ante* merger-partner-perceived profitability is critically affected by their reducing the QV-investment competition an established merger partner faces by eliminating an effective potential competitor, and (5) any QV-investment expansion whose *ex ante* investor-perceived profitability is critically affected by the monopolistic QV-investment incentive the investor in question believed *ex ante* it had to make it (since such incentives reflect the actor’s obtaining private gains that, at best, have no economic-efficiency counterpart by deterring a rival from making a rivalrous QV investment).

I turn next to the concept of an attempt to monopolize. Not surprisingly, a seller is properly said to have unsuccessfully attempted to monopolize when it has committed a monopolizing act or engaged in a monopolizing practice that manifested its specific intent to reduce but did not succeed in reducing the absolute attractiveness of the offers against which it had to compete in circumstances in which the conduct’s profitability would have been *ceteris paribus* critically inflated by its securing this objective.

Finally, I discuss the concepts of exclusionary conduct that forecloses competition. In my judgment, it would be most useful to define exclusionary conduct to be conduct that manifests its perpetrator’s or perpetrators’ specific anticompetitive intent. I have no doubt that that is the way in which U.S. courts, antitrust-enforcement agencies, and antitrust-law scholars have implicitly defined the concept in use. I think that one should also confine statements that conduct forecloses competition to situations in which the conduct manifests specific anticompetitive intent. However, I admit that U.S. antitrust authorities have sometimes stated that conduct has “foreclosed” or would “foreclose” competition when it did not manifest specific anticompetitive intent but would induce exits or deter entry without rendering the perpetrator’s or perpetrators’ business(es) more economically efficient than the businesses of their foreclosed rivals.

Chapter 4
The Actor-Coverage of, Conduct-Coverage of, Tests of Illegality Promulgated by, and Defenses Recognized by U.S. Antitrust Law and E.C./E.U. Competition Law

This chapter has three sections. The first summarizes the actor-coverage of, conduct-coverage of, tests of illegality promulgated by, and the defenses recognized by U.S. antitrust law and points out certain mistakes that U.S. courts and various scholars have made when addressing these issues. The second presents a parallel analysis of the E.C./E.U. competition law. And the third compares the above aspects of U.S. antitrust law and E.C./E.U. competition law. This chapter will not discuss in detail (1) the approaches that U.S. and E.C./E.U. officials and scholars take to market definition, (2) the assumptions they make about the connection between a firm's market share and its monopoly, oligopoly, and overall market power, or (3) the conclusions they have reached about the monopolizing character and/or likely competitive impact of various types of conduct or particular exemplars of specific types of conduct. These issues will be addressed respectively in Chaps. 7, 8, and 10–15. This chapter will also not discuss the institutional framework of U.S. and E.C./E.U. antitrust law (*i.e.*, the nature of their enforcement "agencies" and courts and the roles each such authority plays in the creation and enforcement of competition law), the procedures those various State actors are bound to follow (*inter alia*, the various notification requirements imposed on the law's addressees and the time-constraints imposed on the "agencies'" review of notified mergers), and the "remedial" options available to U.S. and E.C./E.U. antitrust decisionmakers. Section 1 of the Introduction to Part II: Applications and (respectively) Sections 4 and 5 of Chapter 12 delineate the U.S. and E.C./E.U. notification and "agency"-review protocols for horizontal mergers.

1. The Actor-Coverage of, Conduct-Coverage of, Tests of Illegality Promulgated by, and Defenses Recognized by U.S. Antitrust Law

The aspects of U.S. (central-government) antitrust law on which this chapter focuses are created by three statutes and their interpretation and application. The relevant statutes are the Sherman Antitrust Act, the Clayton Antitrust Act, and the Federal

R.S. Markovits, *Economics and the Interpretation and Application of U.S. and E.U. Antitrust Law*, DOI 10.1007/978-3-642-24307-3_4,

Trade Commission Act. As we shall see, on my interpretation, the Sherman Act promulgates a specific-anticompetitive-intent test of illegality, the Clayton Act (with one exception created by a 1936 amendment to Section 2 of the original 1914 Act) promulgates a "lessening competition" test of illegality, and the Federal Trade Commission Act promulgates an "unfair methods of competition" test of illegality. The text that follows will explicitly address only the first two of these three tests of illegality. My decision to ignore the FTC Act's "unfair methods of competition" test of illegality reflects the fact that, with one limited exception that has been of virtually no practical importance, the FTC's antitrust authorization seems to be limited solely to enforcing the Clayton Act. (Although the "unfair methods of competition" language clearly resonates more with the Sherman Act's specific-anticompetitive-intent test of illegality, the FTC in fact is not authorized to enforce the Sherman Act.) The exception in question is that the FTC has been granted statutory authority to define conduct that constitutes illegal price discrimination. The exception has had little practical importance because the FTC has used this special statutory authority to define illegal price discrimination only once and subsequently rescinded the rule it promulgated on that occasion.[56] (I should add that the FTC Act also authorizes the FTC to prohibit methods of competition that are unfair in the sense of giving their perpetrator an advantage not based on its economic-efficiency superiority, regardless of whether the perpetrator's conduct reduced competition or manifested the perpetrator's specific anticompetitive intent.)

A. *The Sherman Antitrust Act*

(1) The Sherman Act as Correctly Interpreted

The Sherman Act has two relevant provisions. Section 1 prohibits "[e]very contract, combination in the form of trust or otherwise, or conspiracy, in restraint of trade or

[56] The FTC's special authority to define illegal price discrimination was granted by 15 U.S.C. § 13(a). For the FTC's decision to rescind its one use of this authority, see 58 Fed. Reg. 35907–01. A 1994 amendment to Section 5 of the Federal Trade Commission Act (which contains "the unfair methods of competition" language to which the text refers) is (largely) consistent with my claim that the FTC is authorized to apply only the Clayton Act's "lessening competition" test of illegality. According to the (admittedly-poorly-drafted) 1994 amendment, the FTC may not deem conduct "unfair unless the act or practice causes or is likely to cause substantial injury to consumers which is not reasonably avoidable by the consumers themselves and not outweighed by countervailing benefits to consumers or to competition." 15 U.S.C. § 45(n). 15 U.S.C. § 21 provides that the FTC does not have jurisdiction to enforce the Sherman Act. Although some authorities believe that this limitation in the FTC's authority has no practical significance in that any act or practice that violates the Sherman Act will also constitute an "unfair method of competition" that violates Section 5 of the FTC Act, I believe that, although the textual and prudential arguments that support this conclusion would be convincing in isolation, they are trumped by 15 U.S.C. § 21's declaration that the FTC does not have jurisdiction to enforce the Sherman Act. See *contra* ELHAUGE AND GERADIN 6.

commerce among the several states, or with foreign nations. . .." Section 2 provides that "[e]very person who shall monopolize, or attempt to monopolize, or combine or conspire with any other person or persons, to monopolize any part of the trade or commerce among the several States, or with foreign nations, shall be deemed guilty of a felony."

(A) The Actor-Coverage of the Sherman Act

Both of the relevant provisions of the Sherman Act cover the conduct of all categories of economic actors—firms, trade associations, and individuals.

(B) The Conduct-Coverage of the Sherman Act

I turn now to the conduct-coverage of the Sherman Act. Section 1 covers conduct that has been agreed to by two or more actors: although its text refers to contracts, combinations, and conspiracies and the concept of a "conspiracy" was well-developed at the time of the Act's passage, the courts have always interpreted the three concepts in question to be variants of the concept of "agreements." Section 2's conduct-coverage is broader than Section 1's in that it covers individual-actor monopolizing conduct and attempts to monopolize as well as multiple-actor monopolizing conduct. With one probable exception and two clear exceptions, the Sherman Act covers all kinds of business conduct.

The possible exception to the rule that the Sherman Act covers all categories of business conduct is unsuccessful attempts to enter into agreements that are anticompetitive in the sense of manifesting what I call specific anticompetitive intent. Such attempts are not covered by Section 1, which makes no reference to attempts, and may not be covered by Section 2 because they are not covered by Section 1 and, given that fact, U.S. courts are likely to be disinclined to read Section 2 to cover them. The conclusion that the Sherman Act does not prohibit unsuccessful attempts to enter into anticompetitive agreements reflects two background facts: (1) the central government of the United States has not passed a general attempt statute—*i.e.*, a statute that makes criminal any attempt whose successful completion has been criminalized, and (2) U.S. courts do not read attempt provisions into criminal statutes that do not contain them. For what it's worth, I can report anecdotally that all U.S. criminal-law professors with whom I have discussed this issue agree that the Sherman Act does not cover unsuccessful attempts to enter into anticompetitive agreements while all antitrust professors with whom I have discussed this issue reject this conclusion (perhaps because they are less familiar with the relevant judicial practice or perhaps because they are less sympathetic to that practice, which they consider to be an undesirable and perhaps unnecessary way to serve the rights-related interest of individuals to have fair notice of the criminal laws that apply to them). I hasten to add that one cannot justify failing to criminalize or prohibit unsuccessful attempts to enter into anticompetitive agreements by claiming that unsuccessful attempts of that sort generate no direct material harm: in particular, one cannot do so because the factual premise of that argument is wrong. The following example illustrates the harmful effect of an unsuccessful attempt to enter into an anticompetitive agreement. Assume that a best-placed firm in an individualized-pricing context has marginal costs of $1, a 10-cent buyer preference advantage, and no ability to obtain an oligopolistic margin naturally. Assume as well that the best-placed firm's rivals must also incur marginal costs of $1 to supply the relevant buyer, that neither the firm in question nor its rivals must incur any contextual marginal costs to charge any relevant price, and that the price the best-placed firm can obtain from the buyer it is best-placed to supply is not affected by any error the firm makes, the buyer makes, or any of its rivals make. On these assumptions, the seller's HNOP would be $1.10, and its (HNOP+NOM) would also be $1.10. Now assume that the firm offers to enter into an anticompetitive agreement with its closest rival for the relevant buyer's patronage—in particular, offers to allow that rival to obtain a higher price than it otherwise could obtain from a different buyer whom that rival is best-placed to supply and the firm in question is second-placed to supply by not beating the rival's oligopolistic price to that buyer in exchange for the rival's allowing it to obtain a higher price from its customer in the same way. Assume that the offer in question was never accepted (*e.g.*, was an offer to enter into a unilateral contract that would be accepted by performance), but that, on the assumption that the offer would be accepted, the firm in question offers its customer a price of $1.14. Now assume that the best-placed firm's rival beats the best-placed firm's $1.14 offer with a $1.03 offer and that the buyer purchases its second-placed supplier's product for $1.03. On these assumptions, the best-placed firm's unsuccessful attempt to enter into an anticompetitive agreement will have cost the buyer in question three cents—the amount by which the buyer's purchase of the best-placed seller's 10-cent-preferred product at $1.10 would have been more attractive to the buyer than the purchase of the undercutting firm's product at a price of $1.03. Still, if I am right, the best-placed seller's unsuccessful attempt to enter into an anticompetitive agreement would not be actionable under the Sherman Act.

The first clear exception to the rule that the Sherman Act covers all categories of business conduct is attempts by firms to influence legislative, administrative, and judicial (government) decisions. So long as a firm "plays fair"—*e.g.*, does not intentionally or perhaps grossly negligently tell untruths or does not induce one or more individuals to argue for the decision the firm prefers without revealing that they are being compensated for doing so, that they are more generally employed by the firm, or that they are in some other way relevantly affiliated with the firm or one of its owners or employees, or (possibly) in an adjudicative context, does not make a claim that is completely baseless, the Sherman Act does not cover attempts by economic actors to influence legislative, administrative, or judicial decisions by engaging in behavior either inside or outside formal government-decision-making processes even if the firm's intent in doing so was specifically anticompetitive in the sense that makes conduct illegal under the Sherman Act (see below). In constitutional-law terminology, this qualification to the general Sherman Act test of illegality constitutes a "saving construction" needed to prevent the Act from prohibiting the firm's exercise (*i.e.*, its owners' exercise) of its (their) First Amendment right to participate in government-decision-making processes as well as the rights-related interest of others to obtain information about public-policy matters and to have government decision-makers be better informed. I should add that this "coverage exception" could alternatively and might better be described as a defense.

The second clear exception to the rule that the Sherman Act covers all categories of business conduct is natural oligopolistic conduct. Such conduct is not covered because it involves no agreement and no attempt to monopolize or act of monopolization.

(C) The Test of Illegality That the Sherman Act Promulgates

As I have already indicated, the Sherman Act's test of illegality is the specific-anticompetitive-intent "test" for monopolization or attempts to monopolize defined in Chap. 3. Thus, covered conduct violates the Sherman Act if and only if its perpetrator's or perpetrators' *ex ante* perception that it would be profitable was critically affected by its or their belief that it would or might reduce the absolute attractiveness of the offers against which it or they would have to compete in some way that would critically inflate the profitability of the conduct in question in an otherwise-Pareto-perfect economy.

(D) The Defenses the Sherman Act Recognizes

I turn finally to the defenses that should be recognized in Sherman Act cases. In legal terminology, something is called a defense if the defendant has the burden of establishing it. In Sherman Act cases, the government clearly has the burden of showing that the defendant(s) believed *ex ante* that the conduct in question would increase the defendant's or defendants' profits by reducing the absolute attractiveness of the offers against which it or they would have to compete in some way that would critically inflate the profitability of the act in question in an otherwise-Pareto-perfect economy (a burden the government may be able to carry by proving that the conduct did have this effect). The defendant(s) can then escape liability by demonstrating that this effect was not critical to its or their *ex ante* perception that the conduct would be profitable—*e.g.*, that the conduct in question's *ex ante* profitability was secured by the Sherman-Act-licit benefits they believed *ex ante* the relevant conduct would yield them (*e.g.*, by generating organizational efficiencies and tax gains, by enabling the owner of a merger partner to liquidate his assets and escape managerial responsibilities, by enabling a firm to enforce its patent rights, or perhaps by enabling a firm to protect its customer lists). Roughly speaking, the burden not only of producing evidence on these latter issues but of persuading the trier-of-fact about them is placed on the defendant(s)—*i.e.*, these facts form the basis of a defense—because (1) defendants are better-placed to establish the relevant facts than the government is to prove the negative and (2) defendants will be guilty in a majority of the instances in which the government can make out its *prima facie* case (so that even if it were no more expensive for the government to prove the negative than for defendants to prove the positive, the trial would generate lower transaction costs if the relevant facts were elements of a defense rather than of the government's *prima facie* case). For example, defendants that have not violated Section 2 because they believed *ex ante* that their conduct's profitability was assured by the Sherman-Act-licit benefits it would generate will usually be better-placed to establish that they held such a belief *ex ante* by demonstrating that their conduct's profitability was in fact assured by the tax advantages, organizational efficiencies, and other relevant benefits it generated than the government will be to establish that the defendants had no such belief *ex ante* by demonstrating that those benefits were too low to make the conduct profitable and that the defendant(s) did not mistakenly critically overestimate them.

(2) Five Errors That Officials and Scholars Have Made When Interpreting the Sherman Act

The U.S. Supreme Court has held that two facts must be established for a firm to be found guilty of monopolization: (1) the [firm's] possession of monopoly power in the relevant market and (2) "the [firm's] willful acquisition or maintenance of that power as distinguished from the power's growth or development as a consequence of a superior product, business acumen, or historic accident."[57] Two general errors that have been made in Sherman Act cases relate to the first of these conditions, and two, to the second. The fact that the first condition is associated with two errors reflects the combination of (1) its having been widely interpreted to require the State or a private plaintiff to demonstrate that the defendant both (A) possessed monopoly or market power prior to engaging in the allegedly-monopolizing conduct and (B) possessed monopoly (or market) power after engaging in the allegedly-monopolizing conduct and (2) the reality that neither of these requirements is appropriate.

None of the arguments that has been made for the "prior possession of monopoly power" condition can bear scrutiny. Thus, as Chap. 11 explains, one cannot justify this requirement by arguing that (1) only firms with pre-existing monopoly power in the "market" in which the allegedly-monopolizing conduct in question took place (A) can finance the short-run loss that monopolization entails, (B) can increase their market power by driving a target rival out, deterring a new entry or established-rival

[57] See United States v. Grinnell Corp. 384 U.S. 563, 570–71 (1966). For recent confirmations of this position, see Verizon Communications, Inc. v. Law Offices of Curtis v. Trinko, LLP, 540 U.S. 398, 407–08 (2004); Spectrum Sports v. McQuillan, 506 U.S. 447, 455–59 (1993); Eastman Kodak v. Image Technical Services, 504 U.S. 451, 481 (1992); and Aspen Skiing Co. v. Aspen Highlands Skiing Corp., 472 U.S. 585, 596 n.19 (1985).

QV-investment expansion, or inducing an established or potential competitor to change the location of an existing or planned QV investment, or (C) can retain in the medium or long run a sufficient percentage of any short-run benefits that their conduct generates in one or more of the above three ways for monopolization to be profitable for them even if it could yield them short-run benefits in the above ways. Indeed, one can also not justify this requirement by arguing that (2) there is a strong positive correlation between a firm's pre-existing monopoly or market power and its ability (A) to finance monopolizing conduct, (B) to obtain short-run benefits from such conduct, or (C) to retain in the medium or long run any benefits such conduct would yield it in the short run. More specifically, as Chap. 11 argues, one cannot justify this requirement in either of the above two ways primarily because there is no such absolute connection or strong positive correlation but secondarily because even if (contrary to my view) the relevant correlation were sufficiently strong and the cost advantage of substituting an analysis of the defendant's market power for an analysis of the monopolizing character of its conduct was sufficiently big for this condition to be cost-effective, moral-rights considerations aside, it would be moral-rights-violative for courts as opposed to legislatures to promulgate this filter. This second, secondary objection reflects the fact that the filter in question is too inaccurate for its legislatively-unauthorized use by a court to be consistent with the litigants' rights to have the country's judges and juries do their best in their individual case to resolve the dispute correctly. (I do not think that a contrary conclusion can be justified by citing the tradition of U.S. courts' controlling their own operations.[58])

I also think that the requirement that the State or private plaintiff establish that the defendant(s) in a Sherman Act monopolization or attempt-to-monopolize case had monopoly or market power after engaging in the allegedly-illegal conduct (to avoid their case's dismissal) is unwarranted. I do not accept either of the two arguments I have heard for the courts' using this filter: (1) the argument that this requirement is justified because the "prior possession of monopoly power" requirement is justified and it is proper to use the post-conduct possession of monopoly power as a surrogate for the pre-conduct possession of monopoly power fails both (A) because the "pre-conduct possession of monopoly power" requirement is unjustified and (B) because the fact that a firm does not have monopoly power post-conduct is compatible with its having had such power pre-conduct since independent intervening events may have eliminated its pre-conduct monopoly power; and (2) the argument that this requirement is justified because, if the defendant does not have monopoly power post-conduct, any attempt that it made to engage in monopolization must have been unsuccessful and the Sherman Act prohibits (or should be interpreted to prohibit) only successful attempts to monopolize fails both (A) because independent events may have deprived defendants of

[58] In part, I reach this conclusion because this type of judicial practice is not self-legitimating or self-validating—*i.e.*, does not render the decisions in question consistent with the society's moral commitments or, relatedly, correct as a matter of law, and, in part, I do so because (by and large) the relevant practices do not sacrifice accuracy or create a bias in favor of one class of litigants (in this instance, defendants) in individual cases.

the monopoly power their successful attempt to monopolize yielded them (and any monopoly power they possessed prior to engaging in such conduct) and (B) because the Sherman Act explicitly covers attempts to monopolize (even when they are unsuccessful) and courts are not authorized to ignore attempt provisions when they think it would be desirable for the legislature to eliminate them.

The third general error U.S. courts have made when interpreting the Sherman Act relates to their operationalization of the world "willful" in the second condition they claim the government must satisfy to obtain a Section 2 conviction. Although U.S. courts have repeatedly correctly distinguished the "willful acquisition or maintenance" of monopoly power from (1) engaging in "competition on the merits" as opposed to engaging in conduct that "*unfairly* tends to destroy competition,"[59] (2) making decisions for "valid business reasons," a "normal business purpose," or "legitimate competitive reasons,"[60] and (3) "honestly-industrial" conduct,[61] they have made many statements about the meaning of the word "willful" that confuses the issue. In particular, U.S. courts have repeatedly said that their references to willfulness or intent do not refer (as I believe they do) to subjective intent but to "objective intent" that can be inferred from the consequences of the firm's conduct. As the authors of a recent text entitled GLOBAL ANTITRUST—LAW AND ECONOMICS have said: U.S. courts that are applying the Sherman Act "do often examine proof of subjective intent in monopolization cases, but not because it is dispositive in its own right—rather they do so because evidence of subjective intent can help the court to *interpret* otherwise ambiguous conduct and its effects. But the ultimate question is an assessment of the conduct and its effects."[62] I find this position at best obfuscating and, on some plausible readings, simply wrong.

U.S. courts need to recognize two things. First, they must recognize that (if one ignores the tax advantages that some business conduct can yield and the possibility that mergers and acquisitions can benefit owners of one of the firms they involve by enabling them to obtain more liquid assets and escape managerial responsibilities) business conduct can be profitable for four reasons: (1) because it enables the actor to extract more seller surplus from a given combination of demand and marginal-cost curves; (2) because it enables the seller to realize at least a normal rate-of-return by improving the combination of demand and marginal-cost curves it faces by improving the seller's product(s), creating a new product, and/or reducing the seller's costs of production, distribution, or finance; (3) because (in the case of some QV investments) it reduces the absolute attractiveness of the offers against which the actor must compete by deterring a rival from making a QV investment in the

---

[59] See Verizon Communications, Inc. v. Law Offices of Curtis v. Trinko, LLP, 540 U.S. 398 (2004).

[60] See Eastman Kodak v. Images Technical Services, 504 U.S. 451, 483 and n.32 (1992) and Aspen Skiing Co. v. Aspen Highlands Skiing Corp., 472 U.S. 585, 605, 608 (1985).

[61] *Id.* at 596 (quoting jury instructions).

[62] EINER ELHAUGE AND DAMIEN GERADIN, GLOBAL ANTITRUST LAW AND ECONOMICS 328 (hereinafter ELHAUGE AND GERADIN) (Hart Publishing, 2007).

relevant area of product-space when this effect does not critically *inflate* the profitability of the investment in question; and (4) because it reduces the absolute attractiveness of the offers against which the actor must compete in one or more ways that inflate the profits yielded by the conduct in question. Second, U.S. courts must recognize that conduct is properly said to constitute an attempt to monopolize if and only if the actor's or actors' *ex ante* perception that it would be at least normally profitable was critically affected by its or their belief that the conduct might increase its or their profits in a way that was inflating by reducing the absolute attractiveness of the offers against which it or they must compete. Conduct that is monopolizing does not constitute "competition on the merits," does "unfairly disadvantage competitors," is not "honestly industrial," is not executed for "valid business" or "legitimate competitive" reasons, and is not engaged in to achieve "a normal business purpose." If U.S. courts kept these possibilities and this definition in mind and rejected obfuscating ideas about the relevance of subjective intent and the usefulness of the peculiar notion of "objective intent," they would be able to interpret and apply the Sherman Act both more easily and more accurately.

The fourth general error that U.S. courts make when interpreting the Sherman Act also relates to the second condition they claim must be satisfied for a defendant to be found to have violated Section 2—more specifically, relates to their (1) statements about the circumstances in which defendants must demonstrate that their monopoly power reflected their "skill, foresight, and industry"[63] to escape Section 2 liability and (2) their assumption that, to prevail in these circumstances, the defendants must establish that their monopoly power was generated by their "skill, foresight, and industry"—*i.e.*, must make out a "skill, foresight, and industry" defense. I disagree with both these contentions. To establish a *prima facie* case of a Section 2 violation, the government must put on either (1) requisitely-convincing documentary evidence or oral testimony that the defendant(s) not only thought *ex ante* that the conduct in question would or might reduce the absolute attractiveness of the offers against which it (they) would have to compete (in one or more ways that the court would recognize would *ceteris paribus* critically inflate the profits yielded by the conduct in question) but would not have engaged in the conduct in question if the defendant(s) had not perceived that it had some prospect of producing such an effect or (2) requisitely-convincing evidence that the profitability of the conduct in question was critically inflated by its reducing the absolute attractiveness of the offers against which the defendant(s) had to compete. Proof that a defendant possessed monopoly power prior to or after engaging in the conduct under investigation is not part of the first, subjective-intent type of evidence just described. Indeed, such proof may not even be part of the second, objective-consequences evidence just described: although conduct that has reduced the absolute attractiveness of the offers against which the defendant must compete will, by definition, have increased its market (economic) power, such conduct may not leave the defendant with enough "monopoly power" in the sense in which U.S. courts understand this term to satisfy this monopoly-power

[63] See United States v. Alcoa, 148 F.2d 416, 430 (2d Cir. 1945).

requirement. And even if the government succeeds in demonstrating that the defendant has monopoly power, the defendant will be able to defeat the inference that it obtained such power by violating Section 2 in ways other than by demonstrating that it obtained such power through "skill, foresight, and industry" since firms can also obtain monopoly power without violating Section 2 through its own good luck, its rivals' bad luck, and (on some definitions of monopoly power) its being particularly adept at converting potential buyer surplus into seller surplus (see Chap. 14) or its being in a position to take advantage of favorable government regulations or tax-code provisions.

The erroneousness of what I am arguing is the fifth general error that U.S. courts,[64] U.S. antitrust-enforcement agencies,[65] and legal/economic[66] antitrust scholars make when interpreting or at least applying the Sherman Act—*viz.*, their assumption that the Act does not distinguish between conduct that increases its perpetrator's or perpetrators' market power as sellers (*inter alia*, their monopoly power) and conduct that increases its perpetrator's or perpetrators' market power as buyers (their monopsony power)—is admittedly constable. The relevant judges, enforcement-agency officials, and scholars all base their legal conclusion on the assumption that the exercise of monopsony power harms the monopsonist's customers in the same way that the exercise of monopoly power harms the customers of the seller that possesses it—*viz.*, by increasing the prices that the relevant power-holder charges for its products. This assumption is based on what I take to be the usually-empirically-incorrect premises (1) that buyers that have market power face an upward-sloping supply curve[67] and suppliers that are price-takers and (2) that the buyers in question will choose to purchase the good involved by offering a single per-unit price for it and (in most cases) buying all the units of that good whose supply that price elicits. It is true that, when these assumptions are accurate, the seller's

---

[64] See Mandeville Island Farms v. American Crystal Sugar, 334 U.S. 219 (1948); United States v. Brown University, 5 F.3d 658, 668 (3d Cir. 1993); Beef Industry Antitrust Litigation, 907 F.2d 510 (5th Cir. 1990); Quality Auto Body v. Allstate Insurance Co., 660 F.2d 1195 (1982); and Weyerhaueser v. Ross-Simmons Hardware Lumber Co., 549 U.S. 312 (2007). I hasten to add that it is critical to distinguish the claims (1) that the non-predatory exercise of buying power by an individual buyer or monopsonist violates the Sherman Act and (2) that non-predatory buyer coops or non-predatory joint-purchasing arrangements of other sorts violate the Sherman Act from the claim (3) that individual-firm or multifirm predatory buying violates the Sherman Act. This last claim, which is clearly correct as a matter of law, will be analyzed in Chap. 11.

[65] See 1992 Horizontal Merger Guidelines at Section 1.0 p. 5: "The exercise of market power by buyers has wealth transfer and resource misallocation effects analogous to those associated with the exercise of market power by sellers."

[66] See Judge (formerly Professor) Richard Posner, writing in Khan v. State Oil Co., 93 F.3d 1358, 1361 (7th Cir. 1996). See, more generally, ROGER BLAIR AND JEFFREY HARRISON, MONOPSONY (Princeton Univ. Press, 1993).

[67] A supply curve is a diagrammatic representation of a schedule that indicates the quantities of a specified good that will be supplied at different prices. The vertical axis in a supply-curve diagram measures some monetary unit (say, dollars), and the horizontal axis, the quantity of the good that will be supplied. When a buyer faces an upward-sloping supply curve, it will have to offer successively higher prices to elicit the supply of additional units of the product in question.

possession of monopsony power will cause it to charge higher prices than it otherwise would for any quantity of its output by raising its marginal costs of production by increasing the cost it has to incur to purchase marginal units of the input on which it is a monopsonist. Under the conditions in question, the firm's monopsony power will produce this result because, in order to purchase a last unit of some input at the price it will have to offer to elicit its supply, the buyer will have to pay higher prices for the intra-marginal units it would otherwise have bought at the lower price it would have to pay to elicit those units' supply. In my judgment, most firms with buyer power do not operate in such conditions—*i.e.*, most such firms face suppliers that are not price-takers and that have some degree of monopoly power themselves. In such a bilateral-monopoly situation, the power of the intermediate buyer (*i.e.*, buyer/producer or buyer/distributor) will be likely to enable it to obtain a lower price for the relevant input (a lower price that applies to each unit of that input it purchases). Under these conditions, the relevant buyer's buying power will reduce the cost of marginal inputs to it and hence its marginal cost of production and thereby lead it to reduce its prices to its customers. To the extent that I am right about this admittedly-contestable empirical issue, the general position of the U.S. courts, the DOJ and FTC, and the economics profession as a whole on the effects and (possibly) Sherman Act legality of conduct that increases its perpetrator's or perpetrators' buyer power is incorrect—"possibly" because the litmus-test for the Sherman Act illegality of conduct may not be its impact on the buyers it affects, because textual and moral arguments that are at least on first consideration plausible can be made for the conclusion that the Sherman Act prohibits one or more buyers from engaging in conduct they would not have perceived to be profitable *ex ante* had they not believed it would or might free them from each other's competition as buyers, regardless of whether that conduct imposes a net equivalent-dollar loss on their and their product rivals' customers. (In the end, I am not convinced by this counterargument because the exercise of buyer power to combat seller power over price that is the only other Pareto imperfection in the economy in question [in an otherwise-Pareto-perfect economy] would increase economic efficiency [if any associated allocative transaction costs could be ignored]—*i.e.*, would yield profits for the perpetrator[s] that would not be critically distorted on the assumptions that the Sherman Act's test of illegality incorporates.)

The sixth and final general error that U.S courts historically made and continue to make to some extent when applying the Sherman Act and that U.S. antitrust-enforcement agencies historically made but have not made for some time when applying the Sherman Act is to assume that the Sherman Act is directed at *intra-brand* competition as well as *inter-brand* competition. The expression "inter-brand competition" refers to the competition that producers of rival products wage against each other. The expression "*intra-brand* competition" refers to the competition that rival distributors of a given brand of product (*i.e.*, of a given product) wage against each other. As Chap. 14 explains, for a variety of reasons, producers of a given brand will often find it profitable to reduce the competition that independent distributors of their product (their brand) wage against each other. More specifically, the producer of a given brand may find it profitable to reduce intra-brand competition between its distributors because such intra-brand competition can reduce the producer's profits *inter alia*

(1) by reducing the price that its brand's ultimate consumers pay for its product below the price that they would have been willing to pay for it had they not been able to buy it more cheaply (or rendering it profitable for the producer to make otherwise-unprofitable changes to prevent this outcome—*e.g.*, to reduce its lump-sum [franchise fees] to its distributors and increase the per-unit price it charges them for its product or to integrate forward into distribution),
(2) by reducing the price the distributors charge for its product and thereby the buyers' perception of the physical quality of its product (when the buyers assume that physical quality and price are positively correlated) or the actual value of the product to buyers (when price is a quality-attribute) or rendering it profitable for the producer to make the otherwise-unprofitable changes delineated at the end of the first item in this list to prevent the preceding outcomes,
(3) by deterring its distributors from making advertising or in-store display-space decisions that would be in the joint interest of the producer and all its distributors by creating a situation in which some of the buyers that are induced to purchase its product by the distributor advertisement or in-store display purchase it from another distributor (say, from a discount house that offers lower prices but supplies the producer with no such advertising or less-good in-store display-space), and
(4) by deterring its distributors from providing pre-sales advise or post-sales warranty-service that would be in the collective interest of the producer and all its distributors, once more by increasing the probability that the buyer that receives the benefit of such advice/service will purchase the good from another distributor (say, once more, from a discount house that offers no such advice or service).

To prevent these sorts of losses, sellers that choose to continue to distribute their goods through independent resellers try to eliminate the intra-brand competition that generates them by contractually obligating the reseller to charge a particular resale price, by controlling the number of independent distributors it uses and their geographic locations, by controlling the geographic territories within which each of its independent distributors can make sales, and by controlling the types of buyers to which its individual distributors can make sales or the named particular buyers to which its independent distributors can make sales.

There are both "ends" and "means" reasons why these efforts of producers to decrease intra-brand competition should not be deemed to violate the Sherman Act—why acts committed with the specific intent to decrease intra-brand competition do not violate the Sherman Act. The "ends" reason is that this conclusion is warranted by the fact that the Sherman Act (indeed, U.S. antitrust law in general) reflects an assumption that it is desirable to allow economic actors that have obtained competitive advantages lawfully to convert as much of these competitive advantages into seller surplus (the difference between total revenue and total variable costs) as they can without violating the Sherman Act's "specific inter-brand anticompetitive intent" test of illegality. That assumption itself reflects two further premises:

(1) it is economically efficient and on that account desirable to allow firms to cash in on their legitimately-obtained competitive advantages because the legitimate choices that yield competitive advantages are economically efficient and desirable and one should therefore not deflate the incentives of actors to make such choices by prohibiting them from making as much profits as they can from the competitive advantages the choices yield them (in ways that do not manifest specific inter-brand anticompetitive intent); and
(2) it is normally morally desirable in itself to allow people to obtain benefits equal to their allocative product and letting them cash in on the competitive advantages their choices yielded allows them to do so.

Although I do not agree with either of these assumptions, I do think that courts are legally obligated to take them into account when interpreting statutes that are based on them.

The "means" reason why the Sherman Act should not be interpreted to prohibit conduct that is specifically intended to reduce intra-brand competition is that efforts to prevent such conduct will usually not end up benefitting relevant consumers because such efforts will tend to lead the producers in question (1) to integrate forward into distribution and place hierarchical controls on its distributive employees that are substantively similar to the contractual controls it was prohibited from placing on its former independent distributors, (2) to lower its lump-sum fees to its distributors and raise the per-unit prices it charges them to induce them to charge (something like) the resale prices it would otherwise have contractually obligated them to charge, (3) to acquiesce in the elimination of the pre-sales advice (which is of value to the consumers), and (4) to provide the warranty-service itself at presumably a higher cost (which will be passed on to buyers), to incur the higher cost of compensating its dealers for providing such service (which will also be passed on to buyers), or to stop providing buyers with warranties (on whose purchase the buyers presumably originally obtained some surplus).

In any event, as Section 3A(2) of Chap. 14 describes, for many years, the U.S. courts (1) concluded that any attempt by a producer to reduce intra-brand competition through vertical price restraints or vertical territorial restraints or vertical-customer-allocation clauses was *per se* illegal under the Sherman Act, (2) then held that, although vertical price restraints were *per se* illegal, the legality of vertical territorial restraints and customer-allocation clauses should be analyzed through a Rule-of-Reason analysis in which the decrease in intra-brand competition that the exemplar of these practices under scrutiny would generate would somehow be balanced against any tendency it had to increase inter-brand competition, and (3) most recently have held that the Sherman Act legality of vertical price restraints as well as that of vertical territorial restraints and vertical-customer-allocation clauses should be assessed through such a Rule-of-Reason analysis. For many years, the U.S. antitrust-enforcement agencies also thought that all intra-brand-competition-reducing vertical restraints were *per se* illegal, but for the last 40 years or so, under the influence of the economic analysis of these practices outlined above, they seem to have concluded that the Sherman Act does not prohibit producers from decreasing intra-brand competition and that, consequently, all vertical restraints that are not designed to facilitate either a producer cartel or a reseller cartel are lawful under the Sherman Act.

B. The Clayton Antitrust Act

(1) The Clayton Act as Correctly Interpreted

(A) The Actor-Coverage of the Clayton Act

Like the Sherman Act, the Clayton Act covers all categories of economic actors—firms, trade associations, and individuals.

(B) The Conduct-Coverage of the Clayton Act

Unlike the Sherman Act, which with two or three minor exceptions covers all categories of business conduct, the Clayton Act covers only a limited subset of business conduct. The Clayton Act has three relevant sections. Section 2 (in its current version, the Robinson–Patman Act[68]) covers price discrimination in the non-economist sense in which the statute defines this concept.[69] Section 3 covers decisions by "any person...to lease or make a sale of goods..., or fix a price charged therefore, or discount from, or rebate upon, such price, on the condition, agreement, or understanding that the lessee or purchaser thereof shall not use or deal in the goods...of a competitor or competitors of the lessor or seller." In terms of standard types of conduct, Section 3 covers not only exclusive dealerships but also contracts that include full-requirements clauses, including tying agreements in which a seller of one commodity obligates a buyer that purchases that commodity

[68] 15 U.S.C. § 13 (1936). The Robinson–Patman Act is an amendment to Section 2 of the Clayton Act.

[69] Two related points should be noted. First, a language point. The Robinson–Patman Act and U.S. lawyers define price discrimination to be the act of charging different prices for "commodities of like grade and quality" and then speak of cost-justified price discrimination (which the Act permits) when the price-differences in question are cost-justified. In the language of economics, the concept of "cost-justified price discrimination" is an oxymoron: if price-differences are cost-justified, there is no price discrimination. Second, the Robinson–Patman Act's reference to "commodities" has caused it to be interpreted not to cover price discrimination on services, and Clayton Act Section 3's reference to "goods" has caused it to be interpreted not to cover otherwise-covered arrangements involving services, land, or inputs. The text will largely ignore these (to my mind, contestable if not wrong) limitations of coverage.

from it to purchase from the seller as well the buyer's full requirements of the second commodity when the seller actually produces and/or meaningfully distributes the second commodity (as opposed to paying someone else to supply the buyer with the second commodity) and reciprocal-trading agreements in which a buyer of one commodity obligates the seller of that commodity to purchase from it the latter's full requirements of a product that the former party actually produces and/or meaningfully distributes. The post-1950 version of Section 7 covers all mergers and acquisitions—*i.e.*, decisions to "acquire...the whole or any part of the stock or other share capital assets of another" entity. Thus, the Clayton Act covers price discrimination as it defines the concept, exclusive dealerships, full-requirements contracts, mergers, and acquisitions.

(C) The Tests of Illegality That the Clayton Act Promulgates

All three relevant sections of the Clayton Act prohibit the conduct they cover when its "effect...may be substantially to lessen competition or tend to create a monopoly" either "in any line of commerce" or "in any line of commerce in any section of the country." For both expositional and, more importantly, policy reasons, I wish that my account of the Clayton Act's abstract test of illegality could start and finish with the preceding sentence. Unfortunately, for reasons that Section 3A1(B) of Chap. 14 explains, it cannot. Although the original 1914 Clayton Act promulgated only the "lessening competition" test of illegality just delineated, the 1936 Robinson–Patman Act revision of Section 2 of the 1914 Clayton Act added to the 1914 Clayton Act's section on "price discrimination" a provision—Section 2(f)—that adds a second test that governs the legality of a subset of "price discrimination" acts—namely, that makes it illegal for a buyer "knowingly to induce or receive a discrimination in price" in the Clayton Act's sense of that concept either when its doing so lessens competition or when its doing so injures one or more of its rivals. I hasten to add that, for reasons that Section 3A(1)(B) of Chap. 14 explains, I doubt that the addition of this second, alternative "injury to competitor" test of illegality has any practical importance: a seller will rarely if ever grant price-concessions to one or more potential customers when its doing so will injure the favored buyer's rivals. To see why, note that (1) a seller will find it profitable to injure one or more of a potential customer's rivals by charging them discriminatorily-high prices only if it would be more organizationally proficient for it to reduce the number of firms authorized to distribute its product to a geographically-defined or a non-geographically-defined set of further-downstream buyers or to reduce the number of final-product producers that use its product as an input to produce goods for a geographically-defined or non-geographically-defined set of further-downstream buyers and (2) in such situations, the seller will find it more practicable and profitable to achieve this result by refusing to deal with the potential customers whose use of its product the seller wants to prevent and, in many cases, giving the potential users of its product that it wants to use its product the exclusive right to resell it or the downstream product it is used to produce to a geographically-defined or non-geographically-defined set of further-downstream buyers (exclusive dealerships that do not violate U.S. antitrust law and are now [in essence] acknowledged to be lawful under U.S. antitrust law). In any event, since I do not think that Section 2(f) of the current Clayton Act or the second, injury-to-buyer-rival test of illegality it promulgates have any practical significance, I will almost always ignore this second test of Clayton Act illegality in the pages that follow (although occasionally, as a reminder, I will refer to the Clayton Act's "lessening competition" test of illegality as its "standard" test of illegality).

How as a matter of law should the Clayton Act's "lessen competition or tend to create a monopoly" test of illegality be interpreted? In my judgment, for Clayton Act purposes, a covered act or practice should be said to have lessened competition or to have tended to create a monopoly if (1) it inflicted a net (on-balance) equivalent-dollar loss on the customers of the perpetrator(s) and the customers of the perpetrator's or perpetrators' rivals and (2) it generated this impact by reducing the absolute attractiveness of the best offer the buyers in question respectively received from any inferior supplier. The preceding sentence's formulation of the Clayton Act's test of *prima facie* illegality (see below) contains two conditions rather than one compound condition. It does so for two reasons. First, I want to highlight the fact that, even if covered conduct does inflict net-equivalent-dollar losses on Clayton-Act-relevant buyers by reducing the absolute attractiveness of the best offer they respectively receive from any inferior supplier (or would inflict a net loss on such buyers if it did not generate any economic efficiencies), it will not violate the Clayton Act's test of *prima facie* illegality if it does not inflict a net-equivalent-dollar loss on those buyers all things considered—*e.g.*, if the equivalent-dollar gains it confers on them by generating relevant economic efficiencies exceed the equivalent-dollar losses it imposes on them or would otherwise impose on them by reducing the absolute attractiveness of the best offer they respectively receive from any interior supplier. Second, I have used the two-condition formulation rather than the one-compound-condition formulation to highlight the difference between the formal structure of the Clayton Act's test of *prima facie* illegality and the effect branch of the test of *prima facie* illegality promulgated by now-Article 101 of the E.U. Treaty. The effect branch of now-Article 101's test of illegality has two components:

(1) a test of *prima facie* illegality—promulgated by now-Article 101(1)—that declares *prima facie* illegal all covered conduct that would inflict a net-equivalent-monetary loss on Clayton-Act-relevant buyers by reducing the absolute attractiveness of the best offer they respectively received from any inferior supplier if their best-placed supplier took advantage of this impact even if it does not inflict a net-equivalent-monetary loss on such buyers, all things considered, because (perhaps to enable themselves to obtain a now-Article 101(3) exemption) the perpetrator decides/perpetrators decide not to take advantage or full advantage of the deterioration in the best offer against which it/they must compete and/or because the relevant buyers secure equivalent-dollar gains from the economic efficiencies the conduct in question generates, and

(2) a defence—created by now-Article 101(3)—that exempts from now-Article 101(1) conduct that yields specified types of economic efficiencies, satisfies various other conditions, and allows relevant consumers a "fair share of the benefit" the conduct generates for its perpetrator(s) and the relevant consumers "combined"—*i.e.*, for the set of actors that consists exclusively of the perpetrator(s) and the relevant buyers.

Thus, the effect branch of now-Article 101's test of *prima facie* illegality has no counterpart to the component of the Clayton Act's test of *prima facie* illegality that states that, to be *prima facie* illegal, conduct must impose a net-equivalent-monetary loss on relevant buyers, all things considered. Even if, contrary to fact, now-Article 101(3) stated that, to be eligible for a now-Article 101(3) exemption, conduct must not impose an equivalent-monetary loss on relevant buyers, this difference between the Clayton Act and the effect branch of now-Article 101's test of illegality would be important because the plaintiff bears the burden of proof on the loss issue when the matter under consideration is whether the conduct violates the Clayton Act's test of *prima facie* illegality whereas the defendant bears the burden of proof on the "net-equivalent-monetary impact on relevant buyers" issue when the matter under consideration is whether the conduct is eligible for a now-Article 101(3) exemption. As we shall see, Article 101's overall test of illegality also diverges from the Clayton Act's overall test of illegality in other ways—*inter alia*, as just indicated, in that the now-Article 101's overall test of illegality (1) makes salient whether relevant buyers obtain a fair share of the resulting benefit whereas the Clayton Act's overall test of illegality makes salient whether relevant buyers have suffered a net-equivalent-monetary loss and (2) does not include the organizational-economic-efficiency defense that I think it correct as a matter of U.S. law to read into the Clayton Act's overall test of illegality.

I want to emphasize another critical substantive feature of my interpretation of the Clayton Act's test of *prima facie* illegality. On that interpretation, the Clayton Act would not be read to prohibit (1) a merger that inflicted a net-equivalent-dollar loss on relevant buyers if it did so by creating a merged firm that was able to discover and take advantage of the fact that the profit-maximizing price for a merger-partner product was higher than the merger partner thought and would have continued to think it was or (2) a full-requirements tie-on or reciprocity agreement that enabled a seller-employer to profit by removing buyer surplus that the seller in question could not otherwise have profited from removing and would not therefore have removed. I hasten to add that this reading is favored by the fact that U.S. industrial policy as a whole as well as the Sherman Act do not prohibit firms from maximizing the profits they can make from a given demand/marginal-cost position even when their efforts to do so inflict equivalent-dollar losses on (reduce the buyer surplus realized by) the actor's customers (so long as those efforts do not entail monopolization as that concept has been defined in Chap. 3). Indeed, U.S. intellectual-property (IP) law is designed to put protected discoverers in a position to profit in this way. Admittedly, U.S. industrial policy does include public-utility rate-of-return regulation and maximum-price regulations that limit the ability of covered firms with presumptively-legitimate competitive advantages to profit from them in ways that would not violate the Sherman Act. But these policies are not part of U.S. competition law: U.S. antitrust law contains no equivalent to the E.U. prohibition of "exploitative abuses" that will be discussed in Sect. 2 of this chapter.

Four additional points need to be made about the Clayton Act's standard test of *prima facie* (see below) illegality. The first three relate to the fact that the Act's relevant provisions prohibit the types of conduct they respectively cover if their "effect. . .*may be substantially* to lessen competition, or tend to create a monopoly" either "*in any line of commerce*" or "*in any line of commerce in any section of the country*" (emphasis added in each case).

The first additional point relates to the words "may be." This language might be read to imply that a private plaintiff or the State need not demonstrate that a defendant's covered conduct was more likely than not to lessen (or to have lessened) competition to win its Clayton Act case—*i.e.*, to imply that the Clayton Act makes covered conduct illegal if the plaintiff can demonstrate that the probability that the conduct will lessen competition exceeds some number that is not higher than 50 %. If this reading were correct, the Clayton Act test would differ from the Sherman Act test on this account since in a Sherman-Act-based civil suit the plaintiff would clearly have to establish more than a 50 % probability that the defendant violated the Sherman Act test of illegality and in a Sherman Act criminal suit the State would clearly have to establish the defendant's guilt beyond a reasonable doubt. However, although such a reading of the Clayton Act's "may be" language is certainly semantically plausible, in practice, courts appear to require private plaintiffs or the State to establish more than a 50 % probability that competition will be or was lessened.

The second additional point relates to the word "substantially." This language might be read to imply that the Clayton Act does not prohibit covered conduct that is requisitely likely to lessen or to have lessened competition if the anticipated (observed) lessening of competition is (was) not substantial. Once more, however, although such a reading is semantically plausible (and would bring the Clayton Act into line with the EC's decision to find a violation of what is now Article 101 of the 2009 Treaty of Lisbon only when covered conduct prevents, restricts, or distorts competition to a more than *de minimis* extent), I know of no Clayton Act case in which a defendant was exonerated because the lessening of competition its conduct was predicted to generate or was observed to have generated was not substantial.

The third additional point relates to the fact that the Clayton Act's various provisions prohibit conduct that is requisitely likely to lessen or to have lessened competition either "in any line of commerce" or "in any line of commerce in any section of the country." This language might be read to have two implications that would clearly be unfortunate as a matter of policy and that I think would not be correct as a matter of law to read it to have. I must admit that a literal reading of those words would yield the first implication: read literally, the language does imply that, even if Clayton-Act-covered conduct is not requisitely likely "to lessen competition or to have lessened competition on balance" in the sense in which I think these expressions should be operationalized in the Clayton Act context in that it does not impose a net-equivalent-dollar loss on Clayton-Act-relevant buyers by reducing the absolute attractiveness of the best offer they respectively receive from any inferior supplier, it would violate the Clayton Act if it were requisitely likely to impose such a loss on such buyers in such a way in one or more product or geographic markets (while being sufficiently likely to have conferred sufficient equivalent-dollar gains on Clayton-Act-relevant buyers in other affected markets not to be requisitely likely to lessen competition or to have lessened competition on balance). Because this literal reading would disserve the proximate goal that the Clayton Act was designed to further and U.S. statutory-interpretation practice deems that fact highly relevant, I think that in the United States such a literal reading would be incorrect as a matter of law. The second implication is more indirect. Some courts, antitrust-enforcement-agency officials, and commentators believe that the statute's "line of commerce" and "section of the country" language—*i.e.*, its invocation of "product markets" and "geographic markets"—implies that U.S. courts and antitrust-enforcement agencies must take a market-oriented approach to the analysis of the Clayton Act illegality of Clayton-Act-covered conduct. Because I believe that market definitions are inherently arbitrary not just at their periphery but comprehensively (see Chaps. 6 and 7) and that market-oriented approaches to antitrust-law analysis inevitably achieve the remarkable double of increasing cost while decreasing accuracy (see Chaps. 10–15), I think that, from a policy perspective, such an interpretation would be highly undesirable. I also do not think that the language in question warrants this interpretation: it is at least as possible to read it to indicate that (1) the Clayton Act forbids covered conduct only if it is requisitely likely to impose more than a *de minimis* net-equivalent-dollar loss on Clayton-Act-relevant buyers in the proscribed way (a reading that I think is incorrect as a matter of law and not entirely attractive from a policy perspective) or (2) the calculation of whether Clayton-Act-covered conduct decreases competition in the Clayton Act sense does not take account of the fact that the resources that the conduct in question prevents being used in a way that benefits Clayton-Act-relevant buyers (*e.g.*, to increase the unit output of the perpetrator[s] and/or its [their] product rivals or to increase the amount of QV investment in the perpetrator's or perpetrators' area of product-space) will be used instead in a way that will increase competition (benefit buyers) in another area of product-space (*e.g.*, to increase the unit output of one or more of the perpetrator's or perpetrators' input rivals or to increase QV investment in an area of product-space in which an input rival of the perpetrator[s] operates)—a conclusion that I think is correct as a matter of law.

The fourth and final additional point that needs to be made about the Clayton Act's standard test of illegality relates to the baseline that should be used to measure competitive impact in the Clayton Act context. Two such baselines need to be distinguished:

(1) a "do-nothing" baseline under which the competitive impact of covered conduct is measured by comparing the state of the world the conduct generates with the state of the world that would have resulted had the perpetrator(s) done nothing and

(2) a "most-procompetitive choice the perpetrator(s) could have made" baseline under which the competitive impact of covered conduct is measured by comparing the state of the world the conduct generates with the state of the world that would have resulted had the perpetrator(s) made the most-procompetitive choice(s) it or they would have found more profitable than doing nothing.

I have no doubt that the Clayton Act should be interpreted to employ a do-nothing baseline. Although, as we shall see, U.S. antitrust officials have sometimes used the "most-procompetitive choice that would have been more profitable than doing nothing" baseline in particular sorts of cases, their choice of this latter baseline is deviant. At the most general level, the courts and their company have always understood that U.S. antitrust law does not require firms to make the most-procompetitive move that would be more profitable than doing nothing. For example, it has never even occurred to anyone that a horizontal merger that (say) increased competition relative to the *status quo ante* would be illegal if the merger partners could have executed other mergers that would have been more profitable than not merging at all that would have been more procompetitive than the merger they actually executed. The next subsection describes three types of cases in which U.S. officials have rejected the correct, do-nothing baseline in favor of "the most-procompetitive choice the perpetrator(s) would have found more profitable than doing nothing" baseline and explains why in those cases this shift in baseline can critically affect the legal outcome.

(D) The Defenses That the Clayton Act Should as a Matter of Law Be Interpreted to Recognize

I turn finally to the defenses that I believe that, properly interpreted, the Clayton Act would be deemed to make available to defendants. In my judgment, there are four such defenses. I have already made reference to the first two, which are spelled out in the statute itself: in "price discrimination" cases, defendants can rebut a *prima facie* case that has been made out against them by demonstrating that the relevant price-difference was cost-justified or that the lower price or superior terms of other sorts offered to the favored buyer were offered "in good faith to meet an equally low price of a competitor, or the services or facilities furnished by a competitor."

The third defense—which is recognized by the 1992 Horizontal Merger Guidelines and by contemporary courts but which, as Chap. 12 explains, was not recognized by U.S. courts in the 1960s and earlier—is a general economic-efficiency defense. Once the government has established a *prima facie* case by proving that—if the conduct in question did not generate any relevant efficiencies—it would (be sufficiently likely to) inflict a (sufficiently-substantial) net-equivalent-dollar loss on Clayton-Act-relevant buyers by reducing the absolute attractiveness of the best offers they respectively received from any inferior supplier, the defendants must be given the opportunity to exonerate themselves by demonstrating that the efficiencies the conduct would generate were sufficiently likely to confer a sufficient equivalent-dollar gain on Clayton-Act-relevant buyers to render it lawful under the Act by preventing the merger from imposing a net-equivalent-dollar loss on Clayton-Act-relevant buyers.

The fourth defense that I believe the Clayton Act should be interpreted to recognize is an organizational-economic-efficiency defense. I should acknowledge at the outset that there is no textual basis in the statute for this defense, which I think should be available to defendants in somewhat-different forms in Section 3 and Section 7 cases. I will first delineate these defenses and then explain why I think they should be read into the statute.

I will start with the Section 3 defense. In my judgment, in Section 3 cases, in order to establish its *prima facie* case, the government or a private plaintiff should be required to demonstrate not (1) that an individual defendant's covered use of exclusive dealerships or full-requirements contractual clauses lessens competition but (2) that a general rule allowing the defendant and all its product rivals to engage in such behavior would lessen competition because (A) the defendant is a well-established firm, (B) the conduct in question was more profitable for the defendant than for its marginal and potential competitors, and (C) the rule allowing all such firms to engage in the relevant conduct would lessen competition on that account in that it would cause one or more marginal competitors to exit (when they would not be replaced by entities that would prevent their exit from reducing competition) and/or would deter the entry of a potential competitor (the expansion of an established rival) whose entry or threat of entry (expansion) would otherwise have increased competition. In my judgment, the contrary conclusion is incorrect as a matter of law because it is inconsistent with the level-playing-field norm of U.S. antitrust law, which implies that firms are entitled to compete on the merits—*i.e.*, because it would imply that the Clayton Act requires courts (1) to prohibit a well-established firm from organizing its business proficiently by engaging in one of the types of conduct that Act covers when such a prohibition would increase competition by helping its marginal competitors survive, its potential competitors to enter, and its established rivals to expand by worsening the array of competitive positions of the well-established firm and concomitantly improving its marginal competitors' competitive-position arrays and its potential competitors' and potential expanders' prospective competitive-position arrays while (2) allowing marginal competitors, potential competitors, and some potential expanders to engage in the conduct in question to help them survive, enter, and expand. To repeat: in my judgment, such pari-mutuel handicapping would be incorrect as a matter of law because it would be inconsistent with the basic norms of U.S. antitrust policy. In any event, in cases in which the government or a private plaintiff can establish a proper *prima facie* Section 3 case against a defendant, I believe that the defendant should be allowed to exonerate itself by demonstrating that the behavior in question increased its profits by increasing its economic efficiency and that, to the extent that the rule in question would worsen the firm's actual and potential competitors' competitive positions, it would do so by increasing its economic efficiency relative to theirs. In brief, I would read this defense into the Clayton Act because doing so makes the Act consistent with the rest of U.S. industrial policy, whose IP law protects discoverers to encourage economically-efficient R&D[70] and allows firms to profit more generally from the competitive advantages their skill, foresight, and industry created.

In my judgment, in the United States, it would also be correct as a matter of law to read a similar organizational-economic-efficiency defense into Section 7 of the Clayton Act. To establish this defense, the defendant would have to prove that its conduct would not have inflicted an on-balance equivalent-dollar loss on its customers and the customers of its product rivals by reducing the absolute attractiveness of the best offers these buyers respectively received from any inferior supplier had it not generated organizational economic efficiencies that harmed the relevant buyers by causing a marginal competitor to exit and/or by raising critically the barriers faced by an otherwise-effective potential entrant or potential expander by worsening the competitive-position array of the marginal competitor and/or the prospective competitive-position array of the potential entrant or expander by improving the defendant's competitive-position array.

(2) Four Errors That Officials and Scholars Have Made When Interpreting the Clayton Act

The first error that courts, academic lawyers, and economists have made when interpreting the Clayton Act relates to the operational definition they have given to its concept "lessen competition." I have already defined how I think this expression should be defined in the Clayton Act context. The operationalizations that others have proposed fail on two accounts. The first is that they focus exclusively on price competition—*i.e.*, ignore QV-investment competition and, relatedly, the combination of price and QV-investment competition. The second is that the various operational definitions they have given to "lessen price competition," which they think are interchangeable in the sense of yielding the same legal conclusions, are incompletely specified, would not yield the same legal conclusions in significant numbers of cases, and are insensitive to the normative assumptions about firm conduct that underlie the Clayton Act (and the Sherman Act).

I will first list the operationalizations in question and then discuss their deficiencies. At various times, courts and academic commentators have proposed that conduct covered by the Clayton Act should be said to have lessened competition if it reduced the unit output of its perpetrator(s), increased its or their price,

[70] For this purpose, the fact that we almost certainly devote too many resources to product R&D from the perspective of economic efficiency is irrelevant. (For an explanation of why we devote too many resources to product R&D from the perspective of economic efficiency, see Richard S. Markovits, *On the Economic Efficiency of Using Law to Increase Research and Development: A Critique of Various Tax, Antitrust, Intellectual Property, and Tort Law Rules and Policy Proposals*, 39 HARV. J. ON LEG. 63 (2002).) The crucial point is that U.S. legislators have protected discoveries at least in part because they believed that they would increase economic efficiency by doing so.

increased its or their P–MC gap, increased its or their (P–MC)/P ratio (which is the so-called Lerner measure of monopoly), imposed a net-equivalent-dollar loss on relevant buyers in any way, or increased seller profits.

I will begin by discussing the poor specification of some of these tests. The unit-output operationalization is ill-specified because those that propose it have not indicated how it would apply to conduct that (1) increases the output of one or more products and decreases the output of one or more other products or (2) changes the attributes of the products to which it relates (or attributes of various services supplied together with "the products" in question). The P, P–MC, and (P–MC)/P operationalizations are ill-specified in that their proponents have not indicated how they would be applied to conduct that affects the price or the marginal cost of more than one product, to conduct that changes the attributes of the product(s) that the perpetrator(s) supply, or to situations in which the relevant seller charges lump-sum fees as well as per-unit prices and/or varies its per-unit prices from unit to unit or buyer to buyer.

Regardless of how these specification-gaps are remedied, the operationalizations in question would at least sometimes produce different legal conclusions. Thus, some acts of price discrimination that (1) increase the seller's average per-unit price, the differences between its average per-unit price and its marginal cost, or its (P–MC)/P ratio where P stands for average per-unit price and (2) inflict an on-balance equivalent-dollar loss on the discriminator's customers by reducing their buyer surplus will (3) increase or at least not decrease the discriminator's unit output. Similarly, some decisions to use tying or reciprocal-trading agreements that contain full-requirements clauses will increase the seller's average-lump-sum-fee *plus* per-unit price, related P–MC gap, and related (P–MC)/P ratio while increasing its unit output, and some will increase all these figures but not inflict an equivalent-dollar loss on the relevant buyers. And again, some conduct that reduces its perpetrator's marginal costs may reduce the perpetrator's price, increase its output, and benefit its customers while increasing its P–MC gap and (P–MC)/P ratio. Indeed, some conduct that reduces its perpetrator's marginal cost and price could reduce its P–MC gap while increasing its (P–MC)/P ratio. And some covered conduct that increases its perpetrator's profits may simultaneously reduce its perpetrator's price, P–MC gap, and (P–MC)/P ratio, increase its perpetrator's unit output, and benefit its perpetrator's customers. I could go on, but this should suffice to establish the legal-outcome inconsistency of the various proposed operationalizations of "lessening competition."

Finally, these operationalizations make no normative or functional sense and are clearly insensitive to the business-conduct norms that underlie U.S. antitrust law. Thus, the unit-output test would make the legality of price discrimination depend on the fortuity of whether the discrimination increased or decreased the discriminator's unit output; the buyer-equivalent-dollar-loss operationalization is insensitive to the premise of U.S. industrial policy that firms are entitled to profit from the competitive advantages they legitimately secured; the various price-related operationalizations are equally insensitive to this normative premise; and the increased-seller-profits operationalization (which has been proposed only in relation to vertical practices) is insensitive both to this normative premise and to the U.S. belief that it is desirable (because economically efficient) to reward economic actors for increasing the efficiency of their operations.

The second mistake that I think has been made in interpreting the Clayton Act relates to its "in any line of commerce" or "in any line of commerce in any section of the country" language. As I have already indicated, because (1) a literal reading of this language would disserve the proximate goal of the Clayton Act of increasing competition by implying the illegality of covered conduct that would increase competition overall but decrease competition in one product or geographic market and (2) except in a few types of cases, U.S. courts ignore the literal meaning of statutes when that meaning disserves the goals of the statute, I think that such a literal reading would be incorrect as a matter of law in the United States. Admittedly, in at least one case, the Supreme Court has stated in dicta that it will be bound by the literal meaning of these words.[71] However, although I acknowledge the contestability of my conclusion, I do think that this literal interpretation is incorrect as a matter of law.

The third error I think U.S. courts, the Department of Justice, and the Federal Trade Commission make when interpreting the Clayton Act relates to the competitive-impact-measurement-baseline issue. Although, in most situations, U.S. officials adopt what I take to be the correct do-nothing baseline, in at least three sorts of cases, they have used or proposed the use of the "most-procompetitive choice the defendant could have made that was more profitable than doing nothing" baseline. The first set of such cases are failing-company cases. The Supreme Court[72] and subsequently the Department of Justice and FTC in their Horizontal Merger Guidelines[73] have stated that, in order to establish a failing-company defense, a failing company that wishes to engage in a merger that would not decrease competition relative to the situation that would prevail if it did nothing must demonstrate that it (1) made a reasonable effort to identify a merger or acquisition whose execution would have been more procompetitive as well as more profitable for it than doing nothing and (2) failed to do so. The second type of such cases are cases involving conglomerate geographic-diversification mergers. Several lower courts seem to assume and the U.S. Supreme Court has intimated[74] that the Clayton Act prohibits

---

[71] The case is Philadelphia National Bank v. United States, 374 U.S. 321 (1963). I describe this position as dicta because the court did not find that the merger involved in the case in question would increase competition in any market: it just noted the possibility that it might.

[72] See Citizen Publishing Co. v. United States, 394 U.S. 131, 136–39 (1969).

[73] See 1992 Horizontal Merger Guidelines at Section 5 and 2010 Horizontal Merger Guidelines at Section 11.

[74] For a relevant lower-court opinion, see United States v. Falstaff Brewing Corp., 332 F. Supp. 970, 972 (1971). In United States v. Falstaff Brewing Corp., 410 U.S. 526, 537–38 (1973), the Supreme Court acknowledged that "[t]here are traces of this view [*i.e.*, that the toe-hold merger doctrine is correct as a matter of law] in our cases, citing Ford Motor Co. v. United States, 405 U.S. 562, 567 (majority opinion) and 587 (Burger, C.J. concurring in part and dissenting in part) (1972), FTC v. Proctor & Gamble, 386 U.S. 568, 580 (majority opinion) and 586 (Harlan, J., concurring) (1976), and United States v. Penn-Olin Chemical Co., 378 U.S. 158, 173 (1964). However, the Court then proceeded to state that it "has not squarely faced the question, for no other reason than because there has been no necessity to consider it" (footnote omitted), denying (at note 14) that "certain language in the Court's opinion in United States v. Continental Can Co., 378 U.S. 441, 464 (1976)" warrants a "contrary" conclusion.

(1) mergers of this type with any size incumbent that would not decrease competition relative to the *status quo ante* unless the diversifying firm can show that it would not have found it profitable to enter the new market on its own (a conclusion that manifests *inter alia* the courts' dubious assumption that such an entry would always be more procompetitive than an entry effectuated through a geographical-diversification merger) and (2) mergers of this type with a medium or large incumbent unless it can show that it had made a reasonable effort to identify a small incumbent with which it could execute a merger or acquisition that would be more profitable than not entering and failed to do so (a conclusion that manifests *inter alia* the courts' dubious assumption that a toehold merger [with a small incumbent] will always or generally be more procompetitive than a merger with a larger incumbent). The third type of such cases are joint-venture cases in which the parents of the joint venture are potential entrants into the market into which their joint venture entered. In one case in which the joint venture clearly would have caused competition to be more intense in the market it entered than it would have been had the joint venture not been formed and neither parent entered on its own, the Supreme Court found the joint venture illegal on the ground that competition would have been increased even more if one of the parents had entered the market in question and the other parent continued to be a perceived potential entrant to that market.[75]

The fourth and most general error that has been made when interpreting the Clayton Act has been made both by the U.S. courts and by U.S.-antitrust-law scholars. Courts and scholars repeatedly claim that, with one possible general exception, the Sherman Act and the Clayton Act promulgate the same test of illegality. (The exception is for current purposes inconsequential: it is sometimes said that the probability of violation that plaintiffs must establish to prevail in Clayton Act cases is lower than the probability of violation that plaintiffs must establish to prevail in Sherman Act cases.) Obviously, I reject the contention that the Sherman and Clayton Acts promulgate the same kind of test of illegality. In my judgment, the texts of these Acts and the history of their passage implies that the Sherman Act promulgates a specific-anticompetitive-intent test of illegality while the Clayton Act promulgates a particular type of competitive-impact test of illegality that is qualified by an organizational-economic-efficiency defense.

I hasten to add that the difference between the Sherman Act's test of illegality and the Clayton Act's test of illegality will sometimes be critical–that conduct that violates the Clayton Act may not violate the Sherman Act and *vice versa* even when both statutes cover the conduct in question. In the one direction, horizontal mergers that violate the Clayton Act may not violate the Sherman Act. To see why, assume a horizontal merger that inflicts a net-equivalent-dollar loss both on the customers of the merger partners by freeing the merger partners from each other's competition

[75] See United States v. Penn-Olin Chemical Co., 378 U.S. 158 (1964). For current purposes, the dubiousness of the relevant Court's belief that the presence of the non-entering parent would increase competition in the market in question even though in fact it would not enter under any foreseeable circumstances is beside the point.

and on the customers of the merger partners' product rivals by increasing (for the preceding reason) the prices the merger partners charge their own customers, hence the amount of price discrimination the merged firm must practice to match any relevant offer its product rivals make to their customers above the amount of price discrimination the merger partners had to practice to match the same offer of their product rivals pre-merger, hence the contextual marginal costs the merged firm would have to incur to match any offer a rival makes above the CMCs its antecedents had to incur to match the offer in question in question—*i.e.*, for reasons unrelated to its yielding organization economic efficiencies. Now, assume, that in addition, the horizontal merger in question yields the merger partners sufficient profits by generating tax benefits, increasing their ability to profit by converting buyer into seller surplus, generating economic efficiencies, and enabling the owner of one of the firms in question to liquidate its assets to be profitable on these accounts alone. On these facts, the merger would violate the Clayton Act but not the Sherman Act. In the other direction, an unsuccessful attempt to drive a rival out by charging the rival's customers discriminatorily-low prices will violate the Sherman Act (because it constitutes an attempt to monopolize) but will not violate the Clayton Act if it has no prospect of reducing competition in any market because it is destined to fail.

I want to close this section by addressing a Clayton-Act-law issue that U.S. courts have failed to address whose correct resolution as a matter of law is contestable. Is it correct as a matter of law to interpret the Clayton Act to be, *inter alia*, a "fence law"? More concretely, as a matter of law, should courts' assessments of the Clayton Act legality (courts' prediction of the competitive impact) of Clayton-Act-covered conduct (most importantly in this context, mergers and acquisitions) take account of their estimates of the likelihood that the conduct would cause its perpetrators and/or its perpetrators' rivals to commit subsequent competition-reducing violations of the Sherman act (in particular, to engage in additional contrived oligopolistic pricing, to create additional retaliation barriers to entry or expansion, and/or to engage in additional predation)? The legal argument against courts' doing so is that it is improper to disadvantage an actor because one thinks it may in the future engage in illegal conduct – that the appropriate government response to any such prospect is to prosecute the perpetrators of such future violations when they occur. The legal argument for the courts' interpreting the Clayton Act to be a "fence law" is that the legislative history of the Clayton Act indicates that it was designed to prevent the development of monopoly (firm economic power?) in its incipiency and that, as we shall see, it is in practice very difficult to detect and prove contrived oligopolistic pricing, contrived QV-investment restrictions, and predation (though, admittedly, this second argument might be characterized as a policy argument rather than as a legal argument). In my contestable judgment, it is legally correct to interpret the Clayton Act to be a fence law. (I should add that this issue does not arise under the Sherman Act. If the defendant's or defendant's *ex ante* perception that their conduct was *ex ante* profitable was critically affected by their belief that it might enable them to commit subsequent Sherman Act violations, that fact would render it violative of the Sherman Act. Indeed, if the defendant or defendants could be shown to have a sufficiently-well-formed intent to engage in the subsequent illegal conduct, its or their engaging in the conduct that would facilitate the subsequent illegal conduct might constitute the kind of concrete step toward committing the subsequent violation that would make the committed conduct illegal on that account even if *ex ante* its perpetrator's or perpetrators' perception of the committed conduct's *ex ante* profitability was not critically affected by a belief that it would increase its or their profits by facilitating subsequent illegal behavior.)

2. The Actor-Coverage of, Conduct-Coverage of, Tests of Illegality Promulgated by, and Defences Recognized by E.C./E.U. Competition Law

The three subsections of this section respectively discuss Article 101 of the 2009 Treaty of Lisbon (formerly Article 81 of the 1957 E.C. Treaty as modified by the 1996 Treaty of Amsterdam), Article 102 of the 2009 Treaty of Lisbon (formerly Article 82 of the 1957 E.C. Treaty as modified by the 1996 Treaty of Amsterdam), and the 2004 E.C. Merger Control Regulation passed by the Council of Ministers.

A. *Article 101 of the 2009 Lisbon Treaty*

The following discussion of Article 101 considers (1) its first paragraph—hereinafter Article 101(1), which articulates the actors whose conduct it covers, the categories of conduct it covers, and the tests of *prima facie* illegality it promulgates; (2) a *de minimis* limitation that relates to the size that firms engaging in Article-101-covered conduct must have for their behavior to be covered by Article 101 (a limitation that in my view has no textual basis but was created by the ECJ and operationalized by the EC); (3) Article 101(3), which declares that Article 101(1) "may. . .be declared inapplicable" to otherwise-covered conduct that satisfies certain conditions; (4) a variety of "block exemptions" granted by the EC under authority delegated to it by the Council of Ministers to secure transaction-cost savings that "exempt" certain categories of conduct or certain categories of conduct engaged in by members of certain industries from Article 101 coverage—in essence, declare them lawful under Article 101, and (5) various discussions by the EC and the E.C./E.U. courts that I believe misinterpret or misapply Article 101.

(1) Article 101(1)

I start by quoting the text of Article 101(1) in full:

> The following shall be prohibited as incompatible with the common market: all agreements between undertakings [an undertaking in European terminology is called a business or firm in the United States], decisions by association of undertakings or concerted practices which

than participation in an anticompetitive agreement: hence, Article 101 does not cover any of the just-listed individual-firm conduct, though it does cover agreements between two or more rivals to secure COMs, erect L barriers, or drive a rival out. More positively, the following types of conduct may properly be classified as a concerted practice or concertation under Article 101(1):

(1) behavior that does not involve the making of any agreement that is designed to increase the prices in a set of across-the-board pricers' HNOP array by inducing its members to announce their prices in the order that will produce this effect and
(2) behavior that does not involve the making of any agreement that is designed to enable rivals to obtain oligopolistic margins naturally in the period in which the behavior took place without creating inter-temporal expectations (the combination of premature price announcements and decisions that increase the cost to sellers of changing their initially-announced prices/decisions—namely, decisions to include their prices in advertisements directed at buyers, to stamp or tag their products with prices, to place the announced price on retail-outlet shelves or induce their independent distributions to do so, to make advance sales at the announced price, *etc*.), and
(3) natural oligopolistic conduct.

Although none of these types of conduct involves an agreement, the fact that each involves consciously-coordinated behavior that is in the individual interests of its separate protagonists and has the object and effect of generating the same consequences as agreements between undertakings that have as their object and effect preventing and restricting competition seems to me to warrant the conclusion that they can rightfully be characterized as concerted practices.

I will now analyze the conduct-coverage implications of the portion of Article 101(1) that begins with the words "in particular." I will start by commenting on the meaning of the expression "in particular" at least in American English in this type of context and the possible implications of that meaning for Article 101(1)'s conduct-coverage. In American English, in this type of context, the words "in particular" indicate that the list that follows these words is comprehensive. If a list is not intended to be comprehensive, in American English, it would be introduced with "for example" or "including." Although I do not know of any instances in which the following language was used for this purpose in a statute or treaty, a list that was not intended to be comprehensive could also (in American English) be introduced with the word "particularly" which, unlike "in particular," means "especially." I believe that "in particular" has the same meaning in this context in British English. If, then, the English version of Article 101(1) were definitive, the fact that its text includes a list of five ways in which conduct can prevent, restrict, or distort competition that is preceded by the words "in particular" would strongly favor the conclusion that Article 101(1) declares covered conduct that has as its object or effect preventing, restricting, or distorting competition *prima facie* illegal only if the conduct is intended to or does have one or more of these effects in one or more of the five listed ways— listed, more specifically, in clauses (a)–(e).

However, at least four arguments disfavor the conclusion that it is correct as a matter of E.C./E.U. law to read the "clauses (a)-(e) list" in Article 101(1) to be comprehensive. Admittedly, two of these arguments—the second and third—depend on my conclusion (see below) that Article 101(1) does cover mergers, acquisitions, and joint ventures (a conclusion the E.C./E.U. antitrust authorities reject in decisions and pronouncements that E.C./E.U. antitrust-law scholars have never questioned). First, the English-language version of the Treaty is no more authoritative than any other E.U.-language version, and the text of Article 101(1) in the E.U.'s other official languages may use, instead of "in particular," language that does not imply that the list it precedes is comprehensive. I have not made a thorough investigation of this issue. However, I can say that, although the Italian and Spanish versions of Article 101(1) use equivalents to "in particular"—use respectively *in particulare* and *en particular* (in the Spanish version, set off by commas), the French and German versions of Article 101(1) use instead of "in particular" words that do not imply that the list that follows is comprehensive—use respectively *notamment*, which may best be translated as "most notably" or "especially," and *insbesondere*, which may best be translated as "especially."

Second, the claim that it is correct as a matter of E.C./E.U. law to conclude that the list in clauses (a)–(e) of Article 101(1) is comprehensive is disfavored by the following inconsistency:

(1) for reasons that I will explain below, the reading of Article 101(1) that deems the "clauses (a)–(e) list" comprehensive implies that only a small percentage of the mergers, acquisitions, and joint ventures that have as an object or effect preventing, restricting, or distorting competition violate Article 101(1)'s test of *prima facie* illegality; and
(2) the text of Article 101(1) that precedes the words "in particular" and the "clauses (a)–(e) list" states that the Article prohibits "*all* agreements between undertakings" (emphasis added) that have as an object or effect preventing, restricting or distorting competition, not just all agreements that have the "clauses (a)–(e)" – listed variants of those objects and effects.

Third, the conclusion that the "clauses (a)–(e) list" is comprehensive is disfavored by the following argument:

(1) on that reading, only a small percentage of the mergers, acquisitions and joint ventures that have as an object or effect preventing, restricting, or distorting competition violate Article 101(1)'s test of *prima facie* illegality;
(2) both the text of the Treaty in general and the history of its promulgation imply that one of its goals was to prevent conduct that imposes equivalent-monetary losses on relevant buyers by preventing, restricting, or distorting competition; and
(3) E.C./E.U. statutory/treaty-interpretation practice (like the practice of continental E.C./E.U. member states [and the practice of the U.S.]) favors interpreting statutes and treaty provisions in the way that promotes the goals of the statute or treaty in question.

And fourth and most contestably, the claim that it is correct as a matter of E.C./E.U. law to conclude that the list in clauses (a)–(e) of Article 101(1) is comprehensive is disfavored by the following argument:

(1) the reading of Article 101(1) that deems the "clauses (a)–(e) list" comprehensive makes Article 101 much less desirable as a matter of policy than the reading that does not deem the "clauses (a)–(e) list" comprehensive; and
(2) at least when the relevant text and "legislative" history is not clear, E.C./E.U. courts (like the courts of the E.C./E.U.'s continental member states [and like the courts of the U.S.]) usually interpret statutes and treaties in the way that makes most policy sense.

For all these reasons, my inclination is to conclude that the list in clauses (a)–(e) of Article 101(1) should not be deemed to be comprehensive. However, I must admit that this conclusion is inconsistent with the conclusion of both E.C./E.U. officials and European E.C./E.U.-competition-law scholars that Article 101(1) does not render *prima facie* illegal mergers, acquisitions, and joint ventures that do have as an object or effect preventing, restricting, or distorting competition—a conclusion that, admittedly, for reasons that I will discuss shortly, would be overbroad even if its implicit assumption that the list in clauses (a)–(e) is comprehensive were correct as a matter of E.C./E.U. law.

I turn now to the specific issue of whether Article 101(1) covers horizontal mergers and acquisitions. If the list in clauses (a)–(e) of Article 101(1) is not deemed to be comprehensive, Article 101(1) clearly would cover mergers, acquisitions, and joint ventures since all such transactions involve agreements between undertakings and the first portion of Article 101(1) states that it covers all agreements between undertakings. Of course, this conclusion leaves unresolved the question whether Article 101(1) would cover mergers, acquisitions, and joint ventures if, contrary to my view, the conclusion that the list in clauses (a)–(e) of Article was comprehensive were correct as a matter of E.C./E.U. law. In order to assess this question, it is necessary to delineate the conditions under which and the various ways in which mergers, acquisitions, and joint ventures can prevent, restrict, or distort competition. Chapters 12–15 analyze these issues in great detail. At this juncture, I will confine my discussion of this issue to the statement that *horizontal* mergers (1) will reduce price competition *inter alia* by freeing the merger partners from each other's competition to the extent that, pre-merger, the merger partners were either the only two best-placed suppliers of given buyers or respectively uniquely best-placed and uniquely second-placed to supply given buyers and (2) may reduce price competition by creating a merged company that engages in more contrived oligopolistic pricing than its antecedents did. I will now use these conclusions to make 8 points or clusters of points that relate to the conditions under which and the frequency with which horizontal mergers that do lessen competition would violate Article 101(1)'s test of prima facie illegality if "the clauses (a)–(e) list" were correctly interpreted as a matter of E.C./E.U. law to be comprehensive:

(1) an agreement to combine undertakings that compete with each other (*i.e.*, a horizontal merger or acquisition) is an agreement that will obviate its participants' agreeing between just themselves to fix purchase or selling prices or any other trading condition; once the participants are combined, they need not agree to abstain from competing against each other on these fronts; if the "clauses (a)–(e) list" were preceded by the work "especially," clauses (a)'s statement that Article 101(1) covers price-fixing and other-term-fixing agreements would imply that it covers horizontal mergers and acquisitions *a fortiori*; admittedly, if a horizontal combination has as one of its objects or effects increasing the extent to which the combined firm relative to its antecedents enters into price-fixing or other-term-fixing agreements with one or more remaining competitors, it might be appropriate to read clause (a) to cover it, but as we shall see horizontal combinations probably tend to create entities that are less prone to engage in such fixes than their antecedents were;

(2) it might be semantically possible but certainly would be peculiar or awkward to say that a horizontal combination "limits or controls" production; admittedly, *inter alia*, horizontal combinations do tend to and are designed to create a combined company that can charge higher prices for the combinants' products than the combinants could charge for them pre-combination (by raising the combined company's HNOPs above the combinants' HNOPs by freeing the combinants from each other's competition for the patronage of buyers they were uniquely equal-best-placed to supply or respectively uniquely best-placed and uniquely second-placed to supply and, derivatively, by enabling the combination to obtain NOMs from buyers from which, pre-combination, the combinants could not obtain OMs naturally) and, except in very unusual circumstances, the resulting increases in prices will tend to reduce the combination's unit outputs below the total unit outputs of the combinants; however, semantically, it still would be peculiar to say that the combination limited or controlled production; undertakings are not normally said to increase price by limiting or controlling production—*i.e.*, by decreasing output: they increase price and a consequence of their doing so is (normally) a decrease in their output;

(3) the expression "limit or control markets" seems redundant to me—*i.e.*, I do not know what it adds to limiting or controlling production (*i.e.*, increasing price), technical development, or investments more generally (including investments that do not generate technical [or commercial] progress). I therefore do not see how a horizontal combination that did not limit or control production, technical developments, or investment could limit or control markets;

(4) although some horizontal combinations may be designed to limit or control technical development—*viz.*, to eliminate a situation in which the combinants would have executed more production-process and/or product research than would have been jointly profitable and/or to reduce the technical research done by remaining rivals by threatening to retaliate against their research efforts or promising to reciprocate to their abstaining from doing such research, I suspect

that the vast majority of horizontal combinations are not designed to and do not limit or control technical development in any way; indeed, I suspect that many such combinations are designed to and do yield outcomes that favor technical progress—*viz.*, are designed to create an entity that can execute given technical research projects more proficiently than the individual combinants could have done and/or to create an entity that will generate more discoveries than the combinants would have done from a given R&D expenditure even though its execution of given R&D projects would not be more proficient than a merger partner's execution of that project would have been because the merged firm's R&D portfolio of some relevant size will be less economically inefficiently duplicative than the combined research portfolio of that size of the merger partners would have been (I should add that this portfolio effect will cause the merger to increase technical progress both directly and by making it profitable for the merged firm to spend more on R&D than would have been profitable for the merger partners to spend);

(5) the points made after (4) are equally applicable to investments that have no prospect of yielding technical (or commercial) discoveries;

(6) although I would understand what was meant by the statement that a horizontal combination enabled its participants to "share markets or sources of supply"—*i.e.*, enabled them not to compete against each other as sellers or buyers, the agreement to combine would more accurately be said to be an agreement (*inter alia*) that would obviate its participants' (now combined into one entity) agreeing to "share markets or sources of supply"; one actor cannot share anything with itself; although some horizontal combinations may have the object or effect of creating an entity that can share markets or supply with remaining rivals to a greater extent than the combinants could do pre-merger, most horizontal combinations do not have such an object or effect—see point (1) in this list;

(7) the vast majority of horizontal combinations are not designed to and do not have the effect of creating an entity that will engage in more price or other-term discrimination than the combinants did; and

(8) the vast majority of horizontal combinations are not designed to and do not have the effect of creating an entity that will include in its contracts with buyers or suppliers more of the "supplementary obligations" with which clause (e) is concerned than the combinants did.

Hence, if it would be correct as a matter of E.C./E.U. law to conclude that list (a)–(e) in Article 101(1) is comprehensive, Article 101(1) would correctly be read as a matter of E.C./E.U. law to cover horizontal combinations if and only if they created a combination that (1) would make more price-fixing, other-term-fixing, or QV-investment-fixing agreements with its remaining rivals than the combinants would have engaged in with each other and their rivals absent the combination and/or (2) would create more market-division agreements or source-of-supply-allocation agreements with its remaining rivals than the combinants would have formed with each other and their rivals absent the combination, or (3) would create an entity that would practice more price discrimination or induce its trading partners to accept more supplementary obligations than its antecedents would have done (despite the fact that horizontal mergers will not tend to have either of these effects). As I have already indicated, I believe that, for two reasons, this result strongly disfavors reading Article 101(1) to make the "clauses (a)–(e) list" comprehensive:

(1) it reveals that the reading is inconsistent with the "all agreements between undertakings" (emphasis added) language of Article 101(1);
(2) it reveals that that reading is inconsistent with the manifest goals of the Treaty; and
(3) at least on the assumption that it would be desirable to prohibit combinations that would not qualify for a now-Article 101(3) exemption if they prevented competition by freeing the combinants from each other's competition but did not create an entity that would enter into more price-and/or-other-conditions-of-sale-fixing agreements and/or more market-division or source-of-supply-allocation agreements than the combinants would otherwise have entered into, it reveals that that reading makes the Treaty far less desirable as a matter of policy.

I want to close this discussion of whether Article 101(1) covers horizontal mergers and acquisitions by making two points about the significance of the first sentence of the preceding paragraph and offering some speculations about why the E.C./E.U. antitrust authorities announced the legally-incorrect conclusion that Article 101(1) does not cover any merger, acquisition, or joint venture and why European academic authorities on E.C./E.U. competition law have almost universally accepted this erroneous legal conclusion. The two points are that the first sentence of the preceding paragraph both (1) implies that the long-standing conclusion (see below) of the EC and the E.C./E.U. courts that Article 101 does not cover *any* merger or acquisition would be incorrect as a matter of E.C./E.U. law even if their (implicit) assumption that the Article's "clauses (a)–(e) list" is comprehensive were correct as a matter of E.C./E.U. law and (2) manifests the fact that, under E.C./E.U. competition law, any tendency of covered conduct to increase the extent to which its perpetrator or perpetrators commit subsequent violations of E.C./E.U. competition law does count against the original conduct's illegality. (As we have seen, by way of contrast, it is not clear that it is correct as a matter of U.S. law to interpret the U.S. antitrust statutes to be fence laws.)

I turn now to the motivation-issue in question. I suspect that the EC and the E.C./E.U. courts reached the legally-erroneous conclusion that now-Article 101 does not cover any mergers, acquisitions, or joint ventures (and that European commentators accepted this conclusion) because they all believed that (1) E.C./E.U. companies needed to merge to increase their proficiency (to take advantage of economies of scale and to combine assets that were complementary for non-scale reasons) *inter alia* to compete more effectively against U.S. (and perhaps Japanese) companies, (2) now-Article 101 would preclude E.C./E.U. companies from executing many desirable mergers because of (A) the difficulty of proving that a merger would generate a kind of economic efficiency whose generation is a prerequisite for a now-Article 101(3) exemption and (B) the difficulty of satisfying and/or the onerousness of satisfying the various other conditions that a merger must satisfy to be eligible for a now-Article 101(3) exemption, and (3) a holding that now-Article 101(1) does not cover mergers would do more good by causing desirable mergers to be executed than harm by causing undesirable mergers to be executed. I disapprove of this legal error for two reasons. First and foremost, I disapprove because it is, to my mind, morally unacceptable for law-interpreting and law-applying institutions to engage in legislation when they have not been authorized to do so. Second, I disapprove for independent policy reasons: although I agree that now-Article 101(3)'s "efficiency defence" is far too restrictive, I suspect that even a legislative decision to allow all mergers would be undesirable on balance—that, jurisprudential (moral) concerns aside, the holding that now-Article 101(1) does not cover mergers did more harm than good.

I will close this discussion of the conduct-coverage of Article 101(1)—correctly interpreted and applied—by comparing Article 101(1)'s and the Sherman Act's conduct-coverage, commenting on the practical significance of the fact that Article 101(1) does not cover certain types of business conduct, and making some observations about some features of and misunderstandings manifest in Article 101(1)'s clauses (d) and (e).

On the assumption that (correctly interpreted) Article 101(1) does cover mergers, acquisitions, and joint ventures, its conduct-coverage differs from the Sherman Act's conduct-coverage in two important respects: (1) Article 101(1) covers (as concerted practices) natural oligopolistic conduct while neither the Sherman Act nor the Clayton Act covers such conduct and (2) Article 101(1) does not cover contrivance that is executed exclusively through the making and possibly the carrying out of threats of retaliation and single-firm predation while the Sherman Act as written does cover both these categories of conduct and the Clayton Act covers them when their execution involves price discrimination in the Clayton Act sense of that concept or prohibitions of the trading partner's patronizing the perpetrator's rivals.

Both these differences are practically important. In my judgment, natural oligopolistic pricing and natural oligopolistic interactions that result in accident-and-pollution-loss-reducing PPR not being executed are both (1) important social phenomena and (2) economically inefficient and *a fortiori* socially undesirable all things considered. The fact that Article 101(1) not only covers but prohibits such conduct (see below) while the Sherman and Clayton Acts do not make E.C./E.U. competition law as written superior to U.S. antitrust law as written. Similarly, in my judgment, contrivance that is executed exclusively through the making and possibly the carrying out of threats of retaliation and single-firm predation are also both (1) important social phenomena and (2) usually economically inefficient ("usually" because contrivance and predation that reduce equilibrium QV investment in the area of product-space in which it is practiced will sometimes increase economic efficiency on that account) and *a fortiori* socially undesirable. Hence, the fact that, as written, Article 101(1) covers neither the indicated variant of contrivance nor single-firm predation while U.S. antitrust law as written does cover both such categories of conduct makes E.C./E.U. competition law as written inferior to U.S. antitrust law as written. Admittedly, this last conclusion would not be justified if these deficiencies of Article 101(1) were remedied by Article 102. Unfortunately, they are not. Although contrived oligopolistic conduct and predatory conduct certainly do constitute exclusionary abuses under Article 102 (see below) and might be characterized as an exploitative abuse under Article 102 (see below), Article 102 covers the conduct only of dominant firms and (by interpretation) firms that are members of a collectively-dominant set of rivals: firms that do not fall into either of these categories may find it profitable to engage in contrived oligopolistic conduct that does not involve any agreement and/or single-firm predation. I hasten to add that, as previously indicated, although the Sherman Act does not leave uncovered single-firm predation by an undertaking that is not "dominant" or a member of a collectively-dominant set of rivals, the U.S. courts have opened up such a gap in coverage by creating a statutorily-unwarranted requirement that, to prevail in a monopolization or attempt-to-monopolize case, private plaintiffs or the State must demonstrate that the defendant possessed market power prior to engaging in the allegedly-predatory conduct.

I now want to make two points about Article 101(1) clause (d)'s coverage of price and other forms of discrimination. First, in combination with the first part of Article 101(1)'s reference to the prevention or restriction of competition, the text of clause (d) indicates that Article 101(1) is concerned with price discrimination that prevents or restricts competition in the market in which the disfavored buyer operates as a seller (in the so-called secondary market) and not price discrimination that lessens competition in the market in which the customers of the customers of the discriminator operate (the so-called tertiary market). In light of the fact that price discrimination is almost certainly most likely to reduce competition in the primary market (in particular, will tend to do so when the discriminatorily-low price manifests either retaliation against legitimate competition or predation) and will rarely reduce competition in the secondary market, this secondary-market focus is regrettable (given that, as we have seen, relevant retaliatory and predatory discrimination is covered by other parts of E.C./E.U. competition law only when practiced by a dominant firm or a member of a collectively-dominant set of rivals). Second, the fact that clause (d) refers to "dissimilar conditions" in "equivalent transactions with *other trading partners*" (emphasis added) implies that Article 101(1) does not apply either (1) to what I would call the competition-distorting (but hard to prevent) practice in which a vertically-integrated concern charges independent buyers of an input (final good) it produces a higher price than the shadow price it instructs its own fabricating (distribution) managers to assume they are being charged when they make various decisions or (2) to vertical mergers, acquisitions, or joint ventures that increase the extent to which the above practice takes place.

Finally, I want to make five comments or sets of comments that relate to clause (e) of Article 101(1)—in particular, to its coverage of agreements between undertakings, decisions by associations of undertakings, and concerted practices either to place other parties under supplementary obligations or to do things that will increase the extent to which the agreement-participants, association-members, or concerted-practice participants place other parties under such supplementary obligations. The first is that the supplementary obligations to which clause (e) refers are created by tying agreements (which obligate a buyer of one product to purchase a second product from the seller in question or from another source the seller identifies), reciprocity agreements (which obligate the seller of one product to purchase a second product from the buyer of the first good or obligate the buyer of one product to sell a second product to the seller of the first good), resale price maintenance (RPM) agreements (which obligate a buyer of a product not to resell it for less than and/or more than some specified price), agreements that contain vertical territorial restraints and customer-allocation clauses (which limit a distributor–buyer to reselling the product the contract involves to buyers in specified territories, to categories of buyers specified on some non-geographic basis, or to named buyers), advertising and shelf-space/other-sorts-of-display-space clauses in contracts of sale (which obligate a distributor–buyer of one product respectively to advertise that product to a specified extent, in specified media, or in particular ways and to provide that product with a specified quantity and quality of shelf-space and other sorts of in-store display-space), complement-specifying clauses in contracts of sale (which obligate the buyer to make available to its customers particular complements of the product in question or complements that meet certain standards and to distribute the good through an outlet that conforms to certain architectural specifications), full-requirements clauses in contracts of sale or purchase (which respectively obligate a buyer to purchase its full requirements of the product in question from the relevant seller and obligate a seller to supply the buyer in question with its total output), boycott provisions in contracts of sale (which obligate the buyer not to patronize specified individual suppliers or categories of suppliers), and single-brand exclusive-dealership agreements (which obligate a buyer not to sell any product that is competitive with the product being supplied).

The second comment is that Article 101(1) does not cover the efforts of producers to influence resellers of their products non-contractually by adopting sales policies of terminating the supply of resellers that do not conform to the producer's resale-price, architectural-layout, advertising, promotion, pre-sales-advise, and/or post-sales-warranty-service preferences, regardless of whether these efforts include warnings of termination or criticisms of non-conformity. However, if you accept my conclusion that (for reasons that Sections 2 and 3B(1) of Chap. 14 as well as the subsequent part of this section explain) the vertical restraints in question rarely violate Article 101, properly interpreted and applied, this sales-policy/contractual-restraint distinction would be unimportant regardless of how it was operationalized if Article 101 were properly interpreted and applied.

The third comment relates to the implicit assumption that clause (e) manifests that at least a substantial number of such supplementary obligations "by their nature or according to commercial usage, have no connection with the subject of. . .[the] contracts" that create them. Since, as Chap. 14 will demonstrate, (1) the overwhelming majority of such supplementary-obligation-creating clauses (A) increase the profits that the contracts in which they are placed yield their participants without reducing the inter-brand competition the relevant producer faces and (B) many such clauses increase economic efficiency as well, it is hard to see how such supplementary-obligation-creating clauses can be said "by their nature...[to] have no connection with the subject of...[the] contracts," and since (2) the overwhelming majority of the sellers the relevant contracts involve would choose to place independent distributors under the supplementary obligations in question if the law did not prohibit their doing so, it is hard to see how, as a matter of "commercial usage," such supplementary-obligation-creating clauses can be said to have "no connection with the subject of...[the] contracts" in which they are included.

The fourth comment or set of comments that I want to make about clause (e) of Article 101(1) relates to the possible reasons for its inclusion. I suspect that the desire of the drafters of clause (e) and ratifiers of the Treaty that included it in what is now Article 101(1) of the Treaty of Lisbon included it because they wanted to prohibit manufacturers from preventing their independent distributors in one then-E.C. member-country from selling the manufacturer's product in another then-E.C. member-country because they thought that the prevented parallel trade would have served one of the Treaty's most important proximate goals—establishing a common market—and the more-ultimate goals that lay behind it—(1) promoting social and political unity (A) by increasing the familiarity that members of each member-country have with the tastes and products of other member-countries and (B) by increasing (business) relations between members of different member-countries and (2) enabling E.C./E.U. companies to take advantage of available economies of scale. I hasten to add that I do not think that prohibiting manufacturers from preventing such parallel trade will achieve these goals: any attempt to prohibit firms from controlling their independent contractors in ways in which they would be allowed to control their own employees will tend to induce them to make lawful moves that will be at least equally inimical to the promotion of inter-common-market-member trade—to execute otherwise-unprofitable (and therefore presumptively-economically-inefficient) vertical integration and instruct their employees not to make sales to buyers in other member-countries, to substitute a pricing-technique that involves lower lump-sum fees and higher per-unit prices for one that involves higher lump-sum fees and lower per-unit prices to render cross-member-country sales unprofitable for independent distributors, to stop discrimination in favor of distributors in poorer-member countries in order to render cross-member-country sales unprofitable for them, or to stop selling their product altogether in member-countries in which they would otherwise have charged discriminatorily-low prices for it.

The fifth comment I want to make about clause (e)—which applies as well to clause (d)—is that to the extent that its policy deficiencies can be attributed to poor draftsmanship (as opposed to an imperfect understanding of the functions and consequences of price discrimination and various supplementary-obligation-creating clauses), their presence would tend to reinforce the inclination of U.S. courts to ignore the words "in particular" when interpreting Article 101(1) if it were part of a U.S. statute or treaty—*i.e.*, to treat the list that follows these words as illustrative rather than comprehensive. However, I do not know whether the same conclusion applies to E.C./E.U. courts.

Some elaboration is necessary: (1) U.S. courts tend to interpret statutes and treaties in the way that (to their mind) best effectuates drafter or legislator/ratifier intent both (A) when the text is not entirely clear and the legislative history does not provide definitive information and (B) even when the text is semantically clear but seems (to the court) to be contrary to drafter/ ratifier intent while (2) the courts of many other countries (such as Great Britain) consider themselves more bound by legislative and treaty texts than U.S. courts do even when the texts are badly drafted and disserve their drafters' or legislators'/ratifiers' goals. I suspect that this difference in interpretive approach reflects the reality that it is far more difficult for the U.S. legislative branch to correct badly-drafted legislation than for (say) the British Parliament to do so. The difference in question reflects a combination of the following facts:

(1) the United States legislature is more effectively bicameral than the British;
(2) the political party that controls the executive branch of the United States government may not control its legislative branch;
(3) the political party that controls one house of the U.S. Congress may not control the other house;
(4) the U.S.' national parties have much less control over their elected government officials than do European national parties (in part because of the difference between parliamentary and congressional government, in part [relatedly] because state parties in the U.S. are stronger relative to national parties in the U.S. than state or constituency parties in Europe are relative to national parties, and in part because of the difference in the relevant countries' voting systems—the absence of party lists in the United States).

Unfortunately, as I have just suggested, I do not know whether E.C./E.U. courts' interpretive practices resemble the practices of U.S. or British courts in this respect. I also do not know whether, all things considered, the structure of the E.C./E.U. legislative and executive branches and the structure of E.C./E.U. political parties favor the "cost-effectiveness" in the E.U. of the U.S. courts' or British courts' relevant interpretive practice.

(C) The Tests of "*Prima Facie* Illegality" Promulgated by Article 101(1)

As already indicated, for conduct that is covered by Article 101 to violate that Article, it must both (1) violate one of the "tests of illegality" Article 101(1) promulgates and (2) fail to quality for the exemption from Article 101(1) that Article 101(3) grants (or at least has been interpreted to grant) all conduct that satisfies the conditions Article 101(3) specifies. For this reason, I use the expression "*prima facie*" tests of illegality to refer to the various tests of illegality that Article 101(1) promulgates.

The discussion that follows assumes that, correctly interpreted as a matter of E.C./E.U. law, Article 101(1) would *not* be read to make the list in clauses (a)–(e) comprehensive. On that assumption, Article 101(1) declares *prima facie* illegal the undertaking-agreements, trade-association decisions, and concerted practices it covers if they have as "their object" or "effect" "the prevention, restriction or distortion of competition within the common market...," regardless of the way they will or may produce these results. I will first discuss the meaning of "preventing or restricting competition" in the above text, then consider together the meaning of "conduct whose 'object' is the prevention or restriction of competition" and "conduct whose 'effect' is the prevention or restriction of competition," and finally analyze the meaning of "conduct whose 'object' or 'effect'" is "the distortion of competition."

The preceding paragraph indicated that I would begin this discussion of Article 101(1)'s tests of illegality by analyzing the meaning of "preventing or restricting competition" as opposed to the meaning of "conduct that has at its object preventing or restricting competition" or "conduct that has the effect of preventing or restricting competition." In fact, however, I do not think that, in the E.C./E.U. competition-law context, it is instructive to parse "preventing or restricting competition" in isolation—*i.e.*, independent of the concepts of "conduct that has preventing or restricting competition as its object or effect." I make this point because several deservedly-respected E.C./E.U. antitrust-law experts have taken the opposite position in conversation with me. More specifically, these experts have argued that, correctly interpreted in the E.C./E.U. competition-law context, (1) conduct should be said to prevent or restrict competition whenever it inflicts (in essence) a net-euro loss on the customers of its perpetrator(s) and the customers of its/their rivals, regardless of its perpetrator's or perpetrators' motive for engaging in the conduct and regardless of the way in which it generates this outcome, and (2) this interpretation should control the interpretations of "conduct that has as its object or effect the prevention or restriction of competition." In the pages that follow, I will argue that conduct should be deemed to have as its object the prevention or restriction of competition only if it manifests its perpetrator's or perpetrators' specific anticompetitive intent and that conduct should be deemed to have the effect of preventing or restricting competition only if it imposes a net equivalent-monetary loss on the customers of its perpetrator(s) and the customers of its/their product rivals "combined" by reducing the absolute attractiveness of the best offer they respectively receive from any inferior supplier. These interpretations imply that conduct that imposes a net-euro loss on relevant buyers but does not manifest its perpetrator's or perpetrators' specific anticompetitive intent (since, for example, they believed *ex ante* that the tax advantages or efficiencies it would generate rendered it profitable) would not violate the object branch of Article 101(1)'s test of illegality even if it did impose a net-euro loss on relevant buyers and that conduct that imposes a net equivalent-euro loss on relevant buyers because it prevents its perpetrator(s) from erroneously charging them unprofitably-low prices, enables its perpetrator(s) to prevent its/their independent distributors from charging ultimate buyers prices that were lower than the prices that would maximize the total profits of the producer(s) and all its/their distributors, or enables its perpetrator(s) to profit by using fancy "pricing techniques" such as tie-ins to remove buyer surplus it/they would otherwise have allowed to escape do not violate the effect branch of Article 101(1)'s test of illegality.

I decided to begin this section with a discussion of the relevant European experts' conclusions about the proper interpretation of "preventing or restricting competition" and that interpretation's implications for the correct way to operationalize the object and effect branches of Articles 101(1)'s test of illegality to put myself in a position to comment on the two beliefs that lead these experts to reach their conclusions on this issue and reject mine. In brief, these experts claim that conduct "prevents" or "restricts" competition in the Article 101(1) sense whenever it imposes a net equivalent-monetary loss on relevant buyers and that this interpretation should control the interpretation of the object and effect branches of Article 101(1)'s test of illegality. More specifically, these experts make two arguments for their interpretation of preventing or restricting competition. The first is that their interpretation is consistent with and my interpretation is inconsistent with the pro-consumer distributive preferences that the 1957 Treaty's competition-law provisions manifest—in particular, both with the fact that now-Article 101(3) provides exemptions for economic-efficiency-generating conduct that violates now-Article 101(1)'s test of *prima facie* illegality only if relevant consumers secure a fair share of the benefit generated by the conduct in question and with the fact that (at least as interpreted) now-Article 102 prohibits dominant firms from perpetrating exploitative as well as exclusionary abuses of their dominant positions. The second is that their interpretations of "preventing or restricting competition" and, derivatively, of the object and effect branches of Article 101(1)'s test of illegality are favored by the fact that clause (e) of now-Article 101(1)—which states that now-Article 101(1) *prima facie* prohibits "agreements between undertakings" that "make the conclusion of contracts subject to acceptance by the other parties of supplementary obligations which, by their nature or according to commercial usage, have no connection with the subject of such contracts"—manifests the assumption of the Treaty's drafters and ratifiers that tie-ins, reciprocity agreements, resale-price-maintenance agreements, vertical territorial restraints and customer-allocation clauses, and single-brand or conventional exclusive dealerships prevent or restrict competition in the Article 101(1) sense of that expression even when they do not reduce inter-brand competition.

I am not convinced by either of these arguments. In my judgment, the first fails for two reasons. One is that it is inconsistent with the text of now-Article 101(1) in that some of the ways in which covered business conduct can inflict equivalent-monetary losses on relevant buyers cannot linguistically be attributed to its preventing or restricting competition even if that expression is deemed to refer to reducing intra-brand as well as inter-brand competition. Thus, mergers that lead to the merged firm's charging higher prices than the mergers partners would have charged by enabling the merged firm to discover and act upon the knowledge that the merger partners had been underestimating their profit-maximizing prices cannot be said to have yielded this outcome by preventing or restricting competition, since the conduct in question does not affect the absolute attractiveness of the offers against which the merged firm must compete: nor can tie-ins or reciprocity agreements that impose equivalent-dollar losses on the seller-employer's customers without altering the absolute attractiveness of the offers against which the seller in question has to compete by making it profitable for the seller to remove buyers surplus whose removal would otherwise have been unprofitable for it. The other reason is that my interpretation is not incompatible with the distributive preferences the treaty manifests: there is no inconsistency between (1) concluding that (A) firms with a dominant position should not commit exploitative abuses of their dominant positions and (B) firms that want to commit covered acts that have as their object or effect inflicting a net-equivalent-monetary loss on relevant buyers by reducing the absolute attractiveness of the best offer they respectively receive from any inferior supplier should not be allowed to engage in that conduct unless it also generates economic efficiencies and affords the relevant buyers a fair share of the benefit it yields them and its perpetrator(s) and (2) concluding that (A) dominant firms that want to commit covered acts that do not constitute exploitative abuses of the buyers involved and do not have as their object or effect inflicting a net-equivalent-dollar loss on relevant buyers by reducing the absolute attractiveness of the best offer they respectively receive from any inferior supplier should be allowed to engage in the conduct in question or that (B) firms that are neither individually dominant nor members of a collectively-dominant set of rivals should be allowed to engage in covered conduct that does not impose an equivalent-monetary loss on relevant buyers by reducing the absolute attractiveness of the best offer they respectively receive from any inferior supplier even if the conduct does inflict a net-equivalent-monetary loss on relevant buyers in one or more other ways. Certainly, there is no reason to believe that the ratifiers of the 1957 Treaty or of the sequels to it that also include now-Articles 101 and 102 would have found (1)(A) and (B) inconsistent with (2)(A) and (B): E.C./E.U. ratifiers seem to think that firms with dominant positions have special obligations to their customers, and from many normative perspectives there is an important difference between profiting by taking better advantage of competitive advantages secured through skill, foresight, industry, or even luck and profiting by committing acts with the specific intent of reducing the competition you face (or, conceivably, profiting at your customers' expense by committing acts that you know will reduce the competition you face even if you would have committed the acts in question anyway).

The second argument that European scholars have made to me orally for their interpretation of preventing or restricting competition and their conclusion about that interpretation's implications for the legally-correct interpretations of the object and effect of branches of Article 101(1)'s test of illegality focuses on the fact that clause (e) of now-Article 101(1) lists as an example of conduct the Article declares *prima facie* illegal conduct that almost always functions exclusively by reducing intra-brand as opposed to inter-brand competition. I do not find this argument convincing because (1) clause (e) is not inconsistent with my proposed reading of the object and effect branches of Article 101(1)'s test of illegality in that conduct covered by clause (e) does sometimes reduce inter-brand competition (though I suspect it does so rarely), (2) it seems highly unlikely that the ratifiers of the 1957 Treaty or even its sequels appreciated the difference between the distributive and economic-efficiency effects of conduct that reduces intra-brand competition on the one hand and of conduct that reduces inter-brand competition on the other, (3) clause (e) manifests other important errors in that, contrary to its declarations, the "supplementary obligations" to which it refers are frequently imposed and are intimately connected to the contracts' in which they are included performing some of their legitimate functions, (4) the position that I acknowledge some Treaty supporters and official interpreters have taken (and that I assume some Treaty ratifiers may also have supported) that it is desirable to interpret clause (e) to prohibit the conduct it covers even when that conduct reduces only intra-brand competition because doing so protects the liberty interests of the businessmen that the conduct in question *ex post* constrains is insupportable (A) because it ignores the fact that the constrained businesspersons have accepted the contractual constraints in question in circumstances in which one could not say that their wills have been overborne, (B) because—point (A) aside—it assumes incorrectly that the relevant businesspersons have a true liberty interest (whose disservice requires special justification) in making the choices that the relevant contractual provisions prohibit them from making (an interest that relates to some choice-option's contributing to their developing a conception of the good or leading a life that is consistent with the conception of the good to which they are individually committed and/or to their fulfilling their moral obligations), and (C) because—as Chap. 14 will show and the EC and E.C./E.U. courts now recognize—prohibitions of the contract clauses in question will lead the businesses that want to include them in their contracts to substitute for them other lawful conduct that will be at least as restrictive of the opportunity-set of the individuals whose alleged liberty interests clause (e) is allegedly designed to protect as the contract clauses that clause (e) covers, and (5) the position (which I acknowledge some Treaty supporters and official interpreters have taken and I assume some Treaty ratifiers may have supported as well) that it is desirable to interpret clause (e) to prohibit the conduct it covers even when that conduct reduces only intra-brand competition because, even then, (i) it may reduce the volume of transactions that take place between member countries and (ii) increases in inter-member transactions are valued for social and political reasons and for their tendency to enable E.C./E.U. firms to take advantage of economies of scale is undercut by the fact (now acknowledged by the EC and the E.C./E.U. courts) that efforts to promote inter-member transactions through clause (e) are likely to be (or at least may well be) counterproductive both because they will tend to lead manufactures to integrate forward into distribution and because, even if they do not lead to such vertical integration, they will lead the firms in question to raise the prices they charge for their goods in poorer member-countries or to stop selling their goods in such countries altogether (thereby reducing both [a] inter-member business relations [the extent to which consumers in each E.C./E.U. member-country learn about other E.C./E.U. countries by consuming their products] and [b] the affected undertakings' sales and abilities to take advantage of economies of scale).

In any event, for the preceding reasons, I reject both the arguments that some E.C./E.U. scholars have made orally to me for interpreting now-Article 101(1) to declare *prima facie* illegal covered conduct that reduces *intra*-brand competition but not *inter*-brand competition. The text that follows will adopt my preferred interpretation.

I will now address in reverse order the interpretation of having as "*their object*" or "*their effect*" the prevention or restriction of competition as these expressions are used in now-Article 101(1). As already indicated, the interpretation of the Article 101(1) concept of "conduct whose *effect* is the prevention or restriction of competition" that is correct as a matter of E.C./E.U. law is conduct that would inflict a net-equivalent-monetary loss on relevant buyers by reducing the absolute attractiveness of the best offer they respectively receive from any inferior supplier if its perpetrator(s) would take full advantage of the reductions it generated in the absolute attractiveness of the best offer that respective relevant buyers received from any inferior supplier and the conduct would not generate any relevant efficiencies. The part of this interpretation that starts with the word "if" in the preceding sentence is required to make the effect branch of now-Article 101(1)'s test of *prima facie* illegality compatible with now-Article 101(3).

I turn now to the expression "their object" in the Article 101(1) text that refers to undertaking-agreements, trade-association decisions, and concerted practices that have as "their object" the prevention or restriction of (inter-brand) competition. Two interpretations seem most plausible. According to the first, the words "their object" refer to "*an* object." According to the second, the words "their object" refer to "*a critical* object"—*i.e.*, an object that critically affected the perpetrator's decision or perpetrators' decisions to engage in the relevant type of Article 101(1)-covered conduct. Some clarification may be useful. On the first interpretation, Article 101(1) would render *prima facie* illegal any covered conduct that was motivated at all by a perpetrator's wish to prevent or restrict competition even if the perpetrator(s) would have engaged in the conduct in question had it or they not perceived *ex ante* that it would or might prevent or restrict competition (though such conduct would not in the end be deemed to violate Article 101 if its perpetrators could show that it qualified for an Article 101(3) exemption—see below). On the second interpretation, Article 101(1) would render *prima facie* illegal only those exemplars of covered conduct that violate the Sherman Act's specific-anti-competitive-intent test of illegality—*i.e.*, only those exemplars of covered conduct whose perpetrator *ex ante* perceived profitability was critically affected by its or their belief that it would or might secure the object of restricting or preventing competition in some way that would render the conduct profitable though economically inefficient in an otherwise-Pareto-perfect economy.

The choice between these two interpretations of Article 101(1)'s "their object" language cannot be based solely on semantic considerations. Read in isolation, the language "their object" could refer either to "an object" or to "a critical object" (of which there might be more than one). In fact, it would be more accurate to say that, semantically, the "their object" language does not fit either the "an object" or the "a critical object" reading particularly well—fits best a "the only object" reading, which clearly is not apposite (since most exemplars of the types of conduct covered by Article 101(1) perform one or more functions other than preventing, restricting, or distorting competition). I am somewhat inclined to conclude that, read in isolation, the "their object" text fits the "a critical object" reading less poorly than it fits the "an object" reading, but the fact that I prefer the "a critical object" reading for policy reasons (see below) makes me distrust "my ear."

I can think of at least three non-semantic arguments that might possibly inform the choice between the "an object" and the "a critical object" reading of "their object." The first of these non-semantic arguments is a consequentialist policy argument that (if valid) would favor the "a critical object" reading of "their object." This argument focuses on the fact that, for four and possibly five reasons, Article 101(3) would not result in the exemption of covered conduct that was rendered desirable by the economic efficiencies it generated despite the fact that it had preventing or restricting competition as "*an* object" when preventing or restricting competition was not "*a critical* object" of the conduct in question. The four definite reasons are:

(1) conduct that is covered by Article 101(1) can generate several types of economic efficiencies that do not appear in the list of categories of economic efficiencies whose generation Article 101(3) states may (in conjunction with other facts) qualify conduct for an exemption from Article 101(1) (see below);
(2) even if the economic efficiencies that conduct generates do fit into one or more of the categories of economic efficiency whose generation Article 101(3) states may result in the relevant conduct's exemption, the conduct in question may fail to qualify for an Article 101(3) exemption because "relevant consumers" did not obtain a "fair share" of "the resulting benefit" (see below);
(3) even if the conduct in question does generate one of the kinds of economic efficiency whose generation renders it eligible for an exemption and does give relevant consumers a fair share of the "benefit" the conduct generates, it may fail to qualify for an Article 101(3) exemption because it affords the perpetrator(s) "the possibility of eliminating competition in respect of a substantial part of the products in question" (I assume: a substantial part of the products in the area of product-space in which the covered conduct takes place); and
(4) even if the conduct in question does generate Article-101(3)-recognized economic efficiencies, does give relevant consumers a fair share of the resulting benefit, and does not afford the perpetrator(s) the just-specified opportunity, the perpetrators might not be able to carry the burden of proof on these issues that Article 101(3) has been interpreted to assign to them.

The policy reason that is only a possible policy reason for preferring the "a critical object" reading of "their object" relates to the requirement of now-Article 101(3) that, to be eligible for an exemption, conduct may not "impose on the undertakings concerned restrictions that are not indispensable to" its generating now-Article-101 (3)-qualifying economic efficiencies or its allowing relevant consumers a fair share of the resulting benefit. This fifth policy reason for reading "their object" to refer to "a critical object" is only a possible reason for doing so because, as I will explain below, this provision is undesirable from a policy perspective if but only if it is interpreted to deny an exemption to the perpetrator(s) only if it/they knew *ex ante* that the restriction(s) it/they was/were creating were not indispensable.

The second non-semantic argument that might bear on the choice between the "an object" and the "a critical object" reading of "their object" favors the "an object reading." This second non-semantic argument focuses on the reality that, if (contrary to fact) now-Article 101(1) referred only to "their object" and not to "their effect," for reasons that Chap. 12 will make clear, an extremely-low percentage of the conduct that would violate Article 101(1)'s test of *prima facie* illegality but would satisfy Article 101(3)'s requirement that it improve production or distribution or promote technical or economic progress would satisfy Article 101(3)'s requirement that relevant buyers obtain a "fair share" of the resulting benefit. (The force of this second non-semantic argument derives from the [not-surprising] fact that an important tenet of legal interpretation is that, *ceteris paribus*, one should not interpret ambiguous or open-textured text in one part of a treaty, statute, or other kind of legal document [say a constitution, corporate charter, or will] in a way that renders another part of that document redundant [or, relatedly, inconsistent with the former text as interpreted].) Fortunately, from my perspective, this argument is not persuasive because, as we have seen, now-Article 101(1)'s test of *prima facie* illegality has an effect branch as well as an object branch and this effect branch would render now-Article 101(3) very much non-redundant even if "their object" is interpreted to mean "*a critical* object."

The third non-semantic argument that can be made in this context is an intellectual/legal-history argument. The drafters and ratifiers of now-Article 101 were aware of U.S. antitrust law, and, although they clearly did not simply want to copy it, they were substantially influenced by it. It seems to me that this argument, which clearly favors the "*a critical* object" reading of "their object" (since on that reading the "their object" branch of now-Article 101(1)'s test of *prima facie* illegality is the same as the U.S. courts' [abstract] specific-anticompetitive-intent rendition of the Sherman Act's test of illegality—*i.e.*, of its interpretation of monopolizing, attempting to monopolize, and agreements in restraint of trade), is completely valid.

All things considered, I think that the interpretation of the "their object" language of now-Article 101(1) that is correct as a matter of E.C./E.U. law would read that text to refer to "*a critical* object." On this interpretation of "their object," the "their object" branch of now-Article 101(1)'s test of *prima facie* illegality adds to the "their effect" branch of now-Article 101(1)'s test of *prima facie* illegality by declaring *prima facie* illegal conduct that was ill-motivated even if it did not succeed in preventing or restricting (or distorting) competition. In so doing, the "their object" branch of now-Article 101(1) replicates what the Sherman Act adds to the Clayton Act in relation to conduct both Acts cover. (Yes, I know that the Sherman Act was passed before the Clayton Act, but that fact is not relevant to the point I am making.) In any event, throughout the rest of this study, I will assume that it is correct as a matter of E.C./E.U. law to interpret the "their object" text of what is now Article 101 (1) of the 2009 Treaty of Lisbon to mean "their critical object."

The preceding analyses focus on the interpretations of "conduct that has the object of preventing or restricting competition" and "conduct that has the effect of preventing or restricting competition" that are correct as a matter of E.C./E.U. law, not on the interpretations that these concepts have actually been given by the EC or the E.C./E.U. courts. E.C./E.U. officials have been no more clear about the meaning of these expressions than U.S. officials have been about the meaning of their U.S. counterparts. Indeed, the EC and E.C./E.U. competition-law courts have obfuscated the relevant issues in precisely the same way that U.S. antitrust-enforcement authorities and U.S. courts have done. As Elhaugin and Geradin have pointed out, according to E.C./E.U. officials, "the term 'object' [in Article 101(1)] does not refer to the subjective intention of the parties but to the objective meaning and purpose of the agreement."[77] Since the "objective meaning and purposes of the agreement" cannot be equated with its "effect," the distinction that E.C./E.U. officials are drawing is clearly obscure and probably incoherent. Of course, it will usually be necessary to infer the objective intentions of the parties to an agreement from its actual or predictable effects—*i.e.*, one will usually not have available statements that the parties made about their subjective intentions. However, that is an evidentiary matter that sheds no light on the conceptual distinction in question.

I turn finally to the meaning of "distorting competition." Although the EC does not distinguish "distorting" competition from preventing or restricting competition, I do think that semantically "distorting" competition is different from "preventing" or "restricting" competition. In particular, I believe that an act or practice *distorts* competition if it causes a seller that is not the most-economically-efficient supplier of a particular buyer to be the buyer's privately-best-placed supplier, if it causes a firm to exit when its operation would be more-economically-efficient than the continuing operation of a surviving QV-investment project or firm, and/or if it deters a potential competitor from entering or an established firm from expanding when the relevant firm's QV-investment project would be more economically efficient than another project that is executed. I should point out that the distinction between reducing (preventing or restricting) competition and distorting competition may have operational significance. For example, a firm's decision to charge discriminatory prices to customers that compete against each other could "distort competition" in the secondary market in the sense in which I have defined this concept even if it does not inflict an on-balance equivalent-monetary loss on the customers of the discriminator's customers or on the customers of the buyers in relation to which the discrimination in question had been practiced.

---

[77] See ELHAUGE AND GERADIN 61, citing CMA CGM-FETTSCA, Case T 213/00, E.U.R. II 913 at Section 183 (2003).

(D) The *de minimis* Limitation to Article 101's Actor-Coverage Created by the ECJ and Operationalized by the EC

The text of Article 101(1) contains no explicit *de minimis* constraint on its actor-coverage. The only textual basis for inferring such a restriction is the provision's reference to "the prevention, restriction or distortion of competition *within the common market*" (emphasis added). However, the European Court of Justice has interpreted now-Article 101(1) not to apply to at least some categories of conduct its text covers if the conduct's perpetrators' absolute size and market shares fall below some critical level,[78] and the EC has concluded that it is authorized to operationalize this conclusion.[79] According to the EC, although now-Article 101 does apply to all "hardcore restrictions"—agreements between competitors to fix prices, limit output, or allocate markets or customers—regardless of the absolute size or market shares of their participants, it does not apply to the other types of agreements its text would otherwise cover if those agreements are of "minor importance,"[80] presumably because they have *de minimis* effects—a condition that the EC deems satisfied if

(1) the agreeing firms have fewer than 250 employees and either an annual revenue less than 50 million euros or an annual balance-sheet total less than 43 million euros, or
(2) the aggregate market shares of the two parties do not exceed:
    (A) ten percent in the case of horizontal agreements or mixed horizontal/vertical agreements;
    (B) fifteen percent in the case of vertical agreements; or
    (C) five percent in the case of agreements having a cumulative effect, which may exist when more than 30 % of the relevant market is covered by parallel agreements having similar effects.[81]

I do not think that now-Article 101(1)'s "within the common market" language implies that its coverage has a *de minimis* restriction. I doubt the legitimacy of a court's reading a *de minimis* restriction into a legislative or Treaty provision whose text (and history) do not warrant such an interpretation. And I believe that many of the agreements that the EC's Notice excludes from now-Article 101 coverage on *de minimis* grounds will have impacts that are too big to be considered *de minimis*.

---

[78] See Volk v. Vervaecke, Case 5/69, E.U.R. 295 (1969).

[79] Commission Notice on Agreements of Minor Importance Which Do Not Appreciably Restrict Competition, OJ C 372/15 (2001).

[80] Commission Notice on Agreements of Minor Importance, OJ C 368/13 at Section 11 (2001).

[81] Commission Notice on Agreements of Minor Importance Which Do Not Appreciably Restrict Competition, OJ C 372/15 (2001).

(E) Misinterpretations/Misapplications of Article 101(1) by the EC and E.C./E.U. Courts

The shortcomings of the EC's and E.C./E.U. courts' interpretations and applications of Article 101(1) are discussed in detail in Chaps. 10, 11, 12, 13, 14, and 15. At this juncture, I will simply list and briefly explain what I take to be the eight most important deficiencies of these institutions' handling of this provision.

First, as I have already indicated, I doubt that the ECJ is authorized to create a *de minimis* limitation to Article 101(1)'s actor-coverage. Nothing in the text of Article 101(1) warrants such a limitation.

Second, the EC's and E.C./E.U. courts' comments on the abstract of "concerted practices" have not been edifying, and its statements about the kinds of conduct that can be characterized as "concerted practices" have not been instructive.

Third, the EC and E.C./E.U. courts have, in my judgment, erred in concluding that Article 101(1) makes *prima facie* illegal conduct that has the object or effect of reducing intra-brand competition and relatedly that Article 101(1) as written prohibits producers from restricting their independent distributors in one member-country from making sales in another member-country. Although clause (e) manifests its drafters' and ratifiers' belief that many of the kinds of conduct that reduce intra-brand competition and prevent "parallel trade" are illegal, it also manifests their misunderstanding of the functions and effects of these practices, and the EC and E.C./E.U. courts are not bound by these mistaken beliefs of the Treaty's drafters and ratifiers.

Fourth, the EC and the E.C./E.U. courts subscribe to the mistaken leverage "theory" of tie-ins and reciprocity—the claim that the exclusive or at least inevitable function and effect of these arrangement is to enable an actor that has economic power in relation to one good to use that power to secure (lever itself into a position of) economic power in relation to a second good.

Fifth and relatedly, the EC and E.C./E.U. courts mistakenly claim that the legality of various vertical practices covered by Article 101(1) depends in part on the market power of the firm engaging in them.

Sixth, the EC[82] and E.C./E.U.[83] courts mistakenly claim that Article 101(1) does not cover mergers, acquisitions, or joint ventures.

Seventh, the EC's and E.C./E.U. courts' delineation of the tests of illegality that Article 101(1) promulgates are far from adequate.

Eighth and finally, I believe that the EC and the E.C./E.U. courts have done a poor job of defining the markets whose definition they assume (incorrectly) can play a significant, constructive role in applying Article 101 (and Article 102).

---

[82] See Reynolds v. Commission, (1987) E.U.R. 4487 (1987).

[83] See BAT, Cases 142 and 156/84 (1984).

(2) Article 101(3)

Now-Article 101(3) provides that the provisions of now-Article 101(1) "may. . .be declared inapplicable" if three conditions are fulfilled: *viz.*, if the undertakings-agreement, trade-association decision, or concerted practice

(1) "contributes to improving the production or distribution of goods or to promoting technical or economic progress, while allowing consumers a fair share of the resulting benefit,"
(2) is the least restrictive means of achieving those objectives ("imposes [only] restrictions which are... indispensable to... those objectives"), and
(3) does not "afford. . .[the relevant] undertakings the possibility of eliminating competition in respect to a substantial part of the products in question."

I want to make ten points about now-Article 101(3) and its application. First, semantically, its language indicates that it does not guarantee the exoneration of firms when the three listed conditions are satisfied: it merely authorizes the EC to declare Article 101(1) inapplicable to defendants when the three conditions are satisfied.

Second, the expression "economic progress" in the first condition listed above is unclear and, on its most persuasive interpretation, the desirability of the "promoting technical or economic progress" condition is dubious. Given the fact that the words "promoting. . .economic progress" immediately follow the words "promoting technical progress" and are immediately followed by a requirement that "consumers... [obtain] a fair share of the resulting benefit," the expression "promoting economic progress" probably should be interpreted to refer to increasing economic efficiency by promoting technical progress. The reason that this interpretation implies that the "promoting technical or economic progress" condition for the now-Article 101(3) exemption will in some cases be undesirable relates to the word "or": that word implies that the fact that a now-Article-101(1)-covered agreement promotes technical progress by increasing the amount of resources its participants devote to production-process research (PPR) and/or technologically-or-commercially-innovative QV-investment creation may result in now-Article 101(1) being declared inapplicable to it if the other conditions for the exemption are satisfied even if the additional production-process and product R&D the agreement induces is *ex ante* economically inefficient.

Third, the expressions "the resulting benefit" and, relatedly, the "share" of the relevant "consumers" that the first condition in question contains are ambiguous, and the resolution of that ambiguity will often critically affect whether now-Article 101(1) "may. . .be declared inapplicable" to the conduct involved in a particular case. More specifically, the text is ambiguous because its words do not indicate (1) whether "the resulting benefit" refers to the benefits (the net-equivalent-monetary gain to the "combination" of perpetrators and the relevant consumers) yielded by the economic efficiencies the conduct in question generated or the benefits yielded by the conduct in question (all its effects taken into consideration) and,

Fourth, the first condition listed above provides no information about the percentage of the equivalent-monetary gains the relevant efficiencies or the conduct that yielded them (all effects considered) yielded the perpetrators and their customers combined that the customers would have to secure from respectively the economic efficiencies the conduct generated or the conduct (all effects considered) for the customers' gains to constitute a "fair share" of the relevant total equivalent-monetary gains.

Fifth, regardless of the percentage of the efficiency-generated gains to the perpetrators and their customers that would constitute a "fair share" of those gains, the requirement that relevant consumers obtain an equivalent-monetary gain from the efficiencies an undertakings-agreement, trade-association decision, or concerted practice yielded or from the conduct in question distinguishes now-Article 101(3) from both the organizational-economic-efficiency defense I think it is legally appropriate to read into the Clayton Act (despite the absence of any Clayton Act textual basis for doing so) and the economic-efficiency defence the EC recognizes in cases that are covered by the European Merger Control Regulation—a defence that efficiency-generating "concentrations" not harm the relevant consumers (see below).

Sixth, semantically, the second condition in the above list seems to make the eligibility of conduct for a now-Article 101(3) exemption depend on the outcome of an *ex post* (time of trial?) enquiry into whether restrictions that the conduct in question imposes were indispensable to its generating qualifying economic efficiencies or its allowing consumers a fair share of the resulting benefit—*i.e.*, does not seem to make the associated exemption-denial depend on whether the perpetrator(s) know or should have known that the restrictions in question were not indispensable to securing those objectives.

Seventh, this second condition is ambiguous as to whether the restrictions to which it refers are restrictions in the opportunity set of one or more relevant actors, restrictions in competition, or restrictions in competition that would result from restrictions in one or more relevant actors' opportunity sets. I will assume that the last of these three interpretations is correct as a matter of E.C./E.U. law.

Eighth, all things considered, this second condition probably would not be undesirable if its operation were limited to two types of situations. Thus, it would not be undesirable if the perpetrator(s) knew *ex ante* that the restrictions in question were not indispensable since in such cases the critical object of the restrictors would have been to restrict competition by restricting one or more relevant actors' opportunity sets. At least, that would be the case if the relevant now-Article 101(3) provision were interpreted to authorize the antitrust-enforcement authorities to declare the restriction illegal but permit the broader conduct with which it was associated. The provision might also not be undesirable if it were interpreted to deny an exemption to the perpetrator(s) if it/they did not know of the existence of the less-restrictive alternative *ex ante* because they did not do a reasonable amount of research into this possibility. In such a situation, imposing a loss on the perpetrator(s) for not doing reasonable research of the relevant kind does seem appropriate (though the fact that such research would have uncovered a less-restrictive alternative is irrelevant to this conclusion). Moreover, although as we shall see, a requirement that actors do a reasonable amount of research into this possibility might do more harm than good by inducing them to do too much such research if (1) they think that triers-of-fact (under the influence of hindsight bias) will tend to conclude that they have done insufficient research of this kind when their research effort was appropriate and (2) they can reduce the probability of such errors by doing too much such research, I am moderately confident that on balance a reasonable-research requirement would be desirable.

Ninth, this provision would be problematic as a matter of policy if it were read to deny an exemption to the perpetrator(s) in cases in which they did do appropriate research but did not discover the relevant information by doing a reasonable amount of research. Read in this way, the provision would almost certainly be undesirable in that it would deny a now-Article 101(3) exemption to one or more otherwise-eligible perpetrator(s) that had done nothing wrong whose conduct was *ex ante* desirable. More specifically, read in this way in such cases, the provision would produce bad results not only

(1) by "punishing" praiseworthy actors but also
(2) by providing perpetrators with an incentive to do more research of this kind than is desirable to the extent that, by doing so, they can reduce the risk that a trier-of-fact (subject *inter alia* to hindsight bias) would conclude that they did not do the amount of relevant research they should have done and possibly
(3) by deterring perpetrators from engaging in *ex ante* desirable conduct (though this depends on how economically efficient the conduct was, the direction in which and extent to which its profitability would have been distorted absent the provision in question, and the *ex ante* distortion that this version of the provision would create in its profitability).

Tenth and finally, the third condition in the preceding condition-list is puzzling in three respects: To start, semantically, the meaning of "the *possibility* of eliminating competition" (emphasis added) is far from clear. Should this condition be read to require that the undertakings-agreement, trade-association decision, or concerted practice in question (1) not make it profitable for the perpetrator(s) to eliminate the relevant competition given the illegality of their doing so, (2) not make it profitable for them to eliminate the relevant competition if it would not be illegal for them to do so, or (3) not create a real prospect of the perpetrators' eliminating the amount of competition referred to? In addition, I have no idea how to operationalize the concept of competition in respect of a substantial part of "the products in question." Finally, if the agreement, decision, or practice in question generates equivalent-monetary gains to its perpetrators and their customers combined, provides the requisite share of those benefits to the relevant consumers, and contains only those restrictions that are indispensable to the generation of the equivalent-monetary benefits in question, why should the fact that in some sense that is not defined it "eliminate[s] competition in respect of a substantial part of the products in question" or *a fortiori* the fact that it "afford[s]...the possibility of eliminating [such] competition" prohibit the EC from declaring Article 101(1) inapplicable?

(3) The Block Exemptions to Article 101(1) the EC Has Granted to Simplify the Implementation of Article 101(3)

The Council of Ministers and the EC (under authority delegated by the Council) have adopted "block-exemption regulations" that declare that, under now-Article 101(3), Article 101(1) is inapplicable to certain types of agreements[84] or agreements in certain sectors.[85] I should say that, although I doubt that the types of agreements to which the EC has granted now-Article 101(3) block exemptions are more likely to satisfy the normal now-Article 101(3) conditions than various other categories of agreements covered by now-Article 101(3) (such as resale-price-maintenance agreements or agreements that contain vertical territorial restraints or vertical-customer-allocation clauses—see Chap. 14) and doubt that agreements in the economic sectors to whose agreements the EC has granted now-Article 101(3) block exemptions are more likely to satisfy the normal now-Article 101(3) conditions than agreements in other economic sectors, I suspect that these block exemptions probably increase the accuracy of the legal decisions that are made because I fear that, like many of their U.S. counterparts, the relevant E.C./E.U. officials do not understand the functions or likely competitive impact of many of the exempted agreements (see Sections 2 and 3 of Chap. 14).

B. Article 102 of the 2009 Lisbon Treaty

(1) The Actor-Coverage of Article 102

The Treaty article that is now-Article 102 of the Lisbon Treaty addresses the behavior of one or more firms that individually have a dominant position ("of one or more undertakings of a dominant position"). The EC and the E.C./E.U. courts interpret Article 102 also to cover the conduct of members of a set of "collectively-dominant

[84] In this category are "transfer of technology" agreements, distribution agreements, specialization agreements, and R&D agreements. See, respectively, Commission Regulation 772/2004 of 27 April 2004 on the Application of Article 101(3) of the Treaty to Categories of Technology Transfer Agreements OJ 123/11 (2004); Commission Regulation 2790/1999 of 22 December 1999 on the Application of Article 101(3) of the Treaty to Categories of Vertical Agreements and Concerted Practices, OJ L 336/21; Commission Regulation 2658/2000 of 29 November 2000 on the Application of Article 101(3) of the Treaty to Categories of Specialization Agreements, OJ L 304/3 (2000); and Commission Regulation 2659/2000 of 29 November 2000 on the Application of Article 101(3) of the Treaty to Categories of Research and Development Agreements, OJ L 304/7 (2000).

[85] In this category are agreements in the motor-vehicle-distribution sector and in the insurance sector. See, respectively, Commission Regulation 1400/2002 of 31 July 2002 on the Application of Article 101(3) of the Treaty to Categories of Vertical Agreements and Concerted Practices in the Motor Vehicle Sector, OJ L 203/30 (2000) and Commission Regulation 358/2003 of 27 February 2003 on the Application of the Treaty to Certain Categories of Agreements, Decisions and Concerted Practices in the Insurance Sector, OJ L 53/8 (2003).

rivals" (whatever that means). I think this interpretation is wrong as a matter of law, but this study will assume its legal correctness. Chapter 8 analyzes the E.C./E.U. competition-law concepts of an individual-firm dominant position and the collectively-dominant position of a set of rivals as well as the protocols that the EC and various E.C./E.U. competition-law courts use to determine whether an individual firm has a dominant position or a group of firms are collectively dominant.

(2) The Conduct-Coverage of Article 102

I start by quoting the text of Article 102 in full:

> Any abuse by one or more undertakings of a dominant position within the internal market or in a substantial part of it shall be prohibited as incompatible with the internal market in so far as it may affect trade between Member States.
>
> Such abuse may, in particular, consist in:
>
> (a) directly or indirectly imposing unfair purchase or selling prices or other unfair trading conditions;
> (b) limiting production, markets or technical development to the prejudice of consumers;
> (c) applying dissimilar conditions to equivalent transactions with other trading parties, thereby placing them at a competitive disadvantage;
> (d) making the conclusion of contracts subject to acceptance by the other parties of supplementary obligations which, by their nature or according to commercial usage, have no connection with the subject of such contracts.

In my judgment, now-Article 102 covers all kinds of conduct in which a dominant firm or the individual members of a set of collectively-dominant firms can engage. Admittedly, now-Article 102 does list four categories of conduct that may violate its prohibition of abuses of a dominant position. But the key word in the preceding sentence is "may": the list is introduced by the statement that "[s]uch abuse, *may*, *in particular* [emphasis added] consist in" the types of conduct then listed, which (semantically) indicates that the list in question should not be read to be comprehensive.

Nevertheless, I will compare Article 102's list of abuses with the list of conduct covered by Article 101. There are three differences between and two overlaps between the items in this list and its counterpart in now-Article 101. The first difference relates to the (a) items in both lists. Item (a) of the now-Article 102 list covers the unilateral imposition of unfair prices or other terms by an individual dominant firm or the members of a collectively-dominant set of rivals (as well as price-fixing or other-term fixing by such collectively-dominant firms, regardless of whether the fixing is achieved exclusively through threats of retaliation) while item (a) in now-Article 101 covers only price or other-term fixing (where the fixed prices or other terms would, I assume, be deemed unfair solely on the ground that they were fixed).

The second difference relates to item (b) in the two lists. Item (b) in the now-Article 102 list covers the unilateral decision of an individually-dominant firm, the unilateral decisions of the members of a set of collectively-dominant rivals, or the concerted decision of the members of a set of collectively-dominant rivals to limit production, markets (does this mean "divide up markets" where the actors are the members of a collectively-dominant set of rivals?), or technical development whereas item (b) in the now-Article 101 list covers undertakings-agreements, trade-association decisions, or concerted conduct that limits production, markets, technical development, and investment more generally. Thus, the list of now-Article 102 does not cover limit QV investments that are not technologically innovative (an omission that would be important if the list were deemed comprehensive but is insignificant given the "*may*. . .consist in" language that introduces it).

The third difference relates to item (c) in the now-Article 101 list. The list in now-Article 102 does not include a counterpart to item (c) in now-Article 101's list—undertakings-agreements, trade-association decisions, or concerted practices to "share markets or sources of supply." In part, this difference can be explained by the fact that now-Article 102 covers the unilateral decisions of an individually-dominant undertaking. But only "in part": now-Article 102 also covers decisions made by a set of collectively-dominant undertakings.

The two similarities in the lists relate to their last two items. Items (d) and (e) in the now-Article 101 list coincide with items (c) and (d) in the now-Article 102 list. The fact that the now-Article 102 list includes price discrimination and the unilateral choice to place buyers under supplementary obligations strengthens my suspicion that these items appear in the Article 101 list not because the consciously-coordinated choice of two or more firms to engage in discrimination or place contract partners under such supplementary obligations is likely to prevent or restrict competition but because the drafters and ratifiers of now-Article 101 (and now-Article 102) did not understand the non-anticompetitive functions that such conduct can perform.

(3) The Tests of Illegality Promulgated by Article 102

As I have already indicated, now-Article 102 prohibits the conduct it covers when that conduct constitutes either an "exploitative" abuse or an "exclusionary" abuse. I will now analyze and comment on these two abuse concepts.

I start with "exploitative abuses." Now-Article 102's list makes it clear that the Article classifies as an exploitative abuse by a dominant individual firm or a collectively-dominant set of rivals a unilateral decision by an individually-dominant firm or one or more members of a collectively-dominant set of firms to charge unfairly-high prices to customers, to impose unfairly-disadvantageous terms of other sorts on customers, to pay unfairly-low prices to suppliers, or to limit production, markets, or technical development in ways that impose net-equivalent-monetary losses on its or their customers. Since now-Article 102's list is not comprehensive, I would not hesitate to conclude that now-Article 102 also prohibits as an exploitative abuse any unilateral decision by an individually-dominant firm or one or more collectively-dominant firms not to make a QV investment or an investment in plant-modernization or new-plant construction that "unfairly" disadvantages their customers. Concerted decisions of all these kinds made by the

members of a collectively-dominant set of rivals could be classified as either an exploitative abuse or an exclusionary abuse. However, the EC has classified such concerted conduct as an exclusionary abuse.[86]

In practice, very few "exploitative-abuse" cases have been brought or won under now-Article 102. Thus, although both the EC[87] and the European Court of Justice[88] have confirmed that now-Article 102 prohibits (as an exploitative abuse) the charging of excessively-high prices, very few "exploitative-abuse" cases have been brought or won, presumably because of the contestability of the operational definition of such concepts as an "excessively-high price," an "unfair price," or an "unfair non-price term or condition."

Operationally, the more important branch of now-Article 102's abuse test of illegality is the "exclusionary-abuse" branch. I will make four sets of points about the correct interpretation of the exclusionary-abuse branch of Article 102's test of illegality. First, conduct of an individually-dominant firm or a set of collectively-dominant rivals should be deemed to constitute an exclusionary abuse of its/their dominant position if it manifests the perpetrator's or perpetrators' specific anticompetitive intent. Of course, since Article 102 is exclusively concerned with the conduct of individually-dominant or collectively-dominant firms, unlike the Sherman Act, it does not prohibit conduct undertaken by non-dominant firms that enable them to secure a dominant position: in the EC authorities' words, to constitute an exclusionary abuse of a dominant position, conduct must have "the effect of hindering the maintenance of the degree of competition still existing in the market or the growth of that competition."[89]

Second, the first point implies that "competition on the merits" cannot constitute an exploitative abuse of a dominant position. Since competition on the merits involves behavior whose *ex ante* perpetrator-perceived profitability was not critically influenced by its/their perception that it would reduce the absolute attractiveness of the best offers against which they would have to compete by deterring a rival from competing, driving a rival out, or deterring a rival QV investment, it cannot violate a specific-anticompetitive-test of illegality.

Third, I need to comment on the text of clause (c) in Article 102. Clause (c) of Article 102 focuses on discriminatory pricing and the inclusion of other sorts of discriminatory terms. The text of clause (c) of now-Article 102—more specifically, its reference to the practice's putting one or more of the discriminator's "trading

---

[86] See DG Competition Discussion Paper on the Application of Article 82 of the Treaty to Exclusionary Abuses at Section 43 at pp. 46–50 and at Section 5.4 at pp. 74–76 (Dec. 2005).

[87] See Tetra Pak II v. Commission of the E.U., OJ L 72/1, pp. 135–38 (1992), stating that then Article 82 of the E.C. Treaty (now Article 102 of the 2009 Lisbon Treaty) prohibits as unfair the practice of renting a machine for a price that equals the sale price of the machine.

[88] See United Brands Co. v. Commission of the E.U., (27/76), 1978 WL 58871 (1978), stating that the article that is now Article 102 of the 2009 Lisbon Treaty prohibits a dominant firm from charging excessive prices, defined to be prices that bear no reasonable relation to the economic value of the product in question.

[89] See Manufacture Française des Pneumatiques Michelin v. Commission (Michelin II), Case T 203/01, E.U.R. II-4071, p. 54 (2003).

parties" (*i.e.*, its customers or possibly [when the discrimination relates to the discriminator's purchasing behavior] its suppliers) at a competitive disadvantage—indicates that the clause is directed at discrimination's causing decreases in secondary-line competition as opposed to decreases in primary-line competition—*i.e.*, of discrimination's decreasing competition in the market(s) in which the discriminator's customers operate as sellers as opposed to its decreasing competition in the market(s) in which the (dominant-firm) discriminator operates as a seller. However, for two reasons, the fact that clause (c) of Article 102 does not cover price discrimination that lessens primary-line competition does not imply that Article 102 does not cover such discrimination. First, because the fact the text of now-Article 102 states that "*abuse may, in particular*, consist in..." (emphasis added) implies that its "clauses (a)–(d) list" is not comprehensive, discrimination that reduces primary-line competition is covered by now-Article 102 even if it is not covered by clauses (a)–(d). Second, because price discrimination that lessens primary-line competition can properly be said to limit primary-line production, such price discrimination is covered by clause (b) of Article 102.[90]

One further point needs to be made (actually reiterated) about the correct handling of price discrimination under Article 102. When discussing the now-Article 101(1) clause, I pointed out that (1) its reference to dissimilar conditions being offered to "other trading parties" excluded from its coverage the practice in which a vertically-integrated concern charges independent producers that purchase an input the vertically-integrated firm produces or independent distributors that purchase a final product the vertically-integrated concern produces a price for the input or final product in question that differs from the shadow price on which it instructs the managers of its own fabricating or distributive "divisions" to base their decisions (presumably the manufacturing division's marginal cost in most situations) and (2) this exclusion is rendered at least somewhat problematic by the tendency of this practice to distort competition in the sense of making the independents worse-placed than the integrated firm for reasons that do not relate to their relative economic efficiency. The earlier discussion also indicated that (for reasons Chap. 14 will explore) it is hard to imagine any useful response the

[90] For the Director General's recognition that clause (c) does not cover price discrimination that reduces primary-line competition, see DG Competition Paper on the Application of Article 82 of the Treaty to Exclusionary Abuses at Section 5.5.3 (Dec. 2005); for scholarship that manifests academics' realization that clause (c) does not cover such discrimination, see Damien Geradin and Nicolas Petit, *Price Discrimination Under EC Law: The Need for a Case-by-Case Approach*, 2 J. OF COMPETITION LAW AND ECON. 479, 487 (2006) and the sources cited therein; for a case in which the ECJ recognized the fact that the clauses (a)–(d) list in Article 102 (then Article 82) is not comprehensive (in the court's terms, is only "indicative"), see Europemballage Corporation and Continental Can Company Inc. v. Commission, ECJ 6-72, ECR [1973] 215 at § 26 (Feb. 21, 1973); for discussions of the fact that the EC and the E.C./E.U. courts have applied Article 102 to cases in which the price discrimination at issue was alleged to have reduced primary-line competition, see Damien Geradin and Nicolas Petit, *Price Discrimination Under EC Law: The Need for a Case-by-Case Approach*, 2 J. OF COMPETITION LAW AND ECON. 479, 488–89 (2006) and the sources cited therein; and for a claim that price discrimination that lessens primary-line competition is covered by clause (b) of Article 102, see *id.*

government could make to this problem. At this juncture I want to point out that, if this practice can be said to increase the dominance of a dominant vertically-integrated firm that engages in it, the "other trading parties" language of clause (c) of now-Article 102 would not pose a barrier to that Article's being applied to the practice, given that the Article's "may...consist in" language implies that the list that language introduces is not comprehensive.[91]

Fourth, all the comments I made about clause (e) of Article 101(1) apply to its counterpart-clause—clause (d)—in Article 102. As I indicated, four points are salient. First, clause (d) of now-Article 102 covers a wide range of supplementary-obligation-creating practices. Second, these types of supplementary-obligation-creating decisions can perform a wide variety of functions other than reducing the absolute attractiveness of the offers against which the firm in question must compete and can have a wide variety of consequences other than reducing competition. Third, some of these supplementary-obligation-creating decisions probably increase economic efficiency while others would decrease economic efficiency by consuming resources to convert buyer surplus into seller surplus if the firm in question would otherwise allow the buyer surplus in question to escape (though the relevant decisions will often be less economically inefficient than the otherwise-unprofitable vertical integration in which the relevant deciders would engage to overcome the buyer-surplus problem in question if they were prohibited from using the above contractual surrogates for vertical integration). Fourth, I doubt that in ordinary language any of these types of arrangements could be said to impose obligations that, "by their nature or according to commercial usage, have no connection with the subject of...[the] contracts" that create them. Since the point of these arrangements is to increase the private proficiency of the relevant sellers' sale of the goods they involve, it is hard to see how, by their "nature," they have "no connection with the subject" of the relevant contracts. And since the relevant sellers would often—indeed, I suspect would usually—place their independent distributors under such supplementary obligations if doing so were not prohibited, it is hard to see how, as a matter of "commercial usage," these arrangements have "no connection with the subject" of the relevant contracts. I have

[91] The text ignores another issue raised by clause (c) of now-Article 102 to which neither the EC nor the E.C./E.U. courts have paid much attention—*viz.*, under what conditions should goods or services be characterized as "equivalent" for the purpose of determining whether clause (c) of now-Article 102 applies to discrimination in the terms on which they are sold. I think there are correct ways of responding to all the questions that others think are connected to this issue. I will discuss three such issues in this note. First, differences in the cost a seller has to incur to supply different buyers with the same good do not in themselves call into question the equivalence of the transactions in question, although such cost differences must be taken into account when deciding whether the terms offered different buyers are discriminatory. As I have already noted, economists have resolved this definitional issue correctly. Differences in prices (or other terms) are properly/usefully deemed discriminatory only if the differences are not cost-justified: the U.S. legal practice of calling term-differences discriminatory and then asking whether the discrimination is cost-justified is cumbersome at best and probably misleading. Second, products that buyers value differently (*e.g.*, high-season, low-season, and intermediate-season plane tickets) are not equivalent and transactions involving them are not "equivalent transactions." Third and relatedly, the act of charging different absolute or percentage markups on different products should not be characterized as discrimination.

chosen to reiterate these points rather than to simply state that they are equally applicable to clause (d) of Article 102 as they were to clause (e) of Article 101(1) because I consider them to be extremely important.

I turn now to the most important nine deficiencies in the way in which the EC and E.C./E.U. courts have interpreted and applied the exclusionary-abuse branch of Article 102. First, neither the EC nor the E.C./E.U. courts have ever explicitly defined the concept of an exclusionary abuse of a dominant position. Second and relatedly, the E.C./E.U. antitrust authorities have made inconsistent statements about whether competition on the merits can ever constitute an exclusionary abuse. In the one direction, the fact that the E.C./E.U. authorities use the word "exclusionary" to refer to those abuses of a dominant position that would be illegal even if they were not exploitative, the fact that exclusionary abuses are said to "foreclose" competition, and various explicit statements made both in the case-law and in EC Discussion Papers suggest that conduct that constitutes competition on the merits should not be found to constitute an exclusionary abuse. In the other direction, the way in which the EC has defined "foreclosure," statements that a dominant firm has a "special responsibility" to maintain or permit the intensification of the competition it faces, an important limitation of the "efficiency defence" the EC recognizes in exclusionary-abuse cases, and the tendency of the EC to focus on the impact of a dominant firm's placing its trading partners under certain types of supplementary obligations as opposed to focusing on the impact of a rule permitting a dominant firm and all its rivals to create such supplementary obligations all imply that the E.C./E.U. authorities believe that conduct that does represent competition on the merits can constitute an exclusionary abuse under now-Article 102 if it decreases or prevents an increase in the competition that a dominant firm or set of collectively-dominant firms faces. Some elaboration is required.

I start with the E.C./E.U. competition-law authorities' use of the expression "exclusionary abuse" and their linking such abuses to conduct that "forecloses" competition. In the usage adopted by U.S. antitrust courts and derivatively by U.S. antitrust scholars, conduct is said to be "exclusionary" or to "foreclose" competition if and only if the speaker or writer believes that it manifests the actor's or actors' specific anticompetitive intent—*i.e.*, does not involve competition on the merits. Because EC antitrust officials and scholars tend to borrow U.S. antitrust language and analyses, it is appropriate to assume as an initial matter that they define the terms "exclusionary" and "foreclose" in the same way that U.S. officials do. Obviously, if E.C./E.U. officials were defining "exclusionary" and "foreclose" in the U.S. way, their use of the expression "exclusionary abuse" and their linking of "exclusionary conduct" with "competition-foreclosing" conduct would imply that competition on the merits—*i.e.*, conduct whose *ex ante* actor-perceived profitability was not critically affected by the actor's or actors' belief that the profitability of the conduct might (in effect) be critically inflated by its reducing the absolute attractiveness of the offers against which it or they have to compete—could not constitute an exclusionary abuse (even if the actor[s] were a dominant firm or member[s] of a collectively-dominant set of firms). However, various statements of the EC about the meaning of "exclusionary" and "foreclose" undercut this argument by indicating that it is not defining these words in the U.S. way. Thus, the 2005 DG Competition Discussion Paper on exclusionary abuses states:

> By foreclosure is meant that actual or potential competitors are completely or partially denied profitable access to a market. Foreclosure thus can be found even if the foreclosed rivals are not forced to exit the market: it is sufficient that the rivals are disadvantaged and consequently led to compete less aggressively. Rivals may be disadvantaged when the dominant company is able to directly raise rivals' costs or reduce demand for the rivals' products. Foreclosure is said to be market distorting if it likely hinders the maintenance of the degree of competition still existing in the market or the growth of that competition and thus has as a likely effect that prices will increase or remain at a supra-competitive level.

My reading of this statement to imply that conduct can be "foreclosing" in the EC sense and hence "exclusionary" in the EC sense if it reduces competition or prevents an increase in competition by increasing the actor's or actors' organizational economic efficiency is supported by the text's describing conduct as market-*distorting* if it is likely to increase or prevent decreases in prices, regardless of whether the conduct generates this effect by increasing the actor's or actors' organizational economic efficiency. This interpretation is confirmed by the Paper's later statement that what it denominates market-distorting foreclosure is more likely in the presence of "network effects and economies of scale and scope."[92] The EC's more-recent communication on exclusionary conduct by dominant undertakings is also consistent with this reading:

> In this document the term 'anticompetitive foreclosure' is used to describe a situation where effective access of actual or potential competitors to supplies or markets is hampered or eliminated as a result of the conduct of the dominant undertaking whereby the dominant undertaking is likely to be in a position to profitably increase prices to the detriment of consumers.[93]

E.C./E.U.-competition-law case-law and DG Discussion Papers also include a number of explicit statements that imply that competition on the merits cannot constitute an exclusionary abuse—in particular, statements that

(1) Article 102 does not prohibit any dominant firm (or set of collectively-dominant firms) from engaging in "normal competition"[94] or from engaging in "genuine competition based on factors such as higher quality, novel products, opportune innovation or otherwise better performance,"[95]
(2) under now-Article 102, "[a] dominant firm is entitled to compete on the merits. Nor does the EC suggest that large producers should be under an obligation to refrain from competing with smaller competitors or new entrants,"[96]

---

[92] DG Competition Discussion Paper on the Application of Article 82 of the Treaty to Exclusionary Abuses at Section 5.1 (Dec. 2005).

[93] EC Guidance on the Commission's Enforcement Priorities in Applying Article 82 of the EC Treaty to Abusive Exclusionary Conduct by Dominant Undertakings, C 45/02 p. 19 (2009).

[94] Hoffman-La Roche & Co. AG v. Commission, E.U.R. 461, p. 91 (1979).

[95] DG Competition Discussion Paper on the Application of Article 82 of the Treaty to Exclusionary Abuses at Section 5.1 (Dec. 2005).

[96] AKZO, OJ L 375, p. 81 (Dec. 12, 1985).

(3) now-Article 102's prohibition of exclusionary abuses implies no more than that "[a]n undertaking in a dominant position cannot have recourse to means other than those within the scope of competition on the merits"[97] or to means "without objective economic justification,"[98]
(4) Article 102 is intended "to ensure that... competitors [of an individually-dominant firm or collectively-dominant set of firms] are... able to expand in or enter the market and compete therein on the merits...,"[99] and
(5) (at least in the pricing context) "in general [I do not know whether this is an important qualification] only conduct which would exclude a hypothetical 'as efficient' competitor is abusive."[100]

Unfortunately, the E.C./E.U. competition-law authorities have also made statements that imply that competition on the merits *can* constitute an exclusionary abuse—not only the previously-referred-to explicit definitions the EC has given to the terms "foreclosure" and "market-distorting" in Article 102 cases and Discussion Papers but also statements in the case-law that "dominant undertakings have a special responsibility not to allow their conduct to impair genuine undistorted competition on a market where competition is already restricted by the fact of the dominant position."[101] Given the way in which the EC has implicitly defined "distorting competition" elsewhere, I do not think that this statement can be reconciled with the statements just listed that indicate that competition on the merits cannot constitute an exclusionary abuse. The EC's position on the economic-efficiency defence that applies in now-Article 102 exclusionary-abuse cases also implies that competition on the merits can constitute an exclusionary abuse.[102] Unlike the specific-anticompetitive-intent test I have argued the U.S.

[97] See Manufacture Française des Pneumatiques Michelin v. Commission (Michelin II), Case T 203/01, E.U.R. II 4071, p. 107 (2003).

[98] *Id.* at p. 110.

[99] DG Competition Discussion Paper on the Application of Article 82 of the Treaty to Exclusionary Abuses at Section 5.1 (Dec. 2005).

[100] *Id.* at p. 5.2.

[101] See Atlantic Container Lines judgment, Case T 191/98, p. 1460 (Sept. 30, 2003).

[102] I should indicate that the EC also recognizes two other "defences" in Article-102 exclusionary-abuse cases. The first, so-called objective necessity defence enables a dominant firm to exonerate itself by demonstrating that the conduct under scrutiny was indispensable (usually for "reasons of safety or health related to the dangerous nature of the product in question") to the permissibility of producing or distributing the product in question. (I assume that this defence would be critical only when the production and distribution of the "product" the conduct in question enables the dominant firm to supply by increasing its safety or healthfulness decreases the competition the dominant firm faces by inducing the exit of a rival product or deterring the introduction of a rival product.) See DG Competition Paper on the Application of Article 82 of the Treaty to Exclusionary Abuses at Section 5.51 (Dec. 2005). The second non-efficiency defence is a "meeting-competition defence." This defence enables a dominant firm to exonerate itself by demonstrating that it engaged in the conduct in question "to minimize the short-run losses resulting directly from competitors' actions...." See *id.* at Section 5.5.2. Although I doubt that the EC had this possibility in mind and admit that the losses the relevant conduct would enable a defendant to avoid would not be just short-run losses, I suspect that this defence would be most relevant to a dominant firm that used tying or

Sherman Act promulgates and the organizational-economic-efficiency defense that I think correct as a matter of U.S. law to read into the U.S. Clayton Act, the economic-efficiency defense that the EC has read into now-Article 102 exonerates dominant firms whose competition on the merits has reduced competition or prevented increases in competition by inducing a rival to exit or deterring an established or potential competitor from making a new QV investment by improving the economic efficiency of the dominant firm's operations and thereby (1) improving the set of competitive positions it enjoys or would enjoy and concomitantly (2) worsening the set of competitive positions its rivals do or would occupy if and only if the net effect of the organizational-economic-efficiency-enhancing conduct in question is to create an on-balance equivalent-monetary gain for the customers of the dominant firm and the customers of their product rivals. As the EC's Discussion Paper states: "If consumers in an affected relevant market are worse off following the exclusionary conduct [note the implicit definition of "exclusionary"], that conduct cannot be justified on efficiency grounds."[103] This conclusion (which, as we shall see in Chap. 12, parallels the conclusion that the U.S. Department of Justice and Federal Trade Commission have reached about efficiency defenses in horizontal-merger cases[104]) implies that, at least in some cases, competition on the merits can constitute an exclusionary abuse under now-Article 102.

In short, the EC and the E.C./E.U. courts have taken inconsistent explicit and implicit positions on whether competition on the merits can constitute an exclusionary abuse of a dominant position.

Third, the European authorities assert that conduct cannot be said to constitute an exclusionary abuse (or an exploitative abuse) unless it does so in a defined market.[105] I hasten to add that U.S. courts also insist that a firm cannot be shown to

---

reciprocity agreements for quality-control purposes or included resale-price-maintenance, vertical-territorial-restraint, or vertical-customer-allocation clauses in its contracts with independent distributors to induce them to make jointly-profitable advertising, door-to-door-sales, pre-sales-advice, and post-sales-service decisions when nondominant rivals were engaging in similar practices for the same reasons. Admittedly, however, the availability of the defence might be affected by the existence of other, less-profitable ways of achieving the same objectives (by the possible non-indispensability of the conduct) or, in some cases, by the fact that the combination of the dominant firm's conduct and its rivals' parallel conduct gave the dominant firm an advantage. For further discussions of this possibility, see the subsequent text of this subsection and Chap. 14 *infra*.

[103] DG Competition Paper on the Application of Article 82 of the Treaty to Exclusionary Abuses at Section 5.5.3 (Dec. 2005). That conclusion also seems to be implied by p. 19 of the 2009 EC Guidance on the Commission's Enforcement Priorities in Applying Article 82 of the EC Treaty to Abusive Exclusionary Conduct, which is quoted in the text to which footnote-number 79 is attached.

[104] See 1992 Horizontal Merger Guidelines at Section 4 and as revised in 1997 and 2010 Horizontal Merger Guidelines at Section 10.

[105] Relatedly, both the EC and E.C./E.U.-competition-law courts have also insisted that a firm cannot be shown to occupy a dominant position (a set of firms cannot be shown to have a collectively-dominant position) without defining the market it dominates (they collectively dominate). See, *e.g.*, AKZO Chemie BV v. Commission, Case C 62/86, E.U.R. I-3359 (1991); Hoffman-La Roche & Co. AG v. Commission, Case 85/76, E.U.R. 461 (1979); and United Brands Co. v. Commission of the E.U., Case 27/76, 1978 WL 58871 (ECJ 1978).

have monopolized or attempted to monopolize or to have decreased competition unless the relevant market (markets) is (are) defined. Since, for reasons that Chap. 6 delineates, I believe that market definitions are inevitably arbitrary not just at their periphery but comprehensively, I find this insistence on identifying one or more relevant markets not just regrettable but fundamentally misguided.

Fourth, the EC and the E.C./E.U. courts have failed to recognize that mergers, acquisitions, and joint ventures can constitute exclusionary (and exploitative) abuses of an individually-dominant or collectively-dominant position.[106] Given that clauses (a)–(d) in Article 102 are introduced by the words "may, in particular," the legally-incorrect conclusion that Article 102 does not cover mergers, acquisitions, or joint ventures is even more surprising than the relevant government authorities' conclusion that Article 101 does not cover such conduct.

Fifth, as Chap. 14 shows, the EC and various E.C./E.U. competition-law courts originally did not comprehend the functions that the relevant sorts of supplementary-obligation-creating clauses perform and although they are catching up with their U.S. counterparts' still imperfect (as well as belated) understanding of the functions that such conduct can perform, their understanding of them is still highly imperfect.[107]

Sixth, as Chap. 14 also shows, although the EC's concern about the possible impact of these arrangements on intra-brand competition may be legally warranted under now-Article 102 (in relation to the application of the exploitative-abuse branch of its test of illegality), (1) the EC's and E.C./E.U. courts' original analysis of this impact[108] failed to take account of the possibility that firms that are prohibited from using supplementary-obligation-creating contractual surrogates for vertical integration may respond to such prohibitions by changing other aspects of their pricing arrangements or by vertically integrating forward into distribution, and (2) although (as I have just asserted) their more-recent pronouncements and decisions have been better-informed, their understanding of the functions and effects of these practices is still highly imperfect.

Seventh, the EC and the E.C./E.U. courts subscribe to the mistaken leverage theory of tie-ins and reciprocity.

Eighth, although the relevant EC statements are ambiguous, several leave the impression that the EC's legal analysis of the impact of supplementary-obligation-creating practices on inter-brand competition will focus on the impact of an individual firm's creating a covered supplementary obligation as opposed to the impact of a legal rule authorizing all members of a group of rivals to create the relevant supplementary obligation. As I indicated when discussing clause (e) of now-Article 101(1), the former focus is inconsistent with the "level playing field"

[106] See Europemballage Corp. & Continental Can, Inc. v. Commission, Case 6/72, G.C.R. 215 (1973).

[107] See, *e.g.*, EC Guidelines on Vertical Restraints, OJ C 291/1 (2000).

[108] *Id.* at Section 1.1.

norm that informs U.S.-antitrust-law analysis,[109] which I think E.C./E.U. competition law is based on as well.

Ninth, for the same reasons that I take the analogous position in relation to Article 101(1), I believe that the E.C./E.U. courts have erred in concluding that the E.C./E.U. commitment to establishing a common market favors interpreting Article 102 to prohibit a dominant producer or the members of a collectively-dominant set of rival producers from using contract clauses or sales policies to prevent its/their independent distributors in one member-country from reselling the producer's/producers' product(s) in another member-country.

However, I hasten to add that the preceding conclusion does not imply that the texts of now-Articles 101 and 102 cover all acts of discrimination (more generally, all kinds of conduct that competition law should prohibit). Competition law should prohibit discrimination that is either (1) predatory or (2) retaliatory against an actor that has failed to cooperate in the discriminator's effort to obtain a contrived oligopolistic margin, a contrived QV-investment restriction, or a contrived reduction in any other form of competition (*i.e.*, whose discriminator-perceived *ex ante* profitability was critically affected by the discriminator's perception that it might reduce the absolute attractiveness of the offers against which it will have to compete by driving a rival out, deterring an expansion or entry, or inducing future cooperation with the discriminator's contrivance efforts)—indeed, should prohibit all variants of strategic behavior, and, to my mind, now-Articles 101 and 102 do not prohibit any type of predation (including predatory discrimination) engaged in unilaterally by an individual firm that is neither dominant on its own nor part of a set of collectively-dominant firms or any attempt at contrivance that does not involve the making of an agreement not to compete. Thus, now-Article 101 does not cover unilateral, individual predation of any kind or contrivance that is attempted or effectuated solely through threatening and/or executing acts of retaliation because it covers only agreements between undertakings, decisions induced by associations of undertakings, and concerted practices. Now-Article 102 does not cover predation or contrivance by any firm that is neither individually dominant nor a member of a collectively-dominant set of product rivals because it applies solely to individually-dominant firms and the members of a set of collectively-dominant rivals. Since (I suspect) firms that are neither individually dominant nor members of a collectively-dominant set of firms would often find it profitable to engage in unilateral predation or contrivance exclusively by threat if the law did not prohibit their doing so, this omission is serious.

[109] Admittedly, in one case, the Supreme Court held that a practice that would be illegal for a well-established firm to use because, by increasing its proficiency, it would weaken the positions of its marginal and potential competitors would be lawful for a marginal or potential competitor to use because, by increasing its proficiency, it would help the firm in question to survive or enter. See White Motor Co. v. United States, 372 U.S. 253 (1963). However, this parimutual-handicapping decision is very much an outlier.

C. The E.C./E.U. Merger Control Regulation (EMCR)[110]

As already indicated, the EC and the E.C./E.U. courts concluded that the Treaty provisions that are now Articles 101 and 102 of the 2009 Treaty of Lisbon do not cover mergers, acquisitions, or joint ventures—an erroneous legal conclusion that European academic experts on E.C./E.U. competition law did not challenge.[111] Starting in 1989, the Council of Ministers responded to the actual and perceived deficiencies of then-Articles 81 and 82 (now-Articles 101 and 102) as bases for merger control by adopting regulations for controlling mergers, acquisitions, and full-function joint ventures (but not partial-function joint ventures, which create entities that [for example] only do research or only serve as a buying-agent for the parents or only perform one part of a more-complex production process).[112] These regulations gave the EC exclusive jurisdiction over mergers and acquisitions between companies whose combined turnover exceeded a specified volume, leaving mergers and acquisitions involving companies with a smaller combined turnover to the control of national authorities (on the questionable assumption that these smaller transactions have no "community dimension"). Puzzlingly (at least to me), the 1989 regulation prohibited only those "concentrations" that "create[] or strengthen[] a dominant position as a result of which effective competition would be significantly impeded in the common market or in a substantial part of it. . .."[113] I say "puzzlingly" because this formulation appears to leave uncovered "concentrations" that would significantly lessen competition without creating a dominant firm, strengthening the dominance of an individual dominant firm, making a set of product rivals collectively dominant, or strengthening the collective dominance of a set of collectively-dominant product rivals. Some Council delegations found this exclusive focus on creating and strengthening dominance undesirable and proposed a U.S.-style "lessening of competition" test. However, other delegations continued to support the dominance-oriented test. A compromise was negotiated that consisted of (1) an Article of the regulation that makes inconsistent references to both tests (perhaps a more generous description would be: that first promulgates a "lessening competition" test and then takes it all back by concretizing that test with the words "in particular as a result of the creation or strengthening of a dominant position") and (2) two supplemental "recitals" that respectively (A) indicate that the "lessening competition" test is different from the dominance-oriented test and is also operative and (B) try to explain away the "now

[110] Council Regulation 139/2004 on the Control of Concentrations Between Undertakings (May 1, 2004). (In E.C./E.U. competition-law parlance, mergers [and acquisitions] are referred to as "concentrations.")

[111] See ELHAUGE AND GERARDIN 875.

[112] Council Regulation 4064/89 on the New Control of Concentrations Between Undertakings, OJ L 395/1 (1989).

[113] See *id.* at Article 2.

you have it, now you don't" aspect or the regulation's text where the "it" is the "lessening competition" test.

Thus, Article 2(3) of the 1994 EMCR states:

> A concentration which would significantly impede effective competition, in the common market or in a substantial part of it, *in particular* [emphasis added] as a result of the creation or strengthening of a dominant position, shall be declared incompatible with the common market.

Supposedly by way of clarification "in the interests of legal certainty" but actually inconsistently with the "now you don't" part of the regulation, Recital 25 states:

> The notion of "significant impediment to effective competition" in Article 2(2) and (3) should be interpreted as extending, beyond the concept of dominance, only to the anticompetitive effects of a concentration resulting from the non-coordinated behavior of undertakings which would not have a dominant position on the market concerned.

Recital 26 then attempts to explain away the apparent internal inconsistency of the regulation's text:

> A significant impediment to effective competition generally results from the creation or strengthening of a dominant position.

Note the difference between the "in particular" language of the regulation and the "generally results from" language of the recital.

Pragmatically, the relevant point is that, since 2004, the EC seems to interpret the EMCR to promulgate a "significant lessening of competition" test of illegality whose "lessening of competition" language appears to be interpreted in the same way that "lessen competition" is interpreted by U.S. authorities in Clayton Act cases.

Moreover, both the economic-efficiency defences and the failing-company defences that the EC recognizes in "concentration" cases seem to be the same as those that the U.S. Department of Justice, the Federal Trade Commission, and U.S. courts recognize in horizontal merger and acquisition cases. Thus, both the EC Guidelines and the DOJ/FTC Guidelines[114] recognize efficiency defenses only if, as a result of the efficiencies (in the EC's words), "consumers will not be worse off as a

[114] See EC Guidelines on the Assessment of Horizontal Mergers at Section VII, OJ C 31/5 (2004), 1992 Horizontal Merger Guidelines as revised in 1997 at Section 4, and 2010 Horizontal Merger Guidelines at Section 10. I hasten to add that this efficiency defence is less generous to defendants than the organizational-economic-efficiency defence that I think legally appropriate to read into the Clayton Act and is also less generous to defendants than the Sherman Act (since, under that statute's test of illegality, mergers and acquisitions will not be illegal if their participants believed *ex ante* that the private benefits the transaction in question would confer on them by generating economic efficiencies, by yielding tax advantages, by enabling one or more participants to liquidate their assets and/or escape managerial responsibilities, and by increasing the ability of the merged firm relative to that of its antecedents to profit by converting buyer into seller surplus would be sufficiently large to render the relevant transaction *ex ante* profitable, regardless of whether it was predicted to, should have been predicted to, or actually did inflict a net-equivalent-dollar loss on the participants' customers and the customers of the participants' product rivals).

result of the merger." And both the EC and the U.S. authorities (both the DOJ/FTC Guidelines and the U.S. courts) recognize the same failing-company defense. In the EC's words, to make out a failing-company defence, the defendant must establish three things:

> First, the allegedly failing firm would in the near future be forced out of the market because of financial difficulties if not taken over by another undertaking. Second, there is no less anticompetitive alternative purchase than the notified merger. Third, in the absence of the merger, the assets of the failing firm would inevitably exit the market.[115]

I should note that, like the failing-company defense recognized by the DOJ/FTC Guidelines and the U.S. courts, this EC failing-company defence adopts a "most-procompetitive move the defendant could make" competitive-impact-measurement baseline as opposed to the do-nothing baseline. I express no opinion on whether the EC's baseline-choice is as inconsistent with the normal E.C./E.U. competition-law competitive-impact-measurement baseline as it is with the normal U.S.-antitrust-law competitive-impact-measurement baseline.

Chapters 12, 13, 14, and 15 will discuss in some detail the various deficiencies of the EC's and the E.C./E.U. courts' interpretations and applications of the EMCR. I will confine myself here to listing what I take to be some of the more serious errors in question. The EC and the E.C./E.U. courts' guidelines and decisions

(1) never operationalize the EMCR's test of illegality,
(2) insist that the market or markets in which covered conduct is alleged to have prohibiting effects be defined,
(3) adopt an abstract definition of an antitrust market that is somewhat different from its U.S. Guidelines' counterpart but has the same faults as the U.S. Guidelines' abstract definition and adopt the same faulty protocol for identifying concrete antitrust markets that the DOJ/FTC Guidelines adopt, though the EC recognizes as the DOJ and FTC do not that this protocol is rendered problematic by the fact that product A's being highly competitive with product B and product B's being highly competitive with product C does not guarantee that product A will be highly competitive with product C (by what the EC terms "chains of substitution" and I term the non-transitivity of the competitiveness of different pairs of products),
(4) promulgate a protocol for analyzing the competitive impact of covered conduct that uses market-aggregated data as "initial indicators,"
(5) assert that a merger partner's possession of a pre-merger market share of 50 % or more favors the conclusion that the merger will lessen competition,
(6) contain confused statements about the nature of "tacit collusion,"
(7) manifest only a partial understanding of the determinants of the impact of mergers, acquisitions, and full-function joint ventures on non-oligopolistic and contrived oligopolistic pricing,

[115] EC Guidelines on the Assessment of Horizontal Mergers at Section VIII, OJ C 31/5 (2004). See also 1992 Horizontal Merger Guidelines at Section 5 and 2010 Horizontal Merger Guidelines at Section 11.

(8) ignore the impact of covered conduct on natural oligopolistic conduct altogether,
(9) manifest only a partial understanding of the determinants of the impact of mergers, acquisitions, and full-function joint ventures on QV-investment competition (though they do pay more attention to this impact than the U.S. Guidelines and court-decisions do),
(10) manifest only a partial understanding of the determinants of the effectiveness of potential competition,
(11) accept limit-pricing theory,
(12) accept the leverage theory of tie-ins and reciprocity,
(13) fail to analyze the determinants of the impact on relevant buyers of any organizational allocative efficiencies the conduct it covers generates, and
(14) are unduly optimistic about the competitive impact of mergers, acquisitions, and full-function joint ventures that are alleged to increase R&D.

3. The Differences Between the Actor-Coverage of, Conduct-Coverage of, Tests of Illegality Promulgated by, and Defenses Recognized by U.S. and E.C./E.U. Competition Law

Sections 1 and 2 of this chapter have distinguished different referents both for the concept "U.S. antitrust law" and for the concept "E.C./E.U. competition law." Section 1 sometimes focused on the meaning one would attribute to the U.S. Sherman and Clayton Acts if one paid attention solely to their texts, sometimes focused on the meaning of those statutes taking into consideration not only their texts but U.S. statutory-interpretation practices and various features of U.S. industrial policy, sometimes focused on the doctrines that U.S. courts have developed and various decision-"Guidelines" the U.S. Department of Justice and Federal Trade Commission have published to operationalize (in some instances to my mind, incorrectly) the relevant statutes' tests of illegality, and sometimes focused on the (to my mind, sometimes-incorrect) conclusions that U.S. courts have reached about the antitrust legality of various specific types of business conduct—conclusions that reflected *inter alia* the incorrect doctrines they developed to operationalize the statutes' tests of illegality and the courts' partly-or-wholly-incorrect understanding of the functions and likely competitive impact of the conduct in question.

Similarly, Section 2's discussion of the content of E.C./E.U. competition law has sometimes focused on the semantic meaning of Articles 81 and 82 of the 1957 E.C. Treaty (now-Articles 101 and 102 of the 2009 Treaty of Lisbon) and of the Merger Control Regulations the Council of Ministers has promulgated, sometimes focused on the (to my mind, often-surprising) ways in which the EC and E.C./E.U. competition-law courts have interpreted those Articles and EMCRs, and sometimes focused on the way in which these authorities have actually applied the Articles in question to particular kinds of conduct (including applications that, to my mind, reflect their peculiar readings of the Treaty and/or imperfect understandings of both the functions of the conduct in question and the consequences of that conduct and of its prohibition).

The fact that Sections 1 and 2 each focused on a number of different "things" creates a risk for the comparative analysis that this section executes. I must be careful not to compare incomparables—not, for example, to compare U.S. law (to my mind) correctly interpreted and applied with E.C./E.U. law (to my mind) incorrectly interpreted and applied. Or, at least, if I do make such comparisons, I must carefully identify the things I am comparing and explicitly state that the things being compared are in important respects different.

Rather than focusing separately on the actor-coverage of, conduct-coverage of, tests of illegality promulgatedly by, and defenses recognized by particular U.S. or E.U. "laws," this section will focus successively on particular types of conduct and examine the way in which each such type of conduct is addressed by U.S. antitrust law and E.C./E.U. competition law. I start with two omissions. First, neither U.S. antitrust law as written nor EC competition law as applied covers decisions to make non-predatory QV investments.

Second, neither U.S. antitrust law as written nor E.C./E.U. competition law as written covers unsuccessful attempts to enter into contrived oligopolistic agreements by firms that are not individually dominant and are not members of a collectively-dominant set of rivals, and U.S. antitrust law as written does not cover such unsuccessful attempts by any category of firm either. The Sherman Act does not cover such attempts by any category of firm because Section 1 does not refer to attempts and, given that fact, the combination of the failure of the United States' government to pass a general "attempt statute" and the decision of the U.S. courts not to correct this omission make it unlikely that U.S. courts would conclude (and incorrect as a matter of U.S. law for the courts to conclude) that Section 2's prohibition of "attempts to monopolize" covers such unsuccessful attempts. Now-Article 101 does not cover any attempts to form a contrived oligopolistic agreement because such attempts involve neither the formation of an agreement nor (in the vast majority of cases) a decision by an association of undertakings nor a concerted practice. Now-Article 102 does not cover unsuccessful attempts to form a contrived oligopolistic agreement when the attempter is not a dominant firm or a member of a collectively-dominant set of rivals.

I next consider all other forms of contrived oligopolistic conduct. The U.S. Sherman Act does cover all other forms of contrived oligopolistic conduct. E.C./E.U. competition law does not. Now-Article 101 does not cover contrivance that is based solely on anticompetitive threats when the rival target of the threat succumbs to it without profiting from it since, in that case, there is no agreement or concerted practice, and now-Article 102 does not cover either this kind of contrivance or any other kind of contrivance when the contriver is neither an individually-dominant firm nor a member of a collectively-dominant set of rivals.

I turn to predatory conduct. Properly interpreted and applied, the U.S. Sherman Act covers and prohibits all forms of predatory conduct, regardless of the monopoly power or dominance of the perpetrator(s) and regardless of whether the predatory conduct is unilateral (single-firm) or concerted. Although some judicial opinions state that, to prove monopolization, a plaintiff must demonstrate that the defendant had monopoly power (prior to or after [?] engaging in the allegedly-monopolizing conduct), this doctrinal position is wrong as a matter of both economics and law and, in practice, is increasingly ignored by the courts. Moreover, the Clayton Act also covers the forms of predatory conduct that its specific provisions address: thus, Section 2 of the Clayton Act covers predatory pricing that involves price discrimination, and Section 3 covers predatory decisions to induce contract partners not to patronize particular suppliers when the effect of these arrangements is to lessen competition. E.C./E.U. competition law does not cover and prohibit some predatory acts. Now-Article 101 does not cover single-firm predation because such conduct involves neither an agreement between undertakings, nor a decision by an association of undertakings, nor a concerted practice, and now-Article 102 does not cover either single-firm or multifirm predation if the firm(s) in question did not individually occupy a dominant position prior to committing the predatory act(s) or was (were) not part of a collectively-dominant set of rivals prior to committing the predatory act(s). To the extent that I am correct in believing that most predatory acts are unilateral and that most predators neither occupied an individually-dominant position nor belonged to a set of collectively-dominant product rivals prior to engaging in predation, this failure of E.C./E.U. competition law to cover unilateral acts of predation by non-dominant firms is a serious deficiency (if I am correct in rejecting the view of many economists that predation is rarely if ever practiced—see Chap. 11).

I move now to horizontal agreements other than mergers, acquisitions, or the creation of new jointly-owned companies (joint ventures). Both U.S. antitrust law (the Sherman Act) and E.C./E.U. competition law fully cover and always prohibit horizontal agreements that (1) contain what the Europeans call "hardcore restrictions"—horizontal agreements that fix prices to be charged third parties, limit output or sales, or allocate markets or customers—and (2) involve no real economic collaboration, regardless of the size or market shares of the participants in the agreements in question. It is slightly more complicated to compare the U.S. and E.U. positions on horizontal agreements that are designed to secure real economic collaboration. As I have already indicated, the EC's so-called de minimis Notice exempts from the coverage of now-Article 101(1) all such horizontal agreements between firms that have (1) fewer than "250 employees and either annual revenue less than 50 million euros or an annual balance-sheet total less than 43 million euros" or (2) an aggregate market share that does not exceed 10 %. U.S. case-law has no similar *de minimis* exclusion. However, Guidelines promulgated jointly by the U.S. Department of Justice (DOJ) and Federal Trade Commission (FTC) in 2000 state:

> Absent extraordinary circumstances, the Agencies do not challenge a competitor collaboration [that is not *per se* illegal] when the market shares of the collaboration and its participants collectively account for no more than twenty percent of each relevant market in which competition may be affected.[116]

[116] United States Department of Justice and Federal Trade Commission, Antitrust Guidelines for Collaborations Among Competitors at Section 4.2 (2000).

When the EC and the U.S. DOJ and FTC do analyze the legality of horizontal competitor-collaboration agreements, they appear to do so in a very similar way—focus on whether, taking the efficiencies the collaboration has been shown to generate and the availability of other significantly less-restrictive means of generating them into account, the collaboration will yield or has yielded an on-balance equivalent-monetary gain to the customers of the collaborators and the customers of their product rivals. As I have already indicated, I think that in those cases in which the collaboration's negative effect on the relevant buyers can be attributed to its driving one or more non-collaborators out or raising the barriers to QV investment faced by one or more potential or established rivals of the collaborators by worsening those rivals' actual or prospective competitive-position arrays by increasing the economic efficiency of the collaborators' operations, the economic-efficiency defense recognized by the DOJ and FTC is less generous to the collaborators than is legally warranted.

I turn now to conglomerate and horizontal mergers, acquisitions, and joint ventures. The comparison of the U.S. and E.C./E.U. law on such transactions must distinguish between the situations that prevailed before and after the passage of the various E.C. Merger Control Regulations (most importantly, before and after the date on which E.C. Merger Control Regulation 139/220 became effective—May 1, 2004). Moreover, the comparison of U.S. and E.C. law on such transactions in the earlier period must also distinguish among what E.C. law, properly interpreted, would have been in that period

(1) if, as I conclude, the "clauses (a)–(e)" list that appears after the words "in particular" in now-Article 101(1) is illustrative rather than comprehensive and if, as I believe, correctly interpreted, now-Article 102 covers such transactions,
(2) if the conclusions just delineated are incorrect but, as I also believe, now-Article 101(1) would in any event declare the indicated transactions *prima facie* illegal if they created a merged company or joint venture that participated in more contrived oligopolistic agreements and joint predation with its rivals than its antecedents would have done or, in the case of an acquisition, resulted in the contriving company's participating in more contrived oligopolistic agreements or joint predation than it otherwise would have done, or
(3) if both the above sets of conclusions are wrong—*i.e.*, if the EC and the E.C./E.U. courts were correct in concluding that neither now-Article 101(1) nor now-Article 102 covers any merger, acquisition, or joint venture.

Obviously, if the legal conclusions articulated in the first two items in the above list are incorrect, the E.C./E.U. law on mergers, acquisitions, and joint ventures prior to the promulgation of any EMCR would have been vastly different from the applicable U.S. law—in particular, would not have covered such transactions at all. In fact, if the legal conclusions articulated in the first item in the above list are incorrect but the conclusion articulated in the second item in that list is correct, the E.C./E.U. competition law that antedated the EMCR would still not cover the overwhelming majority of transactions of these types that U.S. law would deem illegal, though the E.C./E.U. law in question might then declare *prima facie* illegal some such transactions that U.S. law might not declare illegal—*viz.*, mergers, acquisitions, and joint ventures that would increase the incidence of contrivance agreements and joint predation. (U.S. law would not prohibit such transactions if, properly interpreted, the Sherman and Clayton Acts would not be read to be "fence laws"—*i.e.*, to condemn covered conduct on the ground that it is likely to induce subsequent violations of the law.) Moreover, even if one agrees with the conclusions expressed in the first item in the above list, the pre-EMCR E.C./E.U. law on mergers, acquisitions, and joint ventures would differ in at least four important ways from the U.S. law on such transactions. First, if now-Articles 101 and 102 were correctly interpreted to have the same turnover threshold that the EMCR has, that fact would differentiate E.C./E.U. law from its U.S. counterpart. Admittedly, one requirement for Clayton Act illegality is that the conduct *substantially* lessens competition but I am confident that that requirement is easier to satisfy than its EMCR counterpart. (The EMCR assigns jurisdiction over mergers and acquisitions that do not satisfy its size requirements to national authorities on the [to my mind bogus] ground that smaller mergers or acquisitions have no "Community [now Union] dimension.") Second, although now-Article 101(3) does promulgate an efficiency defence, that defence is less generous to defendants than its Sherman Act counterpart, than the related element of the Clayton Act's test of *prima facie* illegality, or than the organizational-economic-efficiency defense I think is correct as a matter of law to read into the Clayton Act. Third, now-Article 101 and now-Article 102 do not (to their credit) contain any text that favors the conclusion that a concentration that does not lessen competition overall is illegal if it lessens competition in any product or geographic market. As we have seen, the Clayton Act's "in any line of commerce or in any section of the country" language does favor this undesirable conclusion (and, as we shall see in Chap. 12, some U.S. case-law does adopt it, though I think these decisions are incorrect as a matter of U.S. law).

The Council of Ministries' Promulgation of the E.C. Merger Control Regulation 139/220 (which took effect on May 1, 2004) vastly reduced the difference between the U.S. and E.C./E.U. law on mergers, acquisitions, and full-function (so-called concentrative) joint ventures. This EMCR promulgates a test of illegality that is basically the same as the Clayton Act's "lessening competition" test. However, the two jurisdictions' laws still differ in relation to these transactions in at least four ways:

(1) the EMCR does not apply to partial-function joint ventures, which would matter less if now-Articles 101 and 102 were deemed to cover such joint ventures (as well as full-function joint ventures and all mergers and acquisitions, an interpretation whose contemporary legal correctness may be disfavored by the passage of the EMCR) but would still matter if now-Article 101 but not now-Article 102 were deemed to cover partial-function joint ventures, given the differences between now-Article 101(3)'s "efficiency defence" and the exonerating role that efficiencies play in U.S. joint-venture law;

(2) the EMCR does not supplement its "lessening competition" test with a Sherman-Act-type specific-anticompetitive-intent test (which would matter less if now-Articles 101 and 102 were deemed to cover mergers, acquisitions, and joint ventures);
(3) it might not be correct as a matter of E.U. law to interpret the EMCR to recognize an organizational-economic-efficiency defense; and
(4) there is no basis for concluding that covered behavior that does not lessen competition overall but does do so in one or more "markets" violates the EMCR.

I address penultimately vertical mergers and their contractual surrogates—simple price discrimination and more complicated pricing-techniques (variants of perfect price discrimination) that are designed to increase the rate at which their seller-employer can convert potential buyer surplus into seller surplus, the various kinds of supplementary-obligation-creating contract clauses that are designed for the same purpose, and the various kinds of supplementary-obligation-creating contract clauses that are designed to achieve a variety of other goals that will be described in more detail in Chap. 14. I should say at the outset that it is far trickier to compare U.S. and E.C./E.U. law on such vertical practices than to compare U.S. and E.C./E.U. law on other kinds of conduct because (1) as we have seen, the expressions "U.S. law" and "E.C./E.U. law" could refer to the relevant law correctly interpreted, the relevant law as interpreted by official interpreters, and the relevant law as applied, (2) some of these referents are hard to pin down in relation to vertical integration and its contract surrogates, and (3) these referents are quite different in relation to vertical integration and its contractual surrogates. Thus, it is not clear whether contemporary U.S. courts will follow some doctrinal positions that the Supreme Court took in earlier cases that relate to the protocol one should use to determine the antitrust legality of some such practices or how long the Supreme Court will stick with its current (to my mind, unjustifiable) position that the legality of some vertical restraints depends on whether they increase inter-brand competition by more than they decrease intra-brand competition. Similarly, it is not clear how the EC (1) will determine if a supplementary obligation, "by [its] nature or according to commercial usage," has "no connection with the subject of the. . .contract[]" that created it or (2) will resolve the inconsistency in its statements that (A) even dominant firms are permitted to compete on the merits and (B) dominant firms have a "special responsibility" to prevent the reduction of or permit the increase of the competition they face.

In any event, it seems to me that there are at least six reasons for believing that the E.C./E.U. law on vertical integration and its contract-clause and sales-policy surrogates may be different from its U.S. counterpart. First, E.C./E.U. competition law (more particularly, the Article that is now-Article 102 of the 2009 Lisbon Treaty) prohibits any individually-dominant firm or any member of a set of collectively-dominant product rivals from committing "exploitative abuses"—*i.e.*, from doing anything that deprives their customers of a "fair share" of the equivalent-monetary gains (the sum of the buyer and seller surplus) their transactions with them generate.

U.S. antitrust law has no similar prohibition. Since most conventional and perfect price discrimination and many of the exemplars of the various types of supplementary-obligation-creating vertical contract-clauses are designed (in the latter cases, sometimes *inter alia*) to increase the rate at which the seller can convert buyer into seller surplus and actually reduce the amount of buyer surplus the buyer secures (as well as the percentage of seller *plus* buyer surplus the buyer secures), E.C./E.U. competition law may, in theory, be more likely to prohibit such conduct when its perpetrator is individually dominant or (by interpretation) a member of a collectively-dominant set of rivals than is U.S. law. (I say "in theory" because the EC and E.C./E.U. courts have rarely enforced the "exploitative-abuse" branch of now-Article 102's test of illegality.)

Second, the fact that E.C./E.U. competition law, unlike U.S. antitrust law, was devised *inter alia* to create a common market in the sense of a single market might be thought to imply that, as a matter of law, now-Article 101 should be read to prohibit an individual firm's limiting the territories within which or customers to which its independent distributors are authorized to resell its products. As I have previously indicated, I think this inference is unwarranted as a matter of law as well as undesirable as a matter of policy, but the E.C./E.U. competition-law tradition may be less supportive of competition on the merits than is the U.S. tradition, and contemporary Europeans may be more likely to be concerned with what they take to be[117] a related "liberty of independent-distributors" issue than contemporary

[117] I say "what they take to be" because, for three reasons, I do not think that such vertical territorial restraints and customer-allocation clauses infringe the "liberty" of independent distributors:

(1) the independent distributors agreed to the restrictions in question under conditions that do not suggest that they were coerced into doing so;

(2) if, as I suspect will often be the case, prohibitions of such clauses may result in the producers' integrating forward into distribution, the clauses might very well increase the set of options available to potential independent distributors; and

(3) I doubt the issue is appropriately characterized as a *liberty* issue in any event.

This third point requires some elucidation. If it is to make a useful contribution to moral and political debate in a liberal, rights-based society, the concept of liberty should be invoked only when the choice that is restricted plays an important role in (1) an individual's choosing the values he wants his life to instantiate or (2) living a life that is consonant with the choice he made. For this reason, prohibitions of an individual's driving north on a one-way-southbound street or prohibitions of an individual's sticking a knife in someone else's gut when there is no justification for his doing so should not be said to restrict his liberty. In my judgment, contractual restrictions on the territories within which an independent distributor can operate or on the buyers to which it can sell are not restrictions on its liberty as that concept should be operationally defined in a liberal, rights-based society (which places a lexically-highest value on individuals' having a meaningful opportunity to lead a life of moral integrity by taking their moral obligations seriously and by taking seriously as well the task of choosing the conception of "the good" to which they personally subscribe and conforming their lives to that choice). Although it may be unwise (as well as incorrect) for me to say this, I suspect that the European proclivity to value the independence of independent distributors is an anachronistic survivor of a feudal past in which an individual was defined by his or her occupation as opposed to (as in a liberal, rights-based society) by his or her moral choices and integrity.

Americans are.[118] If so, at least as a matter of EC and E.U.-court decision-making, the E.C./E.U. competition law on such vertical restraints may be different from the U.S. antitrust law on these practices.

Third, as I suggested earlier, E.C./E.U. competition law may be less committed than is U.S. antitrust law to allowing undertakings in general and especially individually-dominant or collectively-dominant firms to compete on the economic merits when their doing so might reduce competition or prevent increases in competition. To the extent that this is the case in principle or in practice, the legality of those vertical practices that increase the economic efficiency of their employer's operation may be different in the E.U. and in the United States where "legality" could refer either to "legality if the law is correctly interpreted and applied" and/or "legality as the law will be interpreted and applied."

Fourth and relatedly, when the issue is whether a vertical practice violates a "lessening competition" test of illegality (the test of the U.S. Clayton Act, the effect branch of Article 101(1) of the 2009 Lisbon Treaty, and the EMCR), there may be a difference in practice in the analysis of E.U. and U.S. officials (even though I think as a matter of law there should not be). In particular, I fear that E.C./E.U. officials may be more likely than U.S. officials to focus on the impact of an individual defendant's placing its contract partners under supplementary obligations as opposed to the impact of a rule allowing all members of a set of product rivals to do so. I say this despite the fact that the Supreme Court opinion in *White Motor* focused on the former issue in part because I do not think that that case will be followed, in part and relatedly because that opinion's pari-mutuel handicapping is so inconsistent with the deep U.S. commitment to competition on the merits (and level playing fields), and in part because I am less certain that E.C./E.U. competition law as written and *a fortiori* that law's official interpreters and appliers are as committed to competition on the merits as are their U.S. counterparts.

Fifth, positive E.C./E.U. competition law may be more likely to prohibit various supplementary-obligation-creating vertical contract clauses than is positive U.S. antitrust law because E.C./E.U. competition-law appliers may be less conversant with the various functions that such arrangements can perform than are their contemporary U.S. counterparts (whose comprehension is itself admittedly partial and belated).

Sixth and finally, to the extent that tie-ins, reciprocity, vertical price restraints, vertical territorial restraints, and vertical-customer-allocation clauses do inflict equivalent-monetary losses on relevant consumers (and I emphasize that it is not clear that they will, given the way the producers in question will respond to their prohibition), such surrogates for vertical integration will more often violate E.C./E.U. competition law when their employer is individually dominant or a member of a collectively-dominant set of rivals (in particular, the exploitative-abuse branch

[118] Admittedly, some U.S. officials (most prominently, Justice William O. Douglas of the U.S. Supreme Court) have also been concerned with this alleged "liberty of traders" issue.

of now-Article 102) than U.S. antitrust law. I should add that a wide variety of other surrogates for vertical integration not prohibited by U.S. antitrust law might also be condemned under E.C./E.U. competition law as an exploitative abuse of a dominant position if the actor in question had an individually-dominant position or a part of a collectively-dominant position. Thus, the unilateral decision by such an actor to raise its per-unit price and/or lump-sum fee, to practice perfect price discrimination, or to shift to a pricing-technique that combines a lump-sum fee with a per-unit price that exceeds its marginal costs could all, in principle, be deemed illegal as an exploitative abuse of a dominant position. (I would add that a variety of business decisions that do not involve the employment of surrogates for vertical integration could also be deemed exploitative abuses under now-Article 102 if made by an individually-dominant firm or a member of a collectively-dominant set of rivals: *inter alia*, decisions not to make an otherwise-unprofitable quality-or-variety-increasing investment, not to make an otherwise-unprofitable shift to a known, marginal-cost-reducing production process [whose use would make it profitable for it to reduce its prices], and not to engage in [unprofitable] production-process research that would benefit its customers by discovering a less-externality-prone production process it would then be obligated to adopt [because a shift to the discovered process would reduce accident and pollution costs by more than it would increase other production costs][119] could, all in principle, be deemed illegal as an

[119] Some such research may be not only unprofitable but economically inefficient (at least, on otherwise-Pareto-perfect assumptions). But some might be unprofitable but economically efficient on such assumptions. This result may obtain if four conditions are fulfilled:

(1) the producer of the product to whose production process the relevant research relates is liable only for accident losses caused by its negligence;

(2) either because of doctrinal error or because of the difficulty of assessing the negligence of decisions not to execute accident-loss-reducing production-process research, the relevant producer's decision not to do such research will never, in practice, be assessed for negligence;

(3) the relevant potential production-process researcher is a producer of the good to whose production process the relevant research relates; and

(4) if the potential researcher discovers an accident-loss-reducing production process whose use would reduce accident losses by more than it increased other variable costs of production, it would be negligent for it not to shift to the safer production process in question.

Conditions (1) and (2) are fulfilled for most producers in both common-law and civil-law countries. Condition (4) will be fulfilled unless the discoverer can keep its discovery secret. Because information that is relevant to making the kind of discovery in question is often impacted to actors that produce the good in question, condition (3) will frequently be fulfilled, at least when the individual producer/potential researcher is the only producer of the product in question that can finance the necessary research or the number of possible producer-researchers is sufficiently small for each to face a critical natural oligopolistic disincentive in relation to the research (for each to know *inter alia* that if it starts to do such research one or more rivals will follow suit but, if it does not, no-one else will do so either because it would do research if the other did).

I should add that the third sentence in the preceding paragraph states that "this result *may* obtain" (emphasis added) because the fulfillment of the conditions just specified guarantees only that the incentives of the producer to do the relevant production-process research will be deflated. Whether those incentives are critically deflated will depend on the economic efficiency of the relevant research, the market share of the relevant producer/potential researcher, and the weighted-average-expected number of days by which the producer's decision not to do the relevant research will delay the relevant discovery.

exploitative abuse of a dominant position.) Admittedly, the fact that E.C./E.U. officials have been reluctant to condemn as an exploitative abuse by a dominant firm such a firm's decision to charge unfairly-high prices makes it unlikely that they would condemn on this ground the types of choices itemized in the preceding sentence. But it does seem to me that now-Article 102 not just authorizes but requires them to do so if it would be practicable for them to assess the exploitativeness of such choices.

I want to close by pointing out two striking similarities between the U.S. antitrust law and the E.C./E.U. competition law on surrogates for vertical integration. First, despite the fifth dissimilarity in the preceding list, the fact is that the EC and E.C./E.U. courts are rapidly closing the gap between their and their U.S. counterparts' (1) understanding of the legitimate functions that vertical price restraints, vertical territorial restraints, and vertical-customer-allocation clauses can perform and (2) realization that prohibiting such intra-brand-competition-decreasing vertical restraints may not benefit relevant consumers because the producers in question are likely to respond to such prohibitions in lawful ways that are equally inimical to the interests of the consumers in question as the vertical restraints in question would be if, counterfactually, the relevant producer would respond to their prohibition by dropping the vertical restraint and making no other alteration in its behavior. (In fact, if U.S. courts follow the instruction of the Supreme Court to determine the legality of such restraints by balancing their negative impact on intra-brand competition against any positive impact they have on inter-brand competition and the Supreme Court does not change this protocol and declare that the impact of such practices on intra-brand competition is legally irrelevant, I can imagine that in a few years the E.U.'s economic and legal assessment of such practices will be more correct than the U.S.'.)

Second, I suspect that, correctly interpreted, the U.S. and E.C./E.U. law on price discrimination in the sale of final goods to distributors that are horizontal rivals and in the sale of inputs to final-good producers that are horizontal rivals is surprisingly similar. As I indicated, I think that correctly interpreted, the Robinson–Patman Act (unwisely) prohibits such price discrimination if it inflicts an equivalent-dollar loss on the buyer against which discrimination has been practiced by placing it at a competitive disadvantage relative to favored rival resellers (when the product on which discrimination has been practiced is a final good) or final-good producers (when the product on which discrimination has been practiced is an input) even when the discrimination does not lessen competition in the secondary-line market. I think the same legal conclusion is correct in E.C./E.U. competition law in this situation for a different substantive reason: although official interpretations do not seem to differentiate "distorting" competition from preventing or restricting it, what I regard as the natural reading of now-Article 101's separate prohibition of distorting competition might well render illegal a seller's use of discriminatory terms of sale that place disfavored buyers at a competitive disadvantage vis-à-vis favored rivals unrelated to the disfavored buyer's ability to compete on the economic-efficiency merits even if that use does not prevent or restrict competition. I should note, however, because (as Chap. 14 explains) it will rarely if ever be profitable for a producer to discriminate against such retailers and final-good producers when doing so will harm them by putting them at a competitive disadvantage relative to the discriminator's favored customers, I doubt that this possible difference is empirically significant.

* * *

This chapter has delineated and discussed the actor-coverage of, conduct-coverage of, tests of illlegality promulgated by, and defenses or defences recognized by U.S. antitrust law and E.C./E.U. competition law. Chapters 10–15 will supplement this account by describing the conclusions that U.S. and E.C./E.U. authorities have reached about the legality of the kinds of conduct on which they respectively focus.

The Conclusion of this study (which appears at the end of Vol. 2) alternatively summarizes and elaborates on this chapter's discussions of the tests of illegality promulgated by U.S. and E.C./E.U. antitrust law, the errors that U.S. and E.C./E.U. antitrust authorities have made and/or continue to make when interpreting and applying the tests of legality promulgated by the statutes/treaties they respectively are charged with implementing, the relationship between U.S. and E.C./E.U. antitrust law as written (and correctly interpreted and applied) both currently and historically, and the relationship between U.S. and E.C./E.U. antitrust law as actually interpreted and applied both currently and historically.

Chapter 5
Categories of Economic-Efficiency Gains That Are and Are Not Relevant to Conduct's Antitrust Legality

THE WELFARE ECONOMICS OF ANTITRUST POLICY AND U.S. AND E.U. ANTITRUST LAW will list the various narrowly-defined categories of economic inefficiency whose magnitudes both business conduct and antitrust policies can affect that I find useful to distinguish and will explain how such conduct and policies can and when they will increase and decrease each of these narrowly-defined categories of economic inefficiency. This chapter is much less ambitious. Section 1 delineates four broad categories and a few subcategories of economic inefficiency (resource misallocation) whose magnitudes business conduct and antitrust policies can affect. Section 2 lists the various categories of economic-efficiency gains and losses that business conduct can yield whose generation by any exemplar of business conduct is irrelevant to the conduct's antitrust legality and explains why these economic-efficiency effects are irrelevant to the legality of the conduct that generates them under U.S. antitrust law and E.C. competition law. And Sect. 3 lists the various categories of economic-efficiency gains that business conduct can yield whose generation is either directly or indirectly relevant to its antitrust legality and explains briefly why the fact that conduct yields these categories of economic-efficiency gains does favor its legality under the U.S. Sherman Act, the U.S. Clayton Act, Article 101 of the 2009 Lisbon Treaty, Article 102 of the 2009 Lisbon Treaty, and the EMCR.

1. Categories of Economic Inefficiency That Business Conduct and Antitrust Policies Can Affect

For reasons that the antitrust-policy companion to this book will make clear, it is useful to distinguish four broad categories of economic inefficiency (resource misallocation):

(1) pure production-optimum economic inefficiency or resource misallocation, which is present to the extent that a net equivalent-dollar gain could have been generated *inter alia* had the economy's producers produced their actual outputs with different known production processes, had productive inputs other

R.S. Markovits, *Economics and the Interpretation and Application of U.S. and E.U. Antitrust Law*, DOI 10.1007/978-3-642-24307-3_5,

than labor been fully employed (the failure to use the amount of labor whose employment would have been economically efficient is a type of top-level UO-to-UO misallocation between the production of leisure and the production of other goods and services), had a different set of PPR projects been executed with the amount of resources devoted to PPR—*i.e.*, to the extent that PPR-to-PPR misallocation has been generated, and/or had the economy's sellers not priced their products and services in ways that increased the amount of mechanical allocative transaction costs they and their customers generated when devising, assessing, and policing their contracts and/or the amount of allocative delivery costs generated by the distribution of the economy's output to its final consumers (by causing goods to be delivered circuitously through a combination of initial sales and arbitrage);

(2) pure consumption-optimum economic inefficiency or resource misallocation, which is present to the extent that a net equivalent-dollar gain would have been generated had the units of various products that were actually produced been allocated differently among their potential final consumers;

(3) pure top-level-optimum economic inefficiency or resource misallocation, which is present to the extent that a net equivalent-dollar gain would have been generated (A) had more units of one or more products and fewer units of one or more other products been produced without changing the total amount of resources devoted to producing units of known products—*i.e.*, to the extent that UO-to-UO misallocation has been generated (where UO stands for "unit output"), (B) had a different set of QV investments been created with the resources devoted to QV-investment creation—*i.e.*, to the extent that QV-to-QV misallocation has been generated, or (C) had resources been allocated in different proportions between unit-output-increasing and QV-investment-creating uses—*i.e.*, to the extent that QV-to-UO or UO-to-QV misallocation has been generated; and

(4) mixed production-optimum/top-level-optimum economic inefficiency or resource misallocation, which is present to the extent that a net equivalent-dollar gain would have been generated by an appropriate alternative division of the economy's resources between unit-output-increasing and PPR-executing uses or between QV-investment-creating and PPR-executing uses—*i.e.*, to the extent that (A) UO-to-PPR or PPR-to-UO and/or (B) QV-to-PPR or PPR-to-QV misallocation has been generated.

Before proceeding, I want to introduce one further refinement in three of the categories of misallocation to which the preceding list referred. For current purposes, it is important to note that UO-to-UO, QV-to-QV, and PPR-to-PPR misallocation can take place either between or among different areas of product-space (in which case I will refer to the relevant misallocation as *inter-industry* UO-to-UO, QV-to-QV, or PPR-to-PPR misallocation) or within a fairly-narrowly-defined area of product-space (in which case I will refer to the relevant misallocation as *intra-industry* UO-to-UO, QV-to-QV, or PPR-to-PPR misallocation). Thus, if from the perspective of economic efficiency too many resources are allocated to the production of one product variant relative to the amount allocated to the production of a closely-competitive product variant, the misallocation in question will be labeled *intra-industry* UO-to-UO misallocation, and if from the perspective of economic efficiency too many resources are allocated to creating QV investments in one area of product-space relative to the amount allocated to creating QV investments in a fairly-distant area of product-space, the misallocation in question will be labeled inter-industry QV-to-QV misallocation.

2. Categories of Economic-Efficiency Effects Whose Generation Is Irrelevant Under U.S. and E.C./E.U. Competition Law

As I will point out in Chap. 9, many economists and law professors who are conversant with economics mistakenly claim that the U.S. antitrust laws promulgate an economic-efficiency test of illegality. In actuality, however, the impact of business conduct on the extent of many categories of economic inefficiency is irrelevant to its legality under U.S. (and E.U.) antitrust law. More specifically, the facts that business conduct (1) reduces or increases UO-to-UO misallocation by decreasing or increasing price competition, (2) reduces or increases inter-industry QV-to-QV misallocation by decreasing or increasing price competition and/or by decreasing or increasing QV-investment competition, (3) reduces or increases inter-industry PPR-to-PPR misallocation by decreasing or increasing price competition in the ARDEPPSes in which the goods to whose production process the relevant research relates, by decreasing or increasing price competition in the ARDEPPSes producing the goods whose outputs will be reduced if the PPR yields a marginal-cost-reducing production-process discovery, by increasing or increasing PPR competition, and/or by increasing the amount of profits the seller/actor can obtain by selling the right to use production-process discoveries without changing the demand curve for the right to use the discovery in question, (4) reduces or increases UO-to-QV and QV-to-UO, PPR-to-QV and QV-to-PPR, and UO-to-PPR and PPR-to-UO misallocation by decreasing or increasing price competition, QV-investment competition, or PPR competition, and/or by increasing the amount of profits that seller/actors can obtain by selling existing products, newly-discovered products, or the right to use production-process discoveries without changing the DD/MC combination they face when doing so, (5) increases production-optimum misallocation by increasing the allocative mechanical transaction costs a seller generates when pricing its product, (6) increases production-optimum misallocation by raising allocative delivery-costs by increasing the amount of arbitrage in which a relevant seller's customers engage, and (7) increases consumption-optimum or production-optimum misallocation by causing units of a relevant seller's product to be allocated to lower-valuing buyers who are charged lower prices rather than to higher-valuing potential buyers to whom the seller is charging higher prices are all irrelevant to the legality of the conduct under U.S. antitrust law or E.C./E.U. competition law, correctly interpreted and applied. I should add that, although the preceding sentence's assumption that some of the categories of economic inefficiency to which it refers could be increased by increases in price and/or QV-investment competition or could be decreased by decreases in price and/or QV-investment competition does reflect the complicated realities that The General Theory of Second Best highlights—*viz.*, that, in a situation in which one or more optimal conditions cannot be or will not be fulfilled, there is no general reason to believe that fulfilling or more closely approximating the remaining optimal conditions will even tend to bring one closer to the optimum, the legal claim the preceding sentence articulates reflects this reality only to the extent that one or more of the relevant statutes, regulations, or treaty provisions promulgate a lessening-competition or specific-anticompetitive-intent test of illegality and Second-Best Theory reveals that one cannot infer the competitive impact of relevant conduct or the intent of its perpetrator(s) from its impact on UO-to-UO, QV-to-QV, PPR-to-PPR, UO-to-QV and QV-to-UO, PPR-to-QV and QV-to-PPR, and UO-to-PPR and PPR-to-UO misallocation either in the simple way that first-best analyses do or at all.

The preceding claims of legal irrelevance require some explication. I will now explain why the listed types of economic-efficiency gains and losses are irrelevant to the legality of any conduct that generates them under the Sherman Act, the Clayton Act, Article 101 of the 2009 Lisbon Treaty, Article 102 of that Treaty, and the EMCR.

The listed economic-efficiency consequences are irrelevant to the Sherman-Act-legality of any business conduct that generates them because they have no bearing on

(1) whether the Sherman Act covers the conduct in question,
(2) whether the conduct generates Sherman-Act-illicit profits, and
(3) whether the conduct's perpetrator's or perpetrators' *ex ante* belief(s) that it was profitable was critically affected by its or their perception that it might generate Sherman-Act-illicit profits.

The listed economic-efficiency consequences are irrelevant to the Clayton Act legality of any business conduct that generates them because they have no bearing on

(1) whether the Clayton Act covers the conduct in question,
(2) whether the conduct has imposed an equivalent-dollar loss on the combination of the customers of the perpetrator(s) and the customers of its (their) product rivals by reducing the absolute attractiveness of the best offer they respectively received from any inferior supplier, and
(3) when the conducted inflicted an equivalent-dollar loss on Clayton-Act-relevant buyers by reducing the absolute attractiveness of the best offer they respectively received from any inferior supplier, whether the conduct increased its perpetrator's or perpetrators' organizational economic efficiency and, if it did, whether it would not have inflicted such a loss on those buyers in the above way had it not increased its perpetrator's or perpetrators' organizational economic efficiency.

With a number of possible exceptions related to item (5) in the following list, the possible economic-efficiency consequences of business conduct listed previously are irrelevant to whether the conduct that generated them violates Article 101 of the 2009 Lisbon Treaty because they have no bearing on

(1) whether the conduct's perpetrator is a type of actor whose conduct is covered by Article 101,
(2) whether the conduct is a type of conduct covered by Article 101,
(3) whether the absolute size and market shares of the conduct's perpetrators fall below the *de minimis* levels the EC has established,
(4) whether the conduct in question "prevents, restricts or distorts" competition,
(5) whether the conduct "contributes to improving the production or distribution of goods or to promoting technical or economic progress,"
(6) whether the conduct "allow[s] consumers a fair share of the benefits" it yielded in the ways delineated in item (5) in this list,
(7) whether the conduct is the least-restrictive means of achieving the benefits listed in item (5) in this list,
(8) whether the conduct "afford[s]. . .[its perpetrators] the possibility of eliminating competition in respect to a substantial part of the products" it involves, or
(9) whether the type of conduct in question or the industry in which it took place qualifies it for one of the block exemptions the EC has created.

The arguable qualifications that relate to item (5) in the immediately-preceding list are connected to the possibility that any Article 101-covered conduct that decreases inter-industry PPR-to-PPR or UO-to-PPR/PPR-to-UO economic inefficiency and (at least when any additional QV investments that are created are technologically or commercially innovative) and any Article 101-covered conduct that decreases inter-industry QV-to-QV, UO-to-QV/QV-to-UO, or PPR-to-QV/QV-to-PPR economic inefficiency should be construed to have "promote[d] technical or economic progress" in the sense in which Article 101(3) uses this expression. I think that such a construal of this Article 101(3) language would be inapposite. In my judgment, the "promot [ions] of technical or economic progress" to which Article 101(3) refers are increases in economic efficiency that result from (1) increases in the proficiency with which the defendants execute given PPR projects and given technologically-or-commercially-innovative QV-investment projects, (2) increases in the intrinsic economic efficiency of the PPR and technologically-or-QV-commercially-innovative QV-investment projects they undertake, (3) increases in the total amount of resources the perpetrators devote to PPR or technologically-or-commercially-innovative QV investments, and possibly (4) decreases in intra-industry PPR-to-PPR misallocation or in intra-industry QV-to-QV misallocation (where the QV investments in question are technologically or commercially innovative) that are generated by agreements between or among potential innovators that enable them to make the set of PPR or QV-investment research-projects executed in their ARDEPPS more economically efficient without altering the "intrinsic economic efficiency" of the individual projects in the set in question by reducing the duplicativeness of the projects that are executed. *Inter alia*, this interpretation is supported by the related facts that (1) the benefits generated by the relevant promotion of technical or economic progress have always been understood to be the related equivalent-dollar gains obtained by the perpetrators and their

(6) top-level-optimum-economic-efficiency gains business conduct generates by enabling the actor or actors in question to design individual QV-investment-creating projects that are intrinsically more economically efficient,
(7) top-level-optimum-economic-efficiency gains (reductions in intra-industry QV-to-QV misallocation) business conduct generates by reducing the economically-inefficient duplicativeness of the projects in an ARDEPPS' QV-investment-project array, and
(8) top-level-optimum-economic-efficiency gains business conduct generates by enabling a seller to increase economic efficiency by controlling the quality of complements a seller's customers combine with its products and by enabling a seller to induce its distributors to supply buyers with economically-efficient pre-sales advice and post-sales warranty-service (see Chap. 14).

All these categories of economic-efficiency gains are relevant to the Sherman-Act-legality of the conduct that generates them because the profits the relevant conduct's perpetrator(s) realize(s) because it generates them (which will usually not equal the economic-efficiency gains in question) are Sherman-Act-licit profits.

With a few qualifications, all these categories of economic-efficiency gains are relevant to the Clayton Act legality of the conduct that generates them because they all reduce the probability that that conduct will inflict a net equivalent-dollar loss on the combination of the customers of its perpetrator(s) and the customers of its (their) product rivals and because they are exemplars of the organizational-economic-efficiency gains whose generation will render conduct that would otherwise violate the Clayton Act lawful under that Act when their generation was a necessary condition of the relevant conduct's imposing a net equivalent-dollar loss on Clayton-Act-relevant buyers. The qualifications are necessary because (1) efficiencies in the first category listed above will not benefit Clayton-Act-relevant buyers if they are fixed-cost efficiencies, (2) PPR-execution efficiencies and QV-investment-execution efficiencies will not benefit Clayton-Act-relevant buyers if they do not induce the perpetrators to increase the amount of resources they devote to PPR execution or QV-investment creation, (3) PPR-project-design efficiencies will not benefit consumers unless the superior project will reduce marginal costs of production more than the inferior project would do or is more likely than the inferior project to succeed, (4) QV-investment-project-design efficiencies may not create a new QV investment whose use generates more buyer surplus, (5) increases in the economic efficiency of an ARDEPPS' PPR-project array will not benefit Clayton-Act-relevant buyers if they do not reduce marginal costs of production, and (6) increases in the economic efficiency of an ARDEPPS' QV-investment-project array may not benefit Clayton-Act-relevant buyers in part because the greater dispersion of the projects that are created will tend to be associated with a decrease in the intensity of price competition in the relevant area of product-space.

The fact that conduct covered by Article 101 generates one or more of the eight kinds of efficiencies listed in this section will favor its Article 101(1) legality by increasing the probability that its perpetrator(s) would have engaged in it even if it (they) knew that it would not prevent or restrict competition—*i.e.*, by reducing the likelihood that the relevant conduct violated the object branch of Article 101(1)'s test of *prima facie* illegality. The fact that conduct covered by Article 101 of the 2009 Lisbon Treaty generates one or more of the various kinds of efficiencies that appear in the immediately-preceding list also favors the conduct's legality under that treaty-provision by making it less likely that the conduct "distorts" competition and by justifying the conclusion that the conduct did contribute or would contribute to "improving the production or distribution of goods or promoting technical or economic progress" (*i.e.*, by justifying the conclusion that the conduct would satisfy this condition for an Article 101(3) exemption). The fact that business conduct did or would generate the various kinds of economic-efficiency gains just listed also favors its legality under Article 102 by undercutting the claim that the conduct is "exclusionarily" abusive (though the fact that conduct generates some of the economic-efficiency gains just listed does manifest the fact that it falls into the third and fourth categories of conduct that Article 102 implies may be abusive). Finally, with the same qualifications I delineated when discussing the relevance of the economic-efficiency gains in question to the Clayton Act legality of the conduct that generated them, the fact that a merger, acquisition, or joint venture generates one or more of the categories of economic-efficiency gains just listed favors its legality under the EMCR by making it less likely that the conduct imposes a net equivalent-dollar loss on relevant buyers.

* * *

Many economists and legal academics who are conversant with economics claim that the U.S. antitrust laws promulgate an economic-inefficiency test of illegality. This chapter's analysis of the relevance of the various categories of economic-efficiency gains that business conduct can generate refutes this claim and demonstrates that E.C./E.U. competition law also does not make the legality of covered conduct depend exclusively on its economic efficiency (or, for that matter, on the economic efficiency of prohibiting it).

Chapter 6
The Inevitable Arbitrariness of Market Definitions and the Unjustifiability of Market-Oriented Antitrust Analyses

The concrete antitrust-law analyses of every country are virtually always market-oriented—*i.e.*, virtually always derive their legal conclusions from data on parameters such as a firm's market share or the concentration of the market(s) in which it is operating whose definitions assume that markets can be defined non-arbitrarily. Thus, courts, prosecutors, and administrative agencies that are applying treaties that prohibit the abuse of a dominant position or doctrines that assert that the possession of monopoly (or market) power is an element of an actual or alleged antitrust offense (such as engaging in monopolizing conduct) have all assumed that the dominance of any firm or its monopoly or market power should be determined primarily or exclusively by its market share, and courts, prosecutors, and administrative agencies that are seeking to prevent or break up horizontal mergers and acquisitions that manifest their participants' specific anticompetitive intent or lessen competition have primarily or exclusively based their predictions of the competitive impact of such mergers or acquisitions (1) traditionally on the merger partners' individual and combined shares of the relevant markets' sales and the total of the shares of the sales of those markets made by the four or eight firms that had most sales in them and (2) more recently on the post-merger sum of the squares of the market shares of all firms placed within the relevant markets (the post-merger HHIs—Hirschman–Herfindahl Indices—of those markets) and the impact of the merger in question on these HHIs. I hasten to add that the implicit assumption of all such analytic protocols that markets can be defined non-arbitrarily is shared by virtually all industrial-organization economists.

The specific market-oriented approaches to analyzing the antitrust legality of particular types of business conduct are analyzed in more detail in the chapters in Part II that focus on the respective types of conduct in question. This chapter addresses a more general criticism that can be made of all such approaches—*viz.*, that their implicit assumption that markets can be defined non-arbitrarily (or at least sufficiently non-arbitrarily for these approaches to be supportable) is unjustified.

The same two criteria that I previously asserted should be used to evaluate definitions of "the impact of a choice on economic efficiency" should be used to evaluate any formal definition of the concept of a market, any protocol for defining

R.S. Markovits, *Economics and the Interpretation and Application of U.S. and E.U. Antitrust Law*, DOI 10.1007/978-3-642-24307-3_6,

concrete markets, or any actual set of market definitions. The first is an ideal-type criterion: Does the abstract or concrete market definition (or the set of market definitions the relevant protocol would generate) conform with professional and popular usage and understanding (more specifically, does it fit or produce conclusions that fit ideal-type assumptions about the competitiveness of products that are placed in the same market and the difference between the competitiveness of products that are placed in the same market and their respective competitiveness with products that are placed in other markets)? The second is a functional criterion: Will the abstract or concrete market definitions in question or the market definitions that would be generated by the protocol in question make the greatest possible contribution that such definitions could make to a justifiable analysis in which they play a role?

Chapter 6 argues that, regardless of which of these two criteria one uses to evaluate any set of market definitions or protocols for defining markets, market definitions will be arbitrary not just at their periphery but comprehensively. Section 1 demonstrates that, even if one could determine non-arbitrarily the minimum amount of sales any set of products must make to a group of buyers for the products and buyers to constitute a market, there would be at least three reasons why it might not be possible to define markets non-arbitrarily if market definitions are to be assessed by the sort of ideal-type criterion just articulated:

(1) the various popular and professional assumptions in question cannot be operationalized non-arbitrarily;
(2) different sets of market definitions will do best at satisfying the different assumptions in question, regardless of how they are operationalized, and one cannot define non-arbitrarily the metric for measuring how well a set of market definitions satisfies the relevant assumptions overall; and
(3) even if one has defined the preceding metric, more than one set of market definitions may satisfy the relevant assumptions overall equally well.

Section 2 demonstrates that markets cannot be defined non-arbitrarily when a functional criterion is used to evaluate a set of market definitions or a protocol for defining markets. In particular, Sect. 2 demonstrates that, even if one could determine non-arbitrarily the minimum amount of sales that a set of products must make to a group of buyers for the products and buyers to constitute a market, there are at least five reasons why it also will not be possible to define markets non-arbitrarily when the criterion for evaluating a set of market definitions is its ability to play a useful role in a cost-effective protocol for resolving some issue (for example, predicting the competitive impact of a horizontal merger):

(1) no market-oriented approach to any antitrust issue can ever be cost-effective (see below);
(2) even if one can define operationally the proximate goal of a particular antitrust law (say, preventing "decreases in competition" in the sense in which I have defined this concept) and even if the effectiveness of a market definition can be said non-arbitrarily to depend on the extent to which it secures the proximate

goal of the relevant antitrust law, one cannot decide non-arbitrarily whether the metric for that goal's achievement focuses on the number or percentage of errors made in individual cases, on a figure created by weighting the associated incorrect decisions to reflect the specific-deterrent losses they generated, or on a figure created by weighting the associated incorrect decisions to reflect as well the general-deterrent losses they generated;

(3) even if the effectiveness of a market definition can be said non-arbitrarily to depend on the extent to which it secures the ultimate goals of the relevant antitrust law, it would not be possible to establish non-arbitrarily a metric for the securing of the ultimate goals of the U.S. or E.U. antitrust laws because it is not possible to specify non-arbitrarily either the individual goals of U.S. or E.U. antitrust law or the relationship of those individual goals to the maximand of those bodies of law;

(4) it is not possible to decide non-arbitrarily whether the effectiveness of a market definition is a function of the extent to which it secures the proximate or the ultimate goals of U.S. or E.U. antitrust law; and

(5) even if one could define non-arbitrarily a metric for measuring the costs and benefits of a set of market definitions from the perspective of U.S. or E.U. antitrust law, more than one set of market definitions may be equally cost-effective across all cases.

1. The Inevitable Arbitrariness of Classical (Ideal-Type) Market Definitions

Virtually all antitrust analysts have adopted the standard industrial-organization-economics assumption that it is possible to generate non-arbitrary market definitions that will maximize the extent to which popular and professional assumptions about (1) the competitiveness of all pairs of products placed inside a given market (the "insider–insider-competitiveness" assumptions) and (2) the difference between the competitiveness of all pairs of market-insider products and the competitiveness of each product placed in the market in question and its closest competitor in a different market (the "intra-market *versus* inter-market competitiveness-difference" assumption). The relevant insider–insider-competitiveness assumptions are that (1) all pairs of products placed inside a product market are highly competitive with each other in the sense that each is "well-placed" (second-placed or perhaps close-to-second-placed) to obtain a substantial percentage of the customers that every other product in that market is best-placed to obtain and, somewhat relatedly, (2) each product in a given market is approximately equally competitive in the above sense with all other products in that market—that in a market containing products X1–9 products X1 and X2 are well-placed to obtain the same percentage of each other's customers as are products X1 and X3, products X1 and X4, products X8 and

X9, *etc*. The relevant "intra-market *versus* inter-market competitiveness-difference" assumption is that each product will be more competitive with any other product placed inside its market than with any product placed outside its market.

For seven reasons, I reject the proposition that one can define markets non-arbitrarily so as to maximize the extent to which the associated insider–insider-competitiveness figures and the associated intra-market *versus* inter-market competitiveness-difference figures conform with popular and professional assumptions about these figures. First, one cannot generate such a traditional, ideal-type market definition non-arbitrarily because one cannot establish non-arbitrarily the minimum amount of sales that must be made of any set of competitive products to a specified group of customers for the relevant products and buyers to constitute a "market."

The next five reasons for rejecting the claim that ideal-type market definitions can be generated non-arbitrarily all relate to gaps in the specification of the empirical assumptions whose fulfillment is supposed to be maximized by the market definitions in question. These gaps are critical in the current context because they cannot be filled in non-arbitrarily and the way in which they are filled in will almost certainly determine the identity of the market definitions that will yield figures that best conform to the ideal-type empirical assumptions.

More specifically, my second and third reasons for rejecting the claim that the relevant type of market definitions can be generated non-arbitrarily relate to the definition of individual-product-pair "competitiveness" in all three of the above assumptions—*viz*., reflect the fact that there is no non-arbitrary way to define the "competitiveness" of two products. Thus, the second reason is that there is no non-arbitrary way to decide whether the "competitiveness" of two products depends (1) on the volume of sales for which each is the closest competitor of the other for a sale the other is (privately) best-placed to make, (2) on that volume and the amount by which the second-placed member of any product-pair is better-placed than the third-placed supplier of any relevant buyer in relation to a sale the other pair-member is best-placed to make, (3) on "(1)" above and the volume of sales for which each product is close to being the second-placed supplier of a relevant buyer for a sale the other is best-placed to make, or (4) on "(2)" above and the volume of sales for which each product is close to being the second-placed supplier of a relevant buyer for a sale the other is best-placed to make. In brief, one would tend to prefer (3) to (1) or (4) to (2) if one believed that the competitiveness of two products depends not only on the extent to which each reduces the OCAs of the other's producer but also on the extent to which each reduces the profits the other's producer can realize by engaging in contrived oligopolistic pricing. I should add that the unclarity of the notion of "individual-product-pair competitiveness" is also increased by the fact that, even if one could determine non-arbitrarily that one of the operationalizations that appear after "(2)," "(3)," or "(4)" above is the correct operationalization of individual-product-pair competitiveness, there is no non-arbitrary way to decide (A)(i) how those considerations the above correct operationalization deems relevant should be weighted or (ii) whether the expression "close to being" in "(3)" and "(4)" above should be defined to depend on the amount by which the relevant product is worse-than-second-placed in the relevant cases, the number of products that are better-placed than the product in question in the relevant cases, and/or the number of products that are "approximately" as well-placed or better-placed than it is in the relevant cases and (B) if more than one of the considerations listed in "(A)(ii)" should be deemed relevant to the operationalization of the concept of being the "close-to-second-placed supplier of a given buyer," what weight should be given to each of the relevant considerations.

The third reason for rejecting the claim that one can generate non-arbitrary market definitions if the metric for evaluating such definitions is the extent to which they produce figures that conform with popular and professional assumptions about markets relates to a lack of specificity of the notion of overall product-pair competitiveness across all insider–insider product-pairs. Even if individual-product-pair competitiveness could be defined non-arbitrarily or the selection among those definitions of individual-product-pair competitiveness that were not inferior would not affect the identity of the market definitions that would maximize the extent to which the market-definition-based figures conformed with the relevant assumptions, there would be no non-arbitrary way to generate market definitions of this type because there would be no non-arbitrary way to determine whether the all-pairs-of-insiders-are-highly-competitive assumption would be more fulfilled by a division of the economy's products into possibly-partially-overlapping subsets that is associated with a distribution of insider–insider product-pair-competitiveness scores as defined that has a higher mean but higher degree of dispersion (say, variance) and an alternative product division that is associated with a distribution of insider–insider product-pair-competitiveness scores that has a lower mean but lower variance.

The fourth reason why market definitions must be arbitrary if they are to be evaluated by their ability to satisfy popular and professional assumptions about markets relates to the lack of specificity of the notion of the equality of product-pair competitiveness across all insider–insider product-pairs. Even if the minimum size of a market could be specified non-arbitrarily, individual-product-pair competitiveness could be defined non-arbitrarily, and the overall intensity of the competition between all insider–insider product-pairs could be defined non-arbitrarily, there would be no non-arbitrary way to define the inequality of the competitiveness of all insider–insider product-pairs (to determine whether a product division that is associated with a distribution of "differences in insider–insider product-pair-competitiveness scores" that has a lower mean but higher variance conforms with the all-pairs-of-insiders-are-equally-competitive assumption more or less well than a product division that is associated with a distribution of "differences in insider–insider product-pair-competitiveness scores" that has a higher mean but lower variance).

The fifth reason for rejecting the claim that markets can be defined non-arbitrarily under an ideal-type criterion relates to the fact that there is no non-arbitrary way to define the "difference" between the competitiveness of market-insider product-pairs and the competitiveness of the various individual market-insider products with the product placed in a different market with which they are respectively most competitive—*i.e.*, no way to decide whether to define that difference in terms of (1) the absolute difference in the mean of the distribution of intra-market product-pair-competitiveness scores and the mean of the distribution of the relevant inter-market product-pair-competitiveness scores, (2) the difference in the value of some function that reflects the variances (or some other measure of dispersion) as well as the means of the two relevant competitiveness-score distributions, (3) the ratio of the means of the two product-pair-competitiveness-score distributions "(1)" delineates, (4) the ratio of the values of the two more complex product-pair-competitiveness-score distributions "(2)" delineates, or something else.

The sixth reason why one cannot define markets non-arbitrarily so as to maximize the extent to which the market definitions yield figures that conform with popular and professional assumptions relates to the trade-offs that may have to be made when choosing among product divisions that fulfill the three popular and professional empirical assumptions in question to different extents. Although a single set of market definitions might maximize the extent to which the relevant figures conform with all three of the relevant assumptions (assuming that each has been operationally defined), it is certainly not likely that one set of market definitions will be dominant in this sense: if none is, the relevant market definitions will also have to be arbitrary because there is no non-arbitrary way to trade off, for example, an additional "departure" from the assumption that all pairs of market insiders are highly competitive against a reduction in the "departure" from the assumption that all market insiders are equally competitive and/or the assumption that market insiders are far more competitive with each other than the insider products respectively are with the product placed in a different market with which each is most competitive.

The seventh and empirically least-important reason for doubting the feasibility of generating non-arbitrarily the type of product-market definitions on which we are currently focusing is that, if the applicable criterion is ideal-type, even if all the preceding gaps can be filled in non-arbitrarily, it will not be possible to define markets non-arbitrarily if more than one division of the economy's products into possibly-partially-overlapping subsets that satisfy the minimum volume of sales necessary to constitute a market constraint produce relevant figures that conform equally well with each of the three assumptions to the same extent or the three assumptions combined and dominate all other relevant product divisions.

Admittedly, one might argue that in practice the only important part of the preceding analysis is its well-known minimum-size-of-market point—that in practice none of the other potential problems is significant because (1) the same set of market definitions will be optimal from the relevant assumption-conformity perspective regardless of the way in which one operationalizes the concepts to which the relevant market-related assumptions relate or (2) in the antitrust context the same legal conclusions will be generated by all the sets of market definitions among which one can choose only arbitrarily if one is using an ideal-type criterion. However, since no-one has ever provided any reason to believe that either of these claims is correct and there is every reason to believe them to be false, I doubt that one can make this argument unblushingly.

To summarize:

(1) one cannot define markets non-arbitrarily if market definitions are supposed to be evaluated by their ability to produce figures that conform with popular and professional ideal-type assumptions about the competitiveness of products placed in the same market and the difference between the competitiveness of products placed in same *versus* different markets; and
(2) although I have not established that the arbitrary choice among the various market definitions that cannot be dismissed as being worse than optimal using this criterion will often critically affect the outcome of antitrust litigation, I would be very surprised if this were not the case.

2. The Inevitable Arbitrariness of Antitrust (Functional) Market Definitions

For at least five reasons, it will also not be possible to define markets non-arbitrarily if the criterion used to evaluate a set of market definitions is its ability to play a useful role in a cost-effective approach to resolving some antitrust issue under U.S. or E.C./E.U. competition law. The first of these reasons is that no set of market definitions will ever be able to satisfy this criterion because no market-oriented approach to any antitrust issue can ever be cost-effective. Subsequent chapters of this study will establish this conclusion in relation to a variety of antitrust issues in exhaustive and (I fear) exhausting detail. After listing the other four reasons for our inability to define markets non-arbitrarily on a cost-effectiveness criterion, this section will execute a partial analysis of a simplified example that should establish the inevitable cost-ineffectiveness of market-oriented approaches to analyzing the impact of horizontal mergers on the intensity of competition relative to many more-or-less-refined versions of the non-market-oriented approach to these issues I will propose.

The other four reasons are worth listing because a critic could respond by arguing that, even if one could not define a set of most-cost-effective market definitions, one might still be able to define non-arbitrarily a set of least-cost-ineffective market definitions. In fact, for four reasons, it will also not be possible to generate a set of least-cost-ineffective market definitions non-arbitrarily when the effectiveness part of the cost-effectiveness assessment relates to the enforcement of U.S. or E.C./E.U. antitrust law.

The first such reason is that one cannot decide non-arbitrarily whether the relevant definitions' cost-ineffectiveness should be assessed in terms of the proximate goal of the antitrust laws (in the case of the U.S., preventing monopolization and decreases in competition; in the case of the E.U., deterring the restriction, prevention, or distortion of competition in the E.U. unless relevant consumers secure a fair share of any resulting joint benefits to them and the perpetrators and preventing dominant firms from committing exclusionary or exploitative abuses of their position) or in terms of the ultimate goals of the antitrust laws (in the case of the U.S., increasing economic efficiency, improving the distribution of income both by redistributing income from wealthier people to poorer people and by preventing individuals from profiting from their own wrongs, reducing [noneconomic] discrimination by preventing increases in the before-tax incomes of violator managers, derivative increases in the tax rate applied to their marginal incomes, and derivative decreases in the after-tax cost to them of giving up a given amount of taxable income to indulge their prejudices, preventing imbalances in political power by preventing increases in seller concentration that increase such imbalances even in a world in which there are other imperfections in the distribution of political power; in the case of the E.U., the items in the preceding U.S. ultimate-goal list *plus* promoting cross-E.U.-country social and political integration and relevant-independent-distributor and consumer liberty).

The second such reason may not be inevitable but certainly is applicable in the cases of the U.S. and E.U. antitrust law: if one decides that "effectiveness" should be defined in terms of the ultimate goals of the antitrust laws, one will not be able to define markets non-arbitrarily because one will not be able to decide non-arbitrarily which of the possible ultimate goals (some of which I just listed) are the actual goals of the relevant jurisdiction's antitrust laws or the relative weights that should be assigned to those possible goals one concludes are actual goals of the relevant country's antitrust laws. I wrote "may not be inevitable" because the laws and treaties in question were promulgated/ratified by groups of individuals and, for conceptual as well as empirical reasons, it may not be possible to attribute intent to the relevant groups.

The third such reason is salient in rights-based societies that value as a matter of justice legal cases being decided correctly as a matter of law. If one believes as I do that the United States and the E.C./E.U. are rights-based societies/confederations so that the relevant ultimate goal is not the ultimate goal of the relevant statutes'/treaty-provisions' ratifiers but the "goal" of deciding cases correctly as a matter of law under the applicable legislation/treaty, one will not be able to decide non-arbitrarily how to define markets non-arbitrarily if the criterion for evaluation is functional (1) because one cannot determine non-arbitrarily the extent to which a particular set of market definitions or the protocol that generates them disserves justice on this account depends on the number or percentage of incorrect legal conclusions to which they would lead—*e.g.*, the number or percentage of anticompetitive horizontal mergers that would be held lawful and the number of competitively-neutral or procompetitive mergers that would be held illegal—or the number or percentage of incorrect legal conclusions to which they lead weighted by their seriousness and (2) because, if the seriousness of any erroneous legal conclusion is deemed relevant, one cannot decide whether or the extent to which that seriousness depends on (A) the sum of the equivalent-dollar gains that incorrect antitrust-law-case resolutions confer on guilty defendants found innocent or not liable, (B) the sum of the equivalent-dollar losses that incorrect antitrust-law-case resolutions imposed on private parties to the cases in question whose correct legal claims were rejected, (C) the counterpart to the sum delineated after (1) in this list that relates to the guilty-defendant winners of future cases that will be decided incorrectly because of the false resolution of the case at hand, (4) the counterpart to the sum delineated after (2) that relates to the entitled-plaintiff losers of future cases that will be decided incorrectly because of the false resolution of the case at hand, (5) the gains and losses that false-positive findings of guilt or liability will generate by deterring future lawful conduct, and/or (6) the gains and losses that false-negative findings of guilt/liability will generate by inducing future illegal conduct.

The fourth such reason (and fifth reason overall) why one may not be able to define markets non-arbitrarily by applying a least-cost-ineffective criterion is that, even if one could define "effectiveness" non-arbitrarily, more than one set of market definitions may be equally cost-ineffective and the differences among the various equally cost-ineffective sets of market definitions may critically affect the outcome of one or more cases.

I will now try to illustrate my reasons for concluding that no market-oriented approach to assessing the impact of a horizontal merger on competition can be cost-effective by examining two examples that admittedly contain a variety of features that favor my conclusion. I hesitate to include these examples in the text because I do not want to leave the impression that my argument depends on their assumptions. Part II's analyses of the appropriate way to prove the monopolizing character and/or competition-lessening impact of the kinds of conduct with which the two examples are respectively concerned will demonstrate that my argument is not vulnerable to such a special-case attack.

I have included these examples for two reasons: (1) readers of articles I have previously published have found them helpful and (2) the examples give me the opportunity to explain and comment on the difference between traditional, seller-oriented market definitions and the kind of buyer-oriented market definitions whose adoption and use would constitute a half-way move to the kind of non-market-oriented approach to competitive-impact prediction that I recommend.

Both examples involve the retail sale of shoes. For simplicity, I assume that, geography aside, there is only one type of shoe-store and only one type of shoe. In reality, of course, there are many types of shoe-stores (geography aside) and many types of shoes. On particular occasions, some buyers prefer to shop at men's shoe-stores, some at women's shoe-stores, some at children's shoe-stores, and some at family shoe-stores. Some buyers prefer high-priced shoes, some prefer medium-priced shoes, and some low-priced shoes. In each price range, some prefer funky shoes, some prefer Italian shoe-styles, some prefer English shoe-styles, *etc.* In practice, then, shoe-stores differ not only in their geographic location but also in the category or categories of buyers they serve and in the type of shoes they offer to sell them. My examples will ignore all these complexities.

My examples also assume unrealistically that the second-placed supplier and all other relevant suppliers of any buyer whom a shoe-store is best-placed to supply will always be another shoe-store. In our affluent economy, the second-placed supplier of a buyer whom a shoe-store is best-placed to supply may be a dress-store, a restaurant, or a record shop (to name but a few possibilities)—*i.e.*, a potential shoe-buyer who does not "really need" a pair of shoes may be induced to spend the money he or she would otherwise spend on shoes on a sport jacket or dress, a good meal, or a bunch of tapes and records if suppliers of these alternative goods and services charge prices that are closer to their marginal costs than the prices of the shoe-outlet that is best-placed to supply the buyer are to its marginal costs.

My question is: Even on these simplifying assumptions, can one generate a set of market definitions that provides a basis for a cost-effective approach to analyzing the competitive impact of a horizontal merger between retail shoe-outlets in a metropolitan area that consists of a central city (location 1) with 100,000 shoe-buyers and 10 retail shoe-outlets (1A-J) and 10 suburbs, evenly spaced in a circle around the central city (locations 2–11 arranged consecutively in that order), each with 20,000 shoe-buyers and two shoe-stores (respectively stores 2A-B, 3A-B, · · ·11A-B)? I assume that some potential shoe-buyers (pure urbanites) live and work in the central city, others (commuters) live in one of the suburbs but work in the central city, while still others (pure suburbanites) live and work in one of the suburbs. The first example assumes that there are 10 separately-owned shoe-stores in the central city and two separately-owned shoe-stores in each suburb and that no firm owns more than one shoe-store. It also assumes that the only shoe-stores that are well-placed to obtain the patronage of the pure urbanites are the 10 central-city outlets (1A–J). Since these 10 outlets will not normally be equidistant from each pure urbanite, they will not all be equally-well-placed (equal-best-placed) to obtain each such buyer's patronage, but they will be first-placed to tenth-placed to obtain each such buyer's patronage. The shoe-stores that are best-placed and second-placed to obtain the patronage of any pure suburbanite are the stores in the suburb in which he or she lives and works (say XA and XB where X is some number between 2 and 11). Once more, I will assume that XA and XB will not normally be equidistant from any pure suburbanite residing in suburb X so that XA and XB will not normally be equal-best-placed to obtain the patronage of any buyer that works and resides in suburb X. Four additional shoe-stores will be well-placed to obtain the patronage of any such pure suburbanite, the stores in suburbs (X + 1) or (X–1)—except that the third-to-sixth-placed rivals of store 2A or 2B for the patronage of the buyers that store 2A or 2B is best-placed to supply will be stores 3A and B and 11A and B and that the third-to-sixth-placed rivals for the patronage of any buyer that store 11A or 11B is best-placed to supply are stores 10A and B and 2A and B (a complication that I will proceed to ignore for expositional reasons). I will assume in addition that commuters find it more attractive to shop for shoes either in their home suburbs (in the evenings or on holidays and weekends) or in any of the central-city outlets (during their lunch hours or immediately after work) than to shop for shoes anywhere else at any time. On this assumption, the best-placed through twelfth-placed potential suppliers of any commuter that lives in suburb X will be stores XA-B and 1A-J, not necessarily in that order—at least, if any store in the central city is more accessible to a commuter who lives in suburb X than is any store in suburbs (X + 1) and (X–1).

My question is: Can one develop a traditional, seller-oriented market definition or any other kind of market definition that will play a useful role in a cost-effective approach to analyzing the competitive impact of a merger between two shoe-stores in the situation described? Before analyzing this question, two issues must be addressed. First, I should indicate what I mean by a "traditional, *seller-oriented* market definition" and "any other kind of market definition." I will do so by contrasting traditional, seller-oriented market definitions with definitions that I will characterize as being "buyer-oriented." A buyer-oriented market definition would define a market by placing within it all buyers with similar (dollar) preferences and define the seller-side of each buyer-oriented market to include all sellers that were well-placed to obtain the patronage of the buyers in question. A buyer-oriented market-definition approach would equate the number of markets in any given situation with the number of groups of buyers with similar preferences. Individual sellers that were present in at least one of the markets defined in this way might not be present in all of them. The percentage of such markets to which an individual seller was assigned would presumably vary from seller to seller. And the intra-market rivals that any given seller would face would also presumably vary from market to market. In the example described above, the buyer-oriented approach would define 21 different markets: one for pure urbanites; one for each of the 10 sets of commuters, identified by the suburb in which they reside; and one for each of the 10 sets of pure suburbanites, identified by the suburb in which they reside. In a more realistic example that took into account the fact that in addition to location (A) some shoe-buyers prefer (1) respectively high-priced, medium-priced, or low-priced shoes, (2) shoes with particular styles, (3) men's shoe-stores, women's shoe-stores, children's shoe-stores, and family shoe-stores as well as the fact that (B) shoe-stores are more or less specialized along each of the dimensions just described, the number of buyer-oriented market definitions would be far higher.

I do not want to assert that the lawyers, economists, and judges who have tried to define markets in individual cases have ignored the kinds of considerations that would dominate buyer-oriented market definitions. In fact, part of my critique of the current seller-oriented market-oriented approach is that, although it does take many of the relevant facts into consideration, it does not make correct use of the information in question. However, anyone who is familiar with antitrust practice must recognize that individual sellers are rarely, if ever, placed in multiple markets whose seller-sides contain partially-overlapping sets of sellers—*i.e.*, that actual market definitions rarely if ever coincide with those that would be yielded by the approach I am labeling "buyer-oriented." I call the traditional approach "seller-oriented" because it tries to place sellers in markets whose seller-sides are not significantly overlapping. My analysis of any approach that employs seller-oriented market definitions to analyze the situation under consideration assumes that it will reduce the number of markets defined below 21 by placing in each individual market sets of buyers that the buyer-oriented approach would place in different markets.

The second issue that needs to be addressed at this juncture is: What are the various ways in which a horizontal merger between two shoe-stores in such a metropolitan area can affect competition? As Chap. 12 will show, such mergers can affect competition (1) by raising the merged firm's OCAs above the merger partners' (MPs') OCAs both directly and indirectly, (partly relatedly) by raising the merged firm's NOMs above the MPs' NOMs, and by causing the merged firm's COMs to differ from the MPs' COMs, (2) by changing the merged firm's product rivals' (*R*s') OCAs, NOMs, and COMs, and (3) by changing the intensity of QV-investment competition in the areas of product-space in which the MPs and their *R*s operate. Since Chaps. 12 and 13 will analyze the factors that determine the size and magnitude of each of these possible effects in considerable detail, I will confine myself here to one such effect—*viz.*, the extent to which the horizontal merger will decrease price competition by raising the merged firm's OCAs above the MPs' OCAs directly by freeing the MPs from each other's competition. This possible anticompetitive effect of a horizontal merger will be larger (1) the greater the number of times (the more frequently) that pre-merger the MPs were uniquely equal-best-placed to supply a given buyer and, in those instances in which they were, the greater their average OCA over the third-placed supplier of the buyer in question and (2) the greater the number of times (the more frequently) that pre-merger the MPs were respectively (uniquely) best-placed and (uniquely) second-placed to supply a given buyer and, in those instances in which they were, the greater the absolute average difference between the overall competitive disadvantage of the second-placed MP and the overall competitive disadvantage of the third-placed supplier of the buyers in question. The question, then, is: How accurately will different market definitions enable an analyst to predict these factors from data on the MPs' market shares and the pre-merger concentration of one or more relevant markets or from the post-merger HHI(s) of the market(s) in question and the impact of the horizontal merger on the HHI(s) in question.

To permit me to make the relevant market-share and market-concentration calculations, I will have to introduce some additional assumptions. In particular, I will make the following seven assumptions:

(1) each of the 10 central-city shoe-stores is best-placed to supply the same number of pure urbanites (10,000 each);
(2) half of the shoe-buyers who live in a suburb commute to the city (10,000 commuters in each suburb);
(3) for half of the commuters who live in each suburb, a central-city shoe-store is best-placed, and for half, a suburban shoe-store is best-placed;
(4) each central-city shoe-store is best-placed to supply the same number of commuters (one-tenth of the one-half of the 100,000 commuting shoe-buyers or 5,000 commuters);
(5) the two shoe-stores in each suburb are best-placed to supply the same number of customers: each is best-placed to supply 7,500 shoe-buyers (5,000 pure suburbanites and 2,500 of the 5,000 commuters for whom a suburban shoe-store is best-placed);
(6) each central-city shoe-store is best-placed to supply 15,000 shoe-buyers (the difference between the number of buyers that the central-city and suburban shoe-stores are respectively best-placed to supply in equilibrium reflects the higher rents that central-city shoe-stores must pay); and, accordingly,

(7) in the metropolitan area, 10 shoe-stores are best-placed to supply 15,000 buyers each, and 20 shoe-stores are best-placed to supply 7,500 buyers each.

We should now be able to assess the accuracy with which seller-oriented or buyer-oriented market-oriented approaches will be able to predict the extent to which a merger between two shoe-outlets or two shoe-firms in the metropolitan area will reduce competition by increasing the merged firm's OCA above the MPs' OCAs directly by freeing the MPs from each other's price competition. Our conclusion is that, in this situation, no market-oriented approach will be able to predict this effect reasonably accurately for all possible horizontal mergers or overall.

At one extreme, the type of approach to market definition that I have labeled "seller-oriented" could yield the conclusion that there was only one market in this situation—the metropolitan area. On this definition, the 10 central-city shoe-stores would all have 5 % market shares if they made every sale they were best-placed to make (since each is best-placed to serve 15,000 of 300,000 buyers), and the 20 suburban shoe-stores would each have 2.5 % market shares (on the same assumption, since each is best-placed to secure 7,500 of 300,000 buyers). Clearly, one will not be able to predict the frequency with which different shoe-stores were each other's closest competitors from such market-share data in this type of situation. Thus, the fact that two shoe-stores each had a 2.5 % share of the metropolitan market is compatible both with their being each other's closest competitors very often and with their never being each other's closest competitors. For example, mergers between two 2.5 % shoe-stores in the same suburb would combine firms that were either equal-best-placed or respectively best-placed and second-placed to supply the 10,000 pure suburbanites that lived in the MPs' suburb and may have been in such positions in relation to a substantial percentage of the 10,000 commuters that resided in these shoe-stores' suburb—*e.g.*, may well have been in such positions in relation to 15,000 buyers all tolled. At the other extreme, mergers between two 2.5 % shoe-stores in different suburbs (better yet, in far-distant suburbs) will have combined firms that were never equal-best-placed or respectively best-placed and second-placed to supply a given buyer. One simply cannot tell how often two firms were each other's closest competitors for the patronage of a buyer one or both were and no-one else was best-placed to supply from the firms' shares of the metropolitan market. Nor can one tell the average extra disadvantage under which the third-placed suppliers of the buyers in question were operating in their relations with these buyers—*e.g.*, how inconvenient it was for the buyers in question to travel to the next suburb or to buy shoes during their lunch hour or after work in the central city. Market-share data derived from such a metropolitan-wide market definition simply does not tell you what you need to know if your goal is to assess the extent to which a horizontal merger increases the merged firm's OCAs above the MPs' OCAs by freeing the MPs from each other's competition.

Nor can one accurately predict this effect from data on the metropolitan market's post-merger HHI and the effect of the merger on the HHI in the metropolitan market. This conclusion follows from these two facts: (1) the post-merger HHI in the metropolitan market is obviously the same for a merger between two shoe-stores in the same suburb as it is for a merger between two shoe-stores in far-distant suburbs and (2) each of these types of mergers will have the same impact on the metropolitan market's HHI. I should add that the example on which we are focusing also reveals that if the market is defined to include the metropolitan area, the facts that (1) the post-merger HHI in that market was low and (2) the merger had little effect on that HHI are perfectly compatible with the merger's reducing competition considerably by raising the merged firm's OCAs above the MPs' OCAs directly by freeing the MPs from each other's competition. Thus, although the post-merger HHI of the metropolitan market I have described is very low—is 387.5, which equals the sum of the pre-merger HHI ($10[5]^2 + 20\ [2.5]^2 = 250 + 125 = 375$) and the impact of a merger between any two suburban shoe-stores on the metropolitan market's HHI ($12.5 = 5^2–2[2.5]^2$), a merger between XA and XB would reduce competition substantially by raising the merged firm's OCAs above the MPs' OCAs by freeing the MPs from each other's competition.

To get the HHIs up, I will use a second example, which is identical to the first except that it assumes that there is only one central-city firm and one shoe-firm in each suburb (say, while keeping the number of outlets in each location the same). In this case, the metropolitan market would have one urban firm with a 50 % share of the metropolitan market and 10 suburban firms with 5 % market shares so that the pre-merger HHI would be ($[50]^2 + 10[5]^2 = 2{,}750$). In this case, a merger between two suburban shoe-firms (each of which has a market share of 5 %) would increase the HHI by ($[10]^2–2[5]^2 = 50$) points to 2,800. These numbers would lead many to conclude that any such merger was very anticompetitive. In fact, however, a merger between shoe-firms in distant suburbs would still be combining companies that were never uniquely equal-best-placed or respectively best-placed and second-placed to supply the same buyer: the HHI data would therefore be exceedingly misleading, at least on the OCA-impact issue on which I am currently focusing. Of course, a merger between two shoe-firms in non-neighboring suburbs might reduce competition in a number of other ways I am ignoring at this juncture, but Chap. 12 will demonstrate that market-aggregated data based on this metropolitan-wide market definition will not accurately predict these effects either.

Unfortunately, one will not be able to increase the accuracy of the market-oriented approach by picking a different single-market definition since any such alternative would leave some shoe-stores in no market at all and hence would lead to the incorrect conclusion that horizontal mergers that involved them could not reduce competition. Nor would a decision to define two markets—a central-city market and a suburban market be clearly superior. Admittedly, if I return to the first example in which each shoe-store firm owns only one shoe-store, such a two-market market definition would make it highly likely that all firms placed in the central-city market would at least sometimes be each other's closest competitors for buyers whom at least one of the sellers in question was best-placed to supply. However, the two-market market definition would still place into the "suburban market" stores in distant suburbs that were never each other's closest competitors—*i.e.*, would lead to the conclusion that mergers between such distant stores would increase the merged firm's OCAs above the MPs' OCAs directly by freeing the MPs from each other's competition when they would not. And, equally seriously, such a two-market market definition would fail to place in the same market suburban and central-city shoe-stores that were best-placed and second-placed to obtain the patronage of a substantial number of commuters who lived in the suburban shoe-store's suburb in circumstances in which the second-placed shoe-store in question had a substantial advantage over the third-placed supplier of the commuters in question—*i.e.*, would lead to the incorrect conclusion that a merger between such a suburban and such a central-city shoe-store would not increase the merged firm's OCAs above the MPs' OCAs directly by freeing the MPs from each other's competition.

Nor would results clearly be better if the decision-makers defined six markets—one containing the central-city shoe-stores and five containing shoe-stores in two contiguous suburbs. Such a series of market definitions would lead to incorrect legal conclusions because it would ignore the relevance of the central-city shoe-stores for the OCAs of the best-placed suburban suppliers of commuters, would ignore the relevance of some suburban shoe-stores for the OCAs of the central-city shoe-stores that were best-placed to supply some commuters, and would ignore the relevance of the shoe-stores in a neighboring suburb for the OCAs of some suburban shoe-stores that were best-placed to supply some pure suburbanites (at least in the one-firm-per-suburb case).

Perhaps one could imagine a seller-oriented market-definition approach that would yield the conclusion that there were 10 markets, each of which consisted of the central-city shoe-stores and the shoe-stores in one of the suburbs. However, even if contrary to my belief this set of market definitions could be generated by the traditional seller-oriented approach, it would be highly misleading—would imply that the OCAs of the central-city outlet that was best-placed to supply some pure urbanites was more strongly influenced by the operation of the included suburban shoe-stores than it actually was, would imply that the OCAs of the suburban shoe-stores that were best-placed to supply some pure suburbanites were more influenced by the operation of the 10 central-city shoe-stores than they actually were, and would ignore the fact that (at least in the one-firm-per-suburb case) the OCAs of the suburban shoe-stores that were best-placed to supply some pure suburbanites would be influenced by the presence of shoe-stores in neighboring suburbs.

Decision-makers who are required to use seller-oriented market definitions cannot escape from the horns of this dilemma. They must either include in the market firms whose inclusion gives an exaggerated impression of the likely impact of their merging on the merged firm's OCAs relative to the MPs' OCAs or exclude from the market firms whose merger with a market insider will reduce competition by raising the merged firm's OCAs above the MPs' OCAs by freeing the MPs from each other's competition or whose operation will reduce the impact of mergers between market insiders on the difference between the merged firm's and the MPs' OCAs.

For this reason, I can imagine decision-makers shifting to the kind of buyer-oriented market definitions described earlier. However, although such buyer-oriented market definitions would be an improvement over seller-oriented market definitions, analyses based on market-aggregated figures derived from them would still not be so accurate or cost-effective as the non-market-oriented approach I will recommend. For example, in the one-outlet-per-firm case we have been discussing, the market shares of the MPs that were both placed in one of the 11 buyer-oriented markets that would be defined to contain more than two sellers would still not accurately reflect the frequency with which the MPs were respectively best-placed and second-placed or uniquely equal-best-placed to secure the patronage of a given buyer. And again, the combination of the MP-market-share and the market-concentration figures that would apply to any of the 21 markets that would be defined through a buyer-oriented approach would still not accurately indicate the average amount by which the second-placed MP was or the uniquely equal-best-placed MPs were better-placed than the third-placed supplier of the buyers whom the MPs were best-placed and second-placed to supply or uniquely equal-best-placed to supply.

I could go on to explain why the market-aggregated data one would create from buyer-oriented market definitions would also not accurately predict the effect of a horizontal merger on the merged firm's NOMs and COMs relative to those of the MPs, on the OCAs, NOMs, and COMs of the merged firm's rivals, on the intensity of QV-investment competition, or on the extent to which any efficiencies a horizontal merger would generate would increase price or QV-investment competition. However, I will wait until Chap. 12 to do so. A market-oriented approach to horizontal-merger competitive-impact prediction that was based on buyer-oriented as opposed to seller-oriented market definitions would be more accurate and cost-effective than any such approach based on seller-oriented market definitions, but it would not be nearly so accurate or cost-effective as the non-market-oriented approach I will delineate.

Although the analysis I have just executed was partial in the extreme and the cases I have been examining were unrealistically simple, I hope that this exercise gives you some sense of my reasons for concluding that market-oriented approaches to horizontal-merger competitive-impact prediction can never be acceptably accurate or cost-effective. Such approaches always achieve the remarkable double of increasing cost while decreasing accuracy. The market-aggregated figures on which market-oriented approaches base their predictions or assessments have less predictive power than the non-market-aggregated data such approaches collect for the purpose of defining relevant markets: the process of defining such markets and calculating market-aggregated figures generates high costs and negative benefits—*i.e.*, reduces the value of the non-aggregated data that is used to define the markets. Hence, market-oriented approaches to antitrust issues can never be justified functionally.

* * *

Chapter 6 has explained why market definitions must inevitably be arbitrary regardless of whether they are judged by (1) an ideal-type criterion that focuses on the extent to which the market definitions satisfy popular and professional assumptions about (A) the competitiveness of the various product-pairs placed in the same market and (B) the difference between the competitiveness scores of the product-pairs placed in the same market and the competitiveness scores of the pairs of products that consist of one product placed in the market in question and the product placed in another market with which the former product is most competitive and (2) a functional criterion that focuses on whether the market definitions can play a useful role in a cost-effective approach to any antitrust issue. Chapters 7, 8 and 10–15 will criticize the more-specific market-oriented approaches to various antitrust issues that economists, antitrust-enforcement authorities, and judges currently employ.

Chapter 7
Economic (Classical) and Antitrust Markets: Official and Scholarly Proposals*

In 1950, the United States Congress passed the Celler-Kefauver Act[121] to amend the "merger and acquisition" section of the Clayton Act (Section 7) by adding the language "in any line of commerce in any section of the country" to its prohibition of acquisitions of stock or assets whose effect "may be substantially to lessen competition." The addition of this language to the Clayton Act in 1950 by the Celler-Kefauver Act[122] led U.S. antitrust courts and antitrust-enforcement agencies to analyze the legality of all business conduct covered by the Clayton Act by defining relevant product and geographic markets ("lines of commerce" and "sections of the country") and deriving competitive-impact predictions from

*In writing this chapter, I have borrowed substantially from the publications of Dr. Gregory J. Werden, a leading economist at the Antitrust Division of the United States Department of Justice. See, *e.g.*, Gregory J. Werden, *Merger Policy for the 21st Century: Charles D. Weller's Guidelines Are Not Up to the Task* (hereinafter Werden Policy), 33 U. WEST. L. A. L. REV. 57 (2001); Gregory J. Werden, *Market Delineation Under the Merger Guidelines: Monopoly Cases and Alternative Approaches* (hereinafter *Werden Delineation*), 16 REV. OF IND. ORG. 211 (2000); Gregory J. Werden and Luke M. Froeb, *Correlation, Causation, and All That Jazz: The Inherent Shortcomings of Price Tests for Antitrust Market Delineation* (hereinafter *Werden and Froeb Jazz*), 8 REV. OF IND. ORG. 329 (1993); Gregory J. Werden, *Market Delineation Under the Merger Guidelines: A Tenth Anniversary Retrospective* (hereinafter *Werden Retrospective*), 1993 ANTITRUST BULL. 517 (1983); and Gregory J. Werden, *The History of Antitrust Market Delineation* (hereinafter *Werden History*), 76 MARQUETTE L. REV. 123 (1992). I hasten to add, however, that the chapter does not merely replicate Werden's excellent work: it covers some subjects and issues Werden does not address, organizes some of the material both it and Werden's scholarship discuss differently from the way in which Werden does, and makes a significant number of criticisms of and other types of points about some of the positions that economists, legal scholars, and judges have taken on economic-market-definition and antitrust-market-definition issues that Werden did not make and with some of which (I have reason to believe) he would not agree.

[121] 64 Stat. 1125, 1126 (1950).

[122] Admittedly, the first reference to the term "relevant market" in a U.S. federal antitrust case pre-dated the passage of the Celler-Kefauver Act—in particular, was in the Supreme Court's 1948 opinion in United States v. Columbia Steel, 334 U.S. 495, 508 (1948). In fact, the Congress' dissatisfaction with the Court's decision that the acquisition challenged in that case did not violate the Sherman Act led to its passage of the Celler-Kefauver Act.

R.S. Markovits, *Economics and the Interpretation and Application of U.S. and E.U. Antitrust Law*, DOI 10.1007/978-3-642-24307-3_7,

relevant-market-aggregated data—*inter alia*, data on firm market shares, traditional seller-side concentration ratios, and (more recently) HHI figures. Indeed, since that time, U.S. courts have virtually always insisted that a relevant market or set of relevant markets be defined not only in Clayton Act cases but also in Sherman Act Section 2 (monopolization and attempt-to-monopolize) cases. European antitrust institutions—the European Court of Justice (ECJ),[123] the Court of First Instance of the European Communities (CFI),[124] the European Commission (EC),[125] and the courts and antitrust-enforcement agencies of most, if not all, of the member states[126] of the E.C./E.U. have also all adopted market-oriented approaches to antitrust-law analysis.

If the argument of Chap. 6 is correct, the U.S.' and E.U.'s adoption of market-oriented approaches to antitrust-law analysis is misguided. This chapter builds on Chap. 6 by delineating, commenting on, and/or criticizing the ways in which economics and law scholars, judges, and antitrust-enforcement-agency personnel have defined the abstract concepts of "an economic market" and "an antitrust market," the explicit claims and implicit assumptions that such experts have made about the non-arbitrary delimitability of such markets, and the diverse approaches that economists, U.S. courts, the U.S. 1992 Horizontal Merger Guidelines, U.S. antitrust-enforcement-agency personnel operating under these Guidelines, E.C./E.U. courts, and the European Commission have used or proposed using to define relevant economic or antitrust markets.

1. The Definition of "Economic Markets" and "Antitrust Markets"

This section (1) reviews the definition of an "economic market" that I think is best, (2) delineates and criticizes the classical definition of an economic market, (3) discusses the disagreement among economists about whether (even if the classical definition of an economic market is adjusted to take account of my criticisms) any classically-defined economic market exists in the real world, (4) sets forth an alternative, less-encompassing individual-actor-oriented definition of an economic market that was proposed in the 1950s and anticipates the move some antitrust economists have made to substituting the concept of an "antitrust market" for the

[123] See, *e.g.*, ECJ, Europemballage Corporation and Continental Can Company, Inc. v. Commission, 6/27 ECR 19973 215, p. 32, (21 February 1973) and ECJ, United Brands Company and United Brands Continental BV v. Commission, 27/76 ECR 1978, 207, p. 10 (14 February 1978).

[124] See, *e.g.*, CFI, France Télécom v. Commission, T-340/03-WuW/E Eur 1224, 1225 (30 January 2007).

[125] EC Form Relating to the Notification of a Concentration [Merger] Pursuant to Regulation (EC) No. 139/2004, OJ L 133 (30 April 2004).

[126] See, *e.g.*, National Geographic II, BGH (The German Federal Court of Justice), WuW DE-R 1925, p. 19.

traditional concept of an economic market, and (5) considers the supposed functional justification for the concept of an antitrust market.

Chapter 6 argues that, if (contrary to my conclusion) there is a good reason to define economic markets, each such market should be defined to contain (1) a set of buyers defined by the sellers that were well-placed to secure their patronage in relation to a particular purchasing decision, (2) the products to which the purchasing decision in question relates, and (3) the sellers that are well-placed to sell those products to the buyers in question. In Chap. 6, I also assert that, both in their written work and in conversation with me, economists consistently assume that economic markets should be defined to satisfy certain ideal-type criteria: that, ideally,

(1) all seller/product combinations placed in the same economic market should be "highly and equally competitive with each other" (whatever that means) in relation to the buyers placed in that market and
(2) any seller/product combination placed in a given economic market should be substantially more competitive with any other seller/product combination placed in that market (including combinations that include the same seller but a different product) than with any seller/product combination placed in a different market in relation to any buyer (or at least the average buyer) placed in the former market.

The classical definition of an economic market (or of an "industry" as economic markets were originally denominated) is an area of product-space (defined implicitly by both the attributes of the products it contains and the geographic locations of its sellers and buyers) that contains products whose prices tend toward uniformity.[127] This definition would be both defensible and consistent with Chap. 6's formulation if (as the analysts that use the classical definition implicitly assume) the economy's various products could be separated into product sets that are distinct in the following sense:

(1) the members of each such set of products are physically identical and equally attractive to their in-market potential buyers, and all the in-market sellers of the products in question face the same marginal costs (including marginal delivery costs) in relation to the supply of any buyer placed in the market in question, and
(2) the members of the different product-sets the economy contains contain products that are not physically identical and are not equally valued by the buyers in the different markets in which each such set of products would be placed.

[127] See GEORGE J. STIGLER, THE THEORY OF COMPETITIVE PRICE 92 (Macmillan, 1942). See also ALFRED MARSHALL, PRINCIPLES OF ECONOMICS 325 (Macmillan, 8th ed., 1920) and AUGUSTIN COURNOT, RESEARCHES INTO THE MATHEMATICAL PRINCIPLES OF THE THEORY OF WEALTH 51–52 (Nathaniel T. Bacon trans., Augustus H. Kelley reprint, 1971) (1838). These citations (and many that follow) are taken from *Werden History* at 125–26.

However, even if the economy consisted of distinct sets of products whose individual members were equal-best-placed to obtain the patronage of any buyer that might find it beneficial to purchase any of them for a price that would enable its supplier to at least break even on the transaction in question, the first of the above two assumptions that the "classicists" made would not be satisfied for any or virtually any set of products that would be highly and equally competitive for the patronage of a specifiable set of buyers and far more competitive with each other in relation to those buyers than they were with any product not in the set in question. In an economy in which the type of product and geographic differentiation first emphasized in the 1930s by Chamberlin[128] and Robinson[129] are prevalent, the prices of the products placed in an economic market that satisfied the classicists' ideal-type notions would not "tend to uniformity"—instead, would tend to reflect differences in the marginal costs that relevant products' sellers would have to incur to supply relevant buyers and those buyers' preferences among the products in question.

Once economists came to acknowledge the fact that the product and geographic differentiation to which Chamberlin and Robinson called attention were important economic phenomena, they began to disagree about whether economic markets that satisfied the classicists' ideal-type notions existed in the real world.[130] On the one hand, many economic theorists (and lawyers) continued to write and talk as if something like classical economic markets could clearly be delineated non-arbitrarily. Thus, after admitting that the fact that substitutability was a matter of degree implied that few if any groups of products would conform to the classical ideal type of an industry (in modern terms, of a market), which stipulated that industries should contain only products that were "perfect substitutes for each other," Joe Bain argued that this reality required no more than "an adaptation of the [concept of] an industry. . .. The general criterion for inclusion of products in an industry becomes close substitutability, of which perfect substitutability is a special and extreme case."[131] Fritz Machlup responded to the same reality in virtually the same way: after admitting in a discussion of pricing interdependence that "everything in the economy hangs together," he insisted that the concept of an industry (*i.e.*, market) was still useful—in particular, was "an expedient device for ruling out negligible or too uncertain interdependence."[132] The realities of product and geographic differentiation seem to have had no more of an effect on the prominent economists and lawyers who served on the Attorney General's National Committee to study the antitrust laws. Their 1955 report blithely concluded that "[o]ne should

---

[128] See EDWARD H. CHAMBERLIN, THE THEORY OF MONOPOLISTIC COMPETITION (Harvard Univ. Press, 1933).

[129] See JOAN ROBINSON, THE THEORY OF IMPERFECT COMPETITION (hereinafter ROBINSON IMPERFECT COMPETITION) (Macmillan & Co., 1933).

[130] For a thorough discussion, see *Werden History* at 126–31.

[131] JOE S. BAIN, PRICE THEORY 24–25 (H. Holt, 1952). Note the conflation of substitutability and competitiveness.

[132] FRITZ MACHLUP, THE ECONOMICS OF SELLER COMPETITION 213–14 (Johns Hopkins Univ. Press, 1952).

include in a market all firms whose products are in fact good and directly available substitutes for one another in sales to some significant group of buyers and exclude all others."[133] None of these market-concept proponents seems to have been willing to face up to the fact that, if there is no break in the chain of substitutes (in their terms) or in the chain of competitive products (put correctly), there will be no non-arbitrary way to delimit the markets whose usefulness they insist on. I should add that this problem has also been ignored by the substantial number of empirical economists who, both in the 1950s[134] and in the decades that followed,[135] tested price theory by regressing P/MC or rate-of-return data on seller-concentration data and sometimes barriers-to-entry estimates as well without acknowledging the problematic character of (if not the arbitrariness of) the market definitions they created and used.

Of course, as I have already indicated, not all economists thought that the concept of the market need only be tinkered with to produce a construct that was pragmatically useful. Thus, according to Chamberlin, beliefs in "industry or commodity boundaries are a snare and delusion,"[136] a view shared by many others including (more recently) by Franklin Fisher, who insisted that any distinction between firms that are in and out of a particular market is "meaningless."[137]

Other economists took an intermediate position. Thus, after acknowledging that the classical concept of an industry (market) did not match many real-world phenomena, Joan Robinson added that the classical concept will correspond with the real world in a significant subset of cases—*viz.*, in those cases in which "a commodity...is bounded on all sides by a marked gap between itself and its closest substitutes...."[138]

---

[133] ATT'Y GEN'S NAT'L COMM. TO STUDY THE ANTITRUST LAWS 322 (1955). Note again the conflation of substitutability with competitiveness.

[134] See, *e.g.*, JOE S. BAIN, BARRIERS TO NEW COMPETITION 182–204 (hereinafter BAIN BARRIERS) (Harvard Univ. Press, 1956).

[135] For two useful compilations and analyses of the scholarship that addressed this issue, see Richard Schmalensee, *Inter-Industry Studies of Structure and Performance* in HANDBOOK OF INDUSTRIAL ORGANIZATION, vol. 2, 952 (Richard Schmalensee and Robert Willig, eds.) (North-Holland, 1989) and LEONARD WEISS, CONCENTRATION AND PRICE (MIT Press, 1989).

[136] Edward H. Chamberlin, *Product Heterogeneity and Public Policy*, 40 AM. ECON. REV. (PAPERS & PROC.) 85, 86–87 (1950).

[137] Franklin M. Fisher, *Horizontal Mergers: Triage and Treatment*, 1 J. ECON. PERSPECTIVES 23, 27 (1987). See also ROBERT TRIFFIN, MONOPOLISTIC COMPETITION AND GENERAL EQUILIBRIUM THEORY 78–89 (Harvard Univ. Press, 1940).

[138] ROBINSON IMPERFECT COMPETITION at 17. For a more recent claim that, in a significant number of instances, it will be possible to delineate markets non-arbitrarily to contain sets of products that are bounded by such "marked gaps between themselves and their closest substitutes," see Richard Schmalensee, *Another Look at Market Power*, 95 HARV. L. REV. 1789, 1799–1800 (1982). Note that Robinson's reference to "closest substitutes" ignores the distinction between how substitutable two products are for each other and how competitive they are with each other—a distinction made salient by the fact that the firms that are well-placed to supply a particular buyer may have to incur significantly-different marginal costs to do so.

Doubts about the existence of real-world markets that would come close to satisfying anything like the ideal-type notions that underlay the classical conception of a market led many economists to abandon this ideal-type conception of a market in favor of conceptions of markets that they believed could be justified in functional terms. The first such definition that I know of was offered by Edward S. Mason. For pragmatic reasons, Mason abandoned the classical conception of a market, which was not focused on the position of any industrial seller or buyer, in favor of a functional conception that did focus on the position of an individual actor:

> The market and market structure should be defined with reference to the position of a single seller or buyer.... [Such a]...market includes all buyers and sellers of whatever product whose action it considers to influence its volume of sales.[139]

This proposal seems to me to have presaged the replacement of the classical conception of a market by (perhaps one should say the supplementation of the classical conception of a market with) a self-consciously-functional conception of a market—the concept of an "antitrust market." Antitrust markets are markets that have been defined to yield market-aggregated data that will play an important role in an optimal protocol for analyzing the antitrust legality of business conduct. Many advocates of antitrust markets seem to believe that such markets can be delineated in all antitrust cases. Some think that it will be desirable to delimit antitrust markets only in some cases because only in some cases (*viz.*, when the industries in question have "relatively undifferentiated products") will it be cost-effective to use "structural" (market-aggregated) data.[140] The pragmatic argument for "antitrust markets" was first stated by Clair Wilcox years before this terminology was used:

> Whatever the theoretical difficulties, criteria for the guidance of policy must and will be devised, if not by the economist, then by the lawyer and the engineer. If economics does not eventually contribute to this task, then so much the worse for economics.[141]

I remain unconvinced. In the vast majority of cases, there will be no break in the chain of "substitutes" (*i.e.*, competitive products), and, when there is no such break, market delimitations will be arbitrary. Even if products are "relatively undifferentiated" physically, there will usually be significant geographic differentiation. And, for the reasons Chap. 6 elucidated, even in those individual instances in which in some sense a market can be defined non-arbitrarily, market-aggregated data will have less predictive power than the non-market-aggregated data used to generate the market definition in the first place. To make a contribution, economists should stop chasing the market chimera and start developing and testing price-competition

[139] Edward S. Mason, *Price and Production Policies of Large-Scale Enterprises*, 29 AM. ECON. REV. (PAPERS & PROC.) 61, 69 (1939).

[140] George A. Hay and Gregory J. Werden, *Horizontal Mergers: Law, Policy and Economics*, 83 AM. ECON. REV. (PAPERS & PROC.) 173, 176 (1993).

[141] Clair Wilcox, *Discussion*, 40 AM. ECON. REV. (PAPERS & PROC.) 85, 86–87 (1950).

theories and QV-investment-competition theories that do not use market-aggregated parameters—*i.e.*, that do not require any market to be defined. Several economists at the U.S. Antitrust Division[142] have claimed in conversations with me and one has stated in writing[143] that the U.S. antitrust-enforcement agencies' use of market-oriented approaches to antitrust-law analysis is compelled by the "any line of commerce in any section of the country" language of the Celler-Kefauver-Act-amended version of the Clayton Act and the case-law requiring relevant markets to be defined. I disagree with this conclusion. Taken by itself, the current Clayton Act language could legitimately be read to emphasize the fact that, for covered behavior to be illegal, it must be predicted to produce or post-dicted to have produced a *substantial* reduction in competition. Moreover, although, as a pragmatic matter, it may behoove the U.S. antitrust-enforcement agencies to make those market-oriented arguments that U.S. courts have indicated they must make to prevail in individual cases when arguing before courts, if the courts have got the law wrong, the agencies are not obligated to make such arguments and may, in fact, better serve the goals the legislation was designed to achieve in the long run by making justifiable arguments instead of or in addition to incoherent or incorrect market-oriented arguments. In any event, there is no reason why the agencies could not use an appropriate non-market-oriented approach to assess the legality of challenged behavior internally and then cook up a market-oriented argument to be used in the courts.

Indeed, I am far from convinced that the economists (and lawyers) at the U.S. Antitrust Division and Federal Trade Commission who claim that statutory language and case-law compel them to use market-oriented approaches to antitrust-law analysis really do believe this: the Guidelines the agencies have promulgated and

[142] To my knowledge, no judge or practicing lawyer has ever stated that the current Clayton Act does not compel the courts to adopt market-oriented approaches to Clayton Act cases. Indeed, so far as I am aware, only one academic lawyer has taken this position. In the first edition of his highly-respected treatise, Lawrence Sullivan prefaced his discussion of the market-definition cases with the comment: "Market definition is not a jurisdictional prerequisite, or an issue having its own significance under the statute. . . ." (footnote omitted) LAWRENCE A. SULLIVAN, HANDBOOK OF THE LAW OF ANTITRUST 41 (West Pub. Co., 1977).

[143] See *Werden Retrospective* at 521–22:

> The [1992 Horizontal Merger] Guidelines' use of market delineation as the first step of a largely-structural analysis was compelled by case law precedent. Failing to delineate a market would have most likely resulted in the dismissal of any cases filed in court, so the Department of Justice may have had little choice but to delineate markets and assign market shares. Given a choice, many economists would have no doubt preferred to abandon the market delineation-market share approach (footnote omitted).

I question the accuracy of the last sentence in this quotation. Although Werden does recognize that "dispensing with market delineation may be the best course" both in "many" monopolization cases and in "some" horizontal-merger cases (see *Werden Delineation* at 216 and 217 respectively), I doubt his claim that many economists agree with this position, and even Werden thinks that, in relation to the horizontal-merger cases for which a non-market-oriented approach may be best, "the Guidelines' approach is conceptually sound" (*id.* at 217), whatever that might mean.

the approaches their personnel have taken to analyzing the legality of conduct internally have departed from the statutes and case-law too often in too many respects for this claim to be persuasive.[144]

2. The 1992 (U.S.) Horizontal Merger Guidelines' Abstract Definition of and Protocol for Identifying an Antitrust Market[145]

The 1992 Horizontal Merger Guidelines promulgated jointly by the U.S. Department of Justice (DOJ) and Federal Trade Commission (FTC) contain both an abstract definition of the antitrust markets these enforcement-agencies claim they expect to use[146] in horizontal-merger cases and a protocol for identifying the markets that best fit this definition in individual cases. According to the abstract definition, the market for each product of each merger partner involved in a horizontal merger or acquisition consists of that product and the smallest set of other products whose placement under the control of the relevant merger partner would enable the hypothetical combination to profit by raising its prices significantly (by 5 % in most contexts)[147] for the foreseeable future if the price and other

[144] See, *e.g.*, Chap. 12's discussions of the non-market-definition-focused sections of the 1992 Horizontal Merger Guidelines, the non-market-oriented competitive-impact-assessment protocols that the DOJ and FTC have actually been using since the mid-1990's, and the various features of the DOJ/FTC 2010 Horizontal Merger Guidelines that imply that these antitrust-enforcement authorities have actually abandoned market-oriented approaches to competitive-impact prediction. I want to acknowledge that this section draws heavily on *Werden History*.

[145] Although the Guidelines use the word "market" rather than the expression "antitrust market," it is clear that the U.S. antitrust-enforcement agencies believe that the "markets" to which the Guidelines refer are antitrust markets and not economic markets in the sense in which I and others define these two terms. See *Werden Retrospective* at 528–29.

[146] Although, both in conversations with me and in writing, economists at the DOJ have told me that the U.S. antitrust-enforcement agencies and other Executive Branch officials and institutions are not legally obligated to follow the Guidelines, I doubt that this is the case. The United States Supreme Court has held that, although U.S. administrative agencies and other Executive-Branch officials and institutions are not Constitutionally required to publish the decision-protocol they will use to make particular types of decisions, once they have done so, they are Constitutionally bound to follow that protocol. See Accardi v. Shaughnessy, 347 U.S. 260 (1954). For a more recent case that, if anything, expands the reach of this doctrine, see Morton v. Ruiz, 415 U.S. 199 (1974). See also INS v. Yang, 519 U.S. 26 (1996), and, for two dramatic (Watergage-related) cases in which the doctrine played a critical role, see United States v. Nixon, 418 U.S. 683 (1974) (in which the claim at issue was the President's invocation of executive privilege in relation to various tape recordings) and Nader v. Bork, 366F. Supp. 104 (D.D.C. 1973) (in which the firing of the Special Prosecutor Archibald Cox was at issue). I do not think that the DOJ and FTC can avoid this requirement by stating in their Guidelines that they do not consider themselves to be bound by them. The opposite conclusion would defeat the purpose of the prohibition—*viz.*, to give the law's addressees fair notice.

[147] When the 1992 Guidelines speak in general terms, they refer to a "small but significant and non-transitory increase in price." However, they also indicate that the Federal Trade Commission

terms of sale of all product outside this set stayed the same. This definition is said to establish an SSNIP "test" for a candidate market where SSNIP is an acronym for "small but significant non-transitory increase in price." The Guidelines explicitly state that the relevant hypothetical combination may include not only firms "currently producing or selling the relevant product in the relevant area" but firms that would do so "within 1 year and without the expenditure of significant sunk costs of entry and exit, in response to a 'small but significant and non-transitory' price increase."[148] More specifically, when the merger partner (hereinafter MP) practices across-the-board pricing or charges individualized prices that are not significantly discriminatory, the 1992 Guidelines propose that the product in question be placed into a series of markets whose buyer-members consist of those buyers to which the MP in question is charging a given price (or, presumably, very similar prices) and whose seller-members are determined through the protocol just delineated.[149] More operationally, the Guidelines proceed to state that the Antitrust Division and FTC will identify the market its abstract definition assumes is analytically

and Justice Department will normally operationalize this language by using "a price increase of five percent lasting for the foreseeable future." See 1992 Guidelines, Section 1.11. The 1992 Guidelines indicate as well that the normal determinants of the relevant price-increases will be predicted post-hypothetical-combination prices and the actual pre-hypothetical-combination prevailing prices. However, if "circumstances are strongly suggestive of coordinated interaction" (by which I assume they mean contrived oligopolistic pricing), the Federal Trade Commission "will use [as its baseline] a price more reflective of the competitive price." *Id.* I assume that this qualification means that under the protocol the DOJ and FTC will analyze the likely impact of various hypothetical combinations on prices on the sometimes-counterfactual assumption that the merger partners and presumably the other possible combinants did not engage in contrived oligopolistic pricing pre-merger. However, I am not sure what the protocol implies the DOJ and FTC will assume about post-hypothetical-combination prices in the relevant cases—in particular, about the COMs that would prevail after any hypothetical combination was effectuated. Since it would be inaccurate to attribute to the hypothetical combination all the COMs that the combinants would secure post-combination if they would have obtained some COMs pre-combination, I assume that the protocol would count only that amount of the COMs that the combinants would secure post-combination if, counterfactually, they would have obtained no COMs pre-combination. However, since the effect of a given merger on its participants' COMs will depend *inter alia* on how unprofitable contrived oligopolistic pricing was for them pre-merger, I can see no way in which the amount just indicated could be ascertained.

[148] See the 1992 Guidelines, Section 1.32, which discusses "uncommitted" firms that would participate in the relevant market through a "supply response" to the hypothetical price-increase.

[149] See the 1992 Guidelines, Section 1.12. Although this protocol does define markets in a way that clearly is "buyer-oriented" in one sense, it does not indicate that the DOJ and FTC have shifted to "buyer-oriented" market definitions in the sense in which I define that expression. In Chap. 6, I defined a conception of a market to be "buyer-oriented" if, under it, markets are defined so that each includes only buyers that place similar dollar values on the particular product variant they prefer (and only sellers that are well-placed to supply the buyers in question). Section 1.12 obviously involves a partial shift to a buyer-oriented conception of a market. However, the 1992 Guidelines are not fully committed to a buyer-oriented conception of antitrust markets. To see why, note that the 1992 Guidelines will not define separate markets despite the fact that different subsets of relevant buyers place different dollar values on the relevant products if all buyers are charged the same price for any product.

optimal by hypothetically combining with the MP product in question the successive so-called next-best substitutes for this product, where the "next-best substitute" is stipulatively defined to be the product "which, if available in unlimited quantities at constant prices, would account for the greatest value of diversion of demand in response to a 'small but significant and non-transitory' price increase."[150]

This section (1) delineates the respects in which the 1992 Guidelines' account of the abstract market definition the DOJ and FTC will use in horizontal-merger cases is poorly drafted, (2) comments on the 1992 Guidelines' peculiar statement that the DOJ and FTC will calculate the profitability of any price-increase that any set of hypothetical combinants might execute on the assumption that no non-combinant would change its price or other terms of sale in response to the hypothetical combinants' price-change, (3) points out an interesting feature of the concrete market definitions that will conform to the 1992 Guidelines' abstract market definition, (4) explains why the 1992 Guidelines' concrete-market-definition protocol will not always yield concrete market conclusions that fit their abstract market definitions, and (5) explains why a market-oriented analysis that defines markets either in the way that the 1992 Guidelines' abstract definition indicates the DOJ and FTC will define them in horizontal-merger cases or in the way that the Guidelines' concrete-market-definition protocol indicates those "agencies" will define them in such cases will not be the optimal market-oriented approach to analyzing the competitive impact of horizontal mergers.

[150] Although note 9 of Section 1.11 of the 1992 Guidelines clarifies the meaning of "next-best substitute" (the quote in the text comes from this note), the terminology is unfortunate. Economists usually use the word "substitute" to refer to a product that a specific buyer or many buyers find as desirable or almost as desirable as the alternative good in question, ignoring the extent to which the evaluations in question depend on the relative quantities of the two goods owned by the buyer(s) in question. This definition renders irrelevant the prices of the two goods or any related difference in their marginal costs of production (a cost-difference that is relevant to a product's being [in my terminology] "the closest competitor of another good for a particular buyer's patronage"). Since, in the 1992 Guidelines' terminology, how close a "substitute" one good is for another depends to a great extent on the prevailing prices of the goods, the Guidelines' terminology is inconsistent with the standard economics usage just delineated. As my discussion of Joan Robinson's conclusions about the conditions under which it will be possible to define a market non-arbitrarily reveals, this conflation of the "substitutability" of two products with their "competitiveness" also has a long history in economics. I should admit that economists do use an expression that contains the word "substitution"—*viz.*, "the marginal rate of substitution"—to refer to "substitutability" at something like prevailing price levels: in particular, the expression "the marginal rate of substitution between product X and product Y" indicates the rate at which a particular buyer can substitute one good for another at the margin (*i.e.*, given its original purchases of X and Y) and remain equally well-off (remain on the same indifference or revealed-preference curve). Since the original quantities of X and Y owned by the buyer will be determined *inter alia* by the prices of X and Y (the quantities in question will also be determined by the wealth and income of the buyer and by its preferences), this usage of the word "substitution" is more compatible with the 1992 Guidelines' usage than is the standard usage of the word "substitute." Still, I think that the 1992 Guidelines would have better achieved their goal of clarity had they avoided the "next-best substitute" terminology.

A. The Poor Draftsmanship of the 1992 Guidelines' Abstract Definition of an Antitrust Market

The 1992 Guidelines explicitly recognize the importance of clarity. Section 0 states that the Guidelines will specify the approach the DOJ and FTC will take to horizontal mergers as simply and clearly as possible to reduce the uncertainty associated with this part of antitrust law. Obviously, for the Guidelines as a whole to be clear, their protocol for defining antitrust markets must be clear.

There are several reasons to believe that the Guidelines' authors overestimate the clarity of the Guidelines' abstract definition of an antitrust market and their protocol for delineating concrete antitrust markets:

(1) Section 1.522 of the Guidelines suggests that their authors are more optimistic than I about the frequency with which there will be "a wide gap in the chain of demand substitutes at the edge of the product and geographic market"—an alleged empirical reality that would make it far more likely that one could define antitrust markets (indeed, even ideal-type markets) non-arbitrarily;
(2) in conversations with me, economists at the DOJ have denied the empirical importance of situations in which two products that are highly competitive with a common third product are not significantly competitive with each other—a kind of non-transitivity that (as we shall see) vastly complicates the task of identifying the concrete market that best fits the Guidelines' abstract conception of an antitrust market; and
(3) Gregory Werden, an excellent economist who worked at the DOJ for a long time and who, in his own words, is "the person most responsible for the approach to market delineation in the Merger Guidelines"[151] clearly believes that they are sufficiently well-specified "to avoid gerrymandering of markets and provide meaningful guidance by introducing restrictions on the size and shape of markets,"[152] *inter alia* through its "next-best-substitute" protocol[153] and its "Smallest Market principle": indeed, Werden believes that the Guidelines' definition and protocol are capable of yielding "unique relevant markets."[154]

Unfortunately, neither the Guidelines' delineation of its abstract conception of an antitrust market nor its specification of its protocol for delineating the concrete

[151] Private note to the author from Gregory J. Werden (April 1, 1997) accompanying a memo entitled Comments of Gregory J. Werden on—Richard S. Markovits, Two Antitrust Myths: Why It Is Worse-Than-Pointless to Define Markets (a paper I wrote and presented to the economists at the Antitrust Division in 1997).

[152] *Werden Retrospective* at 530.

[153] *Id.* at 531.

[154] *Id.* at 530.

antitrust markets that best fit that abstract conception is clear or well-drafted. This subsection discusses the poor specification of the Guidelines' abstract conception of an antitrust market and the next discusses *inter alia* the poor specification of its concrete-market-delimitation protocol.

I will focus first on across-the-board-pricing contexts and then on individualized-pricing contexts. The analysis that follows assumes that, when the 1992 Guidelines refer to "a price-increase of [at least] 5 % lasting for the foreseeable future"[155] by the hypothetical combinants, the price-increase envisaged is not a price-increase of at least 5 % in the price of each of their relevant products but a set of usually-varying percentage-price-increases that would "average out" to be at least 5 %. Although the 1992 Guidelines never state this assumption explicitly, it is implied by their treating the hypothetical combinants as a single monopolist,[156] by their usual (though not universal) premise that the actors in question are sovereign maximizers,[157] by their reference to the hypothetical monopolist's "rais[ing] the prices of *any or all* of the additional products under its control,"[158] and by their statement that the relevant hypothetical monopolist "will be assumed to pursue maximum profits."[159] On this assumption, the 1992 Guidelines protocol is inadequately specified in at least six different respects.

First, the 1992 Guidelines do not explicitly state whether the DOJ and FTC will define the market to which each merger partner belongs to include the smallest set of sellers (1) that would find it *most profitable* to increase their prices by at least 5 % if they were combined and no remaining rival would respond to their price-changes[160] or (2) that would find it more profitable to raise their prices by 5 % or more than not to raise them at all. Four statements in the Guidelines are relevant in this context. Section 1.11 contains the first: it states than an additional next-best substitute will be added to the relevant MP's market if that MP or a "hypothetical monopolist" formed by combining the MP with higher-ranked next-best substitutes "would not find it profitable to impose. . .an increase in price" of 5 % or more. This statement is ambiguous because it fails to specify whether the profitability of the 5 % price-change is to be calculated by comparing the profits it would yield with the profits that would be yielded by the hypothetical monopolist's second-most-profitable price-change or by comparing the profits it would yield with the profits

---

[155] See the 1992 Guidelines, Section 1.11 at its last paragraph.

[156] See *id.*, Section 1.11 at the paragraph preceding the paragraph in which the textual footnote-number 10 appears.

[157] Thus, the first sentence of paragraph two of Section 0.1 of the Guidelines states: "Throughout the Guidelines, the analysis is focused on whether consumers or producers 'likely would' take certain actions, that is, whether the action is in the actor's economic interest."

[158] See the 1992 Guidelines, Section 1.11 at the paragraph preceding the paragraph in which the textual footnote-number 10 appears.

[159] *Id.*

[160] See the 1992 Guidelines, Section 1.11 at paragraph 2, which explicitly states that the profits that would be yielded by any price-increase the hypothetical combinants execute will be calculated on the assumption that "the terms of sale of all other products are held constant."

the hypothetical monopolist would realize if it did not change its prices at all. The Guidelines' second through fourth relevant statements are in Section 1.21. The first sentence of Section 1.21 states that the relevant (geographic) market definition will turn on whether the hypothetical monopolist "would profitably impose" the relevant price-increase, the second sentence of this paragraph focuses on "what would happen," and the third sentence of this paragraph indicates that the market will be expanded if the relevant "price increases would not prove profitable." The first and third sentences of Section 1.21 are as ambiguous as Section 1.11. However, given the Guidelines' sovereign-profit-maximizing-producer assumption, these two sentences probably do imply that the Guidelines' baseline for calculating the profitability of a price-increase of at least 5 % is the profitability of any other pricing decision (that the market would be further expanded only if the hypothetical monopolist whose members would form the market under consideration would not find a price-increase of at least 5 % *most profitable*). Nevertheless, the Guidelines should have been more explicit. One should not have to make reference to the second section that refers to an idea to understand it, especially when that section itself does not explicitly resolve the ambiguity the first section creates and contains two sentences that contain the same ambiguity. It is especially necessary for texts to be clear when (as here) the protocol they are trying to delineate is not cost-effective since in such cases, the dysfunctionality of the protocol precludes the interpreter from using functional analysis to clarify a poorly-drafted text.

Second, the Guidelines do not explain how one should measure the sales of the sellers placed inside a market (for the purpose of determining whether a particular market definition involved the smallest set of hypothetical combinants) and, relatedly, how one should weight the price-increase on each product that would be most profitable for the hypothetical combinant to make (for the purpose of determining whether the members of a particular hypothetical combination would find an average price-increase of at least 5 % most profitable). For example, the Guidelines do not indicate whether pre-merger sales or post-merger sales should be used for either of these purposes or even whether the same set of sales should be used for the two purposes just listed. Unfortunately, this choice may well determine both (1) whether a given set of hypothetical combinants would find a price-increase of at least 5 % most profitable and (2) which set of hypothetical combinants that would find such a price-increase most profitable is the smallest set of such combinants.

Third, the Guidelines do not specify the minimum amount of sales a set of products must have to constitute a market or what should be done if that minimum is not met by the "market" it defines. A leading economist at the Antitrust Division has told me that if "the smallest market to satisfy the 5 %-price-increase criterion is 'too small,'" the Division will drop the suit. However, like the Guidelines, he did not provide any indication of the way in which this "minimum market size" issue would be handled. Admittedly, the "minimum market share" issue has a textual predicate—*viz.*, the Clayton Act's reference to decreasing competition "in any line of commerce or in any activity affecting commerce in any section of the country." Unfortunately, I see no non-arbitrary way to resolve this issue as a matter of law. (Moreover, the prosecutorial policy-issue depends not only on the volume of sales for which the behavior in question decreased competition but also on the amount by which it decreased competition for those sales [as well as on the amount of sales for which it increased competition and the amount by which it increased competition for those sales].)

Fourth, the Guidelines' definition of its conception of an antitrust market does not specify and probably cannot, even in theory, specify how the DOJ and FTC will calculate the price-increase a hypothetical combination will yield if the combinants' pre-combination prices contain COMs. More specifically, the Guidelines state no more than that, in this kind of situation, the DOJ and FTC "will use a price more reflective of the competitive price"[161]—*i.e.*, will assume that the pre-hypothetical-combination price will be something like the competitive price. I must say that I find this sentence truly bewildering. I would have thought that, when the merger partner and its rivals were obtaining COMs pre-merger, one would analyze the price-effect of different hypothetical combinations by determining their constituent products' pre-merger HNOPs, NOMs, and COMs and predicting each hypothetical combinant's HNOPs, NOMs, and COMs. The Antitrust Division economist to whom I just referred told me that this provision of the Guidelines was included to indicate only that the prevailing price will be ignored when the prevailing collusion would end but for the merger in question. He also indicated that this condition will never be satisfied—that the cases covered by this provision are a null set—and that, if this condition were satisfied, the relevant benchmark would be "the competitive price." Unfortunately, that is not the way the relevant provision reads, the cases it would cover on this (unjustified) interpretation would be a small but not a null set, and—when the relevant condition was satisfied (*i.e.*, when the prevailing COMs would disappear if no merger were executed)—the set of pre-merger prices that the analysis should assume were being charged would not be the competitive prices of the products in question (as my collocutor suggested) but the set of prices that contain the relevant sellers' HNOPs *plus* NOMs: my collocutor's comments reflect his adoption of the standard assumption of most economists that in the general case competitive advantages, contextual marginal costs, and natural oligopolistic margins are zero.

The fifth drafting deficiency of the 1992 Guidelines relates to their statement that "the Agency [*i.e.*, the DOJ and FTC] at times may use a price increase that is larger or smaller than 5 %."[162] I have always assumed that the extent to which the Justice Department and the FTC will in practice be willing to define markets to include sellers whose sales exceed the sales of the smallest group whose combination with the merger partner will make a 5 % price-increase most profitable for the hypothetical combinants if non-combinants do not respond to the price-increases in question

[161] See the 1992 Guidelines in the sentence in which textual footnote-number 10 appears.

[162] See *id.*, Section 1.11, last sentence. See also the 1992 Guidelines, Section 1.11 in the last sentence of the paragraph preceding the paragraph in which note 10 appears, indicating that the relevant market will "generally" be defined in terms of the 5 %-price-increase criterion and indicating that "in most contexts" this criterion will be used.

will increase with the additional price-increase the members of the larger group of combinants would execute and with the additional profits the additional price-increase would yield them. Similarly, I have always assumed that the extent to which the DOJ and FTC will be willing to define markets to include hypothetical combinants whose combination will make a less-than-5 % price-increase most profitable rather than to include hypothetical combinants whose combination would make a price-increase of 5 % or more most profitable will depend on the extent to which doing so would reduce the sales or unit output of the hypothetical-combinant group. However, even if my assumptions are correct (even if, as various economists at the Antitrust Division have confirmed, the Division does make these kinds of trade-offs), the Guidelines' failure to specify this fact is reprehensible. Moreover, there are some grounds for believing that the DOJ and FTC vary the percentage-price-increase not on the basis just described but on an *ad hoc*, result-oriented basis that calls into question the seriousness of its commitment to the Guidelines. Thus, according to Assistant Attorney General James F. Rill (as summarized by Gregory Werden),

> a slightly higher price increase may be used if a merger would not be horizontal [*i.e.*, if neither MP would be placed in the other's market(s)] using a five-percent price increase but would using a slightly higher price increase. A slightly lower price increase may be used if there would appear to be no competitive concern in the market delineated using a five-percent price increase but a serious competitive concern in the market delineated using a slightly lower price increase.[163]

A still different standard for varying the required percentage-price-increase has been suggested by Werden. He would be willing to "go a little further in the candidate market *sequence*"[164]—*i.e.*, to add to the market additional next-best substitutes whose presence in an enlarged hypothetical combination would make a price-increase of more than 5 % profitable—"if doing so would yield...a natural market boundary[—]a political boundary in geographic space or a bright line in product space, [for example,] a 'marked gap in the chain of substitutes.'"[165] Even if the resulting variations in the relevant percentage-price-increase were sensible (and I see no way to determine whether they are), an Executive-Branch decision-making institution should not make them without having specified in advance the criteria it will use to do so.

Sixth and finally, the protocol does not indicate how it will resolve ties: how it will define the relevant market when the combination of different sets of products of the same "size" would make most profitable price-increases of at least 5 %. This "tie-breaker" issue will be more salient if the DOJ and FTC are willing to vary the critical percentage for one or more reasons.

---

163 The quotation comes from Werden's summary of Rill's position in James F. Rill, *Merger Enforcement at the Department of Justice*, 59 ANTITRUST L. J. 45, 49–50 (1990). It is taken from *Werden Retrospective* at 529 n. 31.

164 *Id.* at 531–32 n. 36.

165 *Id.* at 534–35.

The 1992 Guidelines are not better-specified in relation to individualized-pricing situations. To the contrary, all of the drafting deficiencies that the Guidelines have in relation to mergers between across-the-board pricers are present when the MPs are individualized pricers, and three or four additional problems arise in the individualized-pricing context. First, in the individualized-pricing context, the Guidelines do not specify whether the 5 % price-increases to which they refer cover just increases in the price each individualized-pricing combinant charges the customers it is privately-best-placed to supply or whether they cover as well increases in the prices each charges all other buyers for whose patronage it originally bid from a position of competitive inferiority. Second, the Guidelines do not specify how discriminatory the merger partner's prices must be for the protocol to require separate markets to be defined for each set of customers whose members are being charged the same or similar prices. Third, the Guidelines do not specify how uniform the prices charged to a given set of customers must be for them to constitute the buyer-side of a market. Fourth and finally, if the 5 % price-increase on which the protocol focuses covers the prices that an individualized pricer charges buyers it is not best-placed to supply as well as buyers it is best-placed to supply and if the relevant seller's price-increases do not have to be uniform across all the buyers to which the seller makes offers, the Guidelines are also deficient in that they fail to specify how the DOJ and FTC will calculate a given seller's average price-increase—*e.g.*, whether they give more weight to the offers the seller makes to its own customers than to the offers it makes to someone else's customers. I would probably focus on the net equivalent-dollar effect of the price-changes in question on relevant buyers, but nothing in the Guidelines suggests that the DOJ would adopt anything like this kind of approach.

I anticipate that defenders of the 1992 Guidelines' protocol will accuse me of asking for footnotes at a cocktail party. I am doing no such thing. If the Guidelines are to accomplish their self-professed goal of informing the law's addressees of the law's requirement sufficiently clearly to enable them "to avoid antitrust problems when planning mergers,"[166] the Guidelines must be considerably clearer than the preceding discussion reveals them to be. The way in which the gaps I have described are filled in may critically affect the definition of the markets into which the merger partners are placed and derivatively the DOJ's and FTC's conclusions about the legality of the horizontal mergers the MPs wish to execute. This is no trivial matter. Many of the mergers in question would have massive consequences for the owners, employees, and customers of the merger partners and their product rivals as well as for consumers of other products and investors in other areas of product-space. This kind of poor draftsmanship will not do. The poor draftsmanship of the Guidelines cannot be excused by claiming that "[t]he Guidelines are neither a cookbook nor a holy scripture"—*i.e.*, do not purport to provide "specific directions to be followed in precise order" or "the answer to any question if only they are studied sufficiently carefully."[167]

---

[166] See the 1992 Guidelines at paragraph 2.

[167] See *Werden Retrospective* at 535.

B. The Protocol's Assumption That No Market Outsider Will React to Any Hypothetical-Combinant-Group Price-Increases

The Guidelines specify that the DOJ and FTC will calculate the profits any hypothetical combinant could realize by raising its prices by various amounts on the assumption that no firm outside the hypothetically-combined group will alter its prices or any other term of sale in response to any increase in the prices of the hypothetical combinant's products.[168] This assumption is clearly inconsistent with the standard economic assumption that firms engage in profit-maximization, an assumption that the 1992 Guidelines in general adopt.[169] In across-the-board-pricing contexts, the fact that the combinants have unalterably raised their prices by any amount will change the profit-maximizing prices of their non-combinant product rivals. Similarly, in individualized-pricing contexts, any price-increase executed by the hypothetical combinants will change the profit-maximizing prices of the non-combinants. Even if the protocol is read to hypothesize that in individualized-pricing contexts each hypothetical combinant's price-increase relates only to the prices it charges buyers it is best-placed to supply, these price-increases (1) may make it profitable for the non-combinants to lower their prices to buyers one of the hypothetical combinants is best-placed to supply (may raise the immediate gains the non-combinant can obtain by stealing the hypothetical combinant's customer sufficiently to induce it to undercut, to take the risk that the hypothetical combinant will retaliate against its undercutting) and (2) may make it profitable for the non-combinants to raise their prices to buyers they are best-placed to supply by raising the contextual marginal costs the hypothetical combinants would have to incur to undercut them by making the required undercutting prices more discriminatory and by altering the combinants' relevant marginal costs by lowering their unit outputs (a non-combinant price-increase that might in turn increase the prices the hypothetical combinants would find profitable to charge their own customers by raising the contextual marginal costs the relevant non-combinants would have to incur to make given offers to the hypothetical combinants' customers that are lower than the prices the non-combinants are charging their own customers). Moreover, if the Guidelines are read to hypothesize that the hypothetical combinants will unalterably raise their prices not only to buyers that they are best-placed to supply but also to buyers they are not best-placed to supply (including buyers that the hypothetical non-combinants are best-placed to supply), the hypothetical combinant's price-increases will clearly raise the prices that individualized-pricing non-combinants find profitable to charge their own customers whenever one of the combinants was the non-combinant's closest competitor for a relevant buyer's patronage. In fact, the increase in the hypothetical combinant's prices to the non-combinant's customers might raise the prices that a

[168] See the 1992 Guidelines, Section 1.11 paragraph 2.

[169] See the 1992 Guidelines at the first sentence of paragraph 2 of Section 0.1.

non-combinant finds profitable to charge its own customers in other circumstances as well—*viz.*, when the possibility that one or more hypothetical combinants would undercut a contrived oligopolistic price the non-combinant was considering charging (because one or more hypothetical combinants was second-placed or worse-than-second-placed by less than the contemplated COM) originally deterred it from engaging in contrived oligopolistic pricing and the increase in the hypothetical combinant's prices gave the non-combinants a guarantee that their contrived oligopolistic price would not be undercut by any combinant.

In any event, the Guidelines' peculiar assumption that non-combinants will not adjust their prices to any price-increase the hypothetical combinants execute (1) renders unrealistic the calculation that the protocol requires to be made of the profitability of the various price-increases that any set of hypothetical combinants might make, relatedly (2) creates a real possibility that the DOJ and FTC would misidentify the set of hypothetical combinants that was the smallest set of hypothetical combinants whose merger would create a combination that would find a price-increase of at least 5 % most profitable (event if it did not use what I am calling the "protocol" the Guidelines indicate they should use for this purpose), and (3) causes the Guidelines to ignore the effects of the hypothesized combination on the welfare of buyers that non-combinants are best-placed to supply. Although the assumption that non-combinants will not change their prices might reduce the cost of carrying out the thought-experiment the Guidelines indicate the DOJ and FTC will execute to determine whether to challenge a given horizontal merger, this short-cut cannot be cost-effective.

C. Peculiarity of the 1992 Guidelines' Abstract-Market-Definition-Generated Market Definitions

The peculiarity with which this subsection is concerned reflects the following reality: two products' or producers' competitive positions vis-à-vis each other may be "asymmetric" in the sense that the percentage of product or producer X2's customers that product or producer Xl is second-placed or close-to-second-placed to obtain may be far higher than the percentage of product or producer Xl's customers that product or producer X2 is second-placed or close-to-second-placed to obtain so that product or producer Xl may take far more of product X2's customers if X2's prices are raised above the prevailing level and Xl's prices are not than product X2 will take of product Xl's customers if product Xl's prices are raised above the prevailing level and product X2's prices are not. For this reason, the abstract conception of a market that the Guidelines adopt may cause the DOJ and FTC's analysis of a horizontal merger between producers of products X1 and X2 to yield the conclusion that product X1 is in product X2's market (the market that is constructed starting with product X2) but that product X2 is not in product X1's market. This outcome does not surprise me. It reflects facts that suggest that a merger between producers X2 and Xl (*i.e.*, between firms that produce products X2 and Xl) may increase product X2's prices but not product Xl's prices. However, I suspect that this outcome will trouble those who are convinced of the accuracy and cost-effectiveness of market-oriented approaches in general and of the 1992 Guidelines' market-oriented approach in particular.[170] Specifically, such an outcome will seem to be "inconsistent" to such observers since their commitment to market-oriented analysis in part reflects their belief that such asymmetries rarely if ever occur (that products and producers are symmetrically-placed vis-à-vis each other and that each product-pair or firm-pair in a market is equally competitive in both directions with each other product-pair or firm-pair in that market).

D. The Inconsistency of the 1992 Guidelines' Concrete-Market-Definition Protocol and Abstract Definition of an Antitrust Market

The 1992 Guidelines state that the way to generate the smallest sought-after hypothetical-combinant group is to add to each product of an MP those products that were its successive "next-best substitutes," —*i.e.*, that would successively, "if available in unlimited quantities at constant prices,...account for the greatest diversion of demand [from the MP's relevant product] in response to a 'small but significant and nontransitory'...increase [in its price]."[171] In both across-the-board-pricing contexts and individualized-pricing contexts, this protocol will often not yield the concrete market definitions that match the Guidelines' abstract conception of an antitrust market.

One problem with the Guidelines' concrete-market-definition protocol that arises in both types of pricing contexts is the fact that the Guidelines' concept of "next-best substitute" is not the concept that is germane to the relevant competitive-impact analysis. The most important determinant of the impact of one product on the pricing of another is not how "substitutable" the first is for the second even in

[170] Admittedly, not all individuals in this category seem disturbed by this fact. Thus, Werden is not disturbed by the related but somewhat-less-challenging fact that the Guidelines' protocol may define MP1's and MP2's markets very differently though each is in the other's market despite the fact that the two firms produce similar products. See *Werden Retrospective* at 532.

[171] See the 1992 Guidelines, Section 1.11 in the paragraph in which textual footnote-number 9 appears. Some economists at the Antitrust Division apparently assume that Section 1.11 indicates that the market for merger-partner-product A will be defined by adding to A successively (1) A's next-best substitute (say, B), (2) the product X that is the best-remaining substitute of A and B combined, (3) the product Y that is the best-remaining substitute of products A, B, and X combined, *etc*. Although, properly operationalized, this protocol would be more likely to identify the relevant smallest set of hypothetical combinants than adding to A its successive, next-best substitutes (see the text immediately following), the Guidelines adopt the inferior protocol—indicate that to create the market "the Agency will add to the product group the product that is the next-best substitute for the merging firm's product." See the last sentence of paragraph two of Section 1.1 of the 1992 Guidelines.

the Guidelines' sense but how "competitive" the first is with the second in my sense—how frequently and to what extent the first product is the second's closest competitor for the patronage of a buyer the two products' producers are better-placed than anyone else to supply. More specifically, a product A's "next-best substitute" in the Guidelines' sense—the product S that "would account for the greatest value of diversion of demand in response to a 'small but significant and nontransitory' price increase"—may not be the same as A's closest competitor C in my sense for two reasons: (1) since the relevant diversion in demand reflects the pre-existing prices of the products in question, it reflects price-differences that may diverge significantly from the marginal-cost or overall-marginal-cost differences that affect how frequently and to what extent two products are each other's closest competitors and (2) since the diversion in demand in question is measured at pre-existing prices, it does not reflect at all the amount by which the S originally kept the producer of the A from raising its prices by reducing its basic or overall competitive advantage (the amount by which it lowered its HNOP)—*i.e.*, even if it did reveal the number of times the S in question was the A's closest competitor, it would not reveal the amount by which it was the A's closest competitor when it was the A's closest competitor.

The Antitrust-Division economists with whom I have discussed this issue do not admit that my concept of "competitiveness" is different from the Guidelines' concept of substitutability. For the rest of this subsection, I will therefore assume that the Guidelines actually employ my concept of competitiveness: since the errors introduced by the Antitrust Division's use of the concept of substitutability will not in any way tend to offset the errors I am about to discuss, this assumption is—if anything—generous on my part.

In across-the-board-pricing contexts, the smallest set of hypothetical combinants (say, one that contains n products) will frequently include one or more products X other than the MP's relevant product A that do not belong to the set of A's (n-1) closest "substitutes" (even if that term is defined to be the equivalent of my concept of the set of A's [n-1] successively "closest competitors"). In particular, products that do not belong to the set of A's (n-1) "closest competitors" may be part of the smallest hypothetical-combinant group either because they are closely competitive with one or more of A's closest competitors without being close competitors of A and/or because they are close competitors of one or more close competitors of one or more of A's closest competitors (relative to all of A's customers) without being a close competitor of A. In both situations, the products X may belong to the hypothetical-combinant set because their inclusion critically affects the profitability of the hypothetical 5 % price-increase to other members of the smallest set of hypothetical combinants.

An example may clarify this argument. Assume that product A's successive "next-closest competitors" are respectively products B, C, D, E, F, and G. Assume in addition that (1) product C is almost as close a competitor of A as is product B, (2) product G is product C's closest competitor and is a far-closer competitor of product C than is any other product though it is not a close competitor of product A, and (3) that products D, E, and F are all equally product A's next-closest competitor—*inter alia*, all are equally competitive with A—and are also quite competitive with B. In such a case, the smallest combinant-group to include A to meet the 5 %-price-increase requirement might be A–C–G rather than A–B, A–B–C, or A–B–C–D–E–F. The A member of the A–B combination might not find a price-increase of 5 % or more most profitable because such an increase would result in C's taking too many of its customers, and the B member of the A–B combination might not find a price-increase of 5 % or more most profitable because such a price-increase would result in D, E, and F's taking too many of its customers. Since the C member of an A–B–C combination might not be able to profit from raising its prices because such a decision would cause it to lose too many sales to G, a price-increase of 5 % or more might not be most profitable for the members of an A–B–C combination. Although the A member of an A–C–G combination would lose sales to B and a smaller amount of sales to D, E, and F if it raised its prices, it would not lose sales to C, which would find it profitable to raise its prices as well once it was freed from competition with G. The members of an A–C–G combination might therefore find a price-increase of at least 5 % most profitable. Even if the members of an A–B–C–D–E–F combination (but no smaller group containing the merging product and its successive next-closest competitors) would also find a price-increase of at least 5 % most profitable, the smallest combinant group would be A–C–G rather than the smallest group of the merging product and its successive next-closest competitors to find a price-increase of at least 5 % most profitable (assuming that the sales of each of the relevant products were the same).

The 1992 Guidelines' assumption about the members of the smallest set of hypothetical combinants is also wrong in individualized-pricing contexts. In particular, in individualized-pricing contexts as well, the smallest hypothetical-combinant set may include product(s) X that are not closely competitive with A across all A's customers because products X are closely competitive with A's closest competitors or with A's closest competitors' closest competitors. Such products X may be part of the smallest hypothetical-combinant group of (say) t products even though they are not part of the set of A's (t-1) closest competitors because their inclusion increases the likelihood that some other member(s) of the hypothetical-combinant group will be able to profit by raising their prices and, derivatively, that the MP that produces A will be able to profit by raising its prices too if the protocol is interpreted to "require" all hypothetical combinants that engage in individualized pricing to raise their prices not only to their own customers but also to the customers of others and perhaps even if it is not since the prices of the relevant products to buyers in relation to which they are best-placed will raise the CMC their producers must incur to bid for A's producer's customers.

I have devoted attention to this error not only because it is important in itself but also because the mistake that underlies it has more fundamental implications for the 1992 Guidelines' general approach to horizontal-merger competitive-impact analysis. In particular, the mistake that underlies this particular error is the failure to see that (so to speak) being a close competitor (substitute) of a product is not transitive. Thus, the facts that (1) the members of one set of buyers is nearly indifferent between purchasing a low-priced car (C) at its prevailing price and a medium-priced car (B) at its prevailing price and (2) the members of another set of buyers is nearly indifferent between purchasing a medium-priced car (B) at its prevailing price and a high-priced car (A) at its prevailing price do not imply that any buyers are nearly indifferent between purchasing a low-priced car (C) at its prevailing price and the high-priced car (A) at its prevailing price: goods that are close competitors of the same good will often not be close competitors of each other. Obviously, the same phenomenon can arise when the distinction among the goods in question does not relate to their quality and price—*e.g.*, when the relevant differences relate to differences in geographic location or other quality-attributes that do not affect the supply-cost and, relatedly, the quality and price of the goods in question. In any event, this error in the 1992 Guidelines' protocol for identifying the relevant smallest group of hypothetical combinants is also important because the error it manifests relates to a set of empirical realities that undermine the accuracy and acceptability of any market-oriented approach to economic-power assessment or competitive-impact prediction. As we shall see, the 1992 Guidelines acknowledge these empirical realities to some extent (the 2010 Guidelines do so to a far greater extent). However, their authors have failed to grasp not only these realities but the extent to which they render even *antitrust*-market definitions more complicated and cost-ineffective and even-*functionally-ideal* market-oriented approaches to horizontal-merger competitive-impact predation inaccurate and cost-ineffective.

I have always assumed that the DOJ would stop trying to define a product's market by adding to the product its successive "next-best substitutes" if it were convinced that this procedure would not yield the smallest set of products whose combination would produce a firm that would find a price-increase of at least 5 % most profitable—that given the choice between finding markets that (best) fit its abstract conception of an antitrust market and following a protocol that it wrongly believed would yield such concrete markets, the DOJ would abandon the protocol (the means) to make sure that its abstract-definition goal was secured. In fact, the opposite choice strikes me as unthinkable, and not just bizarre. Imagine my surprise, then, when the leading Antitrust-Division economist with whom I discussed this issue stated confidently that, even if I could convince him that the Guidelines' operational protocol would not yield concrete market definitions that matched the Guidelines' abstract conception of an antitrust market, both he and the Division would stick with the protocol (would not abandon the "next-best-substitute" approach to market definition).

E. The Cost-Ineffectiveness of the 1992 Guidelines' Abstract Definition of an Antitrust Market

Section 5 of Chap. 12 will analyze the cost-effectiveness of the 1992 Guidelines' overall approach to predicting the competitive impact of horizontal mergers—*i.e.*, of both its "General Standards," which are market-oriented, and its total approach, which permits the use of various types of non-market-aggregated data to rebut the rebuttable presumptions that some of the "General Standards" establish. Its analysis takes into consideration the possible superiority of approaches to predicting the competitive impact of horizontal mergers that do not presuppose market definitions—that do not make any use of market-aggregated data.

This subsection is more constrained. It assumes *ad arguendo* that the relevant competitive-impact predictions will be based on market-aggregated data and asks whether, given that constraint, the 1992 Guidelines' conception of an antitrust market is functionally ideal—is as cost-effective as any conception of an antitrust market could be when the task at hand is the prediction of the competitive impact of horizontal mergers. I have already pointed out various deficiencies of the 1992 Guidelines' articulation of the DOJ/FTC conception of an antitrust market, explained why (the 1992 Guidelines' claim to the contrary notwithstanding) the DOJ and FTC should not calculate the profitability of the various possible price-increases that any possible set of hypothetical combinants might execute on the unrealistic assumption that no non-combinant would respond in any way to such price-increases, and discussed the misguidedness of the protocol that the 1992 Guidelines claim would yield the concrete market definitions that would accord with the abstract definition they state the DOJ and FTC find optimal. Because I want to focus on what I take to be the essential features of the 1992 Guidelines' market-definition conception, this subsection will focus on a cleaned-up version of the protocol that has none of these inadequacies.

The 1992 Guidelines focus on the possible ways that a horizontal merger may reduce the competitiveness of the merger partners' prices by increasing their BCAs (in my terminology)—*i.e.*, by "lessening of competition through unilateral effects"[172] in their terminology—or by increasing their COMs—*i.e.*, by "lessening of competition through coordinated interaction"[173] (in their terminology). At this juncture, therefore, I want to address two questions. First, will the concrete market definitions that satisfy the criterion established by the 1992 Guidelines' abstract market-definition conception always include MP2's product in MP1's product market whenever the MP1-MP2 merger will (1) increase MP1's BCAs by freeing MP1 from MP2's competition in relation to buyers that MP1 was best-placed to supply and MP2 was second-placed to supply and/or (2) increase MP1's COMs to a significant extent by eliminating the possibility that MP2 might undercut the COM that MP1 would then find profitable to charge? Second, will the concrete market

[172] The enquoted expression is the heading of Section 2.2 of the 1992 Guidelines.

[173] Although the 1992 Guidelines do not explicitly define the expression "coordinated interaction," I do think that its authors intend the expression to refer to what I call contrived oligopolistic pricing (or at least the variant of such conduct that involves the making and enforcement of anticompetitive agreements). Thus, the Guidelines indicate that the behavior in question "includes tacit and express collusion" (*id.* at Section 2.1), and their discussion of the conditions that are conducive to "coordinated interaction" focuses on factors that determine the profitability of contrived oligopolistic pricing in my terminology—*viz.*, factors that influence the ability of firms to make anticompetitive agreements (Section 2.11) and to detect and punish violations of such agreements (Section 2.12). Although the relevant sections of the 1992 Guidelines also use such ambiguous language as "accommodating reactions," which can be part of natural oligopolistic or non-oligopolistic behavior-sequences in my terminology, I attribute the 1992 Guidelines' use of this expression to sloppiness.

definition that satisfy the 1992 Guidelines' market-definition criterion include MP2's product in MP1's product-market only if the MP1-MP2 merger would increase MPl's BCAs and/or COMs in the ways just described? These questions are important in the current context because, if a negative answer must be given to them, that fact suggests that some alternative abstract conception of an antitrust market will probably be more cost-effective in relation to horizontal-merger competitive-impact prediction than the Guidelines' conception.

Unfortunately, a negative answer must be given to both the above two questions. First, the fact that, under the Guidelines' abstract conception of an antitrust market, MP2's product would not be included in MP1's product market does not guarantee that the MP1-MP2 merger will not increase MPl's prices by raising its BCAs and COMs in the manner just described. Thus, if MP2's product were not competitive in my sense with all members of the smallest set of products whose hypothetical combination with MPl's product would enable all the hypothetical combinants to profit by raising their prices by 5 % given the responses that non-combinants would make to such price-increases, the fact that MP2 did not belong to this smallest set might be compatible with its being MPl's closest competitor by a considerable average amount for the patronage of some buyers MP1 was best-placed to supply (where the relevant average equals the average amount by which MP2 is better-placed than the third-placed supplier of buyers MP1 is best-placed to supply and MP2 is either second-placed to supply or equal-best-placed to supply). In particular, such an outcome would be possible if only a few products had to be combined with MPl's product to make the relevant price-increase profitable and MP2's product was less competitive with MPl's product and with the other members of the relevant smallest set of hypothetical combinants than the latter were with each other and with MP1. Indeed, in some cases, MP2's product will not belong in the relevant smallest set of hypothetical combinants despite the fact that it was more competitive with MPl's product than were some members of the smallest hypothetical-combinant set because MP2's product was less competitive with the other members of that set than they were with each other. As we have seen, the fact that MP2's product was not very competitive with the close competitors of MPl's close competitors does imply that MP2's exclusion from the hypothetical-combinant set will reduce the profitability of the 5 % price-increase to the non-MP members of the relevant smallest hypothetical-combinant group to a far lesser extent than would otherwise be the case (and, indeed, will reduce the price-increase the hypothetical combinants would find profitable to a far lesser extent than would otherwise be the case). However, this fact has far less bearing on the effect of the MP1-MP2 merger (as opposed to the hypothetical combination) on the prices that MP1 charges. Indeed, the fact that MP2 is not a close competitor of MPl's close competitors is irrelevant to the impact of an MP1-MP2 merger on MP1's BCAs.[174]

[174] I might add that, although MP2's not being a close competitor of MPl's close competitors makes it less likely that the MP1-MP2 merger will induce the MP1 division of the merged company to increase its COMs (since it makes it less likely that the merged company can use MP2's product to

Second, the implicit assumption of the 1992 Guidelines' concrete-market-definition protocol that any product (whether it is produced by MP2 or someone else) that it places in MP1's market will be significantly competitive with MPl is also unjustified. Since, as Subsection D just explained, the Guidelines' abstract market definition might imply that MP2's product should be placed into MP1's market despite the fact that MP2's product was not closely competitive with MP1's product because it was closely competitive with one or more of those of MP1's close competitors that did belong to the relevant hypothetical-combinant set, the fact that the Guidelines' abstract market definition would require MP2 to be placed into MP1's market would not guarantee that the MP1-MP2 merger would cause MPl to raise its prices by increasing either MP1's BCAs or its COMs.

In short, even if the Guidelines' protocol is cleaned up to eliminate the deficiencies previously discussed, the protocol (1) will sometimes not place MP2 into MP1's market in circumstances in which an MP1-MP2 merger would significantly increase the prices that the merged firm charged for MP1's products above the prices MP1 would have charged for its products and (2) would sometimes place MP2 into MP1's market in circumstances in which the MP1-MP2 merger would not significantly increase the prices the merged firm charged for MP1's product(s) above the prices that MPl would have charged for its products.

I would like to be able to conclude that the preceding arguments demonstrate that the 1992 Guidelines' abstract conception of an antitrust market would not be part of the most-cost-effective market-oriented approach that could be devised for predicting the competitive impact of horizontal mergers. However, for at least three reasons, such a conclusion is not warranted. First, the preceding theoretical argument deals only with possibilities—does not even purport to demonstrate how empirically important the possibilities it explores are. Second, no consistently-applied conception of an antitrust market can avoid making one or both of the two mistakes in question. And, third, since I am unable to describe the approach to market definition that would be functionally ideal in the current context, I cannot show that a cleaned-up version of the Guidelines' abstract antitrust-market conception would not be a component of the market-oriented approach that would be "functionally ideal" in the sense of being less "bad" than any alternative market-oriented approach that could be devised.

Nevertheless, the preceding critique of the Guidelines seems to me to be devastating. But perhaps this assessment is misguided. It assumes that the essential

reciprocate to rivals that have cooperated with MPl and/or to retaliate against rivals that have undercut MP1's contrived oligopolistic prices), MP2's not being a close competitor of MPl's closest competitor may increase the impact of the merger on the COMs that the MP2's division of the merged company obtains if MP1 is often second-placed to obtain the patronage of the buyers that its closest rivals are best-placed to supply and those rivals are often second-placed to obtain MP2s customers even though MP2 is rarely second-placed to supply their customers since in that asymmetric situation MP2 will need to prevent MP1's close competitors from undercutting MP2's contrived oligopolistic offers and will be able to take advantage of (1) any excess reciprocatory power that MPl enjoys in relation to its close rivals and/or (2) any positive difference between the harm-inflicted to loss-incurred ratio for the last act of retaliation that an independent MP1 would find necessary to commit against the rivals in question and the counterpart ratio for an independent MP2.

feature of the 1992 Guidelines' approach to market definition is its instruction that the seller-side of each MP's product-market consists of the smallest set of products to include the MP's product whose combination would enable its members to profit by increasing their prices by 5 %. That essentialist characterization of the Guidelines' market-definition protocol led me to discard the Guidelines' protocol for identifying concrete markets as incorrect. Perhaps I have gotten things backwards. Perhaps (like my Antitrust-Division collocutor) I should have decided that the essential feature of the Guidelines' approach to market definition is its proposal that MP1's market be defined by hypothetically combining MP1's product with its successive "next-best substitutes" until the members of the hypothetical combination could profit by raising their across-the-board prices or their average individualized prices by 5 %. However, not only do I think that my essentialist interpretation of the Guidelines' market-definition protocol is more consistent with the text, I also think that there is no reason to believe that the next-best-substitute approach would be more cost-effective than the approach that really would identify the smallest set of products whose combination with the product in question would enable the hypothetical combinants to profit from 5 % price-increases, much less that the next-best-substitute approach would be functionally ideal, given the constraint that the relevant predictions be based on market-aggregated data.

So far, I have ignored the way in which the Guidelines treat what Section 1.32 refers to as "supply responses"—*i.e.*, the possibility that firms not currently operating in the candidate market might start supplying its buyers within 1 year of its extant sellers' executing "a small but significant and nontransitory" price-increase (the supply-substitutability possibility) as well as the possibility that such a price-increase might induce a new producer to enter more than 1 year later after making investments (*e.g.*, in production and distribution facilities) that take more than 1 year to execute (the entry possibility). I think that the Guidelines' distinction between long-run responses (which involve the incurrence of significant non-recoverable costs) and short-run responses (which [usually] do not) deserves attention. I also agree that, as Section 1.321 recognizes, since these possible responses to price-increases are relevant to the market power of an existing firm and the competitive impact of a merger, either (1) the market-definition component of any market-oriented protocol for assessing monopoly power or predicting the competitive impact of a merger must take account of such responses when identifying the firms that are in the market and calculating all such firms' market shares or (2) these possibilities must be taken into consideration in some other way.

Nevertheless, I find the Guidelines' treatment of these possibilities deficient in at least six important respects. First, the Guidelines' distinction between supply-responses that will be made within 1 year (in which case the relevant sellers will be assigned market shares) and those that will be made in more than 1 year (in which case the relevant sellers' presence will be taken into consideration when analyzing the effects of potential entry) is too simple in that it fails to distinguish situations in which firms not currently supplying the market's buyers could do so immediately and situations in which they could do so not immediately but could do so in less than 1 year. Second, the Guidelines provide no indication of how the DOJ and FTC will calculate the market shares they will assign to "outside" firms capable of supplying inside buyers within 1 year. Third, as I will argue in Chap. 12, the Guidelines do not properly analyze either the conditions under which potential competition will be effective or the way in which it will affect the intensity of competition when it is effective—in particular, do not recognize the difference between increasing price competition directly and increasing QV-investment competition directly (and presumably price competition indirectly). Fourth, although the Guidelines do not elsewhere embrace limit-price theory—*i.e.*, the claim that at least in some circumstances effective potential competition will cause incumbents to lower their prices to deter entry, their treatment of supply responses could be interpreted to imply that their authors agree with this "theory" (which, as Chap. 13 demonstrates, cannot bear scrutiny). Thus, Section 2.212's statement that "[a] merger is not likely to lead to a unilateral elevation of prices of differentiated products if, in response to such an effect, rival sellers likely would replace any localized competition lost through the merger by repositioning their product lines" might be read to imply its author's acceptance of limit-price theory, though I believe that they meant only that any such merger-induced price-increase would be substantially eliminated by repositioning if it did lead to such repositioning. (I should add that I doubt that such repositioning will fully eliminate the price-increase in question and that, regardless of whether it does, it will not prevent the merger from raising prices since any related reduction in the MPs' prices will be offset by increases in the prices charged for the products that were closer in product-space to the products the repositioning eliminated than to the repositioned products.) Fifth, the Guidelines ignore the effects of firms already producing products that would be competitive for the patronage of some of the buyers in the candidate market that have not made any sales or perhaps even any offers to the buyers in question. Sixth, the Guidelines do not discuss the barriers and disincentives that may deter incumbents from responding to the merger by adding to the number of products they offer in the relevant area of product-space. I will return to this subject not just in Chaps. 12 and 13 but also in Section 4 of this chapter in the course of commenting on the U.S. courts' recognition that it might be appropriate to take "supply substitutability" into account when defining markets.

* * *

The 1992 Horizontal-Merger Guidelines' approach to market definition has received substantial praise from highly-respected economists and lawyer-economists.[175] Indeed, I have been chastised for "overlooking" the substantial

[175] According to Ian Ayres, "there is a solid [positive] consensus about the [1984] Guidelines' approach to market definition" (which is identical to the 1992 Guidelines' approach in all respects that are relevant in this context). See Ian Ayres, *A Private Revolution: Markovits and Markets* (hereinafter Ayres), 64 CHI.-KENT L. REV. 861, 865 (1988), citing Lawrence J. White, *Antitrust and Merger Policy: A Review and Critique*, 1 J. ECON. PERSP. 13, 14 (1987), which claims that the 1984 Guidelines' market-definition protocol is its "most important conceptual contribution...," and Franklin Fisher, *Horizontal Mergers: Triage and Treatment*, 1 J. ECON. PERSP. 23, 28 (1987), that describes the 1984 Guidelines' market-definition protocol as "a major step in the direction of sanity." I should add that Ayres clearly shares these views.

contribution that the Guidelines' analysis of market definition made.[176] This subsection has explained why I believe that the Guidelines' approach to market-definition does not deserve the praise it has received.

3. Various Economist-Proposals for Delineating Concrete Classical or Antitrust Markets[177]

Section 2 has already delineated and criticized two approaches to antitrust-market delineation that I assume can be attributed to economists[178]—the approach specified by the 1992 Horizontal Merger Guidelines' abstract market definition and the different approach the Guidelines mistakenly claim will yield the concrete market definitions that best fit their abstract market definition. This section will delineate and comment on six other approaches (approaches three to eight) to market definition that economists have explicitly or implicitly advocated or actually used.

The third approach to antitrust-market definition that economists have proposed builds on Joan Robinson's claim that markets can be defined non-arbitrarily if but only if there are "marked gaps in the chain of substitutes." If one substitutes "competitors" for "substitutes" as I believe should be done, Robinson's position implies that one should approach market definition by investigating the competitiveness of various (presumably-overlapping) pairs of products. If that investigation fails to uncover any gap in the relevant chain of competitiveness, the analyst should conclude that no market can be defined non-arbitrarily. If two relevant gaps are detected, the market consists of those products and sellers that are located between the gaps in question. Although (1) fairly recently, one excellent IO

---

[176] See Ayres at 865.

[177] This section of Chap. 9 makes considerable use of *Werden History* and of *Werden and Froeb Jazz*.

[178] I assume this for a combination of two reasons. First, the authors of not just the 1992 Guidelines but also of their predecessors were clearly influenced by such economists as Edward Mason, Morris Adelman, and Kenneth Boyer. See Edward S. Mason, *Price and Production Policies of Large-Scale Enterprises*, 29 AM. ECON. REV. (PAPERS & PROC.) 61 (1939); Morris A. Adelman, *The Antimerger Act, 1950–1960*, 51 AM. ECON. REV. (PAPERS & PROC.) 236 (1961) and *Comment: Economic Aspects of the Bethlehem Opinion*, 45 VA. L. REV. 681 (1959); and Kenneth D. Boyer, *Industry Boundaries*, in ECONOMIC ANALYSIS AND ANTITRUST LAW 70, 73–74 (Terry Calvani and John Siegfried, eds., 2d ed.) (Little Brown and Co., 1988) (arguing that the best market to define for any firm would include exclusively the "ideal collusive group" to which that firm would belong). Second, from conversations with professionals at the Antitrust Division, I know that the economists on its staff played a leading role in drafting the 1992 Guidelines (though they attribute most of its deficiencies to the late intervention of the Division's lawyers).

(industrial-organization) economist stated his belief that, in many instances, it will be possible to define markets in this way[179] and (2) the 1992 Guidelines' claim that, in most cases, one should use market-aggregated data to predict the impact of a horizontal merger (that most cases should be resolved through the application of its General Standards) seems to manifest an assumption that it will be possible to define markets in this way in most cases, I doubt that relevant gaps will appear in more than a trivial number of cases—*i.e.*, I do not think that, in practice, it will be possible to define markets non-arbitrarily in this Robinsonian way.

The fourth approach to concrete antitrust-market definition that some economists once advocated could be said to represent an operationalization of Robinson's approach had its proponents acknowledged (as they did not) that (as Robinson believed) in most situations there might be no marked gap in the chain of substitutes (*i.e.*, competitors). In 1952, Bain proposed that concrete markets be defined by using the cross-elasticity of demand between various pairs of products—X–e_D (say) between products C and F, which is defined to equal $(\Delta Q_F/Q_F)/(\Delta P_C/P_C)$ where Δ stands for "change in" (*i.e.*, the percentage change in the quantity of F that is sold that would be generated by a small percentage change in the price of C)—to detect what Robinson had called "marked gaps in the chain of substitutes":

> The magnitude of [the] cross-elasticity indicates the degree of substitutability. A low cross-elasticity indicates poor substitutes, a high cross-elasticity indicates close substitutes.[180]

And in the same year, Machlup proposed that concrete markets be defined by investigating both the cross-elasticities of demand and the cross-elasticities between various pairs of products.[181]

As the next section will indicate, for over 50 years,[182] U.S. courts have used the cross-elasticity of demand between one product and another to determine whether to place the latter product into the former product's market in both Sherman Act Section 2 monopolization cases (as part of an analytic protocol in which the courts attempt to infer from the former product's market share whether its producer had monopoly power in the market in question [on the mistaken assumption that possession of monopoly power is an element of the Section 2 offense of monopolizing or attempting to monopolize]) and in Clayton Act Section 7 cases (as part of an analytic protocol courts use to infer from the MPs' market shares and the relevant market's seller concentration the competitive impact of the horizontal merger under investigation). In both types of cases, courts include a second product

---

[179] See Richard Schmalensee, *Another Look at Market Power*, 95 HARV. L. REV. 1789, 1799–1800 (1980).

[180] JOE S. BAIN, PRICE THEORY 50–53 (H. Holt, 1952).

[181] FRITZ MACHLUP, THE ECONOMICS OF SELLER COMPETITION 213–14 (Johns Hopkins Univ. Press, 1952).

[182] The concept (or at least the term) cross-elasticities of demand was first used by a U.S. court in a dictum in Times-Picayune Publishing Co. v. United States, 345 U.S. 594, 612 n. 31 (1953). The first opinion in which a U.S. court actually used the concept to delimit a concrete market was United States v. E.I. du Pont de Nemours & Co., 351 U.S. 377, 380–81 (1956). This approach to market definition continues to be cited approvingly by U.S. courts today.

in the first product's market (when the defendant produced the first product) if the cross-elasticity between the first and second products at their prevailing prices is high and exclude the second product from the first product's market if this cross-elasticity is low. Admittedly, economists[183] (and eventually academic lawyers[184]) came to recognize that this approach is mistaken. The mistake (which came to be known as the *Cellophane* fallacy in honor of the first opinion to actually use cross-elasticity [speculations] to determine markets) was originally said to reflect the fact that the approach measured cross-elasticity at the relevant products' prevailing prices (rather than at their competitive prices) and was later traced to the fact that cross-elasticity figures depend too much on the initial quantities of the two products.[185] Because (speculations about) the cross-elasticity of demand between two products is still used not only by U.S. courts but also by E.C./E.U. courts[186] to determine whether to place the second product in question in the same market as the first product (the product produced by the defendant), I will discuss the two objections to this procedure in some detail.

The first objection has been made in the context of a U.S. case in which the court used the concept of the cross-elasticity of demand to define a market to determine whether a defendant's market share was sufficiently high for it to be found to have monopoly power. (The counterpart E.U. case would be one in which the court wanted to define a market to determine whether a firm's market share was sufficiently high for it to be found to occupy a dominant position.) For current purposes, I will put to one side both the fact that a firm's possession of monopoly power is not an element of any offense under the U.S. antitrust laws if those laws are correctly interpreted and the fact that—even if markets could be defined non-arbitrarily—a firm's market share would not be an acceptably-accurate indicator of its economic power in or dominance of the market in which it was found to be operating.[187] The first objection is that the cross-elasticity figures that are used in antitrust cases, which are calculated or estimated on the assumption that the two products' prices are their current prices, have little bearing on the magnitude that the cross-elasticity of the demand between two products would have if it were measured on the assumption that both products' prices were competetive. Although this claim is correct, it is not the reason why cross-elasticities of demand should not be used to define markets in these cases. As the second objection implies, even if the cross-elasticity of demand between two products at their prevailing prices equaled the

---

[183] See George W. Stocking and Willard Mueller, *The Cellophane Case and the New Competition*, 45 AM. ECON. REV. (1955) and Kenneth D. Boyer, *Industry Boundaries* in ECONOMIC ANALYSIS AND ANTITRUST LAW 70, 74–76 (Terry Calvani and John Siegfried, eds, 2d ed.) (Little Brown and Co., 1988).

[184] See, *e.g.*, RICHARD POSNER, ANTITRUST LAW: AN ECONOMIC PERSPECTIVE 128 (Univ. of Chicago Press, 1976) and Gene C. Schaerr, Note, *The Cellophane Fallacy and the Justice Department's Guidelines for Horizontal Mergers*, 94 YALE L. J. 670 (1985).

[185] The first publication to make this point was Klaus Stegemann, *Cross Elasticity and the Relevant Markets*, 94 ZEITSCHRIFT FÜR WIRTSCHAFTS & SOZIALWISSENSCHAFTEN 151 (1974).

[186] See, *e.g.*, United Brands v. Commission, Case 27/76, E.U.R. 207, 215 (ECJ) (1978).

[187] Both these positions are established in Chap. 8.

cross-elasticity of demand that would exist between them at their competitive prices, it would provide little information on the extent to which the second product's independent existence constrained the pricing of the defendant's product because such demand cross-elasticities are too dependent on the original quantities of the two product involved.

I will now explain the second objection that others have made to the use of cross-elasticities of demand to define markets in U.S. monopolization (or E.C./E.U. abuse of a dominant position) cases.[188] Assume that the product involved in the monopolization case is cellophane—product C—and that the other "product" that might be included in cellophane's market is "other flexible wrapping materials"—product F. The simple way to explain why the cross-elasticity approach to defining markets is unlikely to increase the cost-effectiveness of the market-oriented approach to assessing a firm's monopoly or market control over price (which for this purpose I will assume equals its P/MC ratio) is to show that

(1) P_C/MC_C is inversely related to the absolute value of the elasticity of the demand for C at its profit-maximizing price—hereinafter $e_{D(C)}$—and
(2) the absolute value of the elasticity of the demand for C at its profit-maximizing price is only weakly positively correlated with the cross-elasticity of demand between C and any rival product or product-type such as F ($X\text{–}e_{D(C/F)}$) either at the two products' profit-maximizing prices or at their competitive prices.

These relationships are relevant because they imply that using $X\text{–}e_{D(C/F)}$ to decide whether to place F into C's market (whether to reduce one's estimate of C's monopoly power by reducing C's market share) would increase the accuracy of the resulting estimate of C's monopoly power (P_C/M_C) only slightly even if (contrary to fact) C's market share did strongly correlate with its P_C/MC_C ratio.

I will now explain these two relationships. To see why P_C/MC_C is inversely related to the absolute value of $e_{D(C)}$ at its profit-maximizing price, recall that $e_{D(C)} \equiv (\Delta Q_C/Q_C)/(\Delta P_C/P_C)$ and derive the relevant relationship from two facts: (1) MR_C is defined to equal the derivative of the total revenue (TR) of C with respect to the quantity of C and (2) $MR_C = MC_C$ in equilibrium if C's producer is a sovereign maximizer (because the producer of C will maximize its profits by producing additional units of this product until MR equals MC). More specifically,

(1) $MR \equiv (d[TR]/dQ) = (d[PQ]/dQ) = P(dQ/dQ) + Q(dP/dQ)$ where the "d" is a mathematical symbol indicating that an infinitesimally-small change in the denominator of the ratio in question is being made;
(2) $MR/P = 1 + (dP/P)(Q/dQ) = 1 + (dP/P)/(dQ/Q) = 1 + (1/e) = 1-(1/|e|) = (|e|-1)/|e|$ where $|e|$ is the absolute value of e; and
(3) $P/MR = P/MC = |e|/(|e|-1)$.

Hence, the higher the $|e|$, the lower P/MC. For example, if $|e| = 2$, $P/MC = 2/1 = 2$; if $|e| = 10$, $P/MC = 10/9$; and if $|e|$ is infinite (if demand is perfectly elastic, as it

[188] For this purpose, I will use materials that I have been handing out to students since 1970.

is defined to be in a perfectly-competitive situation, in which the seller will lose all its sales if it raises its price by an infinitesimally-small percentage), $P/MC = 1$.

I will now explain why $e_{D(C)}$ at C's profit-maximizing price will be only slightly and weakly positively correlated with $X\text{–}e_{D(C/F)}$ at C's and F's profit-maximizing prices. The relevant relationship can be established by manipulating the formula for $X\text{–}e_{D(C/F)}$, taking account of the definition of $e_{D(C)}$. Thus,

(1) $X\text{–}e_{D(C/F)} \equiv (\Delta Q_F/Q_F)/(\Delta P_C/P_C)$;

(2) $(\Delta Q_F/Q_F)/(\Delta P_C/P_C) = ([\Delta Q_F/Q_F]/[\Delta Q_C/Q_C])([\Delta Q_F/Q_C]/[\Delta P_C/P_C])$—a result achieved by multiplying the right-hand side of equation (1) by $([\Delta Q_C/Q_C])/([\Delta Q_C/Q_C])$;

(3) $X\text{–}e_{D(C/F)} = ([\Delta Q_F/Q_F]/[\Delta Q_C/Q_C])([\Delta Q_C/Q_C]/[\Delta P_C/P_C]) = (\Delta Q_F/\Delta Q_C)(Q_C/Q_F)(e_{D[C]})$—a result achieved by multiplying the numerator and denominator in the left-hand expression of the first term in Equation (3) by $(Q_C/\Delta Q_C)$ and rearranging terms and substituting $e_{D(C)}$ for the right-hand expression in the left-hand side of equation (3), which it equals by definition.

Thus, even though increases in the absolute value of $e_{D(C)}$ will increase $X\text{–}e_{D(C/F)}$ (thereby strengthening the case for including F in C's market and thereby reducing C's market share and derivatively the probability that the producer of C will be judged to have monopoly power), the overall correlation between $X\text{–}e_{D(C/F)}$ and $e_{D(C)}$ and therefore between $X\text{–}e_{D(C)}$ and P_C/MC_C will be very slight and weak because $X\text{–}e_{D(C/F)}$ will be at least as connected to variations in $\Delta Q_F/\Delta Q_C$ and Q_C/Q_F as to variations in $e_{D(C)}$ since $\Delta Q_F/\Delta Q_C$ and Q_C/Q_F will be likely to vary as dramatically from case to case as $e_{D(C)}$ and variations in these three factors are unlikely to be correlated with each other. It should be obvious that this proof applies not only when $X\text{–}e_{D(C/F)}$ is being measured at the two products' prevailing prices but also when it is being measured at the two products' competitive prices.

However, the most important point to make in the current context relates not to whether the use of data on cross-elasticity of demand can increase or maximize the cost-effectiveness of the market-oriented approach to measuring a firm's monopoly power but to whether, even if it could, that approach could be defended. Assume, for the moment, that a firm's monopoly power should be measured by its P/MC ratio. Surely, it would be both cheaper and more accurate to determine P/MC directly than to do so by defining the market in which the firm should be placed by using cross-elasticity of demand figures (or anything else) to define that market, calculating the firm's market share, and inferring its P/MC ratio from its market share. If further argument is required on this issue, Chap. 8 will supply it.

As I have already indicated, cross-elasticities of demand have been used to define markets not only in monopolization cases but also in horizontal-merger cases. Some economists and lawyers with substantial knowledge of economics have argued that the use of cross-elasticities of demand to define concrete markets can be justified in merger cases though it is indefensible in monopolization cases. Thus, then Professor (now Judge) Richard Posner has argued: "The *Cellophane* fallacy does not arise in a merger case, where the issue is not whether the current price exceeds the competitive level but whether the merger might result in a further deterioration of competitive conditions."[189] In fact, although Posner is correct in pointing out that the fact that cross-elasticities are measured at prevailing rather than competitive prices is not so problematic in merger cases as it is in monopolization (or "abuse of dominant position") cases, both the second objection others made and the more comprehensive objection I made to the use of a market-oriented protocol in which cross-elasticity data is used to define markets are as telling in the horizontal-merger context as they are in the monopolization ("abuse of a dominant position") context. First, cross-elasticity figures do not indicate the extent to which the second product constrains the pricing of the first. Admittedly, the $(\Delta Q_F/\Delta Q_C)$ ratio in the formula for the cross-elasticity of demand (a ratio the Horizontal Merger Guidelines term "the diversion ratio") does indicate the percentage of the sales that C will lose if its price is raised that it will lose to F but it does not tell you the extent to which F matters in those cases—*i.e.*, the extra amount by which C's price could be raised without those sales being lost if F did not exist or was not an independent competitor. Moreover, as we have seen, since (1) $X\text{–}e_{D(C/F)}$ equals not $(\Delta Q_F/\Delta Q_C)$ alone but that expression *times* Q_C/Q_F *times* $e_{D(C)}$, (2) the magnitude of each of these three expressions varies considerably from situation to situation, and (3) the magnitudes of these three expressions are not positively or highly correlated with each other, $X\text{–}e_{D(C/F)}$ is not a good indicator of the diversion ratio—$(\Delta Q_F/\Delta Q_C)$. Second, even if cross-elasticity figures had more bearing on this issue than I believe they have, it would be far more cost-effective to base one's prediction of the impact of a horizontal merger on the relevant HNOP array on estimates of less-aggregated parameters—*e.g.*, in individualized-pricing contexts, on estimates of such things as the frequency with which the one merger partner was uniquely-equal-best-placed or uniquely-second-placed to supply a buyer that the other merger partner was uniquely-equal-best-placed or best-placed to supply and the amount by which, in those cases, the second-placed merger partner or the two uniquely-equal-best-placed merger partners were better-placed than those buyers' third-placed suppliers.

In both monopolization ("abuse of a dominant position") cases and horizontal-merger cases, (1) the use of cross-elasticity of demand data to define markets is unlikely to contribute to the cost-effectiveness of market-oriented analytic protocols, and (2) even if the preceding claim is wrong, market-oriented approaches that make use of data on or speculations about cross-elasticity of demand to define markets will not be as cost-effective as approaches that do not require markets to be defined.

The fifth approach to concrete antitrust-market definition that economists have recommended uses shipment data to delimit geographic markets. More specifically, in 1973, Kenneth Elzinga and Thomas Hogarty proposed that geographic antitrust markets be delimited by calculating two "shipment" ratios for each candidate

---

[189] RICHARD POSNER, ANTITRUST LAW: AN ECONOMIC PERSPECTIVE 125 (Univ. of Chicago Press, 1976).

geographic antitrust market and designating and picking as the actual geographic antitrust market the smallest geographic market for which the value of those two ratios exceeds a number they also specified.[190] Elzinga and Hogarty use the acronym LIFO (little in from outside) to stand for the first of their two ratios: a ratio whose numerator equals the dollar sales of the units of the relevant product that were both produced and consumed within the candidate antitrust market and whose denominator equals the dollar sales of the units of the relevant product consumed in the candidate market, regardless of where they are produced. They use the acronym LOFI (little out from inside) to stand for the second of their two ratios: a ratio whose numerator also equals the dollar sales of the units of the relevant product that were both produced and consumed within the candidate territory but whose denominator equals the dollar sales of all units of the relevant product that were produced in the candidate market, regardless of where they consumed. Elzinga and Hogarty originally proposed that the actual geographic antitrust market be defined to be the smallest candidate market for which both ratios were at least 3/4[191] but subsequently changed their mind and recommended that the actual geographic antitrust market be defined to be the smallest market for which the average of their two ratios was at least 9/10.[192]

I do not think that this type of shipment data can, from a functional perspective, significantly improve the definition of concrete markets in either monopolization ("abuse of a dominant position") cases (in which markets are being defined to facilitate the estimation of the defendant's monopoly or market power) or horizontal-merger cases. I have three objections to this approach to antitrust-market delimitation. First, I see no non-arbitrary way to pick the minimum or average magnitude that a candidate market's LIFO and LOFI ratios must have for it to constitute an antitrust market, no non-arbitrary way to decide whether the size of a candidate market should be measured by the dollar volume of the sales of the relevant product made to buyers located inside it or the dollar volume of the sales of the relevant product made to anyone by producers located within it, and no non-arbitrary way to pick the minimum volume of sales (of either genre) a geographic territory must have for it to qualify as an antitrust market. Second, this use of LIFO and LOFI figures ignores the fact that firms that make no sales (or few sales) in a geographic territory may still considerably constrain the pricing of firms that do make such sales (regardless of whether the latter firms are located in the territory in question). Thus, the only seller of a given product in a given geographic area that is itself located in that area may not be able to raise its prices significantly above its marginal costs because a rival located outside that geographic area can supply an equally-attractive product at only a slightly-higher marginal cost (slightly

[190] Kenneth E. Elzinga and Thomas F. Hogarty, *The Problem of Geographic Market Delineation in Antimerger Suits*, 18 ANTITRUST BULL. 45 (1973).

[191] *Id.* at 73–75.

[192] Kenneth G. Elzinga and Thomas F. Hogarty, *The Problem of Geographic Market Delineation Revisited*, 23 ANTITRUST BULL. 1, 2–3 (1978).

higher because of the slightly-higher delivery costs the rival would have to incur to supply the first firm's customers)—*i.e.*, in the somewhat misleading terminology of antitrust economists, ignore the cross-elasticity of supply or supply-substitutability. My third objection to the Elzinga-Hogarty approach (which may be at least as much an objection to market-oriented approaches to monopoly-power measurement and horizontal-merger competitive-impact prediction as to this shipment-approach to delineating geographic antitrust markets) is that the Elzinga-Hogarty approach is insensitive both (1) to the extent to which all the firms placed within one of their geographic antitrust markets constrain each other's pricing (which is what counts when the market is used to estimate a defendant's market power) and (2) to the extent that two MPs placed within one of their geographic antitrust markets constrained each other's pricing pre-merger (which is one of the most important determinants of the competitive impact of their merger).[193]

A sixth approach to antitrust-market delimitation that has been proposed and employed by some economists to identify concrete markets uses data on the correlation between two products' prices or, more plausibly though still not persuasively, data on the correlation between the movements of two products' prices[194] to determine whether the products should be placed in the same market. The primary proponents of this approach, Stigler and Sherwin, seem to have believed that it and only it should be used to identify antitrust markets.[195] I have four objections to the claim that this approach will yield the concrete market definitions that maximize the cost-effectiveness (in my view, minimize the cost-ineffectiveness) of the market-oriented approach to estimating a defendant's market power or predicting the competitive impact of a horizontal merger. Stigler and Sherwin themselves acknowledge the first (arbitrariness) objection that can be made to their proposal: in their words, there is "no unique criterion" for determining how high the relevant correlation must be for the placement of the one product into the other's market to be warranted.[196] The second objection is limited to the variant of this approach that focuses on correlations between actual prices as opposed to price movements: this variant makes the same error that the classicists (and standard expositors of perfect price competition) make in ignoring the fact that firms that produce product variants of different cost and quality may be highly and equally (indeed, perfectly) competitive with each other and far more competitive

[193] Although Werden has made the second objection to the Elzinga-Hogarty approach, he did not make the first or third. See *Werden History* at 211. Perhaps that is why his overall assessment of the usefulness of shipments data ("as a first cut") is more positive than mine. *Id.* I should note that, except in the context of hospital mergers, the type of shipments data on which the Elzinga-Hogarty test focuses has largely been ignored by U.S. courts, the FTC, and the DOJ.

[194] Technically, correlations between the prices themselves, their first differences, their logarithms, and the first differences of their logarithms.

[195] George J. Stigler and Robert A. Sherwin, *The Extent of the Market*, 28 J. L. & ECON. 555, 556 (1985)

[196] *Id.* at 562.

with each other than with anyone else—*i.e.*, of ignoring the fact that the equilibrium prices of the products in a market that satisfies the classicists' notion of an ideal market may differ substantially from each other in equilibrium. The third (spurious correlation) objection is more general: the movement of two products' prices or the same product's prices in two geographic locations may be highly correlated without their being competitive because (1) the same input or inputs are used to produce both (the marginal or variable costs of both depend on the prices of the same input or inputs) and the price(s) of the relevant input(s) vary or (2) because changes in the GDP and in unemployment-rates have "similar effects" on the demand curves for the products in question. Of course, such spurious correlations can be "controlled for," but doing so is expensive and difficult.[197] The fourth objection to this approach has been clearly and elaborately articulated by Werden and Froeb[198]: the correlation between the price movements of two products will be substantially affected by the elasticities of their demand and supply curves, which will differ significantly for the members of each product pair and among product pairs, and this fact will substantially undercut the connection between the correlation in question and the extent to which the two products are competitive (constrain each other's prices). Although I am not able to make a guess about how often this result obtains that is sufficiently well-informed to be worth writing down, I suspect that in many across-the-board-pricing situations (1) the producer of one product that is highly competitive with the producer of a second product for the patronage of some of the buyers the latter producer is best-placed to supply will respond to a price-increase by the second producer by lowering its price to enable it to obtain a substantial number of the latter producer's customers the former producer could not otherwise have profitably supplied and (2) the anticipation of this response will not make it unprofitable for the latter producer to raise its price in the first place.

A seventh approach to antitrust-market delineation focuses on the speed with which the price of one product adjusts to changes in the price of a second product.[199] I have two objections to this general approach. The first is the familiar objection of arbitrariness: I see no non-arbitrary way to determine the speed of adjustment that should result in two products' being placed in the same antitrust market. The second was (once more) well-articulated by Werden and Froeb (though their comments are

---

[197] Even if the associated costs do not render this approach less cost-effective than some other approach to defining markets for use in monopolization ("abuse of a dominant position") cases and horizontal-merger competitive-impact cases, they would reduce the probability that a market-oriented approach to such cases that used this technique to define the antitrust markets on whose structure it focused would be more desirable than a non-market-oriented approach.

[198] *Werden and Froeb Jazz* at 332–38

[199] See, *e.g.*, Ira Horowitz, *Market Definition in Antitrust Analysis*, 48 SO. ECON. J. 1 (1981); Stephen A. Mathis, Duane G. Harris, and Michael J. Boehlje, *An Approach to the Delineation of Rural Banking Markets*, 60 AM. J. OF AG. ECON. 601 (1978); and Ronald E. Shrives, *Geographic Market Area and Market Structure in the Bituminous Coal Industry*, 23 ANTITRUST BULL. 589 (1978).

addressed at least as much to the issue of whether a market-oriented approach to antitrust issues would be acceptably accurate or cost-effective if it used markets delineated through this technique as to the issue of whether this technique would define markets whose use would maximize the cost-effectiveness [minimize the cost-ineffectiveness] of the market-oriented approach to antitrust-law application):

> [All speed-of-price adjustment] tests [for antitrust markets] are fundamentally flawed.... Neither the rapid adjustment of the price of one product or area to changes in the price of another nor the rapid adjustment of the difference between the two prices is either a necessary or a sufficient condition for either product or area to be in, or not to be in, the relevant market delineated for the other. It is possible that the substitutes for a candidate market are not so good that they would prevent a hypothetical monopolist of the candidate market from raising price significantly, even though the prices of the substitutes adjust instantaneously to price changes in the candidate market, and vice versa. ...[Admittedly,] [s]low price adjustment may have some relevance to market delineation [but only] if it implies that substitution is also slow.[200]

I will count as the eighth and final approach economists have recommended using to delineate concrete antitrust markets two sets of techniques that make use of modern time-series econometrics. The first such approach relies on what is technically known as Granger causality, exogeneity, and measures of feedback.[201] The second relies on the technical time-series concept of co-integration to delimit antitrust markets.[202] According to Werden and Froeb (who are better-placed than I to assess these methods of antitrust-market delineation), the Granger causality/ feedback approach to market definition has "essentially the same" deficiencies as

---

[200] *Werden and Froeb Jazz* at 340. Werden and Froeb have an additional, even more decisive objection to the "relative speed of adjustment" test proposed by Mathis, Harris, and Boehlje, which focuses on the *relative* speeds with which various products' prices adjust to changes in the prices of the product whose antitrust market they are trying to define: even if speed of adjustment were relevant, the *absolute* speed with which one product's price adjusted to a change in the price of another would be relevant, not that absolute speed *relative to* the speed with which other products' prices adjusted to changes in the price of the other product in question. See *Werden and Froeb Jazz* at 340.

[201] See, *e.g.*, C.W.J Granger, *Investigating Causal Relations by Econometric Models and Cross-Spectral Methods*, 37 ECONOMETRICA 424 (1969); John F. Gewecke, *Measurement of Linear Dependence and Feedback Between Multiple Time Series*, 77 J. OF AM. STAT. ASS. 304 (1982); Chris Klein, Edward J. Rifkin, and Noel D. Uri, *A Note on Defining Geographic Markets*, 15 REGIONAL SCI. AND URBAN ECON. 109 (1985); and Phillip A. Cartwright, David A. Kamerschen, and Mei-Ying Huang, *Price Correlation and Granger Causality Tests for Market Definition*, 4 REV. OF IND. ORG. 79 (1989).

[202] See Robert F. Engle and C.W.F. Granger, *Co-Integration and Error Correction: Representation, Estimation and Testing*, 55 ECONOMETRICA 251 (1987); Gary Whalen, Time Series Methods in Geographic Market Definition in Banking (unpublished conference paper, Atlantic Economic Association Meeting) (1990); and Juan J. Dolado, *Co-Integration and Unit Roots*, 4 J. OF ECON. SURVEYS 249 (1990).

the price-correlation approach,[203] and the co-integration approach is based on an empirical assumption that is "often" not satisfied, may result in two products' being placed in each other's markets when neither significantly constrains the pricing of the other, and at best will reveal whether the second product will constrain the pricing of the first product after several years.[204]

I have now reviewed the six major approaches to antitrust-market delineation that economists have recommended that were not adopted by the 1992 Guidelines. All have substantial deficiencies, and none seems likely to yield concrete antitrust-market definitions that will enable market-oriented approaches to market-power assessment and competitive-impact prediction to be significantly less inaccurate and/or costly than I alleged such approaches are in Chap. 6.

4. The U.S. Courts' Handling of the Task of Delimiting Relevant Antitrust Markets

If courts delimited markets in a way that was not result-oriented in a bad sense—*i.e.*, if courts define concrete markets by using a protocol that was result-oriented only in the sense that the concrete market conclusions to which it led caused the courts to reach legal conclusions that were correct as a matter of law (as opposed to legal conclusions that favored the government [private plaintiffs] or alternatively defendants), market delimitation would play a critical role in many antitrust cases. For example, in a horizontal-merger case, the court's relevant-market conclusion would affect the legal outcome in two, admittedly-offsetting but rarely-perfectly-offsetting ways:

(1) in the one direction, the narrower the defined market(s), the less frequently the MPs would be placed in the same market, and the less likely a court that was using a market-oriented approach would be to conclude that the merger violated (say) the Clayton Act because it was requisitely likely to lessen competition; but
(2) in the other direction, the narrower the defined market(s), the higher the MPs' market shares in those markets in which both were placed, the greater the pre-merger and post-merger concentration of the seller-sides of the markets in which both MPs were placed (the higher the post-merger HHI and merger-generated increase in HHI in the markets in which both were placed) and the more likely a court that was using a market-oriented approach would be to conclude that the merger violated (say) the Clayton Act because it was requisitely likely to lessen competition.

---

[203] *Werden and Froeb Jazz* at 343.

[204] *Id.* at 344–45.

In most cases—*viz.*, in those cases in which the parties to the litigation agreed on whether the former effect of a narrower market definition helped the defendant more than the latter effect hurt it, the parties will contest the concrete-market-definition issue. In a few cases—*viz.*, in those in which the State or private plaintiff believes that a narrower (broader) market definition will strengthen its position on balance and the defendant believes that a narrower (broader) market definition will strengthen its position on balance, the parties may well agree to stipulate a market definition that each believes will redound to its interest.

If courts (and antitrust-enforcement agencies) did not deal with the market-definition issue in a purely-result-oriented way in which the desired result was party-oriented as opposed to right-legal-answer-oriented, the subject of this section of Chap. 7 (and of the next two as well) would have great practical importance. However, I must admit that I am not confident that in actual practice much turns on the way or ways in which U.S. (and E.C./E.U.) courts (and antitrust-enforcement agencies) *say* they are determining the relevant markets in antitrust cases. The reason should by now be obvious: there is good reason to believe that U.S. antitrust courts tend to or almost always define markets in a purely-party-result-oriented way. Certainly, many observers both within and without the system believe this to be so. Thus, in 1972, a District Court judge offered this characterization of the lower courts' (and U.S. Government's) treatment of the market-delineation issue:

> Reported cases have largely been limited to government concerns for protection of competition where courts have narrowed and broadened the market without real criteria or consistency.[205]

Although some extrapolation is necessary, Justice Stewart seems to have expressed the same view 5 years earlier in a dissent in a Supreme Court case: "in litigation under §7, the government always wins."[206] (As Werden recognized, Stewart "must" "largely...have had in mind" the fact that the government always wins on market delineation in merger cases.[207]) Both the HARVARD LAW REVIEW and an economist-lawyer team that specialized in antitrust economics reached precisely the same conclusion about the early cases. Thus, the HARVARD LAW REVIEW's account of the 1963 term states that "the Court appears to have taken a [party-] result-oriented approach to definition of the market, gerrymandering the boundaries so as to maximize the prospect of invalidating the challenged acquisition."[208] According to the economist-lawyer team Hale and Hale (who were admittedly criticizing the concept of a submarket [or at least the way in which it was being used by the Court]):

---

[205] Calnetics Corp. v. Volkswagen of Am., Inc., 348 F. Supp 606, 617 (C.D. Cal. 1972), *remanded* 532 F.2d 674, 691 (9th Cir), *cert. denied*, 429 U.S. 940 (1976).

[206] United States v. Von's Grocery Co., 384 U.S. 270, 301 (1966) (Stewart, J., dissenting). In a previous case, the second Justice Harlan also expressed concern that markets were being defined to produce desired (anti-defendant) outcomes. See Brown Shoe Co. v. United States, 370 U.S. 294, 367–68 & n. 3 (1962) (Harlan, J., dissenting in part and concurring in part).

[207] *Werden History* at 169.

[208] *The Supreme Court, 1963 Term*, 78 HARV. L. REV. 143, 274–75 (1964).

"What is objectionable is the broadening and narrowing of product definitions in order to achieve desired results in calculating market shares. . .."[209] My suspicion that product definition by U.S. courts is essentially party-result-oriented is reinforced both by the fact that "the legal tests (for market definition) applied in most of the reported decisions are basically irrational, arbitrary and hopelessly confused"[210] (see below) and by the fact that courts have applied these tests without citing any evidence at all or any evidence that was germane to their application.[211]

Admittedly, the preceding quotations and citations are all 20 to 50 years old. However, I am far from convinced that contemporary U.S. courts execute the market-delineation task in a non-party-result-oriented way.

Indeed, I suspect that currently (as I suspect was true in the past as well) the process of defining markets in a party-result-oriented way begins one stage earlier—with the DOJ and FTC. I have already explained why I am not convinced by Werden's argument that the Guidelines are specified sufficiently clearly "to avoid the gerrymandering of markets": for an analytic protocol to be manipulable, only one of its components must have room for play, and, as I showed, the Guidelines' specification is sufficiently imprecise at several places to give the government substantial wiggle-room. Indeed, I think that, Werden's other claims to the contrary notwithstanding, my conclusion is confirmed by his own statement that the Guidelines are neither a "cookbook" nor a "holy scripture"[212]:

> [T]he competitive analysis prescribed by the Guidelines is not the sequence of discrete steps it may appear to be in the Guidelines, but rather a holistic process. Market delineation is the first step in the paradigm, but *it is neither done in isolation nor completed prior to the analysis of other issues* (emphasis added).[213]

Despite these concerns, I will now discuss two types of markets U.S. courts have concluded could constitute relevant markets and list and evaluate the relevance of the various factors that the U.S. courts claim to have taken into consideration when deciding how to define relevant markets. I do so for five reasons:

(1) I may be wrong about the U.S. courts' delineating markets purely in a party-result-oriented way;

---

[209] G.E. Hale and Rosemary D. Hale, *A Line of Commerce: Market Definition in Anti-Merger Case*, 52 IOWA L. REV. 406, 426 (1966).

[210] G.E. HALE AND ROSEMARY D. HALE, MARKET POWER: SIZE AND SHAPE UNDER THE SHERMAN ACT 111 (Little Brown and Co., 1958).

[211] See *Werden History* at 174, citing numerous cases to support the former of these points (at n. 358) and Reynolds Metals v. FTC, 309 F.2d 223, 229 (D.C. Cir. 1962) (at n. 359) to support the latter.

[212] *Id.* at 535.

[213] *Id.* Werden's position resembles the position taken in 1963 by another economist (Irston R. Barnes) who worked for a U.S. antitrust-enforcement agency. In particular, Barnes also argued that (1) market delineation is not the first independent step in a competitive-impact-analysis protocol and (2) to define markets sensibly, one must first consider the type of competitive effects the merger might have. See Irston R. Barnes, *The Primacy of Competition and the Brown Shoe Decision*, 51 GEO. L. J. 706, 726–27, 729–30 (1963).

(2) even if I am not wrong about this, lawyers and consulting economists may have to couch their arguments in terms to which the courts have indicated they would respond favorably;
(3) lawyers, consulting economists, members of the policy audience, and judges may be able to make constructive use of critiques of the relevant-market "indicators" that U.S. courts claim they employ;
(4) at least two of the concepts the courts claim they use to delimit concrete antitrust markets have analytic value that many economists have failed to recognize; and (to be honest)
(5) readers of this kind of study undoubtedly expect it to cover this subject-matter.

The first new market concept that a U.S. court developed is the concept of a submarket. More specifically, in 1962, in *Brown Shoe Co. v. United States*, the Supreme Court argued that, in antitrust cases, geographic markets within markets (which it called submarkets) could be a relevant market.[214] Economists considered this idea to be not just wrong but absurd. Thus, George Hall and Charles Phillips asserted that the submarket concept was "an intellectual monstrosity" with "little economic justification,"[215] and the economist-lawyer team of Hale and Hale rejected this innovation on the ground that "if one boundary is right, the other must be wrong."[216] I disagree with this assessment of the value of the concept of a submarket. If one assumes *ad arguendo* that the concept of a market and its use in antitrust cases can be defended, so too can the concept of a submarket and its use in such cases. In the terms that were used in Chap. 6, the negative reaction of the economics profession to this concept reflects its support of a seller-oriented conception of antitrust markets. If one adopts the buyer-oriented conception of a market Chap. 6 argues is superior, the concept of a submarket is perfectly intelligible and often at least as useful as the concept of a market. I will use the shoe-store example of Chap. 6 to illustrate this point. Assume the larger geographic territory that might be classified as a relevant market is a metropolitan area that contains a central city and various suburbs. As we saw, on Chap. 6's simplifying assumptions, the set of geographic locations of the shoe-stores that are well-placed to secure the patronage of any commuter will include both the central city and a number of the metropolitan area's suburbs. And as we also saw, on those assumptions, the set of geographic locations of the shoe-stores that are well-placed to secure the patronage of those buyers who live and work in the central city and never visit the suburbs will include only the central city—*i.e.*, will constitute a subset of the set of geographic

---

214 370 U.S. 294, 336–37 (1962).

215 George R. Hall and Charles F. Phillips, *Antimerger Criteria: Power, Concentration, Foreclosure and Size*, 9 VILL. L. REV. 211, 219–20 (1964).

216 G.E. Hale and Rosemary D. Hale, *A Line of Commerce: Market Definition in Anti-Merger Cases*, 52 IOWA L. REV. 406, 426 (1966). The Hales also linked the concept of a submarket to the practice of improperly-resulted-oriented market definition. See also Morris A. Adelman, *The Antimerger Act, 1950–1960*, AM. ECON. REV. (PAPERS & PROC.) 236, 237 (1961) where Adelman refers to the idea of markets within markets as "a pathetic illusion."

locations of the sellers that are well-placed to supply the commuters. There is nothing incoherent about part of the larger geographic antitrust market that is relevant for one group of buyers' being the geographic antitrust market that is relevant for a different group of buyers.

The same conclusion is justified when the markets in question are product markets. The fact that some adults have preferences that result in male shoe-stores, adult shoe-stores, and family shoe-stores all being well-placed to obtain their patronage is perfectly compatible with other buyers' having a strong preference for family shoe-stores over the other two types of shoe-stores. Once one recognizes the possible desirability of using buyer-oriented market definitions, there is nothing monstrous, unjustified, or inconsistent about recognizing as the seller-side of one market a subset of the sellers that are placed in another market.[217]

I do not know whether the *Brown Shoe* Court recognized this possibility: Its discussion of the concept of a submarket was opaque at best. I also do not know whether the other courts that subsequently used the submarket concept did so for party-result-oriented reasons—*viz.*, to generate higher MP-market-share figures and higher seller-concentration figures that would "justify" a conclusion that the merger in question would lessen competition and was therefore illegal. However, I do know that the concept of a submarket would play a useful role in a buyer-oriented-market-oriented approach to antitrust analysis, which would itself be preferable to the seller-oriented-market-oriented approach the courts generally use (though, as Chap. 6 argues, it would still be less cost-effective than a non-market-oriented approach to antitrust-law analysis).

In 1962 and 1963 respectively, a U.S. District Court[218] and the U.S. Supreme Court[219] developed and used a concept that came to be known as a "cluster market" to analyze the competitive impact of a merger between two commercial banks in a case called *United States v. Philadelphia National Bank.* Cluster markets are markets for the purchase and supply of two or more products that are not components of a single more-complicated product (are not, for example, the parts of a car), are not demand-complements of the conventional sort (golf clubs and golf balls), and may not be competitive with each other. The standard example used to

[217] This point also seems to have eluded Richard Posner, at the time (he is now a judge) a legal academic with substantial conversance with economics. See RICHARD POSNER, ANTITRUST LAW: AN ECONOMIC PERSPECTIVE 129 (Univ. of Chicago Press, 1976):

> The "submarket" approach is unsound. If the "outer boundaries" of the market include only the product's good substitutes in both consumption and production…, then a submarket would be a group of sellers from which sellers of good substitutes in consumption or production had been excluded, and these exclusions would deprive any market-share statistics of their economic significance.

I hasten to admit that another leading legal antitrust scholar with substantial knowledge of economics thought the submarket concept (the use of "concentric markets") perfectly appropriate in some cases. See LAWRENCE A. SULLIVAN, HANDBOOK OF THE LAW OF ANTITRUST 42–43 (West Pub. Co., 1977).

[218] United States v. Philadelphia National Bank, 201F. Supp. 148, 363 (E.D. Pa. 1962).

[219] United States v. Philadelphia National Bank, 374 U.S. 321 (1963).

illustrate the concept of a cluster market is the cluster market for different grades of paper. The term "cluster market" derived from the following statement in the Supreme Court's *Philadelphia National Bank* opinion: "the cluster of products (various kinds of credit) and services (such as checking accounts and trust administration) denoted by the term 'commercial banking'...composes a distinct line of commerce."[220]

There are several reasons why at least some buyers may place a positive value on purchasing from one supplier a cluster of products that are not components of the same product, are not conventional complements, and are not or may not be competitive with each other:

(1) purchasing all the products in question from one supplier may reduce shopping time by reducing shopping-travel time and waiting-to-be-served time;
(2) purchasing all the products in question from one supplier may save time and protect privacy interests by reducing the number of people to whom the buyer must communicate "personal" information (*e.g.*, that is relevant to the seller's decision about whether to extend credit or to the seller and buyer's identification of the particular credit arrangement that is in the seller's and buyer's joint equivalent-dollar interest);
(3) purchasing a cluster of products from the same supplier will reduce the amount of time the buyer must allocate to learning how to use the products in question when the members of the cluster that are produced by a given supplier are all best used in the same way but different suppliers' product-lines must be used in different ways.
(4) a buyer may place a positive value on purchasing a cluster of products from the same supplier if each supplier's products have unique aesthetic characteristics and the buyer values aesthetic homogeneity; and
(5) when *ceteris paribus* the seller and buyer would find it individually and mutually profitable to engage in transactions on two or more such products but the value to each of the arrangement in question depends on the other's reliability, purchasing (selling) more than one product from the same seller (to the same buyer) may reduce reliability-investigation costs.

I should add that cluster markets may also be submarkets. Thus, if only some buyers of one of the members of a cluster (say, adult-male shoes) are interested in buying the other members of the cluster (adult-female shoes and children's shoes), the cluster market (for family shoe-stores) will be a submarket (of all shoe-stores that sell adult-male shoes). Similarly, if only some buyers of some set of products that some suppliers supply as a product-line value aesthetic homogeneity, the market for the individual products in the line (whose buyer-members either wish to buy only one member of the line or do not value aesthetic homogeneity) will be a submarket of the cluster market for the whole line (whose buyers want to purchase two or more members of the line and value aesthetic homogeneity or the extra time

[220] *Id.* at 356.

they would have to spend learning how to use different producers' products). All this is obvious once one thinks in terms of buyer-oriented as opposed to seller-oriented markets.

In my experience, economists recognize that, under some conditions, the concept of a cluster market makes economic sense (on the assumption that the concept of a market can be functionally justified) but tend to think that those conditions are virtually never fulfilled. I suspect that this tendency reflects the relevant economists' perception that the conditions that must be fulfilled for the concept of a cluster market to be useful are more restrictive than they in fact are[221] as well as their failure to appreciate the variety of reasons why buyers may place a positive dollar value on purchasing a set of products from the same seller. The only type of market whose characterization as a cluster market economists seem to be willing to accept as useful is one I do not classify to be a cluster market—*viz.*, the market for a set of components of a more complicated product (in Werden's example, for the components of a Honda[222]).

I turn now to the factors that U.S. courts claim influence their delimitation of concrete antitrust markets (to which commentators often refer as market-delineation "tests").[223] I will distinguish 14 such factors or sets of factors.

However, before proceeding, I want to make three admissions. First, my analysis of these factors is going to be primarily linguistic in the sense that it will focus largely on the meaning (in context) of the words the courts use as signifiers of these factors or the courts' verbal definitions of these factors as opposed to the ways in which the courts actually apply these "tests." Second, this feature of my analysis is problematic because U.S. courts often do a better job of defining markets than their description of the tests they are using for this purpose would lead you to expect. Third, many of the critiques that follow are based on the reality that the factor on which the respective tests focus does not perfectly predict the effect to which the tests respectively relate: such a demonstration actually bears more on the cost-effectiveness of the overall market-oriented approach than on the question this section is supposedly addressing—*viz.*, whether U.S. courts have delimited concrete

---

[221] Werden's reaction to the claim that commercial banking constitutes a cluster market is typical: "If, contrary to apparent fact, bank customers insisted on buying all services from a single institution, then the only competitors in the relevant market for each banking service would be full-service banks." *Werden History* at 196. Note the implicit reference to all bank customers and the unnecessarily-restrictive assumption that the buyers in question should "insist on" buying all services from a single institution. In fact, for a cluster market to exist, all that is required is that *some* bank customers *place some positive value* on buying two or more services from a single institution.

[222] *Id.*

[223] I derived my list of indicators or tests primarily from BETTY BOCK, MERGERS AND MARKETS: AN ECONOMIC ANALYSIS OF THE CASE LAW 42–67 (Nat'l Ind. Conf. Bd., 1960), MARK S. MASSEL, COMPETITION AND MONOPOLY: LEGAL AND ECONOMIC ISSUES, Chap. 9 (The Brookings Institution, 1962), and the opinion of the Court in Brown Shoe Co. v. United States, 370 U.S. 294, 325 (1962). The lists in all of these sources are summarized and perspicuously discussed by Werden in *Werden History* 154–57. See also *id.* at 168 and 175–76 for additional tests and critiques of particular tests.

antitrust markets in the way that maximizes the cost-effectiveness (in my judgment, minimizes the cost-ineffectiveness) of the overall market-oriented analysis in which the market-delineation protocol plays a role. Given the failure of the relevant U.S. legislation to state its ultimate goals clearly or to indicate how their achievement should be traded off against not only each other but implementation-cost savings, I doubt that the cost-effectiveness of the U.S. courts' market-definition protocol can be assessed. I should add that even if the preceding problem were not so serious as I believe, I do not possess the information about a large number of parameters one would need to have to evaluate the constrained-optimality of the U.S. courts' approach to concrete antitrust-market delimitation.

The first fact that U.S. courts have indicated influences their concrete-antitrust-market conclusions that I want to discuss is the "peculiar characteristics and uses" test.[224] According to this test, products with the same "peculiar characteristics and uses" should be placed in the same antitrust product market. Although products that have the same peculiar use probably do not face significant competition from products that do not have that use, not all products that have the same peculiar use will be highly competitive for the patronage of any buyer that would profit by purchasing one of them if they were all priced competitively: the average performance of each of the different products that have the relevant peculiar use may be different; the variability of the performance of each of the different products in question may differ from product to product; the producers of the different products in question may face different marginal costs; the different products in question may have different aesthetic attributes to which at least some buyers are responsive; the different products in question may be unequally easy to use; the different products in question may have different longevities; and the different buyers of the products in question may place different monetary values on the average quality of their performances, the reliability of their performance, and (respectively) their aesthetic attributes, longevity, and ease of use. Since, then, not all products that have the same peculiar use will be well-placed to secure the patronage of all buyers that may be able to "profit" by buying one of them, it may not be "optimal" to place all such products in the buyer-oriented markets whose delineation and use would minimize the cost-ineffectiveness of any market-oriented antitrust-law analysis.

The fact that products have the same peculiar characteristics also does not guarantee that they should be placed in the same market even if they also have the same peculiar use—at least unless "having the same peculiar characteristics" is stipulatively defined to entail having the same average performance-capacity, reliability, aesthetic appeal, durability, and ease of use. To the extent that products that share some peculiar characteristics differ along these dimensions, not all of them may be well-placed to secure the patronage of every buyer whose patronage

[224] See, *e.g.*, United States v. E.I. du Pont de Nemours & Co., 353 U.S. 586, 593 (1957) (du Pont-General Motors) and United States v. Brown Shoe Co., 179 F. Supp. 721, 729 (E.D. Mo. 1959), *aff'd*, 370 U.S. 294 (1962).

one of them is best-placed to obtain. Hence, it may also not be cost-effective to place all products that share both the same peculiar characteristics and the same peculiar use in each market in which it is "optimal" to place one or more of them.

Second, some U.S. courts have stated that products that share "distinguishing physical characteristics" should be placed in the same market and should be the only products in those markets in which they are placed.[225] Even if I assume (as no doubt the courts that used this "test" did) that the products in question have the same use, the fact that they have the same distinguishing physical characteristics implies neither that the products in question will all be well-placed to secure the patronage of any buyer for which one of them is best-placed nor that products that do not have those physical characteristics cannot be highly competitive for the patronage of buyers for which one or more of the former products are best-placed or well-placed. The fact that products share physical characteristics does not imply that they have similar performance-capabilities, durability, aesthetic attractiveness, or ease of use; even if the shared physical characteristic has significance for one or more of these value-parameters, the products that share the physical characteristic may vary substantially in other respects that some buyers value; and the cost and value-attributes of one or more products that do not have the shared physical characteristic in question may, in any event, make the latter products highly competitive for the patronage of some or all of the buyers for which the products with the shared physical characteristics are well-placed.

Third, some U.S. courts state that products that have "distinct customers" should be placed in the same market.[226] To the extent that this test implies that courts that are committed to using a market-oriented approach to antitrust-law analysis should use buyer-oriented rather than seller-oriented market definitions, it represents a step in the right direction. However, it is important to emphasize that the fact that one set of products (say, set A) contains all products that are well-placed to obtain the patronage of one group of buyers is perfectly consistent both (1) with only a subset of set A being well-placed to obtain the patronage of another group of buyers and (2) with the set of products that are well-placed to secure the patronage of a third set of buyers' consisting of some or all of the members of product-set A and various additional products: the fact that only producers of glass containers are well-placed to obtain the patronage of buyer-set D and only producers of metal containers are well-placed to secure the patronage of buyer-set E is perfectly compatible with producers of bottles, producers of cans, and producers of plastic or paper containers all being well-placed to secure the patronage of buyer-set F. Hence, in order to assess the competitive impact of a merger between a bottle manufacturer and

[225] See, *e.g.*, Crown Zellerbach Corp. v. FTC, 296 F.2d 800 (9th Cir. 1961), *cert. denied* 370 U.S. 937 (1962).

[226] See, *e.g.*, *id.* and United States v. Bethlehem Steel Corp., 168 F. Supp. 576, 584 and 611 (S.D.N.Y. 1958).

a can manufacturer through a market-oriented protocol, one would have to assess separately its impact in (at least) the three buyer-oriented markets I have just distinguished.[227]

Fourth, a related twosome: at least one U.S. court has argued that market delineation should reflect "the manner in which purchasers choose and buy" the products in question and "the manner in which products are sold."[228] To the extent that one can use these factors to identify buyers with similar preferences, their use by courts to delimit markets seems sound to me with the same caveats just discussed.

Fifth, some U.S. courts have argued that products of a given type that have "distinct prices" should be put into a separate market that only they occupy.[229] However, even if the price of a product is highly correlated with its quality (perhaps because it is highly correlated with its marginal cost), differences in the attributes of products in a given price/cost/quality category may result in not all such products being well-placed in relation to buyers whose patronage one or more of them is well-placed to secure. Moreover, for a variety of reasons, products in different price/quality categories may well be well-placed to secure the patronage of some buyers. I therefore suspect that, in many cases, it would be a mistake to define markets that contain only those products of the type in question that have the same price (cost and quality).

Sixth, some U.S. courts have argued that products of a given type should be separated into different markets according to their costs.[230] The arguments that counsel against putting all products of a given type with the same price into separate markets also undercut the case for putting all products of a given type with the same cost into separate markets.

Seventh, some U.S. courts have argued that all members of a set of "standardized" products should be put into the same market.[231] With two caveats, this suggestion seems perfectly appropriate. The first caveat relates to delivery costs: when different producers of a standardized product face different delivery costs in relation to a given buyer, not all may be well-placed to secure its patronage. (The same point will obtain when the buyer must pick up the good from the factory or depot.) The second caveat relates to the reality that physically-identical products may be valued differently by at least some buyers either because the buyers believe their quality is different or are less certain about the quality of some than of others

[227] US courts have sometimes failed to focus on the fact that different sellers are well-placed to secure the patronage of different sets of buyers (even though their acceptance of the concept of a submarket should have made it easy for them to perceive this reality). See, *e.g.*, United States v. Continental Can Co., 217 F. Supp. 761 (S.D.N.Y. 1963), *rev'd*, 378 U.S. 441 (1964).

[228] Brown Shoe Co. v. United States, 370 U.S. 294, 325 (1962).

[229] See, *e.g.*, In re Reynolds Metals Co., 56 F.T.C. 743 (1960), *aff'd*, 309 F.2d 223 (D.C. Cir. 1962); In re A.G. Spalding & Bros. Inc, 56 F.T.C. 1125 (1960), *aff'd*, 301 F.2d 585 (3d Cir. 1962); Photon Vest Corp. v. Fotomat Corp., 606 F.2d 704 (7th Cir. 1977), *cert. denied* 445 U.S. 917 (1980); and RSR Corp. v. FTC, 602 F.2d 1317 (9th Cir. 1979).

[230] United States v. Corn Products Refining Co., 234 F. 964, 975–76 (S.D. N.Y. 1916).

[231] See United States v. Bethlehem Steel Corp., 168 F. Supp. 576 (S.D.N.Y. 1958).

or because different products may conjure up different associations in the eyes of the buyer in question or others. These realities may also cause some producers of physically-identical products not to be well-placed to secure the patronage of particular buyers. The salience of this possibility is enhanced by the unwillingness of the U.S. courts (in particular, of the Supreme Court) to consider or grasp its implications.[232]

Eighth, some American courts have claimed that market-delineation decisions should be based on product "interchangeability."[233] This concept is inapposite for the same reason that the concept of substitutability (in its general as opposed to its 1992 Guidelines' stipulated sense) is inapposite: it focuses on only half the story, on buyer preferences and not on marginal-cost differences.

Ninth, some American courts claim to have based their concrete market-delineation conclusions on the "cross-elasticities of demand" between various pairs of products, the "sensitivity [of one product's sales] to price changes" of a second product, and/or "the extent to which substitution [between two products] occurs"—three largely-overlapping considerations.[234] Section 3 of this chapter criticized the use of data on cross-elasticities and data on price-movement correlations to define markets not only in horizontal-merger cases but also in monopolization (and abuse of a dominant position) cases. Data on the extent to which one product is substituted for a second product when the second product's price is raised is obviously relevant to the competitive impact of a merger between firms that individually produce one or both of the products in question, though the cross-elasticity of demand between the two products in question is a poor indicator of that determinant of a horizontal merger's relevant competitive impact and is completely insensitive to other determinants of that impact that are at least as important (other less-aggregated parameters that I think it would be much more cost-effective to make the focus of the analysis). In particular, even if (contrary to fact) one could accurately infer ($\Delta X/\Delta Y$) for marginal percentage-price-increases

---

[232] See, *e.g.*, FTC v. Proctor & Gamble Co. (Clorox), 386 U.S. 558 (1967).

[233] See, *e.g.*, United States v. E.I. du Pont de Nemours & Co., 118F. Supp. 41 (D. Del. 1953), *aff'd*, 351 U.S. 377 (1956) and American Crystal Sugar Co. v. Cuban-American Sugar Co., 152F. Supp. 387 (S.D.N.Y. 1957), *aff'd*, 259 F.2d 524 (2d Cir. 1958).

[234] See, *e.g.*, United States v. E.I. du Pont de Nemours & Co. (du Pont-Cellophane), 118 F. Supp. 41 (D. Del. 1973), *add'd*, 351 U.S. 377 (1956); United States v. E.I. du Pont de Nemours & Co. (du Pont-General Motors) 353 U.S. 586 (1957); United States v. Columbia Pictures Corp., 189 F. Supp. 153 (S.D.N.Y. 1960); RSE Corp. v. FTC, 511 F.2d 70 (1970), *cert. denied*, 445 U.S. 927 (1980). I should acknowledge that some courts have focused on "sensitivity to price change" in another sense—*viz.*, in the sense of "the extent to which a buyer would stop purchasing a relevant seller's product if it raised its price by varying amounts." Such information is clearly relevant to the relevant producer's monopoly control over price, and the impact of a horizontal merger on this type of sensitivity to price would clearly be relevant to the relevant merger's impact on price competition. However, once more, this information should be considered directly, not used circuitously to define a market whose definition is then used to generate market-share or market-share and market-concentration figures from which the sought-after assessment or prediction is derived.

of Y from accurate estimates of the cross-elasticity of demand between products Y and X, one could not infer from such cross-elasticity estimates the magnitude of the determinants of the following effects that the merger would have on the P_Y–MC_Y gap (assuming no impact on MC_Y): (1) in individualized-pricing contexts, (A) the determinants of its impact on the average amount by which it would increase Y's BCAs and OCAs when it did have such an impact (by eliminating X as an independent competitor of Y and by altering in various ways the CMCs that Y's other rivals would have to incur to match what would otherwise be Y's HNOP-containing offers to various buyers), (B) the number of times that Y's producer could obtain NOMs and the average magnitude of the new NOMs it could obtain (the determinants of the amount by which the merger would raise Y's BCAs and OCAs and whether X was less likely than Y's other relevant rivals to give Y a chance to rebid), and (C) other determinants of the OMs that Y would find profitable to contrive; (2) in across-the-board-pricing contexts, (A) the determinants of its impact on Y's buyer-by-buyer BPAs and BPDs, (B) the determinants of its impact on X's buyer-by-buyer BPAs and BPDs, relatedly (C) the determinants of the impact the former two impacts have on Y's across-the-board-pricing HNOP by changing the buyer-by-buyer BCA and BCD positions of Y's other rivals, (D) the determinants of its impact on the order in which Y and its other rivals announce their prices, (E) the determinants of the effect that its impact on Y's HNOP will have on its ability to obtain an NOM, and (F) the determinants of its impact on the OMs that Y and X contrive and on the OMs that Y's and X's rivals contrive.

Tenth, some American courts claim that, *ceteris paribus*, products whose production requires large and specialized investment should be placed in a market that only they occupy.[235] I suspect that any such market would sometimes be overinclusive and occasionally be underinclusive—overinclusive because not all members of a set of "similar" products that fit this description will be closely competitive for the patronage of buyers for which one or more of them is best-placed/equal-best-placed and underinclusive because in some situations (simple) products whose production does not require large and specialized investment may be highly competitive with (more complicated) products whose production does require large and specialized investment for the patronage of some buyers.

Eleventh and somewhat relatedly, some U.S. courts have maintained that concrete antitrust markets should contain only products that have similar methods of production or origin.[236] But products made with similar methods of production may have some attributes that make them relatively uncompetitive with each other, products made with different methods of production may be highly competitive with each other, products with different origins (*e.g.*, sugar made from sugar cane and sugar made from sugar beets) may be highly competitive with each other, and products of a given type made from the same basic material may be relatively uncompetitive with each other. Even if one recognizes that perfect fits are unlikely

[235] See United States v. Bethlehem Steel Corp., 168 F. Supp. 576, 594 (S.D.N.Y. 1958).

[236] See In re A.G. Spalding & Bros., Inc., 56 F.T.C. 1125 (1960).

to be available, these factors seem unlikely to be sufficiently-good predictors of the competitiveness of products for market definitions that are based on them to be able to play a constructive role in a cost-effective market-delineation protocol.

Twelfth, some U.S. courts have claimed that "recognition as a separate industry"[237]—*i.e.*, the facts that the general public considers all members of some set of products to belong to a separate industry, that some group of firms or their suppliers or customers make reference to the firms as members of an industry, that the government or the industry uses the product-grouping for statistical purposes, that the firms belong to a trade association whose membership is restricted to them—justifies placing the firms in a single market. Although the fact that a set of firms' customers place them in the same industry may reflect their all being well-placed to supply the buyers in question, it may not, and not only the firms themselves but also their suppliers, their customers, the government, and the general public may place the firms in a single industry for reasons that have little bearing on their being competitive with each other—*e.g.*, because they lobby together, because their demands for inputs vary together (because the demands for their products vary together), because they have similar needs for certain types of delivery services and promptness of supply. Certainly, for both geographic-differentiation and product-differentiation reasons, not all firms that some would place in the same industry will be highly competitive for the patronage of any buyer that one of them is best-placed to supply.

Thirteenth, some U.S. courts have asserted that those firms that make sales across a larger geographic area or advertise in media whose audience lives in a larger geographic area should be placed in the same economic market and should be the only sellers in that market.[238] This proposal obviously will lead to cost-ineffective market definitions when the set of firms that are well-placed to obtain the patronage of all or a significant number of relevant buyers contains those firms that are situated locally and (1) the firms that operate across the larger territory do not operate in all local areas in which other members of their group are operating and (2) some firms that do not operate across a wider geographic area are well-placed to obtain the patronage of some of the buyers in the area in which they do operate. Indeed, even when the firms that operate in the same larger geographic area (say, nationally) all do operate in the more-local area from which buyers select their suppliers, the sellers in question may not all be well-placed to supply some or many of the relevant buyers.

Fourteenth and finally, some U.S. courts have taken what antitrust economists sometimes denominate "supply substitutability" into account when defining markets.[239] This term is currently used to cover three different phenomena, though its employers do not distinguish the first from the second:

---

[237] See United States v. Bethlehem Steel Corp. 168 F. Supp. 576, 594 (S.D.N.Y. 1958).

[238] See United States v. Grinnell Corp., 384 U.S. 563 (1966).

[239] See, *e.g.*, United States v. Bethlehem Steel, 168 F. Supp. 576 (S.D.N.Y. 1958); In re A.G. Spalding & Bros., Inc, 56 F.T.C. 1125 (1960), *aff'd*, 301 F.2d 585 (3d Cir. 1962); and Bowl Am. Inc. v. Fair Lanes, Inc., 299 F. Supp. 244 (D. R.I. 1964), *aff'd in part and rev'd in part*, 384 U.S. 563 (1966).

(1) the ability of one or more firms not currently making any offers to supply a relevant product to the buyers in a candidate market to supply those buyers immediately by shipping in products of the relevant kind they already produce and sell in other geographic areas or by supplying the relevant buyers with appropriate products the sellers in question did not previously produce by making immediate changes in the way they use their existing plant and equipment (*e.g.*, perhaps, to use it to extrude copper wire when previously they used it to extrude aluminum wire),
(2) the ability of one or more firms not currently making any sales of relevant products to the buyers in a candidate market to supply these buyers with competitively-placed products the firms did not previously produce within 1 year (though not quickly enough to satisfy the buyers' immediate needs) without (*inter alia*) buying or constructing specialized equipment or plant, and
(3) the ability of one or more firms not currently making any sales of relevant products to the buyers in a candidate market to supply to these buyers competitively-placed products the firms did not previously produce more than 1 year after the time in question by executing QV-investment-increasing entries or expansions.

In a moment, I will discuss the relevance of these possibilities both for the measurement of a firm's monopoly or market power and for the analysis of the competitive impact of a horizontal merger and, relatedly, for the ability of a market-oriented protocol that does not take account of them when defining markets and hence when calculating market-share and market-concentration figures to accurately assess the monopoly power of a defendant or the competitive impact of a horizontal merger. However, before doing so, I should point out two phenomena or sets of phenomena that analysts of "supply substitutability" do not use this term to cover and that extant approaches to market definition and hence extant variants of the market-oriented approach to market-power or monopoly-power assessment and competitive-impact prediction also ignore:

(1) the fact that the presence of some firms that do not make any sales in a candidate market (indeed, that may not even be making any offers to the buyers in that market) because they are always worse-than-best-placed to supply the buyers in that market may nevertheless constrain the pricing of the best-placed suppliers of those buyers because the "outsiders" in question are second-placed suppliers of some candidate-market buyers or are worse-than-second-placed to supply some such buyers by a sufficiently small amount to inhibit the "insiders'" practice of contrived oligopolistic pricing and
(2) the ability of incumbents in the relevant market to add to the set of products they supply to the candidate market's buyers one or more products that those buyers might be interested in purchasing (or to alter the set of relevant products they produce without changing the number of such products they produce) immediately, in the medium run (within 1 year) perhaps without buying or building any new plant and/or equipment, or in the long run (after the passage of more than 1 year) perhaps after buying or building additional plant and/or equipment.

The failure of the "supply substitutability" analysis to consider the ability of incumbents to alter the set of relevant products they produce in this context is related to the failure of analysts of what I call QV-investment competition to consider the ability of incumbents to expand their QV investments (and, as I suggested in Chap. 2, may be related to the tendency of economists in certain contexts to think of firms non-dynamically—*i.e.*, as entities that are engaged in a fixed set of activities).

I will now discuss the relevance of the three "supply substitutability" phenomena on which current analysts have focused for the monopoly power or market power of a defendant in a U.S. Sherman Act Section 2 "monopolization" case (or E.U. Article 102 "abuse of a dominant position" case) or for the competitive impact of a horizontal merger. In my view, the first of the supply-substitutability phenomena on which contemporary analysts focus—the ability of outsiders to shift immediately to producing products that would be competitive for the patronage of at least some of the buyers in the candidate market—is relevant both (1) to the monopoly power over price a defendant in a Section 2 (or "an abuse of a dominant position") case possesses and (2) to the impact on price competition of (A) horizontal mergers between MPs that do not possess pre-merger and will not possess post-merger the ability to supply an additional product of the relevant kind in a short-run-timely fashion, (B) mergers that will enable one or both MPs to produce a relevant new product in a short-run-timely fashion, and (C) mergers that eliminate as an independent actor a firm not currently selling in the candidate market in question and not currently in a position to compete for the candidate market's buyers' patronage that could supply these buyers in a short-run-timely fashion. I should add that the existence of firms not currently making any sales or even offers in a candidate market that are in a position to supply its buyers immediately—the first of the two possibilities contemporary analysts ignore—will affect the monopoly power of an incumbent and the competitive impact of mergers in precisely the same ways in precisely the same circumstances. The second and third of the "supply substitution" phenomena that contemporary analysts recognize—*viz.*, the possibilities that outsiders could put themselves in a position to produce products that could compete for the patronage of at least some of the buyers in the relevant candidate market not immediately but in less than 1 year or in more than 1 year—are relevant to the monopoly control over QV investment of a defendant in a Section 2 or "abuse of a dominant position" case as well as to (in the varying circumstances stated above) the impact of a merger on QV-investment competition and, derivatively, on the intensity of price competition in the "relevant market" in equilibrium. Again, I should add that the ability of "insiders" (incumbents) to make such QV investments is equally relevant in the same way to the monopoly power of an "insider" or the competitive impact of a merger. The courts therefore are correct in recognizing the legal relevance of supply-substitutability. Unfortunately, however, I see no way to take these possibilities into account when defining concrete antitrust markets that is not circuitous—*i.e.*, that does not involve thinking through the effects of the phenomena in question on the monopoly power of the relevant defendant or the competitive impact of the relevant merger without defining any market, deriving the legal conclusion warranted by the economic conclusion this analysis has generated, and assigning to those firms that have the ability to engage in "supply substitution" putative market shares that will yield the correct legal conclusion, given the rest of the market-oriented decision-protocol the court will use. As Chap. 12 will explain, that is precisely how, according to the 2010 Horizontal Merger Guidelines, the DOJ and FTC will take supply-substitutability into account.

I am therefore not surprised that courts that have tried to take "supply substitutability" into account when defining markets have not done so in a satisfactory way. I should note, however, that the difficulty or impossibility of this task does not justify or even excuse some of the errors U.S. courts have made in this context: for example, even if a machine owned by a firm not currently selling in the relevant candidate market that was originally used for some other purpose could be converted immediately to produce products that would be sold in that market, that fact would be unlikely to justify assigning to the relevant "outside" producers that owned such machines the market shares they would have if all their current sales of products made by the machine had been made in the candidate market.[240]

I want to close this discussion by emphasizing two of the points I made at the outset. Although many of the preceding analyses establish that a market-oriented antitrust-law analysis that incorporates the market-definition "test" in question would produce significantly-inaccurate conclusions about a defendant's monopoly or market power or a merger's competitive impact and this conclusion has same bearing on the issue on which the preceding discussion was supposed to focus—*viz.*, whether the U.S. courts have defined markets in the way that maximized the cost-effectiveness (in my view, minimized the cost-ineffectiveness) of the market-oriented approaches to antitrust-law analysis they were using, the critiques did not focus optimally on this latter issue. Second, U.S. courts often did a better job of examining the relevance of one or more products for the monopoly power of a defendant or the competitive impact of a merger than their pronouncements about the tests they were using to define markets and predict monopoly power or competitive impact would lead you to expect. This reality comes as no purpose to me. In my experience, in the United States, judicial resolutions of cases are often far superior to the justifications the judges offer for their conclusions.

5. The EC's and the E.C./E.U. Courts' Approaches to Delimiting Relevant Antitrust Markets

The European Commission's and the E.C./E.U. courts' approach to market definition very much resembles (and I suspect has been substantially influenced by) their U.S. counterparts' handling of this task. This section will discuss the

[240] See *Werden History* at 191.

relationship between the EC's and the E.C./E.U. courts' approach to market definition and delineation and the U.S. approaches to these issues. I will start by pointing out eight important similarities and then focus on three sets of differences that I take to be equally significant.

The first salient similarity relates to the EC's statements about the nature of the abstract conception of a market that the EC and E.C./E.U. courts should use when applying E.C./E.U. competition law. The U.S. DOJ, FTC, and courts never explicitly address this issue, but the 1992 Guidelines and various court decisions make it abundantly clear that the U.S. antitrust-enforcement agencies and courts will seek to define *antitrust* markets—*i.e.*, markets whose definition can (allegedly) be functionally justified as opposed to classical markets or any other type of ideal-type market. According to the European Commission:

> Market definition is a tool to identify the boundaries of competition between firms. ... The main purpose of market definition is to identify in a systematic way the competitive constraints that the undertakings involved face.[241]

The second similarity between the U.S. and E.C./E.U. approach to market definition/delimitation is at least linguistic and may be substantive. Like their U.S. counterparts, the EC and the E.C./E.U. courts assert that "[a] relevant product market comprises all those products and/or services which are regarded as *interchangeable* or *substitutable* (emphasis added) by the consumer, by reason of the products' characteristics, their prices and their intended uses."[242] As I have said repeatedly, I find the italicized usage regrettable because it appears to imply that the competitiveness of products does not depend on differences in the marginal costs their producers must incur to supply relevant buyers. I hasten to add, however, that the Commission Notice's reference to "their prices" (which are an increasing function of the relevant products' marginal costs) suggests that, in practice, the EC and the E.C./E.U. courts will not make this mistake (just as in practice the *du Pont-Cellophane* Court did not).

Third, the EC approach to market definition resembles the U.S. DOJ/FTC approach in that the EC has also adopted an SSNIP operationalization of the relevant antitrust market.[243]

Fourth, like the U.S. DOJ and FTC, the EC (at least as an initial matter—see below) seems to be assuming that the optimal way to identify the concrete market that satisfies its abstract definition of an antitrust market is to start with the product whose market is to be defined and add to its market its successive next-best substitutes (though the Notice does not use this expression) until the market consists

---

[241] Commission Notice on the Definition of the Relevant Market for the Purposes of Community Competition Law (hereinafter EC 1997 Relevant-Market Notice), OJ C 372 Section 2 (1997).

[242] *Id.* at Section 7 (1997), quoting Section 6 of Form CO With Respect to Regulation (EEC) No. 4064/89. For a U.S. case that states a similar position, see United States v. E.I. du Pont de Nemours Co. (du Pont-Cellophane), 351 U.S. 377, 395 (1956).

[243] EC 1997 Relevant-Market Notice at Sections 15 and 17.

of the smallest set of products whose placement under the control of one firm would make it profitable for that firm to raise its prices to a specified extent for a non-transitory period of time.[244] I will return to this alleged similarity below when discussing the second difference between the E.C./E.U. and U.S. approaches to market definition.

Fifth, like the U.S. antitrust-enforcement agencies and courts, the EC and the E.C./E.U. courts seem convinced that it will always be possible to delimit non-arbitrarily the type of market they are trying to identify.[245] As I have already argued, I disagree even when the type of market one is seeking to delimit is an antitrust market. Even if, contrary to fact, one could estimate all relevant parameters costlessly and accurately, the failure of the promulgators of E.C./E.U. competition law to specify the goals that E.C./E.U. competition law is designed to achieve and the way in which these objectives should be traded off against each other in varying circumstances would preclude a decisionmaker from identifying non-arbitrarily the markets whose use would make the relevant market-oriented approaches as cost-effective as they could be (in reality, as little cost-ineffective as they could be).

Sixth, like their U.S. judicial counterparts, the EC and E.C./E.U. courts think it appropriate to make use of evidence on or speculations about cross-elasticities of demand to define relevant antitrust markets.[246] I disagree. (I should add that the EC also explicitly endorses the use of "tests based on similarity of price movements over time, the analysis of causality between price series and/or similarly of price levels and/or their convergence."[247]) Although, as we saw, many U.S. academic economists favor the use of such approaches, I do not know if DOJ/FTC economists have used them or if the agencies have responded favorably to arguments based on them.

Seventh, I am not sure whether, like the U.S. courts and antitrust-enforcement agencies prior to 2010, the EC makes the mistake of assuming that the fact that a particular business made no sales to a set of buyers implies that the business in question had no impact on competition for those buyers' patronage.[248] Although some statements in the EC's Relevant-Market Notice suggest that the Commission is making this mistake, this inference is somewhat disfavored by its acceptance of limit-pricing "theory." I write "somewhat" because my conclusion that a business that makes no sales to buyers can affect the prices they pay does not reflect my acceptance of limit-pricing "theory" (which I reject). In my view, a seller that makes no sales to any buyer in a set of buyers that would contain the buyers in a

---

[244] *Id.* at Section 17.

[245] *Id.* at *passim*.

[246] *Id.* at Section 39. See also Form CO Relating to the Notification of a Concentration Pursuant to Regulation (EC) No. 139/2004, OJ L 133 at Section 6II (4/30/04). See also United Brands v. Commission, 1978 E.U.R. 207 (ECJ) (1978).

[247] EC Relevant-Market Notice at Section 39.

[248] See, *e.g.*, *id.* at Section 48.

buyer-oriented market because it is never best-placed to supply any of those buyers may still significantly constrain the prices those buyers pay because it is second-placed to supply some of the buyers in question and significantly better-placed to supply them than the firm that is third-placed to supply them. And a potential competitor can be effective even if it does not enter and hence makes no sales to any relevant buyer if its presence induces one or more incumbents to make limit investments to keep it out. Although the failure of the EC to recognize this latter reality does not affect its market definitions in that the EC and the E.C./E.U. courts do not take account of potential competition when defining markets,[249] the failure of the EC and the E.C./E.U. courts to recognize both the fact that potential competition can be effective even when it does not result in entry and the fact that "market outsiders" that make no sales can still be constraining the prices that "market insiders" obtain will distort their competitive-impact predictions.

Eighth, the EC's and the E.C./E.U. courts' treatment of what they call "supply substitutability"[250] and "potential competition"[251] also resemble the treatment that these phenomena receive in the U.S. 1992 and 2010 Horizontal Merger Guidelines. In particular, when a firm not currently supplying buyers in an antitrust market could do so in the short run—*i.e.*, almost immediately without making a "significant adjustment of existing tangible and intangible assets,"[252] the EC states that it will take this reality into account by placing the firm in question into the relevant market and assigning it a market share. By way of contrast, "[w]hen supply side substitutability would imply the need to adjust significantly existing tangible and intangible assets, additional investments, strategic decisions or time delays, it will not be considered at the stage of market definition."[253] Like the U.S. Guidelines, the Commission Notice also indicates that, although potential competition may "represent an effective competitive constraint," such competition will not be taken into account when defining markets but will be considered "if required" "at a subsequent stage" through an investigation of "the condition of entry."[254] I have five somewhat-interrelated comments:

(1) in broad outline, this protocol is identical to the DOJ/FTC 1992 Guidelines';
(2) like the 1992 Guidelines but unlike the DOJ/FTC 2010 Guidelines, the Notice ignores the effect of firms that do not currently make sales to any buyers in the market in question and may not even have made them any offers but still constrain the pricing of market insiders because they are second-placed or not-far-worse-than-second-placed to obtain some relevant buyers' patronage;

[249] *Id.*

[250] *Id.* at Sections 20–23.

[251] *Id.* at Section 24.

[252] *Id.* at Section 20 and n. 4.

[253] *Id.* at Section 23.

[254] *Id.* at Section 24.

(3) like the 1992 and 2010 DOJ/FTC Guidelines, the Notice ignores the impact that the ability of incumbents to expand their QV investments in the relevant area of product-space may have on the area's competitiveness (an omission manifest in Section 24's reference to the condition of entry, which makes it appear [as the EC Guidelines also assume—see Chap. 12]) that the effectiveness of potential competition depends exclusively on the barriers to entry that successive best-placed potential entrants face;

(4) the Notice does provide a clear statement of the way in which the Commission believes courts should respond to a situation in which producers of any member of a technologically-related set of products whose individual members are not highly competitive with each other either produce all of the products in question or could easily do so—*viz.*, define a market to include all the products in question and assign to each producer the share of that supply-side-cluster market that the producer had of the sales of all the products in question.[255] I see no reason why, if this protocol is cost-effective, it should be applied only when *all* producers of any of the products in question either currently produce *all* of the products in question or could shift immediately to producing *all* of the products in question, and I also see no reason to believe that this protocol will yield market-share, market-concentration, and merger-induced change-in-market-concentration figures that will either (A) accurately predict the market power of a defendant and the competitive impact of a horizontal merger or (B) predict these "figures" more accurately than any other protocol one might devise to cover such situations would do; and

(5) the Notice provides even less information about the way the Commission thinks courts should take non-potential-competition supply-substitutability into account when it will take more than 1 year for the potential competitors to enter and, as I have already suggested, what little the Notice (and the EC Guidelines) say about the potential-competition issue is far from encouraging.

Before proceeding to discuss the major differences between the approach to market definition taken by the EC and the E.C./E.U. courts on the one hand and the U.S. DOJ/FTC and courts on the other, I want to comment on a critique of the EC's and the E.C./E.U. courts' position on supply-substitutability that has been made by a prominent European (German) economist/lawyer—Franz Jürgen Säcker—that several European economists have found persuasive.[256] In essence, Säcker's criticism is that, in practice, both the EC and the E.C./E.U. courts pay insufficient

[255] *Id.* at Section 22. For a case in which the Commission did not use this protocol because not all of the relevant producers produced all of the relevant products, see Agfa/Gevaert/du Pont, European Commission Case No. IV/M. 986 p. 26 (2/11/1998).

[256] FRANZ JÜRGEN SÄCKER, THE CONCEPT OF THE RELEVANT PRODUCT MARKET (hereinafter SÄCKER) (Peter Lang, 2008). See also SIMON BISHOP and MIKE WALKER, THE ECONOMICS OF EC COMPETITION LAW: CONCEPTS, APPLICATION AND MEASUREMENT 458 (Sweet & Maxwell, 2000) and MASSIMO MOTTA, COMPETITION POLICY: THEORY AND PRACTICE 104 (Cambridge Univ. Press, 2004).

attention (1) to supply-substitution in circumstances in which the supply response will take longer than 1 year and (2) to potential competition.[257] Säcker believes that long-term competition is particularly important in the E.U. where "in contrast to the USA" "the short merger control time limits [are] not usually determined by public opinion polls or empirical industrial organization studies, but by the know-how of the competition authority or the courts in examination of the normally very informed statements of the parties to the proceedings."[258]

I agree with Säcker's premise that both a firm's monopoly power and a horizontal merger's competitive impact are significantly affected by various factors that have an effect in the medium and long run such as non-immediate supply-substitutability and potential competition. However, I have four objections to Säcker's analysis. The first objection relates to Säcker's argument for these considerations' being more important in the E.U. than in the U.S. The "objection" is that I do not understand his argument. The second objection is that, like virtually all other economists, Säcker has not distinguished QV-investment-competition-related outcomes from price-competition-related outcomes and hence has not developed either (1) definitions for the concepts of (A) a firm's monopoly or market control over QV investment and (B) the impact of any type of conduct on the intensity of QV-investment competition or (2) a conceptual system that would enable him to operationalize such definitions, make the relevant measurements, or execute the associated competitive-impact-analysis. The third objection is that Säcker accepts limit-price theory—*i.e.*, believes that "potential competition can force an undertaking, which from the isolated view of the demand-side seems to be a monopolist, to reduce or refrain from increasing prices that are above marginal cost in order to prevent the market entry of potential competitors."[259] For reasons that Chap. 13 will explain in great detail, except in very special and rare circumstances, I reject this claim. The fourth objection to Säcker's analysis is that, in my judgment, it exaggerates the evidentiary value of testimony from customers and non-defendant participants in the relevant market, of testimony and internal memos from the defendants, and of testimony of the defendant's employees[260]: the customers and rivals of the defendants have an incentive to provide evidence that will benefit them in various ways that will not promote competition and, as I have already suggested, may not in any event be aware of the impact they had on the defendant's decision-making; once it is known that the authorities will make use of such material, defendants will have an incentive to produce memos and e-mails that serve their legal interests and to avoid recorded

---

[257] See SÄCKER at 43–44. Säcker also disagrees with the Commission's refusal to expand the defined market to include all members of a technologically-related set of products when only some of their producers produce all of the products in question.

[258] *Id.* at 25.

[259] *Id.* at 39 and 52.

[260] *Id.* at *passim.*

communications that will disserve their legal interests; the defendants will clearly not have an incentive to provide oral testimony that disserves their legal interests; and defendant-employees that do provide such testimony will often be found to have a grudge against their employer that calls their veracity into question.

I now turn to the three major ways or related sets of ways in which the E.U. approach to market definition differs from the U.S. approach. The first relates to the EC's specification of the abstract (SSNIP) conception of an antitrust market it thinks optimal. The EC's operationalization[261] differs in two respects from the U.S. DOJ/FTC's specification in the 1992 Horizontal Merger Guidelines:

(1) the EC's specification places the magnitude of the minimum price-increase that counts as significant at 5–10 % while the DOJ/FTC indicate that the relevant magnitude will normally be 5 %, and
(2) the EC specifies that one should calculate the price-increase the hypothetical combinants would find most profitable on realistic assumptions about the ways in which the rivals of the hypothetical combinants would respond to various price-increases by the hypothetical combinants while the U.S. Guidelines specify that the profitability of the hypothetical combinants' various possible price-increases should be calculated on the assumption that their remaining rivals would not change any terms of sale in response to them.

These two differences cut in opposite directions: the former tends to make EC concrete market definitions broader than DOJ/FTC market definitions while the latter tends to cause EC concrete market definitions to be narrower than DOJ/FTC concrete market definitions (at least if one assumes, as seems plausible, that the rivals of the hypothetical combinants will tend to increase their prices in response to the combinants' price-increases so that any price-increase that any set of possible hypothetical combinants make will be more profitable on the EC's realistic assumption than on the DOJ/FTC's unrealistic assumption). I do not know which of these tendencies will predominate across all cases, much less whether these differences favor the accuracy or cost-effectiveness of the EC approach or the DOJ/FTC approach.

The second salient difference between the EC's and the U.S. DOJ/FTC's handling of the market-definition issue is potentially much more significant. As I stated earlier, in its 1997 Notice on the Definition of the Relevant Market for the Purposes of Community Competition Law, the European Commission appears initially (at Sections 17–18) to adopt the 1992 Guidelines' next-best-substitute protocol for identifying the concrete markets that best fit its abstract definition of an antitrust market, though its initial treatment of this issue does not state in so many words that the "additional substitutes" that will have to be "included in" the candidate market will be the successive "next-best substitutes" of the product whose market the analysis is trying to delineate. The difference on which I am

[261] EC 1997 Relevant-Market Notice at Section 17.

now focusing appears much later in Section 57 of the Notice. In that section, the Commission states:

> In certain cases, the existence of chains of substitution might lead to the definition of a relevant market where products or areas at the extreme of the market are not directly substitutable. . .. [Such chain-substitution effects may apply] if the distribution of plants is such that there are considerable overlaps between the areas around different plants. . .[or] if products A and C are not direct among substitutes. . .[but] their respective pricing. . .[is] constrained by substitution to B.

The first part of the second sentence in the preceding quotation describes the kind of situation in which it will not be possible to define a classical or any ideal-type of market non-arbitrarily (because there will be no break in the chain of competitors) and in which (for the same reason) it will also be difficult in practice to identify the relevant antitrust market (the concrete market definition that is most cost-effective [least cost-ineffective]). The second part of the second sentence in the above quotation (which though constructed by me out of the Notice's words, does not distort the meaning of the Notice in any way) describes the type of non-transitive case that I argued invalidates the U.S. Guidelines' argument that their next-best-substitute protocol will reveal the concrete market definition that best fits their abstract conception of an antitrust market. The fact that the Notice recognizes the existence of these "chain-substitution effects" and declares that they should be taken into account is important because, at a minimum, it suggests that the EC may abandon its (apparent) support of the U.S. Guidelines' next-best-substitute protocol for delimiting concrete antitrust markets and (if I am being optimistic) may reject its market-oriented approach to assessing a defendant's dominance and predicting a "concentration's" competitive impact as well.

The third difference between the EC Notice's and the 1992 Guidelines' discussion of market definition provides additional (though admittedly modest) support for this optimistic projection. My overall judgment is that the Notice pays more attention to (gives more examples of) the various types of non-market-aggregated parameters on which a non-market-oriented approach to market-power estimation or competitive-impact prediction would focus than do the 1992 Guidelines.

Thus, the only demand-side data that the 1992 U.S. Guidelines refer to (in Section 1.11 on Product Market Definition and Section 1.21 on Geographic Market Definition from which the bracketed material is taken) are:

(1) evidence that buyers have shifted to or considered shifting purchases between products (different geographic locations) in response to relative changes in price or other competitive variables
(2) evidence that sellers base business decisions on the prospect of buyer substitution between products (geographic locations) in response to relative changes in price or other competitive variables,
(3) evidence on the influence of downstream competition faced by buyers in their output markets, and
(4) evidence on the timing and costs of switching products (suppliers).

And the only supply-side data the 1992 U.S. Guidelines refer to (in Section 1.32) are the following "examples of sunk costs": "market-specific investments in production facilities, technologies, marketing (including product acceptance), research and development, regulatory approvals, and testing."

The 1997 EC Notice on the Definition of the Relevant Market for the Purpose of Community Competition Law seems to me to be encouragingly more detailed (though this may be unfair to the U.S. agencies, which may, in practice, consider all the additional parameters the Notice mentions and use all the sources of evidence to which the Notice refers).

In any event, the Notice indicates that the European Commission and E.C./E.U. courts will obtain evidence not only from the defendant in a case but from "the main customers and the main companies in the industry," from "the relevant professional association," and from "companies active in upstream markets."[262] The Commission will sometimes send these sources "written requests" for information about their "perceptions...about responses to hypothetical price increases and their views of the boundaries of the relevant market" and may also discuss these and other relevant issues such as "how negotiations between sellers and buyers take place" with "marketing directors or other officers" of the companies in question.[263] The Commission will also consider "marketing studies" of the parties and their competitors and "consumer surveys on usage patterns and attitudes, data from consumer purchasing patterns."[264] In addition, the Commission will look to (1) data on product attributes and related buyer preferences, (2) "current patterns of purchases,"[265] "substitution in the recent past,"[266] (3) data on "national or local preferences,"[267] (4) data on the need for "a local presence" to sell effectively, on "access to local distribution channels," on regulatory barriers, quotas, and tariffs, on local or national technical standards, packaging regulations, and required administrative authorizations,[268] and on "the actual pattern and evolution of trade flows" and "transport costs,"[269] and (5) data on the "[b]arriers and costs associated with switching demand to potential substitutes" such as "the need to incur specific capital investment or loss of current output in order to switch to alternative inputs...and uncertainty about quality and reputation of unknown supplies."[270]

Although the Notice's presentation of these ideas is somewhat repetitive and (as I have already stated) the absence of a similar level of detail in the 1992 U.S. Guidelines may well be a matter of presentation rather than practice, I hope that the E.U. institutions' use of data on these parameters (like the U.S. institutions' execution of simulation studies that do not use market-aggregated data) will lead

[262] *Id.* at Section 33.
[263] *Id.* at Section 34.
[264] *Id.* at Section 41.
[265] *Id.* at Section 29.
[266] *Id.* at Section 38.
[267] *Id.* at Section 29.
[268] *Id.* at Section 30.
[269] *Id.* at Section 31.
[270] *Id.* at Section 42.

the authorities in question to consider abandoning the market-oriented approach to antitrust-law analysis altogether.

The preceding discussion of E.U. market-definition practice focused exclusively on the EC's relevant Notice. I should admit, however, that "[i]n decisions since the adoption of the [N]otice, the Commission has tended to use the older. . .test,"[271] which focuses more diffusely on demand-side and supply-side substitutability rather than on the Notice's "hypothetical monopolist" test, which the EC took over with some adjustment from the 1992 U.S. Horizontal Merger Guidelines. The CFIs and ECJ have tended to accept the EC's market definitions, although in some cases they have quashed Commission decisions on the ground that the Commission failed to provide adequate justification for its market definition.[272] In a similar vein, in at least one important decision, the CFI correctly held that, because the correct definition of a market may change through time, the EC cannot automatically assume that market definitions generated in earlier cases are appropriate in later cases.[273] I will restrict myself to making two additional, more general points about the relevant EC-court case-law. First, at least in earlier years, the ECJ clearly believed in limit-price theory—*i.e.*, that the threat of entry will deter incumbents from charging as high prices as they would otherwise find profitable to charge.[274] Since, as we have seen, the EC and European economist/lawyers such as Säcker continue to believe in this theory, I assume that the ECJ still does so as well. Second, in some puzzling cases, EC courts have placed a product's complements into the relevant product's product market. Thus, in *Tiercé Ladbroke v. Commission*,[275] the CFI placed live films of horse races provided by satellite into the market for betting services.

* * *

I began this Chapter by asserting that both (A) U.S. courts and antitrust-enforcement agencies and (B) E.C./E.U. courts and antitrust-enforcement authorities are committed to market-oriented approaches to antitrust-law analysis and (2) by pointing out that Chap. 6's demonstration that, regardless of whether ideal-type or functional criteria are used to evaluate them, market definitions are inevitably arbitrary implies that this commitment is unfortunate. I want to close this chapter by listing various pieces of evidence that suggest that the relevant

---

[271] KORAH at 111.

[272] See, *e.g.*, European Night Service v. Commission, T-374/94, ECR II-3141 (1998).

[273] See Coca-Cola Company and Coca-Cola Enterprises, Inc. v. Commission, T-125 and 127/97, ECR II-1733, p. 82 (2000).

[274] See, *e.g.*, Nederlandsche Banden-Industrie Michelin NV v. Commission, 322/81, [1983] ECR 3461, p. 41 (1985), in which the ECJ asserted that, if Goodyear could have built a factory in the Netherlands, its ability to do so would constrain Michelin's pricing and Europeanballage Corporation and Continental Can Co., Inc. v. Commission, 56/72, [1973] ECR 215, pp. 32 and 37 (1973), in which the ECJ argued that, if makers of cylindrical cans could make the differently-shaped cans traditionally used for meats and fish, their ability to do so would deter Continental Can from raising its prices.

[275] T-504/93, ECR II-923 (1997).

courts' and enforcement-authorities' commitment to market-oriented approaches or at least to traditional, seller-oriented-market-definition market-oriented approaches to antitrust analysis may be less total and more short-lived than I initially indicated. Some of the relevant facts have already been discussed, and some, not.

I have already referred to the following eleven relevant facts:

(1) U.S. courts have increasingly made use of the concepts of "submarkets" and "cluster markets"—concepts that involve a shift from seller-oriented to buyer-oriented market definitions that is both desirable in itself and encourages a way of thinking that leads the analyst to realize that market-oriented approaches are (if not arbitrary) cost-ineffective;
(2) some U.S. courts have argued that markets should be defined by sets of "distinct customers";
(3) the 1992 Horizontal Merger Guidelines also accept that, in some situations (*viz.*, when price discrimination is practiced), buyer-oriented market definitions should be substituted for seller-oriented market definitions;
(4) the U.S. 1992 Guidelines acknowledge that, at least in a significant number of cases, the conclusions that one would derive from market-aggregated data alone need to be adjusted to take account of realities that market-aggregated data fail to capture;
(5) sophisticated economists have made telling criticisms of virtually all the approaches to market definition not delineated by the 1992 Guidelines that other economists have proposed or used;
(6) a few judges, some leading academic lawyers, and some respected economists have argued that the U.S. courts and antitrust-enforcement agencies have been defining markets in an illicitly-result-oriented way;
(7) several leading IO economists now acknowledge that, in many or all situations, market definitions will inevitably be arbitrary or "meaningless";
(8) since at least the mid-1990s, the DOJ and FTC have used a variety of approaches that need not be and were not in practice market-oriented (including merger-simulation techniques and inferences from natural experiments) to predict the competitive impact of horizontal mergers;
(9) the EC recognizes a phenomenon that it denominates "chains of substitution," which logically implies not only the unacceptability of the next-best-substitute protocol for identifying antitrust markets but the impossibility of defining economic markets non-arbitrarily and the cost-ineffectiveness of any market-oriented approach to antitrust-law analysis;
(10) the EC's 1997 Relevant-Market Notice already lists a large number of non-market-aggregated parameters from which one could derive market-dominance and competitive-impact conclusions without defining any relevant market; and
(11) the U.S. antitrust-enforcement agencies also already pay attention to such parameters and use simulation techniques for predicting the competitive impact of horizontal mergers that do not require markets to be defined.

Five additional pieces of evidence (not yet mentioned) support my admittedly-optimistic but hopefully-not-Pollyannish view that the U.S.' and E.U.'s commitment to market-oriented approaches to antitrust-law analysis and hence to defining relevant markets may be short-lived (or at least "medium-lived"). First, in a series of post-1992 horizontal-merger decisions, the U.S. DOJ and FTC have used buyer-oriented rather than seller-oriented market definitions.[276] Second, both the DOJ/FTC's joint publication Merger Challenges Data, Fiscal Years 1999–2003 (issued December 18, 2003) and the FTC's publication Horizontal Merger Investigation Data, Fiscal Years 1996–2003 (issued February 2, 2004, and revised August 31, 2004) reveal that the Agencies have often not challenged mergers deemed irrebuttably illegal by the Guidelines' General Standards (*i.e.*, reveal that the Agencies are not really using an exclusively-market-oriented approach even when the Guidelines state that they will). Third, the leading DOJ antitrust economist from whose work this chapter has so profited—Gregory Werden—has written an article in which he states that "in. . .[some] cases, delineating a relevant market may not be the best way to demonstrate monopoly power or determine the impact of allegedly exclusionary conduct"[277] and (2) "[d]ispensing with market delineation also may be the best course in some merger cases"[278] (because market-oriented approaches may be inferior to merger simulations). Fourth, relatively-recent U.S. cases suggest that the U.S. courts are no longer so bound to the market-oriented approach to antitrust-law analysis as they once were. Compare, for example, the claim made in 1963 in *United States v. Philadelphia National Bank* that high and increasing market concentration creates a nearly-conclusive presumption of harm from a merger[279] with the statement made in 1990 in *United States v. Baker Hughes, Inc.* that "concentration simply provides a convenient starting point" for a "totality-of-the-circumstances approach."[280] And fifth and perhaps most significantly, the 2010 U.S. Horizontal Merger Guidelines, which will be discussed in

[276] Thus, the DOJ/FTC Commentary on the Horizontal Merger Guidelines (2006) state at 10 that "[t]he Agencies take into account that all customers in a relevant market are not necessarily situated similarly in terms of their incentives," reiterate at 7 the 1992 Guidelines position that "[i]n cases in which a hypothetical monopolist is likely to target only a subset of customers for anticompetitive price increases, the Agencies are likely to identify relevant markets based on the ability of sellers to price discriminate" (a statement that is admittedly only partially in the right direction in that it implies that the Agencies will not separate out groups of buyers when the relevant companies would not discriminate among or between them), and at 8 describes cases in which "staff. . .define[d] markets based on consumer categories"—*inter alia*, Quest-Unilab (FTC 2003) and Ingersoll-Dresser-Flowserve (DOJ 2000). I should note that this trend is in line with the courts' use of submarkets and cluster markets.

[277] *Werden Delineation* at 216.

[278] *Id.* at 217.

[279] United States v. Philadelphia National Bank, 374 U.S. 321, 362–67 (1963).

[280] United States v. Baker Hughes, Inc., 908 F.2d 981, 984 (D.C. Cir. 1990) (Thomas J., joined by R. Ginsburg, J. and Sentelel, J.). This comparison is taken from Jonathan B. Baker and Daniel L. Rubinfeld, *Empirical Methods in Antitrust Litigation: Review and Critique*, 6 AM. LAW AND ECON. REV. 386, 388 n. 4 (1999).

Section 4D of Chap. 12, no longer promulgate any market-oriented rules that base irrebuttable presumptions of legality or rebuttable presumptions of illegality on post-merger HHI figures and merger-induced increase-in-HHI figures—*i.e.*, largely abandon their predecessors' market-oriented approach to predicting the competitive impact of horizontal mergers.

Obviously, these pieces of evidence fall far short of justifying strong optimism about the prospects for the rejection of market-oriented approaches to antitrust-law analysis:

(1) the EC and E.C./E.U. courts have not yet grasped the implication of their perception that the economy contains a significant number of problem-causing chains of substitution in which transitivity is not present;
(2) the 2010 U.S. Guidelines still insist on the usefulness of a market-oriented approach to analyzing the competitive impact of horizontal mergers and the chief economist of the FTC still insists that in many circumstances market-oriented approaches are worthwhile;
(3) although Werden acknowledges the superiority of non-market-oriented merger simulations over market-oriented approaches to merger-competitive-impact analysis, he continues to insist that the Guidelines approach is "essentially sound"[281]; and
(4) one or even several U.S. judicial opinions calling into question the reliability of the market-oriented approach do not show that the U.S. courts are on the verge of abandoning it.

Still, I do think that we are moving toward using non-market-oriented approaches to antitrust-law analysis. If the argument of this chapter and Chap. 6 is correct, any movement in that direction is to be welcomed (at least if the market-oriented approach is replaced by something like the types of non-market-oriented approaches the rest of this study will delineate).

[281] See *Werden Policy* at 58.

Chapter 8
The Operational Definition of a Firm's Monopoly, Oligopoly, and Total Economic (Market) Power in a Given ARDEPPS

Economists, legislators, antitrust lawyers, judges, and legal scholars often refer to a firm's monopoly power, oligopoly power, and total economic (sometimes called "market") power. However, there is no consensus about the way in which these terms should be operationalized, and discussions of these concepts tend to be rudimentary if not simplistic. This chapter executes tediously-detailed analyses of the concepts of a firm's monopoly, oligopoly, and total economic (market) power.

The exercise is important for a variety of reasons. As an initial matter, lawyers need to understand the concept of a firm's market power or the related concept of a firm's dominant position because the positive law either does or may make a firm's legal position depend on whether it possesses market power or occupies a dominant position. Thus, at the most abstract level:

(1) U.S. courts have concluded that conduct can violate Sherman Act Section 2's prohibition of monopolizing conduct or attempts to monopolize (more generously, that it is advisable for courts to conclude that particular conduct violates Section 2) only if the perpetrator(s) had market power prior to engaging in the conduct under scrutiny;
(2) the 2009 E.C./E.U. Treaty (A) classifies some types of "exclusionary" abuses to be illegal only if these are engaged in by a firm that has a dominant position (or, by interpretation, by a set of rivals that have a collectively-dominant position), (B) has been interpreted to impose "special responsibilities" on firms in dominant positions to help rivals survive, expand, or enter, and (C) prohibits firms with dominant positions from committing "exploitative abuses" of their power by "imposing unfair purchase or selling prices or other unfair trading conditions";
(3) in a significant number of cases, lower U.S. courts have found that the refusal of a defendant found to have a requisite amount of market power in a relevant market to sell to a rival on reasonable terms the right to use an "essential facility" it owns violates the Sherman Act when the court in question would not have deemed that refusal illegal had the defendant not been found to possess the requisite amount of market power;

R.S. Markovits, *Economics and the Interpretation and Application of U.S. and E.U. Antitrust Law*, DOI 10.1007/978-3-642-24307-3_8,

(4) the U.S. Supreme Court, various lower U.S. courts, the EC, and various E.C./E.U. courts have concluded that the decision by a defendant deemed to have market power in a relevant market to use tying or reciprocal-trading agreements is *per se* illegal when such conduct's legality would have been assessed through a fact-sensitive Rule-of-Reason approach had the defendant not been deemed to possess the critical amount of market power; and
(5) although U.S. and E.C./E.U. courts now seem willing to use a (fact-sensitive) Rule-of-Reason approach to assess the legality of a defendant's including vertical territorial restraints or vertical customer-allocation clauses in its contracts with its independent distributors (as opposed to declaring such arrangements *per se* illegal), there is some reason to believe that the Rule-of-Reason approach the courts apply will deem the defendant's market power to be one of the facts that affect the legality of its including vertical territorial restraints and vertical customer-allocation clauses in its contracts with its independent distributors.[282]

Moreover, even if these doctrines and legislative positions did not exist, economists that consult in antitrust cases and antitrust lawyers, judges, and legal scholars would need to understand the differences between a firm's monopoly, oligopoly, and overall market power and the inter-relationships between its monopoly and oligopoly power because this information has implications for the accuracy and practicability of various tests that have been proposed for detecting price-fixing and predatory pricing, for the ways in which horizontal and conglomerate mergers may affect the intensity of competition, and for a number of other concrete issues that Part II will address.

Finally, policymakers and members of the policy audience need to understand the complexity of the definitions of these concepts and the difficulty of measuring the various sorts of economic power a firm might possess because the relevant complexities and difficulties bear on the practicability and desirability both of the above legislation, doctrines, and tests of illegality and of new legislation that has been proposed (*e.g.*, deconcentration statutes that would authorize or require the executive branch of the government to dissolve any firm that has more than some specified amount of "market power").

1. The Definition of a Firm's Monopoly, Oligopoly, and Total Power Over Price, QV Investment, and Price and QV Investment Combined in a Given ARDEPPS

The following analyses of the definition of a firm's monopoly, oligopoly, and total (market) power assume (my own conclusions to the contrary notwithstanding) that markets can be defined non-arbitrarily (though I will frequently substitute the

[282] All these points will be discussed in considerable detail at appropriate junctures of Part II of this study.

acronym ARDEPPS [arbitrarily-designated portion of product-space] for the word "market"). However, even on this assumption, for three reasons, a full account of the definition of a firm's market power will be both complex and annoyingly convoluted. The first such reason is the need to distinguish market power over price from market power over QV investment (and, though I will largely ignore this problem, the related need to develop a conception of overall market power that takes both these dimensions of market power into account).

The second such reason is that, even if one stipulates that (1) a firm's market power over price in a given ARDEPPS relates to its ability to secure prices above its conventional marginal costs in that ARDEPPS (or perhaps above its overall marginal costs in that ARDEPPS)—*i.e.*, to secure supra-competitive prices—at the ARDEPPS' equilibrium QV-investment level and (2) a firm's market power over QV investment relates to its ability to obtain supernormal rates-of-return on its QV investments in the relevant ARDEPPS at the ARDEPPS' equilibrium QV-investment level, the appropriate definition of these two dimensions of a firm's market power would be unclear. Thus, on this stipulation (even if I ignore contextual marginal costs [CMC] for simplicity), a firm's monopoly power over price in a given ARDEPPS could be defined to equal (*inter alia*) its weighted-average P/MC ratio in that ARDEPPS (I ignore the fact that this formulation would be inadequate in cases in which the seller in question engaged in conventional price discrimination or charged its customers lump-sum ["franchise"] fees for the right to purchase its product at a specified per-unit price), its weighted-average (P–MC)/P ratio, its weighted-average (P–MC)/MC ratio, the ratio of its weighted-average per-unit price to its average variable cost (AVC), its weighted-average (P–AVC)/P ratio, its weighted-average (P–AVC)/AVC ratio, or some combination of these metrics. Similarly, even on the above stipulation, a firm's market power over QV investment in a given ARDEPPS could be defined in terms of the most-supernormally-profitable rate-of-return any of its QV investments in the ARDEPPS in question generated, the weighted-average supernormal rate-of-return generated by all of its QV investments in that ARDEPPS, or some combination of these two figures. I hasten to add that—given the fact that the drafters of the statutes, treaty provisions, and other sources of U.S. and E.U. antitrust law have not provided (1) operational definitions of a firm's monopoly, oligopoly, or total market power over price, (2) operational definitions of a firm's monopoly, oligopoly, or total market power over QV investment, (3) operational definitions of a firm's monopoly, oligopoly, or total market power over price and QV investment combined, or (4) clear statements of the individual goals that the relevant bodies of law are designed to achieve or the way in which these goals should be traded off against each other—I see no non-arbitrary way for courts to choose an operational definition of a firm's monopoly or oligopoly control over price, QV investment, or price and QV investment combined. The analysis that follows will ignore this issue.

The third reason why a full analysis of the definition of a firm's market power would be complex and convoluted is that, in particular contexts, the preceding "outcome"-oriented stipulation of the metric for market power may not be appropriate. The problem is that, in some contexts, the appropriate metric for market power may be source-oriented rather than outcome-oriented—*i.e.*, in some contexts, it may be appropriate to define a firm's market power in terms of its monopoly power or its monopoly and oligopoly power combined. The distinction between outcome-oriented and source-oriented definitions of market power is operationally significant because a firm's abilities to secure supra-competitive prices and supernormal profits depend not only on its monopoly and oligopoly control over price and QV investment respectively but also on a number of other factors that should not be characterized as constituents of its monopoly or oligopoly power and do not affect the consequences of its monopoly or oligopoly power—*i.e.*, that are in the above senses independent of its monopoly and oligopoly power. Because the U.S. adjudicators who (to my mind, mistakenly) believe that a firm's market power is relevant to the legality of various kinds of behavior in which it may engage under laws that promulgate specific-anticompetitive-intent or competitive-impact-oriented tests of illegality may believe that a firm's monopoly or monopoly and oligopoly power but not the market power it has from some other source are relevant to the legality of the conduct in question, because the E.C./E.U.-Treaty Article that proscribes firms that occupy an individually-dominant or collectively-dominant position from engaging in conduct that would be lawful for non-dominant firms to engage in may best be interpreted to be defining an individual firm's dominance or a set of product-rivals' collective dominance to equal the sum of the firm's or firms' monopoly and oligopoly power but not the market power it possesses or they possess for other sorts of reasons, and because the legislators that propose or pass deconcentration statutes that authorize or require the executive branch of the government of the country or confederation in question to break up firms with more than some amount of market power may intend to authorize the dissolution of firms that have more than some amount of monopoly or monopoly and oligopoly power, the discussion that follows will not ignore the distinction between outcome-oriented and source-oriented conceptions of market power. Although the associated expositional complications are annoying, their cost must be borne.

A. The Definition of a Firm's Monopoly, Oligopoly, and Total Power Over Price in a Given ARDEPPS

(1) A Firm's Monopoly Power Over Price in a Given ARDEPPS

I turn now to the problems associated with the definition and measurement of the monopoly components of the prices a firm obtains in any ARDEPPS. Parallel analyses apply to individualized-pricing and across-the-board-pricing situations.

(a) An Individualized Pricer's Monopoly Power over Price in a Given ARDEPPS

In individualized-pricing contexts, the monopoly component of the difference between the price a firm obtains from a buyer it is best-placed to supply and the conventional marginal costs it must incur to supply this buyer equals (1) its BCA $\equiv$ BPA + MCA when dealing for the patronage of the buyer *plus* (2) that portion of the contextual marginal costs that the second-placed supplier of the relevant buyer must incur to match the firm in question's HNOP-containing offer to the buyer in question—$CMC_{\#2} \equiv CMC_{\#1} + CCA_{\#1}$—that can be attributed to the firm in question's BCAs *plus* (arguably) (3) any natural oligopolistic margin the firm in question secures from the buyer and that portion (if any) of the contrived oligopolistic margin it secures from that buyer that can be attributed to the BCA and any BCA-generated CCA it enjoys in its relations with the buyer. Although it should be evident that the portion of a firm's ability to secure a price in excess of its conventional marginal costs from a particular buyer that reflects its BCA in its dealings with this buyer should be attributed to its *monopoly* power, the second and third items in the preceding list may require some explanation.

Chapter 2 made four points that are relevant to the second item's inclusion. First, Chap. 2 pointed out that the CMCs that any rival of a best-placed firm must incur to make an offer that matches the firm's HNOP-containing offer to the buyer in question can reflect either or both the fact that the rival's matching-offer price violates a minimum (or conceivably, a maximum) price regulation and/or the fact that the matching-offer price is discriminatory (almost always, is lower than the price the rival charges its own customers, buyers in relation to which it almost always enjoys a BCA). Second, Chap. 2 asserted that, in the vast majority of cases in which $CMC_{\#2} > 0$, the second-placed firm's contextual marginal costs reflect the fact that the offer of the second-placed supplier that will match the best-placed supplier's HNOP-containing offer discriminates against its own customers. Third, Chap. 2 explained that, in the vast majority of individualized-pricing cases, the extent to which the second-placed seller's relevant-matching-offer price discriminates in favor of the buyer to which it is charged and against its own customers increases with the supra-competitiveness of the prices the second-placed seller charges its own customers (the buyers it is best-placed to supply). Fourth and finally, Chap. 2 explained that, to the extent that an individualized-pricing firm is second-placed to obtain the customers of a rival that is sometimes its closest competitor, increases in the firm's BCAs will tend to increase the CMC it must incur to match any offer its rivals make to their customers, hence its rivals' HNOPs and prices to their own customers, hence the CMCs its rivals must incur to match any given offer it makes to its own customers, and, derivatively, its HNOPs (to the extent that the relevant rivals were originally second-placed to obtain its customers). Thus, an individualized-pricing firm's BCAs will increase its HNOP–MC gap not only directly but also indirectly by increasing the contextual marginal costs the second-placed suppliers of its customers must incur to match its HNOP-containing offers.

The third item in the preceding list attributes to an individualized pricer's *monopoly* power over price that portion of its P–MC gap that consists of oligopolistic margins it obtained because of its BCA or BCA-generated CCA. Obviously, if the relevant deconcentration statute either explicitly makes or can best be interpreted to make the authority or obligation of the executive branch to break up a company depend on the sum of the firm's monopoly and oligopoly power, the extent to which a firm's oligopolistic margins are caused by and therefore can be attributed to its monopoly control over price will be of no legal relevance. However, if the relevant deconcentration statute makes the authority or obligation of the executive branch to break up a company depend on the firm's monopoly power over price as opposed to its oligopoly power over price, the connection between the latter and the former will be legally salient. Since, as Chap. 2 pointed out, an individualized pricer will be able to secure an oligopolistic margin naturally from a particular buyer only if it has an OCA in its relations with this buyer, it seems appropriate to attribute the firm's NOMs to its monopoly power over price—at least in all cases in which its ability to secure an NOM is created by its BCA and that portion of its CCA that is caused by its BCA. In those cases in which the ability of a firm to secure an NOM was critically affected by a portion of its CCA that cannot be attributed to its BCA, the attribution of its NOM to its monopoly power is more contestable. It also seems to me that any portion of the COMs an individualized pricer obtains that can be attributed to its BCAs and BCA-generated CCAs should be characterized as deriving from its monopoly control over price. In practice, however, I doubt this possibility's significance: although the profitability of a firm's contriving OMs will tend to increase with its monopoly control over price in that the credibility of its contrived oligopolistic threats and promises will increase with the profits it has to protect against undercutting by inferiors, I suspect that this relationship is almost always more than counterbalanced by the tendency of increases in a firm's OCAs to decrease the profitability of its attempting to contrive oligopolistic margins by increasing the safe profits it must put at risk to do so. I hasten to add that, if this discussion of whether a firm's OMs can be attributed to its monopoly control over price makes you impatient, I share your reaction: even if (contrary to fact) I believed that it would be desirable to prohibit exclusionary and exploitative abuses of a dominant position as opposed to exclusionary conduct by any firm, to make the legality of a firm's conduct more generally depend on its pre-existing market power, or to break up firms that have more than some specified amount of market power, I would not support measuring a firm's market power for these purposes by its monopoly power or exercised oligopoly power as opposed to the sum of its monopoly and exercised oligopoly power—*i.e.*, I would not support distinguishing between monopoly and exercised oligopoly power in these contexts.

I should point out that the preceding operationalization of an individualized pricer's monopoly control over price distinguishes such control not only from that portion of its exercised oligopoly control over price that should not be attributed to its monopoly control over price but also from those sources of its ability to obtain prices above its conventional marginal costs that should not be characterized as constituents of either its monopoly or independent oligopoly control over price: (1) the various determinants other than its own BCAs of the ability of those firms that are second-placed to supply those buyers it is best-placed to supply to secure prices in excess of their conventional marginal costs from those buyers they are best-placed to supply and (2) various relevant errors that its rivals and its customers make.

(b) An Across-the-Board Pricer's Monopoly Power Over Price in a Given ARDEPPS

The analysis of any across-the-board pricer's monopoly control over price parallels the analysis of an individualized pricer's monopoly control over price. When the seller is an across-the-board pricer, the counterpart to the direct effect of the BCA the individualized pricer enjoys in its relations with an individual buyer it is best-placed to supply is the mathematical product of the unit sales the seller in question would make in the relevant ARDEPPS if its rivals charged prices equal to their respective marginal costs and the difference between the price that would be the across-the-board pricer's across-the-board HNOP if its rivals would charge prices equal to their respective conventional marginal costs and the across-the-board pricer's conventional marginal costs—a mathematical product that will increase with the number of unit sales on which the relevant seller enjoys a BCA, its average BCA when it enjoys a BCA, and various attributes of its BCA array that affect its ability to convert potential buyer surplus into seller surplus (attributes that will be explored in Chap. 14). When the seller is an across-the-board pricer, the counterpart to the indirect effect that an individualized pricer's BCAs will have on its HNOP–MC gap by increasing the contextual marginal costs the second-placed suppliers of its customers would have to incur to match its HNOP-containing offers to its customers is the increase in its across-the-board HNOP that its BCAs would cause indirectly by raising its rivals' HNOPs above their MCs (even if they had no BCAs in relation to any relevant buyer). (This indirect effect will be rendered more comprehensible by Chap. 10's discussion of the determinants of the set of prices that the respective sellers in any ARDEPPS will find individually most profitable to charge if none of them engages in any form of oligopolistic pricing.) And the counterpart to the contribution that an individualized-pricing firm's monopoly power over price makes to the NOM and COM it obtains from a given buyer it is best-placed to supply by fulfilling a necessary condition for its obtaining an NOM and making it profitable for it to contrive a COM or increasing the size of the COM that is profitable for it to attempt to contrive is the contribution that the portion of its across-the-board HNOP–MC gap that is attributable directly and indirectly to its BCA array makes to its securing NOMs and COMs.

(2) A Firm's Oligopoly Power Over Price in a Given ARDEPPS

I need to make two points under this heading that apply equally forcefully in individualized-pricing and across-the-board-pricing contexts. The first is that, for the reasons articulated in the note attached to this sentence, I think that a firm's oligopoly control over price should be defined to equal the sum of the COMs it could profitably obtain if the law did not prohibit contrived oligopolistic pricing and the NOMs it could secure.[283] The second is that, to the extent that the analyst has counted

[283] Some U.S. experts argue that the market-power assessments that courts should use when executing antitrust-law analyses should ignore the contrived oligopolistic margins that relevant firms would find it profitable to secure if the law did not prohibit such contrivance. In conversations with me, these scholars have made two arguments to justify this conclusion: (1) firms that value obeying the law in itself or that disvalue engaging in price-fixing independent of its illegality (because they find it immoral) may not on that account take advantage of any opportunity they have to profit by engaging in contrived oligopolistic pricing, and (2) it will always be both feasible and more cost-effective to prevent contrivance by prosecuting and penalizing contrivers than by prohibiting firms that have the opportunity to profit by price-fixing from maintaining or increasing their power to do so by engaging in conduct whose profitability is not critically affected by this effect or by breaking up companies that would find contrivance profitable into component parts that are less able to profit by contriving oligopolistic prices. I am not persuaded by either of these arguments. As to the first, although I grant that some managements would not engage in price-fixing even if it were *ex ante* profitable, I suspect that price-fixing is an important economic phenomenon and doubt the ability of a trier-of-fact to determine whether a particular firm was or was not likely to take advantage of any opportunity to profit by contriving an oligopolistic margin: of course, one might want to discount estimates of the COMs a firm could profitably secure on this moral account. As to the second argument, as Chapter 10 will explain, it will almost always be difficult and expensive and will often be impossible to prove contrived oligopolistic pricing. I would therefore be disposed to count the COMs a firm could profitably obtain if price-fixing were not prohibited as part of its market power when deciding whether it has a dominant position in the course of applying an "abuse of a dominant position" statute or whether it has a legally-significant amount of market power when applying some kindred U.S. legal doctrine or precedent or a deconcentration statute.

I should add that, although no-one has ever argued that a firm's NOMs should not be counted as part of its total market power over price when executing antitrust-law analyses that assume that a firm's pre-conduct possession of market power is relevant to the legality of its conduct or position (because no-one has recognized the difference between natural and contrived oligopolistic pricing), in my view, the argument that might be made for ignoring in this context the NOMs a firm can obtain when measuring its market power in an antitrust-legal-analysis context are weaker than the arguments that have been made for ignoring the COMs that a firm would find profitable to contrive if the law did not prohibit its doing so. Since natural oligopolistic pricing is not prohibited by the antitrust laws of the United States and is prohibited by E.C./E.U. competition law only if it is deemed to constitute a concertation or is practiced by a dominant firm or set of collectively-dominant firms in circumstances in which its practice constitutes an exploitative abuse of a dominant position (a finding that the EC and E.C./E.U. courts rarely make, regardless of the type of conduct under consideration), the only argument for ignoring the NOMs a firm could obtain would have to be based on a claim that managers will be deterred from securing NOMs by a sense that such conduct is immoral. I reject this argument because I doubt that such inhibitions are common. Natural oligopolistic pricing involves no anticompetitive threats or promises and, although I find it socially undesirable, I doubt that managers (who have a duty to serve their company's owners in all lawful ways) would suffer any qualms on this account. Of course, if antitrust law were reformed (as I believe it should be) or Article 101 were interpreted (as I believe it should be) to prohibit natural oligopolistic pricing, one would have to subject the question "Should one count the NOMs a firm could realize if natural oligopolistic pricing were not condemned by law to be part of the firm's total market power over price?" to the same type of enquiry that we just executed in relation to the COMs a firm could profitably obtain if the law did not prohibit its attempting to do so.

as part of a firm's monopoly control over price the part of the COMs it would find profitable to contrive if the law did not prohibit price-fixing and any OMs it could obtain naturally because of its BCAs or OCAs, those portions of its COMs and those NOMs should not be double-counted as part of its oligopoly control over price at least if the firm's total control over price is defined to equal the sum of its monopoly, oligopoly, and other-source control over price.

(3) The Non-Monopoly/Non-Oligopoly Sources of a Firm's Power Over Price in a Given ARDEPPS

As I have already indicated, a firm's ability to secure supra-competitive prices is also affected by various factors other than its own monopoly and oligopoly control over price. Two sets of such factors are worth distinguishing.

The first such set contains factors that clearly are not constituents of a firm's monopoly or oligopoly power. This set contains all the determinants (other than the firm's monopoly and oligopoly control over price) of the supra-competitiveness of the prices its closest rivals charge their own customers. As we have seen, in individualized-pricing contexts, the more supra-competitive those prices, the more discriminatory the prices its rivals must charge the firm's customers to match its HNOP-containing offers to them, the higher those rivals' related CMCs, and the higher the best-placed firm's OCA and HNOP. In across-the-board-pricing contexts, the higher the prices a firm's rivals would charge if it set its price at its MC, the higher its HNOP. The factors that belong in this set include

(1) the BCAs the firm's closest rivals enjoy in their relations with the buyers these rivals are best-placed to supply;
(2) in individualized-pricing contexts, the factors that influence the CCA the firm's closest rivals enjoy in their relations with the buyers those rivals are respectively best-placed to supply (*inter alia*, the BCAs that its respective closest rivals' closest rivals enjoy in their relations with buyers these rivals' closest rivals are best-placed to supply);
(3) in across-the-board-pricing contexts, the factors that would influence the prices each seller's rivals would charge the buyers in relation to which they have a BCA even if the seller in question set a price equal to its marginal costs and they did not engage in oligopolistic pricing (the BCA distribution of each seller's closest rivals, of the closest rivals of each seller's closest rivals, and of the closest rivals of the seller's closest rivals, *etc.*);
(4) in across-the-board-pricing contexts, the order in which a firm's rivals announce their prices (see Chap. 10);
(5) the various factors other than the firm's closest rivals' BCAs that affect their ability to obtain oligopolistic margins naturally—the willingness of its closest rivals' customers to give its closest rivals the chance to rebid when their initial offer is beaten by one or more of these closest rivals' competitive inferiors (the value to these buyers of establishing a reputation of rewarding inferior suppliers for making initially-superior offers), the mechanical cost to the firm's

rivals of changing their initially-announced prices, their ability to determine whether customers that claim to have received superior offers are telling the truth, the extent to which the firm's closest rivals have misrepresented their marginal or incremental costs when bargaining with other buyers, *etc.*;
(6) the various factors other than its own willingness to cooperate that influence the number and magnitude of the COMs its closest rivals obtain from their respective customers; and
(7) various errors that its closest rivals' customers and rivals make that enhance its closest rivals' abilities to charge supra-competitive prices.

The second set of determinants of a firm's ability to secure supra-competitive prices I want to address at this juncture—various mistakes that a firm's potential customers or rivals might make—might be characterized as sources of its monopoly or oligopoly power, though I personally disfavor this classification. I will focus first on relevant-buyer mistakes. The firm's ability to obtain supra-competitive prices will clearly be enhanced if its potential customers overestimate the value of its product to them or underestimate the present value (cost) to them of the payments they will have to make to purchase the good and/or any associated repair-and-maintenance services or other complements. (In the other direction, a firm's ability to obtain supra-competitive prices will clearly be reduced if its potential customers underestimate the value of its product to them or overestimate the present value to them of the payments they will have to make to purchase the good and relevant complements.) Admittedly, a firm's buyer preference advantage and basic competitive advantage could be defined to reflect these types of errors. The conceptual scheme that Chap. 2 delineates does not do so, and, for analytic reasons, I prefer to maintain that scheme's typology. However, I do admit that, to the extent that the authors of the "abuse of a dominant position" treaty article and the future authors of any deconcentration statute that will be passed would be less reluctant to disadvantage firms whose ability to secure supra-competitive prices reflects these sorts of favorable buyer errors than to disadvantage firms whose relevant ability reflects BCAs as I have defined them, one could make a case that such buyer mistakes should be counted as part of a firm's market power when deciding whether an "abuse of a dominant position" treaty article or deconcentration statute is applicable.

The second set of errors that are relevant at this juncture are errors made by a firm's product-rivals. Thus, a best-placed firm's ability to secure supra-competitive prices will be enhanced if its closest rivals for various buyers it is best-placed to supply overestimate their marginal or incremental costs or overestimate the magnitude of the relevant buyer's or buyers' preference(s) for its product and therefore decide not to make an offer. (In the other direction, a firm's ability to secure supra-competitive prices will be reduced if its closest rivals underestimate their marginal or incremental costs.) A firm's ability to obtain supra-competitive prices will also be enhanced if its closest rivals mistakenly assume that the buyers it is best-placed to supply will always give it an opportunity to rebid if they beat its initial offer (or overestimate the probability that they will do so) or underestimate the cost the firm will have to incur to change its initial offer. (Once again, if a firm's closest rivals make the opposite mistake, that error will decrease its ability to secure supra-competitive prices.) And finally, a firm's ability to secure supra-competitive prices will be enhanced as well if its closest rivals mistakenly believe (for reasons for which the firm is not responsible) that it intends to retaliate against their undercutting and/or reciprocate to their cooperation. Admittedly, these types of rival-errors could be classified as sources respectively of a firm's monopoly control over price, ability to secure oligopolistic margins naturally, and ability to secure higher prices because its rivals anticipate its reacting strategically to their response to its initial offer, but I would prefer not to do so.

B. The Definition of a Firm's Monopoly, Oligopoly, and Total Power over QV Investment in a Given ARDEPPS

How should one define a firm's monopoly power over QV investment, a firm's oligopoly control over QV investment, and residually the various sources of its ability to secure supra-competitive rates-of-return that should not be classified as constituents of its monopoly or oligopoly power over QV investment? The discussion that follows is based on two assumptions (in addition to the assumption that markets can be defined non-arbitrarily): (1) that QV investment in any ARDEPPS is in a static equilibrium at the lowest QV-investment level at which such an equilibrium can be established and (2) that the private cost of creating all QV investments in any ARDEPPS is the same. These assumptions are adopted for purely-expositional reasons and will not affect any significant conclusion I reach.

I begin by offering two alternative definitions for a firm's total (market) control over QV investment: (1) the highest supernormal profit-rate the firm realizes on any of its QV investments in that ARDEPPS or (2) the average supernormal profit-rate it realizes on all of its various QV investments in that ARDEPPS. On the highest-supernormal-profit-rate definition, the firm's total (market) power over QV investment equals the difference between the highest supernormal profit-rate generated by any QV investment in the relevant ARDEPPS and the sum of the (Π_D + R + L) barriers the firm faces on its most-supernormally-profitable QV investment in the relevant area of product-space and the *M* incentives or disincentives it had to make that investment. (I ignore the S barrier the firm might face on a QV investment in the relevant area of product-space on the ground that the firm's most-supernormally-profitable QV investment will not be the last QV investment made in the ARDEPPS in question; I ignore the *O* disincentives a firm might face on a QV investment because those disincentives will not be operative on any QV investment that is executed.) On the average-supernormal-profit-rate definition, the firm's total (market) power over QV investment equals the difference between the highest supernormal profit-rate generated by any QV investment in the relevant area of product-space and the average (Π_D + R + L) barriers the firm faces on its various QV investments in the relevant area of product-space. (I ignore the S barriers and *O* disincentives a firm might face on a given QV investment for the same reasons I ignored these concepts when analyzing the highest supernormal profit-rate the firm realized in a specified ARDEPPS; I ignore the *M* incentives and disincentives the firm might have to make particular QV investments because they will already be reflected in the calculation of the [Π_D + R] barriers it faces on its other QV investments in the ARDEPPS in question.)

As we saw in Chap. 2, (1) in those cases in which the ARDEPPS is in a static equilibrium at the lowest QV-investment level that could generate such an equilibrium and the firm that is best-placed to raise ARDEPPS QV investment above this static-equilibrium level is a potential entrant, the highest supernormal profit-rate that is yielded by any QV investment in the relevant ARDEPPS equals the (Π_D + R + S + L) barriers to entry faced by that best-placed potential competitor, and (2) in those cases in which the ARDEPPS is in a static equilibrium at the lowest QV-investment level that could generate such an equilibrium and the firm that is best-placed to raise ARDEPPS QV investment above this static-equilibrium level is an incumbent (a potential expander), the highest supernormal profit-rate that is yielded by any QV investment in the relevant ARDEPPS equals the (Π_D + R + S + L) barriers to expansion that the best-placed expander faces on the expansion in question *minus* the monopolistic QV-investment incentive it has to make it or *plus* the monopolistic or natural oligopolistic QV-investment disincentive it has to make it.

The three categories of sources of a firm's total (market) power over QV investment in a given ARDEPPS are counterparts to the three categories of sources of a firm's market power over price in a given ARDEPPS: (1) the firm's monopoly power over QV investment, (2) its oligopoly power over QV investment, and (3) various factors other than its monopoly and oligopoly power over QV investment that enable it to realize supernormal rates-of-return in that ARDEPPS. I hasten to add that, for several reasons, the ability of a firm to realize supernormal rates-of-return on its QV investments in a given ARDEPPS does not equal any straightforward sum of the various constituents of its monopoly power over QV investment, its oligopoly power over QV investment, and the other possible sources of its ability to realize supernormal profit-rates on the relevant investments:

(1) the various barriers to entry that confront the best-placed potential entrant to the ARDEPPS in question at its static-equilibrium QV-investment level will not affect the ARDEPPS' equilibrium QV-investment level or, derivatively, the firm in question's highest or average supernormal profit-rate in the ARDEPPS if the entry-preventing QV-investment level is lower than the entry-barred, expansion-preventing QV-investment level.

(2) the barriers to expansion, monopolistic QV-investment incentives, and monopolistic or natural oligopolistic QV-investment disincentives that would affect the firm that would be the ARDEPPS' best-placed potential expander at the entry-barred, expansion-preventing QV-investment level will have no effect or a reduced effect on equilibrium QV investment in the ARDEPPS in question and, derivatively, on the relevant firm's highest or average supernormal profit-rate in that ARDEPPS if the entry-preventing QV-investment level exceeds the entry-barred, expansion-preventing QV-investment level;

(3) relatedly, the impact of a firm's monopolistic power over QV investment, its oligopolistic power over QV investment, and the other types of possible

determinants of its ability to realize supernormal profit-rates in a given ARDEPPS will depend on each other; and

(4) relatedly, the impact of each component of a firm's monopoly power over QV investment, of each component of its oligopoly power over QV investment, and of the various other individual possible sources of its ability to secure supernormal rates-of-return on one or more of its QV investments in a given ARDEPPS will depend on the other components of the firm's relevant market power (both the other components in the same category and the other components in different categories).

Nevertheless, the rest of this section's definitional discussion and Section 2's analysis of the connection between a firm's market share and its market power over QV investment will focus on the separate components of these three general categories of the sources of such power.

(1) A Firm's Monopoly Power Over QV Investment in a Given ARDEPPS

I find it useful to distinguish three components of a firm's monopoly power over QV investment in a given ARDEPPS. The first is either (1) the scale barriers to QV investment faced by the potential competitor that is best-placed to enter the ARDEPPS in question at the prevailing static equilibrium (in those cases in which this firm is also better-placed than any incumbent to raise the ARDEPPS' total QV investment above its [lowest] static-equilibrium level) or (2) the scale barriers to QV investment facing the ARDEPPS' best-placed potential expander at its (lowest) static-equilibrium QV-investment level when that firm is also better-placed than any potential competitor to raise the ARDEPPS' QV investment above its (lowest) static-equilibrium level.

The second component of a firm's monopoly power over QV investment is the absolute value of the difference between the (Π_D + R) barriers the firm in question faces on its most-supernormally-profitable or average QV investment in the relevant ARDEPPS and either (1) the (Π_D + R) barriers to entry facing the ARDEPPS' best-placed potential competitor at its static-equilibrium QV-investment level when that firm is better-placed than any incumbent to raise ARDEPPS QV investment above that level or (2) the (Π_D + R) barriers to expansion facing the incumbent that is the ARDEPPS' best-placed potential expander at its static-equilibrium QV-investment level when that established firm is also better-placed to raise ARDEPPS QV-investment above that level than is any potential entrant to the ARDEPPS.

The third and final component of a firm's monopoly power over QV investment—the monopolistic QV-investment disincentives it faces that critically reduce the overall profitability of the expansion in question—is operative only in those cases in which the firm in question is best-placed to raise ARDEPPS QV investment above its static-equilibrium level. I hasten to add that, although in this set of cases these disincentives will always increase the highest and almost always increase the average supernormal profit-rate the firm realizes in the relevant area of product-space, they will reduce the total supernormal profits it realizes in this ARDEPPS (in that, had it not faced such disincentives, it would have found the expansion the disincentives deterred at least normally profitable).

(2) A Firm's Oligopoly Power over QV Investment in a Given ARDEPPS

A firm can properly be said to have exercised oligopoly power over QV investment to the extent that it contrived oligopolistic QV-investment restrictions by creating retaliation barriers to entry and/or expansion and to the extent that it secured QV-investment restrictions through natural oligopolistic interactions that involved its and one or more of its rivals' imposing natural oligopolistic QV-investment disincentives on each other. More specifically, in those cases in which, in equilibrium, a best-placed potential competitor is best-placed to raise the ARDEPPS' total QV investment above its static-equilibrium level, the contrived component of a firm's exercised oligopoly power over QV investment equals any retaliation barrier it erected to the best-placed potential competitor's entering; in those cases in which, in equilibrium, an established rival was best-placed to raise the ARDEPPS' total QV investment above the static-equilibrium level, the contrived component of a firm's exercised oligopoly power over QV investment equals any retaliation barrier it created to the best-placed potential expander's expanding; and in those cases in which, in equilibrium, the firm itself and one or more established rivals are best-placed to raise the ARDEPPS' total QV investment above its static-equilibrium level, the natural component of a firm's oligopoly power over QV investment equals the natural oligopolistic QV-investment incentive it gave its rivals and arguably any additional increase in its highest supernormal profit-rate it secured because they deterred it from expanding as a result of its deterring them from expanding through a natural oligopolistic interaction. I should indicate that note 283's discussion of the appropriateness of considering a firm's contrived and natural oligopolistic power over price when calculating its market power over price for the purpose of applying an "abuse of a dominant market position" doctrine, any kindred legal doctrine, or a deconcentration statute applies *mutatis mutandis* in the current "market power over QV investment" context as well.

(3) The Non-Monopoly/Non-Oligopoly Sources of a Firm's Power Over QV Investment in a Given ARDEPPS

I can think of at least three sources of a firm's ability to realize supernormal profit-rates in a given ARDEPPS that cannot be characterized as constituents or reflections of its monopoly or oligopoly power over QV investment:

(1) any retaliation barriers to entry that one or more of its rivals create for a best-placed potential entrant that was better-placed than anyone else to raise the relevant ARDEPPS' QV investment above its static-equilibrium level (when the firm was not complicitous in the relevant rival's or rivals' relevant conduct) and any retaliation barriers to expansion that one or more of its established rivals created for another incumbent that was better-placed than anyone else to raise the relevant ARDEPPS' QV investment above its equilibrium level (when, again, the firm was not complicitous in the relevant rival's or rivals' relevant conduct);
(2) any natural oligopolistic QV-investment disincentives that two or more of its established rivals generated for each other when they were best-placed to raise ARDEPPS QV investment above its static-equilibrium level; and
(3) any monopolistic QV-investment disincentives an established rival faced that deterred it from making a QV investment that would have raised the relevant ARDEPPS' QV investment above its static-equilibrium level.

I should add that a firm's ability to realize supernormal rates-of-return in a given ARDEPPS will tend to be somewhat reduced by any monopolistic QV-investment incentives one or more of its established rivals have that induce one or more of them to make a QV investment in the relevant ARDEPPS that it or they would not otherwise have made that raised the ARDEPPS' static-equilibrium QV-investment level. Indeed, such critical rival monopolistic QV-investment incentives will usually decrease a firm's supernormal profit-rates even when the QV investment(s) they deter are as large as the QV investments they induce: even when the relevant induced QV investments deter equally-large QV investments by others, they will tend to reduce the supernormal profit-rates realized by the induced investor's rivals (including the firm in question) since the fact that the induced investor had a monopolistic QV-investment incentive to make them will normally reflect the reality that the investment it made was less competitive with its pre-existing projects than the rival investment the induced investment deterred would have been and was therefore likely to be more competitive with the projects of the investor whose market power is at issue than the deterred QV investment would have been.

C. The Definition of a Firm's Monopoly, Oligopoly, and Total Power Over Price and QV Investment Combined in a Given ARDEPPS

I have so far addressed separately the definition or operationalization of the concepts of "a firm's total (market) power over price" and "a firm's total (market) power over QV investment" as these concepts should be understood when applying an "abuse of a dominant position" treaty-article, any kindred doctrine or precedent, or a deconcentration statute. One further concept needs to be considered—*viz.*, "a firm's total (market) power over price and QV investment combined." Unless for some (at best, obscure) reason, the proponents of such doctrines, decisions, and deconcentration statutes believe that one should put special constraints on the conduct of firms or break them up if they have some requisite amount of monopoly, monopoly and natural oligopoly, or monopoly and oligopoly power over *either* price *or* QV investment, the drafters and/or appliers of such doctrines, decisions, and statutes will have to decide what combination of power over price and power over QV investment should result in the firm's enhanced behavioral control or dissolution.

Without knowing the individual goals these doctrines, decisions, and statutes are designed to secure—indeed, without knowing in addition the way in which their authors or ratifiers would want these goals to be traded off against each other—one cannot derive the metric for the combination of these two kinds of power that should be used when applying the doctrines, decisions, and statutes in question even if they would further the individual goals they were designed to secure.

* * *

This section shows that, even if markets could be defined non-arbitrarily, one cannot define a firm's monopoly power, oligopoly power, or total (market) power non-arbitrarily for the purpose of applying an "abuse of a dominant position" treaty-article, any kindred legal doctrine or precedent, or any deconcentration statute that makes the authority or obligation of the government to split up or dissolve a company turn on the company's having some requisite amount of market power unless one can specify not just the individual goals of such doctrines, precedents, and statutes but their objective functions. It also shows that even if one could develop a practicable, non-arbitrary outcome-definition for the concept of a firm's market power over price and QV investment if that sort of definition were the appropriate type to employ when applying the above doctrines, precedents, and statutes, (1) the required type of definition might be source-oriented, and (2) source-oriented definitions might be far more complicated and less practicable to apply. It argues that this last conclusion is salient—that source-definitions may be called for—because (1) the authors, promulgators, and proponents of the legal doctrines, legal precedents, and statutes in question may believe that the desirability of imposing the relevant additional legal duties on companies with dominant positions or the desirability of regulating the prices a company charges or pays or of dissolving a company depends not just on its market power but on the relative extent to which its ability to charge supra-competitive prices and to realize supernormal rates-of-return reflects its monopoly power, its natural oligopolistic power, its exercised contrived oligopolistic power, and various other sorts of considerations or, less likely, (2) because these individuals believe that source-definitions are cheaper to apply acceptably accurately than outcome-definitions.

2. The U.S. Courts' Definitions of a Firm's Market Power and the EC's and the E.C./E.U. Courts' Definitions of a Firm's Market Dominance

A. The U.S. Courts' Abstract and Operational Definitions of a Firm's Market Power

U.S. courts have never separately defined a firm's monopoly, oligopoly, and non-monopoly/non-oligopoly powers. More specifically, although both U.S. courts and U.S. commentators have tended to use the term monopoly power and market power interchangeably, they have never provided an abstract definition of a firm's monopoly power. Moreover, although U.S. courts sometimes refer to a firm's oligopoly power (or ability to secure extra margins by price-fixing), they have never provided an abstract definition of a firm's oligopoly power and have failed to note the existence of what I call NOMs and natural oligopolistic QV-investment disincentives. Finally, U.S. courts have completely ignored the fact that some of the sources of a firm's ability to obtain supra-competitive prices and realize supernormal rates-of-return are sources that cannot properly be said to be constituents of its monopoly or oligopoly power. The abstract definition of a firm's monopoly or market power that U.S. courts use is the definition that the Supreme Court gave to a firm's "monopoly power" in 1956 in the *du Pont-Cellophane* case: according to that definition, a firm's "monopoly power" consists of "the power to control prices or exclude competition."[284] I would like to be able to say that the first part of this oft-relied-upon[285] definition—"the power to control prices"—refers to the relevant firm's monopoly or market power over price, while the second part—"the power to exclude competition"—refers to the relevant firm's monopoly or market power over QV investment. However, although such an interpretation is not linguistically absurd, it is strongly disfavored by two facts:

(1) the fact that, in U.S. antitrust terminology, the words "exclude," "exclusionary," and "exclusion" are used to refer to predatory conduct and conduct that is designed to secure compliance with its perpetrator's efforts to contrive better deals—*i.e.*, are not used to refer to conditions that give a firm monopoly and market control over QV investment such as the Π_D, R, and S barriers that a firm's potential and actual rivals face, which enable the firm to realize supernormal profits by deterring its rivals from making QV investments in its area of product-space—and
(2) the fact that, like economists, U.S. courts have never valued QV-investment competition in itself—have been interested in what I call QV-investment

[284] United States v. E.I. du Pont de Nemours & Co., 351 U.S. 377, 391 (1956).

[285] See, *e.g.*, Eastman Kodak Co. v. Image Technical Services, Inc. 504 U.S. 451, 481 (1992) and United States v. Grinnell Corp., 384 U.S. 563, 571 (1966).

competition only to the extent that the introduction of an additional QV investment into an area of product-space tends to increase the competitiveness of the prices charged for its products.

When U.S. courts have tried to operationalize the concept of a firm's monopoly or market power or to measure an actual firm's relevant power, they have basically ignored the *du Pont-Cellophane* abstract definition of the concept—*i.e.*, they have made no attempt to provide more operational, separate definitions of a firm's power to control prices or exclude competition or to estimate the amount of either of these two types of power that a particular defendant possessed. Instead, with one "qualification," U.S. courts have simply assumed that one can infer a firm's monopoly or market power from its market share. According to the Supreme Court in *Grinnell*: "the existence of such [monopoly] power ordinarily may be inferred from the predominant share of the market...."[286] In *American Tobacco*, the Supreme Court stated that "over two-thirds of the entire domestic field of cigarettes, and...over 80 % of the field of comparable cigarettes" constituted "a substantial monopoly."[287] In *Kodak*, the Supreme Court held that proof that a firm had an 80–95 % market share sufficed to survive a motion of summary judgment on the market-power issue and described the holding of a prior case to be that "over two-thirds of a market is a monopoly."[288] In *du Pont-Cellophane*, the Supreme Court stated that "du Pont produced almost 75 % of the cellophane sold in the United States" and that "[i]f cellophane is the 'market' ..., it may be assumed [du Pont] has monopoly power over that market...."[289] According to Elhauge and Geradin, "lower U.S. courts have generally required a market share of at least 50 % to constitute monopoly power."[290]

I previously stated that U.S. courts have recognized a "qualification" to their general assumption that one can infer a firm's monopoly or market power from its current market share. This "qualification" relates to the possibility that the defendant's current market share may be short-lived—that its market share may decline significantly within a relevant period of time. When this is the case, U.S. courts are willing to take this prospect into account when assessing the firm's power. In some such cases, the relevant firm's market share is expected to decline

---

[286] *Id.*

[287] American Tobacco Co. v. United States, 328 U.S. 781, 797 (1946).

[288] See Eastman Kodak Co. v. Image Technical Services, Inc. 504 U.S. 451, 481 (1992) and American Tobacco Co. v. United States, 328 U.S. 781, 797 (1946). The *Eastman*-Kodak Court also cited United States v. Grinnell Corp., 384 U.S. 563, 571 (1966) for the proposition that a firm's possession of an 87 % market share made it a monopoly.

[289] United States v. E.I. du Pont de Nemours & Co., 351 U.S. 377, 379 (1956).

[290] ELHAUGE AND GERADIN 266–67, citing Einer Elhauge, *Defining Better Monopolization Standards*, 56 STANFORD L. REV. 253, 336 (2003). In a famous, relatively-early case—United States v. Aluminum Co. of American (Alcoa), 148 F.2d 416, 424 (2d Cir. 1945), Judge Learned Hand stated that proof that a firm had a 90 % market share would establish it to be a monopolist, proof that a firm had a 33 % market share would imply that it was not a monopolist, and proof that a firm's market share was 50 % or 64 % would render "doubtful" its characterization as a monopolist.

for reasons unrelated to the prospect of one or more established or potential competitors' making new QV investments in the relevant area of product-space. Cases in this category are ones in which the firm in question is running out of an essential input and cannot obtain the input in question from another source or learn to produce the final product in another way[291] or cases in which the defendant's organizational efficiency and reputation are in a decline that is deemed irreversible.[292] In other cases of this kind, U.S. courts have indicated that, in their judgment, a firm's market share will overstate its market or monopoly power if rival potential QV investors face barriers to entry that are not at least "relatively high."[293] (I hasten to add that the courts have never defined the concept of a barrier to entry and that—on the definition I use—the height of the barriers to entry facing a firm's rivals is far less connected to the likelihood of their making a QV investment in the relevant area of product-space than the U.S. courts seem to believe.) Both in the earlier text in which I first referred to this qualification and in this paragraph, I enquoted the word "qualification" because in actuality this practice of the courts is fully consistent with their basic assumption that one can infer a firm's monopoly or market power at any given time from its market share at that time.

A final point in explanation. The preceding discussion of the official U.S. position on the abstract meaning and operational definition of "a firm's monopoly or market power" has focused exclusively on the U.S. *courts*' relevant statements because the DOJ and FTC have issued no guidelines and made no statements on these issues.

B. The EC's and the E.C./E.U. Courts' Abstract and Operational Definitions of a Firm's Market Dominance

I begin with the EC because, unlike the DOJ and FTC, it has had more to say than its judicial counterparts about the relevant definitional issues. Already in 1972, in *Continental Can*,[294] the EC provided an abstract definition of a firm's dominant position and suggested how it would operationalize that definition:

> Undertakings are in a dominant position when they have the power to behave independently, which puts them in a position to act without taking into account their competition, purchasers, or suppliers. That is the position when, because of their share of the market or of their share of

[291] For a horizontal-merger case in which this possibility was salient, see United States v. General Dynamics Corp., 415 U.S. 486 (1974).

[292] See Boeing-McDonnell Douglas (FTC 1997) as reported in U.S. DOJ/FTC Commentary on the Horizontal Merger Guidelines 16 (2006).

[293] See, *e.g.*, United States v. Microsoft, 253 F.3d 34, 51 (D.C. Cir. 2001) (en banc); Eastman Kodak Co. v. Image Technical Services, Inc. 504 U.S. 451, 469 n.15 (1992); Jefferson Parish Hospital District #2 v. Hyde, 466 U.S. 2, 17 (1984); and United States v. Grinnell Corp., 384 U.S. 563, 571 (1966).

[294] Continental Can—Re Continental Can Company, Inc. and Europemballage, Inc. 1972, OJ L 7/25, CMLR D11, para II.3 (1972).

> the markets combined with the availability of technical knowledge, raw materials or capital, they have the power to determine prices or control production or distribution for a significant part of the products in question. This power does not necessarily have to derive from an absolute domination permitting the undertakings which holds [sic] it to eliminate all will on the part of their economic partners, but it is enough that they be strong enough as a whole to ensure to those undertakings an overall independence of behavior, even if there are differences in the intensity of their influence on the different partial markets.

This discussion of a firm's dominant position is remarkably similar to the U.S. courts' account of a firm's monopoly or market power:

(1) it is "market"-oriented;
(2) it focuses on the ability of a firm to obtain supra-competitive prices: although it recognizes that (in the medium or long run) a firm's ability to obtain such prices may depend on (in my terminology) the (Π_D + R) barriers faced by potential investors in the market in question, it does not value QV-investment competition (quality and variety) in itself;
(3) at least initially, its focus on the ability of a firm to obtain supra-competitive prices is a focus on what I call the firm's OCAs (and NOMs, though I doubt that the EC was aware of the possibility that a firm might be able to obtain an OM naturally) and the absence of any ability of buyers to prevent the firm from taking full advantage of its OCAs (and NOMs)—*i.e.*, the first sentence of the quoted paragraph ignores a firm's ability to obtain COMs or erect L barriers to investment.
(4) somewhat puzzlingly in the last sentence of the quoted passage, the EC shifts its focus from a firm's OCAs and the (Π_D + R) barriers to potential rival investors' creating rival QV investments to the ability of a firm to prevent its product rivals from choosing to compete against it (presumably when it would otherwise be profitable for them to do so), which relates to a firm's ability to contrive OMs and to erect retaliation barriers to potential investors' making rival QV investments; and
(5) the EC attributes a firm's dominance to its market share and possession of technical knowledge, raw materials, and capital, which at least suggests that it might try to operationalize its abstract conception of market dominance by creating a metric that focuses on a firm's market share and the (Π_D + R) barriers faced by the relevant potential investors in its market.

The EC's most recent pronouncements on the concept of market dominance[295] are very similar, though they acknowledge that quality and variety should be valued in itself, state four factors other than market share that should be taken into account when estimating a firm's market dominance, and provide a definition of collective dominance (a concept that had not been developed at the time of *Continental Can*). More specifically, the EC's 2005 Discussion Paper states:

> According to settled case law dominance is a position of economic strength enjoyed by an undertaking which enables it to prevent effective competition being maintained on the

[295] Director General (DG) Competition Discussion Paper on the Application of Article 82 of the Treaty to Exclusionary Abuses, Section 4 (December 2005).

> relevant market by affording it the power to behave to an appreciable extent independently of its competitors, its customers and ultimately of the consumers.
>
> Dominance can exist on the part of one undertaking (single dominance) or two or more undertakings (collective dominance). In the case of collective dominance the undertakings concerned must, from an economic point of view, present themselves or act together on a particular market as a collective entity.[296]

The EC goes on to state:

> Market power is the power to influence prices, output, innovation, the variety and quality of goods and services, or other parameters of competition on the market for a significant period of time.... An undertaking that is capable of substantially increasing price above the competitive level for a significant period of time holds substantial market power and possesses the requisite ability to act to an appreciable extent independently of competitors, customers and consumers.[297]

Note that, like its 1972 *Continental Can* predecessor, this definition focuses on OCAs (and NOMs) and not COMs.

The 2005 Discussion Paper also addresses the appropriate way to determine whether a firm has a dominant position. It begins by indicating that "[h]igher than normal profits may be an indication of a lack of competitive constraints on an undertaking" but that "short-run losses are not incompatible with a dominant position."[298] It then proceeds to state that "[t]he starting point for. . .[the] analysis [of 'the market position of the allegedly dominant firm and its rivals'] is the market shares of the players."[299] "If the undertaking concerned has a high market share compared to other players on the market, it is an indication of dominance, provided that the market share has been held for a long time."[300]

The EC then proceeds to provide a more operational account of the relationship between a firm's market share and its possession of a dominant market position:

> It is very likely that very high market shares, which have been held for some time, indicate a dominant position. This would be the case when an undertaking holds 50 % or more of the market provided that rivals hold a much smaller share of the market. In the case of lower market shares, dominance is more likely to be found in the market share range of 40–50 % than below 40 %, although also undertakings with market shares below 40 % could be

---

[296] *Id.* at Section 4.1. At Section 4.3, the Discussion Paper attempts to clarify how a set of rivals may operate in a collectively-dominant way. Unfortunately, its efforts are not very informative. It begins by stating that the necessary "togetherness" can be achieved through "explicit agreement," "concerted practice," or in some other way, which (unfortunately) it does not define. It points out correctly, that togetherness can be achieved by fixing prices, fixing outputs, or dividing the market, but its efforts to analyze the factors that affect the ability of rivals to achieve togetherness are limited—in particular, are restricted to stating that coordination will be more feasible when the economic environment is "stable" and monitoring participant-behavior is easy.

[297] *Id.*

[298] *Id.*

[299] *Id.* at Section 4.2.1.

[300] *Id.*

considered to be in a dominant position. However, undertakings with market shares of no more than 25 % are not likely to enjoy a (single) dominant position in the market concerned.[301]

The Discussion Paper discusses four factors that the EC believes must be taken into account in addition to market-share data when assessing the dominance of a firm. I will now delineate and evaluate the EC's discussion of the relevance of each of these factors. First, according to the EC,

If market shares have fluctuated significantly over time, it is an indication of effective competition. However, this is only true where fluctuations are caused by rivalry between undertakings on the market. Fluctuations caused, for instance, by mergers are not in themselves indicative of such rivalry.[302]

Although there is something to this point, I suspect that the EC exaggerates the connection between market-share fluctuations and firm dominance. Admittedly, to the extent that market-share fluctuations reflect changes in the preferences of given buyers, market-share fluctuations are likely to be negatively correlated with firm OCAs: the smaller the original OCAs, the smaller the change in tastes that will alter the identity of the best-placed firm and hence (possibly) the market shares of the relevant sellers (if the changes in taste are not random but are toward some firms' products and away from other firms' products). However, to the extent that market-share fluctuations reflect incumbent product-innovations, buyer exits and entries, changes through time in the success of the attempts of some incumbents to contrive oligopolistic margins, and/or (least likely) changes through time in the MCA/MCD positions of different incumbents, the connection between the variability of incumbents' market shares through time and the size of their OCAs will be attenuated. I simply do not know how much one can learn about a firm's market dominance from the variability through time of the market shares of the individual incumbents in any area of product-space. I should add that market-share fluctuations generated by horizontal mergers may favor the conclusion that the merged firm has a dominant position as opposed to simply negating the conclusion that the market-share fluctuation disfavored a finding of market dominance: to the extent that horizontal mergers are motivated by their participants' desire to free themselves from each other's competition, the fact that such mergers have been executed may suggest that the merged firm's OCAs are higher than its antecedents' pre-merger OCAs—*i.e.*, the fact that market-share figures were altered by horizontal mergers may suggest that the merged firm (firms) has (have) higher OCAs than the EC would otherwise have inferred from its (their) market share(s).

Second, the EC recognizes that "[t]he importance of market shares may be qualified by an analysis of the degree of product differentiation in the market."[303] The Discussion Paper's comments on this possibility are not well-developed. They repeat the U.S.' mistake of equating the competitiveness of two products with their

[301] *Id.*

[302] *Id.*

[303] *Id.*

"degree of substitutability" and suggest that the typical situation in which a firm with a 10 % market share will impose a greater competitive constraint on an allegedly-dominant firm with a 50 % market share than does a firm with a 20 % market share is one in which the 10 % and 50 % firms both sell premium products and the 20 % firm sells a bargain brand[304] whereas I suspect that the more typical case in which a low-market-share firm's market share underestimates the constraint it imposes on an allegedly-dominant firm is one in which the low-market-share firm produces a bargain brand: although this statement is not based on any systematic empirical analysis, I suspect that 10 % and 50 % branded products will often not be well-placed to secure the patronage of many of the same buyers—will often appeal to very different segments of the "market's" buyers. However, the more important points are that (1) like the U.S. DOJ and FTC in a different context, the EC does recognize that, in the presence of product differentiation, market-share information may be less significant than it otherwise would be but (2) also like the U.S. DOJ and FTC, the EC is unwilling to face up to the fact that this reality renders cost-ineffective any approach to market-dominance analysis that uses market-share analysis as a starting point (and then adjusts initial conclusions derived from market-share figures to take product differentiation into account). I will return to this issue in Chap. 12.

Third, the EC Discussion Paper states, in addition, that low barriers to expansion and entry may also prevent a firm from charging the supra-competitive prices that its high market share would otherwise enable it to obtain:

> If the barriers to expansion faced by rivals and to entry faced by potential rivals are low, the fact that one undertaking has a high market share may not be indicative of dominance. Any attempt by an undertaking to increase price above the competitive level would attract expansion or new entry by rivals thereby undermining the price increase.
>
> In assessing whether expansion or entry has been, or would have been, or is likely to be timely, the Commission will look at whether any such expansion or entry has been or would have been or will be sufficiently immediate or persistent to prevent the exercise of substantial market power.[305]

I want to make six points about these EC statements:

(1) the EC Paper correctly recognizes that, to the extent that the ability of an incumbent to charge supra-competitive prices causes one or more incumbents to execute a QV-investment expansion and/or one or more potential competitors to enter, the effect of the incumbent's ability to charge such prices on equilibrium prices will be smaller than it would otherwise have been;
(2) in contrast to the EC's statements in its introductory section (Section 4.1), which focus not only on prices and other terms and conditions of sale but also on "innovation" and "the variety or quality of goods and services," its statements in its "Barriers to Expansion and Entry" section (Section 4.2.2) seem to focus solely on the price effects of expansion or entry;

---

[304] *Id.*

[305] *Id.* at Section 4.2.2.

(3) Section 4.2.2 seems to reflect the view (also expressed by the U.S. 1992 Horizontal Merger Guidelines) that the entry and expansion to which, it alleged, higher prices will lead if barriers to expansion or entry are low may eliminate or render sufficiently small to be legally inconsequential the loss that the ability of the relevant incumbent to obtain supra-competitive prices (in the short run) imposes on relevant consumers: for reasons that will be explained in Chap. 12, I think this conclusion is incorrect;
(4) unlike the U.S. Horizontal Merger Guidelines, Section 4.2.2. of the 1995 DG Competition Discussion Paper seems to accept at least some version of limit-price theory—*i.e.*, seems to assume that, when barriers to expansion or entry are low, the threat of expansion or entry will deter an incumbent that has OCAs that would enable it to obtain supra-competitive prices in the short run from charging supra-competitive prices. For reasons that will be explained in Chaps. 11, 12, 13, and 14, I reject this limit-pricing claim in all but a small, special set of circumstances; and
(5) neither in this Discussion Paper nor elsewhere has the EC ever delineated its definition of the concept of "a barrier to entry or expansion." I should admit, however, that the 2005 Discussion Paper [1] enlarges the *Continental Can* opinion's list of factors that can create (in my terminology) (Π_D + R) barriers—*viz.*, enlarges the list to include legal barriers, plant whose relevant post-capacity variable cost or average total cost of operation is higher than that of the most-profitable investment, absolute-cost advantages traceable not only to preferential access to natural resources or essential facilities but also to intellectual-property rights or innovation that is not protected by such rights, superior distribution and sales networks, experience or reputation that cannot be duplicated or replicated at the same cost, first-comer advantages that relate to the costs that buyers must incur to change products or suppliers, [2] recognizes that potential investors may be deterred by what I call scale barriers (S)—*i.e.*, in the Paper's terms, by "economies of scale and scope," and [3] recognizes as well that potential investors may be deterred by retaliation barriers (L)—*i.e.*, in the Paper's terms, by an incumbent's "reputation of responding aggressively to expansion or entry."[306]

Finally, if the expression "a barrier to expansion or entry" is defined in the way that I believe is most useful, the connection between (1) the likelihood that an incumbent's choice to take advantage of its ability to obtain supra-competitive prices in the short run will lead to an established-rival QV-investment expansion or potential-competition entry and (2) the barriers to expansion or entry the relevant rival potential investors face is much more attenuated than the EC appears to believe. As Chap. 2 explained, expansion decisions depend not just on the barriers to QV investment the relevant potential investors face but on those barriers (and sometimes disincentives) relative to

[306] *Id.*

the supernormal profit-rate that the relevant market's most-profitable projects would have generated at the relevant marginal-cost and supra-marginal-cost prices.

Fourth, the 2005 Discussion Paper states that, at least in some cases, buyers will possess purchasing power that will enable them to prevent a firm that would otherwise have been able to obtain prices that were sufficiently supra-competitive to warrant the conclusion that it occupied a dominant position from doing so.[307] Although my impression is that the EC overestimates the frequency with which this outcome obtains, as I will argue in Chap. 12, its belief that buyer power will (if anything) increase the competitiveness of market outcomes is more accurate than the belief of the U.S. DOJ and FTC (and most U.S. economists who have addressed this issue) that buyer power is as likely as seller power to injure final consumers.

Before proceeding to discuss the E.C./E.U. courts' positions on the abstract and operational definitions of market dominance, I want to mention one feature of the EC's operational definition of market dominance that the Commission's case decisions as opposed to its Discussion Paper reference. In both *Michelin I*[308] and *Michelin II*,[309] the Commission's determination of whether the defendant occupied a dominant position turned, in part, on its finding on whether the defendant had engaged in exclusionary abusive conduct. I find this element of the Commission's operational definition (which is kindred to the "power to exclude" element of American courts' definition of market power) unjustifiable for both conceptual and empirical reasons: conceptually because the power to exclude in the sense of the ability to profit by driving a rival out, *etc.*, is different from the power to charge supra-competitive prices and realize supernormal rates-of-return in a given competitive environment and empirically because I believe that (for reasons I stated in Chap. 4) there is not much of an empirical correlation between the latter and the former power.

I turn now to the E.C./E.U. courts' abstract and operational definitions of a dominant market position. As the first sentence of the 2005 EC Discussion Paper's Introduction to its comments on "dominance" states,[310] the position on dominance that the Paper takes is fully in line with settled E.C./E.U. case-law. In 1973, in *United Brands*, the ECJ defined a dominant position to be "a position of economic strength enjoyed by an undertaking which enables it to prevent effective competition being maintained on the relevant market by giving it to behave to a considerable extent independently of its competitors, customers, and ultimately of consumers."[311] And, according to Valentine Korah, in "virtually all its judgments since *United Brands*,"

---

[307] *Id.* at Section 4.23.

[308] Michelin I, Nederlandsche Bandeu-Industrie Michelin v. Commission, 322/81, E.U.R. 3461 (1985)

[309] Michelin II, Case T-203/01, E.U.R. II-4071 (2003).

[310] Director General (DG) Discussion Paper on the Application of Article 82 of the Treaty to Exclusionary Abuses at Section 4.1 (December 2005).

[311] United Brands Company and United Brands Continental BV v. Commission, 27/76, E.U.R. 207, p. 65 (1978)

the ECJ has defined a dominant position in the same way.[312] Thus, in 1999, in *Gencor*, the ECJ stated what it took to be the test for a dominant position in the following words: does the firm have the "power to behave to an appreciable extent independently of [its] competitors or to gain an appreciable influence on the determination of prices without losing its market share."[313] More operationally, E.C./E.U. courts have often determined whether a firm occupies a dominant market position from its market share. In *Hoffman-La Roche*, the ECJ maintained that

> [t]he existence of a dominant position may derive from several factors which taken separately are not necessarily determinative but among these factors a highly important one is the existence of very large market shares.... Although the importance of the market shares may vary from one market to another, the view may legitimately be taken that very large market shares are in themselves, and save in exceptional circumstances, evidence of the existence of a dominant position.[314]

Although, in that case, the market shares that yielded the conclusion that the defendant had a dominant position ranged from about 75 % to about 87 %, in a subsequent case—*Akzo*[315]—the ECJ stated that a market share of 50 % could be considered very large and, except in exceptional circumstances, would create a presumption that its possessor occupied a dominant position. In the other direction, in *Saba II*, the ECJ stated that it was virtually impossible for a firm with a market share of only 10 % to have a dominant market position.[316] In cases in which the defendant's market share fell between 25 % and 50 %, the determination of whether the defendant has a dominant market position appears to be based on both its market share and various overlapping factors that relate to its established rivals' barriers to expansion and its potential competitors' barriers to entry—in particular, on barriers to expansion and entry and (overlappingly) the presence of economies of scale and/or scope and/or network effects and the firm in question's possession of superior technology or control of essential assets.[317]

* * *

Section 2 has explained that U.S. courts have defined a firm's monopoly or market power in terms of its OCAs—*i.e.*, have ignored monopoly or market power over QV investment, oligopoly power over both price and QV investment, and those factors that can give a firm market power over price or QV investment that should not be attributed to its monopoly or oligopoly power. Section 2 has also explained that, except for one reference in the EC's 2005 Discussion Paper to innovation and variety and quality, the EC's and the E.C./E.U. courts' abstract definition of a firm's market

---

[312] See KORAH at 106.

[313] Gencor v. Commission, Case T-102/96, E.U.R. II-753 (1999).

[314] Hoffman-LaRoche & Co. AG v. Commission, E.U.R. 461 (1979).

[315] Akzo Chemie BV v. Commission, Case C-62/86, E.U.R. I-3359 (1991).

[316] Metro v. Commission, Case 75/84, E.U.R. 3021 (1986).

[317] See Damien Geradin, Paul Hofer, Frédéric Louis, Nicholas Petit, and Mike Walker, *The Concept of Dominance*, GOLC Research Paper on Article 82 (2005).

dominance have all the deficiencies of the U.S. courts' abstract definition of monopoly or market power. For the purposes of the next section, however, the more salient point of this section relates to its accounts of the ways in which the U.S. courts on the one hand and the EC and the E.C./E.U. courts on the other hand have operationally defined respectively (1) a firm's monopoly or market power and (2) a firm's dominance of a market. Although, in a few instances, both the U.S. courts and the EC and the E.C./E.U. courts pay some attention to barriers to expansion and entry, (1) in most cases their operational definition of a firm's monopoly/market power or market dominance focuses exclusively on the firm's market share and (2) even when the relevant barriers are considered, they tend to be less important than the firm's market share. This feature of the U.S. and the E.C./E.U. antitrust-enforcement authorities' approach to market-power or market-dominance estimation is unfortunate because, as Sect. 3 of this chapter will show, even if markets are defined optimally from this perspective, one will not be able to estimate a firm's market power over price or QV investment or a firm's dominance of a market either accurately or cost-effectively from its market share (or its market share relative to its rivals' market shares).

3. The Connection Between a Firm's Market Share and Its Various Types of Economic (Market) Power

Section 1 of this chapter argued that a firm's market power or market dominance depends on its power over both price and QV investment and that its power over both price and QV investment can be subdivided into its monopoly power over each, its oligopoly power over each, and its power over each that derives neither from its monopoly power nor from its oligopoly power. Section 2 of this chapter argued that the U.S. courts, the E.C./E.U. courts, and the EC base their estimates of a firm's market power/market dominance primarily on its market share. Section 3 explains why such a market-share-oriented approach to market-power/market-dominance estimation is both inaccurate and cost-ineffective.

A. The Inaccuracy of Any Market-Share-Oriented Approach to Estimating a Firm's Power Over Price

(1) The Connection Between a Firm's Market Share and Its Monopoly Power Over Price

On my definition, a firm's monopoly power over price includes (1) its BCAs, (2)(A) in individualized-pricing contexts, the CCAs it enjoys because its BCAs in relation to its own customers increase the CMCs that the firm's closest rival(s) for its respective customers must incur to match its HNOP-containing offers to its customers by increasing those rivals' HNOP-containing offers to their customers by increasing the CMCs the firm in question must incur to match its rivals' HNOP-containing offers to their customers or (B) in across-the-board-pricing contexts, the amount by which the firm's BCAs in relation to its own customers increase the prices it can charge them by increasing the across-the-board prices its rivals charge by increasing the prices it charges their customers, and contestably (3) any change in the prices it can obtain that are generated by errors its potential customers make when evaluating the value of its product to them or the cost they will have to incur to purchase its product and its product's complements. A firm's market share is not an accurate estimator of any or all of these components of its monopoly control over price.

To start, a firm's market share is not a good estimator of its BCAs. Admittedly, a firm's market share will provide accurate information about the percentage of sales in the defined market that its products in that market are best-placed to make (since sales usually go to the privately-best-placed product). However, a firm's market share will not provide accurate information about its BCAs even if markets are defined with this purpose in mind because (1) a firm's market share provides little or no information about the average amount by which the firm is best-placed when it is best-placed (its average overall or basic competitive advantage when it has one) and (2) this average advantage will vary considerably both from market to market and from product to product within a given market. Thus, a firm that has only 10 % of a market that has been defined in a functionally-ideal way may have far more monopoly control over price than a firm that has 90 % of an equally-large (in terms of sales-volume) market that has been defined in a functionally-ideal way if the former market contains strongly-differentiated products and buyers that have strong preferences for their most-preferred product over their second-most-preferred product while the latter market contains homogeneous products (and locations) among which buyers are indifferent (since the former firm's average overall competitive advantage in those cases in which it is best-placed will be high if it suffers no overall marginal-cost disadvantage while the latter firm's average overall competitive advantage in those cases in which it is best-placed will be low if it does not have substantial average overall marginal-cost advantages when it is best-placed). Indeed, a firm with a 10 % market share in a heterogeneous-product market in which buyer preferences run strong may have more BCAs than even a firm with a 100 % share of an equally-large market since the fact that no-one else has made a sale in the latter firm's market is compatible with the 100 %-market-share seller's having very small average BCAs. For example, this result would obtain if (1)(A) sellers operating in different geographic markets from the alleged monopolist could "export" products to the 100 %-market-share seller's market on short notice or (B) sellers that sold a different product from the product of the 100 %-market-share seller's product could shift on short notice to producing a product that was competitive with the alleged monopolist's (for example, from extruding copper wire to extruding aluminum wire) and (2) these possible suppliers of the alleged monopolist's customers originally made no sales in the 100 %-market-share seller's market because the additional delivery costs they would have to incur or the small cost they would have to incur to convert to producing a different product made them always just slightly worse-than-best-placed to obtain the sales that the 100 %-market-share seller made in the market in question.

The same reasons imply that an individualized pricer's market share will provide little information about the average CCA it enjoys in its relations with buyers it is best-placed to supply because its BCAs increase the CMCs its closest rival(s) for the patronage of these buyers must incur to match its HNOP-containing offers to them. Indeed, because the impact that a firm's BCAs have on its OCAs in this way depends as well on the frequency with which the firm is the closest competitor of rivals that are its closest competitor for the patronage of particular buyers and this factor is likely to vary significantly both from firm to firm within a given ideally-defined market and *a fortiori* between or among different markets that have been defined ideally for the current purpose, I suspect that a firm's market share will provide even less information about its CCAs in its relations with buyers it is best-placed to supply than about its BCAs in its relations with those buyers.

Finally, there is little if any reason to believe that the effect of potential-customer errors on a firm's ability to obtain supra-competitive prices can be estimated from its market share. Indeed, since the ability of a firm to mislead its potential customers into overestimating the value of its product to them and/or underestimating the cost to them of purchasing its product and such complements as replacement parts and maintenance and repair services is at best only slightly positively correlated with its market share and many relevant buyer errors are not seller-induced, I doubt that this component of a firm's monopoly control over price can be accurately estimated from its market share.

I should add that there is no reason to believe that the errors one would make by trying to estimate these individual components of a firm's monopoly control over price from its market share will even tend to counteract each other, much less that they will offset each other perfectly or even substantially. I therefore conclude that one cannot accurately estimate a firm's monopoly control over price from its market share.

(2) The Connection Between a Firm's Market Share and Its Oligopoly Power Over Price

On my definition, a firm's oligopoly control over price equals (1) the NOMs it obtains (though, as I indicated earlier, its ability to obtain NOMs depends in part on its OCAs—*i.e.*, on its monopoly control over price), (2) the COMs it would find profitable to contrive (regardless of whether it chooses to secure them), and (least importantly) (3)(A) in individualized-pricing contexts, any CCA it enjoys because its NOMs and COMs raise the CMCs its closest rival(s) for the patronage of its individual customers must incur to match its HNOP-containing offers to those buyers by raising those rivals' HNOPs to their own customers by raising the CMCs the firm in question must incur to match various offers these rivals might make to their customers and (B) in across-the-board-pricing contexts, any additional margins the firm in question can obtain because its NOMs and COMs raise the prices its rivals charge all buyers by raising the prices it charges all buyers.

I will now discuss the connection between a firm's market share and each of and the combination of all of these components of a firm's oligopoly power over price. I start by examining how accurately one can estimate a firm's NOMs from its market share. I will focus first on situations in which the relevant firm engages in individualized pricing and then on situations in which it sets across-the-board prices. For simplicity, I will limit my analysis to natural oligopolistic pricing that takes place in one pricing-cycle.

Four factors affect the ability of an individualized pricer to obtain an oligopolistic margin naturally:

(1) the willingness of the relevant buyer to give its best-placed supplier an opportunity to rebid if the latter's initial oligopolistic offer is beaten by an undercutting inferior,
(2) the ability of the best-placed supplier to determine that the buyer had actually received the undercutting offer it claimed to have received,
(3) the profits that the best-placed seller would have made by supplying the buyer in question at the price the best-placed seller would have to charge to beat the undercutter's offer had the best-placed seller offered that price originally—profits that would equal the best-placed seller's OCA if the first or final underbid matched this seller's HNOP-containing offer, and
(4) the additional costs that the best-placed supplier would have to incur to change its initial offer—the mechanical cost of the rebid, any costs the rebid generates by encouraging other buyers to intensify their bargaining with the best-placed supplier by suggesting that it can be bid down or by putting the lie to its cost-claims, any costs the rebid imposes on the seller by inducing buyers to expect that it will also reduce its initial price in the future, any costs the rebid generates by angering buyers that paid the best-placed seller the higher price it originally offered the customer in question, and any law-related costs the rebid generates that the same price would not have generated had it been charged initially.

Obviously, the profits indicated after "(3)" must exceed the costs listed after "(4)" for the seller to be able to obtain an NOM.

A seller's market share is a poor indicator of each of these four factors. Thus, a combination of three facts implies that market-share figures will not reveal much about the first-listed determinant of the ability of an individualized pricer to obtain an NOM: (1) the buyer's willingness to give its best-placed supplier the opportunity to rebid will be inversely related to its stake in encouraging its inferior suppliers to undercut any oligopolistic offers it receives from its best-placed suppliers in the future by accepting their undercutting offers, (2) this stake will be higher (A) the greater the extent to which the buyer in question is a repeat buyer of the good concerned and (B) the greater the extent to which sellers in other areas of product-space are aware of how the relevant buyer has behaved in the area of product-space in question, and (3) neither of the factors listed after "(2)" is correlated with the best-placed seller's market share. The best-placed seller's market share will also provide no information about its ability to determine whether the buyer in question is telling the truth about the offers it received. Nor, as was just shown, will the best-placed seller's market share shed much light on its BCAs or OCAs. Finally, although in practice the law-related costs that may be generated by a rebid may be higher than their counterparts for an identical initial bid and the size of the additional costs in question may increase with the pricer's market share (to the extent that enforcement agencies or juries are more likely to pay attention to and think the worse of firms with larger market shares), these facts do not establish any significant connection between a seller's market share and even the law-related-cost component of the cost of changing an initial offer, much less these costs taken as a whole, given that the seller's market share has no bearing whatsoever on the magnitude of the other costs in question.

The preceding analysis implies that one cannot accurately predict an individualized pricer's ability to secure NOMs from data on its market share even if the market definitions that are used have been ideally defined for this purpose.

The same conclusion applies when the firm under investigation is an across-the-board pricer. The across-the-board-pricing analysis differs from the individualized-pricing analysis in three major respects. First, an across-the-board pricer's market share provides less information about its HNOP–MC gap than an individualized pricer's market share does about its OCAs in that the across-the-board pricer's HNOP–MC gap depends on the order in which its rivals announce their prices and is more dependent on the BCA distribution of its product-rivals and its product-rivals' product-rivals. Second, in the across-the-board-pricing context, the costs of changing an initial price are somewhat different. In particular, in such contexts, these costs include (1) the mechanical cost of informing distributors of the price-change, (2) the mechanical cost of the distributors' retagging products, relabeling shelves, and changing computer codes, (3) the cost of changing advertising layouts, and (4) the costs that an across-the-board pricer may incur if its departure from its initially-announced price induces buyers to hold off purchasing its product in future price-rounds in the hope that it will lower its initially-announced price then, too. In the other direction, since across-the-board prices are public, there is no counterpart in across-the-board-pricing contexts for the cost of determining (or not determining) whether buyers have lied about the offers they have received from others. In my judgment, if anything, the above differences suggest that a seller's market share will be even a less-accurate estimator of its ability to obtain NOMs when the firm in question is an across-the-board pricer than when it is an individualized pricer. The third difference between the individualized pricer's situation and the across-the-board pricer's situation relates to the fact that an across-the-board pricer is probably more able than an individualized pricer to put itself in a position to secure NOMs by making premature price announcements (announcements in advance of customer need, made before any advertisements are placed in media that reach final consumers, before any instructions are given or put to use by distributors, or before any sales are executed). This strategy is useful because it enables the seller to delay doing things that increase the cost of its changing its prices until it observes its rivals' announcing non-undercutting prices and doing such things themselves (placing advertisements, instructing distributors, tagging products, making sales). Admittedly, to the extent that a firm's ability to orchestrate such a premature-price-announcement cycle increases with its market share, the firm's market share will bear on its NOMs. I suspect, however, that in practice a firm's ability to make use of premature price announcements has more to do with its overall company reputation than with its position in the "market" concerned. In any event, there is no reason to believe that this point significantly undermines the conclusion that one cannot estimate an across-the-board pricer's NOMs accurately from its market share even if that share relates to a market that has been specifically defined for this purpose.

Once more, I should also point out that there is no reason to believe that the errors that would be generated by market-share-based estimates of each of the determinants of the ability of a firm to obtain an OM naturally would tend to counteract each other, must less that any offsets that are present would be perfect or even substantial. I therefore conclude that one will not be able to estimate a firm's NOMs accurately from its market share.

I turn now to the accuracy with which one will be able to estimate the COMs that a firm would find profitable to contrive from its market share.[318] For reasons of space, I will focus on the connection between *an individualized pricer's* market share and its ability to contrive oligopolistic margins profitably. After delineating the various factors that influence the feasibility and profitability of contrived oligopolistic pricing for an individualized pricer, I will examine the extent to which a firm's market share provides accurate information about the magnitude of these factors.

Before listing the factors in question, I need to discuss two sets of inter-relationships that complicate the analysis of the determinants of the ability of a firm to profit by contriving OMs. The first set of relevant inter-relationships reflects the fact that, to succeed, a contriver must convince the firms whose cooperation it desires to secure that it would be unprofitable for them to undercut its contrived oligopolistic price even though the relevant rivals could profit by undercutting the contriver if the contriver would not react strategically to such conduct. Clearly, the potential undercutter's conclusions about the profitability of undercutting will be affected by (1) its probability-estimate of the likelihood that the contriver will detect the fact that it has been undercut by an inferior (as opposed to having lost a sale because of a spontaneous change in the taste of the relevant buyer), (2) its probability-estimate of the likelihood that the contriver will identify it as the undercutter, (3) its estimate of the amount of harm the contriver will inflict on it through retaliation if the contriver

[318] Because I have defined a firm's oligopoly power over price in terms of the COMs it could profitably contrive as opposed to those it would choose to contrive, the text's list does not include the attitude of the firm's managers to breaking the law by engaging in contrived oligopolistic pricing (which is virtually always relevant in the U.S. [where contrived oligopolistic pricing is virtually always illegal] and frequently relevant in the E.C./E.U. [where contrived oligopolistic pricing violates now-Article 101 if it is arranged through an agreement rather than being effectuated solely through its practitioner's threats and violates now-Article 102 if it is perpetuated by an individually-dominant firm or a set of rivals that would be deemed to be collectively dominant]). However, I do want to point out that there is no reason to believe that a firm's managers' dispreference for breaking the law by engaging in contrived oligopolistic pricing will be correlated in any way with its market share.

does identify it as the undercutter, and (4) its estimate of the amount of benefits the contriver will confer on it by "reciprocating" if but only if it does cooperate by foregoing inherently-profitable undercutting-opportunities to let the potential undercutter secure COMs from the potential undercutter's own customers. Obviously, the preceding analysis implies *inter alia* that the more benefits the contriver can confer on its potential undercutter by reciprocating, the less harm it will have to inflict on it through retaliation should the potential undercutter undercut it to make future undercutting unprofitable for this undercutter and others like it. It also implies that the greater the contriver's effort and success at determining that it has been undercut and identifying its undercutter—*i.e.*, the higher the likelihood that the contriver will withhold reciprocation from and/or engage in retaliation against an undercutter, the smaller the sum of (A) the amount of harm it will have to inflict through retaliation on any undercutter that it has identified and (B) the amount of benefits it will have to withdraw from any identified undercutter by foregoing reciprocation to deter its actual undercutter and other potential undercutters from undercutting it in the future. For expositional reasons, the text that follows will usually ignore these and various related interdependencies.

The second set of inter-relationships that the more detailed analysis that follows will ignore reflects the fact that the profitability of contrived oligopolistic pricing will be heavily affected by the credibility of the contriver's threats of retaliation and promises of reciprocation. That credibility will be determined in part by the contriver's past behavior—*i.e.*, whether it has made and carried out such threats and promises in the past. It will also be determined by the objective profitability of the contriver's carrying out the relevant threats and promises. This objective profitability will in turn depend on (1) the number of customers from which the contriver could contrive oligopolistic margins outside the "market" in question (the number of buyers it was best-placed to supply across the rest of its operations), a factor whose relevance reflects the fact that carrying out its oligopolistic threats and promises in one "market" will enhance its company-wide reputation, (2) the probability that the firm in question will choose to attempt to contrive oligopolistic margins from its customers in other areas of product-space, which will depend *inter alia* on the average amount of safe profits per customer (OCAs) it will have to put at risk to do so and the costs it would have to incur to communicate its contrived oligopolistic intentions, determine that it has been undercut, identify its undercutter, and engage in the required amount of reciprocation and retaliation, as well as (3) the various factors that determine the profits that carrying out oligopolistic threats and promises in the area of product-space will enable the contriver to realize in that area of product-space in the future—(A) the number of customers in that area of product-space the contriver was best-placed to supply and (B) the probability that the firm in question would try to secure COMs from these buyers in the future (itself a function of such factors as [i] the safe profits the contriver would have to put at risk to attempt to secure a COM from its average customer, [ii] the amount of benefits the contriver could confer on cooperators nearly costlessly by reciprocating to their cooperation, and [iii] the amount of harm it would have to inflict on undercutters through retaliation to make their undercutting sufficiently unprofitable for them in order to convince them and their future counterparts that undercutting it would be *ex ante* unprofitable). This set of relationships complicates the analysis of the profitability of contrived oligopolistic pricing because it implies that many determinants of that profitability are relevant twice over—first, in that they affect the profitability of carrying out oligopolistic threats against undercutters and, second, in that they affect the likelihood that the seller's contrived oligopolistic prices will be undercut in the first place by affecting the objective profitability of retaliation and hence the credibility of the retaliatory threat.

I will now list seven sets of determinants of the profitability or probable extent of an individualized pricer's contrived oligopolistic pricing (the number of buyers from which it will try to contrive an OM and the average size of the OMs it attempts to contrive) and analyze their connection to the potential contriver's share of a market that was defined specifically to yield data from which one could infer a firm's "market power." The first such set of determinants relates to the mechanical and law-related costs that a contriver must incur to communicate its contrived oligopolistic intentions to those that would find it inherently profitable to undercut its contrived oligopolistic price. These costs will be higher the greater the number of firms to which the relevant communication must be made—*i.e.*, the greater the number of firms that are either second-placed to obtain the patronage of the buyers from which the contriver (which is best-placed to obtain their patronage) is trying to contrive an OM or worse-than-second-placed by a margin that is smaller than the margin the contriver is trying to contrive. It should be obvious that the potential contriver's market share (the percentage of buyers assigned to the relevant market that the potential contriver is best-placed to supply) has virtually no bearing on this determinant of the relevant communication-costs (the number of rivals that are either second-placed or close to second-placed to obtain the relevant firm's customers). The relevant communication-costs will also be higher if the contriver must communicate linguistically—*i.e.*, cannot communicate its intentions simply by charging a price that would not be profitable for it to charge unless it intended to deter rivals from undercutting it by promising to reciprocate to their cooperation and/or retaliate against their undercutting. A contriver will be able to communicate its intentions in this non-linguistic way (*i.e.*, without incurring mechanical communication-costs or providing any additional evidence of its guilt) if it has a reputation both for contrivance and for not overestimating its HNOPs or NOMs. In particular, a seller that enjoys such reputations will be able to communicate its contrived oligopolistic intentions simply by charging a contrived oligopolistic price because those rivals that would find it profitable to undercut such a price if it would not react strategically to their doing so will assume that it has not erred (or been generous) but rather has made a move that it intends to make profitable for itself by backing it up through reciprocation and/or retaliation. Since the potential contriver's market share will presumably have little bearing on its ability to estimate its HNOPs and NOMs or its reputation for contrivance, market-share data will also have little bearing on this determinant of the communication-costs of contrivance.

The second set of determinants of the profitability or probable extent of a seller's contrivance relates to the seller's ability to determine that it has been undercut by a competitive inferior. The fact that a contriver has lost a customer does not demonstrate that it has been undercut by a competitive inferior: the buyer may simply have had a change in taste, or a new product that was closer to the buyer's preferences may have become available. Moreover, since buyers will sometimes lie to their best-placed supplier about the offers they have received—*i.e.*, will claim to have received superior offers when they have not (to induce their best-placed supplier to grant them a price-concession) or claim to have had a change in taste when they did not (to protect an undercutting inferior), contrivers will not be able to rely fully on buyer reports when trying to ascertain whether they have been undercut by a competitive inferior. For these reasons, contrivers will often try to infer whether inferiors have undercut them from circumstantial evidence about their repeat sales to their old customers, the sales they made to former customers of rivals, and the sales they made to new buyers in the relevant area of product-space. If, at the extreme, the percentage of the buyers in each of these groups to which the contriver would make sales if no inferior engaged in undercutting did not vary from year to year and the current year was in no way different from past years, the contriver could detect the "theft" of even one buyer in any of the above categories by comparing the percentages of the buyers in question to which it made sales in the current year with the percentage of those buyers to which it had made sales in preceding years. This analysis implies that the ability of a contriver to detect undercutting will increase with the constancy of conditions through time and (given the law of large numbers) the number of buyers it is best-placed to supply. The seller's market share is completely irrelevant to the former factor and not much more relevant to the latter: although, obviously, given the number of buyers in a market, the number of buyers a seller is best-placed to supply will increase with its market share, variations in the number of buyers in different markets will largely swamp the preceding consideration. The ability of a contriver to infer undercutting from such circumstantial evidence will also depend on its knowledge of or ability to discover the identity of the determinants of the relevant percentages other than undercutting by competitive inferiors and its knowledge of or ability to discover the magnitudes of these factors both in past periods and in the current period. The seller's market share is completely irrelevant to both these knowledge/ability factors. I therefore do not think that one will be able to infer much about the ability of a seller to infer that it has been undercut (lost a sale to a competitive inferior) from its market share.

The third set of determinants of the profitability or probable extent of contrivance relates to the cost to the contriver of identifying its undercutter. We have already seen that a firm's market share is not a good indicator of one of the most important determinants of this cost—*viz.*, the number of competitive inferiors for which undercutting would be inherently profitable, the number that are not worse-than-second-placed by a larger margin than the COM the seller is trying to contrive. The contriver's market share is almost certainly also a poor indicator of the other determinants of these costs—the contriver's knowledge of the product/service attributes of its rivals and the preferences of its customers (its knowledge of the identity of the competitive inferiors that would be able to profit by undercutting it if it would not react strategically to their undercutting), its knowledge of their dispositions to undercut, and its ability to identify its former customers' new suppliers by observing the delivery vans that bring them supplies or inspecting their input inventories or final products.

The fourth set of determinants of the profitability and probable extent of a firm's contrived oligopolistic pricing relates to the amount of profits the contriver can give to each of its possible undercutters through reciprocation relative to the amount of profits it is asking them to forego by abstaining from undercutting it. Reciprocation is important because it is virtually costless for a firm to reward cooperation by reciprocating in the relevant sense. Since the cooperator would presumably not have given the contriver the opportunity to undercut it profitably unless the contriver had promised not to take advantage of that opportunity, the only cost to the contriver of reciprocating is the cost of foregoing the opportunity to promise cooperation in the future and then welch on this promise. This cost is likely to be low because a firm is unlikely to be able to play that game very often: fool me once, shame on you; fool me twice, shame on me. The first of the two gross factors that are relevant in this context—the profits the contriver is asking each potential undercutter to forego—equals the product of (1) the number of buyers from which it intends to secure a COM despite the fact that the potential undercutter in question is in a position to profit by undercutting it (because the COM exceeds the amount by which the potential undercutter is worse-than-second-placed to supply the buyer in question) and (2) the average difference between the average COM the contriver intends to contrive from the relevant buyers and the average amount by which the potential undercutter is worse-than-second-placed to supply the buyers in question. At least, the profits in question will equal this product if each relevant potential undercutter can assume that its undercutting offer will not be undercut by another undercutter. Obviously, neither of the above factors is sufficiently correlated to the market share of the potential contriver for one to be able to infer this profit figure or its relationship to the benefits the contriver can convey to the potential undercutter in question from even functionally-ideal market-share data that is derived from a functionally-ideal market definition.

If we assume that the potential undercutter cannot obtain the cooperation of any other rival, the second member of this fourth set of determinants—the amount of profits the firm under investigation can give its potential undercutter by promising to reciprocate to this rival's cooperation and carrying out that promise—equals the product of (1) the number of the potential undercutter's customers the firm in question is second-placed to supply and (2) the average advantage the contriver enjoys in relation to those customers over their third-placed suppliers. Since (1) the ratio of the frequency with which a firm is best-placed to the frequency with which it is second-placed varies tremendously from firm to firm within any area of product-space and *a fortiori* from firm to firm across different areas of product-space, (2) the percentage of customers of in-market rivals that any given seller is second-placed to supply varies tremendously from in-market rival to in-market rival, and (3) the average advantage a firm has over the third-placed supplier of buyers it is second-placed to supply varies tremendously from both firm to firm and, for a given firm, with the identity of the best-placed supplier of the buyers in question, a firm's market share provides virtually no information about the amount of benefits it can confer on a given rival by reciprocating to its cooperation. I should add that market-share data reveals no more about the *percentage* of the total (positive and negative) inducements a contriver must offer a given potential undercutter to secure its collaboration that the contriver can provide by reciprocating than about the *absolute amount* of benefits that the contriver can confer on a potential collaborator by reciprocating. I should also add that, in situations in which the collaborator has secured the cooperation of the second-placed supplier of a buyer that the potential reciprocator is third-placed to supply or has secured the cooperation of the third, third and fourth, *etc*., best-placed suppliers of buyers the contriver was second-placed to supply, the contriver's market share will also provide no information about the extra benefits this behavior by the cooperator would enable the contriver to confer on the cooperator through reciprocation.

The fifth set of determinants of the profitability and probable extent of a firm's contrived oligopolistic pricing relates to the ratio of the amount of harm the firm in question can inflict on its target through retaliation to the cost it has to incur to do so—a ratio that will decline as the amount of harm to be inflicted rises. To see why this ratio or ratio-function cannot be inferred from a firm's market share, I will first analyze the harm a contriver can inflict on its undercutter-target by retaliating (by taking one of its target's customers by undercutting its target from a position of inferiority), then analyze the cost to the contriver of an individual act of retaliation, and finally explain why neither the relevant harm nor the relevant cost nor their ratio can be accurately inferred from the contriver's market share. First, if we assume that the undercutter (the retaliator's target) is charging an HNOP to the buyer the contriver is considering stealing as an act of retaliation, an individual retaliatory theft of the customer in question will inflict harm on the target equal to either the OCA the target enjoys in relations with that customer or the sum of this OCA and the portion of the target's contextual marginal costs that are not removed by its losing the sale in question. Second, the cost to the contriver of stealing its target's customer will equal one cent (assuming it has to beat its target's offer by one cent to steal the buyer in question) if the retaliator is the second-placed supplier of the buyer concerned or one cent *plus* the amount by which the retaliator is worse-than-second-placed if the retaliator is not the second-placed supplier of the buyer concerned. (If the buyer in question gives the retaliator's target an opportunity to rebid and the target takes advantage of that opportunity, the harm inflicted on the target will be one cent, and the cost to the retaliator will be the mechanical and contextual cost of making an offer that is rejected—costs I have so far ignored.) If perfect information were costless, a retaliator would create a list of its target's customers ranked by the harm-inflicted to loss-incurred ratio associated with its stealing each and proceed down the list until it has inflicted the requisite amount of harm on the target in question. Third, it should be obvious that the market share of the retaliator is not a good estimator of (1) the harm inflicted by an individual retaliatory theft or the average retaliatory theft a contriver needs to make, (2) the short-run loss the retaliator must incur to execute (the "cost" to it of) an individual retaliatory theft or the average theft the retaliator needs to make, or (3) the harm-inflicted to loss-incurred ratio for either an individual retaliatory theft or all the thefts the retaliator must make to inflict the amount of harm on the target in question that it needs to inflict on the target to deter the target and other potential undercutters from undercutting it in the future. Thus, a contriver's market share is a poor indicator of its target's OCAs either in individual cases or in the target's relations with all buyers the contriver's retaliation would steal. Similarly, a contriver's market share is a poor indicator of the frequency with which it is or is close to being its potential undercutter's closest competitor. And again, a contriver's market share is a poor indicator of two ratios that substantially affect the costs a contriver will have to incur to retaliate sufficiently against an undercutter to deter it and others like it from undercutting the contriver in the future: (1) the ratio of (A) the frequency with which each of the contriver's potential undercutters is in a position to undercut the contriver to (B) the frequency with which the contriver is that potential undercutter's closest rival or is close to being that potential undercutter's closest rival and (2) the ratio of (A) the average amount of profits the contriver is asking a given potential undercutter to forego per customer the undercutter could take from a position of inferiority—the difference between the contriver's average attempted COM for the relevant buyers and the average amount by which the particular potential undercutter was worse-than-second-placed to obtain the relevant buyers' patronage—to (B) the average amount of harm the contriver would inflict on a particular potential undercutter by taking a customer from it through retaliation—the potential undercutter's average OCA in its relations with those of its customers the contriver was well-placed to supply or steal.

The sixth determinant of the profitability and probable extent of a firm's contrived oligopolistic pricing is the reputation of the firm for contrivance. A reputation as a contriver will increase the profitability of contrivance both by enabling the firm to communicate its intentions non-linguistically and by increasing the likelihood that its potential undercutters will cooperate. Once more, I doubt that there is much of a connection between a firm's market share and its reputation for contrivance. Even if larger firms were more likely to be contrivers and to be known as contrivers, the connection would be with the number of buyers the contriver was best-placed to supply across all its operations not just in the market in question, much less with its share of that market. Moreover, I very much doubt that there is a significant connection between a firm's overall size and the objective profitability of contrivance. Admittedly, to the extent that a firm's making good on its promises of reciprocation and threats of retaliation establish a company-wide reputation for contrivance—*i.e.*, enable it to deter undercutting in other areas of product-space and concomitantly to secure COMs in other areas of product-space, the profitability of contrivance will increase with the number of customers the contriver is best-placed to supply across all its operations. On the other hand, for three reasons, it may be less profitable for firms with higher market shares to break the law by contriving: (1) because the antitrust-enforcement agencies may pay more attention to their conduct, (2) because triers-of-fact may be more disposed to find them guilty and disposed to impose higher fines on them/make higher damage awards against them, and (3) because large firms may be receiving more benefits from the government that would be endangered by antitrust convictions or just bad publicity.

I have already mentioned the seventh and final determinant of the likelihood and probable extent of a firm's practice of contrived oligopolistic pricing in any area of product-space—its average OCA in its relations with the buyers in that area of product-space it is best-placed to supply. Although high OCAs may favor contrivance by making the firm's oligopolistic threats and promises more credible, this consideration probably relates more to the firm's overall position and is probably outweighed in any case by the fact that the firm's OCAs in the "market" in question (actually its [OCA + NOM]s) also represent the safe profits it must put at risk in any attempt to contrive an OM—safe profits whose increase makes contrivance less attractive, *ceteris paribus*. Although this argument would imply that COMs would be inversely related to a firm's market share if its market share were directly related to its OCAs, my argument that market share and OCAs are basically uncorrelated implies that one can learn nothing about this determinant of a firm's COMs from its market share.

Once more, there is no reason to believe that the errors one would make if one assumed that the value of each of these determinants of the profitability of a firm's engaging in contrived oligopolistic pricing was positively correlated with its market shares will tend to be offsetting, much less that they will tend to be substantially offsetting. Hence, even if markets are ideally defined to yield market-share data that will illuminate a firm's "market power," one could learn very little if anything about a firm's probable COMs from its share of such a functionally-defined market.

The third component of a firm's oligopolistic power over price that I previously identified is (1) the amount by which an individualized pricer's NOMs and COMs increase its OCAs by increasing its CCAs by raising the CMCs its closest rival(s) for its individual customers must incur to match the firm's HNOP-containing offers to these buyers by increasing the firm's prices to its own customers, hence the CMCs the firm would have to incur to match its closest rivals' HNOP-containing offers, and hence its closest rivals' HNOPs and actual prices to their own customers to the extent that the firm in question was or would otherwise have been their closest rival and (2) the amount by which an across-the-board pricer's NOMs and COMs increase the price it finds most profitable to charge indirectly by increasing the prices its rivals charge to their customers and hence to its customers. A firm's market share is a poor indicator of this component of its oligopoly power over price not only because it is a poor indicator of the firm's NOMs and COMs but also because it is a poor indicator of the frequency with which those rivals whose customers it is second-placed to supply are second-placed to supply its customers.

Once more, there is no reason to believe that the errors one would make if one tried to infer respectively a firm's NOMs, COMs, and this third component of a firm's oligopoly power over price from its market share would tend to offset each other, much less that any offsets that are present would be substantial (or *a fortiori* perfect). Hence, even if markets are ideally defined to yield market-share data that will illuminate a firm's market power, one would not be able to infer a firm's oligopoly power over price from its market share.

(3) The Connection Between a Firm's Market Share and the Non-Monopoly/Non-Oligopoly Sources of Its Power Over Price

Section 8.1 also indicated that a firm's (total) market power over price reflects several factors that cannot be said to increase the firm's monopoly or oligopoly power over price. The most important of these factors are its rivals' BCAs and NOMs and the portion of its rivals' COMs for which its cooperation is irrelevant. In individualized-pricing contexts, these factors will increase the relevant firm's prices by increasing the CMCs its respective closest rivals for its various customers' patronage must incur to match its HNOP-containing offers to these buyers. In across-the-board-pricing contexts, these factors will increase the relevant firm's prices by increasing its rivals' respective prices to their customers (which, in an across-the-board-pricing context, will equal their respective prices to its customers). I also indicated earlier that I would place in this category the factors that enable the firm and its rivals to announce their prices in an order that increases their HNOP arrays when the firms in question set across-the-board prices. It should be obvious that a firm's market share is a poor indicator of its rivals' BCAs and NOMs. I also think that, even in across-the-board pricing situations but also in individualized-pricing contexts, it is a poor indicator of a firm's rivals' COMs. And although a firm's ability to orchestrate a seller-friendly sequence of rival price-announcements may increase with its market share, I do not think that a firm's market share is a good indicator of this price-announcement-sequence determinant of its prices. Once more, since there is no reason to believe that the errors one would make by attempting to infer the various individual non-monopoly/non-oligopoly determinants of a firm's market power over price will substantially or perfectly offset each other, there is every reason to believe that one cannot accurately estimate a firm's non-monopoly/non-oligopoly power over price from its market share.

* * *

Since there is no reason to believe that the errors one would make by attempting to infer a firm's monopoly power over price, oligopoly power over price, and non-monopoly/non-oligopoly power over price from its market share will tend to offset each other, much less that they will offset each other perfectly or even substantially, there is every reason to believe that one cannot accurately estimate a firm's market power over price from its market share.

B. The Inaccuracy of any Market-Share-Oriented Approach to Estimating a Firm's Power Over QV Investment

The fact that a firm charges supra-competitive prices (prices above its marginal costs) for the goods and/or services it sells does not guarantee that it will realize a supernormal profit-rate or any supernormal profits on the associated QV-investment projects. If enough equally-profitable QV-investment projects can be and are introduced into the relevant area of product-space, an equilibrium may be established in which all projects in that area of product-space yield only normal rates-of-return even though the products and services that these projects permit to be supplied are being priced supra-competitively. In my terminology, this equilibrium will be an equilibrium at the actual competitive QV-investment level. For an equilibrium to be established at such a level, all QV investments in the ARDEPPS in equilibrium must belong to the set of most-profitable projects in the relevant ARDEPPS. Traditional economics refers to this equilibrium as the "tangency solution" since in it the demand curve for each product in production is tangent to its producer's average total cost curve at its actual output. Although, traditionally, this equilibrium is said to be generated by "free entry," it can also come about if the relevant established suppliers face no barriers to QV-investment expansion and no QV-investment disincentives over the relevant range of QV investment (though all relevant potential competitors do face barriers to entry) or if the combination of potential competitors that face no barriers and established firms that face no barriers and disincentives (or that have monopolistic QV-investment incentives that perfectly offset the barriers they face) is sufficiently large to generate it.

In practice, tangency solutions rarely if ever obtain. Typically, the level of QV investment in any area of product-space in equilibrium is lower than the level that would result in the most-profitable projects in that area of product-space's generating just a normal rate-of-return over their lifetimes (is lower than the "actual competitive level" of QV investment in the relevant area of product-space). The amount of supernormal profits that a firm will realize in equilibrium on its operations in any given area of product-space will depend on the following four factors or sets of factors: (1) the amount of QV investment it has in that area of product-space, (2) the lifetime equilibrium supernormal rate-of-return that will be generated by the most-profitable projects in that area of product-space, (3) the percentage of the firm's QV investments in that area of product-space that belong to the set of "most-profitable projects," and (4) the extent of the barriers to expansion, monopolistic and oligopolistic QV-investment disincentives, and/or monopolistic QV-investment incentives it faced on the various "less-than-most-profitable" projects it owned in the relevant area of product-space—the extent to which the actual supernormal profit-rate its less-than-most-profitable projects generate in equilibrium is lower than the actual supernormal profit-rate yielded in equilibrium by the most-profitable projects in that area of product-space.

This subsection reviews the monopoly, oligopoly, and other sources of a firm's power over QV investment in a given market and analyzes the accuracy with which one can derive estimates of a firm's monopoly, oligopoly, non-monopoly/non-oligopoly, and (total) market power over QV investment from its market share. The analyses that follow ignore the following fact: since the barriers that will face the successive best-placed potential expanders and entrants in any given market will tend to increase with the number of pre-existing QV-investment projects in the relevant market, a firm's monopoly and oligopoly control over QV investment (and its supernormal profit-rate) will tend to increase with its (and its rivals') monopoly and oligopoly control over price. This relationship reflects the fact that the heights of the $H\Pi_E$, $H\Pi_N$, $I\Pi_E$, and $I\Pi_E$* curves and hence the magnitudes of (1) the entry-preventing, (2) the entry-barred expansion-preventing, and (3) the equilibrium QV-investment levels in any market will all increase with the supra-competitiveness of the prices that will be charged in that market at any given QV-investment level. The analysis that follows also ignores the fact that, to the extent that equilibrium QV investment in the relevant market exceeds the level that would deter the execution of additional QV investments in it, the firm's average supernormal profit-rate and total supernormal profits will be lower than they would otherwise have been.

(1) The Connection Between a Firm's Market Share and Its Monopoly Power Over QV Investment

As Sect. 1 indicated, three components of a firm's monopoly control over QV investment are worth distinguishing:

(1) the difference between the (Π_D + R) barriers faced by the potential investor that was best-placed to raise total QV investment above its equilibrium level in the market in question and the weighted-average (Π_D + R) barriers the firm in question faced on its QV investments in the relevant area of product-space (or perhaps this difference *times* the quantity of QV investments the firm in question made in the relevant area of product-space);
(2) the scale barrier (S) faced by the potential investor that was best-placed to raise total QV investment above its equilibrium level in the relevant area of product-space; and
(3) if the firm in question is best-placed to raise total QV investment above its equilibrium level in the market in question, any monopolistic QV-investment disincentive it faced on the QV investment that would do so.

I will now analyze the accuracy with which one can estimate the relevant (Π_D + R) difference, S barrier, monopolistic QV-investment disincentive, and the sum of these three components of a firm's monopoly control over QV investment in a given market from its market share. The text that follows will assume (realistically) that the firm whose monopoly or total power over QV investment is at issue is the firm with the largest share of the market in question (is the market's leading firm).

To ease the exposition, the text that follows will continue to assume that QV investments are made in the order of their profitability. I start with the relevant (Π_D + R) difference. A firm's market share is a poor estimator of the (Π_D + R)-difference component of its monopoly power over QV investment in a market that has been ideally defined for this purpose because it is a poor indicator of both (1) the difference between the (Π_D + R) barriers that the investor whose QV investment brought total QV investment in the market in question to its equilibrium level faced on that QV investment and the weighted-average (Π_D + R) barriers the firm whose power is being investigated faced on its QV investments in the relevant area of product-space (where the weights assigned to the $[\Pi_D + R]$ barriers the firm faced on its respective relevant QV investments are proportionate to the private cost of creating each) and (2) the difference between the $(\Pi_D + R)$ barriers that the investor that made the least-profitable QV investment in the market in equilibrium faced on that investment and the $(\Pi_D + R)$ barriers that the investor that was best-placed to raise total QV investment in the market in question above its equilibrium level faced on the least-unprofitable QV investment it could make post-equilibrium in that market.

It will be helpful to begin the analysis of the accuracy with which one can estimate the difference between the weighted-average $(\Pi_D + R)$ barriers a market's leading firm faced on its QV investments in the market in question and the $(\Pi_D + R)$ barriers that reduced the supernormal profit-rate generated by the least-profitable QV investment in the relevant market in equilibrium from the leading firm's market share by distinguishing two reasons why a firm may have a high market share: *viz.*, (1) the percentage of buyers the firm is best-placed to supply is higher than the percentage of the market's QV investment it owns and/or (2) it owns a high percentage of the QV investment in the market in question.

When the percentage of buyers the firm is best-placed to supply is higher than the percentage of the relevant market's QV investment it owns, the $(\Pi_D + R)$ barriers that the firm in question faced on the QV investments it owns in the relevant market will tend to be lower than the average $(\Pi_D + R)$ barriers that confront the other firms that owned QV investments in the relevant market in equilibrium[319] and will tend *a fortiori* to be lower than the $(\Pi_D + R)$ barriers that would confront any established firm or potential competitor that might add a QV investment to that market post-equilibrium. Hence, to the extent that the relevant firm's market share reflects the fact that the percentage of its market's buyers that it is best-placed to supply exceeds the percentage of its market's QV investment that it owns, its market share will be positively correlated with the difference between its average $(\Pi_D + R)$ barriers in the market and the $(\Pi_D + R)$ barriers that confronted the firm that made the equilibrating QV investment in the market in question.

However, even if this correlation were stronger than I suspect, the accuracy of any approach to estimating the $(\Pi_D + R)$ difference that is relevant to a firm's monopoly power over QV investment that bases its estimates of this difference on the relevant firm's market share would be undercut to the extent that firms that have high market shares have them because they own a high percentage of the QV investment in the relevant market. To show why market share will not be a good indicator of the relevant $(\Pi_D + R)$ difference, I will first analyze the factors that determine the percentage of a market's QV investment that a particular firm owns and then analyze the extent to which these factors are correlated with the relevant $(\Pi_D + R)$ difference.

---

[319] Admittedly, this correlation may not be present if the average OCA that other QV investors enjoy when they are best-placed is higher than the average OCA that the firm in question enjoys when it is best-placed, but there is no reason to believe that the frequency with which the product created by a QV investment is best-placed will be negatively correlated with the average amount by which it is best-placed when it is best-placed.

The percentage of a market's QV investment that a particular firm owns will be higher (1) the earlier it entered the market in question (put crudely, on whether it is a pioneer or a copy-cat), (2) the greater the extent to which established firms have "insider information" about the availability of possibly-profitable QV-investment opportunities that put them in a position to commit themselves to a QV investment before a potential competitor can commit itself to entering, (3) the less frequently that the barriers to expansion that confront the firm in question critically exceed the barriers that another established firm or a best-placed potential competitor face on a QV investment either would find profitable (a frequency that will be directly related to the rate of growth of equilibrium QV investment in the market in question), and (4) the greater the percentage of the market's QV investment that the firm in question obtained by merger or acquisition.

Admittedly, there are at least five reasons why pioneers probably tend to realize higher-than-average rates-of-return on their QV investments than copy-cats realize on theirs: (1) pioneers are more likely to have made QV investments that yielded patentable discoveries on which they realized an atypically-high supernormal profit-rate; (2) pioneers are more likely to have purchased raw materials or geographic locations at prices that enabled them to realize supernormal rates-of-return on the investments in question; (3) pioneers may have occupied the most profitable non-geographic locations in product-space; (4) pioneers may have profited from the fact that their managers could learn the special features of their market in competition with other neophytes whereas the managers of copy-cats have to compete with old pros; and (5) pioneers may profit more from their reputation as old reliables than they suffer because buyers associate with them deficiencies of early versions of the products in question that neither their products nor the copy-cats' products now have. However, I doubt that the correlations between (1) being a pioneer and having a high market share or (2) being a pioneer and realizing a higher-than-average supernormal profit-rate on one's QV investments are significant and strong enough for market-share-based estimates of the relevant (Π_D + R) differences to be highly accurate on this account.

Moreover, I doubt that the connection in question can be based on an argument that relates to any of the last three determinants of the percentage of a market's QV investment that a particular firm owns. Thus, the importance of insider information does not favor the sought-after market share to (Π_D + R)-difference correlation because the relevant insider information enables a firm to take advantage of the investment opportunity regardless of the relationship between (1) the supernormal rate-of-return it could realize by investing and either (2)(A) the supernormal rate-of-return its pre-existing projects generated or (2)(B) the supernormal rate-of-return that would have been generated by the expansion or new entry the relevant firm's expansion forestalled. Indeed, to the extent that insider information enables a leading firm to make profitable limit investments that yield a lower rate-of-return than the rate yielded by its average QV investment in the relevant area of product-space, there may be an inverse correlation between the importance of the insider information in question and the correlation between the leading firm's market share and the relevant (Π_D + R) differences. Similarly, I doubt that one can establish the hypothesized correlation between a firm's market share and the relevant (Π_D + R) difference by citing the link between a pioneer's market share and the rate at which its market's equilibrium QV investment has grown. Indeed, a slow rate of growth in a market's equilibrium QV-investment level probably cuts against this hypothesis since it will be simultaneously associated with high market shares for pioneers and low (Π_D + R) barriers for the equilibrating QV investor (be it the firm under investigation [which will not have to grow very fast to make the investment in question], one of its established rivals [which will also not have to grow very fast to make the investment in question], or the best-placed potential entrant at the time of analysis [which will have been a higher-ranked potential entrant at an earlier time than would its counterpart in a market whose equilibrium QV-investment level was growing rapidly]). Finally, even if a firm's market share is highly correlated with the percentage of its market's QV investment that it secured through merger or acquisition, (1) that fact would establish the sought-after link between firm market share and the relevant (Π_D + R) differences only to the extent that such mergers increase equilibrium QV investment and (2) the overall amount of horizontal mergers and acquisitions is highly correlated with the amount of such transactions in which the firm under investigation engaged. Neither of these conditions may be fulfilled. As Chap. 12 shows, the effect of horizontal mergers and acquisitions on equilibrium QV investment will vary from transaction to transaction and will depend on the nature of the antitrust regime that is in force. And since many firms in a market other than its leading firm may execute horizontal mergers and acquisitions and the correlation between the leading firm's participation in such transactions and the amount of QV investment transferred in this way will vary substantially from market to market—depending in part on the extent to which the antitrust authorities make it more difficult for a leading firm to participate in such transactions than for a smaller firm to do so, the second of the above two conditions is also unlikely to be fulfilled.

Everything considered, then, I do not think that a firm's market share is an accurate indicator of the difference between the (Π_D + R) barriers that reduced the supernormal rate-of-return generated by the least-profitable QV investment in the relevant market and the weighted-average (Π_D + R) barriers the firm under investigation faced on its QV investments in the market in question. Clearly, there is even less reason to believe that a firm's market share is a good predictor of the (Π_D + R) barriers facing the potential maker of the least-unprofitable QV investment that could be made in the market in question post-equilibrium and the weighted-average (Π_D + R) barriers that the firm faced on its QV investments in the relevant market:

(1) a firm's market share will be uncorrelated with the difference between the (Π_D + R) barriers to the execution of the least-profitable QV investment in the relevant market in equilibrium and the (Π_D + R) barriers to the execution of the least-unprofitable QV investment that could be made in the market in question post-equilibrium, and
(2) there is no reason to believe that the errors that would be generated by any attempt to predict the difference delineated after "(1)" in this list from the market's

leading firm's market share will counteract the errors that would be generated by any attempt to estimate the (Π_D + R) difference on which the preceding discussion focused from the market's leading firm's market share.

A market's leading firm's market share is also unlikely to be an accurate indicator of the scale barriers to investing (S) that reduced the expected supernormal profit-rate of the least-unprofitable QV investment that could be made in the relevant market post-equilibrium. This conclusion reflects three facts: (1) since firm market shares are not highly correlated with production economies of scale relative to the extent of the market, no correlation between market share and scale barriers can be established on this basis; (2) since the ability of a firm to take advantage of distributive economies of scale depends on the volume of all products it distributes through given distributors (the volume of all inside-the-market product variants it distributes through the wholesalers or retailers it uses *plus* the volume of outside-the-market product variants it distributes through a given wholesaler or retailer), neither scale barriers to entry nor, *a fortiori*, such barriers to expansion will be highly correlated with leading-firm market shares; and (3) since the ability of a firm to take advantage of financial economies of scale depends on the extent of its company-wide operations, financial economies of scale will not cause a market's leading firm's market share to be strongly correlated with the scale barriers in those markets.

I also do not think that a firm's market share is an accurate indicator of the extra supernormal profits it realizes because it is in a position to protect the profit-yields of its other QV investments in a given market by not making an additional QV investment in the relevant area of product-space itself in circumstances in which no-one else will add to the market's total QV investment if it does not—*i.e.*, because no other firm could profit by making a QV investment in the relevant market post-equilibrium and it is deterred from doing so by the monopolistic QV-investment disincentive it has to make any such QV investment. Admittedly, the size of the monopolistic QV-investment disincentive a leading firm would have to make such a market-QV-investment-level-increasing QV investment post-equilibrium will tend to increase with its share of the market's equilibrium QV investment and, derivatively, with its market share (though even this correlation is likely to be weak in an economy in which the average competitiveness [however defined] of the product-pairs in a given market [however defined] varies widely from market to market, not all projects in any market are equally competitive, and the average difference in the competitiveness of the product-pairs in different markets varies widely from market to market), but I do not think there is much of a positive correlation between a leading firm's market share and the probability that (1) it but no other firm would find it profitable to make a QV investment in the relevant market post-equilibrium if it did not have a monopolistic QV-investment incentive to do so and (2) it would be deterred from making such an investment by the monopolistic QV-investment disincentive it had to do so. Thus, there is not much of a correlation between a firm's market share and either (1) the probability that it would be better-placed than any other potential investor to raise QV investment in the market in question post-equilibrium or

(2) the probability that the monopolistic QV-investment incentive it would have to make such an investment would be critical.

I have shown that a leading firm's share of a market ideally defined for this purpose is a poor indicator of the (Π_D + R), S, and $M < 0$ components of its monopoly control over QV investment in that market. Since there is no reason to believe that the errors that would be generated by market-share-based estimates of these separate components of a firm's monopoly control over QV investment will tend to counteract each other, much less that the relevant errors will counteract each other close to perfectly or even substantially, the preceding analyses warrant the conclusion that one cannot accurately estimate even a leading firm's monopoly control over QV investment from its share of a market ideally defined for this purpose.

(2) The Connection Between a Firm's Market Share and Its Oligopoly Power Over QV Investment

As Sect. 1 indicated, two components of a firm's oligopoly control over QV investment are worth distinguishing:

(1) the retaliation barriers to entry or expansion (L) the firm would find profitable to erect against a rival that would otherwise have added to the relevant market's total QV investment post-equilibrium and
(2) the natural oligopolistic QV-investment disincentives that the firm in question imposes on one or more rivals and that those rivals simultaneously impose on it in circumstances in which it and/or one or more of the rivals in question would otherwise have added to the relevant market's total QV investment post-equilibrium.

I will now analyze the accuracy with which one can predict the relevant Ls and *O*s from a firm's market share.

I should point out at the outset that, although a firm's profitable erection of retaliation barriers will always increase the amount of supernormal profits it realizes on its QV investments in the relevant area of product-space, the impact that its profitable erection of L barriers has on the weighted-average supernormal profit-rate the firm realizes on its QV investments in the market in question will depend on the circumstances. At least four situations are worth distinguishing. First, when the firm's erection of L barriers reduces equilibrium QV investment in the relevant market by deterring the targeted firm(s) from investing without inducing the firm in question or any other rival to "replace" the deterred investment(s), the firm's erection of the L barriers will increase the supernormal rate-of-return it realizes on each of its QV investments in the market in question. Second, when the firm that has erected the L barriers in question itself "replaces" the QV investments its erection of those barriers deters, its erection of these barriers will (on our assumption that QV investments are made in the order of their profitability) reduce the weighted-average supernormal profit-rate the firm realizes on its QV investments in the relevant market by leading it to make one or more additional QV investments in that area of product-space that are less profitable in themselves than the firm's pre-existing QV investments in that area of product-space unless this effect is outweighed by any difference between the amount by which the firm's induced expansions reduce the profit-yields of its other projects and the amount by which the deterred rival QV investments would have done so. Third, when the firm's erection of the L barriers in question cause non-target rivals to "replace" the QV investments the L barriers in question deterred with alternative QV investments that are (presumably) less competitive with the firm's projects than the deterred QV investments would have been, the firm's erection of the barriers in question will increase the weighted-average supernormal profit-rate of its projects in the relevant market. Fourth, when the firm in question would have made limit investments to deter the rival QV investments its erection of retaliation barriers deterred had it not chosen to erect such L barriers, its erection of the L barriers will also increase the weighted-average supernormal profit-rate it realizes on its QV investments in the relevant area of product-space by obviating its making additional QV investments in that market that, on our assumptions, would be less conventionally profitable than were its pre-existing projects in that market. Although the second possibility in the preceding list would, on some abstract definitions of a firm's oligopoly control over QV investment, create the possibility that a firm's finding it profitable to erect L barriers might decrease the amount of oligopoly power over QV investment it possessed, I will ignore this possibility in the text that follows, or, more precisely, I will proceed on the assumption that a firm's oligopoly power over QV investment is being defined to increase with the profits it can realize by erecting L barriers to expansion or entry. The question is: Can one accurately estimate the probability and likely size of the L barriers a seller (acting alone or with others) creates for its rivals from the seller's share of a market that has been ideally defined for this and related purposes? Once more, I doubt it. In part, my doubts reflect the fact established earlier in this chapter that a seller's market share is a poor indicator of both (1) the extent to which the seller can secure its potential undercutters' cooperation by reciprocating to their collaboration and (2) the loss-incurred to harm-inflicted ratio it would face if it had to inflict enough harm on any target (in this case, an expander or new entrant rather than an undercutter, though this difference is irrelevant) through individualized price retaliation to make the target regret its decision. In part, my doubts reflect the fact that a seller's market share is also a poor indicator of the counterpart ratio it would face if the retaliatory move were a retaliatory across-the-board price-cut or advertising campaign (to which—one could assume counterfactually—no-one other than the target would react). In part, my doubts reflect the fact that a seller's market share is a poor predictor of the extent to which the ratio in question both for it and for the various non-target rivals that have an incentive to join it in creating such L barriers against other potential expanders and entrants (1) will be reduced by retaliation-collaboration between or among these potential beneficiaries of retaliation or (2) will be increased by price wars between them arising from their misunderstanding of each other's conduct (their misperception that the across-the-board price-cuts that particular retaliators made in order to inflict harm on an undercutter were actually designed to steal customers from the non-undercutters in question). And, finally, in part, my doubts reflect the fact that a seller's market share is a poor indicator of the extent to which individual members of the group that is most likely to be able to profit from undercutting (firms with low "market shares" that are second-placed or close-to-second-placed far more often than they are best-placed) can prevent retaliatory responses by not undercutting (the extent to which "not undercutting" is from this group's perspective a public good, which they will under-supply from their group perspective because each member of the group is unable to constrain its fellows to follow its own example and the retaliation will be less profitable for the retaliators than for the firms that have been undercut by the retaliation's target but do not retaliate since those undercut firms that do not participate in the retaliation [which will usually be more costly for the retaliators than for the undercut firms that do not join in the retaliation] will still receive much of the future benefits the retaliation generates for the undercut firms by deterring future undercutting).

The second component of a firm's oligopoly control over QV investment is its "power" to impose natural oligopolistic QV-investment disincentives on rivals that would otherwise find it profitable to make a QV investment post-equilibrium that would raise the relevant market's equilibrium QV-investment level (rivals that would simultaneously impose natural oligopolistic QV-investment disincentives on the firm in question). I see no connection between a firm's market share and either the likelihood that it will impose natural oligopolistic QV-investment disincentives on one or more such rivals or the size of any such disincentives it will impose on any such rival(s) if it does impose such disincentives on one or more such rivals. Thus, I see no connection between a firm's market share and (1) the probability that the firm that would be best-placed post-equilibrium to raise the market's QV-investment level would be an established firm as opposed to a potential entrant, (2) the probability that the firm in question would belong to a set of two or more potential investors that would find it profitable to raise the market's QV-investment level above its equilibrium level if they did not face natural oligopolistic QV-investment disincentives, or (3) the probability that, if the firm in question did belong to such a set of potential-investor incumbents, it and they would impose critical natural oligopolistic QV-investment disincentives on each other.

Moreover, I also see no reason to believe the errors that would be made by any approach that attempts to establish the *O* component of a firm's oligopoly power over QV investment from its market share will offset the errors that would be made by any approach that attempts to predict the L component of a firm's oligopoly power over QV investment from its market share, much less that any related offsets will be perfect or even substantial. I therefore conclude that any approach that attempts to estimate a firm's oligopoly power over QV investment from its market share will be highly inaccurate.

(3) The Connection Between a Firm's Market Share and the Non-Monopoly/Non-Oligopoly Sources of Its Power Over QV Investment

As Sect. 1 indicated, regardless of which plausible definition one adopts of a firm's (total) market control over QV investment in a particular market, that control will have four sources that cannot properly be characterized as constituents of the firm's monopoly or oligopoly control over QV investment:

(1) L barriers that deterred rival potential investors from making and maintaining QV investments that would increase the relevant market's equilibrium QV-investment level that were created exclusively by rivals of the firm in question,
(2) natural oligopolistic QV-investment disincentives that rivals of the firm in question impose on each other that deter them from making QV investments that would raise the relevant market's equilibrium QV-investment level,
(3) monopolistic QV-investment disincentives that deter a rival of the firm in question from making a QV investment that would raise the relevant market's equilibrium QV-investment level, and
(4) any monopolistic QV-investment incentive that induced a rival of the firm in question to make a QV investment that raised the equilibrium QV-investment level in the market in question.

A firm's market share will have no bearing on the first two items in this list and will be connected to the third and fourth items in this list only to the extent that increases in the firm's market share are inversely related to the market share of any established rival that was the market's best-placed potential investor post-equilibrium and, on this account, are possibly inversely related to the absolute magnitude of any monopolistic QV-investment disincentives or incentives the rival in question faces. Since there is no reason to believe that the errors that will be made by any approach that tries to estimate each of the four items in the preceding list from the relevant firm's market share will tend to offset each other, much less that they will offset each other perfectly or even substantially, I am confident that a firm's market share is an inaccurate indicator of its non-monopoly/non-oligopoly power over QV investment.

* * *

I have now shown that a firm's market share will be a poor estimator of its monopoly power, oligopoly power, and non-monopoly/non-oligopoly power over QV investment in a market that has been ideally defined for this purpose. Since there is no reason to believe that the errors that will be made by any approach to estimating respectively a firm's monopoly, oligopoly, and other-source-based power over QV investment that bases its estimates of these powers on the firm's market share will tend to offset each other, much less that any offsets that exist will be perfect or even substantial, the preceding analyses establish that a firm's market share will be a poor estimator of its (total) market control over QV investment.

* * *

Subsections 3A and 3B have respectively shown that a firm's market share is a poor estimator of both its market control over price and its market control over QV investment. Since there is no reason to believe that the errors that will be made by any approach to estimating a firm's market power over price that bases its estimates on the firm's market share will tend to offset the errors that will be made by any approach to estimating a firm's market power over QV investment that bases its estimates on the firm's market share, much less that any offsets that are present will be perfect or even substantial, the analyses of these subsections establish the inaccuracy of any market-share-oriented approach to estimating a firm's market control over price and QV investment combined.

Conclusion

I want to close this chapter with two observations. First, the market-oriented approach that U.S. courts, E.C./E.U. courts, and the EC have taken to market-power and market-dominance estimation is not only inaccurate but unnecessarily expensive. One can estimate a firm's market power not only more accurately but also less expensively by estimating a firm's (P–MC) gaps or gap (or its OCAs, NOMs, and COMs) and its supernormal rates-of-return directly. The market-share-oriented approach that U.S. and E.C./E.U. courts use to estimate a firm's market power or dominance does collect much of the data to which I have just referred in the course of defining the market(s) in which the firm in question is to be placed. However, rather than using such data directly and supplementing it with additional data on supernormal rates-of-return, the market-share-oriented approach uses the data in question to generate market definitions that it then uses to calculate the market shares from which it derives its power estimates. In so doing, the market-share-oriented approach consumes a considerable amount of resources to reduce the value of the data with which it begins. As we shall see in Chap. 12, this conclusion that the market-oriented approach to market-power estimation or market-dominance assessment achieves the remarkable double of decreasing accuracy while increasing cost applies equally forcefully to the market-oriented approach to predicting the competitive impact of horizontal mergers. I hasten to add that both these conclusions were foreshadowed by Chap. 6's demonstration that market definitions are inherently arbitrary.

Second, to the extent that this chapter's placements of the various sources of a firm's market power into monopoly, oligopoly, and non-monopoly/non-oligopoly categories seem awkward, I am not at fault. Economists and lawyers frequently speak of monopoly and oligopoly power but never define such power either abstractly or operationally. Economists and lawyers conflate market power with monopoly power, do not distinguish a firm's power over price from its power over QV investment, and do not recognize that—at least on some plausible definitions—some sources of a firm's market power cannot reasonably be attributed to either its monopoly or its oligopoly power. I have tried to fill in these gaps. If awkward choices must be made to do so, there is no escaping that reality.

Chapter 9
The Need to Analyze Separately the Monopolizing Character, "Abusiveness," Competitive Impact, and Economic Efficiency of Business Choices

Preceding chapters have discussed the concepts of "monopolization," "abusiveness," "competitive impact," and "economic efficiency." This chapter explains why the monopolizing character, abusiveness, competitive impact, and economic efficiency of business conduct must be analyzed separately. Section 9.1 explains why the three concepts that play an important role in U.S. antitrust law and policy discussions—monopolization, competitive impact, and economic efficiency—must be analyzed separately. Section 2 explains why the issue of abusiveness that is salient in E.C./E.U. competition law must be analyzed separately from the monopolization, competitive-impact, and economic-efficiency issues.

1. The Need to Analyze Separately the Monopolizing Character, Competitive Impact, and Economic Efficiency of a Business Choice

Industrial-organization economists and U.S. antitrust-law scholars that are conversant with economics often assume that one need not analyze separately the monopolizing character, competitive impact, and economic efficiency of business conduct. Although these experts rarely make any of the following claims explicitly, they implicitly assume that all conduct that is monopolizing reduces competition and decreases economic efficiency, that all conduct that reduces competition is monopolizing and decreases economic efficiency, and that all conduct that is economically inefficient misallocates resources because it is monopolizing and/or reduces competition. None of these assumptions is accurate:

(1) monopolizing conduct need not reduce competition or decrease economic efficiency;
(2) conduct that reduces competition need not be monopolizing and may not decrease economic efficiency; and

R.S. Markovits, *Economics and the Interpretation and Application of U.S. and E.U. Antitrust Law*, DOI 10.1007/978-3-642-24307-3_9,

(3) business conduct can reduce economic efficiency even if it is not monopolizing and does not reduce competition.

This section explains each of the above three claims or sets of claims and concomitantly the need to analyze separately the monopolizing character, competitive impact, and economic efficiency of business conduct.

I start with the first set of claims in the above list. Monopolizing conduct need not reduce competition because an unsuccessful attempt to monopolize still constitutes monopolizing conduct. Monopolizing conduct need not reduce economic efficiency even if it is successful because other Pareto imperfections (1) may render economically efficient conduct that would be economically inefficient in an otherwise-Pareto-perfect economy if its impact on competition could be ignored and (2) may render economically efficient the reduction in competition that conduct generates. Both claims in the preceding sentence require some explanation.

By definition, monopolizing conduct is conduct that would be economically inefficient in an otherwise-Pareto-perfect economy that is committed by a perpetrator whose *ex ante* perception that it would be profitable is critically affected by its belief that the conduct might reduce the absolute attractiveness of the offers against which it will have to compete. If the perpetrator is a sovereign maximizer and no other Pareto imperfection would distort the private costs or benefits of the conduct in question if it did not reduce the absolute attractiveness of the offers against which the perpetrator had to compete, the perpetrator's belief would imply that the monopolizing act would be not just unprofitable but economically inefficient "in itself" (*i.e.*, if it did not reduce competition by reducing the absolute attractiveness of the offers against which the perpetrator had to compete). However, this conclusion is compatible with the monopolizing conduct's being economically efficient "in itself" in our actual, highly-Pareto-imperfect economy: (1) the perpetrator may have made a mistake—the monopolizing act may have been *ex ante* profitable in itself—or (2) other Pareto imperfections may have made an act that was *ex ante* unprofitable "in itself" and would be economically inefficient "in itself" in an otherwise-Pareto-perfect economy *ex ante* economically efficient "in itself" in the actual, highly-Pareto-imperfect economy. Thus, a monopolizing (predatory) decision to relocate a distributive outlet to drive a rival out that was unprofitable in itself could be economically efficient in itself (*i.e.*, if it did not reduce competition) if the creation and use of the new outlet generated fewer external costs than the maintenance and use of the outlet it replaced would have done. And again, predatory pricing that drives out a rival QV investment that no-one will replace may increase economic efficiency on that account if the profits that the operation (or operation and renewal) of the target investment that was driven out would have generated absent predation would have been critically inflated by the non-internalization of the external costs the target generated and/or by the fact that the private cost the target incurred to purchase the resources it used that it did buy were lower than the allocative cost of its "consuming" them—for example, because it withdrew them from unit-output-increasing uses by imperfect competitors that did not engage in price discrimination.

I am not denying the economic inefficiency of most monopolizing conduct. My point is that such conduct may not be economically inefficient and that—even if as a practical matter there is no need to take account of the possibility that monopolizing conduct may be economically efficient—the prevailing view that all monopolizing conduct is economically inefficient is not only mistaken but manifests a type of error (the failure to take account of the relevance of non-target Pareto imperfections) that in other contexts causes analysts to recommend policies that are less economically efficient and desirable than alternatives that could be devised and implemented. This subject will be considered in great detail in THE WELFARE ECONOMICS OF ANTITRUST POLICY AND U.S. AND E.U. ANTITRUST LAW.

I turn next to the second set of claims listed above. For at least three reasons, conduct that "reduces competition" in the sense of that phrase that is relevant to the application of antitrust laws may not be monopolizing:

(1) conduct that injures relevant buyers by reducing the absolute attractiveness of the best offer they respectively secure from any inferior supplier may not benefit its perpetrator(s) by reducing the absolute attractiveness of the offers against which it or they have to compete because the particular subset of relevant buyers that are injured in this way may not be customers of the perpetrator(s)—may be customers of its/their rivals;
(2) even when the perpetrators do profit from their conduct's injuring relevant buyers by reducing the absolute attractiveness of the best offer the buyers respectively receive from any inferior supplier (because the injured buyers are customers of the perpetrators), the conduct in question may not be monopolizing because the profits in question may not have critically affected the *ex ante* perpetrator-perceived profitability (or, for that matter, the actual profitability) of the conduct under scrutiny; and (least importantly)
(3) even when the profits the conduct in question yielded its perpetrators by reducing the absolute attractiveness of the offers against which the perpetrators had to compete by reducing the absolute attractiveness of the best offer some of its customers received from any inferior supplier did critically affect its *ex post* profitability, the perpetrators may not have believed *ex ante* that they would do so.

The first two of these reasons require some explanation or elaboration. As we will see in Chap. 12, horizontal mergers may injure customers of rivals (*R*s) of the merged firm by reducing the absolute attractiveness of the best offer these buyers respectively receive from any inferior supplier by causing the merged firm to make less attractive offers to them than one or both merger partners made pre-merger when the merger partner(s) in question was (were) the relevant buyers' second-placed suppliers pre-merger by increasing the contextual marginal costs the merged firm would have to incur to offer these buyers the price one or both merger partners offered them pre-merger by increasing the prices the merged firm charged its own customers post-merger above the prices the best-placed independent merger partner charged them pre-merger—*i.e.*, by making the old price the relevant independent merger partner charged a merged-firm rival's customers when it was second-placed to supply them pre-merger more discriminatory for the merged firm than it was for its antecedent. As we shall also see in Chap. 12, horizontal mergers may also injure customers of the merged firm's *R*s by reducing the absolute attractiveness of the best offer these buyers respectively receive from any inferior supplier (1) by raising those *R*s' OCAs sufficiently in the way previously described to permit those *R*s to obtain oligopolistic margins naturally (*i.e.*, to deter both the merged firm and other rivals of the relevant merged-firm rival from making undercutting offers they would otherwise have made) and (2) by raising the oligopolistic margins those *R*s can contrive (*inter alia*, by making the merged firm less willing than its antecedents to beat rival offers that contain a given COM by making the merged firm more vulnerable to retaliation than were its antecedents both by increasing the merged firm's OCAs and NOMs above those of its antecedents and by allowing rivals to retaliate against the merged firm by making low offers to both its antecedents' customers). The preceding arguments will be explained in more detail in Chaps. 11 and 12. I have included them at this juncture, despite the fact that they may be less comprehensible than I will subsequently make them, to explain why the participants in a horizontal merger might not benefit from some of the effects of their merger that would tend to cause it to inflict a net equivalent-dollar loss on relevant buyers by reducing the absolute attractiveness of the best offer these buyers respectively secured from any inferior supplier.

Business conduct that reduces competition in the sense that some antitrust laws make relevant to their legality may also not be monopolizing even when its perpetrator(s) did not profit from the relevant anticompetitive effect because the profits in question may not have critically affected the *ex ante* profitability of the relevant conduct. Thus, a horizontal merger that benefited the merger partners by harming their customers by reducing the absolute attractiveness of the best offer those buyers respectively received from any inferior supplier would not violate a prohibition of monopolizing or attempting to monopolize could not constitute an agreement in restraint of trade if the merger would have been profitable independent of this effect—*e.g.*, if the merger's profitability to its participants was guaranteed by some combination of (1) the tax advantages it would enable the merged firm to secure because one of the merger partners (say, MP1) could use the losses the other merger partner (MP2) had sustained to offset the profits MP1's operations generated when the merger partner that sustained the losses in question (MP2) would not be able to earn profits these losses could be used to offset either within the period in which such losses could be carried forward or as quickly as MP1 and hence the merged firm could do, (2) the advantages it would yield the individual owner of one of the companies in question by enabling him to liquidate his holdings and escape managerial responsibilities even if the "sale price" would not reflect any tendency the merger might have to benefit the merged firm by reducing the attractiveness of the offers its customers received from their inferior suppliers, (3) the private gains it would enable the MPs to obtain by yielding organizational allocative efficiencies (*e.g.*, by reducing the cost the merged firm had to incur to produce the merger partners' products or by enabling the merged firm to make economically-efficient product innovations), and (4) by creating a merged firm that could profit more by converting potential buyer surplus into seller surplus than its antecedents could do.

Finally, I want to explain the third claim I made at the beginning of this section. Business conduct can reduce economic efficiency even if it cannot properly be said to constitute an attempt to monopolize and even if it does not reduce competition in the sense in which antitrust laws use that phrase. Many straightforward pricing practices and many more complicated selling arrangements such as tie-ins, reciprocity agreements, resale-price-maintenance agreements, customer-allocation clauses, and vertical territorial restraints that (1) do not represent attempts to monopolize (because they are made profitable by their ability to enable their employers to take better advantage of a given DD/MC combination and/or to improve their products and are not designed to reduce the absolute attractiveness of the offers their customers receive from independent suppliers) and (2) do not reduce competition (because they do not reduce the absolute attractiveness of the offers that relevant buyers obtain from their inferior suppliers) reduce economic efficiency. In particular, many such practices reduce economic efficiency because they (1) generate allocative transaction costs to convert buyer into seller surplus and (2) (for reasons that THE WELFARE ECONOMICS OF ANTITRUST POLICY AND U.S. AND E.U. ANTITRUST LAW will explain) generate consumption-optimum and production-optimum misallocation as well by increasing the extent to which their practitioners engage in price discrimination in circumstances in which (3) the additional incentives such practices give their employers to create competitive advantages induce them to engage in competitive-advantage-increasing conduct (*e.g.*, creating a QV investment) that either reduces economic efficiency (the most likely outcome) or increases it by less than the amount by which the practices reduce economic efficiency in the two ways delineated earlier in this sentence.

A summary is in order. Why should the monopolizing character, competitive impact, and economic efficiency of any type of business conduct be analyzed separately? One answer is: Different factors determine the monopolizing character, competitive impact, and economic efficiency of given conduct, and, even when the same factor is relevant to more than one of these enquiries, it is relevant in different ways to these separate enquiries. Another answer is: Conduct can reduce competition even though it does not represent an attempt to monopolize; attempts to monopolize may not reduce competition; conduct that reduces competition and successful and unsuccessful attempts to monopolize may not decrease (indeed, may increase) economic efficiency; and conduct that neither reduces competition nor represents a successful or unsuccessful attempt to monopolize may decrease economic efficiency.

2. The Need to Analyze Separately the Abusiveness of the Conduct of a Dominant Firm

As Chap. 4 discussed, E.C./E.U. competition law—in particular, Article 102 of the 2009 Lisbon Treaty—prohibits any individual firm that has a dominant position in a market or any set of product-rivals that is collectively dominant in a market from "abusing" their dominant positions. Two types of "abuses" are distinguished. On the one hand, any dominant firm commits an "*exploitative* abuse" when it takes "unfair" advantage of its (presumptively-lawfully-obtained) dominant position when acting as a seller or buyer by securing terms of sale or purchase that preclude its trading partner from securing a "fair share" of the surplus the transaction in question generates for the seller and buyer in question. On the other hand, any dominant firm commits an "exclusionary" abuse when it uses its presumptively-legitimately-obtained competitive advantage (now the law is unclear) to increase or maintain its dominant position (on my account, by making a choice that not only does not entail "competition on the merits" but manifests the actor's specific anticompetitive intent).

I will now comment briefly on why (1) the exploitative-abusiveness of a dominant firm's behavior must be analyzed separately from the behavior's monopolizing character, competitive impact, and economic efficiency, (2) if the exclusionary-abusiveness of a dominant firm's conduct always involve monopolization or an attempt to monopolize in the Sherman Act sense, it must be analyzed separately from its competitive impact and economic efficiency, and (3) if a dominant firm's conduct can constitute an exclusionary abuse of its dominant position even though it does not entail monopolization or an attempt to monopolize, the way in which "exclusionary abuse" should be defined under Article 102 must be specified, and (regardless of how it is defined) the "exclusionary abuse" of conduct must be analyzed separately from its monopolizing character, competitive impact, and economic efficiency.

I focus first on the exploitative-abuse issue. If one defines "the impact of a choice on the intensity of competition" in the sense in which I have argued it should be defined when applying antitrust statutes or treaties, exploitative abuses will normally have no effect on competition: when a firm that has a dominant position commits an exploitative abuse, it does so by taking "unfair" advantage of an independently-obtained competitive advantage or series of competitive advantages, not by making a choice that reduces the absolute attractiveness of the best offers the relevant buyers respectively receive from any inferior supplier. Similarly, if one defines monopolizing conduct and attempts to monopolize in the sense in which I believe these concepts are used by antitrust statutes and treaties, exploitative abuses will normally not involve an act of monopolization or an attempt to monopolize: exploitative abuses are inherently profitable, do not involve the sacrifice of immediate profits to increase the "abuser's" profits in the long run by reducing the absolute attractiveness of the offers against which the abuser has to compete. Nor is there any reason to believe that exploitative-abuse analysis is coincident with economic-efficiency analysis—*i.e.*, that the prices a dominant seller charges are unfair if and only if its charging them decreases economic efficiency (given its impact on UO-to-UO misallocation, on the economic efficiency of the decisions that would yield firms dominant positions in the future if they made them, *etc.*). I do not know how to operationalize the concept of the "unfairness" of the prices that a dominant seller charges or pays. But I see no reason to believe that monopolization analysis, competitive-impact analysis, or economic-efficiency analysis is an algorithm for determining the unfairness of a dominant firm's prices or other terms of sale or purchase.

I turn next to the concept of a dominant firm's "*exclusionary* abuses." If the exclusionary abuses of a dominant firm all involve monopolization or attempts to monopolize, exclusionary-abuse analysis will be coincident with monopolization analysis but, for the reasons Sect. 1 articulated, will be different from competitive-impact or economic-efficiency analysis. If a dominant firm's competition on the merits constitutes an exclusionary abuse of its dominant position when it enables the firm to maintain or increase its dominance, exclusionary-abuse analysis will be different from monopolization analysis and economic-efficiency analysis and will coincide with competitive-impact analysis only if that analysis is not defined to include an organizational-economic-efficiency defense.

* * *

Chapter 9 has established three sets of conclusions. First, various U.S. experts' claims to the contrary notwithstanding, (1) monopolization, competitive-impact, and economic-efficiency analyses are different, and (2) one cannot infer (A) conduct's monopolizing character from its competitive impact or economic efficiency, (B) conduct's competitive impact from its monopolizing character or economic efficiency, or (C) conduct's economic efficiency from its monopolizing character or competitive impact. Second, (1) exploitative-abuse analysis is different from monopolization, competitive-impact, and economic-efficiency analysis, and (2) one cannot infer the exploitative-abusiveness of a dominant firm's conduct from whether it constituted monopolization, lessened competition, or reduced economic efficiency. Third, (1) the concept of an "exclusionary abuse" may or may not be defined in a way that implies that all exclusionary abuses involve monopolization, (2) if the concept is defined to refer to monopolization by a dominant firm, exclusionary-abuse analysis will coincide with monopolization analysis but differ from competitive-impact and economic-efficiency analysis, and (3) if the concept is not so defined, exclusionary-abuse analysis will almost certainly differ not only from monopolization analysis but also from competitive-impact and economic-efficiency analyses.

Conclusion to Part I

Part I has (1) defined the concepts "the impact of a choice on economic efficiency," conduct that "lessens, prevents, or restricts competition" (as used in antitrust statutes), "monopolizing conduct" or "attempts to monopolize," "agreements in restraint of trade," "conduct whose object is to restrict competition," "exclusionary abuses," "exploitative abuses," and conduct that "distorts competition," (2) listed the various analytically-useful categories of economic inefficiency that are worth distinguishing and explained why the tendency of business conduct to increase or decrease the magnitudes of only a few of them is relevant to the conduct's antitrust-legality under U.S. antitrust law or E.C./E.U. competition law, (3) listed and explained why I reject the various operationalizations of the intensity of competition that industrial-organization economists and legal scholars that know some economics have assumed should be used in antitrust cases, delineated the conceptual schemes I think one should use to determine the impact of a business choice on price and QV-investment competition, and provided some preliminary analyses of the various ways in which horizontal mergers can affect the intensity of price competition, (4) explained the basis of my definition of monopolizing conduct and the substance and point of its various elements, listed several of the kinds of business conduct that may represent an attempt to monopolize, and explained why certain kinds of business conduct that do impose losses on the buyers they directly affect are not monopolizing, (5) delineated and compared the actor-coverage of, conduct-coverage of, tests of *prima facie* illegality promulgated by, and defenses recognized by U.S. antitrust law and E.C./E.U. competition law, (6) explained why—regardless of whether they are evaluated by an ideal-type criterion or a functional criterion—market definitions or protocols for generating market definitions are inevitably arbitrary not just at their periphery but more comprehensively and pointed out that this conclusion implies that the market-oriented approaches that scholars and judges take to a wide variety of antitrust-law-related economic issues should be rejected, (7) delineated and criticized the various attempts of economists and antitrust-enforcement authorities to operationalize both the concept of what they call classical and I call ideal-type market definitions and the concept of what they call antitrust-market definitions and I call functional market definitions, (8) provided operational definitions of (A) a firm's monopoly, oligopoly, other-source, and market power over price and (B) a firm's monopoly, oligopoly, other-source, and market power over QV investment and discussed the independent difficulty of defining a firm's monopoly, oligopoly, and market power over price and QV investment combined, (9) delineated and criticized the ways in which U.S. and E.C./E.U. authorities have measured a firm's market power, (10) explained why a firm's market share is a poor indicator of its market power over price, QV investment, or price and QV investment combined, and (11) explained why the monopolizing character, competitive impact, economic efficiency, exclusionary abusiveness, and exploitative abusiveness of a business choice should be analyzed separately. All the applied analyses that Part II of this study executes will use or reflect the definitions, conceptual schemes, and conclusions Part I has developed.

Part II
Introduction to Part II: Applications

Part II is concerned with applications. This Introduction to Part II has two sections. Section 1 prepares the way for Part II's discussions of U.S. and E.C./E.U. antitrust law by describing the powers of the relevant government enforcement-authorities (prosecutors, administrative agencies, and courts) and the entitlements of victims of antitrust violations to obtain civil redress. Section 2 then summarizes Chaps. 10, 11, 12, 13, 14, and 15 on a section-by-section basis.

1. The Roles and Powers of U.S. and E.C./E.U. Antitrust-Law-Enforcement Actors

A. The Roles, Remedial Powers, and Entitlements of U.S. Antitrust-Law-Enforcement Actors

Fifteen points or clusters of points are salient:

(1) the Sherman Act authorizes the DOJ to seek and the U.S. federal courts to impose criminal sanctions (fines and imprisonment)[320];
(2) with one exception, the Clayton Act authorizes the DOJ to seek only civil sanctions[321];

---

[320] Sherman Act at Sections 1–3. These sections establish the maximum (criminal) fine that can be levied on corporations at $100,000,000. The maximum fine that can be levied on an individual is $1,000,000. Fines on individuals can be combined with prison sentences not exceeding 10 years. See U.S.C. Sections 1–2. General U.S. criminal law authorizes the imposition of an alternative fine equal to the defendant's pecuniary gain or the victims' pecuniary loss. See 15 U.S.C. Section 3571(d).

[321] Clayton Act Sections 12, 15-15c, and 25–26. The exception is Section 3 of the Robinson-Patman Act, which authorizes the imposition of criminal penalties of a fine up to a maximum of $5,000 and a prison sentence of no more than one year for knowingly engaging in price discrimination with an anticompetitive purpose. See 15 U.S.C. Section 13(a). However, this section is seldom enforced.

(3) the Federal Trade Commission Act authorizes the FTC only to issue cease and desist orders and preliminary injunctions,[322] both subject to the approval of the federal courts[323];
(4) the Sherman and Clayton Acts authorize the DOJ to seek and the federal courts to grant preliminary and permanent injunctions, and the Clayton Act and the Federal Trade Commission Act authorize the FTC to issue preliminary injunctions and to request the federal courts to issue injunctions[324];
(5) U.S. antitrust law authorizes the DOJ and FTC to negotiate consent decrees, which the federal courts can overturn only when they conclude that the decrees do not serve the public interest[325];
(6) U.S. antitrust law makes decisions by the DOJ and FTC not to proceed with cases unreviewable by the federal courts[326];
(7) the Hart-Scott-Rodino Act[327] obligates parties planning a merger above a certain size to notify the U.S. antitrust-enforcement "agencies" of their intentions before consummating the merger and to provide the agencies with documents and analyses that relate to the legality of the planned merger; high penalties can be imposed for failures to provide the required notification,[328] and the agencies have been assiduous in their efforts to discover transactions that should have been but were not reported[329]; the DOJ and FTC (which have come to specialize in different industries) have 30 days (15 in cash-tender-offer cases) either to decide whether to challenge the proposed merger or to make a "second request" for additional information; if an agency makes a second request, it can also accept information and analyses from third parties; in addition to deciding to challenge or not to challenge the proposed merger, the agency can decide not to challenge the merger if the parties agree to divest assets in areas of product-space in which the combination as originally proposed seems likely to have legally-problematic effects and/or (conceivably[330]) agree to behave in certain ways;

---

[322] Federal Trade Commission Act Section 5(b). Section 5(l) of the Federal Trade Commission Act authorizes the FTC to levy a civil fine of not more than $10,000 per day for failures to comply with cease and desist orders, injunctions, and other appropriate equitable relief once the relevant "orders" have become final.

[323] The FTC's cease and desist orders are subject to review by federal Courts of Appeal. See 15 U.S.C. Section 45.

[324] See, *e.g.*, 15 U.S.C. Sections 21, 45 and 53(b).

[325] Government consent decrees are effective only after being approved by the courts after entitled parties have been given 60 days notice to comment. See Tunney Act, 15 U.S.C. Section 16(b)–(h).

[326] See In re IBM Corp., 687 F.2d 591, 600–03 (2d Cir. 1982).

[327] 15 U.S.C. Section 18a (1976).

[328] See United States v. Sara Lee Corp., 1996–1 Trade Cas. ¶17,301, 1996 WL 120857 (D.D.C. 1996) for a case in which a $3,100,000 penalty was assessed. See also United States v. Equity Group Holdings, 1991–1 Trade Cas (CCH) ¶ 69,320, 1991 WL 28878 (D.D.C. 1991) for a case in which an $850,000 penalty was assessed for the violation of a consent decree.

[329] See HOVENKAMP HORNBOOK 598.

[330] I say "conceivably" because (for sound reasons) the DOJ prefers to impose structural over conduct conditions. See DOJ, Antitrust Division Policy Guide to Merger Remedies at III.A (October 2004).

(8) both the Sherman Act[331] and the Clayton Act[332] entitle victims of antitrust-law violations that have suffered antitrust injuries to recover not just compensatory damages but treble damages in private antitrust actions even when the government has collected the relevant evidence and won antitrust suits against the perpetrator(s): indeed, the Sherman and Clayton Acts entitle not only non-government actors but also the states' Attorneys General when representing their state in its capacity as a conventional economic agent[333] and foreign government actors to recover treble damages if they are not eligible for foreign-government sovereign immunity in cases brought against them for decisions they made when engaging in commercial activities[334];

(9) U.S. antitrust law also authorizes U.S. states to bring so-called *parens patriae* suits on behalf of those of their residents that or who have not opted out of the state's litigation against violators of the Sherman and Clayton Acts (and either to distribute the treble-damage awards they collect to the actual victims or to deposit those awards in the state treasury)[335];

(10) U.S. law usually makes it possible for class actions to be brought on behalf of legally-entitled victims of antitrust violations[336];

(11) the Sherman and Clayton Acts empower legally-entitled non-government or government victims of their violation to obtain preliminary or permanent injunctions from the courts[337];

(12) U.S. antitrust law authorizes the federal courts to overturn consent decrees if they are not in the public interest, to issue temporary and permanent injunctions, to impose civil fines on violators of the Clayton Act, to impose criminal sanctions (fines and imprisonment) on violators of the Sherman Act, to require violators of the Federal Trade Commission Act or of consent decrees to disgorge the profits the violations yielded them, to offset the anticompetitive

---

[331] See 15 U.S.C. Section 15a.

[332] See Clayton Act Section 4.

[333] See U.S.C. Section 15a.

[334] See, Clayton Act Section 4C(a)(1).

[335] See, *e.g.*, *id.* Few *parens patriae* suits have actually been brought. ELHAUGE AND GERADIN (at 9) attributed this reality to the fact that the relevant statute—15 U.S.C. Section 15c(d)—makes the state liable for the defendant's attorneys fees if the court concludes that the action was brought in bad faith.

[336] For a useful, succinct discussion of antitrust class actions, see ELHAUGE AND GERADIN 23–24.

[337] See 15 U.S.C. Sections 4, 25, 26. The standard for securing injunctive relief is different for the government and private plaintiffs. "In a government case the proof of the violation of law may itself establish sufficient public injury to warrant relief." See California v. American Stores, 495 U.S. 271, 295 (1990). To obtain an injunction, private plaintiffs must demonstrate that the violation is a material causal link to their suffering an antitrust injury—*i.e.*, must establish "threatened loss or damage." See *id.*, 15 U.S.C. Section 26, and Cargill, Inc. v. Montford of Colorado, Inc., 479 U.S. 104, 111 (1986).

effects of a defendant's or the defendants' antitrust violations by requiring them to engage in or refrain from engaging in specified conduct (to divest or create companies, provide access to physical or intellectual property, enter into or modify contracts, reject various otherwise-lawful business opportunities, or forego engaging in otherwise-lawful business practices), and to issue treble (or, in some cases, compensatory) damage awards to antitrust victims that or who have sustained antitrust injuries;

(13) U.S. courts have held that a plaintiff in a private antitrust suit that has established by a preponderance of the evidence that the defendant(s) has (have) violated the antitrust law, that this violation was "a material cause" of the plaintiff's suffering an antitrust injury,[338] and that the plaintiff was either a "direct" victim of the violation or an indirect victim whose legal entitlement would serve the policy objectives of the antitrust laws can recover even if it cannot satisfy normal standards of certainty in relation to the magnitude of its loss[339];

(14) U.S. courts have held that whether an "indirect" victim of an antitrust violation that has suffered an antitrust injury (say, a customer Z of a buyer Y that has had to pay its supplier X a higher price for a good A that Y resells to Z because X has engaged in an illegal price-fix on A) is entitled to sue for and obtain (treble) damages depends on whether (A) a more-directly-injured party would be able to sue the perpetrator if the indirect victim in question could not, (B) allowing the indirect victim in question to sue would make it difficult to prevent the award of duplicative damages, and (C) difficult causality issues would have to be resolved to determine whether the indirect victim really was entitled to recover[340]; and

(15) U.S. courts have failed to recognize that (say) a buyer-victim's losses equal not just the product of the higher price per unit the violation had caused it to pay and the number of units it purchased but that product *plus* the buyer surplus the buyer would have obtained by purchasing at the lower price it

---

[338] For a loss to constitute an "antitrust injury"—the type of injury that can be the basis for a private claim under U.S. antitrust law, it must be an "injury of the type the [U.S.] antitrust laws were intended to prevent and that flows from that which makes the defendants' acts unlawful"—an injury that "reflect[s] the anticompetitive effect. . .of the violation. . .." Brunswick Corp. v. Pueblo-Bowl-O-Mat, Inc., 429 U.S. 477, 489 (1977).

[339] See, *e.g.*, J. Truet Payne Co., Inc. v. Chrysler Motors Corp., 451 U.S. 557, 565–66 (1981); Zenith Radio Corp. v. Hazeltine Research, Inc. (Zenith I), 395 U.S. 100, 123 (1969); Bigelow v. RKO Radio Pictures, 327 U.S. 251, 265 (1946); and Story Parchment Co. v. Paterson Parchment Paper Co., 282 U.S. 555, 563 (1931).

[340] See HOVENKAMP HORNBOOK 621–33 for a cogent discussion of this complex doctrinal/policy issue. The Supreme Court's opinion in Illinois Brick Co. v. Illinois, 431 U.S. 720 (1977) gives a good sense of the relevant analysis. Thus, in *Illinois Brick*, the Court states both (1) (at 737) that in general, indirect purchasers should not be granted the right to sue because (A) direct purchasers will have adequate incentives to bring suit and (B) allowing both direct and indirect purchasers to sue will make it necessary for the courts to resolve the difficult issue of the percentage of any illegally-increased price to the direct purchaser that was passed on and (2) (at 736) that indirect purchasers should be granted standing to sue if they made their purchases under a pre-existing cost-plus contract since in such cases (A) the direct purchaser has no incentive to sue and (B) it will not be difficult to apportion the resulting loss.

would have been charged absent the violation the additional units of the good or service in question it would have purchased at that lower price.

B. The Roles, Remedial Powers, and Entitlements of E.C./E.U. Competition-Law-Enforcement Actors

Ten points or clusters of points are salient:

(1) in 1962, the European Council promulgated Regulation 17,[341] which centralized in the EC the authority to enforce what are now Articles 101 and 102 of the 2009 Lisbon Treaty (though the EC's factual and legal conclusions were always subject to judicial review[342]);
(2) Regulation 17 also required all firms to notify the EC of all agreements covered by what is now Article 101[343];
(3) Regulation 17 gave the EC in addition authority to grant exemptions under now-Article 101(3) for agreements that violated one of now-Article 101(1)'s tests of *prima facie* illegality[344];
(4) Regulation 17 provided that (A) the initiation by the EC of a proceeding under now-Articles 101 and 102 deprives the Member States of competence to deal with the issue in question but (B) if the EC has not initiated a relevant proceeding, the Member States are competent to deal with the relevant matter[345];
(5) in 2003, in response to a request by the EC (which was being overwhelmed by the volume of work that was coming its way), the Council abolished the notification requirement and took advantage of the fact that Member States had created national competition authorities (NCAs) to enforce national competition statutes and the fact that national courts had had experience in applying those laws by authorizing national competition authorities and courts to apply now-Article 101, including now-Article 101(3), and now-Article 102 when (A) the conduct in question has had or will have substantial direct effects on competition within the relevant nation's territory, (B) the national court has the authority to end the violation (say, by issuing a cease and desist order), and (C) the national court has the capacity to collect and assess evidence of the alleged infringement (perhaps with the assistance of other authorities)[346];

---

[341] EEC Council, Regulation No. 17, First Regulation Implementing Articles 85 and 86 of the Treaty (hereinafter Regulation 17), Articles 2–3 and 9 inset 1, English Special Edition: Series I, Chap. 1959–62 at 87 (1962).

[342] *Id.* at Article 9 inset 1.

[343] *Id.*at Articles 4–5.

[344] *Id.* at Article 6.

[345] *Id.* at Article 9 inset 3.

[346] Council Regulation (EC) No. 1/2003 on the Implementation of the Rules of Competition Laid Down in Articles 81 and 82 of the Treaty (December 16, 2002) (hereinafter Regulation 1/2003), OJ L1/1 (2003).

fine up to 10 % of their annual turnovers on undertakings that have failed to comply with a condition for the approval of its merger or joint venture[349];

(10) the EC is authorized to provide business undertakings with guidance letters if they solicit the EC's assessment of the legality of an agreement or practice under now-Articles 101 and 102 if (A) their request for information raises a novel question of law, (B) the information provided by the requestor is sufficient to enable the Commission to assess the legality of the agreement or practice in question, and (C) the relevant question of law bears on the legality of the requestor's conduct; although the EC claims that it is not bound by its guidance letters, the legal relevance of guidance letters is unclear: the EC is bound by a general principle of "legitimate expectations" as well as by Article 340 of the Consolidated Version of the Treaty of European Unity and the Treaty on the Functioning of the European Union[350] (originally Article 288(2) of the 1957 EC Treaty),which entitles parties that have suffered losses from the action of any E.C./E.U. institution to recover those losses in a proceeding before the CFI,[351] though, to my knowledge, no claim for compensation on this basis has ever succeeded[352]; Article 7 of Regulation 1/2003 authorizes the EC to issue cease and desist orders requiring undertakings or associations of undertakings to stop violating now-Articles 101 and 102; the EC can also declare illegal terminated conduct that violated now-Articles 101 and 102; the EC is authorized to employ both behavioral remedies (*e.g.*, in a refusal-to-deal case, to order the refuser to supply the product to the refused party) and structural remedies, though Regulation 1/2003 states that structural remedies can be used (A) only when behavioral remedies would not be equally effective or would be more burdensome for their addressee and (B) only to stop the illegal behavior, not to reverse the anticompetitive consequences of past illegal behavior[353]; although Regulation 17/62 did not explicitly authorize the EC to order interim measures, in 1979 the ECJ interpreted Article 3 of Regulation 17 to empower the EC to order such measures,[354] and this

[349] This account is based on a much-more-detailed description of the protocol in question in Peder Christensen, Kyriakos Founotukakus, and Dan Sjöblom, Mergers 421, 535–92, Chapter 5 in THE E.C. LAW OF COMPETITION (Jonathan Faull and Ali Nikipay, eds., 2d ed., 2007).

[350] 2010/C 83/01.

[351] To succeed, the plaintiff must establish that the EC institution has committed a "sufficiently-serious breach" of a legal rule that caused it to suffer a real and definite harm. As of 2007, no such suit against the EC succeeded.

[352] In part, this fact reflects the reality that the EC has prohibited few mergers (according to ELHAUGE AND GERADIN at 51, only 19 between 1989 and 2007). However, primarily it reflects the fact that E.C./E.U.-court proceedings in merger cases take too long (historically, 21 months on average) for it to be profitable for the merger partners to preserve their ability to merge by not committing relevant resources to other uses in the hope of gaining court-approval.

[353] This reality probably reflects the combination of (1) the legal fact that the E.C./E.U.-institution liability depends on the institution's having committed a "sufficiently-serious breach" of its obligations and (2) the complexity and difficulty of many of the cases in question.

[354] See Camera Care v. Commission, Case C-792/79, ECR 119 at ¶ 18 (1980).

interpretation was codified by Article 8(1) of Regulation 1/2003[355]; the EC is authorized to suspend proceedings it has initiated if the perpetrator(s) of the conduct under investigation terminate that conduct or alter it to make it conform to E.C./E.U. competition law (in the EC's judgment): although many cases brought by the EC are settled in this way without a formal decision, Regulation 1/2003 empowers the EC to bind the parties to such commitments by issuing a formal decision indicating that the parties' fulfillment of the commitments in question would remove all grounds for related action, absent changes in conditions or proof that the Commission's decision was based on incomplete, misleading, or incorrect information supplied by the parties[356]; Article 23(2) of Regulation 1/2003 empowers the Commission to fine a firm up to 10 % of its preceding business year's total turnover for intentionally or negligently infringing now-Articles 101 or 102, violating an interim order, or failing to fulfill a commitment made as part of a settlement arrangement: such fines, which are the EC's primary policy-instrument, are calculated through the use of a far-from-precise protocol that takes account of (A) the seriousness of the infringement (minor, serious, very serious),[357] (B) the duration of the infringement (short, medium, long),[358] (C) the presence of aggravating circumstances (party recidivism, the party's taking a leading role in the violation, the conduct's involving retaliation, the party's refusal to cooperate),[359] (D) the presence of mitigating circumstances (the party's having taken a passive role in the violation, the illegal agreement's never having been implemented, the party's terminating the violation upon the EC's involvement),[360] (E) the party's qualifying for lenient treatment under the terms of the "leniency notice,"[361] (F) the benefits the party obtained from the illegal conduct, the party's ability to pay, and the offensiveness of the party's product-portfolio[362,363];

[355] It appears that, in practice, the interim measures that the EC has ordered have virtually always been ordered at the request of alleged victims rather than by the EC on its own motion. See ELHAUGE AND GERADIN 47.

[356] *Id.* at 47.

[357] See Article 23(3) of Regulation 1/2003.

[358] *Id.*

[359] *Id.* at Section 2.

[360] *Id.* at Section 3.

[361] Commission Notice on the Non-Imposition or Reduction of Fines, OJ C45 (2002).

[362] Commission Guidelines on the Methods of Setting Fines, Section 5, OJ C9 (1998).

[363] In June 2006, the EC issued new Guidelines for its setting of fines that suggest that it intends to increase the fines it levied. Guidelines on the Method of Setting Fines Imposed Pursuant to Article 23(2)(a) of Regulation No. 1/2003 (June 2006). These Guidelines state that (1) fines may be as high as (30 % of the offender's annual sales of the product[s] to which the infringement relates) *times* (the number of years the party's infringement lasted) (so long as the fine does not violate the Council's "10 % of annual turnover" constraint), (2) fines for serious violations such as cartels may be set without regard to the short duration of the infringement, and (3) the upward adjustment for recidivism may be 100 % as opposed to the previous practice of 50 % and the adjustment may be made not just once but for each prior infringement and not just for infringements detected by the

(11) Article 230 of the E.C. Treaty authorizes natural or legal persons to bring annulment proceedings against EC decisions before the CFI (challenging findings of fact) or the ECJ (challenging conclusions of law): appeals against Commission decisions are common in non-merger cases but less common in merger cases,[364] though the rate of merger-case appeals may be increasing[365] as a result of the CFI's adopting a "fast-track" procedure[366] for reviewing merger-case appeals and announcing various substantive decisions in actual merger-appeal cases sharply criticizing the EC for failing to execute appropriate economic analyses[367]; the E.C. Treaty also authorizes the President of the CFI (subject to an appeal to the President of the ECJ) to suspend a contested decision pursuant to Article 242 of the Treaty or to order interim measures pursuant to Article 230 of the Treaty if requested to do so by a plaintiff that can establish a *prima facie* case against the EC decision and demonstrate that the interim relief is necessary to prevent "serious and irreparable harm"; Article 31 of Regulation 1/203 authorizes the CFI and ECJ to "cancel, reduce or increase the fine or periodic penalty imposed" by the EC: in practice, the courts appear to limit their review of the fines the EC has levied to determining whether the EC has followed the required protocol for determining fines—*inter alia*, has taken proper account of the duration and gravity of the offense and the eligibility of the transgressor for leniency[368]: although the CFI has never revised a fine upwards, it has stated its conclusion that it is empowered to do so.[369]

EC but also for infringements of now-Articles 101 and 102 identified by the NCAs. The EC's subsequent decision to levy a fine of 497.2 million euros on Microsoft for its (supposed) abuse of a dominant position may harbinger a substantial increase in the fines the EC levies. See Commission Decision, Microsoft Case COMP/C-3/37/792. Not surprisingly, firms against which historically-unusually-high fines have been levied have begun to challenge those fines before the CFI. See ELHAUGE AND GERADIN 49.

[364] See ELHAUGE AND GERADIN 51.

[365] See *id.* at 52; My-Travel v Commission, Case T-342/99, 5CMLR 221 (2008); and Request, Schneider Electric v. Commission, Case T-351/03 (not yet published).

[366] See Amendments to the Rules of Procedure of the Court of First Instance of the European Communities, OJ L 322/4 (2000).

[367] See Tetra-Laval v. Commission, Case T-5/02, ECR II-43481 (2000); Airtours v. Commission, Case T-342/99, ECR II-2585 (2002); and Schneider Electric v. Commission, Case T-310/01, ECR II-4071 (2002).

[368] See ELHAUGE AND GERADIN 52.

[369] Tokai Carbon Co. Ltd. and Others v. Commission, Joined Cases T-236/01, T-239/01, T-244/01 to T-246/01, and T-251/01, ECR II-1181 at ¶ 165 (2004).

2. A Chapter-by-Chapter (Section-by-Section) Summary of Chaps. 10, 11, 12, 13, 14, and 15

Chapter 10 focuses on natural and contrived oligopolistic conduct of all types. Section 1 analyzes the legality of all such conduct under both U.S. antitrust law and E.C./E.U. competition law if such law is correctly interpreted and applied. Sections 2 and 3 focus on natural and contrived oligopolistic pricing. More specifically, Section 2 analyzes the determinants of the feasibility of natural oligopolistic pricing and the determinants of the profitability of contrived oligopolistic pricing (conventionally called "price-fixing") in both individualized-pricing and across-the-board-pricing contexts. Section 3 (1) delineates the evidence that can properly be used to prove that one or more firms have engaged in contrived oligopolistic pricing, which is almost always prohibited by U.S. antitrust law and is prohibited by E.C./E.U. competition law when it involves agreements or has been practiced by a firm with an individual dominant position or a set of rivals that are collectively dominant, (2) criticizes various "tests" for such pricing that Professor (now Judge) Richard Posner and/or others have proposed, and (3) examines the U.S. and E.C./E.U. case-law on oligopolistic pricing, related types of conduct that can enable sellers to obtain higher prices for given products, oligopolistic output-restricting conduct, and horizontal and vertical "market"-dividing conduct. Section 4 focuses on oligopolistic interactions that affect either (1) the non-price terms in contracts of sale for products with given actual and buyer-perceived physical attributes, performance-characteristics, and images or (2) the various actual and buyer-perceived physical attributes, performance-characteristics, images of the products a set of rivals offers for sale (without causing anyone to create or not create a QV investment). More specifically, Subsection 4(A) lists and, when appropriate, explains both (1) the non-price terms in question—*viz*., credit terms, product-production-date or delivery-date terms, product-installation terms, post-sales-service and replacement-part terms, terms that relate to the provision of product-use instructions, warrantee terms, exculpatory clauses, terms that limit or specify the damages for which the seller will be liable if it fails to fulfill a contractual obligation, and contract-dispute-resolution-process terms—and (2) the actual and buyer-perceived product-attributes in question—*viz*., product-size attributes, actual material product-quality attributes, product-image attributes, and buyer perceptions of product-quality (*e.g*., of product-safety) that can be affected by advertising. Subsection 4(B) distinguishes five functional categories of oligopolistic interactions that can affect such terms of sale, product attributes, product images, or buyer perceptions: (1) contrived oligopolistic interactions that allegedly enable their participants to profit by reducing the attractiveness of the non-price terms of sale they offer buyers and hence the non-cost-of-goods-sold cost to the sellers of the relevant transactions ("allegedly" because I doubt that sellers will ever be able to profit in this way), (2) oligopolistic interactions that are designed to secure product standardization to facilitate the fixing of overall sales-terms, (3) oligopolistic interactions that standardize products when standardization will increase the joint equivalent-dollar gain relevant transactions yield sellers and buyers combined, (4) oligopolistic interactions that reduce image-creating advertising that decreases seller profits (often by more than it benefits buyers), and (5) oligopolistic interactions that reduce advertising that would harm sellers not only because it would be costly but also because it would inform buyers that the sellers' products are less safe than buyers perceive them to be. Subsection 4C then analyzes the legality of these five categories of oligopolistic interactions respectively under U.S. antitrust law and E.C./E.U. competition law as correctly interpreted and applied—*inter alia*, whether they are contrived or natural, whether (if contrived) they always involve an agreement, and whether they are rendered lawful by the non-illicit benefits they yield their perpetrators or by other consequences they have. Next, Subsection 4D summarizes and evaluates the legal correctness of the U.S. and E.U. case-law on such interactions. Section 5 focuses on oligopolistic interactions that can affect the quantity of QV investment in an ARDEPPS, the location of the QV investments in an ARDEPPS, and/or the ownership of the QV investments in an ARDEPPS. Subsection 5A explains that, although one type of predatory behavior that has a relevant effect on QV investment is not oligopolistic, two functional categories of such conduct either can be or inevitably are oligopolistic. Subsection 5B then discusses how and the circumstances in which the total quantity of QV investment in an ARDEPPS can be reduced by natural oligopolistic interdependence and lists the various kinds of contrived oligopolistic conduct that can affect the quantity of QV investment in an ARDEPPS. Subsection 5C analyzes the legality of all types of oligopolistic conduct that relates directly to QV investment under U.S. and E.C./E.U. law properly interpreted and applied. And Subsection 5D reviews the U.S. and E.U. case-law on oligopolistic conduct of the relevant kinds. Section 6 focuses on natural and contrived oligopolistic PPR-related decisionmaking. After pointing out that, with two exceptions, the economic and legal analysis of such decisionmaking is the same as the economic and legal analysis of natural and contrived oligopolistic QV-investment-related decisionmaking, Subsection 6A respectively states and explores the two relevant differences: (1) the fact that the reductions in total PPR that such decisionmaking generates are economically inefficient whereas the reductions in total QV investment that such decisionmaking generates are economically efficient and (2) the fact that, in some circumstances, producers that are liable for the losses they inflict on others by generating accidents and pollution only if they are found to have caused such losses "negligently" (as the common law has defined and applied this concept) may find it jointly profitable not to do presumptively-economically-efficient PPR into less-accident-and-pollution-loss-prone production processes, may sometimes be able to rely on their natural oligopolistic interdependence to achieve this outcome, and may sometimes find it profitable to contrive this outcome. Subsection 6B explains why it may be in the joint interest of potential production-process researchers that also produce the product to whose production-process the PPR in question relates not to do economically-efficient research that is designed to discover presumptively-economically-efficient less-accident-and-pollution-loss prone ways to produce the relevant products, shows why, in some situations, the natural oligopolistic interdependence of such potential production-process researchers may deter them from doing collectively-unprofitable but presumptively-economically-efficient PPR of this kind, and delineates the various kinds of (non-predatory) contrived oligopolistic agreements that may enable such researchers to avoid doing such collectively-unprofitable PPR. Subsection 6C analyzes the legality of all types of PPR-related oligopolistic conduct under U.S. antitrust law and E.C./E.U. competition law if such law is correctly interpreted and applied. And Subsection 6D points out that no U.S. or E.C./E.U. antitrust case addresses such conduct and argues that this reality may reflect the failure of scholars and practicing lawyers to realize that oligopolistic conduct of this kind is possible.

Chapter 11 focuses on predatory conduct. To be predatory in the sense in which I am defining this concept, conduct must satisfy two criteria: (1) it must be designed to benefit its perpetrator or perpetrators (A) by driving out or inducing the relocation of a rival QV investment, (B) by deterring or inducing a change in the location of a prospective new entry or a prospective established-firm QV-investment expansion, or (C) by driving out or inducing the relocation of an extant QV investment and (2) the perpetrator(s) must have attempted to accomplish the goal in question by threatening to make or actually making inherently-unprofitable business choices that will impose losses on the target of the predation if the target does not exit, sell out to the predator, or relocate. On this definition (which I think articulates the standard understanding of the concept), predatory conduct differs from oligopolistic conduct in three respects:

(1) it cannot manifest natural complex interdependence—*i.e.*, there is no such thing as natural predatory behavior;
(2) for linguistic reasons, it must involve the communication and/or carrying out of an anticompetitive threat—*i.e.*, if a sequence of conduct contains only the making and acceptance of an anticompetitive offer (say, an offer to pay a rival not to make a QV investment the rival would otherwise find profitable and an acceptance of that offer by the rival in question), the conduct is, on my definition, contrived oligopolistic, not predatory; and
(3) it is never aimed at changing the pricing and/or other non-investment-related decisions of rivals operating one or more given QV investments (though it can be aimed at altering or preventing a rival's PPR, plant-modernization, or new-plant-construction decision as well as deterring a potential entrant or expander from adding a QV investment to the relevant ARDEPPS or inducing such a firm to change the product-space location of an existing or planned QV investment).

The structure of Chap. 11 is very similar to the structure of Chap. 10. Section 1 defines the concept of predatory conduct, explains why all varieties of such conduct violate the U.S. Sherman Act if that statute is properly interpreted, and argues that, although what is now Article 101 of the 2009 Lisbon Treaty prohibits all agreed-upon multi-firm predation and what is now Article 102 of the 2009 Lisbon Treaty prohibits all predation engaged in by a firm with an individually-dominant position or by one or more members of a set of collectively-dominant rivals, properly interpreted, European competition law does not prohibit individual-firm predation by a firm that is neither individually dominant nor a member of a collectively-dominant set of rivals. Section 2 focuses on predatory pricing. More specifically, Subsection 2A analyzes the determinants of the profitability of predatory pricing.

more employment contracts (partnership agreements) that prohibit the relevant employee (partner) from subsequently working for or becoming a rival after leaving the employer's employ (the partnership) and a decision by the buyer of a business or professional practice to obligate the seller not to work for or become a rival of the buyer. Subsection 9B analyzes the legality under U.S. antitrust law and E.C./E.U. competition law, properly interpreted and applied, of the various sub-types of refusals to deal that Subsection 9A distinguishes. Subsection 9C comments briefly on what I take to be the correct way to structure refusal-to-deal antitrust trials. And Subsection 9D reviews and criticizes the U.S. and E.C./E.U. case-law on refusals to deal. Section 10 focuses on various practices collectively called systems rivalry that are designed to prevent their perpetrator's customers from buying complements of its product from independents and on various types of aftermarket conduct that are also designed to prevent their perpetrator's customers from buying repair and maintenance services or replacement-parts for the perpetrator's basic product from independents. Subsection 10A explains the various functions that systems rivalry and various functionally-identical types of aftermarket conduct can perform. Subsection 10B analyzes the legality of such conduct under U.S. antitrust law and E.C./E.U. competition law, properly interpreted and applied. And Subsection 10C discusses the U.S. case-law, EC position, and E.C./E.U. case-law on such conduct.

I should indicate that Chaps. 10 and 11 have a sub-theme that relates to the justification for the admittedly-complicated conceptual systems Chap. 2 delineated. In particular, Chaps. 10 and 11 justify those conceptual systems (1) by demonstrating that many of the definitional and evidentiary issues the chapters address can be correctly resolved only if one pays attention to the concepts and distinctions that Chap. 2's various vocabulary systems articulate and, relatedly, to the realities that underlie them, (2) by establishing that many of the mistakes that economists and lawyers who are conversant with economics made in the 1960s and 1970s when analyzing various oligopolistic-conduct issues reflect their failure to take account of these distinctions and realities, and (3) by revealing that the errors that scholars made subsequently when analyzing parallel predatory-conduct issues stem from precisely the same omissions.

Chapter 12 focuses on horizontal mergers and acquisitions (hereinafter horizontal mergers). Section 1 delineates the legitimate functions that such mergers can perform for their participants and lists the various ways in which they (1) can reduce the absolute attractiveness of the best offers against which the merged firm will have to compete relative to their counterparts for the merger partners (MPs) and (2) lessen competition in the Clayton Act sense. Section 2 examines in detail (1) the determinants of the extent to which horizontal mergers that yield no efficiencies will generate the two effects just listed and (2) the determinants of the extent to which any static or dynamic efficiencies that a horizontal merger generates will increase the MPs' profits and competition in the Clayton Act sense. More specifically, Section 2 examines in detail (1) the determinants of the extent to which a horizontal merger that yields no relevant efficiencies will generate the two effects just delineated and (2) the determinants of the extent to which any static or dynamic efficiencies that a horizontal merger generates will increase the MPs' profits and competition in the Clayton Act sense. More specifically, Section 2 examines in detail the determinants of the impact that a horizontal merger that generates no relevant efficiencies will have on the OCAs (HNOPs), NOMs, and COMs of both the merged firm relative to the MPs and the merged firm's *R*s in both individualized-pricing and across-the-board-pricing contexts, the determinants of the impact that such a merger will have on QV-investment competition in the ARDEPPS in which it is executed, the determinants of the impact that the static efficiencies a horizontal merger generates would have on the OCAs (HNOPs), NOMs, and COMs of both the merged firm relative to the MPs and the merged firm's *R*s in both individualized-pricing and across-the-board-pricing contexts if those efficiencies would not affect equilibrium QV investment in the relevant area of product-space, and the determinants of the impact that the dynamic efficiencies a horizontal merger generates will have on QV-investment competition in the ARDEPPS in which the relevant merger is executed. More specifically, Sect. 3 explains that the amount by which a horizontal merged between sellers that set individualized prices will directly raise the merged firm's HNOPs above those of the MPs by freeing the MPs from each other's price competition will increase with the frequency with which the MPs were uniquely-equal-best-placed to supply given buyers, the average amount by which in these cases the MPs were better-placed than the third-placed suppliers of the buyers in question, the frequency with which the MPs were respectively uniquely-best-placed and uniquely-second-placed to supply given buyers and the average amount by which in these latter cases the uniquely-second-placed MP was better-placed than the third-placed supplier of the buyers in question. Section 3 also explains that the Sherman-Act-licit profits that the static marginal-cost-related efficiencies a horizontal merger between individualized-pricing sellers yields its participants directly by raising the OCAs of the merged firm above the OCAs of the MPs depends on (1) the size of the marginal-cost reduction the merger yielded, (2) the number of buyers the MPs were best-placed to supply, (3) the number of buyers the MPs were worse-than-best-placed to supply by an amount that was lower than the marginal-cost reduction the merger yielded, and (4) the average amount by which the marginal-cost reduction exceeded the OCD of the better-placed MP when it did exceed that OCD while the equivalent-dollar gains that any marginal-cost reduction generated by a horizontal merger between sellers that practice individualized pricing will confer on Clayton-Act-relevant buyers by improving from their perspective the HNOP-containing offer of their (possibly-changing) best-placed supplier depends on (1) the number of buyers an MP was second-placed to supply, (2) the size of the marginal-cost reduction the merger yielded (up to the point that it exceeds the pre-merger best-placed supplier's OCA), (3) the number of buyers an MP was worse-than-second-placed to supply by an amount that was smaller than the marginal-cost reduction the merger generated, and (4) in these latter cases, the average value of a sum of items equal to the lower of (A) the positive difference between the marginal-cost reduction and the amount by which the relevant MP was worse-than-second-placed to obtain the patronage of a relevant buyer and (B) the pre-merger best-placed supplier's OCA over the pre-merger second-placed supplier (which will be the relevant figure when the efficiency makes the merged firm best-placed). Section 3 analyzes the legality of horizontal mergers under U.S. antitrust law and E.C./E.U. competition law, properly interpreted and applied. Section 4 focuses on the approaches that have been taken to analyzing both the competitive impact and the legality of horizontal mergers by U.S. courts and antitrust-enforcement agencies. Subsection 4A (1) delineates and criticizes the traditional market-oriented (market-share/market-concentration) approach that U.S. antitrust courts took to horizontal-merger analysis, (2) discusses 11 elements of the earlier courts' handling of horizontal mergers that the contemporary antitrust-enforcement agencies respectively have taken over, have rejected, and may or may not have taken over, and (3) reviews briefly the more contemporary lower-court U.S. case-law on horizontal mergers. Subsection 4B focuses on the approaches to horizontal-merger analysis that have been taken by the U.S. Department of Justice (DOJ) and Federal Trade Commission (FTC). More specifically, after discussing the U.S. merger-notification law that imposes severe constraints on the amount of time that the DOJ and FTC have to make an initial assessment of the competitive impact of a proposed merger (which could lead to the relevant agency's making a "second request" for additional information that it could then supplement and process over a longer period of time), Subsection 4B (1) delineates and criticizes in some detail market-oriented and non-market-oriented approaches the DOJ and FTC indicated they would use to predict the competitive impact of horizontal mergers in their 1992 Horizontal Merger Guidelines and 1997 Revision of those Guidelines and the inchoate non-market-oriented approach the DOJ and FTC indicated they would use to predict the competitive impact of horizontal mergers in their 2010 Horizontal Merger Guidelines, and (2) discusses the merger-simulation and inference-from-natural-event approaches that economists both inside the DOJ and FTC and outside the U.S. antitrust-enforcement agencies have taken to this task. Section 5 reviews the market-oriented approach that the EC's Horizontal Merger Guidelines state it will use to predict the competitive impact of horizontal mergers and the E.C./E.U. case-law on horizontal mergers.

Chapter 13 focuses on conglomerate mergers and acquisitions—mergers between firms that are (ideally) never uniquely-equal-best-placed, respectively uniquely-best-placed and uniquely-second-placed, or (perhaps) both well-placed to obtain the patronage of any given buyer. Section 1 explains that the standard Sherman Act specific-anticompetitive-intent test of illegality and the standard Clayton Act lessening-competition test of illegality apply to conglomerate merges and points out that it is correct as a matter of U.S. law to apply the do-nothing baseline when measuring the competitive impact of conglomerate mergers. Section 2 delineates the Sherman-Act-licit and Sherman-Act-illicit ways in which conglomerate mergers that do not eliminate an effective potential competitor can increase their participants' profits and discusses the appropriate structure of trials about the legality of such mergers under the Sherman Act. *Inter alia*, Sect. 2 points out that, particularly when such a conglomerate merger creates a merged company that faces conglomerate rivals that operate in at least one area of product-space in which each MP operates but more generally as well, such conglomerate mergers can yield Sherman-Act-illicit profits by creating a merged firm that contrives more oligopolistic margins, raises more retaliation barriers to entry and expansion, and engages in more predation of other kinds than the MPs would have done. Section 3 delineates the various ways in which conglomerate mergers that do not eliminate an effective potential competitor can decrease and increase competition in the Clayton Act sense and discusses the appropriate structure of trials about the legality of such mergers under the Clayton Act. *Inter alia*, Sect. 3 points out that, particularly when such a conglomerate merger creates a merged firm that faces conglomerate rivals that operate in at least one area of product-space in which each MP operates but more generally as well, such conglomerate mergers can impose equivalent-dollar losses on Clayton-Act-relevant buyers not only by creating a merged firm that engages in more contrivance and predation than the MPs would have done but also by increasing the oligopolistic margins the merged firm's rivals contrive, by causing the merged firm's rivals to confront the merged firm with higher retaliation barriers than those they would have raised against the MPs, and (possibly) by increasing the amount of predation in which the merged firm's rivals engage. Section 4 reviews and criticizes the U.S. case-law and DOJ/FTC positions on the economic effects and antitrust legality of conglomerate mergers that do not eliminate an effective potential competitor. It argues that, although the DOJ and FTC (but not the U.S. courts) used to think that conglomerate mergers could increase price-fixing and both the DOJ/FTC and the U.S. courts used to think that conglomerate mergers could increase predation, their concern was focused solely on the behavior of the merged firm relative to the MPs—i.e., they ignored such mergers' possible effects on the conduct of the merged firm's rivals—and (relatedly) was driven solely by the fear that the merged firm would have deeper pockets that would enable it better to finance strategic behavior—i.e., they ignored the tendency of conglomerate mergers to increase strategic behavior by putting the merged firm and its rivals in a position to engage in cross-ARDEPPS reciprocation and retaliation and by creating a merged firm that can take better advantage of economies of scale in building and maintaining a reputation for engaging in strategic conduct. Section 4 also points out that in at least one case the U.S. Supreme Court ruled against a conglomerate merger on the ground that it would create a merged firm that engaged in more reciprocal trading than the MPs would have done on the insupportable leverage-"theory"-based assumption that reciprocal trading and tie-ins manifest specific anticompetitive intent and lessen competition when engaged in by firms with economic power over one of the products involved. Section 4 points out in addition that, although the U.S. Supreme Court has never disavowed the leverage theory, it has reached conclusions in individual cases that are inconsistent with it and the DOJ and FTC no longer seem to act on it. Finally, Section 4 addresses the toe-hold-merger doctrine, which has been developed and used by several lower U.S. courts. This doctrine proclaims that a geographic-diversification conglomerate merger between a diversifier and a medium or large firm in a geographic area into which the diversifier wants to enter is illegal even if the transaction would not lessen competition relative to the state of the world that would prevail if the diversifier made no attempt to diversify geographically unless the diversifier demonstrates that it made reasonable efforts to identify a small firm with which it could execute a (toe-hold) merger that would have been more profitable than doing nothing to diversify into the relevant geographic area and was unable to do so. Section 4 attacks both (1) this doctrine's two economic assumptions that (A) a toe-hold merger with a small firm will always be or even tend to be more procompetitive than the (presumably-more-profitable) merger with the medium or large firm that was actually proposed and (B) the assumption (A)'s correctness is a sufficient condition for the doctrine's increasing competition and (2) the doctrine's legal assumption that—if its economic assumptions were true (i.e., if it would increase competition)—that fact would imply that it was correct as a matter of U.S. law. Section 5 analyzes the conditions under which potential competition will be effective and describes the competitive impact of effective potential competition. Its conclusions are relevant to (1) the conditions under which and the determinants of the amount by which a conglomerate merger will generate Sherman-Act-illicit profits by eliminating an effective potential competitor and (2) the conditions under which and the determinants of the amount by which a conglomerate merger will inflict a net equivalent-dollar loss on Clayton-Act-relevant buyers by eliminating an effective potential competitor. Section 5 also states and criticizes the positions that some economist-proponents of limit-price "theory" take on the conditions under which potential competition will be effective and the competitive impact that effective potential competition will have. Section 6 analyzes the relevance of the fact that a conglomerate merger eliminates an effective potential competitor to its legality under the Sherman Act and under the Clayton Act, correctly interpreted and applied. It explains that the fact that a conglomerate merger eliminates an effective potential competitor counts against its Sherman Act and Clayton Act legality but is not a sufficient condition for such a merger's being illegal under either statute (since the illicit profits a conglomerate merger generates on this account may not have critically affected an MP's *ex ante* perception of its *ex ante* profitability and since the net equivalent-dollar loss a conglomerate merger imposes on Clayton-Act-relevant buyers on this account may not cause it to impose a net equivalent-dollar loss on such buyers all things considered by reducing the absolute attractiveness of the best offers they respectively receive from any inferior supplier). Section 6 also delineates and criticizes various positions the U.S. courts and/or the U.S. antitrust-enforcement agencies have taken on economics issues that bear on the legality of conglomerate issues. Thus, it points out that U.S. courts claim to have accepted limit-price theory (which they usually refer to as "wings" [as in "waiting in the wings"] theory or "edge" theory), that the U.S. courts do not appear to have understood the economic or legal implications of any variant of that theory (e.g., have not focused on the different positions that various economists have taken on the issue of when limit pricing will be practiced and do not understand that limit pricing is a variant of predatory pricing and, as such, is prohibited by the Sherman Act), that prior to 1992 the DOJ accepted limit-price theory but that the best reading of the 1992 and 2010 Horizontal Merger Guidelines and subsequent agency practice is that the DOJ no longer subscribes to the theory, and that the FTC has been concerned that proposed conglomerate mergers might reduce competition by eliminating an effective potential competitor. Section 7 analyzes the legality of conglomerate mergers under E.C./E.U. competition law both as correctly and as actually interpreted and applied. It explains that conglomerate mergers can violate E.C./E.U. competition law because it violates the specific-anti-competition-intent test of *prima facie* illegality promulgated by the object branch of now-Article 101 and the exclusionary-abuse branch of now-Article 102, the lessening-competition test of illegality promulgated by the effect branch of now-Article 101 and the EMCR, or possibly the exploitative-abuse branch of now-Article 102. It then points out that in practice the EC and the E.C./E.U.-courts have condemned conglomerate mergers that they concluded would create a merged firm that employed more tie-ins, bundling, and/or reciprocity than the MPs would have done if the merged firm would "have a significant degree of market power" "not necessarily amounting to dominance" in one of the markets concerned—a position they take because they subscribe to the leverage theory of tie-ins and reciprocity, which I consider to be in some forms invalid and in other forms of no practical significance. Relatedly, the EC and the E.C./E.U. courts claim that conglomerate mergers can also reduce competition when it generates "portfolio effects," particularly when one of the products involved is a "leading brand"—i.e., when it creates a company that can obtain leverage by refusing to supply two or more products to a buyer. On the positive side, the EC and the E.C./E.U. courts are correctly concerned that conglomerate mergers can increase contrivance by creating a merged firm that can interact with rivals cross-markets (though the EC and E.C./E.U. also think that such mergers will increase contrivance by reducing the number of effective competitors by leading to the use of tie-ins, reciprocity and refusals to deal that drive rivals out [a position I think is wrong] and by making some rivals "more vulnerable" [a position that is unexplained]). Section 7 also lists a number of ways in which conglomerate mergers can reduce competition that the EC and the E.C./E.U. courts have ignored. Finally, Section 7 discusses (1) E.C./E.U.-court holdings that the EC must establish a higher probability than it thought it had to establish that a conglomerate merger would reduce competition to justify a decision to prohibit the merger and (2) E.C./E.U.-court criticisms of the evidence on which the EC based its estimates of the probability that a conglomerate merger would reduce competition.

Chapter 14 analyzes vertical integration and its contractual surrogates. Section 1 describes the spillover effects that the choices of a product's independent final consumers and individual independent distributors can generate. Section 2 delineates the economic functions and examines the probable competitive impact of the various practices I call "surrogates for vertical integration" and comments on some contrary positions on these issues taken by some economists. More specifically, Section 2 reveals that the pricing-techniques, contract-of-sale provisions, and sales/consignment policies that can function as surrogates for vertical integration—multi-part pricing, conventional price discrimination, conventional inter-buyer price discrimination, tie-ins, reciprocity, systems rivalry, resale price maintenance (RPM), vertical territorial restraints and customer-allocation clauses, non-single-brand exclusive dealerships, subsidies to independent-retailer advertising expenses and in-store promotions, slotting arrangements, single-brand exclusive dealerships, long-term full-requirements contracts, and sales and consignment policies that condition the seller's use of an independent retailer or consignee on the latter's making certain choices—can yield their user Sherman-Act-licit profits by reducing (1) the losses it sustains because independent customers secure buyer surplus on their transactions, (2) the costs it finds profitable to incur to convert potential buyer surplus into seller surplus, (3) the losses it sustains because its independent distributors or consignees make decisions related to advertising, in-store promotion-displays and sales efforts, out-of-store sales-efforts, pricing, complement and rival-product sales, and warrantee-servicing that are not in their and the seller's joint interest, and (4) the costs it finds profitable to incur to control these decisions of its independent distributors and consignees. Section 3 analyzes the legality of these surrogates for vertical integration under U.S. and E.C./E.U. antitrust law, properly interpreted and applied, considers the academic commentary on the relevant legal issues, and discusses the U.S. and E.C./E.U. case-law and antitrust-enforcement-agency positions on these practices. *Inter alia*, Section 3 explains why all these surrogates for vertical integration are covered by the Sherman Act and Article 102 of the 2009 Treaty of Lisbon, that all but the relevant sales and consignment policies are covered by Article 101 of the 2009 Treaty of Lisbon, but that only those acts of price discrimination in the economist's sense that also constitute price discrimination in the Clayton Act sense, those tie-ins and reciprocity agreements that impose full-requirements obligations, and single-brand exclusive dealership and full-requirements contracts are covered by the Clayton Act. Section 3 also explains why the level-playing-field norm that clearly underlies U.S. antitrust law and which I think also underlies E.C./E.U. competition law (some official pronouncements and academic commentaries related to the legal obligations of dominant firms under Article 102 notwithstanding) implies that the legally-correct focus when analyzing the legality of any surrogate for vertical integration under the Clayton Act (with the possible, practically-unimportant exception of price discrimination) and under the "effect of preventing or restricting competition" branch of Article 101's test for *prima facie* illegality is the competitive impact not of an individual firm's use of one of these surrogates but of a rule allowing all members of a set of rivals to use it. Section 3 concludes that with rare exceptions (price discrimination that is illegally retaliatory or predatory, tie-ins and reciprocity agreements that function by concealing independent antitrust violations, RPM that is designed to facilitate a retailer horizontal price-fix, and the few single-brand exclusive dealerships and long-term requirements contracts that really are exclusionary), an individual firm's use of any surrogate for vertical integration will not violate the specific-anticompetitive-intent test of the Sherman Act, Article 101, and Article 102 and that in only very rare circumstances will the general availability of any surrogate for vertical integration to all members of a set of product-rivals violate the lessening competition test of the Clayton Act and Article 101 or *a fortiori* violate that test without qualifying for a Clayton Act organizational-economic-efficiency defense or an Article 101(3) exemption. Section 3 also points out that, historically, the U.S. Supreme Court and U.S. lower courts made many mistakes when analyzing the legality of surrogates for vertical integration—*inter alia*, (1) subscribed to a leverage "theory" of tie-ins and reciprocity that claims that when these practices are used by firms that have economic (market) power over one of the products they involve they will inevitably give the firm economic power over the second product they involve as well, (2) claimed that U.S. antitrust law was as concerned with decreases in intra-brand competition as with increases in inter-brand competition, (3) argued that the *per se* illegality of vertical price fixing (RPM) is implied by the *per se* illegality of horizontal price-fixing, (4) used a quantitative-substantiality test to determine the legality of long-term full-requirements contracts, and (5) on at least one occasion claimed that it was legally correct to prohibit well-established firms from using these surrogates (since doing so would help marginal firms survive and potential competitors enter) while permitting marginal and potential competitors to use them (for the same reason). Section 3 then explains that over the past 20–25 years, the U.S. Supreme Court has partially corrected these errors—(1) has found a lawful tie-in lawful despite the fact that the leverage "theory" to which the Court still subscribes implies its illegality (has done so by ignoring the fact that the blanket music-license involved in the relevant case was a tie-in), (2) has held that the legality of an individual seller's use of vertical territorial restraints and customer-allocation clauses and of RPM depends on whether the practices involved in the case in question increase inter-brand competition at least as much as they decrease intra-brand competition (still wrong but less wrong in terms of the outcomes the two doctrines produce), (3) has substituted a still-wrong but less-wrong "qualitative substantiality" test for determining the legality of single-brand exclusive dealerships and long-term full-requirements contracts of other sorts for the more-wrong "quantitative substantiality" test it formerly used for this purpose, and (4) has made no use of the parimutual-handicapping approach to determining the legality of those practices it formerly endorsed. In addition, Sect. 3 notes that, in the past several years the U.S. lower courts have been holding RPM, vertical territorial restraints, and vertical-customer-allocation clauses lawful without comparing their impacts on inter-brand and intra-brand competition and that the U.S. antitrust-enforcement agencies have not reiterated some earlier incorrect pronouncements about the conditions under which long-term full-requirements contracts (and vertical mergers) would be illegal because they would "foreclose competition." Finally, Sect. 3 points out that, historically, the EC and the E.C./E.U. courts made all the mistakes that their U.S. counterparts used to make and that these E.C./E.U. institutions have made much less progress than their U.S. counterparts in correcting these mistakes. Section 3 also points out that the EC and E.C./E.U. courts have made another mistake that they have in one sense been correcting that is different from but related to one of their U.S. counterparts' errors. In particular, the EC and the E.C./E.U. courts have argued that the fact that the Treaty of Rome was designed to promote social and political integration justifies interpreting its competition-law articles to prohibit any firm from barring its independent distributors in one E.C./E.U.-member country from reselling its product(s) in another E.C./E.U.-member country (from engaging in parallel trade). The EC and E.C./E.U. courts have in one sense corrected this mistake not because they have changed their mind about the soundness of their legal conclusion (which I think is wrong as a matter of law) but because they have come to realize that their efforts to increase parallel trade in this way will be unlikely to succeed, given that producers will find it profitable to respond to the relevant prohibitions by making a variety of lawful moves that will probably reduce parallel trade and the extent to which the goods of one E.C./E.U.-member country are sold in other member-countries at least as much as the contractual bans they originally imposed on their distributors did. Section 4 delineates the economic functions and examines the probable competitive impact of vertical mergers and acquisitions and comments on some contrary positions on these issues taken by economists. *Inter alia*, Sect. 4 explains that in addition to performing all the Sherman-Act-licit functions that horizontal and conglomerate mergers can perform, vertical mergers can generate continuous-flow economic efficiencies, eliminate some of the potential-buyer-surplus-related problems that the non-integrated firm would face, and enable the merged firm to profit by substituting a system in which it uses hierarchical controls to influence its own distributive employees for a system in which it used pricing techniques, contract clauses, and sales and consignment policies to control independent distributors and consignees. Section 4 also examines in detail the conditions under which an individual firm's vertical merger (s) or a set of rivals' vertical mergers would correctly be said to have "foreclosed competition." This last analysis includes a discussion of why—for private contextual-cost-related reasons—vertically-integrated firms may find it profitable to supply inputs to their own manufacturing divisions and final goods to their own distributive divisions when an independent supplier could have done so more economically efficient (why vertical integration may distort competition). Section 5 analyzes the legality of vertical mergers and acquisitions under U.S. and E.C./E.U. antitrust law, properly interpreted and applied, considers the academic commentary on the relevant economic and legal issues, and discusses the U.S. and E.C./E.U. case-law and the U.S. and E.C./E.U. antitrust-enforcement-agency positions on the legality of such mergers. *Inter alia*, Sect. 5 criticizes various positions that U.S. courts, the DOJ and FTC, the EC, and E.C./E.U. courts have taken on the conditions under which vertical mergers will foreclose competition, points out that the U.S. courts' historic hostility to vertical mergers seems to be a thing of the past, notes that the DOJ has not reiterated for some time some of the mistaken positions it once articulated, explains that both historically and more recently the EC and the E.C./E.U. courts have tended to conclude that vertical mergers that seem unlikely to me to reduce competition will do so (*inter alia* because they still subscribe to the leverage theory of tie-ins and reciprocity), exaggerated the likelihood that vertical mergers will create merged firms that engage in more predation than the MPs would have done, misanalysed and exaggerated the likelihood that vertical mergers will lead to other sorts of foreclosing conduct, and underestimated their own ability to move against any illegal conduct such mergers makes more feasible and profitable post-merger. Section 5 also points out that the provisions of the EC's 2008 Non-Horizontal Merger Guidelines that relate to vertical mergers are considerably better-informed than the pronouncements and decisions that the EC previously made on such conduct, though they still contain important errors of omission and commission. Section 6 delineates the economic functions and probable competitive impact of vertical integration through internal growth. And Section 7 analyzes the legality of such internal growth under U.S. and E.C./E.U. antitrust law, properly interpreted and applied, and discusses the U.S. and E.C./E.U. case-law on vertical internal growth and the positions that the U.S. and E.C./E.U. antitrust-enforcement authorities have taken on the legality of such internal growth.

Chapter 15 focuses on joint ventures and collaborative arrangements that do not involve the creation of an independent business entity but do perform functions that are the same as or similar to the functions that joint ventures can perform (hereinafter focuses on joint ventures). Section 1 delineates the Sherman-Act-licit and Sherman-Act-illicit functions that can be performed (1) by joint ventures created by agreements that do not impose any problematic restraints on the joint venture and/or its parents and do not limit participation to only some members of a set of competitors and/or deal with non-members in a way that disadvantages them inappropriately and (2) by any problematic restraint-provisions such agreements contain and any participation-limitations or unjustifiably-disadvantageous treatment of non-members the joint venture involves. Section 1's conclusions are relevant to the analysis of the legality of joint ventures under the U.S. Sherman Act, under now-Section 102 of the E.C./E.U. Treaty when at least one of the parents is a dominant firm, (in my view but not the EC's or the E.C./E.U. courts') under now-Section 101 of the E.C./E.U. Treaty, and under the EMCR when the joint venture in question is a full-function joint venture.

Section 2 delineates the various ways in which (1) a joint venture created by an agreement that does not impose any problematic restraints on the parents or joint venture or involve any problematic participation-limitations and/or unjustifiably-disadvantageous treatment of non-members and (2) the restraint-provisions contained in and participation-limitations involved in any actual joint-venture agreement can confer equivalent-dollar gains on and impose equivalent-dollar losses on Clayton-Act-relevant buyers by reducing the absolute attractiveness of the best offer they respectively receive from any inferior supplier. The conclusions of Section 2 are relevant to the analysis of the legality of some joint ventures under the EMCR and of some restrictions imposed by joint-venture agreements under Section 3 of the Clayton Act.

Section 3 analyzes the difficulty of determining whether a joint venture and clauses that restrain the choices that the joint venture and/or its parents can make violate the specific-anticompetitive-intent test of illegality I believe the Sherman Act promulgates. More specifically, Section 3 uses a hypothetical to illustrate the fact that any of the following sets of conclusions could be true about a joint venture created by an agreement that prohibits the joint venture from entering its parents' markets and the parents from entering the joint venture's markets and/or each other's markets:

(1) (A) the joint venture without any of the restraints that the joint-venture agreement might impose on the parents and/or the joint venture is lawful under the Sherman Act because, if the parents did not believe that the joint venture would harm them in any of the ways they could legitimately prevent by including restraints in their joint-venture agreement, they would have concluded *ex ante* that its possible performance of Sherman-Act-licit functions rendered it profitable and (B) the provisions of the joint-venture agreement that imposed restraints on the parents and/or the joint venture are lawful under the Sherman Act because the parents believed *ex ante* that their inclusion in the joint-venture agreement would be rendered profitable by their performance of Sherman-Act-licit functions;

(2) (A) the joint venture without any of the restraints that the joint-venture agreement might impose on the parents and/or the joint venture is lawful for the reasons stated after (1)(A) above but (B) the provisions of the joint-venture agreement that imposed restraints on the parents and/or the joint venture violate the Sherman Act because the parents' *ex ante* belief that they would be profitable was critically affected by the parents' *ex ante* perception that they would or might perform one or more Sherman-Act-illicit functions;
(3) (A) the joint venture without any of the restraints that the joint-venture agreement might impose on the parents and/or the joint venture violates the Sherman Act because the parents' *ex ante* belief that it was profitable was critically affected by their perception that it would or might perform Sherman-Act-illicit functions and (B) the provisions of the joint-venture agreement that imposed restraints on the parents and/or the joint venture also violate the Sherman Act because the parents' *ex ante* belief that they were profitable was critically affected by the parents' *ex ante* belief that they would or might perform Sherman-Act-illicit functions; and
(4) (A) the joint venture without any of the restraints that the joint-venture agreement might impose on the parents and/or the joint venture violates the Sherman Act for the reason stated after (3)(A) above but the provisions of the joint-venture agreement restraining the parents and/or the joint venture are lawful under the Sherman Act for the reasons stated after (1)(B) above.

Section 3 also points out that no easy and cheap-to-apply test can be used to determine whether a joint venture and/or any restraints it imposes on the joint venture and/or the parents violate the Sherman Act: to make such a determination acceptably accurately in the absence of convincing written documents, recordings, and/or eyewitness testimony that establish the parents' specific anticompetitive intent, one would need to know a great deal not only about the Sherman-Act-licit functions that the joint venture and any restrictive provisions the joint-venture agreement contains perform but also about the business opportunities of the parents and the joint venture and the business opportunities of the actual and potential rivals of the parents and joint venture.

Section 4 analyzes the legality of joint ventures and the restrictive provisions that some joint-venture agreements contain under U.S. antitrust law, correctly interpreted and applied. It explains why the Sherman Act and its specific-anticompetitive-intent test of illegality apply to all joint ventures and to all the restrictive provisions that joint-venture agreements contain, argues that the Clayton Act and its "lessening competition" test of illegality do not apply to any joint venture or to any restrictive provision in a joint-venture agreement, and examines the implications of these general legal conclusions for the legality of joint ventures and the restrictive provisions they contain under U.S. antitrust law.

Section 5 reviews the U.S. case-law on joint ventures and the positions that the DOJ and FTC have taken on them. It argues that U.S. courts' and antitrust-enforcement agencies' handling of joint-venture cases and issues has suffered from their failure to understand (1) the determinants of the intensity of QV-investment competition in any area of product-space, (2) the determinants of the profitability of contrived oligopolistic pricing, raising retaliation barriers to entry and expansion, and other sorts of predatory conduct, and (3) at least historically, the functions and effects of various surrogates for vertical integration.

Section 6 analyzes the legality of joint ventures under E.C./E.U. competition law, correctly interpreted and applied. It makes four points or sets of points. First, under E.C./E.U. law correctly interpreted and applied, limited-function joint ventures (*e.g.*, joint ventures created exclusively to do R&D, exclusively to purchase goods or inputs for the parents, or exclusively to market the parents' outputs) are not covered by the EMCR but are covered by now-Article 102 when one or more parents are individually dominant or belong to a collectively-dominant set of rivals and by now-Article 101 regardless of whether a parent occupies a dominant position. Second and relatedly, limited-function joint ventures at least one of whose parents is individually dominant or is a member of a collectively-dominant set of rivals will violate E.C./E.U. competition law, correctly interpreted and applied, if and only if they (1) constitute an exclusionary abuse of the dominant parent's or parents' dominant position (violate a specific-anticompetitive-intent test), (2) lead the dominant parent to engage in an exploitative abuse of its dominant position (an unlikely possibility), or (3) violate the object branch, effect branch, or distorting-competition branch of now-Article 101(1)'s test of *prima facie* illegality and do not satisfy now-Article 101 (3)'s requirements for an exemption. Third, limited-function joint ventures none of whose parents is dominant violate E.C./E.U. competition law if and only if they violate now-Article 101. Fourth, full-function (so-called concentrative) joint ventures violate E.C./E.U. competition law, correctly interpreted and applied, if and only if they (1) violate the EMCR's lessening-competition test, (2) violate now-Article 101, or (3) are perpetrated by at least one firm that is individually dominant or a member of a collectively-dominant set of rivals and violate now-Article 102.

Section 7 analyzes the ways in which the EC and the E.C./E.U. courts have applied E.C./E.U. competition law to joint ventures. It makes three clusters of points.

The first cluster is the most general:

(1) virtually all the relevant Regulations, Notices, Guidelines, and cases deal with the legality of joint ventures under now-Article 101 (because the EMCR was promulgated relatively recently and most joint ventures are not covered by the EMCR [are not full-function, concentrative joint ventures]);
(2) the EC and (since 1998) the E.C./E.U. courts have addressed both the ways in which different types of joint ventures can prevent, restrict, or distort competition in the common market—*i.e.*, can violate now-Article 101(1)'s test of *prima facie* illegality—and the possibility that particular joint ventures and joint ventures of various general kinds will qualify for an economic-efficiency exemption under now-Article 101(3);
(3) often, the EC's and the E.C./E.U. courts' discussions of facts they deem relevant to the now-Article 101 legality of joint ventures do not relate those facts to the component of now-Article-101 legal analysis to which the facts are or are perceived by them to be relevant;

(4) although the EC has frequently concluded that particular joint ventures of all kinds do violate now-Article 101(1)'s test of *prima facie* illegality, it has tended to grant production and R&D joint ventures now-Article 101(3) exemptions, has sometimes granted selling joint ventures now-Article 101(3) exemptions despite its general conclusion that such collaborations basically function as cartels, and has granted now-Article 101(3) exemptions to buying joint ventures created by small-sized and medium-sized enterprises (SMEs) despite its (mistaken) belief that, unless they generate substantial economic efficiencies, they will normally tend to raise the prices ultimate consumers pay—in particular, has granted SMEs such exemptions on the grounds that, when such joint ventures are created by SMEs, they will be more likely to generate economic efficiencies, less likely in any event to impose appreciable losses on consumers, and likely to help their parents compete against larger rivals (a last conclusion that suggests the possibility that the EC and the E.C./E.U. courts may act as parimutual handicappers in cases involving this type of joint venture).

The second cluster of points focuses on the ways in which joint ventures can violate now-Article 101(1)'s test of *prima facie* illegality:

(1) the EC and the E.C./E.U. courts have correctly noted that production and R&D joint ventures can reduce QV-investment competition in the joint venture's market even if they do not result in the parents' contriving QV-investment restrictions; in fact, at least the EC seems to have exaggerated the frequency with which such joint ventures would have this effect both because it has overestimated the likelihood that, absent the joint venture, both parents would have entered the joint venture's market and because it ignored the fact that, in many cases, any reduction in the parents' relevant QV investments would be offset by additional QV investments by non-parents;
(2) the EC and the E.C./E.U. courts have correctly noted that joint ventures can also violate now-Article 101(1)'s test of *prima facie* illegality by increasing the amount of QV-investment contrivance and price-and-other-terms-and-conditions-of-sale contrivance that the parents practice in the joint venture's market and in other markets in which they operate; however, neither the EC nor the E.C./E.U. courts have understood the facts that determine the likelihood that a joint venture will increase contrivance of any kind—more particularly, both the EC and the E.C./E.U. courts have accepted an indefensible, market-oriented approach to this issue that places great weight on the parents' and joint venture's relevant market shares and the concentration of the relevant markets and ignores many other relevant factors, including the fact that most of the feared acts of contrivance would be illegal;
(3) the EC and the E.C./E.U. courts have correctly noted that production and R&D joint ventures can also prevent, restrict, or distort competition in markets that are upstream or downstream from the joint venture's market by leading to "foreclosures" of the parents' rivals; however, neither the EC nor the E.C./E.U. courts have distinguished between joint-venture-induced refusals to deal that are predatory and joint-venture-induced refusals to deal that are inherently profitable; concomitantly neither the EC nor the E.C./E.U. courts have analyzed

whether the fact that a joint venture would reduce or distort competition by creating a joint venture that would find it inherently profitable to refuse to deal with a parent's upstream or downstream rival justifies the conclusion that the joint venture violates now-Article 101(1)'s test of *prima facie* illegality; more generally, the EC's and E.C./E.U. courts' analyses of this "foreclosure" possibility is marred by their use of a market-oriented approach to this issue that assumes that the probability that a joint venture will generate refusals to deal depends primarily on the joint venture's (or the joint venture's and the parents') share of the joint venture's market and the concentration of the seller-side of that market and ignores the fact that the alleged victims of the feared foreclosing acts can make various moves to reduce the harm they suffer;

(4) although for a long while the EC's analyses of the three preceding possibilities were based on general presumptions that I find unwarranted, in part on its own initiative and more recently in response to the E.C./E.U.-courts' criticism of its decisionmaking, the EC has increasingly executed more refined case-by-case analyses of the possibilities in question, though these analyses continue to be vitiated by their market-oriented character; and

(5) the EC and the E.C./E.U. courts also seem to think that agreements that the parents of a production or R&D joint venture enter into to prevent themselves from competing as distributors of the joint venture's output violate now-Article 101(1)'s test of *prima facie* illegality even when the joint venture makes QV investments that in its absence would not have been made at all, as quickly, or as proficiently; I think that prohibitions of such agreements in the stated circumstances are incorrect as a matter of E.C./E.U. competition law for the same reason that decisions prohibiting a manufacturer from preventing its independent distributors or its own distributive employees from competing against each other as distributors of the manufacturer's product are legally incorrect; I also think that prohibitions of such agreements by joint-venture parents may tend to reduce rather than increase competition by deterring prospective parents of such joint ventures from creating them—by deterring such prospective parents from entering the joint-venture's market altogether or by inducing one of them to enter independently with a less-economically-efficient QV investment.

The third cluster of points relates to the EC's and the E.C./E.U. courts' handling of now-Article 101(3) issues:

(1) my admittedly-inadequately-informed impression is that the EC and the E.C./E.U. courts are overly optimistic about whether or the extent to which joint ventures generate economic efficiencies; this optimism is particularly pronounced for R&D joint ventures, but it is also evident when the joint venture in question is a production joint venture (where the perceived economic efficiency often relates to the speed with which the new product will be designed and produced) and is also present when the joint venture is a buying joint venture (where the EC and the E.C./E.U. courts do not seem to realize that the cost-savings that joint buyers can secure exclusively because their collaboration increases their buyer power do not reflect any increase in the economic efficiency of their buying activities);

(2) the EC and the E.C./E.U. courts assume without discussion that any economic-efficiency gains that R&D collaboration generates by enabling the collaborators to reduce the extent to which their R&D is economically-inefficiently-duplicative satisfy now-Article 101(3)'s economic-efficiency-generation requirement (that collaborative R&D that generates such gains can on that account be said to improve production or distribution or promote technical or economic progress) despite the fact that this assumption is unwarranted in cases in which the collaboration that reduces this kind of duplication also reduces the amount of R&D that is executed;
(3) on the whole, the EC and the E.C./E.U. courts have been, to my mind, overly optimistic that relevant consumers will obtain a fair share of the benefit generated by a joint venture that yields qualifying efficiencies;
(4) in my judgment, the EC and the E.C./E.U. courts also misjudge the circumstances in which relevant consumers are not likely to obtain a fair share of the resulting benefit—in particular, seem to think that the probability of such an outcome is critically affected by the joint venture's market share (though I admit that the fact that the block exemption for R&D joint ventures assigns a critical role to whether the joint venture's market share exceeds 25 % may have a different explanation [I am hampered by the EC's failure to explain the basis of this feature of its regulations]);
(5) the EC's practice of prohibiting parents of production and R&D joint ventures from entering into agreements that prevent them from competing against each other as distributors of their joint venture's output may be designed to assure that relevant consumers obtain a fair share of the resulting benefit; however, this response is far too crude to be desirable as a matter of policy; moreover, the EC has also prohibited such arrangements in cases in which the joint venture was not found to and seemed unlikely to have prevented, restricted, or distorted competition—*i.e.*, to have violated now-Article 101(1)'s test of *prima facie* illegality; in such cases, the prohibitions in question would be unauthorized as a matter of law even if they made good policy sense; and
(6) in other joint-venture cases, the EC has solicited and/or accepted decisions by parents to engage in relevant-consumer-benefitting behavior of various sorts that increase the probability that the relevant consumers in question will obtain a fair share of the resulting benefit: this practice is legally warranted.

This summary of Section 7 is unusually detailed and long. I hope it is justified by the fact that it illustrates many of this study's central themes, including (1) the inadequacy of market-oriented analyses of contrivance and predation, (2) the weak relationship between market power and market share, (3) the need to analyze the determinants of the intensity of QV-investment competition and the importance in this connection of considering the investment-positions of all potential QV investors in any area of product-space, (4) the difference between predatory and non-predatory refusals to deal, (5) the difference between legal analysis and policy analysis, and (6) the fact that both legal and policy analyses must take account of the way in which the law's addressees are likely to react to prohibitions of certain kinds of conduct in which they would otherwise engage.

The study's Conclusion has three sections. Section 1 (A) defines the economic concepts that play an important role in the tests of illegality articulated by the U.S. antitrust statutes, the antitrust articles of the E.C./E.U. Treaty, and the European Merger Control Regulation (EMCR) as written and as applied, (B) differentiates subcategories of conduct that U.S. and E.C./E.U. authorities should distinguish but have often failed to distinguish, (C) summarizes my critique of market-oriented approaches to the analysis of antitrust-law issues, and (D) blocks out the basic elements of the non-market-oriented approaches to such issues that I think are warranted.

Section 2 compares post-1950 U.S. antitrust law and pre-EMCR and post-EMCR E.C./E.U. competition law as written. It first analyzes the relationship between the tests of illegality that the two jurisdictions' antitrust laws promulgate. Most importantly, it points out that (1) the Sherman Act's test of illegality is the same as the "object branch" of now-Article 101(1)'s test of illegality and the exclusionary-abuse branch of now-Article 102's test of illegality, (2) the Clayton Act's test of *prima facie* illegality (which does not contain its organizational-economic-efficiency defense) is the same as the EMCR's "impeding effective competition" test of illegality and the "effect branch" of now-Article 101(1)'s test of *prima facie* illegality, and (3) that E.C./E.U. competition law has an "exploitative abuse of a dominant position" test of illegality that has no U.S. counterpart. It then analyzes the relationship between including the actual and alleged differences in the conduct-coverage of U.S. antitrust law and E.C./E.U. competition law as written. Most importantly, it points out (1) that U.S. antitrust law and E.C./E.U. competition law both fail to cover one type of conduct by non-dominant firms—unsuccessful attempts to form contrivance agreements—that they should cover, (2) that the conduct-coverage of U.S. antitrust law and E.C./E.U. competition law differs in four other significant ways—that retaliation-based contrivance by a non-dominant firm and individual-firm predation by a non-dominant firm are covered by U.S. law but not by E.C./E.U. law and that unsuccessful attempts by dominant firms to form contrivance-agreements and a variety of pricing techniques and buyer-unfriendly decisions by dominant firms that are covered by the exploitative-abuse branch of now-Article 101 are not covered by U.S. law, and (3) that contrary to the view of the EC, the E.C./E.U. courts, and Europen E.C./E.U. competition-law experts, mergers and acquisitions were always covered by now-Articles 101 and 102.

Section 3 analyzes the extent to which errors of interpretation and application have made U.S. antitrust law as applied diverge more or less from E.C./E.U. competition law as applied than U.S. antitrust law as written diverges from E.C./E.U. competition law as written. It makes seven points or clusters of points.

The first is:

(1) historically, U.S. and E.C./E.U. authorities have in common made the same two serious errors in applying the antitrust law they are respectively charged with implementing—*viz.*, they both assumed that the law they were supposed to implement was designed to prevent reductions in intra-brand competition as well as reductions in inter-brand competition, and they both assumed that the appropriate approach to take to analyzing the monopolizing/exclusionary

character and competitive impact of covered conduct was a market-oriented approach, and
(2) because both authorities made the same mistakes, these errors did not cause U.S. and E.C./E.U. law as applied to diverge from each other more or less than U.S. and E.C./E.U. law as written diverged from each other.

The second is that, although the U.S. authorities and E.C./E.U. authorities have both sometimes made the parimutual-handicapping mistake of allowing marginal and potential competitors to engage in organizational-proficiency-enhancing conduct while forbidding well-established firms from doing so, it is hard to know whether these errors have made the two jurisdictions' applied law diverge more than their written law diverges because it is difficult to know the frequency with which the two jurisdictions have made this error. The third is (1) that the U.S. authorities' mistaken position that, to prove a monopolization claim, the plaintiff must establish that the defendant had market power before engaging in the allegedly-illegal conduct has made U.S. law as applied more similar to E.C./E.U. as applied than U.S. law as written is to E.C./E.U. law as written but (2) that, if it were ever acted on, the U.S. courts' mistaken claim that conduct that reduces competition in one relevant market but not on balance in all relevant markets combined violates the Clayton Act would make U.S. antitrust law as applied diverge more from E.C./E.U. competition law as applied more than U.S. antitrust law as written diverges from E.C./E.U. competition law as written. The fourth is that, prior to the passage of the EMCR and, to a much lesser extent, even after the passage of the EMCR, the EC's and the E.C./E.U. courts' conclusion that now-Articles 101 and 102 do not cover mergers and acquisitions made E.C./E.U. competition law as applied diverge more from U.S. antitrust law as applied than E.C./E.U. competition law as written diverges from U.S. antitrust law as written. The fifth is that the fact that, over the past 20 years, U.S. authorities have abandoned market-oriented approaches to monopolization and competitive-impact analysis far more than E.C./E.U. authorities have done so has caused U.S. antitrust law as applied to diverge more from E.C./E.U. competition law as applied than U.S. antitrust law as written diverges from E.C./E.U. competition law as written. The sixth point is that the fact that, over the past 20 years, U.S. authorities have stopped declaring conduct that reduces intra-brand competition illegal to a greater extent than E.C./E.U. authorities have done also implies that, on this account over that period, U.S. antitrust law as applied has tended to diverge from E.C./E.U. competition law as applied more than U.S. antitrust law as written diverges from E.C./E.U. competition law as written. The seventh and final cluster of points is (1) that, for a variety of reasons, it is difficult to know whether the divergence of U.S. and E.C./E.U. antitrust law as applied generated by the phenomena on which the fifth and sixth points focus is larger or smaller than the convergence of U.S. and E.C./E.U. antitrust law as applied caused by the promulgation of the EMCR but (2) that if the historic pattern of E.C./E.U. authorities' (after some time-lag) making changes in their positions that resemble the changes that the U.S. authorities have made in their positions, E.C./E.U. competition law as applied will increasingly through time come to resemble U.S. antitrust law as applied.

Chapter 10
Oligopolistic Conduct

This chapter focuses on natural and contrived oligopolistic conduct in the senses in which I have defined these concepts. To my knowledge, no economist has ever offered an explicit definition of "oligopolistic conduct" or recognized my distinction between "natural" and "contrived" oligopolistic conduct. For this reason, I want to begin by setting out the way in which I define "oligopolistic conduct or interdependence," by explaining the relationship between my definitions of these concepts and the way in which economists have implicitly defined them in use (*e.g.*, when labeling certain pricing models *oligopolistic* pricing models), and by specifying my distinction between "natural" and "contrived" oligopolistic conduct.

On my definition, conduct is said to be oligopolistic or to manifest oligopolistic interdependence in two sets of circumstances:

(1) when an actor initiates a behavioral sequence by making a choice it would not have found *ex ante* profitable but for its belief that its rival's response or rivals' responses to that choice would or might be influenced by the rival's or rivals' perception that the initiating actor would or might react to the response(s) in question or
(2) when an actor that is a responder to what it perceives to be an oligopolistic initiative makes a response to the (perceived) initiative that it would not have found *ex ante* profitable but for its perception that the initiator would or might react to its response.

On my definition, then, to be "oligopolistic," conduct must involve an actual or perceived possible three-step sequence.

As I stated in Chap. 2, many pricing models that economists denominate *oligopolistic* pricing models fit this definition. However, economists also use the adjective "oligopolistic" to characterize pricing decisions that manifest a less complicated kind of interdependence—choices that actors make that are influenced by their realization that the payoffs to the various options they have will be affected by (1) decisions that one or more particular, identifiable rivals have already made or (2) the responses that one or more particular, identifiable rivals would make to the relevant actor's choice even if the rival or rivals in question did not believe that the

R.S. Markovits, *Economics and the Interpretation and Application of U.S. and E.U. Antitrust Law*, DOI 10.1007/978-3-642-24307-3_10,

assumption that the EC's and E.C./E.U. courts' extension of now Article 102 to cover the conduct not only of individual firms that are individually dominant but also of two or more firms that are "collectively dominant" is correct as a matter of law.

Six points need to be made about the legality of natural and contrived oligopolistic conduct under U.S. antitrust law. First, no type of natural oligopolistic conduct violates the Sherman Act. This conclusion follows from the fact that natural oligopolistic conduct involves no anticompetitive promises or agreements and no anticompetitive threats—indeed, involves no conduct whose perpetrator-perceived *ex ante* profitability would be critically inflated in an otherwise-Pareto-perfect economy by the perpetrator's belief that it might reduce the absolute attractiveness of the offers against which the perpetrator would compete in the future. I hasten to add that this conclusion should not be conflated with the incorrect conclusion that the Sherman Act does not prohibit oligopolistic conduct that does not involve linguistic communications. When a seller takes advantage of the fact that its rivals know that it rarely if ever overestimates its (HNOP + NOM)s, has no charitable impulses toward them, and (perhaps) has a reputation for contrivance, it may be able to communicate its contrived oligopolistic intentions to the rivals whose cooperation it needs to secure simply by charging a price that exceeds the sum of its HNOP and any NOM it can secure: if the rival will dismiss the possibility that the relevant firm has mistakenly given the rival the opportunity to profit by supplying the firm's customer(s) and realizes that the firm in question is not giving it this opportunity in a fit of generosity, the charging of the contrived oligopolistic price may communicate the pricer's anticompetitive threats and/or offers. If it does, the oligopolistic conduct in question is contrived and, with the qualification the third point I will be making here articulates, is prohibited by the Sherman Act.[370]

Second, with one possible exception to be discussed in the next paragraph, all initiating contrived oligopolistic conduct does violate the Sherman Act. With that possible exception, this conclusion follows from the fact that all initiating contrived oligopolistic conduct involves the communication of anticompetitive promises and/or threats whose perpetrator-perceived *ex ante* profitability would be critically inflated in an otherwise-Pareto-perfect economy by its perceived tendency to reduce the absolute attractiveness of the best offers against which the perpetrator will have to compete in the future.

Third, the exception: correctly interpreted, the Sherman Act probably does not cover unsuccessful attempts to enter into contrived oligopolistic agreements. As Chap. 4 explains, this conclusion reflects the facts that Section 1 of the Sherman Act does not explicitly cover unsuccessful attempts, the United States central government has never passed a general attempt statute (a statute that declares illegal any attempt to do something whose successful completion is illegal), and U.S. courts have consistently refused to read attempt provisions into statutes that do not contain them even when, from a policy perspective, the legislation should cover unsuccessful as well as successful attempts. As Chap. 4 states, I agree with my criminal-law

[370] The text will also examine the relationship between contrivance that does not involve linguistic communications and the "tacit collusion" to which courts and commentators often refer.

and constitutional-law colleagues' rejection of my antitrust-law colleagues' conclusion that the "attempt to monopolize" language of Section 2 can correctly be read to cover unsuccessful attempts to enter into contracts, combinations, and conspiracies in restraint of trade.

Fourth, although I believe that the Sherman Act prohibits firms from accepting a contrived oligopolistic offer to enter into an agreement in restraint of trade, I do not think that the Sherman Act prohibits firms from succumbing to contrived oligopolistic threats. I should add that, in individualized-pricing contexts, in which responders could succumb to contrived oligopolistic threats by allowing the initiator to obtain COMs from the initiator's own customers without taking advantage of any conjoined contrived oligopolistic offer by charging contrived oligopolistic prices to their own customers, it should not be difficult for the State or a private plaintiff to prove that a defendant had not just succumbed to an anticompetitive threat but had accepted an anticompetitive offer. This task will be far more difficult in across-the-board-pricing contexts, in which the same response simultaneously succumbs to the initiator's contrived oligopolistic threat and takes advantage of the initiator's contrived oligopolistic offer (to maintain its contrived oligopolistic price if it is not undermined).

Fifth, I think that Section 2 of the Clayton Act resembles the Sherman Act in that, like the Sherman Act, it does not prohibit natural oligopolistic exemplars of the type of conduct it otherwise does cover—*viz.*, price discrimination. This conclusion reflects the fact that (in my judgment) the Clayton Act prohibits the types of conduct it covers only if that conduct imposes a net equivalent-dollar loss on relevant buyers *by reducing the absolute attractiveness of the best offer these buyers receive from any inferior supplier* and because, when a seller is able to obtain a higher, discriminatory price because of natural oligopolistic interdependence, the relevant buyers' inferior suppliers are not deterred from undercutting its discriminatorily-high, NOM-containing price by the discriminator's discriminatory price or anything else it has done (that is covered by the Act).

Sixth, I do think that Section 2 of the Clayton Act does prohibit contrived-oligopolistic-pricing-generated price discrimination in at least one and possibly two cases. The clear case is one in which the price discrimination involves the retaliatory charging of a discriminatorily-low price to the customers of a firm that has undercut the discriminator's contrived oligopolistic price(s) to its own customer(s). The possibly-contestable case is one in which the price discrimination involves the charging of discriminatorily-high prices to buyers from whom the discriminator is contriving oligopolistic margins. The reason why the coverage of the Clayton Act may be contestable in this second class of cases is that in these cases the cause of the relevant buyers' suppliers' reducing the absolute attractiveness of the relevant offers they (the suppliers) made was not, in general, the price discrimination but the communication of the anticompetitive offers and/or threats that made the price discrimination feasible and profitable (would be the price discrimination only in the unusual case in which the anticompetitive offer and/or threat in question was communicated by the act of charging the price in question, which I am assuming happened to be discriminatory).

I turn now to the legality of natural and contrived oligopolistic conduct under correctly-interpreted and correctly-applied E.C./E.U. competition law. I want to make four points about the E.C./E.U. competition-law legality of natural oligopolistic conduct. First, because no type of natural oligopolistic conduct involves any agreement between undertakings and natural oligopolistic conduct virtually never involves any decision by an association of undertakings, it will be covered by now-Article 101 only if it can be characterized as a concerted practice. Second, as I indicated in Subsection 2A(1)(A) of Chapter 4, because natural oligopolistic conduct of all types involves consciously-coordinated behavior that is in the individual interests of its separate protagonists, it can properly be characterized as a "concerted practice" "between undertakings" and therefore is covered by what is now-Article 101 of the 2009 Treaty of Lisbon. Third, natural oligopolistic conduct does not violate the exclusionary-abuse branch of now-Article 102's test of illegality even if one or more of the perpetrators of the relevant natural oligopolistic conduct occupied an individual or collective dominant position because such conduct is not exclusionary. Fourth, the natural oligopolistic conduct of a firm that is individually dominant or a member of a collectively-dominant set of rivals may cause that firm to violate the exploitive-abuse branch of now-Article 102's test of illegality—*viz.*, will do so if it results in the relevant buyer's securing a less than fair share of the gains its transactions with the seller yield the two of them "combined."

I now want to make four points about the legality of contrived oligopolistic conduct under E.C./E.U. competition law. First, contrived oligopolistic conduct that involves only anticompetitive threats does not violate now-Article 101 because it does not involve an agreement between undertakings, a trade-association decision, or a concerted practice: this point applies to making a contrived oligopolistic threat as well as to succumbing to such a threat. Second, for the same reason, unsuccessful attempts to enter into a contrived oligopolistic agreement would not violate now-Article 101 unless E.C./E.U. written law contains a general attempt-provision or the EC or E.C./E.U. courts are authorized to and actually have promulgated a general attempt-provision or an attempt-provision that applies to all conduct covered by E.C./E.U. competition law. Admittedly, if the attempt to contrive an OM was unsuccessful because the responder initially accepted an anticompetitive offer by the initiator but then welched on its promise of cooperation, both the offer and its acceptance would violate now-Article 101 since the proper characterization of the relevant conduct would be that the parties formed an agreement that one of them subsequently breached. Third, the making of a contrived oligopolistic offer, the acceptance of a contrived oligopolistic offer, and the making of a contrived oligopolistic threat all violate the exclusionary-abuse branch of now-Article 102's test of illegality when the actor in question is either individually dominant or a member of a set of collectively-dominant rivals, but succumbing to a contrived oligopolistic threat does not violate the exclusionary-abuse branch of now-Article 102's test of illegality even when the undertaking that succumbs is individually dominant or a member of a collectively-dominant set of rivals. Fourth, an individually-or-collectively-dominant firm's participation in a natural-oligopolistic-behavior sequence will violate the exploitative-abuse branch of now-Article 102's test of illegality only if it reduces the participant's customer(s)' share of the joint gain their transactions yield them and the participant "combined" below the percentage that is "fair."

2. The Determinants of the Feasibility of Natural Oligopolistic Pricing and the Profitability of Contrived Oligopolistic Pricing

This section is included for five reasons:

(1) an understanding of the determinants of the feasibility of natural oligopolistic pricing is relevant to the determination of whether one or more defendants violated what is now Article 101 of the 2009 Treaty of Lisbon by engaging in a concerted practice that restricted competition;
(2) the determinants of the feasibility of a firm's obtaining an oligopolistic margin naturally and of the size of the one it can obtain naturally are relevant to the determination of the highest price a firm will find profitable to charge if it is not engaging in profitable contrivance as well as of the lowest legitimate price a firm will find profitable to charge (if it is not engaging in profitable predation) and hence to any approach that attempts to determine the contrived-oligopolistic or predatory character of a price "directly" by comparing the seller's actual price with its highest non-contrived-oligopolistic price or lowest non-predatory price;
(3) the determinants of the profitability of contrived oligopolistic pricing bear on the nature of the "structural" evidence that is relevant to the analysis of whether one or more defendants have engaged in contrived oligopolistic pricing—*i.e.*, evidence that relates to whether, if it were not illegal, contrived oligopolistic pricing would be profitable for the defendant(s);
(4) the determinants of both the feasibility of natural oligopolistic pricing and the profitability of contrived oligopolistic pricing are relevant to the approach one should take to predicting the competitive impact of various types of mergers and joint ventures; and
(5) both sets of determinants in question are relevant to the approach one should take to analyzing the economic efficiency and overall desirability of prohibiting various types of mergers and joint ventures as well as a wide variety of other kinds of business conduct.

A. The Determinants of the Feasibility of Natural Oligopolistic Pricing and of the Size of the NOM a Seller Can Secure

(1) In Individualized-Pricing Contexts

For an individualized pricer to be able to obtain an oligopolistic margin naturally from a buyer the firm is privately-best-placed to supply, it must be both possible and inherently profitable for the firm to beat any underbid a rival makes in response to an initial offer that exceeds its HNOP to the buyer in question. At the most abstract level, three categories of factors will determine whether this condition is fulfilled:

(1) factors that affect the willingness of the relevant buyer to give its best-placed supplier an opportunity to beat any superior offer that buyer received from an inferior supplier,
(2) factors that affect the extra costs the best-placed firm would have to incur to reduce its initial price sufficiently for its new offer to be superior to the inferior supplier's initially-superior bid (extra relative to the cost the best-placed firm would have had to incur to make the revised offer initially), and
(3) factors that affect the profits the best-placed firm could have realized initially by supplying the relevant buyer on the terms its revised offer contained

I focus first on the determinants of the probability that the buyer concerned will give an underbid best-placed supplier a chance to rebid. Obviously, unless time is of the essence, *ceteris paribus*, any buyer will find it profitable to give its best-placed supplier a chance to rebid since doing so affords the buyer the opportunity to secure an offer from that supplier that is more attractive than the undercutting offer it received from its inferior supplier and to put pressure on its inferior suppliers to beat its best-placed supplier's initial offer by a sufficiently-large amount to make it inherently unprofitable for the buyer's best-placed supplier to beat their original underbids. However, the relevant *ceteris* are not *paribus*—*i.e.*, other offsetting considerations also come into play. Repeat-player buyers will hesitate to give their best-placed supplier the opportunity to rebid because giving it that opportunity will encourage it to try to obtain oligopolistic margins from them in the future (by reducing the cost of being underbid) and will discourage their inferior suppliers from underbidding their best-placed supplier's oligopolistic prices in the future (given the costliness of the relevant bids). Although I have nothing but armchair empiricism to support this view, I suspect that repeat-player buyers in ARDEPPSes whose sellers are well informed about the relevant buyer-conduct will often find it profitable not to allow a best-placed supplier to rebid when its oligopolistic price has been undercut by an inferior. This claim implies that natural oligopolistic pricing is more likely to be feasible the smaller the extent to which the relevant buyers are repeat-purchasers and the more informed best-placed and inferior suppliers are about the relevant buyer's policies on rebids.

The second set of determinants of the probability that a seller that engages in individualized pricing will be able to obtain an OM naturally from a buyer it is best-placed to supply relates to the profits the seller would have been able to realize at the lower price at which it could beat an inferior rival's undercutting bid had it charged that lower price initially. The members of this set of determinants are its OCA = MCA + BPA + CCA and the amount by which its closest rival's undercutting offer was less attractive to the buyer in question than the best-placed seller's HNOP-containing bid would have them.

The third set of determinants relates to the extra costs the seller would have to incur to change its initially-announced price. In an individualized-pricing context, only three such types of costs are likely to be important: (1) the buyer-expectation-related costs that will arise to the extent that buyers that learn of a seller's rebid will expect it to reduce its initial price to them in the future if they do not receive a superior offer from an inferior supplier (the price-reductions it finds profitable to make on this account or the profits it loses when it loses sales on this account because it refuses to lower its future initially-announced prices); more importantly, (2) the immediate loss the firm will sustain if the buyer in question would have patronized it at its initial price because the buyer had lied about receiving a superior offer from an inferior and the additional buyer-lie-related costs the firm will sustain subsequently if its making an underbid encourages this buyer and/or others to engage in similar ruses in the future; and possibly, (3) goodwill-related costs to the extent that some buyers resent the fact that the firm changed its initial price to others but not to them and are inclined, on this account, not to patronize the seller in the future. Obviously, the existence and size of these costs will be substantially affected by the state of information in the ARDEPPS in question.

(2) In Across-the-Board-Pricing Contexts

The determinants of the feasibility of natural oligopolistic pricing in across-the-board-pricing contexts differ in five respects from their individualized-pricing counterparts. First, in the across-the-board-pricing context, the counterpart to the profits an individualized pricer could have made at the reduced price it would have to charge to beat its undercutting inferior's superior offer to an individual buyer had it charged that buyer that reduced price initially is the profits the initiator would have realized on all its sales had it set its across-the-board price initially at the lower level to which it is non-strategically most profitable for it to reduce its price once its initial price has been undermined. Second, the mechanical cost of changing an initially-announced price is far larger in across-the-board-pricing situations than in individualized-pricing situations. This conclusion reflects the fact that, unlike individualized prices, across-the-board prices are often advertised, tagged on products, marked on shelves, and entered into computers. Third and relatedly, because (unlike a group of individualized-pricing rivals) a group of across-the-board-pricing rivals may be able to put themselves in a position to practice oligopolistic pricing naturally if one of them makes a premature price announcement (a price announcement before any buyer needs to know the price the seller will charge) and it and the others proceed to increase the cost they will individually have to incur to change their initially-announced prices by advertising those prices, tagging their products with those prices, placing those prices on their shelves, entering those prices into their computers, and inducing their independent distributors to take similar action, the feasibility of an across-the-board pricer's engaging in natural oligopolistic pricing depends *inter alia* on the existence of a prominent seller whose own "premature" price announcement and "locking-in" behavior will trigger similar announcements and behavior by others. Fourth, to the extent that not only the initial prices but also price-changes are more public in across-the-board-pricing contexts, the buyer-expectation-related cost of changing an initial across-the-board price is likely to be larger than its counterpart for changing individualized prices. Fifth and finally, because across-the-board prices are public, buyer-lie-related costs and their determinants are unimportant in across-the-board-pricing contexts.

B. The Determinants of the Profitability of Contrived Oligopolistic Pricing and the Magnitude of the COM That Is Most Profitable for a Firm to Attempt to Contrive

(1) In Individualized-Pricing Contexts

To contrive an individualized oligopolistic price, a firm must (1) communicate its intention to engage in a sufficiently-large amount of reciprocation to cooperators and/or retaliation against undercutters (given the *ex ante* probability that it will reciprocate and/or retaliate—*inter alia*, that it will detect such undercutting and cooperation and identify its undercutters) to render otherwise-profitable undercutting unprofitable to rivals—and (2) make such anticompetitive threats and/or promises credible. The credibility of a seller's anticompetitive promises and/or threats at any given time *t* will depend on its reputation for fulfilling its contrived oligopolistic promises and carrying out its contrived oligopolistic threats (a function of its past behavior and the perceived profitability of its fulfilling such promises and carrying out such threats at the time in question).

To maintain or establish its credibility as a contriver, the firm will have to do five things—(1) identify cooperators, (2) reciprocate to cooperators, (3) detect undercutting when it is practiced, (4) identify undercutters, and (5) retaliate against undercutters—to a sufficient extent to render *ex ante* unprofitable undercutting that would otherwise have been *ex ante* profitable for rivals. If an individualized pricer succeeds in its attempt to contrive an oligopolistic price, the associated profits will equal the COM it secures *plus* the benefits its success and any reciprocation its efforts involved confer on it by increasing the credibility of its threats and promises *minus* the sum of the non-legal costs it incurred to make the relevant communications, to identify its cooperators, and to reciprocate to their cooperation and any law-related costs it faces as a result of its contrivance. If a contriver's attempt to contrive an individualized price is unsuccessful, the associated loss will equal the (OCA + NOM)s it could safely have secured without engaging in contrived oligopolistic pricing *plus* the non-legal cost it incurred to make the necessary communications *plus* the non-contextual-cost-related loss it had to sustain to retaliate adequately against its undercutter *plus* any law-related costs it suffered because of its attempted contrivance *plus (minus)* the contrivance-reputation-related cost (benefit) the relevant sequence of events generated. The probability that a given seller's contrived oligopolistic price will be undercut will depend partly on its reputation for carrying out its anticompetitive threats and promises, partly on whether those rivals that could profit by undercutting its offers if it could not react to such conduct believe that the prospective contriver would find it profitable to carry out its anticompetitive threats if it detected their undercutting and identified them as its undercutter, and partly on its individual rivals' perception of the probability that the potential contriver would succeed in determining that it has been undercut from a position of inferiority if it has been and would be able to identify its undercutter.

Of course, whether a firm actually attempts to contrive oligopolistic prices will be substantially affected by the "costs" it has to incur because its managers intrinsically dislike engaging in the practice or violating the law if the practice is prohibited. However, the preceding analysis suggests that a large number of other factors will influence the profitability of attempting to contrive oligopolistic prices. I will now list and explain nine sets of such factors.

The first group of determinants of the profitability of an individualized pricer's contriving oligopolistic prices relates to the reputation of the potential contriver in question and the perceived profitability of its carrying out its contrived oligopolistic promises and threats. As we have seen, the firm's reputation will be determined by its past success at contrivance and record for carrying out any related threats or promises. The perceived profitability of the firm's carrying out its threats and promises in a given situation will depend not only on the cost it must incur to do so (to be discussed below) but also on the volume of transactions on which it can take advantage of the reputational effects of its carrying out its anticompetitive threats and promises. Since a firm's relevant reputation may extend beyond the particular ARDEPPS in which its contrivance is carried out, this argument implies that the profitability of contrivance to a firm may increase not only with the frequency with which it is best-placed in the particular ARDEPPS in question but with the frequency with which it is best-placed in all the ARDEPPSes in which it operates—*i.e.*, in other geographic and product-line ARDEPPSes as well.

The second group of such factors relates to the mechanical and law-related cost of communicating anticompetitive threats and promises. Those costs will depend on three variables. The first is the amount of attention that the antitrust authorities and (to a lesser extent) potential private plaintiffs are paying to the seller or ARDEPPS in question. In this respect, of course, having a reputation for contrivance is a disadvantage, not an advantage. The second is the number of rivals to which the relevant communication must be made: the number of rivals that are second-placed or worse-than-second-placed by a smaller margin than the OM the seller in question wants to contrive (the number of rivals that would find it profitable to undercut its associated oligopolistic-price-containing bid if it could not react to such conduct). The third is the ability of the firm in question to communicate its anticompetitive intentions non-linguistically simply by charging an oligopolistic price. Obviously, such non-linguistic communications will be less expensive mechanically and will be less likely to create legal difficulties for the contriver as well. The ability of a seller to communicate its anticompetitive intentions non-linguistically simply by charging a contrived oligopolistic price will depend on its reputation for contrivance, its reputation for accurately calculating its (HNOP + NOM)s, and the ability of its rivals to realize that they are not best-placed to supply the customer(s) in question: if a firm's rivals realize that it is best-placed to obtain a particular buyer's patronage and that it is unlikely to have overestimated its HNOP + NOM, they will conclude that its charging the buyer in question a price that would enable them to obtain the buyer's patronage on profitable terms if it could not react to their doing so must be intended to communicate its intention to react strategically to their undercutting and/or cooperation.

The third set of determinants of an individualized-price setter's contriving oligopolistic prices contains the factors that affect the cost it must incur to identify those rivals that have cooperated and to which it must reciprocate—the non-undercutting rivals that were second-placed or worse-than-second-placed by a margin that was smaller than the contrived OM it was trying to obtain from the buyer in question. This set of determinants includes (1) the cost to the prospective contriver of determining the difference between the marginal or incremental cost it must incur to supply the buyers it is best-placed to serve and the marginal or incremental cost its various rivals must incur to do so (where the relevant costs include delivery costs, which are a function *inter alia* of geographic proximity), (2) the cost it must incur to determine the strength of its BPAs for its product over it various rivals' products, and (3) the cost it must incur to determine its contextual-marginal-cost advantages over its various rivals in their relations with the buyers in question (*inter alia*, the extent to which its HNOP to the buyer in question would discriminate in its favor or against it, the extent to which its various rivals' respective matching offers to this buyer would contain prices that discriminated in its favor [the extent to which these various rivals' average prices to their own customers exceeded their respective marginal costs]).

The fourth set of determinants of the profitability of contriving individualized oligopolistic prices relates to the amount of benefits the potential contriver can confer on its potential undercutters by reciprocating to a rival's cooperation by abstaining from undercutting the rival when the rival attempts to contain a contrived OM from a buyer the rival is best-placed to supply. Such reciprocation is far cheaper than retaliation and *a fortiori* than paying monetary bribes to competitors. In part, this conclusion reflects the fact that the probability that reciprocation will be detected and cause legal problems is lower than the probability that retaliation will cause such problems, but, primarily, it reflects the fact that the only non-law-related cost of reciprocating is the cost of foregoing the opportunity to make and then welch on a promise of reciprocation—a cost that is probably low, given the fact that one act of welching will probably eliminate opportunities to welch again in the future. In any event, the amount of benefits a seller X1 can confer on a potential undercutter X2 (and hence the profitability of X1's contriving oligopolistic prices) will increase with the frequency with which X1 is X2's closest competitor and the amount by which X1 is better-placed than X2's next-closest competitor when X1 is X2's closest competitor.

The fifth set of determinants of the profitability of charging contrived individualized oligopolistic prices relates to the cost and feasibility of detecting undercutting. Some explanation is necessary.[371] In general, a seller cannot assume that all customers it has failed to retain have been stolen by undercutting competitive inferiors. Buyers that have not been stolen in this sense may shift their patronage if (1) they are dissatisfied with their original supplier's product, (2) their

[371] The textual explanation that follows borrows heavily from George Stigler, *A Theory of Oligopoly*, 72 J. POL. ECON. 44 (1964).

location, needs, or tastes have changed, (3) the producer of a newly-offered product-variant has become their best-placed supplier, or (4) they have adopted a purchasing strategy of switching their suppliers.[372] Moreover, when prices are set on an individualized basis, sellers will be unable to determine whether their defecting customers have been stolen by examining published prices, for actual (as opposed to list) individualized prices almost certainly will not be made public. In such circumstances, sellers also will be unable to rely on direct inquiries to the buyers in question to determine whether their customers have been stolen by inferiors. Buyers may misreport receiving discounts in the hope of obtaining concessions from the inquiring supplier or may deny receiving discounts that were in fact granted to protect their new supplier and avoid a "big-mouth" reputation that would militate against their obtaining similar discounts in the future. As a consequence, sellers that charge individualized prices often will have to infer whether they have in fact been undercut by a competitive inferior from circumstantial evidence.

One of the most important sources of such evidence is the seller's own repeat-sales records. Based on past experience, each seller will establish a probability-distribution estimate of the percentage of its customers that it would expect to lose even if no firm undercut it from an inferior position. The seller will then compare its actual lost sales with such expected lost sales to determine the probability that it has been undercut by one or more worse-placed competitors. Since the number of customers the seller will lose spontaneously does not depend on whether undercutting from a position of inferiority takes place, a seller's ability to detect any given percentage of undercutting will increase with its certainty about the percentage of its customers it would lose if no-one undercut it from a position of inferiority. For example, at one extreme, if the seller correctly assumes that it will lose exactly 20 % of its customers if no-one undercuts it from an inferior competitive position, it will be able to detect even one act of undercutting from an inferior position from circumstantial evidence relating to its repeat sales—*viz.*, from information that it lost 20 % plus one sales. If, at the other extreme, the seller has no information about the percentage of its customers it would lose if no-one undercut it from a position of competitive inferiority either because historically that percentage varied widely for no discernible reason or because current conditions seem likely to differ from past conditions in important ways that the seller cannot measure, its repeat-sales-record information will be useless for this purpose. Accordingly, a seller's ability to detect secret price-cutting (or, more generally, the cost it has to incur to detect any given percentage of such undercutting and hence the profitability of its attempting to contrive individualized oligopolistic prices) will increase with those factors that tend to increase its certainty about its probable repeat-sales percentage: namely, the stability through time of its past repeat-sales

[372] Firms may adopt such a purchasing strategy either to increase their bargaining power or to encourage their inferior suppliers to beat their best-placed suppliers' contrived oligopolistic offers by making it more difficult for their best-placed suppliers to determine that they have been undercut by a competitive inferior.

percentages (which is a function *inter alia* of the number of buyers it supplies[373]), the relevance of its past experience to its present situation, and its ability to identify, measure, and calculate the significance of differences between its current situation and its past situations.[374] I should add that, since sellers can also supplement this kind of circumstantial evidence with similar data on the percentages of established customers of other sellers and new buyers in the ARDEPPS to which they made sales in the period in question relative to the percentages of such buyers they captured in the past, the preceding analysis implies that the profitability of an individualized pricer's contriving oligopolistic prices will also increase with the number of buyers in these two categories, the stability of the seller's repeat-sales percentages to them through time, and the extent to which the current situation is similar to the past or differs from the past in relevant ways that the firm knows or can determine cheaply and accurately.

The sixth set of determinants of the profitability of contrived oligopolistic pricing to an individualized pricer relates to the cost it has to incur to identify its actual undercutter with any degree of accuracy. A seller that realizes that it has been undercut may try to identify its actual undercutter in a number of ways. I should say at the outset that, in practice, a contriver's effort to identify the firm that has undercut it from a position of inferiority is likely to be conjoined with an effort to confirm that its former customers' new supplier was in fact worse-than-best-placed to supply them. A seller that believes it has been undercut by a competitive inferior may find it cost-effective to begin its search for its suspected undercutter by identifying the firms that—absent any change in competitive positions—would have been able to profit by beating its contrived oligopolistic price if it could not react to such a response—its second-placed rival for the buyers it believes it is best-placed to supply and those rivals that are worse-than-second-placed to secure those buyers' patronage by less than the OM it attempted to contrive. Although the probability that a rival had become the best-placed supplier of any former customer of the seller through a spontaneous change in the relevant buyer's "preferences" (or a change in the buyer's loading-dock facilities that

[373] Large numbers promote certainty through the law of large numbers and the central limit theorem.

[374] Recall that the best-placed seller is, by definition, a seller that could make profits by supplying a particular buyer on terms contained in an offer that no rivals can match or better without charging a price below the rival's marginal costs. Of course, rather than incurring such losses, X1 may prefer to deprive X2 of those customers for which X1 is worse-than-second-placed by bribing these buyers to patronize X2's closest rival or by bribing X2's closest rival to undercut X2. If X1 ignored the legal cost of such behavior, the necessary bribe (one cent) would be smaller than the losses X1 would have to sustain to capture these customers for itself. However, this approach has three disadvantages that I think would make it unattractive. First, since the bribe-recipients in question would have to run certain legal risks to accept the bribe, a bribe of more than one cent would, in practice, be necessary. Second, since the bribe would be more obviously illegal than the charging of a sub-marginal-cost price, this approach would involve more legal costs for X1 as well. Third, and finally, since this approach would also create the possibility that the relevant buyer (seller) would accept the bribe and then patronize X2 (not cut its price to X2's customers), it would require the relevant actor to incur certain policing costs as well. Accordingly, in the text that follows, I will assume that a retaliator always will find it cheaper to steal customers for itself than to bribe its undercutting rival's customers not to patronize the undercutter or its target's undercutting rival's rivals to undercut X1's target.

reduced the rival's delivery costs by more than it reduced the relevant seller's) will be directly related to its original supplier-rank (since the rival's original OCD will be inversely related to its original rank, *ceteris paribus*), the fact that second-placed suppliers were often originally at a substantial competitive disadvantage implies that information on the identity of the seller's closest rivals will help it identify rivals that had undercut it from a position of inferiority. Alternatively, a seller may try to identify the rival(s) that has (have) undercut it from a position of inferiority by identifying those of its rivals that secured the patronage of a significantly-higher percentage of its customers that the rivals in question were originally at a small disadvantage to supply than did its other rivals. For this purpose, the seller will have to identify the new suppliers of its former customers by observing deliveries, inspecting former-customer inventories, or examining the products its former customers offer for sale. When such approaches are infeasible or prohibitively expensive, however, the seller may elect to infer those facts from general information about the overall sales of its rivals. Of course, the fact that a particular rival is supplying a higher percentage of the seller's former customers than its previous competitive-position array in relation to the seller's original customers would lead one to expect is perfectly compatible with its not having beaten the seller's offers from a position of competitive inferiority. There may have been a general shift in preferences toward the relevant rival's product or a shift in the preferences of the seller's customers toward the rival's product, the relevant buyers may have changed their loading docks or operating procedures in a way that favored the rival in question, or the rival may have altered its basic product, delivery equipment, or operating procedures in one or more ways that improved its competitive position in relation to the seller's former customers. To determine whether the rival in question has taken the seller's former customers from a position of competitive inferiority, the seller will have to check all of these possibilities out. The seller will be able to discover some of this information by analyzing the relevant rival's or rivals' products to see if they have changed in a way that accounts for their success with its customers and by investigating any change in these rivals' delivery systems or the relevant buyers' loading docks or operating procedures (*e.g.*, the time by which they require delivery) to see whether it accounts for their success. I should add, however, that the seller will frequently not be able to rely on its former customers' accounts of why they shifted to the supplier under suspicion: these buyers will have a stake in protecting suppliers that have given them better deals from a position of inferiority against their best-placed supplier's retaliation. In any event, the profitability of contrived oligopolistic pricing to a given seller will be inversely related to the cost the seller must incur to obtain information of these kinds.

The seventh set of determinants of the profitability of an individualized pricer's contriving oligopolistic prices contains the factors that control the non-contextual losses that retaliation will impose on the retaliator and the contextual costs of retaliation. I will focus first on the determinants of the non-contextual losses that X1 will have to incur to retaliate sufficiently against an undercutter X2 to render undercutting *ex ante* unprofitable for X2 and its counterparts in the future—*i.e.*, the sum of the amounts by which the retaliatory prices X1 would have to charge to achieve this goal would fall below X1's marginal or incremental costs on the transactions in question. Before proceeding to delineate these determinants, it will be helpful to articulate the protocol a contriver X1 would find most-cost-effective to follow if it had to incur no cost to execute the relevant analysis perfectly:

(1) calculate the amount of harm it must inflict on X2 through price retaliation to achieve the relevant goal;
(2) identify X2's individual customers and rank them by the ratio of (the harm it [X1] could inflict on X2 by stealing each such buyer by offering it an inherently-unprofitable low price) to (the [non-contextual] inherent loss X1 would have to sustain to do so); and
(3) go down the list, offering the buyers in question the required retaliatory prices until the total harm inflicted equals the requisite sum.

This protocol implies that the determinants of the non-contextual losses X1 will have to incur to inflict the requisite amount of harm on an undercutter X2 can be placed in two categories:

(1) those that determine the harm-inflicted to loss-incurred ratio for X1's stealing any given customer of X2 and, derivatively, those that affect the non-contextual losses X1 will have to incur to inflict various amounts of harm on X2 by using retaliatory price-cuts to steal two or more of X2's customers and
(2) those that determine the total amount of harm X1 must inflict on X2 to deter X2 and X2's future counterparts from undercutting X1 in the future.

I start with the first set of determinants just listed. For simplicity, I will assume that the target of the retaliation X2 cannot obtain an NOM from the relevant buyer and is not trying to secure a COM from that buyer and that the buyer will purchase one unit of X2's product if offered X2's HNOP price for it or any lower price X2 offers in reaction to X1's conduct or one unit of X1's product if X1 obtains its patronage by beating X2's HNOP-containing offer for X2's product. Unless otherwise specified, I will also assume that if X1 beats X2's HNOP-containing offer to the buyer in question, X1 will make the sale to the relevant buyer on the terms X1 offers. On these assumptions, the harm that a retaliator X1 will be able to impose on its target X2 by stealing any customer of X2 by offering that buyer a retaliatory price-cut equals the amount by which X2's HNOP for that buyer exceeds the marginal costs X2 would have had to incur to supply that buyer. The loss X1 will have to incur to steal any customer of X2 by offering it a retaliatory price will depend on whether X1 is X2's closest rival for the relevant buyer's patronage and, if not, the amount by which X1 is worse-than-second-placed to obtain that buyer's patronage. If, for simplicity, one assumes that X1's undercutting offer beats X2's HNOP-Containing offer by 1 cent, X1 will have to lose 1 cent to take away customers for which it is second-placed and once cent *plus* the amount by which it is worse-placed than X2's closest competitor to take away customers for which it is worse-than-second-placed. Hence, the cost to X1 of taking away any given number of customers from X2 will increase with the amount by which X1 is worse-placed than X2's closest rival for the patronage of those customers that X2 is best-placed to supply. In summary, the cost to X1 of inflicting any given amount of harm on X2 by lowering its prices sufficiently to steal X2's customers will be inversely related to (1) the size of X2's OCAs in its relations with those customers that X2 is best-placed to supply and X1 is, or is close to being, second-placed to supply (which determines the number of customers X1 must steal to do X2 any given amount of harm) and (2) (roughly speaking[375]) the frequency with which X1 is, or is close to being, X2's closest competitor (which determines the average cost to X1 of stealing any given number of X2's customers).

I turn next to the determinants of the amount of harm X1 will have to inflict on X2 to deter X2 and its counterparts from undercutting X1 from a position of competitive inferiority in the future. At least three determinants of this necessary-harm figure merit consideration.

The first is the amount of profits X2 would make by undercutting X1 if X1 did not react to X2's undercutting responses. If I assume, for simplicity, that no-one else would steal the customers of X1 that X2 would steal if X2 did not steal them, that X2 must always beat X1's offer (as opposed to X1's price) to any buyer that X1 was best-placed to supply by 1 cent to steal that buyer, that X2 would always make the sale to any of X1's customers to which X2 made a superior offer on the terms of its initial superior offer, and that each relevant buyer would purchase one unit of X1's product if X1 were not undercut and one unit of X2's product if X2 undercut X1, that sum would equal (1) (the number of X1's customers that X2 is second-placed to supply from which X1 is seeking to contrive an oligopolistic margin) *times* (the average COM X1 is seeking to secure from those buyers *minus* 1 cent) *plus* (2) (the number of X1's customers that X2 is worse-than-second-placed to supply in relation to which the COM that X1 is seeking to obtain exceeds the amount by which X2 is worse-than-second-placed) *times* (the difference between the average COM X1 is trying to obtain from these buyers and the sum of 1 cent *plus* the average amount by which X2 is worse-than-second-placed to obtain the patronage of the buyers in question).[376]

The second determinant of the amount of harm the contriver X1 must inflict on an undercutting X2 is the amount of benefits X1 promised to confer on X2 and would have conferred on X2 by reciprocating had X2 cooperated. The third determinant of the amount of harm X1 would have to inflict on an undercutting X2 through retaliation is the probability that in the future X1 will be able to determine that it has been undercut by an inferior and to identify its undercutter and the extent to which X2 and its future counterparts are risk-averse: the more likely X1's future

---

[375] I write "roughly speaking" because the conclusion that X1 will minimize the cost of inflicting any amount of harm on X2 by stealing those of X2's customers for which the relevant harm-inflicted to loss-incurred ratio is highest implies that, if X2 enjoys an unusually-large OCA in its relations with a particular buyer, X1 may find it cost-effective to steal this customer despite the fact that it is significantly worse-placed than the buyer's second-placed supplier—*i.e.*, despite the fact that it is not "close to being" this buyer's second-placed supplier.

[376] The combination of this paragraph and its predecessor imply that, *ceteris paribus*, the harm-inflicted to loss-incurred ratio for the total amount of harm X1 must inflict on X2 by stealing X2's customers by charging them retaliatory prices to deter X2 and its counterparts from undercutting X1's future contrived oligopolistic prices will be higher the greater the ratio of (the number of buyers X2 is best-placed to supply that X1 is second-placed or close-to-second-placed to supply) to (the number of buyers X1 is best-placed to supply that X2 is second-placed or close-to-second-placed to supply).

prospective undercutters are to escape retaliation, the greater the loss they will have to expect X1 to impose on them if they are identified as its undercutters for them to be deterred, and hence the greater the harm X1 must inflict on any current undercutter it identifies to deter future undercutting.[377] The facts that will affect X2's estimate of its ability to escape detection were considered during the discussion of the cost to X1 of detecting undercutting and identifying its undercutter.

In addition to non-contextual losses, X1 will have to incur certain contextual costs to engage in retaliation: the law-related costs associated with the possibility that the State might prosecute or private plaintiffs might sue X1 for attempting to contrive an oligopolistic margin, any loss X1 sustains because its retaliatory price-cuts alienate some if its other customers because they are associated with its charging the target's customers lower prices than it charged its own, any losses X1 sustains because its retaliation encourages X1's customers to intensify their bargaining by at least appearing to put the lie to X1's cost-claims or to imply that it can be bargained down by buyers they misperceive to be in a similar position to theirs, and any losses X1 sustains because some of X2's customers to which X1 makes retaliatory offers buy X1's product and then resell it to buyers that X1 is best-placed to supply for a lower price than X1 is offering them. These possibilities imply that the profitability of the relevant individual pricer's contriving oligopolistic prices will depend, *inter alia*, on

(1) the reputation that X1 and perhaps its rivals have for contriving oligopolistic margins (which will affect the likelihood that the antitrust authorities will prosecute and private plaintiffs will sue X1 and the likelihood that triers-of-fact will find against X1),
(2) the availability of accounting data or the feasibility of engineering studies that would enable the State or a private plaintiff to establish X1's marginal or incremental costs (and hence the inherent unprofitability of its prices to those of X2's customers to which it offered retaliatory prices),
(3) the likelihood that X1's customers will discover that X1 has offered some of X2's customers lower prices than X1 offered them,
(4) the role that goodwill plays in the relevant area of product-space (in particular, the extent to which X1's customers place a positive value on giving X1 profits),
(5) the extent to which X1 has made statements about its costs to other buyers that are or appear to be inconsistent with the retaliatory prices it is charging some of X2's customers,
(6) the ability of X1's customers to perceive the difference between their position vis-à-vis X1 and the position of X2's target customers vis-à-vis X1 (without having the ability or inclination to relate relevant parts of this information to the State or a private plaintiff),

---

[377] Obviously, this implies that the most-cost-effective strategy for a contriver to employ is to vary its "expenditures" on detection of undercutting and identification of undercutters, on retaliation, and on reciprocation until it secures the same deterrent effect from the last penny it spends on each of these activities.

(7) the ability of those of X2's customers to which X1 offered low, retaliatory prices to identify X1's customers (to which X1 is charging a higher price),
(8) the ability of X1's customers to identify those of X2's customers to which X1 made sales at retaliatory, discriminatorily-low prices, and
(9) the perishability of the product in question and non-perishability-related costs of transporting the good in question from those of X2's customers to which X1 sold it at discriminatorily-low prices to relevant potential patrons of X1.

The eighth set of relevant determinants relates to the histories of a potential contriver's potential undercutters. Obviously, the fact that a potential contriver's potential undercutter has a reputation for succumbing to threats or for making good on reciprocatory promises (in cases in which the potential undercutter has promised to undercut the potential contriver's price to the buyer in question) will increase the *ex ante* profitability of the relevant act of contrivance. So, too, would the fact that the potential contriver's potential undercutter was in a position to profit substantially by developing a reputation for entering into and performing its duties under anticompetitive, contrived-oligopolistic-pricing contracts or the fact that the potential undercutter had itself practiced illegal oligopolistic pricing in the ARDEPPS in question since that fact would make it hesitate to initiate an undercutting-retaliation sequence that would call the authorities' attention to pricing-activities in general in the ARDEPPS.

The ninth and final set of determinants of the profitability of an individualized pricer's contriving an oligopolistic price contains the determinants of the safe profits it has to put at risk to do so—the determinants of its OCAs and NOMs. In this context, it is important to distinguish the (OCA + NOM) the seller enjoys in its relations with the particular buyer in question and the average (OCA + NOM) it enjoys in its relations with the other buyers it is best-placed to supply. It seems clear to me that the profitability of attempting to contrive an OM from a particular buyer is inversely related to the (OCA + NOM) the potential contriver enjoys in its relations with that buyer: the higher the (OCA + NOM) the potential contriver enjoys in its relations with a particular buyer, the greater the safe profits the seller must put at risk to attempt to contrive an OM from that buyer. However, I am not at all sure how the seller's average (OCA + NOM) in its relations with the other buyers it is best-placed to supply cuts: on the one hand, if (contrary to my view) the probability that the seller would try to secure COMs of any size from those other buyers would not be affected by this average (OCA + NOM) figure, the profitability of attempting to contrive an OM from an individual buyer would tend to increase with this other-customer average-(OCA + NOM) figure since the value to the seller of increasing the credibility of its anticompetitive threats and promises by carrying out the anticompetitive threats and promises it made in relation to the individual buyer and hence the credibility and effectiveness of those threats and promises would increase with this other-customer average-(OCA + NOM) figure; on the other hand, if I am right in thinking that the percentage of a firm's customers from which it will attempt to contrive an OM will be inversely related to its average (OCA + NOM) in its relations with those buyers, the profitability of attempting to contrive an OM from an individual buyer will be inversely related to the seller's other-customer average-(OCA + NOM) figure since the value to the seller of maintaining or enhancing its reputation for making good on its anticompetitive threats and promises and hence the credibility of those threats and promises will be inversely related to this other-customer average-(OCA + NOM) figure. My suspicion is that the profitability of attempting to contrive an OM from an individual buyer will be inversely related both to the (OCA + NOM) the best-placed firm in question enjoys in its relations with that buyer and with the average (OCA + NOM) it enjoys in its relations with the other buyers it is best-placed to supply. Obviously, this conclusion implies that the profitability of an individual pricer's attempting to contrive an OM from an individual buyer will be inversely related to all those factors that tend to increase its OCA and NOM in its relations with that buyer and with the other buyers it is best-placed to supply: *inter alia*, the strength of buyer preferences among relevant products with similar marginal costs, the various barriers and disincentives that cause equilibrium QV investment in the relevant ARDEPPS to fall below the actual, competitive QV-investment level, the extent to which buyers are repeat-players and hence have an incentive to deny their best-placed supplier a chance to rebid when its initial bid is beaten, the various factors that would tend to reduce the cost the seller in question would have to incur to reduce its initially-announced price, *etc*.

I suspect that the preceding list of determinants of the profitability of an individualized pricer's contriving an oligopolistic price is far longer than most readers anticipated. It clearly could not have been developed without using the micro-economic conceptual systems Chap. 2 delineated. Admittedly, the additional complexity of my approach will be a practical virtue only if the additional factors my analysis calls attention to are worth considering in real-world contexts—for example, when deciding whether a horizontal merger in an ARDEPPS in which individualized prices are set is likely to increase the incidence of contrived oligopolistic pricing within it or when deciding (in a contrived-oligopolistic-pricing case) whether the defendant could have found contrivance profitable. Most economists would be more likely to be convinced of the usefulness of my conceptual schemes if I used them to create a formal model of the profitability of contriving individual oligopolistic prices. I think such an effort would be premature and that the list and discussion I have provided can improve the accuracy of various legally-relevant predictions. Of course, I am far from being a neutral evaluator.

(2) In Across-the-Board-Pricing Contexts

Rather than analyzing the determinants of the profitability of a seller's attempting to contrive across-the-board prices *de novo*, this subsection concentrates on the difference between these determinants and their individualized-pricing counterparts. Of the nine sets of determinants of the profitability of an individualized pricer's contriving oligopolistic prices that I distinguish, five are either the same or sufficiently similar not to require comment and two have no counterparts in the across-the-board-pricing context: the five relate to (1) the reputation of the contriver, (2) the reputation of the contriver's potential undercutters (in this case, called "potential underminers"), (3) the objective profitability of the contriver's carrying out its anticompetitive threats and promises, (4) the mechanical and law-related costs to the contriver of communicating its anticompetitive intentions to its rivals and their rivals, and (5) the private profits the contriver has to put at risk to practice contrived oligopolistic pricing. And the two relate to (1) the contriver's ability to determine that it has been undercut by an inferior and (2) the contriver's ability to identify its cooperators and underminers (a task that will be simpler in across-the-board-pricing contexts since everyone's prices will be public in such situations). The rest of this subsection will focus on the remaining two sets of determinants: (1) the benefits a contriver can confer on its cooperators by reciprocating to them must be analyzed differently in across-the-board-pricing and individualized-pricing contexts because, in across-the-board-pricing contexts, reciprocation is at least normally not a separate act (in that the oligopolistic price a seller charges its own customers is automatically charged to its rivals' customers) and (2) the cost of retaliation must be analyzed differently in across-the-board-pricing contexts because, in such contexts, price retaliation cannot be directed selectively at the underminer's customers (unless the retaliator finds it profitable to abandon its normal pricing-technique to practice retaliation).

If, in the across-the-board-pricing context, I designate the potential underminer XU, the facts that (1) the initial-price-announcer X1 has charged a primary oligopolistic price (a POP) and (2) some of X1's rivals (say, X2. . .N) have responded with prices that do not undermine X1's POP by rendering it less profitable than X1's HNOP would have been (*i.e.*, with what I call secondary oligopolistic prices or SOPs) will provide XU with considerable benefits even if it chooses to charge a SOP as well: like X1 and X2. . .N, XU will be able to piggyback on its rivals' COMs regardless of whether it undermines them. Of course, since, so to speak, X1. . .N must reciprocate in advance to XU if they want to announce and commit themselves to their own oligopolistic prices, XU may still find it inherently profitable to undermine X1. . .N's oligopolistic prices in the current pricing-round even after XU takes into account the fact that its doing so may make it inherently profitable for X1. . .N to react to its undermining response by lowering their prices in the current pricing-round, by charging less-oligopolistic or non-oligopolistic prices in future pricing-rounds, or by delaying the time at which they announce their prices in future pricing-rounds until after XU has locked itself into its price. Indeed, since this is a discussion of contrived as opposed to natural oligopolistic pricing, we must be assuming that these inherently-profitable reactions will not cost XU more than it could gain by undermining X1. . .N's prices if they could not react to such a response.

By definition, to deter XU from undermining a contrived oligopolistic price in the current pricing-round, X1. . .N must (1) promise to confer enough benefits on XU if it cooperates by charging prices they find too high to be inherently profitable in future pricing-rounds, given the risk of an undermining response, and (2) threaten to impose enough costs on XU if it undermines them through engaging in retaliation of different kinds (inherently-unprofitable price-cutting in current and/or future pricing-rounds, inherently-unprofitable advertising that targets XU's customers, inherently-unprofitable QV investments that target XU's customers, or perhaps inherently-unprofitable delays in the timing of their future price-announcements to make sure that in the future XU has committed itself to a particular price before they lock themselves into prices of their own) so that, taken together, the prospective benefits and costs make it *ex ante* unprofitable for XU to charge an undermining price that it would have found profitable if its rivals could not react strategically to its decision.

With this background, it should be possible to analyze at least some of the factors that will influence the cost of the reciprocation and retaliation that an across-the-board pricer will have to be prepared to carry out to contrive oligopolistic prices. For simplicity, I will proceed on the assumption that such a seller will find it most-cost-effective to rely on across-the-board retaliatory pricing to provide the XUs of its ARDEPPS with the necessary incentives to cooperate—that X1. . .N will not rely on individualized retaliatory pricing, reciprocation, or retaliatory advertising, QV investments, or price-announcement delays to secure cooperation.

First, the cost of the necessary retaliation will be higher (and the profitability of contriving oligopolistic prices will be lower) the greater the profits each relevant XU would realize from charging an undermining price, absent retaliation. Those profits will increase with (1) the ability of the XUs in question to expand their sales without incurring higher marginal costs (a function of their marginal-cost curve [their capacity] and their existing inventory), (2) the ratios of the number of extra sales the XUs would make if they undermined X1. . .N's prices with prices different amounts below their lowest SOP to the number of sales they would have made had they charged their lowest SOP (roughly speaking, the ratios of the number of times they had various low BCDs to the number of times they were best-placed), and (3) the various mechanical, goodwill-related, buyer-expectation-creation-related, and (undeserved[378]) law-related costs XU will have to incur to undermine X1. . .N's contrived oligopolistic prices.

Second, and obviously, the cost of the necessary retaliation will depend on the factors that determine the cost to the individual retaliator of making the price-cuts that, in conjunction with the price-cuts of others that they induce, inflict harm on the underminer that exceed the *extra* profits the underminer's price would have yielded it in their absence (above the difference between the profits it would have earned had it responded with a SOP and the profits its undermining price would yield it if X1. . .N did not react to that price). Unfortunately, these factors are complex to analyze in an across-the-board-pricing situation.

I will begin with four preliminary observations. First, to retaliate effectively, an across-the-board pricer X1 whose non-undermining rivals will not reduce their prices in reaction to XU's undermining offer and its own retaliation will have to reduce its announced price sufficiently to make its undermining rival realize a net loss from any failure to cooperate. Second, in most cases, a potential retaliator in that position will find that it cannot retaliate sufficiently simply by reducing its price until its (P–MC) gap equals its undermining rival's (P–MC) gap. Although such a price-reduction will prevent this rival from taking any sales from the retaliator in the future, it will not cancel out the profits the underminer realized on already-completed "thefts" from the retaliator or on the sales XU did and will continue to take from the retaliator's "innocent" rivals (though such profits will be partially offset by the profits the underminer sacrificed by not extracting the higher SOP it could have obtained from its own customers). Third, to the extent that the initial retaliator's price-reduction induces other rivals to lower their prices (to join in retaliation or even just to lower their

378 "Undeserved" because XU's undermining prices are not illegal.

prices to the lower levels that will be inherently profitable, given the XU's undercutting and X1's retaliation), the retaliator will have to lower its price less than would otherwise be required. Obviously, however, the advantages X1 achieves on this account will be offset by the fact that *X*2. . .N's reactions will hurt X1 in other ways (by causing X1 to lose some customers of its own and perhaps by keeping X1 from taking some of X2. . .N's customers). Fourth, the benefits that retaliation will generate for the retaliator are the same in across-the-board-pricing as in individualized-pricing situations. Retaliation will benefit the retaliator by reducing the probability that any attempt it makes to contrive an OM in the future will elicit an undermining response. By so doing, retaliation will (1) save X1 whatever profits it would have lost as a result of the deterred undermining of the OMs it otherwise would have tried to contrive and perhaps (2) enable X1 to profit by increasing the frequency with which it attempts to contrive OMs and the magnitude of the OMs it attempts to contrive. As in the individualized-pricing context, this suggests that the profitability of contrived oligopolistic pricing to an across-the-board pricer will increase with the frequency with which it can practice such pricing in all the ARDEPPSes in which it is active.

This analysis suggests the advisability of distinguishing five different factors that will influence the net cost a primary oligopolistic pricer will have to incur to impose a given necessary loss on an underminer through across-the-board price retaliation: (1) the mechanical, goodwill-related, buyer-expectation-creation-related, and contextual legal cost such a retaliator will have to incur to change its original price if all other non-underminers maintain their original prices, (2) the losses (gains) such an across-the-board retaliator would incur (realize) if its retaliation would not affect anyone else's short-run price because (A) the profits it would lose at its retaliatory price on those sales it would have made at its original higher price *exceed* (B) the conventional book profits it would realize on the additional sales it would make at its lower, retaliatory price, (3) the net gains the initial retaliator X1 achieves because XU's undermining price and its retaliation against XU induce X1's "innocent" rivals X2. . .N to adjust their prices to a lower, inherently-profitable level and/or to retaliate against XU and/or X1, (4) the various contextual legal costs X2. . .N's price-adjustments impose on X1, and (5) the gains that X1 achieves when it or someone else coordinates its and X2. . .N's price-responses to XU in their mutual interest.

I will not try to get behind these five sets of factors except to explore two public-good-type problems that can prevent across-the-board pricers from being able to contrive oligopolistic margins profitably. For this purpose, I will place the members of any set of across-the-board-pricing rivals into two groups—the prospective contrivers (X1. . .N), which are also the potential retaliators, and the prospective underminers (XU1. . .M), which are also the potential targets of retaliation. Roughly speaking, sellers that are more often best-placed than second-placed or close-to-second-placed are more likely to be contrivers, and sellers that are more often second-placed or close-to-second-placed than best-placed are more likely to be potential underminers (because the conventional book profits the latter's undermining prices would yield them [if their undermined rivals did not react to their undermining response] by increasing their sales will usually exceed the profits their undermining prices cost them by reducing the price at which they make those sales they would have made had they charged a SOP). (I will characterize SOPs as "total" if they maximize the profits of the relevant group of sellers. SOPs will be said to be "partial" if they do not maximize the total profits of the relevant group of sellers but still enable the initiator and cooperators to profit from their contrivance.)

The first public-good-type problem that is relevant in the current context relates directly to the incentives of individual prospective retaliators to retaliate. Even if it would be in the joint interest of all the prospective contrivers to retaliate against any rival that undermined their contrived oligopolistic prices, it might not be in the interest of any individual prospective retaliator to retaliate because any such retaliator will bear a higher percentage of the costs that its retaliation imposes on the prospective retaliator group than of the benefits it confers on this group. This result would be likely to obtain if all products in the relevant area of product-space were equally competitive with each other because in those circumstances the retaliator's share of the retaliation costs borne by the prospective-retaliator group will usually exceed its share of the retaliator-group's total sales (regardless of whether the other members of the prospective-retaliator group find it inherently profitable to adjust their prices to the retaliator's retaliation), while the retaliator's share of the benefits its retaliation confers on the members of the prospective-retaliator group (by deterring future undermining by prospective underminers) equals its share of the prospective retaliators' sales. The associated public-good-type problem is likely to be less severe if the individual members of the prospective-retaliator group are unequally competitive with individual prospective underminers, especially if the members of each prospective-retaliator/prospective-underminer pair are symmetrically competitive with each other. If the percentage of the loss that the undermining price of any underminer XU1 imposes on all prospective retaliators that is borne by a particular prospective retaliator X1 far exceeds X1's share of all the sales made by the members of the prospective-retaliator group (because XU1 is second-placed or close-to-second-placed to supply a higher percentage of the buyers X1 is best-placed to supply than of the buyers that X2. . .N are best-placed to supply) and if the percentage of the loss that X1's retaliation imposed on all X1's rivals (X2. . .N and XU1. . .M) that was borne by XU1 far exceeds X1's percentage of the sales that X1. . .N and XU1. . .M would make if there were no contrivance (because the percentage of the buyers that XU1 is best-placed to supply that X1 is second-placed or close-to-second-placed to supply is far higher than the percentage of the buyers that some member of the sets of sellers X1. . .N and XU1. . .M is best-placed to supply, the public-good-type problem would be far less likely to make it unprofitable for X1 to retaliate against XU1 when X1's retaliation would be profitable for X1. . .N combined: this conclusion primarily reflects the fact that in these circumstances X1's retaliation will be likely to deter undermining that would be disproportionately costly to X1—*i.e.*, the fact that X1's share of the benefits that its retaliation will confer on X1. . .N will be far higher than X1's share of X1. . .N's sales—and secondarily reflects the fact that in these circumstances given across-the-board price-cuts by X1 will inflict higher losses on XU1. I should add that, *ceteris paribus*, the severity of the public-good-type problem that might make it unprofitable for any individual prospective retaliator to engage in retaliation despite the fact that retaliation would be profitable for the prospective retaliators taken as a group will also be inversely related to the "concentration" of the prospective-retaliator group—more specifically, inversely related to the share of prospective-retaliator sales made by the prospective retaliator with the highest share of those sales and directly related to the number of prospective retaliators with substantial shares of prospective-retaliator sales (which will affect the ability of the prospective retaliators to agree on and enforce a coordinated-retaliation strategy).

The second public-good-type problem that is relevant in this context relates directly to the prospective underminers (the prospective targets of the undermined contrivers' retaliation). The basic point is that, to the extent that retaliation affects members of the prospective-underminer group that have not charged undermining prices, abstentions from undermining that would be in the collective interest of the prospective-underminer group taken as a whole may not be profitable for any individual prospective underminer—*i.e.*, the prospective underminers may not be able to abstain from charging undermining prices even though it would be in their collective interest to do so. Once more, the severity of this problem (which can render contrivance that would otherwise be profitable for the prospective contrivers unprofitable for them) will be lower (1) the greater the extent to which the share of the losses that retaliation imposes on the prospective-underminer group that is borne by the actual underminer exceeds that firm's share of the prospective underminers' sales (the greater the extent to which retaliation can be focused on the underminer because its undermining disproportionately injures a prospective contriver whose retaliation will disproportionately affect the underminer) and (2) the greater the concentration of the prospective-underminer group.

3. Contrived-Oligopolistic-Pricing Evidence, Proposed "Tests" for Illegal Price-Fixing, and Relevant U.S. and E.C./E.U. Case-Law

A. The Types of Evidence That Can Help Prove Contrived Oligopolistic Pricing

This subsection delineates and assesses the practicability of using five types of evidence that are actually relevant to whether a defendant has or two or more defendants have engaged in contrived oligopolistic pricing.

(1) Eyewitness Testimony, Audio Recordings, or Documentary Evidence of Contrived Oligopolistic Communications, Statements of Contrived-Oligopolistic-Pricing Intentions, or Admissions of Contrived-Oligopolistic-Pricing Acts

Obviously, direct evidence that a seller has linguistically communicated a contrived-oligopolistic-pricing threat, offer, or acceptance (eyewitness testimony, recordings of spoken messages, documentary proof of written communications) or similar evidence of a defendant's admission of its contrived oligopolistic intent or acts will be relevant to whether the defendant(s) has (have) engaged in contrived oligopolistic pricing. Unfortunately, however, such evidence is rarely available and is often suspect when it is available. Thus, eyewitness testimony by a disgruntled (sometimes fired) employee of a defendant or by a competitor or customer of the defendant(s), who or which may have a financial stake in its (their) conviction, is impeachable on that account. Still, there clearly are cases in which such testimony will be not only available but efficacious. Thus, the lysine cartel was broken up as a result of a combination of (1) testimony by an employee of one of its participants (Archer Daniels Midland) and (2) videotapes the FBI arranged for him to make of subsequent cartel meetings.[379] And the monochloroacetic acid cartel was detected because the management of a company (Clariant) that acquired one of its participants (Hoechst) turned over to the U.S. and E.U. antitrust authorities evidence it found post-acquisition of Hoechst's participation.[380]

(2) Evidence That Permits a "Straightforward" Comparison of a Best-Placed Individualized Pricer's or an Across-the-Board Pricing-Sequence Initiator's Actual Price and the Price That Would Have Been Most Profitable for That Firm if It Could Not Practice Contrived Oligopolistic Pricing Profitably (Its Highest Legitimate Price) and Evidence That Permits a "Straightforward" Evaluation of the Non-Complicity of the Price-Response of a Worse-Than-Best-Placed Individualized Pricer or a Non-Price-Sequence-Initiating Across-the-Board Pricer

(A) Evidence on the Relationship Between (1) the Prices That Individualized Pricers Charged Buyers They Were Best-Placed to Supply, That Firms That Initiated an Across-the-Board Pricing-Sequence Set, That Individualized Pricers Charged Buyers They Were Worse-Than-Best-Placed to Supply When the Buyers' Best-Placed Supplier Had Charged Prices That Contained a Contrived Oligopolistic Margin, and That Across-the-Board Pricers That Had Not Initiated a Pricing-Sequence Charged in Response to an Initiator's Contrived Oligopolistic Price and (2) the Prices These Actors Would Have Found Most Profitable to Charge if They Could Not Practice Contrived Oligopolistic Pricing Profitably (These Actors' Inherently-Most Profitable Prices)—*i.e.*, Evidence That Could Play a Role in the "Straightforward" Assessment of the Contrived Oligopolistic Character of Such Parties' Prices

(1) Evidence on the Relationship Between (A) the Actual Price Charged by an Individualized Pricer to a Buyer It Was Best-Placed to Supply or the Price Charged by a Price-Sequence-Initiating Across-the-Board Pricer and (B) the Price That Would Have Been Most Profitable for Such a Seller to Charge if It Could Not Practice Contrived Oligopolistic Pricing

In a perfectly-informed world in which no actor makes a relevant error, one could prove that an individualized pricer had engaged in contrived oligopolistic pricing

---

[379] See Joseph E. Harrington, Jr., *Detecting Cartels* in HANDBOOK OF ANTITRUST ECONOMICS 213 at 213–14 (hereinafter *Harrington Detecting Cartels*), (Paolo Buccirossi, ed.) (MIT Press, 2008).
[380] See *id.* at 213.

when setting its price to a particular buyer by demonstrating that its actual price to that buyer exceeded its highest legitimate price to that buyer, which would equal the sum of its HNOP and its NOM in its relations with that buyer. As Chap. 2 explained, to determine a best-placed individualized pricer's HNOP to a particular buyer, one would have to determine its MC, CMC, CCA, and BCA = BPA + MCA in its relations with that buyer (where the relevant CCA depends *inter alia* on the prices the seller is charging its other customers and the OCAs and NOMs its closest rivals for the particular buyer's patronage enjoy in their relations with their customers). To determine an individualized pricer's NOM in relation to a particular buyer it is best-placed to supply, one would have to determine not only its OCA in relation to that buyer but also all the other determinants of its NOMs that Subsection 2A(1) of this chapter listed and discussed.

(2) Evidence on the Relationship Between (A) the Array of Across-the-Board Prices That a Set of Across-the-Board-Pricing Rivals Charged and (B) the Prices That Would Have Been Most Profitable for Them to Charge if They Could Not Practice Contrived Oligopolistic Pricing

In a perfectly-informed world, one could prove that an across-the-board pricer that had initiated a pricing sequence had engaged in contrived oligopolistic pricing by demonstrating that its actual price exceeded its HNOP *plus* the extra margin its rivals' independent contrivance would make it profitable for it to charge if it behaved non-strategically *plus* the NOM it could obtain. As Chap. 2 explained, to determine an across-the-board pricer's HNOP, one would have to determine the across-the-board BCA or BCD position of each relevant across-the-board pricer in its relations with each relevant buyer (where the relevant BCA or BCD is calculated on the artificial assumption that each seller's marginal cost for supplying any buyer equals the height of its MC curve at the output it would sell if all relevant sellers charged prices equal to their HNOPs), the direction in which and the extent to which each relevant seller's marginal costs for producing units above and below its "HNOP output" differ from the marginal cost the seller would have to incur to produce the unit of output that would be its marginal unit of output if it and all relevant other sellers charged prices equal to their HNOPs , and the order in which all relevant sellers would announce their prices. (Since this account would require an analyst of a set of across-the-board-pricing sellers' HNOPs to determine their HNOPs—*i.e.*, the outputs they would produce if each of them charged its HNOP—to determine their BCA and BCD positions in relation to relevant buyers in order to determine their HNOPs, it would be better to say that, *inter alia*, to determine a relevant HNOP array one would have to know the BPA/BPD distribution of the relevant sellers in their relations with each relevant buyer and their respective MC curves over the relevant range of outputs.) To determine the extra margin an across-the-board pricer would find profitable to charge because of its rivals' contrivance even if it did not cooperate with them, one would have to know the magnitude of the COMs its rivals would charge if it would not cooperate. And to determine, the extra margin it could obtain because it and its rivals could obtain OMs naturally, one would have to know not only its and their HNOP–MC arrays but also the magnitudes of all the other determinants of their ability to obtain OMs naturally.

In part, I enquoted the word "straightforward" in the heading to this section because the method in question would be extremely complex even in a perfectly-informed world in which no actor makes an error. And in part, I did so because the required analysis will be even more complex in a world in which actors make errors. In such a world, a perfect analysis would have to take account not only of the errors that potential rivals and potential customers of the firm in question might make but also of the errors the defendant might make. When defendants may make errors, the fact that they charged a price above the price that would be most profitable for them to charge if they could not profit from contrived oligopolistic pricing might reflect the fact that they overestimated such things as their OCAs or their and their rivals MCs or their ability to obtain OMs naturally and the fact that defendants charged a price below the price they would find most profitable to charge if they could not practice contrived oligopolistic pricing profitably might be compatible with their having attempted to contrive an oligopolistic price if they had underestimated their OCAs, their and their rivals' MCs, their ability to obtain OMs naturally, *etc.*[381]

(B) Evidence on the "Complicitousness" of the Price Charged by an Individualized Pricer to a Buyer It Was Worse-Than-Best-Placed to Supply or by a Responding (Non-Initiating) Across-the-Board Pricer

The same points that I began the preceding subsection by making about the actual price of a best-placed individualized pricer and of a price-sequence-initiating across-the-board pricer apply *mutatis mutandis* to the actual price charged by an individualized pricer to a buyer it is worse-than-best-placed to supply or by a non-price-sequence-initiating across-the-board pricer: (1) the fact that the price they set respectively in response to the best-placed seller's individualized contrived oligopolistic price or the across-the-board price-sequence-initiating pricer's contrived oligopolistic price is higher than the price that would be profitable for them to charge if their rivals could not react strategically is neither a necessary nor a sufficient condition for their intending to cooperate with the best-placed supplier's or across-the-board pricing-sequence initiator's contrivance because they may have overestimated or underestimated their inherently-most-profitable price-response but (2) in the situation in question, the fact that the price they set is higher than the price that would have been most profitable for them to charge if their rivals

[381] I admit that one might be able to render the "straightforward" method of proving contrived oligopolistic pricing somewhat more practicable by appropriate assignments of the burdens of proof and production on the parameters in question. In my judgment, the burdens of production and persuasion on the actual price and NEHNOP issues should be placed on the State or private plaintiff, and the burdens of production and persuasion on the BEM, REM, own-error margin (hereinafter OEM), and NOM issues should be placed on the defendant(s). If it were not for the risk of holdups and the opposite risk that the private transaction cost of suing might deter a private plaintiff or even the State from bringing justified suits, I would place the burden of paying for the production of evidence on any parameter on the party that was best-placed to produce it. I do not know the relevant strengths of the above two risks in the "price-fixing-suit" context.

could not react strategically is highly probative of their intention to cooperate with the rival in question.

It will also be complex and costly to determine in the "straightforward" way now under consideration whether, in individualized-pricing contexts, a seller's failure to make an offer to a buyer it was worse-than-best-placed to supply was an inherently-profitable or a cooperative response to its best-placed rival's contrived oligopolistic pricing and whether, in both individualized-pricing and across-the-board-pricing contexts, the price a firm charged in response to a rival's contrived oligopolistic pricing was inherently profitable or cooperative—*i.e.*, was higher than the price that would have been most profitable for it to charge if its rivals could not react strategically. This conclusion is warranted when no relevant actor makes a relevant error and, *a fortiori*, when actors can make mistakes.

Individualized pricers have the option of not making an offer to any buyer they are worse-than-best-placed to supply. To determine whether an individualized pricer's decision not to make an offer to such a buyer was inherently profitable or constituted a cooperative response to a best-placed firm's contrived oligopolistic pricing in a world in which no-one ever made a relevant error that was rendered profitable by the prospect of the contriver's possible strategic reactions, one would have to know not only

(1) that the firm in question was worse-than-best-placed to secure the relevant buyer's patronage (its BPA or BPD, MCA or MCD, and CCA or CCD) and
(2) that the price offered that buyer by its best-placed supplier did contain (or was perceived by the inferior to contain) a contrived oligopolistic margin but also
(3) the number the firm in question assigned to the probability that it was not best-placed (or would have assigned to that probability had it done the amount of research into that issue that *ex ante* was inherently profitable for it to do),
(4) partially relatedly, whether the firm in question knew the best-placed firm's price (terms) before deciding whether to make an offer,
(5) the mechanical cost it would have to incur to calculate its costs and make an offer,
(6) the "keeping-in-touch" advantages it might secure by making a plausible offer to a buyer it was currently not best-placed to supply,
(7) the CMC it would have to incur to make an offer that would yield it such "keeping-in-touch" advantages or that might be accepted, and
(8) the number it assigned to the probability that the buyer in question would give the best-placed supplier an opportunity to beat any superior offer it made and that the best-placed firm would find taking advantage of that opportunity inherently profitable (to the probability that the best-placed supplier's price contained a natural but no contrived OM).

The preceding list should suffice to demonstrate that, even in a world in which no-one ever made a relevant error, the "straightforward" method to determine whether an individualized-pricing "responder's" failure to make an offer to a buyer it was not best-placed to supply constituted an inherently-profitable response to its situation or a cooperative response to a rival's actual or perceived contrived oligopolistic pricing that was rendered profitable by the prospect of the contrivance-initiator's strategic reactions will be neither simple nor cheap and may not be practicable in many cases.

Prospects are not better for using the "straightforward" method on which we are now focusing to determine whether the price charged by a competitive inferior in an individualized-pricing context or a non-initiator in an across-the-board-pricing context constituted an inherently-profitable response to the firm's situation or a cooperative response to a rival's actual or perceived contrivance that was rendered profitable by the prospect of the contrivance-initiator's strategic reactions. To determine "straightforwardly" whether the price of an individualized pricer that did not yield a sale was an inherently-profitable price charged by a competitive inferior or a cooperative response by such an inferior to a best-placed rival's actual or perceived contrived oligopolistic pricing, one will have to know even in a world in which no-one ever made a relevant error not just

(1) that the firm in question was worse-than-best-placed to supply the relevant buyer and
(2) that the price of the rival in question contained (or was perceived by the inferior to contain) a contrived oligopolistic margin but also
(3) the marginal cost the inferior in question would have to incur to supply the relevant buyer,
(4) the contextual marginal cost it would have to incur to offer that buyer various prices or to supply that buyer on various terms,
(5) the promotional and learning-by-doing advantages to the inferior of supplying the relevant buyer,
(6) the numbers that the relevant seller assigned (or would have assigned had it done *ex ante* profitable research into this issue) to the probabilities that the different prices it could charge would beat the offer of its competitive superior (in situations in which the inferior is not certain about its BPA or BPD and/or perhaps about the price and other terms of sale the superior has offered), and
(7) the numbers that the relevant seller assigned to the probabilities that the different prices it could charge would deter the relevant buyer from giving its superior supplier a meaningful opportunity to beat the inferior's relevant superior offer and that the best-placed supplier would find taking advantage of such an opportunity inherently profitable.

To determine "straightforwardly" whether the price set by an across-the-board pricer that did not initiate a pricing sequence was inherently profitable or constituted a partial or total SOP to the initiator's contrived oligopolistic price, one would have to know even in a world in which no-one ever made a relevant error not only (1) that the initiator's price contained or was perceived by the responder in question to contain a contrived oligopolistic margin (for which one would need to know the originator's MC curve, its array of BCAs and BCDs in relation to all its rivals, their arrays of BCAs and BCDs vis-à-vis each other, and the order in which they will respond to the initiator's price announcement) but also (2) (even if one did know for other reasons that the initiator's price contained a COM) the relevant responder's MC curve, its array of BCAs and BCDs in relation to both the initiator and its other rivals, any promotional and learning-by-doing incentives it had to charge a lower price, the order in which its rivals would respond to its response to the initiator's price, the subsequent price announcers' BCA/BCD distributions vis-à-vis each other, and whether and the extent to which the subsequent price announcers could obtain NOMs, would choose to cooperate with the initial price announcer's contrivance, and would contrive oligopolistic margins themselves. Even if it would be cost-effective in some circumstances to execute such an analysis, it would clearly be neither simple nor cheap to do so. In fact, I suspect that the "straightforward" approach on which this subsection is focusing would rarely if ever be practicable even in a world in which no-one ever made a relevant error.

Of course, the fact that buyers, rivals, and the responder itself might make relevant errors will further complicate the determination of whether the responder was cooperating with the best-placed individual pricer's or across-the-board price-sequence initiator's attempt to contrive an OM or was simply responding to such a firm's conduct in the way it would have found most profitable to respond if it assumed that this rival would not react to its response strategically. The preceding analysis of the tendency of such errors to complicate the analysis of whether a best-placed individualized pricer or an across-the-board-pricing price-sequence initiator had attempted to contrive an oligopolistic margin applies *mutatis mutandis* in the current context as well.

I should indicate that some studies have attempted to determine whether (in my terms) firms have chosen not to set as attractive a price to the buyers that a rival was best-placed to supply by examining whether the parts of various relevant pairs of firms' prices that could not be explained in conventional-cost and opportunity-cost terms were correlated with each other.[382] This approach will be problematic to the extent that some pairs of firms have unobserved common costs and will fail to detect collusive acts if the colluders learn that it is being used and manipulate their bids to defeat it.

(3) Inter-Temporal and Inter-Regional Evidence That Plays a Critical Role in Two Comparative Protocols for Assessing the Contrived Oligopolistic Character of a Seller's Prices

Obviously, the high cost and inaccuracy of the "straightforward" method of identifying the contrived oligopolistic character of a particular price implies the need to develop other, more-cost-effective methods of determining whether a seller has engaged in contrived oligopolistic pricing. The inter-temporal and inter-regional comparative methods on which this subsection focuses are two such alternatives. These comparative methods have the advantage of obviating the determination of the MC, MCA, BPA, CMC, promotional incentive, learning-by-doing pricing incentive, and NOM figures whose estimation the straightforward method required in individualized-pricing contexts and the BCA-distribution, predicted-order-of-price-announcement, likely-oligopolistic interactions of subsequent price announcers, and

---

[382] See, *e.g.*, Patrick Bajari and Lixin Ye, *Deciding Between Competition and Collusion*, 85 REV. OF ECON. AND STAT. 971 (2003).

promotional-and-learning-by-doing pricing-incentive figures whose estimation the straightforward method required in across-the-board-pricing contexts. Instead of focusing on these figures, the comparative methods focus respectively on inter-temporal or inter-regional contemporaneous *differences* in these determinants of the relevant sellers' highest legitimate prices. To the extent that it is cheaper to estimate these *differences* with the required degree of accuracy than to measure the basic determinants themselves with that degree of accuracy, the comparative methods will be more cost-effective than the straightforward method.

The two comparative methods would try to determine whether a contrived oligopolistic price has been charged by investigating whether the difference (zero to any positive number) between the prices charged for a given set of products at different times or contemporaneously in different regions can be explained by estimated differences in the value of the determinants of the products' highest legitimate prices between the two times in question or between the two regions in question. For example, if the price of some good were higher at t(1) than at t(0) or in region (1) than in region (0) and an analysis of any inter-temporal changes in the determinants of the price of that good that the relevant seller would find most profitable to charge if it could not profit by engaging in contrived oligopolistic pricing led to the conclusion that that price rose less than the actual price rose between the two time-periods in question or an analysis of the inter-regional differences in the determinants of the highest legitimate price of the relevant good led to the conclusion that the highest legitimate price in the high-price region exceeded its counterpart in the low-price region by less than the actual price in the high-price region exceeded the actual price in the low-price region, one could infer either that (1) the higher price contained a COM or (2) that the lower price was below the relevant seller's highest legitimate price (which also equals its lowest legitimate price)—an outcome that could reflect the seller's own error, one or more of its closest rivals' underestimating their own marginal costs, or its attempting to deter a rival from undercutting by charging retaliatory prices, or its engaging in predatory pricing. However, if these latter possibilities seem sufficiently unlikely, a plaintiff could establish the contrived oligopolistic character of at least one of the prices in question by using one of the two comparative methods just delineated. In a similar way, this comparative method could provide evidence of contrived oligopolistic pricing if the actual prices of a given good are the same at two different times or contemporaneously in two different regions when an analysis of the determinants of the relevant highest (lowest) legitimate prices implied that these latter prices were lower at the one time than at the other or in the one region than in the other.

In 1975, I published an article that discussed the possible usefulness of this type of comparative evidence.[383] In the ensuing years, a number of other economists have not only considered this possibility at a theoretical level but used it to assess

[383] See Richard S. Markovits, *Proving (Illegal) Oligopolistic Pricing: A Description of the Necessary Evidence and a Critique of the Received Wisdom About Its Character and Cost*, 27 STAN. L. REV. 307, 310–14 (1975).

whether particular firms had engaged in what I call contrived oligopolistic pricing. Although some of these studies did not focus on what economists call "structural breaks" in firm behavior,[384] others did—*i.e.*, others focus on inter-temporal price-difference associated with the creation or demise of a cartel or a change in the effectiveness of a cartel occasioned by the formation of a trade association[385] or by changes in "market structure" that seem likely to change the profitability of contrived oligopolistic pricing (in their view, the exit of a maverick or the acquisition of a maverick by a likely contriver[386] and, in mine, in addition, in the other direction, the entrance of a producer of a generic or some other product that is second-placed or close-to-second-placed far more often than it is best-placed), changes in the antitrust-enforcement environment that increase or decrease the law-related cost of contrivance,[387] or changes in the economic environment (say, a drop in demand) that led a group of sellers to conclude that it was in their individual interest to develop a more-explicit and better-organized system of collusion.[388]

I should point out that the inter-temporal variant of this comparative approach also covers cases of price-wars (at least price-wars of significant duration). If, as I suspect, unusually-high drops in prices that cannot be explained by unusually-high decreases in costs and/or demand normally manifest the following sequence of pricing conduct—(1) contrived oligopolistic pricing, (2) undercutting or undermining pricing, (3) retaliatory price-cuts aimed at disciplining the undercutters/underminers, and (4) the more general price-cuts that price-wars entail—one could infer contrived oligopolistic pricing from the price-war. I hasten to distinguish this claim from the more general claim that one can infer that a group of rivals have practiced contrived oligopolistic pricing from their prices' being (requisitely) more volatile than are the average set of rivalrous-product prices in the economy: I suspect that, even if contrivance never were practiced, the volatility of the prices of the different sets of rivalrous products one might want to distinguish in an economy would vary too much from set to set for the latter inference to be justifiable.

(4) Other Types of Behavioral Evidence

This subsection discusses seven other types of behavioral evidence that some experts claim can strengthen a contrived-oligopolistic-pricing case: (1) three types of bid-pattern evidence, (2) evidence of two types of inherently-unprofitable individual-firm

---

[384] See Dale R. Funderbunk, *Price-Fixing in the Liquid Asphalt Industry: Economic Analysis Versus the "Hot Document,"* 7 ANTITRUST LAW & ECON. REV. 61, 69 (1974).

[385] See *e.g.*, JOHN M. CONNOR, GLOBAL PRICE-FIXING 194, 223–24, and 234 (Springer, 2d ed., 2007).

[386] See *Harrington Detecting Cartels* at 220.

[387] Michael K. Block, Frederick C. Nold, and Joseph G. Sidak, *The Deterrent Effect of Antitrust Enforcement*, 89 J. POL. ECON. 429 (1981)

[388] See *Harrington Detecting Cartels* at 222.

pricing/bidding behavior, (3) evidence that one or more sellers have made side-payments to one or more of their rivals, (4) evidence that the defendants had the opportunity to set up a contrived-oligopolistic-pricing scheme in face-to-face negotiations; (5) evidence that the defendants had exchanged information whose sharing would facilitate contrived oligopolistic pricing, (6) evidence that the defendants had agreed not to give secret discounts, had agreed not to advertise, or had agreed to offer their customers retroactive rebates equal to any price-cuts they gave future buyers, and (7) evidence that one or more defendants had practiced contrived oligopolistic pricing in the past. It closes by explaining why four additional types of behavioral evidence that other scholars have claimed will either prove that such defendants have contrived oligopolistic prices or strengthen the contrived-oligopolistic-pricing case against them will not do so.

The first type of additional behavioral evidence that some argue can strengthen a contrived-oligopolistic-pricing case focuses on the pattern of bids that the members of a group of rivals have made. Professor Posner pointed out one price-pattern that may suggest that the relevant sellers have engaged in explicit collusion: the fact that all bidders submitted identical bids on non-standard items.[389] If as I suspect in most such situations the relevant sellers would have to incur different costs to supply the buyer in question, their submission of identical bids in a bidding process in which they were supposed to be ignorant of each other's bids would strongly suggest that the sellers in question had engaged in explicit collusion. I should add that, although such an arrangement might appear to disserve the collective interest of the sellers in question by failing to allocate the sale to the lowest-cost potential supplier, no such loss would result if, as is frequently the case, (1) the relevant cost-differences reflected differences in physical proximity to the buyer and hence differences in delivery costs and (2) the buyer would prefer to patronize its most proximate potential supplier, other things being equal, because proximity is positively related to speed of delivery and the cost of arranging face-to-face communication. I hasten to add, however, that such evidence is likely to be available only rarely. Once it is used against a contrived-oligopolistic-pricing defendant, contrived oligopolistic pricers will arrange for their prices not to fall into this pattern.

The second price-pattern that some claim strengthens the case against one or more contrived-oligopolistic-pricing defendants is the pattern in which one seller submitted the low bid and all others set prices that were much higher not only than the low bid but also than the marginal or incremental cost of their performing the job in question. For two reasons, such evidence is also less likely to be helpful than one would wish. First, if such evidence were probative, defendants would be unlikely to supply it: once contrivers know that such evidence will be used against them, they are likely to arrange for their bids not to fall into this pattern. Second, this bid-pattern may be less probative than it appears to be. I have consulted in a case in which this pattern actually had an innocent explanation. The case involved

---

[389] See Richard Posner, *Oligopoly and the Antitrust Laws: A Suggested Approach* (hereinafter *Posner Approach*), 21 STAN. L. REV. 1562 (1969).

the supply of one-pound loaves of white bread to the school system of a city whose individual districts made their own purchasing decisions. Three facts were critical: (1) each school district required its suppliers to deliver the bread to its individual schools before 7 A.M., (2) delivery costs constituted 35–40 % of the variable cost of supplying the bread to a school district, and (3) each baker could supply one school district without putting on an extra truck and driver (by simply having its driver deliver the bread to the schools in that district during the early part of his or her route) but could not satisfy two school districts' time-requirements without putting on an extra truck. As a result, each bakery made a low bid to the school district whose schools it was best-placed (geographically) to supply and higher bids to all other school districts that it could not supply without putting on an extra truck if, as it expected, it obtained the business of the school district to which it made the low offer. Although the resulting bids fit this second suspicious pattern, they did not reflect contrived oligopolistic pricing.

The third price-pattern that some experts believe strengthen a contrived-oligopolistic-pricing case is one in which the identity of the low bidder changed from job (buyer) to job despite the fact that the potential suppliers were equally-well-placed to supply each of the relevant buyers and their doing one job would not affect their competitive positions on other jobs. The same two reasons for doubting that evidence of the bidding-pattern on which the preceding paragraph focused will often be useful in contrived-oligopolistic-pricing cases apply with equal force to the bidding-pattern the preceding sentence described. The innocent explanation for this type of bidding-pattern focuses on the difficulty of estimating at least one part of the cost of performance. If some part of the cost of performance is hard to estimate accurately, random errors by sellers may generate this type of bidding-pattern as the low bidder for each job is the firm that most underestimated the cost of performance. Many years ago, I was a consultant in a price-fixing case involving relocatable school-buildings in which the low bidder for any contract was always the different firm that most underestimated the cost of site preparation.

The second type of behavioral evidence I want to discuss at this juncture resembles the type of evidence the last two subsections considered in that it focuses on the fact that an actor has made bidding or pricing choices (other than charging the allegedly-contrived oligopolistic primary price) that are not inherently profitable. I am considering this evidence under the heading of this subsection because here the fact that a seller charged one buyer an inherently-unprofitable price is being used to prove that the pricer had attempted to secure a contrived oligopolistic price from a different buyer or that one of its rivals had practiced contrived oligopolistic pricing. Thus, evidence that individualized pricer X1 has foregone an opportunity to make an inherently-profitable sale to buyer Y2 that had been charged a contrived oligopolistic price by its best-placed supplier X2 (either by not submitting a bid to Y2 or offering Y2 a price that was higher than the inherently-most-profitable price for X1 to offer Y2) can be used to strengthen the case that X1 had obtained a COM from a buyer Y1 that X1 was best-placed to supply despite the fact that X1's price to Y1 made it inherently profitable for X2 to steal Y1 from X1; evidence that an across-the-board pricer X2 had foregone the opportunity to respond to X1's across-the-board price with a lower price that would have been inherently more profitable than the higher price X2 did set can be used to support the claim that X1 had charged a contrived across-the-board price; evidence that an individualized pricer X1 had stolen a rival X2's customer Y2 by charging it an inherently-unprofitable price can be used to support the claim that X1 had charged a contrived oligopolistic price to one or more other buyers that X1 was best-placed to supply only to have those buyers stolen by X2; and evidence that an across-the-board pricer X1 had reacted to seller X2's response to X1's initiating across-the-board pricing by setting a price that was lower than the price that would have been inherently most profitable for it to set in reaction to X2's response to X1's initial price can be used to support the claim that X1's initial across-the-board price was a contrived oligopolistic price.

I hasten to add, however, that these types of evidence are far from conclusive. Even if I put aside the substantial concern that prices that appear to be inherently unprofitable are in fact inherently profitable (*e.g.*, because the analyst has overestimated the relevant seller's marginal cost; has ignored the promotional-pricing, keeping-in-touch-pricing, and conceivably the learning-by-doing benefits of low prices; in across-the-board-pricing contexts, has "overestimated" the relevant seller's BCA distribution, overestimated the relevant sellers' rivals' BCA distributions, or critically misjudged the order in which its rivals would respond to its prices, *etc.*), inherently-unprofitable prices may be charged by mistake or to retaliate legitimately against a rival that has engaged in illegal retaliatory or predatory conduct. Nevertheless, I do think it appropriate to put the burden of producing evidence on these possibilities as well as the burden of persuasion on them on the defendants.

The third type of behavioral evidence that is relevant in this context is evidence that some members of a set of rivals have made side-payments to other members of the set that cannot be explained in legitimating terms. This type of evidence will be more persuasive to the extent that the payors are more likely to be able to profit from cooperating in a contrived-oligopolistic-pricing scheme (because they are best-placed far more often than they are second-placed or close-to-second-placed) and the payees are more likely to be able to profit by undercutting or undermining contrived oligopolistic prices (because they are best-placed far less often than they are second-placed or close-to-second-placed).

The fourth type of additional behavioral evidence on which I wish to focus at this juncture is evidence that establishes that the alleged contrivers had the opportunity to discuss face-to-face their participation in a contrived-oligopolistic-pricing sequence. Evidence that the alleged contrivers had met as members of a trade association, had discussed the possibility of merging or participating in a merger or joint venture, or had actually participated in a merger or joint venture all fit into this category. The category could also be extended to include evidence that personnel had moved between the allegedly-contriving firms. Of course, this type of circumstantial evidence can provide at best weak support for a contrived-oligopolistic-pricing claim: contrivance can be arranged and executed without any face-to-face communication or, indeed, as we have seen, without any linguistic communication at all, and many if not most social interactions among competitors do not involve their planning illegal activities. Still, if a suspicious pattern of behavior begins soon after the alleged contrivers had the opportunity to communicate face-to-face, evidence of their encounter may have some limited probative value. I should add that the probative value of the relevant evidence would be increased if it could be shown that the merger or joint venture the defendants had discussed or executed reduced competition by freeing them from each other's competition.

The fifth type of behavioral evidence that is relevant to the claim that one or more firms have engaged in contrived oligopolistic pricing is proof that the sellers have exchanged information that will help them profit from such pricing—information about the identity of the seller that supplied particular buyers, the price at which identified or unidentified past transactions took place, the prices offered by specified sellers that were rejected by particular buyers, the marginal or even average variable cost of different, identified sellers, and different sellers' inventories and production plans. As I will explain in more detail below when discussing the legality of such information-exchanges, the exchange of such information will help sellers practice contrived oligopolistic pricing by helping them to determine whether they lost a sale spontaneously or through undercutting by a worse-placed rival, by helping them to identify their actual and prospective undercutters, by helping them to determine their harm-inflicted to loss-incurred ratio for different possible individual acts of price retaliation against specified rivals, and by helping them to determine the extent to which they can reciprocate to the cooperation of specified rivals by not competing hard for the patronage of particular buyers these rivals were best-placed to supply. I should add that, because the exchange of much of this information can also perform legitimate functions (helping firms to determine that their costs are unnecessarily high, enabling firms to avoid underestimating or overestimating their NEHNOPs, *etc.*), such information-exchanges may not be independently illegal, and proof that they took place does not establish that the information-exchangers were planning to or actually did practice contrived oligopolistic pricing. Still, like the "structural" evidence the next subsection will discuss, evidence that such information-exchanges took place is relevant to one or more contrived-oligopolistic-pricing defendants' guilt because it affects the probability that such pricing would be profitable for them.

The sixth type of additional behavioral evidence that some claim strengthen the case against a set of contrived-oligopolistic-pricing defendants is evidence that they agreed (say, at their trade association's insistence, perhaps backed up by the threat of trade-association sanctions) not to grant buyers secret discounts, had agreed not to advertise, and/or had agreed to put price-protection clauses into their contracts with their customers. Obviously, if effective, prohibitions of secret discounts will greatly facilitate the enforcement of contrived-oligopolistic-pricing agreements or the carrying out of contrived-oligopolistic-pricing threats by making it easier for participants both to determine whether lost sales reflect price-cutting as opposed to changes in buyer preferences, needs, or options and to identify the firm that has undercut or undermined the agreed-upon price or set of prices. Because I can see no legitimate function that agreements not to offer secret discounts can perform, their existence clearly shows that their participants intended to fix prices and makes it highly likely that they have actually done so.

Agreements not to advertise facilitate contrived oligopolistic pricing by reducing the incentives firms have to cut prices by precluding them from advertising such price-cuts. Admittedly, however, since firms that undercut or undermine contrived oligopolistic prices usually do so secretly, this type of agreement probably rarely plays a significant role in price-fixing schemes.

Agreements to include price-protection clauses in contracts of sale are more important facilitators of contrivance. Such clauses facilitate the running of contrived-oligopolistic-pricing schemes by reducing the attractiveness of cheating to participants by requiring them to give refunds to previous purchasers of their products any time they cut an individualized price to a rival's customer or cut their across-the-board price. Because I see no legitimate reason for sellers' *agreeing* to include price-protection clauses in their contracts of sale, such agreements do seem to me clearly to evidence contrived oligopolistic pricing. I hasten to add, however, that the same cannot be said for decisions by individual sellers to include such terms in their contracts of sale unilaterally, even if all members of a group of product-rivals decide to do so. Individual decisions to include such clauses can perform legitimate functions. For example, if a seller has reduced its initially-announced prices in one or more-recent pricing-rounds but does not expect to do so in the current pricing-round, it may find it profitable to offer its customers price-protection clauses to deter these buyers from delaying their purchases in the hope of receiving future price-cuts. Indeed, all members of a group of rivals may include such clauses in their contracts independently of each other for this reason. In this type of situation, the independent decisions of a set of rivals to include price-protection clauses in their contracts of sale would not strengthen a contrived-oligopolistic-pricing case against them.

The seventh type of behavioral evidence that some claim strengthen a contrived-oligopolistic-pricing case against one or more defendants is evidence that it or they had practiced contrived oligopolistic pricing in the past, particularly if it or they had done so in the relevant area of product-space or in an area of product-space that was similar in that the magnitudes of the determinants of the profitability of such pricing were similar in the two areas of product-space in question. This type of evidence might be thought to strengthen the case against the defendant(s) in question for two sorts of reasons: (1) because one believes that price-fixers tend to be recidivists and (2) because the fact that defendants previously practiced price-fixing, particularly if they did so in the same or in a similar area of product-space, implies that the practice would be profitable for them. I have my doubts about the recidivist justification: I do not know whether business organizations and their relevant personnel tend to maintain through time the same attitude toward obeying the law (the same proclivity to violate the law). I would guess that, if the previous case of price-fixing led to criminal or civil suits and *a fortiori* criminal convictions or civil fines or liability awards, there would be some tendency of penalized offenders to have learned their lesson or at least to be deterred by the fear that the antitrust-enforcement authorities and potential private plaintiffs would be more likely to pay attention to their conduct than to that of the average firm that had no such record of wrongdoing and that triers-of-fact would be more likely to find them guilty of price-fixing than to find another defendant that had no similar history guilty on otherwise-identical facts.

With one qualification and one major caveat, the second justification for counting against contrived-oligopolistic-pricing defendants evidence of their past price-fixing seems more convincing. Four considerations favor this conclusion:

(1) the fact that the defendants found it *ex ante* profitable to attempt to contrive oligopolistic prices in the ARDEPPS in question or in one or more similar ARDEPPSes in the more-distant past favors the conclusion that they would have found it *ex ante* profitable to attempt to do so in the more-recent past, law-related costs aside;
(2) the fact that the defendants succeeded in contriving oligopolistic prices in the ARDEPPS in question or in one or more similar ARDEPPSes in the more-distant past favors the conclusion that they would have been able to practice such pricing successfully in the relevant ARDEPPS in the more-recent past;
(3) the defendants possession of a reputation for contrived oligopolistic pricing itself tends to increase the profitability of such pricing for them by increasing their ability to communicate their contrived oligopolistic intentions simply by charging a contrived oligopolistic price and by increasing the creditability of their related anticompetitive threats and promises; and
(4) to the extent that the fact that the defendants have practiced contrived oligopolistic pricing in the past implies that they are more likely to be practicing or to be considering practicing contrived oligopolistic pricing elsewhere, that fact may also increase the profitability of their practicing contrived oligopolistic pricing in the ARDEPPS in question by increasing the benefits that contrivance in that ARDEPPS will generate for them by increasing the COMs they obtain elsewhere (because both their successful contrivance in the ARDEPPS in question and their carrying out their related anticompetitive threats and promises will enhance their reputation for contrivance elsewhere).

The qualification derives from the same fact that cut against the recidivism argument: to the extent that the fact that a firm has or a group of firms have contrived oligopolistic prices in the past makes it more likely that its or their later attempts to do so will result in their being prosecuted or sued by the government and sued by private plaintiffs as well as more likely that they will lose such suits, their past contrivance will reduce the profitability of later contrivance in any ARDEPPS both directly and by reducing the extent to which they do or might engage in such behavior in other ARDEPPSes. I simply do not know whether this consideration outweighs the other four.

The caveat is at least as important. At most, this second argument for the relevance of the defendant's or defendants' previous price-fixing would establish a link between their past practice and *the profitability* of their contriving oligopolistic prices subsequently. One obviously cannot prove that a party violated the law by establishing the profitability of its doing so.

Finally, I want to consider two other types of behavioral evidence that a number of scholars (to my mind, mistakenly) have argued should strengthen the case against one or more contrived-oligopolistic-pricing defendants and anticipate the next subsection's explanation of why two additional types of behavioral evidence that Professor/Judge Richard Posner has claimed support an illegal-oligopolistic-pricing claim do not in fact do so. I start with the contention of some scholars that evidence that a group of rivals have tried to standardize the product they sell provides support for the conclusion that they had engaged in contrived oligopolistic pricing. I should indicate at the outset that, although they have never endorsed this position, the U.S. DOJ and FTC have made claims that favor it. Thus, Section 2.12 of their 1992 Horizontal Merger Guidelines states that, when products and the type of pricing that sellers employ are standardized, it is easier for potential contrivers to work out what the Guidelines denominate "terms of coordination," and Section 7.2 of their 2010 Horizontal Merger Guidelines states that "[p]rice transparency can be greater for relatively homogeneous products." For two reasons, I do not think that this last argument justifies the conclusion that proof that a group of rivals has attempted to standardize their products supports the claim that they have engaged in contrived oligopolistic pricing. First, the argument ignores the following facts: (1) to the extent that product-standardization eliminates product-attribute differences that reduced the percentage of the rivals in question that are well-placed to obtain the average relevant buyer's patronage, it will make contrivance less profitable by increasing the number of rivals that are in a position to undercut or undermine a contriver's contrived oligopolistic price and concomitantly the cost to the contriver of making the associated communications and the cost to it of identifying its actual undercutter, and (2) to the extent that product-standardization reduces the average amount by which the average firm that is best-placed to obtain a relevant buyer's patronage is best-placed to do so, reduces the amount by which the average buyer's second-placed supplier is better-placed than its third-placed supplier, and makes information on repeat-sales and past sales-to-new-buyers less relevant to the present, it will also make contrivance less profitable by decreasing the harm-inflicted to loss-incurred ratio for any undercut contriver's inflicting a given loss on its undercutter, by decreasing the extent to which any contriver can reciprocate to its cooperators, and by decreasing the ability of the contriver to determine that it has been undercut by a competitive inferior. Hence, even if product-standardization increased the profitability of contrived oligopolistic pricing more by reducing the average BCA or OCA of the sellers in the relevant area of product-space when they were best-placed (*i.e.*, by reducing the safe profits they must put at risk to contrive an OM), it is not at all clear that product-standardization will increase the profitability of contrived oligopolistic pricing. I hasten to add that Professor/Judge Posner's and the DOJ/FTC's conclusion about the relationship between the extent to which a group of rivals' products are standardized (or heterogeneous) and the profitability of their practicing contrived oligopolistic pricing is the orthodox economics conclusion. Indeed, all other economists who have addressed this issue have concluded that "cartel formation is more likely to exist [*i.e.*, contrived oligopolistic pricing is more likely to be practiced] where there are. . .more homogeneous products. . .."[390]

Second, the argument ignores the wide range of other reasons why a group of rivals may want to standardize their products and the related reality that a large but hard-to-estimate percentage of the attempts by sellers to standardize their products will not reflect the sellers' desire to facilitate their contrived oligopolistic pricing. Admittedly, to the extent that relevant buyers place a positive value on the differentiation of product-attributes that product-standardization eliminates, product-standardization may reduce a group of sellers' profits on that account by reducing the revenues they can obtain without engaging in contrived oligopolistic pricing below the cost-savings that standardization permits. However, product-standardization can also increase the relevant producers' profits in a sufficient number of ways that are legitimate to negate the inference that it was executed to facilitate contrived oligopolistic pricing (even if one assumes, contrary to my own suspicions, that, on balance, it would tend to do so):

(1) even when the only initial difference among the heterogeneous product variants in question to which buyers were not indifferent was their size (square inches, weight, or liquid volume) and the relevant size-differences would not create any competitive advantages (if buyers made no relevant mistakes), by increasing total sales by reducing the cost to buyers of calculating relative prices per inch or ounce or liter: I should add that sellers may want to standardize pricing methods for this reason as well;
(2) when the initial differences among the products did create competitive advantages and disadvantages, by increasing total sales by making it unnecessary for individual buyers to incur the time-and-effort cost of identifying the product variant they should buy or the psychological cost of making uninformed choices;
(3) when the products in question have complements, by increasing total sales by permitting the standardization of complements and thereby eliminating the risk that a buyer that owns the basic product will purchase an incompatible complement or that a buyer that owns the complement will purchase an incompatible basic product (think of the problems of "plug and electrical-outlet incompatibility" in British homes, in which different sorts of electrical outlets can often be found even in the same room); and
(4) when the initial set of diverse products had different methods of use and different use-capabilities, by increasing total sales by permitting standardization of "methods of operation" and "function" and thereby reducing the cost to potential buyers of learning how to use the products and the purposes for which they can and cannot be properly used.

[390] See *Harrington Detecting Cartels* at 213, citing P.A. Grout and A. Sonderegger, *Predicting Cartels* 15 in Economic Discussion Paper (Office of Fair Trading) (2005): "Cartels are far more likely if the product is fairly homogeneous between companies in the market. . .."

been profitable for it to do so (though I admit that this kind of negative evidence is far more probative than its positive counterpart). A defendant may have initiated or illegally participated in contrived oligopolistic pricing even though it was *ex ante* unprofitable for it to do so: to err is human. Still, this type of structural evidence will be useful in conjunction with the other kinds of evidence this subsection has described—or, at least, would be useful if it were ever cost-effective to collect.

If my discussion of "structural evidence" seems less than enthusiastic, that fact reflects less my doubts about the probativeness of such evidence and more my conviction that the relevant facts will be far more difficult to ascertain with requisite accuracy than others suppose. As Chap. 2 and Section 10.2 of this chapter showed, one cannot predict the profitability of contrived oligopolistic pricing from data on the kinds of parameters on which analysis has traditionally focused—*e.g.*, from data on the concentration of and height of the barriers to entry into the market in which the conduct supposedly took place or even from data on a somewhat-more-complicated list of parameters that incorporates some of the added factors that, as we shall see in Chap. 11, the deservedly-highly-respected economists Paul Joskow and Alvin Klevorick think determine the *ex ante* profitability of predatory pricing.[391] Hence, although it will sometimes be cost-effective to supplement the kinds of evidence described in the preceding four subsections with "structural" evidence, I do not think that such evidence will often significantly increase the cost-effectiveness of any attempt to prove contrived oligopolistic pricing.

* * *

This subsection has delineated the various types of evidence that can properly be used to prove that one or more defendants have engaged in contrived oligopolistic pricing and commented on the practicability of using such evidence for this purpose. I have no doubt that—absent reliable evidence that a defendant has made a contrived-oligopolistic communication of an anticompetitive threat or promise, has stated that it intended to engage in such contrivance, or has admitted that it did engage in such contrivance—it will often be impossible and almost always be extremely expensive to prove that a business that has attempted to contrive an oligopolistic price or succeeded in contriving such a price has done so. Of course, if contrived oligopolistic pricing reduces economic efficiency and redistributes income unjustly as much as I think it does, it may well be economically efficient and desirable overall to incur substantial allocative costs to prosecute contrived-oligopolistic-pricing suits. Indeed, given the distributive desirability of punishing contrived oligopolistic pricers, protecting the prospective victims of the future contrived oligopolistic pricing that successful prosecutions will deter, and enabling the victims of past contrived oligopolistic pricing to recover their losses (indeed, in the U.S., treble damages *minus* their lawyer fees and

---

[391] See Paul Joskow and Alvin Klevorick, *A Framework for Analyzing Predatory Pricing Policy* (hereinafter Joskow and Klevorick), 89 YALE L.J. 213 (1979).

other litigation costs) from the contrivers, prosecutions of contrived oligopolistic pricers might be desirable even if they were economically inefficient.

Before proceeding, I want to consider briefly the five types of evidence that can help prove natural oligopolistic pricing—evidence that would be legally relevant under E.C./E.U. competition law if I am correct in concluding that natural oligopolistic pricing is covered as a concerted practice by what is now Article 101 of the 2009 Treaty of Lisbon. All these types of evidence are counterparts to the types of evidence we have just seen can strengthen a contrived-oligopolistic-pricing claim. First, there is eyewitness testimony, audio recordings, or documentary evidence indicating that one or more defendants believed they could obtain oligopolistic margins naturally and/or intended to or actually had obtained NOMs. Second, there is the evidence that can establish that a seller's actual price is higher than its HNOP. Admittedly, persuasive evidence of this kind might not be legally decisive, given the legality under E.C./E.U. law of contrived oligopolistic pricing practiced by a firm that was neither dominant nor a member of a collectively-dominant set of rivals solely through making retaliatory threats. However, in practice, I suspect that such evidence would be legally salient. The only way that a defendant could escape liability if its price were shown to exceed its HNOP would be to demonstrate not only (1) that it was neither individually dominant nor a member of a set of rivals that were collectively dominant but also (2) that its price reflected its securing a COM exclusively by making and possibly carrying out threats of retaliation. I doubt that many defendants would be willing to demonstrate the second of these two facts. Third, with the same qualification, a seller's natural oligopolistic pricing and/or illegal contrived oligopolistic pricing can also be established by the same types of inter-temporal and inter-regional evidence that can be used to establish its practice of contrived oligopolistic pricing. Fourth, a natural-oligopolistic-pricing case can be strengthened or established by evidence that sellers made premature price announcements they would not have found profitable but for the announcements' tendency to enable them to practice oligopolistic pricing naturally. Fifth, "structural" evidence favoring the conclusion that buyers will be likely to give their undercut or undermined best-placed suppliers an opportunity to rebid and that such suppliers will find it inherently profitable to beat their rivals' undercutting or undermining offers can also strengthen a natural-oligopolistic-pricing case.

B. The Types of Evidence That Richard Posner and Other Scholars Argue Can Establish Illegal Oligopolistic Pricing

This subsection is designed to perform three functions: (1) to demonstrate that various methods of proving that one or more defendants have practiced illegal oligopolistic pricing that continue to have some currency cannot bear scrutiny, (2) to provide a basis for my claim that the errors that scholars made when analyzing oligopolistic pricing in the 1960s and 1970s stemmed from the same source as the errors Chap. 11 will demonstrate scholars made when analyzing predatory pricing more recently, and (3) to show that both sets of errors derive from the failure of the scholars in question to take account of many of the concepts and distinctions that Chap. 2 delineated and thereby to justify the admittedly-complex non-standard conceptual systems I have developed to analyze price-theory and competition-theory issues.

The subsection's organization reflects the fact that it is designed to perform the latter two of the above three functions. Rather than addressing each proposed "test" for illegal price-fixing separately, it places several of them into groups defined by the errors that led their supporters to propose them.

(1) Professor Posner's Proposals That Must Be Rejected Because They Ignore the Fact That Firms That Are Not Pure Monopolists Can Enjoy BCAs in Their Relations with Particular Buyers, Can Take Advantage of Their Rivals' CMCs, Can Secure NOMs, and Can Be Affected by Buyer and Rival Errors

Six Posner proposals fall into this category. The first is Professor Posner's claim that U.S. courts can infer that a seller has engaged in illegal oligopolistic pricing from proof that the seller has engaged in systematic price discrimination in the economist's sense.[392] Admittedly, in a world without basic competitive advantages, contextual marginal costs, NOMs, or buyer or seller errors, one could infer that a seller's price contained a COM from the fact that it discriminated against the buyer to which it was charged. Such an inference would be justified because (if we assume for convenience that the relevant marginal costs are equal) the higher of two discriminatory prices will always exceed marginal cost, which will equal the seller's (HNOP + NOM) sum if the seller's basic competitive advantages, its rivals' contextual marginal costs, all error figures, and the seller's NOM all equal zero. In reality, however, competitive advantages are pervasive, variable, and often substantial, and rival contextual marginal costs, the various error margins, and a seller's NOMs may vary among the buyers the relevant seller is best-placed to supply. Indeed, there are good theoretical grounds for believing that price discrimination among buyers the discriminator is best-placed to supply almost always reflects the fact that the relevant seller enjoys different competitive advantages in its relations with the various buyers it is best-placed to supply. Admittedly, some of the price discrimination that sellers practice among buyers they are best-placed to supply will reflect their obtaining a contrived oligopolistic margin from some but not all of their customers or their securing a higher contrived oligopolistic margin from some customers than from others. However, my analysis of the determinants of a firm's contrived oligopolistic margins implies that such margins probably do not vary either frequently or significantly from customer to customer. At least, the proportion of the price discrimination practiced by sellers among buyers they are best-placed to supply that reflects variations in contrived oligopolistic margins is far too small compared to the proportion attributable to variations in competitive advantages, rival contextual marginal costs, various errors, and NOMs to justify

[392] See *Posner Approach* at 1578–79.

inferring the oligopolistic character of a price charged by a best-placed supplier to one of its customers from the fact that it manifested discrimination against the buyer in question.

The preceding paragraph implicitly assumed that the price discriminator was engaged in individualized pricing and was charging discriminatory prices to buyers it was best-placed to supply. Since Posner's price-discrimination "test" does not distinguish between (1) firms that are charging discriminatory prices to classes of buyers and those that are charging such prices to individual buyers or between (2) discriminators whose discriminatorily-low prices are being offered to buyers they are best-placed to supply and those whose discriminatorily-low prices are being offered to buyers they are worse-than-best-placed to supply, its argument should suffice to defeat Posner's price-discrimination proposal.

However, it might be worthwhile to consider the defensibility of the more-limited claim that the fact that a firm has discriminated among classes of customers or has charged discriminatorily-low prices to buyers it is worse-than-best-placed to supply implies that it is engaging in illegal oligopolistic pricing. In fact, neither of these inferences is justifiable. The argument against inferring contrived oligopolistic pricing from price discrimination between or among classes of buyers (that the discriminator is best-placed to supply) is the same as the argument against inferring contrivance from price discrimination between or among individual buyers the discriminator is best-placed to supply: the discrimination is far more likely to reflect the fact that the discriminator's BCAs vary among the classes of buyers in question than that it secured or attempted to secure COMs from one class of buyers but not the other or that the COMs it secured or attempted to secure from one class of buyers were higher than those it secured or attempted to secure from another class of buyers.

One can also not infer that a discriminator was practicing contrived oligopolistic pricing from the fact that the discriminator was charging a discriminatorily-low price to a buyer it was worse-than-best-placed to supply. Admittedly, a seller's charging a buyer it was worse-than-best-placed to supply will manifest its own practice of contrivance if the discriminatorily-low price is a retaliatory price charged to a customer of a rival that rejected the discriminator's contrived oligopolistic offer or did not succumb to the discriminator's contrived oligopolistic threat (*i.e.*, that beat the discriminator's contrived oligopolistic offer). However, even if I ignore the possibility that such discrimination in favor of a buyer the discriminator is worse-than-best-placed to supply may manifest other sorts of illegal retaliation by the discriminator, it will not manifest the discriminator's contrived oligopolistic pricing or other illegal conduct when it manifests the discriminator's (1) taking advantage of its (best-placed) rival's contrived oligopolistic pricing by beating that rival's contrived oligopolistic offer, (2) taking advantage of its best-placed rival's overestimation of that rival's highest non-contrived price, (3) underestimating its own marginal or incremental costs, or (4) retaliating lawfully against a rival's illegal retaliatory or predatory pricing. Once more, I think that the likelihood that one of these benign explanations accounts for a seller's discriminating in favor of a buyer it is worse-than-best-placed to supply is too high for Posner's proposed inference to be justifiable in either a criminal or a civil case.

Of course, it might be possible to modify this price-discrimination test to limit the proposed inference to situations in which the relevant price-differences cannot be explained in benign ways. Indeed, if adjusted in this way, Posner's proposal would be a variant of the two comparative protocols I proposed. However, because I suspect that price discrimination is significantly less likely to be associated with discriminator-contrivance (or contrivance by anyone else) than are inter-temporal and inter-regional price-differences, I doubt that this revised price-discrimination test for contrived oligopolistic pricing would be as cost-effective as my two comparative methods for detecting such pricing.

The second Posner proposal that must be rejected because it ignores the fact that sellers that are not pure monopolists can enjoy BCAs or set supra-competitive prices for other non-contrivance-related reasons is his proposal that the oligopolistic character of one or more sellers' prices can be inferred from inter-temporal price-differences that cannot be explained by differences in marginal costs (or average marginal [*i.e.*, incremental] costs over the relevant range of output) and inter-regional price-equalities that persist in the face of inter-regional marginal-cost differences.[393] According to Professor Posner, when prices differ between regions in which variable costs are the same, one can infer that firms in the region in which the higher prices are charged are practicing oligopolistic pricing—at least when the structure of the higher-priced ARDEPPS is more conducive to such oligopolistic pricing. In fact, however, in a world of monopolistic competition and natural oligopolistic pricing, this inference is not justified, for such differences in prices often reflect differences in other factors that influence the size of the gap between a seller's highest non-oligopolistic price and marginal cost and the size of the error margins and NOMs it obtains: in individualized-pricing contexts, differences in BCAs and rival CMCs and, in across-the-board-pricing contexts, (*inter alia*) differences in BCA distributions and the extent to which the relevant sellers announce their prices in the order that is in their joint interest. Unfortunately, one cannot eliminate this problem by focusing on cases in which the structure of the ARDEPPS in which higher prices are charged is more conducive to contrived oligopolistic pricing because the same structural features that favor contrived oligopolistic pricing may also cause basic competitive advantages to be higher. Accordingly, one cannot infer contrived oligopolistic pricing from the presence of inter-regional and inter-temporal price-differences that cannot be attributed to differences in conventional marginal cost. For these types of comparative methods to work, one must take account of differences in basic competitive advantages, contextual marginal costs, the order in which sellers announce their prices, and NOMs as well as of differences in conventional marginal costs.

The third Posner proposal that falls into this category is the claim that one can infer that one or more sellers are practicing illegal oligopolistic pricing from their failure to reduce their prices when faced with declining demand and rates of capacity-utilization unless the price-increase can be explained by the producers' contemporaneous product-improvements or by actual or planned advertising campaigns that they thought

[393] *Id.* at 1579.

would increase the dollar value that relevant buyers placed on their products.[394] Posner never explains why he thinks this response to declining demand and rates of capacity-utilization implies that the firms in question are practicing contrived oligopolistic pricing. Presumably, he bases this inference on the premises that (in my terms) in the vast majority of cases, a decline in demand will always reduce the relevant firm's HNOPs so that their failure to reduce their prices must betoken the demand decline's increasing their COMs (for some unexplained reason). In fact, it is not clear that demand declines will always or even usually be associated with reductions in HNOPs, and the effect of demand declines on COMs is contestable and certainly contested. I will address each of these issues in turn. First, for two reasons, declines in demand may not reduce the relevant sellers' HNOPs: (1) the decline in demand may be caused by a general macro-economic decline that disproportionately reduces the demand of poor buyers whose original dollar-valuation of both the product in general and of differences between various product-variants was lower than average, and (2) the decline in demand might have led to a reduction in the number of product variants offered for sale or the number of distributive outlets in operation, reductions that would tend to raise the BPAs of the producers of the surviving product variants or operators of the surviving outlets. Second, it is not at all clear why a decline in the demand that a set of rivals faces will cause the firms' COMs to rise. One possible explanation is that firms that are engaging in contrivance may be more inhibited from reducing their prices when their HNOPs fall by the fear that any price-reduction would be more likely to lead to an all-out price-war,[395] though this argument would not account for the relevant sellers' prices' rising in the face of a decline in their HNOPs. Another possible explanation implicitly assumes that (1) decreases in current demand do not affect the likely strength of demand at the future time at which retaliation to current price-cutting would take place and (2) the amount of harm that future retaliation will impose on a current undercutter/underminer will not be geared to the profits the undercutter made by undercutting—*i.e.*, argues on these assumptions that the incentive to undercut will be lower when demand is weaker because the short-run gains from undercutting will be smaller under those circumstances while the loss from retaliation will be the same.[396] I doubt the strength of the former explanation and the premises and hence the conclusion of the latter.

---

[394] *Id.* at 1585–87.

[395] See, *e.g.*, Julio J. Rotemberg and Garth Saloner, *A Supergame-Theoretic Model of Price Wars During Booms*, 76 AM. ECON. REV. 390 (1986).

[396] My objection to the second premise of the second explanation also applies to the analysis of John Haltiwanger and Joseph E. Harrington, Jr., in *The Impact of Cyclical Demand Movements on Collusive Behavior*, 22 RAND J. OF ECON. 89 (1991), which assumes that the profitability of undermining depends not on whether demand is lower-than-average or higher-than-average but on whether demand is on the upswing or downswing (a claim that is most salient in ARDEPPSes subject to seasonal or macro-economic-cyclical movements in demand). Haltiwanger and Harrington's conclusion that collusion is easier in the upswing and more difficult in the downswing regardless of whether current demand is higher-than-average or lower-than-average would be correct if the ratio of the gains from undercutting to the losses the undercutter will suffer from retaliation depended on the relative strengths of near-future *versus* current demand. However, I see no reason to believe that this is the case.

rather than higher-than-average (P–MC) figures, one would not be able to justify inferring contrived oligopolistic pricing from lower-than-average price-change amplitudes even if (contrary to fact) higher-than-average (P–MC) figures primarily reflected higher-than-average COMs.

Fifth and finally, the case for this inference is undermined by the probable tendency of contrived oligopolistic pricing to increase the average amplitude of price-changes in the ARDEPPSes in which it is practiced by leading to occasional or periodic price-wars.

The fifth Posner proposal that falls into this category is related to the fourth: Posner also proposes that courts infer that the constituent firms in an ARDEPPS have practiced illegal oligopolistic pricing from the fact that prices have changed relatively infrequently in the ARDEPPS in question.[398] This claim has three implicit premises: (1) that the NEHNOPs and possible NOMs in any ARDEPPS in which contrived oligopolistic pricing is not practiced will rarely change more frequently than the NEHNOPs and possible NOMs change in ARDEPPSes in which contrived oligopolistic pricing is practiced, (2) that contrivers of oligopolistic prices will adjust their prices less frequently to changes in their NEHNOPs and possible NOMs than will sellers that do not contrive oligopolistic prices because contrivers will hesitate to change their prices for fear that their behaviors may be misunderstood or lead to disagreements that disrupt the established collusion, and (3) that an ARDEPPS' contrived OMs vary insufficiently often fully to offset the tendency of contrivers not to vary their prices so often as non-contrivers (where the latter tendency is implied by the first two premises).

Unfortunately, each of these premises is sufficiently dubious to render this infrequency-of-price-change test unacceptably inaccurate. I simply do not know whether the NEHNOPs of contrived oligopolistic pricers change more or less often than the NEHNOPs of non-contrivers. On the one hand, if contrived oligopolistic pricing tends to be practiced more often the higher the relevant seller's BCAs and the frequency with which BCAs change tends to increase with the size of the BCAs because strong preferences tend to be faddish and less stable (two propositions that may well be true), the NEHNOPs of contrivers will change more often than the NEHNOPs of non-contrivers. On the other hand, if (as I believe) contrived oligopolistic pricing tends to be practiced less often the higher the relevant seller's BCAs and the frequency with which BCAs change tends to increase with the size of the BCAs in question because strong preferences tend to be stable (two propositions that may also be true), the NEHNOPs of contrivers will change less often than the NEHNOPs of non-contrivers. Although I do not know whether the NEHNOPs of contrivers do change more often than the NEHNOPs of non-contrivers, it would be astounding if the NEHNOPs of contrivers in a significant percentage of ARDEPPSes did not change more frequently than the NEHNOPs of non-contrivers in many ARDEPPSes. Indeed, I suspect that this outcome occurs sufficiently frequently to make the Posner-inference now under

---

398 *Id.* at 1580.

consideration unacceptable. Posner's failure to consider this possibility stems from his failure to recognize that sellers that are not pure monopolists can enjoy substantial (and changing) BCAs.

Indeed, this infrequency-of-price-change test would be unacceptable even if the preceding argument could be ignored, for the second explicit premise of Posner's inchoate argument is less important than he believes, and the third implicit premise is clearly false. Thus, although contrivers may hesitate to *reduce* their prices in response to reductions in their NEHNOPs because their price-reductions might be misinterpreted or might cause coordination-difficulties, in our inflationary economy, contrivers are more likely to want to raise their prices in response to increases in their NEHNOPs than they are to want to decrease their prices: since price-increases are less likely to be disruptive of collusion, contrivers are less likely to change prices less often than non-contrivers on this account than Posner implies. Finally, Posner totally ignores the fact that, *ceteris paribus*, contrivers will be more likely to change their prices than non-contrivers because the prices they will want to charge will vary with the determinants of the oligopolistic margin they will find most profitable *ex ante* to try to obtain (as well as with the determinants of their BCAs, their rivals' CMCs, and their own NOMs) and because from time to time contrivers will choose to alter their prices to undercut a rival's COMs or retaliate against an undercutting rival.

A sixth Posner proposal—his recommendation that courts infer contrived oligopolistic pricing from the fact that the sellers have fixed market shares over a substantial period of time[399]—could be discussed under either this heading or the heading that follows. The intuition behind this proposed inference is that contriving oligopolists are less likely to try to increase their market shares by lowering their prices because of fears that such an attempt might trigger a costly price-war that would eliminate both their and their rivals' contrived oligopolistic margins. This argument might be valid were it not for the fact that shifts in market share are more likely to reflect shifts in sellers' BPA distributions (attributable to spontaneous changes in buyer preferences or changes in the product variants that incumbent firms produce) and inter-established-seller differences in the amount of QV investments they make in their ARDEPPS through time than differences in the extent to which individual sellers launch aggressive pricing-campaigns. Posner's failure to recognize that sellers that are not pure monopolists can enjoy BCAs (MCAs and BPAs) in their relations with individual buyers and that QV investment is variable has kept him from recognizing that these facts (and the related possible tendency of contrived oligopolistic pricing to increase the variability of its practitioners' market shares through time by making them hesitate to change their prices in response to changes in their BPA and hence BCA distributions) make his unusually-stable-market-share test too inaccurate for courts to use.

[399] *Id.* at 1582.

(2) Professor Posner's Proposals That Must Be Rejected Because They Ignore Both the Fact That the Equilibrium Level of QV Investment in an ARDEPPS Increases with the Supra-Competitiveness of Its Prices at Various QV-Investment Levels Until Those Prices Reach the ARDEPPS-Profit-Maximizing Level and Relatedly the Determinants of the Intensity of QV-Investment Competition in Any ARDEPPS

Professor Posner made two proposals that must be rejected primarily because they ignore the fact that QV investment is variable (that the set of product-*plus*-service types produced by an ARDEPPS or in the economy as a whole is not exogenously determined). In particular, these proposals must be rejected because they ignore the fact that the practice of contrived oligopolistic pricing in an ARDEPPS will raise the ARDEPPS' equilibrium QV-investment level, that many factors other than the extent to which its constituent firms practice contrived oligopolistic pricing will affect an ARDEPPS' equilibrium QV-investment level, and (in one case) the fact that capacity is a quality-variable when demand fluctuates through time.

The first of Professor Posner's proposals that fails for these reasons is his claim that courts can infer the fact that sellers have engaged in illegal oligopolistic pricing from evidence establishing that they have persistently realized supernormal profits.[400] I should point out at the outset that Posner's specification of this proposal is incomplete in two respects: (1) he does not indicate whether the relevant supernormal profit-rate is the highest supernormal profit-rate the relevant seller or sellers realized on any QV investment in the area of product-space in question or the weighted-average supernormal profit-rate the relevant seller or sellers realized on all their QV investments in the relevant area of product-space, and (2) his articulation of the test leaves the impression that he thinks that the inference should be made from the relevant seller's or sellers' realization of any amount of supernormal profits (earning a profit-rate that was supernormal at all) when I suspect (since the weighted-average investment in most "industries" generates some supernormal profits) that he really intends to recommend that the inference be drawn only when the seller or sellers persistently realized a supernormal profit-rate that was either substantial or higher than its weighted-average, economy-wide counterpart. My critique will consider both the "highest supernormal profit-rate" and the "weighted-average supernormal profit-rate" variants of this Posner proposal and will assume that he is proposing that the inference be drawn only if the relevant persistent supernormal profit-rate was substantial or higher than its weighted-average, economy-wide counterpart. I should also point out at the outset that, for any of the inferences Posner is recommending be made to be justified in a civil case, the relevant supernormal-profit-rate finding must create a greater-than-50 % probability that the sellers in the ARDEPPS in question had practiced contrived (illegal) oligopolistic pricing and that, for any of these inferences to be justified in a criminal case, the relevant supernormal-profit-rate finding must eliminate any reasonable doubt that the ARDEPPS' sellers had practiced illegal oligopolistic pricing.

[400] *Id.*

Professor Posner made no argument for any variant of the claim on which we are now focusing: he simply asserted that the inference in question was justified. In fact, however, this claim would be correct only if at least one of the following two relationships obtained: (1) if the practice of contrived oligopolistic pricing were sufficiently often a cause of one or more sellers' persistent realization of supernormal profits for the inference to be justified on this "causal" basis or (2) if the determinants of whether one or more sellers *would practice* contrived oligopolistic pricing (note: not the determinants of whether such pricing would be profitable for the sellers in question) overlap sufficiently with the determinants of whether one or more sellers will realize persistent supernormal profits for the inference to be justified on this correlational basis. In fact, however, neither of these relationships seems likely to obtain. I will devote more attention to the first, causal argument than to the second, correlational argument, at least in part because putting the correlational argument under too strong a lens would produce too strong a smell of burning straw.

Chapter 2's analysis of QV-investment competition provides the basis for demonstrating the unjustifiability of both the causal argument and the correlational argument for this Posner proposal. I will first review Chap. 2's analysis of the determinants of the highest supernormal profit-rate that will be generated by any QV investment in an ARDEPPS in equilibrium and then examine the implications of this analysis for the causal and correlational arguments for the different variants of this Posner proposal I have distinguished. I will begin by assuming that the relevant situation and associated QV-investment equilibrium is static—*i.e.*, that neither the "ARDEPPS demand" curve nor the marginal, average variable, or average total cost curves for the ARDEPPS' various QV-investment projects vary through time—but will eventually relax this assumption and analyze the significance for this Posner claim of the reality that the equilibrium in most ARDEPPSes is dynamic—that most "ARDEPPS demand curves" vary (usually increase) through time and that many ARDEPPSes' cost curves decrease through time (as the ARDEPPSes' members make production-process-research discoveries).

When the relevant situation and equilibrium are static, the factors that will determine the supernormal profit-rate that the most-profitable projects in a given area of product-space will generate in equilibrium will depend on the nature of the QV-investment equilibrium that will be established. If the equilibrium is established above the ARDEPPS' entry-preventing QV-investment level, the supernormal profit-rate that will be generated by the most-profitable projects in equilibrium will equal the sum of the barriers to expansion and QV-investment incentives and disincentives that just managed to deter the firm that was best-placed in equilibrium to execute an additional QV-investment expansion in the relevant ARDEPPS (if I assume for simplicity—as I will throughout this discussion—that the owners of the relevant ARDEPPS' most-profitable projects had no monopolistic QV-investment incentives to execute them and faced no monopolistic or natural oligopolistic QV-investment disincentives in relation to them); if the equilibrium is established at the ARDEPPS' entry-preventing QV-investment level, the relevant supernormal profit-rate will equal the sum of the barriers to entry confronting the relevant ARDEPPS' best-placed potential competitor; and if the equilibrium is established below the ARDEPPS' entry-preventing QV-investment level, the relevant supernormal profit-rate will equal the sum of the barriers to expansion that just deterred the established firm that was best-placed to expand ARDEPPS QV investment in equilibrium from doing so when the firm that was best-placed to make the least-unprofitable QV investment that could be added to the ARDEPPS was an established firm and will equal the sum of the barriers to entry that just deterred the originally-worse-than-best-placed potential entrant into that ARDEPPS when that firm was in a position to make the least-unprofitable QV investment that could be introduced into the ARDEPPS post-equilibrium.

Now, what does this analysis imply for the viability of the causal argument for any variant of this Posner proposal? Admittedly, these various barriers or barrier-*plus*-(dis) incentive sums will be affected by contrived oligopolistic pricing. *Ceteris paribus*, the higher the COMs in a given area of product-space at any given QV-investment level, the higher its $H\Pi_E$ and $H\Pi_N$ curves at that level, the higher equilibrium QV investment, the higher the barriers likely to be operative in equilibrium, and the higher the supernormal profit-rate yielded by the ARDEPPS' most-profitable projects in equilibrium (or the more likely that an ARDEPPS' most-profitable projects will yield supernormal profits in equilibrium). However, this general connection between the fact that the sellers in an ARDEPPS whose conditions are static are successfully practicing contrived oligopolistic pricing and the highest supernormal profit-rate generated on any QV investment in that ARDEPPS in equilibrium do not justify the causal argument for any of the proposals Posner might be deemed to have made. Thus, the combination of the facts that (1) the best-placed potential entrants into virtually all ARDEPPSes in the economy would face barriers to entry in equilibrium even if the relevant ARDEPPS' incumbents were not practicing contrived oligopolistic pricing successfully and (2) the best-placed potential expander in virtually all ARDEPPSes in the economy would face barriers to expansion in equilibrium even if the relevant ARDEPPS' incumbents were not practicing contrived oligopolistic pricing successfully makes it too likely that one or more QV investments in an ARDEPPS will yield a positive supernormal profit-rate despite the fact that contrived oligopolistic pricing was not being practiced successfully within it for it to be appropriate for courts to infer such contrivance from the fact that one or more QV investments in the relevant ARDEPPS were generating some supernormal profits in equilibrium. (In fact, although this relationship is less relevant, the fact that an ARDEPPS' sellers are securing COMs does not even guarantee that any of its QV investments would yield supernormal profits in a static equilibrium: in theory, the relevant barriers to entry and/or barriers to expansion could be zero in equilibrium even if contrived oligopolistic pricing was being successfully practiced.)

Nor can one rescue the causal argument for Posner's proposal that U.S. courts infer contrived oligopolistic pricing in an ARDEPPS from something related to the supernormal profit-rate yielded by one or more QV investments in the ARDEPPS in question by assuming that he was proposing that such an inference be made only if the highest supernormal profit-rate in the ARDEPPS in equilibrium was absolutely high or higher than its weighted-average, economy-wide counterpart. Indeed, if—as I will assume at the beginning—the practice of contrived oligopolistic pricing is not causally connected to the erection of retaliation barriers to entry or expansion, contrived oligopolistic pricing might not even raise the highest supernormal profit-rate yielded by any QV investment in the ARDEPPS in question in equilibrium: if the same (Π_D + R + S) barriers to entry and expansion applied to each of the additional QV investments that would have to be made to raise total QV investment in the ARDEPPS in question from its no-contrived-oligopolistic-pricing equilibrium to its higher, actual-contrived-oligopolistic-pricing equilibrium, the practice of contrived oligopolistic pricing would not raise the highest supernormal profit-rate generated by any QV investment in the ARDEPPS in equilibrium. Admittedly, in practice, this condition is unlikely to be fulfilled. In most cases, the successful practice of contrived oligopolistic pricing will raise the highest supernormal profit-rate generated by any QV investment in the ARDEPPS in question in equilibrium by causing the (Π_D + R) barriers that face the best-placed potential QV-investment-adder (potential entrant or potential expander) in the actual-contrived-oligopolistic-pricing equilibrium to exceed their counterparts in the no-contrived-oligopolistic-pricing equilibrium: in most cases, the successive QV investments that would be more profitable to add than any alternative QV investment that could be added will be less profitable than their predecessors. However, this reality does not justify the causal argument for this version of the supernormal-profit-related Posner proposal: the highest supernormal profit-rate generated by any QV investment in an ARDEPPS in equilibrium is substantially affected by too many factors other than the ARDEPPS' COMs that vary significantly from ARDEPPS to ARDEPPS (their [NEHNOP–MC]/NEHNOP ratios, their NOM/MC ratios, their sales-to-QV-investment ratios, the rate at which the [Π_D + R] barriers facing successive best-placed potential expanders and entrants on the QV investments they are successively best-placed to make increases once one gets beyond the set of most-profitable QV investments, *etc*.) for any causal argument to be able to justify a court's inferring that an ARDEPPS' incumbents have successfully practiced contrived oligopolistic pricing from the fact that the highest supernormal profit-rate in the ARDEPPS in equilibrium was either substantial or higher than its weighted-average, economy-wide counterpart.

Diagram III illustrates the preceding analysis. The curves in Diagram III have all been defined before except that the various $H\Pi_E$ and $H\Pi_N$ curves now have superscripts "A" or "B." The curves whose labels contain the superscript "B" indicate the relationship between the relevant rate-of-return and ARDEPPS QV-investment level if no contrived oligopolistic pricing were practiced ("B" for "before" the practice of contrived oligopolistic pricing) and the curves whose labels contain the superscript "A" indicate the above relationship if contrived oligopolistic pricing is practiced ("A" for "after" the practice of contrived oligopolistic pricing). For simplicity, Diagram III is constructed on the unrealistic assumption that the practice of contrived oligopolistic pricing will not affect seller risk costs—*i.e*., its construction assumes that neither $N\Pi_E$ nor $N\Pi_N$ nor the difference between them will be affected by the practice of contrived oligopolistic pricing. (In reality, I would expect that such contrivance would tend to increase both $N\Pi_E$ and $N\Pi_N$, though its impact on [$N\Pi_N$–$N\Pi_E$] is less clear.) To ease the exposition, Diagram III is also based on the assumption that potential entrants face no retaliation or scale barriers to entry—more positively, face only risk barriers of MU (equal to the difference between the heights of $N\Pi_N$ and $N\Pi_E$) and

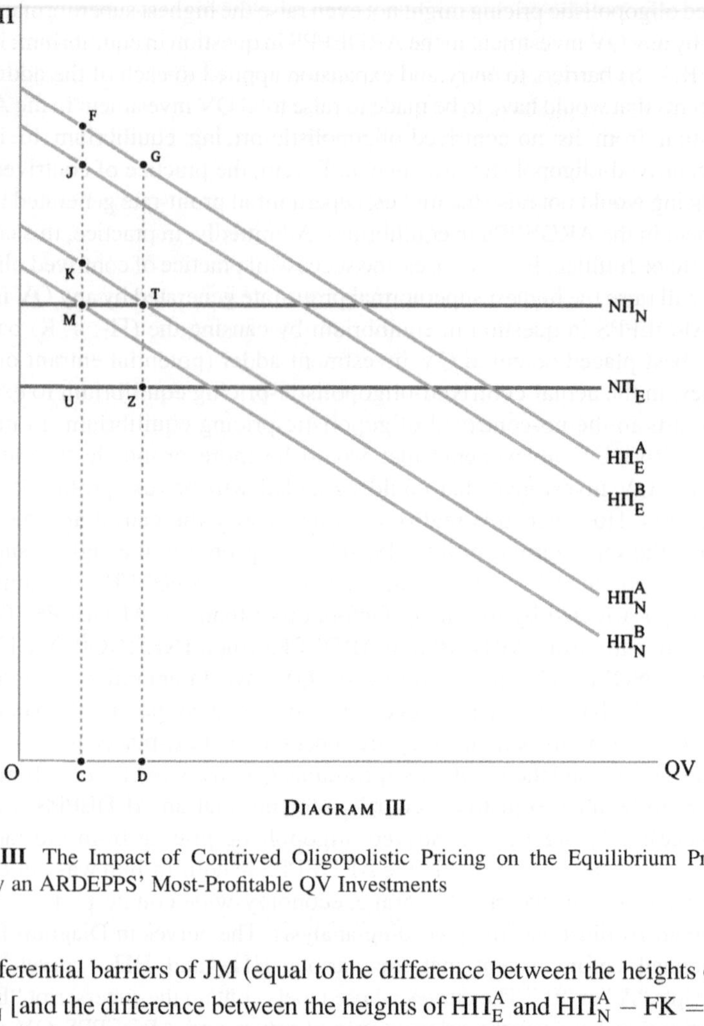

Diagram III The Impact of Contrived Oligopolistic Pricing on the Equilibrium Profit-Rate Yielded by an ARDEPPS' Most-Profitable QV Investments

profit-differential barriers of JM (equal to the difference between the heights of $H\Pi_E^B$ and $H\Pi_N^B$ [and the difference between the heights of $H\Pi_E^A$ and $H\Pi_N^A - FK = JM$]).

The analysis that follows assumes as well that (1) both before and after contrived oligopolistic pricing is practiced, the entry-preventing QV-investment level in the ARDEPPS to which Diagram III relates equals or exceeds the entry-barred, expansion-preventing QV-investment level (which the diagram does not indicate), (2) the no-contrived-oligopolistic-pricing QV-investment equilibrium is at the no-contrived-oligopolistic pricing entry-preventing QV-investment level OC, and the contrived-oligopolistic-pricing QV-investment equilibrium is at the (higher) contrived-oligopolistic-pricing entry-preventing QV-investment level OD, and (3) the barriers to entry that would confront the best-placed potential competitor(s) at the level of QV investment that would be entry-preventing if no contrived oligopolistic pricing were practiced (OC) equal the lower of (A) the barriers to entry that would confront the best-placed potential competitor(s) at the level of QV investment that would be the equilibrium level of QV investment, given the positive amounts of contrived oligopolistic pricing that would actually be practiced at different QV-investment levels (OD) (when a potential entrant would be the best-placed potential QV investor at that QV-investment level), and (B) the sum of the barriers to expansion and $(M + O)$ disincentives or incentives that would confront the best-placed potential expander at that equilibrium QV-investment level OD (when an incumbent is the best-placed potential QV investor at that contrived-oligopolistic-pricing QV-investment equilibrium). This result could obtain because (1) at OC, the number of intrinsically-equally-profitable best-placed QV investments (QV investments associated with the same $[\Pi_D + R]$ barriers) that could be made by potential entrants equaled or exceeded the number of QV investments that would have to be added to the ARDEPPS for its total QV investment to rise from OC to OD; (2) given the barriers to entry facing the ARDEPPS' best-placed, second-placed,. . .*n*th-placed potential competitors, the number of QV investments that its incumbents could make (QV-investment expansions they could execute) for which the sum of the $(\Pi_D + R)$ barriers and $(M + O)$ incentives and disincentives they faced equaled the sum of the $(\Pi_D + R)$ barriers faced by the potential competitor that was best-placed to enter at OC equaled or exceeded the number of QV investments that would have to be added to the ARDEPPS in question for its total QV investment to rise from OC to OD, or (3) the sum of (A) the number of QV investments that could be made by the potential competitor or competitors that were best-placed to enter the ARDEPPS in question at OC that would be as profitable as the most-profitable entry any such firm could execute at OC and (B) the number of QV investments that could be made by the potential expander or expanders that were best-placed to execute an expansion at OC that, given the barriers to entry facing the ARDEPPS' best-placed, second-placed,. . .*n*th-placed potential competitor at OC, would be as profitable as the most-profitable QV investment that any potential competitor could make at OC equaled or exceeded the number of QV investments that would have to be added to the ARDEPPS in question for its total QV investment to rise from OC to OD.

The analysis of Diagram III is also based on an additional assumption that some may find unrealistic—*viz.*, that the decision by firms to engage in contrived oligopolistic pricing will not tend to be conjoined with decisions to contrive oligopolistic QV-investment restrictions by raising the retaliation barriers sufficiently to deter at least some of the new entry or incumbent expansions that successful contrived oligopolistic pricing would otherwise induce. I hasten to note that, for two reasons, I think this assumption is not completely unrealistic. First, successful attempts to engage in contrived oligopolistic pricing that do not lead to public prosecutions or civil suits will increase their practitioners' profits even if the contrivers do not simultaneously raise the operative retaliation barriers to entry and expansion (1) by raising the supernormal profits they realize on their pre-contrivance QV investments in the period before the entries and expansions the contrivance induces are executed even if the resulting increase in QV investment reduces the profit-rates of the original projects to their pre-contrivance levels, (2) by enabling those incumbents that take advantage of the profitable QV-investment opportunities the contrived oligopolistic pricing creates to earn supernormal profits on the additional QV investments they make before the new equilibrium is established and to earn at least normal profits on those investments after the new equilibrium is established even if the profit-rates yielded by the QV investments that were present in the ARDEPPS at its no-contrived-oligopolistic-pricing equilibrium were the same at its contrived-oligopolistic-pricing equilibrium as they were at its no-contrived-oligopolistic-pricing equilibrium, and (3) by enabling the owners of the QV investments that were present in the ARDEPPS in question at its no-contrived-oligopolistic-pricing equilibrium to realize higher supernormal profit-rates on those investments and by enabling the incumbents that the contrived oligopolistic pricing induced to make additional QV investments to earn higher supernormal profit-rates on those QV-investment expansions than previously indicated by causing QV investment to be more restricted (because the operative barriers and disincentives combined are higher at the higher contrived-oligopolistic-pricing equilibrium than at the lower no-contrived-oligopolistic-pricing equilibrium). Second, the determinants of the ability of a set of rivals to contrive oligopolistic prices are quite different from the determinants of their ability to contrive QV-investments restrictions (to create retaliation barriers to entry and expansion). In any event, I will eventually relax this assumption and consider the significance of any tendency of contrived oligopolistic pricing to be conjoined with contrived oligopolistic QV-investment restrictions.

Diagram III reveals that, on its assumptions, although the practice of contrived oligopolistic pricing will raise the height of $\text{H}\Pi_{\text{E}}$ at the original equilibrium QV-investment level OC from JC to FC and the height of $\text{H}\Pi_{\text{N}}$ at QV-investment level OC from MC to KC, respectively, it will not increase the supernormal profit-rate yielded by the relevant ARDEPPS' most-profitable projects in equilibrium, which will remain equal to JU = GZ, because it will increase the equilibrium QV-investment level from OC to OD.

Of course, in practice, not all of the assumptions on which Diagram III is based will always be fulfilled. In situations in which the post-contrived-oligopolistic-pricing entry-preventing QV-investment level is above the post-contrived-oligopolistic-pricing entry-barred, expansion-preventing QV-investment level, contrived oligopolistic pricing will raise the equilibrium highest supernormal profit-rate (*i.e.*, the supernormal profit-rate generated by the ARDEPPS' most-profitable QV investments in equilibrium) if the sum of the barriers facing the first member of the set of successive best-placed potential entrants for which entry is (just) not profitable despite the fact that contrived oligopolistic pricing is being practiced are higher than the barriers to entry that faced the best-placed potential competitor at the no-contrived-oligopolistic-pricing equilibrium. Similarly, in situations in which the entry-barred, expansion-preventing QV-investment level exceeds the entry-preventing QV-investment level, contrived oligopolistic pricing will raise the equilibrium supernormal profit-rate if the sum of the barriers to expansion and *M* or *O* facing the first member of the set of successive best-placed potential expanders for which expansion is (just) not profitable despite the fact that contrived oligopolistic pricing is being practiced exceed the counterpart sum for the first such best-placed potential expander in the no-contrived-oligopolistic-pricing equilibrium. Finally, in situations in which the no-contrived-oligopolistic-pricing equilibrium QV-investment level is below the entry-preventing QV-investment level, the impact of contrived oligopolistic pricing on the equilibrium highest supernormal profit-rate will depend upon whether the best-placed potential investor in each of the two equilibria (the potential investor whose investment would be just unprofitable in the equilibrium in question) is a potential expander or a potential entrant: (1) if the best-placed potential investor in both equilibria is a potential expander, contrived oligopolistic pricing will raise the equilibrium highest supernormal profit-rate to the extent that the sum of the barriers and any *M* or *O* confronting the established firm that would be best-placed to expand in the contrived-oligopolistic-pricing equilibrium exceeds its counterpart for the established firm that would be best-placed to expand in the no-contrived-oligopolistic-pricing equilibrium; (2) if the best-placed potential investor in both equilibria is a potential entrant, contrived oligopolistic pricing will raise the equilibrium highest supernormal profit-rate to the extent that the sum of the barriers to entry that would confront the best-placed potential competitor in the contrived-oligopolistic-pricing equilibrium exceeds its counterpart for the best-placed potential competitor in the no-contrived-oligopolistic-pricing equilibrium; (3) if the best-placed potential investor in the contrived-oligopolistic-pricing equilibrium would be a potential expander (an established firm) while the best-placed potential investor in the no-contrived-oligopolistic-pricing equilibrium would be a potential entrant, contrived oligopolistic pricing will raise the equilibrium highest supernormal profit-rate to the extent that the sum of the barriers and any *M* or *O* confronting the relevant best-placed potential expander in the contrived-oligopolistic-pricing equilibrium exceed the sum of the barriers facing the best-placed potential entrant in the no-contrived-oligopolistic-pricing equilibrium; and (4) if the best-placed potential investor in the contrived-oligopolistic-pricing equilibrium would be a potential entrant while the best-placed potential investor in the no-contrived-oligopolistic-pricing equilibrium would be a potential expander, contrived oligopolistic pricing will raise the highest supernormal profit-rate to the extent that the sum of the barriers to entry facing the best-placed potential entrant at the contrived-oligopolistic-pricing equilibrium exceed the sum of the barriers and any *M* or *O* that would face the best-placed potential expander at the no-contrived-oligopolistic-pricing equilibrium. However, none of these conclusions implies that the causal argument under consideration can justify inferring that a group of rivals has successfully practiced contrived oligopolistic pricing from the fact that the most-supernormally-profitable QV investment in their ARDEPPS yielded a substantially-supernormal profit-rate or a supernormal profit-rate that was higher than its weighted-average, economy-wide counterpart. As I indicated before, even if the extent to which the firms in an ARDEPPS secured COMs were a determinant of the highest supernormal profit-rate any QV investment it contained yielded in equilibrium, this factor would account for too small a percentage of the inter-ARDEPPS variation in highest supernormal equilibrium profit-rates for the causal argument just delineated to justify the inference on which we are now focusing.

The causal argument for Posner's supernormal-profit-rate-related proposal will also not be persuasive if Posner is interpreted to be recommending that U.S. courts infer a group of sellers' successful practice of contrived oligopolistic pricing from the weighted-average supernormal rate-of-return in their ARDEPPS being substantial or higher than its weighted-average, economy-wide counterpart. In fact, the causal argument for this variant of the supernormal-profit-rate-related Posner proposal is substantially weaker than the causal argument for the highest supernormal-profit-rate variant of his proposal. This conclusion reflects the fact that, even when the successful practice of contrived oligopolistic pricing does increase the highest supernormal profit-rate generated in equilibrium in the ARDEPPS in question, it may not increase the weighted-average supernormal profit-rate generated by all the QV investments in the ARDEPPS in question because it will increase the percentage of projects in the ARDEPPS in question in equilibrium that are less than most profitable.[401]

If the practice of contrived oligopolistic pricing by one or more sellers in a given ARDEPPS whose demand and cost functions will not change through time will not cause them to erect higher retaliation barriers to entry into or QV-investment expansion in the ARDEPPS in question, the following three conclusions will be warranted:

(1) for two reasons, one cannot justify a court's inferring that one or more sellers in a given ARDEPPS have successfully practiced contrived oligopolistic pricing in that ARDEPPS from the fact that one or more of its QV investments yielded supernormal profits in equilibrium by arguing that such contrivance will cause such supernormal profits to be generated—*viz.*, (less importantly) (A) because such contrivance may not produce this outcome and (more importantly) (B) because supernormal profits are usually caused by one or more factors other than the relevant seller's or sellers' practice of contrived oligopolistic pricing;

(2) for two reasons, one cannot justify a court's inferring that one or more sellers in a given ARDEPPS have successfully practiced contrived oligopolistic pricing in that ARDEPPS from the fact that the highest supernormal profit-rate yielded by any QV investment in that ARDEPPS is substantial or higher than its weighted-average, economy-wide counterpart by arguing that the successful practice of such contrivance will cause this highest supernormal profit-rate to be higher than it otherwise would be—*viz.*, (A) because this will not always be

---

[401] The following example illustrates this possibility. Assume first (probably counterfactually but irrelevantly and expositionally conveniently) that the normal rate-of-return on all the QV investments in the relevant ARDEPPS both in the no-contrived-oligopolistic-pricing equilibrium and in the contrived-oligopolistic-pricing equilibrium is 10 %. (In reality, contrived oligopolistic pricing will probably increase the normal rate-of-return by increasing uncertainty.) Assume second that in the no-contrived-oligopolistic-pricing equilibrium, the ARDEPPS will contain seven QV investments whose rates-of-return (gross of the normal rate-of-return) are 17 %, 16 %, 15 %, 14 %, 13, 12 %, and 11 % so that the average supernormal profit-rate yielded by the QV investments the ARDEPPS would contain in its no-contrived-oligopolistic-pricing equilibrium is (14 %–10 % = 4 %). Assume third that in the contrived oligopolistic-pricing equilibrium the ARDEPPS will contain ten QV investments whose rates-of-return (gross of the normal rate-of-return) are 18 %, 17 %, 16 %, 15 %, 14 %, 13 %, 12 %, 11 %, 10.5 %, and 10 % so that the average supernormal profit-rate yielded by the QV investments the ARDEPPS would contain in its contrived-oligopolistic pricing would be (13.65 %–10 % = 3.65 %). On these facts, the relevant contrived oligopolistic pricing would increase the supernormal profit-rate generated by the ARDEPPS' most-profitable QV investment in equilibrium (from 7 % to 8 %) while decreasing the average supernormal profit-rate generated by the (changing set of) QV investments in the ARDEPPS (from 4 % to 3.65 %).

the case and (B) because the extent to which the firms in an ARDEPPS have successfully practiced contrived oligopolistic pricing accounts for far too low a percentage of the inter-ARDEPPS variation in highest supernormal profit-rates for such an inference to be justified; and

(3) for two reasons, one cannot justify a court's inferring that one or more sellers in a given ARDEPPS have successfully practiced contrived oligopolistic pricing in their ARDEPPS from the fact that the weighted-average supernormal profit-rate in that ARDEPPS is substantial or higher than its weighted-average, economy-wide counterpart by arguing that the successful practice of such contrivance will raise the weighted-average supernormal profit-rate yielded by all QV investments in that ARDEPPS—*viz.*, (A) because such contrivance is far less likely to raise this weighted-average supernormal profit-rate than it is to raise the ARDEPPS' highest equilibrium supernormal profit-rate and (B) because even if such contrivance does (contrary to my belief) tend to raise this weighted-average supernormal profit-rate, it will account for an even smaller percentage in the inter-ARDEPPS variation in this figure than it does of the inter-ARDEPPS variation in ARDEPPSes' highest supernormal profit-rates.

I now need to examine whether the causal argument for any variant of Posner's supernormal-profit-rate-related proposal would be critically strengthened if I relaxed the assumptions that (1) contrived oligopolistic pricing will not cause its practitioners to erect higher barriers to entry and expansion and (2) the equilibria on which one should focus are static rather than dynamic. I will examine the consequences of relaxing these two assumptions in turn.

I have already explained why the profitability of contrived oligopolistic pricing does not depend on its practitioners' erecting additional retaliation barriers to entry and/or expansion. Of course, this conclusion is perfectly consistent with contrived oligopolistic pricing's increasing the profits that incumbents can realize by erecting additional retaliation barriers. It therefore is plausible to assume that, in the relevant sense, contrived oligopolistic pricing may cause its practitioners to erect higher retaliation barriers. However, the question remains: Will this connection critically strengthen the causal argument for the highest or weighted-average supernormal-profit-rate variant of Posner's supernormal-profit-rate-related proposal?

Admittedly, if contrived oligopolistic pricing does tend to cause its practitioners to erect higher retaliation barriers to entry and expansion, the combination of the two types of barriers in question will tend to raise the highest supernormal profit-rate generated in the relevant ARDEPPS in (the changing) equilibrium not only for the reason that contrived oligopolistic pricing would do so if it were not linked with the erection of additional retaliation barriers but also because (on this assumption) it would be linked to the erection of additional retaliation barriers. For the same reason, if one assumes that contrived oligopolistic pricing tends to cause additional retaliation barriers to be erected, the probability that contrived oligopolistic pricing and the additional retaliation barriers that its practitioners would tend to contrive at the same time would be more likely to raise the weighted-average supernormal profit-rate in the relevant ARDEPPS in (the changing) equilibrium. However, even if I grant that it would be realistic to replace my original, non-linkage assumption with an assumption that sellers that choose to practice contrived oligopolistic pricing are induced by that choice to erect higher barriers to entry and expansion, neither the highest supernormal-profit-rate variant of Posner's supernormal-profit-rate-related proposal nor the weighted-average supernormal-profit-rate variant of that proposal could be justified through an argument that the practice of contrived oligopolistic pricing caused the highest or weighted-average supernormal profit-rate in the ARDEPPS in question to be higher than they otherwise would be. Thus, although on this causal-linkage assumption the practice of contrived oligopolistic pricing would raise the highest equilibrium supernormal profit-rate in the ARDEPPS in question, variations in the COMs that were secured in different ARDEPPSes would still account for too little of the variation in different ARDEPPSes' highest supernormal profit-rates for the causal relationship to justify courts' inferring that the sellers in an ARDEPPS have successfully practiced contrived oligopolistic pricing from the fact that their highest supernormal profit-rate was substantial or higher than its weighted-average, economy-wide counterpart. Similarly, although on this causal-linkage assumption the practice of contrived oligopolistic pricing will be more likely to raise the weighted-average supernormal profit-rate generated by all QV investments in the ARDEPPS in question, I still doubt that all things considered it will tend to do so, and, even if it does, inter-ARDEPPS differences in COMs will account for too small a percentage of inter-ARDEPPS differences in weighted-average supernormal profit-rates for courts to be justified in inferring that an ARDEPPS' sellers have successfully practiced contrived oligopolistic pricing from the weighted-average supernormal profit-rate they realize on their QV investments in the ARDEPPS in question being substantial or higher than its weighted-average, economy-wide counterpart.

Finally, will the causal argument for any variant of Professor Posner's supernormal-profit-rate-related proposals be critically strengthened if we relax our assumption that the relevant ARDEPPS' demand and cost curves do not vary through time in favor of a usually-more-realistic assumption that ARDEPPS demand increases through time and perhaps that ARDEPPS costs decrease through time? In fact, the shift from a static to a dynamic analysis will, if anything, weaken the causal argument for any variant of this Posner proposal by introducing another non-contrivance determinant of the highest supernormal and weighted-average supernormal equilibrium profit-rate in the ARDEPPS—*viz.*, the rate at which the actual, competitive QV-investment level in an ARDEPPS increases through time because "ARDEPPS demand" increases through time and/or ARDEPPS costs decrease through time.

I shift now to the correlational argument for the different variants of Posner's supernormal-profit-rate-related proposal. For this Posner proposal to succeed, (1) there must be a strong, highly-positive correlation between the factors that determine whether the supernormal profit-rate in an ARDEPPS is persistently "substantially" or at least somewhat higher-than-average and the factors that determine the profitability of contrived oligopolistic pricing and (2) the probability that a seller for which (illegal) oligopolistic pricing is *ex ante* profitable will actually choose to practice (illegal) oligopolistic pricing must be over 50 % in a civil suit and high enough to eliminate "any reasonable doubt" of its innocence in a criminal suit. Fortunately, analyses that have already been executed should suffice to establish that the first of these conditions is not fulfilled. Thus, a comparison of (1) this chapter's analysis of the determinants of the profitability of contrived oligopolistic pricing and (2) the combination of Chap. 2's analysis of the determinants of the highest supernormal profit-rate (the intensity of QV-investment competition) in an ARDEPPS and this subsection's comments on the factors that determine the relationship between the highest supernormal profit-rate in an ARDEPPS and its (weighted) average supernormal profit-rate clearly reveals that contrived oligopolistic pricing is too likely to be unprofitable in ARDEPPSes whose highest or weighted-average supernormal profit-rates are high for the correlational argument to work. And, even if this were not the case, my armchair judgment is that the correlational argument would fail because most sellers that could profit *ex ante* by illegally contriving oligopolistic prices do not do so. Hence, I reject the correlational as well as the causal argument for Posner's proposal that U.S. courts infer that the sellers in an ARDEPPS successfully practiced illegal oligopolistic pricing from the fact that they persistently realized substantial or significantly-higher-than-typical supernormal profit-rates on their most profitable or weighted-average QV investments in that ARDEPPS.

So far, my attack on this proposal has focused on the unacceptable inaccuracy of the various supernormal-profit-rate-related contrived-oligopolistic-pricing-proof proposals Richard Posner might have in mind. Another objection can also be made to these Posner proposals. Posner argued that this proposal (like all the others he made) would be cost-effective.[402] Even if one or more variants of this test for contrived oligopolistic pricing would be sufficiently accurate to be morally permissible and legally acceptable, the difficulty and cost of determining real economic profit-rates (in particular, of determining the economic value of a seller's investment and the normal rate-of-return for that investment) might render it cost-ineffective. The methods I have recommended courts use to determine whether sellers have engaged in contrived oligopolistic pricing do not require QV investment to be measured, profit-rates to be calculated, or the normal rates-of-return to be identified, and therefore, unlike this proposed method, my methods avoid the problems that have wreaked such havoc in the regulated-industries context when "fair" rates-of-return had to be calculated.

The second of Posner's proposals that falls into the current category is his claim that it is cost-effective to infer (contrived) oligopolistic pricing from the presence of prolonged "excess" capacity.[403] I should admit at the outset that a large number of

---

[402] See *Posner Approach, passim.*

[403] *Id.* at 1579–80.

economists believe that "there is greater excess capacity under collusion."[404] I will begin by analyzing the accuracy of this proposed inference and then comment on the likely cost-effectiveness of this proposal.

Posner's prolonged-"excess capacity" test for oligopolistic pricing probably would be somewhat more accurate than his persistent-realization-of-supernormal-profits test if the "excessiveness" of capacity could be measured equally accurately as the rate of supernormal profits and its persistence. Since capacity (and inventory) is a type of QV investment in ARDEPPSes in which demand fluctuates through time, the practice of contrived oligopolistic pricing will tend to cause an increase in the "excessiveness" of capacity by increasing equilibrium capacity (QV investment) while decreasing sales (though the effect of the relevant price-increase on units sold will be somewhat offset by the effect of the [average-speed-of-supply-related] quality-increase generated by the associated increase in capacity). However, although the practice of oligopolistic pricing will tend to decrease the rate of capacity-utilization and increase the excessiveness of capacity in the ARDEPPSes in which it takes place, contrived oligopolistic pricing accounts for too low a percentage of all cases in which capacity is excess for the inference Professor Posner recommends to be justified. In part, this conclusion reflects the reality that many other factors tend to cause capacity to be excess: most importantly, (1) imperfections in the price competition faced by the unit-output producers from which the capacity-creator would withdraw the resources it would use to create the capacity (imperfections that are relevant [A] because the private value to unit-output producers of the resources they use to produce their marginal units of output—a function of the marginal revenue the sale of those units will generate—will be less than the allocative value the resources in question will yield in the unit-output producer's employ, a function of the [higher] price for which those output-units will sell and [B] because the private cost to a marginal QV investor of bidding the resources it uses to create its QV investment away from a unit-output producer infinitesimally exceeds their private value to the latter while the allocative cost of the marginal QV investor's bidding the relevant resources away from a unit-output producer equals the [higher] allocative value they would have yielded in the unit-output producer's employ); (2) the BCAs and rival contextual marginal costs that would cause the capacity-creator's product-rivals' prices to exceed their conventional marginal costs even if they did not engage in contrived oligopolistic pricing (factors that are relevant because [A] in effect even if indirectly in practice the capacity-creator will withdraw the resources it "consumes" when it uses its capacity to produce actual units of its good or service primarily from these product-rivals and [B] the fact that these product-rivals' prices are *supra*-competitive implies that the cost of these resources to the capacity-creator will be deflated); (3) the NOMs that sellers in the relevant ARDEPPS are able to obtain;

[404] See *Harrington Detecting Cartels* at 238, citing Timothy F. Bresnahan, *Competition and Collusion in the American Automobile Industry: The 1955 Price War*, J. OF IND. ECON. 457 (1987); Jean-Pierre Benoit and Vijay Krishna, *Dynamic Duopoly: Prices and Quantities*, 54 REV. OF ECON. STUD. 23 (1987); and Raymond Keneckere, *Excess Capacity and Collusion*, 31 INT. ECON. REV. 521 (1990).

(4) the probable fact that accelerated-depreciation and other tax provisions may tend to inflate the private profitability of some QV investments critically; and (5) the fact that the private profitability of marginal QV investments in capacity and inventory will also be inflated by any monopolistic QV-investment incentives the relevant investor has to make them or deflated by any monopolistic or natural or contrived oligopolistic QV-investment disincentives the relevant investor has to make them. In part, this conclusion reflects the related fact that capacity is excess in virtually all ARDEPPSes in the economy in the sense that allocative efficiency would have been higher had marginal and some intra-marginal capacity-creation projects not been executed and the resources released were allocated in the way in which they would otherwise have been allocated—in some combination to various future uses, the production of leisure, the contemporaneous production of additional units of the economy's other products, the creation of some additional QV investments of other types, and some production-process research. In any event, for the above two reasons, no persuasive causal argument can be made for the accuracy of Posner's prolonged-"excess capacity" test for illegal oligopolistic pricing. Moreover, the same two arguments that led me to reject the correlational justification for Posner's persistent-realization-of-supernormal-profits test also apply with equal force in relation to his "excess capacity" test. I should add that it would be no more accurate to infer a group of sellers' participation in (contrived) oligopolistic pricing from the fact that the excessiveness of their capacity was greater than the weighted-average excessiveness of capacity in the economy.

Moreover, even if Posner's prolonged-"excess capacity" test were more accurate than I believe, it would probably not be cost-effective. Posner seems to assume that it will be easy to determine whether capacity is excess. In fact, it is not easy to determine either what capacity and the rate of capacity-utilization are in a given ARDEPPS or what rate of capacity-utilization would be allocatively efficient in that ARDEPPS.

To determine capacity and hence the rate of capacity-utilization, one must determine how much mothballed capacity can be profitably brought back into operation at times of peak demand and how much additional output can be produced at non-prohibitive cost for how long with capacity currently in use by putting on additional shifts (how much current workers will have to be paid to induce them to sacrifice leisure, how many new workers can be trained and added to the workforce, how much down-time is required for machine maintenance and repair, *etc.*). None of these questions is easy to answer.

Nor is it easy to determine the rate of capacity-utilization that is allocatively efficient. Posner seems to have made the traditional economics mistake of ignoring the fact that, when demand fluctuates through time, capacity and inventory are quality-variables because they affect the average speed of supply throughout the fluctuating demand cycle (*inter alia*, the length of supply-delivery delays at times of peak demand). The average rate of capacity-utilization through time that is allocatively efficient will vary from ARDEPPS to ARDEPPS—with the frequency with which quantity demand is higher than average, with the equivalent-dollar value of increases in speed of supply in times of peak or higher-than-average demand, and with the allocative cost of adding to capacity.

It will not be easy or cheap to determine the extent to which capacity is excessive in any ARDEPPS. Posner's prolonged-"excess capacity" test for oligopolistic pricing would probably not be cost-effective even if (contrary to my conclusion) it were acceptably accurate.

(3) Professor Posner's Proposals That Must Be Rejected Because They Ignore the Distinction Between Natural and Contrived Oligopolistic Pricing and in Some Cases the Relevance of the Order in Which Sellers Announce Their Prices to the Set of Highest Prices That Are Not Oligopolistic

I believe that it is essential to distinguish between the legality of a practice or act under the U.S antitrust laws and the desirability of a policy prohibiting the practice or act in question. Professor Posner has tended to treat these two questions as if they were one. In part, this difference in our approach can be traced to his ignoring The General Theory of Second Best: since, unlike Posner, I recognize that resource allocation may be improved by anticompetitive behavior that promotes no production-optimum efficiencies, legal analysis and policy analysis (*inter alia*, the analysis of allocative efficiency) seem far more distinct to me than to him. In part, however, Professor Posner and I disagree on this issue because we disagree both about (1) whether the U.S antitrust statutes promulgate coherent tests of illegality as opposed to authorizing the courts to regulate the conduct they cover "in the public interest" and (2) whether judges are obligated to or should follow the law when they think it is not as desirable as it could be.

In any case, despite my belief that it would be desirable to prohibit natural oligopolistic pricing,[405] for reasons that Chap. 4 explained, natural oligopolistic pricing is not proscribed by the Sherman Act[406] or by any other provision of U.S. antitrust law. Professor Posner's only substantive response to my arguments for this

[405] See Richard S. Markovits, *The Allocative Efficiency and Overall Desirability of Oligopolistic Pricing Suits*, 28 STAN. L. REV. 45 (1976) and THE WELFARE ECONOMICS OF ANTITRUST POLICY AND U.S. AND E.U. ANTITRUST LAW.

[406] In particular, natural oligopolistic pricing does not violate the Sherman Act because it does not involve the making of any anticompetitive threats or offers. However, as Chap. 4 also indicated, although the fact that natural oligopolistic pricing does not involve the making of any agreement between undertakings implies that it is not covered as an illegal agreement between undertakings under what is now Article 101 of the 2009 Treaty of Lisbon, such pricing is covered as a concerted practice under now Article 101—indeed, *prima facie* violates that provision in that its object and effect are to prevent and restrict competition. Moreover, although I do not think that natural oligopolistic pricing would be covered by now Article 102's prohibition of exclusionary abuses even if the perpetrators were individually dominant or members of a collectively-dominant set of rivals, in some cases such pricing would be prohibited by that Treaty provision as an exploitative abuse of a dominant position.

conclusion is an assertion that he knows of no basis in statute or precedent for my position.

The preceding paragraph is relevant at this juncture because at least two and perhaps three of Professor Posner's proposed tests for illegal oligopolistic pricing fail because they do not distinguish between contrived oligopolistic pricing (many of whose constituent moves are illegal under U.S. antitrust law) and natural oligopolistic pricing (all of whose constituent moves are legal under U.S. antitrust law). The first Posner test that falls into this category is his "premature-price-announcement test."[407] Posner states that the type of price announcement that he thinks makes the pricing to which it leads illegal under U.S. antitrust law is a price announcement made "far in advance, without business justification"—the type of price announcement I denominate "premature" (one made earlier than necessary to enable distributors to make proficient purchase, marketing, and store-display decisions and consumers to plan their purchases proficiently). Even if I granted that a court could assess the prematurity of a price announcement acceptably accurately without incurring prohibitive costs (a task that would be relatively simple when the announcement was made at a trade-association meeting or in a trade journal read by fellow sellers and not by distributors or final consumers and much more difficult when it was made publicly or in a journal that at least distributors did read), proof that a seller had made a "premature" price announcement cannot justify a finding of contrived oligopolistic pricing because, although such price announcements may be part of a contrived-oligopolistic-pricing negotiation, they are at least as likely to be designed to perform one of two other legitimate functions.

The first is to enable the announcers to practice oligopolistic pricing naturally by permitting them to reduce the mechanical, goodwill-related, and buyer-expectation-creation-related costs that they would have to incur to react to a rival's undermining response by reducing their initially-announced price. Thus, if a seller announces its intended price before the date on which it and its distributors must place advertisements of its product that include the price-information and before its distributors have to place price-tags on its goods, put prices on their shelves, enter prices into checkout-counter computers, or start to develop product-display and sales-technique plans (which may vary with the price of the good), it can reduce the mechanical cost of changing its initial price by instructing employees of its firm and its independent distributors not to proceed with these tasks until it or they observe its rivals locking themselves into a non-undermining response to its initially-announced price by announcing similar prices (SOPs) and instructing its employees and independent distributors to incorporate them into their advertising, to tag its products accordingly, to place the prices on shelves, to enter them into their computers, and to take account of them when devising display and sales strategies. Similarly, if a seller announces its initial price before it makes actual sales to some buyers and offers its product for sale only after its rivals have locked themselves into SOPs, it can put itself into a position in which it can react to their non-SOP or silence by lowering its

[407] See *Posner Approach* at 1582.

price without alienating (losing the goodwill of) buyers that have purchased its product at its higher, initially-announced price. And, again, if a seller announces its price sufficiently early to be able to lower it in response to its rivals' non-SOPs or silence before it goes public with the price in question, it will put itself in a position to react to undermining responses by lowering its own price without incurring the possible cost of causing buyers to anticipate similar price-reductions in the future—*i.e.*, without creating expectations that will cost it money by causing buyers to delay their purchases in the future (a response that may slow down its future sales and perhaps make it necessary for it to reduce its initially-announced price in the future when it otherwise would not have chosen to do so).

The second legitimate function that premature price announcements can perform is to enable across-the-board pricers to announce their prices in the order that maximizes (or in an order that increases) the magnitudes of the prices in their HNOP arrays—*i.e.*, early enough to enable sellers that are the most likely underminers of higher across-the-board prices (*viz.*, sellers that are, in BCA terms, second-placed or close-to-second-placed far more often than they are best-placed) to lock themselves into prices that would not undermine higher rival prices (by advertising their products at particular prices, tagging their products with those prices, putting those prices on shelves and into computers, and making sales at those prices) early enough to enable those sellers whose higher prices the above sellers might otherwise undermine to delay locking themselves into a price until those potential underminers have locked themselves into a price that would not undermine the latter sellers' higher prices.

The second Posner recommendation that fails for the reasons the current heading articulates is his proposal that U.S. courts infer illegal oligopolistic pricing from the relevant sellers' engaging in public discussions of the right price for their industry.[408] I admit that, in some circumstances, such discussions may represent attempts by contriving oligopolists to settle on a contrived oligopolistic price. However, I doubt that contrivers will often find it profitable to air their dirty laundry in public. In my judgment, most such public discussions that take place before sales of the new models are actually made to the public are designed either to permit oligopolistic pricing to be practiced naturally (in the same way that "premature" price announcements achieve this goal) or to forestall government regulation, while most such discussions that take place after sales have been made perform the latter function. Even if one takes account of the fact that the existence of these two other possible lawful functions may provide a cover that allows contrivers to use public discussions to organize their price-fixing, the percentage of public discussions that betokens contrived oligopolistic pricing is clearly far too low to justify the inference of illegal oligopolistic pricing Posner recommends U.S. courts make. Once more, Posner has been misled by his failure to recognize the fact that U.S. law makes critical the distinction between natural and contrived oligopolistic pricing as well as by his failure to see that the public discussions in question may also serve non-oligopolistic purposes.

[408] *Id.* at 1583.

The third and last Posner test that falls into the category now being considered is his proposal that U.S. courts infer the practice of illegal oligopolistic pricing from the existence of a "recognized price leader" in the ARDEPPS.[409] I do not deny that some recognized price leaders are organizers of contrived-oligopolistic-pricing sequences. Unfortunately for the accuracy of Posner's proposed inference, other recognized price leaders are sellers that make "premature" price announcements that enable themselves and the other incumbents in their ARDEPPS to practice natural oligopolistic pricing, and still others are initial-price-announcers or early-price-announcers for whose announcements most or all of their rivals wait because their early price-announcement increases the height of the prices that the ARDEPPS' constituent firms can charge non-oligopolistically. Once more, my judgment is that the percentage of recognized price leaders that are organizers of or participants in *contrived* oligopolistic pricing is too low for Posner's recommended inference to be acceptable. Obviously, then, this Posner proposal also fails in large part because it ignores the distinction between natural and contrived oligopolistic pricing, the behaviors that make natural oligopolistic pricing feasible, and the legal relevance of the distinction in question.[410]

* * *

Virtually all of Professor Posner's proposed tests for identifying oligopolistic pricing that violates U.S. antitrust law are unacceptable, and the errors that play the most important role in undermining each of his unacceptable proposals are errors that he would have avoided had he paid attention to the distinctions that the conceptual systems Chap. 2 articulated draw and the facts that they emphasize—most importantly, (1) the fact that sellers that are not pure monopolists can enjoy BCAs in their relations with individual buyers and can also increase their prices above the competitive level because their rivals incur contextual marginal costs, (2) the fact that the QV-investment level in each ARDEPPS and the economy as a whole is determined endogenously—in particular, is affected by the extent to which contrived oligopolistic pricing is practiced as well as by the existence of BCAs, CMCs, NOMs, barriers to entry, barriers to expansion, and monopolistic and oligopolistic QV-investment incentives and disincentives, (3) the fact that oligopolistic margins can be obtained naturally as well as through contrivance, and (4) the fact that the Sherman Act prohibits contrived but not natural oligopolistic pricing.

I fear that some economist-readers of this study may be tempted to respond: "Posner committed these mistakes, but he is not a professionally-trained economist, and no well-trained, able economist would ever make such errors." Unfortunately, this understandable reaction is unjustified. As Chap. 11 shows, from the late 1970s until today, some extremely-able, well-trained economists (*inter alia*, Baumol,

---

[409] *Id.* at 1582.

[410] I should admit that Posner's discussion of the premature-price-announcement, "public discussion of the right price," and price-leadership tests for (illegal) oligopolistic pricing acknowledges various practical difficulties with these tests. *Id.* at 1578–93. However, Posner does not anticipate or address the criticisms I have leveled against them.

Joskow, Klevorick, Ordover, and Willig) made mistakes when investigating predatory pricing that are completely analogous to those Posner (and others) made in the 1960s and 1970s when analyzing oligopolistic pricing for precisely the same reasons that Posner made the mistakes he made. That is why this study's positive analyses of oligopolistic and predatory conduct and critiques of the standard literature on these practices confirm the value of the conceptual schemes developed in Chap. 2.

C. The U.S. Courts', the EC's, and the E.C./E.U. Courts' Positions on Oligopolistic Pricing, Horizontal Oligopolistic Output-Restricting Conduct, and "Market"-Dividing Conduct

(1) The U.S. Case-Law on Oligopolistic Pricing

This subsection examines the U.S. courts' positions on five abstract and eight concrete issues related to the question: "What do U.S. courts believe counts as *prima facie* illegal horizontal 'price-fixing' under the Sherman Act?" I start with the five abstract issues.

First, according to U.S. courts, does the Sherman Act classify as *prima facie* illegal horizontal price-fixing parallel pricing by rivals that does not even reflect any individual seller's belief that the payoff to its choice will depend on the choice made by any individual rival? Both perfect competitors and participants in a Chamberlinian large-group monopolistic-competition situation in which all products currently in or that could be introduced into the relevant area of product-space are or would be equally competitive with each other and in which multiple potential entrants face no barriers to entry and/or multiple incumbents face no barriers to expansion or monopolistic or oligopolistic QV-investment disincentives will correctly believe that their pay-offs do not depend on the choices made by any individual rival (since any rival's higher price will be instantly undercut by another equally-well-placed rival and any rival's higher or lower price will cause it to exit and be instantly replaced by an equally-competitive rival), and such firms will make parallel changes in their prices if their costs vary together (say, because they use the same inputs, pay the same prices for those inputs, and those inputs' prices vary through time). Not surprisingly, U.S. courts have never explicitly addressed this issue, but, for two reasons, I am confident that they would not consider such parallel pricing to be prohibited by the Sherman Act: (1) even their early anti-defendant statements about conscious parallel pricing (see below) do not cover this type of conduct, and (2) numerous statements they have made about the kind of pricing that the Sherman Act condemns as *prima facie* illegal price-fixing make it clear that they would not consider "unconscious" parallel pricing to constitute *prima facie* illegal horizontal price-fixing.

The second abstract oligopolistic-pricing-related issue I want to address is: according to U.S. courts, does the Sherman Act classify as *prima facie* illegal horizontal price-fixing consciously-parallel pricing that was triggered by changes in costs or changes in the relevant sellers' BCA-BCD distributions (generated, *e.g.*, by the introduction of an additional QV investment in the relevant area of product-space or the exit and non-replacement of a QV investment in that ARDEPPS) and that partially reflected the seller's recognized simple ("non-oligopolistic" in my sense of that term) interdependence? Although 1939 and 1946 opinions by the U.S. Supreme Court[411] left the impression that it believed that such conscious parallelism did constitute a Sherman Act violation, the Court ruled (in 1954) that this was not the case, holding that "'conscious parallelism' has not yet read conspiracy out of the Sherman Act entirely"[412] and has continued to this day to adhere to this position.[413] Operationally, the U.S. courts' awareness of the distinction between conscious "interdependence" and "collusive (*i.e.*, illegal) price coordination" is manifest by their finding consciously-parallel or consciously-interdependent pricing to be a violation of the Sherman Act only if certain so-called plus factors (which I will discuss below) that they believe increase the probability that the defendants have practiced price-fixing have been shown to be present in the case in question. I admit, however, that (1) both the Supreme Court and some lower federal courts are sometimes not careful to distinguish the important claim that conscious parallelism that reflects only simple interdependence does not violate the Sherman Act from the more banal claim that parallelism that is "not conscious" in the sense that it reflects independent decisionmaking does not violate the Sherman Act and (2) at least some prominent federal judges mistakenly believe that the reason why simple

[411] See Interstate Circuit v. United States, 306 U.S. 208 (1939) and American Tobacco Co. v. United States, 321 U.S. 781, 810 (1946).

[412] See Theatre Enterprises, Inc. v. Paramount Film Distributing Corp., 346 U.S. 537, 541 (1954).

[413] Thus, in 1993, the Supreme Court described conscious parallelism to be the process "not in itself unlawful, by which firms in a concentrated market might in effect share monopoly power, setting their prices at a profit-maximizing, supra-competitive level by recognizing their shared economic interests." Brooke Group Ltd. v. Brown & Williamson Tobacco Corp., 509 U.S. 209, 227 (1993). The Supreme Court addressed the significance of proof that defendants had engaged in "parallel conduct" or made consciously-interdependent decisions more recently in 2007. In Bell Atlantic Corporation v. Twombley, 550 U.S. 544 (2007), the Supreme Court held that proof that Sherman Act defendants had engaged in parallel conduct does not by itself render the plaintiff's claim sufficiently plausible to enable it to obtain discovery—*i.e.*, to survive the defendant's motion to dismiss after pleadings but before discovery. This conclusion extends forward and, if anything, strengthens the Supreme Court's conclusion in 1986 in Matsushita Electrical Industrial Co. v. Zenith Radio Corp., 475 U.S. 574, 588 (1986) that, to avoid summary judgment, Sherman Act plaintiffs must present evidence that "tends to exclude the possibility of independent action" and that proof that defendants have engaged in conduct that is "as consistent with permissible [activity] as with illegal conspiracy does not, standing alone, support an inference of antitrust conspiracy." Contemporary lower federal courts have consistently followed these Supreme Court pronouncements by holding that, taken by itself, convincing proof of parallel conduct or conscious interdependent decisionmaking does not suffice to establish a Sherman Act violation. See, *e.g.*, Blomkest Fertilizer, Inc. v. Potash Corp. of Saskatchewan, Inc., 208 F.3d 1038 (8th Cir. 2000) and In re Petroleum Products Antitrust Litigation, 906 F.2d 432 (9th Cir. 1988).

independent pricing does not violate the Sherman Act (or should not be held to violate the Sherman Act) is the difficulty of enforcing such a prohibition.[414]

The third abstract oligopolistic-pricing-related issue I want to address is: according to U.S. courts, does the Sherman Act classify as *prima facie* illegal horizontal price-fixing conduct that I denominate natural oligopolistic pricing? The simple answer is that, because U.S. courts have not recognized the distinction between natural and contrived oligopolistic conduct, they have never explicitly addressed this issue. However, both (1) the fact that the U.S. courts' general discussions of illegal horizontal price-fixing always focus on oligopolistic pricing that is, in my sense, contrived and (2) the fact that the "plus factors" that U.S. courts say incline them to find illegal consciously-interdependent conduct that they would otherwise find lawful are all factors that the courts believe favor the conclusion that the conduct is "collusive" (in my terms, manifests the kind of complexly-interdependent decisionmaking that is the hallmark of contrived oligopolistic conduct) lead me to conclude that—if they did recognize this distinction—they would reach the legally-correct conclusion that natural oligopolistic pricing is not prohibited by the Sherman Act. (I might add that the fact that, in their 2010 Horizontal Merger Guidelines, the DOJ and FTC recognize for the first time that the category of conduct they denominate "coordinated behavior" includes some exemplars that are not "illegal" makes it more likely that not only they but eventually also the federal courts may fully recognize the distinction between contrived and natural oligopolistic pricing and the fact that, although contrived oligopolistic is almost always illegal under U.S. antitrust law, natural oligopolistic pricing does not violate U.S. antitrust law.)

The fourth abstract oligopolistic-pricing-related issue I want to address is: according to U.S. courts, does the Sherman Act declare *prima facie* illegal variants of what I call contrived oligopolistic pricing that involve explicit anticompetitive threats and/or explicit anticompetitive promises and agreements? U.S. courts have consistently held (explicit) contrived-oligopolistic-pricing *agreements prima facie* illegal under Section 1 of the Sherman Act (though they have never addressed the issue of whether unsuccessful attempts to enter into contrived-oligopolistic-pricing agreements are covered by [presumably Section 2 of] the Sherman Act). However, surprisingly, U.S. courts have never addressed (1) whether an attempt to secure a contrived oligopolistic margin by making an anticompetitive threat but no anticompetitive offer violates Section 2 of the Sherman Act or (2) whether Section 2 of the

[414] See, *e.g.*, the opinion of then-Judge now-Justice Breyer in Clamp-All Corp. v. Cast Iron Soil Pipe Institute, 851 F.2d 478, 484 (1st Cir. 1988). This position is wrong empirically because it would not be unusually difficult for courts to enforce an order that sellers set the price they would find most profitable if their rivals charged prices equal to their respective marginal costs or would not change their initial price in response to the relevant seller's price. And it is wrong legally for two reasons: (1) it assumes incorrectly that, correctly interpreted, the Sherman Act would be read to prohibit pricing that manifests simple recognized interdependence, and (2) it also assumes (to my mind) incorrectly that U.S. (antitrust) courts are authorized to underenforce U.S. antitrust law if there is a good policy reason to do so—more narrowly, if there is a good judicial-error-related or conventional-transaction-cost-related argument for doing so.

Sherman Act covers decisions to respond with a SOP to the POP of a contrived-oligopolistic-pricing initiator that had threatened retaliation (perhaps as well as promising reciprocation) out of fear of retaliation—*i.e.*, by a firm that did not take advantage of any promise of reciprocation in an individualized-pricing situation or could convince the trier-of-fact of its "defensive" motive in an across-the-board-pricing situation, in which rejecting promises of reciprocation is not an option. However, I have no doubt that U.S. courts would conclude that Section 2 of the Sherman Act does make *prima facie* illegal attempts to contrive oligopolistic prices exclusively through threats of retaliation and believe that they would conclude that the Sherman Act does not prohibit succumbing to a contrived oligopolistic threat.

The fifth and final abstract oligopolistic-pricing-related issue I want to address is: according to U.S. courts, does the Sherman Act cover what is conventionally referred to as "tacit collusion"—*i.e.*, conventionally, firms' "reach[ing] an 'understanding' about price even though they do not formally communicate with each other"[415]—or, if the following statement of this issue is different, does the Sherman Act cover contrivance in which the associated anticompetitive threats and/or promises are communicated non-linguistically, simply by setting a contrived oligopolistic price? I have posed this question in the alternative because the referent of "tacit collusion" is unclear. Thus, the Supreme Court has sometimes equated "tacit collusion" with simple recognized interdependence: "Tacit collusion, sometimes called oligopolistic price coordination or conscious parallelism, describes the process, not in itself unlawful, by which firms in a concentrated market might in effect share monopoly power, setting their prices at a profit-maximizing supra-competitive level by recognizing their shared economic interests and their interdependence with regard to price and output decisions."[416] And, despite their failure to recognize the distinction between natural and contrived oligopolistic pricing, various commentators' discussions of "tacit collusion" leave the impression that they believe that "tacit collusion" does not involve the making of an anticompetitive offer or the formation of an anticompetitive agreement (or the making of an anticompetitive threat: like the U.S. courts, commentators ignore the possibility that contrivance can be achieved through threats of retaliation alone). If "tacit collusion" was implicitly being defined to refer to conduct that does not involve the making and acceptance of an anticompetitive offer or the making of and "succumbing to" an anticompetitive threat, I would conclude that the Sherman Act does not prohibit "tacit collusion" and accept that U.S. courts have reached or would reach this conclusion as well. However, in my judgment, in the U.S. courts' usage, the concept of "tacit collusion" covers either exclusively or in part cases in which anticompetitive offers have been communicated or anticompetitive agreements have been reached non-linguistically—*i.e.*, in which offers to enter into unilateral "price-fixing" contracts have been communicated simply by charging a contrived oligopolistic price and those offers have either been accepted by charging a SOP or rejected by charging a price that undercuts or undermines the initiator's POP—and/or

[415] See HERBERT HOVENKAMP, ANTITRUST 98 (hereinafter HOVENKAMP ANTITRUST) (Thomson West, 2005).

[416] Brooke Group Ltd. v. Brown & Williamson Tobacco Corp., 509 U.S. 209, 227 (1993).

anticompetitive threats have been communicated non-linguistically simply by charging a contrived oligopolistic price. If my understanding of the U.S. courts' definition of "tacit collusion" is correct, the Sherman Act would declare tacit collusion *prima facie* illegal, and I would be more prone to read relevant opinions exonerating defendants in "tacit collusion" cases to hold that the State or private plaintiff had failed to establish the requisite probability that an anticompetitive offer and/or threat had been made or that an anticompetitive agreement had been formed—*i.e.*, had failed to prove that the observed behavior was contrived oligopolistic (as opposed to not oligopolistic at all in my sense or natural oligopolistic in my sense).

The consensus view of well-informed U.S.-antitrust-law scholars is that U.S. courts do not believe that the Sherman Act covers "tacit collusion." [417] I am not persuaded that U.S. courts will never hold that the Sherman Act *prima facie* prohibits "tacit collusion" *in the sense in which I think the courts are defining this concept*[418] even if they do support the conclusion that U.S. courts will never hold that the Sherman Act *prima facie* prohibits the "independently-and-unilaterally-adopted" (*i.e.*, parallel but not even simply interdependent) conduct the FTC itself assumed the relevant *du Pont* case involved. To the contrary, I believe that U.S. courts could be persuaded that anticompetitive offers can be made and anticompetitive agreements can be formed non-linguistically and concomitantly that Section 1 of the Sherman Act does cover collusion that is tacit in the sense that it was put into motion through exclusively-non-linguistic communication. I also believe that U.S. courts can be persuaded that the actual or prospective possession of monopoly power is not an element of the Section 2 offense of monopolizing or attempting to monopolize and that anticompetitive threats can also be communicated non-linguistically so that Section 2 of the Sherman Act does cover contrived oligopolistic pricing that involves the non-linguistic communication of relevant anticompetitive threats but not the communication of anticompetitive promises. Indeed, the Court of Appeals opinion Hovenkamp discusses in this context supports my view by pointing out that the FTC was assuming that the defendants had not made "a tacit agreement" and by stating that the FTC had provided no "(1) evidence of anticompetitive intent or purpose on the part of the producer charged, or (2) the absence of an independent legitimate business reason for its conduct."[419]

I turn now to eight concrete issues that are covered by the heading "What conduct is *prima facie* illegal under the Sherman Act?" The first such concrete issue is the *prima facie* legality of rivals' exchanging information about past and present prices, past and present buyers, costs, current inventories, and production plans. Previously, I noted the various ways in which such information-exchanges will facilitate contrived oligopolistic pricing, a reality that accounts for evidence of such exchanges' constituting a

---

[417] See, *e.g.*, Donald Turner, *The Definition of Agreement Under the Sherman Act: Conscious Parallelism and Refusals to Deal*, 75 HARV. L. REV. 655, 670 (1962).

[418] For my reasons for rejecting Turner's arguments for his conclusion, see Richard S. Markovits, *Proving Illegal Oligopolistic Pricing: A Description of the Necessary Evidence and a Critique of the Received Wisdom About Its Character and Cost*, 627 STAN. L. REV. 307, 315–19 (1975).

[419] See E.I du Pont de Nemours & Co. v. FTC, 729 F.2d 128, 139 (2d Cir. 1984).

"plus factor" for the guilt of one or more contrived-oligopolistic-pricing defendants. At this juncture, I want to focus on the following, different two issues: Would it be correct as a matter of law to find that rivals that had agreed to exchange various subsets of the types of information just listed have violated the Sherman Act on that account, and what conclusions have U.S. courts reacted about the Sherman-Act legality of agreements between rivals to exchange different types of such information? My legal analysis will be based on the following legal conclusions or assumptions: (1) the Clayton Act does not cover these sorts of information-exchanges; (2) the Sherman Act does cover them and declares them (*prima facie*) illegal if and only if their participants' *ex ante* perception that they would be profitable was critically affected by their belief that the exchanges in question would or might increase the profits they would realize by contriving oligopolistic prices—*i.e.*, would not declare them illegal if *ex ante* their participants perceived them to be *ex ante* profitable for legitimate reasons (profitable even if they did not increase the profitability of their engaging in contrived oligopolistic pricing, regardless of whether they did in fact expect them to increase the profitability of their participants' engaging in such pricing as well); (3) if the case brought under the Sherman Act is a criminal prosecution, the State must prove the defendant's or defendants' guilt beyond a reasonable doubt; and (4) in appropriate circumstances, in both criminal and civil suits, it is both morally acceptable and legally permissible to establish certain presumptions of guilt that the defendant[s] can rebut. My legal analysis will also be based on a series of armchair-empirical guesses about the likelihoods that the exchange of various sorts of information by rivals would be legitimately profitable.

I will start by setting forth my own admittedly-contestable analysis of the legality of exchanges of various sorts of information under a properly-interpreted-and-applied Sherman Act. I should note that, at least in the United States, such information-exchanges have almost always been organized by trade associations, that some trade associations disseminated the data that was generated to the general public while others did not, and that some of the trade associations gave members no incentives to provide the requested information while others gave their members an incentive to participate by limiting the dissemination of the information generated to members that provided information or by imposing other sanctions on non-participants. The analysis that follows will focus not on such differences but on the nature of the data that is being exchanged.

I will start by considering the legitimate and illegitimate functions of agreements by rivals to exchange information about both past prices and the identities of the sellers and buyers involved in the transactions in question. I can think of five functions that the exchange of this type of information can perform. Two of these functions are legitimate, and three, illegitimate.

The first legitimate function is to help established firms whose projects are doing poorly decide whether to withdraw them and to help established firms that are considering expanding their QV investments to decide whether to expand. Information about the past prices that particular rivals have charged is relevant to these decisions because it indicates the prices against which the relevant QV investments will have to compete in the future.

relevant transactions significantly increases the probability that the profitability of a past-price exchange was critically inflated by its tendency to promote contrived oligopolistic pricing. This conclusion reflects my belief that the omission of information about the identity of the sellers and buyers to which particular past-price information relates will reduce the cost of the information-exchange by far less than it reduces the legitimate benefits generated by the information-exchange (even if one considers the savings anonymity generates for the trade association by reducing the incentives members have to misrepresent the relevant facts and hence the costs the trade association has to incur to check the accuracy of the data its members supply). Although at first thought this conclusion may be surprising, I therefore am more confident that exchanges of information on past prices that do not include information on the identity of the participants in the individual transactions in question should be rebuttably presumed to be illegal than I am that party-identified information-exchanges on past prices should be rebuttably presumed to be illegal.

I turn next to information-exchanges by rivals about future prices that include the names of the sellers that will charge the prices in question. This type of information-exchange can perform two legitimate and one illegitimate function for its participants. First, when the price announcements are "premature" in Posner's sense, they can perform the lawful (though allocatively-inefficient and socially-undesirable) function of enabling sellers to obtain oligopolistic prices naturally. Second, to the extent that the future-price announcements provide some information about the actual height of future prices, they will perform the legitimate function of helping potential exiters and potential expanders make profitable QV-investment decisions. But third, future-price announcements can also be communications through which sellers strive to arrange a contrived-oligopolistic-pricing sequence.

My inclination is to adopt a rebuttable presumption that this type of information-exchange violates the Sherman Act. Defendants should be allowed to rebut this presumption by demonstrating that the future-price-information exchange would be profitable even if it did no more than enable them to obtain oligopolistic prices naturally and/or to make more profitable investment-decisions. These conclusions reflect my judgment that, at least when sellers know past prices, future-price-information exchanges are unlikely to increase their participants' profits significantly by enabling them to make better-informed QV-investment decisions—a conclusion that leads me to believe that the overwhelming majority of this kind of information-exchange would not be profitable if its participants would not use the information in question illicitly.

What of future-price-information exchanges that do not include the names of the sellers that have announced particular future prices? Although the dissemination of information on future-price intentions will be less able to help contrivers arrange their contrivance if the identity of the "intender" is not revealed—*e.g.*, if one cannot tell which of the future-price-intention announcements was made by the ARDEPPS' price leader—I am more confident that future-price-intention information-exchanges may and should be rebuttably presumed to be illegal when the seller in question is not identified than when the relevant seller is identified. Once more, this conclusion reflects the fact that, since the omission of seller-identity information will reduce the private cost of the information-exchange by less than it reduces its legitimate private benefits, exchanges of information on future prices are less likely to be profitable if they do not perform illegitimate functions when the relevant sellers are not identified than when the seller that intends to charge a particular future price is identified. The premise of the preceding sentence reflects the following two "facts": (1) information on future-price intentions will be substantially less valuable to potential exiters and expanders when the identity of the "intender" is not revealed if the QV investment they are considering withdrawing or introducing is unequally competitive with the other QV investments in the ARDEPPS in question and the announced future prices of those other QV investments differ significantly and (2) although intender-identity information may be less relevant to whether exchanges of information on intended future prices enable sellers to obtain oligopolistic margins naturally, it is somewhat relevant in this context as well since some firms are better-placed to initiate and orchestrate natural-oligopolistic-pricing sequences than are others.

I will focus now on exchanges of information among rivals about production and/or delivery costs that specify the seller to which the cost-information in question relates. Seller-identified cost-information exchanges can perform three legitimate and four illegitimate functions. The first legitimate function is to help sellers identify their OCAs in their relations with buyers they are best-placed to supply by enabling them to identify their closest rivals for particular buyers' patronage, the MCs of these rivals, and hence their own MCAs in their relations with the relevant buyers. The second legitimate function is to improve the QV-investment decisionmaking of potential exiters and expanders by helping them identify their actual and prospective closest rivals and their own BCA distributions. The third legitimate function is to inform sellers of the possibility that they may be able to reduce their costs by showing them that various rivals incur lower costs.

In addition, however, such seller-identified cost-information exchanges can also perform four illegitimate functions—*viz.*, can also increase the profitability of contrived oligopolistic pricing in four different ways. First and second, by helping its participants to identify their closest rivals for particular buyers' patronage, such cost-information exchanges can increase the profitability of contrivance by reducing the cost to a contriver of determining the rivals to which it must communicate its anticompetitive intentions as well as the cost to it of identifying the firm that undercut it. Third and relatedly, by improving the exchange-participants' knowledge of the competitive positions of their rivals and of one cause of changes in their rivals' competitive positions, such cost-information exchanges will increase the profitability of contrived oligopolistic pricing by helping participants determine whether they have been undercut by an inferior or lost a sale to a rival that has become their superior in relations with the buyer in question. And fourth, by improving the exchange-participants' estimates of their rivals' competitive positions, such exchanges will increase the profitability of contrived oligopolistic pricing by increasing their ability (1) to determine the combination of the benefits they must promise to confer and the harm they must threaten to inflict on their individual rivals to secure those rivals' cooperation, (2) to calculate the harm-inflicted to loss-incurred ratio for stealing any particular customer of a given rival, and (3) to identify the number of such buyers they must steal to achieve the desired deterrent effect.

I must say that this analysis leaves me in something of a legal quandary. The problem is my uncertainty about how often and to what extent cost-information exchanges benefit their participants by enabling them to see that they could reduce their costs. If I were confident that on the weighted average these benefits were small, I would be tempted to adopt a rebuttable presumption that these kinds of cost-information exchanges are unlawful. But I am not sure about the magnitude of this possible effect. My inclination is therefore to conclude that the State cannot rely on any such presumption to establish the requisite probability that the profitability of such exchanges was actually inflated by their illegitimate functions to win its case. This conclusion is important because defendants will find it difficult to establish the legitimate benefits cost-information exchanges yield them or to demonstrate that contrived oligopolistic pricing would not be profitable for them even if they possessed information on each other's costs (or that they did not in fact engage in contrived oligopolistic pricing after exchanging the information in question).

What of cost-information exchanges in which the seller whose cost-information is provided is not identified? The lack of producer-identification will reduce the ability of cost-information exchanges to perform all its possible functions. Thus, cost-information exchanges are less likely to be profitable for legitimate reasons when the relevant sellers are not identified because the omission of information about the identity of the sellers to which cost-data refer reduces the cost of the exchange by far less than it decreases its legitimate benefits. More specifically, cost-information exchanges will be far less likely to enable sellers to reduce their own costs if the lower-cost rival is not identified when the fact that some rivals have lower costs reflects their having options that other sellers do not have—*e.g.*, reflects the fact that the lower-cost rivals have access to cheaper labor and/or raw materials or have plants whose technology reduces operating costs. However, although I am therefore less confident that cost-information exchanges should be rebuttably presumed to be lawful when the relevant seller is not identified than when it is identified, I still believe that too high a percentage of cost-information exchanges that do not identify the relevant sellers are legitimately profitable for a rebuttable presumption of illegality to be permissible or appropriate.

I turn finally to exchanges of information among rivals about current inventory-positions and future-production plans. Regardless of whether this type of information-exchange identifies the seller to which the information relates, it can perform one legitimate and one illegitimate function. The legitimate function is to help participants to make the output decisions that are in their own interest—to prevent situations from arising in which producers produce too many or too few units of their products because they misapprehend the number of units their rivals will supply. The illegitimate function is to increase the private profitability of contrived oligopolistic pricing by helping sellers that have been undercut identify their undercutters (since the fact that a rival has maintained a large inventory or produced a large output may indicate its intention to increase its undercutting in both individualized-pricing and across-the-board-pricing contexts).

I focus initially on information-exchanges of this type in which the identity of the seller associated with any given inventory-figure or production plan is communicated. In my judgment, this type of information-exchange should not be rebuttably presumed to be illegal under the Sherman Act, regardless of whether the members of the ARDEPPS in question are equally competitive with each other. This conclusion reflects one fact and one assumption: the fact is that, when individual inventory and production-plan figures are linked to specified sellers, the private value of the information in question will not depend on whether the ARDEPPS' sellers are equally competitive with each other. The assumption is that, in the vast majority of situations, the legitimate private value of such information to the participants will exceed the low cost they will have to incur to provide it.

By way of contrast, when an exchange of information about inventories and production plans does not identify the producers to which any set of figures relates, the case for holding it rebuttably illegal seems much stronger to me when the sellers in question are unequally competitive with each other since the legitimate value of such information to participants will be much lower when they are not equally competitive with each other (at least when inventories and production plans vary from participant to participant) and may well be sufficiently low to be lower than the cost of providing the information in question.

I will now describe and evaluate the U.S. case-law on information-exchanges in light of the preceding analysis. My general conclusion is that the U.S. case-law on the type of information-exchanges on which we are now focusing is highly unsatisfactory. Admittedly, the case-law gets some things right: (1) one early opinion recognized that the exchange of information on current inventory and production plans could yield legitimate benefits for its participants by preventing them from producing more units than would be profitable for them to produce,[421] (2) several opinions intimate that exchanges of information on current and future prices could contribute to the formation of a contrived-oligopolistic-pricing agreement, (3) one relatively-modern case recognizes that, in special circumstances, the exchange of sales information may perform the legitimate function of enabling participants to prevent contract fraud by buyers that solicit bids (for cement) for particular projects and accept more than one bid when prices rise (for the purpose of using the "excess cement" they can buy at the low price on other projects),[422] (4) one relatively-modern case considers the possibility that firms may want to exchange price-information to put themselves in a position to make out a "meeting competition in good faith" defense in future price-discrimination suits,[423] (5) the Supreme Court has held that, in information-exchange cases as in all other Sherman Act cases,

[421] Maple Flooring Manufacturers Assn. v. United States, 268 U.S. 463 (1925).

[422] Cement Manufacturers Protective Assn. v. United States, 268 U.S. 588 (1925).

[423] United States v. United States Gypsum Co., 438 U.S. 422 (1978).

"a defendant's state of mind or intent is an element of...[the] offense,"[424] and (6) the lower courts have developed a related (so-called) controlling circumstances exception that recognizes the legality of information-exchanges when they perform legitimate functions.[425] However, the U.S. case-law does not recognize the vast majority of legitimate functions that various sorts of relevant information-exchanges can perform, the vast majority of ways that such information-exchanges can facilitate contrived oligopolistic pricing, or the fact that an exchange's performance of one or more legitimate functions does not render it lawful under the Sherman Act unless its participants believed *ex ante* that it would be rendered profitable by its performance of those functions. Moreover, (1) the opinion that recognizes that the exchange of information about inventories and production plans can enable producers to avoid producing more units than they would find profitable to produce ignores the initial reality that such exchanges can also enable producers to avoid producing fewer units than they would find profitable to produce;[426] (2) the Supreme Court rejected without explanation the contention that price-information exchanges could be legitimated by their participants' need to assess whether a particular price-cut could be defended in "good faith meeting of competition" terms in price-discrimination litigation and refused to endorse the "controlling circumstances" doctrine,[427] (3) several opinions[428] seem to assume that information-exchanges that identify the sellers and buyers to which particular data relate are more likely to be illegal on that account when the reality is the opposite, (4) at least one opinion claims that the exchange of information on past transactions cannot facilitate price-fixing[429] when (as we have seen) that is simply not true, (5) some opinions assume that exchanges of information in which the data that is disseminated is revealed to the public are significantly less likely to violate the Sherman Act when, in reality, public revelation is largely irrelevant (is likely to be a ploy designed to communicate to the public the idea that the participants do not believe that the practice is illegal), (6) virtually all the opinions appear to place considerable weight on dubious evidence that the exchanges increased or stabilized prices (or, in one case, did not increase or stabilize prices), and (7) most opinions seem to rest primarily on the unconsidered conclusion that "[g]enuine competitors do not make daily, weekly, and monthly reports of the minutest details of their business to their rivals."[430]

---

[424] *Id.* at 435.

[425] For a Supreme Court reference to this doctrine, which it traced to Cement Manufacturers Protective Assn. v. United States, 268 U.S. 588 (1925), see United States v. United States Gypsum Co., 438 U.S. 422, 435 (1978).

[426] See Maple Flooring Manufacturers Assn. v. United States, 268 U.S. 563 (1925).

[427] See United States v. United States Gypsum Co., 438 U.S. 422 (1978).

[428] See, *e.g.*, United States v. Container Corp. of America, 339 U.S. 333 (1969).

[429] Maple Flooring Manufacturers Assn. v. United States, 268 U.S. 563 (1925).

[430] American Column & Lumber Co. v. United States, 257 U.S. 377 (1921).

If one is keeping score, the tally is that in four of six of the early information-exchange Supreme Court cases[431] and in the one relatively-modern Supreme Court case that reached the merits[432] the Court ruled against the legality of the information-exchanges in question. The future treatment of information-exchanges by U.S. courts will clearly depend on the way in which the Supreme Court resolves "the more general question going to the existence and proper scope of the so-called controlling-circumstance exception"[433] and perhaps (if I am optimistic about the possible contribution of scholarship) on whether the U.S. courts come to understand the variety of legitimate and illegitimate functions that information-exchanges of different types can perform.

The second type of allegedly-oligopolistic conduct whose *prima facie* legality under the Sherman Act I want to address is "basing-point pricing." Basing-point-pricing schemes designate one or more locations as basing-point bases, specify the price that must be charged for the product at each base, and set the delivered price that must be charged for the product delivered to any location to equal the lowest sum of (1) the basing-point price at any base and (2) the freight cost of transporting the product from that base to the destination-location in question (usually calculated from a specified source such as a particular railroad freight-rate book). Under a basing-point-pricing system, all sellers that bid for any buyer's patronage will have to charge the same delivered price, regardless of any differences in their marginal costs of production or actual delivery costs: sellers whose delivery costs are higher than the applicable freight rate (perhaps because they are located further from the relevant buyer than the most proximate basing point is) will have to "absorb" some of the freight costs in question, and sellers whose delivery costs are lower than the delivery costs from the relevant basing point will have to charge the buyer a delivery fee that exceeds their delivery costs (will have to levy so-called phantom freight charges). Participants in basing-point-pricing schemes secure compliance by making firms that charge lower prices than the scheme prescribes "involuntary basing points"—*i.e.*, by reducing the prices they charge buyers the non-cooperator is best-placed to supply by the difference between the freight charge from the originally-relevant basing point and the (lower) freight charge from the target's location.

It should be obvious that a perfectly-enforced basing-point-pricing scheme will result in all sellers' charging the same price to any buyer (*i.e.*, will fix the price each buyer receives). It may be somewhat less obvious why basing-point pricing would be a privately-cost-effective method of fixing prices if it had no legal advantages (*i.e.*, if it were not less likely than straightforward price-fixing to cause its

[431] The four are Sugar Institute v. United States, 297 U.S. 553 (1930), United States v. American Linseed Oil Company, 267 U.S. 371 (1923), American Column & Lumber Dealers' Association v. United States, 257 U.S. 377 (1921), and Eastern Retail Lumber Association Dealers' Association v. United States, 234 U.S. 600 (1914). The two are Cement Manufacturers Protective Assn. v. United States, 268 U.S. 588 (1925) and Maple Flooring Manufacturers Assn. v. United States, 268 U.S. 563 (1925).

[432] United States v. Container Corp. of American, 393 U.S. 333 (1969).

[433] United States v. United States Gypsum Co., 438 U.S. 422, 450 (1978).

participants to be prosecuted/sued and convicted/found liable). Basing-point-pricing price-fixing schemes appear to be privately-cost-ineffective because (1) to be maximally profitable for a group of sellers, a price-fixing scheme must allocate sales to the seller that is privately-best-placed to make them (*e.g.*, in the case of homogeneous products produced by sellers with identical production costs, to the seller whose delivery cost is lowest) and must preserve the incentive of sellers and buyers to make the location decisions that would be mutually profitable if the sellers were free to charge the prices they wanted and (2) at least at first sight, basic-point-pricing schemes militate against sellers' making sales to the buyer they are best-placed to supply by preventing them from giving the relevant buyers a price-reason to patronize them and militate against sellers' and buyers' making potentially-mutually-profitable location decisions by militating against the seller's supplying the buyer in whose proximity it located (or the buyer's getting a price-concession that reflects the delivery-cost savings its location-decision permitted). In fact, however, these deficiencies of basing-point-pricing price-fixing are less serious than they appear to be at first sight: because, *ceteris paribus*, buyers will prefer to patronize their geographically-most-proximate potential supplier (because it will be easier to have face-to-face discussions with that supplier and that supplier will tend to be able to supply the buyer in question more quickly), the participants in basic-point-pricing schemes will tend to supply the buyers they are best-placed to supply and will be able to secure a buyer's patronage by locating closer to it than any rival is. Admittedly, basing-point-pricing schemes will not involve the amount of price discrimination (in the economist's sense) that its participants would find most profitable, which will reduce both the profits the participants in such pricing schemes realize given their current locations and reduce the profits they can realize by changing their location (as well as the profits they realize because buyers choose to locate closer to their suppliers by reducing buyers' incentives to make such location-decisions). However, at least so long as the law-related costs of participating in basing-point-pricing price-fixing were significantly lower than the law-related costs of participating in more conventional variants of price-fixing, basing-point-pricing price-fixing may well have been more *ex ante* profitable than conventional price-fixing.

For many years, the members of several U.S. industries openly practiced basing-point pricing without encountering any legal difficulties on that account. In 1948[434] and 1949,[435] however, the U.S. Federal Trade Commission and U.S. Supreme Court declared basing-point pricing illegal under U.S. antitrust law, at least if its participants had entered into an agreement to practice basing-point pricing. Moreover, although at least one lower federal court has declared that basing-point pricing is not illegal in the absence of an agreement—*i.e.*, if the various actors made unilateral decisions to

[434] See FTC v. Cement Institute, 333 U.S. 683 (1948).

[435] See Triangle Conduit and Cable Co. v. FTC, 168 F.2d 175 (7th Cir. 1948), *aff'd sub. nom.* Clayton Mark & Co. v. FTC, 336 U.S. 956 (1949).

engage in such pricing[436]—this claim creates an empty economic box since no firm will ever find it profitable to practice such pricing absent an agreement with rivals to do so, a reality that the Supreme Court implicitly recognized in the 1948 case just cited by inferring the existence of a basing-point-pricing agreement from the uniformity of the prices it led its participants to charge.[437]

The fourth type of concrete, allegedly-contrived conduct whose *prima facie* illegality under the Sherman Act I want to consider is participation in agreements to fix (1) the quantity and quality of advertising that changes a product by altering its image directly and/or by changing the characteristics of its actual (or perceived) consumers, (2) warranties, (3) post-sale-service terms, (4) delivery terms, (5) credit terms, (6) buyer/seller dispute-resolution procedures, or (7) any other term or condition of sale that affects the attractiveness of the deal to the buyer to which it is offered. Previously, I explained that such agreements might facilitate the fixing of prices and that some U.S. courts had counted such product-standardizing agreements as a "plus factor" in support of the claim that pricing that was clearly consciously interdependent was "collusive" in their terms or "contrived oligopolistic" in mine. At this juncture, I am arguing something different—*viz.*, that such agreements should be considered to constitute price-fixing in themselves—that there is no good reason to distinguish the fixing of prices (about which buyers care) from the fixing of any other term or condition of sale about which buyers care, at least at the stage of determining whether the agreement constitutes a *prima facie* violation of the Sherman Act.

To my knowledge, no U.S. court has ever condemned as a *de facto* price-fix an agreement among rivals to include terms or conditions of sale in their contracts of sale with their customers that the relevant buyers disvalued. However, I am reasonably confident that U.S. courts would do so if such a case were argued. I am encouraged to reach this conclusion by a 1930 case[438] in which the Supreme Court did declare illegal (as an illegal group boycott) an agreement by film distributors to refuse to supply new theater owners that refused to assume and perform the contractual duties of the prior owners from which they purchased the theaters in question. Admittedly, if (as I believe they were) the new theater owners were legally obligated to fulfill the contractual obligations of the owners from which they bought the theaters, it would be hard to reconcile this decision with the *Cement Institute*[439] holding that it is lawful for rivals to exchange information about past sales including the identity of the buyer they involved to prevent fraud by buyers that solicit bids for concrete for particular jobs and accept more than one of them when concrete prices rise in order to use the "excess" on other projects. However, for present purposes, the more relevant point is that, in this 1930 case, the Court declared illegal an agreement to impose on buyers a non-price term that was disadvantageous to the buyers in question.

[436] Boise Cascade Corp. v. FTC, 637 F.2d 573 (9th Cir. 1980).

[437] FTC v. Cement Institute, 333 U.S. 683, 713 and 715–16 (1948).

[438] United States v. First National Pictures, Inc., 282 U.S. 44 (1930).

[439] FTC v. Cement Institute, 333 U.S. 683 (1948).

The fourth type of price-fixing or price-fixing-related concrete behavior whose *prima facie* legality under the Sherman Act I want to consider is the conduct involved in *National Society of Professional Engineers v. United States*.[440] This case analyzed the Sherman Act legality of an agreement by Society members to obey a provision of its Code of Ethics that prohibited them from submitting any form of price information to a prospective customer until the customer had made a decision to employ the member on condition that a suitable price would subsequently be negotiated. Since even that provisional decision would presumably be made only after discussing the relevant project in some detail with the "job-candidate" and that discussion would presumably be on-balance costly to the prospective employer, I am confident that this pattern of conduct will increase the price of engineering services: the employers will pay more than they would otherwise be willing to pay to avoid having to incur the cost of interviewing additional candidates. Of course, on my understanding, this fact does not imply that the Sherman Act *prima facie* prohibits the conduct in question: if the engineers could show that they would find this conduct desirable for non-financial reasons *ex ante* even if it did not have this effect, it would not be even *prima facie* illegal under the Act, regardless of whether the relevant private benefit was sufficiently connected to a large enough public benefit for the latter to render the conduct lawful under a Rule of Reason analysis even if it were *prima facie* illegal. The defendant engineers argued that they followed this practice to avoid price-pressure that would lead them to reduce "the cost and difficulty" of rendering their service by choosing "to design and specify inefficient and unnecessarily expensive structures and methods of construction." In essence, this argument implies that the engineers found their conduct *ex ante* attractive because it enabled them to do work that they found more satisfying and that would protect "the public health, safety, and welfare," which they claimed would be endangered by the cheaper services they would provide if put in a position in which they had to price their services before being provisionally selected by the prospective employer. I am skeptical of this claim because I reject all three of its premises: (1) the assumption that, as enforced, existing building codes do not protect the public; (2) the assumption that the engineers' prospective employers (A)(i) cannot evaluate the quality of the plans they are offered *ex ante* and either (ii)(a) cannot evaluate the quality of the services provided *ex post* or (b) cannot, for some other reason, recover the losses they sustain because the plans are unnecessarily expensive or dangerous or (B) can pass on the associated loss-risks to another party that will underestimate them and be unable to reduce them or obtain compensation if they come to fruition; and (3) the assumption that the engineers will respond to any reduction in the fees they are paid in the specified, dangerous ways. Moreover, even if these objections to the Society's claims were not valid, I doubt that private parties can legally justify conduct that would otherwise violate the Sherman Act by arguing that it enabled them to perform a police-power function of the State. I would therefore conclude that the Code-of-Ethics-induced behavior involved in this case was *prima facie* illegal under the Sherman Act.

---

[440] 435 U.S. 679 (1978).

The Supreme Court found the conduct in question a violation of the Sherman Act, though it did not engage in the kind of motive analysis I believe it should have executed. Instead, it assumed without real discussion that the conduct was a *prima facie* violation of the Sherman Act and concluded that the statute precluded the defendants from justifying it in public health, safety, and welfare terms even if, in the peculiar circumstances of the case in question, the relevant behavior did promote the public health, safety, and welfare:

> The Sherman Act reflects a legislative judgment that ultimately competition will produce not only lower prices, but also better goods and services. . . .[T]he Rule of Reason does not support a defense based on the assumption that competition is itself unreasonable.[441]

Although I would not have justified the finding of illegality in these terms, I suspect that the Court was really taking the position that private actors cannot legally justify what would otherwise be a Sherman Act violation by claiming the conduct in question manifested their socially-desirable exercise of what is normally the State's police power.

A trade association also required its members to engage in the fifth category of specific conduct that I want to consider that could be found to constitute *prima facie* illegal price-fixing under the Sherman Act. An unreported (because settled) case in which I served as a consultant for defendants involved a provision in the by-laws of a trade association of firms that produced and installed relocatable school-buildings that forbade members to bid for any job offered by anyone that had solicited a round of bids and then rejected all of the bids it received for a period of 6 months after the initial bids were rejected. Virtually all potential suppliers of relocatable school buildings for a significant group of "buyers" were members of the trade association in question. Given that fact and the fact that a 6-month delay would be very costly to the relevant buyers, this practice clearly tended to increase prices by deterring relevant buyers from rejecting all bids made in any round of bidding when none of the bids would otherwise be acceptable to them. Once more, if my interpretation of the Sherman Act is correct, the legally-relevant question is not "Will this practice raise the prices the relevant sellers obtain for their services?" but "Will the practice raise the prices the relevant sellers obtain for their services by reducing the absolute attractiveness of the offers against which they have to compete and, if it does, did this reality critically inflate the sellers' *ex ante* estimates of the profitability of the practice in question—*i.e.*, of the agreement their trade association required them to form—in an otherwise-Pareto-perfect economy?"

In the course of consulting on this case, I developed a competing account of this trade-association by-law that both the sellers in question and (perhaps more importantly) the immediate buyers said was accurate. This explanation focused on the following facts: (1) the relevant buyers were California school districts; (2) the State of California's procurement law forbade State buyers to commit themselves to accept at least one offer made in any round of bidding; (3) California school districts often

---

[441] *Id.* at 695–96.

faced great political pressure to reject all bids for relocatable school-buildings that the relevant personnel found hard to resist even when they knew that the next round of bids would be no better; and (4) the cost of a relocatable-school builder's making a reasonable effort to estimate the cost of performance was approximately 8 % of the cost of doing the work—although it was not difficult or expensive to estimate the cost of building the relocatable school-building, it was both tricky and expensive to estimate the cost of site preparation.[442] I hypothesized that, by reducing the probability that any bidder's bid would be accepted, the California procurement-law provision in question caused bidders to make less of an effort to estimate their performance-costs and hence induced them to include a larger risk premium in their bids. Indeed, I raised the possibility that, by reducing the probability that a school board would reject all offers made in a bidding round by reducing the political pressure their personnel was under to do so, the relocatable school builders' adherence to the rebidding provision of their trade association's by-laws might benefit not only them but also the school districts by encouraging the sellers to prepare more careful bids that would reduce the risk cost of getting the job and hence the bids they made for the work. To my delight and somewhat to my surprise, the procurement officers of several relevant school districts said that they would be willing to testify that this was the case—that they approved of the trade association's rebidding by-law for precisely this reason. If my account is correct and if the relevant seller's perception that it would be *ex ante* profitable for them to adhere to their trade association's rebidding by-law reflected their belief that it would have the effect I just hypothesized, their conduct would not violate the Sherman Act as I believe it is correctly interpreted. I should say that the District Court judge in the case in question ruled without explanation that my account of the relevant practice was irrelevant as a matter of law and, for this reason, did not allow the defendants' lawyers to make this argument or the willing procurement officers to testify.

The sixth type of business conduct that U.S. courts have concluded the Sherman Act condemns in essence as the equivalent of price-fixing is the formation of horizontal agreements to divide up territories, classes of customers, or individual customers. Such market-division agreements have always been deemed *per se* illegal by U.S. courts (indeed, as Chaps. 12 and 14 will discuss, for many years the Supreme Court mistakenly applied this rule to vertical as well as horizontal market-division agreements).[443]

The seventh type of business conduct I want to discuss at this juncture that U.S. courts condemn in essence as the equivalent of price-fixing is the formation of agreements by producers to reduce the quantity of the good they all produce that is

[442] In fact, many of the members of the relevant trade association had gone bankrupt because the jobs tended to go to the firm that most underestimated the cost of site preparation. The suit was against a deep-pocketed conglomerate that had purchased one of the relocatable-school-building "producers" in question and was liable for any damages or fines for which that company was liable, regardless of whether the relevant conduct antedated its purchase by the conglomerate.

[443] The Supreme Court reaffirmed the *per se* illegality of horizontal market divisions in Palmer v. BRG of Georgia, 49 U.S. 46 (1990).

made available for sale. In some cases, such agreements involve nothing more than each seller's reducing its own output. In other cases of this type, each agreeing seller commits itself to buying up the output of one or more non-participants and adjusting its own output to limit the sum of the output it produces and the output of the non-participants whose production it purchases. *Socony-Vacuum*[444] involved this more complex type of output-restriction arrangement. In that case, each major oil refiner agreed to buy up the oil produced by a specified set of independents (its so-called dancing partners) and to limit the sum of that oil and its own oil production that it refined with the goal of increasing the prices of refined-oil products. The Supreme Court condemned the practice as *per se* illegal under the Sherman Act: although, at one stage, the Roosevelt Administration seems to have given its blessing to the majors' efforts to maintain prices, no legislative exemption had ever been secured, and the Court felt in no way bound by the Administration's conduct (no doubt, in part because 1940 was not 1934 and National Recovery Act policies no longer enjoyed the respect they had once been given).

The eighth and final specific business conduct that I want to consider at this juncture is the formation of agreements by rivals to sell their product exclusively or in part through a joint-sales agency. It should be clear that exclusive joint-sales-agency agreements eliminate price and other terms-and-conditions-of-sale competition between or among the sellers they involve. In some cases, U.S. courts have found such arrangements to be prohibited by the Sherman Act,[445] though in others the Supreme Court correctly[446] or incorrectly[447] found that the fact that they generated various allocative benefits rendered them lawful under the Act. These cases and arguments will be discussed in more detail when addressing the questions "Do U.S. courts consider price-fixing to be *per se* illegal under the Sherman Act?" and "If the legality of price-fixing (or its functional equivalents) is sometimes to be determined through a Rule of Reason analysis, under what circumstances will the practice be lawful under the Sherman Act?"

That concludes my analysis of the first U.S. case-law question that I want to address: "What conduct do U.S. courts consider to be *prima facie* illegal horizontal price-fixing (or its equivalent) under the Sherman Act?" I will devote far less space to the second U.S.-case-law issue that needs to be addressed: "What evidence do U.S. courts believe can properly be used to create the requisite probability that one or more defendants have engaged in conduct that the courts think constitutes a *prima facie* price-fixing violation of the Sherman Act?" I will start with the obvious: in the few cases in which it is available, U.S. courts clearly do consider relevant (indeed, often decisive) eyewitness testimony, audio recordings, or documentary evidence of contrived oligopolistic communications, statements of contrived-oligopolistic-pricing intentions, or admissions of contrived oligopolistic pricing. I hasten to add, however,

---

[444] See United States v. Socony-Vacuum Oil Co., 310 U.S. 150 (1940).

[445] NCAA v. Board of Regents of the University of Oklahoma, 468 U.S. 84 (1984).

[446] Broadcast Music, Inc. v. Columbia Broadcasting System, Inc., 441 U.S. 1 (1979).

[447] Appalachian Coals v. United States, 288 U.S. 344 (1933).

that U.S. courts are aware that many relevant written and oral statements are ambiguous and that eyewitness testimony is sometimes unreliable (especially if it comes from a disgruntled [often former] employee, a competitor, or a customer).

U.S. courts also deem relevant evidence that defendants have engaged in consciously-parallel pricing or, less constrainingly, consciously-interdependent pricing. However, as I have already indicated, (1) they recognize that not all or even most such pricing is "collusive"—*i.e.*, constitutes a *prima facie* violation of the Sherman Act—and (2) base their determination of whether particular exemplars of such pricing are "collusive" on evidence of so-called plus factors—*i.e.*, factors that they think increase the probability that pricing found to be consciously interdependent is "collusive" in their terms ("contrived oligopolistic" in mine).

I will now list the various "plus factors" that U.S. courts take into consideration, evaluate their use of these factors, and compare their list of relevant considerations with my and Professor/Judge Posner's proposals. U.S. courts consider six categories of factors or evidence relevant to the determination of whether particular exemplars of consciously-interdependent pricing is "collusive"—*i.e.*, is a *prima facie* violation of the Sherman Act:

(1) "structural"—*i.e.*, non-behavioral—factors that the courts perceive to increase the profitability of contrived oligopolistic pricing (highly-inelastic "industry demand," the fact that the ARDEPPS in question produced a homogeneous product, small number of sellers or high seller concentration, high barriers to entry or infrequent entry in the recent past);
(2) "market"-performance factors—high price, high supernormal profit-rate, and high stability-of-market-share figures, which the courts think favor the conclusion that sellers have engaged in contrived oligopolistic pricing;
(3) information that the sellers that had engaged in consciously-parallel pricing or perhaps only consciously-interdependent pricing had an opportunity to discuss or negotiate a price-fixing arrangement either (preferably) face-to-face or in some other way;
(4) evidence that a defendant had engaged in inherently-unprofitable behaviors that could be part of a contrived-oligopolistic-pricing sequence—*e.g.*, evidence that a relevant seller made no bid when bidding would have been *ex ante* profitable or had offered a higher price than was *ex ante* profitable;
(5) evidence that the defendants had made "premature" price announcements; and
(6) evidence that defendants had made inherently-unprofitable agreements that the courts believe facilitated contrived oligopolistic pricing—agreements to desist from advertising or from granting favorable credit terms (which, to my mind, are independent violations of Section 1), agreements not to grant secret price-discounts or to adhere to list prices, agreements to guarantee buyers rebates on their current purchases equal to any price-cuts the seller gives any buyer in the future, agreements to engage in inherently-unprofitable physical-product standardization, agreements to engage in inherently-unprofitable information-exchanges on costs, past or future prices, identities of past buyers,

inventories and production plans, *etc*., whose dissemination would facilitate contrived oligopolistic pricing.[448]

I will now comment on the actual relevance of each of these sets of factors in turn. When appropriate, I will also comment on the relationship between the factors in each set the courts have considered and the similar factors that I and/or Judge Posner think courts should consider when deciding whether one or more defendants have engaged in *prima facie* illegal contrived oligopolistic pricing.

I begin with "structural" factors. I agree that, at least when the referent of "industry demand" can be identified, its inelasticity is relevant to the potential profitability of contrived oligopolistic pricing to the sellers in the industry, controlling for the "monopolistic" character of their highest non-contrived prices. I say "at least when the referent of 'industry demand' can be identified" because—in the virtually-universal situation in which the relevant products differ in their physical attributes, the images with which they are associated, the reputations of their producers, and the location of their producers—the concrete referent of "industry" and "industry demand" will be problematic whenever the products in question have different costs (and are of different quality) and/or the products in question are not (1) highly and equally competitive with each other and (2) much more competitive with each other than with any product placed outside the industry. Still, as a heuristic matter, I understand what those who refer to "inelastic industry demand" have in mind and agree that the fact that industry demand is inelastic over the relevant range favors the feasibility and profitability of contrived oligopolistic pricing by implying that increases in the prices of all the inside-industry products will not lead to a significant total amount of sales being lost in small separate batches to a large number of relatively-distantly-competitive products whose producers' cooperation would have to be secured for the price-fix to work. However, I do not believe that the other "structural" factors U.S. courts have considered to be "plus factors" really do increase the feasibility and profitability of the ARDEPPS' sellers' price-fixing. Thus, my previous explanation of why product-standardization agreements may not even tend to encourage price-fixing would apply fully to the claim that product homogeneity encourages such pricing even if product homogeneity were defined to exclude geographic-location differentiation: although product homogeneity favors the profitability of contrived oligopolistic pricing by simplifying the negotiation of the prices that each participant can charge and by reducing the safe profits (the BCAs and NOMs) that participants must put at risk to attempt to contrive an oligopolistic price,

[448] See, *e.g*., Blomkest Fertilizer, Inc. v. Potash Corp. of Saskatchewan, 203 F.3d 1028 (8th Cir. 2000), Wallace v. Bank of Bartlett, 55 F.3d 1166 (6th Cir. 1995), Reserve Supply Corp. v. Owens-Corning Fiberglas Corp. 971 F.2d 37 (7th Cir. 1992), Catalono, Inc. v. Target Sales, Inc., 446 U.S. 643 (1980), United States v. General Electric Co., et. al., 197 F.2d 489 (1977), United States v. Container Corp. of American, 393 U.S. 333 (1969), Morton Salt Co. v. United States, 235 F.2d 573 (10th Cir. 1956), and the old information-exchange cases Sugar Institute, Inc. v. U.S., 297 U.S. 553 (1936) (which also involved a trade-association rule prohibiting members from offering secret discounts), Maple Flooring Mfrs. Ass'n v. United States, 268 U.S. 563 (1925), and American Column & Lumber v. United States, 257 U.S. 377 (1921).

it disfavors the profitability of contrived oligopolistic pricing by increasing the percentage of sellers placed in the defined market that are well-placed to obtain the patronage of any relevant buyer to the extent that product heterogeneity is positively associated with the degree to which the products inside the industry are unequally competitive with each other (which I admit it will not be in all cases), by increasing the loss that any undercut contriver will have to sustain to inflict a relevant amount of harm on its undercutter through retaliation, and by reducing the amount of benefits any contriver can confer on cooperating rivals through reciprocation. Partially relatedly, given the fact that the sellers placed in any "market" will rarely be equally competitive with each other or will rarely all be well-placed to obtain the patronage of each individual buyer placed in that market, the number of sellers in any market or, more generally, its seller concentration, however operationalized, will have much less bearing than U.S. courts appear to believe on the feasibility or profitability of an AEDEPPS' incumbents' practicing contrived oligopolistic pricing. And again, given the facts that (1) there would not be much connection between the effectiveness of potential competition at an ARDEPPS' no-contrived-oligopolistic-pricing equilibrium and the height of the barriers to entry facing its best-placed potential entrant even if the ARDEPPS' incumbents could not make new QV investments in it, (2) an ARDEPPS' incumbents can make new QV investments in it, and (3) contrived oligopolistic pricing can be profitable even if it leads to new entry or incumbent expansions (indeed, even if it leads to so much additional QV investment's being made that the highest supernormal profit-rate earned by any project at the contrived-oligopolistic-pricing equilibrium equals its counterpart at the no-contrived-oligopolistic-pricing equilibrium), I do not think that the height of an ARDEPPS' barriers to entry has much bearing on the profitability of contrived oligopolistic pricing to its sellers. Finally and somewhat relatedly, given the last of the three reasons for questioning the "plus factor status" of the height of the barriers to entry into an ARDEPPS and the fact that entry may be infrequent in an ARDEPPS even though potential competition was effective because incumbents had and seized the opportunity to prevent entry by making limit QV investments (*inter alia*, because they learned of particular profitable QV-investment opportunities earlier than any potential entrant did and were able to lock themselves into an expansion before the potential competitor could lock itself into an entry), the fact that entry has been infrequent in an ARDEPPS has little bearing on the ability of its sellers to profit by practicing contrived oligopolistic pricing. And, of course, in any case, the fact that an ARDEPPS' "structure" implies that its sellers could profit by practicing contrived oligopolistic pricing does not prove that they chose to do so in violation of the law.

I turn now to the market-performance factors. I have already explained why an ARDEPPS' (1) weighted-average P–MC, P/MC, or (P–MC)/P figure, (2) highest or weighted-average supernormal-profit-rate, and (3) (weighted-average) market-share-stability figure do not have much bearing either on whether its sellers have practiced contrived oligopolistic pricing or on whether they would find it profitable to do so. From my perspective, it is equally noteworthy that U.S. courts have not considered in price-fixing cases various other market-performance types of evidence that I or Judge Posner argue they should consider. Thus, although the courts have looked to the relevant sellers' supernormal profit-rates (which Professor Posner but not I deem relevant), they have not considered the relevant ARDEPPS' excess-capacity rate or the relevant defendant's or defendants' practice of price discrimination (which Professor Posner but not I consider relevant). Nor have they explicitly acknowledged the relevance of the type of inter-temporal or inter-regional price-comparisons I think are promising or the possible usefulness of comparisons of a defendant's actual prices with its (HNOP + NOM). I hasten to add, however, that a District Court's relatively-recent use of a somewhat controlled inter-"regional" price-comparison to predict the competitive impact of a horizontal merger[449] gives me reason to be optimistic that future courts might be willing to use the kind of controlled price-comparisons that I think would often be cost-effective to use to detect contrived oligopolistic pricing.

I consider next the U.S. courts' consideration of the fact that defendants had actually met and therefore had an opportunity to discuss price-fixing arrangements face-to-face. Although a number of price-fixing opinions do mention this fact, on the whole the courts (like me) do not seem to place much weight on it.

I agree with the courts' consideration as a "plus factor" the fact that one or more defendants have foregone an opportunity to bid that was *ex ante* profitable or have made a bid that was higher than was *ex ante* profitable. However, I am probably even more skeptical than the courts are of their ability to assess the *ex ante* profitability of such decisions, may be more prone than they are to believe that such decisions may have been innocent mistakes, and regret that the courts have not given plaintiffs more of a signal that proof that sellers had made inherently-unprofitable low bids can sometimes strengthen contrived-oligopolistic-pricing cases against either the seller that made the low bid or the seller whose sales the low bid targeted.

I have already indicated why the fact that sellers have made premature price announcements has less bearing on whether they were practicing contrived oligopolistic pricing than Professor Posner and even the courts suppose. The critical fact is that, in many circumstances, sellers make a series of premature price announcements to initiate a sequence of decisions that enable them to practice oligopolistic pricing naturally.

I turn finally to the relevance of evidence that defendants have entered into inherently-unprofitable agreements that concern things other than price for (1) the probability that they had practicing contrived oligopolistic pricing or (2) their disinclination to violate the law. I have already explained why I doubt that agreements to standardize products really do (all things considered) encourage contrived oligopolistic pricing. I have also already explained why, contrary to the courts' apparent belief, such practices as agreements to standardize products and exchange various sorts of information on sales, costs, inventories, and production plans would sometimes or often be profitable independent of any tendency they had to facilitate contrived oligopolistic pricing. Of course, although that fact sometimes or often does critically affect the *prima facie* Sherman Act legality of the agreements

[449] See FTC v. Staples, Inc., 970 F. Supp. 1066 (D.D.C. 1997).

in question, it does not eliminate their relevance to whether the defendants have engaged in price-fixing: to the extent the defendants' participation in these agreements makes it more likely that they would find contrived oligopolistic pricing profitable if they did not have to worry about the consequences of its being illegal, that participation should be considered a "plus factor" in any analysis of whether their consciously-interdependent pricing is actually "collusive" in the sense of being contrived oligopolistic and hence is *prima facie* illegal under the Sherman Act.

The third question about the U.S. case-law on illegal price-fixing that I want to address lies behind the fact that I have so far consistently analyzed the *prima facie* illegality as opposed to the *per se* illegality of various types of pricing under the Sherman Act. This question is actually a pair of related questions: (1) "Is the horizontal fixing of actual or minimum prices *per se* illegal under the Sherman Act or does the legality of such pricing under the Sherman Act depend on the 'reasonableness' of the fixed price or on the court-perceived desirability of some of the court-perceived indirect consequences of the price-fix?"—*i.e.*, "Is the legality of such a price-fix under the Sherman Act to be determined through a Rule of Reason analysis?"—and (2) "If the legality of a price-fix under the Sherman Act does depend on the court-perceived desirability of its court-perceived indirect consequences, what indirect effects must the price-fix be perceived to have for it to be held lawful though *prima facie* illegal under the Sherman Act?"

For many years, the opinion of the Supreme Court in *United States v. Trenton Potteries Co.*,[450] which is usually primarily and correctly cited for the proposition that the reasonableness of the fixed price is irrelevant to the illegality of the horizontal fixing of actual or minimum prices, was also taken to hold more broadly that the horizontal fixing of actual (or minimum) prices was *per se* illegal under the Sherman Act. However, the combination of the Court's opinion in a 1979 case—*Broadcast Music, Inc. v. Columbia Broadcasting System, Inc.*[451]—and its opinions in two early (1918 and 1933) cases that *Broadcast Music* has in a sense revivified—*Board of Trade of City of Chicago v. United States*[452] and *Appalachian Coals v. United States*[453]—has led commentators to question whether the U.S. courts really do think that horizontal actual-or-minimum-price fixing is *per se* illegal or whether, to the contrary, the actual holding of *Trenton Potteries* is the narrower holding that the "reasonableness" of any price (or other term) that is fixed (*i.e.*, the reasonableness of the price's magnitude relative to some cost-figure) is irrelevant to the price-fixing's Sherman Act legality. After briefly reviewing the relevant features of the price-fixes involved in and the opinions written in *Broadcast Music*, *Chicago Board of Trade*, and *Appalachian Coals*, I will list various justifications that have been offered for such price-fixing, comment on their policy-persuasiveness, and discuss whether and

[450] 273 U.S. 392 (1927).

[451] 441 U.S. 1 (1979).

[452] 246 U.S. 231 (1918).

[453] 288 U.S. 344 (1933).

how the U.S. courts have reacted to claims that various alleged effects of the price-fixing involved in individual cases rendered it lawful under the Sherman Act.

Broadcast Music focused on an arrangement in which thousands of performance artists and other performance-right owners assigned to Broadcast Music, Inc. (BMI) the non-exclusive right to license others (primarily, radio and television stations) to play their music through blanket licenses that established prices for playing the music in question. In addition to negotiating the various licensing agreements, BMI undertook to monitor the transmissions of the licensees and non-licensees to ensure that they respectively paid the fees they were contractually obligated to pay and did not play music they had not been licensed to play. For current purposes,[454] the significant feature of this arrangement is that it substantially reduced price competition among the performance artists and performance-right owners in question in relation to the marketing of the covered performances. (I say "substantially reduced" rather than "eliminated" because the owners retained the right to market individual recordings by themselves.) Although BMI had a high share of performance-right-licensing sales, the Supreme Court upheld the arrangement primarily on the ground that the restriction in price competition was necessary for the generation of substantial reductions in the transaction cost of executing the licensing agreements in question and of monitoring the conduct of licensees and non-licensees and secondarily (I think a fig leaf) on the ground that the arrangement between each original performance-right owner was non-exclusive in that the original owners retained the right to make individual licensing agreements. *Inter alia*, then, *Broadcast Music* stands for the proposition that the horizontal fixing of actual prices is not *per se* illegal under the Sherman Act—indeed, will be lawful under that Act—if it is necessary for the generation of large enough (allocative) efficiencies. In my view, this conclusion is correct as a matter of law if it is interpreted to mean that price-fixing is lawful under the Sherman Act if the price-fixers believed *ex ante* that its profitability was secured by its prospective generation of the efficiencies to whose generation it was essential.

Broadcast Music breathed new life into the related but, on the facts, less-defensible holdings of the Court in the pre-*Trenton-Potteries* case *Chicago Board of Trade* and in the Depression-era case *Appalachian Coals*. In *Chicago Board of Trade*,[455] the Supreme Court used a Rule of Reason approach to uphold the Board's "call rule," which "prohibited [its members] from purchasing or offering to purchase during the period between the close of the call [*i.e.*, the Board's normal trading session] and the opening session of the next business day any wheat, corn, oats or rye 'to arrive' at a price other than the closing bid at the call." I would have no objection to the Court's legal conclusion or to the Court's opinion had the Court based its conclusion on either (1) one apparently-uncontestable fact to which it referred that relates to the government's argument and/or (2) one factual conclusion it articulated whose

[454] For other purposes, the significant feature of the relevant arrangement was BMI's use of a tie-in that, according to U.S. judicial doctrine, would be *per se* illegal in the circumstances in question. See Chap. 14.

[455] See Board of Trade of City of Chicago v. United States, 246 U.S. 231 (1918).

accuracy I cannot determine: the apparently-uncontestable fact is that "the government. . .made no attempt to show that the rule was designed to or that it had the effect of limiting the amount of grain shipped to Chicago; or of retarding or accelerating shipment; or of raising or depressing prices,"[456] and the impossible-for-me-to-assess conclusion is that "the rule had no appreciable effect on general market prices; nor did it materially affect the volume of grain coming to Chicago. . . ."[457] Unfortunately, however, the Court's opinion leaves the impression that its conclusion was critically affected by a number of effects of the call rule whose exonerating force is dubious and a number of alleged effects of the rule whose existence is questionable. I will restrict myself here to pointing out two actual effects the Court cited to support its conclusion that, to my mind, would not legitimate the practice if it were *prima facie* illegal and one alleged effect the Court cited to support its conclusion whose existence is questionable. The two actual effects whose policy and legal relevance are dubious are:

(1) the fact that the call rule "tend[s] to shorten the working day or, at least, limit the period of most exacting activity" of Board members[458] and
(2) the fact that the call rule will reduce the market share of the largest firms (which could otherwise take advantage of their larger scale by having employees able to vary the prices they offered outside of official sessions in response to changes in market conditions).

Neither the ability of collusion to benefit colluders without increasing economic efficiency in the process nor the tendency of collusion to prevent larger firms from taking legitimate advantage of their size-related greater efficiency legitimates collusion. The alleged effect whose existence is questionable is to "eliminate[ ] risks necessarily incident to a private market, and thus to enable country dealers to do business at a smaller margin [and] [i]n that way. . .[to] ma[k]e it possible for them to pay more to farmers without raising the price to consumers."[459] This claim fails because it conflates the fact that the call rule will eliminate the "risk" that, in private negotiations over price, country dealers may accept a bid-price that is lower than the price they could have obtained with the claim that the call rule reduces the country dealers' "risk costs," which are caused by the imperfect predictability of their prospective profits.

Appalachian Coals analyzed the legality of an exclusive joint-selling agency for participating Appalachian coal mines that would come into operation only when "firms producing at least 70 % but no more than 80 % of total coal tonnage in Appalachia had joined."[460] Both the trial and the Supreme Court appeal preceded the actual operation of the company. In addition to marketing its participants' coal, Appalachian Coals was supposed to grade the coal they produced. "No attempt was

[456] *Id.* at 238.
[457] *Id.* at 240.
[458] *Id.* at 241.
[459] *Id.* at 240.
[460] See Appalachian Coals v. United States, 288 U.S. 344 (1933).

made to limit production." However, Appalachian Coals was formed to combat two "problems": (1) the fact that coal companies that received orders for coal of a certain size often dumped at low prices the (usually-smaller) lumps of coal they produced jointly with the (usually-larger) lumps of coal for which they had a contract of sale and (2) the coal miners' practice of "pyramiding coal"—*i.e.*, of offering to supply the same physical coal in different venues, thereby making it appear that more coal was available for sale than was actually on supply.

The Supreme Court reversed a District Court ruling against the defendants (grounded on the fact that the joint-sales agency would eliminate competition among its seller-participants) on the grounds that (1) the capacity of Appalachian mines (169,287,640 tons) was considerably below the capacity of all mines in southern West Virginia, Virginia, Eastern Kentucky, and Tennessee (245,233,560 tons) and (2) "[t]he plan cannot be said either to contemplate or to involve the fixing of market prices,"[461] concluding that "[i]f in actual operation. . .[the plan] should prove to be an undue restraint on interstate commerce, if it should appear that the plan is used to the impairment of fair competitive opportunities, the decision upon the present record should not preclude the Government from seeking the remedy which could be suited to such a state of facts."[462]

Admittedly, I do not know enough about coal-transportation costs in 1933 or the location of relevant buyers of Appalachian coal to determine the set of non-Appalachian coal mines that would be well-placed to supply the buyers that Appalachian mines were well-placed to supply. But it seems obvious to me that the joint-sales-agency part of the Appalachian Coals arrangement was designed to benefit its participants *inter alia* by keeping prices up by eliminating competition among them: the coal mines could have set up a joint venture to grade their coal and to prevent the pyramiding of coal (if its prevention were to be deemed lawful because [say] coal pyramiding could be characterized as a type of business fraud) without that venture's also serving as an exclusive joint-sales agent for its participants. The fact that the Appalachian Coals plan limited the company to representing producers whose total tonnage capacity did not exceed 80 % of the tonnage capacity of all Appalachian mines was a legal fig leaf: one does not need to control the prices charged by all producers of a good to increase the market price of the good. The Supreme Court's *Appalachian Coals* opinion seems to me to stand for the proposition that, at least during a depression, a horizontal price-fix that clearly is *prima facie* illegal under the Sherman Act will be judged lawful if it prevents "ruinous competition" that would lead to the bankruptcy of some of the sellers involved, the loss of their employees' jobs, and the concomitant exacerbation of the economic downturn. I would not favor attempts to combat a depression through legislation (such as the then-contemporaneous National Recovery Act of the Roosevelt Administration) that authorized industries to fix prices, but, even if I would, I would deem improper attempts by courts to achieve the same result in the same way by granting (in effect) antitrust-law exemptions to horizontal price-fixers in these circumstances. I am therefore genuinely surprised that such experts as Herbert

---

[461] *Id.* at 373.

[462] *Id.* at 378.

Hovenkamp[463] and one of the authors of the Goetz and McChesney antitrust-law casebook[464] believe that *Appalachian Coals* was or was probably correctly decided.

In any event, I now want to list the various alleged effects of price-raising horizontal fixes of minimum or actual prices that some have argued should lead courts to conclude that the price-fix in question does not violate the Sherman Act. In addition, I will state my own evaluation of these individual claims and report any statements that U.S. courts have made about them. I will begin by pointing out that the U.S. courts have never departed and should never depart from the narrow holding of *Trenton Potteries* that the fact that a horizontal price-fix raised prices to a "reasonable" level (defined implicitly by the price's relationship to the relevant seller's or sellers' marginal or average total cost[s]) does not render it lawful under the Sherman Act. I also think that the U.S. courts will and should adhere to the *Broadcast Music* holding that price-fixing that is necessary to the achievement of real transaction-cost savings does not violate the Sherman Act when, as seems likely to have been the case in *Broadcast Music*, the prospective relevant private savings were sufficient to render the arrangement *ex ante* profitable by themselves. By way of contrast, I think that U.S. courts not only should not but will not follow the *Chicago Board of Trade* dicta that horizontal price-fixing that raises prices is not prohibited by the Sherman Act if the arrangement in question promotes the convenience of the sellers or enables small sellers to prevent large sellers from taking advantage of potential competitive advantages (in this case, in buying) that reflect their economic-efficiency superiority. I admit, however, that my optimism on the latter issue is tempered by the fact that, in a much more-recent case,[465] the Court took a position, which it has never explicitly disowned, that was analogous to the latter *Chicago Board of Trade* position (which I am attacking)—*viz.*, that it may be lawful for small sellers and new entrants to use (presumptively-economically-efficient) vertical territorial restraints that their larger established competitors could not lawfully employ because the former sellers' use of them would help them survive or enter while the latter sellers' use of them would tend to cause the small sellers to exit and deter new entry. In part, my view that these two *Chicago Board of Trade* dicta would no longer be followed reflects (1) the fact that they are inconsistent with the level-playing-field norm of U.S. antitrust law to which U.S. courts often refer approvingly and (2) the fact that U.S. courts have more recently rejected economic-efficiency justifications for price-raising horizontal price-fixing that have a lot more merit (see below). I also believe that, even in a depression, U.S. courts would now reject the "preventing ruinous competition" justification for price-raising horizontal price-fixing that *Appalachian Coals* almost certainly silently endorses: even if (contrary to my own belief[466]) it would be good policy in a depression

[463] See HOVENKAMP ANTITRUST at 110.

[464] See CHARLES J. GOETZ AND FRED S. MCCHESNEY, ANTITRUST LAW: INTERPRETATION AND IMPLEMENTATION 106 (4th ed.) (Foundation Press, 2009).

[465] White Motor Co. v. United States, 372 U.S. 253, 263–64 (1963).

[466] Obviously, because the immediate effect of a price-raising price-fix is to reduce output and hence employment, the argument for a price-fix's preserving employment must be that it does so

to prevent the exit of QV investments and a loss of jobs by authorizing sellers to engage in price-raising horizontal price-fixes, that decision should be made legislatively, not by courts by misinterpreting or misapplying anti-monopolization statutes such as the Sherman Act.

Scholars have also raised the possibility that, properly interpreted, the Sherman Act would be read not to prohibit price-raising horizontal price-fixes when the price-fixers would use the resulting profits to subsidize economically-efficient or socially-desirable activities. Thus, it has been argued that the Sherman Act should not be read to prohibit booksellers from fixing the price of popular commercial books if they would use the proceeds of the price-fix to subsidize their supply of serious literature that is unprofitable for them to distribute. Both I and U.S. courts reject this claim for three reasons: (1) we are skeptical that the price-fixers would actually use the proceeds of their price-fixing to provide socially-desirable services or products that are not profitable for them to supply; (2) even if they would, that fact would not change the reality that their price-fix violated the test of illegality the Sherman Act promulgates; and, relatedly, (3) even if (contrary to fact) it would be desirable to secure the desirable provision of the unprofitable good or service in question by imposing a *de facto* tax on buyers of the price-fixed good, that choice is not one courts are authorized to make in the guise of interpreting or applying an anti-monopolization statute such as the Sherman Act.

I also do not think that U.S. courts should or would declare horizontal price-fixing that *stabilized* prices lawful under the Sherman Act on the ground that it reduced the risk costs the relevant sellers and buyers had to bear below what they would be if they entered into a series of short-term contracts at non-fixed prices. If price-fluctuation-generated risk costs are a problem, the economically-efficient response to that problem is for relevant individual sellers and buyers to enter into long-term contracts that stipulate prices or a price-formula. If seller or buyer error causes that option to be rejected, the economically-efficient response for government to make is to provide the parties in question with better information or, conceivably but doubtfully, to require them to enter into economically-efficient, long-term contracts. Even if horizontal price-fixes that allegedly only stabilize prices—*i.e.*, do not raise weighted-average-expected prices—do not in practice also tend to raise prices, courts would not be authorized in effect to promulgate legislation to respond to this problem by misinterpreting or misapplying an anti-monopolization statute. I admit, of course, that in the unlikely event that one or more defendants could prove that *ex ante* they did not expect their price-fix to raise

by preventing the producer's going bankrupt and shutting down, particularly when its re-entry (or anyone else's entry) may be more difficult than its exit. This possibility cannot be dismissed in the *Appalachian Coals* context since credit may not have been available even to mineowners whose mines were viable over the long run and since water-seepage may render unviable the reopening of a coal mine whose owners could not afford to keep the pumps running when they were shut down. Still, if coal mines should be subsidized for this reason, it would be preferable for the subsidy to come from the government after a government study of the issue rather than from coal consumers after a private price-fix.

prices (since any such increase would not have been ancillary to the price-fix's risk-cost-reducing function) and that they did think it would be profitable despite that fact because it would benefit them by reducing the sum of their and their relevant buyers' risk costs, my interpretation of the Sherman Act would imply that it did not prohibit the price-fix in question. However, if the reason the price-fix was necessary was the buyers' underestimation of the risk cost to them of price instability, I cannot see how defendants could make such a showing.

The next set of supposed reasons for holding a price-raising horizontal price-fix lawful under the Sherman Act was proposed by the United States National Collegiate Athletic Association in the case *NCAA v. Board of Regents of the University of Oklahoma*.[467] In this case, the NCAA tried to justify its fixing of the prices that TV stations had to pay to televise college-football games locally, regionally, and nationally (as well as the frequency with which various teams could appear in local, regional, and national transmissions) by arguing that the price-fix was necessary to enable it to regulate the rules of the game (including the dimensions of the field) and to increase the sports-competitive-equality of the various teams in the Association. In fact, the price-fixing and quantity controls were not necessary to either of these objectives. The latter objective could have been better pursued by controlling the sports budgets of the different educational institutions, in part by subsidizing some of them perhaps *inter alia* to offset differences in recruiting abilities caused by differences in locations, alumni sizes and involvement, sports histories and reputations, media attractiveness, *etc.* I would reject this defense for this reason. Although the Court used the Rule of Reason to evaluate the NCAA's conduct, it quite correctly found against the Association.

The next possible reason why a price-raising horizontal price-fix might not be prohibited by the Sherman Act that I want to discuss turns on an assumption that relevant buyers are not fully sovereign—in particular, cannot evaluate *ex ante* the quality of the service or product various suppliers will provide (and may not even be able to evaluate the quality of the service or product they bought *ex post*). In this "market for lemons"[468] situation, buyers will not be willing to pay a sufficiently-higher price for higher-quality products or services to cover the extra cost of their supply when they would have been willing to do so had they been able to evaluate the quality of the performance they received correctly and, as a consequence, individual sellers acting independently may find it individually most profitable to reduce the quality of the service or product they supply below the level that would be both economically efficient for them to supply and privately profitable for them to supply if buyers could accurately assess the quality of the service or product with which they were supplied. (I acknowledge, of course, that it will usually be both privately profitable and

[467] 468 U.S. 85 (1984).

[468] The reference is to George A. Akerlof, *The Market for "Lemons": Quality Uncertainty and the Market Mechanism*, 84 QUART. J. OF ECON. 488 (1970). In this article, Akerlof argues that, because used-car buyers cannot evaluate the quality of the used cars they are considering buying and therefore tend to undervalue good used cars, dealers tend to market only low-quality used cars and keep the good ones for themselves or friends.

economically efficient for some buyers to purchase lower-quality products or services.) Concomitantly, sellers taken as a group may end up earning lower profits by supplying lower-quality services or products than they could earn by supplying higher-quality services or products if buyers could accurately assess the quality of what they purchased. Sellers that collectively face this problem may therefore find it profitable to induce the government to set and credibly enforce quality-standards or may find it profitable to set and enforce such standards themselves (at least if the setting of such standards induces buyers to increase their valuation of higher-quality product variants). If the government cannot be induced to perform this function or the relevant buyers would not trust the government's and *a fortiori* the industry's own quality-assurances but buyers were perceived by other buyers to be more able to evaluate seller-performance *ex post* than *ex ante*, sellers in this position might also be able to overcome their customers' non-sovereignty more circuitously by fixing the minimum price that anyone could charge for the product or service they supply. In this situation, this strategy would make it more profitable for sellers to forego the cost-savings of lower-quality performance and render the higher-quality performance that would increase the probability that customer-recommendations would yield them additional sales by increasing the profits those additional sales would yield them. I know of no price-raising horizontal-price-fixing case in which the defendants made this "market for lemons" argument, though I suspect that it is the argument that defense lawyers in two cases—*Goldfarb v. Virginia State Bar*[469] and *National Society of Professional Engineers v. United States*[470]—unsuccessfully tried to develop. If my interpretation of the Sherman Act is correct, it should not be held to prohibit price-increasing horizontal price-fixes that sellers executed for this "market for lemons" (buyer non-sovereignty) reason. In these situations, the individual seller's *ex ante* perception that the price-fix would be profitable did not depend critically on any extra profits it expected to realize directly because it reduced the actual absolute attractiveness of the offers against which it had to compete. Indeed, it is not even clear that, in this situation, the price-fix would reduce the actual or buyer-perceived absolute attractiveness of the individual-seller participants' rivals' offers: although it would increase their rivals' prices, it would also increase the quality of the performance their rivals would render and that buyers would expect their rivals would render. In *Society of Engineers*, the Supreme Court rejected a related but (to my mind) critically-different argument the defendants did make by proclaiming that "the Rule of Reason does not support a defense based on the assumption that competition itself is unreasonable."[471] Although clever, this *bon mot* may be too clever by half. Admittedly, a comparative-institutional analysis may lead to the conclusion that a legislature would be better-placed than a court to determine whether this defense really did apply in various commercial contexts, but I do not think that courts are authorized to reject defenses for this reason: the courts should do the best they can and leave it to the legislature to correct their mistakes if they

---

[469] 421 U.S. 773 (1975).

[470] 435 U.S. 679 (1978).

[471] *Id.* at 696.

make them. Of course, one could counter this argument by pointing out that, on my interpretation, Sherman Act analysis proceeds on an otherwise-Pareto-perfect assumption that rules out consideration of these sorts of buyer errors. A more generous (but less accurate) account of the Court's *bon mot* would read it to be making this point.

The penultimate possible reason why a horizontal practice that at first sight appears designed to raise the prices that buyers will agree to pay for a given product or service may not violate the Sherman Act also depends on a buyer error, though, in this instance, the relevant buyer might be said to be an ultimate as opposed to a proximate buyer. The buyer error in question is the error that a state legislature made in promulgating a procurement law that prohibited school districts among others from committing themselves in advance to accepting at least one of the bids made in any round of bids it solicited, thereby exposing the school districts to political pressure from misinformed constituents that tend to think that the bids the school district receive are all too high—*i.e.*, higher than a bid it could get if it requested another round of bids. As I argued earlier, if in these circumstances the cost of calculating the cost of supplying the product or service the school district wants to buy is substantial and big mistakes could be made in estimating these costs, (1) the combination of the state rule in question and the proclivity of powerful political constituencies to underestimate the price the school board will have to pay may actually increase the prices the school boards must pay by deterring suppliers from making careful cost-estimates and thereby inducing them to include substantial risk-premiums in their bids, and (2) an agreement among suppliers not to rebid for a substantial period of time if all bids made in a solicited round of bidding are rejected may actually benefit not only the suppliers but also the buyers by reducing the probability that the buyers will reject all bids, thereby increasing the care with which potential suppliers calculate their bids, thereby reducing the prices they offer the buyer. I have already explained why I believe that such an agreement among potential suppliers should not be held to violate the Sherman Act if it seemed requisitely likely to reduce the prices the relevant buyers will have to pay and indicated that this argument was deemed to be legally irrelevant by the trial-court judge to whom I made it. I suspect that contemporary U.S. courts would also reject it for similar reasons to the ones they gave for rejecting the defenses in *Goldfarb* and *Society of Engineers*.

The final possible justification for a price-raising horizontal price-fix that has been suggested by some scholars is a second-best economic-efficiency argument that applies when the buyers the sellers face have unusual buying power. The argument is that, in this situation, in an otherwise-Pareto-perfect economy the buyers' power would, by itself, cause economic inefficiency and that it might be appropriate for U.S. courts to conclude that seller price-fixing allows sellers to create countervailing power that—by increasing price—will actually increase economic efficiency in the circumstances in question. For reasons that THE WELFARE ECONOMICS OF ANTITRUST POLICY AND U.S. AND E.U. ANTITRUST LAW will discuss in great detail, it is far from clear that, in our actual highly-Pareto-imperfect economy in which the relevant buyers' monopsony power is only one of a myriad of Pareto imperfections distorting the profitability of the various relevant choices that the sellers and buyers in question make, seller price-fixing will actually tend to increase economic efficiency when the sellers face buyers with unusual buying power. However, even if a crude third-best argument could be made for the economic efficiency of seller price-fixing in such cases, I do not think it would be relevant for the analysis of the legality of price-fixes under the Sherman Act, which proceeds on otherwise-Pareto-perfect assumptions. I am unaware of this argument's ever having been made to a U.S. court or of a U.S. court's ever having commented *sua sponte* on the legal relevance of any such argument that might be made. (However, I do believe that an early British restrictive-trade-practices Act did permit sellers to exonerate their price-fix by proving that it was needed to counteract the power of powerful buyers.) I should say that, if contrary to my belief this argument were relevant to the legality of horizontal seller price-fixes under the Sherman Act, it would be equally relevant to the legality of horizontal buyer price-fixes under the Sherman Act when the relevant sellers had an unusual amount of monopoly and oligopoly or market power over price.

The fourth and final question I want to address about the U.S. case-law on (seller) price-fixing is, in fact, a set of two questions: (1) "Do U.S. courts believe that the Sherman Act does not distinguish between horizontal maximum-price fixing and horizontal minimum-price fixing?" and (2) "Do U.S. courts believe that the Sherman Act does not distinguish between the horizontal fixing of minimum prices and the vertical fixing of minimum prices or between horizontal geographic-market divisions and customer allocations on the one hand and vertical territorial restrictions and consumer allocations on the other?" I will address these two questions in turn, first explaining what I take to be the answer to the legal issue in question that is correct as a matter of law and then stating the answers that the U.S. courts have given to each.

With the buyer-error-related exceptions I have just discussed, horizontal minimum-price fixing is always designed to increase its participants' profits by reducing the absolute attractiveness of the offers against which they have to compete. Horizontal maximum-price fixing that is not in fact horizontal minimum-price fixing in disguise is never designed for this purpose. In situations in which the potential customers of a group of rivals will receive insurance reimbursement for their purchases from the sellers in question but their insurance policies impose constraints on the maximum reimbursements the insured can obtain for the goods or services they could purchase from these sellers, the sellers may find it profitable to agree to charge prices to buyers that have such insurance policies that do not exceed the maximum payouts the insurance companies will make for the products or services the sellers supply because such an agreement may enable its participants to make additional sales by preparing the way for them or the insurance company to inform the insured that the participants are suppliers that will charge fees that will not exceed the insurance policy's maximum payouts. Although an individual supplier might be able to profit for similar reasons by committing itself not to charge prices to the insured in excess of the policy limits unilaterally, the agreement will lower the transaction cost per supplier of informing the insured that the suppliers in question have made this commitment. Such horizontal maximum-price-fixing agreements do not violate the test of illegality I believe the Sherman Act promulgates. Unfortunately, in the only case in which the Supreme Court has pronounced on the legality of such a horizontal maximum-price-fixing agreement,[472] it found the agreement *per se* unlawful. The Court's explanation for its conclusion—*viz.*, that maximum-price fixing can easily be a cover for minimum-price fixing and that it will be difficult for courts to determine whether the maximum-price fix allegedly involved in a particular case really is a minimum-price fix—may be consoling but is not convincing: (1) it is simple to tell whether the conditions for legitimate, real maximum-price-fixing agreements are satisfied, and (2) although it is possible that sellers could agree to a nominally-maximum-price fix that was really a minimum-price fix when those conditions are fulfilled, the relevant insurance companies would almost certainly have to be complicitous in such an arrangement (would have to set their maximum payouts above the sellers' non-minimum price-fixed prices), and the insurance companies would not find it spontaneously profitable to cooperate in this way and almost certainly could not be profitably bribed to do so.

The next issues I want to address relate to the U.S. courts' positions on the legality under the Sherman Act of (1) vertical price-fixing agreements between producers and their independent distributors (resale price maintenance—RPM) and (2) the inclusion by producers in contracts with their independent distributors of clauses that limit the territories in which the latter can make sales and/or the customers to which they can make sales. Section 2 of Chap. 14 will examine the actual functions of such RPM agreements, vertical territorial restraints, and vertical customer-allocation clauses and explain why they rarely if ever violate the Sherman Act's test of illegality. For present purposes, the relevant facts are that U.S. courts (1) originally held vertical maximum-price and minimum-price fixes, vertical territorial restraints, and vertical customer-allocation clauses to be *per se* illegal under the Sherman Act, (2) then in 1977 (after a barrage of critiques from economists) explicitly overruled a 10-year-old precedent[473] and declared that the legality under the Sherman Act of any vertical territorial restraint and/or customer-allocation clause would be determined through a Rule of Reason analysis while continuing to insist that vertical minimum-price and maximum-price fixes are *per se* illegal under the Act,[474] (3) next (in 1997[475]) overruled a 29-year-old precedent[476] that held that vertical *maximum*-price fixes were *per se* illegal under the Sherman Act, declaring that the legality of such price fixes under the Sherman Act would henceforth be determined through a Rule of Reason analysis (while reiterating that vertical *minimum*-price fixes were still *per se* illegal); and most recently

[472] Arizona v. Maricopa County Medical Society, 457 U.S. 332 (1982). I should point out that, although the explanation that I have just given fits the case of sellers that supply medical services, dental services, physical-therapy and rehabilitation services, prescription or non-prescription drugs, and various other sorts of medical supplies, it is not limited to suppliers of such services and products—*e.g.*, it applies equally well to sellers that supply car-repair services and products to insured motorists.

[473] United States v. Arnold, Schwinn & Co., 388 U.S. 365 (1967).

[474] Continental T.V., Inc. v. GTE Sylvania, Inc. 433 U.S. 36 (1977).

[475] See State Oil v. Khan, 522 U.S. 3 (1997).

[476] See Albrecht v. Herald Co., 390 U.S. 145 (1968).

(in 2007[477]) declared that the legality under the Sherman Act of vertical *minimum*-price fixes as well as of vertical *maximum*-price fixes would be determined through a Rule of Reason analysis.

"Do U.S. courts believe that the Sherman Act applies to price-fixing by buyers" and "If the U.S. courts do believe that the Sherman Act does apply to price-fixing by buyers, when do they believe that price-lowering price-fixing by buyers will not violate the Sherman Act?" These questions are important both for the legality under the Sherman Act of conventional buyer cooperatives and for the legality under the Sherman Act of various agreements that the constituent teams in professional-sport leagues enter into that reduce the prices they pay for the services of the professional athletes they hire (*inter alia*, agreements to hire league rookies through a draft that permits only one team in the league to bid for the services of any given athlete, agreements to include "reserve clauses" in all contracts between league teams and players that give the hiring team lifetime rights to the relevant-sport-performance services of the player or [more recently] rights to these player-services for a specified number of years, agreements not to bid for free agents, salary-cap agreements that place a maximum limit on the total salaries that any team can pay its players, luxury-tax agreements that require any team whose total player-salaries exceed some specified sum to pay the league a specified percentage of the "excess").

I will first analyze the answers to the two buyer-price-fix legal questions that I think are correct as matters of law and then discuss the U.S. case-law on these issues. My own legal analysis starts with a general legal point about the Sherman Act, then discusses an economic-impact issue that that legal point makes critical, and finally examines the implications of my resolution of the legal and economic-consequences points in question for the resolution of conventional-buyer-cooperative cases and pro-sports-league cases that would be correct as a matter of correctly-interpreted Sherman Act law.

The general point derives from the fact that one of the goals that the Sherman Act was designed to achieve was to improve the buying options available to consumers. There can be no doubt that conventional buyer coops and the various pro-sport-league agreements I just listed reduce competition among buyers, but given the fact that these agreements will tend to reduce the prices the agreeing buyers and (when relevant) their customers pay for the goods and services in question, a plausible functional argument can be made for the conclusion that such agreements are not agreements "in restraint of trade" in the Sherman Act sense of that expression—*i.e.*, do not constitute even *prima facie* violations of the Act. Admittedly, this statutory-goal argument can be countered by a textual argument and perhaps as well by the argument that the Sherman Act was also passed to instantiate the moral position that it is wrong for anyone to profit (and impose losses on others) by engaging in conduct the perpetrator would not have perceived to be profitable *ex ante* had the perpetrator not believed it would yield it private advantages that would have no allocative counterpart in an otherwise-Pareto-perfect economy. (I write "perhaps" because in

[477] See Leegin Creative Leather Prods. v. PSKS, Inc., 551 U.S. 877 (2007).

an otherwise-Pareto-perfect economy, the price-reductions that buyer price-fixing would yield would increase economic efficiency if the allocative transaction cost of arranging and policing the buyer price-fix could be ignored.)

The second set of points I wish to make relates to conventional buyer cooperatives. Such cooperatives come in two forms that are worth distinguishing. Some do nothing more than buy goods or services for their members. Others not only buy products (say fruits, vegetables, grains, meat) for their members but also process them (into cooked or preserved vegetables and fruits, breakfast cereals, crackers, spaghetti sauces) and perhaps advertise the final products. Simple buyer coops can benefit their members by reducing the per-unit mechanical transaction cost of buying the goods in question (by enabling them to take advantage of mechanical-transaction-cost economies of scale), by enabling them to profit by making more perspicuous choices among a given set of supply offers—*i.e.*, by enabling them to take advantage of the fact that one can profitably hire more-cost-effective purchasing agents when making a larger volume of purchases, by enabling them to secure discounts because the larger sales they can offer suppliers reduce the risk costs the suppliers bear, and by enabling them to secure discounts because the coop has more bargaining power than its individual members have. Buyer coops that also process the goods bought and advertise the final products they produce can benefit their members not only in the ways just listed but also by enabling them to profit from the processing and advertising activities as well. Two additional points that are related to the preceding observations should be noted: (1) the elimination of inter-member buyer competition contributes to the ability of simple producer-buyer coops to benefit their members but (2) the elimination of inter-member buyer competition is not necessary for the generation of the additional benefits that complex producer-buyer coops can confer on their members—buyers that purchased their inputs separately could still join together to do R&D, to process their inputs, and to promote their final products (though the buyers might have to agree to purchase only inputs with specified attributes).

Assuming that the Sherman Act does cover price-lowering agreements by buyers not to compete as buyers, what does the preceding analysis imply for the Sherman-Act-legality of price-lowering conventional buyer coops? On my reading of the statute, the Sherman Act does not prohibit a conventional buyer coop if the coop's members would have concluded *ex ante* that the coop's ability to perform the first three functions that I argued simple buyer coops can perform would make it profitable even if it did not benefit them by enabling them to wield additional buying power or to profit by processing and advertising the processed product through the coop. The profits the coop-agreement would enable members to obtain by increasing their bargaining power cannot legitimate the agreement under the Sherman Act (on this interpretation) because (on this interpretation) the Sherman Act deems these benefits illicit, and the profits the coop-agreement would enable members to realize by processing the food (or other things) they bought and advertising the processed output cannot legitimate the agreement under the Sherman Act because the agreement not to compete as buyers was not necessary for these benefits' generation. These conclusions are simply the buyer-price-fix counterparts to the analogous conclusions that I reached about the seller-price-fixing joint-sales arrangement at issue in *Broadcast Music*.

The third set of points I wish to make relates to the various agreements that the individual teams in a professional-sports league make to reduce the price (salaries) they pay the athletes they hire to play the sport in question for them. Seven points are salient in this connection. First, professional-sports leagues themselves are almost always lawful joint ventures: although the teams in any such league could arrange to play games or matches or fixtures outside a league structure, leagues create allocative benefits both by standardizing playing fields and rules of the game and by creating a new product—league competition—whose profitable supply is presumptively economically efficient. Second, at least over significant ranges of sport-competitiveness equality, the allocative efficiency of the league-competition product may very well be a direct function of the competitive equality of the teams in the league. Third, having the various teams in a league be separately owned may contribute to—indeed, may be essential to—the league's profitability and economic efficiency because it critically affects fans' perceptions that the teams really are in sports-competition with each other. Fourth although, in some cases, the financial viability of a league will depend on its constituent teams' not competing against each other as buyers of playing-services, in other cases, it will not. Fifth, although player-salary-reducing league agreements to select league rookies through a draft, to include reserve clauses in player contracts, not to hire free agents, to cap total team salaries, and/or to impose "luxury taxes" on teams whose total player-payroll exceeds the permitted cap will clearly promote the competitive equality of the league's teams relative to an unrestricted player-hiring regime, it will almost never do so relative to other means the league could adopt to achieve this goal that would have less depressing effects on player salaries such as substantial revenue-sharing or national-TV-exposure rules that enable small-market teams to compete more effectively for players by increasing the national-TV exposure their players get and, hence, their players' ability to make money through product-endorsements and guest appearances. Sixth, the relevant player-salary-reducing agreements are not necessary for the other functions the league performs such as standardizing playing-fields and playing-rules and providing league competition. Seventh and relatedly, assuming that the Sherman Act does cover player-salary-reducing professional-sport-league agreements (and that it is proper to consider the individual teams in a sports league to be defendants as opposed to the league itself), the various player-salary-reducing agreements in which professional-sports leagues can require their members to participate will violate the Sherman Act except in the rare instance in which they can be shown to be essential to the financial viability of a league that would be economically efficient in an otherwise-Pareto-perfect economy.

I turn now to the U.S. case-law on buyer agreements. Four cases or sets of cases are relevant. First, in 1948, the Supreme Court held that the Sherman Act applies fully to price-fixing by purchasers:

> The statute does not confine its protections to consumers, or to purchasers, or to competitors, or to sellers. Nor does it immunize the outlawed acts because they are done

> by any of these. The Act is comprehensive in its terms and coverage, protecting all that are made victims of the forbidden practices by whomever they be perpetrated.[478]

This holding has never been reversed or qualified. Moreover, as Chap. 12 indicates, the position that buyer price-fixing is illegal has been implicitly endorsed by the DOJ and FTC in that both the 1992 Horizontal Merger Guidelines used the 2010 Horizontal Merger Guidelines state that the fact that a horizontal merger creates a merged firm that has more buyer power than the sum of the buying power that the two merger partners had individually prior to their merger counts against the merger's legality.

Second, in a number of conventional-buyer-coop cases in which the Government argued that the coop-agreement violated the Sherman Act in that it restricted the territories in which the coop members could operate, neither the Government nor (as a result, I presume) the court even considered the possibility that the agreement of the relevant buyers not to compete against each other as buyers of the products the coop purchased might violate the Sherman Act.[479] Of course, there is no way to tell whether this omission affected the Government's conclusion that this aspect of the agreement in question would pass legal muster for the sort of reason that *Broadway Music* stated seller price-fixes could do so.

Third, a wide variety of joint-venture cases that will be considered in some detail in Chap. 15 have held that competitive restrictions in joint-venture agreements will not be deemed illegal if they are "ancillary" to the purpose of the joint venture without ever defining the relevant concept of "ancillary"—*e.g.*, without indicating whether to be ancillary in the legitimating sense in which these cases implicitly define this concept, the restriction of competition must be essential to the profitability of a joint venture that would be economically efficient on otherwise-Pareto-perfect assumptions.

Fourth, a series of decisions on professional-sport-league player-salary-reducing agreements has held them illegal under the Sherman Act. More specifically, the decisions in question respectively declared illegal under the Sherman Act (1) the National Football League's 1968 rookie-draft procedure (though the relevant decision stated in a dictum that a less-restrictive draft-procedure might be lawful as ancillary),[480] (2) the National Hockey League's reserve-clause agreement,[481] and (3) the NFL's Rozelle Rule, requiring teams that hired a player after his contract with another team expired to compensate the original team with one or more other players or draft choices.[482]

* * *

---

[478] Mandeville Island Farms v. American Crystal Sugar, 334 U.S. 219, 236 (1948).

[479] See, *e.g.*, United States v. Topco Associates, Inc., 405 U.S. 596 (1972).

[480] Smith v. Pro Football, Inc., 593 F.2d 1173 (D.C. Cir. 1978).

[481] Philadelphia World Hockey Club, Inc. v. Philadelphia Club, 351 F. Supp. 462 (E.D. Pa. 1972).

[482] Mackey v. NFL, 543 F.2d 606 (8th Cir. 1976).

This review of the U.S. case-law on the legality of seller horizontal and vertical price-fixing, horizontal output-restrictions, horizontal and vertical market divisions, and of buyer horizontal price-fixing under the Sherman Act has revealed that, although the U.S. courts have resolved many relevant issues correctly from the start and have corrected some mistakes they originally made, there is still considerable room for improvement.

(2) The EC's Positions on (Seller) Oligopolistic Pricing and Various Types of Pricing-Related Conduct That Have Often Been Mischaracterized as Oligopolistic and the E.C./E.U. Courts' Case-Law on All These Types of Conduct

In my judgment, with three clear exceptions, the legality of contrived oligopolistic pricing, natural oligopolistic pricing, parallel pricing that is either not oligopolistic at all in my sense or not contrived oligopolistic in my sense, and various types of non-oligopolistic conduct that are designed to increase the prices its perpetrators can obtain without raising their products' quality is the same under E.C./E.U. competition law as it is under U.S. antitrust law. The first clear exception is that E.C./E.U. competition law does not prohibit contrived oligopolistic pricing that is executed exclusively through threats of retaliation (that does not involve reciprocation-agreements) unless the perpetrator is individually dominant or a member of a collectively-dominant set of rivals (in which case such conduct would constitute an exclusionary abuse of a dominant position, prohibited by now Article 102, and might result in the perpetrator's committing an exploitative abuse of its dominant position as well).

The second clear exception is that what is now Article 101 of the 2009 Treaty of Lisbon does prohibit all natural oligopolistic pricing as concerted practices that have as their object and effect the prevention or restriction of competition.

The third clear exception is that, unlike U.S. antitrust law, E.C./E.U. competition law—in particular, Article 102 of the Treaty of Lisbon—may prohibit as an exploitative abuse of a dominant position four categories of non-oligopolistic or natural oligopolistic conduct if one or more of the perpetrators are individually or collectively dominant and the resulting prices reduce the relevant buyer surplus to an unfair absolute quantity or an unfair percentage of the transaction surplus the relevant sales generated or the maximum amount of transaction surplus the buyers' purchases of the relevant product(s) could have generated:

(1) any conduct that enables across-the-board pricers to announce their prices in an order that is more in their joint interest in that it increases the height of the prices in the group's HNOP array to more-jointly-profitable levels,
(2) natural oligopolistic pricing,
(3) any single-period conduct that enables the pricers to obtain oligopolistic margins naturally in the period in which it takes place without taking advantage of each firm's expectation that its rivals' willingness to charge supra-HNOP prices in the future will depend on whether it undercuts any such prices the rivals

charge in the current period (*e.g.*, the combination of "premature" supra-HNOP-price announcements [made, say, in trade journals before buyers need to know the prices they will have to pay] and other conduct that progressively locks the sellers into supra-HNOP prices [including the prices in advertising that reaches buyers, stamping the prices on products, putting the prices on shelves] that increase the cost they would have to incur to change their price), and

(4) in across-the-board-pricing situations, the following conduct, which might be said to permit its perpetrators to create inter-temporal expectations that enable them to obtain oligopolistic margins naturally—*i.e.*, without anyone's making a threat of retaliation or a promise of inherently-unprofitable reciprocation: one firm's (A) charging a price that is higher than its (HNOP + NOM) and/or (B) recommending to its rivals that they charge prices higher than their (HNOP + NOM)s while indicating that it will do so as well without having much less communicating any intention to retaliate against any rival that undermines its price, without promising to maintain its price in the time-period in question, and without promising to charge prices above its (HNOP + NOM) in future periods if its price in this current period is not undermined.

The fourth type of conduct in the above list is not contrived because it does not rely on threats of (inherently-unprofitable) retaliation or promises of inherently-unprofitable reciprocation to induce rivals to forego charging lower prices that would be profitable for them if the firm charging the higher price did not react strategically to their doing so—because it relies solely on its rivals' expectations that the probability that it will charge prices in excess of its (HNOP + NOM) in the future is positively related to whether and the extent to which the prices of this kind it charges in the current period have been undermined.

If the above exceptions do not play a critical role or are not warranted, the analysis of the legality of contrived oligopolistic pricing, natural oligopolistic pricing, parallel pricing that is not oligopolistic in my sense or is not contrived oligopolistic in my sense, and the various types of price-raising conduct I have just described that is correct as a matter of E.C./E.U. competition law is the same as the analysis of such conduct that is correct under U.S. antitrust law. With this in mind, I will address the way in which the EC and the E.C./E.U. courts have answered six questions that can arise in cases that focus on one or other of the types of pricing-conduct in question.

The first such question is: What position have the EC and the E.C./E.U. courts taken on the legality of explicit horizontal agreements to fix actual or minimum prices under now Article 101 and now Article 102? The answer to this question is clear. Both the EC and the E.C./E.U. courts have always recognized that, with one exception that will be addressed next, horizontal agreements on actual or minimum prices violate what are now Articles 101 and 102 of the Lisbon Treaty, regardless of whether actual prices equaled the agreed-upon "target" or "recommended" prices.[483] By way of

[483] See in general Francois Arbault and Ewoud Sakkers, *Cartels* (Chap. 7) in the EC LAW OF COMPETITION 745–1128 (ed. by Jonathan Faull and Ali Nikpay) (Oxford Univ. Press, 2007). I have relied on this chapter extensively when writing this section. See also ELEANOR FOX, THE COMPETITION

elaboration, I should point out that the EC and E.C./E.U. courts have interpreted their conclusion that now Articles 101 and 102 prohibit horizontal fixes of minimum or actual prices to imply that these Treaty provisions prohibit agreements to use specified pricing formulas,[484] agreements to fix a component of the overall prices charged by a set of rivals,[485] and agreements to fix the maximum rebate that the members of a set of product-rivals can offer any buyer or some set of buyers.[486] The EC and the E.C./E.U. courts also believe that agreements by rivals to run "coordinated price-increase campaigns" qualify as horizontal actual-price-fixing agreements.[487] I should add that, although some "coordinated price-increase campaigns" may manifest anticompetitive agreements, others will not—will violate now Article 101 if and only if they can correctly be said to constitute concerted practices in the now Article 101 sense of that concept. Finally and not surprisingly, the EC and the E.C./E.U. courts have also always understood that the conclusion that now Articles 101 and 102 prohibit the horizontal fixing of actual or minimum prices implies the illegality of horizontal agreements that allocate territories[488] or customers[489] among product-rivals.

LAW OF THE EUROPEAN UNION IN COMPARATIVE PERSPECTIVE: CASES AND MATERIALS 71 (West Pub. Co., 2009). For decisions declaring agreements to set "target prices" illegal even when the prices diverge from actual prices, see Polypropylene, OJ L230/1 (1986); Food Flavour Enhancers, OJ L75/1, p. 94 (2004); Industrial Tubes, OJ L75/1, p. 94 (2004); and Vereiniging von Cementhandelaren, OJ L13/34 (1971). For decisions declaring agreements on "recommended prices" illegal regardless of whether actual prices diverge from the recommended prices, see Welded Steel Mesh, OJ L260/1 (1989). SCK/FNK (Dutch Cranes), OJ L312/79, p. 20 (1995); Joined Cases SCK and FNK v. Commission, T-213/95 and T-18/96, ECR II-1739 (1997); and Fenex, OJ L181/28, p. 61 (1996). I should add that, from the beginning, U.S. courts also declared horizontal price-fixing agreements illegal even when actual prices diverged from the agreed-upon prices. See, *e.g.*, United States v. Trans-Missouri Freight Assn., 166 U.S. 290 (1897) and United States v. Trenton Potteries Co., 273 U.S. 392 (1927).

[484] See Greek Ferries, OJ L109/24 (1999); Roofing Felt, OJ L232/15 (1986); and Agreements Between Manufacturers of Glass Containers, OJ L160/1 (1974). The formulas in question were analogous to but obviously different from basing-point-pricing formulas.

[485] See Building and Construction Industry in the Netherlands, OJ L92/1 (1992); SPO and Others v. Commission, Case T-29/92, ECR II-289, p. 146 (1995); Eurocheque/Helsinki Agreement, OJ L95/50, pp. 46–49 (1992); Industrial Tubes, OJ L125/50 (2004); Ferry Operators-Currency Surcharge, OJ L26/23 (1997); Steel Beams, OJ L1165/1, pp. 244–49 (1994); Alloy Surcharge, OJ L100/55 (1998); Electrical and Mechanical Carbon and Graphite Products, OJ L125/45 (2004); and Krupp Thyssen Stainless and Acciai Speciali Terni v. Commission, Joined Cases T-45/98 and T-47/98, ECR II-3757, p. 15 (2001).

[486] See Agreements Between Manufacturers of Glass Containers, OJ L160/1, p. 36 (1974); Fedetab, OJ L224/29 (1978); Roofing Felt, OJ L232/15 (1986); Quinine, OJ L192/5 (1964); Citric Acid, OJ L239/18 (2002); and Fine Art Auction Houses, OJ L200/92 (2005).

[487] See Quinine, OJ L129/5 (1969); Dyestuff, OJ L195/11 (1969); and ICI v. Commission, Case 48–69, ECR 619, p. 115 (1972).

[488] See Quinine, OJ L192/5 (1969); European Sugar Industry, OJ L140/17 (1973); Vegetable Parchment, OJ L35/1 (1985); Peroxygen Products, OJ L35/1 (1985); Graphite Electrodes, OJ L100/1 (2002); Cement, OJ L343/1 (1994); CEWAL, OJ L34/20 (1993); SAS Maersk Air, OJ L265/15 (2001); Seamless Steel Tubes, OJ L140/1 (2003); and Belgian Beer, OJ L200/1 (2003).

[489] See Polypropylene, OJ L230/1 (1986); Roofing Felt, OJ L232/15, p. 51 (1986); Pre-Insulated Pipes, OJ L24/1 (1999); Luxembourg Brewers, L253/21 (2002); Methylglucamine, OJ L38/18 (2004); and Food Flavour Enhancers, OJ L75/1 (2004).

The second question I wish to address relates to the exception to which my answer to the first question referred: Have the EC or the E.C./E.U. courts ever indicated that under some circumstances horizontal price-fixing agreements or concerted practices that do prevent, restrict, or distort competition would be lawful under E.C./E.U. competition law or indicated the circumstances in which that would be the case? Two such possibilities are conceivable. First, agreements or concerted practices of this kind might not be held to violate now Article 101(1)'s test of *prima facie* illegality if the behavior in question were deemed to be a legitimate attempt to prevent "ruinous competition" or if the prices fixed or secured were deemed "reasonable." Second and relatedly, agreements or concerted practices of this kind might not be held to violate now Article 101 or the exclusionary-abuse branch of now Article 102's test of illegality if the conduct in question satisfied the Article 101(3) conditions of (A) "contribut[ing] to the production or distribution of goods or to promoting technical or economic progress" and (B) allowing relevant consumers "a fair share of the resulting benefits" and their Article 102 counterparts. To my knowledge, the EC and E.C./E.U. courts have never suggested that a horizontal price-increasing price-fix would be deemed not to violate now Article 101(1)'s test of *prima facie* illegality or the exclusionary-abuse branch of now Article 102's test of *prima facie* illegality (when arranged by an individually-dominant firm or a group of collectively-dominant firms) if the price or other terms that were fixed were deemed "reasonable" or "fair": although the fairness of the prices charged is relevant to whether the defendant's conduct constitutes an exploitative abuse of a dominant position, it is not relevant to whether the conduct prevents, restricts, or distorts competition under now Article 101 or constitutes an exclusionary abuse under now Article 102. To the contrary, the EC has clearly stated that *de facto* "ruinous competition" arguments cannot justify price-raising horizontal price-fixes under now Article 101(1)'s test of *prima facie* illegality: "The fact that the. . .[relevant] market was characterized over a period of several years by under-utilization of capacity, with attendant losses by producers, does not relieve the [price-fixing] agreement of its anticompetitive object."[490] However, the EC has held that a fix by buyers (Eurocheque issuers) of the price they would pay other banks that cashed their Eurocheques for a specified service (cashing the Eurocheques) was legitimated under now Article 101(3) by the transaction-cost savings the arrangement generated by obviating individual negotiations between individual issuing and cashing banks on the unproven assumption that the consumers that used Eurocheques obtained a fair share of the resulting benefit.[491] This EC decision is highly analogous to the U.S. Supreme Court's decision in *Broadcast Music*,[492] though the arrangement at issue in *Broadcast Music* allowed individual performance-right holders to market their individual products separately. (The equivalent arrangement in Eurocheque would have been a provision allowing issuing and cashing banks to negotiate their own prices or a provision allowing issuing banks to indicate on the face of their checks the commission

[490] See Polypropylene, OJ L230/1 (1986).

[491] See Uniform Eurocheques, OJ L35/43 (1985).

[492] Broadcast Music, Inc. v. Columbia Broadcasting System, Inc., 441 U.S. 1 (1979).

rate they would pay: admittedly, the latter practice might make it difficult for buyers to evaluate the checks of an issuing bank that did specify a non-standard commission because it would be hard for them to determine how many banks would cash such an issuing bank's checks.)

The third question that needs to be addressed is: What position have the EC and the E.C./E.U. courts taken on "concerted practices" or "concertations"? I have made some suggestions about the categories of conduct that do not involve the creation of any agreement that could be deemed a concerted practice under now-Article 101. Neither the EC nor the E.C./E.U. courts have ever addressed these possibilities. In fact, neither the EC nor any E.U. court has ever defined the concept of "a concertation" explicitly or provided examples of concerted practices that would give some guidance about the nature of such practices. Indeed, the pronouncements the E.C. courts have made on "concertations" are highly confusing and possibly inconsistent or individually incoherent. Admittedly, the E.C./E.U. courts have clearly stated that one cannot prove a concertation by establishing that the firms in question engaged in parallel conduct or even consciously-parallel conduct. Thus, although the EC was originally willing to infer a concertation or concerted practice that would be illegal under now-Article 101 from various forms of parallel conduct (the partially-simultaneous making of identical or parallel quarterly price-announcements or "parallel" decisions to cease supplying a distributor that was engaging in cross-national parallel trade [arbitrage]), the E.C. courts insisted that proof of parallel conduct does not establish a concertation.[493] The E.C.'s and the E.C./E.U. courts' conclusion on this issue is most clearly stated in *Wood Pulp II*: "parallel conduct cannot be regarded as furnishing proof of concertation unless concertation constitutes the only explanation for such conduct" (a stronger requirement than I think appropriate). But exactly what converts behavior that cannot be said to have created an agreement into a concertation remains obscure. Thus, the cases abound with the following sorts of unhelpful statements: concerted practices "do not have all the elements of a contract" but "arise out of conduct that manifests coordination which becomes apparent from the behavior of participants" (*Dyestuffs*). This statement is unhelpful not only (1) because it leaves undefined the concept of "coordination" that would render behavior a concerted practice and (2) because it does not indicate what behavior can render "apparent" the fact that conduct constitutes the kind of coordination that converts behavior into a concerted practice. Moreover, although I agree with the pronouncements in *Wood Pulp II* that now Article 101 "prohibits any form of collusion which distorts competition" and does not "deprive economic operators of the right to adapt themselves intelligently to the existing and anticipated conduct of their competitors," I do not know how to interpret *Wood Pulp II's* claim that what is now Article 101 "does. . .preclude any indirect or direct contact between such operators, the object or effect whereof is either to influence the conduct on the market of an actual or potential competitor or to disclose to such a competitor the

[493] On price announcements, see Wood Pulp II, OJ L85/1 (1985); see also Suiker Unie and Others v. Commission, Joined Cases 40–48, 50, 54–56, 111 and 113–14173, ECR 1663, pp. 173–74 (1975) and Imperial Chemical Indus. v. Commission (Dyestuffs), 1972 ECR 619 (1972). On discontinuance of supply, see Compagnie Royale Asturienne des Mines SA and Rheinzink GmbH v. Commission, Joined Cases 29/83 and 30/83, 1984 ECR 1676 (1984).

course of conduct which they themselves have decided to adopt or contemplate adopting in the market."[494] In particular, I do not know whether the last claim effectively declares that at least some variants of the (ill-specified) conduct to which it refers constitute an illegal concerted practice under what is now Article 101. Further confusion is sewn by the courts' conclusion in some of the relevant cases that the fact that the behavior in question was not perfectly parallel demonstrates that no concertation was present (a conclusion that is not only unwarranted [regardless of how one defines concertation if it is not defined to be consciously-parallel behavior] but is also inconsistent with the courts' correct view that the fact that actual prices deviate from fixed, "target," or "recommended" prices is compatible with an illegal horizontal-price-fixing agreement's having been formed). In practice, the EC and the E.C./E.U. courts seem to be basing their conclusions about whether behavior that does not create or manifest an illegal price-fixing agreement is an illegal concerted practice on whether the relevant market's structure (in my vocabulary, on whether conditions) favor the profitability of price-fixing and whether the defendants have engaged in other behavior that would facilitate price-fixing. This practice resembles the U.S. courts' practice of finding perpetrators of parallel conduct to have violated the Sherman Act if and only if various so-called plus factors are present. I should add that, although the sample of cases on both sides is small, I suspect that contemporary E.C./E.U. courts are *less willing* to find that the combination of (1) proof of parallel behavior and (2)(A) proof of "market structures" (conditions) that favors the profitability of price-fixing and/or (B) proof of other behavior (say, information-exchanges) that facilitate price-fixing establish the illegality of the conduct in question than contemporary U.S. courts are to find that the combination of proof of parallel behavior and proof of analogous "plus factors" establish the Sherman Act illegality of the relevant conduct. I should also add that many U.S. experts such as Fred McChesney of Northwestern have reached the opposite conclusion on this issue. Perhaps the safest conclusion is that the E.C.'s and the E.C./E.U. courts' handling of the concept of a "concerted practice" is equally unsatisfactory as the U.S. courts' handling of the somewhat-related concept of "tacit collusion."

The fourth question that should be addressed under this heading is: What evidence do the EC and the E.C./E.U. courts believe strengthen a horizontal minimum-or-actual price-fixing case against defendants? The answer is that the EC and E.C./E.U. courts believe that the following types of evidence strengthen the case against price-fixing defendants: efforts at standardization (whose relevance I find doubtful since standardization often performs legitimate functions and may not render price-fixing more feasible and profitable, all things considered), evidence of the exchange of sensitive information (which I think strengthens the case that contrived oligopolistic pricing has been practiced even when the exchange is not itself illegal though, as we have seen, the exchange of many types of information that sellers exchange does not facilitate price-fixing and the exchange of some types of information whose exchange

---

[494] Suiker Unie and Others v. Commission, Joined Cases 40–48, 50, 54–56, 111 and 113–14173, ECR 1663, pp. 173–74 (1975).

does facilitate price-fixing performs other legitimate functions as well), evidence of agreements to limit advertising,[495] and evidence that the defendants have divided up territories[496] and/or customers.[497] The EC and E.C./E.U. courts also think that evidence that the defendants had engaged in illegal price-fixing previously favors the conclusion that they subsequently engaged in price-fixing.[498] The EC and E.C./E.U. courts seem to have reached this conclusion because they believe that the defendants' prior participation in price-fixing indicates that the relevant industry has a culture of collusion and has established the necessary communication channels; I think that evidence of past price-fixing is relevant, if at all, because it indicates that contrivance was feasible and presumably profitable in the past and that, at least in the past, the perpetrators were not deterred from engaging in the activity by a preference not to violate the law or not to do something that is immoral. Somewhat relatedly, the EC and E.C./E.U. courts seem to think that evidence that defendants had the opportunity to discuss collusion face-to-face because their managers met as members of a trade association, participated together in policy discussions with government legislators and regulators, or saw each other socially strengthens any contrivance case against them.[499] More persuasively (at least to me), the EC and E.C./E.U. courts give weight in these types of cases to proof that the defendants have allocated market shares,[500] have incurred losses to impose costs on some rivals that can be shown to have not cooperated,[501] have agreed not to compete against a rival in its domestic territory in exchange for the rival's agreeing not to produce a particular product,[502] and have agreed to purchase a bankrupt rival to prevent a new entrant from purchasing it.[503]

The fifth question I need to address is: Has the EC or any E.C./E.U. court ever stated that now Article 101 does not prohibit unsuccessful attempts to enter into price-fixing agreements or unsuccessful or successful attempts to contrive oligopolistic prices exclusively through threats? To my knowledge, neither the EC nor any E.C./E.U. court has ever adverted to either of these issues. The EC has declared illegal an agreement to secure compliance with a price-fixing scheme by cooperatively penalizing non-cooperators,[504] but a finding that such agreements are illegal

---

[495] See Belgian Beer, OJ L200/1 (2003); Electrical and Mechanical Carbon Producers, OJ L125/45 (2004); and Roofing Felt, OJ L232-15 (1986).

[496] See the cases cited at note 488 *supra*.

[497] See the cases cited at note 489 *supra*.

[498] See Agreements Between Manufacturers of Glass Containers, OJ L160/1 (1974); Building and Construction Industry in the Netherlands, OJ L92/1 (1992); and Austrian Banks OJ L56/1 (2004).

[499] See Cartonboard, OJ L243/1 (1994); Cement, OJ L343/1 (1994); and Fine Art Auction Houses, OJ L140/1 (2003).

[500] See Quinine, OJ L192/5 (1969); French-West African Shipowners' Committees, OJ L134/1 (1992); Flat Glass Benelux, OJ L212/13 (1984); Cartonboard, OJ L243/1 (1994); Graphite Electrodes, OJ L100/1 (2002); Citric Acid, OJ L239/18 9 (2002); and Zinc Phosphate, OJ L153/1 (2003).

[501] See Cement, OJ L343/1 (1994) and Pre-Insulated Pipes, OJ L24/1, pp. 98–107 (1999).

[502] Quinine, OJ L192/5, p. 30 (1969).

[503] Roofing Felt, OJ L232/15 (1986).

[504] See Cement, OJ L343/1, p. 25(4) (1991) and Pre-Insulated Pipe Cartel, 99/60 OJ L24/1 (1999).

has nothing to do with the legality under now-Article 101 of contrivance that is practiced exclusively through threats of retaliation.

The sixth and final question I want to address at this juncture is: Have the EC and the E.C./E.U. courts reached any conclusions about the legality of horizontal maximum-price fixes by sellers? As we have seen, horizontal maximum-price fixes can perform some legitimate functions, though there is always a risk that they are in fact minimum-or-actual-price fixes in disguise. In any event, the EC and E.C./E.U. courts believe that the Treaties prohibit horizontal maximum-price fixes by sellers.[505]

This section has focused on *horizontal* price-fixes. As Chap. 14 discusses, *vertical* price-fixes perform entirely-different functions for their employer, rarely reduce inter-brand competition, and even when they do frequently have this impact as a result of their increasing the absolute and relative organizational allocative efficiency of their practitioners. At this juncture, I will say no more than that the EC and E.C./E.U. courts believe that now-Articles 101 and 102 prohibit vertical minimum-price fixes[506] and have moved from a position that these Articles prohibit all vertical territorial restraints and customer-allocation clauses to a more-complicated, mixed position on this issue[507] (much as their American counterparts have done). The EC's and the E.C./E.U. courts' positions on vertical price fixing and vertical territorial divisions and customer-allocation clauses will be discussed in far more detail in Chap. 14.

4. Oligopolistic Decisionmaking on Non-Price Terms in Contracts of Sale or Product-Attributes Whose Alteration Should Not Be Said to Entail the Creation of a QV Investment

A. The Non-Price Contract Terms That Oligopolistic Interactions Can Affect and the Actual and Buyer-Perceived Product-Attributes That Can Be Affected by Oligopolistic Interactions That Do Not Alter Any QV-Investment-Creating Decision

Oligopolistic interactions can affect a large variety of terms of sale other than the prices for which the goods in question can be sold and can also affect the physical attributes, images, and buyer perceptions of the goods sold without inducing or deterring the execution of any QV investment. This subsection will list and (when appropriate) elaborate on (1) the non-price terms of sale that oligopolistic

[505] See Cement, OJ L343/1 (1994).

[506] See Pronuptia GmbH v. Pronuptia de Paris Irmgard Schillgallis, ECR 53 (1986) and Commission Regulation (EC) 2790/1999 of 22 December 1999 on the Application of Art. 81(3) of the Treaty to Categories of Vertical Agreements and Concerted Practices at point 47, OJ L336 (1999).

[507] See Mario Filipponi, Luc Peeperkorn, and Donnecadh Woods, *Vertical Agreements* (Chap. 7) in THE EC LAW OF COMPETITION 1129, 1195–97 (Jonathan Faull and Ali Nikpay, eds.) (Oxford Univ. Press, 2d ed., 2007).

interactions can affect as well as (2) the actual and buyer-perceived product-attributes that oligopolistic interactions can affect without (arguably) changing any QV-investment-creation decision.

The non-price terms of sale (which affect the attractiveness of the relevant transaction to both the buyer and the seller it involves) include credit terms, supply-date or delivery-date terms, product-installation terms, post-sales-service and replacement-part terms, terms that relate to the provision of product-use instruction, warrantee terms, exculpatory clauses (which exempt the seller from liability for losses the buyer sustained because the product in question failed to perform or misperformed through no fault of the seller or because of the seller's negligence, gross negligence, or even willful misconduct), terms that limit or specify the damages for which the seller will be liable if it fails to fulfill its contractual obligations and the buyer sustains any type of loss or specific types of losses as a result, and terms that specify the process through which contract disputes will be resolved. Sales contracts involving sellers that make their choices on them non-oligopolistically—*i.e.*, on the assumption that their payoffs either will not be affected by the response to them of any individual rival or will be affected by only simple (*i.e.*, non-oligopolistic) interdependence—will always include terms on these matters: even if the contract itself does not explicitly address the issue, they will implicitly adopt the term supplied by the law as a default rule. However, for reasons that the next subsection will explain, sellers will sometimes find it profitable to contrive variants of each of these sorts of terms that make their offers less attractive to buyers when they would not have found it profitable to include such terms absent contrivance.

Sellers may also find it profitable to control the unit-size of the products they and their rivals offer for sale or various other physical product-quality attributes. However, as we shall see, the product-attributes they choose to contrive may not be less attractive to buyers than the ones they would otherwise supply—may be inherently-more-attractive, inherently-less-attractive, or inherently-on-balance-neither-more-nor-less-attractive to buyers than the attributes they would have supplied without contrivance.

Finally, sellers may find it profitable to contrive restrictions on individual-product-image-promoting or product-safety-related advertising. Indeed, the amount of money that rivals devote to both these types of advertising may be reduced by natural oligopolistic as well as contrived oligopolistic interdependence.

B. Seven Functional Categories of Oligopolistic Conduct That Affect Terms and Conditions of Sale or Product-Attributes, Buyer-Perceived Product-Attributes, or Product Images Without Altering Any QV-Investment-Creation Decision

The first category of such conduct that some scholars have discussed is the category that is most analogous to straightforward price-fixing. According to these scholars, just as one or more rivals can profit by contriving price-increases, they can profit by contriving reductions in the quality of the credit-terms, supply-dates, product-installation terms, post-sales-service and replacement-part terms, product-use-instruction terms, and -contract-liability and contract-dispute-processing terms they offer buyers. I am not persuaded by this claim. Why will rivals find it profitable to contrive to offer buyers terms of these sorts that differ from the terms they would unilaterally choose to include in their contracts of sale when the latter terms would presumably be inherently profitable for the sellers to offer *inter alia* because, strategic considerations aside, they would be in the joint interest of the relevant seller and buyer combined? Would not the reduction in the price that the relevant buyers would be willing to pay a seller whose offer included less-attractive terms of these sorts exceed the cost-savings the terms enabled the seller to secure?

Those that argue that some non-price-term fixing is functionally perfectly analogous to price-fixing admit that, *ceteris paribus*, sellers would find it more profitable to fix prices than to fix non-price terms. However, they argue that the relevant *ceteris* are not *paribus*: it is easier for participants to detect cheating on the non-price fixes, whose violations leave more public traces (faster delivery-times, product installations, product-use instructions, post-sales service and replacement-part supply, damages payments, the use of particular dispute-resolution processes) than do price discounts and (somewhat inconsistently) that non-price fixes are less likely to lead to prosecutions and suits and convictions than are price-fixes. For two reasons, I am not persuaded. First, I doubt the empirical premises of these defenses: (1) participants in a non-price-term fix will have to determine the prices being charged for credit, post-sales-services, and replacement parts as well as the amounts of damages paid and the types of losses deemed recoverable (which will not be made public if the claims are settled without any claim being filed in a court); (2) non-price terms will be at least as easy for State prosecutors and private plaintiffs to establish as are price-terms; and (3) there is no reason to assume that triers-of-fact will be less inclined to find that fixes of non-price terms have taken place than that price-fixing has been practiced. Second, this defense of the claim that some non-price-term fixes are functionally identical to price-fixes ignores the fact that, to succeed, sellers that fix non-price terms must also fix prices—*i.e.*, that the fix of one or more non-price terms can be defeated by price-reductions that cancel out some or all of the cost-savings that the non-price-term fix generates. Of course, this second objection has a price-fix counterpart: to succeed, sellers that fix prices must prevent not only unauthorized price-reductions but also the inclusion in contracts of sale of non-price terms that are more beneficial to the buyers in question than the terms the relevant sellers would have offered them had prices not been fixed.

Three points related to this fact need to be made. First, because cheating on non-price terms will be more cost-effective than cheating on price terms (given that the fixed non-price term is inherently unprofitable), cheating on non-price terms may pose more of a problem for fixers than cheating on prices. Second, it is important to recognize that fixes of non-price terms that are part of a price-fixing arrangement are being executed by sellers that are, in any case, breaking U.S. antitrust law or E.C./E.U. competition law. Third, estimates of the losses that fixes impose on buyers must take into account the fix's effect on both the price-terms and the non-price terms the buyers are offered.

I have already discussed the second functional category of oligopolistic conduct that relates to neither price terms nor QV-investment or PPR decisions. This category contains contrived oligopolistic interactions that are designed to facilitate contrived oligopolistic pricing by standardizing the non-price terms included in the contracts of sale of given products or services or by standardizing the size and/or other attributes of the set of products whose prices are going to be fixed. I previously indicated why I doubt that such standardization-efforts will increase the feasibility or profitability of contrived oligopolistic pricing.

I have also already discussed the third functional category of the kinds of oligopolistic conduct with which this section is concerned—contrived and natural oligopolistic interactions that are designed to increase the total profits that the participating sellers earn by standardizing products to reduce what might be termed various transaction costs buyers must incur to purchase and use the relevant products and their components: the time and psychological cost that buyers have to incur to choose a product in the relevant category, to learn how to use the products in question (when they do or may wish to use relevant products of more than one producer), and/or to select complements that are compatible with their basic-product choices (and the losses buyers incur when they make wrong choices of these kinds). Standardization that benefits sellers in this way (which can increase, decrease, or leave unchanged the average or weighted-average quality of the directly-affected products) can occur through either natural or contrived oligopolistic interactions. Such standardization will occur naturally even when one or more individual sellers would be able to profit by selling a non-conforming product if its non-conformity would not induce any rival to depart from the relevant standard if each such individual seller believed that its non-conformity would make it inherently profitable for others to deviate and would, on that account, reduce its profits overall: in such a situation, there might be a need for an industry leader to announce the applicable standard or for two or more firms to discuss the standardized product-attributes that would be most profitable for them all to supply but no anticompetitive threats or promises would have to be made. However, if enough sellers believe that their individual deviations would be profitable, even given its effect on the choices others make, to reduce or eliminate the joint gain from standardization, contrivance will have to play a role if those benefits from standardization are to be maximized.

The fourth function that can be performed by the types of oligopolistic conduct on which this section is focusing is to help sellers overcome the inability of buyers to assess the quality of relevant products *ex ante* and possibly *ex post*. As we have seen, when buyers are unable to assess quality, the market for high-quality products may disappear, and, even if no "market for lemons" problem arises, seller profits may be reduced by buyer risk costs. To combat these problems, sellers may want to assure buyers that all products offered for sale meet at least some minimum-quality standard. Natural oligopolistic interdependence will suffice to secure this type of standardization when each relevant seller realizes that any short-run benefit it can achieve by cutting quality will be outweighed by the longer-run losses it suffers because its "cheating" will induce enough of its rivals to abandon the standardization project to cause the "market for lemons" problem to return or at least to increase critically buyer risk costs. When natural oligopolistic interdependence cannot be relied on, sellers that would profit from standardization for these reasons (and cannot induce the government to secure it for them) may be able to contrive it by contracting to standardize their products and/or threatening to retaliate against anyone that fails to conform to the standards they set. In some situations of this kind, trade associations help to secure the desired standardization by specifying quality-standards and issuing seals of approval only to products that satisfy those standards.

A fifth function of contrived oligopolistic efforts to set standards that products must meet or to specify attributes that products must have to get industry certification is to put rivals whose products do not have the relevant attributes at a competitive disadvantage that is not warranted by the actual quality of their products. Obviously, for some sellers to be able to set standards that give them a private advantage that has no allocative counterpart, different physical-product-attributes or different combinations of physical-product-attributes must yield products whose performance is the same or at least whose performance satisfies appropriate minimum standards. When this is the case, sellers of products with a given set of physical attributes can "cook" the "quality" standards their industry promulgates to disadvantage producers whose equally-good or satisfactory products have different physical attributes if the former group of sellers has the requisite control over the standard-setting process.

If the fourth function of the kinds of oligopolistic conduct on which this section is focusing is to help sellers overcome a certain type of buyer ignorance, the sixth function is to help them take advantage of another type of buyer ignorance—the tendency of buyers to underestimate the cost to them of one or more types of non-price contract terms or of some product-attribute (say, product-safety or product-durability). I will focus first on the non-price contract-term possibility and then address the product-safety possibility.

Assume (1) that buyers underestimate the cost to them of contract terms relating to (say) credit, delivery-time, warranties, seller liability for breach, or contract-dispute-resolution processes but (2) that buyers would come to realize their mistakes if the contracts they signed contained (from their perspective) superior terms relating to these issues (*i.e.*, if they had the opportunity to experience the benefits that the superior terms would afford them). In such circumstances, it might be profitable for sellers to contrive to preserve the buyers' ignorance by not supplying them with superior, *de facto* educative non-price terms: each seller might agree to forego the medium-run benefit it could obtain by supplying the superior term in question in exchange for its rivals' agreement to do the same and/or one or more sellers may try to deter rivals from offering the educative terms in question by threatening to retaliate against them if they do so. In fact, in some situations of this type, natural oligopolistic interdependence might suffice to deter any seller from offering an educative, superior term: each seller might be in a position in which it realized that, if it let the cat out of the bag, all its rivals would match its superior term and all would lose the advantage they originally obtained because the relevant ignorant buyers reduced their offer-prices for a contract that contained the inferior term by less than the "cost" the inferior term imposed on the buyers or (more relevantly from the sellers' perspectives) the cost-savings the inferior term's inclusion enabled the sellers to achieve.

Natural and contrived oligopolistic interactions can provide the same sort of benefit to sellers when their customers underestimate the cost to them not of inferior credit, delivery-time, warranties, seller-liability-for-breach, or contract-dispute-processing terms but of various inferior attributes of the product itself—*e.g.*, its lack of durability or its dangerousness—but would come to correct their errors if supplied with products that were superior in these respects, especially if the supplier of such products advertised these attributes of its product variant, thereby calling attention to these issues. In some cases, natural oligopolistic interdependence may suffice to prevent the supply of such educative product-attributes or advertising. In particular, natural oligopolistic interdependence will secure this outcome even if each member of a set of rival producers would find it profitable to make known safety-improvements and advertise them if its choice did not affect the choices of others if the decision of any producer to make these choices would induce enough others to follow suit to leave each of them worse-off. However, when one or more producers would find it profitable to make known safety-improvements or product-durability improvements and advertise that fact even though its decision to do so would induce others to follow suit, one or more producers that would lose money if such decisions were made may find it profitable to deter them from being made by threatening anyone that makes them with retaliation.

I should add that the same analysis will apply when the error that underlies this possibility is being made not by (1) consumers but (2) by courts that are finding producers not liable under a negligence-type product-liability standard because they do not know that a safer product variant whose production would reduce accident-and-pollution losses by more than it would increase other production costs has already been developed or (3) by legislators or administrative-regulation promulgators that have not required producers to shift from producing the more dangerous product variant they currently produce to a known alternative product variant whose production and use would reduce accident-and-pollution losses for which the producer is not currently liable by more than it would increase other production costs because the legislators or administrators are unaware that such a product variant has already been developed.

The seventh and final category of oligopolistic conduct that affects neither prices nor (arguably) QV-investment or PPR decisions relates to image-creating advertising. As I have already indicated, the value of some products to some buyers is a function not only of the products' material attributes and "physical performance" but also of the images the buyer associates with the product in question and/or the assumptions the buyer makes about the inferences third parties will draw about him or her if they believe he or she is a consumer of the product in question. When each member of a set of rivals realizes that (1) it would find it profitable to spend money on image-creating advertising if its decision to do so would not cause others to engage in such advertising but that (2) its advertising would induce others to place counteracting advertisements and (3) it and all other potential advertisers would be better-off if none of them placed such advertisements because (roughly speaking) the advertisements would largely cancel each other out so far as inter-advertiser competition is concerned (*i.e.*, would not significantly improve any advertiser's set of competitive positions relative to those of other advertisers) and would not increase ARDEPPS total sales sufficiently to yield enough profits on that account to outweigh their cost, natural oligopolistic interactions will suffice to deter the relevant sellers from placing such advertisements. When conditions (1) and (3) in the preceding list are satisfied but one or more sellers would be able to gain a sufficient advantage over their advertising rivals if all of them placed such advertisements for the former individual sellers to find such advertising profitable even if it would induce rivals to place similar advertisements, the sellers that would lose from such a wave of advertising will have to contrive restrictions in the advertising in question if such advertising is to be prevented. I should add that, both when the relevant advertising-reduction will result from a natural oligopolistic interdependence and when it will result from contrivance, the private cost of the relevant advertisements to the sellers will exceed the benefits they confer on the relevant buyers even if each buyer is assumed to be a sovereign-maximizer evaluator of the value to it of the advertising of an individual product it buys because the advertising of the products a buyer does not purchase reduces the value to it of the product it does purchase by making it seem less cool or sophisticated or sexy to make the purchase it made as opposed to the purchase it did not make. (If image-creating advertising is classified as a QV investment, this possibility should be considered in Sect. 10.5 of this chapter rather than in this section.)

C. The Legality of Oligopolistic Conduct of the Types This Section Considers That Perform the Seven Functions Just Described Under U.S. Antitrust Law and E.C./E.U. Competition Law, Correctly Interpreted and Applied

(1) The *Prima Facie* and Ultimate Illegality of Each Functional Variant of the Types of Oligopolistic Conduct on Which This Section Focuses Under U.S. Antitrust Law

I start with oligopolistic conduct in this category that is functionally identical to price-fixing—*i.e.*, that tries to fix reductions in the quality of non-price terms in relevant contracts of sale (when the reduction in quality is inherently unprofitable). Since all such conduct is contrived, it will all be *prima facie* illegal under the Sherman Act unless, perhaps, it involves nothing more than an unsuccessful attempt to enter into an anticompetitive agreement to reduce the quality of relevant non-price terms or quality-attributes. Moreover, because contrived oligopolistic pricing whose perpetrator-perceived *ex ante* profitability is critically affected by the perpetrator's belief that it would perform this function will not perform any function that could exonerate its perpetrators under the Sherman Act, oligopolistic conduct in this category will be ultimately as well as *prima facie* illegal under the Sherman Act. Of course, as I have already indicated, I doubt that such non-price-term fixes often take place (though I have no doubt that price-fixers sometimes work to prevent the form of cheating that involves offering superior non-price terms).

For the same reasons, all oligopolistic conduct whose perpetrator-perceived *ex ante* profitability was critically affected by the perpetrator's belief that it would facilitate contrived oligopolistic pricing by standardizing product-attributes and the non-price terms relevant sellers offer buyers is also both *prima facie* and ultimately illegal under the Sherman Act. However, as I indicated in Section 3, the practical importance of this conclusion is vitiated both by the dubiousness of the claim that such standardization will increase the profitability of contrived oligopolistic pricing and by the fact that at least some efforts to standardize product-attributes will increase their perpetrators' profits by reducing the "transaction costs" buyers have to incur to select a product, to learn how to use the product, and to buy compatible product-complements.

As the preceding sentence implies, regardless of whether the conduct in question is natural oligopolistic, conduct that increases its perpetrators' profits by reducing the "transaction costs" that buyers must incur to purchase an ARDEPPS' product are not even *prima facie* illegal under the Sherman Act since the profitability of such conduct is not critically affected by its reducing the absolute attractiveness of the offers against which its individual perpetrators will have to compete—indeed, since such conduct will not even tend to reduce the absolute attractiveness of relevant rival offers. I hasten to add that, even if I believed both that the Sherman Act covers natural as well as contrived oligopolistic conduct and that American courts are authorized to develop and apply overinclusive rules of illegality to obviate their incurring the mechanical and error costs of evaluating individual exemplars of a covered class of conduct, I would think that the percentage of cases of product-standardizing oligopolistic conduct that is explicable in buyer-transaction-cost-reducing terms as opposed to price-fixing-facilitating terms is far too high for a judicial rule prohibiting all product-standardizing oligopolistic conduct to be defensible as a matter of law.

For two reasons, seller efforts to overcome the inability of buyers to evaluate product-quality by guaranteeing that any product sold in their ARDEPPS satisfies some minimum-quality criteria are neither *prima facie* nor ultimately prohibited by the Sherman Act. The more fundamental reason is that, even if oligopolistic efforts to achieve this result are contrived and even if they involve some attempt to prevent firms from offering lower price/quality terms that some buyers may perceive to be more attractive than the offers for the higher-quality products that satisfy the ARDEPPS' minimum-quality standard, individual perpetrators' *ex ante* beliefs that the relevant conduct would be profitable for them will almost never depend on their perception that it would reduce the absolute attractiveness of the offers against which they individually would have to compete. The fundamental reason is that, in many instances, oligopolistic conduct in this functional category will be natural.

Obviously, contrived oligopolistic efforts to set physical-product-attribute standards that will place one or more rivals at a competitive disadvantage that does not reflect their relative economic inefficiency are both *prima facie* and ultimately illegal under the Sherman Act. So, too, are contrived oligopolistic efforts to take advantage of the tendency of buyers to underestimate the cost to them of non-price terms of sale or inferior product-attributes by deterring sellers (1) from supplying educative superior terms of sale or product-attributes and (2) from engaging in educative advertising that calls attention to the issues in question by promoting the superior features of their offers or products, at least if they involve something other than unsuccessful attempts to enter into anticompetitive agreements not to supply such terms or product-attributes or to advertise their supply. Such contrivance violates the Act because its perpetrator-perceived *ex ante* profitability is critically inflated by their belief that it will reduce the absolute attractiveness of the offers against which they will have to compete. Of course, if the relevant sellers rely exclusively on natural oligopolistic interdependence to prevent the supply of the relevant superior terms-of-sale or product-attributes and/or to deter sellers from placing related advertisements, the Sherman Act will not have been violated.

Finally, contrived oligopolistic conduct that is designed to limit the amount of image advertising that a group of competitors place is both *prima facie* and ultimately illegal under the Sherman Act, at least if the conduct involves something other than an unsuccessful attempt to contrive this outcome. Such contrivance is *prima facie* illegal under the Act because its perpetrator-perceived *ex ante* profitability does depend on its reducing the absolute attractiveness of the offers against which its perpetrators must compete when in an otherwise-Pareto-perfect economy this effect would render the conduct *ex ante* economically inefficient. In my judgment, contrived oligopolistic conduct that is designed to achieve this result is ultimately illegal under the Sherman Act as well: even if such conduct is economically efficient because the benefits it yields the advertisers are inflated by their customers' tendency to overvalue it and its tendency to impose external costs on buyers of other products, I do not think that U.S. courts are authorized to consider this possibility when applying the Sherman Act. Of course, reductions in image advertising that reflect natural oligopolistic interdependence create no Sherman Act cause of action.

(2) The *Prima Facie* and Ultimate Illegality of Each Functional Variant of the Types of Oligopolistic Conduct on Which This Section Focuses Under E.C./E.U. Competition Law

I will restrict this discussion to the differences between the legality of the conduct with which this section is concerned under what are now Articles 101 and 102 of the 2009 Treaty of Lisbon and their legality under the Sherman Act. I can think of two definite salient differences and one possible salient difference.

The first definite salient difference is that, unlike the Sherman Act, now-Article 101 does not cover the use of threats of retaliation to contrive non-price terms-of-sale, the supposed-price-fixing-facilitating standardization of terms-of-sale or product-attributes, reductions in the physical quality of products, or reductions in image advertising or the advertising of product-improvements, and although now-Article 102's prohibition of "any abuse...of a dominant position" does cover efforts to secure such results exclusively through threats of retaliation, it applies only to firms that enjoy an individual dominant position or to groups of firms that are collectively dominant, and this type of contrivance can be practiced by one or more firms that (I suspect) should not be said to enjoy respectively an individually-dominant or collectively-dominant position.

The second definite salient difference is that some contrived oligopolistic conduct of the type with which this section is concerned that does not *prima facie* violate the Sherman Act because its perpetrator-perceived *ex ante* profitability was secured by its yielding transaction-cost-reducing standardization or its overcoming the tendency of buyers to undervalue higher-quality relative to lower-quality products (1) will violate now-Article 101 if it (A) is executed through an agreement or trade-association decision, (B) imposes an equivalent-monetary loss on relevant buyers by causing substandard products to exit or not to be introduced, and (C) does not confer "a fair share of the resulting benefit" on relevant consumers and (2) will violate the exploitative-abuse branch of now-Article 102's test of illegality if (A) one or more of its participants are individually dominant or a member of a collectively-dominant set of rivals and (B) for the reason delineated in (1)(B) above, it causes relevant buyers to realize less than a "fair share" of the joint gain their transactions with the perpetrator(s) yielded them and the perpetrator(s) combined.

The third difference on which I want to comment is only a possible difference and might actually be more relevant to the next subsection's discussion of case-law than to this subsection's discussion of the law as correctly interpreted and applied. It relates to the legality under U.S. and E.C./E.U. law of efforts to contrive reductions in image advertising. If it exists, the difference in question relates to the possible divergent evaluations of image advertising by U.S. and E.C./E.U. authorities: U.S. courts are extremely hostile to such advertising (believe that it consumes resources to dupe buyers); I simply do not know what the EC's and the E.C./E.U. courts' attitude toward such advertising is. The U.S. courts' negative assessment of such advertising might tend to make them conclude that contrived efforts to reduce the amount of resources devoted to such advertising do not violate the Sherman Act—specifically, will tend to lead them to conclude that the profits that contrivers obtain by reducing such advertising are Sherman Act licit and legitimating. If the EC and the E.C./E.U. courts had the same attitude toward such advertising, their assessment of it would lead them to conclude that contrived efforts to reduce such advertising would not violate now-Articles 101 and 102: more specifically, would incline them to conclude:

(1) that the profits the perpetrators obtained by reducing such advertising were licit so that their conduct was more likely not to violate the object branch of now-Article 101(1)'s test of *prima facie* illegality or the exclusionary-abuse branch of now-Article 102's test of *prima facie* illegality,
(2) that the reduction in image advertising the conduct generated "improve[d] the distribution of goods" and "promote[d] economic progress," thereby satisfying

one of the requirements for obtaining a now-Article 101(3) exemption from now-Article 101(1), and

(3) that the conduct in question did not really impose an equivalent-monetary loss on the relevant buyers by reducing the absolute attractiveness of the best offer they respectively received from any inferior supplier so that the conduct did not violate the effect branch of now-Article 101(1)'s test of *prima facie* illegality or the exploitative-abuse branch of now-Article 102's test of illegality.

If, however, the E.C./E.U. authorities did not share the U.S. courts' animosity to image advertising, they would on all these accounts be more likely to find contrivance that is designed to reduce such advertising illegal when (I suspect) the U.S. authorities might find it lawful.

D. The U.S. and E.C./E.U. Case-Law on Oligopolistic Conduct That Is Directed at Non-Price Contract-of-Sale Terms, Product-Attributes That Can Be Changed Without Making a QV Investment, or Image-Creating or Educative Advertising

(1) The U.S. Case-Law

I have found little U.S. antitrust case-law on the behaviors on which this section focuses. Three cases or sets of cases are relevant.

First, in *Catalono, Inc. v. Target Sales, Inc.*,[508] the U.S. Supreme Court held that an agreement by beer wholesalers that had previously granted short-term credit to retailers to stop extending any such credit at all (an agreement that resulted in the respondents' uniformly refusing to extend any credit at all) was a form of price-fixing covered and prohibited by the Sherman Act. Second, in *NCAA v. Board of Regents of the University of Oklahoma*,[509] the U.S. Supreme Court made clear in dictum its view that the NCAA's efforts to standardize the product its members supplied by specifying the dimensions of playing-fields and the rules of the game were not prohibited by the Sherman Act. And, in two cases, the U.S. Supreme Court has held that efforts by some seller to manipulate "seal of approval" standards to exclude the plaintiff's product[510] or to manipulate a standards committee into finding a rival's product unsafe[511] were both violations of the Sherman Act. All these decisions are correct as a matter of law.

I should add, however, that U.S. courts have developed a dubious contracts doctrine that invalidates exculpatory clauses included in contracts of sale by "monopolists," which the courts believe have "imposed" these clauses on the

---

[508] 446 U.S. 643 (1980).

[509] 468 U.S. 85 (1984).

[510] Radiant Burners, Inc. v. Peoples Gas & Coke Co., 364 U.S. 656 (1961).

[511] American Society of Mechanical Engineers, Inc. v. Hydrolevel Corp., 456 U.S. 556 (1982).

relevant buyers—the so-called contracts of adhesion doctrine. The premise of this doctrine is that the monopoly power of a seller enables it to make profits by imposing unattractive contract terms on its customers that a non-monopolist would not find profitable to include in its contract of sale because (1) the non-monopolist would have to reduce its price to compensate buyers for the "costs" the terms impose on them and (2) the necessary price-reduction would exceed the savings the term would enable these sellers to secure. This premise is fallacious: a firm's monopoly power does not enable it to impose onerous terms on buyers without reducing the price it charges them by the amount they disvalue the term. The only situation in which it might be economically efficient to invalidate exculpatory clauses would be one in which the relevant buyers critically underestimated the cost those clauses would impose on them, and there is little reason to believe that there is much of a correlation between that condition's being fulfilled and the relevant seller's having monopoly power. (Admittedly, an argument to the contrary could be based on the greater ability of a monopolist to preserve the ignorance of its potential customers, though, as I indicated previously, natural oligopolistic interdependence may suffice to deter non-monopolists from informing buyers of their error.) I hasten to add that I do not mean to imply that the correctness of the doctrine of contracts of adhesion as a matter of law in the U.S. and other common-law countries is determined by its economic efficiency. In fact, if no legislation is on point, I think that the correctness of this doctrine as a matter of law in such countries depends on its consistency with the liberal norm those countries are committed to instantiating in the service of their conception of justice—*inter alia*, on the balance that that norm implies should be struck in such cases between respecting the "autonomy" of the buyer and enforcing the seller's duty of respect and concern for its customer, given the likelihood that triers-of-fact would misdetermine the relevant facts.

(2) EC Positions and the E.C./E.U. Case-Law

The EC and the E.C./E.U. courts have taken positions on three of the types of behavior on which this section is focusing. First, the E.C./E.U. courts have declared agreements or trade-association decisions on non-price terms-of-sale to be *per se* infringements of now-Article 101. Relevant decisions have condemned a cement-dealers' association decision (1) to strictly limit the commercial benefits that sellers could grant purchasers and (2) prohibit sellers from supplying buyers with services whose provision was not "normal,"[512] an agreement among manufacturers of glass containers to charge buyers delivery prices that did not reflect the buyer's proximity to the seller,[513] a decision by an association of agricultural-machinery importers to set delivery and payment terms,[514] an agreement between fine-art auction houses

[512] Vereiniging von Cementhandelaren, OJ L13/34 (1971).

[513] Agreements Between Manufacturers of Glass Containers, OJ L160/1 (1974)

[514] Vimpoltu, OJ L200/44 (1983).

not to give vendors minimum-price guarantees, to charge not less than a specified minimum rate for loans, and to limit credit to trade buyers to 90 days,[515] an agreement between specialty-graphite suppliers to charge specified premiums for non-standard products, to establish common billing conditions, and to use "standard" exchange rates,[516] an agreement among graphite producers to include the same payment terms-and-conditions in their contracts of sale,[517] and an agreement among industrial-tube producers controlling payment, delivery terms, and consignment terms.[518]

Second, E.C./E.U. courts have concluded that now-Article 101 prohibits agreements to limit advertising and other marketing activities.[519]

Third, E.C./E.U. courts have declared illegal under now-Article 101 agreements by sellers to standardize their products on the assumption that such arrangements are designed to facilitate price-fixing.[520] Although I do not know the facts of the cases in question, I suspect that the EC and the E.C./E.U. courts do not fully appreciate the various legitimate functions that product-standardization agreements can perform.

5. QV-Investment-Focused Natural and Contrived Oligopolistic Conduct[521]

A. The Economic Analysis of QV-Investment-Focused Natural and Contrived Oligopolistic Conduct

Chapter 2 discussed the possibility that and the circumstances in which two or more QV investors will be deterred from making QV investments by the natural oligopolistic interdependence of their QV-investment decisions—*i.e.*, when and how such natural oligopolistic interdependence will reduce the quantity of QV investment in an ARDEPPS in equilibrium. As Chap. 2 explained, for natural oligopolistic interdependence to have this effect, four conditions must be satisfied:

[515] Fine Arts Auction Houses, OJ L200/9 (2005).

[516] Specialty Graphites, Decision of 17 December 2002.

[517] Electrical and Mechanical Carbon and Graphite Producers, OJ L125/145 (2004).

[518] *Id.* at OJ L125/150 (2004).

[519] See Belgian Beers, OJ L200/1 (2003); Electrical and Mechanical Carbon and Graphite Products, OJ L125/145 (2004); Vimpoltu, OJ L200/44 (1983); and Roofing Felt, OJ L232/14 (1986).

[520] See Roofing Felt, OJ L232/15 (1986) and Belasco and Others v. Commission, Case 246186, ECR 2117, p. 313 (1989).

[521] A third category of QV-investment-related predatory conduct—the execution of a predatory QV investment—is not oligopolistic. For the correct definition of "predatory QV investment" and a critique of the definition of this concept that other economists have proposed, see Section 5B of Chap. 11.

(1) the barriers to entry facing the best-placed potential competitor at that juncture must be sufficiently high to prevent any new entry from occurring—*i.e.*, to obviate the relevant established firms' making a limit investment to keep any potential competitor out;
(2) the number of established firms that would not be prevented from expanding at the relevant juncture by the barriers to expansion they faced must be small—ideally two but conceivably three or four;
(3) each such established firm must be operating in a situation in which its expansion would make it profitable for one or more of its rivals to expand despite the fact that this rival (these rivals) would not have expanded had the firm in question not expanded (because each's expansion would make the other's expansion profitable by eliminating the loss the other's expansion would otherwise impose on the other by inducing it to expand); and
(4) the profits that each's expansion would therefore take away from itself by inducing one or more rivals to make a QV investment each's rival(s) would not otherwise have created must make it unprofitable for each to make an additional QV investment when it otherwise would have been profitable for each to do so.

I will distinguish three families of contrived-oligopolistic conduct that are QV-investment-related in the sense that they are designed to affect total QV investment in an ARDEPPS, to affect the location of QV investments in an ARDEPPS, and/or to affect the identity of the owners of the QV investments in an ARDEPPS. The first family of QV-investment-related contrived oligopolistic conduct is designed to deter the QV-investment response to a QV investment that causes firms that face natural oligopolistic QV-investment incentives to find unprofitable a QV investment that would otherwise be profitable. A firm that is in this position may attempt to deter the relevant rival response by bribing the rival not to respond to the firm's QV investment with one of its own and/or by threatening to retaliate against the rival should it respond to the firm's QV investment by making a QV investment. I should add that firms that face natural oligopolistic QV-investment disincentives could also overcome the problem they pose by merging or by creating a joint venture to make the one QV investment that would be jointly profitable for the parents to make: the joint venture could deter the parents from adding a second QV investment to the relevant area of product-space either by making it unprofitable for the parents to make such an investment by giving each part-ownership of the joint venture's QV investment or by contractually prohibiting the parents from investing in the joint venture's ARDEPPS.

The second family of QV-investment-related contrived oligopolistic conduct is designed to reduce equilibrium QV investment in the area of product-space in which it is practiced. Conduct in this category includes using threats to create retaliation barriers to entry or expansion and/or paying bribes to potential investors to deter them from making QV investments they would otherwise have found profitable. At the extreme, this category of conduct includes market-division agreements that allocate to different firms the exclusive right to make QV investments in particular areas of product-space. Once more, firms can accomplish these results by participating in mergers or acquisitions or by forming joint ventures that impose restrictions on their parents' investment conduct or rely on the parents' part-ownership of the joint venture to deter them from investing in the joint venture's area(s) of product-space.

The third family of QV-investment-related contrived oligopolistic conduct is designed to affect the location of QV investments in a given area of product-space. Such conduct can be designed either to alter the location of a planned QV investment (new entry or expansion) or to induce the owner of an existing QV investment to substitute for it a QV investment in a different location. Thus, when the positive difference between the amount by which the inherently-most-profitable QV investment a potential entrant or expander could add to an ARDEPPS would increase its supernormal profits and the amount by which an alternative QV investment the potential investor could make would increase its organization's supernormal profit-yield *is lower than* the positive difference between the absolute amount by which the former QV investment would reduce one or more of the investor's rivals' supernormal profits and the absolute amount by which the latter QV investment would reduce the supernormal profits of the same rivals(s), the rival(s) in question may find it profitable to bribe the potential investor to make the inherently-less-profitable QV investment[522] and/or to threaten to retaliate against the potential investor if it makes the QV investment that is more damaging to the rivals in question. Such conduct may also be profitable when the sought-after QV-investment-location change relates to an existing as opposed to a planned QV investment though, when the target QV investment already exists, the conditions for the bribe's profitability are far less likely to be fulfilled—*i.e.*, will probably be fulfilled only when (1) the sought-after relocation is geographic and (2)(A) a low percentage of the value of the original plant/outlet depends on its being used to produce/distribute the product it was originally used to produce or distribute—*i.e.*, the relevant plant or outlet was not specially constructed or adapted for its original use—and (B) a low percentage of the original QV investment consisted of specific-use equipment or any such equipment could be transported cheaply to the new location the briber(s) prefer(s).[523] Under some circumstances, sellers that would

[522] Chapter 11 will consider the efforts of firms to deter or induce the relocation of a new QV investment by threatening retaliation to its execution since such efforts are on my definition predatory as well as contrived oligopolistic.

[523] Before proceeding, I should note that my assumption that the offer and payment of these bribes can be characterized as involving contrived oligopolistic conduct is contestable. In this case, the initiating move may involve nothing more than the communication of a promise to pay a bribe if the offeree makes the choice the offeror wants the offeree to make (which, in practice, may be backed up with a threat of retaliation if the offeree does not "cooperate"). The offeree then accepts or rejects the offer, taking into account the fact that the profitability of these responses will be affected by the offeror's reaction to them. In most other sequences of conduct I described as contrived oligopolistic, the initial move involved not just the communication of an anticompetitive offer and/or threat but an actual business move—*e.g.*, the charging of a POP. I want to assure any reader who, unlike me, thinks this difference critically affects the contrived-oligopolistic status of the bribery on which we are now focusing that my characterization of this conduct has no bearing on any related legal or policy issue.

find it profitable to alter the locations of the QV investments in an area of product-space may choose to accomplish this result through merger or acquisition. Relatedly, sellers that anticipate QV-investment-location problems in a new area of product-space (into which, ideally, only they can profitably invest) may choose to avoid those problems by forming a joint venture that either relies on the parents' part-ownership to deter them from investing in the joint venture's area(s) of product-space or is created by an agreement that contains a clause that prohibits the parents from investing in the joint venture's area(s) of product-space.

I should note that the location-array alterations secured by the conduct on which we are now focusing may be more allocatively efficient as well as more privately profitable for the perpetrators. I want to make four points related to this possibility. First, in some cases, sellers will find it profitable to contrive an economically-inefficient increase in the distance between the product-space locations of the QV investments in their area of product-space because QV investments that are more-widely-spaced will place less competitive pressure on each other: I admit, however, (1) for such conduct to be profitable, the additional profits the increase in diversity yields the investors on this account must exceed the losses it imposes on them as a result of its reducing the economic efficiency of their QV-investment array, and (2) enforcement-costs aside, the relevant sellers would always find it more profitable to fix their prices than to contrive economically-inefficient changes in their QV investments' locations. Second, the real externalities that any firm's efforts to discover a patentable product generates because its research reduces the probability that other firms' efforts to discover the same product (first) will be successful will sometimes make it economically efficient as well as profitable for firms to contrive not just reductions in the total amount of resources they devote to product-R&D QV-investment creation but increases in the diversity of the products their R&D efforts aim at discovering, controlling for the total amount of resources they devote to product R&D.[524] Third, I cannot estimate the percentage of the efforts of firms to contrive alterations in the product-space locations of the QV investments in their area of product-space that is economically efficient, in part because I do not know the percentage of such efforts that focuses on the "location" of product R&D that could yield product patents. Fourth, because defendants in related suits are likely to have far better access to information that is relevant to the economic-efficiency effects of any QV-investment-location change they have arranged than either the State or a private plaintiff will have, I would place the burden of coming forward on this issue on the defendants.

---

[524] This issue will be discussed in detail in THE WELFARE ECONOMICS OF ANTITRUST POLICY AND U.S. AND E.C./E.U. ANTITRUST LAW. For citations to other articles that focus on this possibility, see RICHARD S. MARKOVITS, TRUTH OR ECONOMICS: ON THE DEFINITION, PREDICTION, AND RELEVANCE OF ECONOMIC EFFICIENCY 451–52 at n. 12 (Yale Univ. Press, 2008).

B. The Legality of QV-Investment-Focused Oligopolistic Conduct Under Correctly-Interpreted-and-Applied U.S. Antitrust Law and E.C./E.U. Competition Law

(1) The Legality of QV-Investment-Related Oligopolistic Conduct Under U.S. Antitrust Law, Correctly Interpreted and Applied

Eight points or sets of points are salient. The first three apply equally to non-QV-investment-focused oligopolistic conduct and QV-investment-focused oligopolistic conduct:

(1) natural oligopolistic interactions that decrease equilibrium QV investment in the area of product-space in which they occur are not prohibited by the Sherman Act;
(2) unsuccessful attempts to contrive agreements to alter equilibrium QV investment in any area of product-space and/or to change the locations of the QV investments in an area of product-space are not covered by the Sherman Act; and
(3) the Clayton Act does not cover any variant of QV-investment-focused oligopolistic conduct.

The next three relate to the legality under the Sherman Act of contrived oligopolistic conduct (other than unsuccessful attempts to enter into contrived oligopolistic agreements) that is designed respectively to enable a seller to overcome the natural oligopolistic QV-investment disincentives that are rendering unprofitable a QV investment that would otherwise be profitable, to decrease equilibrium QV investment in the ARDEPPS in which it takes place, and to alter the location-array of the QV investments in a particular ARDEPPS. I will address the Sherman Act legality of these three categories of QV-investment-focused contrived oligopolistic conduct in the above order.

Contrived oligopolistic conduct that is designed to enable a perpetrator to profit by making a QV investment it would not otherwise have found profitable by preventing that investment from inducing a rival to make a QV investment that that rival would not otherwise have made is lawful under the Sherman Act. I admit that such conduct is designed to reduce the absolute attractiveness of the offers against which its perpetrator will have to compete *if it makes a QV investment*. However, for two reasons, this fact does not imply the illegality of such conduct under the Sherman Act. First, since natural oligopolistic QV-investment disincentives deflate the profitability of the QV investments whose profitability they decrease and the fact that those investments would be profitable but for such disincentives implies that they would be economically efficient in an otherwise-Pareto-perfect economy, the profitability of contrived oligopolistic conduct that is designed to overcome the perpetrator's natural-oligopolistic-QV-investment-disincentive problem would not be critically inflated in an otherwise-Pareto-perfect economy—*i.e.*, would not for this reason violate the Sherman Act. Second, in my judgment, this category of QV-investment-focused contrived oligopolistic conduct should not be held to violate the Sherman Act because it furthers the Sherman Act's goal of benefitting the buyers it directly involves—a functional argument whose relevance some would question that favors the conclusion that buyer price-fixing that benefits the ultimate consumers it directly affects should not be deemed to violate the Sherman Act. Before proceeding, I should state that I think that, because natural oligopolistic QV-investment disincentives are generated only rarely and evanescently, I doubt the empirical significance of this category of QV-investment-focused contrived oligopolistic conduct.

Contrived oligopolistic conduct (other than unsuccessful attempts to enter into contrived oligopolistic agreements) that is designed to decrease equilibrium QV investment in the ARDEPPS in which it is practiced violates the Sherman Act. Such conduct is illegal because its perpetrator's or perpetrators' *ex ante* perception(s) that it will be profitable is critically affected by its/their belief(s) that the conduct will reduce the absolute attractiveness of the offers against which it/they will have to compete and would be economically inefficient in an otherwise-Pareto-perfect economy.

The legality under the Sherman Act of contrived oligopolistic conduct that is designed to alter the locations of the QV investments in the ARDEPPS in which it takes place depends on the facts. As we saw, such conduct can increase its perpetrator's or perpetrators' profits in two different ways:

(1) by increasing the difference between the value of their outputs to its consumers and its total cost of production by reducing the extent to which the products on offer are economically-inefficiently-duplicative and
(2) by reducing the competitiveness of the products on offer by placing them further away from each other in product-space.

If the perpetrator(s) of this type of contrived oligopolistic QV-investment-focused conduct believed *ex ante* that, even if it did not benefit them in the second of the two ways just listed, it would be rendered profitable by its performance of the first of the two functions delineated above, the conduct would be lawful under the Sherman Act because the perpetrator's or perpetrators' *ex ante* perception(s) that the conduct was *ex ante* profitable was not critically affected by its/their belief that the conduct would or might reduce the absolute attractiveness of the best offer against which it/they would have to compete: I should add that in these circumstances the conduct in question would also be lawful under the Sherman Act because it would be economically efficient in an otherwise-Pareto-perfect economy. If the conduct's perpetrator's or perpetrators' *ex ante* perception that it would be profitable was critically affected by their belief that it would or might perform the second of the two functions listed above, the conduct would violate the Sherman Act because, in addition to satisfying that condition for Sherman Act illegality, it would in these circumstances be economically inefficient in an otherwise-Pareto-perfect economy.

The final two points I want to make relate to the relevance for the Sherman Act legality of this category of conduct of the economic efficiency of its impact on (1) the total amount of QV investment the ARDEPPS in question will have in equilibrium and (2) the product-space locations of the ARDEPPS' QV investments:

(1) since the economic efficiency of the conduct's impact on total QV investment in the ARDEPPS in which it took place has no bearing on the legitimate profits the conduct conferred or would confer on its perpetrator(s), it has no bearing on the conduct's legality under the Sherman Act; but
(2) since the economic efficiency of the conduct's impact on the locations of the QV investments in the ARDEPPS in which it took place will have some bearing on the extent to which it increases the profits the perpetrator(s) realize by increasing the difference between the value of their output to its consumers and its private cost of production, the economic efficiency of the conduct's impact on the locations of the ARDEPPS' QV investments will (indirectly) be positively correlated with the likelihood that the conduct is lawful under the Sherman Act.

(2) The Legality of QV-Investment-Focused Oligopolistic Conduct Under E.C./E.U. Competition Law, Correctly Interpreted and Applied

I will focus on three possible differences between the U.S. and E.C./E.U. law, correctly interpreted and applied, on the conduct now under consideration. The first two differences can be dealt with quickly.

The first is that individual exemplars of contrived oligopolistic conduct in this category whose first step involves only threats of retaliation are not covered by now Article 101, though they are covered by the Sherman Act. As we have seen, this difference exists in relation to all categories of contrived oligopolistic conduct.

The second is that, although the Sherman Act does not cover natural oligopolistic conduct of this or any other kind, now-Article 101 does cover as "concerted practices" natural oligopolistic conduct of all kinds, including those that are QV-investment-focused.

The third difference, which will take much longer to explore, relates to the legal relevance under U.S. and E.C./E.U. law of any tendency of the conduct on which this section focuses to increase economic efficiency by changing total QV investment in the ARDEPPS in which it takes place or by changing the locations of one or more QV investments in the relevant area of product-space. I will now analyze the possible relevance of any such economic-efficiency increases to the legality under E.C./E.U. law of the conduct that generated them and then compare those relevance-conclusions with their U.S. counterparts, which were delineated in the preceding subsection.

I will start with the significance of a demonstration that the change that relevant conduct generated in the total amount of QV investment made in the ARDEPPS in which it took place increased economic efficiency for the conduct's legality under now-Articles 101 and 102:

(1) since the economic efficiency of the conduct's impact on total QV investment in the ARDEPPS in which it took place has no bearing on the profits it conferred on its perpetrator, it will have no bearing on whether the relevant conduct violated the object branch of now-Article 101(1)'s test of *prima facie* illegality;
(2) since the economic efficiency of the conduct's impact on total QV investment in the ARDEPPS in which it took place has no bearing on its net equivalent-monetary impact on Clayton-Act-relevant buyers, it will have no bearing on whether the relevant conduct violated the effect branch of now-Article 101(1)'s test of *prima facie* illegality;
(3) since the economic efficiency of the increase or decrease in ARDEPPS total QV investment the relevant conduct effectuated has no bearing on whether the conduct improved the production or distribution of goods or promoted technical progress, it would be relevant to whether the conduct satisfied the economic-efficiency-related requirement for a now-Article 101(3) exemption only if it can properly be said to constitute "economic progress" in the sense in which now-Article 101(3) can correctly be deemed to be using this expression: I doubt that it can (I recognize that relevant oligopolostic conduct that increases the amount of QV investment that is made in the ARDEPPS in which it takes place will increase technical progress if the product that is created is technically superior to those already in production, but this possibility is not related to whether the associated increase in total QV investment in the ARDEPPS in question is economically efficient);
(4) since the economic efficiency of the relevant conduct's impact on the total amount of QV investment in the ARDEPPS in which it took place has no bearing on whether relevant buyers obtain a fair share of any net equivalent-monetary gain the conduct confers on relevant buyers and the conduct's perpetrator(s) combined, it is also irrelevant to whether the conduct in question satisfies the "relevant buyer obtain a 'fair share' of the resulting benefit" requirement for a now-Article 101(3) exemption;
(5) since the economic efficiency of the relevant conduct's impact on total QV investment in the ARDEPPS in which it took place is irrelevant to the profits the conduct yields its perpetrator(s), it is irrelevant to whether the conduct would violate the exclusionary-abuse branch of now-Article 102 if one or both perpetrators were individually dominant or members of a collectively-dominant set of rivals; and
(6) since the economic efficiency of the relevant conduct's impact on total QV investment in the ARDEPPS in which it took place is irrelevant to the ratio of the buyer surplus the perpetrator's or perpetrators' customers obtain on their purchases of its/their ARDEPPS products to the sum of the buyer and seller surplus those transactions generate, it is irrelevant to whether the perpetrator(s) has/have violated the exploitative-abuse branch of now-Article 102's test of illegality (which would be of interest if but only if one or more perpetrators were individually dominant or members of a collectively-dominant set of rivals).

All things considered, then, the economic efficiency of the impact of the conduct on which I am now focusing on the total amount of QV investment in the ARDEPPS in which it takes place has no bearing on the conduct's legality under now-Articles 101 and 102, any more than it does on the legality of the same types of conduct under the U.S. Sherman Act.

I turn now to the significance of a demonstration that economic efficiency would be increased by the impact of contrived oligopolistic conduct on the locations of the QV investments in the ARDEPPS in which it took place for the conduct's legality under now-Articles 101 and 102:

(1) since any increases in economic efficiency that are generated by any changes in the locations of the QV investments in the ARDEPPS in which the oligopolistic conduct under review took place will be associated with increases in the licit profits that the conduct yields its perpetrator(s), proof that economic efficiency has been increased by such conduct's impact on the locations of the QV investments in the ARDEPPS in which it took place will favor its *prima facie* legality under now-Article 101 by making it less likely that the conduct had preventing or restricting competition as *a critical object* and will favor its legality under now-Article 102 for the same reason (if one or more of its perpetrators were individually dominant or members of a collectively-dominant set of rivals) by making it less likely that the conduct constituted an exclusionary abuse of a dominant position; and
(2) since any increases in economic efficiency that are generated by any changes in the locations of the QV investments in the ARDEPPS in which the oligopolistic conduct under review took place may be deemed to represent "economic progress" in the sense in which now-Article 101(3) uses this expression, to the extent that such increases in economic efficiency are associated with equivalent-monetary gains for the relevant buyers (because they benefit on balance from the tendencies of the QV-investment-location shifts to [A] increase the sum of the buyer and seller surplus the relevant transactions generate and [B] reduce the relevant buyer surplus to seller surplus ratio), proof that economic efficiency has been increased by such conduct's impact on the locations of the QV investments in the ARDEPPS in which it took place will make it more likely that the conduct will qualify for a now-Article 101(3) exemption when it violates Article 101(1) and may make it less likely that the conduct's perpetrator(s) has/have committed an exploitative abuse of its/their dominant position if it/they occupy such a position.

Hence, the economic efficiency of any QV-investment-location changes that contrived oligopolistic conduct generates probably favor its legality under now-Articles 101 and 102 of the E.C./E.U. Treaty both in some ways that are perfectly analogous to the ways in which those efficiencies favor the legality of such conduct under the Sherman Act and in other ways that have no U.S.-law counterparts.

C. The U.S. and E.C./E.U. Case-Law on QV-Investment-Focused Oligopolistic Conduct

(1) The Relevant U.S. Case-Law

I know of no U.S. case in which two or more defendants have been accused of violating the Sherman Act by allowing the natural oligopolistic QV-investment disincentives they face to deter them from making QV investments or by contriving to make one QV investment between them when they otherwise would have been deterred from making any QV investments by the natural oligopolistic QV-investment disincentives they face. More surprisingly, I also know of no U.S. case in which one or more defendants are accused of violating the Sherman Act by contriving to reduce the total amount of QV investment in an ARDEPPS. Of course, the Supreme Court's longstanding rule prohibiting horizontal market divisions[525] does, in practice, prohibit arrangements that assign to different individual firms the exclusive right to make QV investments in different ARDEPPSes. However, I should add that the horizontal-territorial-division cases have always implicitly assumed that the total amount of QV investment in any market would not be affected and focused on the fact that such arrangements will eliminate the price competition the participants give each other when using their given QV investments.

There is some U.S. case-law on some of the kinds of non-oligopolistic conduct that this section covers. In particular, there is U.S. case-law on (1) joint ventures that may reduce the amount of QV investment made in the joint venture's ARDEPPS by rendering it unprofitable for the parents to make up the difference between the amount of QV investment they would have made in the joint venture's market absent the joint venture and the amount the joint venture makes by giving the parents a stake in the joint venture's profits and (perhaps) by including in the joint-venture agreement a provision barring the parents from making any QV investments in the joint venture's ARDEPPS, (2) joint ventures that partially or totally divide up the parents' ARDEPPSes by including in the joint-venture agreement restrictive clauses barring the parents from making QV investments in each other's ARDEPPSes, (3) mergers and acquisitions in which one merger partner or the acquiring firm retires the QV investment of the other merger partner or the acquired firm, and (4) mergers and acquisitions that are executed to prevent one

[525] The most recent Supreme Court case reaffirming this rule is Palmer v. BRG of Georgia, 498 U.S. 46 (1990). I should add that the text is generous to the Court by implying that the rule in question has always covered only horizontal territorial divisions. In fact, the actual rule originally covered vertical as well as horizontal territorial divisions—a fact that is manifest by the *Palmer* Court's citing a vertical-territorial-division case—United States v. Topco Associates, Inc. 405 U.S. 596 (1972)—to support its claim that the rule in question is longstanding. I should say that the Court's citation of this case is somewhat puzzling, given the fact that, in 1977, it overruled decisions holding vertical territorial restraints *per se* illegal under the Sherman Act and declared that, in the future, the legality of such restraints would be determined through a Rule of Reason analysis. See Continental T.V. v. GTE Sylvania, Inc., 433 U.S. 36 (1977).

merger partner or the acquired firm from making a QV investment that would not be replaced by another firm's QV investment and/or to facilitate the participating firms' eliminating some QV investments or altering the locations of existing or planned QV investments. I will discuss the relevant horizontal-merger and joint-venture case-law in some detail in Chaps. 12 and 15 respectively. *Inter alia*, the horizontal-merger case-law discussion will focus on cases in which a firm has merged with or acquired a rival to shut down its operations.[526]

(2) The EC's and the E.C./E.U. Courts' Positions

I will deal with the EC's and the E.C./E.U. courts' positions on joint ventures and horizontal mergers that affect various QV-investment-related issues in more detail in Chaps. 15 and 12 respectively. However, at this juncture, I do want to record my impression that these E.U. institutions have said more than their U.S. counterparts about the kinds of conduct with which this section is concerned and my suspicion that this reality reflects the fact that the EC and the E.C./E.U. courts are more troubled than are the DOJ, the FTC, and the U.S. courts by conduct that reduces total QV investment in some ARDEPPSes or assigns exclusive rights to make QV investments in particular territories to different undertakings because the EC and the E.C./E.U. courts perceive such conduct to disserve the still-operative goal of the 1957 E.C. Treaty of promoting a common market.

The evidence I would cite in support of my claim that E.C./E.U. authorities have been more active in combatting the kinds of contrived oligopolistic conduct in which firms can engage to reduce total QV investment in an ARDEPPS or to assign exclusive rights to make QV investments in particular ARDEPPSes to particular firms includes

(1) decisions already discussed in which E.C./E.U. courts have found agreements to limit advertising (some of which is a QV investment),[527]
(2) cases in which E.C./E.U. courts have banned agreements dividing up the markets in which individual sellers can make sales when participation in the excluded market would have involved QV investments in wholesaler networkers and may have involved production-facility-creating QV investments,[528]
(3) cases condemning arrangements assigning the right to produce particular classes of products to particular producers,[529]

[526] See Standard Oil Co. of New Jersey v. United States, 221 U.S. 1 (1911) and American Can Co. v. United States, 230 F. 859 (D. Md. 1916), appeal dismissed, 256 U.S. 706 (1921).

[527] See, *e.g.*, Belgian Beer, OJ L200/1 (2003); Electrical and Mechanical Carbon Producers, OJ L/25/45 (2004); and Roofing Felt, OJ L232/15 (1986).

[528] See, *e.g.*, Peroxygen Products, OJ L 34/1 (1985).

[529] See, *e.g.*, Welded Steel Mesh, OJ L 260/1, p. 172 (1989).

(4) production-joint-venture cases in which the court was concerned that the joint venture might reduce competition by deterring the parents from making independent QV investments,[530] and
(5) ancillary-restraint EC Notices and joint-venture cases in which the EC and E.C./E.U. courts seem to be manifesting more skepticism than their U.S. counterparts usually do about whether the collaboration really was necessary, whether the restraints really were ancillary to a useful collaboration, and whether the duration and breadth of the restraints really could be defended.[531]

I hasten to add, however, that the EC's and the E.C./E.U. courts' treatment of the conduct with which this section is concerned have many of the same deficiencies that their U.S. counterparts have:

(1) the E.C./E.U. authorities' definition of "ancillary" is equally unclear;
(2) the E.C./E.U. authorities do not have an adequate conceptual scheme for analyzing the impact of this conduct (or any other type of conduct) on either total QV investment or the intensity of QV-investment competition in an ARDEPPS;
(3) neither the EC nor the E.C./E.U. courts have ever addressed the legal relevance of any tendency of this type of conduct to increase economic efficiency by reducing total QV investment in the ARDEPPS in which it is practiced and, derivatively, in the economy as a whole;
(4) E.C./E.U. institutions have never addressed the legal relevance of the possible economic efficiency of the relocations of QV investments that some conduct covered by this section can effectuate;
(5) E.C./E.U. institutions have never addressed the legality of one or more sellers' bribing another seller not to make a QV investment or to change the location of its planned or extant investment or relatedly of sellers' creating a joint venture or participating in a merger or acquisition to facilitate the payment of such bribes to one or more remaining actual or potential competitors; and
(6) E.U. institutions have never, to my knowledge, addressed the legality of one or more sellers' acquiring or merging with a rival to shut down its operations.

6. PPR-Related Oligopolistic Conduct

This section focuses on (1) the natural oligopolistic interactions that can reduce the amount of PPR executed to discover cheaper ways to produce one or more members of a set of rival products and (2) the various types of oligopolistic contrivance in

[530] See, *e.g.*, Philips/Osram, OJ L 378/37 (1994); Ford/Volkswagen, OJ L 20/14 (1992); and Exxon/Still, OJ L 144/20 (1994).

[531] See Commission Notice on Restrictions Directly Related and Necessary to Concentrations, OJ C/56, 24–31/131 (3/5/05).

which firms can engage to reduce the amount of PPR that is directed at discovering cheaper ways to produce one or more members of a set of rival products, to alter the array of PPR projects that are executed for this purpose (without necessarily changing the total amount of resources devoted to the relevant category or PPR), to allocate among potential production-process researchers exclusive rights to execute particular types of PPR projects that relate to the production process used to produce one or more members of a particular set of rival products or perhaps exclusive rights to do PPR of any type that relates to the production process used to produce particular relevant clusters of products, and to enable themselves to profit by executing one or more PPR projects when they would otherwise execute none because the natural oligopolistic PPR disincentives they faced would make it unprofitable for any of them to execute such a project, given the fact that their doing so would induce one or more others to execute a PPR project the other(s) would not otherwise have executed.

A. The Similarity of and Differences Between Economic Analyses of PPR-Related and QV-Investment-Related Oligopolistic Conduct

To save space, I will simply assert that, with two exceptions, the analyses of Section 5A of this chapter fully apply to PPR. This conclusion should not be surprising, given the fact that a PPR discovery is a product that, for this purpose, is comparable to the products and services that QV investments create. The first difference between the relevant QV-investment and PPR analysis is that—for reasons that I outlined in Chap. 5 and will explain in detail in The Welfare Economics of Antitrust Policy and U.S. and E.U. Antitrust Law—the reductions in PPR that firms contrive or that result from natural oligopolistic interdependence are likely to be economically inefficient whereas the reductions in QV investment that firms contrive or that result from natural oligopolistic interdependence are likely to be economically efficient.

The second difference between the two analyses relates to a special case—the fact that sellers that operate in a legal system that makes them liable for the losses they inflicted by causing accidents and pollution only if their conduct is found negligent (as that concept is defined and applied in the common law) will, under some circumstances, be able to rely on natural oligopolistic interdependence to deter them from doing jointly-unprofitable but *ex ante* economically-efficient research into less-accident-and-pollution-loss-prone production processes, and in other circumstances, will find it profitable to contrive not to do such research. I will now explain these claims.

Common-law courts have never found a producer to be negligent for failing to do research designed to discover production processes whose use would reduce the amount of accident-and-pollution losses their operations generate per unit of output—indeed, have never considered the possibility of applying the negligence standard to decisions not to do any type of research. In some circumstances, this fact will make it unprofitable for a monopolist or a group of sellers whose tort-law or environmental-law liability for the accident-and-pollution losses they generate depends on their being found to have caused such losses negligently to execute PPR projects whose certainty-equivalent private cost is less than the certainty-equivalent amount by which the projects would be expected to reduce allocative production costs (which include the external accident-and-pollution losses the relevant production generates). Specifically, when a monopolist or any group of producers can assume that no outsider will make the relevant discovery if it or they do not (because the relevant research can be profitably performed only by insiders that have the kind of information obtained exclusively by producing and selling the good in question), the monopolist or all insiders taken as a group will not find such product-process-research projects profitable (unless the project would be profitable independent of the effect of the related discovery's use on accident-and-pollution losses) not only because the projects are expensive in themselves but also because the discoveries to which they lead will be costly to the producer(s) in question in that they will make them liable for failing to adopt any otherwise-more-expensive but less-accident-and-pollution-loss-prone production-process that is discovered whose use would reduce accident-and-pollution losses by more than it would increase other costs (since the decision of sellers not to adopt a known, less-accident-and-pollution-loss-prone production-process is assessed for negligence).

The preceding analysis reveals why a pure monopolist that was the only actor in a position to do accident-and-pollution-loss-reducing PPR would find it unprofitable to do such PPR if its tort liability were governed by a common-law negligence rule under which courts did not assess PPR decisions for possible negligence. Of course, the preceding analysis does not imply that individual sellers in an ARDEPPS whose seller-side is not a pure monopoly will not find it profitable to do *ceteris paribus* allocatively-efficient PPR of this kind if no outsider could make the relevant discovery. An individual seller in such a situation that thought that it might make such a discovery first and that no rival could discover an alternative, equally-cost-effective less-accident-and-pollution-loss-prone production process might very well find it profitable to execute any such PPR project that would be *ex ante* allocatively efficient on otherwise-Pareto-perfect assumptions (if IP law would give it protection). Since it will be negligent for producers not to use its discovery—*i.e.*, since producers that do not use its discovery will be liable for any additional accident-and-pollution losses they generate on that account, the discoverer will be able to collect from its product-rivals substantial fees for the right to use its discovery up to the difference between the amount of accident-and-pollution losses their shift to the process it discovered will enable them to avoid and any additional non-accident-and-pollution production-costs their use of the less-accident-and-pollution-loss-prone production-process will impose on them. This prospect may make it profitable for one or more individual members of such an

ARDEPPS to execute such research even though it would be against the collective interest of all members of their ARDEPPS combined if each such member could correctly assume that its decision to do such research would not affect the PPR decisions of its rivals.

This subsection will explain when natural oligopolistic interdependence will suffice to deter the members of an ARDEPPS whose members' tort liability depends on their being found negligent from doing presumptively-economically-efficient accident-and-pollution-loss-reducing PPR and when the members of such an ARDEPPS will find it profitable to contrive reductions in (the elimination of all) such PPR research. I start with the conditions under which natural oligopolistic interdependence will deter the execution of such research.

Natural oligopolistic interdependence will be most likely to deter such research when being the first seller to begin such an accident-and-pollution-loss-reducing-research project does not confer a substantial advantage. This condition is most likely to be fulfilled in two sets of circumstances: (1) when the initial researcher's rivals can begin their research at about the same time that it did (since the initial researcher cannot keep its efforts secret and the relevant research does not require much advanced planning) and (2) when later starters are not at a disadvantage (since it is not costly to accelerate the rate at which such a research project is completed or since the patent that is issued to a first discoverer is unlikely to prevent subsequent discoverers [whose discoveries are likely to be technologically different] from obtaining patents or using their discoveries). In any event, when no seller can obtain an advantage by being the first to initiate such research, each may be deterred from responding to its rivals' decisions not to do such research by initiating such research itself by its realization that its rivals will find it inherently profitable to react to such a decision by executing research-projects themselves that will leave the research-initiator worse-off than it would have been had it not engaged in the relevant research. The preceding analysis implies that the feasibility of natural oligopolistic accident-and-pollution-loss-reducing-research restrictions will primarily depend on the factors that influence the ability of a first researcher to obtain an advantage (its ability to keep its efforts secret, the extra costs later starters would have to incur to accelerate the completion of their projects, the likelihood that researchers that make initial discoveries will be able to block the use or patenting of later discoveries). When the prospect of natural reactions to an individual actor's decision to execute a relevant PPR project does not suffice to deter all sellers from engaging in such research, the producers in a given ARDEPPS may be able to contrive the relevant research-restrictions by bribing rivals that are considering executing such research not to do the research in question or, more likely in such situations, by deterring rivals from executing such mutually-unprofitable PPR by threatening to retaliate against researchers by cutting their prices to the researcher's customers, targeting their advertising on the researcher's customers, placing their QV investments closer in product-space to the researcher's outlets or product variants than would be inherently profitable, or executing inherently-unprofitable competitive research-projects whose discoveries would not be blocked by the initiator's discoveries.[532]

B. The Legality of PPR-Focused Natural-Oligopolistic and Contrived-Oligopolistic Conduct Under U.S. Antitrust Law and E.C./E.U. Competition Law, Correctly Interpreted and Applied

Earlier, I suggested two possible differences between the economic consequences of QV-investment-focused and PPR-focused oligopolistic conduct:

(1) efforts by potential production-process researchers to contrive reductions in the total amount of PPR executed in relation to the production of a given product tend to decrease economic efficiency, while efforts to contrive reductions in the total amount of QV investment executed in any ARDEPPS will tend to increase economic efficiency,[533] and

---

[532] One might wonder why the preceding subsection on QV-investment-focused oligopolistic conduct did not include an analogous discussion of the natural oligopolistic interdependence and contrivance that could enable rival sellers whose tort liability was governed by a negligence standard to increase their collective profits by not doing research designed to discover product variants or (buyer-valued) locations whose use would reduce production and consumption external costs by more than they would increase the sum of other production costs and any positive difference between the value to their buyers of the more-externality-prone and less-externality-prone products or locations in question. The answer is that common-law courts do not assess for negligence the refusal of sellers to shift to producing a "safer" product variant or to shift to operating from a "safer" location and that neither products-liability law nor the doctrine of nuisance uses a negligence standard. I hasten to admit, however, that this subsection's discussion would have a QV-investment-related analogue to the extent that the discovery of the safer product variant might lead U.S. legislatures or health-and-safety regulatory bodies to tax or ban the production of the less-safe products.

[533] Although the policy relevance of this difference is more appropriately considered in the policy-focused companion to this law-study, I do want to make two policy-points here. First, it will almost certainly be more economically efficient to respond to the tendency of developed economies to devote, from the perspective of economic efficiency, too many resources to QV-investment creation and not enough to PPR execution and UO production (1) by decreasing the length and breadth of the IP protection given to patentable product-discoveries and increasing the length and breadth of the IP protection given to production-process discoveries and (2) by raising the effective tax-rate applied to the profits yielded by QV investments of all sorts and lowering the effective tax-rates applied respectively to the profits yielded by PPR projects and the profits yielded by the production of existing products. Second, if the tendency of our economy to generate total-UO/total-QV/total-PPR misallocation of the above kind is not eliminated by the passage and implementation of these or other sorts of policies, there will be a sound economic-efficiency argument both (1) for devoting fewer or no resources to enforcing laws that prohibit contrived-oligopolistic or any other type of conduct that reduces total QV investment in the ARDEPPS in which it occurs and, derivatively, in the economy and (2) for devoting more resources than it would otherwise be economically efficient to devote to enforcing laws that prohibit contrived-oligopolistic or any other type of conduct that reduces total PPR in the PPR ARDEPPS in which it occurs and, derivatively, in the economy.

(2) producers that will be liable in tort law only for losses they are deemed to have caused negligently will be more likely to contrive presumptively-economically-inefficient reductions of PPR into less-accident-and-pollution-loss-prone production processes than presumptively-economically-inefficient research into less-accident-and-pollution-loss-prone product variants and locations.

C. The Legality of PPR-Focused Oligopolistic Conduct Under U.S. and E.C/E.U. Antitrust Law

The relevant analyses are identical to their counterparts for QV-investment-focused oligopolistic conduct.

D. U.S. Case-Law, EC Positions, and E.C./E.U. Case-Law

I know of no DOJ/FTC Guideline, no U.S. case-law, no EC Notice, no EC case decision, and no E.C./E.U.-court case-law that deals with PPR-related natural or contrived oligopolistic conduct. I do not think that this reality reflects the fact that no illegal conduct of this sort occurs in the jurisdictions in question. To the contrary, my guess is that firms engage in a good deal of such conduct and that the absence of any "positive law" on such behavior reflects the failure of economists and lawyers to recognize this category of oligopolistic conduct. However, these economic-consequence differences do not cause the legality of any type of PPR-focused oligopolistic conduct under either U.S. antitrust law or E.C./E.U. competition law to be different from the legality of its QV-investment-focused counterpart under the respective bodies of law.

7. Contrived Oligopolistic Pricing by Economic Actors in Their Capacities as Buyers: Buyer "Price-Fixing"

So far, this chapter has focused on the various types of oligopolistic conduct in which sellers can engage in their capacities as sellers. Economic actors can also engage in oligopolistic conduct in their capacities as buyers—*e.g.*, can engage in oligopolistic conduct (1) to lower the prices they must pay for an input they use to produce a final product or for a final product they resell, or, conceivably, (2) to obtain improvements in various non-price terms of purchase when minimum-price regulations or, possibly, prohibitions of price discrimination preclude them from securing price-concessions that would be more jointly profitable for the buyer(s) involved and their suppliers. Buyer-contrived oligopolistic pricing—which might be called buyer "price-fixing"[534]—can involve (1) two or more actors' agreeing not to compete against each other as buyers—*i.e.*, (1) one buyer's agreeing not to compete against one or more other buyers as purchasers of some good or service in exchange for the other's or others' agreeing not to compete as purchasers of specified products against the first buyer, (2) one buyer's bribing another not to outbid it for a particular set of goods or services, or (3) one buyer's attempting to induce one or more other buyers not to compete against it as purchasers of some good(s) by threatening to react to any such competition by retaliating in one or more ways against the non-cooperator.

To save space, this analysis of buyer price-fixing will be confined to a brief account of the determinants of the profitability of buyer price-fixing, a brief analysis of its legality under the Sherman Act and now-Articles 101 and 102 of the Treaty of Lisbon (correctly interpreted and applied), and a brief summary of the case-law and antitrust-enforcement-agency positions on such conduct in both the U.S. and the E.C./E.U.

A. The Determinants of the Profitability of Contrived Oligopolistic Pricing by Buyers

I will offer no more than a brief outline. The relevant determinants will depend in part on whether the relevant good's sellers are setting individualized or across-the-board prices. In the individualized-pricing situation, the profitability of a given buyer's practicing contrived oligopolistic buying depends *inter alia* on (1) the strength of its reputation for contrivance, (2) the number of buyers that would find it inherently profitable to beat its contrived oligopolistic price to the seller in question (which will affect both the cost it will have to incur to communicate its contrived oligopolistic intentions and to identify any firm that beat its offer from an inferior-buyer position), (3) the various factors that influence its ability to communicate its contrived oligopolistic intentions simply by offering a contrived oligopolistic price (*e.g.*, its reputation for judging accurately the value of the good in question to its buyer rivals), (4) the factors that influence its ability to determine whether its failure to be supplied by a particular supplier reflected its being outbid by a competitive inferior or a change in its position as a buyer (as a result of a change in

[534] The text will ignore the possibility that a best-placed buyer (the buyer that would break even by paying the relevant supplier a price for the good in question that no other buyer could match without sustaining a loss on the transaction) may be able to obtain the product for a price that one or more of its buyer rivals could profit by beating if the best-placed buyer could not react to their response because its buyer rivals know that (1) the relevant supplier will give its best-placed buyer an opportunity to beat any superior offer the supplier receives from an inferior buyer and (2) the best-placed buyer will find it inherently profitable to beat any superior offer an inferior buyer makes (because the buyer surplus the best-placed buyer would have obtained had it made the improved offer originally and had that offer been accepted exceed the special additional cost it would have to incur to change its initial bid).

the valuation of an old rival buyer, the entry of a new buyer that values the seller's product more highly than it does, a change in a rival buyer's delivery arrangements that reduce the costs the seller must incur to deliver the product)—the number of suppliers that supply it, the constancy of the percentage of purchases it is best-placed to make through time, the similarity between current relevant conditions and past relevant conditions, and its ability to measure changes in those conditions, (5) its ability to reciprocate to rival buyers both as a buyer and as a seller, (6) the costs it would have to incur to inflict various relevant amounts of losses on rivals that might outbid it through retaliation both as a buyer and as a seller,[535] (7) the amount of safe buyer surplus it must put at risk to attempt to contrive a lower bid-price, (8) the extent to which its successful attempt to contrive a lower buying price or its making good on contrived-oligopolistic-price-fixing anticompetitive threats and promises will increase the profits it can make through contrivance throughout its organization, *etc*. To save space, I will not outline the determinants of the profitability of buyer price-fixing when the relevant sellers set across-the-board prices.

B. The Legality of Buyer Price-Fixing Under U.S. Antitrust Law and E.C./E.U. Competition Law, Correctly Interpreted and Applied

(1) The Legality of Buyer Price-Fixing Under U.S. Antitrust Law, Properly Interpreted and Applied

Price-fixing by still-independent buyers is covered by the Sherman Act but not by the Clayton Act.[536] Chapter 4's account of the Sherman Act test of illegality focuses on the more common situation in which the allegedly-illegal conduct of the defendants related to behavior in which they engaged in their capacities as sellers. The analogous test of illegality that I believe would be correct as a matter of law to read the Sherman Act to promulgate for conduct committed by actors in their capacities as buyers would be:

---

[535] When I discussed the ability of a seller to reciprocate to its cooperators and to retaliate against its undercutters/underminers, I ignored its ability to reciprocate by not beating their contrived oligopolistic buying-bids and to retaliate by beating their buying-bids. A full analysis of the determinants of the profitability of contrived oligopolistic pricing would take these options into account.

[536] Firms can also execute horizontal and conglomerate mergers or participate in horizontal and conglomerate joint ventures to reduce the competition they give each other as buyers. The fact that horizontal mergers, conglomerate mergers, and horizontal and conglomerate joint ventures reduce the competition their participants give each other as buyers is relevant to their legality under the Clayton Act as well as under the Sherman Act. However, the Clayton Act's applicability will not be explored in this chapter, which is concerned with price-fixing by still-independent buyers. Clayton Act issues will, of course, be analyzed in Chaps. 12 and 13, which focus respectively on horizontal and conglomerate mergers. The Clayton Act does not cover joint ventures.

> Actors violate the Sherman Act if their *ex ante* perception that the conduct under scrutiny was profitable was critically affected by their belief that it would increase their profits by reducing the absolute attractiveness of the offers against which they will have to compete as buyers (in some way that would render their conduct economically inefficient in an otherwise-Pareto-perfect economy).

Under this test, all agreements between or among buyers not to compete against each other when purchasing inputs or final goods and all threats by a buyer to retaliate against a rival buyer's refusal to abstain from outbidding it for a good or service would violate the Sherman Act. However, the preceding statement of the applicable test of Sherman Act illegality and the associated legal conclusion ignore the possible interpretive relevance of a possible difference between one of the consequences of buyer price-fixing and seller price-fixing—*viz.*, the fact that, unlike seller price-fixing (which always inflicts an equivalent-dollar loss on the final consumers who are customers of the price-fixers and the customers of their product-rivals), buyer price-fixing will always confer an equivalent-dollar gain on the final consumers who engage in it and (I suspect) will usually confer an equivalent-dollar gain on the final consumers who are customers of the producers that fix the prices of the inputs they buy as well as on the final consumers who are customers of such price-fixers' product-rivals. If, as I believe, one of the goals of the Sherman Act is to confer an equivalent-dollar gain on Clayton-Act-relevant buyers, a prudential-consequentialist (*i.e.*, functional) argument could be made for the conclusion that the Sherman Act should not be interpreted to prohibit price-fixing by final consumers or by producers/distributors in their capacities as input buyers/buyers of final goods for resale when the latters' price-fixing seems likely to benefit such final consumers. I believe that this functional argument is both legally valid and legitimate, that final-consumer buyer price-fixing does not violate the Sherman Act, and that the price-fixing in which producers/retailers engage when buying inputs/final goods for resale will usually not violate the Sherman Act because it will normally confer an equivalent-dollar gain on the customers of the price-fixers (and the customers of their product-rivals). I hasten to add that the conclusion that buyer price-fixing is not prohibited by the Sherman Act that is favored by the argument that the Act was in part designed to benefit final consumers and that buyer price-fixing will usually if not always benefit final consumers (see below) is consistent with the operational test of illegality I have argued it is correct as a matter of law to interpret the Sherman Act to promulgate: in an otherwise-Pareto-perfect economy (in which the seller power over price that the buyer price-fix was countervailing was the only extant Pareto imperfection [prior to the buyer price-fix]), the buyer price-fix would increase economic efficiency (unless the allocative transaction cost of arranging and policing the buyer price-fix was higher than the economic-efficiency gains the price-reductions it generated would yield).

I anticipate that three objections will be made to this conclusion. I have some sympathy for the first: nothing in the text of the Sherman act suggests that a distinction should be drawn between horizontal seller price fixing and horizontal buyer price fixing. I also have some sympathy for the second: buyer price-fixing is wrongful conduct and, on my interpretation, it would not be prohibited by the Sherman Act. I agree that buyer price-fixing—*e.g.*, bid-rigging by buyer-dealers in auction houses[537]—is wrongful. Even if the auction house itself is not complicitous (has not violated its fiduciary duties to customers that are using its facilities to sell their objects), such buyer price-fixing strikes me not just as improper but violative of moral rights that liberal rights-based States such as the U.S. and the members of the E.C. and E.U. are morally obligated to secure. I must concede that, although U.S. private law (and the private law of some E.C./E.U. countries) does contain doctrines that might be stretched to give seller-victims of buyer price-fixes legal redress,[538] none of these doctrines is perfectly on point. I must also concede that the correctability of this deficiency of the relevant jurisdictions' private law does not undercut this moral argument for interpreting the Sherman Act and Articles 101 and 102 to cover buyer price-fixing.

---

[537] The example has some more pull for me than I suspect it will have for most others: I spend a considerable amount of time in antique markets and auction houses. Indeed, I have been heard to admit that "I believe in flea markets, not in free markets."

[538] The doctrines and cases I have in mind include (1) the doctrine of promissory estoppel (which U.S. courts have developed to legally entitle gift promisees that have reasonably relied on gift promises and sellers that have reasonably relied on statements by buyers that they would enter into contracts with the seller if the seller did certain things or certain conditions were fulfilled to recover their reliance expenditures from the gift promissor or buyer in question [the civil-law counterpart to this doctrine is the doctrine *culpa in contrahendo*]), (2) cases in which buyers who willingly paid a particular price for a good or service have been allowed to recover that portion of the price they paid that the seller charged them because the seller had to incur costs to bribe government officials or buyer agents, (3) the common-law doctrine of payment by mistake, under which buyers who willingly paid a price that was higher than the price the seller would otherwise have charged because the seller or the seller's input-supplier (say, a subcontractor) had mistakenly duplicated an accounting cost-entry, (4) the doctrine of "interference with contractual relations" (which might be stretched to cover buyer price-fixing by arguing that each buyer who willingly participated in such a price-fix was attempting to interfere with the seller's attempt to enter into a contractual relationship with the other buyers whose bidding the contrivers were attempting to control), and (5) the doctrine of promissory fraud (which might be construed to apply on the ground that each buyer is taking advantage of the seller's incorrect assumption that the buyers have not engaged in a price-fix—a mistaken assumption that each price-fix participant could have prevented the seller from making). (In one case, the California Supreme Court allowed a buyer who was purchasing a mink coat for his mistress to rescind the purchase on the ground that it was "fraudulently induced" in circumstances in which he wanted to pay no more than $4000 for the coat but the sale was consummated at the seller's reserve price of $5,000 when the mistress arranged for the seller to "accept" a price of $4,000 in exchange for her making up the $1,000 difference despite the facts that, as Judge Raynor pointed out in dissent, the buyer had "received what he bargained for," "the fair value of the coat was $5,000," and "the coat was of sound quality and came up to. . .[the mistress'] expectations." See Earl v. Sales & Co., 226 P.2d 340 (Cal. 1951).) I want to emphasize that I realize that none of these doctrines is completely on point and that some of the cases in question may have been wrongly decided. I reference them because they do provide some precedential support for a private-law conclusion that seller-victims of buyer price-fixes are legally entitled to recover from the buyer price-fixers the losses the buyer price-fix imposed on the sellers in question—a conclusion that I think is correct as a matter of law in liberal, rights-based societies such as the U.S. and the countries of the E.C./E.U. in that it is favored by an argument of moral principle. For an account of my positions on legitimate and valid legal argument, which underlie this conclusion, see RICHARD S. MARKOVITS, MATTERS OF PRINCIPLE: LEGITIMATE LEGAL ARGUMENT AND CONSTITUTIONAL INTERPRETATION (NYU Press, 1998) and *Liberalism and Tort Law: On the Content of the Corrective-Justice-Securing Tort Law of a Liberal, Rights-Based Society*, 2006 ILL. L. REV. 243 (2006).

The third (economic) objection to my position on the Sherman Act illegality of buyer price-fixing applies only to cases in which the buyers are producers who are fixing the prices of one or more inputs they use to produce their final products or dealers who are fixing the prices of the final products they resell. As I indicated in Chap. 4, both Judge Posner[539] and many other highly-respected industrial-organization economists[540] believe that the exercise of power by producers in their capacities as buyers of inputs or the exercise of power by resellers in their capacities as buyers of the final goods they resell is just as harmful to Clayton-Act-relevant buyers as the exercise of market power by actors in their capacities as sellers. As I also indicated in Chap. 4, I disagree. The argument of these experts assumes that the exercise of such buyer power should be analyzed on the assumption that the buyers in question are functioning as traditional monopsonists (buyers who face an upward-sloping supply curve) in circumstances in which it will not be profitable for them to engage in price discrimination. It is true that, although such monopsonists will pay a lower price for the input or final product they are buying than a non-monopsonist buyer would pay for it, the marginal cost that the monopsonist will have to incur to purchase the last (say, *n*th) unit of the relevant input or product in question will be higher than the marginal cost that a non-monopsonist would have to incur to purchase that *n*th unit because, unlike the perfectly-competitive buyer (whose purchases of additional units of any input or final product will not alter the price it must pay for the intra-marginal units it purchases), the monopsonist's purchase of additional units of the relevant input or final good will increase the price it must pay for (the cost it must incur to purchase) its intra-marginal units if it cannot engage in perfect price discrimination costlessly. It is also true that, if the firm or firms that are exercising buyer power on purchases of inputs or final goods act as classical non-discriminating monopsonists, their exercise of buyer power will inflict an equivalent-dollar loss on their customers and the customers of their product-rivals by raising not just the marginal cost the relevant producer-buyer (distributor-buyer) must incur to purchase the relevant input (final good) but concomitantly the marginal cost it must incur to produce the associated quantity of its final product (the marginal cost of the good it will resell) and hence the price it charges for that final product. However, if producers that fix the price they pay for an input they use or a final good they resell are operating in "bilateral-monopoly" situations in which the relevant suppliers are not perfect competitors, the buyers' price-fix will lower the non-varying price they must pay for each unit of the input or final good whose price is being fixed, and the price-fix in which they engage in their capacities as buyers of inputs or final products (1) will reduce not only the average cost but also the marginal cost to them of buying the input or final product in question and concomitantly (2) will reduce their marginal costs of final-good production or resale and the prices they charge for their final products, thereby conferring an equivalent-dollar gain on their customers and the customers of their product-rivals. Because I believe that the

[539] See Judge Richard Posner, writing in Khan v. State Oil Co., 93 F.3d 1358, 1361 (7th Cir. 1966).

[540] See ROBERT BLAIR AND JEFFREY HARRISON, MONOPSONY (Princeton Univ. Press, 1993).

producers who fix the prices they pay for productive inputs and the distributors that fix the price they pay for the goods they resell are almost always operating in bilateral-monopoly as opposed to classical monopsony situations, I think that the vast majority of input-buyer price-fixes by producers or final-good-buyer price-fixes by resellers further the Sherman Act goal of generating net equivalent-dollar gains for the customers of the price-fixing buyers and the customers of those buyers' product-rivals and hence do not violate the Sherman Act, correctly interpreted.

(2) The Legality of Buyer Price-Fixing Under E.C./E.U. Competition Law, Correctly Interpreted and Applied

I will first address the legality of buyer price-fixing under what is now Article 101 of the 2009 Treaty of Lisbon, correctly interpreted and applied, and then address the legality of buyer price-fixing under what is now Article 102 of that treaty. Although it is clear that now-Article 101 does not cover buyer price-fixing that is executed solely by means of threats or threats and acts of retaliation, it is not clear that now-Article 101 covers buyer price-fixing at all. Admittedly, the conclusion that now-Article 101 does cover buyer price-fixing as well as seller price-fixing is favored by the fact that (1) semantically, now-Article 101(1)'s reference to preventing or restricting competition does not distinguish between seller competition and buyer competition and (2) its "clause (a)–(e)" list of behaviors that now-Article 101(1) deems *prima facie* illegal includes in clause (a) a reference to the fixing of terms of purchase and in clause (c) a reference to "shar[ing] sources of supply"—references that seem to imply that now-Article 101(1) does make buyer price-fixing *prima facie* illegal. However, two arguments can also be made for the conclusion that now-Article 101 does not cover buyer price-fixing. The first of these arguments has two premises:

(1) the E.C./E.U. Treaty has two provisions that manifest the fact that the Treaty's drafters and ratifiers wanted their competition law to benefit relevant buyers—now-Article 101(3), which requires that, for conduct to be eligible for an exemption from now-Article 101(1), it must *inter alia* afford relevant buyers a fair share of the benefit the conduct confers on those buyers and its perpetrator(s) "combined," and now-Article 102, which at least as interpreted promulgates an exploitative-abuse as well as an exclusionary-abuse test of illegality;
(2) price-fixing by final buyers always confers equivalent-monetary gains on relevant buyers and price-fixing by intermediate buyers almost always confers equivalent-monetary gains on relevant final buyers.

The second of these arguments has one premise: there is every reason to believe that, like the U.S. economist/lawyers and antitrust-enforcement officials who have expressed their views on this issue, the E.C./E.U. Treaty's drafters and ratifiers mistakenly believed that buyer price-fixing tends to harm or almost always does harm ultimate buyers. This premise is salient because it suggests that, although the fact that the "clause (a)–(e)" list (which should be interpreted to be illustrative) contains items that reveal that the Treaty's drafters and ratifiers thought that buyer price-fixing was *prima facie* illegal under now-Article 101(1), it might not require that conclusion.

In my view, correctly interpreted as a matter of law, now-Article 101(1) would not be read to declare buyer price-fixing *prima facie* illegal unless the price-fix was designed to drive an established rival out by denying it participation in the fix or to deter the creation of a new QV investment by a potential entrant or expander by denying the relevant potential investor participation in the fix. One might think that this admittedly-contestable general conclusion is not practically important because, if (as I believe) buyer price-fixing virtually always benefits ultimate consumers, such price-fixing will always be eligible for a now-Article 101(3) exemption. In fact, however, this now-Article 101(3) argument ignores (1) the fact that, for conduct to be eligible for an Article 101(3) exemption, it must generate relevant economic efficiencies and (2) the reality that simple buyer price-fixing as opposed to joint-purchasing arrangements (buyer coops) do not generate any economic efficiencies, much less any economic efficiencies that would meet the relevant requirement of now-Article 101(3).

I turn finally to the legality of buyer price-fixing under now-Article 102 of the Treaty. Three points are salient. First, now-Article 102 will not cover buyer price-fixing unless one or more of the perpetrators is individually dominant or a member of a collectively-dominant set of rivals. Second, since buyer price-fixing will always benefit its perpetrator(s) and will virtually always benefit its perpetrator's or perpetrators' customers, it will never or virtually never render a perpetrator guilty of an exploitative abuse under now-Article 102. Third, because (1) the drafters and ratifiers of now-Article 102 were seeking *inter alia* to protect relevant buyers and (2) buyer price-fixing always or virtually always benefits relevant buyers, buyer price-fixing should almost never be deemed to constitute an exclusionary abuse under now-Article 102. I wrote "*almost* never" because I believe that buyer price-fixes that limit the participants in the fix to drive one or more non-participants out or to deter the entry of a potential competitor or the expansion of an incumbent that would not be admitted to the fix could be deemed to constitute an exclusionary abuse.

C. The U.S. Case-Law and DOJ/FTC Position on Buyer Price-Fixing and the EC Position and E.C./E.U. Case-Law on Buyer Price-Fixing

(1) The U.S. Case-Law and DOJ/FTC Position on Buyer Price-Fixing

To my knowledge, only one U.S. case addresses the Sherman Act legality of price-fixing by still-independent buyers that have not formed a joint venture *inter alia* to act as a buyer coop. In 1948, in *Mandeville Island Farms v. American Crystal Sugar*,[541] the Supreme Court held that the Sherman Act does not distinguish

---

[541] 334. U.S. 219 (1948).

between price-fixing by buyers and price-fixing by sellers—in particular, prohibits both:

> The statute does not confine its protection to consumers, or to purchasers, or to competitors, or to sellers. Nor does it immunize the outlawed acts because they are done by any of these. The Act is comprehensive in its terms and coverage, protecting all who are made victims of the forbidden practices by whomever they may be perpetrated.[542]

This holding has never been reversed or qualified. The U.S. DOJ also claims that the Sherman Act prohibits buyer price-fixing in addition to seller price-fixing. However, the DOJ's justification for this conclusion is functional, not textual (as the Supreme Court's was): its position is that price-fixing by buyers (at least by intermediate buyers) is prohibited by the Sherman Act because it is at least as inimical to the interests of final consumers as seller price-fixing is.[543] My disagreement with the DOJ's legal conclusion reflects my disagreement with this economic conclusion.

The DOJ's current position on buyer price-fixing seems inconsistent with the Department's failure to attack the part of the joint venture among about 25 independent small grocery chains involved in *Topco*[544] that involved their agreeing to engage in joint purchasing of inputs and final products, though its decision in *Topco* might reflect (1) its possibly-correct conclusion that the arrangement's legality was secured by Topco's generation of real economies in purchase research, negotiating, and taking delivery, (2) its possibly-correct economic/legal conclusion that the joint-buying arrangement was ancillary to the joint venture's producing final products with the inputs involved, packaging and placing the Topco brand on the final products the joint venture produced and bought, and distributing these products to members—ancillary to these arrangements because the joint-purchasing arrangement facilitated quality-control, (3) (I am speculating) its incorrect legal conclusion that a buyer price-fix that would otherwise be illegal would be lawful if the buyers were small, marginal firms that had to engage in it to survive in competition with larger rivals, and/or (4) (I am speculating again) its possibly-correct economic conclusion that the joint-buying arrangement would not reduce the prices the participants had to pay for the inputs and final products they purchased but was created solely to facilitate quality-control.

By way of contrast, the Supreme Court's decision in *Mandeville Island Farms* and the DOJ's pronouncements on the economic consequences and legality of buyer price-fixes is fully consistent with the U.S. courts' condemnation of the player-salary-reducing arrangements of professional-sport-league joint ventures—in particular, their declaration of the Sherman Act illegality of (1) the National

[542] *Id.* at 236

[543] See 1992 Horizontal Merger Guidelines at Section 1.0 at p. 5. The DOJ and FTC have never addressed the implications of their use of this functional justification for their conclusion that the Sherman Act prohibits buyer price-fixing for the legality under the Sherman Act of price-fixes executed by final consumers.

[544] United States v. Topco Associates, Inc., 405 U.S. 596 (1972).

Football League's 1968 rookie-draft procedure (though the decision stated in dictum that a less-restrictive draft-procedure might be lawful as ancillary),[545] (2) the National Hockey League's reserve-clause arrangement,[546] and (3) the NFL's Rozelle Rule, requiring teams that hired a player after his contract with another team expired to compensate the player's former employer with one or more other players or draft choices.[547] These and many other joint-venture cases whose holdings bear on the legality of buyer-contrived oligopolistic conduct will be discussed in more detail in Chap. 15.

(2) The EC Position and the E.C./E.U.-Court Case-Law on Buyer Price-Fixing

Like its predecessor, this subsection will focus on the EC's and the E.C./E.U. courts' positions on "pure" buyer price-fixing—*i.e.*, on price-fixing by buyers that cannot generate real efficiencies because it does not involve the buyers' combining in any way to do research into the product/supplier that would be most profitable for them to buy/patronize, to negotiate jointly, to take deliveries together, or to jointly produce, package, brand, and/or promote any final product they jointly produce or sell. Chap. 15 will discuss the EC's and the E.C./E.U. courts' positions on buyer price-fixes that are part of more complex, possibly-efficiency-generating arrangements.

Not surprisingly, most of the EC's pronouncements on buyer price-fixing relate to the more complex variants of this practice. However, in its 2001 Guidelines[548] and in a number of its case decisions, the EC takes positions that reveal its view of the now-Article 101 illegality of "pure" buyer price-fixes.

The Guidelines' discussion of buyer power implies that the EC believes that any tendency of buyer price-fixing to reduce the prices that final consumers must pay by reducing the marginal costs of the price-fixers and hence their profit-maximizing prices counts in favor of its Article 101 legality, while any tendency of a buyer price-fix to cause suppliers to exit or to deter new QV investments (investments in branded products and the development of new products) and any tendency of a buyer price-fix to induce the exit of product-rivals of the price-fixers that cannot obtain similar concessions from suppliers count against its Article 101 legality.[549] Although I acknowledge that buyer price-fixes may lead one or more product-rivals of the price-fixers to exit if they cannot participate in the price-fix or secure as large price-reductions in some other way, I suspect that the EC exaggerates the likelihood

[545] Smith v. Pro Football, Inc. 593 F.2d 1173 (D.C. Cir. 1978).

[546] Philadelphia World Hockey Club, Inc. v. Philadelphia Club, 351 F. Supp. 462 (E.D. Pa. 1972)

[547] Mackey v. NFL, 543 F.2d 606 (8th Cir. 1976).

[548] Commission Guidelines on the Applicability of Article 101 of the 1957 E.C./E.U. Treaty to Horizontal Cooperation Agreements, OJ C3/2 (2001).

[549] *Id.* at p. 127.

of this outcome because it underestimates the ability of small rivals of the price-fixers to obtain similar concessions by entering into joint-buying arrangements.

The EC has also taken four other positions that relate to the Article 101 legality of "pure" buyer price-fixes. First, both in its Guidelines[550] and in individual cases,[551] the EC has declared that coordinated buying by buyers whose total share of the purchases made in the market in question is below 15 % do not raise any competitive concern (regardless of whether they attempt to coordinate their buying through joint ventures, other sorts of coop agreements, or solely as independent undertakings). In part because I suspect that any market definition used for this purpose will be arbitrary and in part because I believe that, even if the market definitions that are used in this context are not arbitrary, the defined markets will contain buyers for which some in-market sellers are far better-placed than others and sellers who are more dependent on sales to particular buyers than the buyers' market shares might suggest, I do not think that one can assume that buyers whose total market share as buyers is below 15 % will never be able to secure price-reductions by coordinating their purchasing.

Second, the relevant EC directive suggests that a buyer price-fix that would otherwise violate now-Article 101 may not do so if the buyer coop helps the buyers overcome the countervailing power of their suppliers.[552] I do not understand the legal justification for this conclusion. Certainly nothing in the text of now-Article 101 suggests that the legality of a buyer price-fix will be affected in any way by the market power of the relevant sellers.

Third, in at least one case (which involved a buying pool that adopted formal rules),[553] the EC appears to have characterized as the kind of "improv[ement in] the production or distribution of goods" that can render a buying pool that would otherwise violate now-Article 101(1) lawful under Article 101(3) private benefits that I do not think should be characterized in this way—*viz*., the private benefits the buyer coop generates by enabling its members to obtain "the most advantageous prices" and "security of supply." It should be obvious that any price-reduction the pool enables its members to obtain purely as a result of its buying power (*i.e*., not because of any cost-reductions [say, delivery-cost reductions] its operation

[550] *Id*. at p. 131.

[551] Thus, in Socemas, OJ L201/4 (1968), the EC grounded its conclusion that the members of a buyer coop created to buy food products from other E.C. countries for resale in France did not have sufficient power to reduce competition on the ground that the participants in the coop had a market share of 9 percent of the French food market and that the products they imported through the coop accounted for less than 0.1 percent of their turnover. Similarly, in Intergroup, OJ L212/23 (1975), the EC grounded its conclusion that the SPAR food-wholesaler-and-retailer chains that joined the import-buying buyer-coop Intergroup imported through Intergroup goods that accounted for between 0.06 and 0.89 percent of their turnover and that the retail participants in the coop accounted for less than 4 percent of the total E.C. retail-food turnover (facts that are related to the percentage of the relevant import purchases that Intergroup made).

[552] See Commission Guidelines on the Applicability of Article 101 of the 1957 E.C./E.U. Treaty to Horizontal Cooperation Agreements, OJ C3/2, p. 131 (2001).

[553] National Sulphuric Acid Association, Commission Decision 80/917, OJ L260/24 (1980).

generates) cannot be said to manifest its "improving the production or distribution of goods." And although this conclusion may be more contestable, I also do not think than any additional (buyer) security of supply (or, for that matter, any seller-security in relation to the seller's having buyers for the product it produces) the buyer pool generates "improv[es] the production or distribution of goods" since the associated reduction in the risk costs that the members of the buyer pool and their suppliers bear is presumably counteracted by the pool's increasing the supply-related risk costs that rival-buyers must bear and the sale-related risk costs that other sellers must bear.

Fourth, in a case that involved a buyer's coop as opposed to direct price-fixing by individual buyers but whose relevant point would apply to direct buyer price-fixes as well, the EC argued that the legality of the arrangement was favored by the fact that it was beneficial in that, by helping small wholesalers survive in a procurement market dominated by very large wholesalers, it increased the breadth of product choices available to consumers.[554] I cannot tell whether the survival predicate of this claim was correct in the case in question. However, even if it were correct, I would hesitate to endorse this line of reasoning to the extent that it would sanction the EC's and the E.C./E.U. courts' engaging in the kind of parimutual handicapping that the U.S. Supreme Court indicated was judicially appropriate in *White Motor*. Admittedly, the belief of some E.C./E.U. authorities and of some E.C./E.U. competition-law experts that now-Article 102 imposes an obligation on dominant firms to help smaller rivals survive and prosper favors the conclusion that the kind of parimutual handicapping that I think is wrong as a matter of law in the United States (and undesirable as a matter of policy) may be correct as a matter of E.C./E.U. competition law.

To my knowledge, the E.C./E.U. courts have rarely dealt with buyer price-fixes, regardless of whether the buyers they involve relate to each other solely in their individual capacities or create joint ventures or other types of arrangements to secure their cooperation. However, in the one major case in which an E.C. court has dealt with a buyer coop,[555] a Court of First Instance overturned an EC decision exempting a joint-purchasing arrangement (the European Broadcasting Union—EBU) created by independent broadcasters to buy broadcasting rights to major sporting events on the ground that the sub-licensing scheme the EBU had instituted to allow non-members to broadcast events for which the EBU had purchased broadcasting rights did not give such non-members sufficient access.

* * *

[554] In the case, small wholesalers of pharmaceuticals and pharmaceutical products created a coop to purchase the products in question and create a trademark under which they would resell them. See Orphe, EE1G Orphe, XX Report on Competition Policy 80, point 102 (1990).

[555] M6 and Others v. Commission, Joined Cases T-185/00, T-216/00, and T-300/00, ECR II-3805 (2002).

As I hope is obvious, this chapter's economic and legal analyses of oligopolistic conduct often employed the various complex economics conceptual schemes Chaps. 2 and 5 developed. More specifically, at numerous junctures, the economic and legal analyses of this chapter made critical use of (1) the distinction between natural and contrived oligopolistic conduct, (2) the account of the various non-oligopolistic reasons why a seller's price may exceed its conventional marginal costs, (3) the recognition that firms make decisions not only about price but also about the amount of QV investments they make and the locations of the QV investments they make and about the amount of PPR they execute and the nature of the PPR projects they execute and, relatedly, that the amount and locations of the QV investments and PPR projects in any area of product-space are endogenously determined and influenced in part by natural and contrived oligopolistic conduct, (4) the explanation of why changes in the prices charged by a set of rivals will affect the amount of QV investment that will be present in equilibrium in the area of product-space in which they are operating, (5) the more specific analyses of the factors that determine the additional amount of QV investment that any given increase in price will cause to be introduced into an area of product-space and the impact that the price-increase will have on the highest and weighted-average supernormal profit-rates generated in the area of product-space in question, (6) the recognition that economies can cause economic inefficiency by allocating resources in allocatively-inefficient proportions among unit-output-increasing, QV-investment-creating, and PPR-executing uses, (7) the recognition that economies can also cause economic inefficiency by using the amount of resources they devote to creating QV investments in a given area of product-space to create a less-allocatively-valuable set of QV investments than could have been created with the same amount of resources, and (8) the recognition that economies can cause economic inefficiency as well by using the amount of resources they devote to research into the production processes used to produce a particular product or set of rivalrous products to execute a less-allocatively-valuable set of PPR projects than could have been executed with the same amount of resources.

As I stated in the Foreword to This Law Study, conceptual innovations in economics should be judged by the extent to which they enable their users to identify important questions that would be less likely to be identified without them and by the extent to which they facilitate the analysis both of those questions and of questions that can be articulated without using the distinctions the conceptual innovations highlight. Both this chapter and the preceding paragraph should therefore help to justify the conceptual systems this study develops and employs.

Chapter 11
Predatory Conduct

1. The Definition of Predatory Conduct and Its Legality Under U.S. and E.C./E.U. Antitrust Law, Correctly Interpreted and Applied

To my knowledge, no economist or lawyer has ever explicitly defined the concept "predatory conduct." However, both economists and lawyers have consistently defined "predatory conduct" in use to be a subspecies of the conduct prohibited by the Sherman Act. More specifically, the characterization of conduct as "predatory" has always implied that its perpetrator's (perpetrators') *ex ante* perception that it was *ex ante* profitable was *ceteris paribus* critically inflated by its (their) belief that it would or might reduce the absolute attractiveness of the offers against which it (they) would have to compete by driving an established rival's QV investment out, by inducing an established rival to sell out to the predator(s) at a distressed price, by deterring a potential competitor or established firm from making an additional QV investment in the predator's (predators') ARDEPPS, or (by extension) by inducing the owner of an extant QV investment or the prospective maker of a planned QV investment to change its QV investment's location to a position further away in product-space from the QV investment(s) of the predator(s) where the phrase "*ceteris paribus* critically inflated" indicates that the effect in question would have rendered the relevant behavior *ex ante* profitable though *ex ante* economically inefficient in an otherwise-Pareto-perfect economy.

I turn now to the legality of predation under U.S. and E.C./E.U. law as correctly interpreted and applied. I start with U.S. law. As Chap. 4 indicated, all attempts at predation violate Section 2 of the Sherman Act except for predatory attempts to influence legislative, administrative, and adjudicatory decisions in ways that are not improper, refusals to deal that satisfy the conditions for a choice's being predatory but are legitimated by their enabling the chooser to enforce an independent legal right, and possibly but contestably all individual-firm refusals to deal directly with an actual or potential competitor and refusals to allow a distributor of its product to resell it to an actual or potential rival of the refuser. Although the following

R.S. Markovits, *Economics and the Interpretation and Application of U.S. and E.U. Antitrust Law*, DOI 10.1007/978-3-642-24307-3_11,

conclusion may be contestable, I believe that even unsuccessful attempts to form agreements to engage in concerted predation violate the Sherman Act: although, for reasons I have explained, such unsuccessful attempts are not covered by Section 1's proscription of agreements in restraint of trade, I do think they are covered by Section 2's proscription of attempts to monopolize—that agreements to cooperate in predation are agreements to monopolize though agreements to contrive oligopolistic prices are not.

The Clayton Act does not cover many types of predatory conduct—*e.g.*, does not cover (1) predatory pricing that does not involve "price discrimination" in the Clayton Act sense, (2) the predatory pricing of services regardless of whether it involves Clayton Act price discrimination, (3) predatory advertising, (4) predatory QV investments, (5) predatory investments in PPR, new-plant construction, plant-modernization, and/or worker recruitment and training, (6) predatory buying, (7) direct predatory refusals to deal, (8) predatory wage settlements, (9) predatory "unfair competition," and (10) predatory participation in legislative, regulatory, or adjudicative decision-making process. However, the Clayton Act does prohibit all types of predatory conduct to which it does apply that have the requisite *ex ante* probability of lessening competition. Thus, Section 2(b) of the Clayton Act (the Robinson-Patman Act) prohibits predatory pricing that involves the charging of different prices to "different purchasers of commodities of like grade and quality" that has the requisite probability of lessening competition, and Section 3 prohibits predatory full-requirement contracts on commodities and predatory decisions to condition the sale of a commodity (say, to a distributor) on the buyer's agreeing not to patronize the predator's target when the conduct is requisitely likely to lessen competition. By way of contrast, I do not think that Section 7 of the Clayton Act prohibits acquisitions or mergers that are executed after predation induces its target to sell out at a distressed price or to participate in the merger on distressed terms if, at the time of the merger or acquisition's execution, it was not requisitely likely to reduce competition because, post-predation, the target would have exited had it not participated in the acquisition or merger in question, even though the combination of the predation and the merger or acquisition did reduce competition.

E.C./E.U. law as written does a less of good job of prohibiting predation than does U.S. law as written. Thus, although agreements to cooperate in predation or predatory acts by trade associations are prohibited by now-Article 101 (since they are designed to prevent or restrict [and sometimes to distort] competition), now-Article 101 does not cover individual-firm predatory conduct. And, although (properly interpreted) now-Article 102 does prohibit as an exclusionary abuse of a dominant position any predatory act—whether individual or concerted—by a firm that is either individually dominant or a member of a collectively-dominant set of firms, it does not cover predation by a firm that is neither individually dominant nor a member of a set of collectively-dominant set of firms. If I am right that a firm that could not be said to have a significant amount of market, monopoly *plus* oligopoly, or monopoly power might well find predation profitable, this omission could well be empirically significant.

2. Predatory Pricing

A. The Determinants of the Profitability of Predatory Pricing

This subsection analyzes the private costs and benefits of predatory pricing in both individualized-pricing and across-the-board-pricing contexts and concludes that, in both these contexts, predatory pricing will sometimes be profitable. To ease the exposition, the text will assume (unless otherwise specified) that (1) the goal of the predation is to induce the target to withdraw an existing QV investment and (2) the predation in question is being carried out by one firm rather than by two or more firms acting in concert. The analysis would not have to be altered significantly to cover situations in which the predator was seeking to induce its target to sell to the predator the targeted QV investment at a distressed price or to relocate the QV investment in question. When it seems useful to do so, the analysis will discuss the feasibility and relative profitability of concerted as opposed to single-firm predatory pricing.

(1) The Determinants of the Cost to the Predator of Financing the Cost of Predation and the Determinants of the Ability of the Target to Withstand the Costs the Predation Imposes on It

Almost by definition, firms must sacrifice profits in the short run to practice predation. One of the determinants of the profitability of predation is the cost the prospective predator would have to incur to finance its predation. Obviously, *ceteris paribus*, those costs will increase with the short-run loss the relevant predation entails (a loss whose determinants the next subsection discusses). The relevant finance costs will also depend on the source or sources of the financing and the cost of obtaining financing from each such source. In general, I suspect, it will be cheaper for a firm to finance its predation internally from retained earnings, the profits (including normal profits) it will earn contemporaneously in the ARDEPPS in which the predation is being practiced, and the profits (including normal profits) it will earn contemporaneously in other ARDEPPSes rather than externally from capital raised in debt and equity markets or more privately either by misrepresenting the use to which the relevant funds will be put or by identifying and securing the help of a partner in crime. At a somewhat more concrete level, the cost of financing any given predation-caused short-run loss will depend on such things as the need of shareholders for dividends, the cost to them of securing more pay-outs by changing their investment portfolios, the cost to existing shareholders of issuing new stock, the interest rates the predator must pay on debt both when the creditor knows how its capital will be used and when it does not, and the profits that the predator could have earned on any alternative projects it sacrificed to free up the capital it allocated to predation.

Predatory pricing is also costly for the predator's target. The profitability of waging a predatory-pricing campaign against any given rival depends, in part, on the rival's ability to "finance" internally the short-run losses the predatory-pricing campaign imposes on it as well as on the cost the target will have to incur to obtain external survival-finance. Not surprisingly, the determinants of these parameters are similar to their counterparts for the predator: the amount of retained earnings the target has, the operating profits it is earning contemporaneously in other ARDEPPSes, and the amount of capital it can obtain in debt and equity markets (*inter alia*, its ability to convince external potential financers that its low profits reflect predation that the target can survive or use the law to stop rather than its not having a viable business plan) will all affect the likelihood that any predatory-pricing campaign will succeed and the losses the predator will have to inflict on its target to drive it out and concomitantly the costs the predator will have to incur to do so. I should add that the size of the losses a predator must inflict on a target to drive it out will also depend on the stake the target has in avoiding a (company-wide) reputation for succumbing to predation and (by inference) aggressive retaliation. That stake will depend *inter alia* on the number of other ARDEPPSes in which the target is operating and on the supernormal profits it stands to lose if rivals believe it can be pushed out or pushed around.

(2) The Determinants of the Non-Finance Cost of Predatory Pricing to the Predator

It is worth distinguishing at least four sets of determinants of the non-finance costs a predator must incur to make an established rival withdraw an existing QV investment from its ARDEPPS by practicing predatory pricing. The first relates to the size of the loss the predator must inflict on its target to drive it out altogether (or induce it to sell out to the predator on terms that are favorable to the latter). This set of factors does not depend on whether the predator and its target are pricing individually or on an across-the-board basis. These factors include (1) the amount of conventionally-measured profits the target would make on the QV investment in question absent predation and the extent to which the value of the target's assets would be reduced if it or someone else put them to their next-most-profitable use, (2) the amount of losses the target would sustain on its other QV-investment projects if it succumbed to predation because giving in would give it a reputation for weakness (would label it an easy mark), relatedly (3) the amount of extra profits the predator's target could realize on its other QV investments by resisting predation and thereby establishing a tough "don't tread on me" reputation, and (4) the size of the short-run loss the target is in a position to sustain (the extent of the target's retained earnings, the profits it will earn contemporaneously in other ARDEPPSes, and the ability of the target to obtain "outside" financing from banks, the general debt market, or the equity-capital market—an ability that tends to be reduced by the difficulty of explaining to "outsiders" that the losses the company is experiencing are the result of a predation campaign that is likely to be short-lived rather than of legitimate competition that is likely to be enduring).

The second set of relevant factors relates to the feasibility of practicing predatory pricing on a completely-individualized basis—that is, to the special costs the predator will have to incur to cut prices solely to those buyers that would otherwise have patronized its target. These factors include (1) the cost of identifying these buyers, (2) the mechanical cost of charging them separate prices, (3) the cost of preventing them from reselling or allowing them to resell the goods in question to other buyers that would otherwise have patronized the predator—(a) the difference between the predatory price to the target's customers and the price that would otherwise be the profit-maximizing price to the predator's own customers, (b) the costs the target's customers would have to incur to identify the predator's regular customers or other potential buyers of the predator's product, (c) the costs the target's customers would have to incur to retransport the good in question (the weight, awkwardness, fragility, and perishability of the good), (d) the feasibility or cost to the predator of altering the good supplied to the target's customers to make it unsuitable for the predator's own customers, and (e) the cost to the predator of preventing such resales (the cost of determining that such resales have been made—*e.g.*, the feasibility and cost of placing an identifying mark on the products sold to the target's customers—and the legality of resale bans or related restraints such as resale-price-maintenance clauses), (4) the costs the associated price-cuts impose on the predator by inducing its other customers to intensify their bargaining (by giving them a "fairness" argument for demanding a price-concession, by leaving the impression that other buyers they perceive [incorrectly] to be in a similar position to their own have succeeded in extracting better deals, and by appearing to undermine any claims the predator has made that cost-considerations precluded it from offering them lower prices), and (5) the legal costs the associated price-concessions would have to be expected to generate even if predation were not prohibited (because the concessions would still be discriminatory and would in the unusual circumstances in question actually violate the relevant jurisdiction's antitrust law even if they were not predatory).

The third set of determinants of the cost of predatory pricing to the predator relates to the non-contextual costs the predator must incur to inflict any given amount of harm on its target by engaging in individualized or across-the-board predatory price-cutting. I will focus initially on the non-contextual cost to a predator of inflicting any given amount of harm on its target through individualized predatory pricing. Fortunately, the relevant analysis is identical to Chap. 10's analysis of the harm-inflicted to loss-incurred ratio for retaliatory individualized price-cuts. Thus, if one assumes that the predator's target (1) charges individualized prices, (2) sets its price at its HNOP, (3) sets its price before the predator sets a price to its target's customers, and (4) will not be given the opportunity to beat any lower offer the predator makes, the harm the predator can inflict on the target by charging a predatory price that enables it to steal one of the target's customers will equal the difference between the target's HNOP and its OMC in its relations with the buyer in question while the loss the predator must suffer to inflict this harm will equal 1 cent *plus* the amount by which the predator is worse-than-second-placed to obtain the relevant buyer's patronage. If, on the other hand, the buyer in question gives the predator's target an opportunity to retain its patronage by beating the predator's offer (or at least an opportunity to retain its patronage by beating the predator's offer by some significant amount), the predator's price-cut will have reduced its target's profits by the sum of two amounts: (1) the price-cut the target had to make in response (the amount by which the predator's initial offer beat its target's initial offer *plus* the amount by which the buyer required the target to beat the predator—an amount that reflects the buyer's desire to encourage its inferior suppliers to beat what it may falsely assume was the target's oligopolistic price and to discourage the target from charging oligopolistic prices in the future) and (2) the pricing and contextual marginal costs the target had to incur to respond in this way (*e.g.*, the costs it had to incur because its price-cut led other customers to try to obtain similar concessions, perhaps by claiming that they also had received such concessions from an undercutter). In this case, the loss the predator will have to suffer to inflict the relevant harm will equal the sum of the market-research, mechanical, and contextual marginal costs of making the relevant offer.

The preceding results imply, *inter alia*, that the relevant harm-inflicted to loss-incurred ratio for offering any customer of the target a predatory price will depend on the probability that the relevant buyer will give its best-placed supplier (the target) an opportunity to rebid in this type of case. This probability will depend not only on the relevant buyer's need for speedy delivery but also on whether it is a repeat buyer, on whether the predator's undercutting offer leads the buyer to conclude that its best-placed supplier was trying to secure an oligopolistic price, and on whether information-conditions in the ARDEPPS in question make the buyer conclude that accepting the predator's underbid will benefit it by discouraging its best-placed supplier from pricing oligopolistically in the future and by encouraging its inferior suppliers to beat any future oligopolistic offers its best-placed supplier should make (by giving them the profits it assumes they will make by supplying it and avoiding the necessity of identifying them and thereby exposing them to retaliation).

In any case, *ceteris paribus*, the firm that is practicing individualized predatory pricing will minimize the direct loss it will have to incur to inflict the necessary amount of harm on its target by ranking the target's customers according to the weighted-average-expected or certainty-equivalent predatory-pricing harm-inflicted to loss-incurred ratio applicable to each and making price-cuts to the n highest-ranked customers in question where n is the number of such customers to which such prices must be offered for the requisite amount of harm to be inflicted on the predator's targets. I should perhaps add that predators that have more than one QV investment in the ARDEPPS in which their target is operating will usually find it cost-effective to set predatory prices on more than one product variant. I should also add that predators whose target has some QV investments the predator does not want to drive out as well as one or more QV investments it wishes to eliminate (or buy) will often find it cost-effective to cut their prices to customers of one or more of those of their target's products or outlets the predator is not seeking to eliminate or purchase.

If the predatory pricer finds it prohibitively expensive to individualize its predatory price-cuts, the relevant harm-inflicted to loss-incurred ratio will be the ratio for its privately-optimal across-the-board predatory price-cut. The good news is that

Chap. 10's analysis of the determinants of the harm-inflicted to loss-incurred ratio for across-the-board undermining and (to an admittedly-lesser extent) across-the-board retaliation applies in the current context as well. The bad news is that—as Chap. 10 showed—this analysis is very complex and hard to operationalize. Put crudely, the relevant ratio will be higher *inter alia* (1) the larger the target's average OCA in its relations with buyers it is best-placed to supply and the predator is second-placed or close-to-second-placed to supply, (2) the larger the number of times the predator is second-placed or close-to-second-placed to obtain its target's customers, (3) the smaller the average amount by which the predator is worse-than-second-placed to supply its target's customers when it is close-to-second-placed to supply its target's customers, and (4) the greater the ability of each individual potential predatory pricer to secure the predatory help of other potential predators or, at least, to prevent its predatory price-cutting from inducing rivals it is not seeking to drive out from retaliating against it—an ability whose determinants are the same as their counterparts for retaliation (which were analyzed in Chap. 10). At least in part because I think that predatory pricing is usually practiced on an individualized basis, I will not try to elaborate on this admittedly-partial analysis of the determinants of the varying harm-inflicted to loss-incurred ratio for various amounts of harm inflicted through across-the-board predatory pricing.

The fourth and final set of factors that influence the cost of predatory pricing (or indeed of predation in general) relates to the extra costs the predator may have to incur because its target tries to protect itself by retaliating against the predator's predation. Although such defensive retaliation will usually be costly to the predator's target, retaliation may be profitable for the target both because it may induce the predator to give up and because, regardless of whether it does, it may discourage other potential predators that have not yet invested resources and their reputation in a predation campaign against it from doing so (and, indeed, other potential retaliators to its undercutting from retaliating against it as well). In any event, although defensive retaliation will normally be costly to the target, it will tend to increase the cost the predator has to incur to inflict the necessary amount of harm on its target since the cost to the retaliating predation-target of inflicting some relevant amount of harm on the predator will be far lower than the losses the target would sustain if the predator chose to incur that amount of losses by engaging in additional acts of predatory pricing. The ratio of the harm the predator's target can inflict on the predator to the short-run loss it will have to incur to do so will depend on the same factors that influenced the counterpart ratio for the predator's predatory pricing. Roughly speaking, then, in situations in which individualized retaliation is practicable, the harm-inflicted to loss-incurred ratio for each act of retaliation the predator's target undertakes will be positively related to the size of the overall competitive advantage the predator enjoys in relations with the customer in question and will be inversely related to the amount by which the target is worse-than-second-placed to supply the buyer involved, and the amount of harm the predator's target can inflict on the predator at any given harm-inflicted to loss-incurred ratio will increase with the number of buyers in each such predator-OCA/target-disadvantage-vis-à-vis-the-second-placed-supplier category. Obviously, a complete analysis of this set of factors would include a review of all the determinants of the profitability of individualized retaliation as well as of the cost-effectiveness of product-line or individual-product across-the-board retaliation. Equally obviously, the size of these costs to the predator will also depend on the determinants of the benefits its target can obtain by engaging in defensive retaliation—*inter alia*, the number of non-targeted QV investments it has to protect against predation and the frequency with which it takes advantage of opportunities to undercut rivals that are trying to contrive oligopolistic margins.

(3) The Determinants of the Benefits of Predatory Pricing

It is worth distinguishing three sets of determinants of the amount by which successful predatory pricing will increase the predator's profits in the post-predation period. The first relates to the amount by which successful predation would increase the predator's post-predation profits if (1) reputational consequences could be ignored and (2) the exiting target's assets were not bought up or replaced by any rival of the predator (and the exiting target could not re-enter so easily as it could have continued to operate in the first place). The second relates to the extra profits predation will enable its practitioner to obtain by altering its reputation. And the third relates to the extent to which the profits that predation enables its practitioner to realize in the ARDEPPS directly concerned are reduced by any new QV investments its target's departure would induce other remaining established or potential competitors to make if it did not deter them from doing so.

Three subsets of factors affect the long-run gains predation would generate if it did not affect the predator's reputation or anyone else's QV-investment decisions: those that relate to the predator's HNOP – OMC gaps in individualized-pricing contexts and its HNOP – MC gap if neither it nor any of its rivals engaged in oligopolistic pricing in across-the-board-pricing contexts, those that relate to its natural oligopolistic margins, and those that relate to its contrived oligopolistic margins. I will analyze these three subsets of factors first in individualized-pricing contexts and then in across-the-board-pricing contexts.

If the exit of the predator's target does not induce anyone else to make a QV investment, predation that takes place in an individualized-pricing context will increase the sum of the predator's HNOP – MC gaps in its relations with buyers it is best-placed to supply (in particular, the sum of its OCAs) even if it does not alter its own QV investments by the sum of (1) the amounts by which the target was better-placed than the third-placed suppliers of those buyers that the predator was originally best-placed to obtain and the target was originally second-placed to supply, (2) the amounts by which the predator was better-placed than any remaining rival to obtain the patronage of those buyers that its target was originally best-placed to obtain and the predator was originally second-placed to supply, and (3) the amounts by which the target's exit increases the predator's OCAs by increasing the contextual marginal costs of surviving rivals. Predation will increase the CMCs that the predator's remaining rivals will have to incur to match the predator's HNOP-containing offers to the predator's own customers to the extent that it increases the prices the rivals charge those of their own customers that (1) the predator's target was originally second-placed to supply or (2) the predator was originally second-placed to supply (since by increasing the predator's OCAs and prices to its own customers, predation will increase the CMC the predator will have to incur to beat various offers these remaining rivals might make). (Admittedly, predation will tend to reduce the OMCs the predator's remaining rivals will have to incur to match its HNOP-containing offers to its own customers to the extent that they were originally second-placed to supply the target's customers and their average post-predation HNOP to these buyers is lower than their average HNOP to those buyers they supplied pre-predation, but I assume the effect delineated in the preceding sentence will usually outweigh this effect.) In any event, this increase in the predator's remaining rivals' relevant CMC will raise its OCAs and hence the prices it can obtain from all buyers that (1) these rivals were originally second-best-placed and the predator was originally best-placed to supply, (2) these rivals were originally third-placed, the predator was originally best-placed, and its target was originally second-placed to supply, and (3) these rivals were originally third-placed, the predator was originally second-placed, and the target was originally best-placed to supply. The preceding results imply that, on our current assumptions the gains predation will generate for an individualized-pricing predator in the long run by increasing its OCAs will increase with the following factors: (1) the number of the predator's customers its target was originally second-best-placed to supply, (2) the average amount by which this target was better-placed than any remaining rival to supply those of the predator's customers it was second-placed to supply, (3) the number of the target's customers the predator was originally second-placed to supply, (4) the average amount by which, pre-predation, the predator was better-placed than the third-placed supplier of those of its target's customers that it was second-placed to supply, (5) the frequency with which the predator's target was the closest competitor of another rival of the predator that was either second-placed to obtain one or more of the predator's customers or third-placed to obtain the patronage of one or more buyers that the predator and its target were respectively best-placed and second-placed to supply or *vice versa* (which determines the frequency with which the target's exit will increase the predator's OCA by raising the prices that the non-target rival that would have been its closest competitor for some buyer's patronage post-exit charged its own customers and hence the contextual marginal costs that rival had to incur to match or beat what would otherwise have been the predator's post-exit HNOP), and (6) the amount by which the predator's target was the closest competitor (was better-placed than the next-closest competitor) of the just-described surviving rivals of the predator (which determines in those cases in which it has the following effect the average amount by which the target's exit will increase the predator's OCAs by raising the CMCs of the firms that would otherwise have been the predator's closest competitor for particular buyers' patronage post-exit by raising their OCAs in their relations with their own customers and hence the prices they charge those buyers).

So far, the analysis has implicitly assumed that the predator will not respond to its target's exit by altering the products or distributive services it offers the public—*e.g.*, by changing the location of its distributive outlets. Obviously, even if as we are currently assuming no-one else responded to the target's exit by adding to or changing its QV investments, the profitability of predation will also depend on the extent to which the target's exit enables the predator to increase its profits by increasing its competitive advantages (and perhaps its OMs as well) by altering its QV investments to take advantage of the target's departure.

A comparable analysis can be undertaken for across-the-board-pricing contexts, though, as I have repeatedly emphasized, the relevant points are far more complex to articulate (primarily because they focus on the overall positions of the relevant parties in the ARDEPPS in question rather than on their positions in their relations with specific individual customers). Once more, because I think that predatory pricing is normally individualized, I will deal only briefly with the determinants of the effect of across-the-board predatory pricing on the closest thing to a counterpart to an individualized-pricing predator's HNOP-OMC gaps—the gap between an across-the-board-pricing predator's MC and the prices it would find most profitable to charge if it did not engage in oligographic pricing.

Subsection 1B of Chap. 2 discussed various factors that determine the magnitude of this gap an across-the-board pricer. At this juncture, it may be useful to provide an alternative account of this gap that is misleading in one respect (*viz.*, in that its reference to the "relevance" of the average BCA the relevant firm enjoys when dealing for the patronage of those buyers in relations with which it has a BCA is inexact though informative) and more complete in another respect (*viz.*, in that it recognizes that the NOMs a firm's rivals can obtain and the COMs that its rivals would obtain absent its collaboration will affect the amount by which the MC gap in question exceeds the seller's average [positive] BCA by affecting the amount by which its rivals' across-the-board prices to all buyers would exceed their MCs if it would not collaborate with any attempt they made to contrive oligopolistic prices).

This new account distinguishes two components of this gap:

(1) the gap that would exist if such a predator's rivals charged its potential customers' prices equal to their respective conventional marginal costs and
(2) the additional amount by which the across-the-board-pricing predator's relevant price exceeds its MC because its rivals charge its prospective customers' prices that exceed their respective marginal costs.

As we saw, the first of these two components will tend to increase (put crudely) with the average BCA the seller has when dealing for the patronage of those buyers in relation to which it has a BCA. Roughly speaking, the second component increases with the seller's own average BCA when it has a BCA (which determines the amount by which it would charge supra-marginal-cost prices to buyers in relation to which a rival had a BCA even if its rivals all charged prices equal to their marginal costs), the average BCAs its rivals enjoy when dealing for the patronage of buyers in relation to which they have BCAs, the order in which its rivals lock themselves in to particular prices (by advertising those prices, putting price tags on products and store shelves, and making sales at the prices in question)—in particular, whether rivals that are second-placed or close-to-second-placed more often than they are best-placed lock themselves in to high prices early in a price-round, the average NOM its rivals obtain, and the average COM its rivals would obtain without its collaboration.

In any event, on the assumption that the exit or sell-out of an across-the-board-pricing predator's target would not induce anyone else to alter their QV-investment decisions if the predator did nothing to prevent such a response, the amount by which the predator's successful predation will increase the gap between the price the predator would find most profitable to change if it did not engage in oligopolistic pricing and its marginal cost will be greater

(1) the greater the percentage of the buyers in relation to which (A) the predator had a BCA and (B) the target had the smallest BCD,
(2) the greater the average amount by which the BCD of the target when it had the smallest BCD and the predator had a BCA was lower than the BCD of the firm that had the second-lowest BCD,
(3) the greater the percentage of the buyers in relation to which (A) a close competitor of the predator had a BCA and (B) the target had the smallest BCD,
(4) the greater the average amount by which the BCD of the target when the target had the smallest BCD and a close competitor of the predator had a BCA was lower than the BCD of the firm that had the second-lowest BCD,
(5) the higher the ratio of (the number of buyers in relation to which the target had the lowest BCD or close-to-the-lowest BCD) to (the number of buyers in relation to which the target had a BCA) and the later in any pricing round that the target locked itself into a price,
(6) the lower the willingness of the target to collaborate with the predator's rivals' contrived oligopolistic pricing, and
(7) the greater the extent to which the target's exit enables the predator to increase its BCAs by shifting the product-space location of one or more of its QV investments.

The second set of determinants of the profits that predatory pricing would yield an across-the-board pricer if it did not affect the reputation of the predator for carrying out predatory or retaliatory threats and if the exit of the predator's target would not induce anyone else to make a QV investment in the relevant ARDEPPS relates to any tendency such predation may have to enable the predator to profit by increasing its natural oligopolistic margins. In general, the amount by which predatory pricing increases such a practitioner's profits by enabling it to increase its NOMs will increase with (1) the extent to which the predator's predatory pricing gives it a prominence that enhances its ability to initiate a series of premature price announcements that will make natural oligopolistic pricing feasible, (2) the extent to which the additional sales the predation allows the predator to obtain enables it to take advantage of economies of scale that reduce the per-unit cost to it of changing its initially-announced price (*i.e.*, of changing its advertising, informing its distributors of the price-change, and altering the price tags on its product—all of which possibilities will be more important in across-the-board-pricing situations), (3) the extent to which the predation gives the predator a tough reputation, which reduces the tendency of any change it makes in its initially-announced price to make buyers assume that it will reduce its initially-announced prices in the future as well, and (4) the extent to which it increases the predator's OCAs and concomitantly the frequency with which the cost it must incur to change its initially-announced price falls below the profits it could have made by supplying the buyer in question in an individualized-pricing context and the buyers in question in an across-the-board pricing context at the reduced price at which it could retain the relevant sale or sales after its undercutting rival had beaten its initial offer had it charged the price in question in the first place.

The third set of factors that affect the profits that predatory pricing would generate if it would not increase the credibility of the predator's threats of predation and would not induce anyone else to introduce any new QV investments post-predation relates to the original impact of the target on the ability of the predator to contrive oligopolistic margins. Obviously, predation can contribute to the predator's profits in this way only when contrived oligopolistic pricing is profitable post-predation. Accordingly, the likely impact of predation on the predator's contrived oligopolistic margins will depend on all the factors that influence the profitability of such pricing and not just on the factors that might be affected by predation itself. As Chap. 10 indicated, both the determinants of the pre-predation profitability of the predator's contriving oligopolistic prices and the determinants of the impact of predation on the profitability of the predator's engaging in contrived oligopolistic pricing will depend on whether the predator and its rivals set their prices on an individualized or across-the-board basis. Since the general determinants of the profitability of contrived oligopolistic pricing were examined in exhaustive detail in Chap. 10, I will confine myself here to examining the possible impact of predation on the oligopolistic margins the predator will contrive.

In individualized-pricing contexts, predatory pricing that induces the target to exit or sell out to the predator at a distressed price and thereby simultaneously increases the predator's OCAs, NOMs, and sales will tend to have the following effects on the predator's COMs: (1) increase its COMs by increasing its ability to communicate its intention to engage in contrivance more cheaply simply by charging a contrived oligopolistic price by making the predator's rivals aware of its tendency to make strategic moves; (2) increase its COMs by reducing the number of potential undercutters to which it must communicate its anticompetitive threats and promises (when the target was part of a larger group of firms that were second-placed or close-to-second-placed to obtain the predator's customer) or decrease its COMs by increasing the number of potential undercutters to which the predator must communicate its anticompetitive threats and promises (when the target was originally the predator's closest competitor for a particular buyer's patronage and two or more rivals that were originally much-worse-placed than the target were originally third-placed or close-to-third-placed to secure the relevant buyer's patronage); (3) increase its COMs by increasing its sales and hence its ability to detect secret undercutting from circumstantial evidence about the relationship between the sales it actually made to its own customers, other sellers' customers, and new buyers and the sales it would expect to make to these categories of buyers if no-one engaged in undercutting from a position of competitive inferiority; (4) increase its COMs when it buys out its target by increasing its ability to identify its undercutter by enabling it to pool information about various surviving rivals' positions in relation to its customers and dispositions to engage in undercutting (from a position of competitive inferiority); (5) increase or decrease its COMs by decreasing or increasing the number of independent rivals that would find it inherently profitable to undercut its contrived oligopolistic price (that were worse-than-second-placed by a smaller amount than the COM it was seeking to obtain)—see the entry after "(2)" above; (6) increase its COMs by reducing the cost to it of inflicting any given amount of harm on particular potential undercutters by increasing its potential undercutters' BCAs (by eliminating the target [that was sometimes these rivals' closest competitor], by increasing its own CMCs by raising its OCAs, and by raising other rivals' CMCs by raising their OCAs by eliminating the target, increasing its OCAs, and increasing other rivals' OCAs); (7) increase or decrease its COMs by increasing or decreasing the ratio of the number of times that it is or is close to being a rival's closest competitor to the number of times that the rival is or is close to being its closest competitor; (8) increase its COMs by increasing the amount of benefits it can confer on a potential undercutter by reciprocating to its cooperation by increasing the frequency with which and amount by which it is a given rival's closest competitor (by eliminating the target); (9) increase its COMs by increasing the credibility of its anticompetitive retaliatory threats and reciprocatory promises by demonstrating its commitment to carrying out strategic threats and fulfilling strategic promises; (10) increase its COMs by increasing its average OCA and the number of customers it is best-placed to supply, hence its stake in deterring undercutting, and hence the credibility of its anticompetitive threats and promises; and (11) decrease its COMs by increasing its OCAs and NOMs and hence the amount of safe profits it must put at risk to contrive an oligopolistic margin. Although predatory pricing therefore tends to reduce the predator's COMs in some ways and to increase them in others and although even the sign of the net impact of such pricing on the predator's COMs will no doubt vary from case to case, I suspect that in general predatory pricing will tend to increase the profits the predator realizes by engaging in contrived oligopolistic pricing in individualized-pricing contexts.

For reasons that Chap. 10 should enable you to anticipate, with two exceptions, the analysis of the effect of successful predation on the COMs of across-the-board-pricing predators is similar to its counterpart for individualized-pricing predators. The two exceptions are: (1) those effects that relate to an individualized pricer's ability to determine that it has been undercut and to identify its undercutter are irrelevant in across-the-board-pricing contexts since in such situations sales-transactions are by definition easily observed and (2) in across-the-board-pricing contexts, the exit of the predator's target may also affect the predator's COMs by affecting its ability to induce its rivals not to respond to its retaliation as if that retaliation were an act of general aggressive pricing (as well, perhaps, by increasing its ability to engage in collaborative retaliation).

The second set of benefits predatory pricing can confer on the predator relate to its reputation for engaging in strategic behavior in general and predatory behavior in particular. I have already commented on the tendency of predatory pricing to increase the predator's profits by increasing the credibility of its threats to retaliate against undercutting and reciprocate to its rivals' cooperative pricing-moves. Predatory pricing will also tend to increase the predator's profits to the extent that it reduces the probability that firms whose prices it undercuts or undermines will retaliate against it. Finally, predatory pricing will increase the predator's profits as well to the extent that it increases the credibility of its threats of predation—*i.e.*, to the extent that it induces other rivals it wishes to drive out to exit more quickly or sell out more quickly and more cheaply. Admittedly, the reputational advantages of waging a successful predation campaign will be offset to the extent that such conduct leaves a suspicious trail that increases the probability that enforcement authorities (possible private plaintiffs) will detect, prosecute (sue), and convict (obtain a verdict against) the predator should it choose to engage in similar behavior in the future. On balance, though, I suspect that a successful campaign of predation will tend to raise future profits in the way just described.

Unfortunately, however, I do not have a great deal to say about the factors that determine the extent of such reputational gains. Clearly, they will tend to be larger for companies that sell many products or operate many outlets in the ARDEPPS in question as well as for predators that operate in many different ARDEPPSes (to the extent that predation generates a company-wide reputation that also affects the behavior of the predator's rivals in other ARDEPPSes than those in which it was practiced). In general, the greater the number of occasions on which the predator has the opportunity to profit by engaging in predation or contrived oligopolistic pricing or by undercutting some rival's contrived oligopolistic prices, the greater the extent to which a successful predatory-pricing campaign is likely to increase its profits by enhancing its reputation.

So far, we have assumed that no firm other than the predator would respond to the target's exit by altering the amount or character of its QV investments in the ARDEPPS in question. Obviously, even if the predator's targets cannot reenter, no potential competitor is in a position to enter, and the predator's remaining established rivals do not increase the number of products they offer, outlets they operate, or speed of service they supply, a successful predation campaign will increase the predator's OCAs to a smaller extent and will affect its COMs to a different extent if its remaining established rivals alter their products to bring them closer to the position in product-space previously occupied by the offerings of the predator's target. More importantly, the profitability of predatory pricing will also be inversely related to the amount of additional QV investments that the target's exit would make it profitable for one or more of the predator's established or potential competitors to make if it did not expand and directly related to (1) the extent to which such additional rival QV investments would be further away in product-space from the predator's projects than those of its exited target and (2) the length of time between the date of the target's exit and the date on which such exit-induced rival projects would be operative. In any event, if the target's exit induces such other parties to make additional QV investments, the original increase in the predator's OCAs, NOMS, and COMs will be reduced on that account. And if the predator itself expands its product or distributive line or adds to its capacity or inventory to deter similar QV investments by others, the contribution the predation makes to its supernormal profits post-predation will be reduced on that account since, by definition, such limit investments would not have been profitable but for their tendency to forestall similar investments by others.

In general, the amount by which the profitability of predation is reduced by the tendency of the exit to make it profitable for others to make new QV investments in the relevant ARDEPPS will depend not only on (1) the speed with which the predator's remaining established and potential rivals can react to the target's exit but also on (2) the extent to which the best-placed potential expander or potential competitor are worse-placed to expand in or enter into the part of the ARDEPPS in which the predator's target was operating than the target was to continue its operations and (3) the likelihood that such remaining actual and potential rivals would find it more profitable to enter into a part of the ARDEPPS that was further away in product-space from the predator's projects. I will now address the last two of these three factors in turn.

Two points need to be made about the extent to which the relevant best-placed potential expander or entrant is worse-placed to enter into the target's specific area of product-space than the target was to continue to operate in it. The first is that this factor cannot be equated with the "barriers to expansion or entry" facing the established firm or potential competitor in question, regardless of whether one defines the enquoted expression my way or in the more conventional way popularized by Joe Bain according to which a potential competitor is said to face a barrier to entry to the extent that its post-entry costs will be higher than the technological minimum average total cost of producing a non-differentiated and unpromoted product or to the extent that the entry is expected to reduce prices in the "market" in question.[556] More specifically, this worse-placed-than-the-target factor is not the same as the relevant barriers in my sense in part because those "barriers" do not include the monopolistic QV-investment incentives, monopolistic QV-investment disincentives, and natural oligopolistic QV-investment disincentives that a relevant potential expander might face but primarily because my barriers refer to (A) the difference between (1) the lifetime supernormal rate-of-return that the potential expander or entrant should expect to realize on the relevant QV investment and (2) the lifetime supernormal rate-of-return that would be yielded by the ARDEPPS' most-profitable projects if conditions were static and no entry or expansion took place and not to (B) the difference between the figure delineated after "(1)" above and (3) the supernormal rate-of-return the targeted QV investment would have yielded absent predation from the date on

---

[556] JOE S. BAIN, BARRIERS TO NEW COMPETITION 12–19 (hereinafter BAIN BARRIERS) (Harvard Univ. Press, 1956).

which the predation began. The worse-placed-than-the-target factor is also not the same as the barriers that Bain would say faced the relevant potential entrant or expander: since the target's costs were almost certainly above technological minimum average total cost of production, the relevant QV investor's disadvantage vis-à-vis the target will be smaller than the Bainian barriers to entry or expansion they face.

The second point that needs to be made about the worse-placed-than-the-target factor relates to the fact that the amount by which the relevant investor is worse-placed than the target will tend to increase with the extent to which the target possessed certain assets and attributes (including brand associations and reputations) that the relevant potential investor could not duplicate independently at the same cost or buy from it directly. When such unique assets or attributes do play a role, the profits the predator realizes will be substantially affected by whether it can buy up its target's patents, trademarks, unique locations, or unusually-knowledgeable managers and employees at distressed prices. The predator may be able to make profitable purchases of this kind (1) because it is likely to be aware of the significance of these assets sooner than are its rivals, (2) because the value of these assets may be much lower outside the relevant ARDEPPS, and (3) because the value of such assets to the predator—which includes the amount of extra competitive advantages, NOMs, and COMs they will enable it to secure on its other projects by deterring others from making effective QV investments—may be higher than their value to a target-successor—the amount of profits they would enable the successor to earn directly on the products or services they would enable it to supply in the ARDEPPS.

I want to make only one point about the determinants of the extent to which any exit-induced new QV investment in the ARDEPPS in question is located as close to the predator's projects as were the targeted QV investments. Obviously, *ceteris paribus*, the predator's predation will tend to induce any entering potential competitor or expanding established firm to locate further away from the predator than such a potential QV investor would otherwise find profitable even if it did not deter its entry or expansion.

* * *

Subsection 2C will discuss various arguments that economists and economically-literate law professors have made for their conclusion that predatory pricing would rarely if ever be profitable or practiced even if law-related costs could be ignored. The preceding discussion implies that the profitability of predatory pricing depends on the magnitudes of a large number of parameters. Although I do not have much more than armchair-empirical guesstimates of the values of those parameters, I want to state my own belief that, if predation were not prohibited by the law, it would frequently be profitable. This conclusion reflects my suspicion that sellers (1) often face one or more individual rivals whose operation reduces their BCAs and COMs to an unusual degree—rivals that would be unlikely to be replaced by someone equally as troublesome if they exited (both because the possible target possessed unique attributes that others could not replicate and because the predation would deter potential investors from trying to replicate those attributes [from locating as close to the predator as its target was])—and (2) often are in a position to drive those rivals out at non-prohibitive cost by engaging in individualized predatory price-cutting or a combination of such predatory pricing and predatory advertising (because they are better-placed to harm their target through price-cutting than *vice versa*, because they have more to gain by establishing a reputation for strategic behavior than their target has to gain by establishing a "don't tread on me reputation," and/or because they have a greater ability to withstand financial losses). Although I hesitate to say so, I do think that my experienced guesses on these matters deserve some weight.

B. The Argument That, at Least in Some Circumstances, Established Firms Will Find It Profitable to Practice Predation by Reducing Their Prices to Deter Entry

As I have already indicated, many economists claim that, at least in some circumstances, established firms will find it profitable to deter entry by charging so-called limit prices that are lower than the prices they would otherwise find not only possible but profitable to charge.[557] Although the economists, academic and practicing lawyers, and judges that subscribe to this "limit-pricing" hypothesis have never recognized this fact, limit pricing is, in reality, a variant of predatory pricing.[558] Proponents of limit-pricing theory disagree about the circumstances in

---

[557] Limit-price theory was first articulated in JOHN B. CLARK AND FRANKLIN H. GIDDINGS, THE MODERN DISTRIBUTIVE PROCESS 32 (Ginn & Co., 1888). It was next mentioned in ALFRED MARSHALL, INDUSTRY AND TRADE (Macmillan, 3d ed., 1920). Its real development began with Nicholas Kaldor, *Market Imperfections and Excess Capacity*, 2 ECONOMICA 33 (1935). It was developed further by Robert Triffin, MONOPOLISTIC COMPETITION AND GENERAL EQUILIBRIUM THEORY 122 (Harvard Univ. Press, 1940), PHILIP W.S. ANDREWS, MANUFACTURING BUSINESS 148 (Macmillan, 1949), ROY F. HARROD, ECONOMIC ESSAYS 179 (Macmillan, 1952), and J.R. Hicks, *The Process of Imperfect Competition*, 6 OX. ECON. PAPERS 41 (1954). The early work reached its apotheosis in BAIN BARRIERS and PAULO SYLOS-LABINI, OLIGOPOLY AND TECHNOLOGICAL PROGRESS 33 (Harvard Univ. Press, 1960). In my opinion, much of the subsequent work in this area reinvents the wheel, which it redescribes in game-theoretic or stochastic terms without noticing its deficiencies. See, *e.g.*, Darius Gaskins, *Dynamic Limit Pricing: Optimal Limit Pricing Under Threat of Entry*, 3 J. ECON. THEORY 306 (1971).

[558] Admittedly, if it were true that limit pricers would have to keep their prices permanently lower to deter entry, there might be a policy reason to treat this variant of predatory pricing differently from the way in which the standard type of predatory pricing, which always leads to price increases after the target exits, is treated. (I say "might be" because even on the above assumption the legal relevance of this difference would, at a minimum, be contestable.) In fact, however, the premise that limit pricers would have to keep their prices permanently low to deter entry will often be unrealistic: in the real world, the best-placed potential competitors whose entry the limit pricing would allegedly deter will, over time, come to face higher barriers to entry as they devote the resources they could have used to enter the ARDEPPS in question to other purposes. If this happens, the limit pricers would be able to raise their prices over time to reflect the increase over time in the barriers facing the best-placed potential entrant in the ARDEPPS (whose identity might also change over time). I hasten to add that the preceding discussion assumes *ad arguendo* that limit pricing will succeed in deterring entry, will be more profitable than other methods incumbents can use to deter entry, and will be more profitable than allowing entry to occur—three propositions that (as the text indicates) I believe are false.

which incumbents faced with the threat of entry will find limit pricing profitable. However, the standard version of the theory claims that firms will find it profitable to limit price when the best-placed potential competitor in their ARDEPPS faces substantial or high (as opposed to low to moderate) barriers to entry.

Chapter 13 will criticize limit-price theory in great detail in the course of discussing its implications for the legality of conglomerate mergers that eliminate best-placed or effective potential competitors. At this juncture, I will outline why I think that the limit-pricing variant of predatory pricing will rarely be profitable and list the exceptional conditions under which such pricing might conceivably be profitable.

I doubt the profitability of limit pricing for four reasons. First, I think that, except in unusual circumstances, limit pricing will have little if any effect on the probability of entry. None of the explanations for the alleged deterrent effect of limit pricing that the theory's proponents have offered strikes me as persuasive: thus, I suspect that limit pricing will rarely deceive the relevant best-placed potential competitor (which will often be an established firm working in a related "industry") into underestimating the height of the $H\Pi_E$ curve, will have only a small tendency to increase the risk barrier to entry by making the relevant potential entrant less certain about the prices the incumbents could manage to charge or the incumbents' costs, will rarely significantly increase the retaliation barrier to entry by communicating a threat of retaliation or making that threat more credible (by making retaliation less provable by enabling firms to retaliate simply by maintaining their pre-entry [limit] price), and will be unlikely to increase the profit-differential barrier by increasing the incumbents' goodwill. Second, I think that, even if limit pricing would be not only effective at deterring entry but more profitable than allowing entry to occur, it would be less profitable than other methods of deterring entry: communicating threats linguistically, creating goodwill by offering superior product-quality or service-quality, and (most importantly) making (limit) QV investments. Third, even if (contrary to my own beliefs) limit pricing would deter entry and would be the most-profitable (*i.e.*, least-unprofitable) method of deterring entry (except in unusual circumstances), it would be less profitable than allowing entry to occur. Even on the optimistic assumption that limit pricing that reduced the established firms' supernormal rates-or-return by the absolute percentage X% would reduce the potential entrant's estimate of its post-entry supernormal rate-of-return by X%, the limit-pricing highest supernormal profit-rate would be no higher than the post-entry highest supernormal profit-rate.

I can think of only two circumstances in which limit pricing might be not just more profitable than doing nothing to deter entry but the most-profitable method of deterring entry:

(1) when the possible limit pricer occupied a potentially-highly-profitable market niche whose existence no-one else recognized, the possible limit pricer's operations were far less efficient than the operation that an expanding incumbent or potential competitor could create, and the potential limit pricer could not profitably sell its knowledge of the existence of the profit-opportunity in question (because it could not protect itself against the prospective buyer's using the knowledge it conveyed without paying it for it) or
(2) the limit pricer had reason to believe that, if the profit-opportunity's existence became known, more QV investment would be made in the relevant area of product-space than it could contain in equilibrium, and some time would elapse before the privately-excess investment would be withdrawn or depreciated.

Although I do not deny that these conditions may sometimes be fulfilled, I suspect that they are, at most, rarely fulfilled.

In short, for the above reasons, I think that limit pricing is a theory in search of a phenomenon. In my judgment, the limit-pricing variant of predatory pricing is rarely if ever profitable or practiced.

C. Arguments That Economists or Economically-Literate Legal Academics Have Made for the Unprofitability of Predatory Pricing: Statements and Critiques

(1) The Argument That Predatory Pricing Will Rarely or Never Be Profitable Because the Direct Cost of Predatory Price-Cutting Will Always Be Prohibitive

Some scholars[559] have tried to prove that predatory pricing is rarely if ever practiced by analyzing the direct cost to a potential predator of inflicting sufficient

[559] See, *e.g.*, Frank Easterbrook, *Predatory Strategies and Counterstrategies*, 48 U. CHI. L. REV. 263 (1981). Easterbrook also argues that the probable effectiveness and profitability of predatory pricing will be substantially and often critically reduced by the ability of a target that would operate profitably absent predation to survive by obtaining external financing. See *id.* at 269. For two reasons, this possibility seems less significant to me than to Easterbrook. First, a firm that could have operated profitably had it not been the target of predatory moves might not be able to break even after receiving such external financing once a predatory campaign has been initiated against it. In part, this conclusion reflects the fact that the predator may continue its campaign even after the external financer renders it unprofitable in itself to deter potential external financers of its

harm on its target to drive it out (the loss it would have to incur in the short run to do so) and arguing that it is extremely likely that the target would be replaced too soon for the extra profits the predatory pricing would enable the predator to realize post-exit to compensate it for the pre-exit direct cost of its predation. In my judgment, these analyses are deficient in five major respects.

First, they are usually based on the unrealistic assumption that the predatory price cuts in question will be across-the-board price cuts. In practice, I suspect, most predatory pricing is individualized, and even those sellers whose predation involves reductions in across-the-board prices will tend to reduce their prices primarily on products or in outlets with unusually-high ratios of (1) the number of times the product or outlet in question is at a small BCD in relation to buyers the target is best-placed to supply to (2) the number of times it is best-placed.

Second, because these analyses tend to ignore the reality of monopolistic competition and the related possibility that a particular rival may have a dramatic effect on even a small firm's BCAs, they tend to assume that predatory pricing will be profitable only for firms with large market shares—*i.e.*, only for firms whose across-the-board predatory price-cuts would cost them more relative to the gains they could obtain by driving a rival out than would the across-the-board price-cuts of a seller that faced a lower ratio of (sales the seller could have retained at a non-predatory price) to (extra sales the predator could obtain in both the short run and the long run by charging a predatory price).

Third, because these analyses ignore the fact that the different products within a given area of product-space are not all equally competitive with each other, they ignore the possibility that predation may succeed and be profitable without driving its target out altogether by inducing its target to move its investments further away in product-space from the predator's product variants.

Fourth, and relatedly, these analyses tend to underestimate the probability that predation may be profitable even when the exited firm is replaced because the replacement-investment is further away in product-space from the predator's product variants than were the investments of its target. This result will tend to obtain both (1) when the potential expanders or entrants that make the

future targets from supplying them with capital. (Admittedly, however, one would also have to take account of the offsetting, long-run stake that the external financers may have in developing a reputation for hanging tough to induce predators whose predation led the financer's customers to seek financial help to cease their predation once it has supplied the relevant targets with assistance.) Second, a predation-target to which financing could be profitably supplied if perfect information about its situation were costlessly available may be precluded from securing such financing by the impacted character of the relevant information—by the cost or impossibility of proving the profitability of the relevant loan or capital infusion to an external financer, of demonstrating to an outsider (*inter alia*) that the firm seeking capital would be profitable if predation stopped.

replacement-investments would locate further away in product-space from the predator's QV investments than did the predator's targets for reasons that are unrelated to the predator's possible reactions to their location-decisions (*e.g.*, for reasons that relate to the difference between the Π_D barriers that they and the target would face on different projects) and (2) when the predation induces the replacement-investors to locate their new investments further from the predator's projects than is inherently profitable, by leading them to conclude that the retaliation barrier they face on their investment will increase with its proximity to the predator's projects.

Fifth, these analyses tend to ignore the possibility that predatory pricing may also increase the predator's profits by raising its ability (1) to induce other rivals in the same or other ARDEPPSes to exit, to remain outside the ARDEPPSes in which it operates, or to locate their operations further away from it in product-space, (2) to contrive oligopolistic prices, or (3) to undercut its rivals' contrived oligopolistic prices without inducing its undercut rivals to retaliate against it.

In short, because I believe that these analyses exaggerate the direct costs of predatory pricing and underestimate the weighted-average-expected long-run gains it will generate, I am not persuaded that predatory pricing will rarely be practiced because predatory pricers will rarely be able to recoup the direct cost of their predation in the post-exit period.

(2) The Argument That Predatory Pricing Will Rarely or Never Be Practiced Because It Will Almost Always Be Less Profitable Than Buying the Rival Out[560]

I have two objections to this argument. The first is that it ignores the antitrust-"penalties" cost of such anticompetitive horizontal acquisitions or mergers. Admittedly, predatory pricing is also illegal and costly on that account. However, as Section 3 of this chapter will reveal, it will often be very difficult for the State or a private plaintiff to prove the predatory character of a seller's predatory pricing. In my judgment, it will usually be much easier to demonstrate the illegality of such an acquisition than of the predatory pricing it is designed to obviate and that, concomitantly, the law-related cost of the acquisition is likely to be much higher than the law-related cost of the predatory pricing.

The second objection to this argument is its either/or character. In some cases, sellers will combine predatory pricing with attempts to buy up their target at a distressed price though, admittedly, such attempts will provide the State or a private plaintiff with behavioral evidence to support their predatory-pricing claim.

[560] This argument was first made in John McGee, *Predatory Price Cutting: The Standard Oil (N.J.) Case*, 1 J. LAW & ECON. 137 (1958).

(3) The Argument That Predatory Pricing Will Never Be Profitable Because the Predatory Threat Will Never Be Credible in a Finite Game of Complete and Perfect Information

This is a clever argument that was actually made[561] to criticize the "limit-pricing" hypothesis that predatory pricing can be a profitable response to the threat of entry (or, though its supporters never adverted to this possibility, to the threat of a QV-investment expansion by an established rival). The argument has been summarized in the following way:

> Consider the last entrant. It knows that if it enters and meets predation, it would have been better off to stay out. But it also knows that, if faced by actual entry, the established firm is strictly better off if it behaves nonaggressively. Thus, assuming that both firms will always act in their own best interests, entry will occur in the last market to be threatened and will meet a nonaggressive response. Moreover, this will be the result, no matter what has been the history of play to this point.
>
> Now consider the second-last market to be threatened. If entry were to occur there and if the chain store could deter entry in the last market by adopting predatory practices, it might well adopt such measures. However, as just shown, the outcome in the last market is completely determined, independent of the outcome in the second-last market. Thus, if entry occurs, the chain store will share the second-last market peacefully, and, thus, too, entry will occur in this market.
>
> The induction is inexorable and the conclusion clear: in equilibrium, predation will never be practiced. Moreover, even if (for whatever reason) the chain store were observed to have preyed repeatedly against every previous entrant, the logic still will lead the next entrant to anticipate not that past behavior will be repeated but rather that its entry will meet a nonaggressive response. Repeated observations of behavior which, *a priori*, the entrant expected never to see cannot and do not shake its absolute confidence in its predictions of future behavior.[562]

However, although this ingenious argument is not weakened by the conceptual distinctions this study emphasizes, it is not in the end persuasive. In part, its force is vitiated by its assumption "that it is *common knowledge*. . .that accommodation is the best response to entry and that entry is the best response to accommodation"—an assumption that is unrealistic in the real world in which games of this kind are played by players that do not have "complete and perfect information. . .about the structure of the tree describing the game being played, about the payoffs accruing to all players and about the others' past acts."[563] But, in my judgment, primarily, it is vitiated by its

---

[561] See Reinhard Selten, *The Chain-Store Paradox*, 9 THEORY AND DECISION 127 (1978).

[562] The summary is taken from Paul Milgrom and John Roberts, *Predation, Reputation, and Entry Deterrence*, 27 J. ECON. THEORY 280, 283 (1982).

[563] *Id.*

assumption that the game in question is a finite (time-limited) game and that the equilibrium that will be established is a static equilibrium. Since, in reality, the companies that are players in the relevant game have infinite lives and the equilibria in the ARDEPPSes in which they participate vary through time—are dynamic rather than static, there never will be "a last entrant" and the induction in question will never take place.

I am tempted to respond to this argument with the words that one of my university professors frequently used to criticize my literary interpretations: "ingenious but doubtful."

(4) The Assumption That Predatory Pricing Will Be Profitable Only for (Dominant) Firms with Monopoly Power and Only When "Conditions of Entry" Are Difficult (or "Barriers to Entry" Are High)

Both these assumptions have been adopted by most predatory-pricing analysts—usually without argument. For example, Joskow and Klevorick adopt both in their analysis of the way in which predatory-pricing cases should be handled.[564] In my judgment, both are incorrect.

I will focus first on the claim that predatory pricing will be profitable only for firms with monopoly power or for dominant firms. Strictly speaking, one should distinguish (1) among a firm's monopoly power, oligopoly power, and market power over price and (2) between a firm's power over price and "power over" QV investment. As Chap. 8 argued, a firm's monopoly power over price should be defined operationally in terms of its OCAs; a firm's oligopoly power over price should be defined in terms of its NOMs and COMs; a firm's market power over price should be defined to reflect not only its monopoly and oligopoly power over price but other things that enable it to charge prices in excess of its conventional marginal costs; a firms' monopoly power over QV investment should be defined in terms of the lifetime supernormal profit-rate it can realize on its various QV-investment projects because its ARDEPPS' potential entrants and expanders face Π_D, R, and S barriers; a firm's oligopoly power over QV investment should be defined in terms of the lifetime supernormal profit-rate it can realize on its various QV-investment projects because its ARDEPPS' potential entrants and expanders confront L barriers and natural oligopolistic QV-investment disincentives (*O*) that reflect its ability to expand; and a firm's

[564] See Paul Joskow and Alvin Klevorick, *A Framework for Analyzing Predatory Pricing Policy* (hereinafter Joskow and Klevorick), 89 YALE L. J. 213, 244, 227–31 respectively (1979).

market power over QV investment should be defined to reflect not only its monopoly and oligopoly power over QV investment but other sources of its ability to earn supernormal rates-of-return in the ARDEPPS (other sources that Chap. 8 delineated). When predatory-pricing scholars refer to a potential predator's "monopoly power," they are really referring to the sum of its monopoly and oligopoly power over price—*i.e.*, the gap between its (P = HNOP + NOM + COM) and its OMC (though they ignore CMC and therefore assume that OMC = MC).

The claim that predatory pricing will be profitable only for firms that have considerable "monopoly power" as well as the claim that the profitability of predatory pricing is positively and strongly correlated with the potential predator's total (market) power is unjustified. I have heard economists and economically-sophisticated legal academics make three arguments for using a "prior possession of market power" filter in predation cases. The first focuses on the fact that predation (like all other forms of monopolization) is costly to its practitioner in the short run and claims that firms that do not have market power in the area of product-space in which predation was allegedly practiced could not have financed such conduct (or, at least, were sufficiently unlikely to be able to have financed predation to justify the dismissal of the predation case against them). I reject this argument because a firm that has no market power in the area of product-space in which the predation was alleged to have been practiced could finance the cost of that predation from normal profits earned in the relevant area of product-space, from normal or supernormal profits it was earning in other areas of product-space in which it was operating, from retained earnings regardless of where they were earned or whether they were supernormal when earned, and through external financing obtained without or by informing their source of its illegal intent.

The second and third arguments that have been made for using a "prior possession of market power" filter in predation cases both claim that firms that do not have market power cannot obtain benefits by engaging in predation (or, if I want to be generous, are sufficiently unlikely to be able to obtain benefits from predation to warrant the dismissal of the predation case against them). The first of these arguments asserts that a firm without market power will not be able to benefit even in the short run by driving a rival out because any rival such a firm could drive out would not be better-placed to obtain the perpetrator's customers than a large number of other rivals were and would not be either best-placed to supply any buyer that the perpetrator was uniquely second-placed to supply or equal-best-placed together with the predator and no-one else to supply any buyer. The second of these arguments asserts that, even if a firm without market power could obtain short-run benefits by driving a rival out, it could not retain a significant amount of the benefits in the medium or long run because the QV investment of any rival a firm without market power induced to withdraw would be quickly replaced by an equally-competitive QV investment of another rival.

Admittedly, these two conclusions would be correct if firms without market power always were operating in perfectly-competitive environments. However, in the real world, firms without market power will usually not be perfect competitors, and, when they are not, neither of the claims in question will be justified.

I will start by assessing the short-run-benefit claim. In relation to this claim, the critical facts are: (1) a firm that has no significant BCAs may be in this position because a particular rival (A) was second-placed and far better-placed than any other rival to supply a substantial percentage of the buyers the firm in question was best-placed to supply and (B) was best-placed to supply a substantial number of buyers the firm in question was second-placed and far-better-than-third-placed to supply or equal-best-placed together with the predator and no-one else to supply a significant number of buyers whose third-placed supplier(s) were far-worse-than-best-placed; (2) an across-the-board pricer whose HNOP is close to its MC may be in a position in which a particular rival that is second-placed in BCA terms or close-to-second-placed in such terms far more often than it is best-placed in such terms has substantially reduced its (and its other rivals') HNOPs by refusing to lock itself into a high price early in a pricing round (by announcing and advertising its price, inducing its distributors to tag its product with related resale prices, to place prices for its product on their shelves, and to enter its product's prices into their computers, and to make sales of its product at the announced price); and (3) an across-the-board or individualized pricer that is obtaining low or no COMs may be in a position in which a particular maverick rival kept it (and its other rivals) from obtaining significantly-higher contrived oligopolistic margins by undercutting or undermining its (their) contrived oligopolistic prices. I recognize that the significance of these possibilities depends on the frequency with which they arise or, less demandingly, on the correlation between the extent to which a rival reduces a potential predator's profits on these accounts and the potential predator's pre-existing market power. I can present no empirical evidence on this issue. But, for what it's worth, I am confident that the correlation between a firm's pre-existing market power and its ability to profit in the short run by driving a particular rival out is far too low for the "pre-existing market power" filter to be desirable for this reason even if moral-and-related-legal-rights considerations could be ignored. In any event, it seems clear to me that the proponents of the "pre-existing market power" filter should bear the burden of production and persuasion on this short-run-benefit issue.

I also do not think that one can justify the "pre-existing market power filter" by demonstrating that the percentage of the short-run gains that a predator will be able to obtain by driving a rival out that will be eliminated by the prospect or reality of new entry or established-rival QV-investment expansions will be inversely related to the predator's pre-existing market power. A predator's market power over QV investment is a function of the average amount by which the barriers and QV-investment disincentives it faced on its QV investments in the relevant area of product-space are lower than the barriers faced by the best-placed potential entrant into the area of product-space in question in equilibrium if such a firm is the best-placed potential investor in the relevant area of product-space at its pre-predation equilibrium QV-investment level or the sum of the barriers and disincentives faced by the best-placed established-rival potential expander in the relevant area of product-space at its pre-predation equilibrium QV-investment level if such a firm is the best-placed potential investor in the ARDEPPS in question at this pre-predation-equilibrium, and this difference is at best weakly positively correlated with the determinants of the percentage of the short-run benefits a firm can realize by driving a rival out that it will retain in the medium or long run—*inter alia*, with (1) the weighted-average-expected percentage of the withdrawn investments that other rivals of the predator would replace if it did not replace them itself (with the likelihood that a non-target rival would be better-placed than the predator to replace a withdrawn investment, with the amount by which the barriers or barriers and disincentives that such relevant actual or potential competitors would face would increase as one moved from the first such replacement-investment to subsequent investments, with the number of target QV investments that would be driven out, with the amount by which the predation would raise the retaliation barriers to expansion or entry the predator's relevant rivals faced [which will in part depend on whether they can replace the withdrawn investments with ones that are less competitive with the predator's projects]), with the extent to which any rival that made a replacement-investment would be more willing than the target to collaborate with the predator's contrived oligopolistic pricing and to announce its prices early in an across-the-board-pricing sequence when its doing so would increase the height of the relevant products' HNOP array, and with the ability of the potential predator to reduce the loss that its rivals' ability to profit from making one or more replacement-investments if it does nothing to prevent them from doing so causes it to suffer by making one or more investments to deter them from investing.

Once more, I admit that the force of this critique depends on a large variety of empirical realities. However, in my judgment, the correlation between a firm's pre-existing market power over price and the percentage of the short-run benefits of predation it can retain in the medium and long run is far too weak for the "pre-existing market power" filter to be justified by this correlation. I would argue as well that the proponents of the "pre-existing market power" filter should bear the burden of production and persuasion on this issue.

I should add that, even if I were persuaded to the contrary, I would not attempt to determine a firm's "monopoly power over price" in the way that Joskow and Klevorick appear to favor—*viz.*, by measuring the suspected predator's "market share, the number and size distribution of firms already in the market, the stability of market shares over time, and historical evidence on. . .profits...."[565] I have already explained why market definitions are inevitably arbitrary,[566] why there is little

[565] *Id.* at 226.

[566] See Chap. 6.

correlation between a firm's market share and its BCAs[567] or OMs,[568] why not much can be learned about a group of sellers' BCAs and OMs from the number and size distribution of firms already in their market,[569] why although the stability of market shares may correlate positively with member-firms' COMs it may well not do so[570] and is unlikely in any event to correlate strongly with the relevant sellers' P–OMC gaps,[571] and why a firm's historical supernormal profit-rate says less about its monopoly and oligopoly control over price than about its monopoly and oligopoly control over QV investment (with which its control over price may not be highly correlated).[572] These explanations should suffice for present purposes. Joskow and Klevorick want to "supplement" the other information just delineated with information about the elasticity of demand for the relevant firm's product (presumably at its pre-predation price).[573] Although such information will be relevant only in across-the-board-pricing contexts (in which predatory pricing is least likely), it clearly is relevant to determining the P–OMC gap of the relevant seller in such contexts since a seller's P/MR ratio and hence its P/MC ratio can be calculated from data on the elasticity of demand at its across-the-board price. However, I do not think that it will ever be cost-effective to predict a seller's P–MC gap from the elasticity of demand it faces: it will always be cheaper and more accurate to determine P–MC directly by measuring the seller's P and MC than to do so indirectly by (1) measuring the elasticity of demand it faced at its pre-predation price, (2) calculating its P/MC ratio from the elasticity of its demand, and then (3) calculating the P–MC gap from the ratio by determining the seller's P or MC. In short, even if Joskow and Klevorick were correct in assuming that the profitability of predatory pricing will be highly and strongly correlated with its potential practitioner's P–MC gap, the facts that they think that courts should consider on this account would be either irrelevant or less relevant than other facts that would be cheaper to obtain.

Joskow and Klevorick and many other predatory-pricing analysts also seem to think that such pricing will be profitable only for "dominant" firms[574] (by which I assume they mean firms with large market shares, especially if they are price-leaders). I have indicated that, *ceteris paribus*, the reputational advantages that predatory

---

[567] See Chaps. 8 and 10.

[568] *Id.*

[569] *Id.*

[570] On the one hand, COMs will be positively correlated with market-share stability to the extent that firms that are securing high COMs may hesitate to make additional sales when their marginal costs fall more (rise less) than their rivals' or when buyer preferences shift in their direction out of fear that doing so will disrupt contrived oligopolistic collaboration. On the other, COMs will be negatively correlated with market-share stability to the extent that they are positively correlated with the incidence of rounds of undercutting and retaliation or more all-out price-wars.

[571] Because OCAs vary from ARDEPPS to ARDEPPS and are not highly or strongly correlated with COMs in the ARDEPPSes in question.

[572] See Chaps. 2 and 10.

[573] Joskow and Klevorick at 226–27.

[574] *Id.* at 226.

pricing would generate will increase with the number of sales on which the predator can contrive an OM, the number of sales on which it can undercut a rival's contrived OM, and the number of occasions on which the predator will wish to drive out an established rival, deter the entry of a potential competitor, or induce an expander or new entrant to locate its new QV investment further away in product-space from the predator's projects than they otherwise would have found profitable. Even if (cross markets) these factors were positively correlated with the "market share" of the potential predator in question, any such positive correlation would be at least somewhat offset by the tendency of the law-related costs that a predatory pricer should reckon with incurring to increase with its market share/dominance (a correlation that reflects the tendency of the enforcement authorities to pay more attention to dominant firms and of juries to be more likely to convict such firms or find them liable). Moreover, since markets or ARDEPPSes differ in terms of the number of sales located within them and since potential predators often operate in far more than one ARDEPPS, the correlation between the dominance of a potential predator in the ARDEPPS in which it is accused of practicing predatory pricing and the value to it of developing a reputation for carrying out its strategic threats and promises or resisting the threats of others will be extremely low and weak. Indeed, since the sales that the different sellers that are operating in a given ARDEPPS make in that ARDEPPS will be only slightly correlated with their overall sales and the number of ARDEPPSes in which they operate, I would not expect the private profits that even particular sellers in a given ARDEPPS can realize through predatory pricing to be highly correlated with their *intra*-ARDEPPS sales.

Many economists contend that predatory pricing can be profitable only in areas of product-space in which barriers to entry are high and seem to assume that, when barriers to entry are high, predators will not be prevented from recouping the cost of predation by rivals' making one or more QV investments to replace the QV investment(s) of the exited target. I would reject both these claims even if the economists that made them had explicitly defined the concept of a barrier to entry coherently and consistently or had used it in a coherent and consistent way. (Joskow and Klevorick realize that the conventional "barriers to entry" usage is unsatisfactory. For this reason, they refer to the relevant aspect of the potential predator's situation as "conditions of entry," which they define to refer to factors that reduce the probable profitability of responding to a target's exit by adding a QV investment to the "market" in question or factors that are likely to delay the execution of an exit-induced entry or expansion.[575] My objections also apply to

[575] *Id.* at 227. This usage is itself unfortunate since Bain used the expression "condition of entry" in two senses that differ not only from each other but from Joskow and Klevorick's definition. In particular, Bain used "condition of entry" first to refer to "the maximum gap" between price and marginal cost at which entry may be forestalled for the most-favored established firm or firms in the industry, supposing concurrent price elevations by all established firms. See BAIN BARRIERS at 8. Bain used this expression second to refer to (1) whether entry would take place if limit pricing were not practiced (if not, entry is said to be "blockaded") and (B) whether, if it would, limit pricing would be more profitable than allowing entry to occur (in which case limit pricing would

formulations of the positions I am criticizing that substitute Joskow and Klevorick's concept of "conditions of entry" for any variant of the concept of "barriers to entry.") I will focus first on the negative claim that recoupment will not be possible if barriers to entry are not high and then on the positive claim that recoupment will not be prevented by rival QV investments when barriers to entry are high.

First, recoupment may be possible when "barriers to entry are not high" if that statement is read (as Joskow and Klevorick in effect propose) to imply that an exiting target will be quickly replaced by a new entrant if nothing is done to prevent that outcome:

(1) in cases in which the predation results in the predator's buying the target at a distressed price and the substitution of the predator for the target does not raise prices in the ARDEPPS sufficiently to increase its equilibrium QV-investment level, the combination of the predation and the purchase will yield recoupment directly while deterring new entry by maintaining the ARDEPPS' pre-predation QV-investment level;
(2) in cases in which the predation results in the predator's buying the target at a distressed price and the substitution of the predator for the target does raise prices sufficiently in the ARDEPPS to increase its equilibrium QV-investment level, if the predator can take advantage of the associated investment opportunity because the sum of the barriers to expansion and (positive or negative) disincentives it faces are not critically higher than those facing the best-placed potential entrant to the ARDEPPS in question, both the purchase and the subsequent expansion will yield the predator profits;
(3) in cases in which the predation causes the target to exit without selling its business to anyone that will continue to operate it in the ARDEPPS in question, the predation will yield the predator profits even if the target's exit would otherwise lead to an immediate new entry if the predator can profit by making a limit QV investment to deter the new entry and can lock itself into such an investment before any potential competitor can make a similar move (conditions that I suspect will normally be fulfilled since there is no reason to believe that the barriers to expansion facing predators will be higher than the barriers to entry facing best-placed potential competitors, since predators will normally have a monopolistic QV-investment incentive to make the limit investment in question, and since predators will normally "learn of" this investment opportunity before any potential competitor does [since the predator knows of its plan to engage in predation before anyone else does]);

be practiced and entry is said to be "effectively impeded") or less profitable than allowing entry to occur (in which case limit pricing would not be practiced and entry is said to be "ineffectively impeded").

(4) in many cases in which the predation causes the target to exit and the target's exit causes an equally-large QV investment to be made immediately by a potential competitor, the predation will yield the predator profits because the new QV investment's general array of competitive positions is inferior to the target's array of competitive positions, because the new entry is further away in product-space from the predator's QV investments than was the target's QV investment, and/or because the new entrant is more willing to cooperate in contrived oligopolistic interactions than was the target; and
(5) regardless of whether the predation enables the predator to earn additional profits in the ARDEPPS in which it took place, it may increase its profits elsewhere by enhancing its reputation for both predation and contrivance.

I turn now to the positive claim that recoupment will not be prevented by one or more rivals' replacing the target's QV investment(s) with one or more new QV investments of its (their) own if barriers to entry are high in the sense that the target's exit will not lead to a new entry either at all or for a considerable period of time. Although this claim may seem to be tautologous, it is not: it ignores the possibility that the target's QV investment may be replaced by a QV-investment expansion by an existing rival of the predator. For the relevant positive claim to be true, it must be revised to refer to the condition of entry (expansion) (in Joskow and Klevorick's sense) facing best-placed rival potential expanders as well as the condition of entry facing best-placed potential competitors.

In sum, the arguments of those economists that think that high barriers to entry are critical for recoupment are undermined by their making a large number of the mistakes I claim economists virtually always make when discussing (in other terms) what I call QV-investment competition—*viz*., by their ignoring

(1) the fact that not all QV investments in any area of product-space are equally competitive with each other,
(2) the ability of a predator to expand to take advantage of any QV-investment opportunity its predation creates,
(3) the fact that not only the predator and its potential competitors but also its established rivals may choose to respond to the exit of the predator's target by adding a QV investment to the relevant area of product-space, and
(4) the fact that predation can also increase the predator's profits outside the ARDEPPS in which it is practiced by enhancing the predator's reputation for predation and contrivance.

* * *

In short, I am not persuaded by any of the arguments other scholars have made about the frequency with which sellers would find predatory pricing profitable if it were not illegal or, given that it is illegal, about the circumstances in which such pricing would be profitable.

D. The Evidence That Can and Cannot Be Used to Prove Predatory Pricing

(1) The Operational Definition of a Predatory Price and the Five Types of Evidence That Can Properly Be Used to Prove That a Defendant Has Engaged in Predatory Pricing

(A) The Operational Definition of a Predatory Price

In my terminology, a seller is properly said to have practiced predatory pricing when it has set a price that is below the price it perceived to be inherently-most-profitable in order to increase its profits strategically by reducing the absolute attractiveness of the offers against which it must compete by inflicting harm on its target and thereby (A) inducing the target to withdraw or change the location of a QV investment it has made or to sell an extant QV-investment project to the predator at a distressed price and/or (B) deterring the target from making an additional QV investment or a QV investment as close in product-space to the predator's projects as the target would otherwise have found profitable. This definition requires ten sets of elaborations.

First, I should emphasize that, like my definition of oligopolistic pricing, this definition of predatory pricing focuses on the subjective intent of the relevant actor. Thus, in my terminology, a seller that has set its price to achieve a predatory strategic goal will have engaged in predatory pricing even if the price it set was not below its actual inherently-most-profitable price because it had overestimated that price. Similarly, in my terminology, a seller whose pricing was not designed to secure a predatory strategic goal would not have engaged in predatory pricing even if its price was below its actual, inherently-most-profitable price if its price reflected its underestimating its inherently-most-profitable price.

Second, and relatedly, on my definition, the predatory character of the pricing of a seller that has made no mistake depends on the price's total non-strategic profitability not just on its short-run profitability. Thus, the inherent profitability of a decision to charge a lower price will reflect not just its short-run profitability but also any contribution it makes to the seller's long-run profits by increasing the demand for its product by giving more buyers the experience of consuming it, by enabling it to make profitable aftermarket sales or other types of complement sales, by reducing its future costs of production and/or distribution by giving it more experience in producing and distributing the product, by increasing the likelihood that buyers that do not purchase from it in the short run may turn to it down the road by inducing them to think about buying its product and perhaps to discuss its product and their needs with it, by reducing the probability that contrivers that it has undercut will retaliate against its undercutting in the future (when the lower price in question manifests its defensive retaliation against such a contriver's retaliation), and/or by reducing the probability that predators will target it in the future (when the lower price in question manifests its defensive retaliation against predation).[576] In short, on my definition of predatory pricing, the predatory character of a price depends on the individual-product promotional, product-line promotional, institutional (seller-company) promotional, network-expansion, aftermarket-complement, learning-by-doing, keeping-in-touch, and defensive-retaliation advantages the lower price confers on the pricer as well as on its short-run profitability. Before proceeding, I should point out that single-product promotional pricing, product-line promotional pricing, network-expanding pricing, learning-by-doing pricing, and possibly even institutional (seller-company) promotional pricing all have an effect other than providing legitimate benefits for the seller that engages in them that complicates the analysis of their legality under the specific-anticompetitive-intent test I claim the Sherman Act promulgates. All such pricing also denies benefits to the pricer's product-rivals and by doing so (1) reduces the absolute attractiveness of the offers they will make to the perpetrator's potential customers even if the rivals do not exit on this account and (2) may cause a rival to exit when it will not immediately or ever be replaced by a firm that is equally competitive with the perpetrator's product as the exiting rival was/would be and may critically raise the barriers to QV investment faced by an otherwise-effective potential QV investor. Thus, to the extent that such pricing reduces the pricer's established or prospective rivals' sales, it will prevent the rivals from learning by doing; to the extent that the pricing in question prevent the rivals from making a sale, it will prevent them from obtaining related promotional advantages on the product they would otherwise have sold or on all products they offered for sale; to the extent that the pricing in question prevents a rival from selling a first item in its product-line to one or more buyers, it will prevent the rival from obtaining product-line promotional advantages when trying to sell additional items in that line to the relevant buyer(s); and to the extent that the pricing in question reduces the size of the networks of the rivals of the pricer at the same time that it increases the size of the pricer's network, it will reduce the absolute attractiveness of the pricer's rivals' products and offers on that account at the same time that the associated expansion in the size of the pricer's network increases the absolute attractiveness of its product. Of course, under the specific-anticompetitive-intent test I believe the Sherman Act promulgates, the gains the relevant pricer anticipates its pricing will yield it by depriving its rivals of these benefits will render its pricing illegal if and only if the pricer's *ex ante* conclusion that its pricing would be profitable was critically affected by the pricer's belief that it would or might increase the pricer's profits in one or more of these ways. Indeed, the "if" part of the preceding sentence is itself inaccurate: on my understanding of the Sherman Act's test of illegality, in situations in which (in an otherwise-Pareto-perfect economy?) it would be most economically efficient to have only one product-line or one network, the fact that a seller would not have found its pricing *ex ante* profitable but for the pricer's belief

[576] Decisions to charge lower prices may also be profitable for strategic, non-predatory reasons when they are made by contrivers to retaliate against undercutters (underminers). The text ignores this possibility because such non-defensive retaliation is as illegal as predatory pricing.

that it would or might cause all its rivals to exit when they would not be replaced by anyone else would not render it Sherman-Act-violative or, more generally, in situations in which the economically-efficient number of product-lines or networks is smaller than the number of extant product-lines or networks, the fact that a seller's belief that its pricing was *ex ante* profitable was critically affected by its perception that it would or might induce one or more exits that would increase the economic efficiency of its ARDEPPS' product-line or network array would not render the pricing Sherman-Act-violative.

Third, when determining whether the price a seller is charging is inherently profitable, one must use appropriate cost-figures to calculate both the profits that were yielded by the price it did charge and the profits that would have been yielded by other prices it could have charged. The simple label for the appropriate cost-figure is "avoidable costs," but this expression does not itself indicate how four significant complications should be dealt with. I will now address each in turn:

(1) When the relevant seller has only a given amount of goods for sale or is running up against a rigid capacity-constraint, the appropriate cost-figure will be not the cost of production (or production and delivery) but the opportunity cost of foregoing the sale that would have to be sacrificed to make the sale in question when the relevant opportunity cost exceeds the cost of production and delivery. Those opportunity costs are the revenue the alternative sale would yield *minus* any cost of locating the alternative buyer *minus*, when relevant, any positive difference between the cost of delivering the good to the alternative buyer and delivering it to the buyer in question *plus* any promotional benefits a sale to the alternative buyer would yield.

(2) When the relevant good is in inventory and cannot be immediately sold to an alternative buyer for a known price if it is not sold to the buyer in question, the appropriate cost-figure (if, for simplicity, I ignore risk costs) will be not the cost of production and, if relevant, delivery but the present value of the weighted-average-expected amount of revenue the seller will anticipate obtaining for the good by selling it to someone else or to the buyer in question subsequently if the seller does not sell it now to the buyer in question (a sum that will reflect *inter alia* the good's physical perishability as well as the possibility that its value may increase or decrease through time as a result of changes in the tastes and/or the wealth/income positions of its potential buyers) *minus* the weighted-average-expected storage-costs the seller will anticipate having to incur if the seller does not sell the good now *minus* any positive difference between the delivery costs it will expect to incur if it sells the good later and the delivery costs it would have to incur if it sold the good now to the buyer in question *plus* the weighted-average-expected amount of promotional benefits the seller should anticipate future sales generating.

(3) When the relevant seller's plant will deteriorate if not used, the cost of maintaining it during a shutdown is lower than the cost of making it operational after it has been shut down (*e.g.*, if the "plant" is a mine that will flood if the pumps are not kept running and the cost of making a flooded mine operational is higher than the cost

of keeping the pumps running), and it would be profitable in the long run to keep the plant in operation (*e.g.*, to keep the pumps running), the cost of operating the plant as opposed to shutting it down should be reduced by the difference between the profits the associated maintenance expenditures enable the seller to make in the post-hypothetical-shutdown period and any profits the seller could have made by operating the plant in the post-hypothetical-shutdown period if the plant had not been maintained in the interim (the difference between the cost of making the plant operational if it has not been maintained during the shutdown and the lower cost of maintaining it during the shutdown *minus* any loss the investor would have had to incur to resume its business after the shutdown if the plant had not been maintained during the shutdown).

(4) In all circumstances, the determination of whether particular types of costs are "avoidable" and hence should be taken into account will depend on the conduct in which the seller in question will have to engage to make the sale in question: if the seller in question would have to build new plant or buy new equipment to supply the relevant buyer with the good or goods for which the buyer is offering a price, the cost of buying or renting the relevant plant and buying the relevant equipment will be avoidable in the context in question (and should be considered to be variable costs in this context) even if, in other contexts, the same type of costs are considered to be fixed costs; if a binding price is set prior to incurring the advertising costs, the advertising costs are avoidable and variable, but if the advertising predates the setting of a binding price, the advertising costs are not avoidable and are fixed.

Fourth, on my definition, a decision to charge a price that is lower than the price that would be the most-profitable price for the seller to charge, strategic considerations aside, and is aimed at driving a target out is not predatory or, perhaps more to the point, does not violate the Sherman Act test of illegality if its attractiveness to the pricer was secured by its satisfying the pricer's desire to inflict harm on its target (if the price was charged out of spite). I hasten to add, however, that such pricing may violate the Clayton Act if it involves Clayton Act discrimination on a commodity and is requisitely likely to reduce competition, will violate now-Article 101 of the (2009) E.U. Treaty if it is executed concertedly by two or more "undertakings" or by a trade association (if its effect is to restrict or distort competition, independent of whether that effect was its object), and will violate now-Article 102 of the (2009) E.U. Treaty if it is executed by a firm with an individually-dominant position or one or more firms that belong to a set of collectively-dominant rivals and the "abuse" language of that Article can properly be interpreted to cover not just exclusionary abuses and exploitative abuses of buyers but also abuses of rivals in the sense of conduct that drives them out for reasons unrelated to their relative economic efficiency. Moreover, it seems to me that, even if such spiteful attempts to drive a rival out is not an antitrust violation, it is or should be a business tort.

Fifth, it is important to note that, when it is costly to calculate and communicate a bid, a decision to make a bid will be predatory when (if I ignore risk costs) (1) the cost of making the bid is higher than the profits the bidder believes it will make if the bid is accepted *times* the probability the bidder assigns to the bid's being accepted and (2) the bidder makes the bid anyway to reduce the price its target would charge or could obtain in the hope that the reduction in the profits the target realized would lead the target to exit, *etc*.

Sixth, it is also important to note that, when a best-placed seller is uncertain about its HNOP + NOM (to simplify, I ignore the complications the second point in this list discussed), its decision to charge a price to a buyer it is best-placed to supply that is lower than its certainty-equivalent inherently-most-profitable price to that buyer will be predatory if it made that decision to reduce the probability that a target rival will make the sale to prevent that firm from making a profit in the hope of driving the target out. Note that the price in question is predatory despite the fact that it is being charged to a buyer the predator is best-placed to supply and exceeds the predator's OMC.

Seventh, in across-the-board-pricing situations, decisions by sellers not to take advantage of their abilities to obtain OMs naturally will be predatory if motivated by a desire to drive a rival out or induce it to relocate.

Eighth and somewhat relatedly, in across-the-board-pricing contexts, decisions by sellers not to make premature price announcements and do the other things that would enable them to profit by putting themselves in a position to obtain oligopolistic margins naturally will be predatory if motivated by a desire to drive a rival out or induce it to relocate.

Ninth, decisions by across-the-board pricers not to announce their respective prices in the order that would maximize the height of the prices in their HNOP array will be predatory if motivated by a desire to drive a rival out or induce it to relocate.

Tenth, as the preceding analyses imply, the lowest non-predatory price a perfectly-informed seller can charge (its lowest legitimate price—LLP) will equal the highest non-contrived price such a seller can charge (its highest legitimate price [HLP]). More concretely, if I ignore the complications introduced by promotional pricing, learning-by-doing pricing, keeping-in-touch pricing, and defensive retaliation, such a seller's LLP and HLP will both equal its (HNOP + NOM).

(B) The Five Types of Evidence That Can Properly Be Used to Prove the Predatory Character of a Seller's Pricing

Unless otherwise indicated, this subsection proceeds on the simplifying assumptions that the alleged predator has not made a relevant mistake, has not been engaging in promotional, learning-by-doing, or keeping-in-touch pricing, and has not been retaliating defensively or acting out of spite and that its pricing has not increased the profits it earns in aftermarkets or when selling other complements. I do not deny the importance of these possibilities, which I would handle by making them the basis of defenses—*i.e.*, by allowing defendants to exonerate themselves by explaining their prices in these terms while assigning all the burdens of proof on these issues to the alleged predator.

Chapter 10 delineated five types of evidence that can be used to establish that a seller has engaged in contrived oligopolistic pricing. Since (1) a seller's lowest legitimate price is the same as its highest legitimate price and (2) a predatory price is a price (charged for predatory reasons) that is lower than the lowest (and highest) legitimate price the seller can charge while a contrived oligopolistic price is a price that is higher than the highest (and lowest) legitimate price the seller can charge, it should be no surprise that the same types of evidence that are relevant to proving contrived oligopolistic pricing are relevant to proving predatory pricing.

(i) Direct Evidence of the Alleged Predator's Admitted Intention to Practice or Actual Practice of Predatory Pricing

In a few cases, it may be possible to prove that a defendant has practiced predatory pricing by putting on testimony of witnesses that heard the defendant admit its intention to practice or its actual practice of such predation, by introducing audio or video recordings of incriminating statements about its pricing that the defendant made, or by providing documentary evidence in which the defendant's predatory intentions, plans, or practices were recorded. In fact, a predatory-pricing case may also be improved by evidence of this kind that relates to non-pricing predatory conduct since actors that are practicing one type of predation are more likely on this account to be practicing other types of predation. However, predators (even those engaged in concerted predation) will rarely leave a trail of such written evidence, audio and video recordings will almost never be available, and the testimony of the relevant witnesses will often be unreliable since the witnesses in question will frequently be disgruntled current or former employees of the alleged predator or employees or owners of the alleged target of predation (who are testifying about predatory threats made to induce the target to exit, to deter the target from expanding, or to induce it to sell out, perhaps at a distressed price). Of course, even if such testimony cannot be treated as conclusive, it can affect a trier-of-fact's estimate of the probability that the defendant has engaged in predatory pricing. Moreover, in a few cases, more reliable oral testimony, recorded conversations, and written memoranda will be available. Thus, when a predator attempts to deter (1) financial institutions or input suppliers from extending credit to its target or (2) distributors from committing themselves to handle the target's product, more reliable testimony will be available since such suppliers or distributors will have less to gain from the relevant testimony and less reason to take revenge on the alleged predator. In addition, when predators communicate their intentions over the phone or orally, recordings may be available, and when they do so in e-mails, the messages may be recoverable from the target or from the predator's computer's hard drive. Moreover, in a surprisingly-large number of cases, managers keep memos that they have been instructed to destroy that discuss predatory (or other anticompetitive) plans or keep notes of meetings in which anticompetitive plans have been discussed. Still, in the vast majority of cases, such direct evidence of predatory intent or conduct will not be available.

(ii) Direct Comparisons of the Alleged Predator's Actual Prices with the Lowest Legitimate Price (LLP) It Can Charge

Taken together, Section 1 of Chap. 2's analysis of the various components of a seller's P–MC gap and Section 2 of Chap. 4's conclusions about the legality of natural and contrived oligopolistic pricing under U.S. and E.C./E.U. antitrust law determine the lowest legitimate price for a conventional, sovereign profit-maximizer to charge in different situations. I will now analyze in the following order the LLP that (1) a perfectly-informed across-the-board pricer can charge, (2) the LLP that an imperfectly-informed across-the-board pricer can charge, (3) the LLP that a perfectly-informed individualized pricer can charge a buyer it is best-placed to supply, (4) the LLP that an imperfectly-informed individualized pricer can charge a buyer it is best-placed to supply, (5) the LLP that a perfectly-informed individualized pricer can charge a buyer it is worse-than-best-placed to supply, and (6) the LLP that an imperfectly-informed individualized pricer can charge a buyer it is worse-than-best-placed to supply.

In across-the-board-pricing contexts, the lowest legitimate price (LLP) for a perfectly-informed, conventional profit-maximizer (that is not practicing individual-product promotional, product-line promotional, institutional [seller-company] promotional, network-expanding, learning-by-doing, or keeping-in-touch pricing and is not engaging in legitimate, defensive retaliation) equals its across-the-board (HNOP + NOM) in the U.S. and its HNOP in the E.C./E.U. If a seller that is setting profit-maximizing across-the-board prices in the U.S. is uncertain about its (HNOP + NOM) sum or a seller that is setting such prices in the E.C./E.U. is uncertain about its HNOP, the calculation of its LLP is somewhat more complicated. In particular, to determine the LLP of such a seller, one must first determine the amount of research it would find *ex ante* inherently profitable to do into the determinants of its LLP, then generate the probability-distribution estimates of the profits that each relevant price it could charge would yield that would be generated by the research into these issues that would be *ex ante* most profitable for it to execute, and finally determine the price it would find inherently most profitable *ex ante* (the price that would maximize its certainty-equivalent legitimate profits) by combining the weighted-average-expected profit figures one could generate from stage two's probability-distribution estimates with risk-cost estimates that reflect information about the seller's risk-averseness as well as about the dispersion of the various stage-two probability distributions.

In individualized-pricing contexts, the LLP for a given seller to charge a given buyer depends (1) on whether the seller is best-placed or worse-than-best-placed to supply the buyer in question as well as (2) on how certain one assumes the seller in question is about various relevant facts (*e.g.*, in the U.S., about the probability that it [if it is best-placed] or its competitive superior [if it is not] will be able to obtain an NOM). The lowest legitimate price for an individualized pricer to charge a buyer it is best-placed to supply will be clear if it is certain about all the relevant facts—*viz.*, will equal its (HNOP + NOM) for that buyer in the U.S. and its HNOP in the E.C./E.U. However, this result is not interesting in the current context because a best-placed seller will never charge its own customer a predatory price in the situation described: since it can obtain the relevant buyer's patronage at its lowest legitimate price, it will have no reason to charge predatory prices to its own customers in these circumstances. By way of contrast, the lowest legitimate price for an individualized pricer to charge a buyer it is best-placed to supply when it is uncertain about some of the relevant facts is of interest in the current context because an imperfectly-informed best-placed individualized pricer may choose to reduce its price below the level that would maximize its certainty-equivalent profits to reduce the weighted-average-expected profits a target rival can obtain by undercutting it (because it has unintentionally charged a price that exceeds its [HNOP + NOM] in the U.S. or its HNOP in the E.C./E.U.). Unfortunately, to determine such a best-placed seller's lowest legitimate price, one would have to know the amount of research that would be *ex ante* inherently profitable for it to do into the determinants of its lowest legitimate price (the cost of improving its probability-distribution estimates of the relevant factors to any give extent and the legitimate benefits of doing so), the probability-distribution estimate it would generate of its LLP–OMC gap if it undertook the *ex ante* inherently-profitable amount of research into the gap's determinants, and the extent of the risk costs it would bear at different prices.

The lowest legitimate price for an individualized pricer to charge a buyer it is worse-than-best-placed to supply will always be relevant in a predatory-pricing context because a worse-than-best-placed individualized pricer will always have the opportunity to inflict harm on a best-placed individualized pricer by stealing the customer in question. Unless the best-placed supplier of a given buyer either has made an error (about its and its closest rival's costs, its OCA, its REM, its BEM, and/or [in the U.S.] its NOM) or has attempted to contrive an oligopolistic margin, the underbid of a perfectly-informed worse-than-best-placed individualized pricer will always be predatory, retaliatory, mistaken, or purely tortious. In most cases in which the best-placed seller has neither erred nor attempted to contrive an OM, the strategic, erroneous, or tortious character of the inferior's undercutting bid will be manifest by the fact that the sum of the price in the undercutting bid that the inferior made and any promotional, network-expanding, aftermarket/other-complement, learning-by-doing, and keeping-in-touch benefits the sale it would generate will yield will be lower than the overall marginal cost it had to incur to make the relevant bid and sale. When the perfectly-informed inferior is undercutting a bid that contains a natural oligopolistic margin, the strategic, erroneous, or tortious character of its price will be reflected by the fact that the pricing costs it has to incur to make the bid in question will exceed any keeping-in-touch benefits its bid will yield (since the latter are the only benefits its bid will yield in a natural-oligopolistic-pricing situation, given that in such a context the best-placed supplier will in the end obtain the patronage of the buyer in question). (Undercutting an NOM-containing rival bid with predatory intent is clearly illegal in the U.S. since the rival's natural oligopolistic pricing is lawful. I also think that undercutting a rival's NOM-containing bid with predatory intent is illegal in the E.C./E.U as well. However, I admit that the fact that the rival's natural oligopolistic pricing is illegal in the E.C./E.U. might be deemed to render such undercutting lawful in the E.C./E.U. despite the undercutter's predatory intent. I would not declare predatory undercutting lawful under E.C./E.U. law under these circumstances, though I would declare lawful an undertaking's reporting its rival's illegal conduct to the authorities even if the reporting was done with predatory intent.) When a worse-than-best-placed individualized pricer sets its price to a given buyer without perfect information about its OMC, BPD, or (in the U.S.) the ability of the best-placed seller to obtain an OM naturally (whether the best-placed firm will be given an opportunity to rebid if its initial offer is beaten and whether the best-placed firm will find it inherently profitable to take advantage of any such opportunity to rebid it is given), the worse-than-best-placed seller's underbid will be strategic, mistaken, or tortious if it is lower than the price that would maximize its certainty-equivalent profits: unfortunately, to calculate this lowest legitimate price, it will be necessary to determine the amount of research into the relevant issues that would be *ex ante* inherently profitable for the competitive inferior to do, the probability-distribution estimate of the profits it would anticipate realizing at each price it might charge the relevant buyer that the inherently-profitable amount of research into the relevant issues would generate, and the risk costs it would incur at each price. Once again, a seller might find it profitable overall to charge a price below such a lowest legitimate price because the predatory or retaliatory benefits that doing so would generate by reducing its target's profits exceed the inherent cost (the sacrifice in immediate certainty-equivalent returns) of doing so.

The preceding description of the factors that determine the LLPs that different sellers can charge particular buyers in various circumstances should have made clear the low cost-effectiveness of direct comparisons of actual prices and LLPs in predatory-pricing contexts. Thus, just as Chap. 10 argued that it will usually be prohibitively expensive to prove that a perfectly-informed seller's across-the-board price exceeds its highest legitimate price (HLP) in contrived-oligopolistic-pricing suits by comparing its actual price with its (HNOP + NOM) sum in the U.S. or with its HNOP in the E.C./E.U., it will rarely be cost-effective to prove that an across-the-board pricer's price is lower than its LLP in predatory-pricing suits by comparing its actual price with its (HNOP + NOM) sum in the U.S. or with its HNOP in the E.C./E.U. Obviously, it will be even less cost-effective to base assessments of the predatory character of a seller's pricing on such a comparison when the relevant seller is not perfectly informed. Indeed, although the problems created by the possibilities that the seller in question may be engaging in promotional pricing of any sort, network-expanding pricing, learning-by-doing pricing, keeping-in-touch pricing, or defensive retaliation or may be trying to raise the profits it makes in aftermarkets or by selling other complements can probably be minimized by placing on defendants the burdens of producing and paying for the evidence on these possibilities, the probable fact that these types of pricing will be more likely to play a significant role in predatory-pricing suits than in contrived-oligopolistic-pricing suits suggests that this type of proof is even less likely to be cost-effective in the former than in the latter context.

Admittedly, if I am correct that predatory pricing is almost always practiced on an individualized basis, the preceding paragraph's conclusion will not be highly relevant. It undoubtedly is substantially more cost-effective to determine the predatory character of an individualized pricer's price by comparing its actual price with its LLP than to use this method in across-the-board-pricing contexts. Although, theoretically, a best-placed individualized pricer may charge predatory prices to its own customers when it is uncertain about the height of its LLP, most predatory individualized prices will be charged to buyers the seller is worse-than-best-placed to supply. When the relevant sellers are perfectly informed in a non-natural-oligopolistic-pricing situation, one can establish a *prima facie* case of predatory pricing by showing that the price charged (the incremental revenue the relevant sale would yield when more than one unit was sold to the relevant buyer) was lower than the sum of the seller's conventional and contextual marginal (incremental) costs. When the relevant sellers are perfectly informed in a natural-oligopolistic-pricing situation, one can determine the inherent profitability of an undercutting price that would have been profitable if, contrary to fact, it yielded a sale by comparing the contextual and pricing costs of the bid in question with the keeping-in-touch-pricing benefits it generated. As we saw, when the competitive inferior must make its bid in a situation in which it is uncertain about whether the best-placed firm will overestimate its HNOP or (in the U.S.) can obtain an oligopolistic margin naturally, it will be more complicated to estimate its LLP. Still, in all such individualized-pricing situations, I suspect it will be more cost-effective to compare a potential predator's price with its LLP than will be the case in across-the-board-pricing contexts. Obviously, however, such comparisons will be expensive and more-or-less-inaccurate in individualized-pricing as well as in across-the-board-pricing contexts.

Before proceeding to the next type of evidence that may be useful in predatory-pricing cases, one additional point should be made. The preceding discussion did not comment in any detail on the relationship between the LLP for a particular seller and its conventional marginal cost, conventional average variable cost, or conventional average total cost. These issues will be addressed in more detail in Subsection A(2) of this chapter, which analyzes *inter alia* various predatory-pricing presumptions that others have urged courts to adopt that focus on the relationship between the alleged predator's prices and various costs.

(iii) Inter-Temporal and Inter-Regional Analyses of the Relationship Between Actual-Price Differences and Estimated-LLP Differences

These two types of comparative evidence are analogous to their contrived-oligopolistic-pricing counterparts. If one can prove, for example, that (1) a seller's actual price to a particular buyer (or across-the-board price) at time t(1) is lower than its price to which buyer (its across-the-board price) at time t(0) by more than its relevant LLP at t(1) seems likely to be below its relevant LLP at t(0), (2) a seller's relevant actual price at t(1) exceeds its relevant actual price at t(0) by less than its relevant LLP at t(1) seems likely to exceed its relevant LLP at t(0), (3) a seller's actual price to one buyer is lower than its contemporaneous price to another buyer in the same or a different region (or a sellers' across-the-board price in one region is lower than its contemporaneous across-the-board price in another region) by more than the former LLP seems likely to be below the latter, or (4) a seller's actual price to one buyer (actual across-the-board price in one region) exceeds its actual price to another buyer (actual, contemporaneous across-the-board price in another region) by less than the former LLP seems likely to exceed the latter or equals its price to another buyer when the former LLP exceeds the latter LLP, this comparative evidence will imply either that the former price is sub-LLP or that the latter price is contrived oligopolistic. As in the contrived-oligopolistic-pricing-suit context, these difference-focused comparative methods are likely to be more cost-effective than the straightforward method the preceding subsection described because it is easier to estimate inter-temporal, inter-buyer, or interregional differences in MCs, MCAs, BPAs, CMCs, *etc.*, than to estimate those parameters themselves.

(iv) Behavioral Evidence

I have already discussed the possibility that a private plaintiff or the State may be able to support its claim that a seller has engaged in predatory pricing by introducing eyewitness testimony, audio recordings, and/or documentary evidence that the defendant admitted its intention to engage in or its actual practice of predatory conduct. In some cases, other types of behavioral evidence can be used to support a predatory-pricing accusation. For example, in some situations, evidence establishing that the defendant tried to acquire the alleged target prior to initiating or after initiating its alleged predatory-pricing campaign will support a predatory-pricing claim, particularly if the price the defendant offered was clearly a distressed price. In other cases, the predatory-pricing claim will be strengthened by evidence that the alleged predatory pricer may have tried to engage in other types of predation as well: for example, may have tried to induce potential capital-suppliers, input-suppliers, or customers of the target not to deal with the target. For two reasons, this type of behavioral evidence will be relevant regardless of whether it would support a finding of predation on its own. First, evidence suggesting that a defendant may have engaged in one kind of predation may increase the persuasiveness of ambiguous evidence suggesting that it engaged in another kind of predation. Second, evidence suggesting that a seller may have engaged in one kind of predation may affect a trier-of-fact's conclusion about the amount of harm the seller inflicted on its target by engaging in a given amount of another type of predation (since the consequential damages that result from a given direct profit-loss may increase with the other losses the relevant target sustained). In addition, the claim that a particular defendant has engaged in predatory pricing may be strengthened by behavioral evidence indicating that the alleged target has undercut the alleged predator's presumably-contrived oligopolistic prices in the past since that fact increases the probability that the alleged predator would find it profitable to eliminate the alleged target.

The relevance of the final type of behavioral evidence that can be used to bolster a predatory-pricing claim is admittedly contestable. I think that a predatory-pricing case will be somewhat though not substantially strengthened by a demonstration that the following sequence of behaviors took place: (1) a new QV investment was made in an ARDEPPS by an expanding established firm or new entrant; (2) the alleged predator cut its price; (3) the QV investment in question was withdrawn or sold at a distressed price to the alleged predator; and (4) the alleged predator raised its price. This sequence of events does not prove predatory pricing because it is fully consistent with the alleged predator's always charging legitimate prices. Thus, the alleged predator's initial price-cut may be a perfectly-legitimate response to the new QV investment's lowering its LLP by reducing its OCAs and hence its HNOP and/or lowering its NOMs (in the U.S.) and COMs as well (since a reduction in a seller's OCAs may preclude it from obtaining an oligopolistic margin naturally). Correspondingly, the alleged predator's "reversal" of its price-cut after the new QV investment has been withdrawn or sold out to it may reflect nothing more than the increase in its HNOP, NOM (in the U.S.), and/or COM that resulted from the elimination of the new QV investment as a source of independent competition. Since, I suspect, most new QV investments that fail after provoking price-cuts that are reversed after they are withdrawn or sold were not targets of predation of any kind, this type of evidence cannot be used to establish a presumption of predatory pricing. One still needs to show that the price-cut in question was to a sub-LLP level. Nevertheless, although the following conclusion is contestable, I do think that evidence of this sequence of behaviors does legitimate a trier-of-fact's raising his or her estimate of the probability that the alleged predator's price was predatory when independent evidence suggests that the defendant's prices were sub-LLP: that the percentage of reversed price-cuts that are independently suspicious that really were predatory that were part of this type of behavior-sequence is higher than the percentage of suspicious price-cuts or reversed price-cuts that really were not predatory that were part of this type of behavior-sequence.

(v) "Structural" Evidence

The phrase "structural evidence" is something of a misnomer in that it implies the existence of non-arbitrarily-definable markets whose "structures" will affect the profitability of predatory pricing. For reasons that Chap. 6 articulated, I do not believe that markets can be defined non-arbitrarily or that it will ever be cost-effective to base an analysis on market-aggregated data (*e.g.*, on data on a "market's" "structure"). Nevertheless, I will continue to use the phrase "structural evidence" in the now conventional sense of evidence that relates to the probability that and extent to which the alleged predatory pricer would find it profitable to practice predatory pricing against the alleged target if the law did not prohibit its doing so (or, perhaps, more relevantly, evidence about the probable profitability of the alleged predatory pricing, given the relevant law and law-enforcement practices).

Section 1(A) of this chapter analyzed the determinants of the profitability of predatory pricing in exhaustive and exhausting detail. I will not repeat its specific findings here. For present purposes, it should suffice to reiterate its general conclusion that the determinants of the profitability of using predatory pricing to drive out existing QV investments are far more complicated and difficult to measure empirically than many seem to suppose. This conclusion has two implications that are relevant in this context. First, the use of so-called structural evidence is less likely to be cost-effective than many appear to believe. And second, given the difficulty that both a court and one or more potential predators will have in making accurate estimates of the determinants of the profitability of the latter's trying to drive a particular rival out through predatory pricing, it seems inappropriate to reject a predatory-pricing claim on a finding that the alleged pricing seems less than 50 % likely to be *ex ante* profitable.

* * *

By using one or more of the five types of evidence just described, a private plaintiff or the State will sometimes be able to establish a *prima facie* case that a defendant has engaged in predatory pricing. I do not mean to imply that the task will usually be easy or cheap, and I do not mean to deny that it will often be impossible or prohibitively expensive to establish the liability or guilt of a firm that has practiced predatory pricing. Nevertheless, I do think that it will sometimes be possible to prove predatory pricing by submitting the kinds of comparative and behavioral evidence that have just been described even if direct comparisons of actual prices and LLPs and structural evidence are as cost-ineffective as I believe.

(2) Seven Presumptions That Academic Economists or Economist-Lawyers Have Proposed Courts Use to Resolve Predatory-Pricing Cases: Statements and Critiques

(A) The Presumptions That Are Implicit in the Two-Tier Approach to Predatory-Pricing Cases That Joskow and Klevorick Recommend Courts Adopt

Joskow and Klevorick argue that courts should adopt a two-tier approach to predatory-pricing suits.[577] Under this approach, unless the private plaintiff or the State can demonstrate that predatory pricing was sufficiently likely to be profitable for the defendant and sufficiently likely to be sufficiently misallocative if practiced to make it *ex ante* economically efficient for the court to receive evidence about the alleged predator's allegedly-predatory pricing, the court will rule in favor of the defendant prior to receiving any evidence about its allegedly-predatory conduct. In one sense, this approach could be described as a *de facto* irrebuttable presumption of the non-predatory character of pricing practiced in situations in which these showings cannot be made.

Five objections can be made to this two-tier approach or, more precisely, to the *de facto* irrebuttable presumption of non-predation it in effect establishes in various circumstances. The first is that, even if it would be economically efficient for legislatures to adopt this proposal, it would be inconsistent with our rights-commitments for courts to do so. As Chap. 9 explained, neither U.S. antitrust law nor E.C./E.U. competition law promulgates an economic-inefficiency test of illegality. This fact has two moral-rights-related implications: (1) the U.S. or E.C./E.U. courts' adoption of the Joskow and Klevorick two-tier approach would violate the moral right of all citizens to be the authors of the laws that subsequently constrain them because it would entail the courts' usurpation of legislative power and (2) to the extent that the U.S. or E.C./E.U. courts' adoption of the Joskow and Klevorick two-tier approach would result in the courts not investigating in some cases the predatory character of conduct that was, in fact predatory, it would violate the moral right of the plaintiff-victims of the illegal predation in question to an adjudicatory process that was requisitely likely to secure their legal rights.

[577] See Joskow and Klevorick, *passim*.

The second is that, even if it would not violate anyone's rights for courts to adopt the Joskow and Klevorick presumption and even if their doing so would increase economic efficiency, it would not be desirable overall for courts to adopt this presumption if the distributional consequences of the presumption were sufficiently undesirable from the relevant value-perspective for the presumption to be undesirable overall despite its allocative efficiency. This consideration is salient because the court cases that correctly find firms guilty of predatory pricing are distributively desirable both (1) from a variety of normative perspectives that pay no attention to the relationship between the conduct of affected parties and the resources and opportunities that are available to them—*e.g.*, in that (I suspect) the deterrence of predation and the requirement that predators pay damages to their victims will tend to redistribute income from individuals who are richer to individuals who are poorer—and (2) from normative perspectives that assert that the resources and opportunities available to individuals should match the moral quality of their conduct (which would imply that predators should not profit from [indeed, should be punished for] their wrong and the victims of predation should be able to obtain redress). (I should add that, in my judgment, one of the "goals" of the Sherman Act is to effectuate the latter kind of "historic" distributive norm.)

The third objection is an act-rule objection. I suspect that, even if each individual court that adopted the Joskow and Klevorick two-tier approach increased allocative efficiency in each individual case in which it did so, the rule itself might be misallocative. This conclusion is possible because the misallocation that the approach generates in the average case it causes to be dismissed by encouraging predatory pricing by potential predators in situations in which the rule will cause cases to be dismissed is higher than the misallocation it causes in individual cases, each of which must be considered to be marginal. This result reflects the difference between the anti-deterrent effect of the marginal and average two-tier dismissals *per se*, not any difference in the cases themselves. Hence, even if Joskow and Klevorick did concern themselves with the anti-deterrent effect of their two-tier proposal, its adoption would misallocate resources unless individual courts were instructed to base their decisions on the potential misallocative effects of the average rather than the marginal "incorrect" dismissal.

This subsection is primarily concerned with the fourth and fifth objections that can be made to Joskow and Klevorick's two-tier proposal—the micro-economic and welfare-economics objections that Joskow and Klevorick have mis-specified the determinants of the probable profitability and *ex ante* allocative inefficiency of predatory pricing. According to Joskow and Klevorick, both the probability that a defendant would have found it profitable to engage in the predatory pricing of which it is accused and the allocative inefficiency of its having engaged in the alleged predatory pricing will be (1) directly related to its short-run monopoly power (over price) and (2) inversely related to (A) the favorability of the "condition of entry" in their sense—the length of time a potential entrant would require to replace an exiting target—and (B) the absolute and relative contribution of small firms to technological innovation in the area of product-space in question.[578] In practice, Joskow and

[578] *Id.* at 242–49.

Klevorick (1) seem to measure the alleged predator's short-run monopoly power by its market share, the extent to which the firm has functioned as a price leader, the stability through time of the number and size distribution of the sellers in the alleged predator's "market"—*i.e.*, ARDEPPS, the magnitude of its supernormal profits, and the length of the period of time during which those profits have not declined; (2) clearly measure the condition of entry by the capital required to enter the relevant "market," the importance of product differentiation to the alleged predator and in the alleged predator's market (whether the alleged predator has BPAs based on advertising as manifest by its ability to obtain a "premium price" that does not reflect any physical superiority of its product and how much money the alleged predator has spent on "image" advertising), the ability of potential entrants to buy critical assets or hire critical employees (say, from the target), the extent to which outsiders will exaggerate the riskiness of operating in the relevant market, the frequency of entry in the past 10 years, and the characteristics of any new entrants (whether they were large, diversifying firms); and (3) explicitly measure the contribution of small firms to technological innovation by the importance of technological innovation in the "market" in question and the percentage of its technological innovations made by small firms.

I will begin with the micro-economic critique of this analysis of the determinants of the profitability of predatory pricing. Rather than repeating the analysis of this issue that Section 1A of this chapter executed and comparing it with Joskow and Klevorick's analysis, I will confine myself to stating my major objections to their position:

(1) (A) the profitability of predatory pricing depends on the factors that determine the amount by which the possible target reduced the possible predator's OCAs, NOMs, and COMs, not on the size of the possible predator's OCAs or market share pre-predation, and

(B) the correlation between the former factors and the possible predator's pre-predation OCAs or market share is extremely low—for example, the producer of a specialized product or of a generic alternative to a set of highly-advertised products may find it profitable to practice predation against the only other producer of a similar specialized or generic product since that rival's operation prevented it from having the substantial OCAs it otherwise would enjoy despite the fact (actually, because of the fact) that the predator in question did not have substantial OCAs (or a substantial share of anything that would be called a "market") pre-predation;

(2) a firm's OCAs, NOMs, and COMs are not in any case highly correlated with its market share;

(3) the fact that a firm is a price leader is also unlikely to be strongly correlated with the ratio of its OCAs, NOMS, and COMs either to those of its product-rivals or to those of the weighted-average firm in the economy;

(4) given the fact that, regardless of how they are defined, "markets" differ in terms of the importance of locational and product differentiation within them, the percentage of their constituent members that are second-placed or close-to-second-placed to obtain the patronage of any buyer any market-insider is best-placed to supply, and the frequency with which insiders are competitive with each other, there is very little correlation between the number and size

distribution of the constituent firms of a "market" or the stability of these figures through time and its constituent firms' OCAs, NOMs, and COMs;

(5) the amount of supernormal profits a seller obtains has more to do with its total power over QV investment than with its monopoly (and oligopoly) power over price—a fact that is important because there is not much of a correlation between a firm's monopoly (and oligopoly) power over price and its total power over QV investment;

(6) given the fact that most alleged predators (indeed, most firms) are conglomerates that are active in many different ARDEPPSes and the fact that predatory pricing is likely to affect the predator's company's reputation in all the ARDEPPSes in which it is operating or may become active, there is also not much of a correlation between a company's share of any particular market in which it is operating as a seller and the extent to which its predatory pricing in that market will increase its profits by changing its reputation;

(7) Joskow and Klevorick exaggerate the extent to which capital requirements, product differentiation, unique assets, and potential-investor misperceptions of risk will determine the likelihood that and the delay after which an exiting target's QV investment will be replaced by an investment that is as competitive with the predator's QV investment

   (A) because they ignore the significance of the fact that the most-likely source of the replacement will be an expanding established rival of the predator,
   (B) because they (apparently) underestimate the extent to which the fact that most potential competitors are large conglomerates operating in allied fields reduces the importance of these factors even when the most-likely source of the replacement QV investment is a potential competitor, and
   (C) because they (again, apparently) ignore or underestimate the importance of the possibility that replacement-investments may be further away in product-space from the predator's projects than were the withdrawn projects of the predator's target;

(8) Joskow and Klevorick probably overestimate the importance of the frequency with which exiting has occurred in the relevant "market" in the preceding decade because new entrants are more likely to exit than incumbents, and Joskow and Klevorick probably underestimate the frequency with which the failure of potential competitors to enter reflects not the fact that they face high barriers to entry in my sense or long delay-times but the fact that their presence has induced the established firms in the ARDEPPS in question to make sufficient limit investments to deter their entry; and

(9) the frequency with which small firms in the relevant ARDEPPS have made technological innovations may have less to do with the likelihood that the exiting target will be replaced by a QV investment by another firm that will be equally damaging to the predator than Joskow and Klevorick may believe it has (they are, in fact, silent on this issue) not only because that investment may be made by a large, expanding established firm but also because the innovation

that can reduce the barriers a potential expander or entrant faces is as likely to be non-technological as technological.

The fifth objection to Joskow and Klevorick's two-tier proposal focuses on its welfare-economics claim that the amount of misallocation that predatory pricing generates will be (1) directly related to the predator's pre-predation monopoly control over price and the contribution that small firms made to technological innovation in the ARDEPPS in question, (2) inversely related to the condition of entry, and (3) primarily determined by the preceding three factors.[579] Unfortunately, to assess this claim properly, one would have to execute the kind of third-best-allocative-efficiency analysis of anti-predatory-pricing policies that I will execute in THE WELFARE ECONOMICS OF ANTITRUST POLICY and U.S. and E.U. ANTITRUST LAW. I will restrict myself here to a few comments on the short-run and long-run allocative-efficiency consequences of predatory pricing. I hope that they will be at least somewhat comprehensible and informative.

I will focus separately on the short-run and the long-run economic-efficiency effects of predatory pricing. The short-run economic-efficiency effect of predatory pricing depends on whether the predator steals its target's customer or simply reduces the price the target obtains from its customer. If the predatory pricing results in the predator's supplying its target's customer, its short-run effect will be misallocative. This conclusion reflects not only the allocative transaction cost generated by the predator's bid but also the fact that the predator's being privately-worse-placed than its target to supply the buyer in question creates a presumption that it is also allocatively-worse-placed than its target to supply that buyer. If the predatory pricing simply reduces the price its target obtains from the relevant buyer (because that buyer gives the target the opportunity to rebid, the target does rebid, and the buyer accepts the target's improved offer), the economic efficiency of the associated short-run impact of the predatory pricing will depend on whether the target's price-reduction increases its unit sales, on whether any such increase in its unit sales increases or decreases economic efficiency, and on whether any related increase in economic efficiency exceeds the allocative transaction costs the predatory pricing generates. In virtually all cases, the reduction in the target's price will either leave the buyer's unit purchases of the target's product unchanged or cause the buyer to increase its unit purchases of the target's product. On the assumption that the resources that would be used to produce any additional units of output the predation causes its target to produce in the short run will be withdrawn from the production of other goods, any increase in the unit purchases of the target's product that the predatory pricing causes will increase/decrease economic efficiency will depend on whether the post-predation P/MC^* ratio of the target's product "diverges" less/more from the post-predation weighted-average P/MC^* ratio of the products from whose production the resources used to produce the extra units of the target's product are withdrawn than the no-predation P/MC^* ratio of the target's

[579] *Id.* at 231–34.

product would have diverged from the weighted-average no-predation P/MC^* ratio of the products from whose production the resources used to produce the extra units of the target's product would have been withdrawn where the asterisks next to the MCs in question indicate that the MCs have been adjusted to take account of externalities, taxes on the margin of income, and various other Pareto imperfections so as to make the ratio of the two MC^* figures equal the marginal or incremental rate at which the goods whose unit outputs are being reduced by the predatory pricing can be transformed into the target's product. In the situation now under consideration, the predatory pricing will generate allocative transaction costs both directly to the extent that it involves the predator's making a bid and/or calculation it would not otherwise have made and indirectly by causing the relevant buyer to ask the target (its best-placed supplier) to rebid and by causing the target to rebid.

Successful predatory pricing will have three sets of long-run allocative-efficiency effects. First, *ceteris paribus*, it will tend to affect the magnitudes of a wide variety of various categories of economic efficiency by decreasing price competition in the long run: in particular, predatory pricing will tend on this account (1) to increase the amount of misallocation that individuals generate by misallocating time to leisure, do-it-yourself labor, and crime as opposed to legitimate market labor; (2) to increase the amount of X-inefficiency caused by the taxation of marginal income—in particular, by increasing the misallocation that the predator's managers and employees generate by substituting non-taxable work-related benefits for taxable income by reducing the after-tax cost to them of giving up a given amount of taxable income by increasing the salaries and wages that would be offered to them and hence the tax-rate that would be applied to their marginal salaries and wages; (3) to change in a direction that cannot be predicted on an *a priori* basis and that I cannot usefully predict in any other way the amount of misallocation the economy generates by allocating too many resources to unit-output production in some areas of product-space relative to the amount it allocates to unit-output production in other areas of product-space, controlling for the total amount of resources it allocates to unit-output production; (4) by changing in a direction that cannot be predicted on an *a priori* basis and that I cannot usefully predict in any other way the amount of economic inefficiency the economy generates by allocating too many resources to QV-investment creation in some areas of product-space, controlling for the total amount of resources devoted to QV-investment creation in the economy as a whole; (5) to increase the amount of misallocation the economy generates by raising the percentage of the economy's resources devoted to QV-investment creation while reducing the percentages of the economy's resources devoted respectively to production-process research and the production of units of the smaller set of products that would be produced if predatory pricing did not reduce price competition; and (6) by reducing the real incomes of the poor (of poor consumers) and thereby (A) generating externality-related misallocation by displeasing on balance (my perhaps-optimistic assumption) those who are concerned about the income of others and (B) increasing both (i) the amount of misallocation poor consumers generate by making misallocative, externality-generating choices (*e.g.*, driving breakdown-prone, dangerous cars or living in fire-and-disease-spreading housing-units)—choices that poor consumers make because they are in their individual interest—and (ii) investment-in-human-capital-related misallocation by reducing the investment made in poor adults and, more importantly, in the children of the poor. Second, predatory pricing may misallocate resources in the long run in addition by substituting a less-economically-efficient QV investment (by the predator or someone else) for the target's eliminated QV investment. Third, and in the other direction, to the extent that successful predatory pricing reduces QV-investment competition in the ARDEPPS in which it is practiced—*i.e.*, to the extent that the target's QV investment is not replaced even by QV investments that are further away in product-space from the predator's projects than were the project(s) of its target, the predatory pricing will increase allocative efficiency by reducing the percentage of the economy's resources devoted to QV-investment creation.

What is the connection between these five sorts of possible allocative-efficiency effects and the three factors (or sets of factors) on which Joskow and Klevorick's first tier focuses? Before proceeding, I want to reiterate that the analysis that follows will be far more comprehensible to readers who have previously read the policy companion to this law book.

Joskow and Klevorick's first factor is the predator's pre-predation monopoly power over price (which can be read to refer to its total control over price)—*i.e.*, the predator's P/MC ratio or its (P–MC)/P ratio. This factor has no bearing whatsoever on the short-run misallocation predatory pricing will generate to the extent that it results in the predator's taking sales from its target. If the relevant MC ratios equaled the relevant MC^* ratios, the predator's P/MC ratio would have some bearing on whether any increase the predatory pricing generated in the target's short-run unit output when the predation simply reduced the price the target obtained for its product would increase or decrease economic efficiency. In particular, if, in addition to assuming that the relevant MC ratios equal their MC^* counterparts, I assume plausibly that the P/MC ratios of predators and their targets are highly positively correlated, any increase in the target's short-run unit output the predatory pricing caused will be more likely to be economically efficient the greater the ratio of the predator's P/MC ratio to its weighted-average economy-wide counterpart to the extent that some of the resources used to produce the extra units of the target's output are withdrawn from the production of products that are not closely competitive with the target's product. (This last qualification is necessary because it seems likely that the P/MC ratios of products that are highly competitive are similar.) Of course, the importance of this conclusion (which implies that predatory-pricing prosecutions or suits will be less allocatively efficient [not more allocatively efficient as Joskow and Klevorick suppose] when the predator's P/MC ratio is higher than its weighted-average economy-wide counterpart) is undercut by the reality that the relevant MC ratios will not equal their MC^* counterparts.

I turn now to the relevance of the predator's P/MC ratio to its long-run economic-efficiency effects—*i.e.*, to the extent to which it increases or decreases long-run economic efficiency by decreasing price competition in the long run, by substituting for the target's QV investment a less-economically-efficient QV investment of the predator or someone else, and by reducing QV-investment competition. I will not analyze here the connection between (1) the ratio of the predator's P/MC ratio to its weighted-average economy-wide counterpart and (2) each of these long-run economic-efficiency impacts of its predatory pricing. (I will do so in the policy companion to this book.) At this juncture, I will state only that, with three counteracting exceptions, the above ratio of ratios has no bearing on the economic inefficiency of the predator's predatory pricing. The three exceptions are:

(1) the higher the ratio in question, the greater the extent to which the predatory pricing will cause misallocation in the long run between leisure and unit-output-producing market labor devoted to the production of the good in question;
(2) the higher the ratio in question, the greater the extent to which the predatory pricing will cause misallocation in the long run between do-it-yourself labor and unit-output-producing market labor devoted to the production of the good in question; and
(3) the higher the ratio in question, the greater the extent to which the predatory pricing will generate misallocation in the long run by causing goods that are distantly competitive with the good in question to be substituted for it.

The second factor that Joskow and Klevorick claim determines the allocative-efficiency consequences of predation is the "condition of entry," which they define in a special way to refer to the likelihood that the exit of the target will be followed by a new entry after various lapses of time. As I have already indicated, their analysis of the determinants of this factor is misguided in that it ignores the possibility that the target might be replaced by an expanding established rival of the predator, underestimates the importance of the fact that most potential competitors are large conglomerates that are already operating in allied fields, ignores the possibility that even if the target's investment is not replicated its exit might induce new entries or established-firm expansions that are further away in product-space from the predator's projects than were those of its target, and focuses on the barriers to entry (in my sense) that potential competitors face rather than on the relationship between those barriers and the highest rate-of-return the established firms could realize on their most-profitable projects post-predation if nothing else changed. However, in the discussion that follows, I will assume that the "condition of entry" is defined to indicate the probability that the target's QV investments will be replaced if it exits.

Joskow and Klevorick seem to think that the less attractive the condition of entry in their sense, the more misallocative the predator's predatory pricing. In fact, this conclusion is highly contestable. Admittedly, the less likely the target is to be replaced or the greater the delay in its replacement, the greater the extent to which the predatory pricing will decrease price competition in the long run and misallocate resources thereby. However, in the other direction, the less likely the target is to be replaced or the greater the delay in its replacement, the greater the extent to which the predatory pricing will reduce resource misallocation by decreasing the misallocation associated with the total amount of QV investment in the economy. Even if, on balance, improvements in the condition of entry are associated with decreases in the misallocativeness of the relevant predatory pricing, the connection is clearly far weaker than Joskow and Klevorick suppose: like everyone else, Joskow and Klevorick have been misled by their failure to see that we currently devote too many resources to QV-investment creation from the perspective of allocative efficiency.

This failure also undermines Joskow and Klevorick's analysis of the relevance of the contribution that small firms in the ARDEPPS in question have made to technological innovation. Although Joskow and Klevorick's discussion of this factor[580] is somewhat opaque, the innovativeness of small firms in the ARDEPPS in question could be relevant in three ways: (1) the greater the contribution of small firms to technological innovation, the more attractive the condition of entry because the greater the ability of potential competitors or, indeed, even small established firms to make innovations that will make it profitable for them to replace the target's QV investments with projects of their own; (2) the greater the technological contribution of small firms, the greater the likelihood that the target was a technological innovator and the greater the allocative cost of its elimination; and (3) the greater the technological contribution of small firms, the greater the extent to which the predation will decrease allocative efficiency by deterring non-targets from making technological innovations. Even if all three of these empirical propositions are correct, their implications for the economic efficiency of predation are not clear. Thus, the allocative-efficiency implications of the last two propositions is uncertain because they fail to distinguish between product-innovation and production-process innovation. This failure may be critical because (in my view[581]) the profitability of product-innovations is inflated (is higher than their allocative efficiency) while that of process-innovations is deflated (is lower than their allocative efficiency)—*i.e.*, because the product-innovations that predatory pricing deters may well be allocatively inefficient. Nor is the impact of the first proposition in the preceding list clear. Indeed, the preceding paragraph's analysis implies that the misallocative effect of predatory pricing may be either directly or inversely related to the contribution of small firms in the ARDEPPS in question to technological innovation.

All told, then, my analysis rejects both (1) Joskow and Klevorick's claim that the misallocativeness of a seller's predatory pricing will be primarily determined by (A) its pre-predation monopoly control over price, (B) the attractiveness of entry post-predation, and (C) the contribution of small firms in its ARDEPPS to technological innovation and (2) their claim that the misallocativeness of a seller's predatory pricing will be strongly directly related to the first and third factors just listed and will be strongly inversely related to the second of these factors.

Admittedly, other economists who have recommended two-tier approaches have proposed that courts focus on somewhat different factors in the first tier of their recommended approach. Thus, Ordover and Willig recommend that in the first tier judges focus on (1) the horizontal concentration of the relevant market, (2) "entry hurdles," (3) re-entry barriers, and (4) such other structural factors as the

[580] *Id.*

[581] See TRUTH OR ECONOMICS at 165–237.

comparative size and financial standing of the predator and its target or potential entrants.[582] In my judgment, the same kinds of objections can be made to this proposal as to Joskow and Klevorick's.

The point of the preceding analysis is not just that (1) Joskow and Klevorick and (2) Ordover and Willig have misspecified the first tier of their respective two-tier proposals but that—even if the criterion they use to evaluate approaches to determining the legality of allegedly-predatory conduct were legitimate—it would be far more complicated and costly to filter out predation cases that are not "worth considering" than they suppose. In fact, in many if not most situations, I suspect that it would be far less expensive to determine whether plaintiff has established the requisite probability that predation has been practiced than to determine the allocative efficiency of making that determination and penalizing predators.

(B) The Irrebuttable Presumption That Pricing Cannot Be Predatory If Its Alleged Target's Investments Would Be Quickly Replaced After Its Exit

Many economists have argued that the courts should refuse to consider the possibility that one or more sellers' prices were predatory unless the plaintiff can demonstrate that the defendant could recoup the cost of predation by raising its prices in the long run if the alleged predation succeeded in driving its alleged target out. More specifically, they urge, in effect, that the courts establish an irrebuttable presumption that one or more sellers' prices are not predatory in all cases in which the plaintiffs cannot prove that the alleged target's investments would not be replaced if the target exited.[583] I have five objections to this irrebuttable presumption.

First, even if predation that induces the predator's target to exit will cause that target's QV investments to be replaced by new-entry-created or rival-expansion-created QV investments that are as close in product-space to the predator's projects as were those of the exited target, the presumption ignores the possibility that the predation might increase the predator's profits in the long run if the replacement QV investments were made by firms that were more willing to accept contrived oligopolistic offers or succumb to contrived oligopolistic threats than was the predator's target or if the predation made the predator's contrived oligopolistic threats and promises more credible.

Second, the presumption ignores the possibility that predation may be profitable if it induces its target to relocate further away in product-space from the predator's projects rather than to exit altogether. Third, and relatedly, it ignores the possibility that predation may also be profitable if an exiting target's investments are replaced

[582] See Janusz Ordover and Robert Willig, *An Economic Definition of Predation*, 91 YALE L.J. 8, 12–13 (1981).

[583] See, *e.g.*, *id.* The U.S. Supreme Court has adopted this presumption in several cases. See, *e.g.*, Brooke Group Ltd. v. Brown & Williamson Tobacco Corp., 504 U.S. 209 (1993) and Matsushita Electric Industrial Co. v. Zenith Radio Corp., 475 U.S. 574 (1986).

by investments by others that are further away in product-space from the predator's projects than were the exited projects of the predator's target.

Fourth, this irrebuttable presumption is based on one of the two following incorrect assumptions: (1) that no-one engages in predation that turns out to be unprofitable because the exited investment is replaced too quickly with projects that are too close to being as competitive with the predator's investments as were its target's investments or (2) that mistaken predation that lowers prices in the short run without raising them in the long run generates no antitrust injury. The first of these assumptions is simply empirically wrong. The second is wrong because it ignores the interest of the predator's target. Even if predatory pricing benefits each of the customers of the predator and its product-rivals because the investment that is driven out is immediately replaced by an identical investment and the predatory effort does not increase contrived oligopolistic pricing, the predation would still generate an antitrust injury by inflicting losses on the predator's target—losses that were not deserved, that could not be attributed to the target's relative allocative inefficiency. In my judgment, the Sherman Act does have an "unfair competition" strain in these sorts of cases—is designed *inter alia* to protect competitors against suffering unfair losses as a result of a rival's attempts to profit by engaging in predation regardless of whether those attempts are privately misguided. I also think that it is probably appropriate to interpret now-Article 102's "abuse" language to cover predation that injures the predator's target even though it does not succeed in reducing competition.

Fifth and finally, even if I thought that this irrebuttable presumption was legally sound, I would be skeptical of its cost-effectiveness. The courts have adopted this presumption because they think it will be cheaper and more cost-effective to determine whether replacement-investments would preclude an alleged predator from recouping the immediate cost of its predation than to assess the predatory character of the defendant's allegedly-predatory pricing directly (or in any other acceptable way). Even though, for reasons that the pages that follow articulate, I reject the various price–cost predation-presumptions that others have recommended, I am not persuaded that the presumption now under consideration would be cost-effective even if it were established by legislation and constitutional. Primarily, my skepticism reflects the difficulty of determining whether predation could succeed by inducing its target to relocate in the general area of product-space in question as well as the difficulty of determining whether the replacement-investments that would be made would be as close to the predator's own projects as were the exited investments of its target—*i.e.*, reflect the fact that the projects in any area of product-space are not equally competitive with each other. Secondarily, my skepticism reflects my optimism about the cost-effectiveness of several of the methods of establishing the predatory character of a seller's pricing that I have proposed.

In any event, for the above five reasons, I would reject the irrebuttable presumption that the pricing of one or more sellers cannot be predatory if their alleged target's investment would be replaced if the target withdrew.

(C) The Irrebuttable Presumption That Prices That Are Below Conventional Marginal (or Average Variable) Cost Are Predatory

Both Areeda and Turner[584] and Joskow and Klevorick[585] appear to believe that all prices below conventional marginal cost must be illegitimate (or indeed predatory) and should be irrebuttably presumed to manifest behavior that violates the antitrust laws. Since average variable (average direct) costs are easier to ascertain than marginal costs and probably do approximate them until production exceeds full capacity, many courts that have recommended or adopted this presumption have in fact assumed that, operationally, an irrebuttable presumption of predation should be made against any seller whose prices fall below its conventional average variable cost.[586]

I also believe that most prices below the seller's conventional marginal costs are illegitimate. In fact, in several ways, my analysis reinforces this conclusion in both individualized-pricing and across-the-board-pricing contexts. Thus, my analysis implies that a worse-than-best-placed supplier's individualized price may be predatory even when it exceeds its conventional marginal costs when the price is lower than its overall marginal costs—the sum of its conventional and contextual marginal costs. Similarly, my analysis implies that a best-placed, imperfectly-informed individualized pricer's price may be predatory even if the price exceeds its overall marginal costs if the price is lower than the price that would maximize the pricer's certainty-equivalent profits, strategic considerations aside, given its uncertainty about the height of its inherently-most-profitable price. In particular, an uncertain best-placed individualized pricer's decision to charge a price that was below its inherently-most-profitable price would be predatory even if the price exceeded the pricer's overall marginal costs if it charged the price to reduce the certainty-equivalent profits a target rival should expect to make from the best-placed seller's errors in the hope of driving the target out, of deterring it from entering, or of inducing it (or someone else) to locate its project further from the predator's QV investments. Indeed, my analysis also implies that not only sub-conventional-marginal-cost prices but also *supra*-conventional-marginal-cost across-the-board prices are more likely to be predatory than standard economic analysis suggests by revealing that an across-the-board pricer's lowest legitimate price typically exceeds its marginal costs by far more than its average BCA when it is best-placed—in particular, exceeds its MC as well by the across-the-board equivalent to an individualized pricer's closest rival's contextual marginal costs (roughly speaking,

---

[584] See PHILIP AREEDA & DONALD TURNER, ANTITRUST LAW (hereinafter AREEDA & TURNER) vol. 3, 711a (Little Brown, 1978). These authors limit this conclusion to cases in which the price in question is also below average total cost. *Id.* at 711d and 715b. This limitation is illogical. It would be justified only if all those but only those sub-marginal-cost prices that exceeded average total cost represented legitimate promotional or learning-by-doing pricing. There is no reason to believe that either of these conditions is fulfilled.

[585] Joskow and Klevorick at 252

[586] See *id.* at 251 note 76.

exceeds its MC *inter alia* by the difference between the prices its rivals offer its customers and the marginal costs its rivals would have to incur to supply them).

However, despite this fact, I reject the conclusion that all sub-marginal-cost prices should be irrebuttably presumed to be predatory or prohibited by the antitrust laws for two different reasons: (1) because sub-marginal-cost prices can be legitimately profitable when they generate promotional-pricing, learning-by-doing pricing, keeping-in-touch pricing, and legitimate-defensive-retaliation benefits and (2) because prices that are too low to be legitimately profitable may not be predatory or violative of the antitrust laws—may be mistaken or simply tortious (motivated purely by spite). Even if the mistake possibility is highly unlikely, the others must be taken into account. Promotional pricing, learning-by-doing pricing, and keeping-in-touch pricing are all clearly legitimate—indeed, are all procompetitive. Defensive retaliation must be distinguished from predation because it is not illegal for a target of a contriver's retaliation or a predator's predation to try to protect itself by retaliating against the predator or the retaliating rival whose contrived oligopolistic prices it had undercut. And tortious pricing-campaigns that are designed to injure or drive out a rival must be distinguished from predation (1) because they may be neither predatory (since they may be motivated by pure spite—*i.e.*, by a desire to injure the competitor and not competition) nor monopolizing (since they may do nothing more than injure the competitor—*i.e.*, since they may not in fact reduce competition, may simply reduce the target's profits without driving it out or force the target out in circumstances in which it will be immediately replaced by an equally-effective rival) and (2) because the *fora*, penalties, and damage awards that are available when the defendant's behavior is neither predatory nor monopolizing—*i.e.*, in business-tort actions—are quite different from their antitrust counterparts.

Hence, although I would certainly agree that sub-marginal-cost pricing is usually either predatory or illegally retaliatory and would think it appropriate to allow the State or a private plaintiff to establish a *prima facie* case of predatory pricing by proving that the defendant's price was below its conventional marginal costs, I do not think that all sub-marginal-cost prices should be irrebuttably presumed to violate the antitrust laws. Defendants that have been shown to have charged prices below their conventional marginal costs must be given the opportunity to exonerate themselves by establishing the requisite probability that their prices were promotional, motivated by a desire to learn by doing or to keep in touch, mistaken, legitimately retaliatory, or motivated by pure spite.

(D) The Partially-Rebuttable Presumption That Supra-Marginal-Cost Prices That Are Below Average Total Cost Are Predatory

Joskow and Klevorick argue that, except when the market in question contains "substantial excess production capacity" that the defendant has not created to deter entry, a dominant firm that responds to entry by reducing its prices below its average total costs should be presumed to have engaged in predatory pricing (if the market's characteristics seem to favor the profitability of predatory pricing while making any such pricing that is practiced particularly undesirable).[587] Although Joskow and Klevorick seem to be focusing on the situation of a dominant seller operating in an across-the-board-pricing market that had recently been entered, nothing they say is inconsistent with this proposal's applying to non-dominant sellers, to individualized-pricing markets, or to markets in which entry has not recently taken place—*e.g.*, to individualized-pricing markets in which one or more established firms have recently added to their QV investments or indeed to individualized-pricing markets in which no new QV investment has recently been made.

I should emphasize at the outset that I am far more skeptical about the cost-effectiveness of comparisons of a seller's price with its average total cost than Joskow and Klevorick and others appear to be: the task of estimating the economic value of a firm's fixed assets and of allocating the overhead costs of a multi-product or diversified firm has always seemed forbidding to me. But assume for the moment that ATC can be determined sufficiently accurately sufficiently cheaply to make comparisons of P and ATC a potentially-cost-effective option. Are prices that were below average total costs (for significant periods of time?) sufficiently likely to be predatory to justify Joskow and Klevorick's partially-rebuttable presumption? In my judgment, this question must be given a negative answer both in the across-the-board-pricing context on which Joskow and Klevorick appear to have focused and in situations in which prices are set on an individualized basis.

Joskow and Klevorick do admit that a sub-ATC price may be legitimately profit-maximizing when the alleged predator is operating in a declining market or when a potential competitor has recently entered at a scale that would result in capacity's being "underutilized" if price equaled average total cost. They also admit that this result may obtain when the dominant firm had followed "a conscious strategy of carrying excess capacity so as to deter entry,"[588] though they believe that such a firm should not be allowed to justify its sub-average-total-cost price as being legitimately profit-maximizing in this case.

However, the real point is that, for a variety of reasons, particular QV investments may not be capable of yielding normal rates-of-return at particular stages of their existence. For example, this result could obtain (1) because a decrease in ARDEPPS demand reduced equilibrium QV-investment level below the ARDEPPS' current, actual QV-investment level, (2) because a new entrant or expanding established firm mistakenly raised ARDEPPS QV investment above its equilibrium level, (3) because a new entrant or expanding established firm made a QV investment it knew would raise ARDEPPS QV investment above its current, static-equilibrium level in the belief that growth in ARDEPPS demand, the exit of other QV investments, or the superiority of its own QV investment would enable it to realize at least a normal rate-of-return on its project over its whole life, (4) because the QV investment that was yielding subnormal profits had been a mistake, or (5) because, even if the ARDEPPS' equilibrium QV-investment level would not increase in the future, the QV

[587] See *id.* at 252–54.

[588] *Id.* at 253.

investment that was yielding subnormal profits in the period in question would yield at least a normal rate-of-return over its lifetime. Joskow and Klevorick's declining-industry case corresponds to the first possibility just listed; their large-scale-of-entry case relates to the second but misstates the conditions under which it will occur since it will not always be profitable to set a price below ATC when MC is less than ATC where demand intersects ATC, since the same problem can arise from established-firm QV investments as from new entries, and since Joskow and Klevorick incorrectly imply that in all these cases capacity will be underutilized in an economic sense when in fact their argument implies neither this (since capacity that is usually not utilized may be economically efficient when demand fluctuates through time) nor that the capacity in question will be underutilized in a technological sense (since the relevant product should be defined to reflect average speed of supply); and their limit-investment-in-capacity case incorrectly assumes that a defendant should be barred from proving that its prices are inherently profitable when it has made limit investments in capacity. This latter assumption is unjustified for two reasons: (1) because limit investments will usually not raise QV investment in the ARDEPPS in question in that they will deter others from making equally-large or indeed even larger QV investments and (2) because, as we shall see in Section 4 of this chapter, limit investments will usually not be predatory or illegal—*i.e.*, because on both these accounts the principle that underlies Joskow and Klevorick's assumption (the principle that "a man should not profit from his own wrong") does not imply that a limit investor ought to be barred from justifying its sub-ATC price by demonstrating that it was inherently profitable.

In any case, I tend to think that one or more of these conditions are fulfilled quite often and correspondingly that even across-the-board sub-ATC prices are frequently inherently profitable. It is also important to note in this connection that, even if sub-ATC prices are not profit-maximizing in the short run, they may be inherently profitable if they help the investor increase the demand for its product and/or decrease the cost of producing its product in the long run (*i.e.*, if they perform promotional or learning-by-doing functions) or perhaps if they protect the pricer against future predation or illegal retaliation (*i.e.*, if they are defensively retaliatory). And, as we have seen, prices that are too low to be inherently profitable in the conventional sense of that phrase may still not violate the antitrust laws—*viz.*, may be mistaken or motivated by spite. For all these reasons, then, I believe that the probability that a seller that is charging a supra-marginal-cost across-the-board price that is below its average total cost is not violating the antitrust laws is too high for Joskow and Klevorick's partially-rebuttable presumption of predation to be justified.

Obviously, all the arguments that led me to conclude that many sellers whose across-the-board prices do not cover their average total cost are not violating the antitrust laws will also apply to individualized-pricing sellers that are failing to realize a normal rate-of-return. Of course, in individualized-pricing contexts, the real issue is usually whether the prices an accused seller is offering buyers that one or more of its rivals are privately better-placed to supply are predatory. As we have seen, the lowest legitimate price that a seller that is not trying to engage in promotional pricing, to learn by doing, to keep in touch, or to practice defensive retaliation could offer someone else's customer in an individualized-pricing context will virtually always exceed the seller's conventional marginal costs. However, the fact that a seller X has offered to supply someone else's customer at a price that is lower than X's ATC certainly does not make it likely that its offer was predatory. Indeed, I suspect that many individualized pricers offer many of their own customers prices that fail to cover their average total costs. Accordingly, I do not think that the State or a private plaintiff can establish a presumption that a seller has engaged in predatory pricing simply by showing that the accused offered to supply some buyers (or indeed some rival's customers) at a price below its ATC.

I should not end this discussion of Joskow and Klevorick's proposal that prices that are above marginal cost but below average total cost be rebuttably presumed to be predatory without mentioning the fact that this recommendation conflicts with Areeda and Turner's proposal that prices that are above marginal cost (which they recommend be assumed to equal average variable cost, which they think is more measurable) but below average total cost be rebuttably presumed to be non-predatory.[589] As the preceding critique of Joskow and Klevorick's proposal implies, I agree with Areeda and Turner's position on this issue.

(E) The Rebuttable Presumption That Prices That Equal or Exceed Average Total Cost Are Not Predatory

Although Joskow and Klevorick recognize that a price above average total cost might still be predatory,[590] they propose that "a price decrease to a point above average total cost. . .be presumed to be legal unless the price cut were reversed either fully or to a significant extent within a reasonable period of time—for example, 2 years."[591] The next subsection analyzes the reversed-price cut presumption. This subsection focuses on the P > ATC presumption that the reversed-price–cost presumption can override.

Once more, Joskow and Klevorick seem to be focusing on a situation in which the accused has responded to entry by reducing its price. However, their argument

[589] See AREEDA & TURNER, vol. 3, 711a (1978).

[590] See Joskow and Klevorick at 254. Once more, however, the example they offer of such a supra-ATC predatory price is a limit-pricing example, indeed a limit-pricing example that again puts too much stress on the profits the new entrant can make just after entry. See *id.* at 254–55 note 85. Since I think that limit pricing is rarely if ever practiced and doubt that the returns a new entrant can realize in the "immediate post-entry" period would often be critical in any case (since most entrants are large conglomerates that are perfectly able to finance short-run losses), I question the appositeness of this example. I should add that, although Joskow and Klevorick never addressed the following admittedly-probably-rare possibility, I am certain that they would grant that prices that exceed average total cost may well be predatory if they are below marginal cost, a possibility that can occur when the seller in question is operating above full capacity—*i.e.*, where MC > ATC.

[591] *Id.* at 255.

would seem to be equally applicable to situations in which no entry or indeed QV-investment expansion had recently taken place as well as to situations in which the allegedly-predatory pricing-act was not a price cut but a failure to increase price(s) when changes in conditions would appear to have raised the alleged predator's LLP or a choice to increase price(s) by less than the relevant changes in conditions would appear to require. Joskow and Klevorick also appear to be focusing on the pricing behavior of dominant firms, though once more I can think of no reason to limit their proposal to such sellers.

Joskow and Klevorick's argument for this presumption that all prices that equal or exceed ATC are legal is based on four premises: (1) although "a dominant firm's price cuts to levels below average total cost. . .almost always reflect a departure from short-run profit maximization,"[592] a price cut to a point above ATC is unlikely to be predatory (at least this premise is implied both by their conclusion and by their introducing their admission that *supra*-ATC prices might be predatory with the tell-tale adverbial phrase "at least in theory")[593]; (2) no "simple formula that the courts could utilize effectively"[594] could enable the courts to distinguish legitimately-competitive price cuts from their predatory counterparts; (3) "no practical way exists to distinguish a predatory price cut to a point above average total cost from one that is a short-run profit-maximizing response to the growth of competition"[595]; and (4) any attempt to draw the necessary distinction "runs the serious risk of restricting truly competitive price cuts."[596]

In brief, (1) I disagree with Joskow and Klevorick's optimism about the legitimacy of prices that exceed ATC because any across-the-board pricer whose projects are more profitable than an established rival's and whose legitimate (*i.e.*, non-strategic) profit-maximizing price exceeds its ATC may be able to profit by driving such a potential target out by charging *supra*-ATC prices that are lower than its legitimate profit-maximizing price—*i.e.*, because in my judgment, for this reason, the percentage of *supra*-ATC prices that are predatory is too high for Joskow and Klevorick's irrebuttable presumption to be justicizable; (2) I agree that no "simple" formula can be developed to test the predatory character of a price that exceeds ATC; (3) I regard as conclusory Joskow and Klevorick's assertion that "no practical way" exists to distinguish those prices in excess of ATC that are predatory and non-predatory; and (4) I believe that their conclusion that any attempt to draw the relevant distinction would produce an unacceptable probability of false findings of predation is both gratuitous and incorrect: there is absolutely no reason why a court that started with a reasonable assumption about the likelihood that a price that exceeds ATC would be predatory should be likely to be misled by a plaintiff's attempt to demonstrate that such a price was below the lowest legitimate

---

[592] *Id.* at 254–55.

[593] *Id.* at 254.

[594] *Id.* at 255.

[595] *Id.*

[596] *Id.*

price the relevant seller could charge by introducing any of the various types of evidence I have described. It may be that, from the perspective of allocative efficiency, the cost of establishing predation in such cases will be prohibitive, but judges are not authorized to exclude cases on the ground that their adjudication would not be economically efficient, and such case-dismissals might not be overall-desirable (rights-considerations aside) in any event.

(F) The Presumption That Predation Was Practiced or the Claim That There Is a Substantial Likelihood That Predation Was Practiced When a (Dominant?) Seller Significantly or Fully Reversed a Price Cut Within 5 (or 2) Years of Having Made It (When the Price-Cut Was Followed by the Withdrawal of a New Entrant's or Expanding Established Firm's New QV Investment?)

Both William Baumol[597] and Joskow and Klevorick[598] adopt some version of an "unsustained price reduction" test for predatory pricing.[599] Baumol proposes that courts presume that any post-entry price-reduction by a dominant firm (that is followed by the exit of the new entrant) and that is not sustained for 5 years should be presumed to be predatory. I have already explained why any such test should not be limited to dominant firms or to situations in which a QV investment has been executed and withdrawn by a new entrant as opposed to by an expanding incumbent. Baumol's proposal is unwarranted both because it ignores the fact that the creation and withdrawal of an additional QV investment in an ARDEPPS will lead respectively to a decrease and increase in its pre-existing products' LLPs and because, as Joskow and Klevorick acknowledged,[600] in many situations the reversal of the price-cut in question will have been caused by increases in the alleged predator's LLP that are unrelated to the exit of the alleged target.

Joskow and Klevorick's version of this presumption, which in their words is "essentially the one advocated by Baumol,"[601] is used to reverse their normal presumption that prices above ATC are not predatory. According to Joskow and Klevorick, if a (dominant?) seller executes a price-cut to some level above its ATC that is followed by a rival's withdrawal of QV investment,[602] its decision to reverse this cut "either fully or to a significant extent. . .within 2 years"[603] should establish a rebuttable presumption that its initial price-cut was predatory. In essence, then,

---

[597] William Baumol, *Quasi-Permanence of Price Reductions: A Policy For Prevention of Predatory Pricing*, 89 YALE L.J. 1, 4–6 (1979).

[598] See Joskow and Klevorick at 255.

[599] See *id.* for their formulation of this test.

[600] *Id.*

[601] *Id.*

[602] I interpret Joskow and Klevorick's statement that this "test" would come into play only after "the 'predatory process' [has] run its course" to imply this requirement. See *id.*

[603] *Id.*

Joskow and Klevorick have altered Baumol's proposal by reducing the period in which price-cut reversals would be presumed to be predatory from 5 years to 2 years and by allowing the alleged predator to rebut the presumption of predation by showing that its price-increase was due to a rise in its LLP that was independent of the exit of the new entrant.

Although the latter change is an improvement, essentially the same objections can be made to Joskow and Klevorick's proposal as to the Baumol proposal: (1) if it is cost-effective, it should not be restricted to dominant firms; (2) if it is cost-effective, it should not be restricted to situations in which a new entry has been executed and withdrawn: since a high percentage of the new entrants in the kinds of ARDEPPSes in which predation may be practiced are large conglomerates that are no more vulnerable than expanding established firms or, indeed, than established firms that have not expanded and since in many areas of product-space the percentage of new entries that fail that were not the target of predation is high, a reversed price-cut is not sufficiently more likely to have been predatory when the initial price-cut was preceded by a new entry and followed by the new entrant's exit to justify restricting this Joskow-and-Klevorick presumption to situations in which an originally-potential competitor has made and then withdrawn a QV investment; and (3) since the execution and withdrawal of a QV investment by an originally-potential competitor will respectively reduce and increase the LLPs of the established firms in the ARDEPPS in question, the fact that a price-cut that was made after a new entry has taken place was reversed after the new entrant exited is too unlikely to be associated with predation to warrant a rebuttable presumption that the pricer in question had practiced predation both in general and when the reversed price-cut resulted in the seller's charging a price that exceeded its average total cost.

(G) The Irrebuttable Presumption That Any Dominant Firm That Responds to Entry by Increasing Its Output (by More Than 10 %) Within 12–18 Months of the Entry's Occurrence Has Practiced Predatory Pricing

Baumol's proposed presumption was actually a response to the related proposal of Oliver Williamson that is delineated in the above heading.[604] Admittedly, any such post-entry increase in an established-firm's output is suspicious: although one would expect a new entry to cause each established firm to reduce its prices by reducing its LLPs, one would also expect any additional quantity-sales each such firm would obtain on this account in comparison with the *status quo ante* to be lower than the amount of sales it would lose to the new entrant. Nevertheless, even within the 12–18-month period on which the Williamson proposal focuses, the

---

[604] See Oliver Williamson, *Predatory Pricing: A Strategic and Welfare Analysis*, 87 YALE L.J. 284 (1977). Williamson also proposed that prices that do not cover average total cost be deemed to be predatory. *Id.* at 296 and 333–34.

probability that independent reductions in costs or independent increases in ARDEPPS demand would cause the established firms in a recently-entered ARDEPPS to increase their outputs by more than 10 % is simply too high not only for the irrebuttable presumption Williamson proposes to be acceptable but even for a rebuttable presumption to be acceptable. Indeed, the difficulty and expense of proving the relevant cost-decreases and/or demand-increases reinforce my inclination to think that even a rebuttable presumption of predation is inappropriate in the circumstances on which we are now focusing.

* * *

In short, for a variety of reasons, I would reject all the presumptions that academic economists or economist-lawyers have proposed courts adopt in predatory-pricing cases. Some must be rejected because they are allegedly justified by allocative-efficiency considerations that are not supposed to determine judicial decisions of the kinds in question (and because the proposals are less likely to increase allocative efficiency than their proponents claim). Some must be rejected because they will not reduce costs as much as their proponents assume. But most must be rejected because they overestimate the probability that the defendants to which they apply have in fact engaged in predatory pricing and/or underestimate the feasibility of a defendant's exonerating itself by establishing facts that demonstrate that its pricing was not predatory.

The only proper way to prove predatory pricing is to use one or more of the five types of evidence that Subsection A(1) of this chapter described. Although antitrust-law presumptions are desirable if authorized and cost-effective, most of those that have been proposed in the predatory-pricing-suit context should be rejected.

E. The U.S. Case-Law, EC Position, and E.C./E.U. Case-Law on Predatory Pricing

(1) The U.S. Case-Law on Predatory Pricing

I will make 11 points or cluster of points about the relevant case-law. The first point is that the U.S. case-law on predatory pricing seems to reflect an effort by the courts to strike an appropriate balance between underdeterring predatory pricing by failing to convict or find liable defendants that have, in fact, engaged in predatory pricing and deterring legitimate price competition by convicting or finding liable defendants accused of predatory pricing whose pricing was, in fact, legitimately competitive. In my view, even if one could delineate an uncontestable standard for evaluating any such balance from a "policy" perspective, U.S. courts would not be authorized to handle predatory-pricing cases in this way. The duty of U.S. courts is to find the defendant(s) guilty in any criminal predatory-pricing cases if and only if its (their) guilt has been established beyond a reasonable doubt and to find the defendant(s) liable in civil predatory-pricing cases if and only if its (their) liability has been established by a preponderance of the evidence. U.S. courts are not authorized to develop the decision-protocol for deciding predatory-pricing cases whose use will maximize economic efficiency or some other objective function that takes account of one or more relevant, defensible distributive norms when the use of that protocol will not result in the courts' deciding each such case as accurately as it can. If it would be desirable for the United States to have an operational decision-rule to determine the prices that are illegally low that was underinclusive, overinclusive, or partially underinclusive and partially overinclusive from the perspective of the goal of prohibiting predatory pricing, the Congress not the courts should promulgate it.

The second point is that the way in which the U.S. courts strike the balance between underdeterring predatory pricing and deterring legitimate price-reductions is significantly influenced by the justices' and judges' belief that "predatory pricing schemes are rarely tried, and even more rarely successful." U.S. courts seem to have been persuaded that this is the case by the economics scholarship on this point that I criticized earlier in this chapter. Although I cannot provide empirical evidence to support my contrary conclusion, I believe that predatory pricing is practiced far more often than U.S. courts recognize.

The third point is that Section 1 of Chap. 4's general account of the way in which U.S. courts have applied Section 2 of the Sherman Act is fully consistent with the approach that U.S. courts have taken to Sherman Act predatory-pricing cases. In particular, U.S. courts insist that, to win a Section 2 predatory-pricing case, the State or private plaintiff must demonstrate *inter alia* (1) that, prior to engaging in the conduct alleged to be predatory, the defendant(s) had monopoly or market power in the area of product-space in which the alleged predation supposedly took place (was planned) and (2) that the pricing in question either succeeded in driving out a rival or created a "dangerous probability" of generating such an outcome. As Chap. 4 indicated, I reject the requirement that defendants be shown to have had market power prior to engaging in the conduct alleged to be predatory because—far from being a necessary condition for a defendant's having predatory intent or its conduct's yielding it profits by driving a rival out, deterring a rival QV investment, or inducing a rival to relocate an extant or planned QV investment—the defendant's prior possession of market power in the area of product-space in which the alleged predation took place is not even strongly or significantly correlated with its having such an intent or its conduct's yielding profits in one or more of these ways. As Chap. 4 also stated, although "structural" evidence that really does establish that an attempt at predation was unlikely to be successful or profitable in the circumstances of a given case clearly does disfavor the conclusion that the defendant had engaged in predatory pricing (because, in general, firms engage in predation only when it would be profitable for them to do so), I do not think it appropriate for a court to make proof that the conduct alleged to be predatory either succeeded in increasing its perpetrator's profits by driving a rival out or created a dangerous probability of the perpetrator's profits being increased in this way a necessary condition for Sherman Act liability: given that firms can violate the Sherman Act by attempting to monopolize by engaging in predatory conduct that has little or no probability of success, subjective evidence (see below) that firms had predatory intent or objective evidence (see below) that firms had charged prices that were lower than their LLPs and had not done so for any legitimate reason should be considered to justify a conviction even if the defendant had no chance of driving any rival out or profiting from doing so.

The fourth point is that the Supreme Court has concluded that predatory pricing is covered by the law of monopolization as opposed to the law of attempts to monopolize. I have never understood the point of distinguishing "attempts to monopolize" and "monopolization" and have therefore always dismissed as pointless the Court's development of separate doctrines to deal with "attempts to monopolize" and "monopolization." However, if Herbert Hovenkamp is correct in concluding that "the market power requirement [for proving a "dangerous probability" of success] for the attempt offense is much less than it is for the offense of monopolization,"[605] I will have to revise my assessment (for consequential as opposed to truth-related reasons) of the Court's distinguishing "attempt to monopolize" cases from "monopolization" cases: to the extent that it is easier for plaintiffs in "attempt to monopolize" cases than for plaintiffs in monopolization cases to satisfy the Court's mistaken requirement that, to win, non-State plaintiffs or the State must establish that the defendant(s) had market power prior to engaging in the allegedly-illegal conduct, I am pleased that the Court classifies some of the conduct in question as "attempts to monopolize" rather than as monopolization. Of course, since the Court has classified predatory pricing to involve monopolization as opposed to an attempt to monopolize, this second-best argument for paying attention to the distinction in question does not apply when predatory pricing is at issue.

The fifth point or cluster of points relates to the U.S. courts' comments on the relevance of "intent" evidence in monopolization/attempt-to-monopolize cases in general and in predation/predatory-pricing cases in particular. I think that specific-anticompetitive-intent is almost always a critical issue in monopolization cases. The U.S. courts do not seem to accept this conclusion. In my view, some of the positions that U.S. federal courts have taken on the relevance of "intent" in Section 2 cases are simply wrong, and some are critically ambiguous. The position that is wrong is the statement of Judge Learned Hand that one can "disregard any question of intent" in monopolization cases because "no monopolist monopolizes unconscious of what it is doing."[606] This argument is wrong because it assumes incorrectly as a matter of law that the monopolization that the Sherman Act prohibits is charging supra-competitive prices (and/or perhaps realizing a supernormal profit-rate). Even if firms never do those things unconsciously, that fact would have no bearing on the legal salience of whether a defendant had the kind of specific anticompetitive intent that I think is almost always critical for the illegality of its conduct under the Sherman Act. The position that is ambiguous is the Supreme

[605] See HOVENKAMP ANTITRUST at 151.

[606] United States v. Aluminum Co. of American (Alcoa), 148 F.2d 416, 432 (2d Cir. 1945).

Court's oft-reiterated 1966 pronouncement that a critical element of the offense of monopolization (or attempting to monopolize) is "the willful acquisition or maintenance of [market] power."[607] It seems to me that on its most plausible interpretation this language implies that the Court's position is coincident with my claim that a critical element of the offense of monopolization or attempting to monopolize is the perpetrator's specific anticompetitive intent. However, I have to admit that, semantically, one could interpret "willful acquisition or maintenance of [market] power" to include choices made with the knowledge that they would create market power that did not manifest specific anticompetitive intent, indeed (conceivably) that did not manifest the chooser's belief that the choice in question would or might reduce the absolute attractiveness of the offers against which it would have to compete. Somewhat more concretely, the Supreme Court has drawn a distinction between "subjective evidence of intent"—*i.e.*, defendant statements or writings indicating that the defendant was (consciously) engaging in predation—and "objective evidence of intent"—*i.e.*, evidence that the defendant's conduct would not have been profitable had it not increased the defendant's profits by achieving predatory goals (evidence from which one could infer the defendant's subjective predatory intent if the defendant could not create a requisite probability that it had simply made a mistake). The Court seems to have drawn this distinction because it believes that "objective evidence of intent" is more relevant than "subjective evidence of intent." I acknowledge both that evidence of what the federal courts denominate "objective evidence of intent" does have substantial probative value and that statements by defendants that plaintiffs have argued constitute subjective evidence of predatory intent are often ambiguous. Thus, as Judge Frank Easterbrook (an economically-sophisticated former Professor of Law at the University of Chicago) pointed out in a 1989 decision, the defendant's statement to the plaintiff—"We are going to run you out of the egg business. Your days are numbered."—is as consistent with the defendant's intending to engage in legitimate competition as with its intending to practice predatory pricing.[608] Nevertheless, I am worried by the courts' "preference for" objective evidence of intent over subjective evidence of intent not only because some subjective evidence of intent is highly probative but also because I fear that in practice courts may be placing undue weight on some kinds of evidence that are part of the evidence they denominate "objective evidence"—*viz.*, (1) evidence that the defendant's conduct will drive a rival out or critically raise the barriers to QV investment facing an otherwise-effective potential QV investor and (2) evidence that in so doing the conduct in question will raise the defendant's profits. More specifically, I am concerned that the courts believe that such "objective evidence" suffices to establish perpetrator liability when, in fact, it

---

[607] See United States v. Grinnell Corp., 384 U.S. 563, 570–71 (1966). See also Wheeling-Pittsburgh Steel Corp. v. Mitsui & Co., 35 F. Supp. 2d 597 (S.D. Ohio 1999); Coastal Fuels of Puerto Rico, Inc. v. Caribbean Petroleum Corp., 79 F.3d 182 (1st Cir. 1996); and Rebel Oil Co., Inc. v. Atlantic Richfield Co., 51 F.3d 1421 (9th Cir. 1995).

[608] See A.A. Poultry Farms, Inc. v. Rose Acre Farms, Inc., 881 F.2d 1396, 1402 (7th Cir. 1989).

does not since it does not establish that the actual profitability (and *a fortiori* that the defendant's *ex ante* belief that the conduct in question was profitable) was critically affected by its generating these effects (by the defendant's belief that it would or might generate these effects)—*i.e.*, I am concerned that in practice the courts' preference for "objective evidence of intent" manifests their failure to understand that the actual test of illegality is a subjective specific-anticompetitive-intent test of illegality.

The sixth point that should be made is that the doctrine that U.S. courts have developed to deal with Clayton Act (Robinson-Patman Act) predatory-price-discrimination claims is different from the doctrine that it uses to resolve Sherman Act Section 2 cases. I wish I could say that the relevant differences in doctrine can be explained entirely by the difference in the tests of illegality that the two statutes promulgate. Regrettably, the U.S. case-law on Robinson-Patman Act predatory-pricing price-discrimination claims does not seem to clearly distinguish between the Clayton Act's competitive-impact test and the Sherman Acts' specific-anticompetitive-intent test. In any event, the U.S. judicial doctrine that applies to Robinson-Patman Act predatory-pricing price-discrimination cases does differ from the doctrine that applies to Sherman Act Section 2 predatory-pricing cases in two significant respects. First, the State or private plaintiffs can win Robinson-Patman Act cases without demonstrating that the defendant had monopoly or market power in the market in which the allegedly-predatory pricing took place prior to engaging in the conduct in question—*i.e.*, the courts do not carry over to the Clayton Act this mistaken requirement that Sherman Act plaintiffs demonstrate the defendant's prior possession of monopoly power. Second, according to the applicable judicial doctrines, the State or a private plaintiff can win a Robinson-Patman Act suit by establishing that the price discrimination in which the defendant(s) engaged created a "reasonable possibility" of a substantial injury to competition whereas the State or a private plaintiff can win a Sherman Act Section 2 suit only by establishing the existence of "a dangerous probability" that the conduct in question will succeed. In the Supreme Court's words, it

> interprets Section 2 of the Sherman Act to condemn predatory pricing when it poses a dangerous probability of actual monopolization..., whereas the Robinson-Patman Act requires only that there be a "reasonable possibility" of substantial injury to competition before its protections are triggered.[609]

As Chap. 4 indicated, I think that this difference is warranted by a combination of the texts of the relevant statutes, the rule that, to prevail in a civil suit, the plaintiff must establish its case by a preponderance of the evidence, and the rule

---

[609] See Brooke Group Ltd. (Liggett) v. Brown & Williamson Tobacco Corp., 509 U.S. 209, 225 (1993), citing Spectrum Sports, Inc. v. McQuillan, 506 U.S. 447, 459 (1993) for the relevant element of the Sherman Act test and Falls City Industries, Inc. v. Vanco Beverages, Inc., 460 U.S. 428, 434 (1983) for the relevant element of the Robinson-Patman Act point. Later in Brooke Group, the Court substituted the expression "reasonable prospect" for "a reasonable possibility." See Brooke Group Ltd. (Liggett) v Brown & Williamson Tobacco Corp., 509 U.S. 209, 242 (1993).

that, to prevail in a criminal suit, the State must prove guilt beyond a reasonable doubt.

The seventh point relates to the U.S. Supreme Court's position on the extent to which one can infer predatory pricing from various sorts of price/cost comparisons. I will start by providing two quotations from the Supreme Court's 1993 opinion in *Brooke Group* and then comment on these two statements or sets of statements. In the first quotation, the Court declares that, to win a Section 2 Sherman Act predatory-pricing suit, the State or private plaintiff must demonstrate that the defendant had willfully obtained or maintained (attempted to obtain or maintain) market power by charging prices below "an appropriate measure of its rival's costs."[610] In the second, the Court states:

> Although *Cargill* and *Matsushita* reserved as a formal matter the question "'whether recovery should *ever* be available. . .when the pricing is above some measure of incremental cost,'" *Cargill* (quoting *Matsushita*), the reasoning in both opinions suggests that only below-cost prices should suffice, and we have rejected elsewhere the notion that above-cost prices that are below general market levels or the costs of a firm's competitors inflict injury to competition cognizable under the antitrust laws. *See Atlantic Richfield Co. v. USA Petroleum Co.*, 495 U.S. 328 (1990).... As a general rule, the exclusionary effect of prices above a relevant measured cost either reflects the lower cost structure of the alleged predator, and so represents competition on the merits, or is beyond the practical ability of a judicial tribunal to control without courting intolerable risks of chilling legitimate price-cutting. "To hold that the antitrust laws protect competitors from the loss of profits due to such price competition would, in effect, render illegal any decision by a firm to cut prices in order to increase market share. The antitrust laws require no such perverse result."[611]

I have three comments. First, the Court would have done well to have focused separately on the relevance of (1) the relationship between an alleged predator's price and an appropriate measure of the alleged target's costs and (2) the relationship between an alleged predator's price and various types of costs the alleged predator itself had incurred or would incur. Second, when consumers whose patronage an alleged target is best-placed to obtain have a buyer preference for the alleged predator's product over the alleged target's product (which is more than offset by the target's MCA over the alleged predator), the alleged predator can also practice predation by charging prices that exceed the alleged target's marginal or average total cost. Third, the Court must determine the "appropriate measure" of both "the rival's" (*i.e.*, the alleged target's) costs and the alleged predator's costs and must also analyze the relevance of the fact that the alleged predator's price is "below general market levels." All things considered, I find the Supreme Court's comments on the possible relevance of price/cost comparisons to the resolution of predatory-pricing cases jumbled, insufficiently-well-defined, and ill-considered.

---

[610] See *id.* at 222.

[611] See *id.*, citing Matsushita Electric Industrial Co., Ltd. v. Zenith Radio Corp., 475 U.S. 574 (1986) and Cargill, Inc. v. Monfort of Colorado, Inc., 479 U.S. 104 (1986).

The eighth point or cluster of points that should be made relate to the way in which the U.S. Courts of Appeal have operationalized these Supreme Court price/cost "guidelines." Because the lower courts' positions were really responses to proposals made by two Harvard Law School professors (Philip Areeda and Donald Turner[612]), one of whom (Turner) was a Ph.D. economist as well as a lawyer and had served as head of the U.S. Antitrust Division, I will begin this discussion by summarizing their proposals.

The Areeda-Turner test for predatory pricing had three prongs, two of which incorporated a pragmatic recommendation. The pragmatic recommendation was that average variable cost (AVC) be substituted for marginal cost (MC): the proffered justification was that AVC tends to be close to MC at the relevant output-levels and is much easier to estimate than MC. The three prongs (which were said to apply only to firms with pre-existing monopoly power in the market in which the pricing in question took place) were:

(1) a price above "full cost" (*i.e.*, average total cost) should be irrebuttably presumed to be non-predatory and therefore lawful;
(2) a price above average variable cost but below average total cost should be rebuttably presumed to be non-predatory and lawful (rebuttably in that the presumption can be rebutted by subjective evidence of predatory intent and/or proof that the relevant price was inherently unprofitable); and
(3) a price lower than average variable cost should be irrebuttably presumed to be predatory and therefore illegal.

The U.S. Courts of Appeal initially embraced the Areeda-Turner predatory-pricing tests.[613] However, over time, they at least partially rejected all four parts of the Areeda-Turner approach.

The first part of the Areeda-Turner approach that U.S. courts began to question was the way in which Areeda and Turner proposed to measure AVC, which they thought should be substituted for MC. Disagreement centered on how courts should respond to the difficulty of determining whether advertising and research costs should be considered to be fixed or variable costs. (Courts were also uncertain about how joint costs should be handled.) It seems to me clear that, for the purpose of determining whether a seller's pricing is predatory, research costs are fixed costs, advertising costs are variable costs only when the issue is whether the combination of the advertising campaign used to make certain sales and the pricing of the goods sold was inherently profitable or predatory (a question that requires the analyst to take account of any long-run benefits the advertising generated as well as the short-run consequences of the advertising and the immediate sales it generated), and joint costs should be handled by (1) assigning all of them to each product whose production/distribution yielded them but (2) crediting to each such product the

[612] See Philip Areeda and Donald Turner, *Predatory Pricing and Related Practices Under § 2 of the Sherman Act*, 88 HARV. L. REV. 697 (1975).

[613] See, *e.g.*, Pacific Engineering & Production Co. of Nevada v. Kerr-McGee Corp., 551 F.2d 790 (10th Cir. 1977).

profits one would calculate the sale of the associated units of the other products involved yielded if none of the joint costs were assigned to those other products' production and distribution. In any event, some circuits rejected Areeda and Turner's response to this problem—a proposal that certain categories of such costs always be considered variable and other categories of such costs always be considered fixed—in favor of a case-by-case approach.[614] On a related but different issue, at least one circuit supplemented the Areeda-Turner position on variable costs by deciding (correctly) that, when a seller has limited capacity, the incremental cost of its making one sale depends not only on the standard variable cost it had to incur to supply the buyer in question but also on the opportunity cost of its doing so—the profits it could otherwise have made by using the capacity in question to supply another buyer.[615]

Some circuits also rejected the second part of Areeda and Turner's proposal—*viz.*, their recommendation that prices above the seller's average total cost always be irrebuttably presumed to be non-predatory. In particular, some circuit courts held that prices above average total cost might be predatory "limit pricing" aimed at deterring new entry.[616] I think that these courts were right to reject this prong of the Areeda-Turner proposal. Although I doubt the empirical importance of limit pricing, I agree that supra-ATC pricing can be predatory and disagree with the Supreme Court's conclusion that attempts to identify instances of supra-ATC pricing that is predatory will disserve the antitrust law's goal of promoting competition (as well as with its implicit assumption that, if this were true, that fact would justicize the courts' adoption of an irrebuttable presumption that supra-ATC prices were non-predatory). I know of no Court-of-Appeals case that has addressed this issue since the Supreme Court commented in *Brooke Group* about how courts should respond to above-"cost" pricing.

Although, initially, U.S. courts adopted the third part of the Areeda-Turner proposal—*viz.*, that prices above AVC but below ATC be rebuttably presumed to be non-predatory[617]—after *Brooke Group*, circuit courts have split on whether lower courts can find predatory prices that exceed incremental costs but are lower than average variable costs.[618]

---

[614] See, *e.g.*, William Inglis & Sons Baking Co. v. ITT Continental Baking Co., Inc., 668 F.2d 1014 (9th Cir. 1981), *cert. denied*, 459 U.S. 825 (1982).

[615] United States v. AMR Corp., 335 F.3d 1009 (10th Cir. 2003).

[616] See Transamerica Computer Co. v. IBM Corp., 698 F.2d 1377 (9th Cir. 1983), *cert. denied*, 464 U.S. 955 (1983).

[617] See, *e.g.*, Morgan v. Ponder, 892 F.2d 1355 (8th Cir. 1989); McGaite v. Propane Gas Co., 858 F.2d 1487 (1988); Southern Pacific Communications Co. v. AT&T, 740 F.2d 980 (D.C. Cir. 1984); and Northeastern Telephone Co. v. AT&T, 651 F.2d 76 (2d Cir. 1981).

[618] Compare Spirit Airlines v. Northwest Airlines, 431 F.3d 917 (6th Cir. 2005) and Concord Boat Corp. v. Brunswick Corp., 207 F.3d 1039 (2000), holding that prices above average variable costs can be predatory, with United States v. AMR Corp., 335 F.3d 1009 (10th Cir. 2003), Stearns Airport Equipment Co. v. FMC Corp. 170 F.3d 518 (5th Cir. 1999), and Adro, Inc. v. Philadelphia Newspapers, Inc., 51 F.3d 1191 (3d Cir. 1995), holding that *Brooke Group* precludes finding prices above AVC predatory.

Finally, some U.S. courts have also rejected the fourth part of the Areeda and Turner proposal—*viz.*, the proposal that prices below average variable cost be irrebuttably presumed to be predatory. Indeed, even the Supreme Court has implicitly recognized that such prices may not be predatory if they are promotional[619] or motivated by spite.[620]

The ninth point or cluster of points I want to make about the U.S. case-law on predatory pricing does not really relate to any part of the Supreme Court's general guidelines for resolving predatory-pricing cases. Rather, it relates to a separate Supreme Court claim that a seller may practice predation by varying the price it charges for a given product in different geographic markets according to the strength of the competition it faces in the markets in question. I have no doubt that, in some instances, inter-market price-differences may reflect predatory pricing. Indeed, one of the types of evidence that I have argued can be used to prove predatory pricing—inter-regional price-comparisons—typically focuses on this sort of price-difference. However, my analysis reveals that inter-regional price-differences will manifest the practice of either predatory or contrived oligopolistic pricing only if the price-differences in question cannot be legitimized (do not reflect differences in MCs, CMC, BPAs, and/or NOMs). (I should add that my analysis also shows that the absence of inter-market price-differences will manifest predatory or contrived oligopolistic pricing when differences in MCs, CMC, BPAs and/or NOMs imply that the LLPs in the different markets in question should differ by more than their actual prices differ.) The Supreme Court's position (in a case called *Utah Pie*[621]) is mistaken because it counts in favor of the conclusion that a seller has practiced predatory pricing the fact that its prices vary from market to market according to the size of its OCAs (according to the strength of the competition it faces)—*i.e.*, because it fails to recognize the legitimating force of the fact that inter-market price-differences can be explained in OCA terms. I hasten to add that this holding had some significant precedential support. In an important District Court case in which a renowned judge was aided by a famous Harvard economist who acted as a court master, the judge held that a defendant in a Section 2 monopolization case could not defend its possession of monopoly power by demonstrating that that power was "thrust upon it" or achieved through "skill, foresight, and industry" because the company partly secured it by varying the markups it charged for its different products according to the strength of the competition it faced on them.[622] The bad news is that the Supreme Court has still not overruled its decision in *Utah Pie*. The good news is that, more recently, the Supreme Court pointedly refused to endorse its *Utah Pie* holding in a paragraph that manifested its desire to avoid

---

619 See Brooke Group Ltd. v. Brown & Williamson Tobacco Corp., 509 U.S. 209, 231, 238–39, 241–42 (1993). See also A.A. Poultry Farms, Inc. v. Rose Acre Farms, Inc. 881 F.2d 1396, 1400 (7th Cir. 1989).

620 Brooke Group Ltd. v. Brown & Williamson Tobacco Corp., 509 U.S. 209, 225 (1993).

621 Utah Pie Co. v. Continental Baking Co., 386 U.S. 685 (1967).

622 See United States v. United Shoe Machinery Corp., 110 F. Supp. 295 (D. Mass. 1953). The judge was David Wyzanski; the court master was Carl Kaysen.

making decisions that would kill legitimate price-cutting[623] and that various Courts of Appeal have implicitly questioned the viability of the *Utah Pie* holding.[624]

The tenth point or cluster of concrete points I want to make about the U.S. case-law on predatory pricing relates to the recoupment part of the Supreme Court's predatory-pricing-case guidelines—*i.e.*, to the Supreme Court's statement that, to prevail in a Section 2 Sherman Act predatory-pricing case or a Robinson-Patman Act predatory-price-discrimination case, the State or a private plaintiff must show that the defendant's conduct (1) either had succeeded in driving a rival out or created a requisite probability of that result's obtaining (a "dangerous probability" in a Sherman Act case and a "reasonable possibility" in a Robinson-Patman Act case) (2) in circumstances in which any such outcome would create a requisite probability that the defendant's profits would rise sufficiently for the predation to be profitable. In my judgment, U.S. courts have made at least seven mistakes when operationalizing the recoupment part of the Supreme Court's predatory-pricing-case guidelines. First, U.S. courts have always mistakenly assumed that the only way in which predatory pricing can add to the predator's long-run profits is to enable the predator to earn additional profits in the market in which the predation was practiced: in fact, predation can also enable the predator to obtain additional profits in other "markets" by strengthening its reputation for predation and, by analogy, contrived oligopolistic conduct. Second, like Judge Easterbrook when he was a professor, U.S. courts have always implicitly mistakenly assumed that predatory pricing always involves across-the-board as opposed to individualized or somewhat-selective price-cuts. Third, when discussing the profitability of predatory pricing, U.S. courts have always mistakenly assumed that all products in a given market would be approximately equally competitive with each other: this assumption underlies both their failure to see that predation can succeed by inducing rivals to change the location of their extant or planned QV investments and their belief that predation cannot be profitable in unconcentrated markets because too little of the negative effects of the across-the-board price-cuts the courts assumed predation would entail would be experienced by any one rival of the predator. Fourth, the second and third mistakes just listed have led U.S. courts to mistakenly conclude that predatory pricing can be profitable only for firms with high pre-existing market shares. Thus, in *Cargill*, the Supreme court stated in dicta that a 21 % market share was too low for predation to be profitable.[625] Fifth, U.S. courts have tended to assume mistakenly that predatory pricing cannot be profitable unless "barriers to entry" are high.[626] I have already explained why this contention is wrong when criticizing various presumptions recommended by economists: the effectiveness of the potential competitors that might replace the exited target

[623] See Brooke Group Ltd. v. Brown and Williamson Tobacco Corp., 509 U.S. 209, 220–22 (1993).

[624] See, *e.g.*, A.A. Poultry Farms, Inc. v. Rose Acre Farms, Inc., 881 F.2d 1396, 1404 (7th Cir. 1989).

[625] Cargill, Inc. v. Monfort of Colorado, Inc., 479 U.S. 104, 119 n.15 (1986).

[626] See, *e.g.*, American Academic Suppliers v. Beckley-Candy, 922 F.2d 1317 (7th Cir. 1991).

depends not on the height of the barriers to entry they face but on the relationship between the barriers to entry they face and the sum of the barriers to expansion and QV-investment (dis)incentives that would face the established firm in the relevant ARDEPPS that would be best-placed to expand at the ARDEPPS' entry-barred, expansion-preventing QV-investment level. Sixth, U.S. courts seem to assume that firms that would not find it individually profitable to engage in predatory pricing on their own are exceedingly unlikely to be able to profit by agreeing to coordinate their predation: according to the Supreme Court, agreed-upon joint predation is "incalculably more difficult to execute" because "[i]n order to succeed, the conspirators must agree on how to allocate present losses and future gains among the firms involved, and each firm must resist powerful incentives to cheat on whatever agreement is reached."[627] In my judgment, although the difficulties the Court lists are substantial, its conclusion ignores the ability of joint predation to increase the harm-inflicted to loss-incurred ratio (particularly when the predatory price-cuts are individualized) as well as the fact that the price-cuts of those conspirators that play their part will substantially reduce the incentives of individuals to cheat when the predatory price-cuts are across-the-board price-cuts. Seventh and finally, it seems to me that, at least when the relevant price-cuts would be across-the-board, this last point also undercuts the Supreme Court's claim[628] that attempts to engage in joint predatory pricing without verbal communication are substantially less likely to be successful or profitable than attempts to enter into explicit joint-predatory-pricing agreements.

The eleventh and final point or cluster of points I want to make about the U.S. case-law on predatory pricing relates to "price squeezes." In economics, the expression "price squeeze" is used to refer to the pricing practice in which a vertically-integrated firm charges independent buyers that compete with it in a downstream market a price for an upstream product (input) that both it and its non-integrated downstream rivals use to produce the downstream product that makes it "difficult for" the independent non-integrated concern(s) to survive. The concept of a price squeeze became important in U.S. antitrust law when, in the 1945 *Alcoa* case, Judge Learned Hand stated in what I take to be dicta that price squeezes violate Section 2 of the Sherman Act (entail monopolizing or an attempt to monopolize) whenever (1) the firm conducting the squeeze had monopoly power in the upstream market, (2) the upstream price charged was "higher than 'a fair price,'" and (3) the combination of the upstream price and the downstream price the

---

[627] See Brooke Group Ltd. v. Brown & Williamson Tobacco Corp., 509 U.S. 209, 227 (1993).
[628] *Id.*

firm charged precluded the non-integrated rival from making "a living profit."[629] I will focus first on the U.S. case-law on price squeezes and then on various economic points made about the practice.

I want to make five points about the U.S. case-law on price squeezes. First, price-squeeze doctrines that were very similar to Hand's were, for many years, used by various circuits to condemn price squeezes under the Sherman Act.[630] Second, although economists and economically-sophisticated legal scholars have long recognized the resemblance of (illegal) price squeezes to predatory pricing[631] and even those judges that were skeptical of the claim that price squeezes violate the Sherman Act and questioned whether courts should try to identify those price squeezes that do violate the Act recognized that the objection to them was that they were "exclusionary" in the pejorative antitrust sense,[632] the courts never linguistically classified price squeezes as a variant of predatory pricing.[633] Third, the decisions condemning particular price squeezes as violations of Section 2 of the Sherman Act were always inconsistent with the antitrust doctrine that "[a]s a general rule, businesses are free to choose the parties with whom they will deal,

---

[629] See United States v. Aluminum Co. of America, 148 F.2d 416, 437 (2nd Cir. 1945). Hand's comments on the legality of Alcoa's alleged price squeeze were inconsistent. Thus, he states: ". . .perhaps it ought not to be considered as a separate wrong; moreover, we do not use it as part of the reasoning by which we conclude that the [*i.e.*, Alcoa's] monopoly was unlawful. But it was at least an unlawful exercise of Alcoa's power. . .." *Id.* The conclusion that Hand thought that price squeezes that satisfied the three criteria listed in the text violated Section 2 of the Sherman Act is also supported by the fact that his discussion of Alcoa's price squeeze is in a section of the opinion entitled "Alcoa's Unlawful Practices" and by his statement "That it was unlawful to set the price of 'sheet' [the downstream product] so low and hold the price of ingot [the upstream product] so high, seems to us unquestionable, provided, as we have held, that on this record, the price of ingot must be regarded as higher than a 'fair price.'" *Id.* at 438. (Earlier in the opinion, Hand had also found that Alcoa had monopoly power.) My conclusion that Hand's price-squeeze legal conclusion is dicta reflects the fact that, in the context of the opinion, price squeezes need not have been independently illegal for Alcoa's use of them to have militated against a finding that it had not violated the Sherman Act because its monopoly power had been "thrust upon it" or had been achieved through "skill, foresight, and industry." Indeed, even if price squeezes were "honestly industrial," a finding that they had helped Alcoa obtain or preserve its monopoly power would favor the conclusion that Alcoa had violated Section 2 of the Sherman Act so long as the price squeeze was not economically efficient.

[630] See, *e.g.*, Bonjorno v. Kaiser Aluminum & Chem. Corp., 752 F.2d 802, 809–10 (3d Cir. 1984); City of Kirkwood v. Union Electric Co., 671 F.2d 1173, 1176 n.4, 1178–79 (8th Cir. 1982); and City of Mishawaka v. American Electric Power Co., 616 F.2d 976, 985 (7th Cir. 1980).

[631] See, *e.g.*, CHARLES J. GOETZ AND FRED S. MCCHESNEY, ANTITRUST LAW: INTERPRETATION AND IMPLEMENTATION 491 (Foundation Press, 2009).

[632] See Judge (now Justice) Breyer's opinion for the first-circuit Court of Appeals in Town of Concord v. Boston Edison Co., 915 F.2d 17, 18–19 (1st Cir. 1990).

[633] Indeed, the only case I know in which a court recognized that the State's or a private plaintiff's price-squeeze argument was really or also a predatory-pricing argument is the recent case in which the Supreme Court held that price-squeeze claims cannot be brought under Section 2 of the Sherman Act. See Pacific Bell Telephone Company, dba AT&T California, et al. v. LinKline Communications, Inc., et al., 129 S.Ct. 1109, 1120–21 (2009) (hereinafter Pacific Bell).

as well as the prices, terms, and conditions of that dealing."[634] This third point reflects the fact that price squeezes could be said to be a (usually-gentler) variant of a refusal to deal. I should add that U.S. courts now reject their former (incorrect) position that individual refusals to deal cannot be predatory. Fourth, in 2009, in a case I am calling *Pacific Bell*, the Supreme Court rejected the price-squeeze doctrine (in essence declared price squeezes [including those that would violate Hand's test of illegality] *per se* lawful under the Sherman Act). (In essence, this case resolved a disagreement in the circuits about whether an earlier decision confirming that a firm with no antitrust duty to deal with its rivals at all is under no obligation to provide those rivals with a "sufficient" level of service if it does sell some services to some or all of them[635] implies that such firms have no antitrust duty to avoid executing price squeezes.) Fifth, the rationale for the *Pacific Bell* rejection of Hand's price-squeeze doctrine was (1) in part, the difficulty of articulating a price-squeeze doctrine in a way that provides sufficient guidance to the law's addressees, (2) in part, the difficulty that judges would have in applying the Hand test (of determining the "fairness" of a price and of ascertaining whether the vertically-integrated firm's two prices precluded its non-integrated rivals from making "a living profit"), (3) in part, the difficulty of devising a suitable remedy for a price-squeeze violation, (4) in part, the Court's perception that, in addition to being impracticable, Hand's test required courts to regulate prices in a way that was inconsistent with the American society's commitment to a "free-market system" as manifest in the general structure not only of its antitrust law but also of its industrial policy as a whole, and (5) in part, the Court's perception that the Hand price-squeeze doctrine is economically inefficient for a variety of reasons that I will discuss, among other matters, in the next paragraph.

I will now make seven points that relate either to the economics of price squeezes or to the economic analysis of price squeezes. First, regulations that impose on vertically-integrated concerns (1) duties to sell their upstream products to independent downstream rivals on terms the integrated concern would not find legitimately profitable and/or (2) duties to charge prices for its downstream products that are higher than the prices they would find most legitimately profitable to charge may decrease economic efficiency by deterring firms from engaging in economically-efficient vertical integration by reducing the amount by which the integration increases the firm's operating profits (when *ex ante* the profitability of vertical integration is uncertain). Second, the claim that prohibitions of price squeezes are economically inefficient because constraints on the prices that a vertically-integrated concern can charge downstream rivals for its upstream product

[634] See Pacific Bell at 1118, citing United States v. Colgate & Co., 250 U.S. 300, 307 (1919). I hasten to add that exceptions to that general rule have been made by circuit courts in so-called essential-facilities cases (see Subsection 5B of this chapter) and by the Supreme Court in a prominent, fairly-recent case. See Aspen Skiing Co. v. Aspen Highlands Skiing Corp., 472 U.S. 585 (1985).

[635] See Pacific Bell at 1119, articulating the holding of Verizon Communications, Inc. v. Law Offices of Curtis v. Trinko, LLP, 540 U.S. 398, 410 (2004) (hereinafter Trinko).

will reduce economic efficiency by deterring vertically-integrated firms from doing economically-efficient upstream-product R&D by deflating the profits they can earn by doing such research is problematic for two reasons: (1) it ignores the fact that the price-squeeze doctrine focuses on the relationship between the integrated firm's upstream-product price and downstream-product price, not on the height of its upstream-product price in isolation, and (2) it ignores the possibility that the other Pareto imperfections in the system may inflate the profitability of upstream-product R&D to both vertically-integrated and non-vertically-integrated potential researchers. Third, the claim that any doctrine that causes vertically-integrated firms to raise their downstream-product price will not only harm the directly-affected buyers on that account but will also cause UO-to-UO misallocation (misallocation that results when goods in production are produced in economically-inefficient proportions—when economic efficiency would be increased if more units of some products were produced and fewer units of other products were produced [controlling for the total amount of resources allocated to the production of units of extant products]) on that account ignores The General Theory of Second Best. Fourth, the conclusion that "successive (independent) monopolies (as opposed to a single-firm, vertically-integrated monopoly) injure consumers" because the downstream price charged by the downstream monopoly will be higher than the downstream price charged by a vertically-integrated monopoly—"a proposition on which there is unanimous agreement"[636] (if you ignore me)—is certainly exaggerated in terms of both the magnitude and the universality of the effect in question in that the argument from which it is derived assumes, often unrealistically, that an independent upstream producer will engage in single-pricing: if at the other extreme the upstream producer will sell its product by charging the relevant buyer a lump-sum fee for the right to purchase as much of the product in question as that buyer wishes at a price equal to the price at which the buyer's demand curve cuts the seller's marginal-cost curve from above, successive monopolies will have no effect on the price charged downstream-product buyers.[637] Fifth, the assumption that an upstream-product producer will always find it more profitable to supply its upstream product to a non-integrated downstream-product producer than to produce the downstream-product itself when the independent can produce the downstream product more efficiently would be incorrect in its universality even if the independent's and upstream-product producer's production of the downstream product would generate the same externalities and the costs of the inputs they both would buy to produce the downstream product would not be

---

[636] See Town of Concord v. Boston Edison Co., 915 F.2d 17 (1st cir. 1990), quoting Fishman v. Estate of Wirtz, 807 F.2d 520, 563 (7th Cir. 1986) (Easterbrook, J. dissenting and collecting authorities).

[637] The determinants of the profitability of both this form of perfect price discrimination and the most-profitable combination of supra-marginal-cost per-unit prices and lump-sum fees for a seller to charge will be analyzed in Chap. 14. Chapter 14 will also explain that the argument that modern economists have made for the ability of tie-ins to generate leverage also implicitly assumes (unrealistically) that, absent the tie-in, the relevant seller would single-price the tying product.

distorted by other types of Pareto imperfections because (1) even in the short run, the upstream producer might not be able to remove all buyer surplus from the independent, (2) in the long run—*i.e.*, after the upstream-product producer had withdrawn from downstream-product production, the independent might be able to secure additional supplies by taking advantage of any bilateral-monopoly situation that arose, and (3) the upstream-product producer might be concerned that the experience of producing and selling the downstream product might critically reduce the barriers to upstream-product-market entry facing the independent downstream-product producer. Sixth, and relatedly, a vertically-integrated concern that is the only producer of an upstream product may find it profitable to refuse to deal with an independent downstream-product producer or to subject such a rival to a price squeeze to raise the operative barriers to entry by making it necessary for a new entrant to enter at both levels or to find (risk not finding) another independent that would be willing to enter (that had simultaneously entered) at the other level when such choices would otherwise not be profitable for the integrated concern in question. Seventh, it is far from clear that price squeezes that reduce the number of producers operating in a given area of product-space will, on that account, reduce the amount of product R&D or PPR done in that area of product-space, and there is a good chance that any related reduction in the amount of product R&D done in any area of product-space will be economically efficient.

In short, in my judgment, the U.S. case-law on predatory pricing is highly unsatisfactory. I regret to say that, to a substantial extent, its deficiencies reflect the courts' accepting various positions that economists have taken on related issues.[638]

(2) The EC Position and the E.C./E.U.-Court Case-Law on Predatory Pricing

I will make 20 points or sets of related points about the European Commission's and the E.C./E.U. courts' positions on predatory pricing. First, both the EC and the E.C./E.U. courts clearly consider predatory pricing to be an exclusionary abuse that is prohibited by now-Article 102 of the 2009 Treaty of Lisbon[639] when engaged in by

[638] The text has focused exclusively on the case-law interpreting and applying to allegedly-predatory pricing Section 2 of the Sherman Act's proscription of monopolization and attempts to monopolize and the Clayton Act's proscription of "price discrimination" that is requisitely likely to lessen competition. The Sherman Act also prohibits "conspiracies" to monopolize. As Herbert Hovenkamp has stated: "Proof of conspiracy to monopolize does not require the plaintiff or prosecutor to show a 'dangerous probability of success.'" The violation is established merely by the proof of an agreement and an overt act carried out in furtherance of the scheme. American Tobacco Co. v. United States, 328 U.S. 761 (1946). See HOVENKAMP ANTITRUST at 162–63.

[639] For example, it is notable that the predatory-pricing case brought against the Associated Central West Africa Lines (Cewal) shipping conference for using so-called fighting ships that charged lower than normal prices to shippers that would otherwise have patronized a non-member (G & C) was brought under now-Article 102 of the Treaty and not under now-Article 101. See Joined Cases C-395/96 P & C-396/96P, Compagnie Maritime Belge Transps. SA v. Commission, 2000 E.U.R.

one or more firms with individually-dominant positions or one or more members of a set of firms that are collectively dominant.[640]

Second, to my knowledge, neither the EC nor any E.C./E.U. court has ever declared agreements by separate firms to engage in joint predatory pricing (or any other type of joint predation) or decisions by a trade association to have one or more of its members engage in predatory pricing (or any other type of predation) to be a violation of what is now Article 102 of the 2009 Treaty of Lisbon. Although this "omission" would have little or no practical significance if the EC and the E.C./E.U. courts were correct in assuming that predatory pricing would never be profitable for any firm that was not individually dominant or any set of firms that were not collectively dominant[641]—*i.e.*, if virtually all predatory conduct were covered by now-Article 102, this assumption is incorrect.

Third, unlike the U.S. courts, the ECJ has concluded that predatory pricing or any other type of predatory conduct (engaged in by an individually-dominant firm or two or more members of a set of collectively-dominant rivals) is illegal when it can be shown to have reduced competition or created a risk that competition would

---

I-1365 (E.U.J.) and Joined Cases T-24/95, T25/93, T26/93 & T-28/93, Compagnie Maritime Belge Transps. SA v. Commission, 1996 E.U.R. II (CFI).

[640] Admittedly, the EC and E.C./E.U. courts sometimes do state that the concept of an exclusionary abuse is an "objective" concept that does not require any proof of intent—*i.e.*, covers pricing that is not predatory if it enhances or maintains the dominant position of an individually-dominant firm or collectively-dominant set of rivals. See Hoffmann-La Roche v. Commission, Case 85/76, ECR 46, p. 91 (1979). However, I do not think they really mean it: What they really mean is that exclusionary abuses can be established purely through what they call "indirect evidence" (which the U.S. courts call "objective evidence") that the conduct in question would not have been profitable had it not secured a predation-related result such as driving a rival out—*i.e.*, without producing persuasive "direct evidence" (which the U.S. courts call "subjective evidence") of predatory intent. This interpretation is favored by the EC's and the E.C./E.U. courts' repeated insistence that abusive behavior be distinguished from competition on the merits and by their conclusion that defendants can exculpate themselves by demonstrating that their conduct was efficient, was a reaction to the buyer's breach of contract, or was required to secure the public health. See Carles Estera Mossa, Stephen A. Ryan, Svend Albaek, and Maria Luisa Tierno Centella, *Article 102* in THE EC LAW OF COMPETITION 313, 351 (ed. by Jonathan Faull and Ali Nikpay) (Oxford Univ. Press, 2d ed., 2007). It is also supported by such Commission statements as "[t]he predatory nature of charging lower prices to all or certain customers is found in the predator making a sacrifice by deliberately incurring short run losses with the intention to eliminate or discipline rivals or prevent their entry." See DG Competition Discussion Paper on the Application of Article 102 of the Treaty to Exclusionary Abuses, Section 6.1 (2005). (The EC's inclusion of the words "or discipline" in the preceding sentence manifests the fact that it defines the concept of predation more broadly than economists do to include retaliation that is part of oligopolistic contrivance.)

[641] See DG Competition Discussion Paper on the Application of Article 102 of the Treaty to Exclusionary Abuses, Section 6.1 (2005): "In a competitive market with many competitors the exclusion of some of them will, in general, not lead to a sufficient weakening of competition so as to allow the predator to recoup the 'investment.'"

be reduced even when there is no evidence that the perpetrator(s) had "a realistic chance of recouping losses" once its rivals have been eliminated.[642]

Fourth, the EC and the E.C./E.U. courts assume that predation properly so-called (and retaliation to non-cooperation with contrivance) will be profitable for and practiced only by firms with pre-existing monopoly power.[643] I disagree.

Fifth, the EC and the E.C./E.U. courts appear to believe that, even when the alleged predator is a dominant firm or two or more members of a set of collectively-dominant rivals, recoupment will not be possible and (presumably) predation will therefore not be practiced unless there are high barriers to entering the relevant area of product-space.[644] As I argued earlier, high barriers to entry are neither a necessary nor a sufficient condition for the profitability of predatory pricing.

Sixth, unlike the U.S. courts (which have ignored this possibility), the EC and the E.C./E.U. courts recognize that predatory pricing (and other types of predation) can increase the predator's profits by enhancing its reputation for predation (and contrivance) not just in the area of product-space in which the predation in question took place but in all areas of product-space in which the predator operates.[645]

Seventh, the EC has emphasized in the way that the U.S. courts have not that pricing that would otherwise appear to be predatory may have been rendered inherently profitable by the promotional[646] and/or learning-by-doing[647] benefits it conferred on the seller.

Eighth, at least in principle, the EC and the E.C./E.U. courts recognize that low prices that were set to meet competition in good faith are not predatory when, on this account, they are inherently profitable.[648] I write "at least in principle" because, as I will indicate below, in practice, the EC and the E.C./E.U. courts may have failed to accept valid "meeting competition in good faith" defenses by dominant firms that had made selective price-cuts.

Ninth, to my knowledge, the EC and the E.C./E.U. courts have never mentioned the possibility that pricing that would otherwise have been inherently unprofitable may have been rendered legitimately profitable by the keeping-in-touch benefits it conferred on the pricer or may have been legitimately defensively retaliatory.

Tenth, like the U.S. courts, the EC and the E.C./E.U. courts have never recognized the possibility that firms that are uncertain of their HLP may practice predation by charging supra-avoidable-cost prices that are lower than their *ex ante*

---

[642] See Tetra Pak International SA v. Commission of the European Communities (Tetra Park II), Case C-333/94P, ECR I-5951, p. 44 (1995).

[643] See DG Competition Discussion Paper on the Application of Article 102 of the Treaty to Exclusionary Abuses, Section 6.1 (2005).

[644] *Id.* at Section 6.2.2.2 at p. 122: proof of dominance and high entry barriers suffices to establish "the possibility to recoup."

[645] See *id.* at p. 119 and Section 6.2 at p. 101.

[646] See *id.* at Sections 6.1 at p. 95 and 6.21 at p. 110.

[647] See *id.* at Section 6.2.5 at p. 131.

[648] See *id.* at Section 6.2.5 at p. 132.

legitimate certainty-equivalent, profit-maximizing price to prevent a target from profiting from their *ex post* mistakes and have never recognized that firms may practice predation by failing to make premature price announcements that would enable them to obtain oligopolistic margins naturally or by failing to announce their across-the-board prices in the order that would maximize the height of the prices in their HNOP array.

Eleventh, unlike the U.S. courts, the EC has explicitly recognized that, when relevant, the assessment of the inherent profitability of a firm's prices must take account of the fact that the goods involved had already been produced and were perishable, of the goods' possible declining value for other reasons, of the fact that the goods are expensive to store, and/or of the fact that the cost of continuing to operate a plant or mine that had been operated continuously may be lower than the start-up cost of reopening a closed plant or mine.[649]

Twelfth, unlike the U.S. courts, the EC has explicitly recognized that the probable success and related profitability of predation will depend on the relative abilities of the potential predator and its potential target to finance respectively their predation and survival efforts internally from retained earnings as opposed to from external sources and that, controlling for any such difference, the probability that an alleged predator has actually engaged in predation will be higher if it is aware of the advantages of internal over external financing.[650]

Thirteenth, like the U.S. courts, the EC and the E.C./E.U. courts seem to be assuming that all products that are in any given "market" are equally competitive with each other and that all buyers in any given market will have many suppliers that are either equal-best-placed or close-to-best-placed to supply them. This assumption is manifest in (1) those institutions' failure to realize that a predator can recoup its "predation investment" by inducing established rivals to move their existing QV investments further away in product-space from the predator's projects and inducing potential expanders and entrants to locate their planned QV investments further away in product-space from the predator's projects and (2) their assumption that, "in general," in markets with many competitors the exclusion of some of them will not enable a predator to recoup its predation investment.[651]

Fourteenth, like the U.S. courts, the EC seems to think that collaborative predation (by members of a collectively-dominant set of rivals) is unlikely to be practicable (in the EC's view, because of the difficulty such firms will have in distinguishing predation against an outsider from internal aggressive competition and because the firms in question "usually lack a [legal] mechanism to share the financial burden of the predatory action").[652] However, the EC's doubts seem less strong than those of the U.S. courts—*viz.*, lead it to state only that predation by a

---

[649] See *id.*

[650] See *id.* at Sections 6.1 and 6.2.2 at p. 111.

[651] See *id.* at Section 6.1 at p. 97.

[652] See *id.* at Section 6.1 at p. 98.

collectively-dominant set of rivals is less likely than predation by an individually-dominant firm.

Fifteenth, the EC and the E.C./E.U. courts agree with the U.S. courts that prices below average avoidable cost (which they are also willing to assume equal average variable cost) should be rebuttably presumed to be predatory and that prices above average avoidable cost but below average total cost should be rebuttably presumed to be not predatory.[653]

Sixteenth, the EC rejects the U.S. courts' conclusion that courts should irrebuttably presume that prices above average total cost are not predatory. Thus, the EC indicates that it would find that a dominant firm that had charged prices above its average total cost had violated now-Article 102 on the ground that its pricing constituted abusive predatory pricing if (1) the price in question resulted from a price-cut that was designed to "prevent entry or eliminate entrants by pricing below the average total cost of the entrant," (2) the price-cutter was an "incumbent dominant company. . .[that had] a clear strategy to exclude," and (3) the entrant was less efficient only because the incumbent had non-replicable advantages (which, in my terms, gave rise to a Π_D barrier to entry) or there were relevant economies of scale that the entrant could take advantage of only after the passage of some time.[654] I want to note three other points about this passage. To start, the reference to "preventing entry" implies that the EC accepts the limit-pricing hypothesis, which I believe is justified only under very unusual conditions that are unlikely to be fulfilled in the general run of cases to which the EC's position applies.[655] In addition, I want to point out that there is no basis in the Treaty for the ECs limiting now-Article 102's prohibition to situations in which the target entrant is not less-economically-efficient than the predator[656]: the fact that the new entrant or prospective entrant faced higher Π_D barriers than the predator faced on its weighted-average QV investment in the area of product-space in question has no bearing on whether the dominant firm's conduct was predatory and little bearing on the economic efficiency of prohibiting its predatory pricing. Finally, and relatedly, the fact that the new entrant's disadvantage could be traced exclusively to the predator's non-replicable advantages and the inability of the new entrant to take as much advantage of economies of scale in the immediate post-entry period as the predator could do does not suggest that the new entrant was as efficient as the predator: to the contrary, in most cases, these sources of disadvantage will suggest that the new entrant was less efficient than the predator.

[653] See *id.* at Section 6.2.2.

[654] See *id.* at Section 6.24 at p. 129.

[655] The EC also accepts the limit-pricing hypothesis in *id.* at Section 6.2 and in Deutsche Post AG, Commission Decision 2001/354/EC, OJ L 125/27 (2001).

[656] See Joined Cases C-395/96P and C-396/96, Compagnie Maritime Belge Transps. SA v. Commission, E.U.R. I-1365 (I.C.J.) (2000) and Joined Cases T-24/93, T-26/93, & T-28/93, Compagnie Maritime Belge Transps. SA v. Commission, ECR II-1201 (1996).

Seventeenth, in at least one case,[657] the EC held that a statutory monopolist that was able to earn supernormal profits on the services it was given the exclusive right to supply but was simultaneously obligated to supply violated the Treaty by pricing other services below long-run average incremental costs (LRAIC) where LRAIC was defined to include many fixed costs that were not, in fact, variable during the time-period covered by individual price announcements. (I hasten to add that the Commission was very careful not to include as an investment cost joint costs the defendant had to incur to fulfill its statutory obligation to render some services, regardless of the profitability of the defendant's doing so.) Although it might be predatory for such a firm to charge a price below LRAIC as defined (just as it might be predatory for any firm to charge a price above its average total cost), the conclusion that such a firm's charging a price below LRAIC as defined is always predatory or should always be irrebuttably presumed to be predatory by the EC or an E.C./E.U. court is not defensible.

Eighteenth, although in several cases including the *CEWAL* "fighting ships" case[658] the Commission and E.C./E.U. courts clearly were correct in finding price discrimination to be a predatory abuse of now-Article 102, in other cases in which the Commission and E.C./E.U. courts found price discrimination to be a predatory abuse under now-Article 102, this conclusion is far more open to question. Thus, in *Irish Sugar*,[659] the Commission and the reviewing court dismissed the defendant's claim that its granting price-concessions to buyers on the Irish border that were also receiving offers from non-Irish suppliers was "defensive" in nature—*i.e.*, that the price-concessions were made in good faith to meet competition—on the irrelevant ground that the defendant did not offer similar concessions to non-border buyers and could not have earned normal profits had it done so. Once more, I acknowledge that the border rebates may have been predatory: my complaint is that the opinion provided no relevant evidence for its implicit conclusion that the reduced border prices were not inherently profitable and cited an irrelevant fact to justify its position.

Nineteenth, in other cases, the Commission and the E.C./E.U. courts condemned as predatory abuses under now-Article 102 so-called target rebates (rebates based on the buyer's making a specified amount of purchases) and other sorts of rebates that covered buyer purchasing-conduct over a long reference-period on no better evidence than they had in *Irish Sugar*—in those cases on the one-year length of the reference-period or the non-uniformity and/or secrecy of the scheme.[660]

---

[657] Deutsche Telekom, Case COMP/C-1/37451, OJ L263 (2003).

[658] CEWAL & Ors, OJ L34/20 (1993); on appeal Compagnie Maritime Belge Transps. SA v. Commission, ECR II-1201 (1996).

[659] Irish Sugar PLC v. Commission, Case T-228/97, E.U.R. II-2969 (CFI) (1999).

[660] See, *e.g.*, Coca-Cola, Case COMP/39.116, decision of 6/22/2005; Coca-Cola, IP/88/615 (1988); NV Nederlandse Banden—Industrie Michelin v. Commission (Michelin I), E.U.R. 3461, p. 73 (1983); and Hoffmann-La Roche v. Commission, 85–76 (ECJ 1979). See also the "top-slice rebate" cases such as the ICI Soda-Ash cases.

Twentieth and last, unlike the U.S. courts that finally decided to declare price squeezes *per se* legal under the Sherman Act, E.C./E.U. courts continue to consider them to be contrary to now-Article 102 when their perpetrator is a firm with an individually-dominant position.[661]

This completes my discussion of the U.S. and E.C./E.U. courts' case-law on predatory pricing and the EC's position on such pricing. The economics and law of the prices charged in long-term requirements contracts will be discussed in Section 6 of this chapter and the economics and law of price discrimination and the prices charged in tying and reciprocal-trading agreements will be discussed in Chap. 14.

3. Predatory QV Investments

A. *The Definition of a Predatory QV Investment*

(1) The Correct Definition of the Concept of a Predatory QV Investment and a Related Explanation of When and How a QV Investment Will Be Predatory

A predatory QV investment is simply a QV investment whose execution satisfies the general definition of predatory conduct. Thus, a QV investment is predatory if and only if it was made by an investor whose *ex ante* perception that it would be profitable was *ceteris paribus* critically inflated by its belief that the investment would or might increase its profits by reducing the absolute attractiveness of the offers against which it would have to compete by inducing a rival to remove a QV investment from the area of product-space in which it would be located, by deterring a potential entrant or expander from adding a QV investment to the relevant area of product-space, by inducing the owner of one or more extant QV investments in that area of product-space to relocate one or more of its QV investments further away in product-space from the predator's QV investment(s), and/or by inducing a prospective QV investor to locate its investment further away in product-space from the predator's QV investment(s) in circumstances in which these effects would not only critically increase but would critically inflate the QV-investor's *ex ante* estimate of the profitability of the QV investment in question

[661] See, *e.g.*, Deutsche Telekom, Case COMP/C-1/37451, 37.578, 37.579, OJ L263 (2003) and Industrie des Poudres Sphériques SA v. Commission, Case T-5/97, p. 178 (2000).

in an otherwise-Pareto-perfect economy—*i.e.*, would induce the investor to perceive that investment to be *ex ante* profitable even though it would have been *ex ante* economically inefficient in an otherwise-Pareto-perfect economy. As I indicated in Chap. 4, this last clause must be included because (1) no act can be properly characterized as "predatory" unless its *ex ante* actor-perceived profitability would have been *critically inflated* by the actor's belief that it might reduce the absolute attractiveness of the best offers against which it would have to compete in one or more of the just-listed ways in an otherwise-Pareto-perfect economy (as opposed to simply being critically increased by such an actor-belief) and (2) the set of QV investments whose *ex ante* investor-perceived profitability was *critically increased* by the investor's *ex ante* belief that they would reduce the absolute attractiveness of the best offers against which it would have to compete in one or more of the above-listed ways includes many QV investments whose *ex ante* investor-perceived profitability was not *ceteris paribus critically inflated* on this account (either was not inflated at all on this account or would not have been critically inflated for this reason in an otherwise-Pareto-perfect economy). In Chap. 4, I also stated that the preceding discussion implies, that, in my terminology, a QV investment will be predatory if and only if, had the relevant investor thought in these terms, it would have concluded *ex ante* that its QV investment's profitability would have been critically inflated in an otherwise-Pareto-perfect economy by the monopolistic QV-investment incentive it believed it had to make it. In other words, assuming for simplicity that the QV investment in question would deter a rival from adding a QV investment to the relevant area of product-space, a QV investment will be predatory if made by a QV investor whose *ex ante* conclusion that its QV investment was certainty-equivalent profitable was critically affected by its belief that the investment would reduce its other QV-investment projects' profit-yields (relative to the *status quo ante*) by less than those projects' profit-yields would otherwise have been reduced by the rival QV investment(s) the QV investment in question would deter in that (1) its predatory QV investment was further away in product-space from its other projects than the QV investment(s) it would deter would be, (2) the deterred QV investment would reduce the NOMs and COMs the relevant QV investor would secure because the maker of the deterred QV investment would not cooperate with the predator's efforts to secure oligopolistic margins and the deterred QV investment would cause other rivals of the predator to cooperate less than they would if the predator made the QV investment in question, and/or (3) in across-the-board-pricing situations, the substitution of the predator's QV investment for the rival investment it would deter would increase the extent to which the firms in the relevant ARDEPPS announced their prices in the order that would enable them to maximize the height of their HNOP array. (To see why, in an otherwise-Pareto-perfect economy, the profit-yield of a QV investment will be inflated to the extent that the QV investment increases the profit-yields of the investor's other QV investment[s], note that there is no reason to believe that the substitution of the firm's QV investment for the rival project it replaced will have increased the economic efficiency of the array of locations of the QV investments in the area of product-space in question—*i.e.*, will have reduced intra-ARDEPPS QV-investment misallocation in this way. To see why, in an otherwise-Pareto-perfect economy, the profit-yield of a QV investment will be inflated to the extent that its substitution for a rival QV investment increases the NOMs and COMs the investor obtains when using its other QV investment[s], note that, in such an economy, the associated increase in the investor's prices will generate economic inefficiency [as will any associated increase in the NOMs and COMs of the investor's rivals]. To see why, in an otherwise-Pareto-perfect economy, the profit-yield of a QV investment will be inflated to the extent that its substitution for a rival, actual or planned QV investment increases the HNOPs of the investor on its other QV investment[s] in the same ARDEPPS [as well as the HNOPs of its fellow across-the-board-pricing rivals] by increasing their ability to make their price announcements in the order that maximizes the prices in their HNOP array, note that, in such an economy, the increase in prices the QV investment generates in this way will also be misallocative. To see why, in an otherwise-Pareto-perfect economy, the profit-yield of a QV investment that increases equilibrium QV investment in the relevant ARDEPPS will be inflated to the extent that [1] the amount by which the investment in question increases the profit-yields of the investor's other QV investment[s] by inducing actual rivals to change the locations of their extant QV investments or potential independent investors to change the location of their future QV investments *exceeds* [2] the amount by which it reduces the profit-yields of the investor's other QV investment[s] by cannibalizing its [their] sales, note both that, once more, there is no reason to believe that the change in the locations of the relevant rival QV investments will be economically efficient and that, in such an economy, the additional QV investment that a QV investment that does not cause a rival QV investment to exit or deter the execution of a new QV investment by a rival will add to the relevant area of product-space would, in any event, be economically inefficient.)

Chart II has been designed to illustrate the correct definition of a predatory QV investment and to set up my critique of the different definition of this concept proposed by two deservedly-highly-respected economists, Janusz Ordover and Robert Willig.[662] Both Chart II itself and its analysis employ the concept of a limit (QV) investment as well as that of a predatory QV investment. As I have indicated previously, in my vocabulary, the statement that a QV investment is a "limit investment" indicates that, *ex ante*, the investor that made it would not have found it *ex ante* profitable had it not believed that the investment would or might

[662] See Janusz Ordover and Robert Willig, *An Economic Definition of Predation: Pricing and Product Innovation* (hereinafter Ordover and Willig), 91 YALE L.J. 8 (1981).

deter a potential or established competitor from making a QV investment (or, by extension, that it would or might induce an established rival to withdraw or change the location of a QV investment or a potential competitor to change the location of a planned QV investment).

Chart II is designed to illustrate the conditions under which a QV investment made by an investor that believed *ex ante* that it would or might deter an established or potential competitor from adding a new QV investment to the relevant area of product-space would or might induce a rival to withdraw an existing QV investment in the relevant area of product-space or would or might induce a rival to change the product-space location of an existing or future QV investment in the relevant area of product-space to one that was less proximate to the investor's other QV investments in that area of product-space would be a predatory QV investment and/or a limit QV investment. To ease the exposition, I will assume that the QV investor believes *ex ante* that the QV investment in question will deter a rival entry or expansion that would have been executed in its absence. *Mutatis mutandis*, the analysis that follows will be equally applicable to QV investments made by investors that believe *ex ante* that they will drive out extant rival QV investments or induce rivals to change the location of their extant or planned QV investments.

Chart II has seven rows and five columns. Each row of Chart II provides a different type of profit information about the QV investments described in Chart II's columns. The entries in Row (1) indicate the amount of operating profits the relevant QV investor perceives *ex ante* the investment would have to be expected to yield on the weighted average to be just normally profitable—*i.e.*, just sufficiently profitable to make the potential investor willing to make the investment in question. For simplicity, Chart II assumes that that amount is the same ($100) for each of the QV investments it describes. The entries in Row (2) indicate the amount of non-distorting profits the investor expects *ex ante* its investment to generate—the nominal profits it expects it to generate (the difference between the revenues it expects *ex ante* to realize by selling the product the investment will create or by operating the distributive outlet the investment will create and the variable[663] cost of producing the relevant product or running the relevant outlet) *plus* the non-distorting contribution it expects *ex ante* the investment to make to the profit-yields of its other QV investments by reducing the costs it has to incur to establish or operate them and/or increasing the demand that buyers have for the products or distributive services they enable it to supply. Row (3) indicates the amount by which the investor expects *ex ante* that the relevant QV investment would reduce its other QV investments' profit-yields both directly by taking sales from them and indirectly by inducing its rivals to alter their conduct non-strategically if the investment in question would not deter any established or potential competitor from making a new QV investment

[663] I am implicitly counting the fixed cost of producing the product in question or building the outlet in question as part of the QV investment concerned. Nothing turns on this classification. If these fixed costs are counted as operating costs, operating profits will be lower but so too will be the magnitude of the QV investment in question and concomitantly the amount of operating profits that would constitute a normal rate-of-return on it.

Chart II Some examples of QV investments made by an investor that believed *ex ante* that they would or might deter an established or potential competitor from making an additional QV investment but would not induce an established rival to withdraw an existing QV investment or an established or potential rival to change the location of an existing or future QV investment that will be respectively non-predatory/non-limit QV investments, non-predatory/limit QV investments, and predatory/limit QV investments

		Non-predatory, non-limit QV investments		Non-predatory, limit QV investments		Predatory, limit QV investments
Col/Row	Investor QV-investment profit-expectations	IA	IB	IIA	IIB	III
(1)	Investor-perceived normal profits	$100	$100	$100	$100	$100
(2)	Investor-expected nominal profits *plus* investor-expected non-distorting contributions to profit-yields of investor's other projects	$150	$150	$110	$110	$ 90
(3)	Amount by which the investor expects the QV to reduce its other QVs' profit-yields in comparison with the *status quo ante* by cannibalizing its other products' sales and inducing reductions in extant-rival-product prices—the monopolistic QV-investment disincentive the investor would perceive that it faced if it did not believe that the QV would deter a rival QV	$ 30	$ 30	$ 30	$ 30	$ 30
(4)	Profits the investor would expect the QV to yield if it would not deter a rival QV	$120	$120	$ 80	$ 80	$ 60
(5)	Certainty-equivalent amount by which the investor believes the rival QV its relevant QV will deter would reduce the investor's other QVs' profit-yields in comparison with the *status quo ante*	$ 20	$ 40	$ 20	$ 40	$ 50
(6)	QV investor's perceived monopolistic QV-investment incentive	–$ 10	+$ 10	–$ 10	+$ 10	+$ 20
(7)	Actual certainty-equivalent profits the investor expects the relevant QV to yield—*i.e.*, the certainty-equivalent contribution the investor expects the QV will make to its overall profits	$140	$160	$100	$120	$110

(and would neither induce any such rival to relocate its future QV investments nor induce an established competitor to withdraw or relocate an existing QV investment). Row (4) indicates the profits the investor would expect *ex ante* the indicated QV investment to yield if it would not deter a rival QV investment (given that it would also not induce a rival to withdraw a QV investment or relocate an existing or future QV investment). The entry in Row (4) of any column equals the entry in Row (2) *minus* the entry in Row (3) of that column. If the entry in Row (4) of any column equals or exceeds the entry in Row (1) of that column—*i.e.*, if the amount of profits the investor expected *ex ante* that the QV investment in question would yield if it would not deter a rival from making an additional QV investment (or induce a rival to withdraw an existing QV investment or to relocate an existing or future QV investment) is at least normal, the investment will not be a limit investment. The entries in Row (5) of Chart II indicate the certainty-equivalent amount by which the investor believes *ex ante* the rival QV investments its investment would or might deter would have reduced its other QV investments' profit-yields in comparison with the *status quo ante*—the weighted-average amount by which it expected those deterred rival QV investments would have reduced its other projects' profit-yields *minus* the risk costs it will incur because it is uncertain about the rival QV investments its investment would actually deter and/or the amount by which they would have reduced its other QVs' profit-yields. The entries in Row (6) indicate the monopolistic QV-investment incentive (or disincentive when they are negative) the investor believes *ex ante* it has to make the indicated QV investment. The entry in Row (6) of any column equals the entry in Row (5) *minus* the entry in Row (3) of that column: the QV investor will perceive itself *ex ante* to have a monopolistic QV-investment incentive to make a particular QV investment if and to the extent that it believes *ex ante* that the QV investment in question will reduce its other QV investments' profit-yields in distorting ways in comparison to the *status quo ante* by less than those profit-yields would otherwise be reduced by the rival QV investments it believes that its contemplated QV investment will deter. The entries in Row (7) of Chart II indicate the total certainty-equivalent amount by which the investor believes *ex ante* its contemplated QV investment will increase its organization's profits (gross of capital costs). The entry in Row (7) of any column equals the sum of the entries in Rows (2) and (6) of that column—the sum of the non-distorted profits the relevant QV investor expects *ex ante* the investment in question to yield and the distorting monopolistic QV-investment incentive it believes *ex ante* it has to make the investment in question. The entry in Row (7) of any column also equals the sum of the entries in Rows (4) and (5) of that column—the sum of the profits the relevant QV investor would expect *ex ante* the investment described to yield if it would not deter a rival from making a QV investment and the amount by which the QV investor expects *ex ante* the investment in question to raise its other QV investments' certainty-equivalent profit-yields by deterring a rival from making a QV investment. Presumably, the potential investor will make the investment whose profit information is discussed in any column if and only if the entry in Row (7) of that column is at least as high as the entry in Row (1) of that column—*i.e.*, if and only if it believes *ex ante* that the certainty-equivalent profits it anticipates the QV investment's yielding at least equal the profits it believes *ex ante* will constitute a normal rate-of-return on it. On what I take to be the correct definition of "a predatory QV investment," a QV investment whose profit information is described in a column of Chart II will be predatory if and only if the entry in Row (2) of that column is lower than the entry in Row (1) of that column but the entry in Row (7) of that column equals or exceeds the entry in Row (1) of the column—*i.e.*, if and only if the investor's *ex ante* belief that the relevant QV investment would be at least normally profitable was critically affected by its belief that it had a monopolistic QV-investment incentive to make it (if and only if it would not have perceived the investment to be at least normally profitable but for its perception that the investment would or might yield it some purely-private, distorting profits *ex post*).

Chart II contains five columns. The information in each column describes a particular QV investment, defined by the various profit-expectations the investor that made it or contemplated making it had about it. The first two columns (IA and IB) provide information about QV investments that are neither predatory QV investments nor limit QV investments. The second two columns (IIA and IIB) provide information about QV investments that are not predatory QV investments but are limit QV investments. The last column (III) provides information about a QV investment that is not only a limit QV investment but also a predatory QV investment.

We should now be able to explain why the preceding characterizations of the five QV investments described in Chart II are correct. The QV investments whose profit data are presented in Columns IA and IB are not predatory QV investments because the profits the relevant investor would have expected them to yield *ex ante* if it did not think it had a monopolistic QV-investment incentive to make them—the amounts indicated in Row (2)—are at least as high as (in fact, exceed) the amount of profits the investor perceived to be normal for the QV investments in question—the amounts indicated in Row (1). The QV investments described in Columns IA and IB are non-limit QV investments because, as a comparison of the entries in Rows (4) and (1) of Columns IA and IB respectively reveal, the relevant investor would have expected these QV investments to yield at least normal profits *ex ante* even if it had not believed that they would or might deter a rival QV investment in the relevant area of product-space ($120 > $100). I chose to provide two examples of non-predatory, non-limit QV investments to emphasize the fact that a QV investor's *ex ante* belief that it has a monopolistic QV-investment incentive to make the investment in question is not a sufficient condition for its being either a predatory or a limit QV investment. Thus, although the investor whose investment is described in Column IB believed *ex ante* that it had a monopolistic QV-investment incentive to make the investment in question, that investment is neither a predatory nor a limit QV investment.

The QV investments described in Columns IIA and IIB are non-predatory, limit QV investments. They are limit QV investments because, as a comparison of the entries in Rows (4) and (1) of Columns IIA and IIB respectively reveal, the investor would not have expected *ex ante* that these investments would yield at least normal returns had it not expected them to deter the investor's rivals from making an additional QV investment ($80 < $100). Note that the limit-investment status of the QV investments covered by Columns IIA and IIB does not depend on whether their deterrent effect critically reduces the monopolistic QV-investment disincentive the relevant investor believed it faced *ex ante*—say, from (–$30) to (–$10), as in Column IIA—or converted what it perceived *ex ante* would otherwise have been a monopolistic QV-investment disincentive into a monopolistic QV-investment incentive—say, changed the relevant distortion from (–$30) to (+$10), as in Column IIB. A QV investment is a limit investment if and only if the investor's *ex ante* assessment of the certainty-equivalent profit-consequences of its deterrent effect—indicated in Row (5)—raises the actual profits the investor expected *ex ante* the investment to yield—indicated in Row (7) and equal to the entry in Row (4) *plus* the entry in Row (5)—from below normal to normal or above normal—*i.e.*, cause the entry in Row (7) to equal or exceed the entry in Row (1) despite the fact that the entry in Row (4) is lower than the entry in Row (1). On the other hand, the QV investments described in Columns IIA and IIB are not predatory QV investments because the investor's *ex ante* estimate of the gross profits they would yield would constitute at least a normal rate-of-return on the investments in question even if the investor did not believe *ex ante* that it had a monopolistic QV-investment incentive to make them. In both cases, this conclusion is guaranteed by the fact that the profits that the investor would have expected them to yield *ex ante* if the investor did not think it had a monopolistic QV-investment incentive to make them—the entry in Row (2), $110—were at least normal—equaled or exceeded the entry in Row (1), $100. I chose to include two examples of non-predatory, limit QV investments in Chart II to emphasize the fact that a QV investor's *ex ante* belief that it had a monopolistic QV-investment incentive to make the investment in question is neither a sufficient condition for the investment's being predatory nor a necessary condition for its being a limit investment. I will now discuss each of these points in turn.

As Column IIB manifests, so long as any monopolistic QV-investment incentive the investor believed *ex ante* that it had to make the relevant QV investment is not critical to its investor-perceived *ex ante* profitability—so long as the investor believed *ex ante* that the legitimate profits the investment would yield, an amount indicated in Row (2), would constitute at least a normal rate-of-return on the investment, the QV investment will not be predatory. Thus, although the investor whose *ex ante* perceptions are recorded in Column IIB believed it had a $10 monopolistic QV-investment incentive to make the QV investment described in Column IIB, that investment was not predatory because its investor's *ex ante* conclusion that the investment would be at least normally profitable was not critically affected by this belief: the fact that the investor perceived *ex ante* that the investment would yield undistorted profits ($110) that were at least normal (in this case, exceeded $100) implies that the investor would have perceived the investment to be (at least normally) profitable *ex ante* even if the investor believed *ex ante* that its tendency to deter a rival QV investment would do no more than eliminate or adequately reduce the monopolistic QV-investment disincentive the relevant investor would otherwise have had to make it (as did the non-predatory, limit investment described in Column IIA).

The QV investment described in Column IIA illustrates the fact that an investor's *ex ante* belief that it had a monopolistic QV-investment incentive to make a particular QV investment is not a necessary condition for its being a limit QV investment. So long as the investor would not have believed *ex ante* that its investment would be at least normally profitable had it not believed it would or might deter a rival QV investment (or induce a rival to withdraw an existing QV investment or relocate an existing or future investment), the investment is a limit investment even if the investor did not believe *ex ante* that it had a monopolistic QV-investment incentive to make it. Thus, although the investor that made the QV investment described in Column IIA did not believe *ex ante* that it had a monopolistic QV-investment incentive to make it (indeed, believed *ex ante* that it faced a monopolistic QV-investment disincentive of $10 on the investment in question), that investment was a limit investment because the investor would have perceived the investment to be subnormally profitable *ex ante* but for its expectation that the investment would or might deter an established-rival QV-investment expansion or potential-competitor new entry: because the entry in Row (4)—$80—is lower than the entry in Row (1)—$100.

The QV investment described in Column III is a predatory, limit QV investment. A comparison of the entries in Rows (4) and (1) of Column III reveal that it is a limit investment (since $60 is less than $100). The entries in Rows (1), (2), (6), and (7) reveal that it is a predatory QV investment. Specifically, this conclusion reflects the facts that the undistorted profits the investor expected the investment to yield *ex ante*—$90, see the entry in Row (2)—were subnormal—were less than $100, see the entry in Row (1)—while the actual certainty-equivalent profits the investor expected the investment to yield *ex ante*—$110, see the entry in Row (7)—were rendered at least normal by the monopolistic QV-investment incentive the investor believed *ex ante* that it had to make the investment—$20, see the entry in Row (6). Column III manifests two things about predatory QV investments. First, a QV investor's *ex ante* belief that it has a monopolistic QV-investment incentive to make a particular QV investment is a necessary condition for its being predatory. Second, a QV investment's being a limit investment is also a necessary condition for its being a predatory QV investment: unless the QV investor's *ex ante* belief that the investment would be at least normally profitable was critically affected by its *ex ante* belief that the investment would or might deter a rival QV investment (or would or might cause a rival to withdraw an existing QV investment or relocate an existing or future QV investment), the investment's profitability could not be critically affected by the investor's *ex ante* belief that it would on one or more of these accounts have a monopolistic QV-investment incentive to make the investment in question.

I want to close this discussion by making two points. The first is that in some situations an incumbent's QV investment will deter a rival entry or expansion not only by increasing the total amount of QV investment in the relevant area of product-space and occupying the most-profitable unoccupied location in product-space but also by reducing the probability that public authorities will permit a potential expander or entrant to create an essential part of the QV investment it might otherwise make. For example, an incumbent's decision to build an additional railroad bridge over a river one had to cross to reach a particular urban terminus might deter an entry by a potential competitor by making it less likely that the city government would authorize the construction of another bridge over the river by increasing the aesthetic cost of that bridge's construction or the amount of additional navigation costs its existence would cause river-traffic to incur. (The construction of additional petroleum storage facilities may also militate against the relevant city government's granting a potential expander or entrant permission to create such facilities for similar reasons with the same consequence.) Although the fact that a particular QV investment "raised potential investors' costs" (in fact, precluded rival investment) in this way does not guarantee that the investment that had this consequence was predatory, the fact that some QV investments will deter rival expansions or entries may critically affect their efficaciousness. It may be that some of the investments in what have been deemed to be "essential facilities" in essential-facilities cases were predatory because they were efficacious *inter* alia for this sort of reason.

The final point I want to make is that, in my judgment, a substantial number (though a low percentage) of the QV investments in developed economies are predatory. I acknowledge that no QV investment made by a new entrant is predatory. I also admit that the vast majority of QV investments made by expanding incumbents are not predatory: few such investments are made to drive out a rival QV investment, and most earn significant supernormal conventional book profits. However, I do think that a substantial percentage of the least-profitable QV investments in the economy's various areas of product-space that are made by expanding incumbents are predatory: this conclusion reflects my belief that a high percentage of those investments are made by firms that realize that (1) their QV investments will deter an established rival or potential competitor from introducing an additional QV investment into the relevant area of product-space, (2) their QV investment will reduce the profit-yields of their other QV investment(s) in the relevant area of product-space by significantly less than those profit-yields would otherwise have been reduced by the rival QV investment the investment in question would deter, and (3) the associated monopolistic QV-investment incentive will often exceed the supernormal profits these QV investments yield, all things considered—*i.e.*, the least-profitable QV investments in question would have been *ex ante* subnormally profitable but for the monopolistic QV-investment incentive their respective makers had to make them.

(2) Ordover and Willig's Incorrect Definition of the Concept of a Predatory QV Investment

In a highly-regarded article,[664] the economists Janusz Ordover and Robert Willig claim that a QV investment made by an investor that anticipated *ex ante* that it would or might cause an existing rival QV investment to be withdrawn will be predatory if and only if the investor would not have found that investment to be (normally) profitable *ex ante* had it not believed that the investment would or might cause an existing rival QV investment to be withdrawn. This subsection

[664] Ordover and Willig, *passim*

(1) demonstrates the erroneousness of Ordover and Willig's claim, (2) examines the implications of Ordover and Willig's position on the predatoriness of any QV investment made by an investor that believed *ex ante* that the investment would or might induce an active product-rival to exit for the conclusion they would reach about the circumstances in which such a QV investment made by an investor that believed that it would or might deter the execution of a new entry or established-rival QV-investment expansion in the area of product-space in which it was made would properly be said to be predatory and explains why this latter position is also incorrect,[665] and (3) comments on various other aspects of Ordover and Willig's position on predatory QV investments and on other claims that Ordover and Willig make in the course of their analysis of the circumstances in which QV investments should be deemed predatory.

Ordover and Willig not only recognize that QV investments can be predatory but assert and purport to demonstrate that "even genuine innovations—new products that in some ways are superior to existing products in the eyes of both engineers and consumers—are in some circumstances anticompetitive"[666]—*i.e.*, predatory. However, they restrict their analysis of this possibility to cases in which the QV investment is made by an investor that believed *ex ante* that it would or might induce a rival QV investment to be withdrawn and conclude that a QV investment made by an investor that had such a belief *ex ante* should be deemed predatory if and only if the investor's *ex ante* perception that the investment in question was at least normally profitable *ex ante* was critically affected by its belief that the investment would or might induce such an exit.[667] This conclusion clearly differs from mine. My position is that a QV investment made by an investor that believed *ex ante* that it would or might lead to the withdrawal of a rival QV investment is predatory if and only if the investor's *ex ante* perception that it was at least normally profitable was critically affected by its *ex ante* belief that it had a monopolistic QV investment incentive to make it. (To see the difference between my position and Ordover and Willig's, note that their position will yield the conclusion that some QV investments in this category made by investors that own no other QV investment whose profit-yield might be increased by the substitution of the QV investment in question for a rival QV investment it caused to be withdrawn will be predatory even if the investor in question has no plan to wage any subsequent fight to the death unfairly.) In my terminology, Ordover and Willig have made the

---

[665] Although Ordover and Willig recognized that such QV investments might be predatory, they chose not to directly address the circumstances in which they would be predatory. *Id.* at 10 n.8.

[666] See *id.* at 8–9.

[667] Ordover and Willig's more felicitous formulation of their conclusion—*viz.*, that such a QV investment is predatory if and only if it "would be unprofitable without the exit it causes, but profitable with the exit"—is objective, *ex post*, and hence non-probabilistic. However, they recognize that something like my more awkward formulation is in fact more realistic. Thus, they admit that their formulation is based on what they recognize to be the unrealistic assumption that "businessmen know how their actions affect their profitability and the profitability of their rivals. . . ." See *id.* at 9, 13 n. 19, and 14 n. 20.

mistake of assuming that all QV investments that are expected to lead to the withdrawal of an extant QV investment that are limit QV investments are predatory. Ordover and Willig have either (1) forgotten the fact that, to be predatory, conduct must be *ex ante* economically inefficient on otherwise-Pareto-perfect assumptions (on the actor's perception of the relevant facts) and/or (2) failed to realize that the fact that a QV investment's profitability will be *increased* by its tendency to drive a rival QV investment out does not imply that that investment's profitability will be *inflated* by its tendency to drive a rival QV investment out since, on otherwise-Pareto-perfect assumptions, the exit of the rival QV investment will increase the economic efficiency of the QV investment in question by precisely the same amount that it increases its profit-yield.

Since few QV investments cause rival QV investments to be withdrawn while many QV investments (in particular, many QV investments that bring the QV-investment level in the relevant area of product-space to the level that would be an equilibrium level if underlying conditions would not change) do deter a new entry or a QV-investment expansion by an established rival, it is somewhat surprising that Ordover and Willig chose not to analyze the conditions under which a QV investment that (in their words) "merely deters entry"[668] should be deemed "predatory." Although Ordover and Willig were clearly reluctant to articulate this conclusion (perhaps because they intuited that it could not be correct), their position on the circumstances in which a QV investment in the relevant category made by an investor that believed *ex ante* that it would or might induce the withdrawal of an established rival QV investment should be deemed predatory clearly implies that a QV investment in this category made by an investor that believed *ex ante* that it would or might deter a new entry (or established-rival QV-investment expansion) should be deemed predatory if this belief critically affected the investor's *ex ante* perception that the investment would be at least normally profitable.

As I have already indicated, in my judgment, this position conflates predatory QV investments with limit QV investments. The fact that a particular QV investment is a limit QV investment—a QV investment whose investor-perceived *ex ante* profitability depends on the investor's perception that it would or might deter a potential or actual competitor from making a QV investment in the area of product-space in which the QV investment in question is located—does not make the QV investment predatory because it does not imply that the QV investor perceived itself to have a monopolistic QV-investment incentive to make the QV investment in question, much less that it perceived itself to have a critical monopolistic investment incentive to make that investment. The fact that a QV investment is a limit investment is compatible with its reducing or eliminating the monopolistic QV-investment disincentive the QV investor would otherwise have perceived itself to be confronting without inducing it to think that it had a monopolistic QV-investment incentive to

[668] See *id.* at 10 n. 8. Ordover and Willig's only comment on the relevant issue is the unexplained assertion that "the profit benchmark that is appropriate to test for predation against actual entrants may not be the benchmark to test for entry deterrence." See *id.* at 10 n. 9.

make the QV investment in question. Indeed, even when the relevant QV investor (accurately) perceives itself to have a monopolistic QV-investment incentive to make a particular limit investment, its perception that it has such an incentive might not be critical: it might perceive the nominal profits of the investment in question (or the sum of the nominal profits it believed the investment would generate and the non-inflating contribution it believed the investment would make to its other projects' profit-yields by generating joint-cost economies and/or enhancing the perceived value of its other products to their potential consumers or distributors) to be at least normal.

Finally, I want to comment briefly on five other aspects of Ordover and Willig's discussion of the proper way to define or determine the legality of predatory QV investments. First, like most economists who analyze business conduct that is covered by antitrust laws (and, more surprisingly, like many law professors who specialize in antitrust and know some economics), Ordover and Willig do not distinguish between the analysis of the legality of a business practice under the current antitrust laws and the analysis of the economically-efficient way to "regulate" the business practice in question. As I argued in Chaps. 5 and 9, I think this distinction is both real and important. Second, Ordover and Willig assume that—if it would be economically efficient to require the plaintiff or the State in a predatory-QV-investment suit to establish the possible profitability of the alleged predation before putting on more specific evidence relating to the predatory character of the conduct in question—this two-step approach would be authorized by current law.[669] As I argued when criticizing Joskow and Klevorick's two-step approach to predatory-pricing cases, I do not think that current law authorizes the courts to proceed in this way. Third, Ordover and Willig's analysis of the factors that determine the possible profitability of predation is deficient in many respects: (1) assumes that markets can be defined non-arbitrarily[670]; (2) assumes that for predation to be profitable in the market in which the allegedly-predatory QV investment has been made, that market must be "horizontally concentrated"—a proposition I would reject even if I thought that markets could be defined non-arbitrarily both because in our monopolistically-competitive world "monopoly power" (*inter alia*, competitive advantages) can be present in unconcentrated markets and because in our monopolistically-competitive world monopoly power can be substantially increased by the removal of a particular rival QV investment even if the exit causes a new QV investment to be made in the relevant area of product-space since that new investment may be further away in product-space from the predator's projects than was the project that was withdrawn; and (3) uses the insufficiently-specified concepts of "entry hurdles" and "reentry barriers" to analyze the potential profitability of predation.[671] Fourth, Ordover and Willig assume incorrectly that their definition of predatory QV investment would deem

[669] Ordover and Willig borrow this position from Joskow and Klevorick.

[670] See Ordover and Willig, *passim*.

[671] See *id.* at 11 n. 3.

predatory all QV investments that are allocatively inefficient and would deem non-predatory all QV investments that are economically efficient,[672] a conclusion that is almost certainly incorrect in our highly-Pareto-imperfect world in which the private cost of creating and producing units of new products and the private variable cost of producing units of old products are distorted by imperfections in price competition, externalities, taxes on the margin of income, *etc.*, and the benefits of introducing a new product are distorted by human error and buyer surplus. And fifth, Ordover and Willig assume incorrectly or state misleadingly that all choices that increase allocative efficiency will yield a "social optimum,"[673] will increase "welfare,"[674] and hence will be "socially desirable."[675]

B. The Legality of Predatory QV Investments Under U.S. and E.C./E.U. Antitrust Law, Correctly Interpreted and Applied

(1) U.S. Law

Any decision by an individual firm to make a predatory QV investment or any decision by two or more firms to execute a joint venture to make a predatory QV investment violates the Sherman Act, properly interpreted and applied. Both types of decisions violate Section 2 of the Sherman Act, and the joint-venture decision violates Section 1 as well. (For reasons that Chap. 4 discussed, joint ventures that create predatory QV investments that do not achieve their predatory objectives or planned predatory joint ventures that have no chance of achieving those objectives may not violate the Sherman Act.) Decisions by two or more firms to execute a predatory joint venture and decisions by individual firms to make a predatory QV investment do not violate the Clayton Act because none of that Act's provisions covers such conduct. I should add that, although, *ceteris paribus*, Section 7 of the Clayton Act does prohibit one or more firms from reducing competition by acquiring or merging with a rival and eliminating its QV investments, the "investments" that the firms in question are making are not "predatory QV investments" in my terms since to be a "predatory QV investment" in my terms an investment must be real—*i.e.*, must create a QV investment—and the merger-investments to which the previous sentence referred do not do so.

---

[672] See *id.* at 24–25.

[673] *Id.* at 19.

[674] *Id.* at 25.

[675] *Id.* As Chap. 1 indicated, the statement "X increases allocative (economic) efficiency" entails no more than that the equivalent-dollar gains it confers on its beneficiaries exceed the equivalent-dollar losses it imposes on its victims. For a demonstration of why economically-efficient choices may be unjust or undesirable from various defensible value-perspectives even if they do not violate anyone's moral rights, see TRUTH OR ECONOMICS at Chap. 4.

(2) E.C./E.U. Law

Correctly interpreted and applied, what is now Article 102 of the 2009 Treaty of Lisbon clearly does prohibit any individually-dominant firm, any member of a collectively-dominant set of rivals, or two or more such firms from making a predatory QV investment. Whether such investments are made by a now-Article-102-covered individual actor or by one or more covered actors through a joint venture, they constitute an exclusionary abuse in violation of now-Article 102. Now-Article 101 also prohibits the predatory QV investments to which it applies—*viz.*, those made at the behest of a trade association (regardless of whether one or more of the investors in question is a dominant firm or a member of a set of collectively-dominant rivals) and those made as a result of an agreement by two or more firms whether through a joint venture or some other scheme that involves one firm's making the investment in question and one or more of its rivals' agreeing to bear some of the costs of its doing so. However, now-Article 101 does not prohibit individual firms from making predatory QV investments in the absence of such a compensation scheme because it does not cover such conduct.

C. The Evidence That the State or a Private Plaintiff Should Be Required to Introduce to Establish a Prima Facie *Predatory-QV-Investment Claim and the Evidence That a Defendant Should Be Allowed to Use to Exonerate Itself*

I will first discuss the various categories of evidence that can help the State or a private plaintiff establish a *prima facie* predatory-QV-investment case and then discuss the various categories of evidence that can enable a defendant against which such a case has been made to exonerate itself. After that, I will briefly discuss which party should bear the burden of persuasion on various issues that are relevant to the resolution of a predatory-QV-investment claim, which party should bear the burden of producing various types of relevant evidence, and which party should bear the cost of producing each such type of evidence.

The predatory character of a QV investment can be established through either or both subjective (U.S. usage) or direct (E.C./E.U. usage) evidence of predatory intent or "objective" (U.S. usage) or "indirect" (E.C./E.U. usage) evidence of predatory intent—*i.e.*, evidence that the investment in question was not inherently profitable, that the investor did have a monopolistic QV-investment incentive to make it, and that that incentive rendered the QV investment profitable overall. In a few cases, subjective or direct evidence of intent will be available—*i.e.*, defendant memoranda, audio or audio-visual recordings of defendant *ex ante* statements of anticompetitive intent or *ex post* admissions of guilt, admissions of guilt by defendant wrongdoers who feel contrite or hope to receive more-favorable treatment from the prosecution, testimony of innocent (or guilty) whistleblowers, testimony of potential customers of the alleged predators that were told of the defendant's predatory plans by indiscreet sales-personnel who were trying to persuade them not to patronize another supplier (the target) by persuading them that the target would not be able to supply them in the medium or long run, and/or testimony of predation victims that were told of the company's predatory plans in the course of negotiations to buy them out at a distressed price (ideally substantiated by evidence demonstrating that the defendant had indeed offered to buy the alleged target out for a price that was lower than the value the target would have if it were not a predation-target). Private plaintiffs or the State may be able to secure internal memos that contain statements of predatory intent far more often than one might suspect. Although one might think that such memos would be destroyed prior to or early on in any litigative process, companies often have one or more executives or employees who do not follow shredding instructions for any one of a number of reasons: because they fear that such evidence-destruction is illegal, because they disapprove of their company's predatory conduct or fear the legal repercussions of being found to have participated in such conduct and want to distance themselves from it, because they like to keep complete files for the sake of doing so, or because they are disorganized or careless. Moreover, to the extent that the relevant memos were typed onto computers and circulated through e-mail, they may be recoverable because it is far more difficult to remove traces of them from a computer system than many seem to suppose. (Of course, the company's files may also contain a number of self-serving memos that were included precisely to "demonstrate" the company's innocent intent in case of litigation.) Unfortunately, the testimony of employees will be impeachable to the extent that they can be shown to be disgruntled, and the testimony of targets is rendered suspect by their financial stakes in the defendant being found guilty or liable.

The requisite predatory intent can also be established through objective or direct evidence that the QV investment alleged to be predatory was not (would not be) inherently profitable, that the investor did have a monopolistic QV-investment incentive to make it, and that this incentive rendered the QV investment profitable overall. The objective evidence that is relevant to the inherent unprofitability of the investment is evidence on (1) the profits it would be said to yield or be predicted to yield by a conventional analysis that focused on the profits yielded directly by the use of the product-design, outlet, or capacity it created—*i.e.*, that ignored the effect of the use of the QV investment in question on the profits yielded by the investor's other QV-investment projects, (2) the impact the creation and use of the QV investment would have on the profits yielded by the investor's other projects by reducing the cost of creating and using them or by increasing the demand for them (by increasing the extent to which the investor offered a full line or improving the reputation of the investor [the assumptions buyers made about the physical quality of its products and/or the image-benefits of consuming its brand]), and (3) the amount of profits that would be normal for the QV investment in question—the magnitude of the investment and the normal rate-of-return applicable to it. The objective evidence that is relevant to whether the investor had a QV-investment incentive to make the investment and the magnitude of any such incentive it had to make it is evidence about (1) whether the investment in question would (A) induce an established rival to withdraw a QV investment, (B) deter a potential or actual competitor from making a QV investment in the relevant area of product-space that would have been more proximate to the investor's other QV investments than the QV investment in question was, would have militated against contrived oligopolistic-pricing by more than the investment in question did, and/or would have militated against natural oligopolistic pricing or the profit-maximizing timing of price-announcements by more than the investment in question did, and/or (C) induce an incumbent to substitute for its extant QV investment or a prospective investor to substitute for its planned QV investment one that would reduce by less the BCAs, NOMs, and COMs the investor enjoyed or could obtain when using its other projects and (2) if it did (would), the amount by which it did (would) increase the profit-yields of the investor's other QV investments on these accounts.

At least three types of studies could produce evidence on these two sets of issues:

(1) studies of the relevant parameters done or commissioned by the defendant *ex ante*;
(2) studies done or commissioned by the private plaintiff or State of the predictions that the defendant should have made *ex ante* that derive their conclusions from investigations of the *ex ante* situation; and
(3) when the suspect QV investment has actually been made, studies done or commissioned by the private plaintiff or State of the predictions the defendant should have made *ex ante* that derive their conclusions from investigations of the actual *ex post* magnitudes of the relevant parameters.

I now want to comment on each of these three types of studies. First: defendant studies. As Ordover and Willig note: "The defendant's investment planning process may be the most useful source of data concerning the firm's expectations. Decisions to commit substantial funds to R&D projects [or QV investments in general] are likely to be supported by internal analyses of prospective costs and financial benefits."[676] Since internal financial analysts have a stake in giving accurate, honest reports and company files are not always purged of tell-tale evidence (and even when they are, original memos appear surprisingly often in an orderly manager's personal files or the hard drive of the company's computer system), internal memoranda and e-mails may demonstrate that the alleged predator's QV-investment decision was critically affected by its hope and expectation that the investment would or might alter one or more rivals' QV-investment decisions in ways that would increase the profit-yields of its other QV investments. Of course, in this context, too, the courts will have to be sensitive to the possibility that an actual predator may include in its files misleading reports of these kinds to justify its behavior. Second: State or private-plaintiff studies that focus on the information that would have been available to the defendant *ex ante*. Obviously, even when the QV investment in question does not involve any technological research or the

[676] See Ordover and Willig at 27.

creation of a product that really is significantly different from any known alternative, this second type of study will be difficult to execute, and its conclusions (perhaps especially about the normal rate-of-return) will be far from precise or fully reliable. Third: State or private-plaintiff studies that focus on the actual consequences of QV investments that have been made. Although this third type of study will be based on harder data (except about the normal rate-of-return) than the second type of study, its usefulness is undermined by the fact that its conclusions will be relevant only to the extent that the investor is well-informed *ex ante*. Obviously, to the extent that part or all of the suspect QV investment is technologically and/or commercially innovative, the difficulty and reliability of the type of *ex ante* study listed second and the unreliability of the inference made in the type of *ex post* study listed third will be greater.

If the evidence that the private plaintiff or the State has submitted is sufficient to enable it to survive a defendant motion for a directed verdict or for dismissal, the defendant can use at least six types of evidence or arguments to exonerate itself. First, the defendant can rebut the subjective or direct intent-evidence the private plaintiff or State introduced in various ways: for example, by putting on witnesses that deny that the alleged oral statements were ever made, by showing that the oral and written statements in question could have had or did have a different meaning from the one attributed to them by the other side, by pointing out that—even if the written or oral statements in question did show that their makers believed the company had a monopolistic QV-investment incentive to make the QV investment in question—it did not show that they believed that this incentive was critical to the *ex ante* profitability of that investment because they might have believed or actually did believe *ex ante* that that investment would be profitable for legitimate reasons (that the combination of the profits it would be calculated to generate if its effects on the profit-yields of the investor's other projects were ignored and the profits it would yield the investor by reducing the cost the investor would have to incur to create and use its other QV investments and by increasing the demand for the other products the QV investor would sell by increasing their absolute attractiveness to relevant buyers would constitute at least a normal rate-of-return on the QV investment whose predatory character is at issue), by demonstrating that—even if those that made the suspect choice did believe at one point in time that its profitability would be or was critically inflated by a monopolistic investment incentive—they did not believe that to be the case at the time at which they committed themselves to making the suspect QV investment, by submitting documentary evidence that contradicts or is inconsistent with the other side's intent claims, by attacking the motives or general credibility of the other side's witnesses, and/or by demonstrating that the memos, e-mails, or oral statements the other side cited were made by people who did not have authority to make the allegedly-predatory decisions.

Second, the defendant can rebut the other side's objective or indirect evidence on the legitimate profitability of the allegedly-predatory QV investment by establishing the requisite probability (50 % in a civil suit and whatever probability is required to establish reasonable doubt in a criminal case) that the private plaintiff's or State's legitimate-profit-rate calculation was wrong even on the assumption that it took account of all relevant possibilities. More specifically, the defendant might respond to this "subnormal legitimate profitability" evidence in at least the following four ways:

(1) the defendant might provide evidence that it had criticized its own internal or commissioned studies (on which the State or private plaintiff had relied) or that the people that made the suspect decisions did not believe the studies in question or perhaps made their choice without knowledge of the conclusions these studies reacted;
(2) the defendant could criticize at trial various aspects of the other side's study of the *ex ante* situation;
(3) the defendant could criticize the other side's analysis of or conclusions about the *ex post* figures from which it derived its *ex ante* claims or argue that, for various reasons, it was not able *ex ante* to predict these figures accurately and actually underestimated the size of the investment in question, underestimated the normal rate-of-return for that investment, overestimated the nominal profits it would yield, overestimated the profits the investment would enable it to earn on its other QV investments by overestimating the amount by which the investment would reduce the cost of creating and using those QV investments and/or the amount by which it would increase the demand for its other products, overestimated the amount by which the investment would reduce its other projects' profit-yields relative to the *status quo ante*, and/or underestimated the amount by which the rival QV investment(s) the investment would deter would reduce its other products' profit-yields relative to the *status quo ante*;
(4) the defendant might argue that the QV investment's legitimate future returns were expected to be higher than its current or recent past returns—that demand for the product or outlet the investment created was expected to rise either because consumers were in the process of learning about their attractiveness or because overall demand for the products in the relevant area of product-space was expected to rise during its lifetime, that the company had adopted policies that had reduced the QV investment's short-run yield to a misleadingly-low level (had charged prices that were lower than the prices that would maximize the profits the investment would yield in the short run in order to promote the product or had engaged in other promotional activities that are expensed in the short run but expected to bear fruit in the long run), or that the investment would increase the profits yielded by the investor's other projects by progressively-larger amounts by reducing its costs or increasing the demand for its products progressively over time.

I turn now to the three burden-allocation issues. For convenience, I will assume that the suit in question is to be decided by a Sherman-Act-type test of illegality. To establish a *prima facie* case in a predatory-QV-investment suit to be decided by the application of the basic Sherman Act test of illegality, the State or private plaintiff should be required to produce (1) evidence of predatory intent that would be requisitely persuasive if not undermined by the defendant's subjective/direct evidence or (2) evidence that the nominal profits yielded by the QV investment under scrutiny were subnormal and that the investor had a monopolistic QV-investment incentive to make it (because it might or did lead to the exit of an extant QV investment, the deterrence of a prospective QV investment, or the relocation of an extant or prospective QV investment in circumstances in which, on these accounts, the QV investor would have a monopolistic QV-investment incentive to make the QV investment in question) that would be requisitely persuasive if not undermined by the defendant. Once the State or private plaintiff established its *prima facie* case (put in enough evidence to avoid a summary judgment or directed verdict), the defendant(s) in a predatory-QV-investment case should be allowed to exonerate itself (themselves) (1) by contradicting the State or plaintiff's subjective/direct intent-evidence, (2) by showing that the State had misestimated the nominal profit-yield of the investment in question or had mistakenly concluded that the defendant had a monopolistic QV-investment incentive to make the QV investment under scrutiny, (3) by showing that the QV investment in question was rendered profitable by the legitimate contributions it made to the profits the defendant's (defendants') other QV investments yielded (by reducing the cost of creating or using them and/or by increasing the demand for the product or services they created), and/or (4) by showing that it (they) had believed *ex ante* that the QV investment in question would be legitimately profitable even though it found out *ex post* that the investment was not legitimately profitable.

In my opinion, the State or private plaintiff should have the burden of persuasion as an initial matter on the facts necessary for a *prima facie* case to be established. Once the State or private plaintiff has carried that initial burden, the defendant(s) should have the burden of persuading the trier-of-fact that the probability that those facts obtained was not requisitely high. In my judgment, the defendant(s) should also have the burden of persuasion on the joint-cost and joint-benefit issues as well as on the mistake issue. I would place on the defendant(s) the burden of producing all cost-data that relates to the cost of creating and using the suspected QV investment but would require the State or private plaintiff to pay for the production of that data. I would place on the State or private plaintiff the burden of producing and paying for all data that relates to the monopolistic QV-investment incentive the defendant(s) was (were) alleged to have to make the QV investment under scrutiny. And I would place on the defendant(s) the burden of producing and paying for data on any joint economies it (they) alleged the QV investment in question generated and any exonerating mistakes it (they) made.

D. The U.S. Case-Law, EC Position, and E.C./E.U. Case-Law on Predatory QV Investments

(1) The U.S. Case-Law

The U.S. case law on possibly-predatory QV investments is sparse. This subsection comments on the judicial opinions written in the four best-known cases to have focused on the possible illegality of QV investments. Unfortunately, in my judgment, the opinions in all four of these cases contain significant errors.

The first member of this dubious quartet is *United States v. Aluminum Co. of America* (*Alcoa*).[677] In *Alcoa*, Judge Learned Hand argued that the fact that Alcoa's QV investments in capacity deterred others from constructing aluminum-refining capacity made the monopolistic position he found Alcoa to be occupying illegal under Section 2 of the Sherman Act. I hasten to admit that Hand's opinion does not explicitly find that Alcoa's capacity-investments were themselves illegal (predatory) or, indeed, were even "not honestly industrial,"[678] whatever that might mean. However, Hand did say that Alcoa's decisions to build new capacity were "effective exclusions,"[679] and, in U.S. antitrust jargon, the statement that a choice is "exclusionary" does imply that it is illegal. At a minimum, it also seems fair to conclude that, in Hand's view, Alcoa's construction of this capacity defeats the claim that its (alleged) monopoly power was "thrust upon it,"[680] that its high market share was "not inevitable" [681] (whatever that might mean). I have no doubt that Alcoa's capacity-expansions did deter rivals from building aluminum-refining plants and were made more profitable by that fact. However, nothing in the *Alcoa* opinion suggests that Alcoa's capacity-expansions were even non-predatory limit investments, much less predatory limit investments. Thus, nothing in the opinion suggests (1) that Alcoa would not have found its expansions profitable even if they had not deterred any rival QV investment, (2) that Alcoa actually had a monopolistic QV-investment incentive to make the QV investments in question (though I suspect it did), or (3) that any monopolistic QV-investment incentives Alcoa had to make the relevant investments critically affected Alcoa's *ex ante* perception that they were at least normally profitable (which I doubt they did). I do not think that Hand's opinion in *Alcoa* can be read to assert that any QV investment that deters a rival QV investment is predatory and Sherman-Act-violative on that account or that Alcoa's capacity-expansions were predatory in the correct sense of "predatory"—assertions that, in my view, are respectively wrong and highly unlikely to be true. However, Hand does seem to believe that Alcoa's capacity-expansions delegitimate what he takes to be its monopoly power, and this position is also indefensible.

Chronologically, the second major federal case that is relevant in this context is *United States v. United Shoe Machinery*.[682] In his opinion for the (federal) District Court in this Sherman Act case, Judge Wyzanski argued that, although United Shoe's decisions to do research designed to discover superior shoe-manufacturing

---

[677] 148 F.2d 416 (2d Cir. 1945). For other cases that seem to have raised similar issues, see American Tobacco Co. v. United States, 328 U.S. 781 (1946) and du Pont v. Federal Trade Commission (du Pont-Ethyl), 488 F. Supp. 747 (1980).

[678] See United States v. Aluminum Co. of American (Alcoa), 148 F.2d 416 at 431.

[679] *Id.*

[680] *Id.* at 429.

[681] *Id.* at 431.

[682] 110 F. Supp. 295 (D. Mass. 1952).

machines and to produce machines that could perform every function involved in shoe manufacturing (by inference, to make the QV investments that enabled the company to produce each such machine) were not predatory or immoral—indeed, were "honestly industrial,"[683] they did not legitimate United's (alleged) monopoly position (could not be said to justify the conclusion that United's position was entirely [or even primarily] attributable to its social efficiency[684] and disproved the claim that United's position was "inevitable"[685])—indeed, favored the conclusion that United's overall position was illegal.

The third major federal antitrust case on QV investments is *Union Leader*,[686] a case involving a decision by a newspaper published in one town to publish a second paper in another town that had its own local journal in circumstances in which the profitability of the relevant investment depended on its driving the second town's original newspaper out of business. The court assumed that in such fight-to-the-death cases the defendant's conduct will violate Section 2's prohibition of monopolizing or attempting to monopolize if and only if it conducted the relevant fight to the death unfairly—*i.e.*, by making competitive moves other than the QV investment itself that gave it a competitive (survival) advantage unrelated to its investment's relative allocative efficiency. This position ignores the possibility that the QV investment may itself be predatory—that the investor's *ex ante* belief in the investment's normal profitability was critically affected by its perception that the substitution of the QV investment in question for its exited rival's QV investment would or might increase the profit-yield of the investor's other QV investments without increasing the allocative-efficiency contribution of its operations (*e.g.*, because the investor's new QV investment was further away in product-space from its other QV investments than was the rival QV investment whose exit its QV investment would induce and because it would in any event price all its products to maximize the total returns of its organization). I should say that the court's failure to address this possibility may not have made any difference—may have reflected the fact that the possibility was not a reality in the case in question.

The fourth important U.S. case that contains statements that bear on the circumstances in which a QV investment should be deemed predatory is *Transamerica Computer Co. v. IBM*.[687] In this case, the plaintiff argued that any assessment of the predatory character of IBM's pricing and investment decisions should take account *inter alia* of their impact on the profits yielded by IBM's other products—*i.e.*, on the so-called impact costs of these decisions. Unfortunately, neither the plaintiff's proposal that the court take account of "impact costs" nor the court's account of the plaintiff's proposal defined the "impact costs" in the way

[683] *Id.* at 331 and 345.

[684] *Id.* at 345.

[685] *Id.* at 331 and 345.

[686] Union Leader Corp. v. Newspapers of New England, 180 F. Supp. 125 (D. Mass. 1959), aff'd in part and rev'd in part, 284 F.2d 582 (1st Cir. 1960), cert. denied, 365 U.S. 833 (1961).

[687] 459 F. Supp. 626 (1978).

they would have to be defined for "impact cost" analysis to yield correct conclusions about the predatory character of the QV investments under scrutiny—*i.e.*, focused on whether a seller's new investment affected the profit-yields of its old QV investments not only by cannibalizing the sales of its pre-existing products but also by affecting various rivals' relevant pricing and investment decisions. Thus, according to the court, when the decision to be evaluated was the introduction of a new product, the relevant "impact costs" were "the reduction in anticipated future profits of an existing product line caused by the introduction of a new product line."[688] In any event, in the end, the court decided to reject the "impact cost" approach altogether—in particular, to exclude evidence on any determinant of such "impact costs" as a matter of law. The court attempted to justify this decision on the inaccurate and/or irrelevant grounds[689] that

(1) the consideration of such evidence "could be a disincentive to research and innovation,"[690]
(2) such evidence is speculative,[691]
(3) impact costs are not reflected in conventional profit and loss statements,[692] and
(4) consideration of such evidence would lead courts to require businesses to maximize their profits, which would cause them to ignore their social responsibilities.[693]

To summarize: few cases have focused on the possible antitrust illegality of QV investments, and all the opinions in the major cases that have addressed this issue have made critical mistakes.

[688] *Id.* at 631.

[689] *Id.*

[690] In fact, it would deter R&D that might lead to predatory QV investments but encourage the predator's rivals to do R&D.

[691] In fact, such evidence is no more speculative than the other kinds of evidence the courts admit in such cases.

[692] This accounting practice is totally irrelevant to whether courts should consider these costs, given the fact that, regardless of the way in which accounts are kept, businessmen clearly do consider such costs.

[693] Five objections can be made to this contention. First, the consideration of such costs would actually militate against businesses' increasing their profits by engaging in predation. Second, the prohibition of businesses' sacrificing short-run profits to obtain profits in the long run by deterring entries or expansions does not prohibit them from sacrificing profits in the public interest. Third, there is no reason to believe that predators will spend their ill-gotten gains in the public interest. Fourth, even if they do, the tendency of the exclusion of such evidence to increase the expenditures of this kind that the predators make would be more or less offset by the predation's tendency to decrease the expenditures of this kind that would otherwise have been made by the predator's victims had they profited from making the QV investments the predator's predatory QV investments deterred. Fifth, the impact of an antitrust ruling on the extent to which its addressees make charitable contributions or other types of non-profitable expenditures in the public interest is irrelevant to its correctness as a matter of law in any event.

(2) The EC Position and the E.C./E.U. Case-Law

To my knowledge, neither the EC nor any E.C./E.U. competition-law court has ever addressed the legality of predatory QV investments as I have defined this concept. Admittedly, both the EC and the E.C./E.U. courts have declared illegal as "exclusionary abuses" decisions by an individually-dominant firm or a member of a collectively-dominant set of rivals to acquire a majority or minority stake in a rival, to merge with a rival, to acquire a bankrupt firm to prevent its assets from being acquired by an outsider, or to buy up a rival to retire its plant and equipment but since none of these behaviors involves the creation of a new QV investment, none of the "investments" in question is the type of real investment that, on my definition, can be predatory.

4. Predatory Cost-Reducing Investments

Predatory cost-reducing investments include (1) predatory investments in cost-reducing plant-modernization, cost-reducing new-plant construction, cost-reducing equipment, and/or cost-reducing employees (specifically, predatory investments in their training and/or recruitment) that does not involve the making of any production-process discoveries and (2) predatory investments in cost-reducing PPR.

A. The Definition of a Predatory Cost-Reducing Investment

A predatory cost-reducing investment is simply a cost-reducing investment whose execution satisfies the general definition of predatory conduct. Thus, a cost-reducing investment is predatory if and only if it was made by an investor whose *ex ante* perception that it was profitable was *ceteris paribus* critically inflated by its belief that it had a monopolistic incentive to make the investment because it would or might induce a rival to withdraw an extant QV investment, deter a rival from adding to the amount of QV investment in the relevant area of product-space, induce an existing rival to change the location of an extant QV investment, induce a prospective QV investor to change the location of its planned QV investment, and derivatively change not only the investor's OCAs but also (possibly) its NOMs, COMs, and in the case of a cost-reducing investment made in an ARDEPPS in which prices were set across-the-board the height of its rivals' HNOPs.

I will now explain (1) when and why investors in cost-reducing investments in (A) plant-modernization, new-plant construction, equipment, and/or employees (specifically, investments in their recruitment and/or training) that does not involve the making of any production-process discoveries and (B) PPR that is not designed to discover less-accident-and-pollution-loss-prone production processes will have a monopolistic incentive to make the investments in question, (2) when and why investors in PPR that is designed to discover less-accident-and-pollution-loss-prone production processes will have such an incentive to make the investments in question, and (3) when the fact that the maker of a cost-reducing investment believes that it has a monopolistic incentive to make the investment in question will render the investment predatory.

A firm will have a monopolistic incentive to make a cost-reducing investment that will not reduce the accident-and-pollution losses its production of any relevant amount of its product generates in the same circumstances in which a firm will have a monopolistic QV-investment incentive to make a QV investment—*viz.*, when the cost-reducing investment in question induces a rival to withdraw a QV investment, deters a rival from making a new QV investment that would increase equilibrium QV investment in the ARDEPPS in question, induces a rival to move to a location further away in product-space from the other projects of the maker of the cost-reducing investment, or induces a prospective QV investor to make a similar change in the location of a planned QV investment. As we saw when discussing QV investments that affect rival decisions in these ways, investments that have these effects (1) will increase the suspect investor's HNOPs by eliminating a rival QV investment that was either best-placed to supply a buyer that one of the suspect investor's projects was second-placed to supply or that was second-placed to supply a buyer that one of the suspect investor's projects was best-placed to supply, by causing a rival to substitute for such a QV investment one that was not best-placed to supply buyers that one of the suspect investor's projects was originally second-placed to supply or that was worse-placed to supply one or more of the suspect investor's customers than the rival's original investment was when that original rival investment was second-placed to obtain the suspect investor's customers, and by increasing the extent to which its rivals announce their across-the-board prices in a sequence that increases their HNOP array, (2) will sometimes increase the suspect investor's NOMs by increasing its OCAs, increasing its prominence in a way that enhances its ability to initiate a series of relevant premature price announcements, and/or by preventing the entry of a rival that does not know how to behave in the ways that would enable itself and its rivals to obtain OMs naturally, and (3) will sometimes increase the suspect investor's COMs by eliminating non-cooperators, preventing the entry of new firms that would be less good at contrivance or less willing to cooperate in contrivance, and changing the suspect investor's and its rivals BCA/BCD distributions in ways that facilitate contrivance. Makers of cost-reducing investments may have a monopolistic incentive to make them because cost-reducing investments that reduce the marginal cost the investor has to incur to produce the unit of output that was its last unit of output pre-investment can make it inherently profitable for the investor's rivals to make the same sorts of alterations in their investment decisions that predatory QV investments can render profitable for them to make—in the case of predatory cost-reducing investments, by improving the investor's competitive-position arrays and concomitantly worsening its rivals' actual and prospective competitive-position arrays.

More specifically, a cost-reducing investment in plant-modernization, new-plant construction, equipment, and/or employees (specifically, investments in their recruitment and/or training and an investment in cost-reducing PPR that is not directed at discovering a less-accident-and-pollution-loss-prone production process but that reduces the investor's marginal costs) may alter the investor's rivals' QV-investment and/or pricing decisions because it (1) will reduce the number of buyers that rival products are best-placed to supply—in particular, will do so by the number of customers for whose patronage the relevant rival-product originally was best-placed and the investor's product originally was worse-than-best-placed by less than the marginal-cost reduction the investment generated (in which case the associated loss in competitive advantages will equal [the number of customers in question] *times* [the rival product's pre-investment average competitive advantage in relation to those buyers]) and (2) will reduce the amount by which a rival product that is still best-placed post-investment is best-placed to the extent that the investor (A) originally was second-placed and at a disadvantage that was bigger than the marginal-cost reduction (in each such case, the reduction in the rival's competitive advantage will equal the reduction in marginal costs) and/or (B) originally was worse-than-second-placed by a margin that was lower than the marginal-cost reduction (in each such case, the reduction in the rival's competitive advantage will equal the difference between the marginal-cost reduction and the sum by which the investor was originally worse-than-second-placed). Obviously, such cost-reducing-investment-induced decreases in competitive advantages may make it profitable for a rival of the cost-reducing investor to withdraw an existing product without replacing it and may make it unprofitable for an actual or potential rival of the cost-reducing investor to make a new QV investment in the relevant area of product-space that the rival would otherwise have found profitable. Indeed, since the amount by which any given cost-reducing investment will reduce the sum of the competitive advantages that will be enjoyed by producers of any product that competes with or would compete with the cost-reducing investor's products will depend on the attributes of that rival product (on the pre-investment actual or prospective competitive position of the cost-reducing investor in relation to buyers whose patronage the other product in question was or would be best-placed to secure), cost-reducing investments may also make it profitable for an established rival of the investor to relocate an extant QV investment further from the investor's QV investment or for an established or potential competitor to place a new QV investment further from the investor's QV investment than the rival would otherwise have chosen to do. Moreover, any associated changes in the identities of the owners of the QV investments in the cost-reducing investor's ARDEPPS and any associated changes in the BCA/BCD distributions of the cost-reducing investor and its rivals may also benefit the cost-reducing investor by increasing the NOMs and COMs it can obtain as well as by increasing its HNOP in an across-the-board-pricing context by increasing the extent to which the cost-reducing investor's rivals announce their prices in a sequence that increases the height of their and its HNOP array.

A firm may also have a monopolistic investment incentive to do production-process research that is designed to discover a less-accident-and-pollution-loss-prone way to produce a product it produces. For a firm to have such an incentive to do such PPR, one or more of the following four sets of conditions must be fulfilled:

(1) (A) there is some possibility that the relevant PPR will discover a production process that will reduce the sum of the non-accident-and-pollution-loss marginal costs generated by the production of the good to whose production the discovery relates and the accident-and-pollution losses that production of

marginal units of this good generates below the pre-discovery non-accident-and-pollution-loss costs generated by the production of marginal units of the good in question, and

(B) various factors that will be discussed when explaining the non-predatory functions of certain types of systems rivalry make it inherently profitable for the discoverer to charge a supra-marginal-cost (*i.e.*, positive as opposed to zero) price for the right to use the discovery to produce a marginal unit of output;

(2) (A) there is some possibility that the relevant PPR will discover a production process that will reduce the sum of the non-accident-or-pollution-loss marginal costs of producing a relevant quantity of the good in question and the accident-and-pollution losses that the production of marginal units of the good in question will generate while increasing the non-accident-or-pollution-loss costs of producing marginal units of the good in question,

(B) the relevant producers are liable for the accident-and-pollution losses they generate only if their generation of those losses was negligent, and

(C) by increasing the non-discoverers' production costs by rendering negligent their continued use of their original, less-safe but otherwise-less-expensive production-process, the discovery makes it unprofitable for some established producers to continue to produce existing products or for established or potential competitors to introduce new products;

(3) (A) there is some possibility that the relevant PPR will discover a production process that will reduce the sum of the non-accident-and-pollution-loss total cost of producing a relevant quantity of the product in question and the total accident-and-pollution losses the production of those units generated, and

(B) various factors that will be discussed below make it inherently profitable for the discoverer to put a positive price on the right to use the discovery to produce marginal units of output; and/or

(4) (A) there is some possibility that the relevant PPR will discover a production process that will reduce the sum of the non-accident-and-pollution-loss total cost of producing a relevant quantity of the product in question and the total accident-and-pollution losses the production of the units in question generated or would generate while increasing this sum above the pre-discovery non-accident-and-pollution-loss total cost of producing the relevant quantity of the good in question,

(B) the relevant producers are liable for the accident-and-pollution losses they generate only if their generation of those losses was negligent, and

(C) the associated increase in the total cost these producers would have to incur to produce the relevant output critically reduces the profits they can earn by continuing to produce an existing product or introducing a new product into the relevant area of product-space.

I have now explained the circumstances in which the maker of a cost-reducing investment will have a monopolistic incentive to make the investment in question. I should add that, to the extent that the preceding discussion left the impression that production-process researchers can have a monopolistic incentive to do their research only if they also produce the good to whose production process the PPR relates, this impression is inaccurate. Independent research organizations can also have what might be called a derivative monopolistic incentive to do PPR that a producer/potential researcher would have a monopolistic incentive to execute if it could carry out such research proficiently: to the extent that such a producer/potential researcher would have such an incentive, the incentive's existence would affect the payment the producer/potential researcher in question would be willing to make to the independent *ex ante* to induce the latter to do the research as well as the payment the producer/potential researcher would be willing to make to the latter *ex post* for the discovery.

Of course, the fact that the maker of a cost-reducing investment has a monopolistic incentive to make it does not render that investment predatory. For a cost-reducing investment to be predatory, the investor must believe *ex ante* (1) that it has a monopolistic incentive to make the investment in question (regardless of whether it actually has such an incentive) and (2) that that incentive renders the cost-reducing investment in question *ex ante* profitable despite the fact that it would otherwise be *ex ante* unprofitable.

I want to close this subsection with a set of speculations about the percentage of cost-reducing investments that are predatory that parallel the speculations I made about the percentage of QV investments that are predatory. In my judgment,

(1) the vast majority of cost-reducing investments are not predatory;
(2) because the conditions under which the maker of a cost-reducing investment will have a monopolistic investment incentive to execute it are more restrictive than the conditions under which the maker of a QV investment will have a monopolistic investment incentive to execute it, I suspect that the percentage of cost-reducing investments in any given supernormal-profit class that are predatory is lower than its counterpart for non-systems-rivalry QV investments in that supernormal-profit class;
(3) the percentage of cost-reducing investments in any given supernormal-profit class that is predatory is inversely related to the supernormal profits that define the class in question; and
(4) a non-trivial percentage of cost-reducing investments is predatory.

B. The Legality of Predatory Cost-Reducing Investments Under U.S. Antitrust Law and E.C./E.U. Competition Law, Correctly Interpreted and Applied

The preceding section's analysis of the legality of predatory QV investments under U.S. antitrust law and E.C./E.U. competition law is fully applicable to the legality of predatory cost-reducing investments.

C. The Evidence That the State or a Private Plaintiff Should Be Required to Introduce to Establish a Prima Facie *Predatory-Cost-Reducing-Investment Claim and the Evidence That a Defendant Should Be Allowed to Use to Exonerate Itself*

I would place on the State or private plaintiff the burden of persuasion on the issue of whether the cost-reducing investment under scrutiny reduced the investor's marginal costs. I would place on them as well the burden of paying for the production of evidence on this issue. However, I would place the burden of producing that evidence on the defendant. I would also place on the State or private plaintiff the burden of persuasion on all other issues that relate to the defendant's having a monopolistic incentive to make the cost-reducing investment in question as well as the burden of producing evidence on the associated facts and paying for that evidence-production. In addition, I would place on the State or private plaintiff the burden of persuasion on the inherent nominal unprofitability of the cost-reducing investment under scrutiny. I would place on the defendant the duty of producing the evidence that is relevant to this issue but place the burden of paying for that evidence on the State or private plaintiff. Finally, I would place on the defendant all three burdens that relate to any claim it makes that its decision to make the investment in question was mistaken or that the nominal profitability of the investment in question understated its actual profitability because the experience of executing the cost-reducing investment in question would reduce the cost of or increase the proficiency of the investor's future cost-reducing investments. (Admittedly, this learning-by-doing possibility seems even more remote to me in the cost-reducing-investment context than in the QV-investment context. Moreover, I see no counterpart in the cost-reducing-investment context to the tendency of some QV investments to increase the demand for the investor's other products by filling out its line, increasing its reputation for producing physically-superior goods, or improving the image or increasing the status value of its products.)

D. The U.S. Case-Law, EC Position, and E.C./E.U. Case-Law on Predatory Cost-Reducing Investments

There is none; there is none; there is none. I do not think that the failure of U.S. and E.C./E.U. institutions to address this phenomenon reflects either the phenomenon's empirical insignificance or the impracticability of predatory-cost-reducing-investment suits. As I have already indicated, I believe that a substantial number of such investments are predatory and that suits against firms that engaged in this type of predation would be practicable (are certainly as practicable as predatory-QV-investment suits).

Instead, I think this enforcement failure reflects the fact that economists, legal academics who are conversant with economics, and legal practitioners have failed to realize that cost-reducing investments can be predatory.

5. Predatory Buying

A seller's purchasing offer or purchase is predatory if the seller's *ex ante* perception that it was profitable was critically affected by the seller's belief that it would or might reduce the absolute attractiveness of the best offers against which it would have to compete by inducing one or more rivals to exit and/or by deterring one or more rival QV investments by raising the price that one or more target rivals must pay for an input or precluding the rival(s) from purchasing the input.

A. The Definition of Predatory Buying

A decision by an established firm to purchase or bid for an "input" that an established rival would use in its current operations or that a potential expander or entrant would use to create or use its prospective QV investment is predatory if the buyer/bidder perceived *ex ante* that its purchase would not be profitable but for its tendency to drive a rival out, to deter an actual or potential competitor from making an additional QV investment in the relevant area of product-space, or to induce an actual or potential rival to relocate its existing or planned QV investment(s) further away in product-space from the buyer/bidder's projects by bidding up the price the relevant rival would have to pay for the input in question or precluding that rival from purchasing it (if it is a patent or other essential, unique asset, by buying it before the rival could attempt to do so and refusing to sell it to the rival when the rival wanted to purchase it). A wide variety of types of inputs may be predatorily purchased or bid for: intellectual property (*e.g.*, patents), scientists and managers (who can be put on long-term contracts of employment or employment contracts of any length if they include clauses that prohibit the relevant employees from competing against the employer or working for a competitor of the employer), other sorts of employees (either by bidding up wages or, more cost-effectively, by granting wage or other labor-conditions concessions to unions on condition that the terms of the labor agreement also apply to the target rival, whose employees the union in question also represents[694]), plant and equipment, or various kinds of

---

[694] Three related points are worth noting. First, in some cases—*viz.*, when the firm bidding up the price of the relevant labor or granting the wage concession to a union uses less of the relevant type of labor per unit of output than its rival does, such concessions may yield it profits by giving it a marginal cost advantage even if it does not drive the target out. Second, one cannot assume that an employer's decision to pay workers more than it has to pay them to get them to sign on is either anticompetitive or inexplicably charitable. Paying employees, managers, and suppliers more than

variable-cost inputs other than labor. Predatory buying can be engaged in either by an individual incumbent or concertedly by two or more incumbents. The assets that are bought predatorily can be owned either by their individual purchasers or collectively (*e.g.*, in a patent pool under whose rules incumbents but no outsider can make use of the intellectual property in the pool[695]).

B. The Legality of Predatory Buying Under U.S. Antitrust Law and E.C./E.U. Competition Law, Correctly Interpreted and Applied

(1) U.S. Law

Predatory buying violates the Sherman Act. However, it is not covered by any provision of the Clayton Act. I might add that it does not seem to me to constitute a type of unfair method of competition that would violate Section 5 of the Federal Trade Commission Act.

(2) E.C./E.U. Law

Predatory buying in which the predator actually makes a purchase always violates what is now Article 101 of the 2009 Treaty of Lisbon since it always involves an agreement that prevents, restricts, and distorts competition. Predatory buying in which the predators simply bid up the price of the good or service in question without actually purchasing it is not covered by now-Article 101, strictly interpreted, if it is engaged in by an individual firm but would be prohibited by now-Article 101 if it was organized by a trade association or involved a concerted effort by two or more predators.

---

one needs to pay to secure "their services" may be inherently profitable if such "generosity" elicits superior performance or increases the demand for the payor's products by pleasing buyers that value patronizing firms that treat their employees generously. (Ben and Jerry's ice-cream company illustrates the latter possibility.) Third, as I will point out in Section 8, the Supreme Court has held in one case that a wage settlement that raised the costs of the perpetrator's rivals by more than it raised its own costs violated the Sherman Act. See United Mine Workers v. Pennington, 381 U.S. 567 (1965). I would say that some wage settlements can be predatory even if they do not raise the defendant's cost by more than they raise its rivals' costs.

[695] I want to add three points. First, the intellectual property in most patent pools continues to be owned by the individual members of the pool as opposed to by the pool itself. Second, the property in many if not most patent pools was not acquired predatorily. Third, although many patent pools either place restrictions on the licensing of the intellectual property they contain to outsiders or require outsiders to pay higher license fees to use the intellectual property in the pool than insiders must pay to use such property (in many cases, charge outsiders a positive fee to do so when insiders license each other to use their patents without paying any fee at all), the associated refusals-to-deal and price-discrimination provisions are often not predatory.

Both when it does result in a purchase agreement and when it does not, predatory buying will violate now-Article 102—as an exclusionary abuse—when the predator is or at least one of the predators are individually dominant or members of a collectively-dominant set of rivals.

C. The U.S. Case-Law, EC Pronouncements, and E.C./E.U. Case-Law

(1) The U.S. Case-Law

In 2007, the U.S. Supreme Court recognized that the legality of bidding and pricing practices under Section 2 of the Sherman Act should be analyzed in the same way.[696] In essence, this decision affirmed lower-court cases declaring illegal under the Sherman Act decisions by businesses to hire away one or more employees or managers of a rival when done with predatory intent.[697] And, in one case, a U.S. Court of Appeals recognized that the combination of (1) a decision to accumulate patent rights that the accumulator does not use and (2) decisions to refuse to license others to use them and to attack others for infringing the patents in question can constitute an attempt to monopolize.[698] However, the prevailing case-law is that the accumulation and subsequent non-use of patents does not violate the U.S. antitrust law.[699] In my view, a firm's purchase of a patent or exclusive right to use the patent can be predatory even if it does use the patent itself (*inter alia*, if the firm's *ex ante* perception was that the benefits it would obtain by using the patent would not render the purchase profitable), and the fact that a firm has not in the end used a patent it purchased (or obtained through its own research) does not imply that its purchase of the patent or the combination of its execution of the research that yielded a patentable discovery and its successful effort to patent that discovery was predatory (the purchase or research may simply have been *ex post* unprofitable).

(2) EC Pronouncements and E.C./E.U. Case-Law

I know of no EC position or E.C./E.U. case-law on predatory bidding or purchasing.

---

[696] See Weyerhaeuser Co. v. Ross-Simmons Hardwood Lumber Co., Inc., 539 U.S. 312 (2007).

[697] The first case in this line is Albert-Pick Barth Co. v. Mitchell Woodbury Corp., 57 F.2d 96 (1st Cir. 1932), *cert. denied*, 286 U.S. 552 (1932).

[698] See Kobe, Inc. v. Dempsey Pump Co., 198 F.2d 416, 423–24 (10th Cir.), *cert. denied* 344 U.S. 867 (1952).

[699] See, *e.g.*, Continental Paper Bag Co. v. Eastern Paper Bag Co., 210 U.S. 405 (1908).

6. Predatory Advertising

A. The Definition of Predatory Advertising and the Conditions Under Which Advertising Is Predatory

Advertising is predatory when the advertiser's *ex ante* perception of its profitability was critically affected by its belief that the advertising would or might increase its profits by causing a rival QV investment to be withdrawn, by deterring an established rival's expansion or a potential competitor's entry, by inducing the owner of a QV investment in the relevant area of product-space to relocate further away in product-space from the predator's QV investments, and/or by inducing a prospective QV investor to make a similar change in the location of its planned QV investment. For advertising to achieve one or more of these results, it must be directed at actual or potential buyers of the extant or planned target QV investment. For advertising to be predatory, the advertiser must believe *ex ante* not only (1) that it will or may generate one of these effects and (2) that it will or may increase its profits by doing so but also (3) that the advertisement would not otherwise be profitable and (4) that the profits it will yield by producing these effects renders it *ex ante* profitable, all things considered, though inherently unprofitable.

B. The Legality of Predatory Advertising Under U.S. Antitrust Law and E.C./E.U. Competition Law, Correctly Interpreted and Applied

(1) U.S. Law, Correctly Interpreted and Applied

Predatory advertising carried out by a single firm violates Section 2 of the Sherman Act, properly interpreted and applied. Predatory advertising that results from an agreement (by two or more firms to engage in such advertising or by one or more firms to engage in such advertising and one or more other firms to share the cost of the predatory advertising) violates Section 1 of the Sherman Act. Unsuccessful attempts to enter into predatory-advertising agreements do not violate Section 1 of the Sherman Act, whether such unsuccessful attempts violate Section 2 of the Sherman Act is open to question. Predatory advertising is not prohibited by any provision of the Clayton Act because no provision of that Act covers advertising.

(2) E.C./E.U. Law, Correctly Interpreted and Applied

Predatory advertising by an individually-dominant firm or by one or more members of a collectively-dominant set of rivals is prohibited as an exclusionary abuse by what is now Article 102 of the 2009 Treaty of Lisbon. Any agreement by two or more firms to engage in predatory advertising and any decision by a trade association to practice such advertising or to orchestrate its practice by one or more of its members violates what is now Article 101 of the 2009 Treaty of Lisbon. However, the unilateral decision of a firm that is neither individually dominant nor a member of a set of collectively-dominant rivals to engage in predatory advertising is not prohibited by E.C./E.U. competition law.

C. The U.S. Case-Law, EC Pronouncements, and E.C./E.U. Case-Law

I know of no U.S. case, no EC discussion paper, or no E.C./E.U. case that addresses the legality of predatory advertising. I should say, however, that in a few cases, the U.S. Supreme Court has manifested considerable hostility to what I assume to have been non-predatory advertising that was designed to yield the advertiser a buyer preference advantage in circumstances in which its product was assumed by the Court to be physically identical to its rivals' products and the product in question (in one relevant case, bleach) did not seem likely to play a role in the fantasy-life, self-image, or reputation (status) of its consumers.[700] Although I would not place much weight on these cases, they do favor the conclusion that U.S. courts would be open to considering the possibility that a defendant's advertising might be predatory (that they would not be deterred from doing so by a concern that, regardless of how this type of claim was resolved but certainly if false-positive findings of predatory advertising were made, predatory-advertising suits would chill advertising that benefitted consumers and increased economic efficiency).

[700] See Federal Trade Commission v. Proctor & Gamble Co. (Clorox), 386 U.S. 568 (1967). See also the following statement in United States v. International Telephone and Telegraph Corporation, 324 F. Supp. 19 (D. Conn. 1970), citing FTC v. Procter & Gamble Co., 386 U.S. 568 (1967), General Foods Corp. v. FTC, 386 F.2d 936 (3rd Cir. 1967), cert. denied, 391 U.S. 919 9 (1968), United States v. Ingersoll-Rand Co., 320 F.2d 509 (3rd Cir. 1963), Allis-Chalmers Mfg. Co. v. White Consolidated Industries, Inc. 414 F.2d 506 (3rd Cir. 1969), cert. denied, 396 U.S. 1009 (1970), and United States v. Wilson Sporting goods Co., 288 F. Supp. 543 (N.D. Ill. 1968): "The law is well settled that when a company which is the dominant competitor in a relatively oligopolistic market is acquired by a much larger company, such acquisition violates Section 7 of the Clayton Act if the acquired company gains marketing and promotional competitive advantages from the merger which will further entrench its position of dominance by raising barriers to entry to the relevant markets and by discouraging smaller competitors from aggressively competing. The effect of such a merger will be substantially to lessen competition."

I should add that the cases do not seem to distinguish between situations in which the relevant marketing and promotional advantages reflect real (*i.e.*, economic or socially-valuable) economies and situations in which they do not (in which they reflect, for example, nothing more than the fact that the merged firm has greater bargaining power than its antecedent[s]). Although the U.S. courts' attitudes toward many business practices have changed since 1970, I do not think that their attitudes toward advertising have altered during the period in question.

7. Predatory "Unfair Competition" and Predatory Unfair or Improper Participation in Government Decision-Processes

A. Predatory "Unfair Competition"

(1) The Antitrust Definition of "Unfair Competition" and the Conditions Under Which Such Unfair Competition Is Predatory

A seller engages in "unfair competition" in the sense in which that concept is defined in antitrust law when it commits one or more acts in the following non-exhaustive list that are designed to yield it a competitive advantage over a rival that has no allocative-efficiency counterpart (that make it privately-better-placed than the rival [if the private placement of sellers is based on the relevant buyer's perceptions of the relative attractiveness of the relevant seller's products] without making it allocatively-better-placed than the rival):

(1) knowingly, recklessly, or negligently misrepresenting the quality of its own product (an act that may violate an administrative regulation of the sort that the U.S. Food and Drug Administration promulgates);
(2) claiming that its product is actually the product of its rival (palming-off or passing-off);
(3) knowingly, recklessly, or negligently making false statements about a rival's product (which may constitute the common-law tort of unfair competition or commercial disparagement);
(4) knowingly, recklessly, or negligently influencing a trade association to give a target-rival's product an undeservedly-low rating or to withhold a seal of approval by inducing the trade association to use criteria that unjustifiably disadvantage the rival or by causing the trade association to misfind relevant facts;
(5) deterring a potential supplier of a target from selling to it or entering into a long-term supply contract with it by knowingly, recklessly, or negligently claiming falsely that the target was a poor credit risk (was on the verge of bankruptcy or was likely to be caught up in damaging commercial or patent litigation—which might also constitute the tort of commercial falsehood);
(6) bribing a rival's supplier or employee to perform less well than the supplier or employee otherwise would or a rival's supplier not to perform at all (which constitutes the tort of interference with a contract);
(7) intimidating or harassing a rival's customers or employees;
(8) illegitimately obstructing access to a rival's business (which may be an actionable violation of its property rights);
(9) bribing the agent of a buyer not to patronize the target rival or to purchase from the unfair competitor; and
(10) deterring a potential customer of a target from patronizing the target or entering into a long-term purchase-contract with the target by knowingly,

recklessly, or negligently claiming falsely that the target's production would violate the actor's or someone else's patent (which might constitute the tort of commercial falsehood).

Although I am certain that some conduct in which firms can engage that will give them a private advantage that has no allocative counterpart (*e.g.*, bargaining effectively to secure a discount that rivals are unable to obtain that does not reflect the lower cost of supplying the bargainer or any other economic-efficiency-based private benefit the bargainer's patronage affords the relevant supplier) will not be deemed to constitute "unfair competition" in the antitrust sense of this expression, I suspect that the preceding list is not comprehensive.

As I indicated in parentheticals attached to some items in the preceding list, many of the types of conduct that constitute "unfair competition" in the antitrust sense of that concept also violate administrative regulations, tort law, or property law. However, for current purposes, the relevant point is that if, *ex ante*, the actor that engaged in such conduct believed (1) that it would not be profitable but for its tendency to increase its profits by driving a target out, deterring a prospective QV investor from making a QV investment in the perpetrator's relevant area of product-space, inducing an established rival to move to a product-space location that was less competitive with the unfair competitor's products, and/or induce a prospective investor in the ARDEPPS in question to make such a change in the location of its planned QV investment in the relevant area of product-space, (2) that it would increase the actor's profits in one or more of these ways, and (3) that the associated profit-yield rendered the relevant conduct *ex ante* profitable, the conduct in question would be predatory. (I should add that all such conduct also constitutes an unfair method of competition under the U.S. Federal Trade Commission Act, distorts competition in the now-Article 101 sense of that phrase, and constitutes an exclusionary abuse of a dominant position under now-Article 102 when perpetrated by a firm that is individually dominant or belongs to a set of collectively-dominant rivals.)

(2) The Legality of Predatory and Non-Predatory Unfair Competition Under U.S. Antitrust Law and E.C./E.U. Competition Law, Properly Interpreted and Applied

(A) U.S. Antitrust Law

I will focus on the Sherman Act, Clayton Act, and Federal Trade Commission Act in that order. An individual firm's practice of predatory unfair competition always violates Section 2 of the Sherman Act, and any agreement by two or more firms to practice predatory unfair competition violates Section 1 of the Sherman Act (though an unsuccessful attempt to form an agreement of this kind does not violate Section 1 or [I believe] derivatively Section 2 of the Sherman Act). Unfair competition will clearly be predatory when its perpetrator-perceived *ex ante* profitability depended on its driving an extant QV investment out, deterring a new QV investment, inducing an establish rival to change its location, or inducing a potential QV investor to change the location of a planned QV investment. Moreover, although unfair competition cannot be correctly characterized as predatory when its practitioner did not believe *ex* ante that it would or might induce any such change in an actual or potential competitor's QV-investment decision, it may still violate the specific-anticompetitive-intent test of illegality I claim the Sherman Act promulgates if its perpetrator-perceived *ex ante* profitability was critically inflated by the perpetrator's belief that it would increase its profits by reducing the relevant-buyer-perceived absolute attractiveness of the offers rivals make without changing the QV investments they own. Thus, knowing or negligent false communications to a rival's potential suppliers about its credit-worthiness, trustworthiness, or vulnerability to patent-infringement suits that make them less inclined to deal with the target will violate the Sherman Act even if they are not predatory if the perpetrator's (perpetrators') *ex ante* perception that such conduct was profitable was critically affected by its belief that the conduct would or might reduce the absolute attractiveness of the offers the target will make by worsening the deals the target can make with suppliers. Similarly, perpetrator efforts to make it more difficult for suppliers and employees to gain access to a target's place of business, to harass them in other ways, to bribe them to perform less well than they otherwise would, or to tell lies about the target that will deter potential suppliers from contracting with it or potential employees from working for it will violate the Sherman Act even if they are not predatory if the perpetrator's *ex ante* perception that such conduct was profitable was critically affected by its belief that the conduct would or might reduce the absolute buyer-perceived attractiveness of the offers the target will make by worsening the deals the target can make with its suppliers and employees. And again, perpetrator efforts to make it more difficult for potential customers of the target to gain access to the target's place of business will violate the Sherman Act even if they are not predatory if the perpetrator's *ex ante* perception that such conduct was profitable was critically affected by its belief that the conduct would make the target's offers (which, in this context, include shopping convenience) less objectively attractive. Moreover, if my original statement of the Sherman Act test of illegality can properly be revised to refer to "reducing the buyer-perceived absolute attractiveness of the perpetrator's rivals' offers or the buyer-perceived relative attractiveness of the perpetrator's rivals' offers given the objective absolute attractiveness of the perpetrator's own offers," unfair competition that is not predatory will also violate the Sherman Act if its perpetrator-perceived *ex ante* profitability was critically affected by the perpetrator's belief (1) that it would or might reduce the buyer-perceived absolute attractiveness of the target's offers by knowingly or negligently falsely disparaging the target's products, causing the target to be given an unjustifiably-low evaluation by a trade association or independent rating service, or calling into question the target's survival prospects and/or (2) that it would or might reduce the buyer-perceived relative attractiveness of the target's offers by knowingly, recklessly, or negligently exaggerating the quality of the perpetrator's own product or by passing them off as the target-rival's product.

The Clayton Act does not prohibit unfair competition in the antitrust sense of that concept, regardless of whether the conduct in question is predatory because no provision of the Clayton Act covers any of the types of conduct that can properly be said to constitute unfair competition.

However, the Federal Trade Commission Act does prohibit all types of unfair competition. In particular, Section 5 of that Act declares: "Unfair methods of competition in or affecting commerce...are hereby declared unlawful." It is important to note, however, that private plaintiffs cannot recover damages under the Federal Trade Commission Act and that the FTC is not authorized to impose prison terms or fines in its initial intervention. All the FTC can do on its own is issue an injunction (called a "cease-and-desist order"). I should add that the FTC does have the authority to bring an action in court to levy fines for violation of an existing cease-and-desist order or for a "knowing violation" of the Federal Trade Commission Act—in practice, for the commission of an act previously found illegal by the Commission.

(B) E.C./E.U. Competition Law

Properly interpreted and applied, what is now Article 102 of the 2009 Treaty of Lisbon prohibits all acts of unfair competition committed by a firm that is individually dominant or a member of a collectively-dominant set of firms. Indeed, because now-Article 102 prohibits exploitative as well as exclusionary abuses, its coverage of such conduct (unlike the Sherman Act's) is clearly comprehensive (though, properly interpreted and applied, the Sherman Act's coverage is not limited to behavior by dominant firms).

Because, by definition, both predatory and non-predatory unfair competition always prevents, restricts, and distorts competition, now-Article 101 also prohibits firms from agreeing to engage in unfair competition or a trade association from itself engaging in such conduct or orchestrating its members' doing so. However, now-Article 101 does not cover single-firm unfair competition.

(3) The U.S. Antitrust-Law Case-Law, EC Position, and E.C./E.U. Competition-Law Case-Law on Unfair Competition

(A) The U.S. Case-Law

To my knowledge, only three lines of U.S. cases have focused on the kinds of predatory unfair competition with which this section is concerned. The most famous case in this category is *Union Leader Corp. v. Newspapers of New England.*[701] *Union Leader* analyzed the Sherman Act legality of a competitor's using unfair methods in a fight to the death with a rival in a situation in which only

[701] 180 F. Supp. 125 (D. Mass. 1959), *aff'd* in part and *rev'd* in part, 284 F.2d 582 (1st Cir. 1960), *cert. denied*, 365 U.S. 833 (1961).

one of the contestants could survive financially. In *Union Leader*, the District Court judge (Wyzanski) held that, in such a situation, any attempt by a contestant to win by engaging in an "unfair practice not honestly industrial"[702]—a practice that would give it an advantage not based on its merits—was predatory and therefore prohibited by the Sherman Act. In Wyzanski's words, "[i]n a situation in which it is inevitable that only one competitor can survive, the evidence which shows the use, or contemplated use, of unfair means is the very same evidence which shows the existence of an exclusionary intent."[703] Wyzanski's opinion in *Union Leader* found two of the tactics that the defendant had employed to be unfair: (1) paying secret "consulting fees" to merchants to "talk up" the defendant's newspaper relative to its opponents' (a finding that is persuasive) and (2) making secret offers to publish some advertisements at preferential rates below those appearing on published rate-cards (a legal finding that is dubious at best). But the accuracy of Wyzanski's conclusions about whether the defendant in *Union Leader* had waged unfair competition is not the point: for current purposes, the important point is that Wyzanski recognized that unfair competition can be predatory and therefore violative of the Sherman Act in fight-to-the-death situations and that (although Wyzanski did not address this issue) there is no economic or legal reason to limit that holding to such situations.

The second line of relevant "unfair competition" cases condemned under the Sherman Act business decisions (already discussed under the heading "predatory buying") to hire one or more employees or managers away from a rival when done with what I would deem predatory intent.[704] Although the relevant courts did not use the expression "unfair competition" to describe the relevant conduct, they clearly had this notion in mind.

The third line of relevant "unfair competition" cases deals with trade association seals of approval. In the first such case of which I am aware, the Supreme Court held in 1961 that it would be *per se* illegal for a trade association to arbitrarily deny a seal of approval to a product (in the instant case, a gas heater) when doing so would cause the product to exit (in the instant case, because the trade association's denial of the seal of approval resulted in member gas utilities' refusing to supply gas to facilities that used the heater denied approval).[705] In 1988, the U.S. Supreme Court stated that a refusal to certify a product would also violate the Sherman Act under a Rule-of-Reason analysis when the standard-setting organization had been captured by a group intent on keeping a superior product off the market in circumstances in

---

[702] *Id.* at 585.

[703] *Id.* at 140.

[704] See Albert-Pick Barth Co. v. Mitchell Woodbury Corp., 57 F.2d 96 (1st Cir. 1932), *cert. denied* 286 U.S. 552, (1932).

[705] Radiant Burners, Inc. v. Peoples Gas Light & Coke Co., 364 U.S. 565 (1961). As lower courts recognized, this ruling did not imply the illegality of denying a certificate of approval non-arbitrarily without any intent to force the denied product out. See Eliason Corp. v National Sanitation Foundation, 614 F.2d 126 (6th Cir. 1980), *cert. denied* 449 U.S. 826 (1980).

which the non-certification would lead government regulators to prohibit the installation of the product in question.[706]

(B) The EC Position and E.C./E.U. Case-Law

I do not believe that the EC or any E.C./E.U. court has ever taken a position on the legality of predatory or non-predatory unfair competition under E.C./E.U. competition law.

B. Predatory Participation in Legislative, Administrative, and Adjudicative Decisionmaking

(1) The Definition of Predatory Participation in Legislative, Administrative, or Adjudicative Decisionmaking

A firm's participation in legislative, administrative, or adjudicative decisionmaking is predatory if, *ex ante* the firm would not have found that participation profitable or desirable (even if not conventionally profitable) had it not believed that the participation would or might induce a target rival to remove and not replace an extant QV investment, deter an established or potential competitor from making a new QV investment in the relevant area of product-space, induce an established rival to substitute for its original QV investment a QV investment that is less competitive with the perpetrator's QV investments, and/or induce a prospective QV investor to locate its planned QV investment further away in product-space from the perpetrator's QV investments. I hasten to add that, although some predatory participation in government-decisionmaking processes may raise the target's costs by more than they raise the predator's costs or, more generally, may worsen the target's competitive-position array relative to the predator's,[707] participation in government-decisionmaking processes can be predatory even if it does not have such an effect—can, for example, critically increase the predator's long-run profits

[706] Allied Tube & Conduit Corp. v. Indian Head, Inc. 486 U.S. 492 (1988).

[707] For example, (1) a tariff will increase the target's cost more than it increases the perpetrator's if the perpetrator does not use the input on which the tariff is levied or produces it itself or has entered into a long-term supply contract with an independent supplier and cannot take advantage of the tariff by reselling its inputs without incurring significant costs; (2) a zoning ordinance will increase a potential-entrant's or potential-expander's costs by more than it increases the perpetrator's costs if the perpetrator's production-facility is grandfathered in or is located outside the area to which the zoning regulation applies while the target has good reason to locate in the area in question; and (3) an environmental regulation will increase a target's costs by more than it increases the perpetrator's if the target but not the perpetrator generates the pollutant to whose generation the environmental regulation applies or the environmental regulation makes location relevant and the locations of the target and perpetrator differ in relevant ways.

by driving a rival out or deterring a rival QV investment even if it has the same impact on the predator's and the target's short-run profits if the rival's position is more fragile than the predator's and the gain the behavior in question yields the predator on this account critically affects the predator's *ex ante* perception of the relevant conduct's profitability. Thus, a firm may find it profitable to secure one or more of these outcomes by supporting legislation that, *inter alia,* would ban imports, raise tariffs, limit the number of sellers that can operate in the relevant area of product-space, impose operating fees (*e.g.*, fees for taxi medallions), or create standards of eligibility that one or more target established firms or potential entrants cannot meet (when they will not be replaced by other firms that would be equally competitive with the perpetrator). Indeed, firms may find it possible to secure some of these results by supporting such legislation even if they do not succeed in securing the legislation's passage: their efforts may nevertheless drive rivals out or deter new entries or established-rival expansions by making it necessary for a target actual or potential competitor to incur prohibitively-costly expenses to prevent the passage of legislation that would otherwise require it to exit or prevent it from expanding or entering.

A firm's participation in administrative-agency-decisionmaking processes may also be predatory, regardless of whether the process in question is legislative or adjudicative in character (involves rule-making or case-resolution). To the extent that "rule-making" is a legislative activity, the argument of the preceding paragraph is fully applicable. Firm participation in administrative case-processing can also be predatory. Thus, a firm may behave predatorily when it opposes an actual or potential rival's being licensed to be a commercial trucker or aviator or to operate along a particular route, a rival's being authorized to operate a radio or TV station in a particular location, a rival's product being declared safe and useful, a rival's being given a small business loan, a rival's being allowed to open up a mining operation or construct and operate a particular type of plant in a specified location, a rival's being allowed to use a particular production process that generates specifiable amounts of particular pollutants in a give location, *etc*.

Finally, a firm's participation in the adjudicative process can also be predatory. More specifically, if, *ex ante*, a firm would not have found it profitable or desirable overall (1) to bring a particular suit against an actual or potential rival, (2) to devote as much time and money to that suit as it did, or (3) to induce someone else to sue the perpetrator's rival by providing the other party with relevant information or financial support, by volunteering to testify in someone else's suit against a rival, or by devoting more time and money to preparing such testimony than it would have found profitable to do had it not believed that its doing so would or might (1) induce the defendant (and/or others) to withdraw a QV investment that was competitive with the perpetrator's QV investment, (2) deter the defendant and/or others from making a new QV investment that would have been competitive with the perpetrator's QV investments, and/or (3) induce the defendant and/or others to alter their product-space locations to make them less competitive with the perpetrator's QV investments, the conduct in question will be predatory.

Before proceeding to analyze the legality of predatory participation in government-decisionmaking processes, I need to emphasize one feature of the preceding account of such conduct. On my account, which proceeds straightforwardly from the general definition of predatory conduct, the predatory character of a firm's participation in any legislative, administrative, or adjudicative process does not depend on whether the firm knowingly, recklessly, or negligently made misstatements of fact, misrepresented its own motives or financial interest in the government decision in question, made secret payments to people to provide formal and/or written testimony or to make public comments on the relevant issues outside official processes, bribed government staff members or decisionmakers, or promised to reward them for cooperating by providing them with attractive post-government-service employment. A firm's participation in a government-decisionmaking process can be predatory even if it in one sense "plays fair."

(2) The Legality of Predatory Participation in Legislative, Administrative, and Adjudicative Processes Under U.S. Antitrust Law and E.C./E.U. Competition Law, Properly Interpreted and Applied

In my judgment, so long as a firm "plays fair"—*inter alia*, does not knowingly, grossly negligently (recklessly), or perhaps negligently make untrue statements in government processes or in public outside those processes, does not misrepresent its financial interest in the outcome of a government-decisionmaking process, does not induce others to make false statements in official or non-official public fora and/or to participate in the discussion of the merits of a government decision inside or outside official fora without revealing or while misrepresenting their relationship to the firm or someone connected to the firm or their own stake in the proceedings in question, does not bribe government staff or decisionmakers, does not offer to reward such individuals' cooperation with post-government-service employment, and does not knowingly, recklessly, or negligently make unjustified legal claims in court or knowingly, recklessly, or negligently induce others to make such legal claims, its predatory motivation does not render its participation in legislative, administrative, or adjudicative decisionmaking processes illegal under either U.S. antitrust law or E.C./E.U. competition law. To the extent that the texts of the relevant statutes and treaty, their legislative histories, and the other sorts of things that influence their correct interpretation and application favor a different conclusion, those considerations must be overridden to vindicate the moral and constitutional right of the firms (*i.e.*, their owners and other interested affiliates) to participate fairly in these government-decisionmaking processes and the moral and constitutional right of others to be informed and to have the government's decisions be informed by the firm's fair participation.

With the important, qualified exception just stated, the analysis of the legality of this variant of predatory conduct under U.S. antitrust law and E.C./E.U. competition law, properly interpreted and applied, is the same as the analysis of all other types of predatory conduct under these bodies of law. With the identical, important, qualified exception, the analysis of the antitrust legality of participation in government-decisionmaking processes that is not predatory but was committed with specific anticompetitive intent (that the firm would not have found profitable or desirable *ex ante* had it not believed that it would or might reduce the absolute attractiveness of the offers against which it would have to compete by causing rivals whose QV-investment choices it did not affect to make objectively-less-attractive offers to its actual or potential customers) is also the same as the analysis of the antitrust legality all other types of non-predatory conduct committed with specific anticompetitive intent.

(3) The U.S. Case-Law, EC Position, and E.C./E.U. Case-Law on Participation in Government-Decisionmaking Process That Is Either Predatory or Engaged in with a Non-Predatory Specific Anticompetitive Intent

(A) The U.S. Case-Law

Three major U.S. decisions analyze the antitrust legality of the kind of participation in government-decisionmaking processes with which this section is concerned and the related so-called petitioning immunity from antitrust liability—*Eastern Railroad Presidents Conference v. Noerr Motor Freight* (hereinafter *Noerr*),[708] *California Motor Transport Co. v. Trucking Unlimited* (hereinafter *California Motor Transport*),[709] and *Professional Real Estate Investors v. Columbia Pictures Industries* (hereinafter *PRE-Columbia*).[710]

The allegedly-illegal conduct in *Noerr* was the organization and execution of a publicity campaign by a public-relations firm at the behest of an association of presidents of eastern railroads that was designed "to foster the adoption and retention of laws and law-enforcement practices destructive of the trucking business, to create an atmosphere of distaste for the truckers among the general public, and to impair the relationship between the truckers and their customers."[711] The publicity campaign used the so-called third-party technique, in which "propaganda actually circulated by a party in interest...[was given] the appearance of being spontaneous declarations of independent groups."[712] According to the Supreme Court, the relevant propaganda involved "deception of the public, manufacture of bogus sources of reference, [and] distortion of public sources of information."[713] Nevertheless, the Supreme Court concluded that the defendants' conduct did not violate the Sherman Act, holding that actions that involve "attempts to influence the

708 306 U.S. 127 (1961).

709 404 U.S. 508 (1972).

710 508 U.S. 49 (1993).

711 365 U.S. 127 at 129.

712 *Id.* at 140.

713 *Id.* at 140, citing the District Court opinion in Noerr Motor Freight, Inc. v. Eastern Railroad Presidents Conference, 155 F. Supp. 768 (1957).

passage or enforcement of law"[714] cannot violate the antitrust laws even if they "fall short of the ethical standards generally approved in this country"[715] unless the claim that they are "directed toward influencing governmental action" is a "mere sham."[716]

California Motor Transport—which involved an alleged conspiracy of the defendants to institute federal and state proceedings to resist and defeat applications by respondents to acquire operating rights or to transfer or register those rights—not only confirmed *Noerr* but extended its basic holding to representations made to administrative agencies and courts, citing a previous Supreme Court case and a Court of Appeals case that were on point.[717] In fact, the Court's opinion in *California Motor Transport* seems to me to have broadened *Noerr* in a second way as well by taking positions that imply that virtually no representation to a court will ever fall within *Noerr's* "sham" exception. Thus, according to the *California Motor Transport* Court, the conduct of the alleged conspirators in that case would be considered to be a sham only if they "sought to bar their competitors from meaningful access to adjudicatory tribunals and so to usurp that decision-making process"[718] or, again, only if they sought "to harass and deter their competitors from having 'free and unlimited access' to the agencies and courts."[719] It is hard to imagine conduct less culpable than kidnapping a target and/or its lawyers that would literally "bar" the target from "meaningful access" to the relevant adjudicatory tribunal or deny the target "free and unlimited access" to such a tribunal. Certainly, if this language is to be interpreted literally, it is difficult to reconcile it with the actual decision of the *California Motor Transport* Court, which remanded the case for consideration of the "sham-ness" issue.

The relevant portion of *PRE-Columbia* represents an attempt to eliminate the resulting confusion. Unfortunately, the Court's *PRE-Columbia* opinion leaves the criteria for "sham-ness" in adjudicatory contexts critically unclear. In *PRE-Columbia*, the behavior alleged to be a sham was an unsuccessful copyright-infringement suit in which the accused motion-picture studios attempted to prevent PRE from renting to hotel guests in their rooms videodiscs of films on which the studios held copyrights. The suit (whose initiation was allegedly predatory) was unsuccessful because the District Court and Court of Appeals concluded that the showing of a videodisc in a hotel room does not constitute a public performance and therefore does not violate the copyright holder's "exclusive right 'to perform the copyrighted work[s] publicly.'"[720] In holding that Columbia's suit did not violate the Sherman

---

[714] *Id.* at 135.

[715] *Id.* at 140.

[716] *Id.* at 144.

[717] 404 U.S. 508 (1972). The Supreme Court held that a firm's "conspiracy with a licensing authority to eliminate a competitor may...result in an antitrust transgression," citing Continental Ore Co. v. Union Carbide & Carbon Corp., 370 U.S. 690 at 707 (1962).

[718] *Id.* at 512.

[719] *Id.* at 515.

[720] 508 U.S. 49 at 53.

Act, the Supreme Court rejected PRE's argument that in an adjudicatory context *Noerr's* sham exception should be made to turn on "subjective intent alone"[721]—rejected, for example, the contention that suits brought by plaintiffs that manifested an "indifference to outcome" or suits that would not "have been brought but for [a] predatory motive" should be considered to be a sham.[722] Instead, the Court adopted an "objective" test of "sham-ness," holding that "an objectively reasonable effort to litigate cannot be sham regardless of subjective intent"[723] and that to be a sham a lawsuit (1) "must be objectively baseless in the sense that no reasonable litigant could realistically expect success on the merits"[724] and (2) "must conceal 'an attempt to interfere directly with the business relationships of a competitor'" (citing *Noerr*) "through the 'use [of] the governmental process as opposed to the outcome of that process as an anticompetitive weapon'"[725] (citing *City of Columbia v. Omni Outdoor Advertising*[726]). Although, as I will explain, the *PRE-Columbia* Court proceeded to confuse the issue by stating later in the opinion that "sham litigations must constitute the pursuit of claims so baseless that no reasonable litigant could realistically expect to secure favorable relief"[727] and by suggesting that to have such a realistic expectation the plaintiff must have only "some chance of winning,"[728] it exonerated Columbia on the ground that (as the District Court and Court of Appeals had found) it had "probable cause to sue PRE for copyright infringement."[729]

The Supreme Court's *PRE-Columbia* opinion contains inconsistent statements on each of two sham-exception-related issues. First, in one place, the *PRE-Columbia* opinion states that initiating a lawsuit cannot be held to be a Sherman Act violation if the objective probability that the plaintiff should win "on the merits" was sufficiently high while in another place it states that initiating a lawsuit cannot violate the Sherman Act if the objective probability of the plaintiff's "winning" or "secur[ing] favorable relief" was sufficiently high. In practice, the probability of a plaintiff's "winning" or "securing favorable belief" is affected not only (A) by the probability that it should, as a matter of law, prevail on the substantive merits but also (B) by the probability that the plaintiff will be able to win on procedural grounds, (C) (perhaps relatedly) by the probability that the plaintiff will be able to spend more money on the lawsuit than the defendant or be more adept than the defendant at choosing and supervising its lawyers, (D) by the probable effects on its chances of any lack of competence on the part of the judge who will hear the case, (E) by the probable effect on its chances of any tendency of the relevant judge to be influenced by extra-legal considerations such as his or her own policy-preferences,

[721] *Id.* at 58.
[722] *Id.* at 56.
[723] *Id.* at 57.
[724] *Id.* at 59.
[725] *Id.* at 67.
[726] 499 U.S. 365 at 380 (1991).
[727] 508 U.S. 49 at 61.
[728] *Id.* at 62.
[729] *Id.*

desire for judicial promotion, desire to obtain some other type of political post, desire to obtain a position in the private sector, desire to help a political candidate (such as an incumbent that appointed the judge), and/or desire to secure bribes—regardless of whether the alleged predator did anything other than bring the suit to take advantage of these tendencies, and/or (F) by the probable effect on its chances of any tendency of a relevant jury to misfind the facts—regardless of whether the alleged predator did anything reprehensible in this connection such as bribing or threatening a juror, knowingly, recklessly, or negligently giving false testimony, or inducing someone else to commit perjury. This list certainly suggests that in most cases the probabilities on which the Court's two formulations of its "sham-ness" test focus—"the probability of winning on the merits" and "the probability of winning"—will be significantly different.[730]

The second inconsistency in the *PRE-Columbia* Court's various formulations of its test for "sham-ness" relates to the objective probability of the plaintiff's "winning" or "winning on the merits" that the Court says will remove a suit from the "sham" category. In one place in its *PRE-Columbia* opinion, the Court indicates that a suit cannot be sham if the plaintiff could "realistically expect" to win while in another place in this opinion the Court states that the plaintiff's suit will not be sham if it has "some chance of winning." Since in ordinary language the words "realistically expect" to win seem to me to require more than "have some chance of winning," I am uncertain about the probability of winning that the Court thinks prevents a plaintiff's suit from being sham.

Although my conclusions about the antitrust legality of predatory and non-predatory anticompetitive-intent-motivated participation in government-decisionmaking processes resembles the U.S. Supreme Court's in that, like the Court's, my approach provides firms with a petitioning immunity, I think the legally-correct approach to such conduct is less protective of defendants than the Supreme Court's in two respects: (1) in adjudicatory contexts, the legally-correct approach would define sham-ness in terms of the conclusion the defendant should have reached about the objective merits of its suit or claim as opposed to the conclusion it should have reached about the probability that it would win and (2) in all sorts of cases of this kind, the legally-correct approach would not grant a defendant petitioning immunity if it did not "play fair." In this respect, my

[730] I should note that there is also a substantial difference between the "probability of a plaintiff's winning on the merits" and the "strength of its case on the merits." Because competent, assiduous decision-makers can disagree in good faith on the facts and/or the law and because such disagreements may be more important in some cases than in others, a plaintiff in one suit that might be estimated (on the average by a randomly-selected panel of experts) to have the better case by a 90–10 margin (if 100 points are assigned to the two sides) may be uncertain of victory while a plaintiff in another suit that might be estimated by the members of such a panel to have the better case by a 51–49 margin might be absolutely certain of victory on the merits in the above sense. In other words, even in a world in which judicial decisions are made on the merits, there may be a substantial difference between "the strength of a plaintiff's case" and "the probability of its being successful on the merits." I should also note that the preceding discussion assumes that there are internally-right answers to the relevant legal questions—an assumption that I support but a high percentage of contemporary American legal academics believe is often not correct.

conclusions about the legally-correct approach to these cases parallel the approach the *Union Leader* court deemed legally correct to take to the efforts of firms to win "fights to the death" when only one contestant can survive economically even if all behave perfectly properly.[731]

I should add that, with one admittedly-significant exception, the fair-play variant of the "petitioning immunity" doctrine that I think is correct as a matter of law is consistent with surrounding law—in particular, with current common-law torts doctrines, common-law and statutory whistleblower-protection rules, and federal procedural rules. The exception is the common-law tort doctrine that gives participants in a wide variety of judicial proceedings and in legislative proceedings (in some jurisdictions including proceedings in such subordinate bodies as municipal councils)—*i.e.*, witnesses, parties, counsel, and judges—"absolute immunity" from defamation claims based on any defamation they published at any stage of such a proceeding or process, even if *ex ante* they knew their statement to be false and were motivated by ill-will toward the plaintiff so long as their statement is "relevant" or "pertinent" to some issue before the court or legislative body in question.[732] Indeed, "most [U.S.] courts have adopted what appears to be a standard of good faith [on the issue of relevance], requiring only that the statement have some reasonable relation or reference to the subject of inquiry, or be one that 'may possibly be pertinent,' with all doubts resolved in favor of the defendant...."[733] I admit that this "absolute immunity defense" is inconsistent with the "fair play" variant of the "petitioning immunity" doctrine I find legally correct.

I will now discuss the various bodies of surrounding law that are consistent with the "fair play" requirement that I think is legally correct. Thus, the various "misuse of legal procedure" tort doctrines all favor a "fair play" requirement. In particluar, the common law of torts contains a tort of "malicious prosecution," which lies against anyone that institutes a proceeding of a criminal character,[734] "assists another person to begin such a proceeding, ratifies it when it is begun on defendant's behalf, or takes any active part in directing or aiding the conduct of the case"[735] if (1) "the criminal proceeding was initiated or contrived by the defendant without 'probable cause'" with "malice in fact"—*i.e.*, "for the purpose of obtaining any private advantage"[736] (not necessarily just to indulge his hatred of the defendant or out of spite[737]).[738]

[731] See Union Leader Corp. v. Newspapers of New England, 180 F. Supp. 125 (D. Mass. 1959).

[732] See PROSSER AND KEETON ON THE LAW OF TORTS 816–21 (West Pub. Co., 5th ed., 1984).

[733] *Id.* at 818.

[734] *Id.* at 870.

[735] *Id.* at 872.

[736] *Id.* at 876.

[737] *Id.* at 883.

[738] Defendants in "malicious prosecution" suits can escape liability by proving that the "plaintiff was in fact guilty of the offense with which the plaintiff was charged," regardless of whether the defendant was found "not guilty" in the case that gave rise to the tort action. *Id.* at 885.

In addition, in the United States, the traditional "malicious prosecution" tort has led to the development of a tort that covers the wrongful initiation of civil suits. "Most American courts now impose liability for malicious civil claims brought without probable cause," though "a very large minority" hold that a victim can recover only if he "can show a 'special grievance,' such as interference with its person or property...."[739]

American courts also recognize a tort of "abuse of process," which is committed by someone that misuses or misapplies "a process justified in itself for an end other than that which it was designed to accomplish."[740] Admittedly, for this tort to lie, the defendant, in addition to initiating the process, must have committed "some definite act or threat not authorized by the process" such as attempting to induce the surrender of property or the payment of money (to which the defendant may have been entitled) "by the use of the process as threat or a club."[741] Still, it seems to me that this "abuse of process" tort supports the "fair play" requirement that I think is legally correct to build into any "petitioning immunity" doctrine.

The predation standard I am proposing is also consistent with various U.S. whistleblower-protection laws—*i.e.*, with the various U.S. common-law "public policy exceptions" to an employer's normal common-law power to fire employers at will,[742] with the various anti-retaliation provisions that have been attached to

[739] *Id.* at 889.

[740] *Id.* at 897.

[741] *Id.* at 898

[742] See, *e.g.*, Palmateer v. International Harvester Co., 421 N.E.2d 353 (Ill. 1978) (holding actionable the discharge of an employee who provided information to police investigating the alleged criminal violations of a co-worker); Palmer v. Brown, 424 Kan. 893, 752 P.2d 685 (1988) (holding actionable the discharge of an employee for failing to promise not to report a superior's fraudulent Medicaid billing practices); Harless v. First Nat'l Bank, 162 W.Va. 116, 246 S.E.2d 270 (1978) (holding actionable the discharge of an employee for attempting to report illegal bank overcharges to banking authorities); Sheets v. Teddy's Frosted Foods, Inc., 179 Conn. 471, 427 A.2d 385 (1980) (holding actionable the discharge of an employee for insisting that the employer comply with state drug-labeling requirements); and Adler v. American Standard Corp., 538 F. Supp. 572 (D. Md. 1982) (holding actionable the discharge of an employee for threatening to expose the employer's antitrust violations). *Cf.* Peterman v. Teamsters Local 396, 174 Cal. App. 2d 184, 344 P.2d 25 (1959) (prohibiting the discharge of an employee who declined to commit perjury before a legislative committee); Trombetta v. Detroit, Toledo & Ironotn Railroad Co., 81 Mich. App. 489, 265 N.W.2d 385 (1978) (protecting an employee who refused to alter state-mandated pollution-control reports); and Sabine Pilot Service v. Hauck, 687 S.W.2d 733 (Tex. 1985) (holding that public policy prohibits employers from firing employees who refuse to commit illegal acts). Most but not all states have some form of public-policy exception, which often includes some whistleblower protections, but the doctrines are often quite narrow and the employee's burden is heavy. *See* STUART H. BOMPEY, MAX G. BRITTAIN, JR. & PAUL I. WEINER, WRONGFUL TERMINATION CLAIMS: A PREVENTIVE APPROACH (hereinafter BOMPEY *et al.*) 51–52 (Practicing Law Institute, 2d ed., 1991). For a review of the case-law, *see id.* at 46–53.

federal regulations of the terms and conditions of employment,[743] with the various non-retaliation provisions that have been attached to federal and state regulations of non-employment-related employer conduct (such as pollution),[744] and with the

[743] Among the many federal anti-retaliation provisions are the following: National Labor Relations Act of 1935, 29 U.S.C. §158(a)(4) (1994) (prohibiting employer discrimination against employees who file charges under the NLRA or testify in NLRA proceedings); Age Discrimination in Employment Act of 1967, 29 U.S.C. §623 (1994) (forbidding employer discrimination against employees who oppose or report age discrimination); Fair Labor Standards Act, 29 U.S.C. §§201, 215(a)(3) (1994) (prohibiting retaliation against employees who file a complaint or participate in proceedings); Occupational Safety and Health Act of 1970, 29 U.S.C. § 660(c) (1994) (prohibiting employer retaliation against employees who report employer violations of safety standards); Employee Retirement Income Security Act of 1974, 29 U.S.C. §§1140, 1141 (1994) (prohibiting discrimination against employees who claim benefits under the Act or participate in an investigation against their employer); Federal Mine Safety and Health Act of 1977, 30 U.S.C. §815(c) (1994) (prohibiting the discharge of employees who participate in proceedings against their employer for health-and-safety violations); Migrant and Seasonal Agricultural Worker Protection Act of 1983, 29 U.S.C. §1855 (1994) (prohibiting discrimination by an employer against migrant workers who file complaints or participate in an investigation under the statute); Employee Polygraph Protection Act of 1988, 29 U.S.C. § 2002 (1994) (prohibiting employers from retaliating against employees who bring or participate in actions under the Act); and Title VII of the Civil Rights Act of 1964, 42 U.S.C. § 2000e-3 (1994) (prohibiting discrimination against or the discharge of any employee for reporting employer violations of the Act). For a partial listing of state anti-retaliation provisions, see BOMPEY *et al.* at 8–11. Among federal statutes, see Water Pollution Control Act of 1948, 33 U.S.C. §1367 (1994) (prohibiting retaliation against employees for reporting their employer's water pollution); Title III of the Federal Property and Administrative Services Act of 1949, 41 U.S.C. §251 *et seq.* (1994) *amended by* 108 Stat. 3243, 3365 (1994) (prohibiting retaliation against employees of civilian contractors who report contract violations); Atomic Energy Act of 1954, 42 U.S.C. §5851 (1994) (prohibiting an employer from discharging any employee who reports nuclear-safety violations); Clean Air Act of 1955, 42 U.S.C. §7622 (1994) (prohibiting retaliation against employees for reporting employer violations of clean-air standards); Solid Waste Disposal Act of 1965, 42 U.S.C. § 6971 (1994) (prohibiting retaliation against employees for reporting an employer's violation of solid-waste-disposal regulations); Safe Drinking Water Act of 1974, 42 U.S.C. § 300j-9 (1994) (prohibiting employers from firing employees who report violations of this Act); Toxic Substances Control Act of 1976, 15 U.S.C. § 2622 (1994) (prohibiting retaliation against employees for initiating or testifying in proceedings against the employer); Surface Mining and Reclamation Act of 1977, 30 U.S.C. § 1293 (1994) (prohibiting retaliation against employees for reporting employer violations of surface-mining guidelines); Comprehensive Environmental Response, Compensation and Liability Act of 1980, 42 U.S.C. § 9610 (1994) (prohibiting an employer from firing any employee for reporting or participating in investigations of CERCLA violations); Asbestos Hazard Emergency Response Act of 1986, 15 U.S.C. § 2651 (1994) (prohibiting retaliation against employees for reporting a potential violation of the statute by a state or local educational agency); Department of Defense Authorization Act of 1987, 10 U.S.C. § 2409 (1994), *amended by* 108 Stat. 3243, 3364 (1994) (prohibiting retaliation against employees of contractors of Dept. of Defense, Coast Guard, and N. A.S.A. for reporting violations of contract law); and Major Fraud Act of 1988, 18 U.S.C. § 1031(g) (1994) (prohibiting retaliation against employees for participating in a prosecution of an employer accused of defrauding the United States). For a partial listing of similar state provisions, see BOMPEY *et al.* at 10 n. 32.

[744] Among federal statutes, see Water Pollution Control Act of 1948, 33 U.S.C. §1367 (1994) (prohibiting retaliation against employees for reporting their employer's water pollution); Title III

various broader "whistleblower-protection" statutes that a few states have enacted to protect against employer retaliation against any employee who has reported to the public authorities his employer's violation of one or more specified laws.[745] All these doctrines and laws are consistent with the "fair play" variant of the "petitioning immunity" doctrine in that the protection they afford is not available to employees who have intentionally given false reports (who did not act in "good faith").[746] Indeed, at least as interpreted, some of the doctrines and statutes in question appear to withdraw protection from employees whose false reports were made not intentionally or in bad faith but "unreasonably,"[747] which I assume means recklessly in regard to the truth or perhaps even negligently. This requirement that the report in question be reasonable and made in good faith is obviously consistent with the "fair play" component of the "petitioning immunity" doctrine that I think antitrust law should as a matter of law be interpreted to recognize.

I might add that the conclusion that the initiation of a lawsuit should not be deemed to violate the Sherman Act unless there is no chance of winning on the merits is consistent with the Federal Rules of Civil Procedure, which authorize judges to impose sanctions on plaintiffs (*e.g.*, to require plaintiffs to pay defendants' lawyers'

of the Federal Property and Administrative Services Act of 1949, 41 U.S.C. §251 et seq. (1994) *amended by* 108 Stat. 3243, 3365 (1994) (prohibiting retaliation against employees of civilian contractors who report contract violations); Atomic Energy Act of 1954, 42 U.S.C. §5851 (1994) (prohibiting an employer from discharging any employee who reports nuclear-safety violations); Clean Air Act of 1955, 42 U.S.C. §7622 (1994) (prohibiting retaliation against employees for reporting employer violations of clean-air standards); Solid Waste Disposal Act of 1965, 42 U.S.C. § 6971 (1994) (prohibiting retaliation against employees for reporting an employer's violation of solid-waste-disposal regulations); Safe Drinking Water Act of 1974, 42 U.S.C. § 300j-9 (1994) (prohibiting employers from firing employees who report violations of this Act); Toxic Substances Control Act of 1976, 15 U.S.C. § 2622 (1994) (prohibiting retaliation against employees for initiating or testifying in proceedings against the employer); Surface Mining and Reclamation Act of 1977, 30 U.S.C. § 1293 (1994) (prohibiting retaliation against employees for reporting employer violations of surface-mining guidelines); Comprehensive Environmental Response, Compensation and Liability Act of 1980, 42 U.S.C. § 9610 (1994) (prohibiting an employer from firing any employee for reporting or participating in investigations of CERCLA violations); Asbestos Hazard Emergency Response Act of 1986, 15 U.S.C. § 2651 (1994) (prohibiting retaliation against employees for reporting a potential violation of the statute by a state or local educational agency); Department of Defense Authorization Act of 1987, 10 U.S.C. § 2409 (1994), *amended by* 108 Stat. 3243, 3364 (1994) (prohibiting retaliation against employees of contractors of Dept. of Defense, Coast Guard, and N.A.S.A. for reporting violations of contract law); and Major Fraud Act of 1988, 18 U.S.C. § 1031(g) (1994) (prohibiting retaliation against employees for participating in a prosecution of an employer accused of defrauding the United States). For a partial listing of similar state provisions, see BOMPEY *et al.* at 10 n. 32.

[745] See, *e.g.*, MICH. COMP. LAWS ANN. § 15.362 (West, 1981); CONN. GEN. STAT. ANN. § 31–51 (West, 1983); ME. REV. STAT. ANN. the. 26, § 832 (1984). For a description of these laws and an analysis of their impact, see Terry Morehead Dworkin and Janet P. Near, *Whistleblowing Statutes: Are They Working?*, 25 AM. BUS. L.J. 241 (1987).

[746] See, *e.g.*, Palmer v. Brown, 752 P.2d 685 at 689 (1988).

[747] See, *e.g.*, Schriner v. Meggini's Food, 3 IER Cas. (BNA) 129 at 132 (Neb. 1988).

costs)[748] if and only if the plaintiff's pleading, motion, or other submission to the court was "frivolous"[749] or was "presented for any improper purpose, such as to harass or to cause unnecessary delay or needless increase in the cost of litigation..."[750]

I want to make one final point that relates to the sham-ness as opposed to the "fair play" criterion that courts might use to determine whether predatory participation in government decisionmaking-processes constitutes a Sherman Act violation. Assume that in principle an actor has no First Amendment right to make an argument for a particular public decision the actor knew was based on false empirical premises or was critically logically flawed. It might be legitimate for the courts to be more willing to assess for shamness arguments that are allegedly relevant to the determination of the answer to a legal-rights question that is correct as a matter of law than to assess for shamness arguments that are allegedly relevant to the determination of the answer to a policy question that is most desirable (assuming that no extant legal right might be violated): courts may feel that they are better-placed to assess legal arguments than policy arguments. To the extent this is so, courts would be right to be more ready to declare predatory participation in adjudicative processes a Sherman Act violation than to declare predatory participation in legislative processes a Sherman Act violation.

(B) The EC Position and the E.C./E.U. Case-Law

I know of no EC discussion paper or E.C./E.U. case that deals with the legality of predatory participation in legislative processes or non-predatory participation in such processes that is motivated by the actor's specific anticompetitive intent. However, the EC and an E.C./E.U. court of first instance (CFI) have addressed the legality under now-Article 102 of predatory abuses of the adjudicative process, and the EC has addressed the legality under now-Article 102 of a predatory abuse of an administrative process.

Both the EC and the CFI have declared that, because access to courts is a fundamental right, a dominant firm's initiation of a legal proceeding can constitute an exclusionary abuse under now-Article 102 "only in wholly-exceptional circumstances."[751] According to the EC and CFI, two conditions must be fulfilled for the initiation of an adjudication (by a dominant firm or one or more members of a set of collectively-dominant rivals) to violate now-Article 102:

(1) the dominant undertaking could not reasonably have believed that the defendant had violated the asserted legal right, and

---

[748] Fed. Rules Civ. Proc. Rule 11(c) (1994).

[749] Fed. Rules Civ. Proc. Rule 11(b)(2) (1994).

[750] Fed. Rules Civ. Proc. Rule 11(b)(1) (1994).

[751] The quotation is from a CFI opinion. See ITT Promedia NV v. Commission, T-111/96, p. 60 (1998). See also the unpublished opinion of the EC in ITT Oromedia Belgacom, IV/35.258 (1996), cited in ITT Promedia NV v. Commission, T-111/96, p. 55 (1998).

(2) the dominant undertaking must have initiated the legal action "to eliminate competition."[752]

I want to make two points about these two criteria:

(1) it is not clear whether the second condition is that the defendant would not have initiated the suit in question but for its belief that the suit would or might eliminate competition (a condition that might not be satisfied even if the dominant firm believed that the suit would eliminate competition and placed a positive value on that consequence), and
(2) the conditions focus exclusively on the initiation of the suit as opposed to the way in which the dominant firm prosecuted the suit.

In one case,[753] the EC also addressed the possibility that participation in an administrative process by a dominant firm or member of a collectively-dominant set of rivals might constitute an exclusionary abuse prohibited by now-Article 102. In that case, the Commission based its decision against the defendant on the unfairness (my term) of the defendant's conduct before the regulatory body—*viz.*, on its making misrepresentations before a number of national patent offices and its misuse of rules and procedures before national medicines agencies that must authorize the marketing of medicinal products with the intention of blocking or delaying the marketing of a generic substitute for one of its products.

8. Predatory Efforts to Raise Rivals' Costs (in Various Ways Not Yet Covered)

A. The Definition of Predatory Efforts to Raise Rivals' Costs and Some Additional Variants of This Type of Conduct

This section is redundant. I have already discussed a number of types of conduct in which one or more firms may engage to drive rivals out, deter them from entering or expanding, or worsen their competitive positions without driving them out by raising their rivals' costs: (1) bidding up the prices of material inputs or intellectual property the rival required or buying up inputs that could not be replicated and refusing to sell them to the rival; (2) obstructing a rival's place of business; (3) discouraging a rival's potential suppliers from supplying it or a rival's potential employees from working for it; (4) inducing a rival's independent suppliers or employees to provide inferior performances; (5) bringing unjustified legal suits, making unjustified legal claims, or spending additional money in the pursuance of such claims to secure legal outcomes (say, production-process-patent-infringement

[752] See *id.* at pp. 72–73 and 93.

[753] Astra Zeneca, IP/05/737 (2005).

conclusions) that will raise the rival's costs and/or to increase the transaction costs it is profitable for the rival to incur to defend itself; (6) participating in administrative processes to influence the decisionmakers to promulgate zoning, environmental, IP, food-and-drug regulations or to make decisions in zoning, environmental, IP, and food-and-drug cases that will raise the rival's costs; and (7) participating in legislative processes to secure legislation that will deny the rival access to foreign imports, raise the cost of these imports to it, or subject it to environmental regulations or taxes that will increase its costs. Many of these behaviors will at least sometimes increase the target rival's costs by more than they increase their perpetrator's costs,[754] but even when they do not, they may benefit the perpetrator sufficiently by driving the rival out or deterring a new entry or QV-investment expansion by an incumbent to more than cover their cost. In particular, this result will obtain if the highest supernormal profit-rate generated in the ARDEPPS at the post-conduct lower-QV-investment equilibrium is higher than it was at the pre-conduct higher QV-investment equilibrium—an outcome that may obtain because lumpiness can cause equilibrium QV investment to exceed the quantity of such investment that will deter any new QV investment from being made. I have included this section despite its redundancy because economists are accustomed to thinking of "raising rivals' costs" as one category of predatory conduct.

B. U.S. and E.C./E.U. Law, Correctly Interpreted and Applied

(1) U.S. Law, Correctly Interpreted and Applied

If the types of conduct in question are inherently unprofitable, they will be predatory if their perpetrator's *ex ante* perception that they would be profitable, all things considered, was critically affected by its belief that they would or might increase its profits by driving a rival out, deterring a QV-investment-increasing new entry or incumbent QV-investment expansion, or inducing a rival to move to a product-space location that is less competitive with the predator's. If the types of conduct in

[754] For example, (1) a tariff will increase the target's cost more than it increases the perpetrator's if the perpetrator does not use the input on which the tariff is levied or produces it itself or has entered into a long-term supply contract with an independent supplier and cannot take advantage of the tariff by reselling its inputs without incurring significant costs; (2) a zoning ordinance will increase a potential-entrant's or potential-expander's costs by more than it increases the perpetrator's costs if the perpetrator's production-facility is grandfathered in or is located outside the area to which the zoning regulation applies while the target has good reason to locate in the area in question; (3) an environmental regulation will increase a target's costs by more than it increases the perpetrator's if the target but not the perpetrator generates the pollutant to whose generation the environmental regulation applies or the environmental regulation makes location relevant and the locations of the target and perpetrator differ in relevant ways; and (4) the cost to the perpetrator of raising its rival's costs in the first four ways listed in the text is lower than the amount by which this conduct will raise its rival's costs.

question were inherently unprofitable, they will also manifest specific anticompetitive intent when they are not predatory if their perpetrator's *ex ante* perception that they were profitable was critically affected by its perception that they would or might increase its profits without affecting any rival's QV-investment decision by improving its competitive advantages by raising various target-rivals' marginal costs by more than they raised its own. All this is standard. However, it may be worth noting that, because efforts to raise rivals' costs by granting concessions in wages and other terms of employment or by hiring the target's employees, managers, and suppliers involve agreements, such conduct is covered by Section 1 of the Sherman Act as well as by Section 2 and because "unsuccessful" attempts to hire a target's employees, managers, and suppliers that raise a rival's costs by making it pay these parties more do not involve the formation of any agreement they will not be covered by Section 1 of the Sherman Act and may not be covered by Section 2 of the Sherman Act either.

(2) E.C./E.U. Law, Corrrectly Interpreted and Applied

The relevant analysis is virtually the same as Subsection 7A(2)(B)'s analysis of the E.C./E.U.-competition-law legality of the rival-cost-raising variants of unfair competition. However, it may be worth noting that, because efforts to raise rivals' costs by granting concessions in wages and other terms of employment or by hiring the target's employees, managers, and suppliers involve agreements, such conduct is covered by now-Article 101 (as well as by now-Article 102 when it is perpetrated by a dominant firm or a member of a collectively-dominant set of rivals).

C. The U.S. Case-Law, EC Position, and E.C./E.U. Case-Law on These Variants of Rival-Cost-Raising Conduct

(1) The U.S. Case-Law

In a 1965 case, *United Mine Workers v. Pennington,*[755] the Supreme Court concluded that a wage settlement that raised the costs of the perpetrator's rivals by more than it raised the perpetrator's own costs violated the Sherman Act. U.S. case-law contains other opinions that endorse the view that, in some situations, a firm's efforts to raise its rival's or rivals' costs in other ways will violate the Sherman Act (though, in some of these cases, the illegality of the particular conduct in which the defendant engaged is, at a minimum, contestable).[756]

---

[755] 381 U.S. 657 (1965).

[756] See, *e.g.*, United States v. Microsoft Corp., 253 F.2d 34, 66 (D.C. Cir. 2001) and Reazin v. Blue Cross and Blue Shield of Kansas, 899 F.2d 951 (10th Cir. 1990).

(2) The EC's Discussion Papers and the E.C./E.U. Case-Law

I know of no EC discussion paper or E.C./E.U. case that analyzes the legality of the types of rival-cost-raising conduct on which this section has focused.

9. Predatory "Refusals to Deal," Broadly Understood

This section uses a definition of "refusals to deal" that is broad in two ways. First, the definition is "broad" in that it includes not only (1) unilateral or concerted decisions by one or more firms (A) not to sell to or buy from a specified actor or category of actors and, relatedly, (B) not to sell to or buy from anyone that sells to or buys from a specified actor or category of actors but also (2) unilateral or concerted decisions by one or more firms not to participate in a joint venture or joint-sales relationship with a specified rival or set of rivals, (3) decisions by a joint venture, the parents of a joint venture, or the participants in a patent pool not to allow any or certain specified rivals to take part in the joint venture or patent pool, (4) unilateral or concerted decisions by one or more firms to enter into full-requirements contracts or exclusive-dealership arrangements with their customers/dealers that are designed to legally obligate these "buyers" not to deal with the seller's rivals, (5) unilateral or concerted decisions by one or more firms to execute as lessors long-term leases that contain terms that make it unprofitable for the lessees to patronize any rival of the lessor for the duration of the lease, and (6) any decision by an employer or by a member of a partnership to include in a contract of employment or partnership agreement a provision prohibiting the employer/partner from selling his services to a product-rival (or from competing directly with his employer/partner on his own) and any decision by the buyer of a business or professional practice to include in the contract of sale a provision barring the seller from selling his services to a product-rival of the buyer or competing against the buyer directly himself. Second, the definition of "refusals to deal" it uses is also broad in that it defines the conduct to cover not only decisions not to consider dealing with another party but decisions not to engage in a transaction with one or more specified parties after giving the possibility of doing so due consideration.

I turn now to the concept of a *predatory* refusal to deal. The definition of a predatory refusal to deal can be derived directly from the general definition of predatory conduct. Thus, one or more firms should be said to have refused to deal predatorily if, *ex ante*, they would not have expected their refusal to deal to be profitable but for their belief that it would or might increase their profits in the long run by reducing the absolute attractiveness of the offers against which they will have to compete by inducing an established rival to withdraw a QV investment, by deterring such a rival or a potential competitor from introducing a new QV investment, or by inducing such firms to locate their QV investments further away in product-space from the predator's QV investments than they otherwise would have found profitable when the fact that the conduct in question will have one or more such effects would critically inflate its profitability in an otherwise-Pareto-perfect economy. Derivatively, one or more sellers should be said to have predatorily induced someone else to refuse to deal with a particular party if *ex ante* the inducing firm would not have found it profitable to induce the relevant refusal to deal but for its belief that doing so would or might increase the inducer's profits by reducing the absolute attractiveness of the offers against which the inducer had to compete in one or more of the ways just listed when this effect would critically inflate the profits of the conduct in question in an otherwise-Pareto-perfect economy.

Both Subsection 9A and Subsection 9B will focus on two different sets of conduct-types that, on my broad definition, involve refusals to deal: one set that I characterize as "straightforward" refusals to deal and a second set that covers the securing of contractual commitments that either prohibit a contract partner from dealing with an actual or potential competitor of the perpetrator or make it unprofitable for the contract partner to do so. Each of these two subsections (1) explains the legitimate functions that the types of conduct on which it focuses can perform and how and when these types of conduct will be predatory, (2) analyzes the legality of these variants of refusals to deal under U.S. antitrust law and E.C./E.U. competition law, properly interpreted and applied, and (3) describes and comments on the U.S. case-law, EC position, and E.C./E.U. case-law on the relevant types of conduct.

A. Two Categories and Numerous Subcategories of Predatory and Non-Predatory Refusals to Deal

(1) "Straightforward" Refusals to Deal with a Buyer or Supplier That the Refuser Does Not Perceive to Be an Actual or Potential Product-Rival, with a Buyer or Supplier That the Refuser Does Perceive to Be an Actual or Potential Product-Rival, or with a Buyer or Supplier That Deals with a Buyer or Supplier That the Refuser Believes to Be an Actual or Potential Product-Rival

(A) Straightforward Refusals to Deal with a Buyer or Supplier That the Refuser Does Not Perceive to Be an Actual or Potential Product-Rival

It may seem peculiar to start with refusals to deal with such parties, given that refusers cannot have a predatory motivation to refuse to deal with them. I do so both because the various reasons why refusals to deal with such actors may be profitable may also be operative when the refuser does believe that the refused party is an actual or potential rival and because a significant number of refusal-to-deal antitrust cases involve refusals to deal with such parties.

If I define refusals to deal with a party to include failures to engage in a transaction with the party, an individual firm may find a unilateral or concerted refusal to deal with a party it does not consider to be an actual or potential product-rival legitimately profitable or attractive overall for at least the following 11 reasons:

(1) (the conventional marginal or incremental cost a refusing seller would have to incur to supply the refused buyer *minus* any learning-by-doing cost-savings the seller could obtain by supplying the buyer in question) was higher than (the conventional [see below] marginal or incremental revenue the seller could obtain by supplying the refused buyer and any promotional advantages it could secure by supplying that buyer) or (the conventional [see below] dollar value to a refusing buyer of any amount of the refused seller's good or service) was lower than (the conventional marginal or incremental cost to the refused seller of supplying that amount of the product to the refusing buyer in question);
(2) a transaction that would otherwise have been mutually profitable was rendered unprofitable by the pricing costs and contextual marginal costs the parties would have to incur to participate in it;
(3) the refuser found an otherwise-profitable transaction unprofitable or unattractive overall because it (A) believed that the refused party (or perhaps one of its employees) had violated a previous contract with the refuser or an understanding that it had with the refuser, had committed a tort against the refuser, had violated an intellectual-property right or other type of property right of the refuser (say, by revealing commercial information to which the refuser had a proprietary right), or had violated a legal obligation not to compete with the refuser and (B) either thought that the refusal to deal would or might induce the legal-right violator to desist from the violation and/or pay restitution and/or placed a negative value on any profits the transaction would have given the violator;
(4) the refuser disliked the refused party for some other reason and found a conventionally-profitable transaction with the refused party unattractive overall because it placed a positive value "out of spite" on depriving the refused party of profits or placed a negative value on giving the refused party any profits;
(5) the refuser found a conventionally-profitable transaction with the refused party unattractive overall because the refuser believed that boycotting the refused party was sufficiently likely to help the refuser achieve sufficiently-important political goals for the refusal to deal to be attractive overall;
(6) the refuser believed *ex ante* that the refused party had a bad economic or political reputation and thought that the cost any business association with the refused party would impose on it by tarnishing its economic or political reputation and/or increasing the likelihood that it might be investigated, prosecuted, or sued civilly exceeded the profits the transaction would otherwise have yielded it;
(7) the refuser believed *ex ante* that an otherwise-profitable sale of an input to the refused party would be rendered unprofitable by the loss of reputation it would suffer if it engaged in the transaction in question because (A) the refuser's product was an input that the buyer would use to produce a low-quality product and the buyer's customers and others would incorrectly attribute the

buyer's product's poor performance at least in part to the quality of the refuser's input or (B) the refuser's product was a final good that the buyer wanted to use together with one or more inferior or otherwise-unsuitable complements, put to an inappropriate use, or improperly employ for an appropriate use and others who would observe the poor performance-outcome or would be told of it by the potential buyer would attribute that outcome to the refuser's product rather than to the buyer's mistaken conduct;

(8) the refuser turned down a deal that would have been more profitable than no deal in the hope that the other party would eventually accept a deal that would be more favorable to the refuser or with the expectation that the refusal would improve the deals it could strike with this and other parties in the future by enhancing its reputation as a tough bargainer;

(9) the refuser (A) turned down an otherwise-profitable deal to supply repair-and-maintenance information and equipment and/or replacement parts to an independent provider of repair and maintenance services for the refuser's durable machine or to supply product information to an independent potential supplier of physical complements to its basic product or (B) included a clause in its contracts of sale for its durable machine or basic product obligating its customers to purchase their full requirements of associated repair-and-maintenance services or physical complements from it to enable it to meter price its machine or basic product—*i.e.*, to lower the lump-sum fee it charges but require its customers to purchase their full requirements of such complements from it for more than their normal market prices when the value of the machine or basic product to a buyer is highly positively correlated with the amount of repair-and-maintenance services or physical complements it uses (see Chap. 14);

(10) the refuser turned down a deal that would otherwise have been profitable because the refusal was rendered profitable by a price-fixing conspiracy in which all participants committed themselves to accepting only certain prices or certain non-price terms or in which each buyer was assigned to a particular seller; and

(11) the refuser turned down a deal that would otherwise have been profitable because the refusal was rendered profitable by a vertical territorial restraint or customer-allocation clause to which it had agreed.

(B) Straightforward Refusals to Deal with a Buyer or Supplier That the Refuser Does Perceive to Be an Actual or Potential Product-Rival

In addition to the 11 reasons just listed, a firm may find it profitable to refuse to deal with a buyer or seller it perceives to be an actual or potential product-rival for at least the following five reasons:

(1) the refuser may believe that, by depriving the refused party of the profits the refuser could not otherwise prevent the refused party from realizing on the relevant transaction, the refusal to deal would cause the refused party to exit

from or deter it from entering or expanding its QV investments in the refuser's area of product-space by making it more difficult for the refused party to finance its original operation or new investment by making use of retained earnings and perhaps by securing external financing;

(2) when the refuser is a seller and the good or service the seller refuses to sell is an input that is "consumed" by the use of an existing QV investment and/or would be "consumed" by the creation and/or use of a new QV investment, the refusal to deal may yield the refuser profits by inducing an exit or deterring a new QV investment by making it impossible or more costly for the owner of the extant QV investment to continue to use it or for the maker of any new QV investment to create and use it: this second reason is really a variant of the first, which I would not distinguish from the first but which some may believe should be distinguished from the first when the refused good is "essential" to the survival of an existing competitor of the refuser or to the ability of a potential competitor to enter or an established rival to expand its QV investments in the refuser's area of product-space;

(3) when the refused good is a product a refused potential entrant or (possibly) a refused potential expander might choose to produce itself, the refusing seller may find it profitable to reject an otherwise-profitable transaction to prevent such a potential buyer from reducing the $(\Pi_D + R)$ barriers to entry or expansion it faced by examining the product in question: even if the potential entrant or expander in question could produce the relevant product more proficiently than the refuser, it might not be profitable for the refuser to license the other firm to do so because once the other firm was in operation and the refuser had partially or totally withdrawn from production, the other firm might enjoy bargaining power that would enable it to secure sufficiently-favorable license-terms to make its original entry or expansion unprofitable for the original producer;

(4) when the refused good is a replacement part, a physical product used to maintain or repair a durable good, or information about how to maintain or repair a durable good or the refusal takes the form of a provision in the contract of sale of the machine that requires the buyer to purchase all its repair-and-maintenance services from the seller, the producer of the durable good may find it profitable to reject an otherwise-profitable sale to a buyer that runs a repair-and-maintenance service or to prohibit its customers from patronizing such a service-provider to deter the service-provider from entering the durable-good-production market by preventing it from reducing the $(\Pi_D + R)$ barriers it faced by examining and working with the durable product, learning the identity of the basic product's buyers, and interacting with them (though such refusals may also be designed to enable the refuser to use a form of meter pricing to sell its durable machine—*i.e.*, to lower its price for the machine in exchange for the buyer's agreeing to purchase its repair-and-maintenance services from the buyer for a supra-normal-market price when the buyer's quantity demand for repair-and-maintenance services increases with its use of the machine and hence the value of the machine to it and the difference between the contract price for repair-and-maintenance services and the normal price of such services

divided by the number of uses after which such services are required is the meter rate); and

(5) when the refused "good" is information about the refuser's "basic product" that will enable an independent complement-producer to create a useful complement for the basic product or the refusal takes the form of a provision in the contract of sale for the basic product that requires the buyer to purchase all its complements from the seller, the producer of the basic product may find it profitable to reject an otherwise-profitable transfer of relevant information to such a potential complement-producer or to prohibit its customers from patronizing such an independent complement-producer to deter the independent complement-producer from entering the basic-product market by preventing the complement-producer from reducing the (Π_D + R) barriers it faced by working with the durable product, learning the identity of the basic product's buyers, and working with them (though, once more, such refusals may also be designed to enable the refuser to meter price its basic product when the value of its basic product to any buyer increases with the number of units of one or more complements the buyer combines with it—*e.g.*, when the value of a camera to its buyers increases with the amount of film and developing services they combine with it).

I now need to address whether refusals to deal that owe their existence to the refuser's *ex ante* perception that they would or might increase its profits in one of the above five ways are predatory. Since I am assuming that the refusal-perpetrator's *ex ante* perception that these refusals were profitable was critically affected by its belief that they would or might increase its future profits by inducing the exit of an extant rival QV investment or preventing the introduction of a new rival QV investment, such refusals will be predatory if their tendency to induce exits and deter new QV investments not only critically increases their profitability but would critically *inflate* their profitability in an otherwise-Pareto-perfect economy. In my judgment, refusals to deal whose *ex ante* actor-perceived profitability is *critically increased* by their tendency to induce rival exits and deter new rival QV investments in one or more of the five ways just described are not predatory because the profits they are expected to yield on this account would not *critically inflate* their *ex ante* actor-perceived profitability in an otherwise-Pareto-perfect economy because, in such an economy, this tendency of the refusals in question would increase economic efficiency at the same time that they increased refuser profits by preserving the incentives of future potential investors to make economically-efficient QV investments that create products whose profitability they will want to preserve by refusing to sell them to actual and potential rivals.

(C) Straightforward Refusals to Deal with a Buyer (or a Seller) That Deals with a Firm with Which the Refuser Does Not Want the Refused Firm to Deal

A firm may want another firm with which it could deal not to engage in transactions with a third firm for suitably-adjusted variants of any or all of the last four reasons discussed in Subsection 9A(1)(A) or for a suitably-adjusted variant of any of the five reasons discussed in Subsection 9A(1)(B). The analysis of any decision by a firm not to deal with another firm if, contrary to the former firm's wishes, the latter firm dealt with a third firm is identical to the analysis of the straightforward refusals to deal with which Subsections 9A(1)(A) and 9A(1)(B) were concerned.

(2) Provisions in Vertical Contracts Between Sellers and Buyers in Which Sellers (Buyers) Either Prohibit Buyers (Sellers) from Dealing with an Actual or Potential Rival of the Seller (Buyer) in Question or Incur Costs to Make It Unprofitable for the Buyer (Seller) in Question to Deal with the Seller's (Buyer's) Actual or Potential Rival

(A) Long-Term Full-Requirement Contracts

A long-term full-requirements contract is an agreement in which a buyer agrees to purchase its full requirements of some product during the period in question from a particular seller.[757] Long-term full-requirements contracts can perform many legitimate business functions. More specifically, even when such contracts are not part of a tying or reciprocal-trading agreement, they can increase their participants' profits by reducing their contracting costs, encouraging them to adapt their operations in each others' interests, minimizing the sum of their conventional risk costs, and relatedly putting them in a better position to make long-term investments by providing them respectively with an assured source of "sales" and an assured source of supply. Moreover, as Chap. 14 explains, when incorporated into an appropriate tying or reciprocity agreement, long-term full-requirements contract-clauses can enable their employer to reduce the cost it must incur to control the quality of the complements its customer combines with its product or the quality of the goods with which its supplier supplies it, to reduce the cost a seller must incur to implement a meter-pricing scheme, or to reduce the amount of transaction surplus (buyer *plus* seller surplus) it must destroy to remove a given amount of its customer's buyer surplus through non-marginal-cost per-unit pricing.[758]

As we have seen in relation to other sorts of practices, the fact that a long-term full-requirements contract can generate legitimate profits can critically affect its predatory status: if *ex ante* the defendant in a "long-term full-requirements contract" case perceived that the contract's profitability was guaranteed by the legitimate profits it anticipated its yielding, the contract would not be predatory even if (1) it would also increase its employer's profits by reducing the absolute attractiveness of the offers against which it had to compete by driving a rival out or deterring

[757] Although in some circumstances long-term supply contracts in which a seller agrees to supply its full output to a particular buyer for a specified period may also be predatory, the text will not deal with this relatively-unimportant possibility.

[758] See Chap. 14 for a detailed explanation of these claims and a discussion of the other non-monopolizing functions that tie-ins and reciprocity can perform.

an entry or expansion and (2) the relevant employer was aware that the agreement would produce this effect and valued it partially on this account.

Although I suspect that the vast majority of long-term full-requirements contracts are not predatory (and that only a few such agreements do reduce the absolute attractiveness of the offers against which their employer has to compete), I have no doubt that the defendant-perceived *ex ante* profitability of some long-term-requirements contracts is critically affected by their perceived tendency to deter an entry or expansion or drive an established project out. I will now explain when and how such agreements can increase their employer's profits in these illegitimate ways.

In appropriate circumstances, one or more sellers X or X1...N that want to prevent a new entry or a QV-investment expansion by an established rival (or conceivably but less likely, that want to drive out an existing QV investment) will be able to do so by inducing enough of the potential entrant's or expander's prospective customers (the established project's actual patrons) Y1...N to agree not to deal with the target for a critical period of time by inducing them to commit themselves to buying their full requirements of the product their target would produce for the period in question from them (*i.e.*, from X or X1...N) to preclude the prospective QV investor from being able to break even on its entry or expansion or the owner of the extant QV investment in question from being able to break even on that investment's continued operation. This section explores the effectiveness and profitability of such predatory long-term full-requirements contracts. For convenience, it will focus exclusively on contracts of this type that are designed to deter a new entry or an incumbent's QV-investment expansion.

To be effectively predatory, long-term full-requirements contracts must lock up enough existing buyers to prevent any new product or outlet from generating normal profits. This requirement does not imply that such contracts can be predatory only if the number of uncommitted buyers operating in the ARDEPPS in question is too low to support the established project or new QV investment that was the alleged target of the supposed predation. In our monopolistically-competitive world, an individual QV investment will not be able to compete effectively for all the uncommitted buyers in an ARDEPPS. This fact implies both that the execution of a new QV investment in the relevant part of the ARDEPPS in question may be precluded despite the fact that the number of buyers left uncommitted in the ARDEPPS as a whole would be sufficient to support the relevant new venture if it could appeal to all of them and that an individual established seller may be able to prevent an invasion of its portion of the relevant area of product-space by locking up an appropriate percentage of those buyers that have preferences for products with the set of attributes that its goods and services or, more to the point, the target QV investment of its target rival possess.

Admittedly, the fact that the established firms have locked up the required existing buyers would not even tend to deter a potential entrant or expander that was indifferent between selling to independent buyers and entering at both levels. In reality, of course, the potential entrant or expander will almost never find the two-level entry as attractive as a one-level entry—will not have the knowledge or skills necessary to enter profitably into the downstream business, will face capital or managerial constraints that make the second QV investment unprofitable, or will be deterred from investing in the downstream market by the fact that its QV investment there would raise QV investment in that ARDEPPS above its equilibrium level.[759] For all these reasons, then, long-term full-requirements contracts that do lock up potential existing customers of new QV investments will tend to discourage (will reduce the profitability of) entry or expansions though they may not succeed in deterring them if the QV investments in question would have been sufficiently profitable in their absence.

The fact that one or more long-term full-requirements contracts can effectively deter the execution of new QV investments raises a second issue: since, other things' being equal, the QV investment such contracts would deter would benefit the buyers in the market in question, how can it be profitable for the alleged predators to pay the buyers enough to get them to agree to the contracts in the first place? The answer is that the buyers will be tyrannized by their small decisions. Thus, each of the individual buyers whose individual demand the predator does not have to lock up to prevent an established rival from surviving or an established or potential competitor from making a new QV investment may agree to enter into a long-term full-requirements contract for a very small payment that does not cover the loss it will sustain when enough buyers commit themselves to the predator to drive out the established QV investment or deter the new QV investment because each assumes that, even if it does not lock itself in, enough of its fellow-buyers will enter into such contracts to deter the new QV investment in question. In other words, because in this situation a refusal to commit provides a kind of public good to all buyers taken as group, such refusals will be undersupplied from the perspective of the group of buyers taken as a whole if that group is insufficiently concentrated and its members are unable to bind each other contractually not to enter into long-term full-requirements contracts. Hence, in this type of situation, an individual predator or group of predatory sellers will be able to induce the relevant buyers to commit themselves to refusing to deal with the prospective owner of a new QV investment (or the owner of an established project) for a price that leaves the buyers worse-off as a group than they otherwise would have been.

Long-term full-requirements contracts that sellers find profitable for the reason just described are predatory. *Ex hypothesis*, the contracts in question would not have been profitable but for their tendency to increase the relevant sellers' long-run profits by deterring a new QV investment (or driving out an existing QV investment), and, in an otherwise-Pareto-perfect economy, the profits they yield the relevant seller on this account would have no economic-efficiency-gain counterpart. Indeed, I also think that buyers that have accepted this kind of offer, knowing that their contractual partner has made it to deter a new QV investment (or drive out

[759] I should note in addition that the dual-investment strategy will not be available at all when the relevant buyers are final consumers. I admit, however, that this point is not likely to be empirically significant: the buyers involved in long-term full-requirements contracts are virtually always manufacturers or distributors.

an existing QV investment), have engaged in (*i.e.*, been complicitous in) predation.[760] This may seem a harsh judgment since the buyers in question will have lost from the whole sequence of events, but each buyer will have accepted a payment in exchange for agreeing to help the predator achieve its illegal goal: the appropriate response for such a buyer is to go to law, not to bail itself out (no matter how partially) at its colleagues' expense by becoming its abuser's accomplice.

(B) Long-Term Exclusive Dealerships

The expression "exclusive dealership" is used to refer to arrangements that have one or both of the following features: (1) the seller agrees both to give a distributor the exclusive right to distribute its product in a given geographic area or to some specified set of customers and to (usually) supply the distributor with the latter's full requirements of the product(s) in question on specified terms and/or (2) the seller conditions its agreement to supply a distributor on the distributor's agreeing not to distribute any rival product (in which case the exclusive dealership is functionally equivalent to an agreement in which the dealer commits itself to taking its full requirements of the product in question from the participating supplier—*i.e.*, not to buy from any other potential supplier—for the duration of the dealership-agreement). (Europeans refer to exclusive dealerships that have the second characteristic as "single-brand" exclusive dealerships.) Long-term exclusive dealerships can yield legitimate profits in a wide variety of ways. In particular, dealerships that are exclusive in both the ways just described can generate legitimate profits *inter alia*

(1) by reducing the private transaction costs the relevant buyer and seller must incur to sell and buy the products in question,
(2) by reducing the total risk costs the buyer and seller bear because of uncertainties about supply and demand,
(3) relatedly, by enabling the buyer and seller to plan their investments more profitably,
(4) if the exclusive territories or customer-sets are defined appropriately, by enabling the seller to induce its distributors to make more-jointly-profitable advertising decisions, pre-sales-advice decisions, and post-sales-service decisions (by preventing positive and negative inter-distributor spillover effects),[761]
(5) by encouraging the manufacturer to inform the distributor and the distributor to inform the manufacturer of useful sales-techniques by precluding respectively

[760] Admittedly, it may be difficult in practice to establish the requisite probability that the buyer in question did not assume that the small price-concession it received reflected its supplier's desire to secure the long-run advantages some long-term full-requirements contracts generate by reducing contracting costs, encouraging participants to adapt their operations in their joint interest, lowering conventional risk-costs, and relatedly by facilitating long-term investments by providing an assured market.

[761] This possibility will be explained in more detail in Chap. 14.

the distributor from using those techniques to sell a rival product and the manufacturer from teaching those techniques to a distributor-rival of the distributor, and

(6) by preventing the distributor from making jointly-non-optimal decisions to sell a product produced by the manufacturer's rival.

In the other direction, regardless of whether they are arranged by a single producer or a group of established producers, exclusive dealerships that preclude the dealers from distributing the products of anyone else can also raise the seller's profits by inducing exits and deterring QV-investment expansions and entries in the same way that and in the same circumstances in which other types of long-term requirements contracts can do so.

An exclusive-dealership contract will be predatory when the seller's *ex ante* perception that it was certainty-equivalent profitable was critically increased by its belief that the exclusive-dealership arrangement would or might increase its profits by inducing the exit of an established rival QV investment or deterring the creation of a new rival QV investment by locking up a potential customer of the investor in question. If one assumes that the seller in question has not made a mistake, an exclusive-dealership arrangement will be predatory only if (1) the legitimate gains it yielded did not outweigh its costs and (2) it locked up a sufficient percentage of some target's potential customers to create some possibility that it would induce the target's exit or deter the target's entry or QV-investment expansion (because of the relative unattractiveness to the target of integrating forward or investing on two levels).

(C) Long-Term Leases

One or more sellers of durable products may also practice predation by entering into long-term leases with their customers that obligate the buyers to pay rents that do not vary with usage in the last years of the leases, especially if they renew the old leases or execute new leases (to begin at the expiration of the old leases) sufficiently in advance of the expiration of the old leases (*i.e.*, before any potential competitor or rival potential expander can secure enough sales to make its prospective entry or expansion profitable) to lock up enough buyers to preclude any potential competitor from being able to execute a profitable entry and any established rival firm being able to execute a profitable expansion. Such leases will deter entry or expansions better than would outright sales of the durable product (say, a machine) since the buyer of a machine could, so-to-speak, free itself up to patronize a new entrant or expanding incumbent by reselling the machine it had purchased. Such leases will be particularly effective at deterring entry if they contain penalty clauses that make the rent the lessee must pay the lessor in the last years of its operation vary inversely with the number of times it uses the machine—*i.e.*, if, far from enabling the lessee to save money on its lease, a lessee's decision to use a new entrant's machine increases the payments it must make to the lessor of its old machine.

Of course, long-term leases of machines may also be profitable for perfectly-legitimate reasons. They may enable sellers to make sales to buyers that could not finance the outright purchase of the machine, increase the seller's ability to prevent its machines' being misused by including "proper use" clauses in the lease (when the seller fears that the reputation of its product would be damaged if it performed badly because of misuse), increase the seller's ability to prevent others that want to copy its machine from gaining access to it, and enable the seller to prevent its old machines' being sold in competition with its new machines on terms that reduce the profits its legitimately-obtained competitive advantages can yield. If the defendant involved in a particular long-term-lease case perceived the lease's *ex ante* profitability to be guaranteed by its performance of such legitimate functions, the lease would not be predatory. Of course, even if a seller's decision to lease its machine were not predatory, its adoption of an early-renewal policy or inclusion of a penalty-for-"underuse" clause might be predatory. I hasten to add, however, that one cannot infer predation from the fact that the rent that the lease requires the lessee to pay for a machine in the last year(s) of the lease exceeds the dollar value to the lessee of being able to use the machine during those years: the portion of the rent that a lessee must pay that does not vary with the frequency with which the lessee uses the machine may not critically affect the profitability to the lessee of substituting a new entrant's machine for the leased machine, and (even if it does) rent schedules that include late-year rental payments that exceed use-value may manifest not predation but the lessor's having given a loan to the lessee (by setting the earlier years' rental-payments below use-value), a loan that the lessee is being required to repay in the final years of the lease by paying rentals in excess of use-value.

(D) "Refusal-to-Deal" Provisions in Employment Contracts, Partnership Agreements, and Contracts for the Sale of Businesses or Professional Practices

Employment contracts often contain provisions forbidding the employee from (1) selling (communicating) information he has obtained in the course of his employment to any of his employer's actual or potential competitors and/or (2) working for any such rival of his employer (or competing against his employer by entering his employer's line of business on his own) for some stated period of time after leaving his employer's employ. (The restriction in the last parenthetical involves a refusal to deal in that it prohibits the employee from dealing for the patronage of his employer's potential customers as an independent competitor.) Partnership agreements often impose perfectly-analogous restrictions on the individual partners. Contracts for the sale of businesses (particularly of professional practices or other sorts of personal-service-rendering businesses) also often impose analogous restrictions on the seller of the business in question—*e.g.*, often forbid the seller to enter into the same business for a stated number of years in the geographic areas in which its former business operated.

Such arrangements can be perfectly legitimate and have no anticompetitive consequences. Employment-contract restrictions in the legal right of the employee to work for a rival of his employer can be included in employment contracts solely to make it profitable for the employer to teach the employee various things and to give the employee various learning experiences when it is economically efficient for the employer to do so and the restriction imposes no costs on the employer's rivals because, if the employer could not restrict his employees in this way, the potential employee would not be employed by the employer in question or would not be taught anything valuable by the employer in circumstances in which *ex ante* the employee did not have any attributes that made it profitable for the employer's rivals to hire him. Partnership-agreement restrictions in the legal right of the partners to compete against each other or to communicate valuable business information to rivals of the partnership will also be perfectly legitimate and have no anticompetitive consequences in analogous circumstances. I should add that, in both these types of cases, the restrictions in question are legitimated not only by their economic efficiency but by the fact that they enable the employer that or partner who would be hurt by the employee's or partner's subsequent competition or communication to a rival to protect its moral and related legal right to the information that the restricted employee/partner learned from the employer/partner. A similar argument can be made for the possible pure legitimacy of restrictions in sales of businesses. To the extent that the buyer of a business or professional practice is buying, among other things, the goodwill of the seller, a restriction in the legal right of the seller to compete against the buyer can both (1) protect the moral and legal right of the buyer to that goodwill and (2) increase economic efficiency by permitting the transfer of businesses from owners who place a lower value on them to buyers who value them more highly and by providing prospective sellers of businesses economically-efficient incentives to create goodwill.

Admittedly, however, the restrictions with which this subsection is concerned can also be purely predatory or anticompetitive. Thus, a potential employer that or partner who will not convey any information to an employee or partner that will increase the latter's productivity in the business in question and will not provide the employee/partner with any learning experiences that will have such an effect can include such restrictions in an employment contract or partnership agreement (1) purely to drive a rival out or prevent a rival's entry or expansion by precluding the rival from hiring the restricted employee or partner (in which case the restrictions will be predatory), (2) purely to reduce the ability of an established or potential competitor to compete against it by precluding such a rival from hiring the employee/partner in question (in which case the restrictions will be anticompetitive though not predatory), or (3) purely to prevent the restricted employee or partner from competing against it directly (in which case the restriction can probably not be said to be predatory [since the deterred rival has been paid not to compete] but clearly will be anticompetitive). Similarly, a buyer of a business that has no goodwill may restrict the seller's legal right to compete with the buyer purely to reduce the competition it faces (in which case the restriction will clearly be anticompetitive though, once more, the fact of the payment disfavors calling it predatory).

Moreover, it should also be obvious that many restrictions of these types will fall between these two extremes—will be neither purely-legitimate nor purely-anticompetitive shams. In these cases, the restrictions will both promote legitimately-profitable and presumptively-economically-efficient communications or sales (and concomitantly protect information in which the employer/partner has a proprietary interest or goodwill that the buyer has purchased) and benefit the restrictor relative to the *status quo ante* by removing as a direct or indirect source of competition an individual who would otherwise have been able to subject the restrictor to some competitive pressure.

It should be no surprise that I would consider these restrictions to be predatory or anticompetitive only if the restrictor's *ex ante* perception that the restriction was profitable (given the price he had to pay to the employee, partner, or business-seller to secure that party's agreement to it) was critically affected by the restrictor's *ex ante* belief that it would or might reduce the absolute attractiveness of the offers against which it would have to compete by precluding the restricted employee, partner, or business-seller from competing against it directly or indirectly by working for or communicating to a rival in the way that party would have done had it not worked for, become a partner of, or sold out to the restrictor in question.

(E) Vertical Territorial Restraints and Customer-Allocation Clauses in Distributorship Agreements

Distributors may be obligated to refuse to deal by vertical-territorial-restraint clauses or customer-allocation clauses in their distributorship agreement, which respectively limit the territory within which they may make a sale or the customers or classes of customers to which they may make a sale. As Chap. 14 will demonstrate, such vertical territorial restraints and customer-allocation clauses are normally legitimately profitable and rarely reduce competition (*inter alia*, are rarely predatory).

B. The Legality of Predatory Refusals to Deal Under U.S. Antitrust Law and E.C./E.U. Competition Law, Correctly Interpreted and Applied

(1) U.S. Antitrust Law, Correctly Interpreted and Applied

I will focus first on the Sherman Act and then on the Clayton Act. The text of the Sherman Act would appear to cover all refusals to deal with the possible exception of unsuccessful attempts to arrange multi-firm refusals to deal (group boycotts). However, Chap. 4 argued that it would be correct as a matter of law to recognize a broader exception to this coverage-conclusion whose contestable premise is that U.S. law does not impose a duty on a firm to help its actual or potential rivals obtain information, skills, or financing that would enable them to improve their actual or prospective competitive-position arrays. As I indicated in Chap. 4, this premise is consistent with the Clayton Act's do-nothing baseline for assessing the competitive impact of mergers, acquisitions, and joint ventures—*i.e.*, with the fact that, with a few, deviant exceptions that I think are wrong as a matter law (I recognize the difficulty these "exceptions" pose for me), the Clayton Act has always been understood to prohibit firms from engaging in such conduct only when the conduct is requisitely likely to reduce the intensity of competition below what it would have been had the defendant done nothing (as opposed to requiring firms that engaged in such conduct to choose the most-procompetitive exemplar of that type of conduct they could have discovered with reasonable effort that would have been more profitable for them than engaging in no conduct of the relevant kind). As I also indicated in Chap. 4, this premise is also manifest in the statements of U.S. judges that firms are entitled to choose their trading partners, in the claim by the U.S. Supreme Court that it never endorsed the "essential facilities" doctrine when in fact it created it and extended it in two fairly-recent cases, and in the seemingly-foolish Sherman Act opinions in which the Supreme Court declared it to be illegal for a seller to contractually obligate its distributors to do certain things or to inform them that it will discontinue supplying them if they do not follow certain "recommendations" while declaring it lawful for a seller to cease supplying a distributor that makes decisions the seller dislikes without explicitly informing the distributor either *ex ante* or *ex post* of the supply policy in question. On the other hand, as Chap. 4 indicated as well, this premise is disfavored by Section 3 of the Clayton Act in at least some of its applications. In any event, because I acknowledge the contestability of this possible exception and recognize that most experts would reject it, I will analyze the legality of various relevant categories of refusals to deal under the Sherman Act in the pages that follow both on the assumption that this broader coverage-exception is not correct as a matter of law and on the assumption that it is correct as a matter of law.

Full-requirements contracts, exclusive dealerships, vertical territorial restraints and customer-allocation clauses in distribution agreements, and restrictive covenants in contracts of sale of some businesses or professional practices[762] are also covered by Section 3 of the Clayton Act. In particular, Clayton Act Section 3 prohibits (1) leases or contracts of sale for "goods, wares, merchandise, machinery, supplies or other commodities" that obligate the buyer to refuse to deal with one or more competitors of the seller or (2) communications that indicate the seller's

[762] The reason why Section 3 covers some but not all contracts for the sale of businesses or professional practices is that its coverage is limited to leases or contracts for the lease or sale of "goods, wares, merchandise, machines, supplies, or other commodities...." Whether Section 3 covers restrictive covenants in the contract of sale of a business or professional practice therefore depends on whether the business or professional practice that is being sold owns one or more assets of any of these types and on whether those assets are being sold together with the other valuable assets of the business or professional practice in question (customer lists, goodwill, employee know-how). I should note, relatedly, that Section 3 clearly does not cover employment contracts or partnership agreements that do not involve the sale or lease of any of the types of assets in the above list.

intention not to renew a contract or lease if the buyer deals with one or more specified competitors of the seller if the arrangement is sufficiently likely to lessen competition or tend to create a monopoly. I would also read Section 3 of the Clayton Act to cover long-term leases that make it unprofitable for the lessee to patronize the lessor's competitors for the duration of the lease. Properly interpreted, Section 3 of the Clayton Act prohibits all full-requirements contracts, exclusive-dealership agreements, and long-term leases that I would deem predatory except for those that *ex ante* did not have the requisite probability of reducing competition. Properly interpreted, Section 3 of the Clayton Act will not prohibit contracts and leases of these sorts that are not predatory because *ex ante* the sellers they involve correctly perceived that their legitimate functions made them certainty-equivalent profitable unless (1) contrary to my own suspicion, such arrangements are more profitable for successful well-established firms than for marginal or potential competitors, (2) these differences in their profitability makes it sufficiently likely that their availability to all firms will reduce competition by causing a marginal established firm to exit or by deterring a potential entrant or expander firm investing, and (3) one rejects my conclusion that an organizational-economic-efficiency defense that would apply in this sort of case should be read into the Clayton Act. Chapter 14 will explain these points in detail. Section 3 also prohibits any predatory refusal to deal that is secured by a vertical territorial restraint or customer-allocation clause in a distributorship agreement. Chapter 14 will also explain in some detail why virtually all such restraints and clauses are non-predatory (and do not reduce competition).

(2) E.C./E.U. Competition Law, Correctly Interpreted and Applied

As I indicated in Chap. 4, E.C./E.U. competition law—in particular, Articles 101 and 102 of the 2009 Lisbon Treaty—may differ from U.S. antitrust law in ways that render illegal under E.C./E.U. competition law, properly interpreted, some refusals to deal that would be lawful under U.S. antitrust law, properly interpreted. I will first address the three features of Article 102 that distinguish it in relevant ways from U.S. antitrust law and then address the two features of Article 101 that are most salient in the current context.

The first significant feature of Article 102 is the fact that it prohibits dominant firms from engaging in exploitative as well as exclusionary abuses—*i.e.*, is the fact that it rejects the U.S. position that firms that have obtained competitive advantages lawfully may exploit them fully. Since, as E.C./E.U. competition-law-enforcement institutions recognize, it is extremely difficult in practice to determine whether the terms that a dominant firm is offering are unfair (*i.e.*, are illegally exploitative), this element of Article 102 may favor the conclusion that Article 102 can properly be given a fence-law interpretation under which it would be deemed to prohibit firms from engaging in what I take to be non-predatory refusals to deal whose profitability is critically increased by their tendency to deter rivals from making new QV investments or to withdraw extant QV investments in one or more of the five ways

Subsection 9A(1)(B) listed (*viz.*, by not helping the rivals compete against the refuser)—*i.e.*, to prohibit dominant firms from acting in a way that increases their power to "impose unfair. . .purchase or other unfair trading conditions" (since it will be difficult to determine whether they have exercised this power).

The second feature of Article 102 that is relevant in the current context is its listing as a (possible) example of an abuse the inclusion in contracts of provisions that impose "supplementary obligations [on buyers], which by their nature or according to commercial usage, have no connection with the subject of the contracts." At least, this feature of Article 102 would arguably (see below) be relevant if, as I suspect, the drafters and ratifiers of the 2009 Lisbon Treaty (or, perhaps, of the 1957 Treaty in which this provision originally appeared if the 2009 drafters and ratifiers had no position on these issues) believed that it covered full-requirements tie-ins, exclusive dealerships, and contract terms that preclude buyers from reselling the good they brought to an actual or potential rival of the seller to be abusive.

The third feature I am going to attribute to Article 102 that distinguishes it from U.S. law in a way that is salient in the current context may be a feature of its interpretation rather than of the Article itself: the EC, the E.C./E.U. courts, and European E.C./E.U.-competition-law scholars have frequently stated that now-Article 102 imposes an obligation on dominant firms to help rivals—to stimulate the growth of competition in the "markets" they dominate. To the extent that the "legislative history" of now-Article 102 broadly conceived supports this interpretation, that fact would also favor the conclusion that—when the relevant refuser is a firm that is individually dominant or is a member of a set of collectively-dominant rivals—its refusal to help its actual or potential rivals in one or more of the ways Subsection 9A(1)(B) delineated by dealing with them constitutes an exclusionary abuse under now-Article 102.

Now-Article 101 also contains three provisions that favor the conclusion that it prohibits some refusals to deal that U.S. law does not prohibit. All these provisions have counterparts in now-Article 102. The first feature of now-Article 101 that is relevant in this context is its listing as an example of the kind of conduct that prevents, restricts, or distorts competition an agreement between undertakings "to make the conclusion of contracts subject to acceptance by the other parties of supplementary obligations which, by their nature or according to commercial usage, have no connection with the subject of such contracts"—a provision that would "possibly" (see below) be relevant if the drafters and ratifiers of the 2009 Lisbon Treaty or of the 1957 Treaty of Rome considered the prohibitions of dealing in full-requirements contracts and exclusive dealerships to have "no connection with the subject of such contracts." The second provision of now-Article 101 that is relevant in this context is Section 3(b), which states that, even if covered conduct can be shown to increase economic efficiency, it is prohibited by now-Article 101 if it "afford[s]. . .[the] undertakings the possibility of eliminating competition in respect of a substantial part of the product in question." The third feature of now-Article 101 that is relevant in this context is its statement in Section 3 that, even if covered conduct increases economic efficiency and does not violate Section 3(b), it will violate Article 101 if it does not "allow[ ] consumers a fair share of the resulting benefit."

I have two final comments. The first relates to my previous statement that the provisions in now-Articles 101 and 102 condemning the imposition of "supplementary obligations hav[ing] no connection with the subject of such contracts" would *possibly* favor the conclusion that they prohibit the full-requirements clauses in full-requirements contracts and the prohibition-of-dealing clauses in exclusive-dealership contracts. I wrote "possibly" because these provisions of now-Articles 101 and 102 would support this conclusion only if (1) the drafters and ratifiers of the Treaty believed that such clauses impose supplementary obligations "having no connection with the subject of the contracts" and (2) their misunderstanding of the functions and consequences of such contract terms should affect the interpretation and application of the Treaty. I have no idea what the relevant drafters and ratifiers believed about such clauses, but I am extremely reluctant to accept the conclusion that their misunderstandings should affect the interpretation and application of the Treaty that is correct as a matter of law. No matter what these actors thought, as Chap. 14 demonstrates, the relevant restrictions in full-requirements contracts and exclusive dealerships are intimately connected to the functioning of the contracts that impose them. In my judgment, the drafter and/or ratifier intent that is binding is their "abstract" or "conceptual" intent, not their incorrect concretizations of the abstract position they thought they were putting into law. I want to emphasize that my position on this issue does not reflect my considered conclusion that prohibitions of non-predatory full-requirements contracts and exclusive dealerships are undesirable or any disposition on my part as an American to react skeptically to any non-U.S. regulation that differs from its U.S. counterpart.

The second final comment relates to the claim that now-Article 102 was intended to impose a duty on dominant firms to help their actual or potential competitors. I want to point out that the imposition of such a duty on dominant firms might disserve two other goals that now-Article 102 has always been understood to have—(1) benefitting the customers of a perpetrator and the customers of its product-rivals and (2) promoting economic efficiency. Even if the imposition of a duty on dominant firms to help rivals would benefit relevant consumers and increase economic efficiency in the short run, it might injure relevant consumers and decrease economic efficiency overall by deterring firms from making otherwise-profitable QV and cost-reducing investments that would benefit relevant buyers and increase economic efficiency by reducing the profits such investments will yield when they are successful and by inducing currently-dominant or prospectively-dominant firms to divest part of their operations when it would not otherwise be profitable for them to do so because the undivested firm was more organizationally economically efficient than its successor operations would be to avoid being classified as dominant to escape the special duties of a dominant firm.

C. The Way in Which Predatory Refusal-to-Deal Cases Should Be Structured

I will restrict myself to three points. To shorten the exposition, I will assume that the refuser is a seller. First, I would place on the State or private plaintiff the burden of persuading the trier-of-fact that (1) (the sum of the "conventional" marginal or incremental revenue the refused deal would have generated for the refusing seller and any promotional advantages the refusing seller would have obtained by supplying the refused buyer) would have exceeded (the "conventional" marginal or incremental cost the refusing seller would have had to incur to supply the buyer in question *minus* any learning-by-doing cost-savings that the refusing seller would have achieved by supplying the refused buyer), (2) the refusal would tend to increase the refuser's profits by inducing an established rival to exit, deterring a rival from making a new QV investment, or inducing a rival to change the location of an extant or planned QV investment, and (3) the tendency of the refusal to increase the refuser's profits in the above way would critically inflate its profitability in an otherwise-Pareto-perfect economy. Second, I would place on the defendant the duty of persuading the trier-of-fact that (1) the refusal was rendered inherently profitable by the contextual costs, pricing costs, and reputational costs it would have had to incur to engage in the transaction in question and/or by its tendency to enable it to enforce its legal rights, (2) the refusal related to a possible deal with an independent supplier of repair-and-maintenance services for the refuser's durable machine or physical complements of the refuser's basic product and was motivated by the refuser's desire to practice meter pricing on the durable machine or basic product in question, (3) the refusal was motivated by spite, the refuser's principled negative valuation of giving the refused party profits, or the refuser's desire to achieve a more general political goal, or (4) the refusal was mistaken. (Of course, refusers can also prevail by undermining the opposing party's evidence on the issues on which they bear the burden of persuasion.) Third, I would place the burden of production on the defendant in relation to those facts and only those facts that it was better-placed to provide: facts about the defendant's conventional costs and revenues and facts that form the basis of the defenses listed in the second point; because an innocent defendant would be no better-placed than the State or private plaintiff to provide facts about the exit-deterring, new-QV-investment-preventing, or QV-investment-relocating effects of its refusal, I would place the burden of production on those issues on the State or private plaintiff. Although, *ceteris paribus*, it will tend to be economically efficient to require the party that has the duty to produce evidence to pay for its production, the *ceteris* are not always *paribus*, and fairness has a role to play as well: these considerations incline me to shift the cost of production to the State or private plaintiff if the suit fails, certainly if their decision to bring the suit appears *ex post* to have been unwarranted *ex ante*.

D. The U.S. Case-Law, EC Position, and E.C./E.U. Case-Law on Refusals to Deal

(1) The U.S. Case-Law

Because, on my definition, the concept of a "refusal to deal" covers a large number of categories of conduct to which economists and lawyers justifiably give separate designations, to save space, I will report usually briefly on only a small sample of the U.S. cases on the categories of refusals to deal I have distinguished. The case-law on some of these categories of "refusals to deal" will also be discussed in Chap. 14, which analyzes vertical integration and its contractual surrogates. I will begin with some general comments on the case-law and then focus more specifically on the case-law that focuses on (1) "straightforward" refusals to deal and (2) vertical contracts between one party and its customer or supplier that either (A) prohibit the non-arranging party from dealing with an actual or potential rival of the arranger or certain potential customers of the arranger or (B) make it unprofitable for the non-arranger to deal with an actual or potential rival of the arranger.

My first general comment is that U.S. courts have not been consistent in their conclusions about whether refusals to deal in a particular category are *per se* illegal or illegal only if a Rule-of-Reason analysis leads to that conclusion. Thus, as Mr. Justice Brennan stated in his opinion for the Supreme Court in *Northwest Wholesale Stationers*, "[e]xactly what types of activity fall within the forbidden category [of group boycotts] is. . .far from certain."[763]

My second, somewhat-related general comment is that—although the case-law contains many statements that either do imply or have been read to imply that unilateral refusals to deal do not violate the Sherman Act but concerted refusals to deal often do violate the Sherman Act—it also contains (1) statements that recognize that unilateral refusals to deal can violate the Sherman Act[764] and conclusions that particular unilateral refusals to deal do violate the Sherman Act[765] and (2) general statements that concerted refusals to deal can be lawful under the Sherman

---

[763] Northwest Wholesale Stationers v. Pacific Stationery & Printing Co., 472 U.S. 284, 294 (1985), quoting LAWRENCE A. SULLIVAN, THE HANDBOOK OF THE LAW OF ANTITRUST 229–30 (West Pub. Co., 1977): "[T]here is more confusion about the scope and operation of the *per se* rule against group boycotts [*i.e.*, concerted refusals to deal] than in reference to any other aspect of the *per se* doctrine."

[764] Thus, in one of the earliest "refusal to deal cases," the Supreme Court indicated that it agreed with the common-law rule on refusals to deal, which it summarized in the following way: "[i]*n the absence of any purpose to create or maintain a monopoly*," "a seller may exercise its own independent discretion as to parties with whom it will deal" (emphasis added). United States v. Colgate & Co., 250 U.S. 300, 307 (1919).

[765] See, *e.g.*, Aspen Skiing Co. v. Aspen Highlands Skiing Corp., 472 U.S. 585 (1985) and Lorain Journal Co. v. United States, 342 U.S. 143 (1951).

Act[766] and more-specific statements and conclusions that, in specified circumstances, they would be or were lawful under the Sherman Act.[767] I suspect that the confusing character of the U.S. courts' statements on these issues reflects the combination of (1) the judges' intuition that the Sherman Act does not impose a duty on any firm to help its actual rivals survive or expand their QV investments in its area of product-space or to help its potential competitors enter its area of product-space and (2) the judges' discomfort with this conclusion. This ambivalence is most clearly manifest in the so-called essential facilities cases—in particular, in the Supreme Court's refusal to acknowledge that it has ever required a seller that owns a so-called essential facility to give rivals access to it on fair terms when in fact the Supreme Court (in essence) created the doctrine in question and not only followed it but appears to have extended it in two more-recent cases (see below).

My third general comment relates to the U.S. courts' application of their correct conclusion that individual or concerted refusals to deal that are executed to help their participants secure unlawful objectives (or induce unlawful conduct) are illegal while individual or concerted refusals to deal that are executed to help their participants secure lawful objectives (or induce lawful conduct) are legal. In particular, in some cases, U.S. courts have misapplied this rule because they have misjudged the legality of the kinds of behavior that particular refusals to deal were executed to induce. Chapter 14 will analyze in more detail the economic functions and legality of the relevant kinds of behavior—vertical territorial restraints, vertical customer-allocation clauses, and resale price maintenance.

The fourth general comment is that, in some refusal-to-deal cases, U.S. courts have drawn some silly distinctions that are as daft as the distinctions they have drawn in some cases involving contractual surrogates for vertical integration.[768]

---

[766] See, *e.g.*, St. Paul Fire & Marine Insurance Co. v. Barry, 438 U.S. 531, 542 (1978): "concerted refusals to deal are not inherently destructive of competition." See also Northwest Wholesale Stationers, Inc. v. Pacific Stationery & Printing Co., 472 U.S. 284, 295 (1985):

> Wholesale purchasing cooperatives such as Northwest are not a form of concerted activity characteristically likely to result in predominantly anticompetitive effects.... The act of expulsion from a wholesale cooperative does not necessarily imply anticompetitive animus and thereby raise a probability of anticompetitive effect.... Nor would the expulsion characteristically be likely to result in predominantly anticompetitive effects, at least in the type of situation this case presents. Unless the cooperative possesses market power or exclusive access to an element essential to effective competition, the conclusion that expulsion is virtually always likely to have an anticompetitive effect is not warranted.

[767] See Dr. Miles Medical Co. v. John D. Park & Sons, 220 U.S. 373 (1911).

[768] The first of these latter distinctions is the distinction between a manufacturer's contractually controlling the price a distributor may charge for a product it has purchased from the manufacturer (which control was deemed illegal) and a manufacturer's contractually controlling the price a distributor may charge for a product the manufacturer has consigned to it (which contract was deemed lawful). See United States v. Colgate & Co., 250 U.S. 300 (1919) and United States v. General Electric Co., 272 U.S. 476 (1926). The second of these latter distinctions is the distinction between a manufacturer's (1) merely stating its intention not to deal with distributors that charge low prices for its product and ceasing to supply distributors that charged such low

I have in mind the distinction—made by the Supreme Court in *Cement Manufacturers' Protective Association v. United States*[769]—between exchanging information that would help to enable the exchangers to identify buyers that committed contract fraud against them (in the instant case, by soliciting binding bids for the supply of cement to be used for a specified job and accepting more than one bid to use on other jobs as well if the price of cement rose), which the Court deemed lawful by itself, and exchanging such information as part of a scheme in which the exchangers agreed to sanction those that had committed frauds against them by jointly refusing to deal with them (which the Court deemed illegal, though it would not have considered illegal a series of independent [unilateral] decisions by the individual cement manufacturers to boycott the offending buyers).

(A) The U.S. Case-Law on "Straightforward" Refusals to Deal

Two lines of cases deal with what I am calling "straightforward" refusals to deal. The first, primary line analyzes the legality of the conduct in question under conventional Sherman Act doctrine, which makes refuser "intent" the determinant of legality. The second, secondary line of cases analyzes the legality of the refusals to deal of certain types of actors under a so-called essential facilities or bottleneck doctrine in which intent does not play a critical role.

I need to elaborate on the preceding two sentences in two ways. The first elaboration relates to the relevant concept of intent and is anticipated by my enquoting "intent" in the second sentence of the preceding paragraph. Although U.S. courts have (to my mind, correctly as a matter of law) always required what I and they call "a specific intent to destroy competition or build monopoly" for a finding that a defendant has engaged in an "attempt to monopolize," they have insisted that only "general intent," not specific intent, is necessary for a finding that a defendant has violated Section 2 by completing the offense of monopolization.[770] If the courts are defining "general intent" so that a perpetrator is said to have the requisite "general intent" if *ex ante* it assigns a requisite number to the probability that the conduct in question will reduce the absolute attractiveness of the offers against which it will have to compete (and possibly if in addition the perpetrator desires to engage in the conduct on that account as well), I find this "general intent" conclusion incorrect as a matter of law: if *ex ante* the perpetrator believed that its conduct would be profitable even if it would not reduce the absolute attractiveness of the offers against which it would have to compete, the fact that it also believed that its conduct would increase its profits by reducing the absolute attractiveness of the offers against which it would have to compete is irrelevant to its conduct's

---

prices (which was deemed lawful) and (2) warning or threatening non-compliers explicitly (which was deemed illegal). See U.S. v. Parke, Davis & Co., 362 U.S. 29 (1960). 268 U.S. 588 (1929).

[769] 268 U.S. 588 (1929).

[770] See, *e.g.*, Times-Picayune Publishing Co. v. United States, 345 U.S. 594, 626 (1953).

legality under the Sherman Act, regardless of whether the conduct has already succeeded in reducing the absolute attractiveness of the offers against which the perpetrator must compete. With one partial exception, the discussion that follows will ignore this error—*i.e.*, in particular, will assume that the courts are applying the specific-anticompetitive-intent test in all refusal-to-deal cases that they are using an "intent" doctrine to decide (in all monopolization cases as well as in all attempt-to-monopolize cases).

The second elaboration relates to my assertion that there are two lines of "straightforward"-refusal-to-deal cases. In fact, as will be discussed, it is difficult to determine whether some relevant cases were resolved through the application of the "intent" doctrine or the application of the "essential facilities" doctrine.

I will report separately on six functional sub-categories of "straightforward" refusals-to-deal cases, distinguished by the motive of the refuser, that the courts were clearly using the conventional "intent" doctrine to resolve. The first such sub-category contains cases in which the refuser's motive was to reject deals that were inherently unprofitable. U.S. courts have rightly declared such refusals to deal to be lawful, even when the rejected party had a longstanding contractual relationship with the refuser.[771]

The second functional sub-category of "straightforward" refusals to deal are refusals to engage in otherwise-profitable deals to prevent entry or drive out existing rivals. As we shall see, although some of these cases were clearly resolved by the application of the legally-correct specific-anticompetitive-intent doctrine, the court that decided other of these cases seems likely to have been employing some variant of the "essential facilities" doctrine to resolve them without acknowledging this fact in its opinion.

I now want to discuss, in chronological order, seven U.S. cases that the deciding court purported to be resolving by applying the specific-anticompetitive-intent doctrine that involved refusals to deal that either (1) were assumed by the courts to have been motivated by a desire to induce one or more rivals to exit, to deter one or more rival QV investments, or simply to worsen the competitive-position array of one or more rivals or (2) might have been so motivated. The first such case, decided in 1914, is *Eastern Retail Lumber Dealers' Association v. United States*.[772] The Supreme Court's decision prohibited under the Sherman Act an agreement among retail lumber detailers to identify and refuse to deal with lumber wholesalers that also dealt directly with non-distributor buyers on the assumption that the retailers made this decision to deter the entry of the lumber wholesalers into the

---

[771] Thus, in Paschall v. Kansas City Star Co., 727 F.2d 962 (8th Cir. *en banc*), *cert. denied*, 469 U.S. 872 (1985), the Eighth Circuit held that a newspaper did not violate the Sherman Act by ceasing to deal with its independent carriers after concluding that self-delivery would be more profitable, and in Packard Motor Car Co. v. Webster Motor Car Co., 243 F.2d 418 (D.C. Civ. 1957), the D.C. Court of Appeals ruled that Packard did not violate the Sherman Act by terminating the franchise of a longtime Baltimore dealer when it discovered that it would be more profitable to reduce to one the number of dealer-distributors it used in the Baltimore area.

[772] 234 U.S. 600 (1914).

retail lumber-distribution business. If this were the motivation of the retailers or if the boycott had been arranged to deter the wholesalers from defeating a price-fix by the retailers, the conclusion that their agreement violated the Sherman Act was clearly correct.

The second case in this category I want to discuss, decided in 1941, is *Fashion Originators' Guild of American (FOGA) v. Federal Trade Commission.*[773] In *FOGA*, the Supreme Court correctly condemned an agreement among producers of designer clothes to boycott any retailer that sold copies produced by so-called style pirates. The objective of this concerted refusal to deal was obviously to deter such piracy—*i.e.*, to drive one or more style pirates out and deter the entry of new style pirates. Since the members of FOGA did not have intellectual-property rights in their designs and therefore could not justify their boycott as a method of protecting their legal rights, the Court's decision was clearly correct. (Had the designers succeeded in their efforts to obtain IP protection for their designs, their group boycott might well have been lawful—*i.e.*, might well have been a lawful attempt to protect their legal rights. However, the designers had failed to obtain the IP protection they sought.)

The third case that belongs in this category is the 1945 case *Associated Press (AP) v. United States.*[774] In *AP*, the Supreme Court decided that a joint venture of about 1,200 newspapers that was organized primarily to obligate its members to supply each other exclusively and without charge with the stories they wrote and secondarily to write stories itself for publication by its members was lawful in itself but violated the Sherman Act by adopting by-laws that forbade members from selling their stories to non-members and giving each member the power to condition any rival's joining the joint venture on the rival's receiving a majority vote of existing members and paying a hefty fee.

I want to make six points about the Court's legal conclusions in *AP* or the arguments that may have led the Court to reach them. First, the Court's conclusion that the by-law that relates to the entry of new members is illegal would be wrong as a matter of law (if the specific-anticompetitive-intent variant of the "intent" branch of the Sherman Act test of illegality were exclusively correct and/or applicable and the "essential facilities" doctrine were legally incorrect or inapplicable) if AP's members' *ex ante* belief that these rules were profitable reflected their perception that the rules would increase their profits by inducing members to write additional jointly-profitable stories and/or by reducing the transaction costs that members had to incur to prevent members that were their rivals from publishing a version of their stories at the same time that the writer did so and claiming to have discovered the information the stories contained themselves if such "simultaneous publication" by story-writer rivals were forbidden. The Court's failure to recognize this point appears to reflect its failure to recognize the legitimate-private-gain economic-efficiency-related justification for the by-laws that empower members to make it

[773] 312 U.S. 457 (1941)

[774] 344F.3d 229 (2d Cir. 2003), *cert. denied*, 543 U.S. 881 (2004)

more difficult for their rivals to secure membership in AP: if a newspaper knows that it cannot beat one or more of its rivals to the publication of an original story by writing the story itself (because it is obligated to supply any story it writes to all AP members [including the story-writer's rivals] as soon as the story is completed and the rivals are entitled to publish the story immediately as well), the incentives of newspapers to write original stories may be critically deflated. Admittedly, this problem with open membership might be overcome by a rule prohibiting members that are direct rivals of a story-provider from publishing the story for some period of time after the writing newspaper published it. However, this response might not be practicable: it may be too difficult or costly to refute a rival's claim to have discovered and written the story independently.

Second, the by-law provision prohibiting members from supplying their own stories to non-members does probably violate the Sherman Act. It cannot be justified by arguing that it is necessary to prevent members that are not rivals of a story-writer member from reselling the story to a rival story-writer since all cross-sales could be forbidden without prohibiting member story-writers from selling their own stories to non-members. This by-law provision appears to manifest specific anticompetitive intent. Each member agrees not to supply stories to the other members' rivals in exchange for the other members' agreeing not to supply stories to its rivals.

Third, the Court's conclusion that the joint venture itself was lawful might be incorrect. In particular, the AP joint venture would itself be illegal if its members' *ex ante* belief that it was profitable was critically affected by their perception that its by-law prohibiting sales of stories to non-members critically affected its profitability—*i.e.*, if *ex ante* they did not think that the joint venture was rendered *ex ante* profitable by its eliminating the transaction costs its members would otherwise have to incur to buy and sell stories from and to each other (given the by-law provisions that enabled them to prevent the arrangement from deterring them from writing jointly-profitable stories), by the profits they would make by financing journalism by AP itself, and by the profits they would make by building up the reputation of AP and garnering the benefits of being associated with such a highly-reputed organization.

Fourth, it is important to note that, for the AP joint venture itself to violate the Sherman Act, it is not necessary for the arguments that claim it generates various Sherman-Act-licit benefits to be pure shams: even if the licit benefits in question were real, the joint venture would be illegal if *ex ante* the parents did not believe that those licit benefits would have sufficed to render the joint venture profitable, all things considered—*i.e.*, if *ex ante* the parents believed that the joint venture's profitability was critically affected by its by-law prohibiting them to sell their stories to non-members (*i.e.*, to those of each other's rivals that were not members).

Fifth, even if it were true that, all things considered, it would be desirable to require AP (and similar joint ventures) to open up their membership on non-discriminatory terms, that fact would in itself be irrelevant to the legality under the Sherman Act of their not doing so (though it would, of course, be relevant to whether Congress should pass legislation requiring joint ventures like AP to open up their membership).

Sixth and finally, because I think that the membership by-laws of AP were Sherman-Act-licit and doubt that the Court did not understand their legitimating basis, I suspect that the *AP* opinion's conclusion that the membership by-laws were illegal did not manifest its trying to apply but misapplying the Sherman Act's standard specific-anticompetitive-intent test—in particular, suspect that it manifested the Court's subscription to some variant of the "essential facilities" doctrine that is inconsistent with the standard specific-anticompetitive-intent test (though, as I shall point out below, this conclusion is contestable and the *AP* ruling on the membership by-laws may simply reflect the Court's belief that it is authorized to regulate such practices in the public interest or the Court's willingness to usurp power when it believes that its exercise of the power in question would serve the public interest [if one ignores the "cost" of a nation's courts' usurping power]).

The fourth case I want to discuss at this juncture is *Lorain Journal*.[775] In this 1951 case, the Supreme Court found illegal under the Sherman Act a newspaper's refusal to sell advertising space to any buyer that also advertised on a local radio station. Both the Court and commentators have always assumed that Lorain Journal had the specific anticompetitive intent to preserve its monopoly over advertising by driving out the radio station.[776] Although the Court's legal conclusion would clearly be correct if this motivational assumption were accurate, that assumption is, in fact, contestable. If the newspaper believed that (1) the value of newspaper advertising to different possible advertisers varied significantly, (2) it would be prohibitively costly or infeasible to determine the value that particular prospective advertisers placed on advertising space and/or to vary straightforward prices from customer to customer, (3) the buyer surplus that the vast majority of advertisers that advertised both in the newspaper and on the radio obtained on its newspaper-space purchase exceeded the buyer surplus it obtained on its radio-time purchase, and (4) in part for the above reasons, a decision to forbid newspaper advertisers to advertise on the radio would increase the "demand curve" for newspaper advertising—*e.g.*, would enable the newspaper to sell more advertising space at given prices—even if its refusal to deal would not drive the radio station out—indeed, even if its policy increased the demand curve the radio station faced when selling radio advertising time more by inducing some advertisers that would otherwise have divided their advertising between the newspaper and the radio to shift entirely to the radio than it reduced the radio-station's advertising sales by inducing some such advertisers to shift entirely to newspaper advertising (a possible though admittedly-unlikely outcome). I should add that, the Court's and a leading U.S. antitrust-law expert's (Herbert Hovenkamp's) position to the contrary notwithstanding, for the exclusionary account of the boycott to be justified, it is not necessary for the newspaper to have a "dominant position in the market" prior to engaging in its refusal to deal[777]: even if other newspapers were being published, the relevant advertisers may have

---

[775] Lorain Journal Co. v. United States, 342 U.S. 143 (1951)

[776] *Id.* at 149–50.

[777] See HOVENKAMP ANTITRUST at 251.

been obtaining more buyer surplus on their purchases of advertising from the Lorain Journal than they obtained from their purchases of advertising from the radio station. Indeed, there is not much reason to believe that this condition would be less likely to be fulfilled in a "market" in which more than one newspaper was being published.

The fifth opinion that belongs in this category that I want to discuss is the Supreme Court's 1973 opinion in *Otter Tail Power Company v. United States.*[778] In *Otter Tail*, the Supreme Court found that a public utility that was an integrated producer, wholesaler, and retailer of electrical power had violated the Sherman Act "by attempting to prevent communities in which its retail distribution franchise had expired from replacing it with a municipal distribution system" by "refus[ing] to sell power at wholesale to proposed municipal distribution systems where it had been [performing the retail distribution function]...[and] refus[ing] to 'wheel' power to such systems, that is to say to transfer by direct transmission or displacement electric power from one utility to another over the facilities of an intermediate utility."[779] Since, as we have seen, producers or wholesalers (like the Otter Tail Power Company) will find it profitable to retail their product through independents that are better-placed to retail it than they are unless some special conditions are fulfilled, the first question that needs to be addressed is: "Why did the Otter Tail Power Company find it profitable to refuse to deal with municipalities that wanted to engage in retail power distribution?" I doubt that Otter Tails' refusal to deal was rendered profitable by a concern that its loss of the relevant retail-power-distribution jobs would make it less proficient at retail power-distribution over time—*i.e.*, by a concern that its loss of these jobs would in this way enable the relevant municipalities and other customers to extract better terms from Otter Tail than they would otherwise be able to secure. I am certain that Otter Tail's refusal to deal with the municipalities in question was not rendered profitable by any tendency of the municipalities' performance of the retail-power-distribution function to facilitate their entry into the power-production or wholesale power-distribution business (*i.e.*, to make them an effective potential entrant into one or both of those businesses): municipalities do not enter those businesses, and engaging in retail power-distribution would not in any case teach the retailer much about electrical-power production or wholesaling or enable them to learn the identities of or make a good impression on such businesses' buyers. I suspect that Otter Tail found the refusal to deal that *Otter Tail* focused on inherently profitable because the rate regulations under which it operated constrained its wholesale pricing of power more than they constrained its retail pricing of power. If that were the case, Otter Tail might find it more profitable to retail itself all the power it produced or obtained even if its refusal to deal would not affect the number of municipalities that choose to enter the retail power-distribution business. If this last explanation of Otter Tail's

---

[778] 410 U.S. 366 (1973).

[779] The quotation is actually from the District Court opinion in the case. See United States v. Otter Tail Power Co., 331F. Supp. 54, 57–58 (D. Minn. 1971).

conduct is correct, its refusal to deal would not violate the specific-anticompetitive-intent branch of the federal courts' refusal-to-deal doctrine. I also do not think that the Supreme Court's conclusion that Otter Tail Power's refusal to deal violated the Sherman Act can be justified in *Union Leader* "fair fight to the finish" terms: it is not clear that that doctrine applies when the contestants are a municipality that controls the ultimate outcome and a private firm as opposed to two private firms, and, if I am right that Otter Tail Power's refusal to deal with the municipality-retailers reflected the fact that the opportunity cost to Otter Tail Power of selling them power exceeded the highest price they would find profitable to pay Otter Tail Power for power or the highest price Otter Tail Power was allowed to charge for power as a wholesaler, it is not clear that Otter Tail Power's refusal to deal could be characterized as unfair. In any event, although (as I will admit below) sound counterarguments can be made to this conclusion, my view is that the Supreme Court's *Otter Tail* discussion was really based on the "essential facilities" doctrine—*i.e.*, did not manifest the Court's mistaken application of the specific-anticompetitive-intent doctrine.

The sixth opinion that belongs in this category is the Supreme Court's 1985 opinion in *Aspen Skiing Co. v. Aspen Highland Skiing Corp.*[780] *Aspen Skiing* was concerned with the legality under the Sherman Act of seven decisions of the Aspen Skiing Co. (denominated "Ski Co." by the Court), which owned three of the four developed downhill-skiing mountains in or near Aspen, Colorado and accounted for more than 75 % of the ski-run sales in the Aspen (sub)market: Ski Co.'s decision

(1) to offer its one other rival in that area—the owner of the fourth developed ski-mountain in that area, Aspen Highlands Skiing Corp. (denominated "Highlands" by the Court)—participation in a joint-sales arrangement for marketing a 6-day, all-mountain ski-pass at a price below the price of daily tickets on terms that were worse than the terms on which Highlands had formerly participated in this joint-sales arrangement with Ski Co. (in particular, to offer Highlands a share of the total revenue yielded by the ski-pass' sales that was lower than the percentage that ski-pass-buyer uses of Highlands' mountain constituted of their uses of all four mountains);
(2) to discontinue its joint-sales arrangement with Highlands altogether;
(3) to offer a three-mountain ski-pass ticket that permitted use of all three of its facilities;
(4) to refuse to accept the payment-tokens for use of Ski Co. facilities that Highlands provided buyers of the all-mountain, 6-day ski-pass Highlands sold on its own (initially, coupons or vouchers guaranteed by deposits in an Aspen bank, which local merchants were willing to redeem at full value, and then American Express travelers checks and money orders);
(5) to refuse to sell Highlands any tickets for Ski Co.'s lifts either at the tour operator's discount or at retail;

[780] 472 U.S. 585 (1985).

(6) to raise its single-ticket price to a level that precluded Highlands from being able to sell all-mountain ski-passes at a profit; and
(7) to place advertisements for its facilities at the Aspen-skiing destination that left the impression that there were only three skiing mountains (its own) in Aspen.

More precisely, the Supreme Court had to decide whether to reverse the Court of Appeals decision[781] not to overturn the trial court's rejection of Ski Co.'s motion for judgment notwithstanding the verdict after the jury had found Ski Co. guilty of monopolization under Section 2 of the Sherman Act consequent to receiving an instruction that Ski Co.'s refusal to deal "does not violate Section 2 if valid business reasons exist for that refusal." The question for the Court was whether, taken as a whole and viewed in the light most favorable to Highlands, the evidence in the record was sufficient to support the jury's verdict in Highlands' favor on the monopolization charge.

I should say that I find the basic charge to the jury and various elaborations of that charge the trial judge provided far from perfectly informative. In part, my confusion reflects my inability to grasp the court's understanding of the difference between the offense of "monopolization" and the offense of "attempting to monopolize"; in part, my confusion reflects my uncertainty about the meaning of the concept of "a general intent to monopolize" that the court claimed is all a defendant must have for a finding of monopolization to be justified (a "general intent" that differs from the specific anticompetitive intent that the courts agree in general is a necessary condition for a finding that a defendant has attempted to monopolize); and in part, my confusion derives from statements by the trial court and by courts in general that leave the impression that they believe (incorrectly in both cases) (1) that a defendant should not be deemed to have a specific anticompetitive intent if the conduct at issue provided the defendant with some Sherman-Act-licit benefits and (2) that the only benefits that can prevent an inference of specific anticompetitive intent are private benefits that the conduct in question generated because it promoted economic efficiency. However, although the Court of Appeals stated that the Ski Co.'s motion for a directed verdict and motion for a judgment notwithstanding the verdict preserved its right to challenge the instructions the jury received as well as its right to challenge the adequacy of the evidence for its liability under the law as correctly construed, it rejected Ski Co.'s argument that "the verdict cannot be construed as based on a finding that [defendant's] refusal to cooperate was intended, or was motivated by a purpose or desire, to achieve or maintain monopoly power" because the trial court "instructed the jury that no such finding was necessary" on the grounds that (1) "[t]here was no proper or timely objection to the formulation of the intent instruction, as required by Rule 51 [or the Federal Rules of Civil Procedure]" and (2) "[u]nder § 2 general intent is all that is required to support a monopolization claim. . . ."[782] I do not find these responses satisfactory.

[781] Aspen Skiing Co. v. Aspen Highlands Skiing Corp., 738 F.2d 1509 (10th Cir. 1984).
[782] *Id.* at 1521 n. 16, quoting Brief of Defendant-Appellee, Cross-Appellee at 47 n. 34.

The relationship between Rule 51 and the court's earlier statements about the preserving effects of motions for a directed verdict or for judgment notwithstanding the verdict are hard to fathom. And although the court's claim that only general intent is required for a finding of monopolization is undoubtedly correct as a matter of precedent, on the most plausible interpretations of "general intent" and "monopolization," the claim is wrong as a matter of law, correctly construed, and inapplicable to the case in question in that Highlands had not exited and had not been shown to be at risk of failure.

In any event, the Court of Appeals proceeded to assess the sufficiency of the evidence for the jury's verdict under both an "essential facilities" or "bottleneck" doctrine and under an "intent" doctrine that made critical the Ski Co.'s "intent to create or maintain a monopoly" without clarifying whether the intent in question was a specific anticompetitive intent or an expectation that the effect in question would eventuate even if the possibility of its doing so did not critically affect Ski Co.'s *ex ante* perception that its conduct was profitable.[783]

The Supreme Court affirmed the Court of Appeals' judgment on the ground that the evidence in the record construed most favorably in support of Highlands' position was adequate to support the verdict under the intent instructions given by the trial court, indicating at footnote 44 that for this reason the Court found it unnecessary "to consider the possible relevance of the 'essential facilities' doctrine...."[784] The Court's opinion did not shed any clarifying light on the difference between "general intent" and "specific anticompetitive intent," the difference between "monopolization" and "an attempt to monopolize," or the reason why only "general intent" must be established to prevail in a monopolization case while specific anticompetitive intent must be established in an "attempt to monopolize" case.

More specifically, the Court

(1) seemed to think that the fact that Ski Co. had decided to change its conduct in relation to Highlands was suspicious,
(2) stated that, although the Ski Co. advertising that left the impression that Aspen had only three skiing mountains (its own) would not in itself sustain a finding of illegality, it was "consistent with" (supported?) such a finding,
(3) did not comment on Ski Co.'s decision to charge high prices for single-day tickets for its facilities,
(4) implied that Ski Co.'s sale of a three-mountain 6-day ticket priced below the total price of daily tickets manifested a "deliberate effort to discourage its customers from doing business with" Highlands,
(5) stated that Ski Co.'s refusal to accept Highlands' coupons as payment for daily tickets "supports the inference that Ski Co. . . .was willing to sacrifice short-run benefits and consumer goodwill in exchange for a perceived long-run impact on

[783] *Id.* at 1520–22.

[784] Aspen Skiing Co. v. Aspen Highlands Skiing Corp. 472 U.S. 585, 611 and at n. 44.

its smaller rival" Highlands, given that the coupons were "no more burdensome than the credit cards accepted at Ski Co. ticket windows"—*i.e.*, were not "administratively cumbersome"—and that Ski Co. accepted coupons in other areas in which it and rivals sold interchangeable lift tickets,

(6) rejected the claim that Ski Co.'s refusal to deal with Highlands was motivated by Ski Co.'s desire to dissociate itself from what it considered to be Highlands' inferior services on the grounds that (A) the claim of Highlands' inferiority was supported by "little more than vague insinuations. . .[that were] sharply contested by various witnesses," (B) the fact that Ski Co. was willing to associate with what it considered to be inferior products elsewhere (a persuasive point), and (C) the fact that consumers could make up their own minds on matters of quality (a largely-irrelevant point),

(7) rejected the claim that the original arrangement in which revenues were shared based on usage was rendered impracticable by the difficulty of monitoring usage, and

(8) ignored Ski Co.'s argument that it wanted to stop co-marketing four-mountain passes with Highlands because it feared that its participation in such an arrangement might cause it legal difficulties—a claim that Ski Co. bolstered by pointing out that in 1975 the Colorado Attorney General had filed a complaint against Ski Co. and Highlands alleging that their negotiations about the four-mountain ticket provided them with the opportunity to engage in price-fixing (a complaint that resulted in a consent decree that permitted them to continue to offer their four-mountain ticket if they announced their own prices unilaterally before negotiating the cooperative-marketing deal).[785]

To be honest, I do not know what to make of the Supreme Court's *Aspen Skiing* opinion. Ski Co.'s conduct may well have been predatory, and, more to the point, the evidence on the record may well have been more than adequate to support a jury verdict that it was predatory. Still, the trial-court judge's instructions to the jury were far from clear and may have permitted the jury to base its verdict on a conclusion that Ski Co. owned an essential facility that it had a duty to share with its smaller rival. (I agree with the Court of Appeals that, for "essential facilities" doctrine purposes, the fact that the essential facility was horizontally rather than vertically related to the refused party's business is irrelevant.) The fact that the Supreme Court did not address the various ambiguities in the trial court's "intent" instruction, the fact that the Supreme Court's opinion makes reference to the fact that "[t]he development of any major additional facilities is hindered by practical considerations and regulatory obstacles,"[786] and the fact that the Supreme Court's opinion states that the legality of Ski Co.'s conduct depends not only on its impact on Highlands but also on "its impact on consumers"[787] all favor the conclusion

---

[785] *Id.* at 591 n. 9. For the early members of this list, see *id.* at 604–07.

[786] *Id.* at 588 and n. 6.

[787] *Id.* at 605.

that—despite note 44 and the fact that Ski Co.'s conduct had not caused Highlands to exit and had not been shown to create a significant risk that Highlands will exit—this opinion may manifest the 1985 Court's subscription to some variant of the "essential facilities" doctrine.

The seventh and final case I want to consider at this juncture is the 2003 case *United States v. Visa U.S.A., Inc.*[788] *Visa U.S.A.* focused on the conduct of an "open" joint venture formed by approximately 1,000 banks to increase the profits they could make by selling (issuing) general-purpose credit cards to their customers and "acquiring" card-paid transactions of merchants ("open" in the sense that there is no limit to the number of banks that can join as issuers and/or acquirers). The Second Circuit affirmed the trial court's conclusion that, although the joint venture was itself lawful, its by-law provision restricting members to issuing Visa cards and MasterCard cards and "acquiring" Visa-card and MasterCard-card transactions violated Section 1 of the Sherman Act by excluding American Express and Discover from a segment of the market for network services.

I will first analyze the legality under the Sherman Act of the joint venture and the by-law that restricts the members of the joint venture to patronizing Visa and MasterCard, ignoring the fact that MasterCard and Visa U.S.A. are non-profit organizations, and then consider the possible relevance of this fact.

The first step in any analysis of the legality of the joint venture itself under the Sherman Act is to list the various functions that the joint venture in question could be performing. Since the joint venture may be able to obtain more attractive terms from credit-card-network companies such as Visa U.S.A. and MasterCard to the extent that its substitution for its parents benefits the credit-card-network companies it patronizes, the following list of functions includes functions the joint venture performs for the credit-card-network companies it patronizes as well as functions it performs directly for the joint venture's parents:

(1) reducing the mechanical transaction costs that the parent-banks and the credit-card-network companies with which they deal must incur to transact business with each other by enabling them to take advantage of transaction-cost-related economies of scale,
(2) enabling the credit-card-network companies to avoid incurring the searching-for-customer costs, advertising costs, and other kinds of sales-effort costs they would otherwise have had to incur to make the sales they made to the joint venture,
(3) reducing the risk costs that the patronized credit-card-network companies incur because they do not know how many sales they will make (when the joint venture will concentrate its purchases more than its parents would have done and the risk-cost-related benefits that any amount of assured sales will yield a credit-card-network company increases more than proportionately with the amount of sales that are assured),

[788] 344 F.3d 229 (2d Cir. 2003), on appeal from 163 F. Supp. 2d 332 (2003)

(4) creating a joint-venture buyer that has more bargaining power than the sum of the bargaining power that its parents had when acting separately, and
(5) enabling the parents of the joint venture to avoid being tyrannized by their small decisions into accepting payments for agreeing to patronize only one or a small number of specified credit-card-network companies when their doing so would be against their collective interest given the price-concessions they could have individually obtained for restricting themselves in this way because their acceptance of these restrictions would or might induce the exit of one or more non-patronized credit-card-network companies that would not be immediately replaced by an equally-effective competitor and/or would or might critically raise the barriers to QV investment confronting an otherwise-effective potential QV investor in the credit-card-network business.

If, *ex ante*, the joint venture's parents believed that its *ex ante* profitability would be secured by its ability to perform one or more of the first three functions in the preceding list, the joint venture would clearly be lawful under the Sherman Act. I should add that the fact that the banks did not agree to restrict themselves to dealing with only one credit-card-network company is perfectly compatible with the preceding condition's being fulfilled: the fact that the banks found that the benefits they could obtain by giving their customers the option of choosing between two credit cards or choosing to take out both credit cards through the bank exceeds the cost such an arrangement generates by reducing the scale of the joint venture's transactions with each of the credit-card-network companies with which its parents can deal is perfectly compatible with the joint venture's profitability's being secured by the three benefits it generated by executing transactions with Visa and MasterCard that are still larger than the transactions that the individual parents would have executed with them.

If *ex ante* the joint venture's parents believed that its *ex ante* profitability was critically affected by its creating a joint-buyer that had more buying power than the sum of any buying power the parents had when acting separately, the legality of the joint venture under the Sherman Act would depend on whether the Sherman Act should be interpreted (as I believe it should be) to permit buyer price-fixing and (by implication) any joint venture or merger or acquisition whose participant-perceived *ex ante* profitability was critically affected by the participants' beliefs that it would or might enhance their buying power as opposed to being interpreted (as a literal reading of its text suggests it should be and the U.S. courts, the U.S. antitrust-enforcement agencies, and many distinguished scholars claim it should be) to prohibit buyer price-fixing and (by implication) any joint venture or merger or acquisition whose participant-perceived *ex ante* profitability was critically affected by the participants' beliefs that it would or might enhance their buying power.

If, *ex ante*, the joint venture's parents believed that its *ex ante* profitability was critically affected by the price-reductions the joint venture would secure because their agreement to restrict themselves to issuing Visa and MasterCard credit cards and "acquiring" Visa-card or MasterCard-card transactions would or might reduce the absolute attractiveness of the offers against which the Visa and MasterCard networks would have to compete by driving out an established competitor of Visa and MasterCard that would not be immediately replaced by an equally-effective competitor and/or by critically raising the barriers to QV investment facing an otherwise-effective rival potential QV investor in the credit-card-network area of product-space, the legality of the joint venture under the Sherman Act would depend on (1) whether the lower-QV-investment equilibrium that the joint venture's Visa and MasterCard generated was in the joint interest of all credit-card-network companies and all their customers (would be economically efficient in an otherwise-Pareto-perfect economy) and (2) whether, if it were, that fact would render the restrictions on the members of the joint venture lawful under the Sherman Act. I have no doubt that the first of these conditions will sometimes be fulfilled—that the decrease in the number of credit-card-network brands and/or "models" that might be generated by the kind of refusals to deal at issue in *Visa U.S.A.* will sometimes increase economic efficiency and on that account be in the net equivalent-dollar interest of the credit-card-network companies and their customers. Moreover, I believe that the "*ceteris paribus* critically inflated" part of the test of illegality the Sherman Act promulgates implies that, if this effort by Visa and MasterCard to reduce the amount of QV investment in the credit-card-network business would increase economic efficiency by creating something like an economically-efficient natural duopoly, that fact would render the conduct in question lawful under the Sherman Act. I acknowledge that I am discomfited with this conclusion—that I feel some sympathy for the conclusion that natural-duopoly or natural-monopoly arguments are relevant for the Congress but not for the courts.

So far, I have implicitly ignored the fact that both the Visa U.S.A. card-network and the MasterCard card-network are non-profit organizations. I do not think that any of the preceding conclusions need to be altered to reflect the fact that the networks in question are non-profit organizations. The fact that these card-network companies are non-profits does not alter (1) their interest in making arrangements of this kind that increase their profits or (2) the fact that they will share with the banks the joint gains these arrangements generate for themselves and the banks.

The District Court that ruled on this case found the restriction the joint venture at issue imposed on its members illegal on the ground that (1) it harmed competition in the market for network services by excluding American Express, Discovery, and presumably other potential network creators from a significant segment of the relevant market and (2) those costs were not outweighed by the "procompetitive effects" the exclusionary rules generated "by promoting 'cohesion' within the MasterCard and Visa U.S.A. networks." The Court of Appeals affirmed on the ground that the District Court's finding was "reasonable." I do not understand the meaning of "cohesion" in the current context. In any event, I think that the courts in question applied the wrong decision-rule in this case: if *ex ante* the joint venture's participants believed that the *ex ante* profitability of both the joint venture itself and the restrictions its by-laws imposed on the credit-card networks its members could patronize was assured by the prospect of their performing Sherman-Act-licit functions (some of which may not be economic-efficiency-related), the joint venture and the restrictions would be lawful under the Sherman Act even if they also increased the members' profits by reducing the absolute attractiveness of the offers against which the Visa U.S.A. and MasterCard networks had to compete. (I should add that the fact that the restrictions may have generated economic-efficiency gains related to the first three private gains in the preceding list of functions may imply that they would survive a Clayton Act challenge [had the case been brought under Section 3 of the Clayton Act] even if they did impose a net equivalent-dollar loss on Clayton-Act-relevant buyers by driving rivals of Visa U.S.A. and MasterCard out or preventing the entry of other credit-card networks because in those circumstances the perpetrators could establish an organizational-economic-efficiency defense for their conduct.)

The third functional category of refusals-to-deal cases whose legality U.S. courts have analyzed by applying an "intent" doctrine are refusals to deal designed to effectuate or implement a price-fix or non-price-term fix. As already indicated, the Supreme Court's conclusion that the boycott that was at issue in *Eastern Retail Lumber Dealer's Association* may have reflected its belief that the defendant retailers' boycott of wholesalers that also sold at retail was designed to prevent the wholesalers in question from defeating the retailers' price-fix by integrating forward into retail (though I must admit that I have doubts that retail lumber distributors were capable of fixing prices successfully). In other cases, U.S. courts have made clear that their conclusion that the concerted refusals to deal at issue violated the Sherman Act was based on a finding that the boycotts were executed to help their participants execute a horizontal fix of price or non-price terms. Thus, in *Federal Trade Commission v. Superior Court Trial Lawyers Association,*[789] the Supreme Court found illegal a collective decision by trial lawyers not to represent indigent defendants in order to increase the state-paid compensation the lawyers would receive for providing such representation. Relatedly, in *Paramount Famous Lasky v. United States,*[790] a U.S. court condemned the efforts of film distributors to induce their film-exhibitor customers to consent to the use of a particular type of commercial dispute-resolution process by agreeing not to deal with any buyer that did not grant its consent.

A fourth functional category of refusals to deal that U.S. courts have used standard intent doctrine to analyze are refusals to deal that the refusers engage in to secure their legal rights. In my judgment, such refusals to deal are lawful under the Sherman Act if the refuser believes (the refusers believe) *ex ante* that it (they) really had the legal entitlement in question and do not violate the Sherman Act in any event unless the refuser's (refusers') *ex ante* perception that the refusals are profitable was critically affected by its (their) belief that they would or might drive a rival out, deter a new QV investment, or induce a relevant change in the location of an extant or planned QV investment. The U.S. courts' performance in these cases has been uneven. As we saw, *FOGA* correctly condemned a group refusal to deal that would have been a lawful means of enforcing a legal right had the boycotters

---

[789] 493 U.S. 411 (1990).

[790] 282 U.S. 30 (1930).

not known *ex ante* that they did not, in fact, have the legal right in question—*viz.*, the right that their clothing designs not be pirated. Another Supreme Court decision incorrectly declared *per se* illegal under the Sherman Act the efforts of several Los Angeles automobile dealers to induce General Motors to pressure dealers to stop reselling its cars to discounters by threatening to stop supplying them.[791] This decision reflected the Court's failure to see that (for reasons that Chap. 14 will explain) GM had a legal right to adopt and enforce a resale-price-maintenance policy and that the dealers had the right to pressure GM to enforce the policy in question. I should add that this case is perfectly consistent with an earlier Supreme Court decision in which the Court incorrectly ruled that a decision by a retailer (with alleged monopsonistic power) to induce a manufacturer to stop supplying a rival in order to drive it out would be *per se* illegal if the relevant facts could be established in circumstances in which, in all likelihood, both the retailer's request and the manufacturer's decision to discontinue supplying the retailer's rival reflected their desire to enforce a resale-price-maintenance policy that the refused retailer was violating.[792] Because by the time in question the courts had come to acknowledge that vertical territorial restraints did not always violate the Sherman Act, other cases have ruled that the Sherman Act legality of decisions to terminate relationships with dealers that have violated such restraints should be analyzed under the Rule of Reason[793]: since, as Chap. 14 will demonstrate, such restraints virtually never violate the Sherman Act (or the Clayton Act), any associated refusals to deal should almost never be deemed to violate the Sherman Act either. Still other cases in this category have, to my mind, incorrectly condemned under the Sherman Act an agreement by movie distributors not to supply new owners of existing theaters until the new owners have agreed to fulfill the contractual obligations they assumed from their theater's previous owners[794] and an attempt by a business to induce the potential suppliers of a rival not to deal with it because the rival had obtained information from a former manager of the defendant to which the defendant thought it had a proprietary right.[795]

The fifth functional category of refusals to deal are refusals to deal designed to protect the reputation or goodwill of the refuser. I have already suggested the possibility that the Aspen Skiing Company's refusal to deal with Aspen Highland Skiing Corporation may have reflected, at least in part, its desire not to have its reputation for supplying a high-quality product damaged by association with the supplier of an inferior product. In 1961, in *Molinas v. National Basketball*

[791] United States v. General Motors Corp., 384 U.S. 127 (1966).

[792] See Klor's, Inc. v. Broadway-Hale Stores, Inc., 359 U.S. 207 (1959). As I will indicate in the text that follows, the request of the large retailer that asked the manufacturer to stop supplying its rival in *Klor's* is often assumed to have been motivated by spite.

[793] See Business Electronics Corp. v. Sharp Electronics Corp., 485 U.S. 717 (1988) and Monsanto Co. v. Spray-Rite Service Corp., 465 U.S. 752 (1984).

[794] United States v. First National Pictures, 282 U.S. 44 (1930).

[795] Copperweld Corp. v. Independence Tube Corp., 467 U.S. 752 (1984).

Association,[796] a U.S. District Court ruled *inter alia* that the NBA's decision to protect its reputation for supplying non-fixed basketball games by issuing a lifetime suspension against a plaintiff who had placed bets in favor of a professional team for which he was playing was not a Sherman Act violation even though he had been given neither notice nor a hearing prior to the suspension. Two years later, in *Silver v. New York Stock Exchange*,[797] the Supreme Court implicitly upheld the right of the New York Stock Exchange to maintain its reputation by excluding a broker who had (presumably) behaved improperly from telephone access to the Exchange in a decision that declared *per se* illegal failures of the Exchange to provide due process to those against whom it exercised this power. (In the instant case, the Exchange had not even told Silver why he was being excluded.[798]) I hasten to add that, unless the Exchange's members' *ex ante* perception that they would profit from the Exchange's not providing procedural protections to members when deciding whether to exclude them from participating in the Exchange was critically affected by these members' belief that this decision would or might reduce the absolute attractiveness of the offers against which they would have to compete, the Exchange's failure to provide such procedural protections would not violate the Sherman Act.

The sixth and final functional category of refusals to deal that have been handled through the application of an intent doctrine are refusals to deal that are engaged in for non-profit reasons—out of spite or to secure various political objectives for non-financial reasons. Although the conduct at issue in *Klor's* is often described as an attempt by a defendant to induce a supplier to boycott the plaintiff out of spite, the court in that case never addressed this possibility, and other explanations seem more convincing. As I indicated earlier, there is some reason to believe that the refused retailer was targeted because it was violating the manufacturer's resale-price-maintenance policy and, even if this were not the case, the fact that the market was unconcentrated and the plaintiff was small is perfectly consistent with the defendant's having a profit incentive to drive it out unrelated to resale price maintenance in that the plaintiff may have been more competitive with the defendant than with other rivals and may have been likely to be replaced by someone less competitive with the defendant. The main case dealing with politically-motivated

---

[796] 190 F. Supp. 249 (1961).

[797] 373 U.S. 341 (1963).

[798] In a subsequent decision, the Court indicated that the *per se* character of its approach in *Silver* reflected the fact that the Exchange had "a dominant position in securities trading markets" and the fact that the Exchange had been given a statutory power of self-regulation. See Northwest Wholesale Stationers, Inc. v. Pacific Stationary & Printing Co., 472 U.S. 284 (1985). In *Northwest Wholesale Stationers*, the Court held that even an unexplained expulsion of a member from the type of association involved in that case would be evaluated through the Rule of Reason if the association that had expelled the member had no market power. Regardless of the desirability of requiring due process in such contexts, I find it difficult to justify the conclusion that antitrust law requires this outcome.

boycotts—a 1980 Court of Appeals case—held quite correctly that the Sherman Act does not prohibit refusals to deal that are politically motivated.[799]

Section 10 of this chapter addresses the U.S. case-law on refusals by a manufacturer to deal with independent suppliers of maintenance-and-repair services that are motivated by the manufacturer's lawful desire to prevent its customers from buying from others complements of its product.

The preceding discussion of the U.S. courts' handling of "refusal to deal" cases focused on their application to such cases of the "intent" doctrine or doctrines they use to resolve monopolization or "attempt to monopolize" cases in general. U.S. courts also sometimes have used another doctrine—the "essential facilities" or "bottleneck" doctrine—to resolve "refusal to deal" cases. Although as I indicated earlier the Supreme Court explicitly stated that its affirmance of the Court of Appeals decision in *Aspen Skiing* was not based on the "essential facilities" doctrine (on which the Court of Appeals had partially but not critically relied) and although in 2004 the Court declared that it had "never recognized" the "essential facilities" doctrine crafted by lower courts,[800] the Supreme Court actually originated the doctrine in 1912 and has made at least one and perhaps as many as three more-recent decisions that may best be accounted for by the Court's subscription to the doctrine. In any event, the lower federal courts have based a host of decisions on the doctrine.

I will now delineate the doctrine, discuss the case in which the Supreme Court first used it, indicate why I believe that the Court's decisions in some more-recent cases were actually based on some variant of the doctrine, and finally describe the lower federal courts' use of the doctrine. I should say at the outset that the "essential facilities" doctrine has never been given a definitive formulation. As actually employed, the doctrine asserts that the Sherman Act imposes a legal obligation on at least *some actors* that own an *essential facility to make it available* to rivals. Proponents of or commentators on this "essential facilities" doctrine disagree about the denotation of all three italicized expressions in the preceding sentence. Some but not all think that the only actors that have a duty to make an essential facility available to their rivals are joint venturers (as opposed to individual monopolists), monopolists, owners that have received government subsidies, and/or public utilities. I see no basis for interpreting the Sherman Act to impose an obligation on firms to provide their rivals on reasonable or "non-discriminatory" terms with access to a valuable asset the firms have created or purchased or to supply to their rivals on reasonable or non-discriminatory terms valuable services the firms have learned to supply proficiently when the potential suppliers' ownership of the asset or ability to supply the service proficiently resulted from their participation in a joint venture as opposed to resulting from actions the firm took on its own or from the firm's participation in a different kind of cooperative arrangement or in a merger

---

[799] See Missouri v. National Organization for Women, Inc., 620 F.2d 1301 (8th Cir. 1980), *cert. denied*, 449 U.S. 842 (1980).

[800] See Verizon Communications, Inc. v. Law Offices of Curtis V. Trinko, LLP, 540 U.S. 398, 411 (2004).

or acquisition. I also see no basis for concluding that the Sherman Act imposes such a "sharing obligation" on firms that have market or monopoly power or on firms that have received government subsidies. Although I recognize that the common law imposes on public utilities a general duty to serve, that fact does not imply that the Sherman Act imposes such a duty on regulated public utilities—a legal conclusion that is salient *inter alia* because the Sherman Act entitles victims of violations to treble damages and because federal courts have jurisdiction over Sherman Act suits but not over most violation-of-the-duty-to-serve public-utility suits. Some but not all proponents and commentators think that, for a facility to be "essential" in the doctrinal sense, access to it must be essential to the attractiveness or feasibility of entry or the survival of an extant QV investment—*i.e.*, the plaintiff must not be able (1) to enter or survive without it or an equivalent, (2) to obtain it from someone else at non-prohibitive cost, or (3) to create it itself at non-prohibitive cost. Finally, some but not all proponents and commentators think that the doctrine permits the owner of a facility to charge buyers the highest price they would be willing to pay for it, while others believe that the doctrine requires each affected owner to charge non-owners a "non-discriminatory price" (*i.e.*, a price equal to the "cost" the owner had to incur to create or obtain the facility in question) or a reasonable or fair price. Finally, some but not all proponents of and commentators on the essential-facilities doctrine believe that the doctrine precludes owners of an essential facility from denying others access to it only if their refusal to deal was "anticompetitively motivated" in some (regrettably) undefined sense of that expression—a version of the doctrine that would render it otiose if "anticompetitive" were defined in the way that I think is appropriate in the Sherman Act context.

The "essential facilities" doctrine was first promulgated by the Supreme Court in 1912 in *United States v. Terminal Railroad Association of St. Louis*.[801] The Terminal Railroad Association of St. Louis was a joint venture formed by several railroad companies, bridge operators, and freight-transfer companies that owned the only two bridges that crossed the Mississippi River at St. Louis, the only ferry-service across the river at St. Louis, and every terminal connecting the bridges and ferry to railroads terminating on either side of the river. The Supreme Court concluded that the joint-venture parents' decision to combine the assets assigned to the joint venture did not violate the Sherman Act because it yielded various economic efficiencies. However, it also concluded that, given the fact that the facilities of the joint venture were the only reasonable means of entering (actually, also of leaving) the city and the fact that the terminal company was "not an independent corporation at all" (why this fact should be of any significance much less "of the utmost significance" is never explained), one feature of the by-laws of the joint venture and various decisions the joint venture made under them did violate the Sherman Act. The offending feature of the by-laws was the provision requiring unanimous consent of all members of the association for any non-member to be allowed to join it or use its facilities. The offending decisions were pricing

[801] 224 U.S. 383 (1912).

decisions that imposed discriminatory burdens on short-haul traffic and on certain non-member railroads and merchants. The Court remanded the case with instructions to the lower court either to dissolve the association or to secure the agreement of its members to admit any existing or future non-member on "just and reasonable terms" and to give non-members access to its facilities on such terms as well—*i.e.*, either to dissolve the association or to secure the agreement of the joint venture to act as a "bona fide agent and servant of every railroad line which shall use its facilities." As I have already indicated, although I might well favor legislation requiring the kind of joint venture or collaborative arrangement Terminal Railroad constitutes to conform to the *Terminal Railroad* remedy, I do not think that the *Terminal Railroad* decision is correct as a matter of law. However, for present purposes, the relevant fact is that, the Court's claim to the contrary in *Trinko* notwithstanding, in *Terminal Railroad* it did far more than endorse the "essential facilities" doctrine: in essence, it created it.

Although the Supreme Court has never explicitly invoked the "essential facilities" or "bottleneck" doctrine it created in *Terminal Railroad* to explain or justify any later decision it made, the Court's decisions in *AP*, *Otter Tail*, and perhaps *Aspen Skiing* may best be accounted for in "essential facilities"-doctrine terms. I acknowledge that in none of these cases was there evidence establishing that the refused party's survival was endangered by the refusal to deal that was at issue: no argument was made in *AP* that newspapers could not survive if they were not members of AP; several of the municipalities to which Otter Tail Power refused to supply power obtained power from other sources; and although Highlands' profits were reduced by the Ski Co.'s refusal to deal with it, no evidence suggested that Highlands' survival was put at risk by that refusal to deal. Still the conclusion that the Court's *AP* and *Otter Tail* decisions reflected its belief that joint ventures or firms that were in AP's and Otter Tail Power's positions do have a duty to cooperate with rivals is favored by the fact that its decisions against AP and Otter Tail Power could not be justified on any intent-doctrine basis, and the conclusion that the Court's *Aspen Skiing* decision reflected its subscription to some variant of the "essential facilities" doctrine (its statement to the contrary notwithstanding) is favored (though admittedly much less strongly) by the facts that (1) the Court tried to justify the conclusion that Ski Co. had acted illegally by pointing out that its conduct was against the interest of consumers (which is not in itself relevant to conduct's illegality under the Sherman Act), (2) the Court made statements that imply (incorrectly as a matter of law) that the only kind of justification that Ski Co. could offer for its conduct that would tend to legitimate it under the Sherman Act would be a demonstration that the conduct yielded the Ski Co. private benefits by generating increases in economic efficiency, (3) partially relatedly, the Court failed to take account of the possibility that Ski Co. may have wanted to terminate its cooperation with Highlands to avoid legal problems (to avoid creating a risk that it might be prosecuted for price-fixing with Highlands), (4) the Court pointed out that physical conditions and government regulations either precluded or made it difficult for Highlands or anyone else to create facilities that would replace Ski Co.'s withdrawn facilities, and (5) (perhaps least persuasively) the Court failed to address the confusing character of the trial court's instructions to the jury (which were confusing in part because of deficiencies in the Court's own "intent" doctrines and in part because of uncertainties about the substantive content and legal status of the "essential facilities" doctrine).

The "essential facilities" doctrine has been applied by a large number of lower federal courts, though far from all "essential facilities" claims have been upheld.[802] Limitations of space preclude me from discussing this case-law in any detail here.

(B) The U.S. Case-Law on Refusals to Deal Secured Through Provisions in Contracts Between Sellers and Buyers, Employers and Employees, and Partners

(i) Long-Term Full-Requirements Contracts

The leading U.S. case on long-term full-requirements contracts is *Tampa Electric Co. v. Nashville Coal Co.*[803] *Tampa Electric* addressed the legality under Section 3 of the Clayton Act of a contract in which an electricity-generating company agreed to purchase from a particular coal-supplier its full requirements of fuel for two new coal-fueled-generator units for 20 years. The contract also stipulated a price formula and a minimum amount of coal that the buyer must purchase in each year. Another provision stated that Tampa Electric would be bound to purchase from Nashville Coal its full requirements of coal for any additional coal-fueled units it constructed during the first 10 years of the contract's duration on the terms the contract stated. The Supreme Court overturned rulings by the District Court and Court of Appeals that the contract violated the Clayton Act, replacing its own previous "quantitative substantiality" test of illegality (it was estimated that Tampa Electric would buy $128,000,000 of coal under the contract) with what came to be called a "qualitative substantiality" test. The Court noted the various ways in which such long-term requirements contracts could increase economic efficiency—*i.e.*, that it would reduce risk for both parties and decrease selling expenses, declared that "a mere showing that the contract itself involves a substantial number of dollars is ordinarily of little consequence,"[804] stated that the critical question was whether "the opportunities for other traders to enter into or remain in. . .[the relevant] market..[was] significantly limited,"[805] and found that the sales covered by the

[802] See, *e.g.*, Florida Fuels, Inc. v. Krueder Oil Co., 717 F. Supp. 1528 (S.D. Fla. 1989); Consolidated Gas Co. of Fla. v. City Gas Co. of Fla., 665 F. Supp. 1493 (S.D. Fla. 1987); Fishman v. Wirtz, 807 F.2d 520 (7th Cir. 1986); U.S. Football League v. National Football League, 1986–2 Trade Cas. 67218 (S.D.N.Y. 1986); MCI Commun. Corp. v. AT&T, 708 F.2d 1081 (7th Cir. 1983), cert. denied, 464 U.S. 891 (1983); United States v. AT&T, 552 F. Supp. 131 (D.D.C. 1982), aff'd mem. Sub nom.; Maryland v. United States, 460 U.S. 1001 (1983); and Hecht v. Pro-Football, Inc., 570 F.2d 982 (D.C. Cir. 1977), cert. denied 436 U.S. 956 (1978). But see Interface Group v. Massachusetts Port Auth., 816 F.2d 9 (1st Cir. 1987) and Garshman v. Universal Resources Holding, Inc., 824 F.2d 223 (3d Cir. 1987).

[803] 365 U.S. 320 (1961).

[804] *Id.* at 329.

[805] *Id.* at 328.

contract constituted too small a percentage (9.77 %) of the relevant sales made in the relevant market (which encompassed not just Florida and Georgia but parts of Pennsylvania, Virginia, West Virginia, Tennessee, Alabama, Ohio, and Illinois) for the contract to violate Clayton Act Section 3. *Tampa Electric's* conclusion was right, though it is important to emphasize that the critical fact is not the percentage of "market" sales that is locked in but whether enough sales of the right kind are left unlocked-in to permit the survival or profitable entry of alleged targets.

(ii) Long-Term Exclusive Dealerships

Two initial points. First, from an economic perspective, there is no good reason to distinguish the analysis of long-term full-requirements contracts from long-term exclusive dealerships. Second, the concern is with *long-term* full-requirements contracts and *long-term* exclusive dealerships because, as the U.S. case-law recognizes,[806] individual short-term arrangements of these sorts (as opposed to a series of consecutive short-term arrangements negotiated in advance that cover a long period of time) cannot exclude.

As the discussion of long-term full-requirements contracts indicated, the first canonical U.S. Supreme Court decision on long-term exclusive dealerships (*Standard Stations*[807]) was at least read to promulgate a "quantitative substantiality" test of illegality. *Standard Stations* found that the Standard Oil Company's assignment of exclusive dealerships to retailers of its gasoline and various accessories violated Section 3 of the Clayton Act. The standard reading of *Standard Stations—i.e.*, the claim that it promulgated a "quantitative substantiality" test of illegality—is based on the fact that the case found illegal the defendant's "foreclosing" 7 % of the relevant market by arranging exclusive dealerships. However, this account ignores the fact that the Court was also influenced by its conclusion that, taken together, the exclusive-dealership arrangements of all major refusers foreclosed about 65 % of the relevant market. The opinion did recognize the salience of such issues as whether the effect of the exclusive dealerships "has been to enable the established suppliers individually to maintain their own standing and at the same time collectively, even though not collusively, to prevent a late arrival from wresting away more than an insignificant portion of the market."[808] Still, because the opinion's conclusion that exclusive dealerships would be sufficiently likely to lessen competition to violate the Clayton Act when they "foreclosed" "competition...in a substantial share of the line of commerce affected"[809] did not focus on the percentage of dealers in that market that would have to distribute the product of a new

---

[806] See, *e.g.*, Omega Environmental, Inc. v. Gilbarco, Inc. 127 F.3d 1157 (9th Cir. 1997) and Paddock Publications, Inc. v. Chicago Tribune Co., 103 F.3d 42 (7th Cir. 1996).

[807] Standard Oil Co. v. United States (Standard Stations), 337 U.S. 293 (1949).

[808] *Id.* at 309.

[809] *Id.* at 314.

entrant or non-major established firm for such a firm to be financially viable, it is fair to characterize its test of illegality to be quantitative as opposed to qualitative.

In any event, as the preceding subsection indicated, in 1961, the Supreme Court replaced *Standard Station*'s "quantitative substantiality" test of illegality with *Tampa Electric*'s "qualitative substantiality" test. Although I am not entirely satisfied with the way in which U.S. courts have analyzed whether the long-term dealerships or full-requirements contracts that have been the focus of particular cases will lessen competition in the Clayton Act sense or are predatory (*inter alia*, whether they will induce exits or deter entry or expansions, whether they were perceived by their arrangers *ex ante* to be inherently profitable, or whether they could be defended on organizational-economic-efficiency terms),[810] U.S. courts are at least trying to base their legal conclusions in these cases on correct analyses of the relevant practices' tendency to deter new entries or drive out established QV investments and correctly assess the relevance of some of the determinants of the likelihood that the practice will reduce competition in these ways.[811]

---

[810] For example, the conclusion of some courts that exclusive dealing cannot be unlawful in markets in which barriers to entry are low is simply mistaken: in some situations, an exclusive-dealing-generated increase in the barriers to entry a best-placed potential competitor faced to a level that would still be considered to be low may deter its entry and reduce the intensity of QV-investment competition and, derivatively, of price competition on that account. See, *e.g.*, CDC Technologies, Inc. v. IDEXX Laboratories, Inc., 186 F.3d 74 (2d Cir. 1999). Equally mistaken is the conclusion of some courts that exclusive dealerships can be illegal only if employed by sellers with pre-existing market power: a firm without market power could use exclusive dealerships to drive out the rival that deprived it of market power or to deter the execution of new QV investments that would preclude it from obtaining market power as a result of changes in market conditions. See, *e.g.*, Muenster Butane, Inc. v. Stewart Co., 651 F.2d 292, 298 (5th Cir. 1981) and Cowley v. Braden Industries, Inc. 613 F.2d 751, 755 (9th Cir. 1980).

[811] For example, lower courts have almost always recognized that exclusive dealerships whose duration is one year or less will almost never reduce competition by deterring new QV investments or inducing exits. See, *e.g.*, Omega Environmental v. Gilbarco, 127 F.3d 1157, 1164 (9th Cir. 1997), cert. denied, 525 U.S. 812 (1998); Paddock Publications v. Chicago Tribune Co., 103 F.3d 42, 47 (7th Cir. 1996), cert. denied, 520 U.S. 1264 (1997); Roland Machinery Co. v. Dresser Industries, Inc., 749 F.2d 380 (7th Cir. 1985); Barry Wright Corp. v. ITT Grinnell Corp., 724 F.2d 227, 236–38 (1st Cir. 1983); and Western Parcel Express v. United Parcel Service, Inc., 190 F.3d 974, 976 (9th Cir. 1999). At least two lower courts have recognized that the dealer's theoretical right to terminate will not eliminate the risk of competition's being reduced if termination is in practice infeasible or impracticable. See United States v. Dentsply, Inc., 2000–2001 Trade Cas. (CCH) p. 73,247 at 90, 139–41 (D. Del. 2001), rev'd, 2005 WL 426818 (3d Cir. 2005) and Minnesota Mining & Manufacturing Co. v. Appleton Papers, Inc., 35 F. Supp. 2d 1138, 1144 (D. Minn. 1999). Lower courts have also recognized that exclusive dealing that leaves a channel of distribution open is unlikely to reduce competition. See, *e.g.*, United States v. Microsoft Corp., 87 F. Supp. 2d 30, 53 (D.D.C. 2000), aff'd in part, rev'd in part, and remanded 253 F.3d 34, 69 (D.C. Cir. 2001), cert. denied 534 U.S. 952 (2001) and Seagood Trading Corp. v. Jerrico, Inc., 924 F.2d 1555, 1572–73 (11th Cir. 1991).

(iii) Long-Term Leases

I have already discussed Judge Wyzanski's discussion of long-term leases in *United Shoe*. Wyzanski recognized that such leases could be honestly industrial (not predatory) but incorrectly thought that any competitive advantage they yielded their employer could not legitimate its monopoly power. He also did not realize (1) that long-term leases could be predatory, (2) that, even in situations in which such leases could be employed for non-predatory reasons, minimum-use clauses that were predatory could be incorporated into them, and (3) that the charging of fees in the last years of the lease that exceed the value the lessor obtains from the leased machine or building in those years is often not predatory (often manifests the lessor's requiring the lessee to repay in the last years of the lease the loan the lessor extended to it by charging a rental in the early years of the lease that was lower than the value the lessor obtained by using the leased machine or building in the early years of the lease—*i.e.*, the price the lessor could have paid for using the machine in the early years of the lease and remainded equally well-off if it did not have a budget-constraint). I do not know of any other discussion of the economics or antitrust-legality of long-term leases in U.S. antitrust cases.

(iv) Resale-Price-Maintenance Provisions, Vertical Territorial Restraints, and Vertical Customer-Allocation Clauses in Distributorship Agreements

Resale-price-maintenance clauses in distributorship agreements prevent distributors from reselling the manufacturer's product at a reduced price to other distributors that operate discount houses, and vertical territorial restraints and vertical customer-allocation clauses in distributorship agreements explicitly prohibit the distributors from dealing with buyers operating in various geographical areas, with named buyers, or with buyers in specified other categories. Many practicing lawyers and U.S. judges and some U.S. antitrust-law scholars believe that such clauses in distributorship agreements violate the Sherman Act on that account. For reasons that many other economists understand and Chap. 14 of this study will explain, this legal conclusion is unwarranted. Chapter 14 will discuss in some detail the U.S. case-law on RPM, vertical territorial restraints, and vertical customer-allocation clauses. At this juncture, I will confine myself to stating (1) that for nearly a century, U.S. courts held all such clauses *per se* illegal under the Sherman Act, (2) that, subsequently, the Supreme Court held that, although resale-price-maintenance provisions that set minimum resale prices are *per se* illegal under the Sherman Act, the legality of vertical territorial restraints and vertical customer-allocation clauses and of resale-price-maintenance clauses that set maximum prices under that statute must be determined on a case-by-case basis through the application of the Rule of Reason, and (3) that, most recently, the Supreme Court has held that the Sherman Act legality of RPM that sets minimum resale prices, of RPM that sets maximum resale prices, and of vertical territorial restraints and vertical customer-allocation causes must be determined by the application of the Rule of Reason.

(v) Clauses in Employment Contracts, Partnership Agreements, or Contracts for the Sale of Businesses or Professional Practices Obligating the Employee, Partner, or Seller Not to Reveal Associated Information to a Competitor of the Employer, Partner, or Buyer and Not to Compete Against the Employer, Partner, or Buyer

In 1711, in *Mitchel v. Reynolds*,[812] an English court declared enforceable a covenant in a contract of sale of a bakery prohibiting the seller to compete against the buyer for a limited amount of time by re-entering the baking business in the area in which the bakery was located. From its earliest days, the Sherman Act case-law has always deemed lawful reasonable restrictions of this kind in contracts for the sale of a business, employment contracts, and partnership agreements. Thus, in 1898, in *Addyston Pipe & Steel*,[813] in dicta, Judge (subsequently Chief Justice) William Howard Taft stated that "[r]estrictions in the articles of partnership" on the subsequent business activity of its members are not prohibited by the Sherman Act. Subsequent cases have confirmed that, so long as the duration and geographic scope of such restrictions are reasonable, such restrictions are lawful as "ancillary" to a legitimate transaction. Thus, in a 1985 case, Judge Easterbrook declared:

> If A hires B as a salesman and passes customer lists to B, B's reciprocal covenant not to compete with A is "ancillary." At the time A and B strike their bargain, the enterprise (viewed as a whole) expands output and competition by putting B to work. The covenant not to compete means that A may trust B with broader responsibilities, the better to compete against third parties. Covenants of this type are evaluated under the Rule of Reason as ancillary restraints, and unless they bring a large market share under a single firm's control they are legal.[814]

And in a 2002 case, a Missouri District Court held that a covenant not to compete in the sale of a medical clinic was lawful because it was ancillary to the total sale-arrangement—*i.e.*, because it was "necessary to promote the enterprise and productivity of. . .[the] arrangement."[815]

(2) The EC Position and the E.C./E.U. Case-Law

(A) The EC Position

I have many objections to important parts of both the EC position and the E.C./E.U. case-law on refusals to deal. Once more, my objections do not manifest the inability of an American to understand arguments for legal or policy conclusions that differ from their U.S. counterparts. Before getting to the E.C./E.U. case-law, I will try to

---

[812] 98 S.C. Eng. Rep. 347 (1711).

[813] United States v. Addyston Pipe & Steel Co., 85 F.271 (6th Cir. 1898).

[814] Polk Bros. v. Forest City Enterprises, 776 F.2d 185, 189 (1985), citing *Addyston Pipe & Steel.* Note Easterbrook's need to justify his claim that the arrangements on which he was focusing would increase competition by saying that it would increase output.

[815] See Woman's Clinic, Inc. v. St. John's Health System, 252 F. Supp. 2d 857 (W.D. Mo. 2002).

explain my objections by stating and criticizing the EC's position on "refusals to supply," as presented first in a 2005 Discussion Paper and then in a 2009 Guidance communication.

The relevant 2005 Discussion Paper begins by proclaiming that "[u]ndertakings are generally entitled to determine when to supply and to decide not to continue to supply certain trading partners. This is also true for dominant companies."[816] Although the courts of at least the continental members of the E.C./E.U. often derive legal rights from moral rights, the Discussion Paper leaves the impression that the EC believes that the general legal entitlement derives not from a moral right of undertakings (*i.e.*, their owners) to take advantage of the competitive advantages they created through (in American terms) "skill, foresight, and industry" but from the policy goals of maintaining or increasing competition, benefitting consumers, and increasing economic efficiency. I should add that the EC seems to be no more aware than American scholars, lawyers, and public officials that these three goals are not only different but may favor different decisions.

The 2005 Discussion Paper then focuses on two types of refusals to deal—decisions to terminate an existing supply relationship[817] and refusals to start supplying an input.[818] The 2005 Discussion Paper states that the EC supports a rebuttable presumption that decisions to terminate an existing input-supply relationship violate now-Article 102 when the refusing undertaking is dominant and the refusal is likely to have a negative effect on competition,[819] which it subsequently equates with making consumers worse-off.[820] More specifically, according to the 2005 EC Discussion Paper:

> . . .[I]f there are several competitors in the downstream market and the supplier of the input is not itself active in that market, the impact of the termination may be small [*i.e.*, too small for the termination to be illegal] unless the exclusion is likely to lead to collusion. However, if the input owner is itself active in the downstream market and terminates supplies to one of its few competitors, it will normally be presumed that there is a negative effect on competition on the downstream market. . ..[821]

The Discussion Paper then proceeds to state that the defendant in any such termination-case can overcome the presumption of illegality by demonstrating that its termination has made (will make) "consumers" "better off" because the terminated buyer "is not able to provide the appropriate commercial assurances that it will fulfill its obligations" or because the refusing undertaking intends to replace the terminated buyer by integrating forward and will perform the relevant job more efficiently than the terminated buyer did.[822]

---

[816] DG Competition Discussion Paper on the Application of Article 102 of the Treaty to Exclusionary Abuses, Section 9.1 at p. 207 (2005).

[817] *Id.* at Section 9.2.1.

[818] *Id.* at Section 9.2.2.

[819] *Id.* at Section 9.2.1.1.

[820] *Id.* at Section 9.2.1.4.

[821] *Id.* at Section 9.2.1.3.

[822] *Id.* at Section 9.2.1.4.

I have nine criticisms to make of this EC position on the legality under now-Article 102 of the input-supply-termination decisions of dominant firms. First, the EC's analysis of the usual impact of input-supply terminations by sellers that intend to vertically integrate forward into the downstream market ignores the fact that, *ceteris paribus*, the potential consumers of any product are likely to be benefitted by the substitution of a vertically-integrated downstream producer or distributor for an independent downstream producer or distributor: although I believe that economists vastly exaggerate the extent to which a downstream imperfection in price competition will raise the prices charged for a good produced by an imperfectly-competitive upstream producer (because they assume that the upstream seller will engage in single pricing when, in most cases, it will charge downstream producers or distributors a lump-sum fee plus a per-unit price that is lower than the conventional profit-maximizing per-unit price), I agree that the downstream imperfection in price competition will tend to cause prices to be higher than they would be if the upstream seller were vertically integrated forward and equally efficient at the downstream task as were the independent(s) that would otherwise perform the downstream functions. This conclusion reflects the fact that, for reasons that Chap. 14 will explain, the most-profitable pricing strategy for a non-integrated firm will usually combine a lump-sum fee with a per-unit price that exceeds its marginal cost at the associated output.

Second and relatedly, the error just discussed implies that the Discussion Paper's statements about possible defences is deficient in that it ignores the fact that, for the above reason, even if the downstream operation of a refusing undertaking that replaces the terminated downstream buyer with a business of its own is not more proficient than was the operation of the terminated independent, the substitution will tend to benefit relevant buyers by causing a reduction in the price of the downstream product.

Third, the 2005 Discussion Paper does not justify its claims that (1) the fact that a dominant firm at one time found it profitable to supply someone implies that, at that time, it considered it "efficient" to do so and (2)(A) the fact that the supplied buyer is likely to have made an investment in the supply relationship (B) "creates a rebuttable presumption that continuing these relationships is procompetitive,"[823] and these claims are, in fact, not justifiable: (1) even if the fact that the refuser originally found it "efficient" (*i.e.*, profitable) to supply the refused party did imply that its doing so benefitted relevant consumers, there would be little reason to believe that its continuing to do so when it no longer found that conduct profitable would benefit consumers, and (2) the buyer's investment in the supply relationship favors the EC's conclusion only to the extent that termination will deter buyers in the future from creating similar investments and that effect will hurt consumers more in the long run than the prohibition of the termination will hurt them in the short run by preventing vertical integrations that would benefit them.

[823] *Id.* at Section 9.2.1 at p. 217.

Fourth, the 2005 Discussion Paper's list of defences ignores the defense that—even if the prohibition of the termination would benefit the relevant buyers if it would have no effect on the QV-investment, PPR, and plant-modernization and new-plant-construction decisions of prospective investors that would want to be able to protect their competitive advantages by terminating input-supply relationships—it might very well not do so, given its likely impact on such investment decisions. Admittedly, the Discussion Paper does admit in Section 9.1 that "[t]he knowledge that they may have a duty to supply against their will might lead companies not to invest in the first place or to invest less"[824] and does include a discussion of the relevance of this reality to the desirability of declaring refusals to supply an input violative of now-Article 102. But a similar point should have been made in relation to terminating an existing supply relationship.

Fifth, although the 2005 Discussion Paper correctly states that prohibitions of input-supply terminations (or of refusals to start supplying inputs) may produce increases in follow-on research and development, it does not discuss the incentives of original investors to deal with follow-on researchers, the circumstances in which "transaction costs" broadly understood might result in an original investor's making negative supply-decisions that prevented jointly-profitable or efficient follow-on R&D from being performed, the feasibility of addressing such refusals to deal separately and independently under E.C./E.U. competition law, or the possibility of altering IP law to reduce the inefficiency that refusals to deal with follow-on researchers cause.

Sixth, more generally, the 2005 Discussion Paper does not address the difficulty of (1) measuring any short-run gains that prohibitions of supply relationships would confer on relevant consumers and any net losses it would impose on them by deterring relevant investments and comparing their present value or (2) measuring the relevant short-run and long-run economic-efficiency effects of such prohibitions and comparing their present value.

Seventh and relatedly, the 2005 Discussion Paper does not discuss the comparative institutional case for assigning to a competition-law/competition-policy commission or court the job of revising IP law to benefit Clayton-Act-relevant consumers or increase economic efficiency. Obviously, I doubt that the EC and E.C./E.U. courts are as well-suited to perform these tasks as other institutions that could be designed for this purpose would be.

Eighth, the 2005 Discussion Paper does not justify its implicit assumption that dominant firms have a duty to help their actual and potential competitors compete against them—an assumption that is hard to reconcile with its statement that "[u]ndertakings [including dominant companies] are generally entitled to determine to supply and to decide not to supply certain trading partners."

And ninth, relatedly, finally, and in some ways, most fundamentally, the 2005 Discussion Paper does not discuss whether now-Article 102's prohibition of dominant firms' engaging in exploitative abuses covers a dominant firm's choosing

[824] *Id.* at Section 9.1 at p. 213.

not to help a rival compete against it even if the prices or other conditions of sale the dominant firm is currently securing or will be able to secure after refusing to deal would not themselves be deemed illegally exploitative. Relatedly, the 2005 Discussion Paper does not discuss the possibility that, even in those cases in which the resulting prices and other terms of sale would violate now-Article 102, now-Article 102 might not properly be read to prohibit conduct that (1) could lead to their being secured but might not do so because the dominant firm might choose not to exercise its power but (2) would confer other benefits on their perpetrator.

The 2005 Discussion Paper's statement of and comments on its proposed regime for initial refusals to supply differs in only three respects from its termination-of-supply counterparts:

(1) because the factual predicates of the argument for presuming terminations of supply to be illegal are not fulfilled in refusal-to-start-supplying cases, the EC does not argue that a presumption of illegality can be justified in such cases by (A) the refuser's initial view that supply was "efficient" and (B) the supply-relationship investment of the refused buyer;
(2) for no explained reason, the EC says that, in refusal-to-start-supplying cases, it is "more likely that there is a negative effect on competition on the downstream market [only] if. . .the input owner is itself active in the downstream market and excludes use of its few competitors"[825] whereas the EC stated that, in supply-termination cases "it will normally be presumed that there is a negative effect on competition on the downstream market"; and
(3) the EC discussion of defences in "refusal to start supplying" cases adds to the list of defences it indicated it would recognize in cases in which a dominant defendant was accused of illegally terminating a supply relationship not only the defence that the refusal to start supplying was required to make an (economically-efficient or buyer-benefitting) investment profitable but also a defence that the refused buyer did not have the technical ability to use a refused essential facility properly (so that, once more, relevant buyers were not harmed by the supply refusal and/or economic efficiency would not be sacrificed).[826]

I have four comments, all of which relate to the first of these defences:

(1) if the claim is that now-Article 102 prohibits refusals to start supplying when the prohibition is economically efficient, the defendant should have the opportunity to prove that the investment that created the product it might be required to supply was economically efficient and that a duty to supply the resulting product would have rendered the investment *ex ante* unprofitable;
(2) although the 2005 Discussion Paper is correct in stating that the investment defence is less likely to be established if the investment that created the product whose starting supply was refused was made by a public authority or was made

[825] *Id.* at Section 9.2.2.4.
[826] *Id.* at Section 9.2.2.5.

by an actor that had a legal obligation to make it, (A) even public authorities have budget constraints and their willingness to invest may, therefore, depend on the profits they can make by marketing their discoveries, and (B) I do not understand the meaning of the concept "investments 'primarily. . .made for reasons not related to the market' in which the refused company would use the refused input" (for which the Discussion Paper also claims no investment-related defence will be established)[827];

(3) if the claim is that now-Article 102 prohibits refusals to start supplying when a decision to supply would benefit relevant consumers over the long haul, the defendant should have to prove not only that its refusal made a relevant investment (*ex ante*, see below) profitable but that the investments its refusal's prohibition would deter would have benefitted relevant consumers more than they were harmed in the short run by the refusal in question; and

(4) the defendant should be required to show not that its refusal to start supplying critically increased the *ex post* profitability of a relevant investment but that a rule permitting it to refuse to start supplying would critically increase the *ex ante* profitability of its investment.[828]

The relevant 2009 EC Guidance Communication is its Communication entitled Guidance on the Commission's Enforcement priorities in Applying Article 82 (now-Article 102) of the EC Treaty to Abusive Exclusionary Conduct by Dominant Undertakings.[829] The relevant paragraphs of the Communication (pp. 75–90) focus not only on literal refusals to supply downstream rivals but also (see p. 80) on decisions to charge high prices that will prevent equally-efficient downstream competitors of the integrated dominant undertaking that is charging those prices from trading profitably (so-called constructive refusals to supply). On the other hand, as p. 77 indicates, paragraphs of the Communication that explicitly address "refusals to supply" do not address "halting supplies in order to punish customers that do not agree to tying arrangements,. . .[that] are aimed at preventing the purchaser from engaging in parallel trade or from lowering its resale price. . .." Instead, these paragraphs focus on the refusal to grant access to an essential facility, an essential network, or an essential piece of intellectual property (see p. 78), regardless of whether the relevant refusal is a refusal to initiate supply or a refusal to continue supplying a potential buyer or licensee (see p. 79).

---

[827] *Id.*

[828] I also want to comment on the EC Discussion Paper's treatment of two other "refusal to start supplying" issues. First, Section 9.2.2.6 leaves the impression that refusals to license the use of intellectual property is less likely to be found to constitute an abuse under now-Article 102 than the refusal to supply other sorts of goods or facilities. Except to the extent that investments that yield intellectual property are less likely to be made by government authorities, I see no reason to think that this fact has any legal relevance. Second, Section 9.2.3's discussion of refusals to supply information needed for interoperability are wrong for reasons that Subsection 10B of this chapter will explain.

[829] C 45/02 (2009).

identity of potential buyers and the provision of information to those potential buyers that may make them actual buyers.

Fourth, the 2009 Communication also ignores the fact that the imposition of a duty to supply on dominant firms may reduce economic efficiency and harm consumers by deterring firms from securing dominant positions by making economically-efficient choices and/or by inducing firms that have dominant positions to make economically-inefficient decisions to divest part of their operations to render themselves non-dominant.

Fifth, although the Communication does indicate (under the heading of "efficiencies") that its enforcement decision will depend on whether it concludes that the long-run loss the imposition of a duty to supply will impose on consumers by deterring firms from developing new products that they will then be obligated to supply to downstream rivals will exceed the loss that refusals to supply will impose "directly" on Clayton-Act-relevant buyers, the trade-off this statement indicates the Commission will make is between these two sets of effects on relevant consumers' equivalent-dollar welfare—*i.e.*, does not value in itself the impact of the Commission's decision on economic efficiency.

Sixth, even if all the Commission's comments on the factors that determine the magnitude of the "direct" losses that refusals to supply will impose on Clayton-Act-relevant buyers and the magnitude of the investment-incentive-related losses that prohibitions of refusals to supply will impose on other consumers were correct, those comments do not come close to providing a basis for a protocol for making the relevant trade-off.

Seventh, the Communication's comments on the factors that determine the investment-disincentive losses that prohibitions of refusals to supply will generate (1) fail to note the importance of whether the refusing seller's control over the essential intellectual-property right, raw material, or other input resulted from its own efforts on the one hand or a merger, acquisition, joint venture, or patent pool on the other, (2) exaggerates the degree to which terminations of supply are less likely to critically affect investment incentives than *de novo* refusals to supply (both because terminations that reflect, say, changes in the original buyer's ability to enter the upstream market, changes in relevant elements of the legal environment, or changes in the extent of relevant-seller ignorance may be as valuable to refusing suppliers as are *de novo* refusals to supply and because the amount of supernormal profits the relevant investments would be expected by the potential investor to yield if it were allowed to refuse to supply will not be highly sensitive to whether a proposed refusal to supply was a termination or a *de novo* refusal), and (3) assume incorrectly that investments that were subsidized by the government or made under the protection of special or exclusive rights will tend to be more supernormally profitable than other investments if the investor were allowed to refuse to supply.

Eighth, the Communication's reference to "the elimination of effective competition" is ambiguous and, on one interpretation, unacceptably underoperationalized. As to the ambiguity, it is not clear whether the phrase refers simply to "reducing competition" or to "reducing competition below some level deemed to be 'effective.'" As to specification, in the latter case, the Communication makes no effort to specify the level of competition that constitutes "effective competition."

Ninth, for reasons that this chapter explores and Chaps. 6 and 8 foreshadow, the correlation between the likelihood that or the extent to which a refusal to deal will eliminate effective competition in either of the two senses delineated above will increase with the refuser's market share is very low.

Tenth, although the impact of a foreclosing refusal to deal on price competition will increase with the frequency with which the foreclosed buyers were equally-best-placed or uniquely-second-placed to obtain the patronage of downstream buyers that the refuser was best-placed to supply and the average amount by which the relevant foreclosed buyer was better-placed than the third-placed supplier of the refuser's customers in those instances in which the foreclosed buyer was equally-best-placed or uniquely-second-placed to supply a buyer the refuser was equally-best-placed or uniquely-best-placed to supply, these factors are far from perfectly correlated with the substitutability of the refused buyer's product with the refuser's product (since substitutability does not take account of relevant marginal-cost differences).

Eleventh and finally, the Communication's comments on the relevance of the Community's having already imposed a legal obligation on the dominant undertaking to supply are not clear. I take the EC to be stating that in that situation it is bound by the relevant public authority's "balancing of incentives" and that that balancing implies that the refusal to supply violates not only the specific Community law imposing a duty to supply on the defendant in the "antitrust case" in question but also now-Article 102 (if the defendant is individually dominant or a member of a set of collectively-dominant rivals). If that is the import of p. 82 of the 2009 Communication, I concur.

(B) The E.C./E.U. Case-Law

(i) "Straightforward" Refusals to Deal

I turn now to the E.C./E.U. case-law on refusals to deal. I focus first on the case-law on the various functional variants of what I earlier labeled "straightforward" refusals to deal and then consider the case-law on refusals to deal required or made profitable by various types of vertical contracts.

I know of only one E.C./E.U. case that, to my mind, focuses on the legality of a firm's refusing a deal that was inherently unprofitable because the conventional incremental cost the refuser would have had to incur to participate in it was lower than the conventional incremental revenue the deal would yield it. That case[830] declared illegal as an exclusionary abuse United Brands' decision to reduce supplies to an existing distributor because it was spoiling United Brands' bananas, taking part in a competitor's advertising campaign, and making less effort to sell United Brands' product than United Brands thought appropriate. The ECJ ruled against United Brands because, in the ECJ's view, United Brands had failed to employ less-restrictive means of protecting its interests such as complaining about

[830] United Brands Company, OJ L95/1 (1976)

poor performance before cutting off an existing supplier and because the ECJ valued the interest of distributors in exercising individual judgment. I think that, so long as the distributorship-arrangement a dominant undertaking makes does not have the object or effect of reducing the inter-brand competition it faces for reasons that do not reflect the arrangement's increasing its relative economic efficiency, its choice of distributor-arrangements cannot properly be said to constitute an exclusionary abuse of its dominant position. I also do not believe that distributors have a right-related interest in making choices against the interests of their suppliers or that E.C./E.U. competition law is designed *inter alia* to secure any such distributor "interests."

To my knowledge, no E.C./E.U. case has addressed the legality of a refusal to deal motivated by the fact that the contractual marginal and pricing costs of arranging and participating in the deal were prohibitive or by the fact that the deal would have critically-bad reputational consequences. I also know of no E.C./E.U. case that focuses on the antitrust legality of refusals to deal that were motivated by spite or non-commercial objectives. In the absence of any evidence to the contrary, I assume that such cases do not exist because the EC and the E.C./E.U. courts would conclude that refusals to deal of these sorts do not violate E.C./E.U. competition law.

However, a substantial number of E.C./E.U. cases have condemned refusals to deal that structure or police horizontal price-fixes. I include in this category cases condemning horizontal territorial allocations (and the associated refusals of participants to deal with buyers not in their assigned territories),[831] cases condemning horizontal customer allocations (and the associated refusals of participants to deal with buyers not assigned to them),[832] cases condemning horizontal allocations of market shares (which, at a minimum, prohibit participants from dealing for the patronage of additional buyers once they have obtained their agreed-on market share),[833] and cases condemning group boycotts of firms that violated price-fixing agreements as well as of their subcontractors.[834]

As the EC's 2005 Discussion Paper and 2009 Communication would lead one to expect, E.C./E.U. case-law has also developed and applied (without using this

---

[831] See, *e.g.*, Kronenbourg/Heineken (French Beer), OJ L184/57 (2005); Belgian Beer, OJ L200/1 (2003); Seamless Steel Tubes, OJ L140/1 (2003); Graphite Electrodes, OJ L100/1 (2002); SAS/ Maersk Air, OJ L265/15 (2001); Cement, OJ L343/1 (1994); CEWAL, OJ L34/20 (1993); Peroxygen Products, OJ L35/1 (1985); Vegetable Parchment, OJ L70/54 (1978); Sukie Unie and others v. Commission, ECR 1663 (1975); European Sugar Industry, OJ L140/17 (1973); and Quinine, OJ L192/5 (1969).

[832] See, *e.g.*, Food Flavour Enhancers, OJ L75/1 (2004); Methylglucamine, OJ L38/18 (2004); Luxembourg Brewers, OJ L253/21 (2002); Pre-Insulated Pipes, OJ L24/1 (1999); and Roofing Felt, OJ L232/15 (1986).

[833] See, *e.g.*, Zinc Phosphate, OJ L153/1 (2003); Citric Acid, OJ L239/18 (2002); Graphite Electrodes, OJ L100/1 (2002); Cartonboard, OJ L243/1 (1994); French-West African Shipowner's Committees, OJ L134/1 (1992); Flat Glass Benelux, OJ L212/13 (1984); and Quinine, OJ L192/5 (1969).

[834] See Pre-Insulated Pipes, OJ L24/1, pp. 98–107 (1999).

terminology) the kind of "essential facilities" doctrine that U.S. lower courts use but which the U.S. Supreme Court (incorrectly [and, I suspect, disingenuously]) claims it has never endorsed. As the E.C./E.U. competition-law expert Valentine Korah has stated, the case-law seems to support the conclusion that a dominant firm has (1) a duty to supply a former customer when the latter requires access to survive and the fulfillment of that duty would prevent the dominant firm from "extending its dominance to a neighboring market"[835] and (2) a duty to supply an undertaking, "not necessarily an existing or former customer, who intends to make a new product for which there is actual or potential demand, provided that the input is essential for producing such a product. . .."[836] More particularly, specific cases have also held that a dominant ice-cream manufacturer has a duty to allow its distributors to stock rivals' products in freezers it provided,[837] that three (presumably-collectively-dominant) TV stations have a duty to provide programming schedules to a firm that wanted to produce a comprehensive (all-station) TV guide for which there was consumer demand,[838] and that dominant producers of desirable products have a duty to enable independent producers of its product's complements to produce compatible complements[839] and possibly to supply replacement parts to independent service organizations (ISOs).[840] Section 10 of this chapter will discuss in detail both the economics and the law of these latter two types of refusals to deal.

(ii) Refusals to Deal Secured Through Provisions in Contracts Between Sellers and Buyers, Employers and Employees, and Partners

(a) Long-Term Leases of Durable Products I know of no E.C./E.U. case that directly addresses long-term leases of durable products of the type that the U.S. Judge Wyzanski addressed in *United Shoe*.

(b) Long-Term Full-Requirements Contracts Although these sorts of arrangements are normally discussed in Europe under the heading of exclusive dealing, in the U.S. they would be treated separately. In the E.C./E.U., the relevant practice is defined to include not just full-requirements contracts but also requirements that a buyer make a substantial, specified amount of relevant

---

[835] See VALENTINE KORAH, AN INTRODUCTORY GUIDE TO EC COMPETITION LAW AND PRACTICE 184 (hereinafter KORAH) (Hart Publishing, 2007), citing Tetra Pak II, OJ L72/1 (1991); Telemarketing, ECR 3261 (1985); and Commercial Solvents, OJ L299/51 (1973).

[836] See *id.*, citing IMS, OJ L59/18 (2001); Oscar Bronner v. Mediaprint, ECR I-7817 (1998); and Magill TV Guide (Re the): ITP, BBC, and RTE v. Commission, OJ L78/43 (1989), on appeal Radio Telefis Eireann and Others v. Commission, ECR II-485 (1991) and Radio Telefis Eireann and Others v. Commission, ECR I-743 (1995).

[837] Van den Bergh Foods Ltd. v. Commission, Case T-65/98 (2003).

[838] See Magill TV Guide (re the): ITP, BBC, and RTE v. Commission, OJ L78/43 (1989).

[839] Microsoft, available in English at CMLR 965 (2005).

[840] See Volvo AB v. Erik Veng (Case 238/87), ECR 6211 (1988), 4 CMLR 122 (1989) and Hugan/Lipton, OJ L22/23 (1978).

purchases from a seller. The EC seems more likely to find that such arrangements violate E.C./E.U. competition law than U.S. courts are to find them violative of U.S. antitrust law—in part because the EC seems to think that the Treaty is designed to prevent for its own sake buyers' surrendering their "freedom" to turn elsewhere for supply, in part because the EC may underestimate the legitimate value of long-term supply relationships to both buyers and sellers, and in part because the EC appears to use a quantitative as opposed to a qualitative test of illegality (see below). Thus, in *Soda Ash*, the EC limited contracts that specified a fixed tonnage of supply to two years in circumstances in which (I am confident) no U.S. court would have done so.[841]

(c) Long-Term Exclusive Dealerships (Single-Branding Constraints) Earlier, I indicated that Americans use the expression "exclusive dealership" ambiguously to refer both (1) to arrangements in which a seller gives a distributor an exclusive right to distribute one or more products in a specified territory or to a specified set of buyers and (2) to arrangements in which a seller prohibits a distributor of one or more of its products to sell any rival product. Europeans avoid this linguistic confusion: they refer to the second arrangement just described as "single-branding." In the useful European terminology, this subsection is concerned with the case-law on single-branding.

There may be a disagreement between the EC and the E.C./E.U. courts (the CFIs and ECJ) on single-branding. Roughly speaking, the EC seems to be using something more like the U.S. "quantitative substantiality" test to determine their legality, to be skeptical of the economic-efficiency (objective) justifications defendants have offered for their engaging in such conduct, and to be concerned about distributors' surrendering their freedom.[842] The ECJ seems more inclined to use something akin to the contemporary U.S. courts' "qualitative substantiality" test of illegality—*i.e.*, to focus not on the share of buyers foreclosed but on whether existing single-branding arrangements render entry unprofitable.[843] However, I am not confident of this assertion: the ECJ also does sometimes seem to assume that the fact that a single-brand exclusive-dealing arrangement forecloses a substantial share of a market implies that it violates E.C./E.U. competition law.[844]

The EC's most recent pronouncements on single-brand exclusive dealing (and on stocking obligations, conditional rebates, and other pricing schemes that have the effect of preventing the reseller's rivals from making sales to the buyer in question), contained in pp. 33–46 of its 2009 Communication entitled Guidance on the Commission's Enforcement Priorities in Applying Article 82 of the EC Treaty

---

[841] Solvay (Soda Ash) OJ L152/21 (1991), CMLR 645 (1994).

[842] See, *e.g.*, Hachette, 8th Annual Competition Report, pp. 114–15 and IRI/Nielson, 1996 Annual Competition Report, p. 63.

[843] See, *e.g.*, Delimitis, C-234/89, ECR I-935 (1991).

[844] See BPB Industries Plc & Anor v. Commission, Case T-65/89, ECR I-865, p. 68 (1993); BPB Industries Plc a British Gypsum Ltd. v. Commission, ECR II-389, p. 68 (1993); and Hoffmann-La Roche & Co. AG v. Commission, Case 85/76, ECR 461 (1979).

to Abusive Exclusionary Conduct by Dominant Undertakings, include a claim that I know is wrong as a matter economics that the EC thinks has important legal implications. The relevant economics claim (made in pp. 36 and 39) is that if a seller produces a "must stock item," it can always profit by using its position on that product as "leverage" to obtain various sorts of concessions from the buyer—*e.g.*, to induce the buyer not to purchase products of rivals—or at least it can always reduce the cost of obtaining the relevant concessions by using its competitive advantages on such products for this purpose. This leverage theory is wrong because it ignores the fact that, if the producer has charged a price for its "must stock item" that takes full advantage of its competitive advantages on that product, it will not be able to use those advantages again to induce the buyer to make decisions that are costly to the buyer but beneficial to the seller: one cannot have one's cake and eat it, too. Put another way, this leverage theory is wrong because, in order to use the competitive advantages it enjoys on a "must stock item" to induce a buyer to do something the buyer finds costly to do, the seller must forego profits it could otherwise have made directly by charging the conventional profit-maximizing price for the "must stock item" and, unless special conditions are satisfied (conditions that will be discussed in great detail in Chap. 14 in the context of analyzing the functions of tie-ins and reciprocity), it will be no more profitable for a seller to induce its buyer not to deal with a rival (or make any other decision costly to the buyer) by reducing the price of the "must stock item" than by paying the buyer straightforwardly in cash to forego the choices the buyer would otherwise have preferred to make. As previously stated, the EC believes that the supposed ability of producers to use their position on "must stock items" to generate leverage has significant implications for its analysis of the legality of single-brand exclusive dealerships or other seller conduct designed to prevent rivals from supplying the seller's customers. In particular, the EC claims (at p. 36) that when "the dominant undertaking is an unavoidable trading partner" [*i.e.*, sells a must stock item] for all or most customers, even an exclusive purchasing arrangement of short duration can lead to anticompetitive foreclosure. This position is an incorrect qualification to the EC's correct, more general position that the risk that an exclusive-purchasing arrangement will reduce inter-brand competition will increase with the duration of the exclusive-purchasing obligation.

(d) Restrictions on Dealing Created by Resale-Price-Maintenance Provisions, Vertical Territorial Restraints, and Vertical-Customer-Allocation Clauses in Distributorship Agreements As Chap. 14 will explain, the EC position and the E.C./E.U. case-law on resale price maintenance, vertical territorial restraints, and vertical customer-allocation clauses are complicated. Much like their U.S. counterparts, the EC and the E.C./E.U. courts seem to be increasingly aware of the legitimate economic functions of these vertical practices. I will examine the developing law on these practices in Chap. 14. For present purposes, I will confine myself to pointing out that any decision that such a practice violates E.C./E.U. competition law will concomitantly condemn the refusals to deal they encourage.

would set the price of XC at its average total cost. Since, *ex hypothesis*, the average total cost that the independent producers of XC will incur to produce it are lower than the average total cost that the producer of X had to incur to produce it, the perfectly-competitive independent producers of XC will charge a lower price for XC than I am assuming the producer of X would charge for it. On the assumption that X and XC are always consumed in one-to-one proportions (regardless of their relative prices), the replacement of X's producer as a producer of XC by perfectly-competitive independent producers of XC would enable X's producer to increase its profits by raising its price for X by the difference between its and the independents' average total cost for producing XC without suffering any loss of unit-sales on X or any loss of profits on XC (whose price I am assuming would have been a break-even price). In fact, unless some relevant *ceteris* are not *paribus*, the conclusion that the producer of X will profit from its replacement by more-privately-proficient, independent producers of XC will also obtain when the independent producers of XC are not perfectly competitive so long as the producer of X maintains its ability to produce the needed quantity of XC at the average total cost it would have had to incur to produce that quantity prior to the independent's or independents' entries. Of course, to the extent that the producer of X would have to incur significant costs to maintain its original ability to produce XC or to restore its ability to do so after exiting from XC production, independent producers of XC that were not perfectly competitive might be able to impose losses on the producer of X by charging prices for their XC that were higher than the average total cost the producer of X originally had to incur to produce it or by putting the producer in X in a position in which its least-unprofitable move would be to incur costs to maintain its original ability to produce XC.

I will now list and explain the five functions or clusters of related functions that systems rivalry can perform—the reasons why firms may find it profitable to engage in the practice. The profitability of using systems rivalry to perform the first three functions I will discuss critically depends on a legal fact—*viz.*, the fact that, in both the U.S. and the E.C./E.U., the tying agreements that would otherwise usually be a more profitable way of achieving the seller's relevant goals are mistakenly deemed illegal.

The first function that systems rivalry can perform is preventing X's buyers from combining X with inferior XCs whose use would impose losses on the producer of X because of errors made either by buyers of the inferior, independently-produced XC or by potential buyers of X that observed how it performed for a buyer of X that had purchased an inferior XC or were spoken to by a complaining buyer of X that had purchased an inferior XC and was dissatisfied with the way in which X and the inferior XC performed together. X's customers may choose to purchase an inferior, independently-produced XC for either or both of two reasons. The first is that some of X's buyers are not sovereign maximizers—*i.e.*, may make such a purchase by mistake. For example, if they have the opportunity to do so, some of X's buyers may choose to combine X with a low-price/low-quality (inferior) complement XC despite the fact that the cost-savings they thereby achieve are lower than the equivalent-dollar loss they sustain because the X/inferior-XC combination generates lower equivalent-dollar value for them than would the combination of X and a higher-quality complement. To the extent that the penny-pinching buyers in question attribute the poor performance of the X/inferior-XC combination to X, their choice may harm X's producer by reducing their future demand for X. Moreover, to the extent that these buyers communicate their mistaken evaluation of X to other potential buyers of X or to the extent that these other potential buyers of X observe the poor performance of the penny-pinchers' X/inferior-XC combination themselves and attribute it to X, X's buyer's mistaken complement-purchase will also harm X by reducing the demand that other buyers have for X in the future. Second, even if none of X's customers' purchases of an inferior complement XC is mistaken from that buyer's own perspective, a decision by a buyer of X to increase its own profits by combining a cheaper, inferior complement with X may harm X's producer on balance if other buyers that would prefer to pay more for superior performance attribute the relatively-poor performance of the X/inferior-XC combination used by the penny-pinching buyer of X to X rather than to the complement that that buyer combined with X. In both sets of circumstances, X's producer may therefore find it profitable to prevent its customers from purchasing inferior complements such as Y.

Admittedly, in some instances, the producer of X may be able to accomplish this objective without engaging in conduct that is conventionally said to involve systems rivalry—*e.g.*, by warning X's buyers of the associated risks and/or by contractually obligating its customers to use complements with specified quality-attributes. Unfortunately, neither of these strategies is foolproof or costless: the warnings may not be heeded by sovereign, maximizing penny-pinchers or by some buyers that are error-prone; the list of required complement-attributes may be costly to provide and difficult to comprehend; and the requirement that complements of specified quality be used may in any event be costly or impossible to enforce. When one or more of these conditions is satisfied, the most-profitable way for X's producer to deal with its customers' tendency to harm it by selecting complements to its primary product whose use is not in its interest (and may not be in theirs) may be to practice systems rivalry: (1) to threaten to cease supplying buyers of X that do not buy their XC from it or from an independent supplier that it has recommended to them and to carry out those threats; (2) to cease supplying buyers that do not purchase XC from it or a suitable (from its perspective) substitute for XC from an independent without ever explaining the basis of this decision; (3) to require its customers to purchase their full requirements of XC from it or from someone it designates (to enter into full-requirements tie-ins with its primary-product customers); (4) to introduce a variant of X (X*) with which the inferior XCs are incompatible; or (5) to combine (4) with decisions to keep secret information about X* that would enable the manufacturers of inferior XCs to alter their products to render them compatible with X^* and/or to withdraw the original X from the market (even if it would not otherwise have been profitable to do so). Of course, none of these types of systems rivalry will be costless, and some may be (incorrectly) deemed to constitute antitrust violations. Thus, as Chap. 14 explains, a decision by a producer of X to refuse to supply X to buyers that combine it with an inferior XC might (incorrectly) be deemed to constitute an illegal refusal to deal under Section 3 of the Clayton Act, an act of monopolization that violates Section 2 of the Sherman Act, or an exclusionary abuse of a dominant position that violates what is now Article 102 of the 2009 Lisbon Treaty if the producer of X has an individually-dominant position or is a member of a set of collectively-dominant rivals in the "market" in which X is sold. Similarly, as Chap. 14 will also explain, a decision by a producer of X to try to induce its customers to buy XCs of appropriate quality by conditioning its obligation to supply them with X on their agreeing to purchase their full requirements of XC from it or an authorized alternative supplier would almost certainly be declared illegal in the U.S. as a violation of Section 3 of the Clayton Act or Section 1 of the Sherman Act if the producer of X was deemed to have market power in the market for X and would almost certainly be declared illegal both under what is now Article 101 of the 2009 Lisbon Treaty and under what is now Article 102 of the 2009 Lisbon Treaty if the producer of X was deemed to be a dominant firm. Hence, even if such quality-control tie-ins would not be prohibitively expensive to enforce, they might be a less profitable way of overcoming this problem than systems rivalry would be if its practitioners were not equally likely to be convicted of an antitrust violation for engaging in systems rivalry.

A second function of systems rivalry is increasing the profitability of one technique a seller can use to reduce the sum of the transaction costs it has to incur and gross (*i.e.*, pre-tax) transaction surplus it must destroy in the process of converting a given amount of buyer surplus into as much seller surplus as possible—*viz.*, meter pricing. Meter pricing is the practice in which a seller of a durable good or idea makes its customers pay each time they use its good or idea. To see why such pricing may be profitable, assume that the relevant seller produces a differentiated durable good X[846] whose equivalent-dollar value to each of those buyers it is best-placed to supply varies with the frequency with which the buyer in question will use X. If the relevant seller could costlessly buy or construct, install, and inspect a meter on X that could not be tampered with, there are a number of reasons why it might be able to profit by reducing the lump-sum fee it charges for X and requiring each of its purchasers to pay a meter rate in addition to the reduced lump-sum fee each time the buyer uses X. In particular, although the charging of such a *supra*-marginal-cost per-use price (meter rate) will reduce the maximum amount of profits the seller can secure (will reduce

[846] The text will focus on situations in which the metered good is a durable machine. Meter pricing can also be profitable when the "metered good" is a franchise idea—when the customers are owners of sales-outlets that distribute a product or service the franchise-creator (say, McDonald's or Arby's) designed and advertised. In such cases, the "seller" (or the franchisor) is likely to implement meter pricing by charging end-product royalties (where the royalty paid is the meter rate) or using tie-ins in which the franchisee is required to buy its full requirements of one or more of the goods it distributes (say, potatoes, ketchup, and/or hamburger meat) from the franchisor for more than the product's or products' normal price (so that the difference between the contract price and the normal price of the tied good[s] is the meter rate). (The tie-in may be performing a complement-quality-control as well as a metering function.) (End-product royalties may also be used when the seller's good is a conventional input or intermediate product—say, buttons—that the buyer uses to produce a conventional final good—say, shirts.) Meter-pricing tie-ins will tend to be more profitable than end-product-royalty schemes to the extent that it is cheaper to enforce the full-requirements provision of the tie-in than to prevent final-sales-reporting fraud and to the extent that the tie-in also enables the tying seller to control the quality of the complementary inputs its customer uses. For a detailed analysis of meter-pricing tie-ins, see Chap. 14 *infra*.

gross transaction surplus) by deterring the buyer from using the machine as often as the seller would use it if the seller were vertically integrated forward into the buyer's business and as privately proficient at carrying out that business as was the buyer,[847] the switch from the outright sale of its durable product to such a meter-pricing arrangement may well increase the seller's profits on balance because the shift will tend to increase its profits

(1) by obviating its incurring the cost of doing research into the frequency with which particular buyers would expect on the weighted average to use its machine in order to prevent itself from losing profits because it underestimates the frequency with which particular buyers expect to use its machine and hence charges them less than they would be willing to pay for the machine and because it overestimates the frequency with which particular buyers expect to use its machine and hence charges them a price that results in its losing their patronage,
(2) by reducing the loss it sustains
    (A) because the seller underestimates the frequency with which its customers will use its product—*i.e.*, because of seller pessimism, which will cause the seller to charge them lump-sum fees that are lower than the lump-sum fees they would have been willing to pay (will cause the seller to offer terms that on this account will yield it lower profits than the meter-pricing system will generate)—and
    (B) because its potential customers underestimate the frequency with which they will use its product—*i.e.*, because of buyer pessimism, which will reduce the lump-sum fee they are willing to pay *ex ante* to purchase the product outright below the total lump-sum *plus* per-unit charges they will willingly pay for using the product *ex post* when they realize how frequently they can benefit by using X,
(3) by reducing the loss it sustains because it overestimates the frequency with which particular buyers will use its machine and hence charges them a price that results in its losing their patronage,
(4) when the buyer or buyers in question are uncertain about the frequency with which they individually will use its machine, by shifting from the buyers to the seller the risk that they will use it less often than they individually expect to use it on the weighted average (to the extent that the seller is less risk-averse than the buyers are or to the extent that the metering arrangement removes more risk from the buyers than it imposes on the seller because the overall usage of the machine by all of its buyers will vary less than will its usage by each individual

[847] The amount of transaction surplus a seller will have to destroy to remove a given amount of buyer surplus through *supra*-marginal-cost pricing will be inversely related to the relevant good's transaction-surplus-maximizing (TSM) output (the output at which the relevant demand curve cuts the relevant marginal-cost curve from above) and the (absolute value of the negative) slope of the demand curve over the relevant range of output below the TSM output and will be directly related to the positive slope of the relevant marginal-cost curve over the relevant range of output below the TSM output. For an analysis of this issue, see Chap. 14 *infra*.

buyer—*i.e.*, because, unlike its individual buyers, the seller does not have to be concerned with variations in the individual buyers' respective shares of the sales all its customers make "combined" of the product they use its machine to produce)—a possibility whose salience can be traced to the fact that the risk costs a seller's customers will bear under their deal will reduce dollar for dollar the lump-sum fee they can profitably pay the seller for the right to purchase its product on the specified terms, and

(5) by reducing the cost to the seller of preventing or allowing buyer arbitrage—*i.e.*, the costs and losses the seller incurs because its customers may find it profitable to use its machine to perform services for another of the machine's potential buyers (by raising the cost to the seller's customers of marginal uses of the machine, thereby lowering the difference between [A] the average per-use charge the seller is trying to secure from other potential customers—the sum of the average lump-sum fee *plus* per-use charge for using the product—and [B] the cost the seller's actual customers would have to incur to resell the seller's machine's services to others—the price the seller charges its customers for their marginal uses of its machine).[848]

In some situations (at least if the law allowed them to do so), sellers that want to engage in meter pricing will find it more profitable to use so-called meter-pricing tie-ins rather than actual meters to effectuate such a scheme. If, for example, the buyer must use one unit of a complementary good (say, buttons) each time it uses the relevant (button-fastening) machine, the seller can practice meter pricing without using a meter by requiring any buyer of the seller's primary product X to purchase the buyer's full requirements of the complementary good from the seller as well for a per-unit price that exceeds the complement's normal market price. In effect, the difference between the contractual and market price for the complement is the meter rate. Such a meter-pricing tie-in will tend to be more profitable than the use of an actual meter (1) the more expensive it is to construct, install, and inspect a meter, (2) the greater the impracticability of maintaining a meter (think, for example, of maintaining a meter on a riveting machine), (3) the easier it would be to tamper with the meter and the more difficult it would be to detect such tampering, and (4) the cheaper it would be for the producer of X to alter the variant of the complement it supplies its customers (notching the buttons in a difficult-to-copy way) to facilitate detecting customer violations of their full-requirements obligations by inspecting their inventories of XCs or the final product (to identify the XCs they have actually used).

---

[848] Because U.S. courts have tended to hold price discrimination illegal even when it is not sufficiently likely to reduce competition in the Clayton Act sense to warrant the conclusion that it violates that Act, it is important to note that the profitability of meter pricing does not depend on its generating price discrimination. Thus, the preceding analysis implies that a seller may find it profitable to engage in meter pricing even if it has only one customer or even if all its customers are identical in all relevant respects. Admittedly, however, since the first and part of the third function of meter pricing listed above will be more important when different potential customers value the seller's machine differently because they do not expect to use it the same number of times, meter pricing will tend to be more profitable when it produces results that are *ex post* discriminatory.

For two reasons, sellers that would find it profitable to use meter-pricing tie-ins might find it more profitable to engage in systems rivalry, and sellers that would not find it profitable to meter price through meter-pricing tie-ins might find it profitable to meter price through systems rivalry. First, as Chap. 14 will discuss, the law-related cost of the systems rivalry might be lower than that of the meter-pricing tie-ins. The salience of this possibility reflects the fact that both U.S. and E.C./E.U. courts have incorrectly concluded that in many situations meter-pricing tie-ins violate respectively U.S. antitrust law and E.C./E.U. competition law. Obviously, this possibility will be less relevant if systems rivalry is declared illegal, though it would continue to have some significance if it were less difficult for the State or private plaintiffs to win meter-pricing tie-in cases than to win predation cases against actors that have engaged in systems rivalry that does not involve the execution of tie-ins (*e.g.*, against actors that made a QV investment that created a new variant of the primary product [with which the complements of independent complement-producers are incompatible] that might be profitable without regard to any tendency it had to deter such independent complement-producers from introducing a new primary product, to induce them to change the product-space location of the new primary product they would introduce, to induce them to exit from the primary-product-production or complement-production business, and/or, for that matter, to deter such parties from selling complements to the investor's primary-product customers). Second, law-related costs aside, some non-tie-in variant of systems rivalry might be more profitable than meter-pricing tie-ins because it eliminates the possibility of buyers' cheating by substituting lower-priced complements purchased on the open market for the tied complement supplied by X's producer at a price that includes a meter charge.

The third function of systems rivalry that should be distinguished also relates to the need of a seller with competitive advantages to reduce the sum of the transaction cost it incurs and gross transaction surplus it destroys in the process of creating seller surplus by eliminating any given amount of buyer surplus. In particular, in some situations, systems rivalry will enable a seller to reduce the extent to which its practitioner's *supra*-marginal-cost per-unit pricing of its primary product destroys gross transaction surplus in the course of converting buyer surplus into seller surplus. Systems rivalry can perform this function when the primary product is an input or intermediate good against which substitution is possible or a final good that can be consumed in varying proportions with its complements. More specifically, in either of these situations, systems rivalry can perform this function by enabling a seller that wants to charge a *supra*-marginal-cost price for its primary product to prevent its *supra*-marginal-cost pricing of that product from inducing its customers to substitute complements XC of its product X for X when such substitutions would reduce gross transaction surplus. For expositional reasons, the text that follows will assume that the relevant product X is an input or intermediate good that is used by its purchaser in combination with a complement XC to produce some final good A.

I have already explained why a seller of some durable product X might find it profitable to charge a *supra*-marginal-cost meter rate for using X. For similar reasons, sellers of non-durable products may also find it profitable to charge *supra*-marginal-cost prices for each unit of their product its purchasers buy (as

(1) deterring one or more independent producers of complements of the investor's original primary products from introducing a rival primary product;
(2) causing an independent complement-producer that will introduce a new primary product to introduce a "commercially-inferior" product variant that is less-well-placed to secure the primary-product customers of the systems-rivalry practitioner than the new product the independent complement-producer would otherwise have introduced would have been;
(3) causing an independent complement-producer that already produced a primary product to withdraw that product or to accelerate its exit from that line of business; and/or
(4) in cases in which the systems-rivalry practitioner already sold complements of the primary product not only to its own primary-product buyers but also to buyers of its rivals' primary products or thought there was some possibility that it might do so in the future, inducing the independent complement-producer to stop producing the relevant primary product's complements altogether or to accelerate its exit from this line of business.

Systems rivalry can reduce the profits that an independent complement-producer would expect to be able to realize by introducing a primary product in at least the following five ways:

(1) by depriving the independent complement-producer of the profits the perpetrator would not have found legitimately profitable to prevent the complement-producer from securing by supplying complements to the perpetrator's primary-product customers in circumstances in which the independent complement-producer (A) would have used these profits to finance a primary-product-creating QV investment and (B) could not secure external financing for this project as cheaply;
(2) by depriving the independent complement-producer of the opportunity to learn things about the primary product by working with the perpetrator's primary product that would have enabled the independent complement-producer to make a more profitable primary-product-creating QV investment;
(3) by depriving the independent complement-producer of the opportunity to learn things about the attributes that increase a primary product's attractiveness by talking with the primary-product producer's customers;
(4) by depriving the independent complement-producer of the opportunity to identify the perpetrator's customers, to learn things about the particular delivery needs of the perpetrator's customers, to increase its ability to communicate with these buyers, to impress these buyers with its reliability, and to make these buyers place a positive value on giving it profits—*i.e.*, of the opportunity to increase the profitability to the independent complement-producer of its prospective primary-product-creating investment in all these ways; and
(5) by depriving the independent complement-producer of any other joint economies it could realize by supplying complements to the perpetrator's primary-product buyers and introducing a new primary product itself—*e.g.*, joint economies in identifying buyers that would be interested in purchasing

complements of the practitioner's primary product and might be interested in purchasing primary products produced by the independent complement-producer.

Moreover, even if systems rivalry does not deter one or more independent complement-producers from introducing a primary product, it might in each of the above ways cause them to introduce a primary product that was worse-placed to obtain its practitioner's primary-product customers. More specifically, by reducing (1) the funds an independent complement-producer can devote to creating a new primary product, (2) the information it can secure by working with the system-rivalry practitioner's product and the systems-rivalry practitioner's primary-product customers, and (3) the opportunity it has to identify these buyers, to convince them of its reliability, to establish good communication with them, and to make them like it, systems rivalry can cause an independent complement-producer that does introduce a new primary-product to introduce one that is worse-placed to supply the systems-rivalry practitioner's customers than the one the independent complement-producer would otherwise have introduced.

Relatedly, in some circumstances, systems rivalry can induce an independent complement-producer to withdraw a primary product it also produced or to accelerate its exit from this line of business by depriving that firm of the profits it would otherwise have made by supplying complements to the practitioner's customers—profits that (1) the systems-rivalry practitioner would not have found legitimately profitable to eliminate in any other way and (2) the independent would have used to finance its continuing production of the primary product. For systems rivalry to cause the independent's exit from primary-product production or to accelerate that exit, the independent's primary-product business must be yielding operating losses in the short run or perhaps operating profits that constitute a subnormal short-run return on the amount of money the independent could obtain by selling its related assets to someone that would use them for another purpose. Systems rivalry will be more likely to drive the independent out of primary-product production if the independent complement-producer's primary-product business' expected long-run returns were subnormal but might succeed even if the operating profits its primary-product-production project would yield in the long run would constitute a rate-of-return on its investment that would be normal but for the systems rivalry if the systems rivalry critically raises the normal rate-of-return for the independent complement-producer's primary-product project, as it might if (1) the target could not self-finance and (2)(A) impacted information and/or the risk costs that external financers would have to incur to finance firms that may be targets of predation and/or (B) the mechanical transaction cost of obtaining external financing would preclude the independent complement-producer from obtaining external financing to sustain an investment that would yield normal returns in the long run if the independent complement-producer could finance the primary-product project itself.

Finally, systems rivalry can induce an independent complement-producer to exit or to accelerate its exit from the complement-production business in the same ways that it can induce or accelerate an independent complement-producer's exit from primary-product production.

B. The Legality of Systems Rivalry Under U.S. Antitrust Law and E.C./E.U. Competition Law, Correctly Interpreted and Applied

(1) U.S. Antitrust Law, Correctly Interpreted and Applied

For a combination of two reasons, I do not think that systems rivalry ever violates the Sherman Act as properly interpreted and applied. First, the vast majority of systems rivalry is practiced by sellers whose *ex ante* perception that it would be profitable reflected their belief that it would perform one or more of the first four functions in Subsection A's list—all of which are perfectly legitimate: the fact that the first three functions in question can also be performed by tie-ins that U.S. courts are likely to conclude violate the Sherman Act and (in some cases) the Clayton Act does not imply that these functional variants of systems rivalry violate U.S. antitrust law, properly interpreted and applied, because the judicial decisions in question are incorrect as a matter of law.[849] Second, in my judgment, even those exemplars of systems rivalry perpetrated by a firm whose *ex ante* perception that the conduct in question would be profitable was critically increased by the firm's belief that it would or might perform one or more of the functions in the fifth set of functions Subsection A described do not violate the Sherman Act because the contrary conclusion would, in effect, impose a positive duty on investors whose QV investments have put them in a position to secure supra-competitive prices and realize supernormal profits to help their rivals undermine their position and would thereby deter their economically-efficient QV investments in an otherwise-Pareto-perfect economy—because for this reason, in such an economy, the tendency of the conduct in question to deter new rival QV investments from being made or induce extant rival QV investments to be withdrawn would not inflate though it would increase its certainty-equivalent profit-yield. This latter argument is supported not only by the general fact that neither U.S. antitrust law nor other parts of U.S. industrial policy have been understood to impose a duty on firms with OCAs and the ability to realize supernormal profits to help actual and potential rivals compete with them but also by the fact that, with a few deviant exceptions, U.S. antitrust law has not been interpreted to require firms to choose the most-procompetitive option that would be more profitable than doing nothing, that U.S. law recognizes a business' propriety interest in its customer lists—for example, by prohibiting current and former employees from revealing such information to others,[850] and that U.S.

[849] The text ignores the fact that, in the U.S. legal system, lower courts are bound to follow higher-court precedents even if those precedents are wrong as a matter of law.

[850] See, *e.g.*, RESTATEMENT OF AGENCY at § 395, Using or Disclosing Confidential Information, Comment (B) and at § 396, Using Confidential Information After Termination of Agency (1933) and RESTATEMENT OF UNFAIR COMPETITION (THIRD) § 42, Breach of Confidence by Employees, Comment f, *Customer lists*: "The general rules that govern trade secrets are applicable to the protection of information relating to the identity and requirements of customers. Customer identities and related customer information can be a company's most valuable asset and may represent a considerable investment of resources.... [However,] [a] customer list is not protectable as a trade secret...unless it is sufficiently valuable and secret to afford an economic advantage to a person that has access to the list." See also Lynch v. Evans, 2000 WL 3363253 (S.D. Iowa) and Nutronics Imaging, Inc. v. Danan and Danan Nutronics Imaging, Inc., 1998 WL 426570 (E.D. N.Y.).

law recognizes as well a business' proprietary interest in a wide range of other sorts of information not protected by patent or copyright law.

Many exemplars of systems rivalry that do not involve the execution of a QV investment and many exemplars of systems rivalry that do involve the execution of a QV investment involve conduct that is covered by Section 3 of the Clayton Act. Thus, Clayton Act Section 3 clearly covers (1) a decision by a perpetrator to refuse to deal with (sell to) a potential buyer that patronizes an unauthorized independent complement-producer, (2) a decision by a perpetrator to contractually forbid its customers to buy from an independent complement-producer, and/or (3) tie-ins that obligate the perpetrator's primary-product customers to purchase their full requirements of complements from it or someone it specifies. Moreover, although the Clayton Act does not explicitly cover systems rivalry that consists solely of the creation of a product variant with which the original complements made by independent complement-producers are not compatible, decisions to keep the attributes and features of the new product variant secret, decisions to withdraw the old product variant, and/or decisions to disparage the product and delivery-reliability of independent complement-producers, it seems plausible to me to conclude that—since such choices are devised to circumvent the Act's provisions on refusals to deal and tie-ins—those provisions should be interpreted to apply to them as well.

However, although it is conceivable that some exemplars of systems rivalry do violate Section 3 of the Clayton Act, I suspect that systems rivalry rarely does violate the Clayton Act and that it will be extremely difficult to prove the Clayton Act illegality of the few exemplars of this practice that do violate it. This conclusion reflects the following "facts":

(1) for reasons that Chap. 14 will explore, when the legality of this kind of vertical practice under the Clayton Act is at issue, the relevant question is the impact not of an individual seller's engaging in the conduct in question but the impact of a rule allowing all members of a set of relevant rivals to engage in it;
(2) such a rule will tend to injure relevant buyers by reducing the absolute attractiveness of the best offer they respectively receive from any inferior supplier only if the conduct is more profitable for well-established firms than for marginal established firms or potential entrants or expanders;
(3) there is no reason to believe that the conduct in question will tend to be more profitable for well-established firms than for marginal firms and potential entrants and expanders: indeed, if anything the latter sorts of firms are more likely to be vulnerable to buyers' using inferior complements and less likely to be able to overcome through forward vertical integration the problems that underlie the second and third functions in Subsection A's list; and
(4) in some cases in which the general availability of the practice will injure Clayton-Act-relevant buyers in the relevant way, the defendants may well be able to make out an organizational-economic-efficiency defense: for example, such a defense may be available for systems rivalry that is designed to prevent losses caused by buyer errors that cause them to make choices that are presumptively economically inefficient as well as unprofitable for them, for

systems rivalry that reduces the cost of implementing meter pricing and perhaps increases the extent to which such pricing is practicable, and for systems rivalry that reduces jointly-privately-unprofitable and presumptively-economically-inefficient product or input substitutions.[851]

---

[851] Of course, even if system rivalry does not violate the U.S. antitrust laws, it might violate other sorts of legal norms. I can think of five relevant possibilities.

First, some systems rivalry may violate a supply contract between a particular independent complement-producer and the primary-product producer that is engaging in systems rivalry—*e.g.*, a contract in which the primary-product producer agreed to purchase all or a specified quantity of the complement-producer's output. Although obviously one would have to know the details of any written contract and the substance of any oral agreement between the parties about the way in which ambiguous or vague terms in their written contract would be interpreted to determine the primary-product producer's liability, I suspect that the primary-product producer would often be unable to argue successfully that its development of a new product variant with which the complement-producer's product was not compatible relieved it of its duty to purchase the agreed-upon output of the complement-producer, regardless of whether it coupled the new product variant's introduction with a withdrawal of those of its original products with which the complement-producer's product was compatible. Certainly, the primary-product producer would be unlikely to succeed if the systems rivalry hindered the complement-producer's efforts to develop a complement that was compatible with the new primary product by preventing the latter from obtaining information about the primary product's attributes and features that would facilitate the independent's development of a compatible complement. If the complement-producer prevailed in such a contract suit, it would in theory be entitled to full expectation damages—*i.e.*, to recover not only its reliance costs but also the profits it expected to realize on the purchases the primary-product producer was obligated to make. However, in long-term full-requirements supply-contract cases, courts tend not to allow suppliers to recover the part of their expectations that the courts deem "speculative."

Second, some systems rivalry may violate what is somewhat misleadingly called a "promissory estoppel" right of an independent complement-producer. A complement-producer might be entitled to recover on this basis if it had reasonably relied on statements of a primary-product producer that had "encouraged it to believe" that it would eventually be given a supply contract. Even if a court found that no supply contact had been formed (that is why I enquoted "promissory estoppel" in the first sentence of this paragraph) and even if the court found that the primary-product producer had not behaved wrongfully (*inter alia*, had not acted in bad faith and had not made an outright misrepresentation), it might well rule that the independent complement-producer was entitled to recover the losses it sustained by reasonably relying on the primary-product producer's encouraging statements. Once more, in cases like this, God is in the details: the more misleading or arguably-intentionally-misleading the primary-product producer's statements, the closer those statements came to constituting an offer, and the more reasonable the complement-producer's reliance, the more likely the complement-producer will be able to recover on a promissory-estoppel basis. (The canonical promissory-estoppel case that deals with situations that seem analogous to the one I am positing is Hoffman v. Red Owl Stores, Inc., 26 Wis. 2d 683, 133 N.W.2d 267 (1965).) Although, in theory, complement-producers that win systems-rivalry cases on a promissory-estoppel basis would be entitled to expectation damages, in practice, courts do not always award such damages in these cases—not only exclude expectations that are "speculative" but grant awards that are closer to reliance damages (indeed, may exclude from recovery certain types of reliance damages—*e.g.*, the opportunity costs the supplier incurred in reliance [the profits the plaintiff did not earn because it sacrificed other opportunities to prepare itself to supply the defendant]).

Third, when the independent complement-producer can convince a court that the primary-product producer was guilty of negligent misrepresentation, it will be able to recover "the loss" that systems rivalry imposed on it in a tort suit. Although, in theory, an independent complement-producer that wins a negligent-misrepresentation systems-rivalry suit will be entitled to recover

(2) E.C./E.U. Competition Law, Correctly Applied and Interpreted

Now-Article 102 covers all variants of systems rivalry that are perpetrated by an individually-dominant firm or a member of a set of collectively-dominant rivals. Now-Article 101 covers systems rivalry that is executed through full-requirements tie-ins.

My account of the functions that systems rivalry can perform and my related conclusion that systems rivalry virtually never violates the Sherman Act favor the conclusion that systems rivalry cannot properly be condemned as an exclusionary abuse under now-Article 102. I wrote "*favor* the conclusion" rather than "*establish* the conclusion" because the conclusion that now-Article 102 prohibits systems rivalry is favored by (1) the view that now-Article 102 obligates dominant firms to help rivals compete against them and (2) the facts that (A) one of the goals that now-Articles 101 and 102 were designed to achieve was creating a single common market and (B) systems rivalry may prevent inter-E.U.-country trade by preventing independent complement-producers in one E.U. country from supplying

---

only its loss (in essence, reliance damages—though that is a contract remedy), there is some reason to believe that, in practice, courts tend to award successful plaintiffs in cases in which the misrepresentation was worse-than-normally-negligent something closer to expectation damages.

Fourth, when an independent complement-producer has been induced to sell its business at a distressed price to a primary-product producer that has threatened to practice systems rivalry (that would not otherwise be profitable) or has actually practiced systems rivalry in circumstances in which it was not otherwise profitable (behavior that could be said to communicate a threat to continue practicing such system rivalry), the complement-producer may be able to win a restitution suit that would entitle it to void the contract (to rescission) or to force the primary-product producer to disgorge the profits it secured by making the relevant threat. (The relevant RESTATEMENT provision that addresses this possibility does so under the heading "duress by threat." See RESTATEMENT (SECOND) OF CONTRACTS § 175 (1979).) I should say, however, that the RESTATEMENT does contain some provisions under this heading that call into question whether this kind of action would be available to the independent complement-producer in the situation I described. Thus, the RESTATEMENT says that such an action in restitution would lie only if the defendant's conduct involved "a breach in the duty of good faith and fair dealing under a contract"—see *id.* at § 176(1)(d)—and/or a "threat" whose "effectiveness...[was] significantly increased by prior unfair dealing by the party making the threat"—see *id.* at § 176(2)(b)—language that would appear to require the fulfillment of something like the conditions for a promissory-estoppel claim to lie. On the other hand, the RESTATEMENT contains another provision that suggests that such an action in restitution will frequently be available to independent complement-producers in the situation I described: "[a] threat is improper if the resulting exchange is not on fair terms, and what is threatened is otherwise a use of power for illegitimate ends"—see *id.* at §176(c)(2).) In theory, this remedy of disgorgement may result in a successful plaintiff's being awarded damages that are greater than its actual loss—damages that equal the profits the defendant realized on the transaction in question (though in some cases [most often when the defendant's conduct was not truly egregious] courts require the defendant to disgorge only those profits it realized because of its wrongdoing [allow the defendant to keep the profits it realized for independent reasons related to its own skill]).

Fifth and finally, when the systems-rivalry practitioner has wrongfully disparaged the independent complement-producer's product or its performance-reliability, the independent complement-producer will be able to recover its loss in tort in a suit for disparagement or, in some instances, for tortious interference with contractual relations.

secret the attributes or features of the new products that independents would have to know to produce complements that were compatible with them). I will now explain why Kodak and IBM would find it profitable to meter price their new products and how their ability to practice meter pricing would be enhanced by a decision to keep their products' attributes and features secret as long as possible.

In Eastman Kodak's case, these conclusions are suggested by the following facts:

(1) the value of Kodak's new camera to any buyer will increase with the number of times the buyer uses it;

(2) in this situation, Kodak may find it profitable to meter-price the camera—to reduce the lump-sum fee it charges for the camera and to make the customer pay an additional fee each time it uses the camera (at least, Kodak will find that such a pricing strategy will tend to increase its profits by obviating its doing research into the frequency with which different potential buyers would use the camera, by preventing it from losing profits by charging different customers too low or too high a lump-sum fee, by helping it overcome buyer pessimism, by enabling it to shift use-intensity risk from the buyers to itself, by obviating its incurring additional transaction costs at the checkout counter, and conceivably by reducing the incentives of Kodak-camera buyers to engage in arbitrage by selling to others the right to take pictures with their camera);

(3) in theory, Kodak could practice meter pricing when selling its camera by installing a meter on its camera and sending people around periodically to read the meter and extract payments from its customers;

(4) in practice, this method of implementing a meter-pricing system would almost certainly be prohibitively expensive—meters are expensive to build and install, meters can be tampered with, and it will in any case be expensive to send around meter-readers and to extract payments from buyers after the meter has been read;

(5) Kodak could also use full-requirements tie-ins to implement a meter-pricing strategy—*i.e.*, could require its camera-buyers to purchase from it either all the photo-finishing services they buy to develop the pictures they take with the new camera at a price that exceeds the normal market price for photo-finishing services or all the film they use with the new camera for a price that exceeds the normal market price for the film (in each instance, the difference between the contract price and the normal market price for the tied "good" will equal the meter rate if the price in question is quoted per picture);

(6) however, this method of implementing a meter-pricing system also has its drawbacks—such tie-ins might well be (incorrectly) held to violate the U.S. antitrust laws, and (if compatible complements were available from independent suppliers) the full-requirements provisions they contain would be difficult to enforce in any event;

(7) if Kodak could preclude anyone else from supplying photo-finishing services or film for use with its new camera, it could practice meter pricing without using a tie-in by leaving camera buyers contractually free to buy film or photo-finishing

services from anyone and offering to supply such services or film to its camera buyers at a price above the competitive price for such services or goods; and

(8) by keeping secret the attributes of its new camera that independent photo-finishing-equipment manufacturers, photo-finishers, and film manufacturers would need to know to produce compatible complementary products or services, Kodak was putting itself in a position to practice meter pricing without using either a meter or a full-requirements meter-pricing tie-in.

It is also possible that Kodak was keeping the relevant attributes of its new camera secret to prevent its camera-customers from purchasing from others (usually inferior) complements whose use would lower Kodak's camera's performance, damage its reputation, and hence lowering the profits Kodak could make by selling the camera.[855] On my reading of the Sherman Act, if *ex ante* Kodak believed that its systems rivalry was rendered profitable by the practice's increasing the profits the company could make through meter pricing and/or by its controlling the quality of the complements Kodak's customers combined with its camera, those facts would render Kodak's systems rivalry lawful under the Sherman Act even if *ex ante* Kodak also believed that its systems rivalry would deter independent complement-producers from entering Kodak's primary-product market or induce one or more primary-product producers that could produce complements for Kodak's primary product to exit the primary-product or complementary-product market. Readers who do not accept this conclusion and suspect that Kodak's conduct was designed, perhaps *inter alia*, to deter such entries or induce such exits may find some solace in the absence of any evidence suggesting either that the disadvantaged complement-producers had any intention of entering the camera-production business or were induced by Kodak's conduct to exit the camera-production business or even the film-production or film-processing business.

The same functional explanation seems likely to account for IBM's decision to introduce a new CPU and to withhold information about its new product's characteristics. In IBM's case, the counterpart to the predicate that the value that a potential buyer places on a new camera *ex ante* will increase with the frequency with which the buyer expects to use the camera is the fact that the value that a potential buyer of a new CPU places on this product *ex ante* will increase with the number of functions the buyer anticipates using it to perform and hence with the number of peripherals the buyer expects to use and actually will use in conjunction with it. This functional hypothesis and its associated corollaries that IBM's systems rivalry was neither predatory nor Sherman-Act-violative is confirmed by the absence of any evidence suggesting either that the disadvantaged peripheral-manufacturers had any intention of entering the mainframe or CPU manufacturing business or that IBM had made any attempt to buy them out. In short, I am confident that neither Kodak's nor IBM's practice of systems rivalry violated the Sherman Act.

---

[855] This possibility is suggested by evidence that Kodak was concerned about certain deficiencies of its new camera prior to introducing it. See *Berkey Photo* at 278.

Although the opinions in both of these cases reached the correct conclusion about the legality of the defendants' systems rivalry, the respective courts' analyses of this issue were far from perfect. I will touch briefly upon six features of the opinions in question.

First, both opinions reiterate the current, respectively mistaken and ambiguous positive-law (doctrinal) account of the elements of the Section 2 crime of monopolization:

(1) the defendant's possession of monopoly power in the relevant market and
(2) the defendant's "willful acquisition or maintenance of that power" through acts that, even if "otherwise lawful, were unreasonably restrictive of competition."[856]

The first of these elements is mistaken because it is irrelevant. The second is ambiguous because it is unclear whether "willful" implies specific anticompetitive intent or just knowledge of possible consequence and positive valuation of any such outcome.

Second, both the *Berkey Photo* and the *IBM* opinions[857] recognize that proof that the product innovations on which the cases focused were profitable independent of any consequences those innovations had for the conduct or survival of various independent complement-producers defeats the claim that the product innovations were themselves predatory and hence Sherman-Act-violative.

Third, the *Berkey Photo* and *IBM* opinions both state[858] that the antitrust laws allow firms or actors that have made some valuable discovery (*e.g.*, have discovered a product-attribute that buyers will value, a production-process attribute that will render a production-process that incorporates it more privately-cost-effective, or the identity of economic actors that will want to purchase a particular product at a price that will enable its producer to profit by supplying them) to keep that information to themselves in order to increase economic efficiency by maintaining the incentives of potential discoverers to make the relevant discoveries.

Fourth, the *Berkey Photo* and *IBM* opinions both fail to analyze the functions that systems rivalry in general can perform or the functions that the particular exemplars of systems rivalry with which they were respectively concerned did perform. In part, this deficiency of the opinions reflects the two courts' conclusion that the product-innovations in question were profitable independent of their consequences for the survival or behavior of any independent supplier of complements for the defendants' original primary product. However, in part, it may also reflect the courts' disinclination to articulate and then find legitimate functions that are also performed by tie-ins and reciprocity agreements that the Supreme Court has declared illegal.

---

[856] See *IBM* at 735–76. See also *Berkey Photo* at 744.

[857] See *Berkey Photo* at 278 and *IBM* at 744.

[858] See *IBM* at 281–83 for a lengthy discussion and *Berkey Photo* at 744.

Fifth, because these possibilities did not arise in the cases in question, neither the *Berkey Photo* opinion nor the *IBM* opinion directly addressed the legality under the Sherman Act of systems rivalry committed by a perpetrator whose *ex ante* perception that it would be at least normally profitable was critically affected by its belief that the systems rivalry would or might (1) deter an independent complement-producer from introducing a primary product, (2) induce an independent complement-producer that also produced one or more primary products to exit from the primary-product business, (3) cause an independent complement-producer to introduce a less-well-placed primary-product variant or a primary-product variant that was less competitive with the perpetrator's primary product(s) because it was more distant in product-space from them, or (4) when the perpetrator also produced complements that it sold or might sell to buyers of other companies' primary products, induce an independent complement-producer to withdraw from the complement-producing business.

The sixth and final feature of these opinions that is worthy of note is their failure to recognize the possibility that, regardless of whether the systems rivalry on which they focused was predatory, it might violate the Clayton Act because a rule allowing all members of the relevant set of product rivals to engage in systems rivalry would inflict a net equivalent-dollar loss on the customers of the practitioners and the customers of their product-rivals by reducing the absolute attractiveness of the best offer they respectively received from any inferior supplier.

(B) The U.S. Case-Law on Systems Rivalry That Does Not Involve the Making of a QV Investment

Here are the facts of the leading Supreme Court case on systems rivalry that does not involve the making of a QV investment—the 1992 aftermarket-conduct case, *Kodak-ITS*.[859] Beginning in the 1980s, Eastman Kodak allowed independent service organizations (ISOs) such as Image Technical Services (ITS) to repair and service Kodak's high-volume photocopiers and micrographic equipment. Starting in 1985, Kodak reversed course and adopted various policies devised to make it more difficult for ISOs to supply purchasers of Kodak copiers and micrographic equipment with repair-and-maintenance services. In particular, to achieve this result, Kodak (1) stopped selling replacement parts to ISOs, (2) required the independent manufacturers of replacement-parts for Kodak machines (so-called original equipment manufacturers—OEMs) to sell such parts only to Kodak, (3) pressured Kodak-machine owners that were allowed to service their own machines not to resell replacement-parts to ISOs, (4) pressured independent distributors of Kodak replacement-parts to supply them only to Kodak-machine buyers—*i.e.*, not to sell them to ISOs, and (5) refused to sell replacement-parts to some buyers unless they agreed to purchase their repair-and-maintenance services from Kodak as well.

[859] 504 U.S. 451 (1992).

As a result of this change in Kodak policy, ISOs (A) found it more difficult, more expensive, or impossible to obtain replacement parts for Kodak machines, (B) lost profits, and (C) in some instances, exited. Concomitantly, at least some of the customers of the affected ISOs were put in a position in which their best option was to purchase repair-and-maintenance services from Kodak in deals that were less attractive than those they had previously struck with an ISO. The ISOs sued, alleging that Kodak's tying its sales of replacement parts to buyers to their purchase of repair-and-maintenance services was a violation of Section 1 of the Sherman Act (was a contract in restraint of trade) and that all the policies just described constituted attempts to monopolize in violation of Section 2 of the Sherman Act (in my terms, were predatory).

My analysis of the legality of Kodak's conduct under the Sherman Act is based on the following two economic propositions:

(1) Kodak's *ex ante* perception that its relevant conduct was profitable was based on its belief that it would perform one or more of three legitimate functions I will delineate below; and
(2) there was no evidence to support the claim that Kodak's conduct would deter any ISO or OEM from entering the market in which Kodak's primary product was sold or that any such entry would harm Kodak.

I have two related comments:

(1) because Kodak's lawyers did not explain the actual legitimate functions of Kodak's conduct, much less provide evidence to support these explanations, the first proposition reflects nothing more than my surmise: I will return to this "failing" of Kodak's lawyers at the end of this subsection; and
(2) because I believe that the Sherman Act does not prohibit a firm from engaging in systems rivalry to deter complement-producers from entering its primary-product market, I do not believe that the second proposition is legally relevant: I include it because I anticipate that some readers will be unconvinced by my arguments for the legal proposition just articulated.

The three uncontestably-legitimate functions that Kodak's systems rivalry could have performed are:

(1) increasing the cost-effectiveness of Kodak's efforts to prevent its products' reputation from being harmed by its customers' purchase of inferior or improper replacement-parts or repair-and-maintenance services;
(2) enabling Kodak to implement a meter-pricing system on Kodak's primary products without using physical meters, full-requirements meter-pricing tie-ins, or end-product-royalty schemes by putting it in a position to obtain *supra*-marginal-cost prices for its replacement-parts and repair-and-maintenance services by precluding ISOs from undercutting such prices (since both the value of the machine to a given buyer and the amount of replacement-parts and repair-and-maintenance services that any buyer purchases will increase

[proportionately?] with the frequency with which the buyer uses the machine); and

(3) putting Kodak in a position to coordinate the *supra*-marginal-cost pricing respectively of replacement-parts, repair-and-maintenance services, and machine uses to prevent buyers from making jointly-privately-unprofitable substitutions of one or more of these things for the other.

I hasten to add that the claim that Kodak's conduct was designed to perform one or more of the above three legitimating functions is not undermined either by the fact that Kodak allows some buyers to service the machines it buys from Kodak or by the fact that at an earlier date Kodak allowed ISOs to service its machines. Some buyers may be less likely to service Kodak's machines unsatisfactorily than are others, and Kodak may have learned through time that allowing its customers to service the machines they bought from it reduces its profits by damaging the reputation of its machines and/or may have over time become more able to service its machines proficiently itself.

The Supreme Court case was an appeal by Kodak of a Court of Appeals decision[860] overturning a District Court grant of summary judgment in Kodak's favor.[861] The Supreme Court approached the case as a tie-in case and not as a systems-rivalry case, a fact made important by the hostility that the Court has shown to tie-ins and the more-favorable attitude lower courts have manifested to systems rivalry. More specifically, in the Supreme Court majority's view, the correct response to the summary-judgment motion turned *inter alia* on the answers to the following questions:

(1) Could a reasonable trier-of-fact find that replacement-parts and repair-and-maintenance services were separate products (whose joint sale constituted a [possibly-illegal] tie-in)?
(2) Could a reasonable trier-of-fact find that Eastman Kodak had market power over the so-called tying product (the replacement-part) even if one assumed (as the Court believed it had to in the context of this appeal) that Kodak had no monopoly power in the high-volume-photocopier and micrographic-equipment markets?
(3) Could a reasonable trier-of-fact conclude that Kodak's conduct represented an attempt to maintain its monopoly control over its parts and strengthen its monopoly control over aftermarket services? and
(4) Could a reasonable trier-of-fact conclude that Kodak did not have valid business reasons for all the conduct that would otherwise be found to violate Section 1 or Section 2 of the Sherman Act?

The Supreme Court answered each of these questions in the affirmative and for this reason upheld the Court of Appeals' reversal of the District Court's summary judgment in Kodak's favor. The Supreme Court's opinion in *Kodak-ITS* was based

[860] Image Technical Services, Inc. v. Eastman Kodak Co., 903 F.2d 612 (9th Cir. 1990).
[861] Image Technical Services, Inc. v. Eastman Kodak Co., 1988 WL 156332 (N.D. Cal. 1988).

But for one fact, I would have some sympathy for the Court. At least in part, the inadequacy of the Court's response to Kodak's "free-riding" argument reflected Kodak's lawyers' failure to do a good job of explaining the possible functions of their client's conduct or of connecting that conduct to the incentives that Kodak and other potential investors have to make QV investments that would be profitable if their owners could fully exploit the competitive advantages they gave them. However, my sympathy for the Court is substantially diminished by my suspicion that the Court's poor past performance militated against Kodak's lawyers' making the arguments that the Court needed to hear: I suspect that the reason that Kodak's lawyers did not explain the functions that Kodak's conduct performed and perhaps did not ask their clients the questions that would have enabled the lawyers to understand those functions themselves was that the body of applicable antitrust law the Court has developed led the lawyers to believe that the Court was unwilling to rethink its incorrect conclusion that meter pricing and the various other types of complicated pricing strategies that tie-ins can implement are prohibited by our antitrust laws.

The most disturbing feature of the opinions in *Kodak-ITS* is not so much the errors they contain but the fact that they manifest the tendency of doctrinal errors to deter lawyers from making the correct arguments that might lead the Justices to correct their mistakes: in this case, to induce the defendant's lawyers to substitute a weak, inventory-cost argument and a poorly-formulated and probably-inapplicable "prevent ISOs from free riding on the defendant's capital investment" argument for the argument that should have won the day—*viz.*, the argument that (1) the conduct that was alleged to be illegal was devised to enable the defendant in question not only to protect its product's quality-reputation but also to enable it to practice meter pricing or coordinate its *supra*-marginal-cost pricing of two or three "products" and that (2) the antitrust laws do not prohibit firms from preserving their competitive advantages or exploiting them more fully by using fancy pricing-techniques such as meter pricing and (jointly-suboptimal-substitution-preventing) "coordinated *supra*-marginal-cost pricing" because, (perhaps dubiously and certainly contestably) like our intellectual property laws, our antitrust laws are based on the premise that it is socially desirable to allow commercial discoverers and innovators to exploit the demand-curve/marginal-cost-curve combinations they face.

(2) The EC Position and E.C./E.U. Case-Law

In a series of decisions starting in 1984, the EC concluded that the variant of systems rivalry in which a dominant firm modifies its primary product in a way that renders independently-produced complements incompatible with it and/or refuses to provide independent producers of complements information about the dominant firm's primary product that they must have to develop compatible

decision by Kodak (if Kodak did make it). My point is that the Court clearly did not understand it either.

complements is prohibited by now-Article 102 as an exclusionary abuse of a dominant position if the perpetrator has such a position. Thus, in 1984, in the E.C./E.U. *IBM* case,[867] the Commission required IBM to supply technical information to manufacturers of such peripheral products as printers sufficiently in advance of its marketing of its new primary products to enable them to compete with IBM in the peripheral market. Similarly, in 1980, in *Decca Navigator System*,[868] the Commission concluded that the decision of a dominant manufacturer of maritime navigational systems to modify the electronic signals its equipment generated in a way that caused independently-produced system-components to be unreliable without informing independent component-producers of the change constituted an exclusionary abuse of a dominant position under now-Article 102. Most recently, in 2006, in *Microsoft*,[869] the EC concluded that Microsoft committed an exclusionary abuse of its dominant position by refusing to disclose certain information about the Microsoft PC operating system and server to independent operating-system manufacturers to which it had previously supplied such information when the information in question would help the independents manufacture products with some innovative features that were fully compatible with the Microsoft primary product. In the course of this decision, the Commission found that Microsoft's conduct was illegal even though it did not prevent these rivals from producing compatible products and that Microsoft could not justify its conduct by arguing that it enables the company to protect its IP rights or was necessary for it to have efficient incentives to innovate. The Commission also indicated that, as an overwhelmingly-dominant firm, Microsoft had more of a special responsibility to help its rivals than would a dominant firm that was less dominant, citing *Compagnie Maritime Belge*[870] to support this conclusion. The EC's *Microsoft* decision was subsequently upheld by the CFI.[871]

If it were not for the possibility that the drafters and ratifiers of what is now Article 102 of the 2009 Treaty of Lisbon may have intended it to impose a duty on dominant firms to help their actual and potential competitors,[872] I would find this line of cases not only ill-advised as a matter of policy but incorrect as a matter of law. As I indicated previously, in part, I reach this conclusion because of doubts about the wisdom of imposing such duties on companies that have secured dominant positions. And in part, I do so because I doubt the wisdom of assigning to antitrust commissions and antitrust courts the task of making the trade-offs that need to be made if IP law is to be adjusted desirably.

* * *

[867] Undertakings offered by IBM, 14th Report on Competition Policy, pp. 94–95 (1984).

[868] Decca Navigator System, OJ L43/27, pp. 108–10 (1988).

[869] Microsoft, Commission Decision COMP/37.792 (2006).

[870] Compagnie Maritime Belge, C-395/96P, ECR I-1365 pp. 132 and 137 (2000).

[871] Microsoft v. Commission, Case T-201/04 (2007).

[872] DG Competition Discussion Paper on the Application of Article 102 of the Treaty to Exclusionary Abuses, Section 9.1 at p. 207 (2005).

GPSR Compliance

The European Union's (EU) General Product Safety Regulation (GPSR) is a set of rules that requires consumer products to be safe and our obligations to ensure this.

If you have any concerns about our products, you can contact us on ProductSafety@springernature.com

In case Publisher is established outside the EU, the EU authorized representative is:

Springer Nature Customer Service Center GmbH
Europaplatz 3
69115 Heidelberg, Germany

Batch number: 10269235

Printed by Printforce, the Netherlands